Microsoft® Excel 365 Complete

IN PRACTICE

2019

©Chris Ryan/Getty Images

Microsoft® Excel 365 Complete

IN PRACTICE

2019

Kathleen Stewart
MORAINE VALLEY COMMUNITY COLLEGE

Randy Nordell
AMERICAN RIVER COLLEGE

©Chris Ryan/Getty Images

McGraw Hill

MICROSOFT EXCEL 365 COMPLETE: IN PRACTICE, 2019

This book is printed on acid-free paper.

4 5 6 7 8 9 LMN 21 20

ISBN 978-1-260-81841-3 (bound edition)
MHID 1-260-81841-1 (bound edition)
ISBN 978-1-260-81884-0 (loose-leaf edition)
MHID 1-260-81884-5 (loose-leaf edition)

Managing Director: *Terry Schiesl*
Portfolio Manager: *Wyatt Morris*
Product Developers: *Alan Palmer*
Marketing Manager: *Corban Quigg*
Content Project Managers: *Harvey Yep*
Buyer: *Susan K. Culbertson*
Design: *Egzon Shaqiri*
Content Licensing Specialists: *Shawntel Schmitt*
Cover Image: *©Deklofenak/Getty Images*
Compositor: *SPi Global*

Library of Congress Control Number: 2019943402

mheducation.com/highered

dedication

Thank you to the members of my writing team for your collegiality and encouragement on this work. I also want to thank the development, editing, production, and marketing staff at McGraw-Hill for your efforts and support on this series. And I am indebted to reviewers, instructors, and students who have made comments, critiques, and suggestions.

—Kathleen Stewart

Bob and Lanita, thank you for generously allowing me to use the cabin where I completed much of the work on this project. Don and Jennie, thank you for teaching me the value of hard work and encouraging me throughout the years. Kelsey and Taylor, thank you for keeping me young at heart. Kelly, thank you for your daily love, support, and encouragement. I could not have done this without you. I'm looking forward to spending more time together on our tandem!

—Randy

brief contents

contents

WINDOWS & OFFICE

EXCEL

about the authors

KATHLEEN STEWART, M.S. Ed., M.B.A.

Kathleen Stewart is retired from her role as professor and department chairperson for the Information Management Systems Department at Moraine Valley Community College in Palos Hills, Illinois. She has a master's degree in occupational education from Southern Illinois University in Carbondale and an M.B.A. from Loyola University in Chicago. She has authored Microsoft Office texts for many years for McGraw-Hill and has been involved in corporate training in the Chicago area. When not occupied by a writing project, she enjoys traveling, working on her golf game, literacy tutoring, and exploring cultural activities in the city.

RANDY NORDELL, Ed.D.

AMERICAN RIVER COLLEGE

Dr. Randy Nordell is a Professor of Business Technology at American River College in Sacramento, California. He has been an educator for over 25 years and has taught at the high school, community college, and university levels. He holds a bachelor's degree in Business Administration from California State University, Stanislaus, a single subject teaching credential from Fresno State University, a master's degree in Education from Fresno Pacific University, and a doctorate in Education from Argosy University. Randy is the lead author of the *Microsoft Office 365: In Practice, Microsoft Office 2016: In Practice,* and *Microsoft Office 2013: In Practice* series of texts. He is also the author of *101 Tips for Online Course Success* and *Microsoft Outlook 2010.* Randy speaks regularly at conferences on the integration of technology into the curriculum. When not teaching and writing, he enjoys spending time with his family, cycling, skiing, swimming, backpacking, and enjoying the California weather and terrain.

preface

What We're About

We wrote *Microsoft Excel 365 Complete: In Practice, 2019 Edition* to meet the diverse needs of both students and instructors. Our approach focuses on presenting Excel topics in a logical and structured manner, teaching concepts in a way that reinforces learning with practice projects that are transferrable, relevant, and engaging. Our pedagogy and content are based on the following beliefs.

Students Need to Learn and Practice Transferable Skills

Students must be able to transfer the concepts and skills learned in the text to a variety of projects, not simply follow steps in a textbook. Our material goes beyond the instruction of many texts. In our content, students practice the concepts in a variety of current and relevant projects *and* are able to transfer skills and concepts learned to different projects in the real world. To further increase the transferability of skills learned, this text is integrated with SIMnet so students also practice skills and complete projects in an online environment.

Your Curriculum Drives the Content

The curriculum in the classroom should drive the content of the text, not the other way around. This book is designed to allow instructors and students to cover all the material they need to in order to meet the curriculum requirements of their courses no matter how the courses are structured. *Microsoft Excel 365 Complete: In Practice, 2019 Edition* teaches the marketable skills that are key to student success. McGraw-Hill's Custom Publishing site, **Create,** can further tailor the content material to meet the unique educational needs of any school.

Integrated with Technology

Our text provides a fresh and new approach to an Excel applications course. Topics integrate seamlessly with SIMnet with 1:1 content to help students practice and master concepts and skills using SIMnet's interactive learning philosophy. Projects in SIMnet allow students to practice their skills and receive immediate feedback. This integration with SIMnet meets the diverse needs of students and accommodates individual learning styles. Additional textbook resources found in SIMnet (Resources and Library sections) integrate with the learning management systems that are widely used in many online and onsite courses.

Reference Text

In addition to providing students with an abundance of real-life examples and practice projects, we designed this text to be used as a Microsoft Excel 365 reference source. The core material, uncluttered with exercises, focuses on real-world use and application. Our text provides clear step-by-step instructions on how readers can apply the various features available in Microsoft Excel in a variety of contexts. At the same time, users have access to a variety of both online (SIMnet) and textbook practice projects to reinforce skills and concepts. Both SIMnet and this text are updated with the most current Excel 365 features. For the most current updates, please refer first to SIMnet.

instructor walkthrough

Textbook Learning Approach

Microsoft Excel 365 Complete: In Practice, 2019 Edition uses the *T.I.P. approach:*

- **T**opic
- **I**nstruction
- **P**ractice

Topic

- Each Office application section begins with foundational skills and builds to more complex topics as the text progresses.
- Topics are logically sequenced and grouped by topics.
- Student Learning Outcomes (SLOs) are thoroughly integrated with and mapped to chapter content, projects, end-of-chapter review, and test banks.
- Reports are available within SIMnet for displaying how students have met these Student Learning Outcomes.

Instruction (How To)

- *How To* guided instructions about chapter topics provide transferable and adaptable instructions.
- Because *How To* instructions are not locked into single projects, this textbook functions as a reference text, not just a point-and-click textbook.
- Chapter content is aligned 1:1 with SIMnet.

Practice (Pause & Practice and End-of-Chapter Projects)

- Within each chapter, integrated Pause & Practice projects (three to five per chapter) reinforce learning and provide hands-on guided practice.
- In addition to Pause & Practice projects, each chapter has 10 comprehensive and practical practice projects: Guided Projects (three per chapter), Independent Projects (three per chapter), Improve It Project (one per chapter), and Challenge Projects (three per chapter). Additional projects can also be found in the Library or Resources section of SIMnet.
- Pause & Practice and end-of-chapter projects are complete content-rich projects, not small examples lacking context.
- Select auto-graded projects are available in SIMnet.

Chapter Features

All chapters follow a consistent theme and instructional methodology. Below is an example of chapter structure.

Main headings are organized according to the ***Student Learning Outcomes (SLOs).***

SLO 1.1

Creating, Saving, and Opening a Workb

In Microsoft Excel, the file that you open, edit, and save is a
tains ***worksheets***, which are comparable to individual pages in
is also referred to as a ***spreadsheet*** or a ***sheet***, and you can use th
text also uses the terms "workbook" and "file" interchangeably

Microsoft Excel (Excel) is spreadsheet software for creating an
A workbook consists of rows and columns to organize data, perfo
reports, and build charts. With Excel, you can create simple to complex
workbooks. This chapter presents basic procedures for creating and editin

STUDENT LEARNING OUTCOMES (SLOs)

After completing this chapter, you will be able to:

- **SLO 1.1** Create, save, and open an Excel workbook (p. E1-3).
- **SLO 1.2** Enter and edit labels and values in a worksheet (p. E1-7).
- **SLO 1.3** Use the SUM function to build a simple formula (p. E1-19).
- **SLO 1.4** Format a worksheet with font attributes, borders, fill, cell s (p. E1-22).
- **SLO 1.5** Modify columns and rows in a worksheet (p. E1-30).
- **SLO 1.6** Insert, delete, and move worksheets in a workbook (p. E1-
- **SLO 1.7** Modify the appearance of a workbook by adjusting zoom views, and freezing panes (p. E1-41).
- **SLO 1.8** Review and prepare a workbook for final distribution by sp setting properties, and adjusting page setup options (p. E1

A list of Student Learning Outcomes begins each chapter. All chapter content, examples, and practice projects are organized according to the chapter SLOs.

EXCEL

CASE STUDY

Paradise Lakes Resort (PLR) is a vacation company with properties located throughout northern Minnesota. PLR staff use Excel to track revenue, monitor expenses, maintain employee records, and perform similar tasks. In the Pause & Practice projects for Chapter 1, you create, edit, and format a workbook that displays categories of revenue for one week.

Pause & Practice 1-1: Open, edit, and save a workbook.

Pause & Practice 1-2: Use *SUM* and format data in a worksheet.

Pause & Practice 1-3: Edit columns, rows, and sheets in a workbook.

Pause & Practice 1-4: Finalize a workbook for distribution.

The *Case Study* for each chapter is a scenario that establishes the theme for the entire chapter. Chapter content, examples, figures, Pause & Practice projects, SIMnet skills, and projects throughout the chapter closely related to this Case Study content. The three to five Pause & Practice projects in each chapter build upon each other and address key Case Study themes.

How To instructions enhance transferability of skills with concise steps and screen shots.

ANOTHER WAY

The *Function Library* group on the *Formulas* tab has an *AutoSum* button. You can also enter =SUM() in a cell by pressing **Alt** and the **+/=** key on the top keyboard row.

HOW TO: Use the SUM Function

1. Click the cell for the total.
2. Click the **AutoSum** button [*Home* tab, *Editing* group] (Figure 1-20).
3. Press **Enter** to accept the range and complete the function.
   - Drag the pointer to select a different range before pressing **Enter**.
   - If the row or column of values to be added is adjacent to the formula cell as shown in Figure 1-20, you can double-click the **AutoSum** button to insert and accept the function.

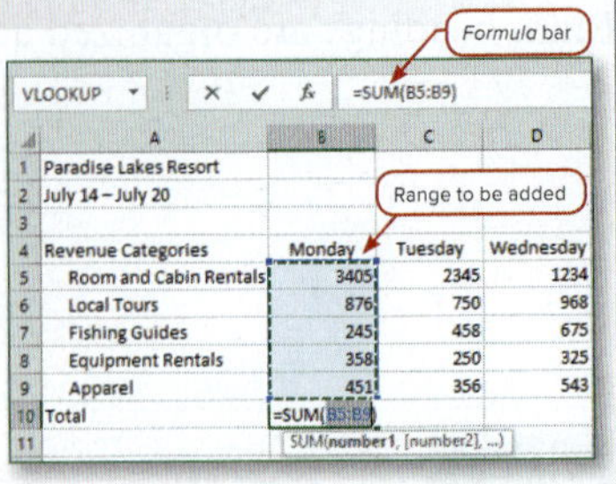

Figure 1-20 *SUM* function

How To instructions are easy-to-follow concise steps. Screen shots and other figures fully illustrate How To topics.

Students can complete hands-on exercises in either the Office application or in SIMnet.

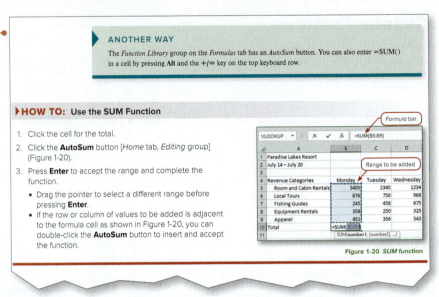

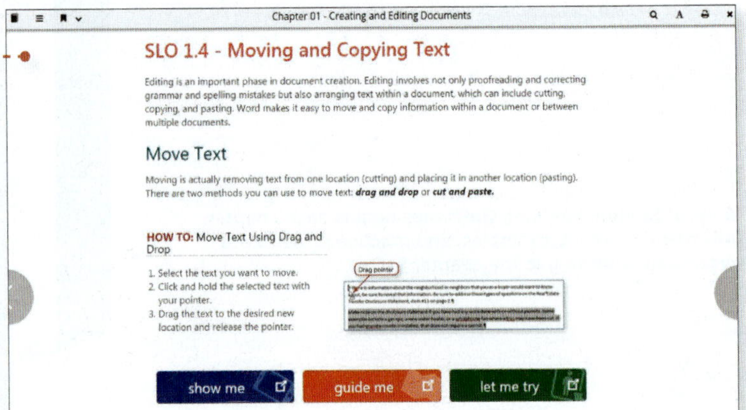

Paradise Lakes Resort (PLR) is a vacation company with properties located throughout northern Minnesota. PLR staff use Excel to track revenue, monitor expenses, maintain employee records, and perform similar tasks. In the Pause & Practice projects for Chapter 1, you create, edit, and format a workbook that displays categories of

Pause & Practice 1-1: Open, edit, and save a workbook.

Pause & Practice 1-2: Use *SUM* and format data in a worksheet.

Pause & Practice 1-3: Edit columns, rows, and sheets in a workbook.

Pause & Practice 1-4: Finalize a workbook

Pause & Practice projects, which each cover two to three of the Student Learning Outcomes in the chapter, provide students with the opportunity to review and practice skills and concepts. Every chapter contains three to five Pause & Practice projects.

MORE INFO

The *AutoSave* feature turns on by default when you save a file to *OneDrive*, and changes made to the file are automatically saved as you work. *AutoSave* displays in the upper-left corner of the title bar.

More Info provides readers with additional information about chapter content.

Another Way notations teach alternative methods of accomplishing the same task or feature, such as keyboard shortcuts.

ANOTHER WAY

Press **Esc** to leave the Excel *Home* page and open a blank workbook.

Marginal notations present additional information and alternative methods.

End-of-Chapter Projects

Ten learning projects at the end of each chapter provide additional reinforcement and practice for students. Many of these projects are available in SIMnet for completion and automatic grading.

- ***Guided Projects (three per chapter):*** Guided Projects provide guided step-by-step instructions to apply Excel features, skills, and concepts from the chapter. Screen shots guide students through the more challenging tasks. End-of-project screen shots provide a visual of the completed project.
- ***Independent Projects (three per chapter):*** Independent Projects provide students further opportunities to practice and apply skills, instructing students what to do, but not how to do it. These projects allow students to apply previously learned content in a different context.
- ***Improve It Project (one per chapter):*** In these projects, students apply their knowledge and skills to enhance and improve an existing document. These are independent-type projects that instruct students what to do, but not how to do it.
- ***Challenge Projects (three per chapter):*** Challenge Projects are open-ended projects that encourage creativity and critical thinking by integrating Excel concepts and features into relevant and engaging projects.

Appendix

- ***Office 365 Shortcuts:*** Appendix A covers the shortcuts available in Microsoft Excel and within each of the specific Office applications. Information is in table format for easy access and reference.

Additional Resources in SIMnet

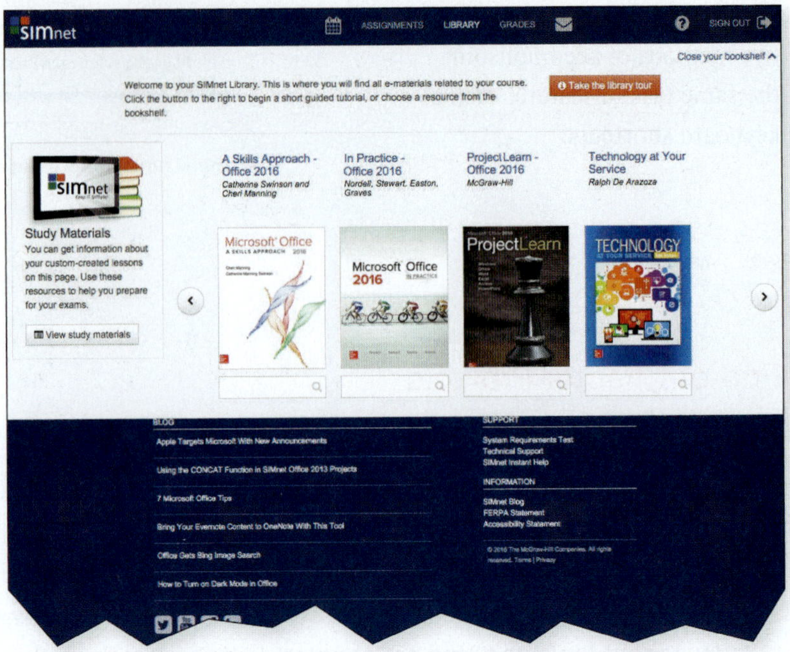

Students and instructors can find the following resources in the Library or Resources sections in SIMnet.

Student Resources

- ***Data Files:*** Files contain start files for all Pause & Practice, Capstone, and end-of-chapter projects.
- ***SIMnet Resources:*** Resources provide getting started and informational handouts for instructors and students.
- ***Check for Understanding:*** A combination of multiple choice, fill-in, matching, and short answer questions are available at the end of each SIMbook chapter in SIMnet to assist students in their review of the skills and concepts covered in the chapter.

Capstone Projects

- ***Integrating Applications:*** Projects provide students with the opportunity to learn, practice, and transfer skills using multiple Office applications.
- ***Integrating Skills:*** Projects provide students with a comprehensive and integrated review of all of the topics covered in each application (Word, Excel, Access, and PowerPoint). Available in individual application texts.

Appendices

- ***Business Document Formats:*** Appendix B is a guide to regularly used business document formatting and includes numerous examples and detailed instructions.

Instructor Resources

- ***Instructor's Manual:*** An Instructor's Manual provides teaching tips and lecture notes aligned with the PowerPoint presentations for each chapter.
- ***Test Bank:*** The extensive test bank integrates with learning management systems (LMSs) such as Blackboard, WebCT, Desire2Learn, and Moodle.
- ***PowerPoint Presentations:*** PowerPoint presentations for each chapter can be used in onsite course formats for lectures or can be uploaded to LMSs.
- ***SIMnet Resources:*** These resources provide getting started and informational handouts for instructors.
- ***Solution Files:*** Files contain solutions for all Pause & Practice, Capstone, Check for Understanding, and end-of-chapter projects.

acknowledgments

REVIEWERS

Lori Mueller
Southeast Missouri State University
Scott Straub
College of Western Idaho
Philip Reaves
University of Western Georgia
B. Bhagyavati
Columbus State
Carolyn E. Johnson
Northern Oklahoma College
Dona Gibbons
Troy University
Denise Sullivan
Westchester Community College
Suzanne Marks
Bellevue College
Phyllis Fleming
Middlesex County College
Salli DiBartolo
Eastern Florida State College
Teresa Roberson
Northwest-Shoals Community College
Amy Chataginer
Mississippi Gulf Coast Community College
Dr. Lucinda Stanley
Wor-Wic Community College
Bill Dorin
Indiana University Northwest
Anita Laird
Schoolcraft College
Sue Bajt
Harper College
Ralph Argiento
Guilford Technical Community College
Annette D. Rakowski
Bergen Community College
Beth Deinert
Southeast Community College
Jo Stephens
University of Arkansas Community College Batesville
Terry Beachy
Garrett College
Vincent Kayes
Mount Saint Mary College, Newburgh
Kimberly Madsen
Kellogg Community College
Nicolas Rouse
Phoenix College
Barbara Hearn
Community College of Philadelphia
Terribeth Gordon
University of Toledo
Stacy Martin
Southwestern Illinois College
Dr. Hamid Nemati
University of North Carolina at Greensboro
Beverly Amer
Northern Arizona University
Michael L. Matuszek
San Antonio College
Sandra Metcalf
Grayson College
David Cook
Stephen F. Austin State University
Donnie W. Collins
Andrew College
Frank Whittle
Dutchess Community College
Robert LaRocca
Keiser University
Adnan Turkey
DeVry University
Sheryl S. Bulloch
Columbia Southern University
Richard Flores
Citrus College
Dmitriy Chulkov
Indiana University Kokomo
Mary Locke
Greenville Technical College
Sherrie Drye
North Carolina A&T State University
Andrew Smith
Marian University Indianapolis
Crystal Theaker
Chandler-Gilbert Community College
Pam Cummings
Minnesota State Community and Technical Colleg
Tina LePage
Chandler-Gilbert Community College
Darenda Kersey
Black River Technical College
Amy Rutledge
Oakland University
Brian Fox
Santa Fe College
Trey Cherry
Edgecombe Community College
Gigi N. Delk
The University of Texas at Tyler
Dr. Richard A. Warren
Vernon College
Debra Morgan
Eastern Washington University.
Pamela Bilodeau
Olympic College
Jim Hughes
Northern Kentucky University
Diane Shingledecker
Portland Community College
Hyo-Joo Han
Georgia Southern University
Becky McAfee
Hillsborough Community College Home
Karen Donham
University of Arkansas at Monticello
Craig Bradley
Shawnee Community College
Elodie Billionniere
Miami Dade College
Joan Rogers
Hillsborough Community College
Genalin F. Umstetter
Delta College
Michael Kato
University of Hawaii
Ann Konarski
St. Clair County Community College
Dr. Mark W. Huber
University of Georgia
Kathleen Morris
The University of Alabama
Rebecca Leveille
American River College
Dory Eddy
Colorado Christian University
Masoud Naghedolfeizi
Fort Valley State University
Joe Vargas
Santa Barbara Business College
Donna Kamen
Truckee Meadows Community College
David Sanford
Northwood University Home
Ken Werner
Alaska Vocational Technical Center
Gigi Simonsen
Northeast Community College
Paula Gregory
Yavapai College
Mordechai Adelman
Touro College
Ron Oler
Ivy Tech Community College of Indiana
Sandra LaFevers
Joliet Junior College
Sherilyn Reynolds
San Jacinto College
Melissa Nemeth
Indiana University
Barbara Garrell
Delaware County Community College
Astrid Todd
Guilford Technical Community College
Deedee Flax
Dodge City Community College
Elizabeth P. Sigman
Georgetown University
Preston Clark
Cornell University
Sara Rutledge
Mount Aloysius College
Robyn Barrett
St. Louis Community College
William Neiheisel
Gwinnett College
Sheila Gionfriddo
Luzerne County Community College
Teodoro Llallire
Fairleigh Dickinson University
Tracy Driscoll
Bishop State Community College
Sam McCall
St. Philip's College
Joyce King
Bay College
John Schrage
Southern Illinois University Edwardsville
John Maloney
Miami Dade College
Lisa Friesen
Southwestern Oklahoma State University
Shelley Ota
University of Hawaii
Heidi Eaton
Elgin Community College

LaVaughn Hart
Las Positas College
Sandy Keeter
Seminole State College
Kathy J. Schaefer
Southwest Minnesota State University
Edward Hall
Seward County Community College
Saiid Ganjalizadeh
The Catholic University of America
Melinda Norris
Coker College
Phillip Dickson
Black River Technical College
Kathy Powell-Case
Colorado Northwestern Community College
Marianne Daugharthy
College of Western Idaho
Ann Taff
Tulsa Community College
Lydia Slater
Rock Valley College
Seyed Roosta
Albany State University
Pamela Silvers
Asheville-Buncombe Technical Community College
Phillip Davis
Del Mar College
Logan Phillips
Tulsa Community College
Dianne Hill
Jackson College
Jeff Harper
Indiana State University
Carla K. Draffen
West Kentucky Community & Technical College
Colin Onita
San Jose State University
N. T. Izuchi
Quinsigamond Community College
Camille Rogers
Georgia Southern University
Luy Parker
California State University, Northridge
Homer Sharafi
Prince George's Community College
Bill Courter
Jackson College
Robert Wardzala
University of Findlay
Lindsey Huber
Northern State University
David Rosenthal
Seton Hall University
Sandro Marchegiani
University of Pittsburgh
Linda Johnsonius
Murray State University
Barbara Bracken
Wilkes University
Marie Hassinger
Susquehanna University
Rich Cacace
Pensacola State College
Arcola Sullivan
Copiah-Lincoln Community College
Angela Mott
Northeast Mississippi Community College
Tony Hunnicutt
College of the Ouachitas
Stephen D. Ross
Mississippi Delta Community College
Alex Morgan
De Anza College
Aaron Ferguson
University of Maryland University College
Patricia White
University of Maryland University College
Anne Acker
Jacksonville University
Pam Shields
Mt. Hood Community College
Nancy Lilly
Central Alabama Community College
Mandy Reininger
Chemeketa Community College
Alison Rampersad
Lynn University
Jeanine Preuss
South Puget Sound Community College
Timothy J. Lloyd
University of Maryland University College
Betsy Boardwine
Virginia Western Community College
Meg Murray
Kennesaw State University
Lynne Lyon
Durham College
Peter Meggison
Massasoit Community College
Sujing Wang
Lamar University
Alla Zakharova
University of South Alabama
Rachel E. Hinton
SUNY Broome Community College
Rhoda A. M. James
Citrus College
Gena Casas
Florida State College at Jacksonville
James D. Powell
College of the Desert
Sue Joiner
Tarleton State University
Dawn Nelson
University of Dubuque
Carlos Jimenez
El Paso Community College
Diane Smith
Henry Ford College
Steven Brennan
Jackson College
Mehran Basiratmand
Florida Atlantic University
Sharolyn Sayers
Milwaukee Area Technical College
Charles Wunker
Webber International University
Doreen Palucci
Wilmington University
Kristy McAuliffe
San Jacinto College
Rob Lemelin
Eastern Washington University
Nancy Severe
Northern Virginia Community College
Julie Becker
Three Rivers Community College
David Childress
Kentucky Community & Technical College System
Carolyn Kuehne
Utah Valley University
Carolyn Carvalho
Kent State University
Irene Joos
La Roche College
Dr. Shayan Mirabi
American InterContinental University
Zhizhang Shen
Plymouth State University
Kirk Atkinson
Western Kentucky University: WKU
Nisheeth Agrawal
Calhoun Community College
Dr. Bernard Ku
Austin Community College
Jennifer Michaels
Lenoir-Rhyne University
William Barrett
Iowa Western Community College
Naomi Johnson
Dickinson State University
Gilliean Lee
Lander University
Clem Lundie
San Jose City College
Cynthia C. Nitsch
MiraCosta College
Beth Cantrell
Central Baptist College
Bernice Eng
Brookdale Community College
Paul Weaver
Bossier Parish Community College
William Penfold
Jamestown Community College
Kathrynn Hollis-Buchanan
University of Alaska
Carmen Morrison
North Central State College
Marie Campbell
Idaho State University
Jpann G. Becento
Navajo Technical University
Annette Yauney
Herkimer College
Judy Jernigan
Tyler Junior College
Elise Marshall
University of North Florida
Karen Waddell
Butler Community College
Allison Bryant
Howard University
William Spangler
Duquesne University
Henry Bradford
Massasoit Community College
Julie Haar
Alexandria Technical & Community College
Martha Balachandran
Middle Tennessee State University
Cheryl Jordan
San Juan College
Mary Kennedy
College of DuPage
Pengtao Li
California State University Stanislaus
Odemaris Valdivia
Santa Monica College
Joyce Quade
Saddleback College
Pam Houston
Oglala Lakota College
Marc Isaacson
Augsburg University
Penny Cypert
Tarrant County College

Manuel T. Uy
Peralta Colleges
Bonnie Smith
Fresno City College
Brenda Killingsworth
East Carolina University
Ember Mitchell
Dixie State University
Emily Holliday
Campbell University

Holly Bales
International Business College in Indianapolis
Elizabeth Sykes
Golden West College

TECHNICAL EDITORS

Karen May
Blinn College
Andrea Nevill
College of Western Idaho
Richard Finn
Moraine Valley Community College
Chris Anderson
North Central Michigan College
Gena Casas
Florida State College
Leon Blue
Pensacola State College
Amie Mayhall
Olney Central College
Patrick Doran
University of Wisconsin Milwaukeex

Thank you to the wonderful team at McGraw-Hill for your confidence in us and support throughout this project. Alan, Wyatt, Tiffany, Corban, Debbie, Harvey, and Julianna, we thoroughly enjoy working with you all! A special thanks to Debbie Hinkle for her thorough and insightful review of the series. Thank you to all of the reviewers and technical editors for your expertise and invaluable insight, which helped shape this book.

—Randy, Kathleen, Annette, and Pat

Intro Chapter

WINDOWS & OFFICE

Windows 10, Office 365/2019, and File Management

CHAPTER OVERVIEW

Microsoft Office 2019 and Windows 10 introduce many new and enhanced features. Office 2019 includes the Office features added to Office 365 since the release of Office 2016. The integration of Office 2019 and Windows 10 improves file portability and accessibility when you use *OneDrive*, Microsoft's free online cloud storage. Office 2019, Office 365, Office Online, Office mobile apps, and Windows 10 enable you to work on tablet computers and smartphones in a consistent working environment that resembles your desktop or laptop computer.

STUDENT LEARNING OUTCOMES (SLOs)

After completing this chapter, you will be able to:

- **SLO Intro. 1** Explore select features of Windows 10 (p. Intro-2).
- **SLO Intro. 2** Use basic features of Microsoft Office and navigate the Office working environment (p. Intro-12).
- **SLO Intro. 3** Create, save, close, and open Office files (p. Intro-19).
- **SLO Intro. 4** Customize the view and display size in Office applications and work with multiple Office files (p. Intro-28).
- **SLO Intro. 5** Print, share, and customize Office files (p. Intro-32).
- **SLO Intro. 6** Use the *Ribbon,* tabs, groups, dialog boxes, task panes, galleries, and the *Quick Access* toolbar (p. Intro-37).
- **SLO Intro. 7** Use context menus, mini toolbar, keyboard shortcuts, and function keys in Office applications (p. Intro-41).
- **SLO Intro. 8** Organize and customize Windows folders and Office files (p. Intro-46).

CASE STUDY

Throughout this book, you have the opportunity to practice the application features presented in the text. Each chapter begins with a case study that introduces you to the Pause & Practice projects in the chapter. These Pause & Practice projects give you a chance to apply and practice key skills in a realistic and practical context. Each chapter contains three to five Pause & Practice projects.

American River Cycling Club (ARCC) is a community cycling club that promotes fitness. ARCC members include recreational cyclists who enjoy the exercise and camaraderie as well as competitive cyclists who compete in road, mountain, and cyclocross races throughout the cycling season. In the Pause & Practice projects, you incorporate many of the topics covered in the chapter to create, save, customize, manage, and share Office files.

Pause & Practice Intro-1: Customize the Windows *Start* menu and *Taskbar*, create and save a PowerPoint presentation, create a folder, open and rename an Excel workbook, and use Windows 10 features.

Pause & Practice Intro-2: Modify an existing document, add document properties, customize the *Quick Access* toolbar, export the document as a PDF file, and share the document.

Pause & Practice Intro-3: Copy and rename files, create a folder, move files, create a zipped folder, and rename a zipped folder.

SLO INTRO. 1

Using Windows 10

Windows 10 is an ***operating system*** that controls computer functions and the working environment. Windows 10 uses the familiar ***Windows desktop***, ***Taskbar***, and ***Start menu***. The Windows operating system enables you to customize the working environment and to install applications (apps), such as Microsoft Office. Visit the ***Microsoft Store*** to download additional apps similar to how you would add an app to your smartphone. Your ***Microsoft account*** stores your Microsoft settings, enabling you to download apps from the Microsoft Store, and to connect to Microsoft Office, *OneDrive*, and *Office Online*.

Windows 10

The Windows 10 operating system controls interaction with computer hardware and software applications (apps; also referred to as programs). ***Windows 10*** utilizes a ***Start menu*** where you select and open an app. Alternatively, you can open apps using the ***Taskbar***, the horizontal bar that displays at the bottom of the Windows desktop. When you log in to Windows 10 using your Microsoft account, your Microsoft account synchronizes your Windows, Office, and ***OneDrive*** cloud storage among computers.

Microsoft Account

In Windows 10 and Office 365/2019, your files and account settings are portable. In other words, your Office settings and files travel with you and are accessible from different computers. You are not restricted to using a single computer. When you sign in to Windows 10 using your Microsoft account (user name and password), Microsoft uses this information to transfer your Windows and Office 2019 settings to the computer you are using. Different types of Microsoft accounts exist: Personal, Education, and Business.

Figure Intro-1 Create a Microsoft account

Your Microsoft account not only signs in to Windows and Office but also to other free Microsoft online services, such as *OneDrive* and ***Office Online***. As a student, you can get a free education Microsoft account at https://products.office.com/en-us/student/office-in-education. Also, you can create a free personal Microsoft account at https://signup.live.com (Figure Intro-1).

> **MORE INFO**
>
> You will use your Microsoft account for projects in this text.

Windows Desktop and Taskbar

The Windows desktop is the working area of Windows. When you log in to Windows, the desktop displays (Figure Intro-2). The *Taskbar* displays horizontally at the bottom of the desktop. Click an icon on the *Taskbar* to open apps and folders (see Figure Intro-2). Pinning is used to add shortcuts to the *Taskbar* or the *Start* menu. You can pin the *Settings, File Explorer,* and other frequently used apps to the *Taskbar* (see "Customize the Taskbar" later in this section).

Figure Intro-2 Window desktop and *Taskbar*

Start Menu

Windows 10 utilizes a redesigned *Start* menu (Figure Intro-3) that you open by clicking the ***Start* button** located in the bottom left of the *Taskbar.* From the *Start* menu, you open apps, files, folders, or other Windows resources. The *Start* menu is divided into two main sections. The left side of the *Start* menu displays the *Account*, *Documents*, *Pictures*, *Settings*, and *Power* buttons. This section also displays *Recently added* and *Most used* items, as well as an alphabetical listing of all apps installed on your computer. The right side of the *Start* menu displays tiles (large and small buttons) you click to open an application or window.

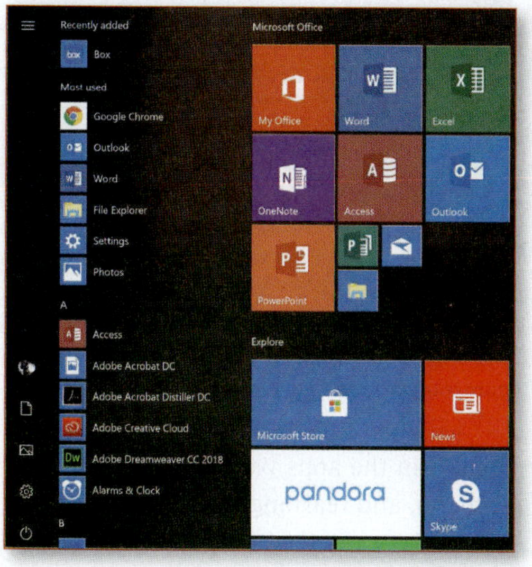

Figure Intro-3 Windows *Start* menu

You can customize which apps and items appear on either side of the *Start* menu, arrange and group apps on the *Start* menu, resize the *Start* menu, and display the *Start* menu as a ***Start* page** when you log in to Windows. See "Customize the Start Menu" later in this section for information about customizing the *Start* menu.

Add Apps

Windows 10 uses the term ***apps*** generically to refer to applications and programs. Apps include the Windows 10 Weather app, Microsoft Excel program, Control Panel, Google Chrome, or *File Explorer.* Many apps are preinstalled on a Windows 10 computer, and additional apps can be installed on your computer. Install an app, such as Office 2019 or Quicken, by downloading it from a web site. These apps are referred to as ***desktop apps*** or ***traditional apps***.

The ***Microsoft Store*** app is preinstalled on Windows 10 computers. Install apps such as Netflix, Yelp, and Spotify from the Microsoft Store. These apps are referred to as ***modern apps*** and look and function similar to apps you install on your smartphone. Many apps in the Microsoft Store are free, and others are available for purchase.

HOW TO: Add an App from the Microsoft Store

1. Click the **Start** button to open the *Start* menu.
2. Click the **Microsoft Store** button (tile) to open the Microsoft Store app (Figure Intro-4) and click the **Apps** tab.
   - If the *Microsoft Store* tile is not available on the *Start* menu, locate the *Microsoft Store* button in the alphabetic listing of all apps.
3. Search for and select an app in the Microsoft Store (Figure Intro-5).
   - The Microsoft Store includes different categories of apps.
   - You can search for apps by typing keywords in the *Search* box in the upper-right corner.
   - When you select an app, information about the app displays.
4. Click the **Get**, **Buy**, or **Free trial** button to install the app.
   - You must have a payment method stored in your Microsoft account to purchase apps from the Microsoft Store.
5. Click **Launch** to open the installed app.
   - When you install an app, the app displays in the *Recently added* area on the *Start* menu and *All apps* list of applications.

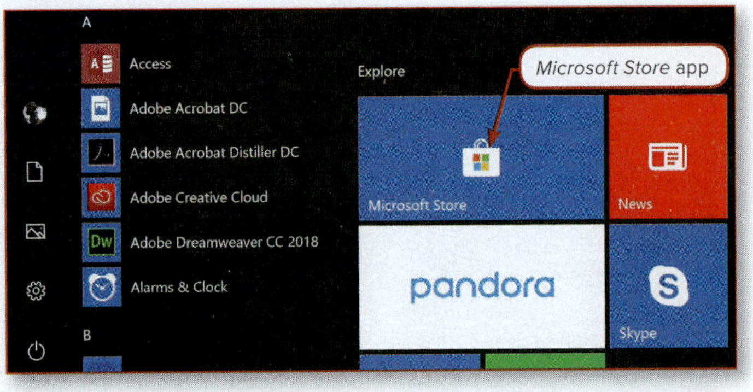

Figure Intro-4 *Microsoft Store* app on the *Start* menu

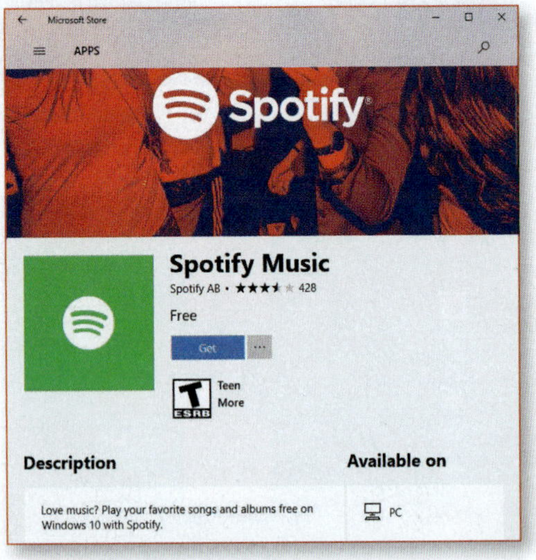

Figure Intro-5 Install an app from the Microsoft Store

Customize the Start Menu

When you start using Windows 10 or after you have installed apps, you can customize what appears on your the *Start* menu. When you ***pin*** an app to the *Start* menu, the corresponding app tile remains on the right side of the *Start* menu. Pin the apps you most regularly use, unpin the apps you don't want displayed on the *Start* menu, and rearrange and resize app tiles to your preference.

▸HOW TO: Customize the Start Menu

1. Click the **Start** button to open the *Start* menu.
2. Move an app tile on the *Start* menu by clicking and dragging the app tile to a new location. The other app tiles shuffle to accommodate the placement of the moved app tile.
3. Remove an app tile from the *Start* menu by right-clicking the app tile and selecting **Unpin from Start** from the context menu (Figure Intro-6).
   - The app tile is removed from the right side of the *Start* menu, but the program or task is not removed from your computer.
4. Pin an app tile to the *Start* menu by right-clicking the app in the alphabetic listing of apps in the *Start* menu and selecting **Pin to Start** (Figure Intro-7).
   - Drag the newly added app tile to the desired location on the *Start* menu.
5. Resize an app tile by right-clicking the app tile, selecting **Resize**, and selecting **Small**, **Medium**, **Wide**, or **Large**.
   - Some apps only have *Small, Medium,* and *Wide* size options.
6. Turn on or off the live tile option by right-clicking the app tile, selecting ***More***, and selecting **Turn Live Tile on** or **Turn Live Tile off**.
   - Live tile displays rotating graphics and options on the app tile. When this option is turned off, the name of the app displays on the tile.
7. Uninstall an app by right-clicking the app you want to uninstall and selecting **Uninstall**.
   - Unlike the unpin option, this option uninstalls the program from your computer, not just your *Start* menu.
   - The *Uninstall* option is not available for some pre-installed Microsoft Windows apps.
8. Resize the *Start* menu by clicking and dragging the top or right edge of the *Start* menu.
9. Customize *Start* menu settings by clicking the **Start** button, selecting **Settings** button (Figure Intro-8) to open the *Settings* window, clicking the **Personalization** button, and clicking the **Start** option at the left (Figure Intro-9).
   - Click the **X** in the upper-right corner to close the *Settings* window.

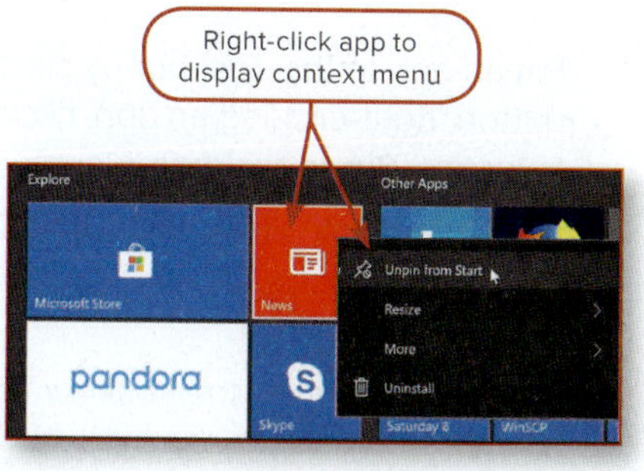

Figure Intro-6 Unpin an app from the *Start* menu

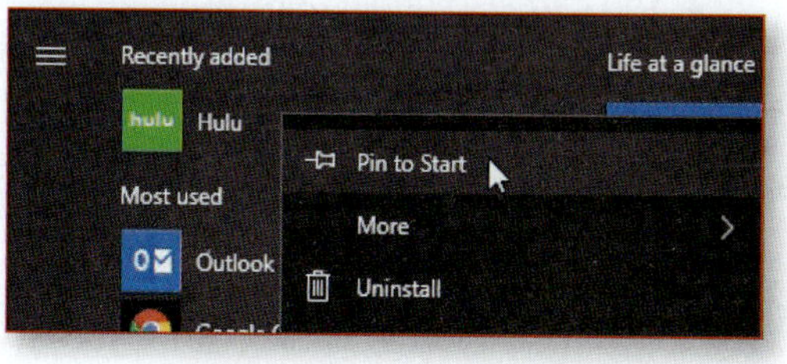

Figure Intro-7 Pin an app to the *Start* menu

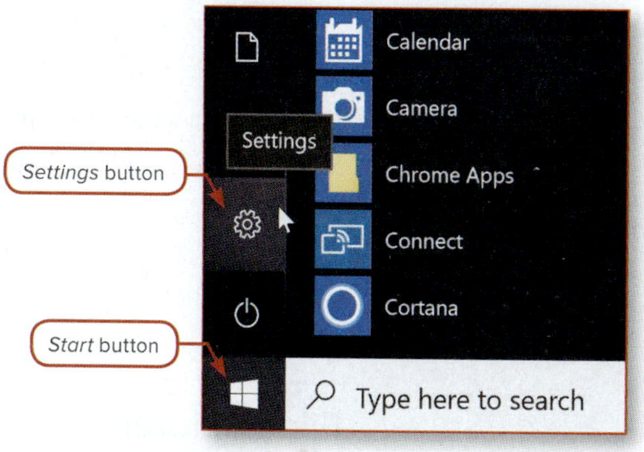

Figure Intro-8 *Settings* button on the *Start* menu

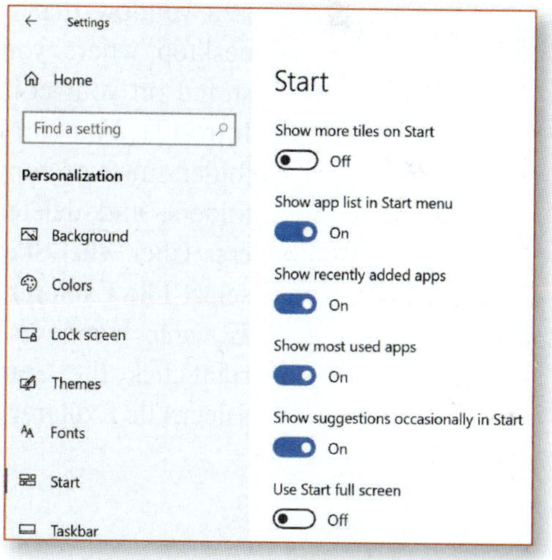

Figure Intro-9 Use full screen *Start* menu

Customize the Taskbar

The *Taskbar* is the horizontal bar located at the bottom of the Windows desktop, and you can quickly open an app by clicking an icon on the *Taskbar* rather than opening it from the *Start* menu. You can customize the *Taskbar* by pinning, unpinning, and rearranging apps. The right side of the *Taskbar* is the *System Tray,* which displays smaller icons of system applications that automatically run in the background of the Windows operating system.

HOW TO: Customize the Taskbar

1. Pin an app to the *Taskbar* by clicking the **Start** button, right-clicking an app, clicking **More**, and selecting **Pin to taskbar** (Figure Intro-10).
   - You can also pin an app to the *Taskbar* by right-clicking an app from the alphabetic listing of apps in the *Start* menu.
2. Unpin an app from the *Taskbar* by right-clicking an app icon on the *Taskbar* and selecting **Unpin from taskbar** (Figure Intro-11).
   - You can also unpin apps from the *Taskbar* by right-clicking an app in the *Start* menu, clicking **More**, and selecting **Unpin from taskbar**.
3. Rearrange apps on the *Taskbar* by clicking and dragging the app to the desired location on the *Taskbar* and releasing.

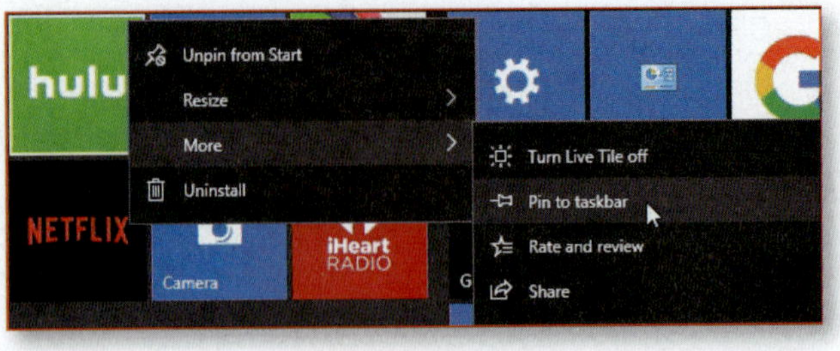

Figure Intro-10 Pin an app to the *Taskbar*

Figure Intro-11 Unpin an app from the *Taskbar*

> **MORE INFO**
>
> If using a touch screen, press and hold an app on the *Start* menu or *Taskbar* to display the app options.

File Explorer

The *File Explorer* in Windows 10 is a window that opens on your desktop where you browse files stored on your computer (Figure Intro-12). You can open a file or folder, move or copy items, create folders, and delete files or folders. Click the **Start** button and select **File Explorer** to open a *File Explorer* window. Alternatively, right-click the **Start** button and select **File Explorer**.

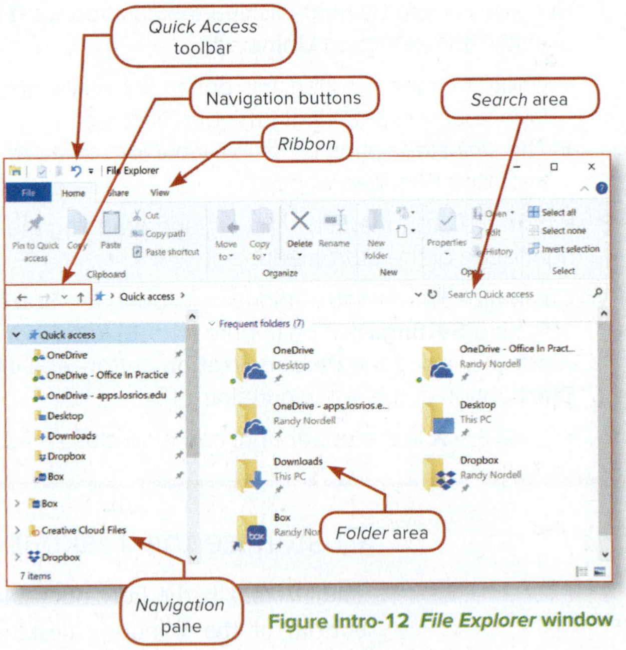

Figure Intro-12 *File Explorer* window

> **MORE INFO**
>
> You can pin the *File Explorer* to the *Taskbar* for easy access to this window.

The *File Explorer* has different areas:

- ***Navigation pane***: The *Navigation* pane displays folders on the left. The ***Quick access*** area at the top of the *Navigation* pane displays shortcuts to favorite folders. You can pin or unpin folders in the *Quick access* area of the *Navigation* pane.
- ***Navigation buttons***: The navigation buttons (*Back, Forward, Recent location,* and *Up*) are located directly above the *Navigation* pane and below the *Ribbon.* Use these buttons to navigate a File Explorer window.
- ***Folder pane***: When you select a folder in the *Navigation* pane, the contents of the folder display in the *Folder* pane to the right of the *Navigation* pane. Double-click a folder or file in the *Folder* pane to open it.
- ***Ribbon***: The *Ribbon* is located near the top of *File Explorer* and includes the *File, Home, Share,* and *View* tabs. When you click a tab on the *Ribbon,* the *Ribbon* displays the options for the selected tab. Other contextual tabs display when you select certain types of files. For example, the *Picture Tool Manage* tab opens when you select a picture file in the *Folder* pane.
- ***Quick Access toolbar***: The *Quick Access* toolbar is above the *Ribbon.* From the *Quick Access* toolbar, click the **New Folder** button to create a new folder or click **Properties** to display the properties of a selected file or folder. You can add buttons, such as *Undo, Redo,* and *Rename,* to the *Quick Access* toolbar.
- ***Search***: The *Search* text box is located on the right of the *File Explorer* window below the *Ribbon.* Type key words in the *Search* text box to find files or folders.

OneDrive

OneDrive is a cloud storage area where you store files in a private and secure online location that you access from any computer. With Windows 10, the ***OneDrive folder*** is one of your storage location folder options, similar to your *Documents* or *Pictures* folders (Figure Intro-13). You can save, open, and edit your *OneDrive* files from a *File Explorer* folder. Your *OneDrive* folder looks and functions similar to other Windows folders. *OneDrive* synchronizes your files so when you change a file stored in *OneDrive* it is automatically updated on the *OneDrive* cloud.

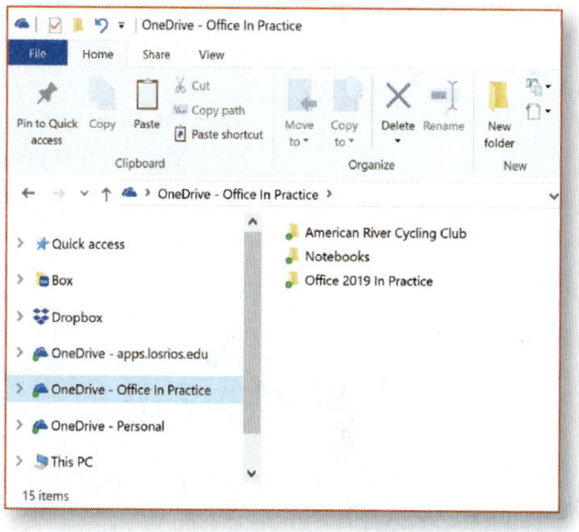

Figure Intro-13 ***OneDrive* folder in a *File Explorer* window**

When you store your files in *OneDrive,* you have the option of storing the files on *OneDrive* only (in the cloud) or syncing the files to your computer so they are saved on both your computer and on the cloud. You can customize which *OneDrive* folders and files are cloud only (not stored on your computer) and which folders and files are synced to your computer.

▸HOW TO: Customize OneDrive Settings

1. Open a *File Explorer* window using one of the following methods:
   - Click the **Start** button and select the **File Explorer** button.
   - Click the **File Explorer** button on the *Taskbar* (if available).
   - Right-click the **Start** button and select **File Explorer**.

2. Right-click the **OneDrive** folder in the *Navigation* pane of the *File Explorer* window and select **Settings** to open the *Microsoft OneDrive* dialog box.
   - Alternatively, right-click the **OneDrive** icon (if available) in the *System Tray* (right side of the *Taskbar*) and select **Settings**.
3. Click the **Account** tab and click the **Choose folders** button to open the *Sync your OneDrive files to this PC* dialog box (Figure Intro-14).
   - Check the **Sync all files and folders in OneDrive** box to sync all files and folders to your computer.
   - You can also select only those folders to sync in the *Or sync only these folders* area by selecting or deselecting the check boxes. Use this option to save storage space on your computer.
4. Click **OK** to close the *Sync your OneDrive files to this PC* dialog box and click **OK** to close the *Microsoft OneDrive* dialog box.

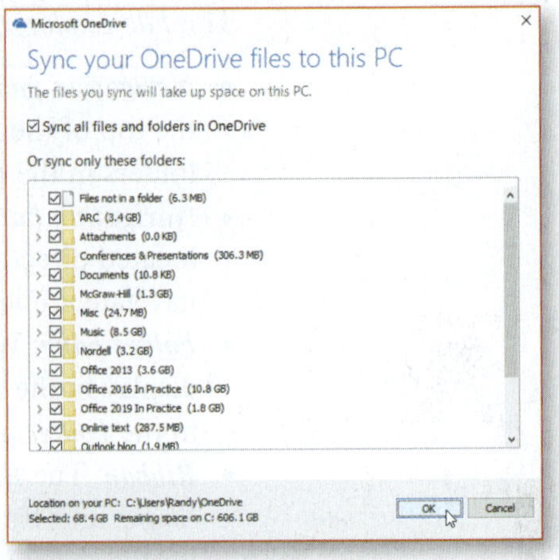

Figure Intro-14 Customize *OneDrive* folders to sync to your computer

OneDrive Online

In addition to the *OneDrive* folder on your computer, you can also access your *OneDrive* files online using an internet browser such as Microsoft Edge, Google Chrome, or Mozilla Firefox. When you access *OneDrive* online using a web browser, you can upload files, create folders, move and copy files and folders, and create Office files using *Office Online* (*Office Online* is discussed in *SLO Intro.2: Using Microsoft Office 2019*).

> **MORE INFO**
>
> *OneDrive* online may display differently and include different features depending on the type of Microsoft account you have: personal, education, or business.

HOW TO: Use OneDrive Online

1. Open an internet browser window and navigate to the *OneDrive* web site (www.onedrive.live.com), which takes you to the *OneDrive* sign-in page.
   - Use any internet browser to access *OneDrive* (Microsoft Edge, Google Chrome, Mozilla Firefox).
2. Click the **Sign in** button in the upper-right corner of the browser window.
3. Type your Microsoft account email address and click **Next** (Figure Intro-15).
4. Type your Microsoft account password and click **Sign in**. The *OneDrive* page displays.
   - If you are on your own computer, check the **Keep me signed in** box to stay signed in to *OneDrive* when you return to the page.
   - The different areas of *OneDrive* are listed under the *OneDrive* heading on the left (Figure Intro-16).
   - Click **Files** to display your folders and files in the folder area.
   - At the top of the page, buttons and drop-down menus list the different actions you can perform on selected files and folders.

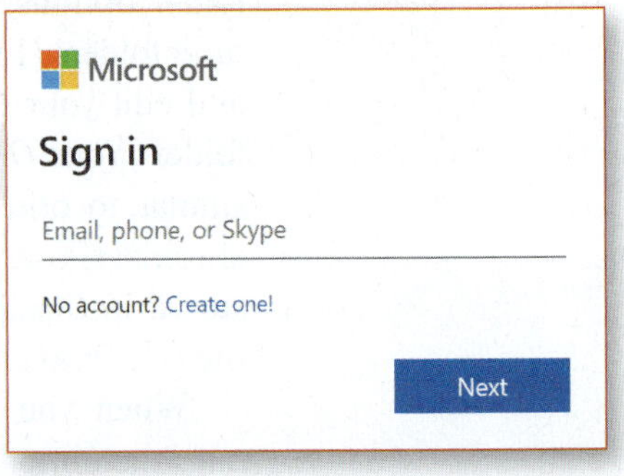

Figure Intro-15 Log in to *OneDrive* online

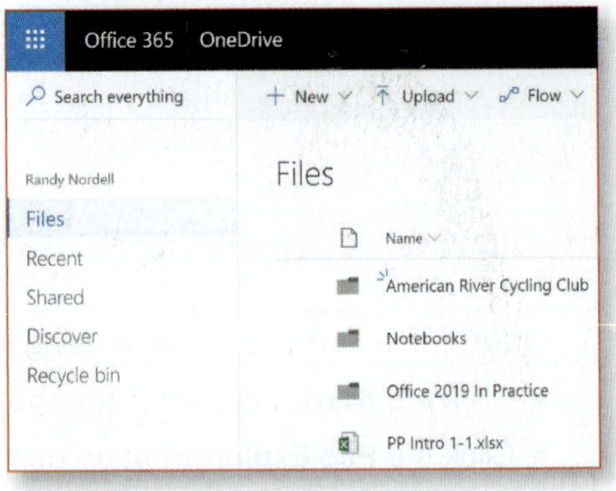

Figure Intro-16 *OneDrive* online environment

Cortana

In addition to using the search tools in *File Explorer,* you can also use ***Cortana***, which is the Windows search feature. While the search feature in *File Explorer* searches only for content on your computer, *Cortana* searches for content on your computer, on the internet, and in the Microsoft Store. You can either type keywords for a search or use voice commands to search for content.

When you open *Cortana,* other content, such as weather, upcoming appointments, and popular news stories, displays in the *Cortana* pane.

HOW TO: Search Using Cortana

1. Click the **Cortana** search area on the *Taskbar* to open the *Cortana* pane (Figure Intro-17).
   - If the *Cortana* search area is not on the *Taskbar,* click the **Start** button, right-click **Cortana** in the list of apps, and select **Pin to taskbar**.
2. Type keywords for your search in the **Type here to search** area at the bottom of the *Cortana* pane.
   - You can also click the microphone icon and speak to enter keywords as the search.
   - Content from your computer, the internet, and the Microsoft Store displays in the *Cortana* pane (Figure Intro-18).
   - The search results are grouped into categories such as *Best match, Photos, Search suggestions, Store,* and *Places.* These categories vary depending on the search results.
3. Click a result in the *Cortana* pane to view a file, search the internet, or view apps in the Microsoft Store.
   - The buttons at the top of the *Cortana* pane filter your search by *Apps, Documents, Email,* and *web.*
   - The *More* button displays a drop-down list of additional filter options.
4. Click the **Menu** button at the top left to display other content options in the *Cortana* pane (see Figure Intro-18).
   - The other content options are *Home, Notebook,* and *Devices.*

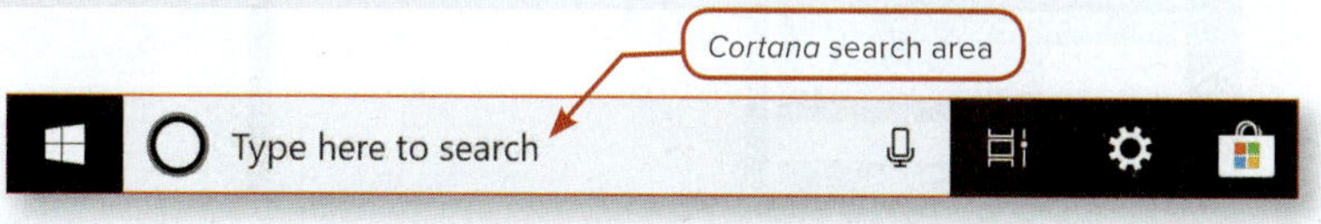

Figure Intro-17 ***Cortana*** **search area on the** ***Taskbar***

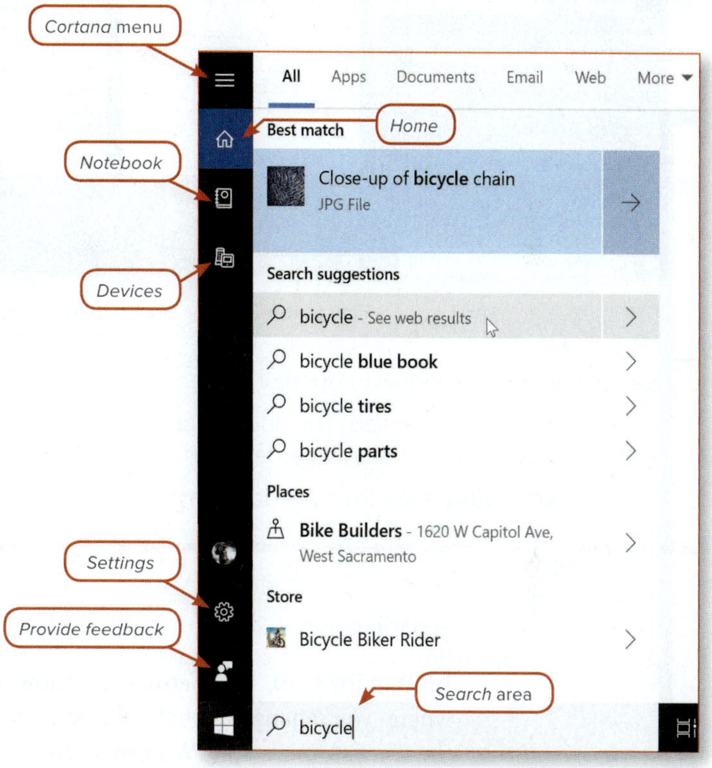

Figure Intro-18 Use ***Cortana*** **to search your computer, the internet, and the Microsoft Store**

Task View

Task View displays all open apps and windows as tiles on your desktop, and you can choose which item to display or close. This feature is very helpful when you have multiple items open and need to select or close one. Additionally, *Task View* displays a timeline of tasks you've worked on in Windows. Scroll down in *Task View* to display previous days.

▶HOW TO: Use Task View

1. Click the **Task View** button on the *Taskbar* (Figure Intro-19).
   - All open apps and windows display on the desktop (Figure Intro-20).

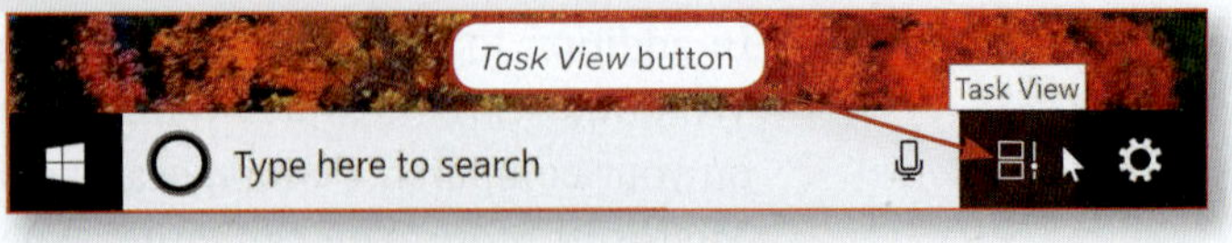

Figure Intro-19 ***Task View*** **button on the** ***Taskbar***

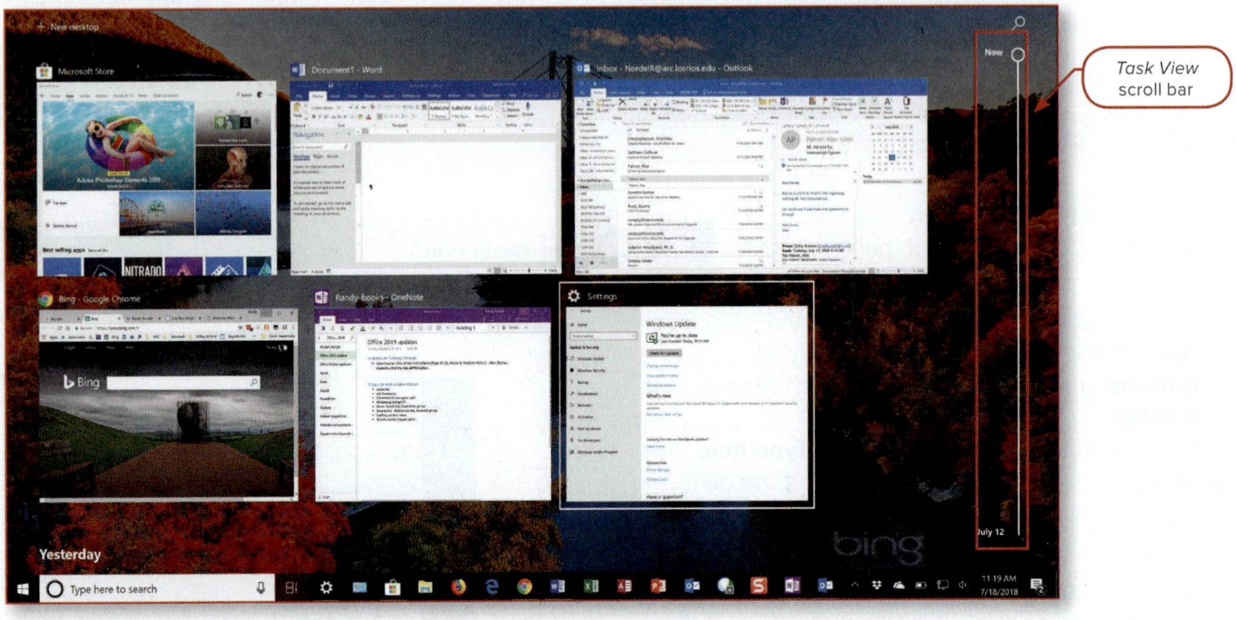

Figure Intro-20 ***Task View*** **with open apps and windows displayed on the desktop**

2. Select the app or window to open or close.
   - Click a tile to open an app. The app opens and *Task View* closes.
   - Click the **X** in the upper-right corner of an app to close an app. *Task View* remains open when you close an app.
3. Scroll down to view tasks from previous days.

Settings

In Windows 10, the ***Settings*** window is where you change global Windows settings, customize the Windows environment, add devices, and manage your Microsoft account. Click the **Settings** button (Figure Intro-21) on the *Taskbar* or *Start* menu to open the *Settings* window (Figure Intro-22). The following categories are typically available in the *Settings* window. *Settings* categories and options may vary depending on the version of Windows you are using and updates to Windows.

- ***System***: Display, notifications, and power
- ***Devices***: Bluetooth, printers, and mouse

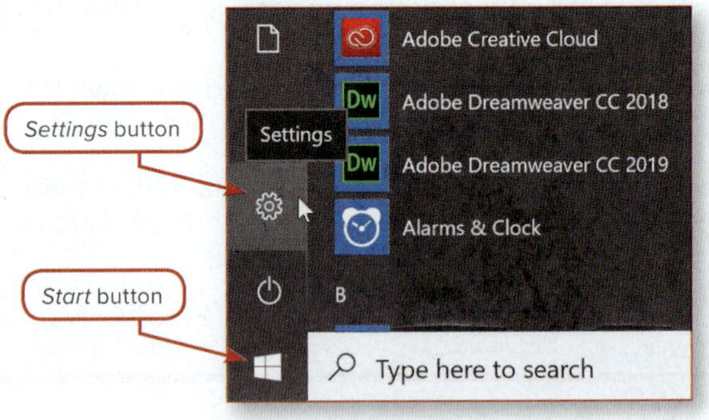

Figure Intro-21 ***Settings*** **button on the Start menu**

- ***Phone***: Link your Android and iPhone
- ***Network & internet***: Wi-Fi, airplane mode, and VPN
- ***Personalization***: Background, lock screen, and colors
- ***Apps***: Uninstall, defaults, and optional features
- ***Accounts***: Your account, email, sync, work, and family
- ***Time & Language***: Speech, region, and date
- ***Gaming***: Game bar, DVR, broadcasting, and Game Mode
- ***Ease of Access***: Narrator, magnifier, and high contrast
- ***Cortana***: Cortana languages, permissions, and notifications
- ***Privacy***: Location and camera
- ***Update & Security***: Windows Update, recovery, and backup

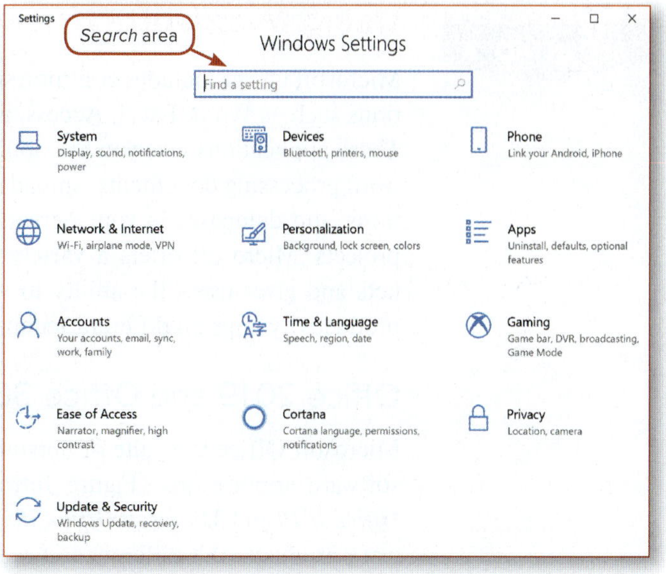

Figure Intro-22 ***Settings*** **window**

MORE INFO

If you can't find an item in *Settings,* use the *Search* dialog box (*Find a setting*) to type keywords. If *Settings* is not available on the *Taskbar,* you can find it in the list of apps on the *Start* menu.

Action Center

The ***Action Center*** in Windows 10 provides a quick glance of notifications and buttons to open other commonly used settings and features in Windows. The *Action Center* displays notifications such as emails and Windows notifications. Click an action button to turn on or off features or open other windows or apps such as the *Settings* menu (*All Settings* button) or OneNote (*Note* button). Click the **Action Center** button on the right side of the *Taskbar* (last button in the *System Tray*) to open the *Action Center* pane, which displays on the right side of your screen (Figure Intro-23).

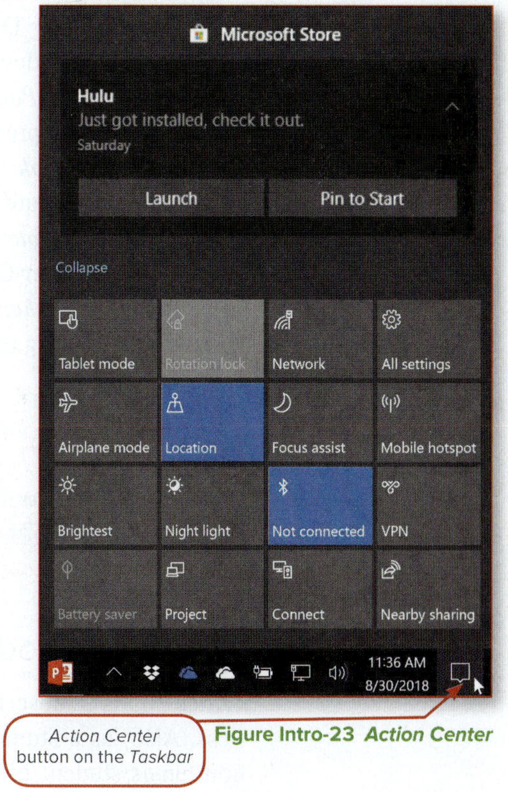

Figure Intro-23 ***Action Center***

ANOTHER WAY

Windows+A opens the *Action Center.* The *Windows* key is typically located near the bottom-left corner of the keyboard.

SLO INTRO. 2

Using Microsoft Office

Microsoft Office includes common software applications such as Word, Excel, Access, and PowerPoint. These applications give you the ability to work with word processing documents, spreadsheets, presentations, and databases in your personal and business projects. Microsoft offers a variety of Office products and gives users the ability to work with these productivity apps on different technology devices.

Figure Intro-24 Microsoft Office application tiles on the *Start* menu

Office 2019 and Office 365

Microsoft Office is a suite of personal and business software applications (Figure Intro-24). ***Microsoft Office 2019*** and ***Microsoft Office 365*** are similar software products; the difference is how you purchase the software. Office 2019 is the traditional model of purchasing the software, and you own that software for as long as you want to use it. Office 365 is a subscription that you pay monthly or yearly, similar to how you purchase Netflix or Spotify. If you subscribe to Office 365, you automatically receive updated versions of the applications when they are released.

The common applications typically included in Microsoft Office 2019 and 365 are described in the following list:

- ***Microsoft Word***: Word processing software used to create, format, and edit documents such as reports, letters, brochures, and resumes
- ***Microsoft Excel***: Spreadsheet software used to perform calculations on numerical data such as financial statements, budgets, and expense reports
- ***Microsoft Access***: Database software used to store, organize, compile, and report information such as product information, sales data, client information, and employee records
- ***Microsoft PowerPoint***: Presentation software used to graphically present information in slides such as a presentation on a new product or sales trends
- ***Microsoft Outlook***: Email and personal management software used to create and send email and to create and store calendar items, contacts, and tasks
- ***Microsoft OneNote***: Note-taking software used to take and organize notes, which can be shared with other Office applications
- ***Microsoft Publisher***: Desktop publishing software used to create professional-looking documents containing text, pictures, and graphics such as catalogs, brochures, and flyers

MORE INFO

Office 365 includes regular updates that include new and enhanced features, while Office 2019 does not include these regular updates. So, differences in features may exist between the Office 2019 and Office 365.

Office 365 Products, Versions, and Update Channels

Office 365 is a subscription to the Office applications and can be purchased for home or business. Also, as a student, you can get Office 365 for education free (https://products.office.com/en-us/student/office-in-education). The Office applications that come with an Office 365 subscription can vary depending on the Office 365 product subscription you have. With an Office 365 subscription, you can install the Office applications (both PC and Mac) on multiple computers and mobile devices.

Another advantage of an Office 365 subscription is regular updates that enhance the functionality of the apps. The version and build of your Office 365 is determined by the update channel, which is the frequency of updates. This is typically set by your school or business. If you have Office 365 Home or Personal, you determine the update channel. If you have an Office 365 for education or business, the college or business determines the update channel. The following are common update channels:

- ***Semi-annual Channel***: Receives updates two times a year in January and July
- ***Semi-annual Channel (Targeted)***: Receives new feature updates earlier than the Semi-annual Channel. These semi-annual updates are rolled out in March and September.
- ***Monthly Channel***: Receives new feature updates as soon as they are available, which is typically every month

HOW TO: View Your Office 365 Product Information

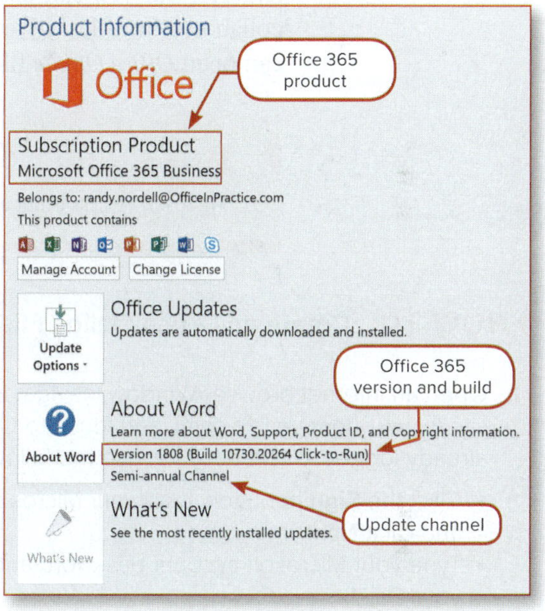

Figure Intro-25 ***Product Information*** **displayed in the** ***Account*** **area on the** ***Backstage*** **view**

1. Open an Office application and open a blank or existing file if necessary.
2. Click the **File** tab to open the *Backstage* view.
3. Click **Account** at the left to display *User Information* and *Product Information*.
   - The *Product Information* area displays the Office 365 product installed on your computer (Figure Intro-25).
   - The *About [Application]* area displays the version, build, and update channel.
   - The *Version* number indicates the year and month of the most recent update. For example, "Version 1808" means 2018 and the eighth month (August).
4. Click the **Update Options** button to select an update option: *Update Now, Disable Updates, View Updates,* or *About Updates*.
   - Click the **Update Now** button to manually check for Office 365 updates.
5. Click the **What's New** button to view the new features included in the most recent Office 365 updates for your update channel.
6. Close the **Back** arrow to close the *Backstage* view and return to the file.

Office Desktop Apps, Office Mobile Apps, and Office Online

Office desktop apps are the full-function Office 2019 or 365 programs installed on your computer (PC or Mac). Both Office 2019 and Office 365 are considered Office desktop apps. Because of the increased popularity and capabilities of tablets and mobile devices, Office software is also available for both tablets and smartphones. ***Office mobile apps*** are the Office 365 programs that can be installed on tablets or other mobile devices. Office mobile apps do not have the full range of advanced features available in Office desktop applications, but Office mobile apps provide users the ability to create, edit, save, and share Office files using many of the most common features in the Office suite of programs.

MORE INFO

Office mobile apps are also referred to as ***Office universal apps***.

The ***Office Online*** apps are free online apps from Microsoft that work in conjunction with your Microsoft account and *OneDrive* (Figure Intro-26). With *Office Online*, you can work with Office files online through a web browser, even on computers that do not have Office 2019 or 365 installed. Click the **App** launcher in the upper-left corner of *OneDrive* to display the *Office Online* applications. This list of *Office Online* apps may display differently depending on the type of Microsoft account you are using.

Figure Intro-26 *Office Online*

You can access *Office Online* from your *OneDrive* web page to create and edit Word documents, Excel workbooks, PowerPoint presentations, and OneNote notebooks. *Office Online* is a scaled-down version of Office and not as robust in terms of features, but you can use it to create, edit, print, share, and collaborate on files. If you need more advanced features, you can open *Office Online* files in the desktop version of Office.

MORE INFO

Microsoft Access is not available in *Office Online* or as an Office mobile app.

HOW TO: Create an Office Online File

1. Open an internet browser Window, navigate to the *OneDrive* web site (www.onedrive.live.com), and log in to *OneDrive*. If you are not already logged in to *OneDrive*, use the following steps.
   - Click the **Sign in** button, type your Microsoft account email address, and click **Next**.
   - Type your Microsoft account password and click **Sign in** to open your *OneDrive* page.
2. Click the **New** button and select the type of *Office Online* file to create (Figure Intro-27).
   - A new file opens in the *Office Online* program.
   - The new file is saved in your *OneDrive* folder (both online and on your computer).

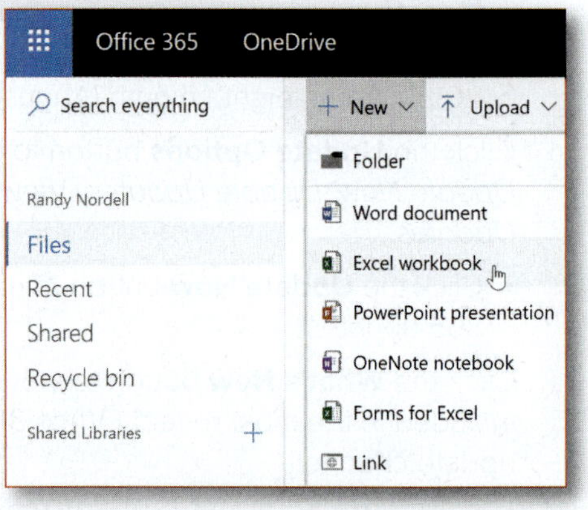

Figure Intro-27 Create an *Office Online* file from your online *OneDrive* page

3. Rename the file by clicking the file name at the top of the file, typing a new file name, and pressing **Enter** (Figure Intro-28).
   - You can also click the **File** tab to open the *Backstage* view, select **Save As**, and choose **Save As** or **Rename**.
   - Click the **Open in *[Office application]*** button (for example, **Open in Excel**) to open the file in the Office desktop application (see Figure Intro-28).
4. Close the browser tab or window to close the file.
   - *Office Online* automatically saves the file as you make changes.

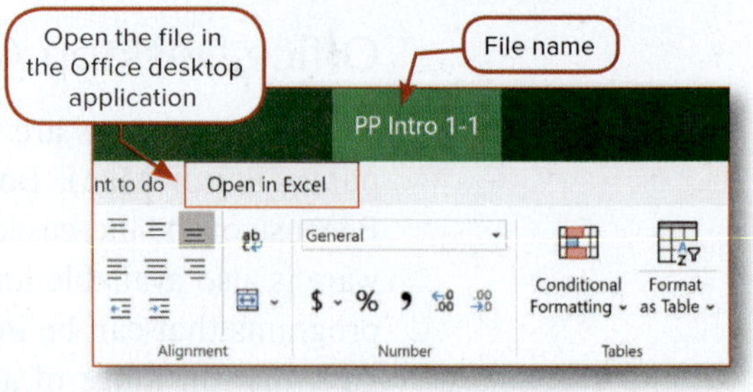

Figure Intro-28 Rename an *Office Online* file

Open an Office Desktop Application

When using Windows 10, you open an Office desktop application by clicking the application tile on the *Start* menu or the application icon on the *Taskbar*. If your *Start* menu and *Taskbar* do not display the Office applications, click the **Start** button and select **Word**, **Excel**, **Access**, or **PowerPoint** from the alphabetic list of apps to launch the application (Figure Intro-29).

You can also use *Cortana* to quickly locate an Office desktop app (Figure Intro-30).

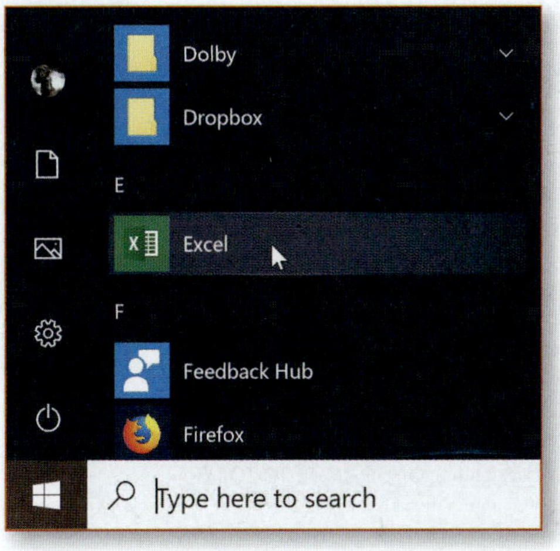

Figure Intro-29 Open an Office desktop app from the *All apps* area on the *Start* menu

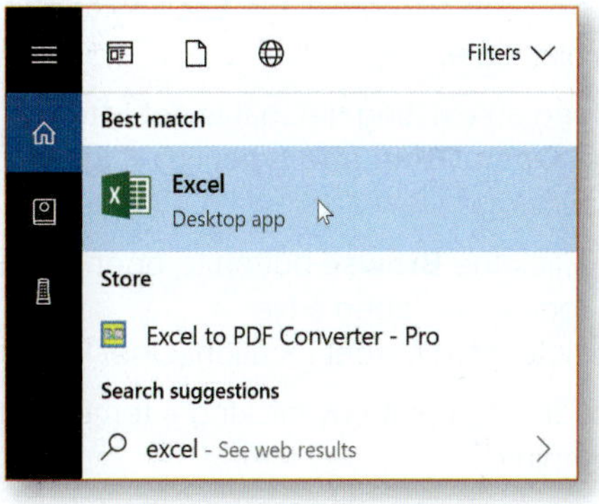

Figure Intro-30 Use *Cortana* to find and open an app

MORE INFO

Add commonly used apps to your Windows *Start* menu and/or *Taskbar* to save time. See the "Customize the *Start* Menu" and "Customize the *Taskbar*" sections in *SLO Intro.1: Using Windows 10.*

Office Start Page

Most of the Office applications (except Outlook and OneNote) display a ***Start page*** when you launch the application (Figure Intro-31). From this *Start* page, you can create a new blank file (for example, a Word document, an Excel workbook, an Access database, or a PowerPoint presentation), create a file from an online template, search for an online template, open a recently used file, or open another file. These options vary depending on the Office application.

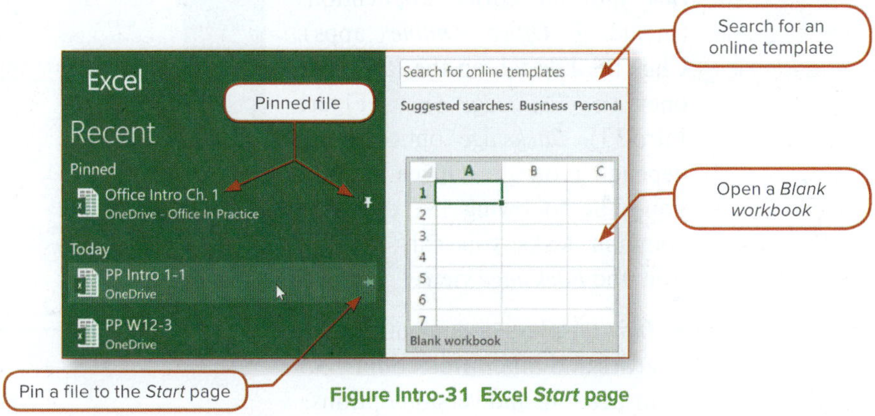

Figure Intro-31 Excel *Start* page

▸HOW TO: Use the Office Start Page

1. Open an Office application from the *Start* page or *Taskbar.*
2. Open a file listed in the *Recent* area on the left side of the *Start* menu by clicking the file name. The file opens in the working area of the Office application.
   - The *Recent* area on the left side of the *Start* page displays recently used and pinned files.
3. Open a new blank file by clicking the **Blank *[file type]*** tile (*Blank workbook, Blank document,* etc.) to the right of the *Recent* area (see Figure Intro-31).
   - You can also press the **Esc** key to exit the *Start* page and open a new blank file.
4. Open an existing file that is not listed in the *Recent* area by clicking the **Open Other *[file type]*** link (Figure Intro-32). The *Open* area on the *Backstage* view displays.
   - Click the **Browse** button to open the *Open* dialog box where you can locate and open a file.
   - Select a different location (*OneDrive* or *This PC*) and select a file to open.

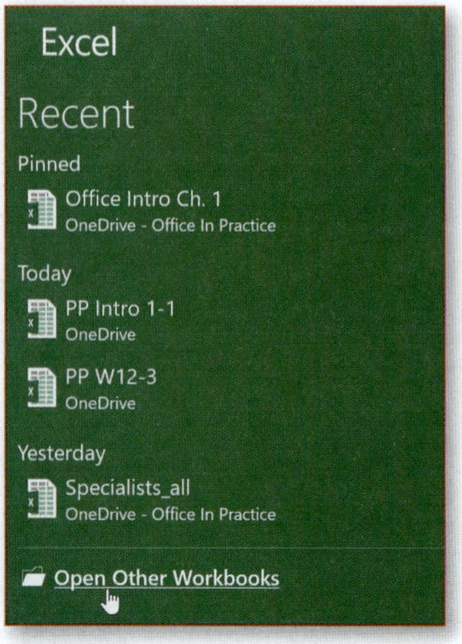

Figure Intro-32 *Open Other Workbooks* link on the *Start* page

5. Open a template by clicking a template file on the right or searching for a template.
   - Search for a template by typing keywords in the *Search* area on the *Start* page.
   - Click a link to one of the categories below the *Search* area to display templates in that category.
6. Pin a frequently used file to the *Start* page by clicking the **pin** icon (see Figure Intro-31).
   - The pin icon is on the right side of items listed in the *Recent* area and at the bottom right of templates displayed in the *Templates* area (to the right of the *Recent* area).
   - Pinned files display at the top of the *Recent* area.

MORE INFO

In Access, you have to open an existing database or create a new one to enter the program.

Backstage View

Office incorporates the ***Backstage* view** into all Office applications (including *Office Online* apps). Click the **File** tab on the *Ribbon* to open the *Backstage* view (Figure Intro-33). *Backstage* options vary depending on the Office application. The following list describes common tasks you can perform from the *Backstage* view:

- ***Info***: Displays document properties and other protection, inspection, and version options.

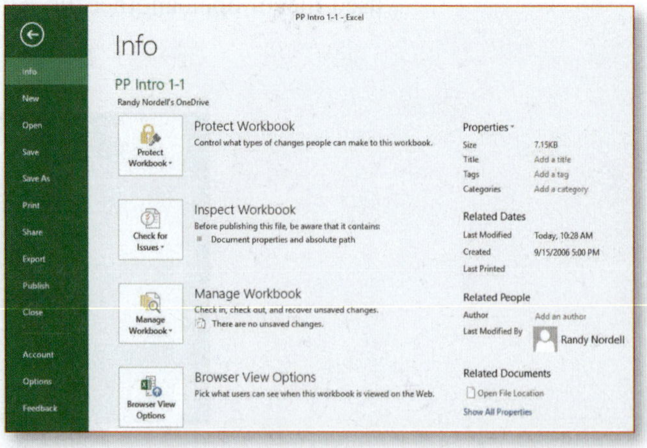

Figure Intro-33 *Backstage* view in Excel

- ***New***: Creates a new blank file or a new file from a template or theme.
- ***Open***: Opens an existing file from a designated location or a recently opened file.
- ***Save***: Saves a file. If the file has not been named, the *Save As* dialog box opens when you select this option.
- ***Save As***: Opens the *Save As* dialog box.
- ***Print***: Prints a file, displays a preview of the file, or displays print options.
- ***Share***: Invites people to share a file or email a file.
- ***Export***: Creates a PDF file from a file or saves it as a different file type.
- ***Close***: Closes an open file.
- ***Account***: Displays your Microsoft account information.
- ***Options***: Opens the *[Application] Options* dialog box (for example, *Excel Options*).

MORE INFO

Options on the *Backstage* view vary depending on the Office application you are using.

Office Help—Tell Me

In all the Office 2019/365 applications, ***Tell Me*** is the help feature (Figure Intro-34). This feature displays the commands in the Office application related to your search. The *Help* feature in older versions of Office displayed articles describing the feature and how to use it. The *Tell Me* feature provides command options that take you directly to a command or dialog box. For example, if you type *PivotTable* in the *Tell Me* search box in Excel, the results include the option to open the *Create PivotTable* dialog box, as well as other options such as *Recommended PivotTables* and *Summarize with PivotTable*.

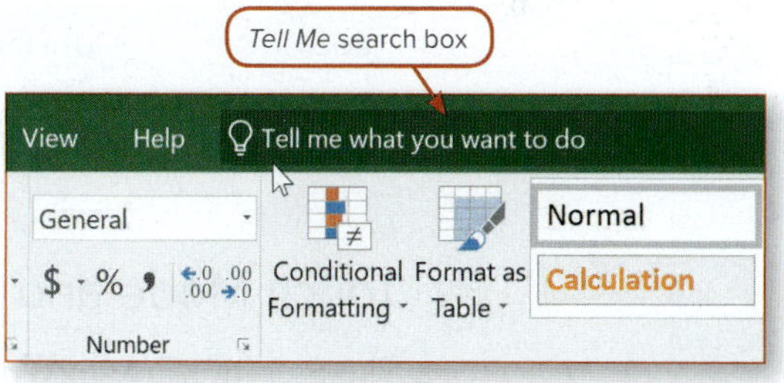

Figure Intro-34 ***Tell Me*** **search box**

HOW TO: Use Tell Me

1. Place the insertion point in the **Tell me what you want to do** search box at the top of the *Ribbon* (see Figure Intro-34).
2. Type keywords for the command or feature for which you are searching.
3. Select an option from the search results list (Figure Intro-35).
   - When you select a search result, it may apply a command, open a dialog box, or display a gallery of command choices.

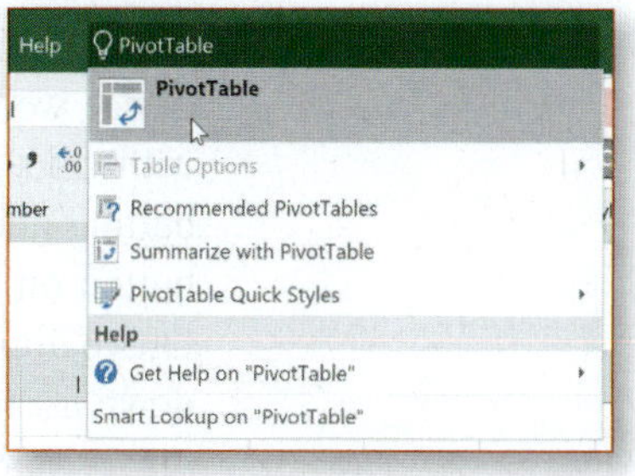

Figure Intro-35 ***Tell Me*** **search results**

ANOTHER WAY

Alt+Q places the insertion point in the *Tell Me* dialog box.
The previous *Help* feature is still available in Office. Press **F1** to open the *Help* pane on the right.

Mouse and Pointers

If you are using Office on a desktop or laptop computer, use your mouse (or touchpad) to navigate around files, click tabs and buttons, select text and objects, move text and objects, and resize objects. Table Intro-1 lists mouse and pointer terminology used in Office.

Table Intro-1: Mouse and Pointer Terminology

Term	Description
Pointer	Move your mouse to move the pointer on your screen. A variety of pointers are used in different contexts in Office applications. The following pointers are available in most of the Office applications (the appearance of these pointers varies depending on the application and the context used): • ***Selection pointer:*** Select text or an object. • ***Move pointer:*** Move text or an object. • ***Copy pointer:*** Copy text or an object. • ***Resize pointer:*** Resize objects or table columns or rows. • ***Crosshair:*** Draw a shape.
Insertion point	The vertical flashing line indicating where you type text in a file or text box. Click the left mouse button to position the insertion point.
Click	Click the left mouse button. Used to select an object or button or to place the insertion point in the selected location.
Double-click	Click the left mouse button twice. Used to select text.
Right-click	Click the right mouse button. Used to display the context menu and the mini toolbar.
Scroll	Use the scroll wheel on the mouse to scroll up and down through your file. You can also use the horizontal or vertical scroll bars at the bottom and right of an Office file window to move around in a file.

Touch Mode and Touch-Screen Gestures

The user interface in Windows 10 and Office 2019 has improved touch features to facilitate the use of Windows and the Office applications on a tablet computer or smartphone. On tablets and smartphones, you can use a touch screen rather than using a mouse, so the process of selecting text and objects and navigating around a file is different from a computer without a touch screen.

In Office 2019/365, ***Touch mode*** optimizes the Office working environment when using a computer with a touch screen to provide more space between buttons and commands. Click the **Touch/Mouse Mode** button on the *Quick Access* toolbar (upper left of the Office app window) and select **Touch** from the drop-down list to enable *Touch* mode (Figure Intro-36). To turn off *Touch* mode, select **Mouse** from the *Touch/Mouse Mode* drop-down list.

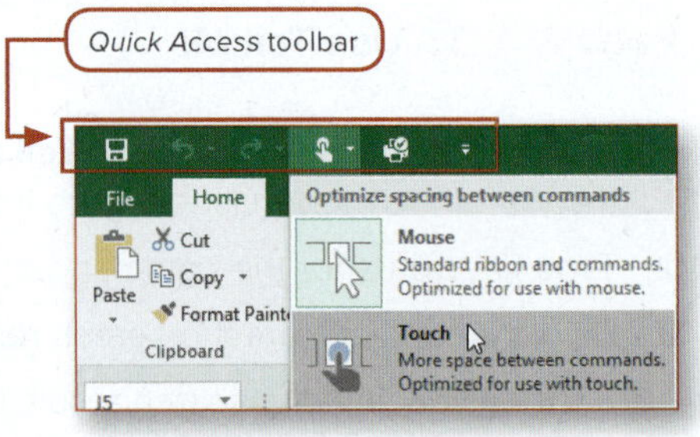

Figure Intro-36 Turn on *Touch* mode

> **MORE INFO**
>
> The *Touch/Mouse Mode* button displays on the *Quick Access* toolbar when using a touch-screen computer.

Table Intro-2 lists common gestures used when working on a tablet or smartphone (these gestures vary depending on the application used and the context).

Table Intro-2: Touch-Screen Gestures

Gesture	Used To	How To
Tap	Select text or an object or position the insertion point. Double tap to edit text in an object or cell.	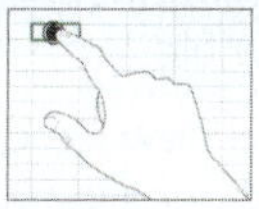
Pinch	Zoom in or resize an object.	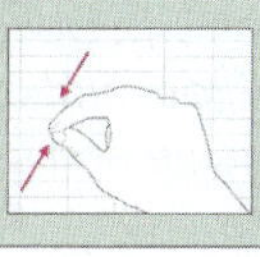
Stretch	Zoom out or resize an object.	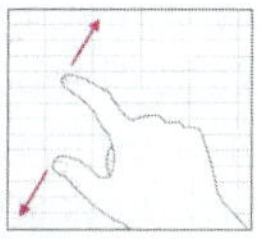
Slide	Move an object or selected text.	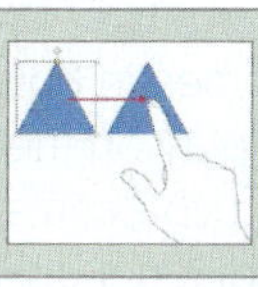
Swipe	Select text or multiple objects.	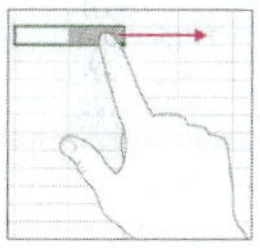

MORE INFO

Window 10 has a ***Tablet mode*** that optimizes all of Windows and apps for touch screens. When you turn on the *Tablet mode* feature in Windows, the *Touch mode* in Office apps turns on automatically. Click the **Action Center** button on the Windows *Taskbar* and click the **Tablet mode** button to turn on this feature in Windows.

SLO INTRO. 3

Creating, Saving, Closing, and Opening Office Files

Creating, saving, opening, and closing files is primarily done from the *Start* page or *Backstage* view of the active Office application. Both the *Start* page and the *Backstage* view provide many options and a central location to perform these tasks. You can also use shortcut commands to create, save, and open files.

Create a New File

When you create a new file in an Office application, you can create a new blank file or a new file based on a template (in PowerPoint, you can also create a presentation based on a theme). On the *Start* page, click **Blank *[file type]*** to create a new blank file in the application you are using (in Word, you begin with a blank document; in Excel, a blank workbook; in Access, a blank desktop database; and in PowerPoint, a blank presentation).

▸HOW TO: Create a New File from the Start Page

1. Open an Office application. The *Start* page displays when the application opens (Figure Intro-37).
2. Click **Blank *[file type]*** to open a new file.
   - The new file displays a generic file name (for example, *Document1, Book1,* or *Presentation1*). You can rename and save this file later.
   - When creating a new Access database, you are prompted to name the new file when you create it.
   - A variety of templates (and themes in PowerPoint only) display on the *Start* page, and you can search for additional online templates and themes using the *Search* text box at the top of the *Start* page.

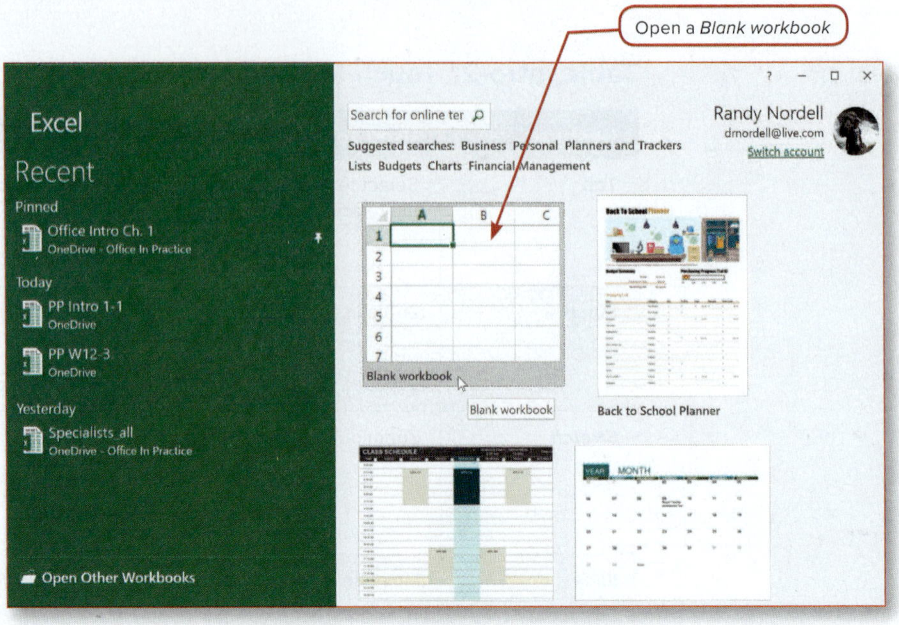

Figure Intro-37 *Start* page in Excel

MORE INFO

Esc closes the *Start* page opens a blank file in the Office application (except in Access).

If you have been using an application already and want to create a new file, you create it from the *Backstage* view. From the *Backstage* view, the new file options are available in the *New* area.

▸HOW TO: Create a New File from the Backstage View

1. Click the **File** tab to display the *Backstage* view.
2. Select **New** on the left to display the *New* area (Figure Intro-38).
3. Click **Blank *[file type]*** to open a new blank file or select a template or theme to use.
   - The new file displays a generic file name (*Document1, Book1,* or *Presentation1*). You can name and save this file later.
   - When you are creating a new Access database, you are prompted to name the new file when you create it.

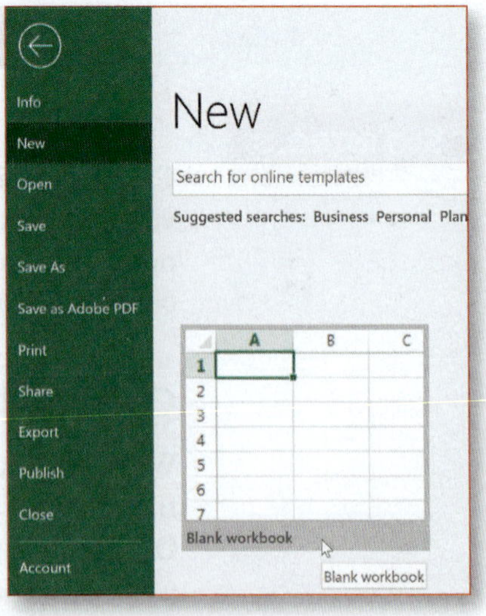

Figure Intro-38 *New* area on the *Backstage* view in Excel

> **ANOTHER WAY**
>
> **Ctrl+N** opens a new file from within an Office application. In Access, **Ctrl+N** opens the *New* area in the *Backstage* view.

Save a File

In Access, you name a file as you create it, but in Word, Excel, and PowerPoint, you name a file after you have created it. When you save a file, you type a name for the file and select the location to save the file. You can save a file on your computer, an online storage location such as *OneDrive,* or portable device, such as a USB drive.

HOW TO: Save a File

1. Click the **File** tab to display the *Backstage* view.
2. Select **Save** or **Save As** on the left to display the *Save As* area (Figure Intro-39).
   - If the file has not already been saved, clicking *Save* or *Save As* takes you to the *Save As* area on the *Backstage* view.
3. Click the **Browse** button to open the *Save As* dialog box (Figure Intro-40).
   - Alternatively, type the file name in the *Enter file name here* text box and click **Save**. To change the save location, click the **More options** link to open the *Save As* dialog box or select a save location at the left (*OneDrive* or *This PC*) and select a folder from the list of folders (see Figure Intro-39).
4. Select a location to save the file in the *Folder* list on the left.
5. Type a name for the file in the *File name* area.
   - By default, Office selects the file type, but you can change the file type from the *Save as type* drop-down list.
6. Click **Save** to close the dialog box and save the file.

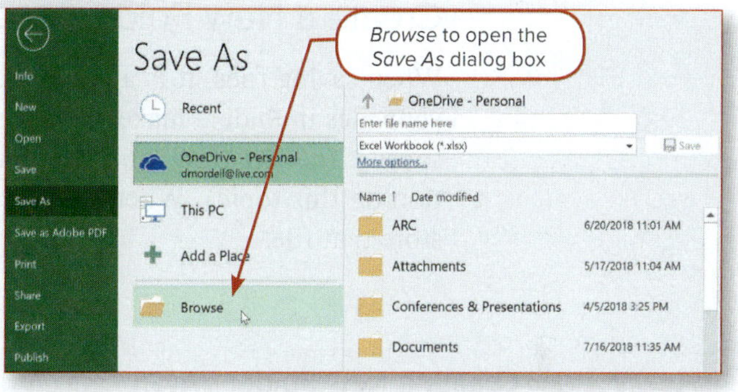

Figure Intro-39 ***Save As*** **area on the** ***Backstage*** **view in Excel**

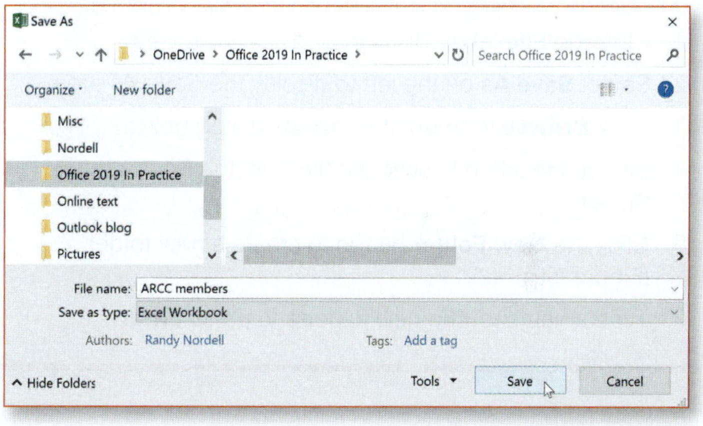

Figure Intro-40 ***Save As*** **dialog box**

> **ANOTHER WAY**
>
> **Ctrl+S** opens the *Save As* area on the *Backstage* view when a file has not been named. If a file has already been named, **Ctrl+S** saves the file without opening the *Backstage* view. **F12** opens the *Save As* dialog box.

> **MORE INFO**
>
> If you save a file in *OneDrive,* you have access to that file from any computer with internet access. Also, you can share and collaborate on files stored in *OneDrive. OneDrive* is one of the folders in the *Save As* dialog box.

AutoSave

AutoSave is a new feature that automatically saves a file that is stored on *OneDrive,* Microsoft's cloud storage area. The *AutoSave* feature turns on by default when you save a file to *OneDrive,* and changes made to the file are automatically saved as you work on a file.

Office 2019 Note: The *AutoSave* feature is not available in Office 2019.

This feature displays in the upper-left corner of the file (Figure Intro-41). Click the **AutoSave** button to turn it on or off. When *AutoSave* is on, the save options on the *Backstage* view change from *Save* and *Save As* to ***Save a Copy.***

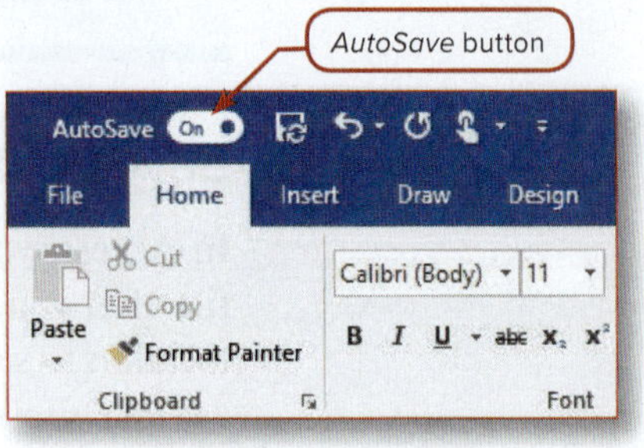

Figure Intro-41 *AutoSave* feature

Create a New Folder When Saving a File

When saving files, it is a good practice to create folders to organize your files. Organizing your files in folders makes it easier to find files and saves time when you are searching for a specific file (see *SLO Intro.8: Organizing and Customizing Folders and Files* for more information on this topic). When you save an Office file, you can also create a folder in which to store that file.

HOW TO: Create a New Folder When Saving a File

1. Click the **File** tab to display the *Backstage* view.
2. Select **Save As** on the left to display the *Save As* area.
3. Click **Browse** to open the *Save As* dialog box.
4. Select a location to save the file from the *Folder* list on the left.
5. Click the **New Folder** button to create a new folder (Figure Intro-42).
6. Type a name for the new folder and press **Enter**.

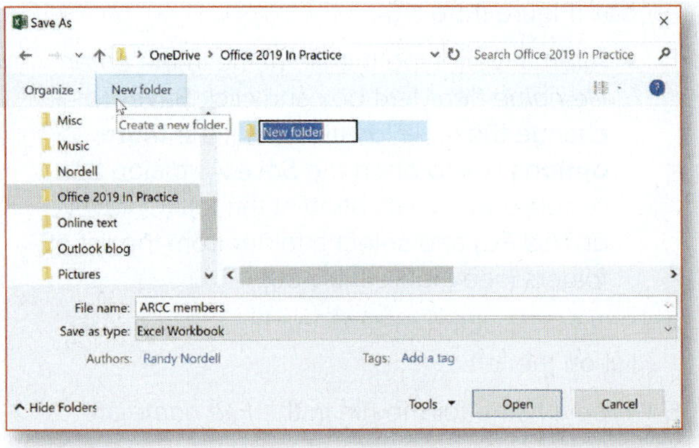

Figure Intro-42 Create a new folder

ANOTHER WAY

F12 opens the *Save As* dialog box (except in Access). On a laptop, you might have to press **Fn+F12**. See more about the *Fn* (Function) key in *SLO Intro. 7: Using Context Menus, the Mini Toolbar, and Keyboard Shortcuts.*

Save As a Different File Name

After you have saved a file, you can save it again with a different file name. If you do this, you preserve the original file, and you can continue to revise the second file for a different purpose.

▸ HOW TO: Save As a Different File Name

1. Click the **File** tab to display the *Backstage* view.
2. Select **Save As** on the left to display the *Save As* area.
3. Click the **Browse** button to open the *Save As* dialog box (see Figure Intro-42).
4. Select a location to save the file from the *Folder* list on the left.
5. Type a new name for the file in the *File name* area.
6. Click **Save** to close the dialog box and save the file.

MORE INFO

If *AutoSave* is turned on, ***Save a Copy*** is the save option on the *Backstage* view rather than *Save* and *Save As*.

Office File Types

By default, Office saves a file in the most current file format for that application. You also have the option of saving files in older versions of the Office application. For example, you can save a Word document as an older version to share with or send to someone who uses an older version of Word. Each file has an extension at the end of the file name that determines the file type. The ***file name extension*** is automatically added to a file when you save it. Table Intro-3 table lists common file types used in the different Office applications.

Table Intro-3: Office File Types

File Type	Extension	File Type	Extension
Word Document	*.docx*	Access Database	*.accdb*
Word Template	*.dotx*	Access Template	*.accdt*
Word 97-2003 Document	*.doc*	Access Database (2000-2003 format)	*.mdb*
Rich Text Format	*.rtf*	PowerPoint Presentation	*.pptx*
Excel Workbook	*.xlsx*	PowerPoint Template	*.potx*
Excel Template	*.xltx*	PowerPoint 97-2003 Presentation	*.ppt*
Excel 97-2003 Workbook	*.xls*	Portable Document Format (PDF)	*.pdf*
Comma Separated Values (CSV)	*.csv*		

Close a File

You can close a file using the following different methods:

- Click the **File** tab and select **Close** on the left.
- Press **Ctrl+W**.
- Click the **X** in the upper-right corner of the file window. This method closes the file and the program if only one file is open in the application.

When you close a file, you are prompted to save the file if it has not been named or if changes were made after the file was last saved (Figure Intro-43). Click **Save** to save and close the file or click **Don't Save** to close the file without saving. Click **Cancel** to return to the file.

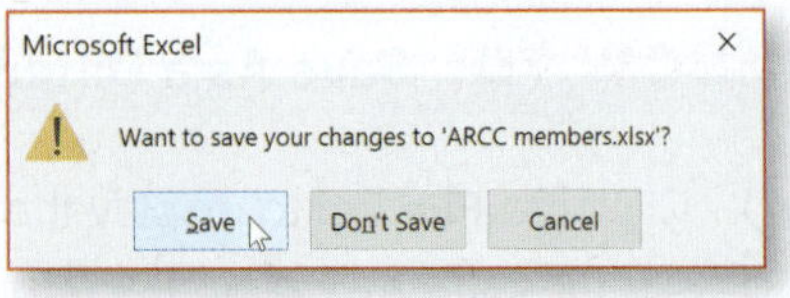

Figure Intro-43 Prompt to save a document before closing

Open an Existing File

You can open an existing file from the *Start* page when you open an Office application or while you are working on another Office file.

▸HOW TO: Open a File from the Start Page

1. Open an Office application to display the *Start* page.
2. Select a file to open in the *Recent* area on the left (Figure Intro-44).
   - If you select a file in the *Recent* area that has been renamed, moved, or is on a storage device not connected to the computer, you receive an error message.
3. Alternatively, click **Open Other *[file type]*** (for example, *Open Other Presentations*) to display the *Open* area of the *Backstage* view (see Figure Intro-44).
   - Click the **Browse** button to open the *Open* dialog box (Figure Intro-45).
   - Select a location from the *Folder* list on the left.
   - Select the file to open and click the **Open** button.
   - If the file opens in *Protected View*, click the **Enable Editing** button to enable you to edit the file.

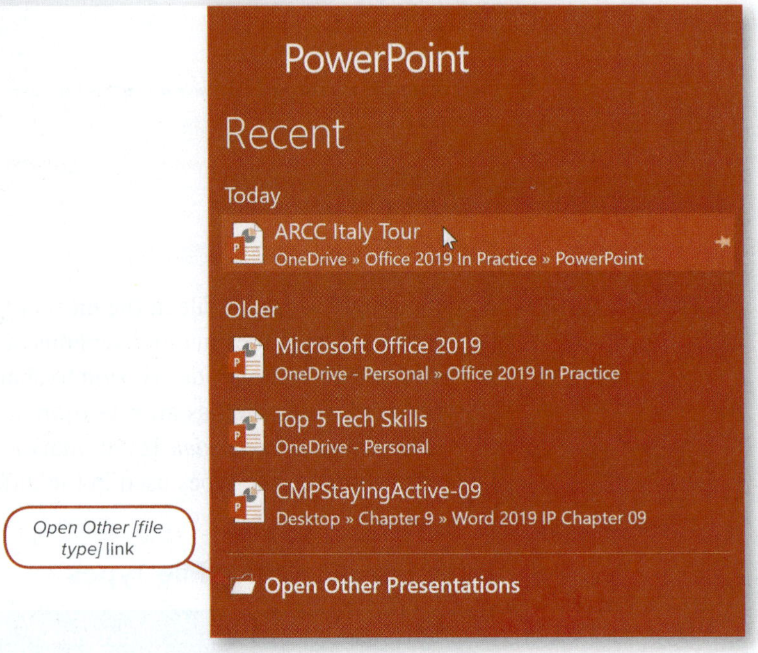

Figure Intro-44 Open a *Recent* file from the *Start* page

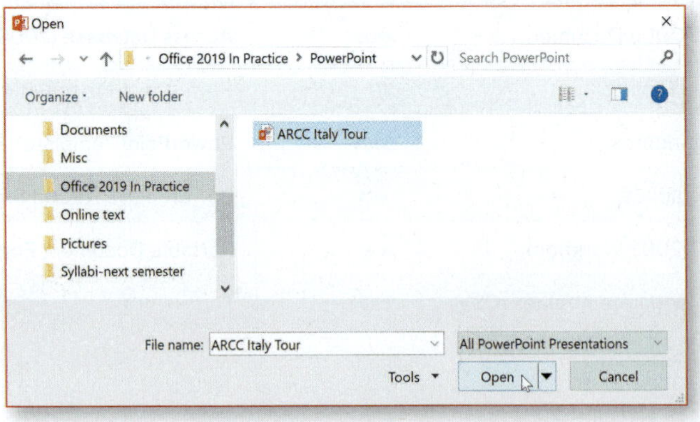

Figure Intro-45 *Open* dialog box

When working on a file in an Office application, you might want to open another file. You can open an existing file from within an Office application using the *Open* area on the *Backstage* view.

MORE INFO

When opening a file from an online location, Office may open the file in *Protected* view. If the file opens in *Protected View,* click the **Enable Editing** button to edit the file.

HOW TO: Open a File from the Backstage View

1. Click the **File** tab from within an open Office application to display the *Backstage* view.
2. Click **Open** on the left to display the *Open* area on the *Backstage* view (Figure Intro-46).
3. Click the **Browse** button to open the *Open* dialog box.
   - Alternatively, select a file to open from the list of *Recent* files on the right of the *Open* area on the *Backstage* view.
4. Select a location from the *Folder* list on the left.
5. Select the file to open and click the **Open** button.
   - If the file opens in *Protected View,* click the **Enable Editing** button to enable you to edit the file.

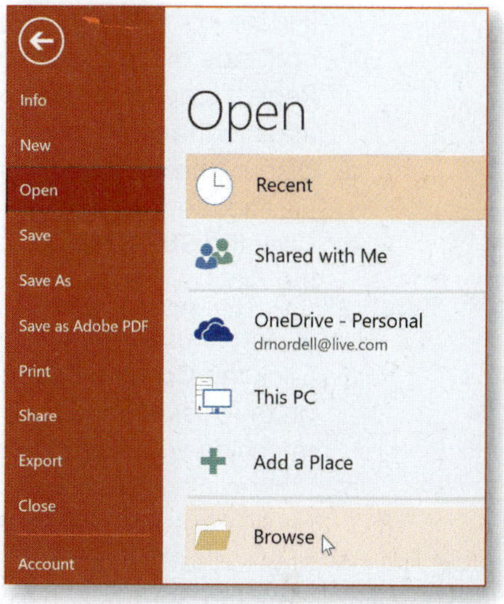

Figure Intro-46 ***Open*** **area on the** ***Backstage*** **view**

ANOTHER WAY

Press **Ctrl+F12** to open the *Open* dialog box when you are in the working area of an Office application (except in Access). On laptops, you might have to press **Fn+Ctrl+F12**.

You can also open a file from a *File Explorer* folder. When you double-click a file in a *File Explorer* folder, the file opens in the appropriate Office application. Windows recognizes the file name extension and launches the correct Office application.

PAUSE & PRACTICE: INTRO-1

For this project, you log in to Windows using your Microsoft account, customize the Windows *Start* menu and *Taskbar,* create and save a PowerPoint presentation, create a folder, open and rename an Excel workbook, and use Windows 10 features.

File Needed: ***ARCC2020Budget-Intro.xlsx*** *(Student data files are available in the* Library *of your SIMnet account.)*
Completed Project File Names: ***[your initials] PP Intro-1a.pptx*** and ***[your initials] PP Intro-1b.xlsx***

1. Log in to Windows using your Microsoft account if you are not already logged in.
   a. If you don't have a Microsoft account, you can create a free account at https://signup.live.com.
   b. If you are using a computer on your college campus, you may be required to log in to the computer using your college user name and password.
2. Pin the Office apps to the *Start* menu. If these apps tiles are already on the *Start* menu, skip steps 2a–e. You can pin other apps of your choice to the *Start* menu.
   a. Click the **Start** button at the bottom left of your screen to open the *Start* menu.
   b. Locate *Access* in the alphabetic list of apps, right-click the **Access** app, and select **Pin to Start** (Figure Intro-47). The app displays as a tile on the right side of the *Start* menu.
   c. Repeat step 2b to pin **Excel**, **PowerPoint**, and **Word** apps to the *Start* menu.
   d. Display the *Start* menu and drag these Office app tiles so they are close to each other.
   e. Click the **Start** button (or press the **Esc** key) to close the *Start* menu.

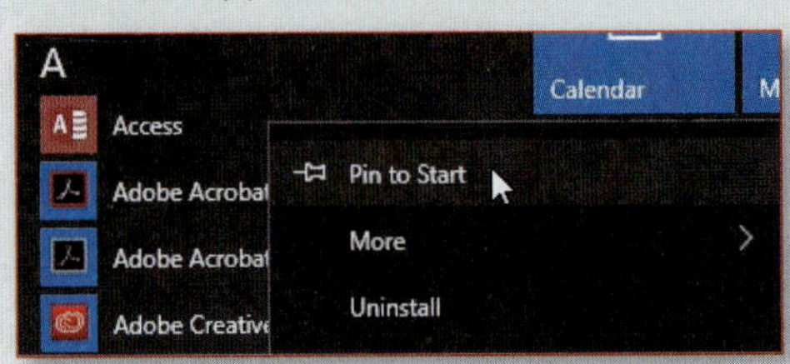

Figure Intro-47 Pin *Access* to the *Start* menu

3. Use *Cortana* and the *Start* menu to pin Office apps to the *Taskbar.*
   a. Click the **Cortana** button (to the right of the *Start* button) on the *Taskbar* and type Access. *Cortana* displays content matching your search.
   b. Right-click the **Access** option near the top of the *Cortana* pane and select **Pin to taskbar** (Figure Intro-48). The app pins to the *Taskbar.*
   c. Click the **Start** button to open the *Start* menu.
   d. Right-click the **Excel** tile on the right side of the *Start* menu, click **More**, and select **Pin to taskbar**. The app pins to the *Taskbar.*
   e. Use either of the methods described above to pin the **PowerPoint** and **Word** apps to the *Taskbar.*
   f. Drag the Office apps on the *Taskbar* to rearrange them to your preference.

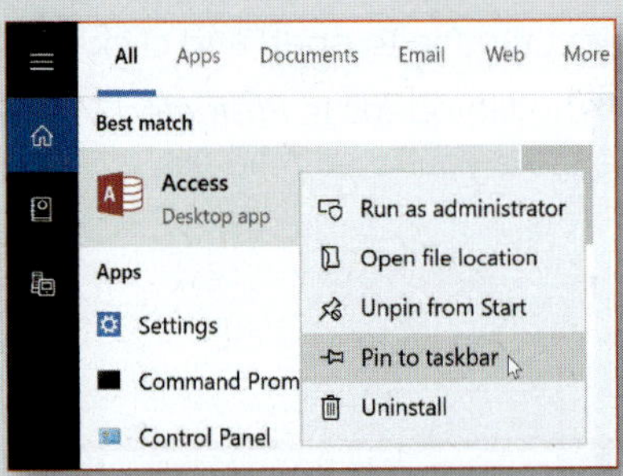

Figure Intro-48 Use *Cortana* to find an Office app and pin it to the *Taskbar*

4. Create a PowerPoint presentation and save the presentation in a new folder.
   a. Click the **PowerPoint** app tile on your *Start* menu to open the application.
   b. Click **Blank Presentation** on the PowerPoint *Start* page to create a new blank presentation.
   c. Click the **Click to add title** placeholder and type American River Cycling Club to replace the placeholder text.
   d. Click the **File** tab to open the *Backstage* view and click **Save As** on the left to display the *Save As* area.
   e. Click **Browse** to open the *Save As* dialog box (Figure Intro-49).
   f. Select a location to save the file from the *Folder* list on the left. If the *OneDrive* folder is an option, select **OneDrive**. If it is not, select the **Documents** folder in the *This PC* folder. You can also save to a portable storage device if you have one.
   g. Click the **New Folder** button to create a new folder.

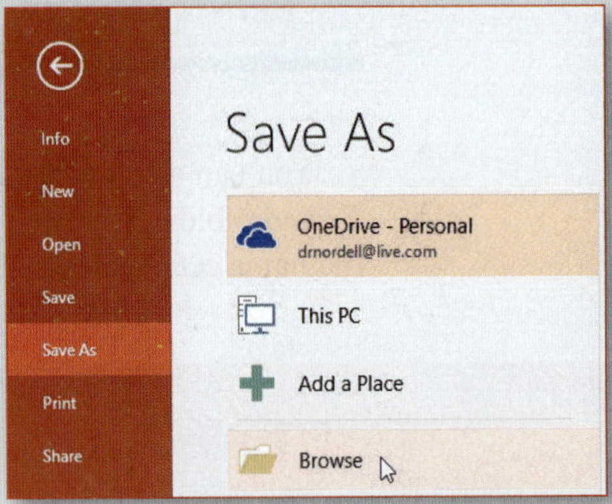

Figure Intro-49 *Save As* area on the *Backstage* view in PowerPoint

h. Type American River Cycling Club as the name of the new folder and press **Enter** (Figure Intro-50).

i. Double-click the ***American River Cycling Club*** folder to open it.

j. Type [your initials] PP Intro-1a in the *File name* area.

k. Click **Save** to close the dialog box and save the presentation. Leave the file and PowerPoint open. If you saved your file to OneDrive, you may receive a notification about automatic saving.

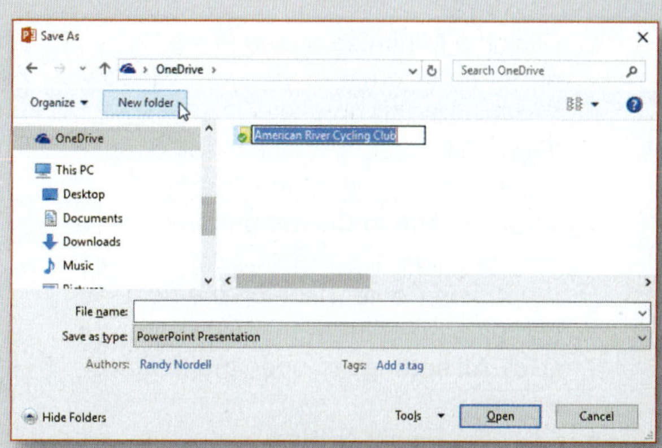

Figure Intro-50 Create a new folder from the *Save As* dialog box

5. Open an Excel file and save as a different file name.
   a. Click the **Excel 2019** app button on the *Taskbar* to open the *Start* page in Excel.
   b. Click the **Open Other Workbooks** link on the bottom left of the Excel *Start* page to display the *Open* area of the *Backstage* view.
   c. Click **Browse** to open the *Open* dialog box (Figure Intro-51).
   d. Browse to your student data files and select the ***ARCC2020Budget-Intro*** file.
   e. Click **Open** to open the workbook. If the file opens in *Protected View,* click the **Enable Editing** button.
   f. Click the **File** tab to open the *Backstage* view.
   g. Click **Save As** on the left to display the *Save As* area and click **Browse** to open the *Save As* dialog box. If this file is stored on OneDrive, click **Save a Copy** rather than *Save As*.
   h. Locate the ***American River Cycling Club*** folder (created in step 4h) in the *Folder* list on the left and double-click the folder to open it.
   i. Type [your initials] PP Intro-1b in the *File name* area.
   j. Click **Save** to close the dialog box and save the workbook. Leave the file and Excel open.

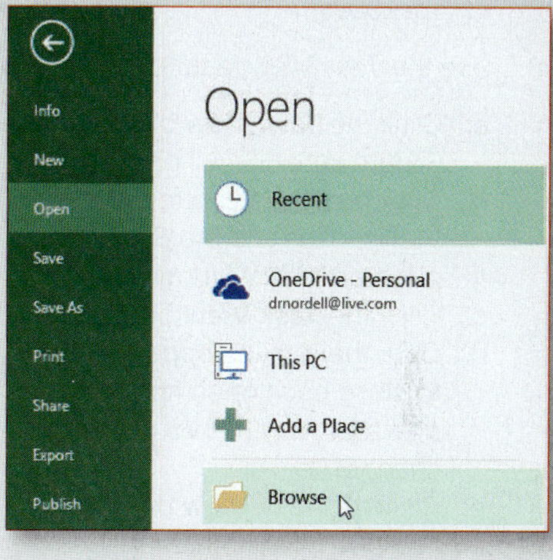

Figure Intro-51 *Open* area on the *Backstage* view

6. Use the *Tell Me* feature in Excel to find a command.
   a. Click the **Tell Me** search box on the *Ribbon* of the Excel window and type PivotTable (Figure Intro-52).
   b. Click **PivotTable** to open the *Create PivotTable* dialog box.
   c. Click the **X** in the upper-right corner of the *Create PivotTable* dialog box to close it.

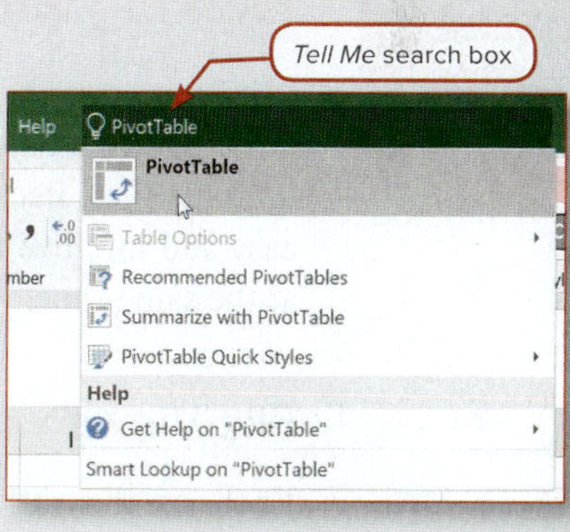

Figure Intro-52 Use the *Tell Me* feature to find a command

7. Open the *Microsoft Store* app, the *Action Center*, and the *Settings* window.
   a. Click the **Cortana** search area and type Microsoft Store.
   b. Click **Microsoft Store** at the top of the *Cortana* pane to open the *Microsoft Store* app.
   c. Click the **Apps** tab in the top left and browse the available apps in the Microsoft Store.

d. Click the **Minimize** button in the upper-right corner of the *Store* window to minimize this app (Figure Intro-53). The app is still open, but it is minimized on the *Taskbar.*

e. Click the **Action Center** button on the right side of the *Taskbar* to display the *Action Center* pane on the right (Figure Intro-54).

f. Click **All settings** to open the *Settings* window.

g. Click the **Find a setting** search box, type Printer, and view the search results.

h. Click the **Minimize** button to minimize the *Settings* windows to the *Taskbar.*

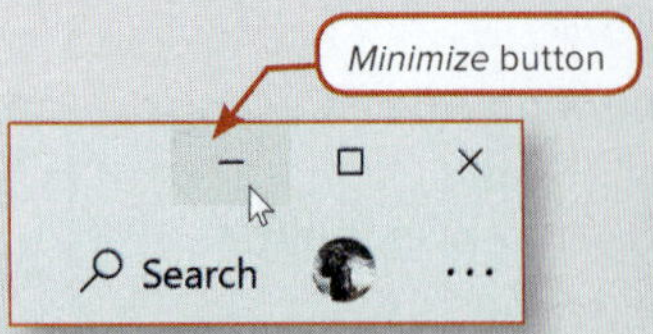

Figure Intro-53 *Minimize* button on an app window

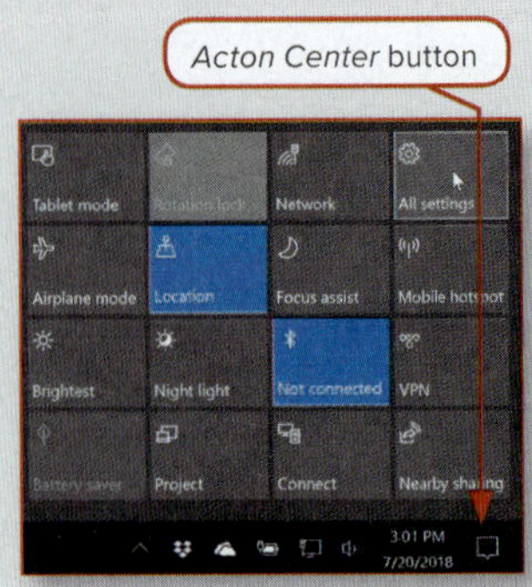

Figure Intro-54 Windows 10 *Action Center*

8. Use the *Task View* feature to open and close apps and windows.

a. Click the **Task View** button on the left side of the *Taskbar* (Figure Intro-55). All open apps and windows display tiled on the Windows desktop.

b. Click the **Store** app to open it. *Task View* closes and the *Store* app displays on your Windows desktop.

c. Click the **Task View** button again.

d. Click the **X** in the upper-right corner to close each open app and window. You may be prompted to save changes to a file.

e. Click the **Task View** button again or press **Esc** to return to the desktop.

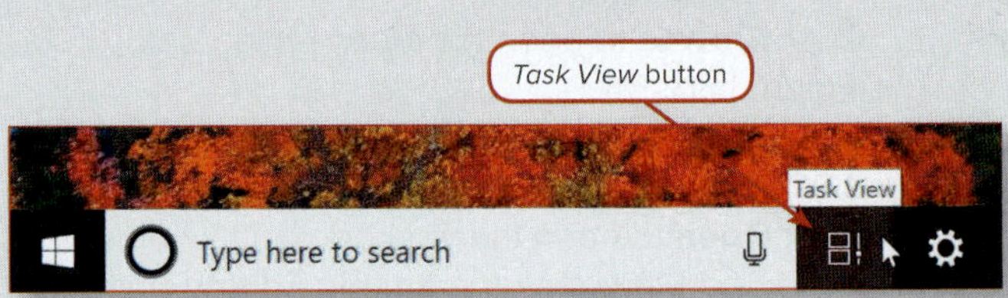

Figure Intro-55 *Task View* button on the *Taskbar*

SLO INTRO. 4

Working with Files

When you work with Office files, a variety of display views are available. You can change how a file displays, adjust the display size, work with multiple files, and arrange windows to view multiple files. Because most people work with multiple files at the same time, Office makes it easy and intuitive to move from one file to another or to display multiple document windows at the same time.

File Views

Each of the different Office applications provides you with a variety of ways to view your document. In Word, Excel, and PowerPoint, the different views are available on the ***View tab*** (Figure Intro-56). You can also change views using the buttons on the right side of the ***Status bar*** at the bottom of the file window (Figure Intro-57). In Access, the different views for each object are available in the *Views* group on the *Home* tab.

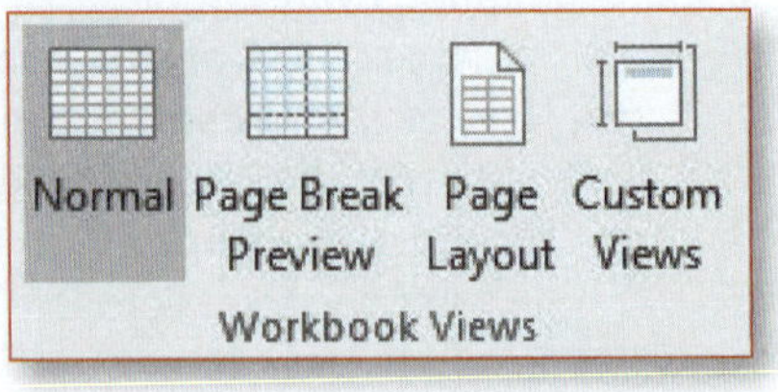

Figure Intro-56 *Workbook Views* group on the *View* tab in Excel

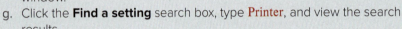

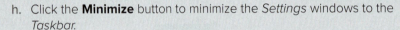

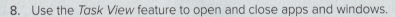

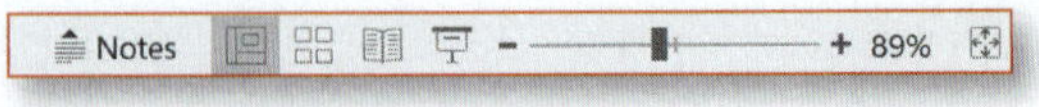

Figure Intro-57 PowerPoint views on the *Status* bar

Table Intro-4 lists the views that are available in each of the different Office applications.

Table Intro-4: File Views

Office Application	Views	Office Application	Views
Word	*Read Mode* *Print Layout* *web Layout* *Outline* *Draft*	**Access** *(Access views vary depending on active object)*	*Layout View* *Design View* *Datasheet View* *Form View* *SQL View* *Report View* *Print Preview*
Excel	*Normal* *Page Break Preview* *Page Layout* *Custom Views*	**PowerPoint**	*Normal* *Outline View* *Slide Sorter* *Notes Page* *Reading View* *Presenter View*

Change Display Size

Use the ***Zoom*** feature to increase or decrease the display size of your file. Using *Zoom* to change the display size does not change the actual size of text or objects in your file; it only changes the size of your display. For example, if you change the *Zoom* level to 120%, you increase the display of your file to 120% of its normal size (100%), but changing the display size does not affect the actual size of text and objects in your file. Decrease the *Zoom* level to 80% to display more of your file on the screen.

You can increase or decrease the *Zoom* level several different ways. Your *Zoom* options vary depending on the Office application.

- ***Zoom level** on the Status* bar (Figure Intro-58): Click the + or − button to increase or decrease *Zoom* level in 10% increments.
- ***Zoom group** on the View tab* (Figure Intro-59): The *Zoom* group includes a variety of *Zoom* options. The options vary depending on the Office application.
- ***Zoom dialog box*** (Figure Intro-60): Click the **Zoom** button in the *Zoom* group on the *View* tab or click the **Zoom level** on the *Status* bar to open the *Zoom* dialog box.

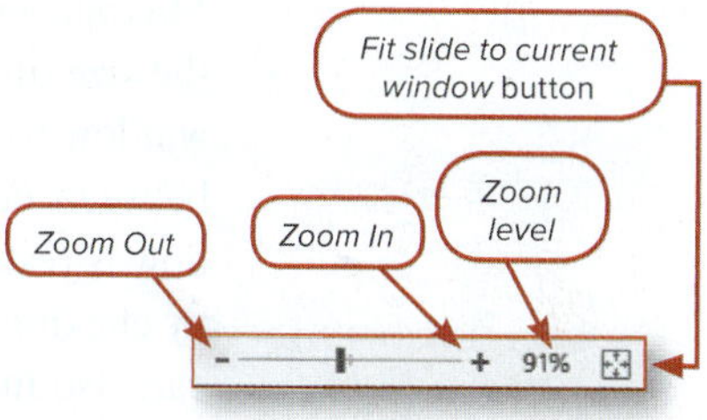

Figure Intro-58 *Zoom* area on the *Status* bar in PowerPoint

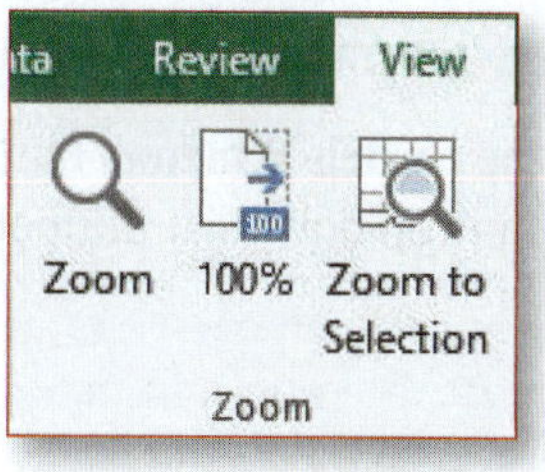

Figure Intro-59 *Zoom* group in Excel

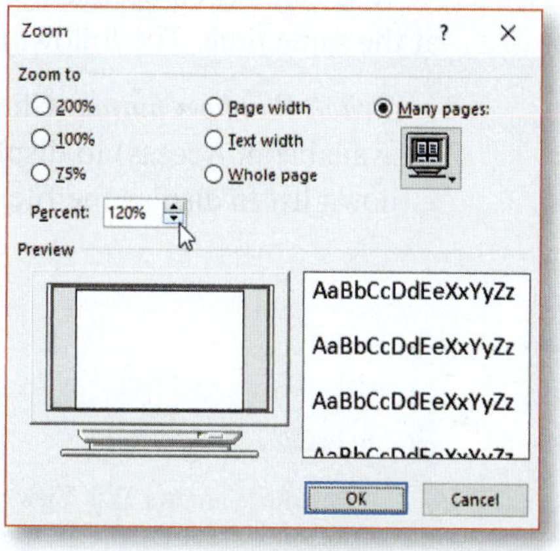

Figure Intro-60 *Zoom* dialog box in Word

MORE INFO

The *Zoom* feature is only available in Access in *Print Preview* view when you are working with reports.

Manage Multiple Open Files and Windows

When you are working on multiple files in an Office application, each file is opened in a new window. ***Minimize*** an open window to place the file on the Windows *Taskbar* (the bar at the bottom of the Windows desktop), ***restore down*** an open window so it does not fill the entire computer screen, or ***maximize*** a window so it fills the entire computer screen. The *Minimize*, *Restore Down/Maximize*, and *Close* buttons are in the upper-right corner of a file window (Figure Intro-61).

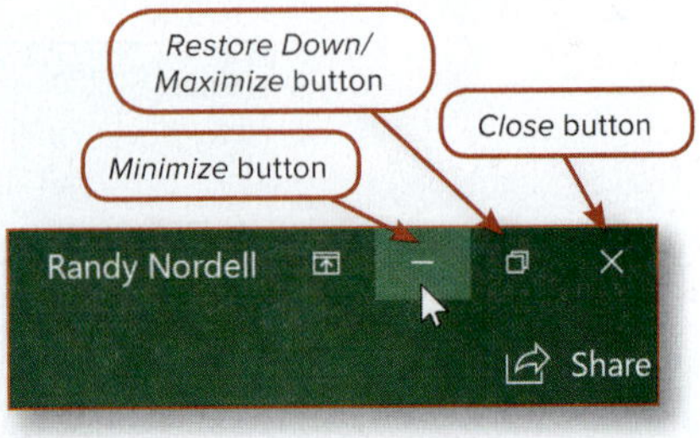

Figure Intro-61 Window options buttons

- ***Minimize***: Click the **Minimize** button (see Figure Intro-61) to hide the active window. When a document is minimized, it is not closed. It is reduced to a button on the *Taskbar* and the window does not display. Place your pointer on the application icon on the Windows *Taskbar* to display thumbnails of open files. Click an open file thumbnail to display the file (Figure Intro-62).

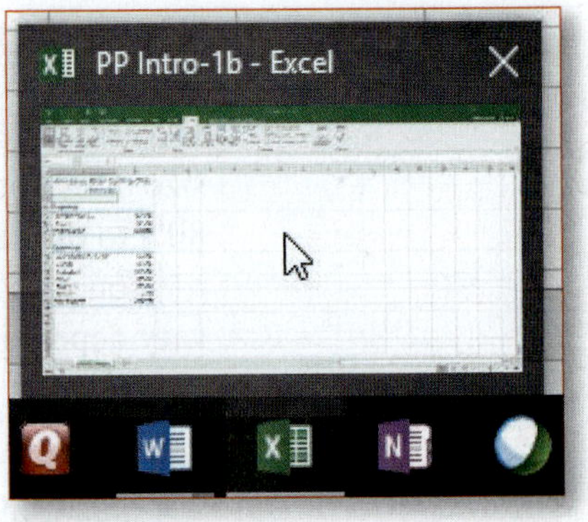

Figure Intro-62 Display minimized file on the *Taskbar*

- ***Restore Down/Maximize***: Click the **Restore Down/Maximize** button (see Figure Intro-61) to decrease the size of an open window or to maximize the window to fill the entire screen. This button toggles between *Restore Down* and *Maximize*. When a window is restored down, change the size of a window by clicking and dragging a border of the window. You can also move the window by clicking and dragging the title bar at the top of the window.
- ***Close***: Click the **Close** button (see Figure Intro-61) to close the window. If there is only one open file, the Office application also closes when you click the *Close* button on the file.

You can switch between open files or arrange open files to display more than one window at the same time. The following are several methods to do this:

- ***Switch Windows button***: Click the **Switch Windows** button [*View* tab, *Window* group] (not available in Access) to display a drop-down list of open files. Click a file from the drop-down list to display the file.

ANOTHER WAY

Click the Windows **Task View** button on the *Taskbar* to tile all open windows and apps on the desktop.

- ***Windows Taskbar***: Place your pointer on an Office application icon on the Windows *Taskbar* to display the open files in that application. Click a file thumbnail to display it (see Figure Intro-62).
- ***Arrange All button***: Click the **Arrange All** button [*View* tab, *Window* group] to display all windows in an application. You can resize or move the open file windows.

Snap Assist

The ***Snap Assist*** feature in Windows provides the ability to position an open window to the left or right side of your computer screen and fill half the screen. When you snap an open window to the left or right side of the screen, the other open windows tile on the opposite side where you can select another window to fill the opposite side of the computer screen (Figure Intro-63).

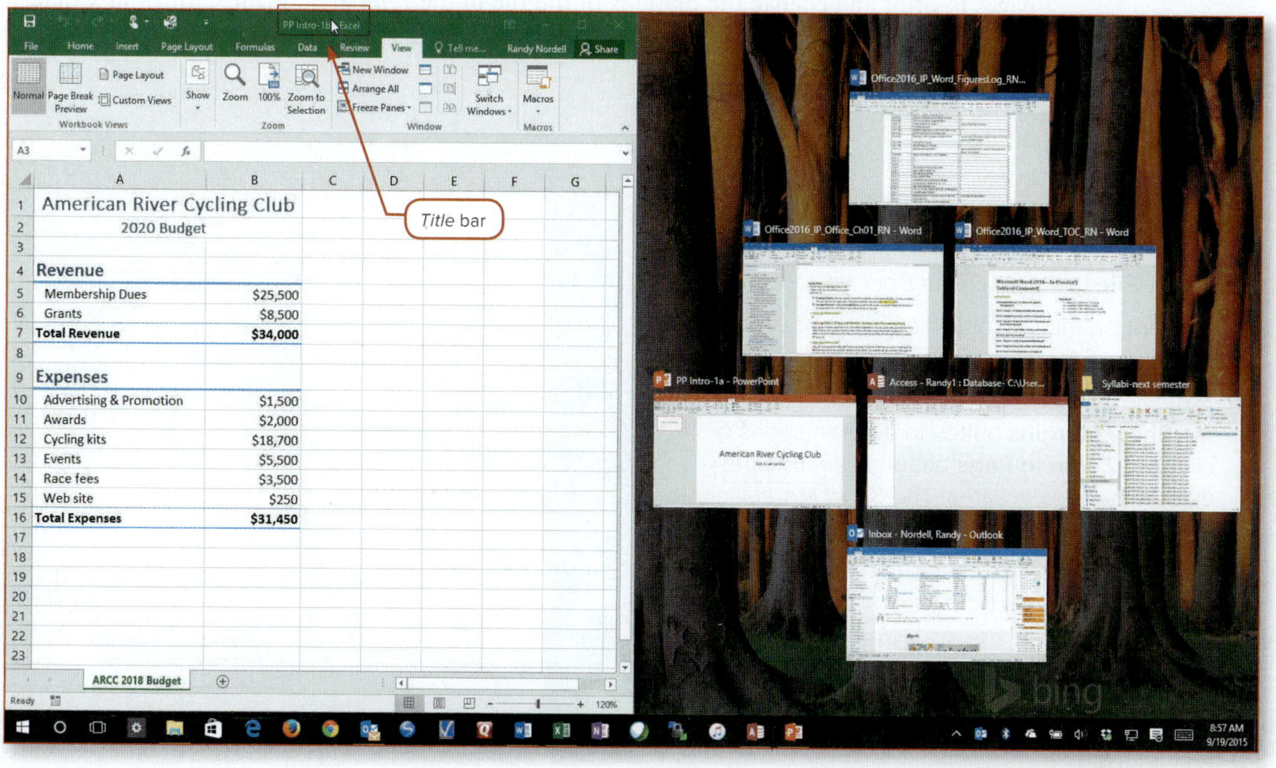

Figure Intro-63 Windows *Snap Assist* feature

▶HOW TO: Use Snap Assist

1. Click the **title bar** of an open window.
2. Drag it to the left or right edge of the computer screen and release the pointer.
   - The window snaps to the side of the screen and fills half of the computer screen (see Figure Intro-63).
   - The other open windows and apps display as tiles on the opposite side.
   - If you use a touch-screen computer, press and hold the title bar of an open window and drag to either side of the computer screen.
3. Select a tile of an open window or app to fill the other half of the screen.

MORE INFO

Snap Assist also enables you to snap a window to a quadrant (quarter rather than half) of your screen. Drag the **title bar** of an open window to one of the four corners of your computer screen.

SLO INTRO. 5

Printing, Sharing, and Customizing Files

Use *Backstage* view in any of the Office applications, to print a file and to customize how a file is printed. You can also export an Office file as a PDF file in most of the Office applications. In addition, you can add and customize document properties for an Office file and share a file in a variety of formats.

Print a File

Print an Office file if you need a hard copy. The *Print* area on the *Backstage* view displays a preview of the open file and many print options. For example, you can choose which page or pages to print and change the margins of the file in the *Print* area. Print settings vary depending on the Office application you are using and what you are printing.

HOW TO: Print a File

1. Open the file you want to print from a Windows folder or within an Office program.
2. Click the **File** tab to open the *Backstage* view.
3. Click **Print** on the left to display the *Print* area (Figure Intro-64).
   - A preview of the file displays on the right. Click the **Show Margins** button to adjust margins or click the **Zoom to Page** button to change the view in the *Preview* area. The *Show Margins* button is only available in Excel.
4. Change the number of copies to print in the *Copies* area.
5. Click the **Printer** drop-down list to choose from available printers.
6. Customize what is printed and how it is printed in the *Settings* area.
   - The *Settings* options vary depending on the Office application and what you print.
   - In the *Pages* area (*Slides* area in PowerPoint), select a page or range of pages (slides) to print.
   - By default, all pages (slides) are printed when you print a file.
7. Click the **Print** button to print your file.

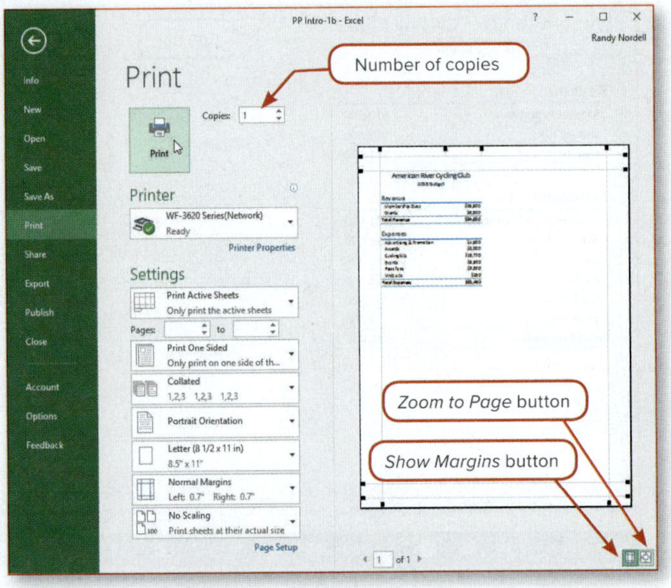

Figure Intro-64 ***Print* area on the *Backstage* view**

ANOTHER WAY

Press **Ctrl+P** to open the *Print* area on the *Backstage* view.

Export as a PDF File

Portable document format, or ***PDF***, is a specific file format that is often used to share files that are not to be changed, or to post files on a web site. When you create a PDF file from an Office application file, you are actually exporting a static image of the original file, similar to taking a picture of the file.

The advantage of working with a PDF file is that the format of the file is retained no matter who opens the file. PDF files open in the Windows Reader app or Adobe Reader, which is free software that is installed on most computers. Because a PDF file is a static image of a file, it is not easy for other people to edit your files. When you want people to be able to view a file but not change it, PDF files are a good choice.

HOW TO: Export a File as a PDF File

1. Open the file you want to export as a PDF file.
2. Click the **File** tab and click **Export** to display the *Export* area on the Backstage view (Figure Intro-65).
3. Select **Create PDF/XPS Document** and click the **Create PDF/ XPS** button. The *Publish as PDF or XPS* dialog box opens.
   - XPS (XML Paper Specification) format is an alternative to a PDF file. XPS is a Microsoft format and is not widely used.
4. Select a location to save the file.
5. Type a name for the file in the *File name* area.
6. Click **Publish** to close the dialog box and save the PDF file.

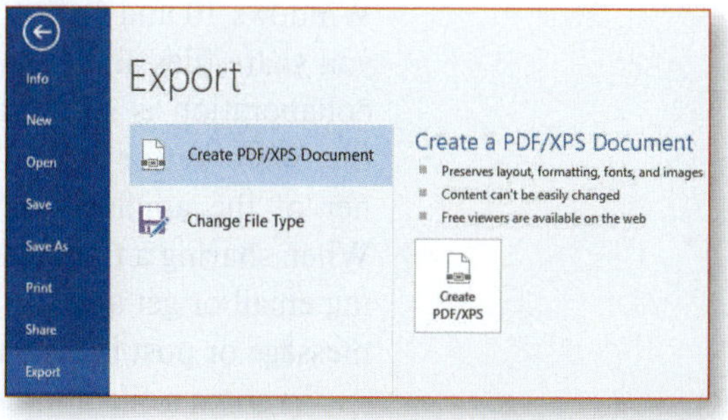

Figure Intro-65 *Export* a file as a PDF file

MORE INFO

Microsoft Word can open PDF files, and you can edit and save the file as a Word document.

If Adobe Acrobat is installed on your computer, ***Save as Adobe PDF*** displays as an option on the *Backstage* view.

Document Properties

Document properties are hidden codes in a file that store identifying information about that file. Each piece of document property information is called a ***field***. You can view and modify document properties in the *Info* area of the *Backstage* view.

Some document properties fields are automatically generated when you work on a file, such as *Size*, *Total Editing Time*, *Created*, and *Last Modified*. Other document properties fields, such as *Title*, *Comments*, *Subject*, *Company*, and *Author*, can be modified. You can use document property fields in different ways such as inserting the *Company* field in a document footer.

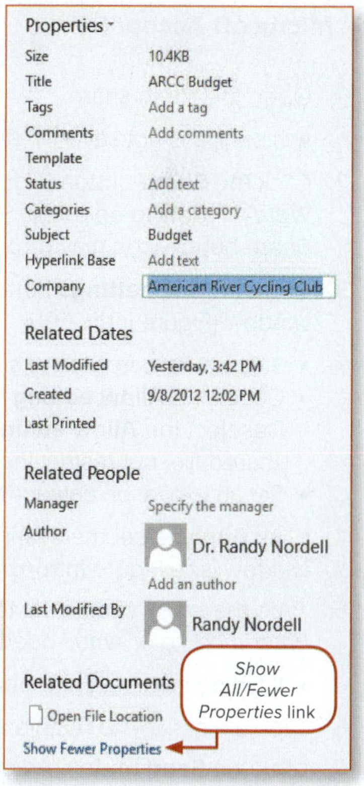

Figure Intro-66 Document properties

HOW TO: View and Modify Document Properties

1. Click the **File** tab and click **Info** (if not already selected). The document properties display on the right (Figure Intro-66).
2. Click the text box area of a field that can be edited and type your custom document property information.

3. Click the **Show All Properties** link at the bottom to display additional document properties.
   - Click **Show Fewer Properties** to collapse the list and display fewer properties.
   - This link toggles between *Show All Properties* and *Show Fewer Properties*.
4. Click the **Back** arrow to return to the file.

Share a File

Windows 10 and Office have been enhanced to help you share files and collaborate with others. Because collaboration is so important and commonly used, the ***Share*** button is available in the upper-right corner of the application window, except on Access. When sharing a file with others, you can send a sharing email or get a sharing link to paste into an email message or post in an online location.

To share a file, it must first be saved in *OneDrive*. If you try to share a file that is not saved in *OneDrive*, Word prompts you to save your document to *OneDrive* before sharing it. Depending on the type of Microsoft account you're using, the sharing options display in a ***Send Link*** window (education and business Microsoft accounts) (Figure Intro-67) or the ***Share*** pane (personal Microsoft account). The *Send Link* window or *Share* pane displays a variety of sharing options.

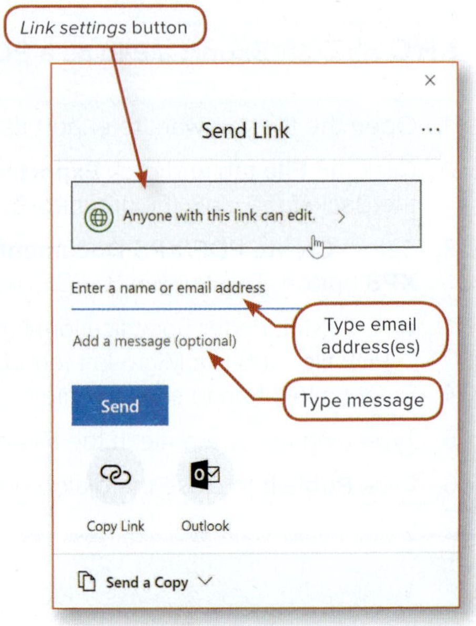

Figure Intro-67 *Send Link* window

▸HOW TO: Share an Online File (Education and Business Microsoft Accounts)

1. Open the file to share.
   - If the file is not saved in *OneDrive*, save the file to *OneDrive*.
2. Click the **Share** button (Figure Intro-68) in the upper-right corner of the Word window to open the *Send Link* window (see Figure Intro-67). The *Share* button icon may display differently in Office 2019.
3. Click the **Link settings** button (see Figure Intro-67) to open the *Link settings* window (Figure Intro-69).
   - Select who can use the sharing link.
   - Check the **Allow editing** box to enable recipients to edit the shared file. Deselect the **Allow editing** box to enable recipients to open and view the shared file, but restrict them from editing it.
   - Set an expiration date for the sharing link if desired (optional).
4. Click **Apply** to set the sharing link options and to return to the *Send Link* window (see Figure Intro-67).
5. Type the email address of the person with whom you are sharing the file in the *Enter a name or email address* area.
   - If typing multiple email addresses, separate each with a semicolon.
6. Type a message to recipient(s) in the *Add a message* area. This is optional.
7. Click the **Send** button. An email is sent to people you invited.
8. Click the **X** to close the confirmation window.

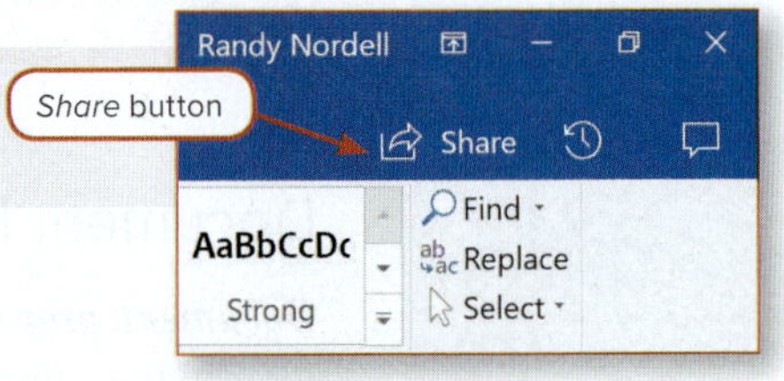

Figure Intro-68 *Share* button

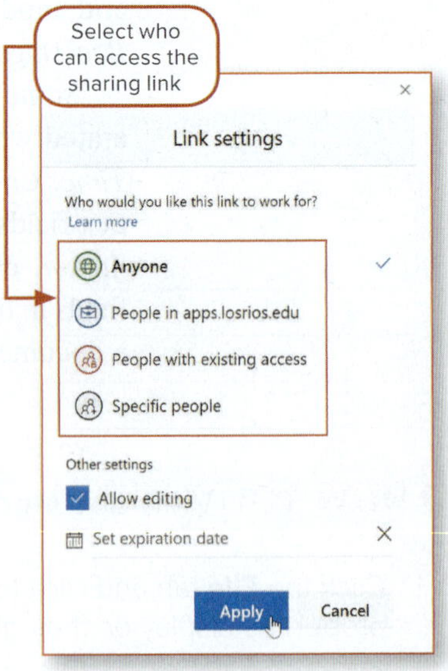

Figure Intro-69 *Link settings* window

If you're using a personal Microsoft account, the *Share* pane opens at the right after you click the *Share* button.

▶ HOW TO: Share an Online File (Personal Microsoft Account)

1. Open the file to share.
   - If the file is not saved in *OneDrive,* save the file to *OneDrive.*
2. Click the **Share** button in the upper-right corner of the Word window to open the *Share* pane to the right of the Word window (Figure Intro-70). The *Share* button icon may display differently in Office 2019.
3. Type or select the email address of the person with whom you are sharing the file in the *Invite people* area.
4. Select **Can edit** or **Can view** from the *Permission* drop-down list.
   - *Can edit* enables users to edit a shared document.
   - *Can view* enables users to open and view a shared document but restricts users from editing the document.
5. Type a message to recipient(s) in the *Message* area.
6. Click the **Share** button. An email is sent to people you invited.
7. Click the **X** to close the *Share* pane.

Figure Intro-70 Share a *OneDrive* file

Creating a sharing link (hyperlink) is another way to share a file with others rather than sending an email through Word. You can create and copy a sharing link and email the sharing link to others. You have the option of creating an ***Edit link*** or a ***View-only link***.

▶ HOW TO: Create a Sharing Link (Education and Business Microsoft Accounts)

1. Open the file to share.
   - If the file is not saved in *OneDrive*, you are prompted to save the file to *OneDrive*.
2. Click the **Share** button in the upper right of the Word window to open the *Send Link* window.
3. Click the **Link settings** button to open the *Link settings* window (see Figure Intro-69).
   - Select who can use the sharing link.
   - Check the **Allow editing** box to enable recipients to edit the shared file. Deselect the **Allow editing** box to enable recipients to open and view the shared file, but restrict them from editing it.
   - Set an expiration date for the sharing link if desired (optional).
4. Click **Apply** to set the sharing link options and to return to the *Send Link* window.
5. Click the **Copy Link** button to open the window that displays the sharing link (Figure Intro-71).
6. Click the **Copy** button to copy the sharing link.
7. Click the **X** to close the confirmation window.
8. Paste the copied sharing link in an email, Word document, or other online location.

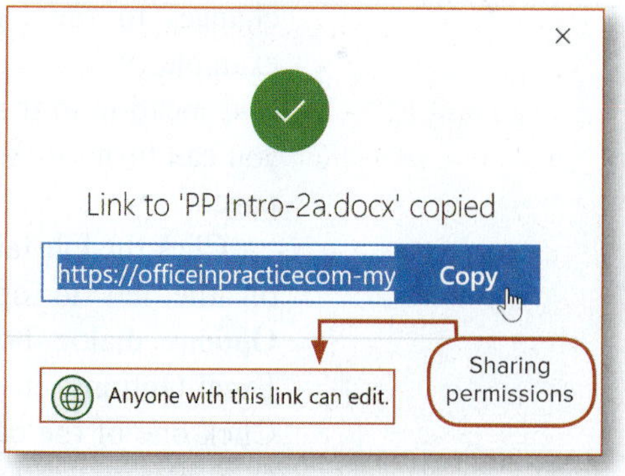

Figure Intro-71 Copy sharing link

If you're using a personal Microsoft account, the *Share* pane opens at the right after you after you click the *Share* button.

▸HOW TO: Create a Sharing Link (Personal Microsoft Account)

1. Open the file to share.
   - If the file is not saved in *OneDrive*, you are prompted to save the file to *OneDrive*.
2. Click the **Share** button in the upper right of the Word window to open the *Share* pane to the right of the Word window.
3. Click **Get a sharing link** at the bottom of the *Share* pane (see Figure Intro-70).
4. Click the **Create an edit link** or **Create a view-only link** button (Figure Intro-72) to create a sharing link.
   - *Can edit* enables users to open, view, and edit a shared document.
   - *Can view* enables users to open and view a shared document but restricts users from editing the document.
5. Click the **Copy** button to copy the sharing link (Figure Intro-73).
6. Click the **Back** arrow to the left of *Get a sharing link* at the top of the *Share* pane to return to the main *Share* pane, or click the **X** to close the *Share* pane.
7. Paste the copied sharing link in an email, Word document, or other online location.

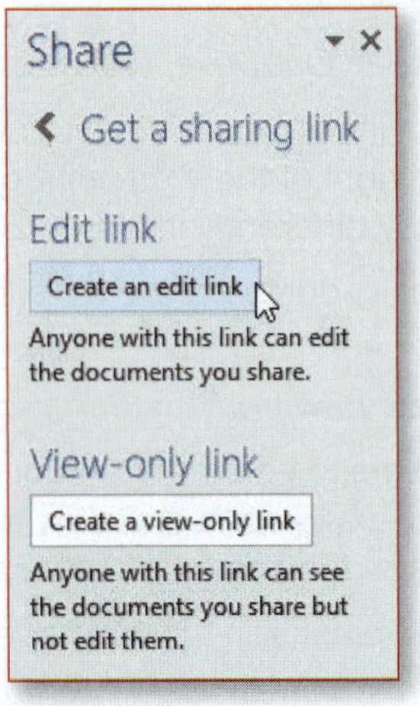

Figure Intro-72 Create a sharing link

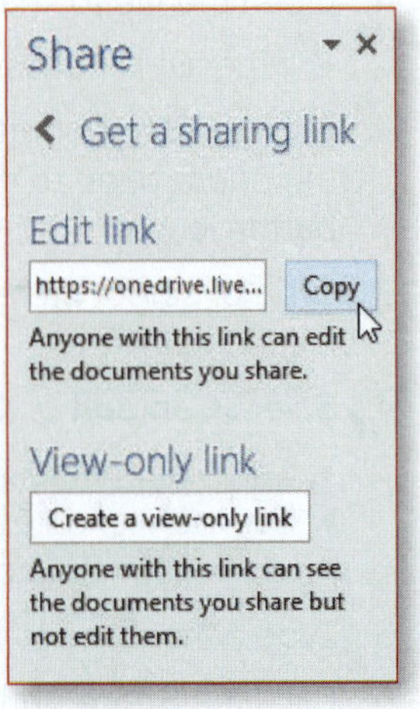

Figure Intro-73 Copy a sharing link

ANOTHER WAY

You can also share a file through email by clicking the **Send as attachment** link at the bottom of the *Share* pane. The email share options require the use of Microsoft Outlook (email and personal management Office application) to share the selected file through email.

Program Options

Use program options to apply global changes to the Office program. For example, you can change the default save location to the *OneDrive* folder or you can turn off the opening of a *Start* page.

Click the **File** tab and select **Options** on the left to open the ***[Program]* Options** dialog box (Word Options, Excel Options, etc.) (Figure Intro-74). Click one of the categories on the left to display the category options on the right. The categories and options vary depending on the Office application.

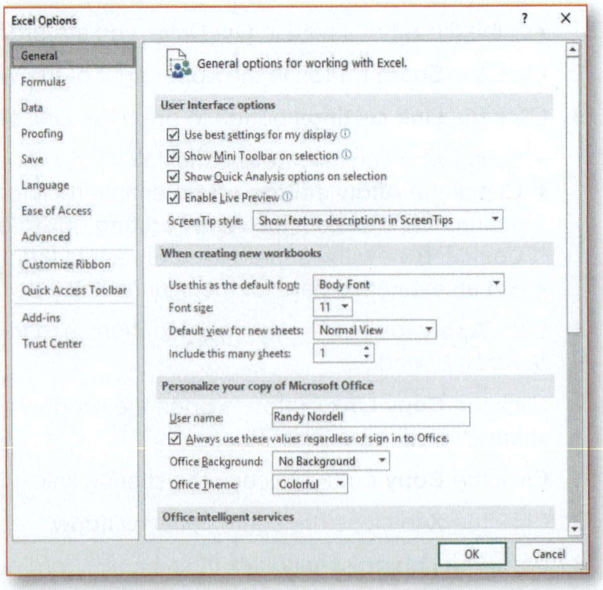

Figure Intro-74 *Excel Options* dialog box

SLO INTRO. 6

Using the Ribbon, Tabs, and Quick Access Toolbar

Use the *Ribbon*, tabs, groups, buttons, drop-down lists, dialog boxes, task panes, galleries, and the *Quick Access* toolbar to modify your Office files. This section describes different tools used to customize your files.

The Ribbon, Tabs, and Groups

The ***Ribbon***, which appears at the top of an Office file window, displays the many features available. The *Ribbon* is a collection of ***tabs***. Each tab includes ***groups*** of commands. The tabs and groups available vary for each Office application. Click a tab to display the groups and commands available on that tab.

Some tabs always display on the *Ribbon* (for example, the *File* tab and *Home* tabs). Other tabs are contextual, which means that they only appear on the *Ribbon* when you select a specific object. Figure Intro-75 displays the contextual *Table Tools Fields* tab that displays in Access when you open a table.

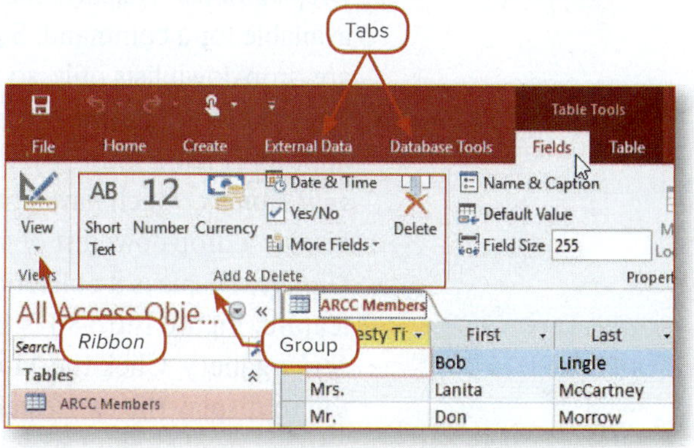

Figure Intro-75 Contextual *Table Tools Fields* tab displayed

> **MORE INFO**
>
> The *Ribbon* may appear slightly different depending on the version of Office you are using.

Ribbon Display Options

The *Ribbon* displays by default in Office applications, and you can customize the appearance of the *Ribbon*. The ***Ribbon Display Options*** button is in the upper-right corner of an Office application window (Figure Intro-76). Click the **Ribbon Display Options** button to select one of the three options:

- ***Auto-Hide Ribbon***: Hides the *Ribbon*. Click at the top of the application to display the *Ribbon*.
- ***Show Tabs***: Displays *Ribbon* tabs only. Click a tab to open the *Ribbon* and display the tab.
- ***Show Tabs and Commands***: Displays the *Ribbon* and tabs, which is the default setting in Office applications.

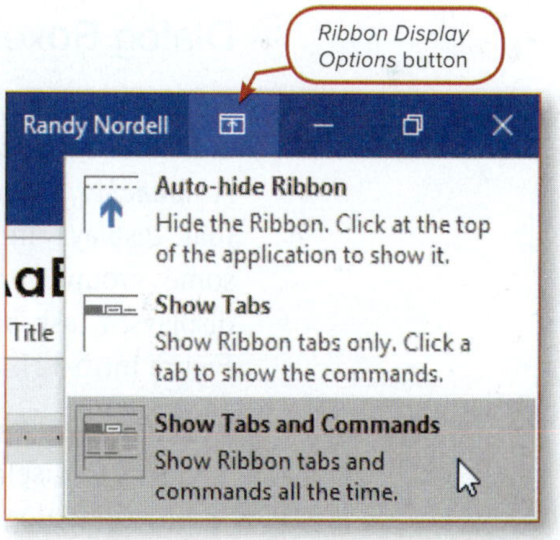

Figure Intro-76 *Ribbon Display Options*

> **MORE INFO**
>
> **Ctrl+F1** collapses or expands the *Ribbon*. Also, double-click a tab name on the *Ribbon* to collapse or expand it.

Buttons, Drop-Down Lists, and Galleries

Groups on each of the tabs contain a variety of ***buttons***, ***drop-down lists***, and ***galleries***. The following list describes each of these features and how they are used:

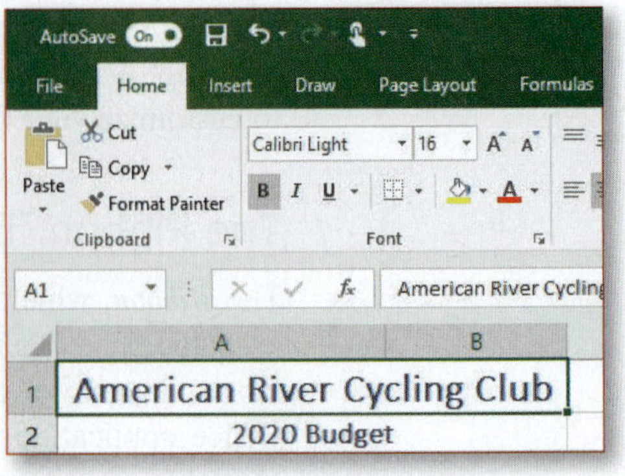

Figure Intro-77 ***Bold*** **button in the** ***Font*** **group on the** ***Home*** **tab**

- ***Button***: Applies a feature to selected text or an object. Click a button to apply the feature (Figure Intro-77).
- ***Drop-down list***: Displays the various options available for a command. Some buttons are drop-down lists only, so when you click these buttons a drop-down list of options appears (Figure Intro-78). Other buttons are ***split buttons***, which have both a button you click to apply a feature and an arrow you click to display a drop-down list of options (Figure Intro-79).
- ***Gallery***: Displays a collection of option buttons. Click an option in a gallery to apply the feature. Figure Intro-80 is the *Styles* gallery. Click the **More** button to display the entire gallery of options or click the **Up** or **Down** arrow to display a different row of options.

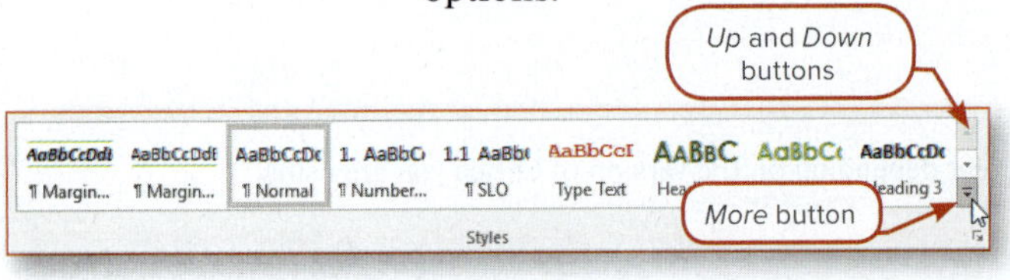

Figure Intro-80 ***Styles*** **gallery in Word**

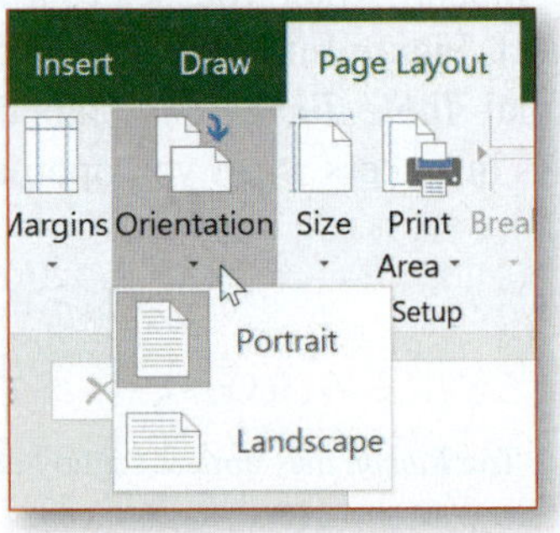

Figure Intro-78 ***Orientation*** **drop-down list**

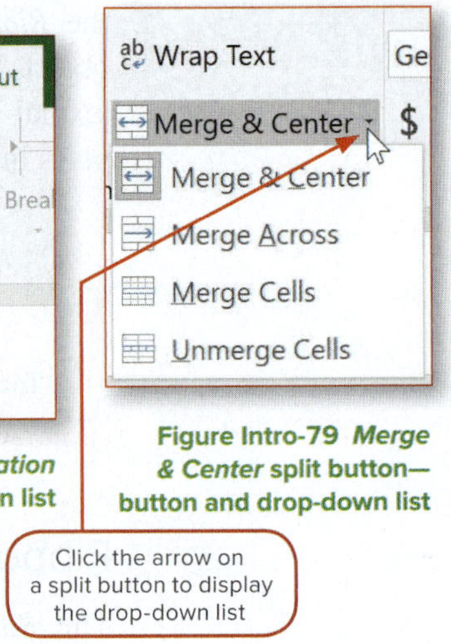

Figure Intro-79 ***Merge & Center*** **split button—button and drop-down list**

Dialog Boxes, Task Panes, and Launchers

Office application features are also available in a ***dialog box*** or ***task pane***. A ***launcher***, which is a small square that displays in the bottom right of some groups, opens a dialog box or displays a task pane when clicked (see Figure Intro-82).

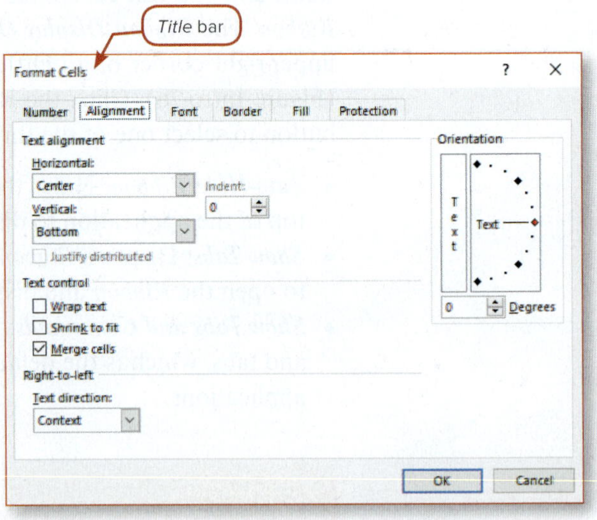

Figure Intro-81 ***Format Cells*** **dialog box**

- ***Dialog box***: A new window that opens to display additional features. Move a dialog box by clicking and dragging the title bar. The title bar appears at the top of the dialog box and displays the title. Figure Intro-81 shows the *Format Cells* dialog box that opens after you click the *Alignment* launcher in Excel.
- ***Task pane***: Opens on the left or right of an Office application window. Figure Intro-82 shows the *Clipboard* pane, which is available in all Office applications. Task panes are named

according to their purpose (for example, *Clipboard* pane or *Navigation* pane). You can resize a task pane by clicking and dragging its left or right border. Click the **X** in the upper-right corner to close a task pane.

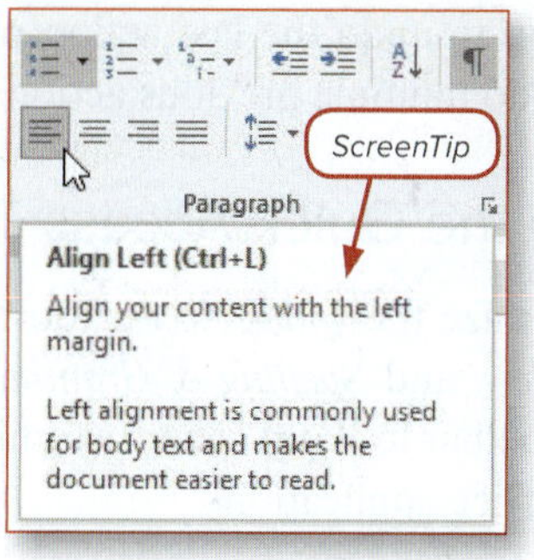

Figure Intro-83 ***Align Left* *ScreenTip***

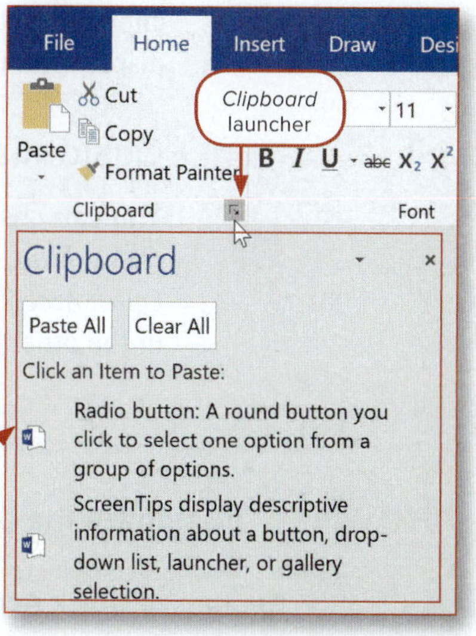

Figure Intro-82 ***Clipboard* pane**

ScreenTips

ScreenTips display descriptive information about a button, drop-down list, launcher, or gallery selection. When you place your pointer on an item on the *Ribbon*, a *ScreenTip* displays information about the selection (Figure Intro-83). The *ScreenTip* appears temporarily and displays the command name, keyboard shortcut (if available), and a description of the command.

Radio Buttons, Check Boxes, and Text Boxes

Dialog boxes and task panes contain a variety of options you can apply using ***radio buttons***, ***check boxes***, ***text boxes***, ***drop-down lists***, and other buttons (Figure Intro-84).

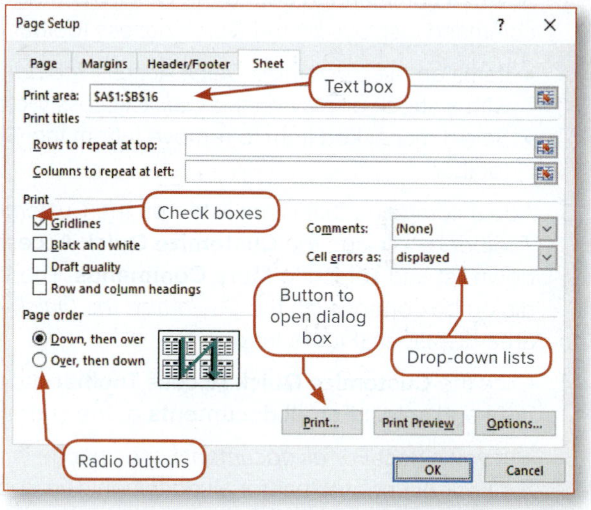

Figure Intro-84 ***Page Setup* dialog box in Excel**

- ***Radio button***: A round button you click to select one option from a group of options. A selected radio button displays a solid dot inside the round button. Radio buttons are mutually exclusive.
- ***Check box***: A square button you click to select one or more options. A check appears in a selected check box.
- ***Text box***: An area where you type text.

A task pane or dialog box may also include drop-down lists or other buttons that open additional dialog boxes. Figure Intro-84 shows the *Page Setup* dialog box in Excel, which includes a variety of radio buttons, check boxes, text boxes, drop-down lists, and command buttons that open additional dialog boxes (for example, the *Print* and *Options* buttons).

Quick Access Toolbar

The ***Quick Access toolbar*** is located above the *Ribbon* on the upper left of each Office application window. It contains buttons to apply commonly used commands such as *Save*, *Undo*, *Redo*, and *Open*. The *Undo* button is a split button (Figure Intro-85). You can

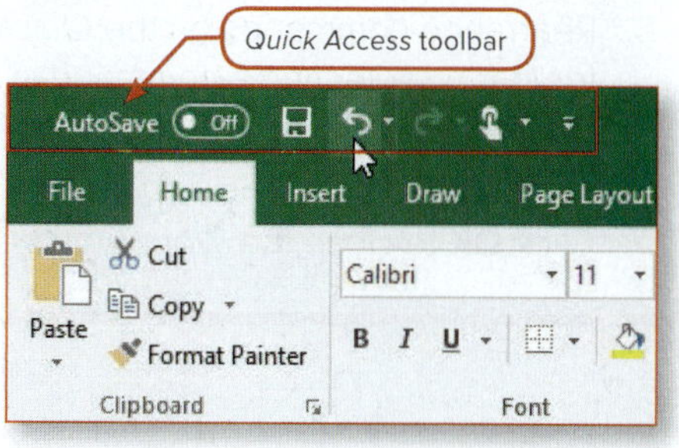

Figure Intro-85 ***Quick Access* toolbar**

click the button to undo the last action performed, or you can click the drop-down arrow to display and undo multiple previous actions.

Customize the Quick Access Toolbar

You can customize the *Quick Access* toolbar to include commands you regularly use, such as *Quick Print*, *New*, and *Spelling & Grammar*. The following steps show how to customize the *Quick Access* toolbar in Word. The customization process is similar for the *Quick Access* toolbar in the other Office applications.

▸HOW TO: Customize the Quick Access Toolbar

1. Click the **Customize Quick Access Toolbar** drop-down list on the right edge of the *Quick Access* toolbar (Figure Intro-86).
2. Select a command to add to the *Quick Access* toolbar. The command displays on the *Quick Access* toolbar.
   - Items on the *Customize Quick Access Toolbar* drop-down list with a check display on the *Quick Access* toolbar.
   - Select a checked item to remove it from the *Quick Access* toolbar.
3. Add a command that is not listed on the *Customize Quick Access Toolbar* by clicking the **Customize Quick Access Toolbar** drop-down list and selecting **More Commands**. The *Word Options* dialog box opens with the *Customize the Quick Access Toolbar* area displayed (Figure Intro-87).
4. Click the **Customize Quick Access Toolbar** drop-down list on the right and select **For all documents** or the current document.
   - If you select *For all documents*, the change is made to the *Quick Access* toolbar for all documents you open in Word.
   - If you select the current document, the change is made to the *Quick Access* toolbar in that document only.
5. Select the command to add from the alphabetic list of commands on the left and click the **Add** button.
   - If you can't find a command, click the **Choose commands from** drop-down list and select **All Commands**.
   - The list on the right contains the commands that display on the *Quick Access* toolbar.
6. Rearrange commands on the *Quick Access* toolbar by selecting a command in the list on the right and clicking the **Move Up** or **Move Down** button.
7. Click **OK** to close the *Word Options* dialog box.

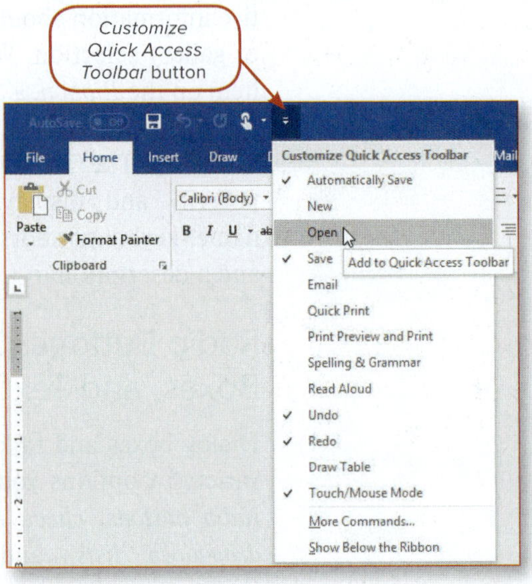

Figure Intro-86 Add a command to the *Quick Access* toolbar

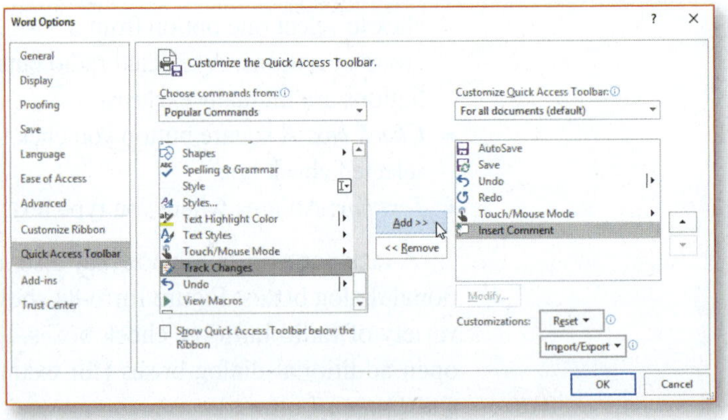

Figure Intro-87 Customize the *Quick Access* toolbar in the *Word Options* dialog box

> **ANOTHER WAY**
>
> To remove an item from the *Quick Access* toolbar, right-click an item and select **Remove from Quick Access Toolbar**.

SLO INTRO. 7

Using Context Menus, the Mini Toolbar, and Keyboard Shortcuts

Most of the commands used for formatting and editing your files display in groups on the tabs. But many of these features are also available using context menus, the mini toolbar, and keyboard shortcuts. Use these tools to quickly apply formatting or other options to text or objects.

Context Menu

A ***context menu*** displays when you right-click text, a cell, or an object such as a picture, drawing object, chart, or *SmartArt* (Figure Intro-88). The context menu is a vertical list of options, and the options are contextual, which means they vary depending on what you right-click. Context menus include options that perform an action (*Cut* or *Copy*), open a dialog box or task pane (*Format Cells* or *Insert*), or display a drop-down list of selections (*Filter* or *Sort*).

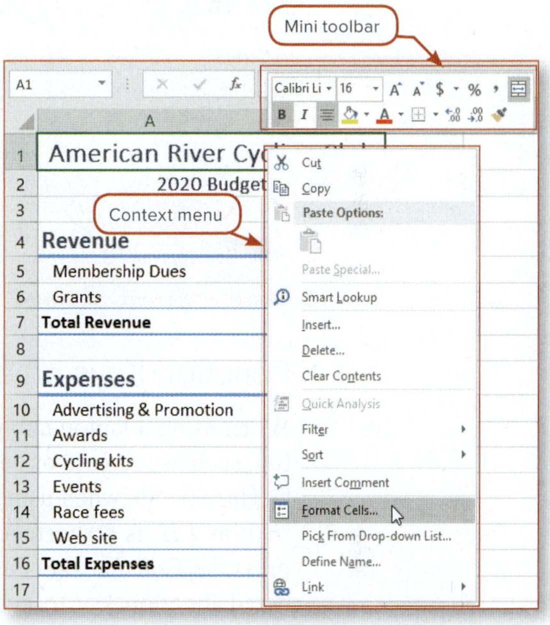

Figure Intro-88 Context menu and mini toolbar

Mini Toolbar

The ***mini toolbar*** is another context menu that displays when you right-click or select text, a cell, or an object in your file (see Figure Intro-88). The mini toolbar is a horizontal rectangular menu that lists a variety of formatting options. These options vary depending on what you select or right-click. The mini toolbar contains a variety of buttons and drop-down lists. The mini toolbar typically displays above the context menu, and it automatically displays when you select text or an object, such as when you select a row of a table in Word or PowerPoint.

Keyboard Shortcuts

You can also use a ***keyboard shortcut*** to quickly apply formatting or perform commands. A keyboard shortcut is a combination of keyboard keys that you press at the same time. These can include the **Ctrl**, **Shift**, **Alt**, letter, number, and function keys (for example, **F1** or **F7**). Table Intro-5 lists common Office keyboard shortcuts.

Table Intro-5: Common Office Keyboard Shortcuts

Keyboard Shortcut	Action or Displays	Keyboard Shortcut	Action or Displays
Ctrl+S	Save	**Ctrl+Z**	Undo
F12	*Save As* dialog box	**Ctrl+Y**	Redo or Repeat
Ctrl+O	*Open* area on the *Backstage* view	**Ctrl+1**	Single space
Shift+F12	*Open* dialog box	**Ctrl+2**	Double space
Ctrl+N	New blank file	**Ctrl+L**	Align left
Ctrl+P	*Print* area on the *Backstage* view	**Ctrl+E**	Align center
Ctrl+C	Copy	**Ctrl+R**	Align right
Ctrl+X	Cut	**F1**	*Help* pane
Ctrl+V	Paste	**F7**	*Spelling* pane
Ctrl+B	Bold	**Ctrl+A**	Select All
Ctrl+I	Italic	**Ctrl+Home**	Move to the beginning
Ctrl+U	Underline	**Ctrl+End**	Move to the end

MORE INFO

See *Appendix A: Microsoft Office Shortcuts* (online resource) for additional Office keyboard shortcuts.

Function Keys on a Laptop

When using a laptop computer, function keys perform specific Windows actions on your laptop, such as increase or decrease speaker volume, open Windows *Settings*, or adjust the screen brightness. So, when using a numbered function key in an Office application, such as *F12* as a shortcut to open the *Save As* dialog box, you may need to press the ***Function key*** (**Fn** or **fn**) on your keyboard in conjunction with a numbered function key to activate the Office command (Figure Intro-89). The *Function key* is typically located near the bottom left of your laptop keyboard next to the *Ctrl* key.

Figure Intro-89 Function key

PAUSE & PRACTICE: INTRO-2

For this project, you work with a document for the American River Cycling Club. You modify the existing document, add document properties, customize the *Quick Access* toolbar, export the document as a PDF file, and share the document.

File Needed: ***ARCCTraining-Intro.docx*** *(Student data files are available in the* Library *of your SIMnet account.)*
Completed Project File Names: ***[your initials] PP Intro-2a.docx*** and ***[your initials] PP Intro-2b.pdf***

1. Open Word and open the ***ARCCTraining-Intro*** file from your student data files. If the file opens in *Protected View*, click the **Enable Editing** button.

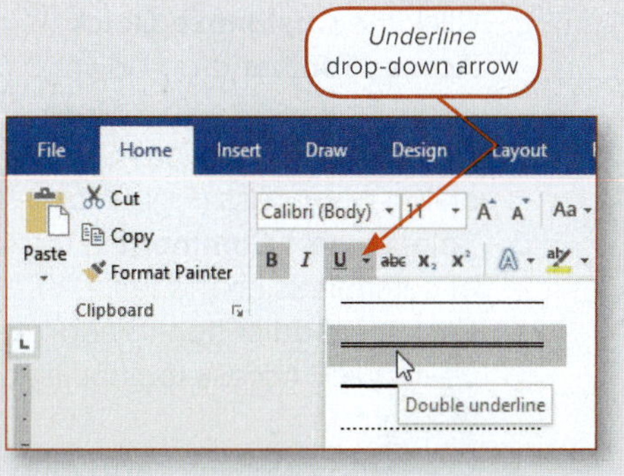

Figure Intro-90 Apply *Double underline* to selected text

2. Save this document as [your initials] PP Intro-2a in the *American River Cycling Club* folder in your *OneDrive* folder.
   a. In *Pause & Practice Intro-1*, you created the *American River Cycling Club* folder in *OneDrive* or other storage area. Save this file in the same location.
   b. If you don't save this file in *OneDrive*, you will not be able to complete steps 7 and 9 in this project.
3. Use a button, drop-down list, and dialog box to modify the document.
   a. Select the first heading, "**What is Maximum Heart Rate?**"
   b. Click the **Bold** button [*Home* tab, *Font* group].
   c. Click the **Underline** drop-down arrow and select **Double underline** (Figure Intro-90).
   d. Click the **launcher** in the *Font* group [*Home* tab] to open the *Font* dialog box (Figure Intro-91).
   e. Select **12** from the *Size* area list or type 12 in the text box.
   f. Click the **Small caps** check box in the *Effects* area to select it.
   g. Click **OK** to close the dialog box and apply the formatting changes.
   h. Select the next heading, "**What is Target Heart Rate?**"
   i. Repeat steps 3b–g to apply formatting to selected text.

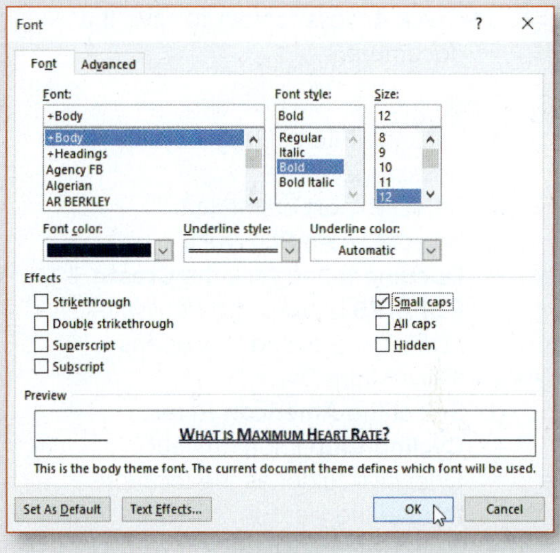

Figure Intro-91 *Font* dialog box

4. Add document properties.
   a. Click the **File** tab to display the *Backstage* view.
   b. Select **Info** on the left (if not already selected). The document properties display on the right.
   c. Click the **Add a title** text box and type ARCC Training.
   d. Click the **Show All Properties** link near the bottom to display additional document properties.
   e. Click the **Specify the subject** text box and type Heart rate training.
   f. Click the **Specify the company** text box and type American River Cycling Club.
   g. Click the **Back** arrow on the upper left to close the *Backstage* view and return to the document.
5. Customize the *Quick Access* toolbar.
   a. Click the **Customize Quick Access Toolbar** drop-down arrow and select **Open** if it is not already selected (Figure Intro-92).
   b. Click the **Customize Quick Access Toolbar** drop-down arrow again and select **Spelling & Grammar**.

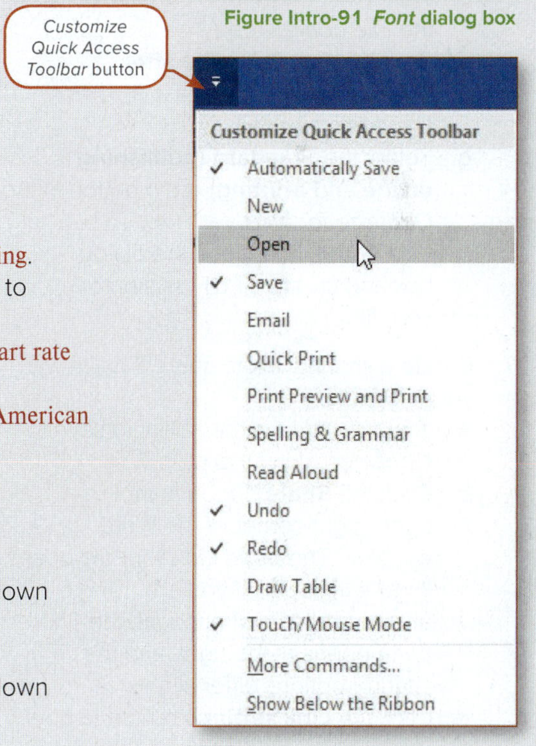

Figure Intro-92 *Customize Quick Access Toolbar* drop-down list

c. Click the **Customize Quick Access Toolbar** drop-down arrow again and select **More Commands**. The *Word Options* dialog box opens (Figure Intro-93).
d. Select **Insert Comment** in the list of commands on the left.
e. Click the **Add** button to add it to your *Quick Access* toolbar list on the right.
f. Click **OK** to close the *Word Options* dialog box.
g. Click the **Save** button on the *Quick Access* toolbar to save the document.

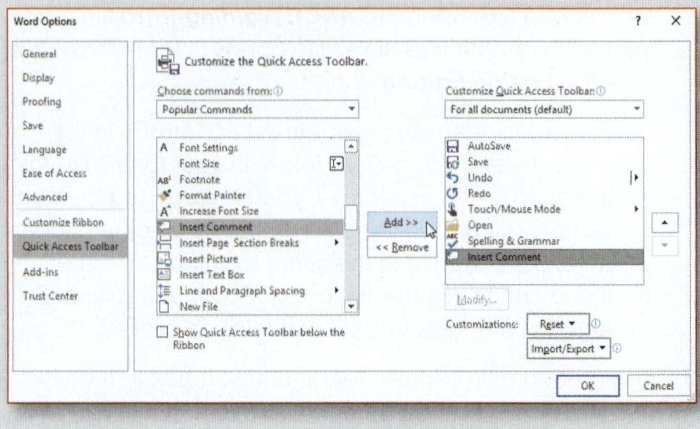

Figure Intro-93 Customize the *Quick Access* toolbar in the *Word Options* dialog box

6. Export the file as a PDF file.
   a. Click the **File** tab to go to the *Backstage* view.
   b. Select **Export** on the left.
   c. Select **Create PDF/XPS Document** and click the **Create PDF/XPS** button. The *Publish as PDF or XPS* dialog box opens (Figure Intro-94).
   d. Select the **American River Cycling Club** folder in your *OneDrive* folder as the location to save the file.
   e. Type [your initials] PP Intro-2b in the *File name* area.
   f. Deselect the **Open file after publishing** check box if it is checked.
   g. Select the **Standard (publishing online and printing)** radio button in the *Optimize for* area.
   h. Click **Publish** to close the dialog box and create a PDF version of your file.

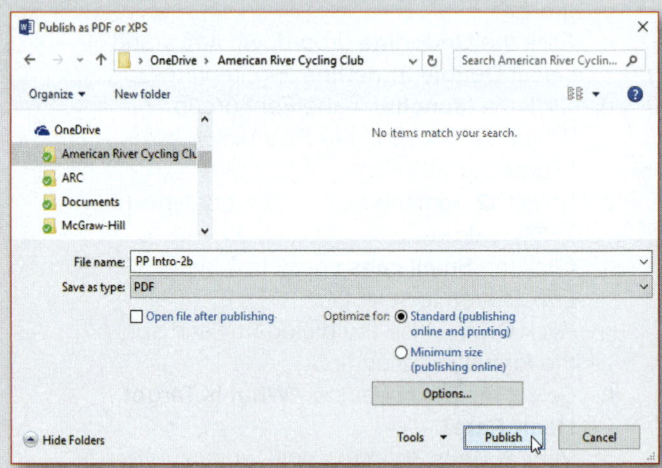

Figure Intro-94 *Publish as PDF or XPS* dialog box

7. Create a sharing link to share this file with your instructor.
   a. If you don't have the ability to save to *OneDrive*, skip all of step 7.
   b. Click the **Share** button in the upper-right corner of the Word window. The *Send Link* window opens (Figure Intro-95). If you are using a personal Microsoft account, the *Share* pane opens at the right, and the sharing options differ slightly.
   c. Click the **Link settings** button to open the *Link settings* window.

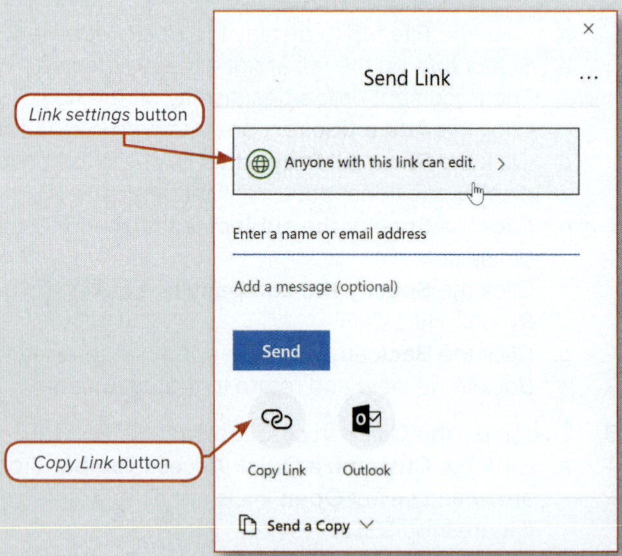

Figure Intro-95 *Send Link* window

d. Click the **Anyone** button and check the **Allow editing** box (if necessary) (Figure Intro-96).

e. Click **Apply** to return to the *Send Link* window.

f. Click the **Copy Link** button to create a sharing link.

g. Click **Copy** to copy the sharing link and click the **X** in the upper-right corner to close the sharing link window (Figure Intro-97).

h. Use your email account to create a new email to your instructor. Include an appropriate subject line and a brief message in the body.

i. Press **Ctrl+V** to paste the sharing link to your document in the body of the email and send the email message.

8. Save and close the document (Figure Intro-98).

Link to 'PP Intro-2a.docx' copied

https://officeinpracticecom-my | Copy

Anyone with this link can edit.

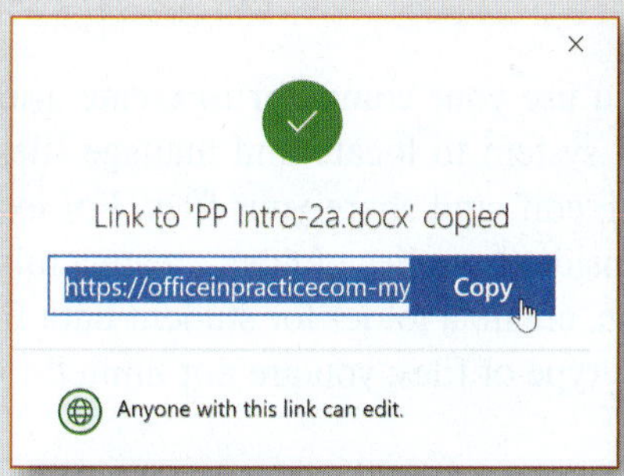

Figure Intro-97 Copy a sharing link

Link settings

Who would you like this link to work for?
Learn more

Anyone ✓

People in apps.losrios.edu

People with existing access

Specific people

Other settings

☑ Allow editing

Set expiration date ✕

Apply Cancel

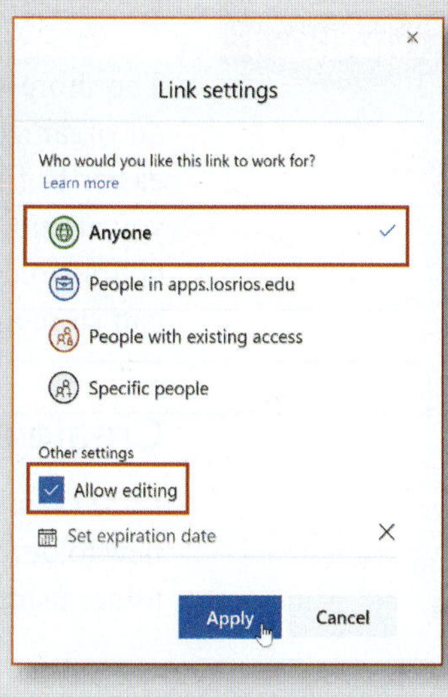

Figure Intro-96 *Link settings* window

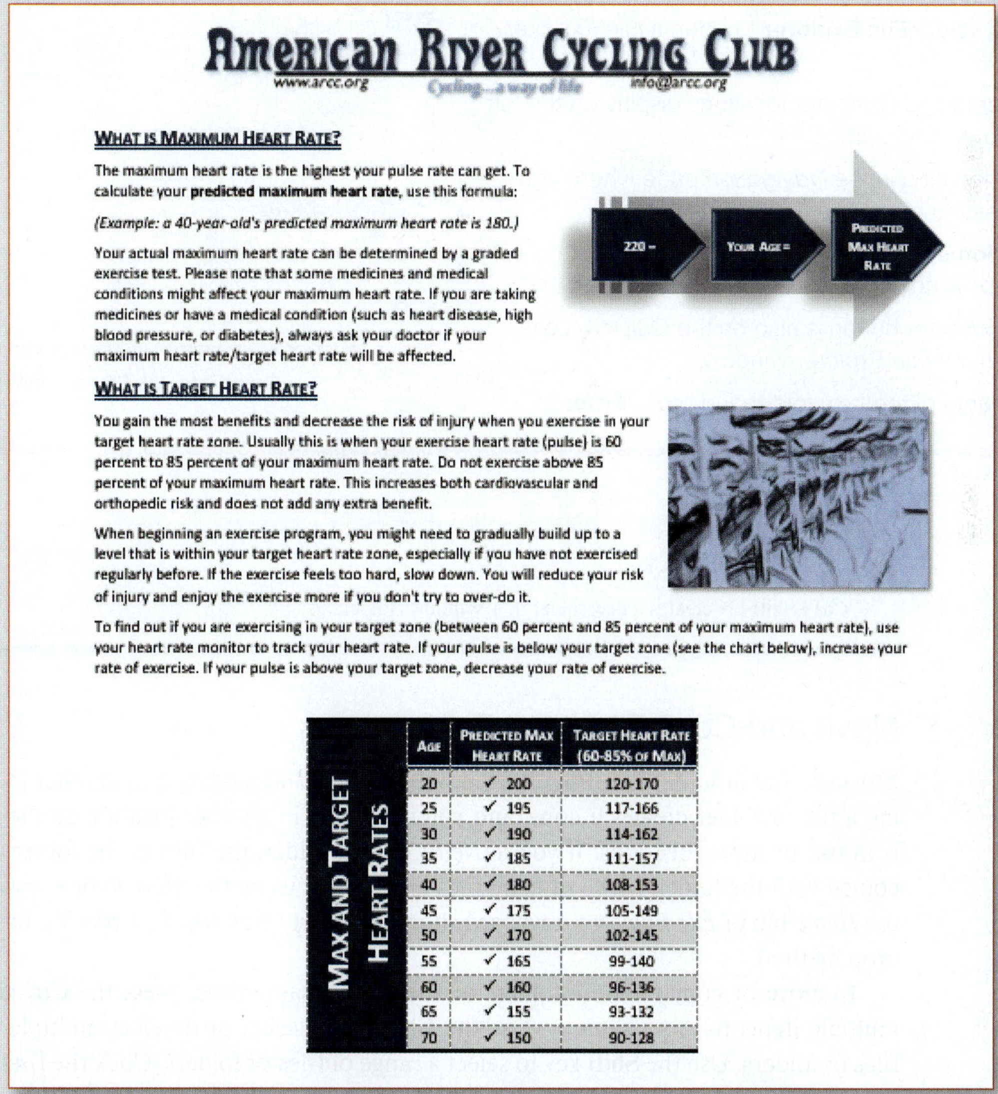

American River Cycling Club

www.arcc.org Cycling...a way of life info@arcc.org

What is Maximum Heart Rate?

The maximum heart rate is the highest your pulse rate can get. To calculate your **predicted maximum heart rate**, use this formula:

(Example: a 40-year-old's predicted maximum heart rate is 180.)

Your actual maximum heart rate can be determined by a graded exercise test. Please note that some medicines and medical conditions might affect your maximum heart rate. If you are taking medicines or have a medical condition (such as heart disease, high blood pressure, or diabetes), always ask your doctor if your maximum heart rate/target heart rate will be affected.

220 – Your Age = Predicted Max Heart Rate

What is Target Heart Rate?

You gain the most benefits and decrease the risk of injury when you exercise in your target heart rate zone. Usually this is when your exercise heart rate (pulse) is 60 percent to 85 percent of your maximum heart rate. Do not exercise above 85 percent of your maximum heart rate. This increases both cardiovascular and orthopedic risk and does not add any extra benefit.

When beginning an exercise program, you might need to gradually build up to a level that is within your target heart rate zone, especially if you have not exercised regularly before. If the exercise feels too hard, slow down. You will reduce your risk of injury and enjoy the exercise more if you don't try to over-do it.

To find out if you are exercising in your target zone (between 60 percent and 85 percent of your maximum heart rate), use your heart rate monitor to track your heart rate. If your pulse is below your target zone (see the chart below), increase your rate of exercise. If your pulse is above your target zone, decrease your rate of exercise.

	Age	Predicted Max Heart Rate	Target Heart Rate (60-85% of Max)
Max and Target Heart Rates	20	✓ 200	120-170
	25	✓ 195	117-166
	30	✓ 190	114-162
	35	✓ 185	111-157
	40	✓ 180	108-153
	45	✓ 175	105-149
	50	✓ 170	102-145
	55	✓ 165	99-140
	60	✓ 160	96-136
	65	✓ 155	93-132
	70	✓ 150	90-128

Figure Intro-98 PP Intro-2a completed

SLO INTRO. 8

Organizing and Customizing Folders and Files

The more you use your computer to create and edit files, the more important it is to create an organized system to locate and manage files. Use ***folders*** to store related files to make it easier to find, edit, and share your files. For example, you can create a folder for the college you attend. Inside the college folder, create a folder for each of your courses. Inside each of the course folders, create a folder for student data files, solution files, and group projects. Folders can store any type of files; you are not limited to Office files.

Create a Folder

In *SLO Intro. 3: Creating, Saving, Closing, and Opening Office Files*, you learned how to create a new folder when saving an Office file in the *Save As* dialog box. You can also create a Windows folder using *File Explorer*. You can create folders inside other folders.

HOW TO: Create a Windows Folder

1. Click the **File Explorer** on the *Taskbar* or click the **Start** button and select **File Explorer** to open a *File Explorer* window.
   - Your folders and computer locations display on the left in the *Navigation* pane.
2. Select the location in the *Navigation* pane where you want to create a new folder.
3. Click the **Home** tab and click the **New folder** button [*New* group]. A new folder is created (Figure Intro-99).
   - The *New Folder* button is also on the *Quick Access* toolbar in the *File Explorer* window.
4. Type the name of the new folder and press **Enter**.

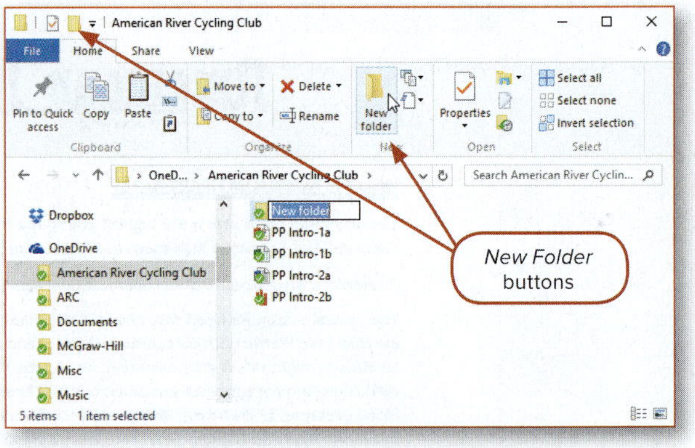

Figure Intro-99 Create a new Windows folder

> **ANOTHER WAY**
>
> Ctrl+Shift+N creates a new folder in a Windows folder.

Move and Copy Files and Folders

Moving a file or folder is cutting it from one location and pasting it in another location. Copying a file or folder creates a copy, and you can paste in another location so the file or folder is in two or more locations. If you move or copy a folder, the files in the folder are moved or copied with the folder. Move or copy files and folders using the *Move to* or *Copy to* buttons on the *Home* tab of *File Explorer*, keyboard shortcuts (**Ctrl+X, Ctrl+C, Ctrl+V**), or the drag-and-drop method.

To move or copy multiple folders or files at the same time, press the **Ctrl** key and select multiple items to move or copy. Use the **Ctrl** key to select or deselect multiple non-adjacent files or folders. Use the **Shift** key to select a range of files or folders. Click the first file or folder in a range, press the **Shift** key, and select the last file or folder in the range to select all of the items in the range.

▸HOW TO: Move or Copy a File or Folder

1. Click the **File Explorer** on the *Taskbar* or click the **Start** button and select **File Explorer** to open a *File Explorer* window.
2. Select a file or folder to move or copy.
   - Press the **Ctrl** key or the **Shift** key to select multiple files or folders.
3. Click the **Home** tab in the *File Explorer* window.
4. Click the **Move to** or **Copy to** button [*Organize* group] and select the location where you want to move or copy the file or folder (Figure Intro-100).

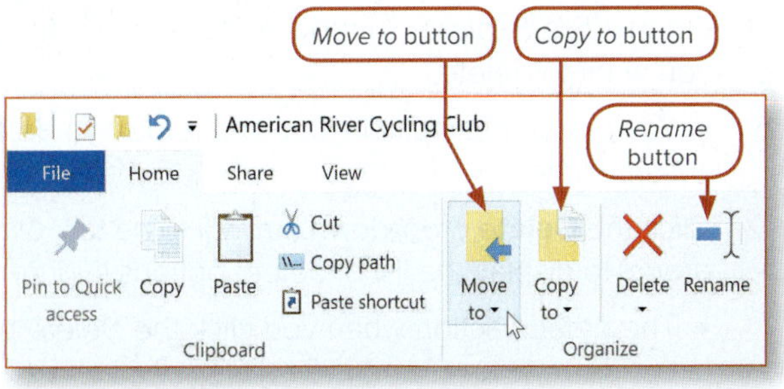

Figure Intro-100 Move or copy a selected file or folder

   - If the folder is not available, select **Choose location** to open the *Move Items* or *Copy Items* dialog box.
   - To use keyboard shortcuts, press **Ctrl+X** to cut the file or folder or **Ctrl+C** to copy the file or folder from its original location, go to the desired new location, and press **Ctrl+V** to paste it.
   - To use the drag-and-drop method to move a file or folder, select the file or folder and drag and drop to the new location.
   - To use the drag-and-drop method to copy a file or folder, press the **Ctrl** key, select the file or folder, and drag and drop to the new location.

ANOTHER WAY

Right-click a file or folder to display the context menu and select **Cut**, **Copy**, or **Paste**.

Rename Files and Folders

You can rename a file or folder in a *File Explorer* window. When you rename a file or folder, only the file or folder name changes. The contents of the file or folder do not change.

▸HOW TO: Rename a File or Folder

1. Click the **File Explorer** on the *Taskbar* or click the **Start** button and select **File Explorer** to open a *File Explorer* window.
2. Select the file or folder you want to rename.
3. Click the **Rename** button [*Home* tab, *Organize* group] (see Figure Intro-100).
4. Type the new name of the file or folder and press **Enter**.

ANOTHER WAY

Select a file or folder to rename, press **F2**, type the new name, and press **Enter**. You can also right-click a file or folder and select **Rename** from the context menu.

Delete Files and Folders

You can easily delete files and folders. When you delete a file or folder, it is moved from its current location to the ***Recycle Bin*** on your computer. The *Recycle Bin* stores deleted items. If a file or folder is in the *Recycle Bin*, you can restore it to its original location or move it to a different location. You also have the option to permanently delete a file or folder. If an item is permanently deleted, you do not have the restore option.

▸HOW TO: Delete Files and Folders

1. Open a *File Explorer* window and select the file or folder you want to delete.
   - You can select multiple files and folders to delete at the same time.
2. Click the **Delete** drop-down arrow [*Home* tab, *Organize* group] to display the list of delete options (Figure Intro-101).
   - The default action when you click the *Delete* button (not the drop-down arrow) is *Recycle*.
3. Delete a file by selecting **Recycle**, which moves it to the *Recycle Bin*.
   - *Recycle* deletes the item(s) and moves it (them) to the *Recycle Bin*.
   - When you *Recycle* an item, you are not prompted to confirm the deletion. To change the default setting, select **Show recycle confirmation** from the *Delete* drop-down list. A confirmation dialog box displays each time you delete or recycle an item.

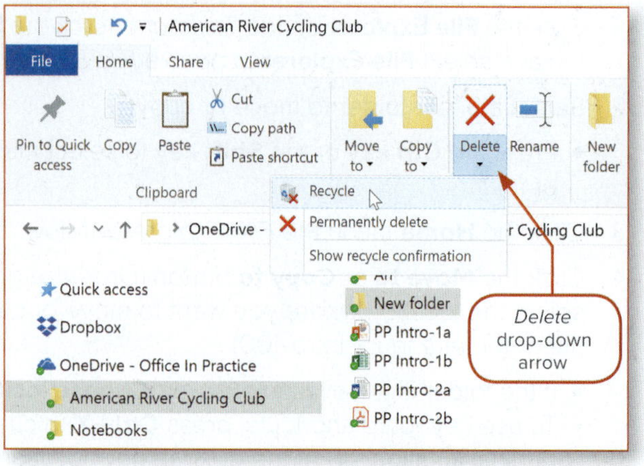

Figure Intro-101 Delete selected folder

4. Delete a file permanently by clicking the **Delete** drop-down arrow and selecting **Permanently delete**. A confirmation dialog box opens. Click **Yes** to confirm the deletion.
   - *Permanently delete* deletes the item(s) from your computer.

ANOTHER WAY

Press **Ctrl+D** or the **Delete** key on your keyboard to recycle selected item(s).
Press **Shift+Delete** to permanently delete selected item(s).

Create a Zipped (Compressed) Folder

If you want to share multiple files or a folder of files with classmates, coworkers, friends, or family, you can ***zip*** the files into a ***zipped folder*** (also called a ***compressed folder***). For example, you can't attach an entire folder to an email message, but you can attach a zipped folder to an email message. Compressing files and folders decreases their size. You can zip a group of selected files, a folder, or a combination of files and folders, and then share the zipped folder with others through email or in a cloud storage location such as *OneDrive*.

▸HOW TO: Create a Zipped (Compressed) Folder

1. Open a *File Explorer* window.
2. Select the file(s) and/or folder(s) you want to zip (compress).
3. Click the **Zip** button [*Share* tab, *Send* group] (Figure Intro-102). A zipped folder is created.
   - The default name of the zipped folder is the name of the first item you selected to zip.

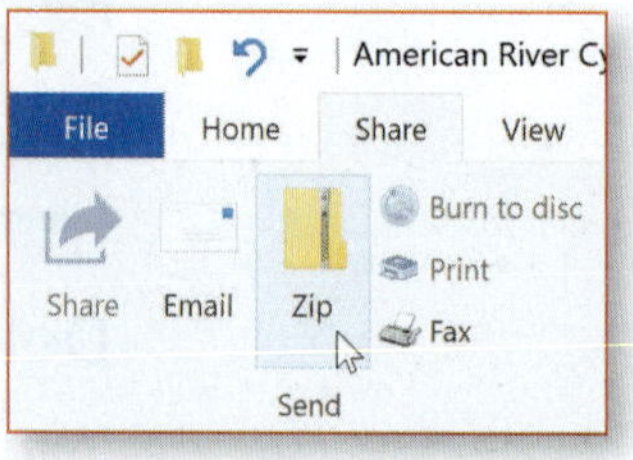

Figure Intro-102 Create a zipped folder

4. Type a name for the zipped folder and press **Enter**. Alternatively, press **Enter** to accept the default name.
   - The icon for a zipped folder looks similar to the icon for a folder except it has a vertical zipper down the middle of the folder.

> **ANOTHER WAY**
>
> Right-click a selected file(s) and/or folder(s), click **Send to**, and select **Compressed (zipped) folder**.

Extract a Zipped (Compressed) Folder

If you receive a zipped folder via email or download a zipped folder, save the zipped folder to your computer and then ***extract*** its contents. Extracting a zipped folder creates a regular Windows folder from the zipped folder.

HOW TO: Extract a Zipped (Compressed) Folder

1. Select the zipped folder to extract.
2. Click the **Compressed Folder Tools** tab.
3. Click the **Extract all** button (Figure Intro-103). The *Extract Compressed (Zipped) Folders* dialog box opens (Figure Intro-104).
4. Click **Extract** to extract the folder.
   - Both the extracted folder and the zipped folder display.
   - If you check the **Show extracted files when complete** check box, the extracted folder will open after extracting.

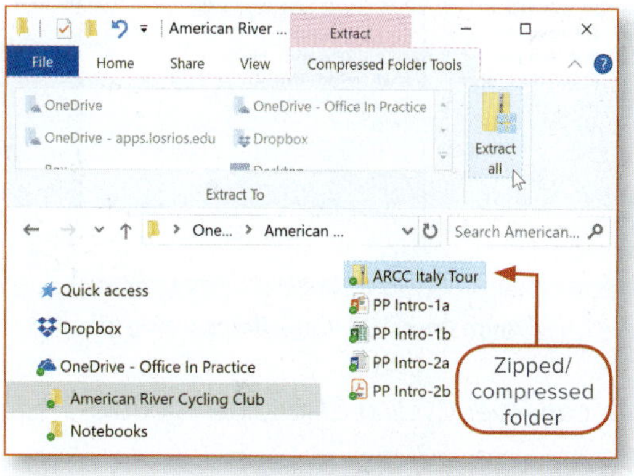

Figure Intro-103 Extract files from a zipped folder

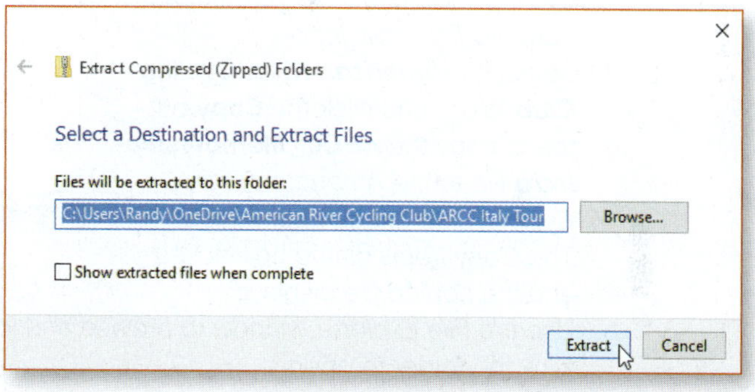

Figure Intro-104 *Extract Compressed (Zipped) Folders* dialog box

> **ANOTHER WAY**
>
> Right-click a zipped folder and select **Extract All** from the context menu.

PAUSE & PRACTICE: INTRO-3

For this project, you copy and rename files in your *OneDrive* folder on your computer, create a folder, move files, create a zipped folder, and rename a zipped folder.

Files Needed: ***[your initials] PP Intro-1a.pptx***, ***[your initials] PP Intro-1b.xlsx***, ***[your initials] PP Intro-2a.docx***, ***[your initials] PP Intro-2b.docx***, and ***ARCC_Membership-Intro.accdb*** *(Student data files are available in the Library of your SIMnet account.)*
Completed Project File Names: ***[your initials] PP Intro-1a.pptx***, ***[your initials] PP Intro-1b.xlsx***, ***[your initials] PP Intro-2a.docx***, ***[your initials] PP Intro-2b.docx***, ***[your initials] PP Intro-3.accdb***, and ***ARCC Italy Tour-2020*** (zipped folder)

1. Copy and rename a file.
   a. Click the **File Explorer** on the *Taskbar* or click the **Start** button and select **File Explorer** to open a *File Explorer* window. If *File Explorer* is not available on the *Taskbar* or *Start* menu, use *Cortana* to find and open a *File Explorer* window.
   b. Browse the *File Explorer* window to locate your student data files.
   c. Select the ***ARCC_Membership-Intro*** file.
   d. Click the **Copy to** button [*Home* tab, *Organize* group] and select **Choose location** from the drop-down list to open the *Copy Items* dialog box.
   e. Browse to locate the *American River Cycling Club* folder you created in *Pause & Practice: Intro-1*.
   f. Select the ***American River Cycling Club*** folder and click the **Copy** button to copy the ***ARCC_Membership-Intro*** file to the *American River Cycling Club* folder (Figure Intro-105). The *Copy Items* dialog box closes and the copied file displays.

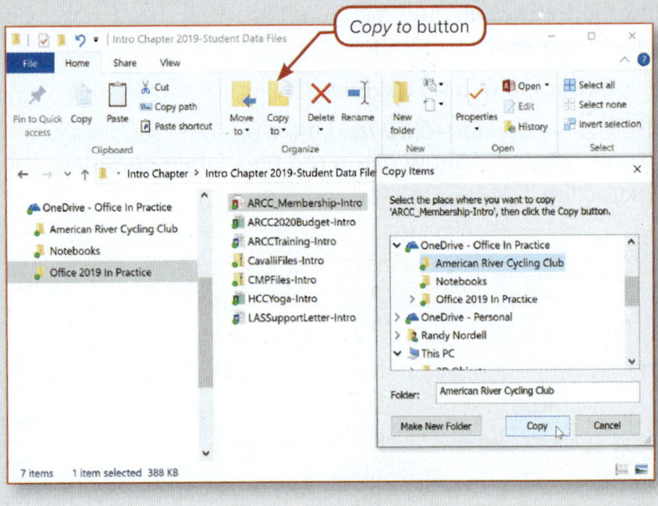

Figure Intro-105 ***Copy Items*** **dialog box**

   g. Use the *File Explorer* window to browse and locate the *American River Cycling Club* folder. Double-click the folder to open it.
   h. Click the ***ARCC_Membership-Intro*** file in the *American River Cycling Club* folder to select it.
   i. Click the **Rename** button [*Home* tab, *Organize* group], type [your initials] PP Intro-3 as the new file name, and press **Enter** (Figure Intro-106).

2. Create a new folder and move files.
   a. With the *American River Cycling Club* folder still open, click the **New folder** button [*Home* tab, *New* group] (see Figure Intro-106).
   b. Type ARCC Italy Tour as the name of the new folder and press **Enter**.
   c. Select the ***[your initials] PP Intro-1a*** file.

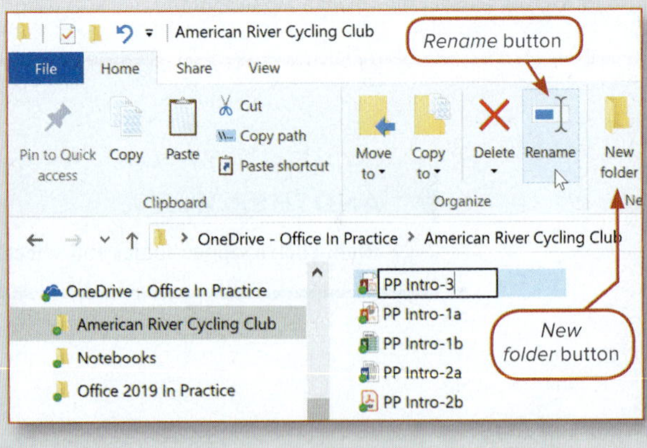

Figure Intro-106 Rename a file

d. Press the **Ctrl** key, select the ***[your initials] PP Intro-1b***, ***[your initials] PP Intro-2a***, ***[your initials] PP Intro-2b***, and ***[your initials] PP Intro-3*** files, and release the **Ctrl** key. All five files should be selected.
e. Click the **Move to** button [*Home* tab, *Organize* group] and select **Choose location** to open the *Move Items* dialog box (Figure Intro-107).
f. Browse to locate the *ARCC Italy Tour* folder in the *Move Items* dialog box.
g. Select the ***ARCC Italy Tour*** folder and click the **Move** button to move the selected files to the *ARCC Italy Tour* folder.
h. Double-click the ***ARCC Italy Tour*** folder to open it and confirm the five files are moved.
i. Click the **Up** or **Back** arrow above the *Navigation* pane to return to the *American River Cycling Club* folder (see Figure Intro-107).

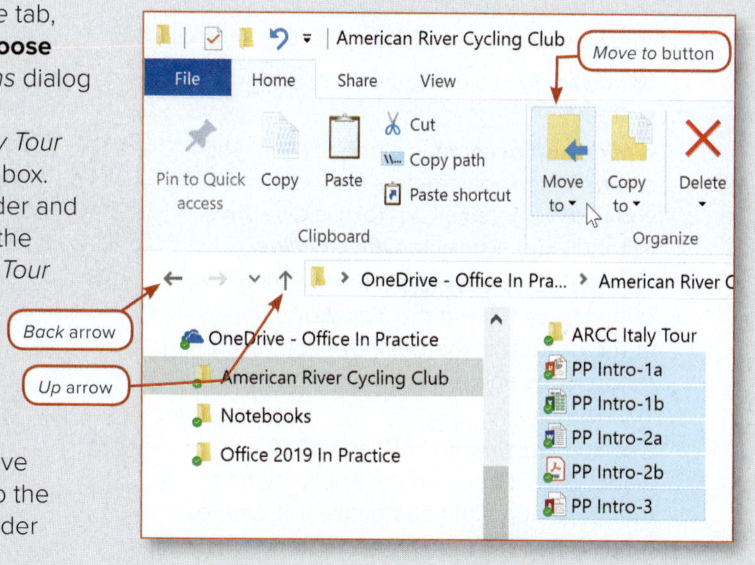

Figure Intro-107 Move selected files to a different folder

3. Create a zipped folder.
   a. Select the ***ARCC Italy Tour*** folder.
   b. Click the **Zip** button [*Share* tab, *Send* group]. A zipped (compressed) folder is created.
   c. Place the insertion point at the end of the zipped folder name, type -2020, and press **Enter** (Figure Intro-108).

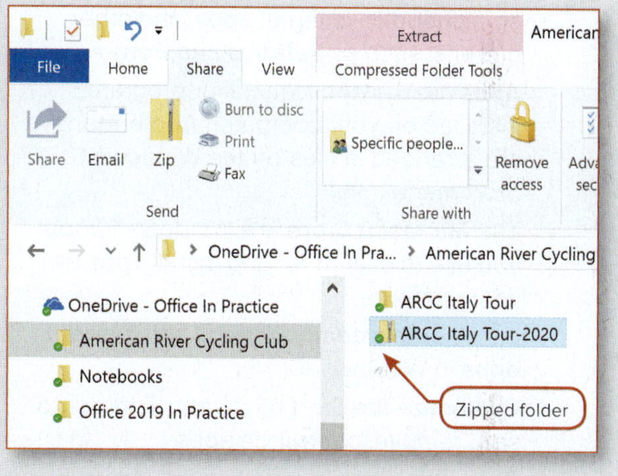

Figure Intro-108 Create a zipped folder

4. Email the zipped folder to your instructor.
   a. Use your email account to create a new email to send to your instructor.
   b. Include an appropriate subject line and a brief message in the body.
   c. Attach the ***ARCC Italy Tour-2020*** zipped folder to the email message and send the email message.

Chapter Summary

Intro. 1 Explore select features of Windows 10 (p. Intro-2).

- ***Windows 10*** is a computer operating system.
- A ***Microsoft account*** is a free account you create. When you create a Microsoft account, you receive an email address, a ***OneDrive*** account, and access to ***Office Online***.
- The ***Windows desktop*** is the working area of Windows 10, and the ***Taskbar*** displays at the bottom of the desktop. You can rearrange icons and pin applications to the *Taskbar*.
- Use the ***Start menu*** in Windows 10 to select a task. You can pin applications to the *Start* menu and customize the arrangement of apps.
- The left side of the ***Start menu*** displays ***Recently added*** apps, ***Most used*** apps, an alphabetic listing of apps, and other buttons, such as ***Settings*** and ***Power***.
- ***Apps*** are the applications or programs installed on your computer. App buttons are arranged in tiles on the Windows 10 *Start* menu.
- The ***Microsoft Store*** is a Windows 10 app you use to search for and install apps on your computer.
- Install both ***traditional apps*** and ***modern apps*** in Windows 10.
- Customize the *Start* menu and *Taskbar* to add, remove, or arrange apps.
- *File Explorer* is a window that displays files and folders on your computer.
- *OneDrive* is the cloud storage area where you can store files in a private and secure online location.
- The ***OneDrive folder*** in Windows 10 is one of your file storage location options.
- Access *OneDrive* folders and files using an internet browser window.
- ***Cortana*** is a search tool in Windows 10 used to locate information on your computer and the internet.
- ***Task View*** displays all open apps and windows as tiles on your desktop. Select an app or window to display or close.
- Use the ***Settings*** window to customize the Windows environment.
- The ***Action Center*** displays notifications and buttons to open many common Windows settings and features.

Intro. 2 Use basic features of Microsoft Office and navigate the Office working environment (p. Intro-12).

- ***Office 2019/365*** is application software that includes ***Word***, ***Excel***, ***Access***, ***PowerPoint***, ***Outlook***, ***OneNote***, and ***Publisher***.
- ***Office 2019*** and ***Office 365*** include the same application products, but they differ in how you purchase them. Office 365 includes features that may not be available in Office 2019.
- ***Office desktop apps*** are the full-function Office 2019 or 365 products you install on your laptop or desktop computer.
- ***Office universal apps*** are a scaled-down version of Office applications installed on a tablet or mobile device.
- ***Office Online*** is free online software that works in conjunction with your online *Microsoft* account.
- A ***Start page*** displays when you open each of the Office applications. You can open an existing file or create a new file.
- The ***Backstage view*** in each of the Office applications performs many common tasks such as saving, opening an existing file, creating a new file, printing, and sharing.
- ***Tell Me*** is the Office help feature that displays Office commands related to specific topics.
- Use the mouse (or touchpad) on your computer to navigate the pointer on your computer screen. Use the pointer or click buttons to select text or objects.
- When using Office 2019/365 on a touch-screen computer, use the touch screen to perform actions. You can choose between ***Touch Mode*** and ***Mouse Mode*** in Office applications.

Intro. 3 Create, save, close, and open Office files (p. Intro-19).

- Create a new Office file from the *Start* page or *Backstage* view of the Office application.

- Assign a file name when you save a file for the first time.
- ***AutoSave*** is a new feature that automatically saves a file stored in *OneDrive*.
- Create folders to organize saved files, and you can save a file as a different file name.
- Office applications use a variety of different file types.
- Close an Office file when finished working on it. If the file has not been saved or changes have been made to the file, you are prompted to save the file before closing.
- Open an existing file from the *Start* page or from the *Open* area on *Backstage* view in each of the Office applications.

Intro. 4 Customize the view and display size in Office applications and work with multiple Office files (p. Intro-28).

- Each Office application has a variety of display views.
- Select an application view from the options on the ***View tab*** or the view buttons on the ***Status bar***.
- The ***Zoom*** feature changes the display size of your file.
- ***Minimize***, ***restore down***, or ***maximize*** an open Office application window.
- Work with multiple Office files at the same time and switch between open files.
- ***Snap Assist*** enables you to arrange an open window on one side of your computer screen and select another window to fill the other side of the screen.

Intro. 5 Print, share, and customize Office files (p. Intro-32).

- Print a file in a variety of formats. The *Print* area on the *Backstage* view lists print options and displays a preview of your file.
- Export a file as a ***PDF (portable document format)*** file and save the PDF file to post to a web site or share with others.
- ***Document properties*** store information about a file.
- Share Office files in a variety of ways and enable others to view or edit shared files. To share a file with others, save the file in *OneDrive*.
- Program options are available on the *Backstage* view. Use program options to apply global changes to an Office application.

Intro. 6 Use the *Ribbon,* tabs, groups, dialog boxes, task panes, galleries, and the *Quick Access* toolbar (p. Intro-37).

- The ***Ribbon*** appears at the top of an Office window. It contains ***tabs*** and ***groups*** with commands to format and edit files.
- The ***Ribbon Display Options*** provides different ways to display the *Ribbon* in Office applications.
- A variety of ***buttons***, ***drop-down lists***, and ***galleries*** display within groups on each tab.
- ***Dialog boxes*** contain additional features not always displayed on the *Ribbon*.
- Click the ***launcher*** in the bottom-right corner of selected groups to open a dialog box.
- A ***ScreenTip*** displays information about commands on the *Ribbon*.
- Dialog boxes contain ***radio buttons***, ***check boxes***, ***drop-down lists***, and ***text boxes***.
- The ***Quick Access toolbar*** contains buttons that enable you to perform commands and displays in all Office applications. It is located in the upper left.
- Add or remove commands on the *Quick Access* toolbar.

Intro. 7 Use context menus, mini toolbar, keyboard shortcuts, and function keys in Office applications (p. Intro-41).

- A ***context menu*** displays when you right-click text or an object. A context menu contains different features depending on what you right-click.
- A ***mini toolbar*** is another context menu that displays formatting options.
- Use ***keyboard shortcuts*** to apply features or initiate commands.
- Numbered ***function keys*** perform commands in Office applications. On laptops, you may have to press the **Function key (Fn** or **fn)** to activate the numbered function keys.

Intro. 8 Organize and customize Windows folders and Office files (p. Intro-46).

- ***Folders*** store and organize files.
- Create, move, or copy files and folders. Files stored in a folder are moved or copied with that folder.
- Rename a file to change the file name.
- A deleted file or folder moves to the ***Recycle Bin*** on your computer by default. Alternatively, you can permanently delete files and folders.
- ***Zip*** files and/or folders into a ***zipped (compressed) folder*** to email or to share multiple files as a single file.
- ***Extract*** a zipped folder to create a regular Windows folder and to access its contents.

Check for Understanding

The SIMbook for this text (within your SIMnet account) provides the following resources for concept review:

- Multiple-choice questions
- Short answer questions
- Matching exercises

For these projects, you use your *OneDrive* to store files. If you don't already have a Microsoft account, see *SLO Intro.1: Using Windows 10* for information about creating a free personal Microsoft account.

Guided Project Intro-1

For this project, you organize and edit files for Emma Cavalli at Placer Hills Real Estate. You extract a zipped folder, rename files, manage multiple documents, apply formatting, and export as a PDF file.
[Student Learning Outcomes Intro.1, Intro.2, Intro.3, Intro.4, Intro.5, Intro.6, Intro.7, Intro.8]

Files Needed: ***CavalliFiles-Intro*** (zipped folder) *(Student data files are available in the* Library *of your SIMnet account.)*
Completed Project File Names: ***PHRE*** folder containing the following files: ***BuyerEscrowChecklist-Intro***, ***CavalliProspectingLetter-Intro***, ***[your initials] Intro-1a.accdb***, ***[your initials] Intro-1b.xlsx***, ***[your initials] Intro-1c.docx***, ***[your initials] Intro-1d.docx***, and ***[your initials] Intro-1e.pdf***.

Skills Covered in This Project

- Copy and paste a zipped folder.
- Create a new folder in your *OneDrive* folder.
- Extract a zipped folder.
- Move a file.
- Rename a file.
- Open a Word document.
- Use *Task View* to switch between two open Word documents.
- Turn off *AutoSave*.
- Save a Word document with a different file name.
- Change display size.
- Use a mini toolbar, keyboard shortcut, context menu, and dialog box to apply formatting to selected text.
- Export a document as a PDF file.

---

1. Copy a zipped folder and create a new *OneDrive* folder.
   a. Click the Windows **Start** button and click **File Explorer** to open the *File Explorer* window. If *File Explorer* is not available on the *Start* menu, use *Cortana* to find and open the *File Explorer* window.
   b. Browse in the *File Explorer* window to locate your student data files.
   c. Select the ***CavalliFiles-Intro*** zipped folder from your student data files and press **Ctrl+C** or click the **Copy** button [*Home* tab, *Clipboard* group] to copy the folder.
   d. Select your ***OneDrive*** folder on the left of the *File Explorer* window, and click the **New folder** button [*Home* tab, *New* group] to create a new folder. If you don't have *OneDrive* available, create the new folder in a location where you store your files.
   e. Type PHRE and press **Enter**.
   f. Press **Enter** again to open the *PHRE* folder or double-click the folder to open it.
   g. Press **Ctrl+V** or click the **Paste** button [*Home* tab, *Clipboard* group] to paste the copied ***CavalliFiles-Intro*** zipped folder in the *PHRE* folder.
2. Extract a zipped folder.
   a. Select the ***CavalliFiles-Intro*** zipped folder.
   b. Click the **Compressed Folder Tools Extract** tab and click the **Extract all** button (Figure Intro-109). The *Extract Compressed (Zipped) Folders* dialog box opens.
   c. Uncheck the **Show extracted files when complete** box if it is checked.
   d. Click the **Extract** button. The zipped folder is extracted, and the *PHRE* folder now contains two *CavalliFiles-Intro* folders. One folder is zipped and the other is a regular folder.

e. Select the zipped ***CavalliFiles-Intro*** folder and click the **Delete** button [*Home* tab, *Organize* group] to delete the zipped folder.

3. Move and rename files.
   a. Double-click the **CavalliFiles-Intro** folder to open it.
   b. Click the first file, press and hold the **Shift** key, and click the last file to select all four files.
   c. Press **Ctrl+X** or click the **Cut** button [*Home* tab, *Clipboard* group] to cut the files from the current location (Figure Intro-110).
   d. Click the **Up** arrow to move up to the *PHRE* folder.
   e. Press **Ctrl+V** or click the **Paste** button [*Home* tab, *Clipboard* group] to paste and move the files.
   f. Select the ***Cavalli files-Intro*** folder and press **Delete** to delete the folder.
   g. Select the ***CavalliPHRE-Intro*** file and click the **Rename** button [*Home* tab, *Organize* group].
   h. Type [your initials] Intro-1a and press **Enter**.
   i. Right-click the ***FixedMortgageRates-Intro*** file and select **Rename** from the context menu.
   j. Type [your initials] Intro-1b and press **Enter**.

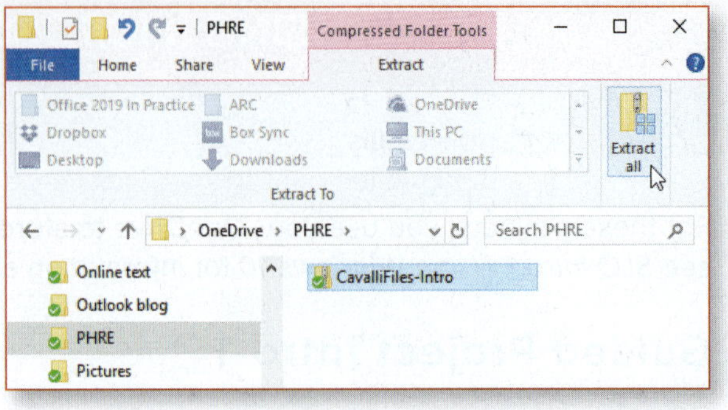

Figure Intro-109 Extract a zipped folder

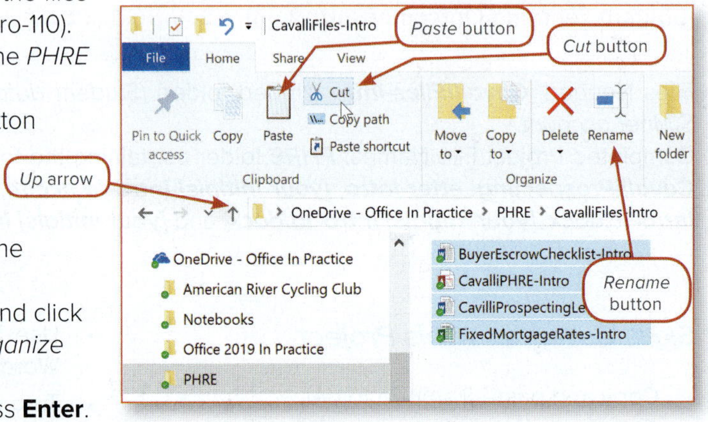

Figure Intro-110 *Cut* files to move from a folder

4. Open two Word documents and rename a Word document.
   a. Click the ***BuyerEscrowChecklist-Intro*** file, press the **Ctrl** key, and click the ***CavalliProspectingLetter-Intro*** file to select both files.
   b. Press the **Enter** key to open both files in Word. If the files open in *Protected View*, click the **Enable Editing** button.
   c. Click the **Task View** button on your *Taskbar* (Figure Intro-111). All open windows display as tiles on your desktop.
   d. Select the ***BuyerEscrowChecklist-Intro*** document.
   e. Click the **AutoSave** button [*Quick Access* toolbar] to turn *AutoSave* off (if *AutoSave* is on).
   f. Click the **File** tab to open the *Backstage* view and select **Save As** on the left.
   g. Click the **Browse** button to open the *Save As* dialog box.
   h. Type [your initials] Intro-1c in the *File name* text box and click **Save**. The file is saved in the *PHRE* folder.
   i. Click the **X** in the upper-right corner of the Word window to close the document. The *CavalliProspectingLetter-Intro* document remains open.

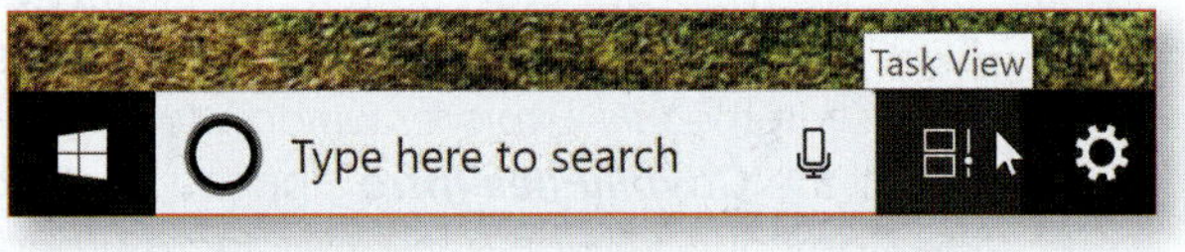

Figure Intro-111 *Task View* button on the *Taskbar*

5. Change display size and edit and rename a Word document.
   a. Press the **Task View** button on your *Taskbar* and select the ***CavalliProspectingLetter-Intro*** document.

b. Click the **Zoom In** or **Zoom Out** button in the bottom right of the document window to change the display size to **120%** (Figure Intro-112).

Figure Intro-112 Use *Zoom* to change the display size to 120%

c. Select "**Placer Hills Real Estate**" in the first body paragraph of the letter. The mini toolbar displays (Figure Intro-113).

d. Click the **Bold** button on the mini toolbar to apply bold formatting to the selected text.

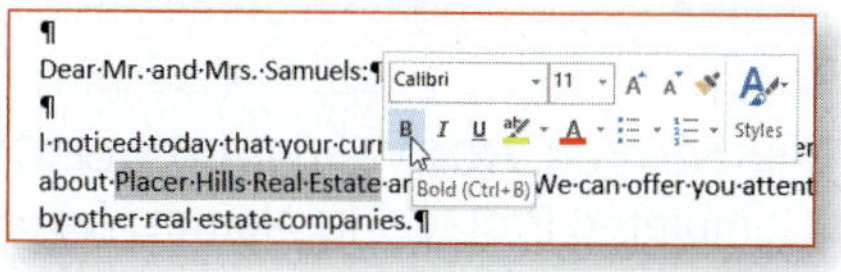

Figure Intro-113 Use the mini toolbar to apply formatting

e. Select "**Whitney Hills resident**" in the first sentence in the second body paragraph and press **Ctrl+I** to apply italic formatting to the selected text.

f. Select the text that reads "**Emma Cavalli**," below "Best regards,".

g. Right-click the selected text and select **Font** from the context menu to open the *Font* dialog box.

h. Check the **Small Caps** box in the *Effects* area and click **OK** to close the *Font* dialog box.

i. Select "**Emma Cavalli**" (if necessary) and click the **Bold** button [*Home* tab, *Font* group].

j. Click the **File** tab and select **Save As** on the left. If the file is saved in *OneDrive* and *AutoSave* is turned on, select **Save a Copy**.

k. Type [your initials] Intro-1d in the *File name* text box and click **Save** (Figure Intro-114).

Figure Intro-114 *Save* area on the *Backstage* view.

6. Export a Word document as a PDF file.

a. With the ***[your initials] Intro-1d*** still open, click the **File** tab to open the *Backstage* view.

b. Select **Export** on the left, select **Create PDF/XPS Document** in the *Export* area, and click the **Create PDF/XPS** button (Figure Intro-115). The *Publish as PDF or XPS* dialog box opens.

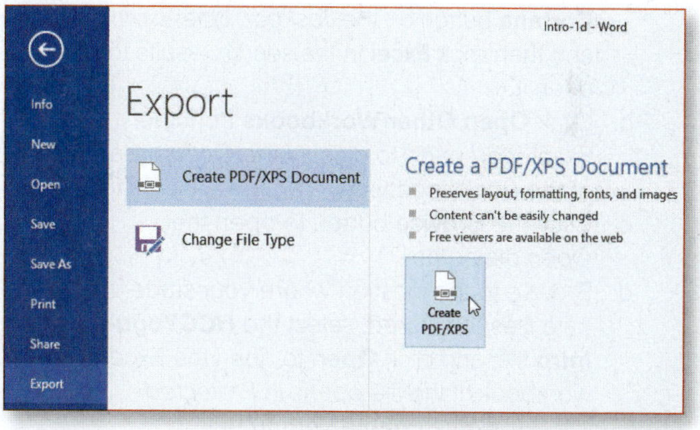

Figure Intro-115 Export as a PDF file

c. Deselect the **Open file after publishing** check box if it is checked.

d. Select the **Standard (publishing online and printing)** radio button in the *Optimize for* area.

e. Type [your initials] Intro-1e in the *File name* text box, select a location to save the file, and click **Publish**.

f. Click the **Save** button on the *Quick Access* toolbar or press **Ctrl+S** to save the document.

g. Click the **X** in the upper-right corner of the Word window to close the document and Word.

7. Your *PHRE* folder should contain the files shown in Figure Intro-116.

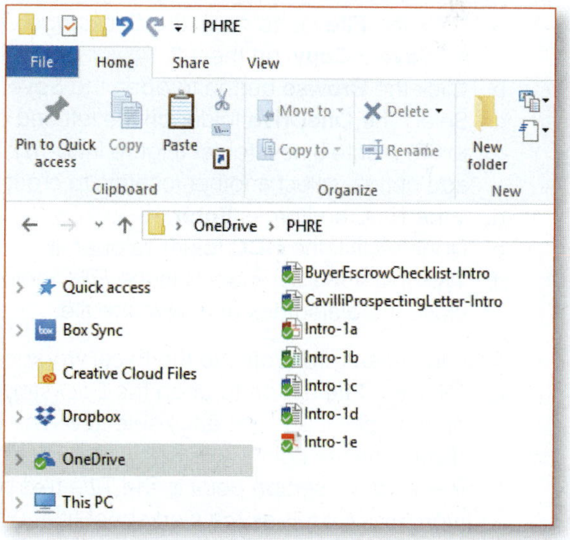

Figure Intro-116 Intro-1 completed

Guided Project Intro-2

For this project, you modify an Excel file for Hamilton Civic Center. You create a folder, rename a file, add document properties, use *Tell Me* to search for a topic, share the file, and export a file as a PDF file.
[Student Learning Outcomes Intro.1, Intro.2, Intro.3, Intro.5, Intro.6, Intro.7, Intro.8]

File Needed: ***HCCYoga-Intro.xlsx*** *(Student data files are available in the* Library *of your SIMnet account.)*
Completed Project File Names: ***[your initials] Intro-2a.xlsx*** and ***[your initials] Intro-2b.pdf***

Skills Covered in This Project

- Open Excel and an Excel workbook.
- Create a new folder.
- Save an Excel workbook with a different file name.
- Add document properties to a file.
- Use *Tell Me* to search for a topic.
- Open a Word document.
- Share a file.
- Export a file as a PDF file.

1. Open Excel and open an Excel workbook.
   a. Click the Windows **Start** button and click **Excel** to open this application. If Excel 2019 is not available on the *Start* menu, click the **Cortana** button on the *Taskbar*, type Excel, and then click **Excel** in the search results to open it.
   b. Click **Open Other Workbooks** from the Excel *Start* page to display the *Open* area of the *Backstage* view.
   c. Click the **Browse** button to open the *Open* dialog box.
   d. Browse to the location where your student data files are stored, select the ***HCCYoga-Intro*** file, and click **Open** to open the Excel workbook. If the file opens in *Protected View,* click the **Enable Editing** button.

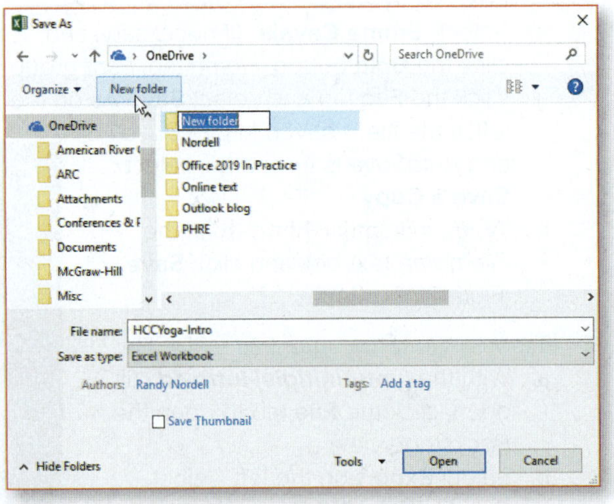

Figure Intro-117 Create a new folder from the *Save As* dialog box

2. Save a file as a different file name in your *OneDrive* folder.
   a. Click the **File** tab to open the *Backstage* view and select **Save As** (or **Save a Copy**) on the left.
   b. Click the **Browse** button to open the *Save As* dialog box.
   c. Select the **OneDrive** folder on the left and click the **New folder** button to create a new folder (Figure Intro-117). If *OneDrive* is not a storage option, select another location to create the new folder.
   d. Type HCC and press **Enter**.
   e. Double-click the **HCC** folder to open it.
   f. Type [your initials] Intro-2a in the *File name* area and click **Save** to close the dialog box and save the file.
3. Add document properties to the Excel workbook.
   a. Click the **File** button to open the *Backstage* view and select **Info** on the left if it is not already selected. The document properties display on the right.
   b. Place your insertion point in the *Title* text box ("Add a title") and type Yoga Classes as the worksheet title.
   c. Click the **Show All Properties** link at the bottom of the list of properties to display more properties (Figure Intro-118).

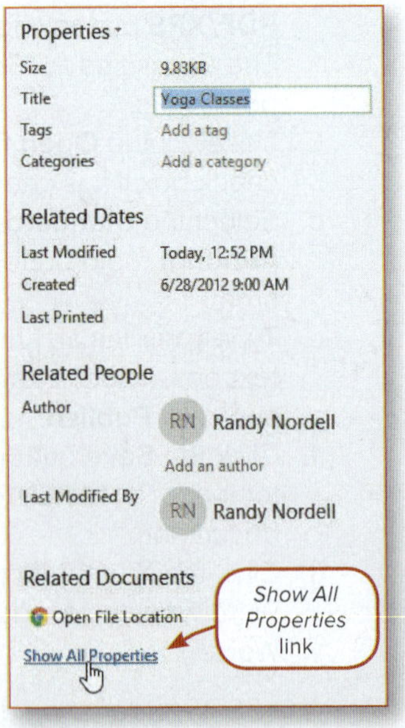

Figure Intro-118 Add document properties

d. Place your insertion point in the *Company* text box and type Hamilton Civic Center as the company name.
e. Click the **Back** arrow in the upper left of the *Backstage* window to return to the Excel workbook.

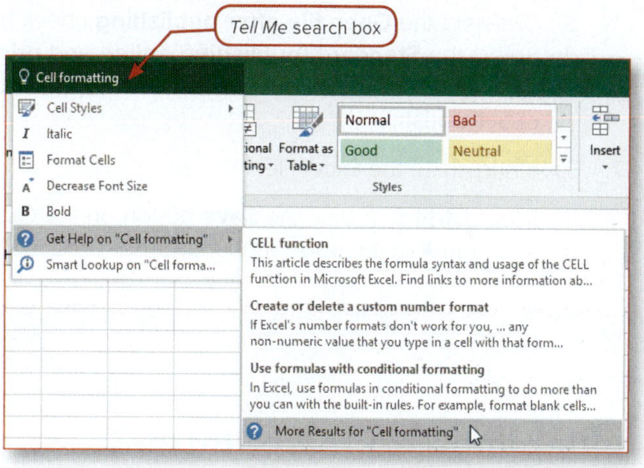

Figure Intro-119 Use *Tell Me* to search for a topic

4. Use *Tell Me* to search for a topic.
   a. Click the **Tell Me** search box at the top of the *Ribbon* and type Cell formatting (Figure Intro-119).
   b. Select **Get Help on "Cell formatting"** and click **More Results for "Cell formatting"** to open the *Help* pane at the right.
   c. Click the first result link to display information about the topic.
   d. Click the **Back** arrow to return to the search list.
   e. Click the **X** in the upper-right corner to close the *Help* pane.

5. Share an Excel workbook with your instructor. If your file is not saved on *OneDrive*, skip step 5.
   a. Click the **Share** button in the upper-right corner of the Word window to open the *Send Link* window (Figure Intro-120). If you're using a personal Microsoft account, the *Share* pane displays at the right, and the sharing options differ slightly.
   b. Click the **Link settings** button to open the *Link settings* window (Figure Intro-121).
   c. Click the **Anyone** button and check the **Allow editing** box (if necessary).
   d. Click **Apply** to close the *Link settings* window and return to the *Send Link* window.
   e. Type your instructor's email address in the *Enter a name or email address* area (see Figure Intro-120).
   f. Type a brief message to your instructor and click the **Send** button.
   g. Click the **X** in the upper-right corner of the confirmation window to close it.

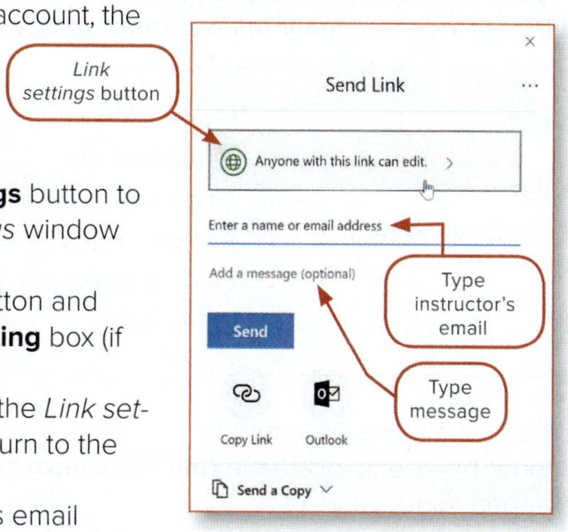

Figure Intro-120 *Send Link* window

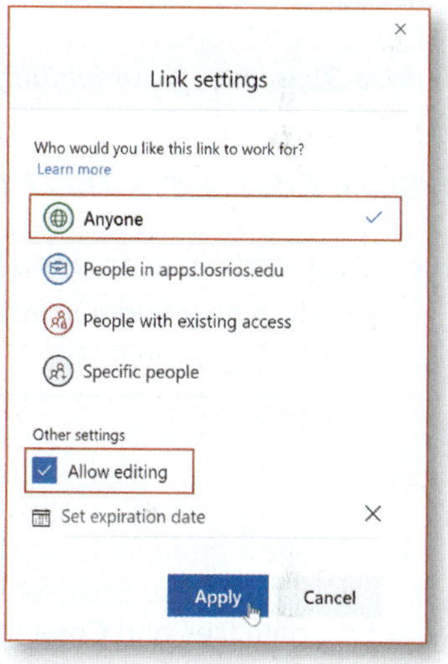

Figure Intro-121 *Link settings* window

6. Export an Excel file as a PDF file.
   a. Click the **File** tab to open the *Backstage* view.
   b. Select **Export** on the left, select **Create PDF/XPS Document** in the *Export* area, and click the **Create PDF/XPS** button (Figure Intro-122). The *Publish as PDF or XPS* dialog box opens.

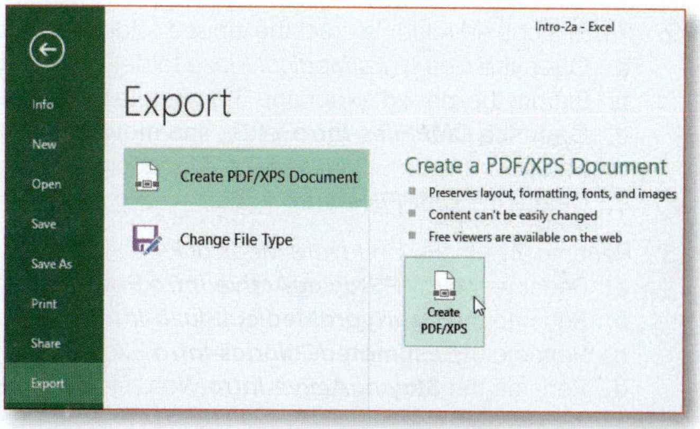

Figure Intro-122 Export as a PDF file

c. Deselect the **Open file after publishing** check box if it is checked.
d. Select the **Standard (publishing online and printing)** radio button in the *Optimize for* area.
e. Type [your initials] Intro-2b in the *File name* text box, select a location to save the file, and click **Publish**.

7. Save and close the Excel file.
   a. Press **Ctrl+S** or click the **Save** button on the *Quick Access* toolbar to save the worksheet.
   b. Click the **X** in the upper-right corner of the Excel window to close the file and Excel.

Independent Project Intro-3

For this project, you organize and edit files for Courtyard Medical Plaza. You extract a zipped folder, delete a folder, move files, rename files, export a file as a PDF file, and share a file.
[Student Learning Outcomes Intro.1, Intro.2, Intro.3, Intro.5, Intro.8]

File Needed: ***CMPFiles-Intro*** (zipped folder) *(Student data files are available in the* Library *of your SIMnet account.)*
Completed Project File Names: ***[your initials] Intro-3a.pptx***, ***[your initials] Intro-3a-pdf.pdf***, ***[your initials] Intro-3b.accdb***, ***[your initials] Intro-3c.xlsx***, and ***[your initials] Intro-3d.docx***

Skills Covered in This Project

- Copy and paste a zipped folder.
- Create a new folder in your *OneDrive* folder.
- Extract a zipped folder.
- Delete a folder.
- Move a file.
- Rename a file.
- Open a PowerPoint presentation.
- Export a file as a PDF file.
- Open a Word document.
- Share a file.

1. Copy a zipped folder and create a new *OneDrive* folder.
   a. Open a *File Explorer* window, browse to locate the ***CMPFiles-Intro*** zipped folder in your student data files and **Copy** the zipped folder.
   b. Go to your *OneDrive* folder and create a new folder named Courtyard Medical Plaza within the *OneDrive* folder. If *OneDrive* is not a storage option, select another location to create the new folder.
2. Paste a copied folder, extract the zipped folder, and move files.
   a. Open the *Courtyard Medical Plaza* folder and **Paste** the zipped folder.
   b. Extract the zipped folder and then delete the zipped folder.
   c. Open the ***CMPFiles-Intro*** folder and move all of the files to the *Courtyard Medical Plaza* folder.
   d. Return to the *Courtyard Medical Plaza* folder to confirm the four files were moved.
   e. Delete the ***CMPFiles-Intro*** folder.
3. Rename files in the *Courtyard Medical Plaza* folder.
   a. Rename the ***CMPStayingActive-Intro*** PowerPoint file as [your initials] Intro-3a.
   b. Rename the ***CourtyardMedicalPlaza-Intro*** Access file as [your initials] Intro-3b.
   c. Rename the ***EstimatedCalories-Intro*** Excel file as [your initials] Intro-3c.
   d. Rename the ***StayingActive-Intro*** Word file as [your initials] Intro-3d.

4. Export a PowerPoint file as a PDF file.
   a. Open the ***[your initials] Intro-3a*** file from the *Courtyard Medical Plaza* folder. The file opens in PowerPoint. If the file opens in *Protected View,* click the **Enable Editing** button.
   b. Export this file as a PDF file. Don't have the PDF file open after publishing and optimize for **Standard** format.
   c. Save the file as [your initials] Intro-3a-pdf and save in the *Courtyard Medical Plaza* folder.
   d. Close the PowerPoint file and exit PowerPoint.
5. Share a file with your instructor. If your files are not saved in *OneDrive*, skip step 5.
   a. Return to your *Courtyard Medical Plaza* folder and open the ***Intro-3d*** file. The file opens in Word. If the file opens in *Protected View*, click the **Enable Editing** button.
   b. Click the **Share** button in the upper-right corner of the Word window to open the *Send Link* window. If you're using a personal Microsoft account, the *Share* pane displays at the right, and the sharing options differ slightly.
   c. Click the **Link settings** button to open the *Link settings* window, click the **Anyone** button, check the **Allow editing** box (if necessary), and click **Apply** to close the *Link settings* window and return to the *Send Link* window.
   d. Type your instructor's email address in the *Enter a name or email address* area.
   e. Type a brief message to your instructor and click the **Send** button.
   f. Click the **X** in the upper-right corner of the confirmation window to close it.
6. Save and close the document and exit Word.
7. Close the *File Explorer* window containing the files for this project (Figure Intro-123).

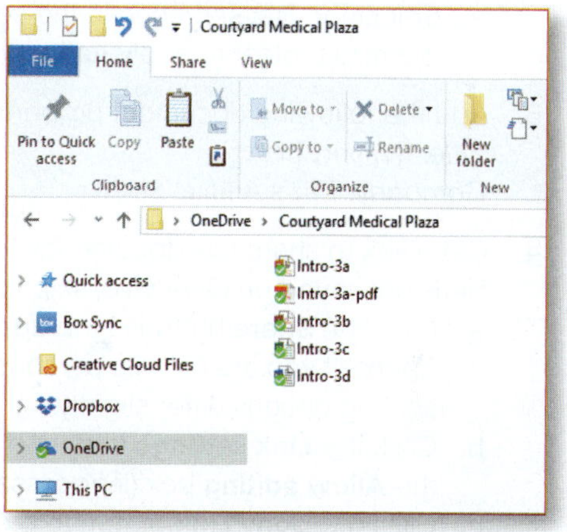

Figure Intro-123 Intro-3 completed

Independent Project Intro-4

For this project, you modify a Word file for Life's Animal Shelter. You create a folder, rename a document, add document properties, modify a document, create a sharing link, export a document as a PDF file, and create a zipped folder.
[Student Learning Outcomes Intro.1, Intro.2, Intro.3, Intro.5, Intro.6, Intro.7, Intro.8]

File Needed: ***LASSupportLetter-Intro.docx*** *(Student data files are available in the* Library *of your SIMnet account.)*
Completed Project File Names: ***[your initials] Intro-4a.docx***, ***[your initials] Intro-4b.pdf***, and ***LAS files*** (zipped folder)

Skills Covered in This Project

- Open a Word document.
- Create a new folder.
- Save a file with a different file name.
- Apply formatting to selected text.
- Add document properties to the file.
- Create a sharing link.
- Export a file as a PDF file.
- Create a zipped folder.

1. Open a Word document, create a new folder, and save the document with a different file name.
   a. Open Word.
   b. Open the ***LASSupportLetter-Intro*** Word document from your student data files. If the file opens in *Protected View*, click the **Enable Editing** button.
   c. Open the **Save As** dialog box and create a new folder named LAS in your *OneDrive* folder. If *OneDrive* is not a storage option, select another location to create the new folder.
   d. Save this document in the *LAS* folder and use [your initials] Intro-4a as the file name.
2. Apply formatting changes to the document using a dialog box, keyboard shortcut, and mini toolbar.
   a. Select "**To:**" in the memo heading and use the launcher to open the *Font* dialog box.
   b. Apply **Bold** and **All caps** to the selected text.
   c. Repeat the formatting on the other three memo guide words "**From**:", "**Date**:", and "**Subject**:".
   d. Select "**Life's Animal Shelter**" in the first sentence of the first body paragraph and press **Ctrl+B** to apply bold formatting.
   e. Select the first sentence in the second body paragraph ("**Would you again consider** . . . ") and use the mini toolbar to apply **italic** formatting.
3. Add the following document properties to the document:
   Title: Support Letter
   Company: Life's Animal Shelter
4. Get a link to share this document with your instructor and email your instructor the sharing link. If your file is not saved on *OneDrive*, skip step 5.
   a. Click the **Share** button in the upper-right corner of the Word window. The *Send Link* window opens. If you are using a personal Microsoft account, the *Share* pane opens at the right, and the sharing options differ slightly.
   b. Click the **Link settings** button to open the *Link settings* window, click the **Anyone** button, check the **Allow editing** box (if necessary), and click **Apply** to return to the *Send Link* window.
   c. Click the **Copy Link** button to create sharing link.
   d. Click **Copy** to copy the sharing link and click the **X** in the upper-right corner to close the sharing link window.
   e. Use your email account to create a new email to your instructor. Include an appropriate subject line and a brief message in the body.
   f. Press **Ctrl+V** to paste the sharing link to your document in the body of the email and send the email message.
   g. Click the **Task View** button on the Windows *Taskbar* and select the ***Intro-4a*** document to display this document.
   h. Use the **Save** command on the *Quick Access* toolbar to save the file before continuing.
5. Export this document as a PDF file.
   a. Export this file as a PDF file. Don't have the PDF file open after publishing and optimize for **Standard** format.
   b. Save the file as [your initials] Intro-4b and save in the *LAS* folder.
   c. Save and close the document and exit Word.
6. Create a zipped folder.
   a. Use *File Explorer* to open the **LAS** folder in your *OneDrive* folder.
   b. Select the two files and create a zipped folder.
   c. Name the zipped folder LAS files.
7. Close the open *File Explorer* window (Figure Intro-124).

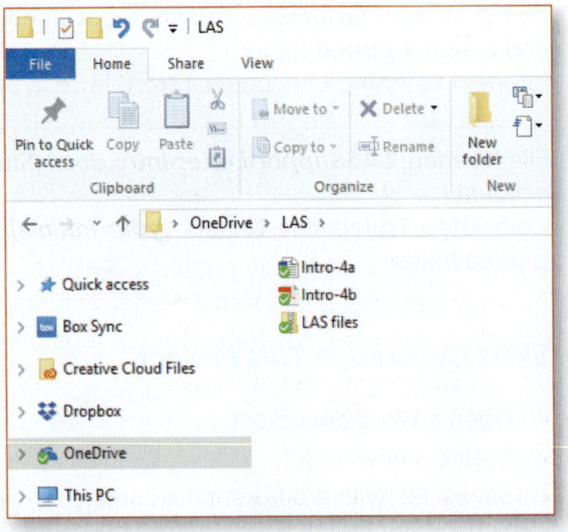

Figure Intro-124 Intro-4 completed

Challenge Project Intro-5

For this project, you create folders to organize your files for this class and share a file with your instructor. [Student Learning Outcomes Intro.1, Intro.5, Intro.8]

Files Needed: Student data files for this course
Completed Project File Name: Share a file with your instructor

Using *File Explorer*, create *OneDrive* folders to contain all of the student data files for this class. Organize your files and folders according to the following guidelines:

- Create a *OneDrive* folder for this class.
- Create a *Student data files* folder inside the class folder.
- Copy and paste the student data files in the *Student data files* folder.
- Extract student data files and delete the zipped folder.
- Create a *Solution files* folder inside the class folder.
- Inside the *Solution files* folder, create a folder for each chapter.
- Create a folder to store miscellaneous class files such as the syllabus and other course handouts.
- Open one of the student data files and share the file with your instructor.

Challenge Project Intro-6

For this project, you save a file as a different file name, customize the *Quick Access* toolbar, share a file with your instructor, export a file as a PDF file, and create a zipped folder.
[Student Learning Outcomes Intro.1, Intro.2, Intro.3, Intro.5, Intro.6, Intro.8]

File Needed: Use an existing Office file
Completed Project File Names: ***[your initials] Intro-6a*** and ***[your initials] Intro-6b***

Open an existing Word, Excel, or PowerPoint file. Save this file in a *OneDrive* folder and name it [your initials] Intro-6a. If you don't have any of these files, use one from your Pause & Practice projects or select a file from your student data files.

With your file open, perform the following actions:

- Create a new folder on *OneDrive* and save the file to this folder using a different file name.
- Customize the *Quick Access* toolbar to add command buttons. Add commands such as *New*, *Open*, *Quick Print*, and *Spelling* that you use regularly in the Office application.
- Share your file with your instructor. Enable your instructor to edit the file.
- Export the document as a PDF file. Save the file as [your initials] Intro-6b and save it in the same *OneDrive* folder as your open file.
- Zip the files in the folder.

Source of screenshots Microsoft Office 365 (2019): Word, Excel, Access, Powerpoint.

Microsoft® Office

IN PRACTICE

excel

CHAPTER 1

Creating and Editing Workbooks

EXCEL

CHAPTER OVERVIEW

Microsoft Excel (Excel) is spreadsheet software for creating an electronic workbook. A workbook consists of rows and columns to organize data, perform calculations, print reports, and build charts. With Excel, you can create simple to complex personal or business workbooks. This chapter presents basic procedures for creating and editing an Excel workbook.

STUDENT LEARNING OUTCOMES (SLOs)

After completing this chapter, you will be able to:

SLO 1.1 Create, save, and open an Excel workbook (p. E1-3).

SLO 1.2 Enter and edit labels and values in a worksheet (p. E1-7).

SLO 1.3 Use the SUM function to build a simple formula (p. E1-19).

SLO 1.4 Format a worksheet with font attributes, borders, fill, cell styles, and themes (p. E1-22).

SLO 1.5 Modify columns and rows in a worksheet (p. E1-30).

SLO 1.6 Insert, delete, and move worksheets in a workbook (p. E1-36).

SLO 1.7 Modify the appearance of a workbook by adjusting zoom size, changing views, and freezing panes (p. E1-41).

SLO 1.8 Review and prepare a workbook for final distribution by spell checking, setting properties, and adjusting page setup options (p. E1-47).

CASE STUDY

Paradise Lakes Resort (PLR) is a vacation company with properties located throughout northern Minnesota. PLR staff use Excel to track revenue, monitor expenses, maintain employee records, and perform similar tasks. In the Pause & Practice projects for Chapter 1, you create, edit, and format a workbook that displays categories of revenue for one week.

Pause & Practice 1-1: Open, edit, and save a workbook.

Pause & Practice 1-2: Use *SUM* and format data in a worksheet.

Pause & Practice 1-3: Edit columns, rows, and sheets in a workbook.

Pause & Practice 1-4: Finalize a workbook for distribution.

Creating, Saving, and Opening a Workbook

In Microsoft Excel, the file that you open, edit, and save is a ***workbook***. Each workbook contains ***worksheets***, which are comparable to individual pages in a Word document. A worksheet is also referred to as a ***spreadsheet*** or a ***sheet***, and you can use these terms interchangeably. This text also uses the terms "workbook" and "file" interchangeably.

Create a New Workbook

By default, a new workbook includes one worksheet, but a workbook can include multiple sheets. The worksheet ***tab*** is located near the bottom left of the workbook window and is labeled *Sheet1*.

When you first open Excel, the ***Excel Home page*** displays and you can create a new blank workbook, open a recently saved workbook, or create a workbook from an Excel template (a model workbook). Click **Blank workbook** to start a new blank workbook. You can also select *Blank workbook* from the *New* area in the *Backstage* view.

> **ANOTHER WAY**
>
> Press **Esc** to leave the Excel *Home* page and open a blank workbook.

HOW TO: Create a New Workbook from the Backstage View

1. Click the **File** tab to display the *Backstage* view.
2. Select **New** on the left to display the *New* area in the *Backstage* view (Figure 1-1).

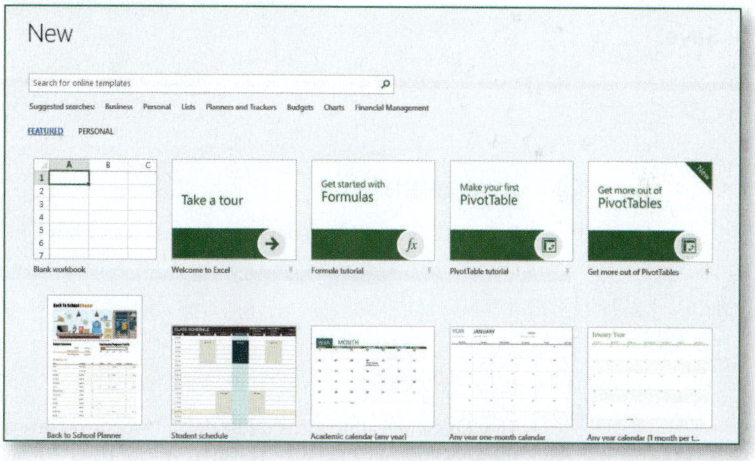

Figure 1-1 *Backstage* view for creating new workbooks

- Templates display with a thumbnail preview and name.
- Available templates update regularly so your screen may not match the figure.

3. Click **Blank workbook** to create a new blank workbook.

> **ANOTHER WAY**
>
> Press **Ctrl+N** to open a new workbook.

Save and Close a Workbook

When you open a blank workbook, Excel automatically assigns a file name, such as *Book1*, but you should type a descriptive file name for the workbook in the *Save As* area. Save a workbook on your computer, in a *OneDrive* folder, or on external media.

HOW TO: Save a New Workbook

1. Click the **File** tab to display the *Backstage* view.
2. Select **Save As** on the left to display the *Save As* area.
   - Press **Ctrl+S** to open the *Save As* area in the *Backstage* view for a workbook that has not yet been saved.
3. Select the location to save your workbook.
   - Click **Recent** to display a list of recently used folders.
   - Click **OneDrive** to see your cloud folder names.
   - Click **This PC** to save the file to the *Documents* or another folder on the computer.
   - Click **Add a Place** to select a commonly used cloud location.
   - Click **Browse** to open the *Save As* dialog box for further navigation (Figure 1-2).
4. Click a folder name to open it and type the file name in the file name box.
5. Click **Save**.

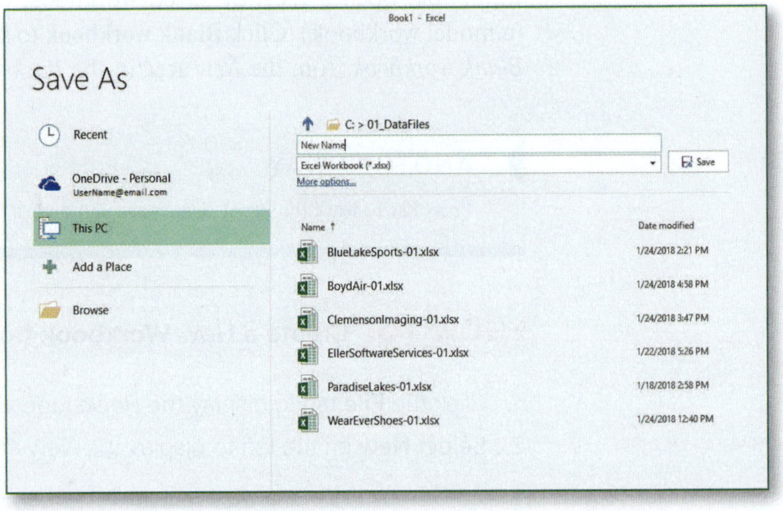

Figure 1-2 *Save As* **area in** *Backstage* **view**

> **ANOTHER WAY**
>
> Press **F12 (FN+F12)** to open the *Save As* dialog box.

> **MORE INFO**
>
> The *AutoSave* feature turns on by default when you save a file to *OneDrive*, and changes made to the file are automatically saved as you work. *AutoSave* displays in the upper-left corner of the title bar.

You can re-save a workbook with the same file name by pressing **Ctrl+S** or by clicking the **Save** button in the *Quick Access toolbar*.

To close a workbook, click the **File** tab and choose **Close**. Press **Ctrl+W** or **Ctrl+F4** to close a workbook, too. These commands leave Excel running with a blank screen so that you can open another file or start a new workbook.

Click the **X** (*Close* button) in the upper-right corner of the window to close a workbook. If the workbook is the only one open, this command closes the file and exits Excel. If multiple workbooks are open, clicking the *Close* button closes only the active workbook.

Open a Workbook

A workbook can be opened from the *Home* page, the *Open* area in the *Backstage* view, or the *Open* dialog box. When a workbook is opened from an internet or unrecognized source, it opens in ***Protected View***. Click **Enable Editing** when you know that it is safe to work with the file.

HOW TO: Open a Workbook

1. Click the **File** tab to open the *Backstage* view.
2. Click **Open** to display the *Open* area.
   - Recently used workbook names are listed on the right.
   - Click *Folders* to display a list of recently used folders (Figure 1-3).
   - *Shared with Me* lists workbooks that others have shared with you.
   - *OneDrive* lists your cloud folder names.
   - The *This PC* option lists recently used folder names on the computer.
   - Click **Add a Place** to identify a new cloud location or click **Browse** to locate a folder.
3. Select the location and folder where the workbook is stored.
4. Locate and click the workbook name.
   - The workbook opens.

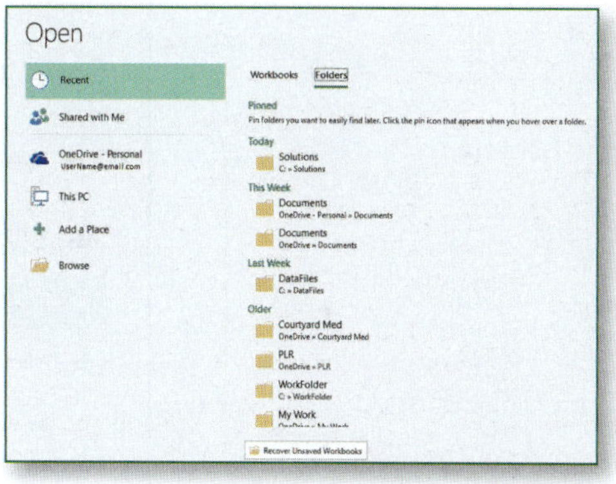

Figure 1-3 ***Open*** **area in** ***Folders*** **view**

ANOTHER WAY

Ctrl+O displays the *Open* area in the *Backstage* view. **Ctrl+F12** displays the *Open* dialog box.

MORE INFO

From an *Explorer* window, double-click a workbook file name to launch Excel and open the workbook.

Save a Workbook with a Different File Name

To preserve an existing workbook, open and save it with a different file name, creating a copy of the original file with a new name. Follow the same steps that you would when saving a new workbook.

HOW TO: Save a Workbook with a Different File Name

1. Click the **File** tab to open the *Backstage* view.
2. Click **Save As** to display the *Save As* area.
   - When *AutoSave* is active, click **Save a Copy** to open the *Save As* area.
   - The current folder name displays.
3. Navigate to and select the folder name.
4. Type or edit the workbook name in the file name area.
5. Click **Save** to save the file and return to the workbook.

Workbook File Formats

Excel workbooks are saved as ***.xlsx*** files, indicated as *Excel Workbook* in the *Save As* area and dialog box. You can save a workbook in other formats for ease in sharing data. For example, save a workbook in *Excel 97-2003* format so that a coworker with an earlier version of Excel can use the data, or create a PDF file to display data for users who do not have Excel.

The *Save As* area and the *Save As* dialog box list available formats (Figure 1-4). Table 1-1 lists common formats for saving an Excel workbook.

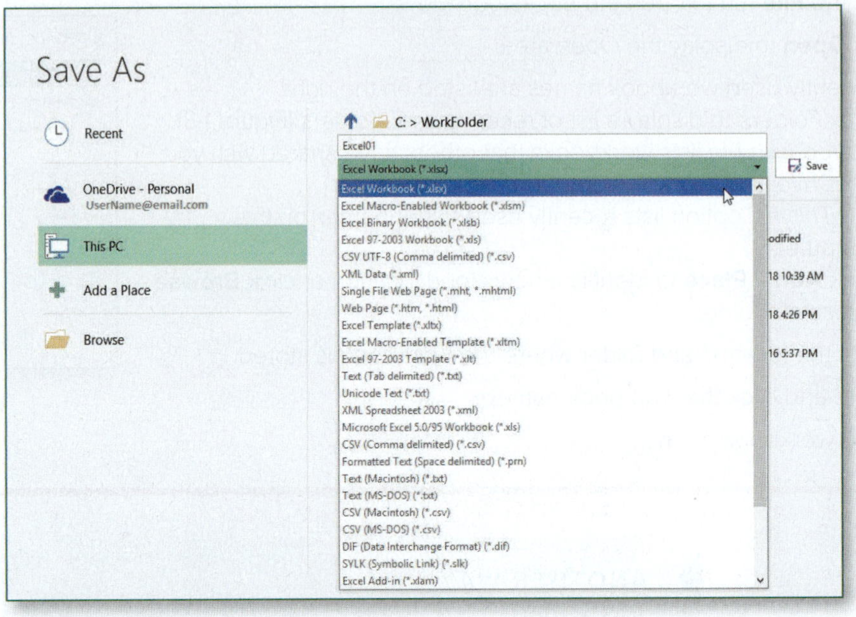

Figure 1-4 Workbook file formats

Table 1-1: Common Save Formats

Type of Document	File Name Extension	Uses of This Format
Excel Workbook	.xlsx	Excel workbook compatible with versions 2010 and later.
Excel Macro-Enabled Workbook	.xlsm	Excel workbook with embedded macros.
Excel 97-2003 Workbook	.xls	Excel workbook compatible with older versions of Microsoft Excel.
Excel Template	.xltx	Model or sample Excel workbook stored in the Custom Office Templates folder.
Excel Macro-Enabled Template	.xltm	Model or sample Excel workbook with embedded macros stored in the Custom Office Templates folder.
Portable Document Format (PDF)	.pdf	An image of the workbook for viewing that can be opened with free software.
Text (tab-delimited)	.txt	Data only with columns separated by a tab character. File can be opened by many applications.
Comma Separated Values (CSV)	.csv	Data only with columns separated by a comma. File can be opened by many applications.
OpenDocument Spreadsheet	.ods	Workbook for the Open Office suite as well as Google Docs.
Web Page	.htm, .html	Excel workbook formatted for posting on a web site that includes data, graphics, and linked objects.

SLO 1.2

Entering and Editing Data

A worksheet consists of columns and rows. Column labels are letters and row labels are numbers. Enter data in a ***cell***, which is the intersection of a column and a row. Each cell is identified with a ***cell reference*** (or ***cell address***), the column letter and row number that represents the location of the cell. Cell A1 is the intersection of column A and row 1. A rectangular group of cells is a ***range***. The range address **A1:B3** identifies six cells in two columns and three rows.

A worksheet displays column and row headings as well as gridlines to help you identify the location of data. You can change the gridlines and headings options from the *View* tab if you prefer to see a cleaner background for your work. The *Gridlines* and *Headings* settings in the *Show* group are toggles that display or hide these features.

> **MORE INFO**
>
> From the *View* tab, you can also display or hide the formula bar and the ruler.

Enter Labels and Values

Data in a worksheet cell is text, a number, or a formula. A ***label*** is text that displays a name, a title, or similar descriptive information. Labels are not included in calculations. A ***value*** is a number that can be used in a calculation or is the result of a calculation. A ***formula*** is a calculation or expression that displays a result.

When you type data that includes alphabetic characters and numbers, Excel treats that data as a label. Examples include a street address or an ID such as ABC123. When you type data with numbers that are not used in calculations, enter the data as a label by typing an apostrophe (') before the data. Examples of this type of data include a telephone or Social Security number without hyphens.

> **MORE INFO**
>
> If you type a Social Security number *with* hyphens, Excel identifies it as a label.

When a label in a cell is longer or wider than the cell, the label spills into an empty adjacent cell. If adjacent cells are not empty, the label is truncated or cut off in the cell, but the entire entry is visible in the ***Formula bar***. The *Formula* bar appears below the *Ribbon* and displays the contents of the selected cell. When a value is too large for the width of the cell, the cell displays a series of # symbols or shows the value in exponential notation (part of the number with E+n as in 1235E+4). To see all cell contents, simply widen the column.

To enter data, click the cell with the pointer to select and activate the cell. The pointer appears as a solid, white cross (a thick plus sign) when selecting data in the worksheet. The ***active cell*** displays a solid border, and its address appears in the ***Name box*** (Figure 1-5).

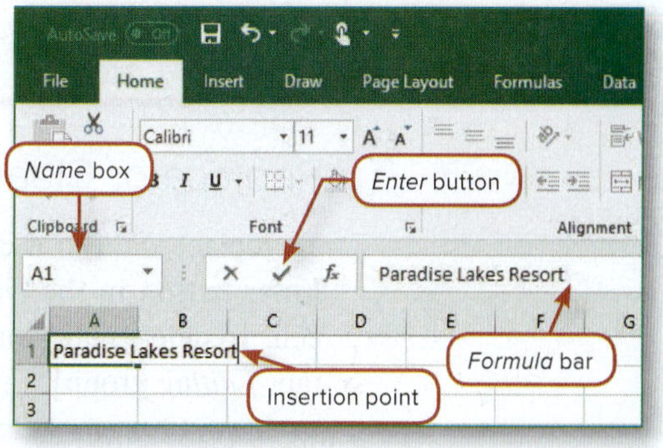

Figure 1-5 Entering data

▸ HOW TO: Enter Data into a Workbook

1. Select the cell and type the data. When you type, an insertion point displays.
   - The label or value appears in the cell and in the *Formula* bar.
2. Press **Enter** to complete the entry and activate the cell below.
   - Press **Tab** to complete the entry and activate the cell to the right.
   - Press any keyboard directional arrow key to complete the entry and activate the cell in the direction of the arrow.
   - Press **Ctrl+Enter** to complete the entry and keep the current cell active.
   - Click the **Enter** button in the *Formula* bar to complete the entry and keep the cell active.

Edit Cell Contents

You can edit cell data as you type or after the entry is complete. To edit as you type, press the **Backspace** key to delete characters to the left of the insertion point, or use arrow keys to move the insertion point and press the **Delete** key to erase characters to the right of the insertion point. To edit a completed entry, start *Edit* mode by double-clicking the cell or by pressing **F2 (FN+F2)**. The word "Edit" appears in the *Status* bar to alert you that data entry is in progress. Position the insertion point either in the cell or in the *Formula* bar, edit the entry, and press any completion key.

When using keyboard function keys, you may need to press the **FN** key with the function key to access the command. This depends on the type of computer as well as the keyboard. This text will show a shortcut like this **F2 (FN+F2)** as a reminder to note your keyboard layout.

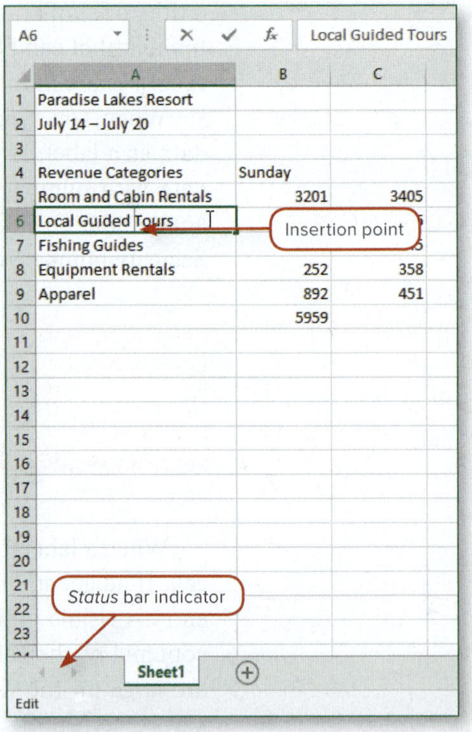

Figure 1-6 *Edit* mode

▸ HOW TO: Edit Cell Contents

1. Double-click the cell to be edited.
   - You can also click the cell and press **F2 (FN+F2)** to start *Edit* mode.
2. Position the insertion point in the cell or the *Formula* bar (Figure 1-6).
3. Edit the data.
4. Press **Enter**.

Replace or Clear Cell Contents

To replace data in a cell, select the cell and type the new data. Then press **Enter**, click the **Enter** button in the *Formula* bar, or press any completion key. The new data displays in the cell. To delete data from a cell, select the cell and press **Delete** or click the **Clear** button [*Home* tab, *Editing* group]. From the *Clear* button options, you can choose *Clear All, Clear Formats,* or *Clear Contents* (Figure 1-7). Pressing the **Delete** key removes the contents and preserves formatting.

▸HOW TO: Clear Cell Contents

1. Select the cell or cells.
2. Press **Delete** on the keyboard.
    - Click the **Clear** button [*Home* tab, *Editing* group] and choose an option.
    - *Clear All* removes formatting and content.
    - *Clear Formats* only clears formatting and keeps data.
    - *Clear Contents* deletes content but keeps formatting.

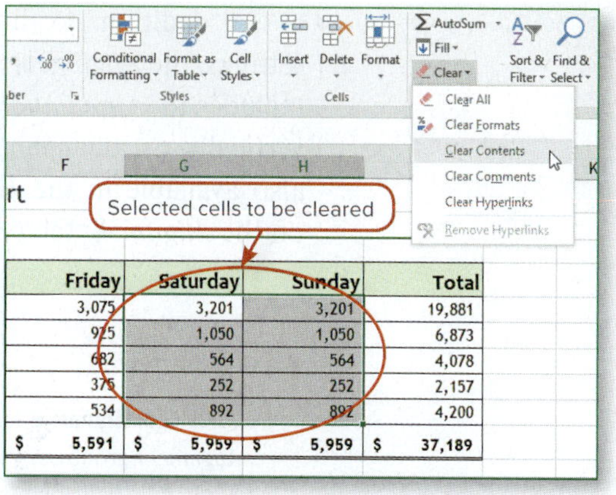

Figure 1-7 *Clear* button options

Align and Indent Cell Contents

Excel recognizes a combination of letters, numbers, spaces, and other characters as a label. Labels are aligned on the bottom left of the cell. When you type only numbers into a cell, Excel identifies the entry as a value. Values are aligned on the right and bottom of the cell.

You can change the vertical and horizontal ***alignment*** of data in a cell from the *Alignment* group on the *Home* tab (Figure 1-8). Horizontal alignment choices are *Align Left, Center*, and *Align Right*. Vertical alignment options are *Top Align, Middle Align*, and *Bottom Align*.

An ***indent*** moves cell contents away from the left edge of the cell. In Figure 1-8, labels in rows 5:9 are offset from the label in row 4. The *Increase Indent* button [*Home* tab, *Alignment* group] moves cell contents one space to the right if the data is left-aligned. Remove an indent by clicking the *Decrease Indent* button [*Home* tab, *Alignment* group].

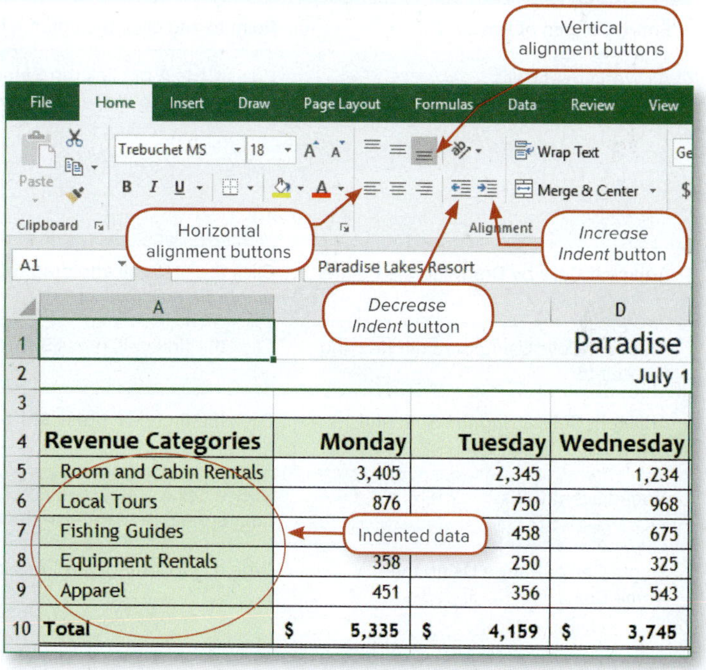

Figure 1-8 Alignment and indent options

▸HOW TO: Align and Indent Text

1. Select the cell.
2. Click a horizontal text alignment button [*Home* tab, *Alignment* group].
    - *Center* positions a label midway between the left and right boundaries of the cell.
    - *Align Left* starts a label at the left boundary of the cell.
    - *Right Align* positions a label at the right cell boundary.
3. Click a vertical text alignment button [*Home* tab, *Alignment* group].
    - *Middle Align* positions data midway between the top and bottom cell boundaries.
    - *Top Align* places data at the top cell boundary.
    - *Bottom Align* aligns data at the bottom boundary of the cell.
4. Click an indent button [*Home* tab, *Alignment* group].
    - The *Increase Indent* button moves data toward the right cell boundary.
    - The *Decrease Indent* button moves data toward the left cell boundary.

In addition to horizontal and vertical settings, the *Alignment* group on the *Home* tab includes the *Orientation* button to display data vertically or at an angle. These settings are also available in the *Format Cells* dialog box on the *Alignment* tab (Figure 1-9).

> **MORE INFO**
>
> Click the **Alignment** launcher [*Home* tab, *Alignment* group] or press **Ctrl+1** to open the *Format Cells* dialog box.

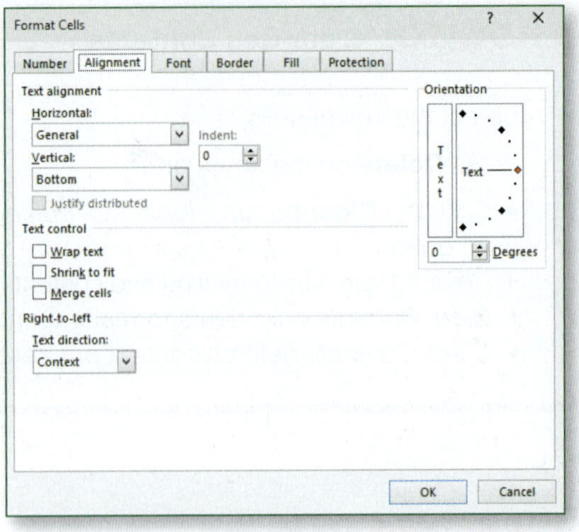

Figure 1-9 *Alignment* tab, *Format Cells* dialog box

Select Cells

As you format or edit a worksheet, the first step is to select the cell or cells to be edited. Select a single cell by clicking it. Select a range by clicking the first cell and dragging the pointer in any direction to select adjacent cells. Table 1-2 outlines basic selection methods.

Table 1-2: Selection Methods

Selection	Instructions
Entire Column or Row	Point to and click the column heading. Point to and click the row heading.
All Worksheet Cells	Press **Ctrl+A** or click the **Select All** button (above the row 1 heading and to the left of the column A heading). 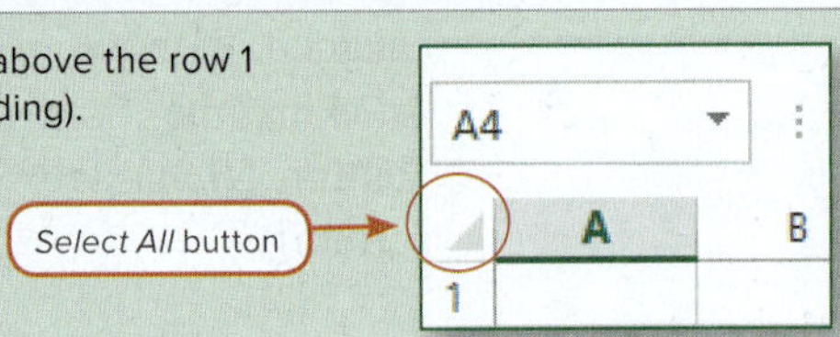
Adjacent Cells by Dragging the Pointer	Click the first cell and drag the selection pointer over the cells to be included. Release the pointer.
Adjacent Cells Using the Shift Key and the Pointer	Click the first cell, press **Shift**, and click the last cell in the range.
Adjacent Cells Using the Shift and Arrow Keys	Click the first cell, press **Shift**, and press any arrow key.
Nonadjacent Cells	Click a cell or select the first range, press **Ctrl**, and select the next cell or range. Release the pointer first; then release the **Ctrl** key.
Single Cell or Range Using the *Name Box*	Type a cell or range address in the *Name* box and press **Enter**. 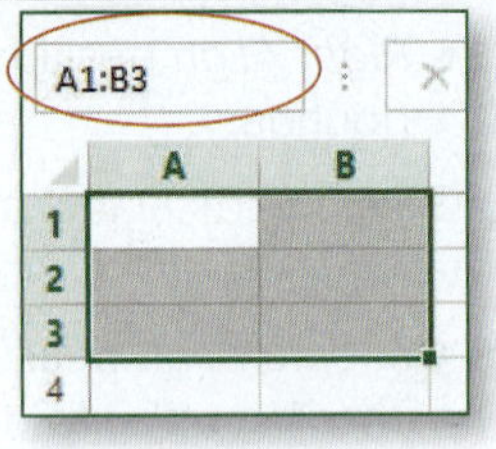

You can see selected cell ranges in Figure 1-10.

To deselect a range of cells, click a cell that is not in the selection. To remove a selected cell from a selected range, press **Ctrl** and click the cell to be deselected.

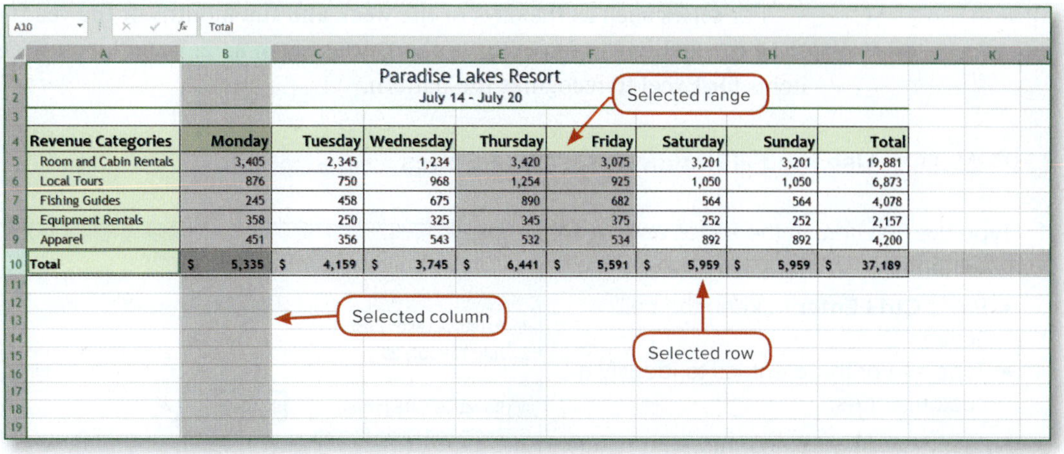

Figure 1-10 Selected cells in a worksheet

> **MORE INFO**
>
> To enter data column by column, select the entire cell range, type the first entry, and press **Enter**. Continue to type each entry and press **Enter**. The insertion point moves down each column and to the top of the next column based on the selected range.

The pointer changes shape depending on the current task or mode. Table 1-3 describes the shapes and indicates when they appear.

Table 1-3: Pointer Shapes

Pointer Icon	Pointer Use
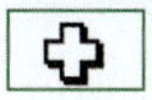	***Selection pointer*** (thick, white cross or plus sign) selects a cell or range; the selection pointer appears when you move the pointer over a cell.
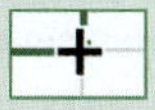	***Fill pointer*** (crosshair or thin, black plus sign) copies cell contents or completes a series; it appears when you place the pointer on the *Fill Handle*, the tiny square in the bottom-right corner of a selected cell or range.
	***Move pointer*** (solid, white arrow with a black four-pointed arrow) moves data; it appears when you place the pointer on the border of a selected cell or range.
	***Resize pointer*** (two-pointed arrow) adjusts a formula cell range or an object; it appears when you place the pointer on a selection handle in a formula range or on a sizing handle for a selected object.

The Fill Handle

A ***series*** is a list of labels or values that follows a pattern. An example of a label series is the days of the week or the months of the year. A series of values is 1, 3, 5, 7, 9. Excel recognizes patterns and can complete most series with the ***Fill Handle***. If no recognizable series exists, the *Fill Handle* copies the data.

The *Fill Handle* is a small square in the lower-right corner of the cell or selected range. Drag this handle across the cell range for the series or to copy data. When you release the pointer, the data is completed, and the *Auto Fill Options* button displays near the end of the series. This button provides choices for how to complete the series, but you usually do not need to make any changes.

For series such as the days of the week and the months of the year, you only need to enter the first item in the series. For other series, such as 2, 4, 6, 8, you need to enter at least two items for Excel to recognize the pattern.

▸HOW TO: Use the Fill Handle to Create a Series

1. Type the first item in the series and press **Enter**.
   - Press **Ctrl+Enter** to keep the cell active.
   - Type two or three entries to identify a custom series.
2. Select the cell with the entry.
   - Select all cells with data that identify the pattern.
3. Point to the *Fill Handle* to display the *Fill* pointer (thin, black plus sign) (Figure 1-11).
4. Click and drag the *Fill* pointer through the last cell for the series.
   - A series can be horizontal or vertical.
   - You can double-click the *Fill* pointer to complete data down a column if other columns are already completed to the last row.
5. Release the pointer.
   - The series is complete and the *Auto Fill Options* button appears.
6. Click the **Auto Fill Options** button.
   - Choose an option as desired (Figure 1-12).
   - *Auto Fill* options depend on the data type.
7. Continue to the next task.
   - The *Auto Fill Options* button disappears when you enter data in a cell or give a command.

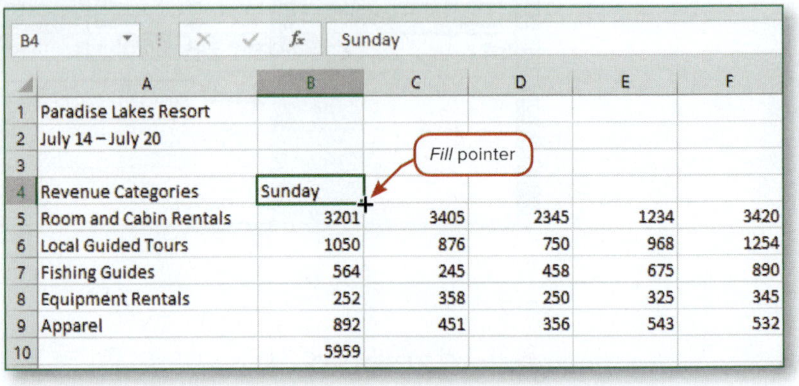

Figure 1-11 Use the *Fill Handle* to complete a series

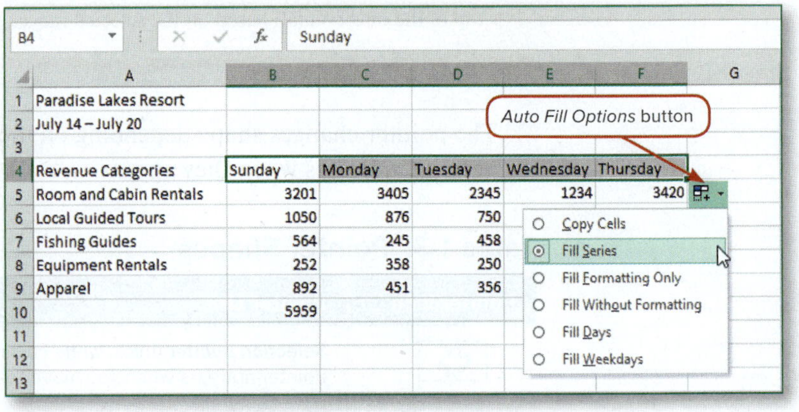

Figure 1-12 Completed series with *Auto Fill Options* button

AutoComplete

AutoComplete is an Excel feature that displays a suggested label in a column when the first character or two that you type matches a label already in the column. *AutoComplete* enables you to quickly and accurately complete repetitive data. It works only for data that is alphanumeric, not for a column of values.

In a column that lists city names, for example, a particular city name might be repeated many times. The first time it appears, you type it as usual. For the second and succeeding occurrences of the name, Excel completes the label as soon as you type the first character. If the *AutoComplete* suggestion is correct, press **Enter**. If the suggestion is not correct, continue typing the label as needed.

Excel usually makes a suggestion after you type a single character in a cell in the column. If the column has more than one entry that begins with that character, type a second character and *AutoComplete* displays another suggestion. Press **Enter** to accept.

MORE INFO

In a column of data, right-click a cell and choose **Pick From Drop-down List** to display a list of all labels already used in the column.

HOW TO: Use AutoComplete

1. Type the first character in a label.
   - A suggested label appears in the cell.
   - Type a second and third character when many labels begin with the same letter.
   - Type uppercase or lowercase characters to display an *AutoComplete* suggestion.
2. Press **Enter** to accept the *AutoComplete* suggestion (Figure 1-13).
   - Continue typing to ignore an *AutoComplete* suggestion.
   - Press **Enter** to complete a new label.

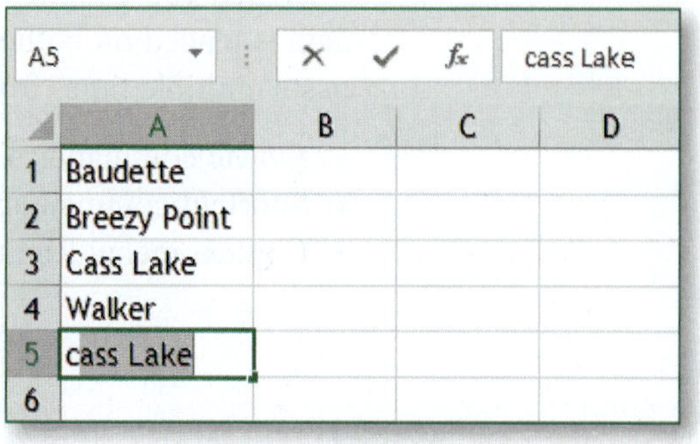

Figure 1-13 ***AutoComplete*** **suggestion**

Cut, Copy, and Paste Cell Contents

Excel has the same *Cut*, *Copy*, and *Paste* commands as other Windows applications. Use the ***Cut*** command to move data from one location to another. The ***Copy*** command duplicates cell contents to a different location. The ***Paste*** command places cut or copied data in the selected location. Data is cut or copied from a ***source cell*** or range and is pasted in a ***destination cell*** or range. When you cut or copy data, it is stored on the Windows *Clipboard* as well as the *Office Clipboard*.

Move or Cut Cell Contents

Move data using drag and drop, keyboard shortcuts, or *Cut* and *Paste* commands in the *Clipboard* group on the *Home* tab. Drag and drop is quick when you want to move or copy cells within a visible range on the worksheet. When you use the drag-and-drop method, the source data is not stored on either clipboard.

HOW TO: Move Data Using Drag and Drop

1. Select the cell(s) to be moved. Point to a border of the selection to display a move pointer (black four-pointed arrow with white arrow).
2. Click and drag the selection to the new location (Figure 1-14).
   - A preview selection shows the destination address.
   - The pointer displays a white arrow as you drag.
3. Release the pointer.

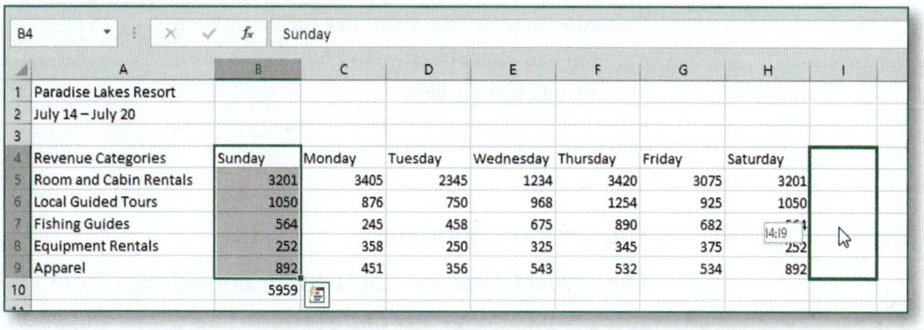

Figure 1-14 Drag and drop to move data

> **MORE INFO**
>
> Add an external mouse to a computer with a touchpad for ease in selecting cells and dragging and dropping data.

When you use the *Cut* command from the *Ribbon* or the keyboard shortcut, the selected data is placed on both clipboards. You can paste once from the Windows *Clipboard.* You can paste multiple times from the *Office Clipboard.* Use one of three methods to cut data:

- *Ribbon* commands: **Cut** and **Paste** buttons [*Home* tab, *Clipboard* group]
- Shortcut commands: **Ctrl+X** to cut and **Ctrl+V** to paste
- Context menu: Right-click and select **Cut**; right-click and select **Paste**

HOW TO: Move Data Using Cut and Paste

1. Select the cell or range to be moved.
2. Click the **Cut** button [*Home* tab, *Clipboard* group].
   - A moving border surrounds the source cell(s) (Figure 1-15).
3. Select the destination cell for data that was cut.
   - Select the top-left cell in a destination range.
4. Click the **Paste** button [*Home* tab, *Clipboard* group].
   - If the destination cell(s) are not empty, pasted data overwrites existing data.

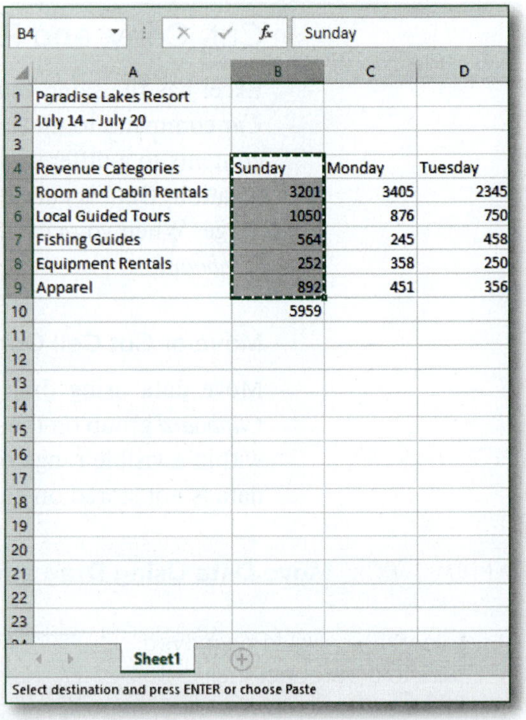

Figure 1-15 Cut data has moving border

> **MORE INFO**
>
> After cutting data, right-click the destination cell and select **Insert Cut Cells** to avoid overwriting existing data.

The Office Clipboard

The ***Office Clipboard*** stores cut or copied data from Office applications and the data are available for pasting in any application. The *Office Clipboard* holds up to 24 items with each cut or copied item appearing, in turn, at the top of the pane. Click the **Clipboard** launcher to open the *Clipboard* task pane.

▸HOW TO: Use the Office Clipboard

1. Click the **Home** tab.
2. Click the **Clipboard** launcher to open the *Clipboard* pane (Figure 1-16).
3. Click **Clear All** to empty the *Clipboard.*
   - The button is gray if the clipboard is empty.
4. Select data to be cut or copied.
5. Click the **Copy** or **Cut** button [*Home* tab, *Clipboard* group].
   - Use any *Cut* or *Copy* command from the *Ribbon* or keyboard.
   - Each item moves to the first position in the *Clipboard* pane.
6. Select a destination cell.
7. Click the item icon in the *Clipboard* to paste it.
   - You can paste an item multiple times in different locations.
8. Click the **Close** button to hide the *Clipboard.*

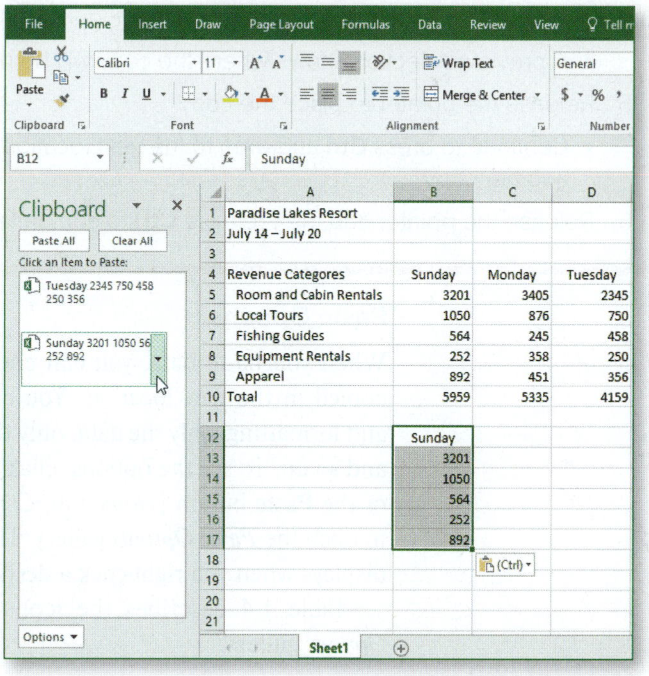

Figure 1-16 ***Clipboard*** **pane**

> ### MORE INFO
> To remove an item from the *Clipboard* task pane, click its drop-down arrow and choose **Delete**.

Copy Cell Contents

Copying data places a duplicate on the *Clipboard* so that it can be pasted in another location. When you use a *Ribbon*, keyboard, or context menu command, you can paste the data multiple times. You can copy data using the drag-and-drop method and paste it multiple times, even though the copied data is not placed on the *Clipboard.*

The *Copy* command stores data on the *Clipboard*, and the *Paste* command duplicates *Clipboard* contents in the worksheet.

- *Ribbon* commands: **Copy** and **Paste** buttons [*Home* tab, *Clipboard* group]
- Shortcut commands: **Ctrl+C** to copy and **Ctrl+V** to paste
- Context menu: Right-click and choose **Copy**; right-click and choose **Paste**

▸HOW TO: Copy Data Using Drag and Drop

1. Select the cell(s) to be copied.
2. Point to a border of the selection to display the move pointer.
3. Press **Ctrl** to display the copy pointer.
   - The copy pointer is a white arrow with a tiny plus sign.

4. Drag the selection to the desired location (Figure 1-17).
    - A preview selection shows where the copy will be pasted.
5. Release the pointer to place the copy.
    - Continue to press **Ctrl** and drag to the next location for another copy.
6. Release the pointer and then release **Ctrl** to complete the task.

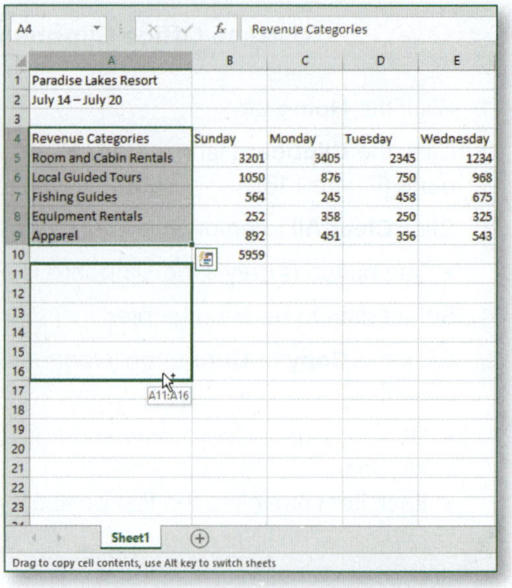

Figure 1-17 Copy data using drag and drop

Paste Options

When you paste data, you can choose how it is copied in the new location. You can paste data and formatting, only the data, only the formatting, and so on. To see the options, click the lower half of the **Paste** button [*Home* tab, *Clipboard* group] to open the ***Paste Options*** gallery. The gallery also displays when you right-click a destination cell.

Table 1-4 describes the icons in the *Paste Options* gallery:

Table 1-4: Paste Options

Group	Paste Icon	Paste Option	Description
Paste		*Paste*	Copies all data and formatting; this is the default option.
		Formulas	Copies all data and formulas, but no formatting.
		Formulas & Number Formatting	Copies all data and formulas with formatting.
		Keep Source Formatting	Copies all data and formatting; same as *Paste*.
		Match Destination Formatting	Copies data and applies formatting used in the destination.
		No Borders	Copies all data, formulas, and formatting except for borders.
		Keep Source Column Widths	Copies all data, formulas, and formatting and sets destination column widths to the same width as the source columns.
		Transpose	Copies data and formatting and reverses data orientation so that rows are pasted as columns and columns are pasted as rows.
		Merge Conditional Formatting	Copies data and *Conditional Formatting* rules. This option is available only if the copied data has conditional formatting.
Paste Values		*Values*	Copies only formula results (not the formulas) without formatting.
		Values & Number Formatting	Copies only formula results (not the formulas) with formatting.
		Values & Source Formatting	Copies only formula results (not the formulas) with all source formatting.

Other Paste Options		*Formatting*	Copies only formatting, no data.
		Paste Link	Pastes a 3-D reference to data or a formula.
		Picture	Pastes a picture object of the data. Data is static, but the object can be formatted like any object.
		Linked Picture	Pastes a picture object of the data. The copied data is dynamic and reflects edits made in the source data. Format the picture like any object.

MORE INFO

The *Paste Special* command opens a dialog box with additional options to paste comments, data validation, themes, and arithmetic operations.

PAUSE & PRACTICE: EXCEL 1-1

In this project, you open an Excel workbook that tracks revenue for one week at Paradise Lakes Resort. You add labels and values to complete the report; align labels; and edit, cut, and paste data. Your worksheet will have deliberate spelling errors for checking in a later Pause & Practice exercise.

File Needed: ***ParadiseLakes-01.xlsx***
Completed Project File Name: ***[your initials] PP E1-1.xlsx***

1. Open a workbook.
   a. Click the **File** tab and click **Open**.
   b. Navigate to the folder where your data files are stored.
   c. Click the name of the folder to open it.
   d. Locate the file name ***ParadiseLakes-01*** and click to open it.
   e. Click **Enable Editing** if the workbook has opened in *Protected View* (Figure 1-18).

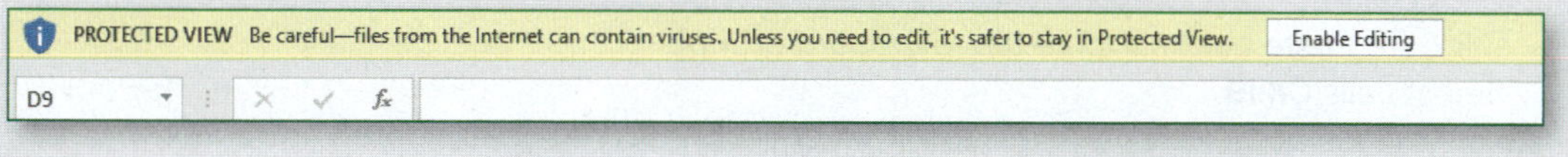

Figure 1-18 Workbook opened in *Protected View*

2. Save the workbook with a different name.
   a. Click the **File** tab and choose **Save As**.
   b. Click **Browse** to open the *Save As* dialog box.
   c. Navigate to and select a location to save the workbook.
   d. Change the file name to [your initials] PP E1-1 in the *File name* area.
   e. Click **Save** to save the file and close the *Save As* dialog box.

3. Enter data.
   a. Click cell **A1** and type Paradise Lakes Resort.
   b. Press **Enter**.
   c. Click cell **A10**, type Total, and press **Enter**.
   d. Type the values shown below in cells **G5:H9**.

	G	H
5	3075	3201
6	925	1050
7	682	564
8	375	252
9	534	892

4. Use the *Fill Handle* to complete a series.
   a. Click cell **B4**.
   b. Point to the *Fill Handle* (small square in the lower-right corner) until the *Fill* pointer (thin, black plus sign) appears.
   c. Click and drag the *Fill* pointer to reach cell **H4**.
   d. Release the pointer.
5. Edit worksheet data.
   a. Click cell **B10**.
   b. Press **Delete** to remove the contents.
   c. Double-click cell **A4** to start *Edit* mode.
   d. Click to position the insertion point and delete the "i" in "Categories" to create a deliberate spelling error.
   e. Press **Enter** to accept the edit.
   f. Click cell **A9** and type Aparel with the error. You will correct errors in *Pause & Practice 1-4*.
   g. Press **Enter** to replace the entry.
6. Indent and align text.
   a. Select cells **A5:A9**.
   b. Click the **Increase Indent** button twice [*Home* tab, *Alignment* group].
   c. Select cells **B4:H4**.
   d. Click the **Center** button [*Home* tab, *Alignment* group].
7. Cut and paste data.
   a. Select cells **B4:B9**.
   b. Click the **Cut** button [*Home* tab, *Clipboard* group].
   c. Click cell **I4**.
   d. Click the **Paste** button [*Home* tab, *Clipboard* group].
   e. Select cells **C4:I9**.
   f. Point to any border of the selected range to display a black, four-pointed arrow with a white arrow.
   g. Drag the range to start in cell **B4** and release the pointer.
   h. Click cell **A1**.
8. Save and close the workbook (Figure 1-19).
   a. Press **Ctrl+S** to save the workbook with the same file name.
   b. Click the **Close** button in the upper-right corner to exit Excel.

	A	B	C	D	E	F	G	H
1	Paradise Lakes Resort							
2	July 14 – July 20							
3								
4	Revenue Categores	Monday	Tuesday	Wednesday	Thursday	Friday	Saturday	Sunday
5	Room and Cabin Rentals	3405	2345	1234	3420	3075	3201	3201
6	Local Tours	876	750	968	1254	925	1050	1050
7	Fishing Guides	245	458	675	890	682	564	564
8	Equipment Rentals	358	250	325	345	375	252	252
9	Aparel	451	356	543	532	534	892	892
10	Total							

Figure 1-19 PP E1-1 completed

SLO 1.3

Using the SUM Function

A ***formula*** calculates a result for numeric data in a cell. A ***function*** is a built-in formula. ***SUM*** is a function that adds the values in a cell range. The terms "formula" and "function" are used interchangeably.

To use the *SUM* function, click the cell where you want to show a total. Then click the **AutoSum** button [*Home* tab, *Editing* group]. Excel inserts the function =SUM() with a suggested range of cells to be added between the parentheses. If that range is correct, press **Enter**, **Ctrl+Enter**, or click the **Enter** button in the *Formula* bar to complete the function. If the suggested range is not correct, select a different range or choose cells individually and then press a completion key. The sum is shown in the cell, and the function is visible in the *Formula* bar.

ANOTHER WAY

The *Function Library* group on the *Formulas* tab has an *AutoSum* button. You can also enter =SUM() in a cell by pressing **Alt** and the **+/=** key on the top keyboard row.

HOW TO: Use the SUM Function

1. Click the cell for the total.
2. Click the **AutoSum** button [*Home* tab, *Editing* group] (Figure 1-20).
3. Press **Enter** to accept the range and complete the function.
   - Drag the pointer to select a different range before pressing **Enter**.
   - If the row or column of values to be added is adjacent to the formula cell as shown in Figure 1-20, you can double-click the **AutoSum** button to insert and accept the function.

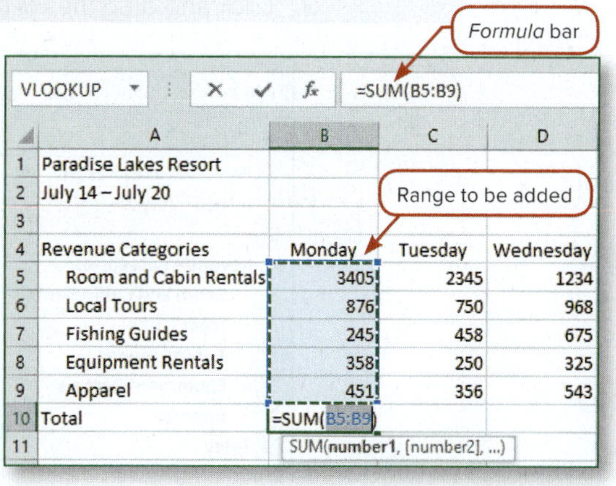

Figure 1-20 *SUM* function

MORE INFO

Display formulas instead of results by clicking the **Show Formulas** button on the *Formulas* tab or by pressing **Ctrl+~**.

Function Syntax

An Excel function has ***syntax***, the required elements and the order of those elements for the function to work. Every function starts with the equals sign [=] followed by the name of the function and a set of parentheses. Within the parentheses, you enter the argument(s). An ***argument*** is the cell reference or value required to complete the function. A function can have a single argument or multiple arguments. In =SUM(B5:B9), the argument is the range B5:B9. Multiple arguments in a function are separated by commas. This function includes three arguments: =SUM(B5, B10, B15).

SUM(B5:B9)

SUM(B5, B10, B15)

Copy the SUM Function

Copy the *SUM* function using regular copy and paste commands, as well as the *Fill Handle*. When *SUM* is used to total data in rows or columns, enter the formula in the first column or row and copy it to the other locations. In Figure 1-21, for example, the same function is used in cells B10 through H10, each with its own argument. The formula in cell B10 is =SUM(B5:B9), the formula for cell C10 is =SUM(C5:C9) and so on. When a function is copied into adjacent cells, use the *Fill Handle*. Excel copies the formula and adjusts each argument based on the location in the worksheet.

HOW TO: Use the Fill Handle to Copy a Function

1. Click the cell with the function to be copied.
2. Point to the *Fill Handle* in the lower-right corner.
3. Click and drag the *Fill* pointer across the cells where the function should be pasted (Figure 1-21).

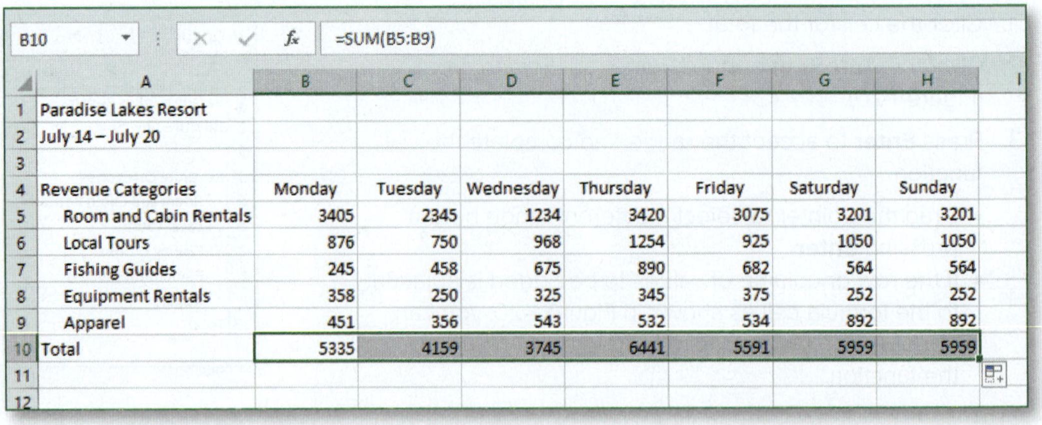
B10 =SUM(B5:B9)

	A	B	C	D	E	F	G	H
1	Paradise Lakes Resort							
2	July 14 – July 20							
3								
4	Revenue Categories	Monday	Tuesday	Wednesday	Thursday	Friday	Saturday	Sunday
5	Room and Cabin Rentals	3405	2345	1234	3420	3075	3201	3201
6	Local Tours	876	750	968	1254	925	1050	1050
7	Fishing Guides	245	458	675	890	682	564	564
8	Equipment Rentals	358	250	325	345	375	252	252
9	Apparel	451	356	543	532	534	892	892
10	Total	5335	4159	3745	6441	5591	5959	5959
11								
12								

Figure 1-21 Use the *Fill Handle* to copy a function

ANOTHER WAY

Use regular copy and paste commands to copy a function or formula to any location on the worksheet.

Edit the Function Argument

If you edit a value in a cell that is referenced in a formula or function, the results are automatically recalculated. If you must change a cell or range argument in a function, however, you use *Edit* mode to enter new references. In *Edit* mode, you can make a change in the *Formula* bar or in the cell. You can often use the ***Range Finder*** to drag or select a new range, too. The *Range Finder* is an Excel feature that highlights and color-codes formula cells as you enter or edit a formula or function.

HOW TO: Edit an Argument Range in the Formula Bar

1. Select the cell with the function.
2. Click the argument cell range in the *Formula* bar.
   - The *Range Finder* highlights the argument range in the worksheet.
   - The range is color-coded in the *Formula* bar to match the highlighted range (Figure 1-22).
3. Type the new cell references in the *Formula* bar.
4. Press **Enter**.
   - Click the **Enter** button in the *Formula* bar to complete the edit.

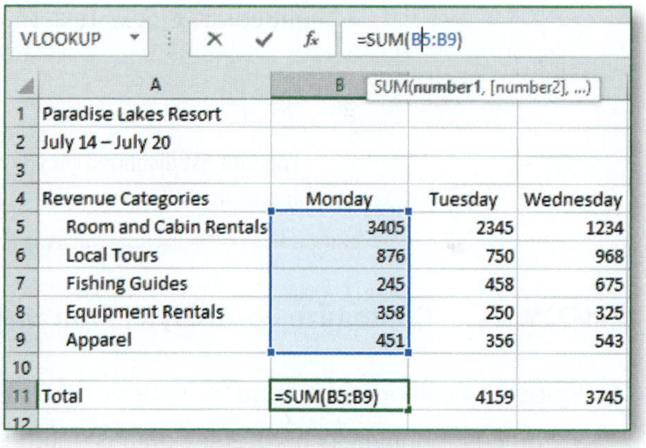

VLOOKUP
=SUM(B5:B9)
SUM(number1, [number2], ...)
Paradise Lakes Resort
July 14 – July 20
Revenue Categories
Monday
Tuesday
Wednesday
Room and Cabin Rentals
3405
2345
1234
Local Tours
876
750
968
Fishing Guides
245
458
675
Equipment Rentals
358
250
325
Apparel
451
356
543
Total
=SUM(B5:B9)
4159
3745

Figure 1-22 Argument range is color-coded

You can drag a *Range Finder* handle to select a different argument range, expanding or shrinking the number of included cells. This is easy to do when the formula cell is not adjacent to the range.

ANOTHER WAY

Double-click the cell with the function and edit the argument in the cell.

HOW TO: Edit an Argument Range by Dragging

1. Double-click the cell with the function.
   - *Edit* mode starts (Figure 1-23).
2. Drag the selection handle down to expand the argument range.
   - Drag the selection handle up to shrink the argument range.
3. Press **Enter** to complete the change.
   - Click the **Enter** button in the *Formula* bar.

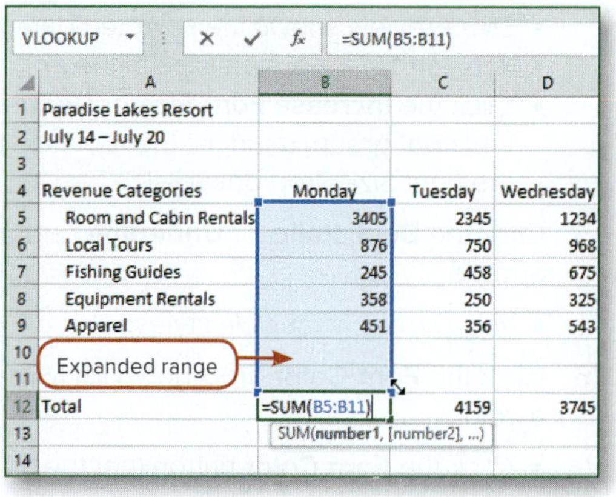

Figure 1-23 Edit an argument range by dragging

SLO 1.4

Formatting a Worksheet

A new workbook uses a default ***theme*** named *Office* which is a collection of fonts, colors, and special effects. The default theme applies the 11 point Calibri font and the *General* number format to all cells. You can change the theme as well as individual font attributes, or you can add fill and borders to highlight or emphasize data.

Font Face, Size, Style, and Color

A ***font*** is a type design for alphanumeric characters, punctuation, and keyboard symbols. ***Font size*** specifies the size of the character, measured in ***points*** (pt.). A point is equal to 1/72 of an inch. The ***font style*** refers to the thickness or angle of the characters and includes settings such as **bold**, underline, or *italic*. ***Font color*** is the hue of the characters in the cell. Apply any of these font attributes to a single cell, a range of cells, or selected characters in a cell.

Default font attributes for Excel workbooks are:

- Font: Calibri
- Font size: 11 point
- Font color: Black, Text 1

MORE INFO

The font list displayed on your computer depends on your Windows installation and other installed applications.

HOW TO: Customize Font, Style, Font Size, and Font Color

1. Select the cell or range to be formatted.
   - You can format cells before any data is entered.
   - You can select a range of characters in the *Formula* bar.
2. Click the **Font** drop-down list [*Home* tab, *Font* group].
   - A list of available fonts displays.
3. Point to a font name.
   - *Live Preview* shows the selected data with the new font applied (Figure 1-24).
4. Click the **Font Size** drop-down list [*Home* tab, *Font* group] and select a size.
   - *Live Preview* shows the selected data in the new size.
   - You can type a custom size in the *Font Size* area.
   - Click the **Increase Font Size** or **Decrease Font Size** button [*Home* tab, *Font* group] to adjust the font size to the next or previous size in the *Font Size* drop-down list.
5. Click the **Bold**, **Italic**, or **Underline** button [*Home* tab, *Font* group] to apply a style.
   - You can apply multiple styles.
6. Click the **Font Color** drop-down list [*Home* tab, *Font* group] and select a color.
   - Click the **Font Color** button (not the arrow) to apply the most recent font color shown on the button.

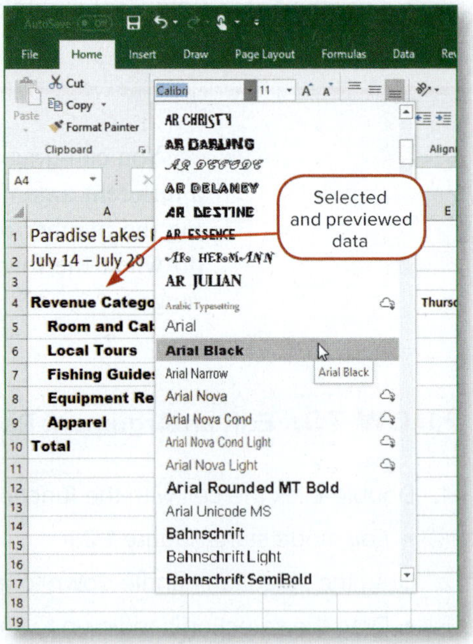

Figure 1-24 ***Live Preview*** **when selecting a font name**

The ***mini toolbar*** includes common commands from the *Font*, *Alignment*, and *Number* groups. It appears when you right-click a cell or selected range (Figure 1-25).

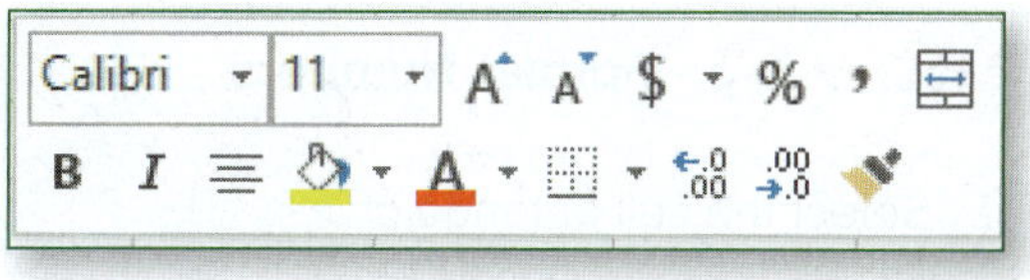

Figure 1-25 Mini toolbar

The *Format Cells* dialog box includes basic format settings and more. It has six tabs: *Number*, *Alignment*, *Font*, *Border*, *Fill*, and *Protection*.

- Mini toolbar: Right-click a cell or selected range.
- *Format Cells* dialog box: Click the **Font** launcher in the *Font* group, press **Ctrl+1**, or right-click a selected cell and choose **Format Cells** (Figure 1-26).

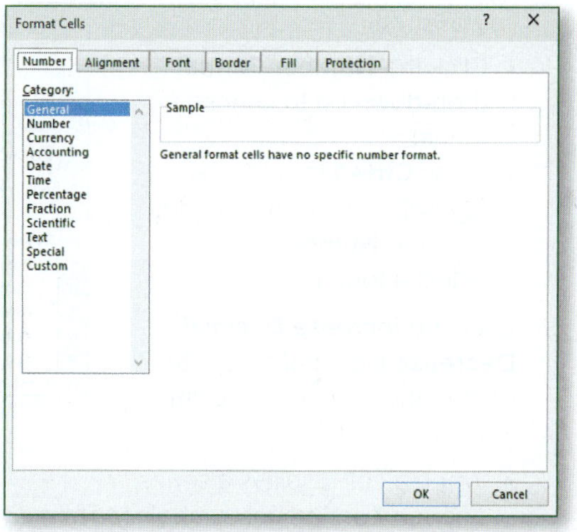

Figure 1-26 *Format Cells* dialog box

The Format Painter

The ***Format Painter*** copies formatting attributes and styles from one cell to another cell or range. You can apply your custom formats without having to redefine each attribute, saving time and ensuring consistency in format.

▸HOW TO: Use the Format Painter

1. Select a cell that contains the formatting you want to copy.
2. Click the **Format Painter** button [*Home* tab, *Clipboard* group].
   - The pointer changes to a thick, white cross with a tiny paint brush.
   - Double-click the **Format Painter** button to lock it for painting formats to multiple areas in the worksheet.
3. Click the cell or drag across the range to be formatted (Figure 1-27).
4. Release the pointer.
   - The *Format Painter* is no longer active.
   - If the *Format Painter* command is locked, click the **Format Painter** button or press **Esc** to turn off the command.

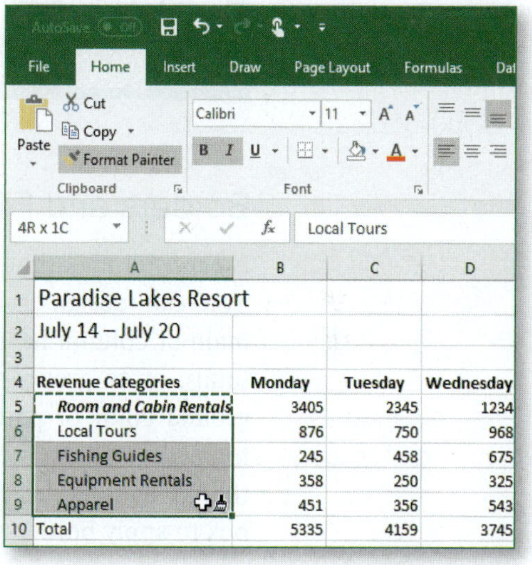

Figure 1-27 Copy formats to a range using *Format Painter*

Number Formats

You can format values with currency symbols, decimal points, commas, percent signs, and more so that data are quickly recognized and understood. The *Number* group on the *Home* tab includes command buttons for *Accounting*, *Percent*, and *Comma* styles, as well as command buttons to *Increase Decimal* or *Decrease Decimal*. Dates and times are values, and *Date* and *Time* formats are included in the *Number* group. From the *Format Cells* dialog box, you can apply and customize these number formats or create your own format.

HOW TO: Format Numbers

1. Select the cell or range of values.
2. Click a command button [*Home* tab, *Number* group] (Figure 1-28).
   - Click the **Number Format** drop-down list to choose a format.
   - Press **Ctrl+1** to open the *Format Cells* dialog box and click the **Number** tab to select a format.
3. Click the **Increase Decimal** or **Decrease Decimal** button to control the number of decimal places.
   - When a cell displays a series of pound or number symbols (#####), widen the column to see the value.

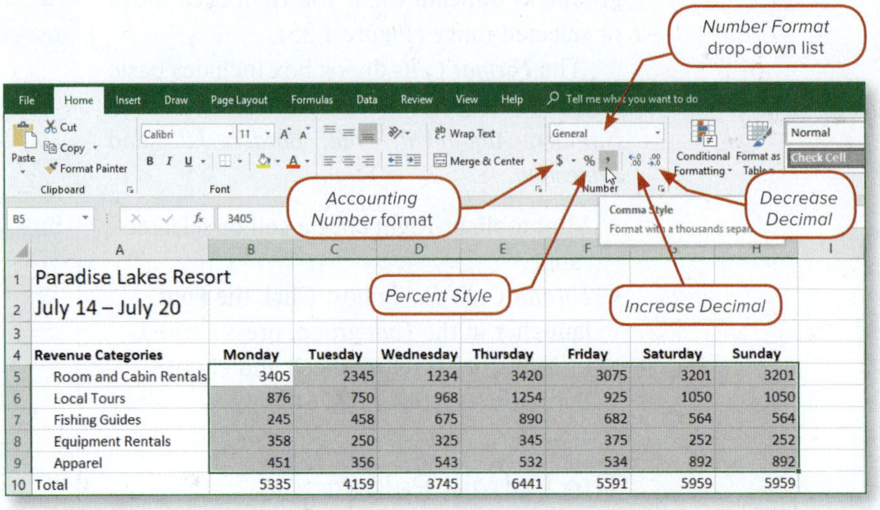

Figure 1-28 ***Number*** **group on the** ***Home*** **tab**

ANOTHER WAY

Click the **Number** launcher [*Home* tab] to open the *Format Cells* dialog box.

Borders and Fill

A ***border*** is an outline for a cell or a range. You can design a border to separate main or column headings, to emphasize totals, or to group data. ***Fill*** is a background color or pattern and is used to highlight or draw attention to data. Use the *Ribbon* or the *Format Cells* dialog box to apply borders and fill color.

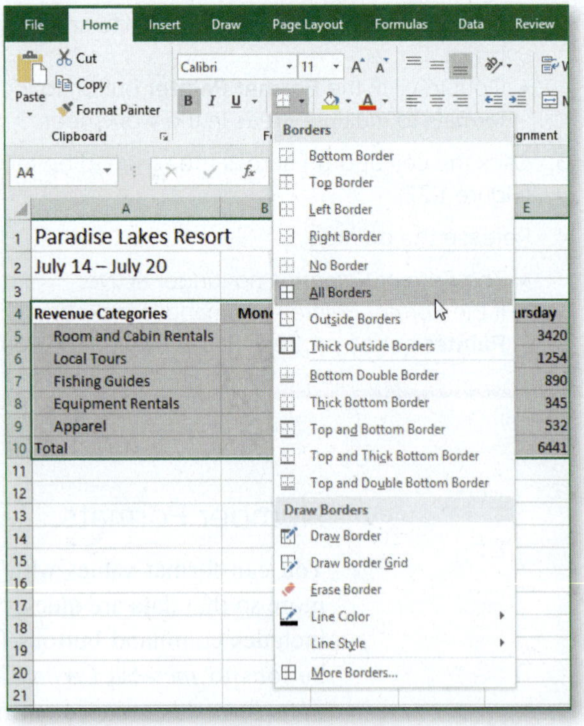

Figure 1-29 ***Borders*** **drop-down list**

HOW TO: Add Borders and Fill Using the Ribbon

1. Select the cell or range.
2. Click the arrow next to the **Borders** button [*Home* tab, *Font* group].
   - The **Borders** button shows the most recently used border style.
3. Select a border option from the list (Figure 1-29).
   - To remove a border, choose **No Border**.

4. Click the arrow for the **Fill Color** button [*Home* tab, *Font* group].
   - Click the **Fill Color** button to apply the most recently selected color.
   - To remove a fill, choose **No Fill**.
5. Select a color tile in the palette (Figure 1-30).
   - *Live Preview* displays the cell or range with the color applied.
   - Click **More Colors** to build a custom color.

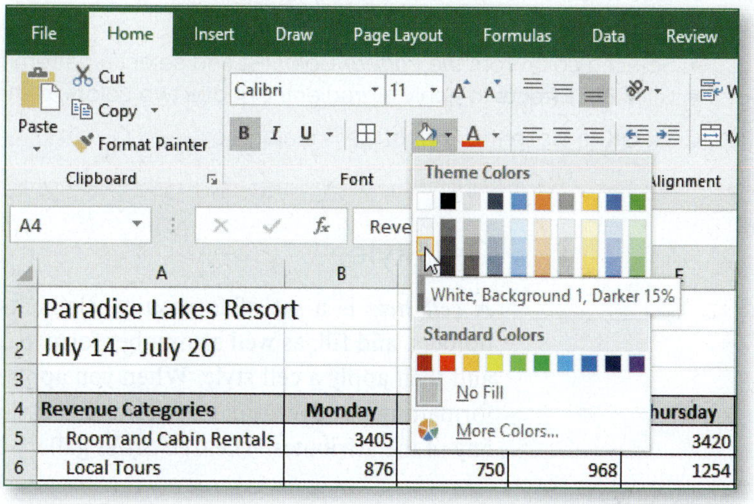

Figure 1-30 *Fill Color* palette

The *Format Cells* dialog box has a *Border* tab and a *Fill* tab. From the *Border* tab, choose a different line style, a different color, or different positions for the border. From the *Fill* tab, you can design patterned or gradient fills. A ***pattern*** fill uses crosshatches, dots, or stripes. A ***gradient*** is a blend of two or more colors. Use fill choices carefully, because they affect the readability of your data.

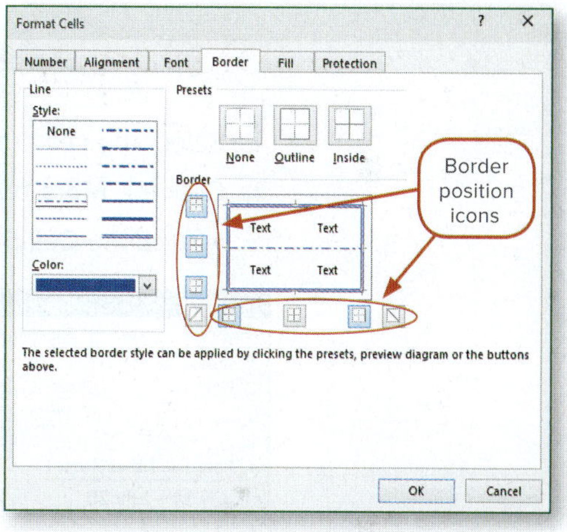

Figure 1-31 Build a custom border in the *Format Cells* dialog box

▸HOW TO: Add Borders and Fill Using the Format Cells Dialog Box

1. Select the cell or range.
2. Click the **Font** launcher [*Home* tab, *Font* group] to open the *Format Cells* dialog box.
   - Press **Ctrl+1** to open the *Format Cells* dialog box.
   - Right-click a cell in the range and select **Format Cells**.
3. Click the **Border** tab (Figure 1-31).
   - Click **None** to remove all borders.
4. Choose a color from the *Color* drop-down list.
   - Select the color before choosing a line style or location.
5. Select a line style in the *Style* area.
6. Click **Outline** in the *Presets* area to apply an outside border.
   - The *Preview* area shows the border.
   - Build a custom border by clicking the desired icons in the *Border* area or by clicking the desired position in the *Preview* area.
7. Click the **Fill** tab (Figure 1-32).

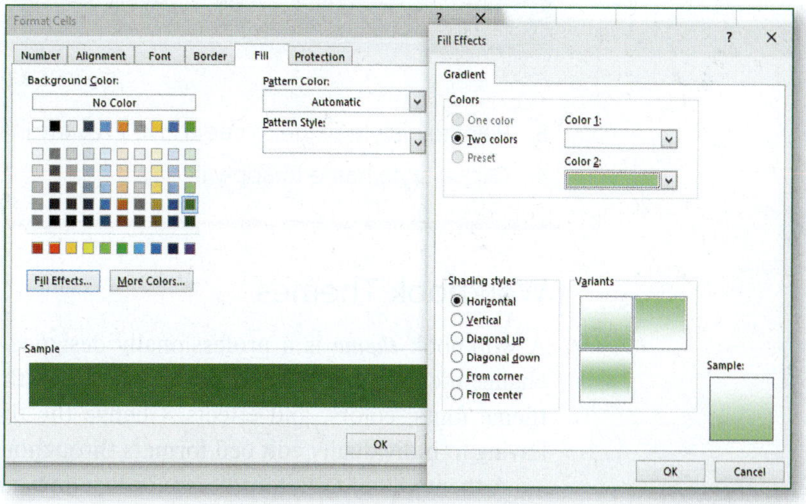

Figure 1-32 *Fill* tab in the *Format Cells* dialog box and *Fill Effects* dialog box

8. Select a color tile in the *Background Color* area.
   - Select a color from the *Pattern Color* list and select a pattern from the *Pattern Style* list.
   - Click **Fill Effects** to apply a gradient. Choose two colors, a shading style, and a variant.
9. Click **OK** to close the *Format Cells* dialog box.

Cell Styles

A ***cell style*** is a set of formatting elements that includes font style, size, color, alignment, borders, and fill, as well as number formats. Like other formatting, you select the cell or range and then apply a cell style. When you apply a cell style, the style format overwrites individual formatting already applied. After a cell style is applied, however, you can individually change any of the attributes. The *Cell Styles* gallery is located in the *Styles* group on the *Home* tab.

MORE INFO

Your screen size and settings determine if you see part of the *Cell Styles* gallery in the *Ribbon* or only the *Cell Styles* button.

HOW TO: Apply Cell Styles

1. Select the cell or range.
2. Click the **More** button in the *Cell Styles* gallery.
   - Click the **Cell Styles** button [*Home* tab, *Styles* group] to open the gallery (Figure 1-33).

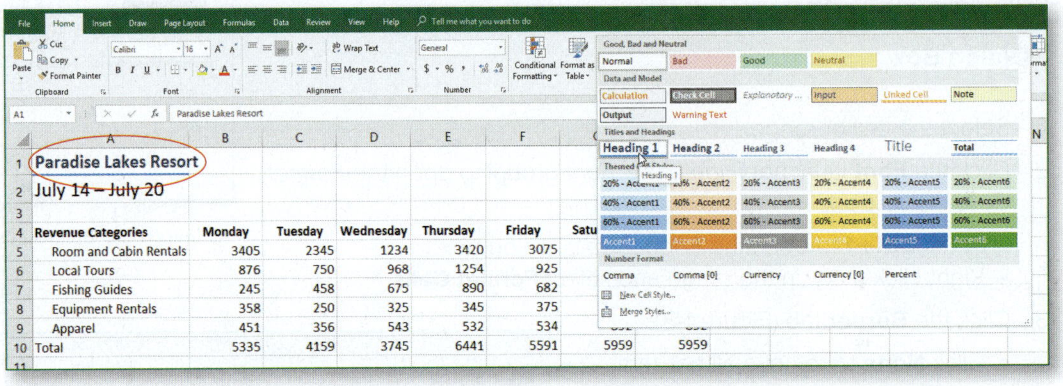

Figure 1-33 ***Cell Styles*** **gallery and *Live Preview* for selected cells**

3. Point to a style name to see a *Live Preview* in the worksheet.
4. Click a style name to apply it.

Workbook Themes

A workbook ***theme*** is a professionally designed set of fonts, colors, and effects. When you change the workbook theme, data formatted with theme settings are reformatted with the new theme fonts, colors, and effects. Change the theme to quickly restyle a worksheet without having to individually edit cell formats throughout the sheet.

A theme includes a font name for headings and one for body text. You can see the names of *Theme Fonts* at the top of the *Font* list. *Theme Colors* are identified in the color palettes for the **Fill** and **Font Color** buttons [*Home* tab, *Font* group]. Cell styles use font and color settings from the theme.

The *Themes* gallery lists built-in themes, and additional themes are available online. You can also create and save your own theme.

HOW TO: Change the Workbook Theme

1. Click the **Theme** button [*Page Layout* tab, *Themes* group].
   - The *Themes* gallery opens.
2. Point to a theme name.
   - *Live Preview* displays the worksheet with new format settings (Figure 1-34).
3. Click a theme icon to apply a different theme.
   - Display the **Font** button list [*Home* tab, *Font* group] to see the theme font names at the top of the list.
   - Display the **Font Color** and **Fill Color** button galleries [*Home* tab, *Font* group] to see new theme colors.

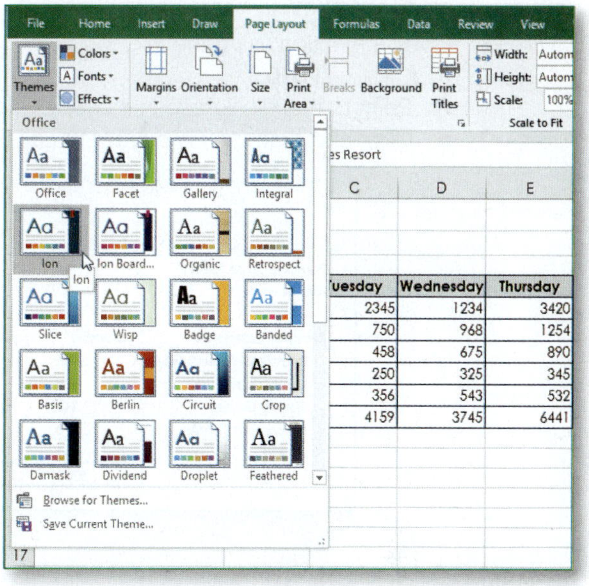

Figure 1-34 *Themes* gallery and a *Live Preview* in the worksheet

MORE INFO

Rest the pointer on the **Themes** button [*Page Layout* tab, *Themes* group] to see the name of the current theme. Rest the pointer on the **Fonts** button [*Page Layout* tab, *Themes* group] to see font defaults for the theme.

PAUSE & PRACTICE: EXCEL 1-2

In this project, you open the workbook you created in *Pause & Practice 1-1*. You add totals using *SUM* and copy the function using *AutoFill*. Your format changes result in truncated or cutoff data; you learn how to adjust column widths in the next learning objective and repair this problem in the next Pause & Practice project.

File Needed: ***[your initials] PP E1-1.xlsx***
Completed Project File Name: ***[your initials] PP E1-2.xlsx***

1. Open a workbook and save it as a different name.
   a. Click the **File** tab and choose **Open**. Locate the folder where your file is stored.
   c. Open ***[your initials] PP E1-1***. (Click **Enable Editing** if the workbook has opened in *Protected View*.)

b. Press **F12 (FN+F12)** to open the *Save As* dialog box.
c. Locate the folder where your files are saved.
d. Edit the file name to [your initials] PP E1-2 and click **Save**.

2. Calculate daily totals using *SUM*.
   a. Click cell **B10**.
   b. Click the **AutoSum** button [*Home* tab, *Editing* group].
   c. Press **Enter** to accept the suggested range and to complete the formula.

3. Copy a function using the *Fill Handle*.
   a. Click cell **B10**.
   b. Point to the *Fill Handle* in the lower-right corner of the cell.
   c. Click and drag the *Fill* pointer to cell **H10** (Figure 1-35). Release the pointer.

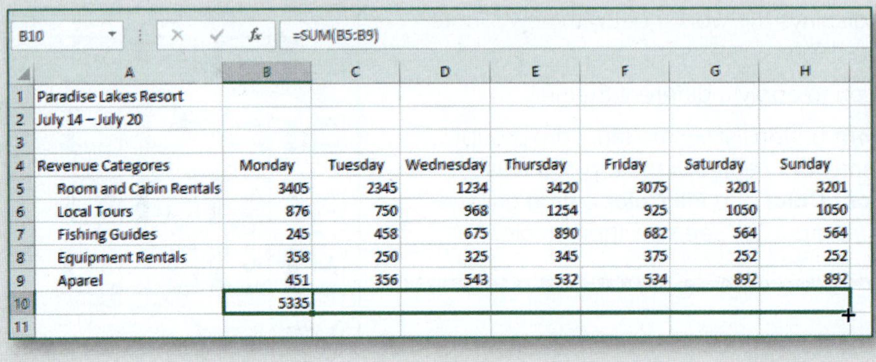

Figure 1-35 Copy a function with the *Fill* pointer

4. Calculate sales category totals.
   a. Click the empty cell **J5**.
   b. Double-click the **AutoSum** button [*Home* tab, *Editing* group] to accept and complete the formula.

5. Edit the argument cell range.
   a. Click cell **J5**.
   b. Click the *Formula* bar showing the range **B5:I5**.
   c. Change the range to display **B5:h5**. When you type the "h," you will see a *Formula AutoComplete* list. Ignore the list (Figure 1-36).
   d. Press **Enter** to accept the new range.

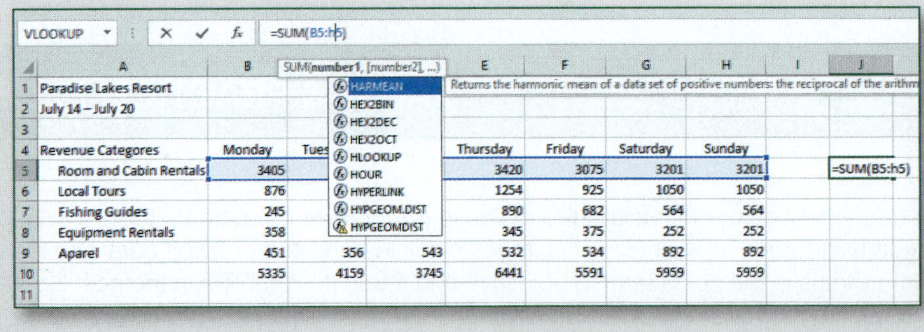

Figure 1-36 Edit the cell reference in the *Formula* bar

6. Copy a function using the *Fill Handle*.
   a. Select cell **J5** and point to the *Fill Handle*.
   b. Click and drag the *Fill* pointer to cell **J10**. Release the pointer.

7. Drag and drop to move a cell range.
   a. Select cells **J5:J10**.
   b. Point to any border of the selected range to display the move pointer.

c. Drag the range to cells **I5:I10**.
d. Type Total in cell **I4**.

8. Apply cell styles.
   a. Select cell **A1** and click the **Cell Styles** button or the **More** button [*Home* tab, *Styles* group] to open the *Cell Styles* gallery.
   b. Click **Title** in the *Titles and Headings* group.
   c. Select cell **A2** and click the **Cell Styles** button or the **More** button [*Home* tab, *Styles* group].
   d. Select **Heading 2** in the *Titles and Headings* group.
   e. Select cells **A10:I10** and open the *Cell Styles* gallery [*Home* tab, *Styles* group].
   f. Select **Total** in the *Titles and Headings* group.
   g. Select cells **A4:A10**, press **Ctrl**, and select cells **B4:I4** to add them to the selection.
   h. Open the *Cells Style* gallery and select **Light Blue, 20% - Accent1** in the *Themed Cell Styles* category.
   i. Click cell **F1** to deselect cells and view the styles.

9. Change the theme and apply font attributes.
   a. Click the **Themes** button [*Page Layout* tab, *Themes* group] and choose **Facet** from the gallery.
   b. Select cell **A4** and click the **Home** tab.
   c. Click the **Font** drop-down list [*Font* group] and select **Candara** in the *All Fonts* section.
   d. Click the **Font Size** drop-down list and select **16 pt**.
   e. Click the **Bold** button [*Font* group].
   f. Select cells **A5:I10**.
   g. Click the **Font Size** drop-down list and choose **12 pt**.

10. Use the *Format Painter*.
    a. Click cell **A4**.
    b. Click the **Format Painter** button [*Home* tab, *Clipboard* group].
    c. Drag to paint cells **B4:I4** and release the pointer (Figure 1-37).

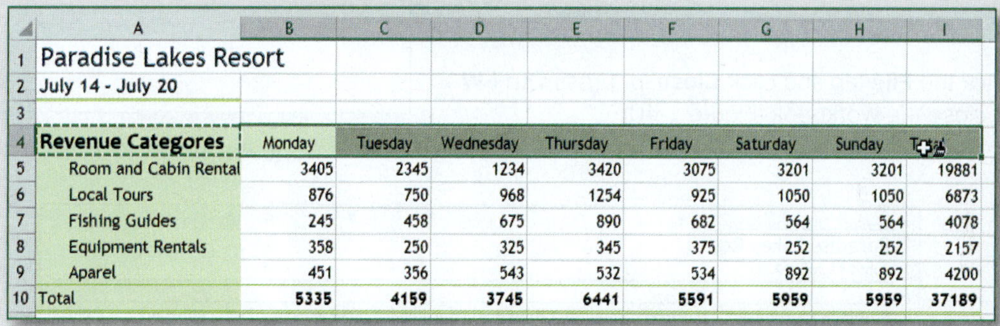

	A	B	C	D	E	F	G	H	I
1	Paradise Lakes Resort								
2	July 14 - July 20								
3									
4	Revenue Categores	Monday	Tuesday	Wednesday	Thursday	Friday	Saturday	Sunday	T[illegible]
5	Room and Cabin Rental	3405	2345	1234	3420	3075	3201	3201	19881
6	Local Tours	876	750	968	1254	925	1050	1050	6873
7	Fishing Guides	245	458	675	890	682	564	564	4078
8	Equipment Rentals	358	250	325	345	375	252	252	2157
9	Aparel	451	356	543	532	534	892	892	4200
10	Total	5335	4159	3745	6441	5591	5959	5959	37189

Figure 1-37 Paint the format from cell A4

11. Apply number formats and align text.
    a. Select cells **B5:I9**.
    b. Click the **Comma Style** button [*Home* tab, *Number* group] and leave cells B5:I9 selected.
    c. Click the **Decrease Decimal** button [*Home* tab, *Number* group] two times while cells B5:I9 are selected.
    d. Select cells **B10:I10**.
    e. Click the **Accounting Number Format** button [*Home* tab, *Number* group]. You may see a series of # symbols in the cells.
    f. Click the **Decrease Decimal** button [*Home* tab, *Number* group] two times.
    g. Select cells **B4:I4**.
    h. Click the **Align Right** button [*Home* tab, *Alignment* group]. Not all labels are visible with this alignment setting.
    i. Apply **Bold** to cell **A10**.

12. Add borders.
    a. Select cells **A4:I10** and click the **Border** button arrow [*Home* tab, *Font* group].
    b. Select **All Borders**. The border format from the *Total* cell style in row 10 is overwritten with the *All Borders* format.
    c. Select cells **A10:I10** and press **Ctrl+1** to open the *Format Cells* dialog box.
    d. Click the **Border** tab.
    e. Click the bottom border icon in the *Border* preview area to remove the border (Figure 1-38).
    f. Click the double solid line style (second column, seventh style).
    g. Click the bottom border position in the preview area to reset the border (Figure 1-39).
    h. Click **OK** to close the *Format Cells* dialog box and to apply the new border.
    i. Select cells **A2:I2** and open the *Format Cells* dialog box.
    j. Click the **Border** tab and click the bottom border position two times to remove the bottom border.
    k. Click the **Color** drop-down list, and select **Dark Green, Accent2, Darker 25%** (sixth column).
    l. Select the thick, solid line style (second column, fifth style).
    m. Click the bottom border location in the preview area to reset the border.
    n. Click **OK** and then click cell **A1**.
13. Click the **Save** button in the *Quick Access* toolbar.
14. Click the **File** tab and click **Close**, or press **Ctrl+W** to close the workbook (Figure 1-40).

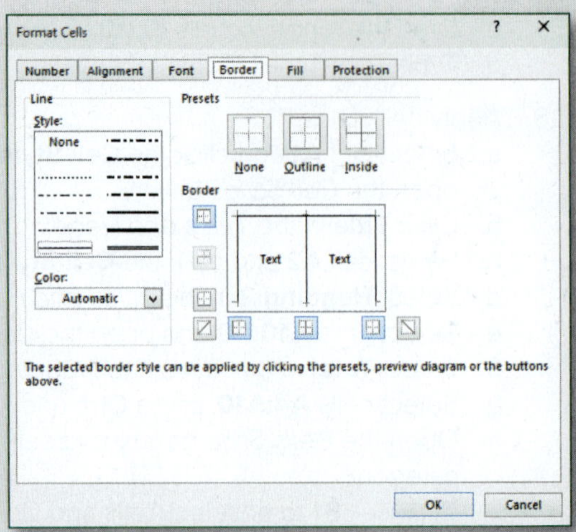

Figure 1-38 Remove the bottom border

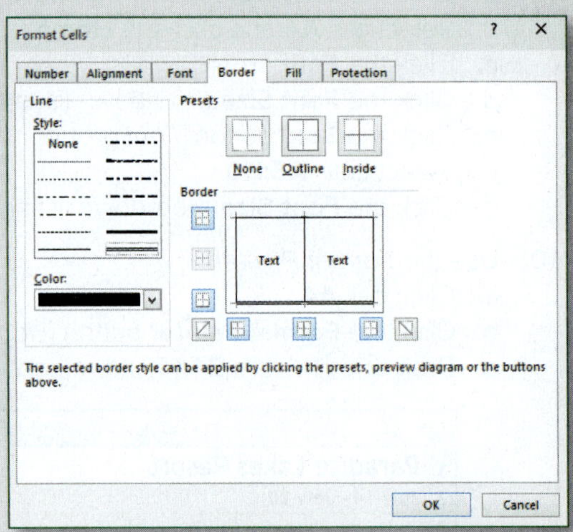

Figure 1-39 Reset the bottom border

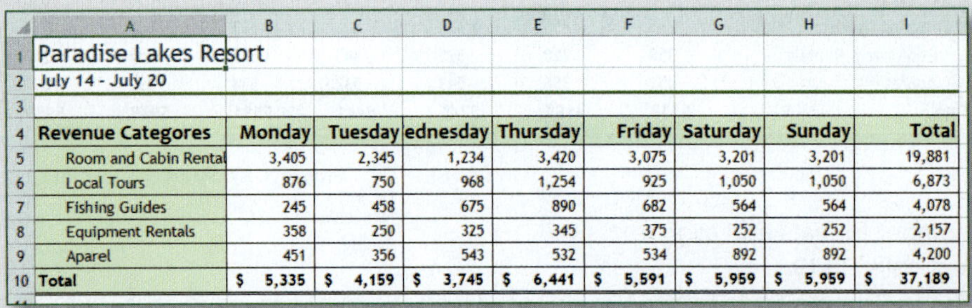

	A	B	C	D	E	F	G	H	I
1	Paradise Lakes Resort								
2	July 14 - July 20								
3									
4	Revenue Categores	Monday	Tuesday	ednesday	Thursday	Friday	Saturday	Sunday	Total
5	Room and Cabin Rental	3,405	2,345	1,234	3,420	3,075	3,201	3,201	19,881
6	Local Tours	876	750	968	1,254	925	1,050	1,050	6,873
7	Fishing Guides	245	458	675	890	682	564	564	4,078
8	Equipment Rentals	358	250	325	345	375	252	252	2,157
9	Aparel	451	356	543	532	534	892	892	4,200
10	Total	$ 5,335	$ 4,159	$ 3,745	$ 6,441	$ 5,591	$ 5,959	$ 5,959	$ 37,189

Figure 1-40 PP E1-2 completed

SLO 1.5

Modifying Columns and Rows

A worksheet includes a default number of rows and columns, each in the default width and height for the workbook theme. Over 1 million rows and more than 16,000 columns are available for use. You can modify the width of a column, insert columns, change the height of a row, delete a column, and apply other changes to the worksheet.

> **MORE INFO**
>
> Unused rows and columns are ignored when you print a worksheet with default print settings.

Adjust Column Width and Row Height

The default width for a column in a worksheet using the Office theme is 8.43 characters (64 pixels) in the default font. Change column width to any value between 0 and 255 characters. The default height of each row is 15 points (20 pixels). A ***pixel*** measures one screen dot. You can change column width or row height by dragging the border between column or row headings, by using the context menu or by selecting a command from the **Format** button list [*Home* tab, *Cells* group]. You can adjust one or more columns or rows at the same time.

HOW TO: Change Column Width or Row Height

1. Select one or more cells in the same column.
   - The cells need not be in adjacent rows.
2. Click the **Format** button [*Home* tab, *Cells* group].
3. Select **Row Height**.
   - The *Row Height* dialog box opens.
4. Enter a height in points and click **OK**.
   - The row height adjusts for the rows in which you selected cells.
5. Select one or more cells in the same row.
   - The cells need not be in adjacent columns.
6. Click the **Format** button [*Home* tab, *Cells* group].
7. Select **Column Width**.
   - The *Column Width* dialog box opens.
8. Enter a new width in characters and click **OK** (Figure 1-41).

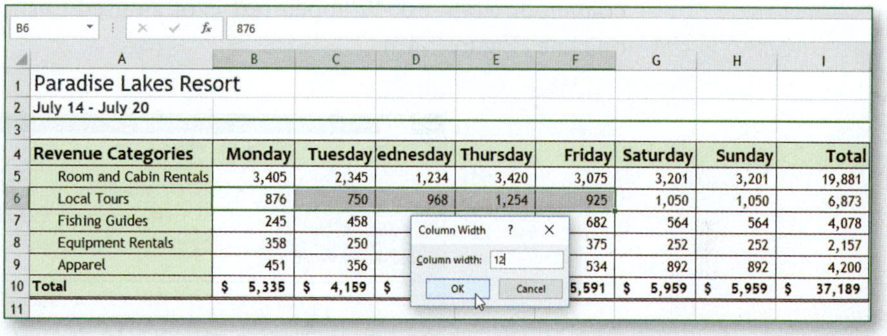

Figure 1-41 Change the column width for columns B:F

> **MORE INFO**
>
> To set a custom column width for a new worksheet, click the **Format** button [*Home* tab, *Cells* group] and select **Default Width**.

You can quickly change column widths and row heights using the worksheet headings. Point to the border between two column or row headings and click and drag to set a new width or height. When you point to a border, the pointer changes to a resize arrow, and you will see a *ScreenTip* with the setting as you drag. You can use this method with multiple columns or rows, too. Drag across the headings to select the number of columns or rows to adjust, and then click and drag any border in the selected group.

AutoFit Columns and Rows

The ***AutoFit*** feature resizes column width or row height to fit the width or height of the longest or tallest entry. The quickest way to *AutoFit* a column is to double-click the right border of the column heading (Figure 1-42). To *AutoFit* a row, double-click the bottom border of the row heading. You can *AutoFit* multiple columns or rows by first selecting them and double-clicking any border within the selection. You can also use the *AutoFit Column Width* or the *AutoFit Row Height* commands on the **Format** button in the *Cells* group on the *Home* tab.

▸HOW TO: AutoFit Column Width or Row Height

1. Point to the border to the right of the column heading or below the row heading.
   - Drag to select more than one column or row.
2. Double-click the resize arrow.
   - All selected columns and rows adjust to the longest or tallest entry.

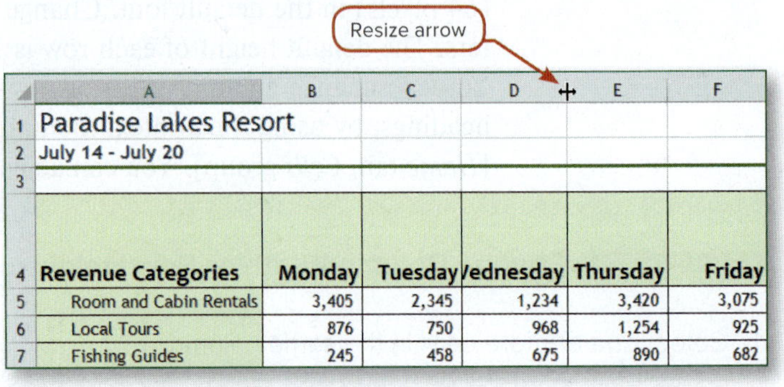

Figure 1-42 Double-click a column border to *AutoFit* its width to the longest item

Wrap Text, Merge Cells, and Center Across Selection

When a label is too long for the column width, it spills into an empty adjacent cell. If the adjacent cell is not empty, a long label may be cut off within the cell. You can widen the column or wrap text. Wrapped text is often used to show lengthy column titles on more than one line (Figure 1-43).

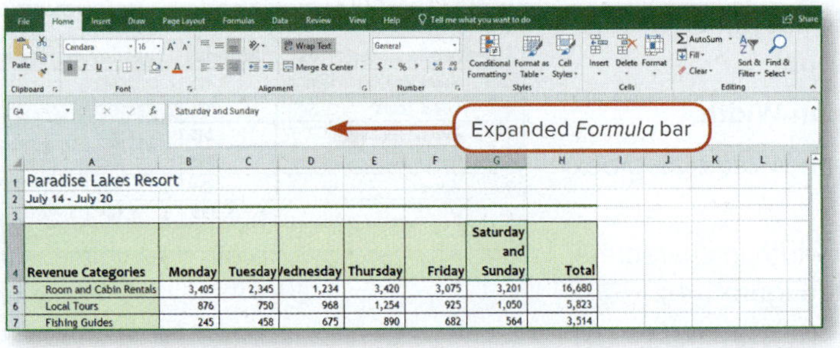

Figure 1-43 Label in cell G4 wraps to two lines; *Formula* bar expanded

The ***Wrap Text*** command displays a label on multiple lines within the cell, splitting the label between words to fit the width of the column. You control where the label splits by inserting a manual ***line break***. Press **Alt+Enter** after the word where you want a new line to start. When using multi-line labels, expand the *Formula* bar by clicking the expand or collapse button at the right edge of the *Formula* bar.

> **MORE INFO**
>
> After using the *Wrap Text* command, you may need to adjust the column width or row height to better display the label.

▸HOW TO: Wrap Text in a Cell

1. Select the cell with the label.
2. Click the **Home** tab.
3. Click the **Wrap Text** button in the *Alignment* group.
   - To control the split, edit the cell and click at the desired location. Press **Alt+Enter** to insert a manual line break and then press **Enter** to finish.
4. Adjust the column width and row height as desired.

> **ANOTHER WAY**
>
> As you type a label, press **Alt+Enter** at the point where a new line should start, finish the label, and press **Enter**. The *Wrap Text* command is automatically enabled.

The ***Merge & Center*** command combines two or more cells into one cell and centers the data within the combined cell. This command is a quick way to center a main label over multiple columns. Because the result is one large cell, you can format the area with special fill effects. When you use *Merge & Center*, the data must be in the upper-left cell of the selection.

The *Merge & Center* button [*Home* tab, *Alignment* group] includes options to merge cells without centering and to unmerge cells.

▸HOW TO: Merge and Center

1. Select the cells to be merged and centered.
   - You can merge and center the cells first and then enter the data.
2. Click the **Home** tab.
3. Click the **Merge & Center** button [*Alignment* group] (Figure 1-44).

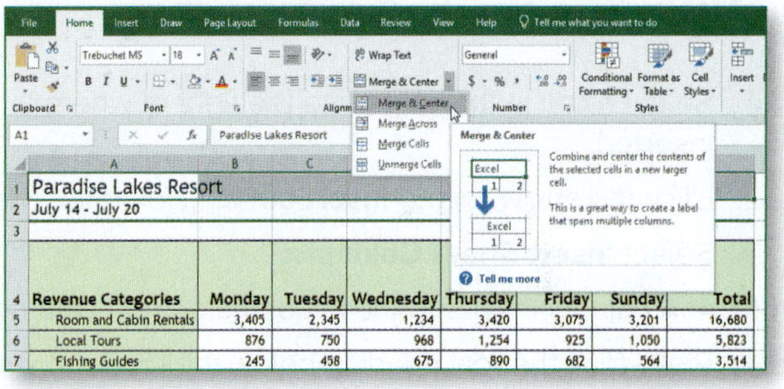

Figure 1-44 Select cells to merge and center

The ***Center Across Selection*** command horizontally centers multiple rows across multiple columns. When you have two or three rows of labels to center, select the entire range and center them with one command. This command does not merge cells, and you can still insert and delete rows and columns in the centered area.

The *Center Across Selection* command is on the *Alignment* tab in the *Format Cells* dialog box.

Insert and Delete Columns and Rows

You can insert or delete rows or columns in a worksheet. When you do, Excel moves existing data to make room for new data or to fill the gap left by deleted data. Functions or formulas are automatically updated to include an inserted row or column, and they reflect deleted rows or columns in the argument or range.

▶HOW TO: Center Across a Selection

1. Select the cell range that includes the data to be centered.
   - Select all rows with data to be centered.
   - Select columns to identify the range over which the labels should be centered.
2. Click the **Alignment** launcher [*Home* tab, *Alignment* group].
3. Click the *Horizontal* drop-down arrow and choose **Center Across Selection** (Figure 1-45).
4. Click **OK**.

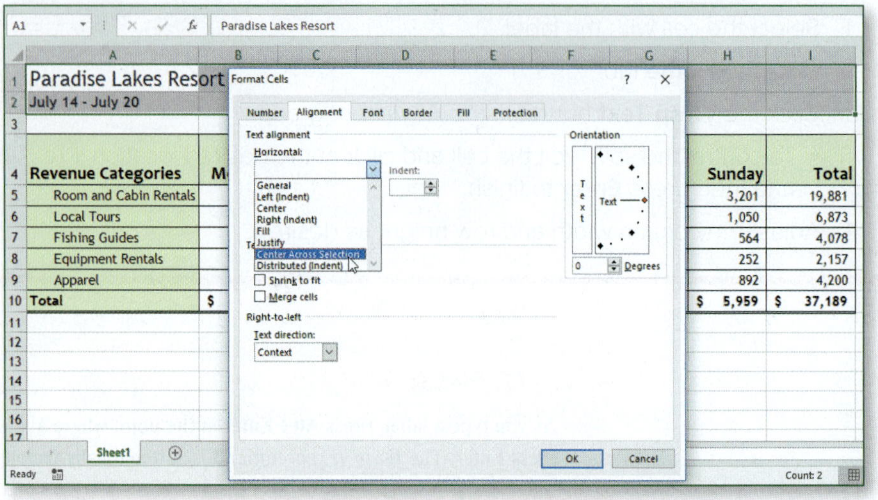

Figure 1-45 Selection A1:I2 identifies area for centering

You can insert rows and columns from options on the *Insert* button [*Home* tab, *Cells* group]. A second way is to right-click a column or row heading and choose *Insert* from the context menu. To insert multiple columns or rows, first select the number of columns or rows that you want to insert. For example, if you want to insert two columns to the left of column A, select columns A:B. Then use any *Insert* command to insert two new columns.

▶HOW TO: Insert a Column or a Row

1. Select a cell in the column to the right of where a new column is to be inserted.
2. Click the arrow on the **Insert** button [*Home* tab, *Cells* group].
3. Select **Insert Sheet Columns**.
   - A column inserts to the left of the current column.
4. Right-click the row heading below the row where a new row should appear.
5. Choose **Insert** from the context menu (Figure 1-46).
   - A row appears above the selected row.

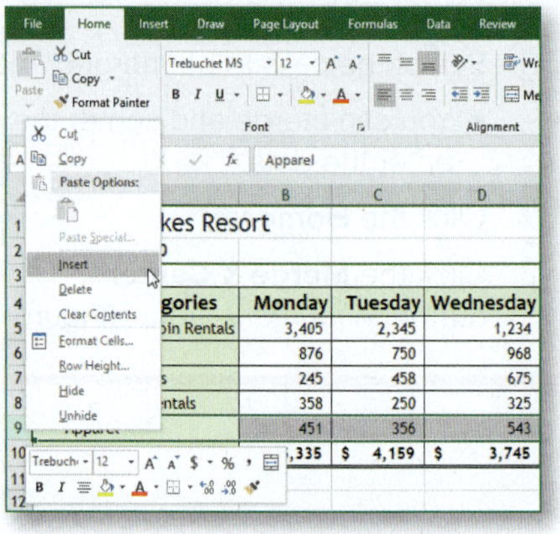

Figure 1-46 Insert a row above row 9

ANOTHER WAY

Select a cell and press **Ctrl+plus sign** (+) in the numeric keypad. Choose **Entire Column** or **Entire Row** and press **Enter**. Press **Ctrl+minus sign** (−) in the numeric keypad to delete a column or row.

When you delete a column or row, data are deleted and the remaining columns and rows shift to the left or up. Most functions or formulas are updated if you delete a row or column that is within the argument range.

> **MORE INFO**
>
> Select a row or column heading and press **Ctrl+plus sign** (+) or **Ctrl+minus sign** (−) in the numeric keypad to insert or delete a row or column.

Delete rows and columns using the **Delete** button [*Home* tab, *Cells* group] or from the context menu. To delete multiple columns or rows, select them and use the **Delete** command.

HOW TO: Delete Columns or Rows

1. Select a cell in the column to be deleted.
2. Click the arrow on the **Delete** button [*Home* tab, *Cells* group].
3. Select **Delete Sheet Columns**.
   - The entire column is deleted.
   - Remaining columns shift to the left.
4. Right-click the row heading for the row to be deleted.
   - The context menu opens.
5. Choose **Delete**.
   - The entire row is deleted.
   - Remaining rows shift up.

> **MORE INFO**
>
> Delete or insert cells with the *Insert Cells* or *Delete Cells* commands [*Home* tab, *Cells* group]. Be careful with these commands, because they shift data and can affect formulas or the position of data in a worksheet.

Hide and Unhide Columns and Rows

If a worksheet has more data than necessary for your current task, hide data to optimize screen space. In a checkbook register with data for several years, you might want to hide rows from two years ago so that you only see the current year's data. You should not delete the old data because it is necessary for record-keeping.

Hidden rows and columns are available and included in calculations and can be shown whenever necessary. The ***Hide*** and ***Unhide*** commands apply to columns or rows; you cannot hide cells. When a column or row is hidden, a tiny gap displays between the column or row headings. In addition, column or row headings are not consecutive, so you can quickly identify what is hidden.

HOW TO: Hide and Unhide Columns or Rows

1. Click the row or column heading of the row or column to be hidden.
   - Select multiple row or column headings as desired.
   - Rows or columns need not be adjacent.

2. Right-click one of the selected row or column headings.
   - The context menu opens.
3. Select **Hide** (Figure 1-47).
   - The entire row or column is hidden.
   - Formula references to hidden cells are maintained.
4. Drag across the column or row headings for the hidden columns or rows.
   - Drag from the column to the left of a hidden column to one column to the right of a hidden column.
   - Drag from the row above hidden rows to one row below hidden rows.
5. Right-click one of the selected row or column headings.
   - The context menu opens.
6. Select **Unhide**.

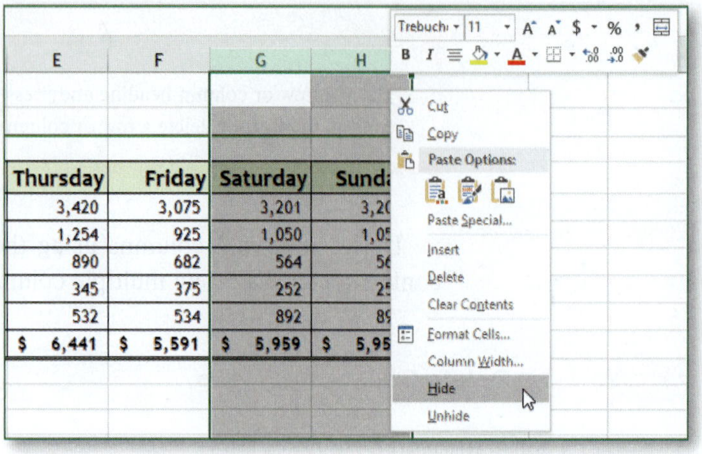

Figure 1-47 Hide two columns

> **ANOTHER WAY**
>
> To hide or unhide columns or rows, select the column or row headings, click the **Format** button [*Home* tab, *Cells* group], choose **Hide & Unhide**, and select the desired command.

SLO 1.6

Inserting, Deleting, and Moving Worksheets

Each worksheet in an Excel workbook has a worksheet tab near the bottom left of the Excel window that displays the name of the sheet. A new workbook starts with one sheet, but the number of worksheets is limited only by the size of memory on the computer. You can insert and delete sheets, rename them, and change the tab color. You can also hide, copy, or move sheets.

Insert and Delete Worksheets

You can keep related worksheets in a single workbook for ease in managing your files and tasks. For example, a monthly workbook could include revenue and expense, payroll, and customer data sheets. When a workbook includes multiple worksheets, activate a sheet by clicking its tab name.

Insert worksheets using the **Insert** button [*Home* tab, *Cells* group] or by simply clicking the **New Sheet** button to the right of the tab names. You can also right-click an existing sheet tab and choose **Insert** to open an *Insert* dialog box. Inserted worksheets are named *SheetN*, where *N* is the next available number.

To delete the active worksheet, right-click the sheet tab and select **Delete**. You can also click the arrow on the **Delete** button [*Home* tab, *Cells* group] and select **Delete Sheet**.

> **MORE INFO**
>
> Press **Ctrl+Page Down** to move to the next worksheet in the tab order. Press **Ctrl+Page Up** to move to the previous sheet.

▶HOW TO: Insert and Delete Worksheets

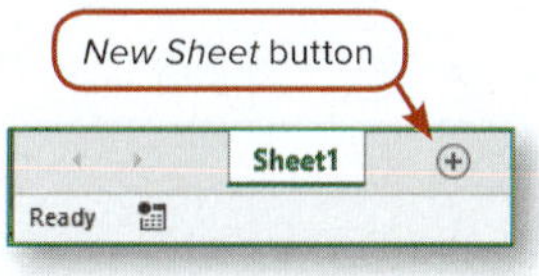

Figure 1-48 *New Sheet* button

1. Click the **New Sheet** button (plus sign) to the right of the worksheet tabs (Figure 1-48).
   - A new sheet inserts to the right of the active sheet.
2. Click the arrow on the **Insert** button [*Home* tab, *Cells* group].
3. Select **Insert Sheet**.
   - A new sheet inserts to the left of the active sheet.
4. Right-click a tab and select **Insert**.
   - The *Insert* dialog box opens.
5. Select **Worksheet** and click **OK**.
   - The new sheet inserts to the left of the active sheet.
6. Right-click a sheet tab and choose **Delete**.
   - The sheet is deleted.
7. Click the arrow on the **Delete** button [*Home* tab, *Cells* group] and select **Delete Sheet**.
   - The sheet is deleted.

ANOTHER WAY

Press **Shift+F11** to insert a worksheet to the left of the active sheet.

MORE INFO

To delete or insert multiple sheets, select multiple tabs. Then right-click one of the selected tabs and choose **Delete** or **Insert**.

Rename Worksheets and Change Tab Color

New worksheets are named *Sheet1*, *Sheet2*, and so on, but you can rename a worksheet to identify its contents and purpose. The tab width adjusts to display the name, so if you use lengthy names, you limit the number of tabs visible at the same time. When you cannot see all the tabs, use the ***tab scrolling buttons*** located to the left of the leftmost tab name. Move forward and backward through the tabs, or right-click a tab scrolling button to display the *Activate* dialog box with a list of existing worksheet names (Figure 1-49). The tab scrolling buttons are enabled when needed.

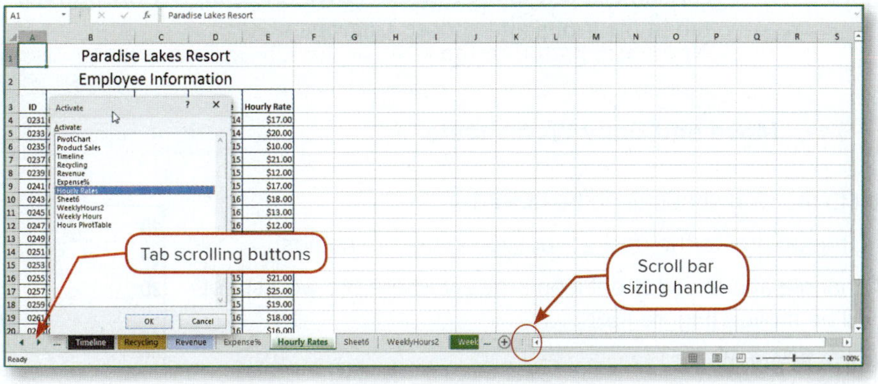

Figure 1-49 *Activate* dialog box and tab scrolling buttons

> **MORE INFO**
>
> The number of tab names visible at one time depends on the width of the horizontal scroll bar. Resize the scroll bar by dragging the sizing handle at the left of the scroll bar.

Apply a ***tab color*** to further distinguish a particular sheet. The color palette includes tiles for theme and standard colors, as well as an option to build a custom color.

HOW TO: Rename a Worksheet and Apply a Tab Color

1. Double-click the worksheet tab.
   - Right-click the tab and select **Rename**.
2. Type the new name on the tab and press **Enter**.
   - Click the **Format** button [*Home* tab, *Cells* group] and select **Rename Sheet**.
3. Right-click the worksheet tab.
4. Choose **Tab Color** from the context menu to open the palette (Figure 1-50).
   - Click the **Format** button [*Home* tab, *Cells* group] and select **Tab Color**.
5. Select a color.
6. Click another tab to better see the tab color.

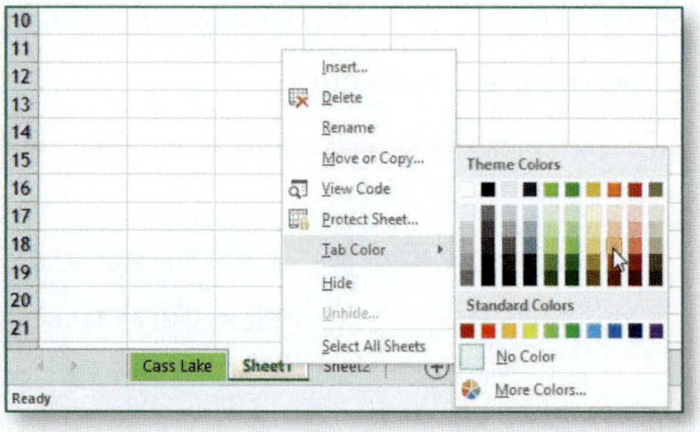

Figure 1-50 Change the tab

Move and Copy Worksheets

Rearrange (move) tabs to display the worksheets in your preferred left-to-right order. You can also move worksheets to another workbook.

Copy a worksheet to create an exact duplicate of the data and formatting. When you copy a worksheet, the copy is named with the same name as the original followed by a number in parentheses (for example: *January (2)*).

When moving sheets within a workbook, simply drag the tab to the desired location. When moving or copying to another workbook, however, use the ***Move or Copy*** dialog box.

You can move or copy multiple sheets. Select sheet names using **Ctrl** or **Shift**. The word *[Group]* displays in the title bar. After you complete the move or copy command, right-click any tab in the group and choose **Ungroup**.

HOW TO: Move and Copy Worksheets

1. Point to the worksheet tab to be moved.
2. Drag the pointer to the desired location in the tab names.
   - A triangle and a worksheet icon preview where the worksheet will be moved (Figure 1-51).
3. Release the pointer.
4. Right-click the worksheet tab to be copied.

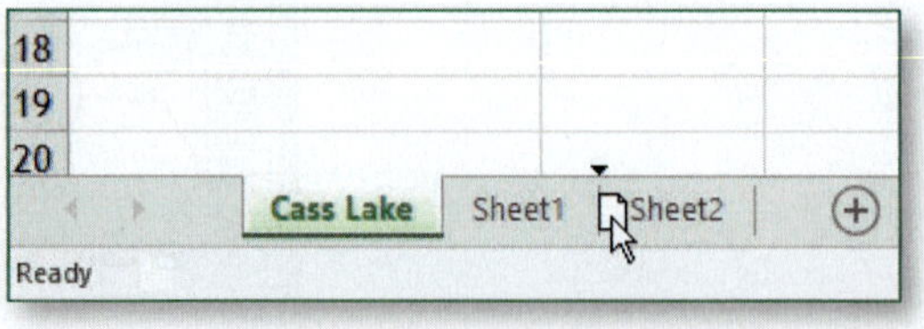

Figure 1-51 Drag a sheet tab to a position

5. Select **Move or Copy**.
   - The *Move or Copy* dialog box opens.
   - Click the **Format** button [*Home* tab, *Cells* group] to select **Move or Copy Sheet**.
6. Click the **To book** drop-down arrow and choose a workbook name.
   - To copy the sheet in the same workbook, choose its name.
   - To copy the worksheet into a different workbook, choose its name; the workbook must be open.
7. Choose a sheet name in the *Before sheet* list.
   - Choose **(move to end)** to place the copied sheet as the last tab.
8. Select the **Create a copy** box (Figure 1-52).
9. Click **OK** to close the dialog box.
   - The copied worksheet has the same name as the original followed by *(2)*.
10. Rename the copied sheet as desired.

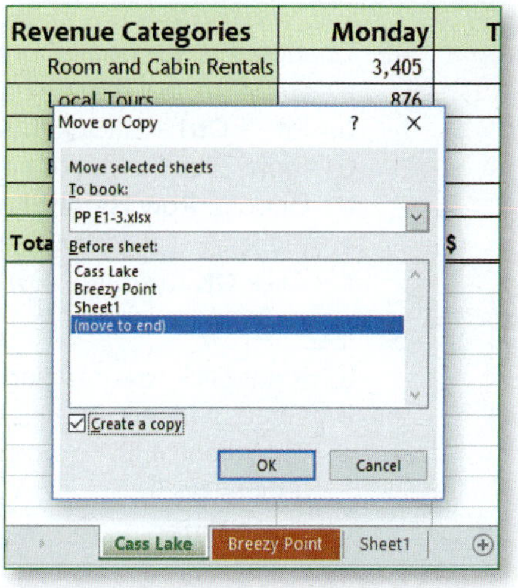

Figure 1-52 ***Move or Copy* dialog box**

ANOTHER WAY

To copy a worksheet by dragging, press **Ctrl** and drag the tab to the desired location for the copy.

PAUSE & PRACTICE: EXCEL 1-3

In this project, you open ***[your initials] PP E1-2*** and adjust column heights and row widths, insert a row, merge and center cells, and add borders. You also copy and rename sheets, apply tab colors, and delete worksheets.

File Needed: ***[your initials] PP E1-2.xlsx***
Completed Project File Name: ***[your initials] PP E1-3.xlsx***

1. Open the ***[your initials] PP E1-2*** workbook completed in *Pause & Practice 1-2*.
2. Save the file as [your initials] PP E1-3. (If your file is saved in *OneDrive* and *AutoSave* is on, select **Save a Copy**.)
3. Change the width of columns B through I.
   a. Point to the column **B** heading to display a down-pointing arrow.
   b. Click and drag to reach column I.
   c. Click the **Format** button [*Home* tab, *Cells* group].
   d. Select **Column Width** from the menu.
   e. Enter 14 in the *Column Width* dialog box.
   f. Click **OK** to set the new width for the selected columns.

4. Change the row height for rows 4 and 10.
   a. Click the row **4** heading.
   b. Press **Ctrl** and click the row **10** heading. Two rows are selected.
   c. Right-click the row **4** heading.
   d. Choose **Row Height** from the context menu.
   e. Enter 24 as the new height.
   f. Click **OK** to set the row height for both rows.

5. Insert a row.
   a. Right-click row heading **9**.
   b. Choose **Insert**. The inserted row is row 9, and the remaining rows have shifted down.
   c. Type Food & Beverage in cell **A9**. The format of the other rows applies to the new row. (Figure 1-53).
   d. Press **Enter**.

	A	B	C	D	E	F	G	H	I
1	Paradise Lakes Resort								
2	July 14 - July 20								
3									
4	**Revenue Categores**	**Monday**	**Tuesday**	**Wednesday**	**Thursday**	**Friday**	**Saturday**	**Sunday**	**Total**
5	Room and Cabin Rental	3,405	2,345	1,234	3,420	3,075	3,201	3,201	19,881
6	Local Tours	876	750	968	1,254	925	1,050	1,050	6,873
7	Fishing Guides	245	458	675	890	682	564	564	4,078
8	Equipment Rentals	358	250	325	345	375	252	252	2,157
9	Food & Beverage								
10	Aparel	451	356	543	532	534	892	892	4,200
11	**Total**	**$ 5,335**	**$ 4,159**	**$ 3,745**	**$ 6,441**	**$ 5,591**	**$ 5,959**	**$ 5,959**	**$ 37,189**

Figure 1-53 New row and label

6. Hide a row.
   a. Select cell **A9**.
   b. Click the **Format** button [*Home* tab, *Cells* group].
   c. Select **Hide & Unhide** in the *Visibility* category.
   d. Select **Hide Rows**. The selected row is hidden.

7. Center titles across a selection.
   a. Select cells **A1:I2**.
   b. Click the **Alignment** launcher [*Home* tab, *Alignment* group].
   c. Click the *Horizontal* drop-down arrow and choose **Center Across Selection**.
   d. Click **OK**.

8. Rename a worksheet and change the tab color.
   a. Double-click the **Sheet1** tab name.
   b. Type Cass Lake.
   c. Press **Enter**.
   d. Right-click the **Cass Lake** tab name and select **Tab Color**.
   e. Select **Green, Accent1, Darker 50%** (fifth column).

9. Copy and rename a worksheet to create a formatted worksheet for the Breezy Point data.
   a. Right-click the **Cass Lake** tab.
   b. Choose **Move or Copy**. The *Move or Copy* dialog box opens.
   c. Choose **(move to end)** in the *Before sheet* list.
   d. Select the **Create a copy** box.
   e. Click **OK**. The copied sheet is named *Cass Lake (2)*.
   f. Double-click the **Cass Lake (2)** tab, type Breezy Point, and press **Enter**.
   g. Right-click the **Breezy Point** tab and choose **Tab Color**.

h. Format the tab color to **Orange, Accent4, Darker 25%** (eighth column).
i. Select cells **B5:H10** and press **Delete** (Figure 1-54).
j. Press **Ctrl+Home**.

	A	B	C	D	E	F	G	H	I
1	Paradise Lakes Resort								
2	July 14 - July 20								
3									
4	Revenue Categores	Monday	Tuesday	Wednesday	Thursday	Friday	Saturday	Sunday	Total
5	Room and Cabin Rentals								
6	Local Tours								
7	Fishing Guides								
8	Equipment Rentals								
10	Aparel								
11	Total	$ -	$ -	$ -	$ -	$ -	$ -	$ -	$ -

Figure 1-54 Data deleted on copied sheet

10. Click the **Cass Lake** tab and press **Ctrl+Home**.
11. Press **Ctrl+S** to save the workbook.
12. Click the **File** tab and click **Close** to close the workbook (Figure 1-55).

	A	B	C	D	E	F	G	H	I
1	Paradise Lakes Resort								
2	July 14 - July 20								
3									
4	Revenue Categores	Monday	Tuesday	Wednesday	Thursday	Friday	Saturday	Sunday	Total
5	Room and Cabin Rental	3,405	2,345	1,234	3,420	3,075	3,201	3,201	19,881
6	Local Tours	876	750	968	1,254	925	1,050	1,050	6,873
7	Fishing Guides	245	458	675	890	682	564	564	4,078
8	Equipment Rentals	358	250	325	345	375	252	252	2,157
10	Aparel	451	356	543	532	534	892	892	4,200
11	Total	$ 5,335	$ 4,159	$ 3,745	$ 6,441	$ 5,591	$ 5,959	$ 5,959	$ 37,189
12									

Figure 1-55 PP E1-3 completed

SLO 1.7

Modifying the Appearance of a Workbook

You can adjust how you view data in a worksheet. You can select a view, zoom in or out on the data, freeze parts of the screen, split the worksheet into two panes, and switch between multiple open windows.

Workbook Views

The *View* tab has a *Workbook Views* group with three main views or layouts for working in an Excel worksheet. The views are ***Normal***, ***Page Break Preview***, and ***Page Layout***. You can also create ***Custom Views***.

- *Normal* view is the default and is used to create and modify a worksheet.
- *Page Break Preview* displays printed pages with dashed or dotted lines to mark where new pages start.
- *Page Layout* view opens the header and footer areas, indicates margin areas, and shows rulers.
- *Customs Views* enable you to name and save display and print settings, such as hidden columns or selected cells.

Buttons for *Normal* view, *Page Layout* view, and *Page Break Preview* appear on the right side of the *Status* bar.

MORE INFO

Use the **Ribbon Display Options** button (on the right of the workbook title bar) to hide the *Ribbon* for maximum screen space in any workbook view.

HOW TO: Switch Workbook Views Using the Status Bar

1. Click the **View** tab.
   - The *Normal* button is activated in the *Workbook Views* group.
2. Click the **Page Layout** button in the *Status* bar.
   - This view displays the header, the footer, and margin areas (Figure 1-56).

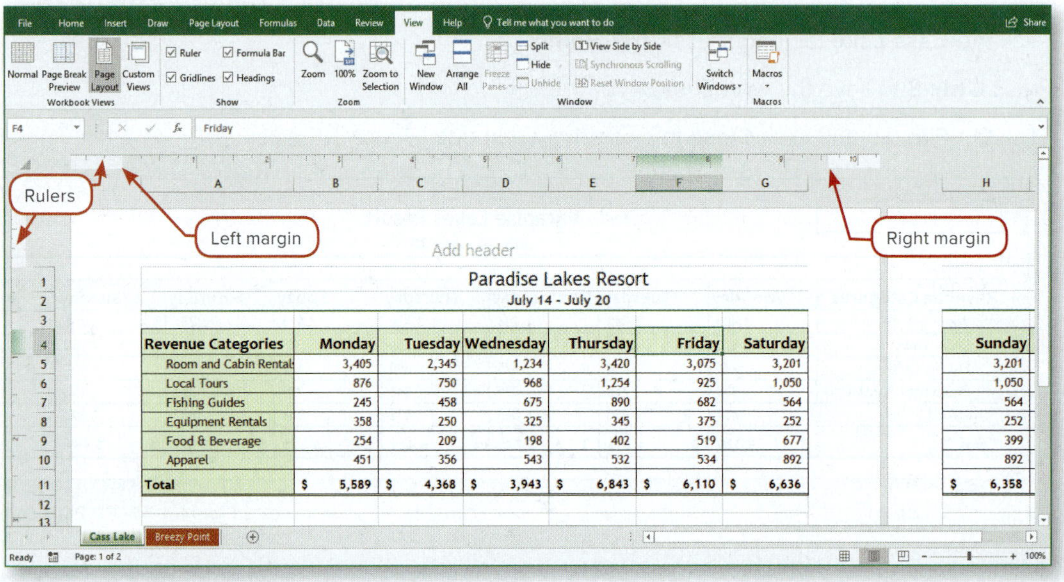

Figure 1-56 ***Page Layout*** **view**

3. Click the **Page Break Preview** button in the *Status* bar.
   - If the data does not fit on a single page, a dashed line indicates where the second page will start (Figure 1-57).

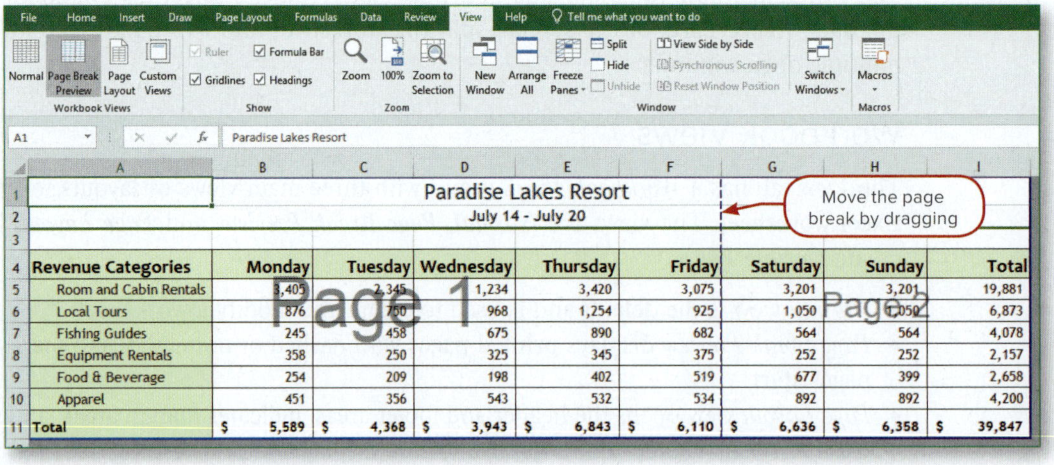

Figure 1-57 ***Page Break Preview***

4. Click the **Normal** button in the *Status* bar.

Zoom Options

You can change a sheet's magnification to see more of the data at once (zoom out) or to scrutinize content more carefully (zoom in). Use the *Zoom* group on the *View* tab or the *Zoom* controls in the *Status* bar.

The *Status* bar controls include a **Zoom In** button, a **Zoom Out** button, and the **Zoom** slider. The slider is the vertical bar in the middle of the horizontal line which you drag to change the magnification level.

HOW TO: Change Zoom Levels

1. Click the **Zoom In** button in the *Status* bar.
   - The magnification increases in 10% increments with each click.
2. Click the **Zoom Out** button in the *Status* bar.
   - The magnification decreases in 10% increments with each click.
3. Drag the **Zoom** slider in the middle of the horizontal line to the left or right to set a value (Figure 1-58).
   - The magnification percentage displays to the right of the line.
4. Click the **Zoom** button [*View* tab, *Zoom* group].
   - The *Zoom* dialog box includes preset values.
5. Click a radio button to choose a *Magnification* level.
   - Select **Fit selection** for a selected range to fill the screen.
   - Choose **Custom** to enter any magnification value.
6. Click **OK**.

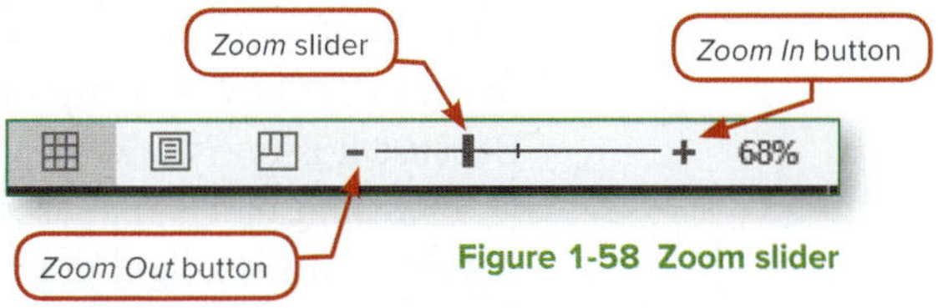

Figure 1-58 Zoom slider

ANOTHER WAY

The *Zoom* group [*View* tab] has ***100%*** and ***Zoom to Selection*** buttons.

Freeze Panes

In a worksheet with many rows and columns of information, it is not possible to see all the data at once. As you scroll to see information on the right, related labels or values on the left scroll out of view. The ***Freeze Panes*** command locks rows or columns in view so that you can position data for easy review. The worksheet is divided into two or four panes (sections) with a thin, black border to indicate the divisions.

The active cell becomes the top-left corner of the moving pane. For example, if you select cell B5 and select the *Freeze Panes* command, column A and rows 1:4 are stationary.

HOW TO: Freeze and Unfreeze Panes

1. Select a cell in the worksheet.
   - Click a cell one row below the last row to be frozen.
   - Click a cell one column to the right of the last column to be locked.
2. Click the **Freeze Panes** button [*View* tab, *Window* group].
   - Select **Freeze Top Row** to lock row 1 in view, regardless of the active cell.
   - Choose **Freeze First Column** to keep the first column in view, regardless of the active cell.

3. Select **Freeze Panes**.
   - All rows above and all columns to the left of the active cell are locked in position.
   - A thin, black border identifies frozen rows and columns.
4. Scroll the data in any direction (Figure 1-59).
5. Click the **Freeze Panes** button [*View* tab, *Window* group].
6. Select **Unfreeze Panes**.
   - The black border is removed.

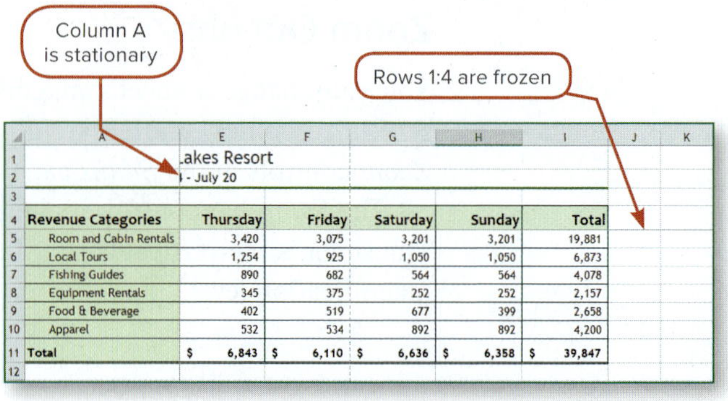

Figure 1-59 ***Freeze Panes*** **results when cell B5 is selected and columns B:D are scrolled left**

Split a Worksheet into Panes

The ***Split*** command divides a worksheet into two or four display panes. Each pane shows the same sheet, but you can arrange each pane to show different rows and columns or the same rows and columns. Only one active cell displays, and you may not see it in all the panes. Because it is one worksheet, an edit can be made in any pane.

The panes are split based on the position of the active cell when you select the command. A ***splitter bar*** is a light gray bar that spans the window, either horizontally, vertically, or both. You can drag a splitter bar to resize the panes.

HOW TO: Split a Worksheet

1. Select the cell for the location of a split.
   - Click a cell in column A (except cell A1) to split the worksheet into two horizontal panes.
   - Click a cell in row 1 (but not cell A1) to split the worksheet into two vertical panes.
   - Click a cell to split the worksheet into four panes.
2. Click the **Split** button [*View* tab, *Window* group].
3. Drag a splitter bar to resize a pane (Figure 1-60).
4. Click the **Split** button [*View* tab, *Window* group] to remove the split.

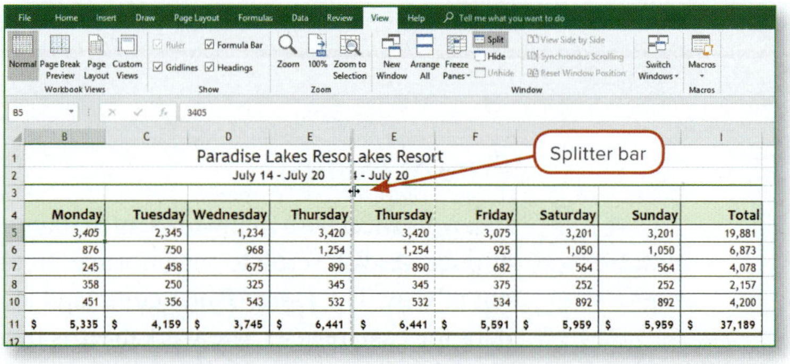

Figure 1-60 Split worksheet

> **ANOTHER WAY**
>
> Remove a window split by double-clicking the splitter bar.

Hide or Unhide Worksheets

A ***hidden worksheet*** is a worksheet whose tab does not display. It is part of the workbook and can be referenced in calculations. A worksheet might be hidden to prevent accidental changes to it, or it might hold data that should not be easily visible. Hide a worksheet using the **Format** button [*Home* tab] or by right-clicking the sheet tab. You cannot hide a worksheet if it is the only sheet in the workbook.

> **MORE INFO**
>
> The command to print an *Entire Workbook* does not print a hidden worksheet.

HOW TO: Hide and Unhide Worksheets

1. Right-click the sheet tab to hide.
   - Press **Ctrl** to select multiple sheets, then right-click any one of the selected tabs.
2. Select **Hide**.
   - The worksheet tab is hidden.
3. Right-click any worksheet tab.
4. Select **Unhide**.
   - The *Unhide* dialog box opens.
5. Select the tab name to unhide (Figure 1-61).
6. Click **OK**.

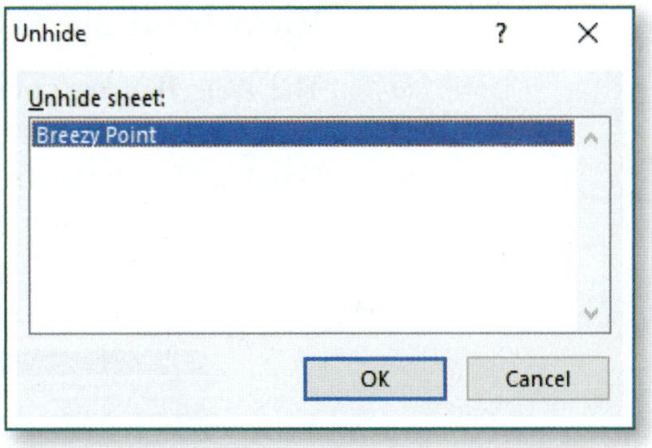

Figure 1-61 *Unhide* dialog box

> **MORE INFO**
>
> The *Hide* command on the *View* tab hides a workbook. A hidden workbook can be used to store programming routines such as macros or external reference data that should be protected from viewing or accidental editing.

Switch Windows Command

The ***Switch Windows*** command changes or cycles through open workbooks. You can switch windows from the *Ribbon*, from the Windows taskbar, or with the keyboard shortcut **Ctrl+F6**. When you click the **Switch Windows** button [*View* tab, *Window* group], a menu lists the names of open workbooks. To use the Windows taskbar, point to the Excel icon to see a thumbnail with the file name of each open workbook, and click the one to be edited. The keyboard shortcut toggles between the last two viewed workbooks.

When only two workbooks are open, you can view them side by side. The *View Side by Side* button is grayed out when only one workbook is open. For side-by-side viewing, you can scroll the windows together or separately. *Synchronous Scrolling* moves both workbooks in the same direction at the same time. This is especially helpful when worksheets have the same types of data in the same locations. Synchronous scrolling is automatically enabled when you choose the *View Side by Side* command.

> **MORE INFO**
>
> If three or more workbooks are open when you select the *View Side by Side* command, the *Compare Side by Side* dialog box opens with the names of open workbooks. The one you select displays side by side with the active workbook.

▸HOW TO: Switch Windows Using the Ribbon

1. Open two or more workbooks.
2. Click the **Switch Windows** button [*View* tab, *Window* group].
   - The names of open workbooks display.
3. Click the name of the workbook to view.

View Multiple Worksheets

The ***New Window*** command opens a new separate window with the same workbook. The new window displays the workbook name in the title bar followed by a colon and number. Combined with the ***Arrange All*** command, you can position different parts of the workbook to make comparisons or monitor changes as you work. Figure 1-62 shows different sheets in the same workbook.

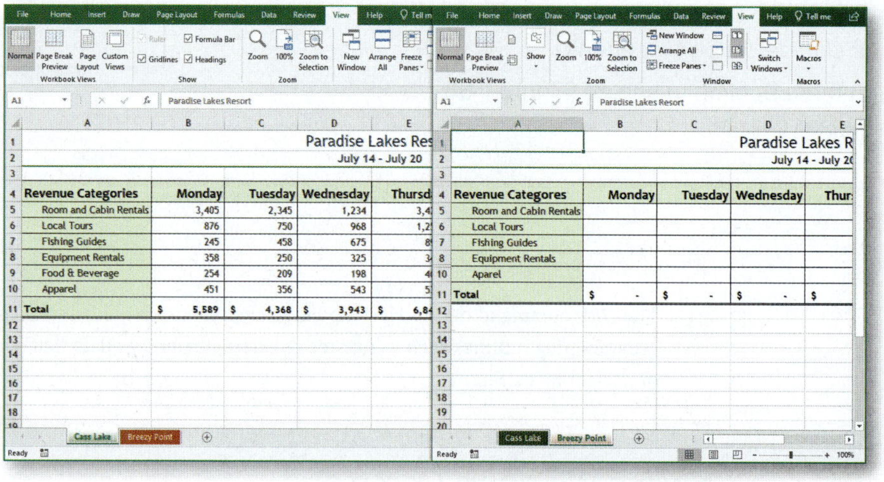

Figure 1-62 Two windows for a workbook

> **MORE INFO**
>
> Open as many windows as needed and arrange them all.

▸HOW TO: View Multiple Worksheets at the Same Time

1. Click the **View** tab and click the **New Window** button [*Window* group].
   - A second window opens for the same workbook and is active.
   - Both windows are maximized.
2. Click the **Arrange All** button [*View* tab, *Window* group].
   - The *Arrange Windows* dialog box opens.
3. Choose an option for arranging the windows.
   - The active window displays on the left (vertically tiled) or at the top (horizontally tiled).
   - If several workbooks are open but only the active workbook has multiple windows, choose **Windows of active workbook** so that only those windows display.

4. Click **OK**.
   - The active window is arranged on the left or at the top.
5. Click the **Maximize** button in either title bar.
   - The window is full size.
6. Click the **Close** button (**X**) in the title bar to close the window.
   - The other window displays at its tiled size.
7. Click the **Maximize** button.

SLO 1.8

Finalizing a Workbook

Before you distribute your work to others, make sure that it is ready for sharing. A quick spell check can help locate and correct misspelled labels. Enter document properties or insert headers and footers to help identify your work. You can control how your worksheet prints by setting margins, changing the orientation, or adjusting page breaks.

Check Spelling

The ***Spelling*** command scans a worksheet and locates words that do not match entries in the main Office dictionary; it also finds duplicate words. The dictionary is shared among all Office applications, and you can add labels to it, such as unusual or technical words. You can spell check the entire worksheet or a selected range.

The *Spelling* dialog box includes options for handling an error, as shown in Table 1-5.

Table 1-5: Spelling Dialog Box Options

Option	Action
Ignore Once	Skips the occurrence of the label.
Ignore All	Skips all occurrences of the same spelling of the label.
Add to Dictionary	Adds the label to the default dictionary.
Change	Changes the label to the highlighted entry in the *Suggestions* box.
Change All	Same as *Change,* but changes the same label throughout the worksheet.
Delete	Appears for *Repeated Word.* Click to delete one occurrence of the label.
AutoCorrect	Adds the label to the *AutoCorrect* list.
Options	Opens the *Excel Options* dialog box to the *Proofing* tab for changing default settings.
Undo Last	Reverses the most recent correction.
Cancel	Discontinues spell checking.

HOW TO: Spell Check a Worksheet

1. Press **Ctrl+Home** to move to cell **A1**.
   - Start at the beginning of the worksheet.
   - Select a range to limit spell checking to that group of cells.

2. Click the **Review** tab and click the **Spelling** button [*Proofing* group].
   - The first error is located.
   - A list of suggested corrections displays.
3. Select the correct spelling in the list.
   - If no acceptable suggestions display, click the **Not in Dictionary** box and type the correct spelling of the label.
4. Click **Change** to replace the misspelled label (Figure 1-63).
5. Click **OK** when spelling is complete.

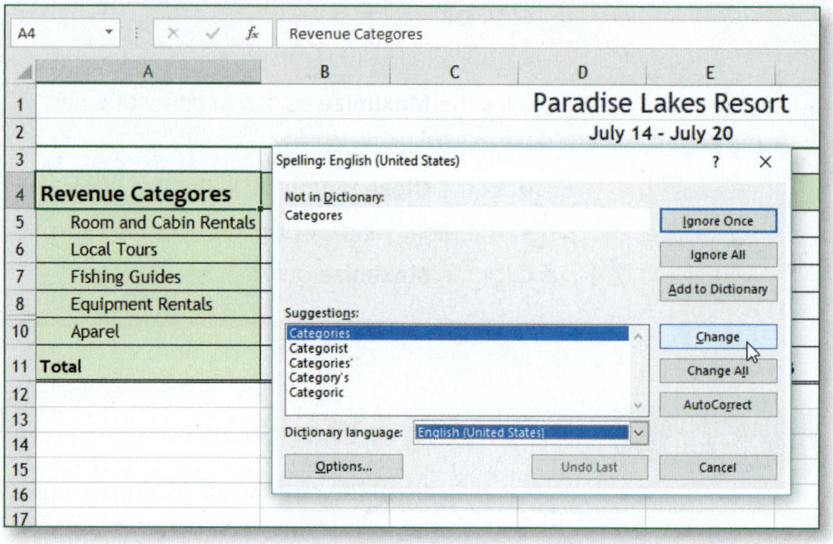

Figure 1-63 ***Spelling* dialog box**

Document Properties

A ***document property*** or ***metadata*** is a field of information. Metadata are settings and content including the author name, the date the file was created, the type and size of file, and more. Certain properties cannot be edited such as dates and file size; these settings are automatically updated. You can edit other document properties, including *Title*, *Author*, and *Subject*. A partial list of properties is available in the *Backstage* view on the right in the *Info* pane.

▸HOW TO: Add Document Properties in Backstage View

1. Click the **File** tab to display the *Backstage* view.
2. Select **Info** if it is not already selected.
   - Property field names are listed.
3. Click an entry box to enter or edit an item (Figure 1-64).
4. Return to the workbook and save the file.

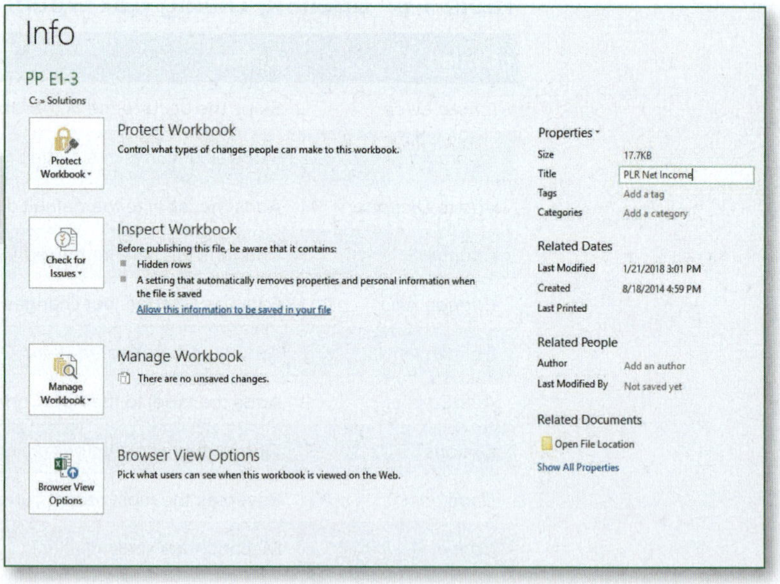

Figure 1-64 Workbook properties

The Properties Dialog Box

You can review all properties in the *Properties* dialog box. The *General*, *Statistics*, and *Contents* tabs list metadata. The *Summary* tab includes properties such as the title, subject, and keywords. Keywords are used in file search commands. On the *Custom* tab, choose additional properties and type default values.

▸ HOW TO: Open the Properties Dialog Box

1. Display the *Backstage* view and click **Info**.
2. Click the **Properties** button.
3. Select **Advanced Properties**.
   - The *Properties* dialog box opens (Figure 1-65).
4. Click a tab to view or edit a property.
5. Click **OK** to close the dialog box.

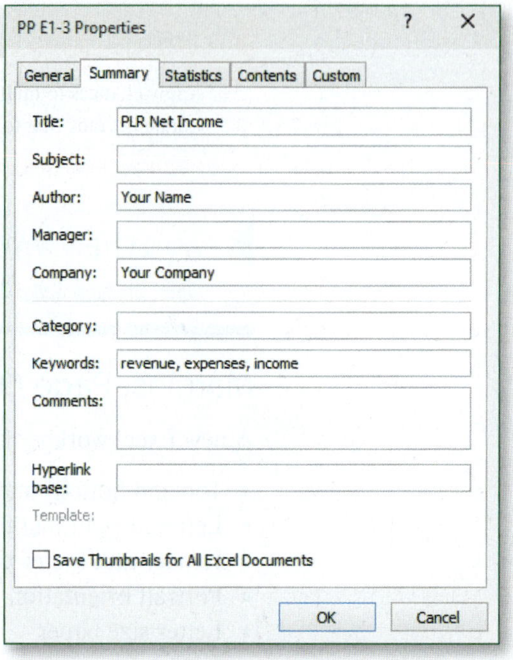

Figure 1-65 ***Properties*** **dialog box**

The Page Setup Dialog Box

The *Page Setup* dialog box offers several command groups for controlling how a worksheet prints. The commands are from the *Sheet Options*, *Scale to Fit*, and *Page Setup* groups on the *Page Layout* tab, as well as commands for setting headers and footers. The ***Page Setup*** launcher [*Page Layout* tab, *Page Setup* group] opens the dialog box.

> **ANOTHER WAY**
>
> Open the *Page Setup* dialog box by clicking the launcher in the *Scale to Fit* or the *Sheet Options* group on the *Page Layout* tab.

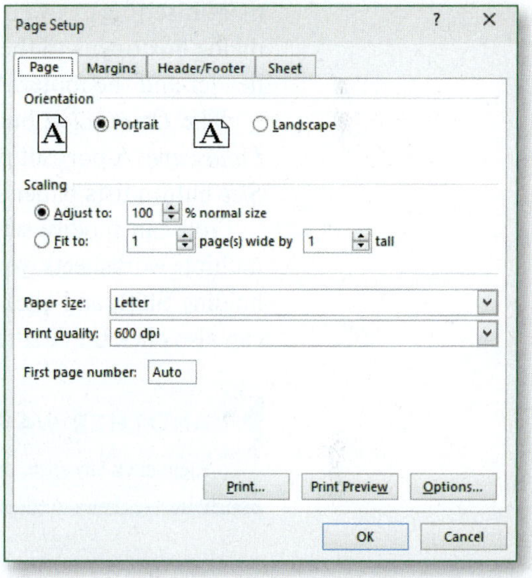

Figure 1-66 ***Page*** **tab in the** ***Page Setup*** **dialog box**

Each tab in the *Page Setup* dialog box includes a *Print*, a *Print Preview*, and an *Options* button (Figure 1-66). The *Options* button opens the *Printer Properties* dialog box. Table 1-6 summarizes commands on each tab in the *Page Setup* dialog box:

Table 1-6: Page Setup Dialog Box Options

Tab	Available Settings
Page	Set the *Orientation* to *Portrait* or *Landscape*. Use *Scaling* to shrink or enlarge the printed worksheet to the paper size. Choose a *Paper size* or set *Print quality*. Define the *First page number*.
Margins	Adjust *Top*, *Bottom*, *Left*, and *Right* worksheet margins. Set *Header* and *Footer* top and bottom margins. *Center on page* horizontally and/or vertically.
Header/Footer	Choose a preset header or footer layout. Create a custom header or footer. Specify first and other page headers. Set header and footers to scale with worksheet and to align with margins.
Sheet	Identify a *Print area* other than the entire worksheet. Identify *Print titles* to repeat on each page. Print *Gridlines*, *Row and column headings*, *Comments*, and *Error messages*.

MORE INFO

Apply changes to multiple worksheets at the same time using the *Page Setup* dialog box. Select the worksheet tabs first to group the worksheets.

ANOTHER WAY

Open the *Page Setup* dialog box by clicking the *Page Setup* link in the *Print* area on the *Backstage* view.

Margins, Page Orientation, and Paper Size

A new Excel workbook uses the following default settings:

- Top and bottom margins: 0.75″
- Left and right margins: 0.7″
- Header and footer margins: 0.3″
- Portrait orientation
- Letter size paper

The **Margins** button [*Page Layout* tab, *Page Setup* group] lists *Normal*, *Wide*, and *Narrow* for margin settings as well as *Custom Margins*. When you select **Custom Margins**, the *Page Setup* dialog box opens to the *Margins* tab. Here you set any value for any margin area, including the header and the footer. You can also center the page horizontally or vertically from this tab.

The *Orientation* button [*Page Setup* group, *Page Layout* tab] has two choices, *Portrait* or *Landscape*. A portrait page is taller than it is wide. A landscape page is wider than it is tall. The *Size* button lists paper sizes, but your printer must be able to accommodate the size.

You can modify settings for one worksheet or for several worksheets at a time. To format multiple worksheets, you need to group the worksheet tabs. Do this by clicking the first tab name, holding **Shift**, and clicking the last tab name to select all sheets between those two names. You can also click the first tab name, press **Ctrl**, and click nonadjacent sheet names to create a group.

ANOTHER WAY

Right-click any sheet tab and choose **Select All Sheets** to group all sheets in the workbook for formatting.

HOW TO: Set Margins, Page Orientation, and Paper Size

1. Click the **Margins** button [*Page Layout* tab, *Page Setup* group].
2. Select **Custom Margins** to open the *Page Setup* dialog box (Figure 1-67).
   - The dialog box opens to the *Margins* tab.
3. Type each margin setting as desired.
   - Use the spinner buttons to change the margin value.
4. Select the **Horizontally** box in the *Center on page* area.
   - This command centers the data between the left and right margins.
   - You can also vertically center the data on the page.

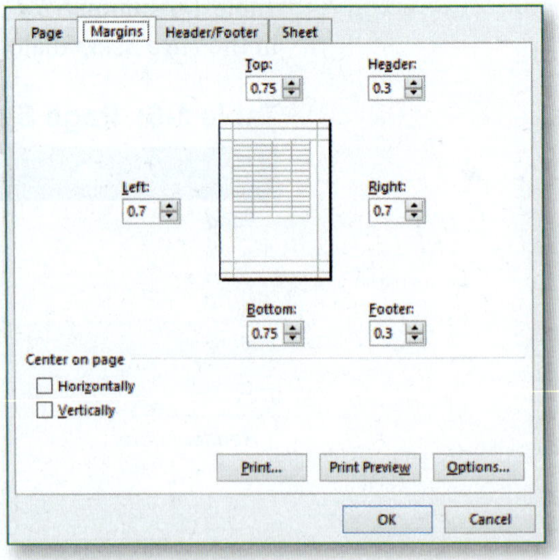

Figure 1-67 *Margins* tab in the *Page Setup* dialog box

5. Click the **Page** tab in the *Page Layout* dialog box.
6. Select the radio button for **Portrait** or **Landscape**.
7. Click the **Paper size** arrow and select a paper size.
   - The default paper size is 8½ × 11" (called *Letter*).
8. Click **OK** to close the dialog box.

MORE INFO

Top and bottom margins must be greater than header and footer margins. If they are not, worksheet data prints over header and footer text.

ANOTHER WAY

In *Page Layout* view, you can set margins using the ruler. Display the rulers by clicking the *View* tab and selecting the *Ruler* box [*Show* group]. Point to a margin boundary to display a two-pointed arrow and drag the pointer to a new setting.

Headers and Footers

A ***header*** is information that prints at the top of each page. A ***footer*** is data that prints at the bottom of each page. Use a header or a footer to display identifying information such as a company name or logo, page numbers, the date, or the file name.

Each header or footer has left, middle, and right sections. Information in the left section is left aligned, data in the middle section is centered, and material in the right section is right aligned. You can select a predefined header and footer, or create your own.

MORE INFO

Predefined headers and footers include one, two, or three elements, separated by commas. One element prints in the center section. Two elements print in the center and right sections. Three elements use all three sections.

Headers and footers are not visible in *Normal* view, but they can be viewed in *Page Layout* view or *Print Preview*. Insert and edit headers and footers in *Page Layout* view.

HOW TO: Insert a Header and Footer Using the Ribbon

1. Select the worksheet.
   - Select more than one worksheet to apply the same header or footer.
2. Click the **Insert** tab.
3. Click the **Header & Footer** button [*Text* group].
   - The view changes to *Page Layout* view.
   - Three header sections display at the top of the worksheet.
   - The *Header & Footer Tools Design* tab is active.
4. Click a header section.

5. Click an element name in the *Header & Footer Elements* group [*Header & Footer Tools Design* tab].
   - A code is inserted with an ampersand (&) and the element name enclosed in square brackets (Figure 1-68).
   - You can type your own label in a section.
   - You can select and delete codes and text in a section.
6. Click the **Go To Footer** button [*Header & Footer Tools Design* tab, *Navigation* group].

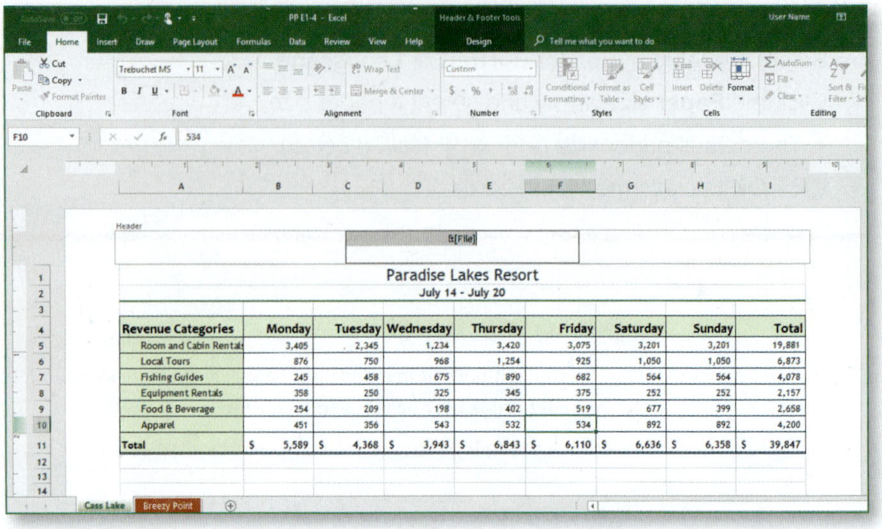

Figure 1-68 ***Header*** **section in** ***Page Layout*** **view**

7. Click a footer section.
8. Click an element name in the *Header & Footer Elements* group [*Header & Footer Tools Design* tab].
   - The related code is inserted.
   - You can type your own label in a footer section.
   - You can select and delete codes and text in a section.
9. Click any worksheet cell.
   - The header and footer appear as they will print.
   - The *Header & Footer Tools Design* tab no longer displays.
10. Click the **Normal** button in the *Status* bar.
    - The header and footer are not visible in *Normal* view.

ANOTHER WAY

To insert a built-in header or footer, click the **Header or Footer** button [*Header & Footer Tools Design* tab, *Header & Footer* group] and select an option.

MORE INFO

In a typed header or footer label such as "Research & Development," type two ampersands in the section like this: Research && Development. This distinguishes the required ampersand from the one used in an element code such as &[Date].

You can also use the *Page Setup* dialog box to insert a header or a footer. A *Header & Footer* tab includes the preset headers and footers, as well as a *Custom Header* or *Custom Footer* option.

HOW TO: Insert Headers or Footers on Multiple Sheets

1. Select a single tab or multiple worksheet tabs.
   - Click the first worksheet tab for the group, press **Shift**, and click the last tab.
   - Click a worksheet tab, press **Ctrl**, and click a nonadjacent tab.
   - Right-click any tab and click **Select All Sheets**.

2. Click the **Page Setup** launcher [*Page Layout* tab, *Page Setup* group.
   - The *Page Setup* dialog box opens.
3. Click the **Header/Footer** tab.
4. Click the arrow for the *Header* or the *Footer* text box (Figure 1-69).
   - A list of built-in header or footer layouts opens.
   - Choose **(none)** to remove a header or footer.
5. Choose a predefined header or footer.
   - The header or footer displays in the preview area.
6. Click **Custom Header** or **Custom Footer** to open the *Header* or *Footer* dialog box (Figure 1-70).
7. Click a section.
8. Click a button to insert an element.
   - Point to a button to see its *ScreenTip*.
   - The text or code appears in the section.
9. Click **OK** to close the *Header* or *Footer* dialog box.
   - The custom header or footer displays in the preview area.
10. Click **OK** to close the *Page Setup* dialog box.
11. Right-click a sheet tab and choose **Ungroup Sheets**.

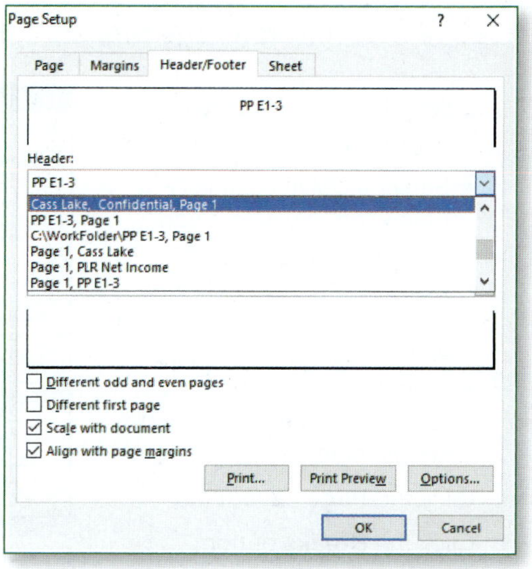

Figure 1-69 Select a built-in header or footer in the *Page Setup* dialog box

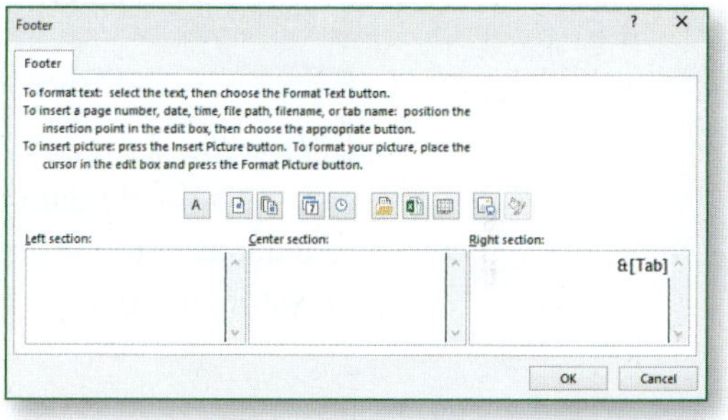

Figure 1-70 Custom *Footer* dialog box

Remove a header or footer in *Page Layout* view or from the *Page Setup* dialog box. To remove headers and footers from multiple worksheets, select the sheet tabs so that they are grouped. In *Page Layout* view, click the header or footer section and delete labels and codes. From the *Page Setup* dialog box, simply select *(none)* from the *Header* or *Footer* drop-down list.

HOW TO: Remove Headers and Footers

1. Select the worksheet(s).
2. Click the **Page Setup** launcher [*Page Layout* tab, *Page Setup* group].
3. Click the **Header/Footer** tab.
4. Click the **Header** or **Footer** drop-down list and select **(none)**.
5. Click **OK** to close the *Page Setup* dialog box.
6. Ungroup sheets if needed.

Page Breaks

A ***page break*** is a printer code that starts a new page. When worksheet data spans more than one printed page, automatic page breaks are inserted based on the paper size, the margins, and scaling. Automatic page breaks readjust as you add or delete data. You can insert manual page breaks, too. Manual page breaks do not adjust as you edit worksheet data.

In *Page Break Preview*, an automatic page break displays as a dotted or dashed blue line. A manual page break appears as a solid, blue line.

▶HOW TO: Insert a Page Break

1. Select the cell for the location of a page break.
   - Select a cell in column A below the row where you want to start a new page.
   - Select a cell in row 1 to the right of the column where you want to start a new page.
   - Select a cell below and to the right of where new pages should start.
2. Click the **Page Layout** tab.
3. Click the **Breaks** button.
4. Select **Insert Page Break** (Figure 1-71).
   - A manual page break displays as a thin, solid line in the worksheet in *Normal* view.

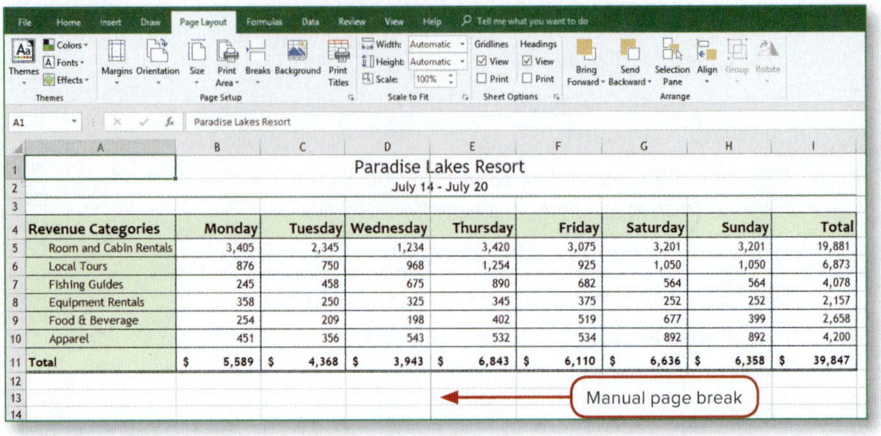

Figure 1-71 Page break inserted after Column D

Preview and Move a Page Break

In *Page Break Preview*, move an automatic or a manual page break by dragging its blue line. You can see how the data displays and evaluate the new printed pages. Depending on the amount of data, as you move a page break, another automatic break may be inserted. When you move an automatic page break, it becomes a manual page break.

> **MORE INFO**
>
> To move a page break in *Normal* view, you must delete the existing break and insert a new one; you cannot drag the line.

▶HOW TO: Preview and Move a Page Break

1. Click the **Page Break Preview** button in the *Status* bar.
   - Adjust the zoom size in *Page Break Preview*.
2. Point to the page break (dashed or solid, blue line) to display a two-pointed arrow.
3. Drag the pointer to a new location (Figure 1-72).
   - If you drag an automatic page break, it converts to a manual break.
4. Release the pointer.
   - A manual page break appears as a solid, blue line.
   - Another automatic page break may be inserted if the data requires it.
5. Click the **Normal** button in the *Status* bar.

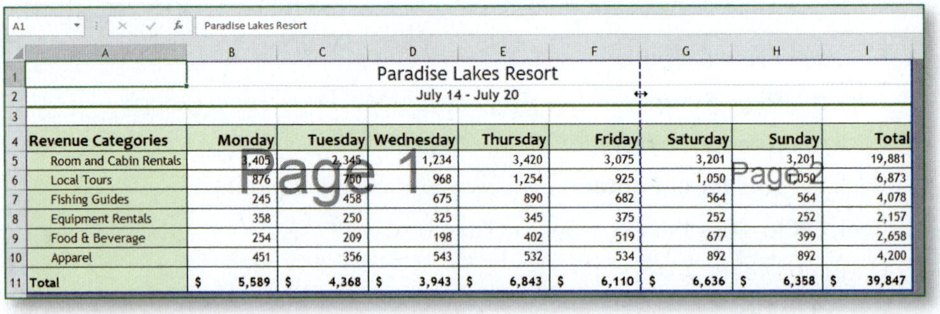

Figure 1-72 Drag a page break line to a new position

Remove a Manual Page Break

You can remove a manual page break in *Normal* view or *Page Break Preview*. Click a cell immediately to the right of or below the break and then click the **Remove Page Break** button [*Page Layout* tab, *Page Setup* group]. When you delete a manual page break, Excel may insert a new automatic page break.

> **MORE INFO**
>
> Insert a manual page break before an automatic page break to "delete" the automatic break.

HOW TO: Remove a Manual Page Break

1. Click the **Page Break Preview** button in the *Status* bar.
2. Click a cell immediately to the right of or below the page break to be removed.
3. Click the **Breaks** button [*Page Layout* tab, *Page Setup* group].
   - Select **Reset All Page Breaks** to remove all manual page breaks.
4. Click **Remove Page Break** (Figure 1-73).
   - An automatic page break is inserted if required.

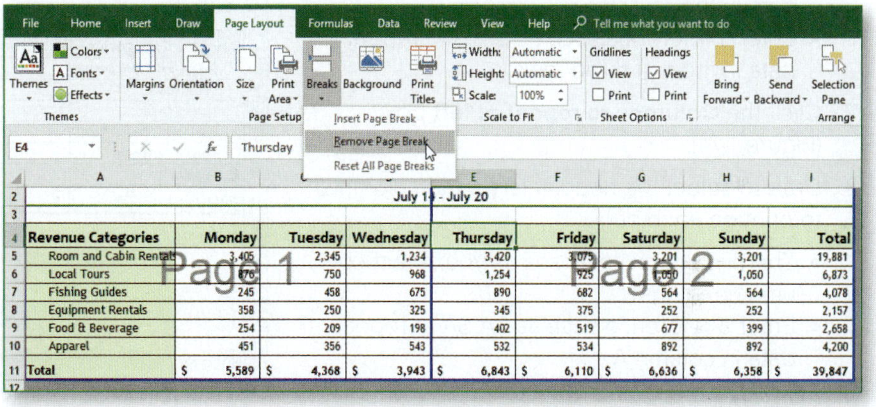

Figure 1-73 Remove a manual page break

> **ANOTHER WAY**
>
> In *Page Break Preview*, drag a manual page break off the page to the right. Excel inserts an automatic page break if required by the margins and other settings.

Customize Print Settings

You can print the entire workbook, the current worksheet, or a selected cell range by making a choice in the *Settings* area in the *Backstage* view for the *Print* command. The *Sheet Options* and *Page Setup* groups on the *Page Layout* command tab include additional options for repeating titles, displaying a background image, and printing gridlines, column letters, and row numbers.

Gridlines, the vertical and horizontal lines that form the columns and rows, are a visual guide to your working on the sheet. Row and column headings serve a similar purpose–to help you navigate in a worksheet. By default, the gridlines and headings do not print, but you can print them using an option on the *Page Layout* tab.

A ***print title*** is a row or column of data that is repeated on each printed page. For example, print main labels from rows 1:3 and from column A on each printed page of a 20-page worksheet.

▶HOW TO: Print Gridlines, Print Titles, and Column and Row Headings

1. Click the **Page Layout** tab.
2. Select the **Print** box under *Gridlines* in the *Sheet Options* group.
3. Select the **Print** box under *Headings* in the *Sheet Options* group.
4. Click the **Print Titles** button [*Page Layout* tab, *Page Setup* group].
   - The *Page Setup* dialog box opens to the *Sheet* tab.
5. Click the **Rows to repeat at top** box.
6. Drag to select the heading(s) for the row(s) to print on each page.
   - The row reference(s) displays in the text box.
   - The **$** symbol is an identifier to include all data in the row(s).
   - Enter a reference such as $1:$3 to repeat data in the first three rows.
7. Click the **Columns to repeat at left** box (Figure 1-74).
8. Drag to select the heading(s) for the column(s) to print on each page.
   - The dialog box collapses as you select column headings.
   - Enter a reference such as $A:$A to repeat data in column A.
9. Click **OK**.

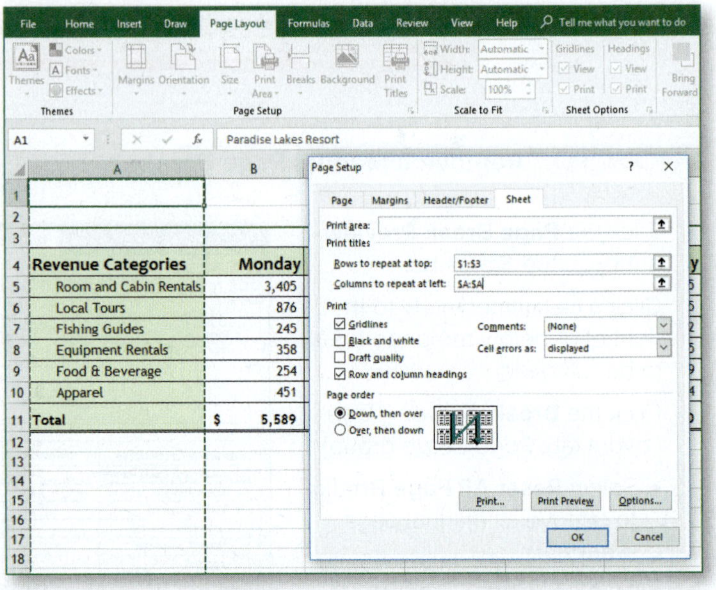

Figure 1-74 ***Sheet*** **tab in the** ***Page Setup*** **dialog box**

ANOTHER WAY

Print *Gridlines* and *Row and column headings* by selecting an option in the *Page Setup* dialog box.

Scale to Fit

The ***Scale to Fit*** command enlarges or shrinks printed data to fit a specific number of pages or a particular paper size. You can scale printed data as a percentage of normal size or by setting the number of pages. Normal size is how the data would print in the current font size and is shown as *Automatic* in the *Scale to Fit* group [*Page Layout* tab].

▶HOW TO: Scale to Fit

1. Click the **Page Layout** tab.
2. Click the **Width** drop-down list [*Scale to Fit* group] and select an option.
3. Click the **Height** drop-down list [*Scale to Fit* group] and select an option (Figure 1-75).
   - Click the **Scale** button spinner arrows to set a percentage of the normal size.

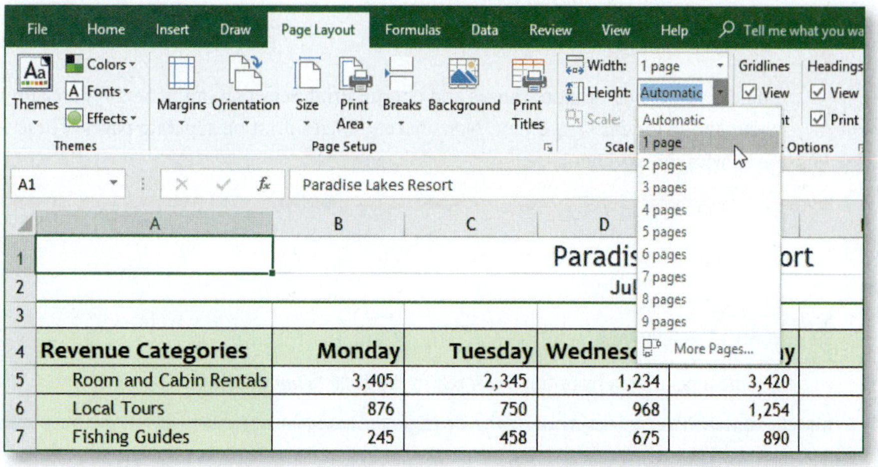

Figure 1-75 *Scale to Fit* options

ANOTHER WAY

Click the **Scale to Fit** launcher [*Page Layout* tab, *Scale to Fit group*] to open the *Page Setup* dialog box and set options in the *Scaling* area.

Print Area

A ***print area*** is the data that prints from a *Print* command. The default print area is the entire worksheet, but you can identify any range of cells as a print area. You can add adjacent data to a print area, and you can clear a print area to return to the default.

HOW TO: Set and Clear a Print Area

1. Select the cells to print.
   - You can select nonadjacent ranges but they print on separate pages.
2. Click the **Page Layout** tab.
3. Click the **Print Area** button [*Page Setup* group] (Figure 1-76).
4. Select **Set Print Area**.
   - You can see the print area in the *Backstage* view for the *Print* command and in *Page Break Preview*.
   - A print area is saved with the workbook.
5. Click the **Print Area** button [*Page Layout* tab, *Page Setup* group].
6. Select **Clear Print Area**.
   - All print areas are cleared.
   - The default print area is reset to print the entire sheet.

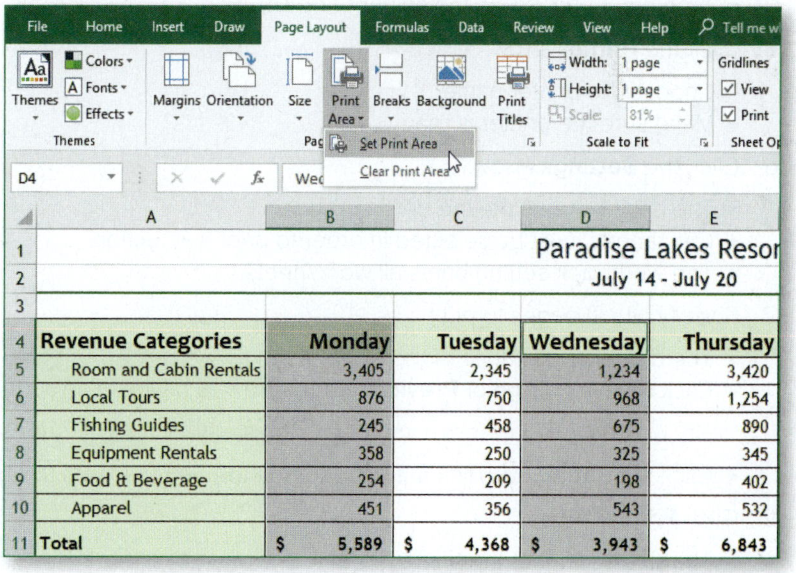

Figure 1-76 Nonadjacent print areas

MORE INFO

You can select one or more ranges and choose **Print Selection** in the *Settings* area for the *Print* command in the *Backstage* view. Nonadjacent ranges print on separate pages. These selections are not saved with the workbook.

ANOTHER WAY

Define a print area from the *Sheet* tab in the *Page Setup* dialog box.

Print a Worksheet or Workbook

The *Print* command in the *Backstage* view provides a preview so that you can make changes before actual printing. The *Show Margins* button toggles the display of margin and column markers. Drag the column and margin markers to new settings. The *Zoom to Page* button toggles between two zoom settings for the preview.

HOW TO: Preview and Print a Worksheet

1. Click the **File** tab and select **Print**.
   - Click **Print Preview** in the *Page Setup* dialog box to open the *Print* command in the *Backstage* view.
2. Click **Show Margins** to display margin and column markers.
3. Click **Zoom to Page** to toggle between zoom sizes.
4. Set the number of *Copies*.
   - Type a number or use the spinner arrows.
5. Click the **Printer** arrow.
   - Choose the printer name.
   - Make sure the printer is ready.
6. Click the **Settings** arrow.
   - The active sheets are the default.
   - Cell ranges must be selected in order to print a selection.
   - The workbook setting prints all worksheets.
7. Specify which pages to print.
   - The default is all pages of the worksheet.
   - Click the **Next Page** or **Previous Page** arrow to navigate through multiple pages.
8. Verify orientation, paper size, margin settings, and scaling (Figure 1-77).
   - Click the **Page Setup** link at the bottom of the *Settings* area to open the *Page Setup* dialog box.
9. Click **Print**.
   - The data is sent to the printer.
   - The *Backstage* view closes.

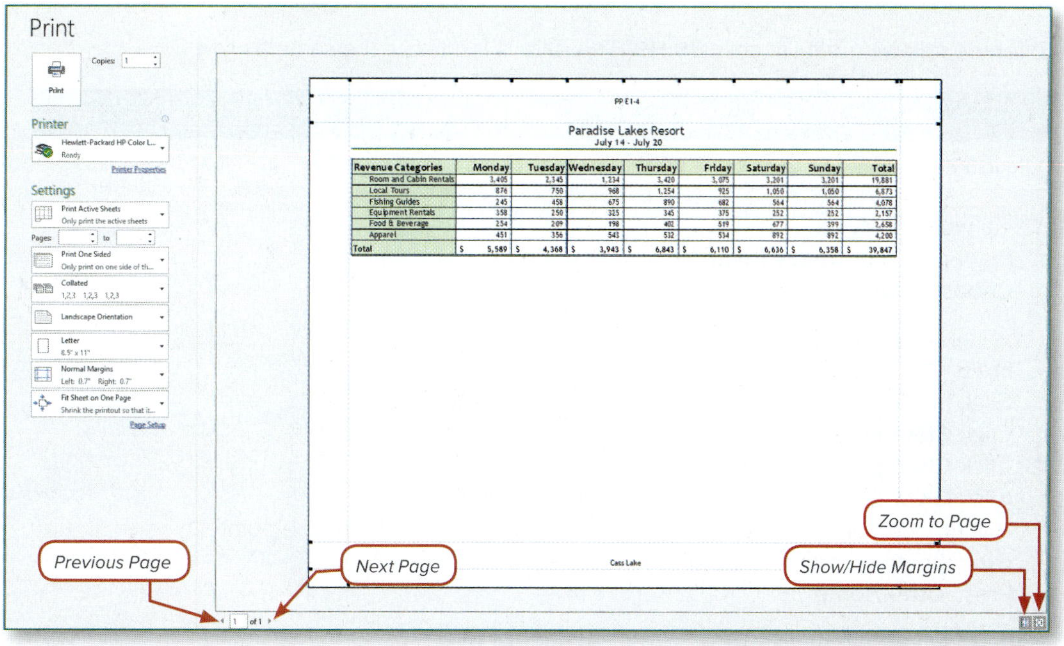

Figure 1-77 ***Backstage*** **view for** ***Print***

ANOTHER WAY

Press **Ctrl+P** to open the *Print* command in the *Backstage* view.

PAUSE & PRACTICE: EXCEL 1-4

In this project, you open ***[your initials] PP E1-3.xlsx*** to unhide a row, add data, and hide a sheet. You also spell check a worksheet, set document properties, and finalize the workbook for distribution.

File Needed: ***[your initials] PP E1-3.xlsx***
Completed Project File Name: ***[your initials] PP E1-4.xlsx***

1. Open ***[your initials] PP E1-3*** completed in *Pause & Practice 1-3*.
2. Save the workbook as [your initials] PP E1-4. (If your file is saved in *OneDrive* and *AutoSave* is on, select **Save a Copy**.)
3. Select the **Cass Lake** worksheet.
4. Unhide row 9.
   a. Click and drag to select row headings **8:10**.
   b. Right-click either of the selected row headings.
   c. Choose **Unhide** from the context menu.

5. Enter the following data in cells **B9:H9**. The data is formatted the same as row 8.

	B	C	D	E	F	G	H
Food & Beverage	254	209	198	402	519	677	399

6. Hide a worksheet.
   a. Right-click the **Breezy Point** tab.
   b. Choose **Hide**.
7. Check spelling and adjust column width.
   a. Press **Ctrl+Home**.
   b. Click the **Spelling** button [*Review* tab, *Proofing* group].
   c. Click **Change** to accept the suggested correction for "Categores."
   d. Click **Change** to accept the suggested correction for "Aparel."
   e. Click **OK** when spell checking is finished.
   f. Point to the border between columns A and B to display the resize pointer.
   g. Drag the pointer to set the width to 25.63 (210 pixels).
   h. Press **Ctrl+Home**.
8. Enter document properties.
   a. Click the **File** tab to display the *Backstage* view.
   b. Click the **Show All Properties** link at the bottom of the properties list.
   c. Click the *Title* text box and type PP Excel 1-4.
   d. Type Draft in the *Status* text box.
   e. Click the *Subject* text box and type Weekly Revenue (Figure 1-78).
   f. Click the **Show Fewer Properties** link at the bottom of the properties list.
   g. Return to the worksheet.

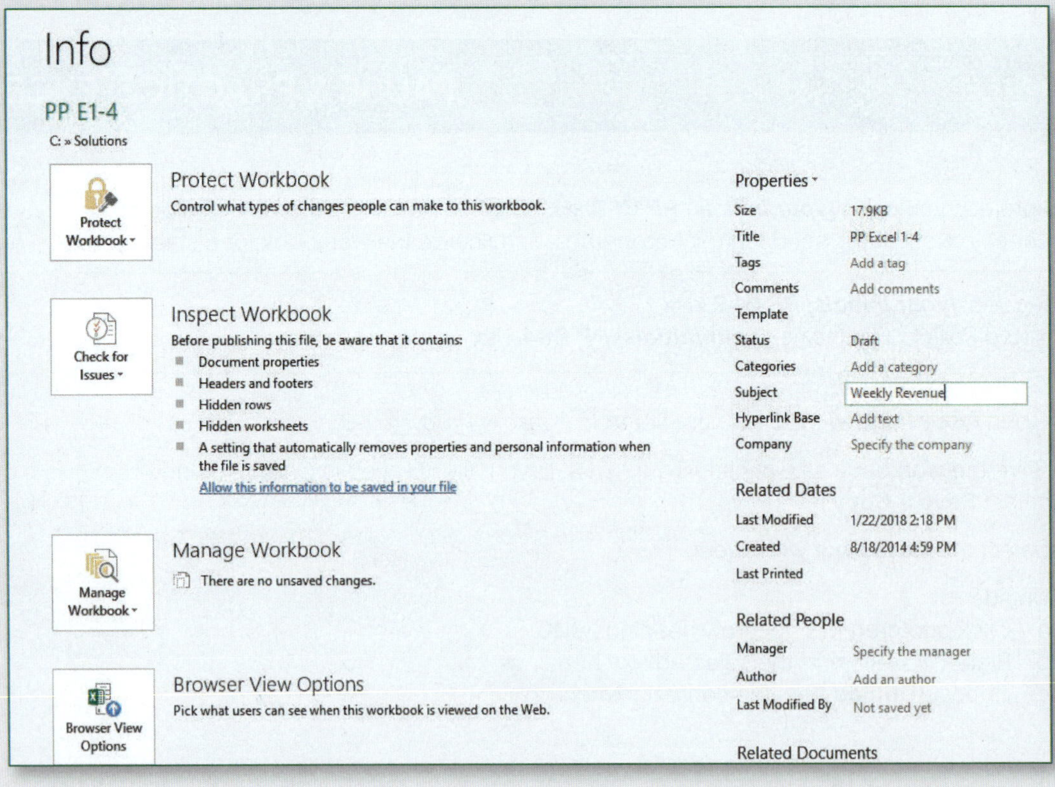

Figure 1-78 Properties in *Backstage* view

9. Change page setup options.
   a. Click the **Page Layout** tab.
   b. Click the **Orientation** button and select **Landscape**.
   c. Click the **Page Setup** launcher to open the *Page Setup* dialog box.
   d. Click the **Fit to** button on the **Page** tab.
   e. Set **1** page wide and **1** page tall.
   f. Click the **Margins** tab.
   g. Select the **Horizontally** box in the *Center on page* area.
   h. Do not close the dialog box.

10. Add a header and footer.
   a. Click the **Header/Footer** tab.
   b. Click the **Header** drop-down list and select ***[your initials] PP E1-4***. The file name displays in the preview center section.
   c. Click the **Footer** drop-down list and select **Cass Lake** to insert the sheet name in the center section of the footer.
   d. Click **OK** to close the *Page Setup* dialog box.

11. Preview and print the worksheet.
   a. Click the **File** tab and select **Print**. *Print Preview* displays how the worksheet will print.
   b. Return to the worksheet, or select the printer and click **Print** if you are instructed to do so.

12. Save and close the workbook (Figure 1-79).

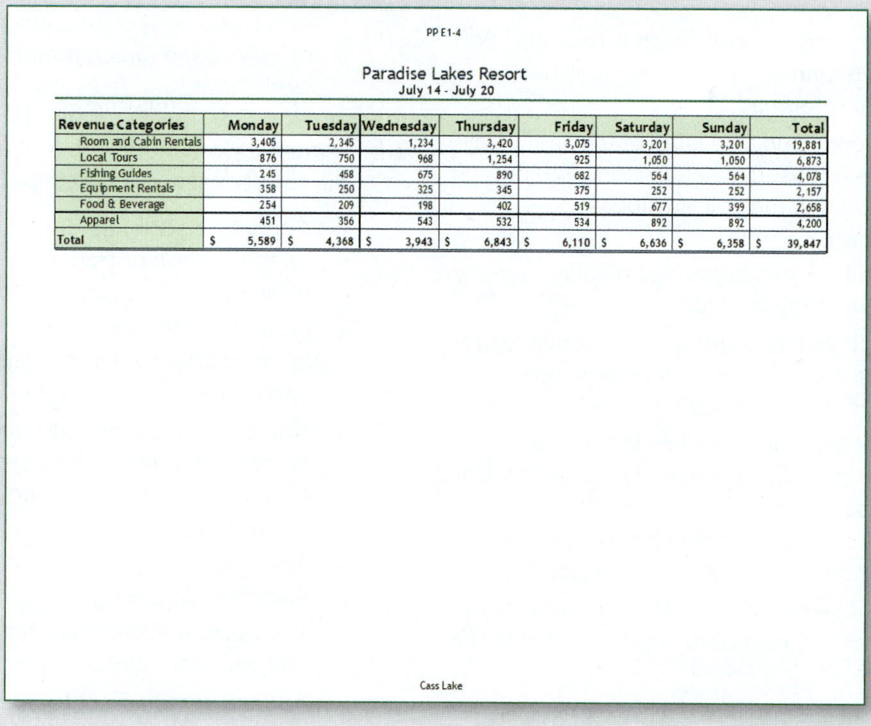
PP E1-4

Paradise Lakes Resort
July 14 - July 20

Revenue Categories	Monday	Tuesday	Wednesday	Thursday	Friday	Saturday	Sunday	Total
Room and Cabin Rentals	3,405	2,345	1,234	3,420	3,075	3,201	3,201	19,881
Local Tours	876	750	968	1,254	925	1,050	1,050	6,873
Fishing Guides	245	458	675	890	682	564	564	4,078
Equipment Rentals	358	250	325	345	375	252	252	2,157
Food & Beverage	254	209	198	402	519	677	399	2,658
Apparel	451	356	543	532	534	892	892	4,200
Total	$ 5,589	$ 4,368	$ 3,943	$ 6,843	$ 6,110	$ 6,636	$ 6,358	$ 39,847

Cass Lake

Figure 1-79 PP E1-4 completed

Chapter Summary

1.1 Create, save, and open an Excel workbook (p. E1-3).

- A new Excel workbook has one worksheet and is named *BookN*, with numbers assigned in order throughout a work session.
- Save a workbook with a descriptive name that identifies the contents and purpose.
- Create a new workbook from the *Excel Start* page or from the *New* command on the *File* tab.
- A workbook opened or copied from an online source opens in ***Protected View***.
- An Excel workbook is an ***.xlsx*** file, but it can be saved in other formats for easy sharing of data.

1.2 Enter and edit labels and values in a worksheet (p. E1-7).

- Data is entered in a ***cell*** which is the intersection of a column and a row. Each cell has an address or reference.
- Data is recognized as a label or a value. Labels are not used in calculations. A label is left-aligned in the cell; a value is right-aligned.
- A ***formula*** is a calculation that displays a value as its result in the worksheet.
- Press **F2** (**FN+F2**) or double-click a cell to start *Edit* mode. After making the change, press **Enter** to complete the edit.
- Horizontal alignment options for cell data include *Align Left*, *Center*, and *Align Right*. Data can also be indented from the cell border. Vertical alignment choices are *Top Align*, *Middle Align*, and *Bottom Align*.
- A group or selection of cells is a ***range***. Use the pointer and keyboard shortcuts to select a range.
- Use the ***Fill Handle*** to create a series that follows a pattern. The *Fill Handle* copies data when no pattern exists.
- ***AutoComplete*** supplies a suggestion for a column entry that begins with the same character as a label already in the column.
- Cut, copy, and paste commands include drag and drop, as well as regular Windows ***Cut, Copy***, and ***Paste*** buttons on the *Home* tab, context menus, and keyboard shortcuts.

1.3 Use the *SUM* function to build a simple formula (p. E1-19).

- A ***function*** is a built-in formula. Results appear in the worksheet cell, but the function displays in the *Formula* bar.
- The ***AutoSum*** button [*Home* tab, *Editing* group] inserts the *SUM* function in a cell to add the values in a selected range.
- Each function has ***syntax*** which is its required parts in the required order. A function begins with an equals sign (=), followed by the name of the function. After the name, the function ***argument*** is shown in parentheses.
- Change a function argument by entering new cell references in the *Formula* bar or by dragging the range border in the worksheet.
- When you copy a function, Excel adjusts cell references to match their locations in the worksheet.

1.4 Format a worksheet with font attributes, borders, fill, cell styles, and themes (p. E1-22).

- Apply font attributes from the *Font* group on the *Ribbon* or from the *Format Cells* dialog box.
- Font attributes include the ***font*** name or face, the ***font size***, font styles such as bold, italic, and underline, and the ***font color***.
- Number formats include decimals, commas, currency symbols, and percent signs. They also determine how negative values appear in the worksheet.
- Apply number formats from the *Ribbon* or the *Format Cells* dialog box.
- The ***Format Painter*** copies formatting from one cell to another.
- Add borders or fill color to cells for easy identification, clarification, and emphasis.
- A ***cell style*** is a preset collection of font, font size, alignment, color, borders, and fill color and is based on the theme.
- A ***theme*** is a collection of fonts, colors, and special effects for a workbook.
- Use themes and cell styles to quickly format a worksheet with consistent, professionally designed elements.

1.5 Modify columns and rows in a worksheet (p. E1-30).

- The default column width and row height depend on the font size defined by the workbook theme.
- Change the width of a column or the height of a row by dragging the border between the headings.
- ***AutoFit*** a column or row by double-clicking the border between the headings.
- The ***Format*** button [*Home* tab, *Cells* group] includes commands to change ***row height*** and ***column width***.
- Insert or delete a column or a row by right-clicking the column or row heading and choosing *Insert* or *Delete*.
- The ***Insert*** and ***Delete*** buttons [*Home* tab, *Cells* group] include commands for inserting and deleting rows and columns.
- Display a label on multiple lines in a cell using the ***Wrap Text*** command to split the label.
- The ***Merge & Center*** command combines two or more cells into one and centers the data within that new cell.
- Use the ***Center Across Selection*** command to center multiple rows of data across the same range.
- Hide one or multiple rows or columns, but they are still available for use in a formula.

1.6 Insert, delete, and move worksheets in a workbook (p. E1-36).

- The number of worksheets in a workbook is limited only by the amount of computer memory.
- Click the ***New Sheet*** button next to the worksheet tabs to insert a new sheet in a workbook.
- The ***Insert*** and ***Delete*** buttons [*Home* tab, *Cells* group] include options to insert and delete worksheets.
- Double-click a worksheet tab, type a name, and press **Enter** to rename a sheet.
- Apply a ***tab color*** to distinguish a particular sheet by changing the background color.
- Move a worksheet tab to another location in the list of tabs by dragging it to that location.
- Create an exact duplicate of a worksheet in the same or another workbook with the ***Move or Copy*** command or the context menu.

1.7 Modify the appearance of a workbook by adjusting zoom size, changing views, and freezing panes (p. E1-41).

- View a workbook in three ways: ***Normal***, ***Page Layout***, and ***Page Break Preview***.
- Switch views using the *Status* bar buttons or from the *Workbook Views* group on the *View* tab.
- Adjust the zoom size to display more or less data on screen. Zoom controls are available in the *Status* bar and from the *View* tab.
- Use the ***Freeze Panes*** command to lock selected rows or columns on screen to scroll data while keeping important data in view.
- Use the ***Split*** command to divide the screen into multiple sections to see different areas of a large worksheet at once.
- Hide a worksheet from view and unintended editing.
- When multiple workbooks are open, the ***Switch Windows*** command lists the open workbook names.
- Switch among open workbooks using the Windows taskbar.
- The ***New Window*** command displays the same workbook in a second window. Use this command with the ***Arrange All*** command to view different areas or sheets of a workbook at the same time.

1.8 Review and prepare a workbook for final distribution by spell checking, setting properties, and adjusting page setup options (p. E1-47).

- Spell checking a workbook follows the same steps as other Office applications.
- A ***document property*** is ***metadata*** stored with the file.
- Several properties are supplied by Excel and cannot be edited. Other document properties are added or edited by the user.
- Several properties are visible and are edited in the *Info* area in the *Backstage* view.
- Open the *Properties* dialog box to build or edit properties.
- The *Page Layout* tab includes commands to set page margins and orientation.
- Add ***headers*** and ***footers*** to print at the top and bottom of each page.

- Excel inserts automatic page breaks when a worksheet fills more than one printed page.
- Insert manual ***page breaks*** to change where a new page starts.
- Print ***gridlines*** as well as row and column headings from commands on the *Page Layout* tab or in the *Page Setup* dialog box.
- Use the ***Print*** area in the *Backstage* view to make additional changes to the printed worksheet. Changes include choosing to print only a selection or the entire workbook.

Check for Understanding

The ***Online Learning Center*** for this text (within your SIMnet account) provides the following resources for concept review.

- Multiple-choice questions
- Short answer questions
- Matching exercises

Guided Project 1-1

Life's Animal Shelter (LAS) maintains data in an Excel workbook to track daily expenses for categories that include supplies, animal food, and wages. You will create a new workbook for the current week, enter and format the data, and prepare the workbook for distribution.
[Student Learning Outcomes 1.1, 1.2, 1.3, 1.4, 1.5, 1.6, 1.7, 1.8]

File Needed: None
Completed Project File Name: ***[your initials] Excel 1-1.xlsx***

Skills Covered in This Project

- Create and save a workbook.
- Enter labels and values.
- Use the *Fill Handle*.
- Set column widths and row heights.
- Merge and center labels.
- Apply a workbook theme and cell styles.
- Apply font attributes and insert borders.
- Use *SUM* and set number formatting.
- Copy and rename worksheets.
- Set worksheet tab color.
- Change page setup options.
- Use spell check.
- Adjust zoom size and freeze panes.

1. Create and save a workbook.
   a. Create a new **Blank workbook**.
   b. Click the **Save** button on the *Quick Access* toolbar to open the *Save As* area.
   c. Navigate to and select the folder to save the workbook.
   d. Name the workbook [your initials] Excel 1-1 and click **Save**.
2. Rename the sheet and set the tab color.
   a. Double-click the **Sheet1** tab name.
   b. Type Week 1 and press **Enter**.
   c. Click the **Format** button [*Home* tab, *Cells* group].
   d. Select **Tab Color** in the *Organize Sheets* category.
   e. Select **Blue Accent1, Darker 50%** (fifth column).
3. Enter data with deliberate errors.
   a. Type Life's Aminal Shelter with the spelling error in cell **A1**, and press **Enter**.
   b. Type Setember 1 through 7 with the spelling error in cell **A2**, and press **Enter**.
   c. Type Expens Categories in cell **A4**, and press **Enter**.
   d. Type Monday in cell **B4**, and press **Enter**.
4. Adjust column width.
   a. Point to the border between the column **A** and column **B** headings to display a two-pointed arrow.
   b. Double-click to *AutoFit* column **A**.
5. Enter labels and values into the worksheet.
   a. Type *Pet nutrition* information in row 5 as shown in Figure 1-80.
   b. Type *Veterinary supplies* information in row 6 as shown in Figure 1-80.
   c. Type *Shelter supplies* information in row 7 as shown in Figure 1-80.
   d. Type *Salaries and wages* and *Utilities (prorated)* information in rows 8 and 9 as shown in Figure 1-80.

6. Use the *Fill Handle* to fill a series and copy data.
   a. Select cell **B4**.
   b. Click and drag the *Fill* pointer to cell **H4**.
   c. Select cells **B8:B9**. One *Fill Handle* displays in cell B9.
   d. Click and drag the *Fill* pointer to cell **H9**. When no discernible pattern exists, the *Fill Handle* copies data.
   e. Point to the border between the column **D** and column **E** headings to display a two-pointed arrow.
   f. Double-click to *AutoFit* column **D**.

	A	B	C	D	E	F	G	H
1	Life's Aminal Shelter							
2	Setember 1 through 7							
3								
4	Expens Categories	Monday						
5	Pet nutrition	55.25	47.5	38.55	27.45	42.5	35.25	51.75
6	Veterinary supplies	27.85	32.35	35	25	28.5	38.75	44.85
7	Shelter supplies	78	56.45	65.35	55	70	60.25	45.35
8	Salaries and wages	475						
9	Utilities (prorated)	45						
10								

Figure 1-80 Labels and values to be entered with errors in cells A1:A2 and A4

7. Merge and center labels.
   a. Select cells **A1:H1** and click the **Merge & Center** button [*Home* tab, *Alignment* group].
   b. Select cells **A2:H2** and click the **Merge & Center** button [*Home* tab, *Alignment* group].
   c. Select cells **B4:H4**.
   d. Click the **Center** button [*Home* tab, *Alignment* group].

8. Choose a workbook theme.
   a. Click the **Themes** button [*Page Layout* tab, *Themes* group].
   b. Choose **Integral** from the gallery.
   c. Click the **Home** tab. All labels and values are set in the **Tw Cen MT** font.

9. Apply cell styles.
   a. Select cell **A1** and click the **Cells Styles** button or the **More** button [*Home* tab, *Styles* group].
   b. Select **Title** in the *Titles and Headings* category. For the *Integral* theme, a title is formatted in the *Tw Cen MT Condensed* font, 18 points.
   c. Select cell **A2** and click the **Cells Styles** or the **More** button [*Home* tab, *Styles* group].
   d. Select **Heading 2** in the *Titles and Headings* category. The second level heading uses *Tw Cen MT* bold, 13 points. Both styles use a dark blue color.
   e. Select cells **A4:A9**.
   f. Press **Ctrl** and select cells **B4:H4**. Two ranges are selected.
   g. Click the **Cells Styles** or the **More** button [*Home* tab, *Styles* group].
   h. Select **Light Turquoise, 40% - Accent1** in the *Themed Cell Styles* category.
   i. Click the **Bold** button [*Home* tab, *Font* group].
   j. Select cell **A10**.
   k. Type Total and press **Enter**. The format from the column is automatically applied.

10. Apply font attributes.
    a. Select cells **A4:H10**.
    b. Click the **Font size** drop-down list [*Home* tab, *Font* group] and select **12**.
    c. Change the font size for cell **A2** to **14**.
    d. Select cells **A5:A9**.
    e. Click the **Increase Indent** button [*Home* tab, *Alignment* group] two times.
    f. Select cell **A10** and click the **Align Right** button [*Home* tab, *Alignment* group].

11. Use the *SUM* function and copy a formula.
    a. Select cell **B10**.
    b. Click the **AutoSum** button [*Home* tab, *Editing* group] and press **Enter** to accept the suggested range.
    c. Select cell **B10** and drag the *Fill* pointer to cell **H10**.

12. Apply number formatting.
    a. Select cells **B5:H10**.
    b. Click the **Accounting Number Format** button [*Home* tab, *Number* group]. Column widths are adjusted to accommodate the values.
    c. Click the **Decrease Decimal** button [*Home* tab, *Number* group] two times. Column widths do not adjust.

13. Change row heights.
    a. Click the heading for row **4**.
    b. Press **Ctrl** and click the row **10** heading. Two rows are selected.
    c. Right-click the row **4** heading.
    d. Choose **Row Height** and type 25 as the new height.
    e. Click **OK**.
    f. Click the heading for row **5** and drag down to select rows **5:9**.
    g. Point to the bottom border of the row **9** heading to display the resize arrow.
    h. Drag the pointer down to reach a height of **21.00** (**28 pixels**) and release the pointer (Figure 1-81).

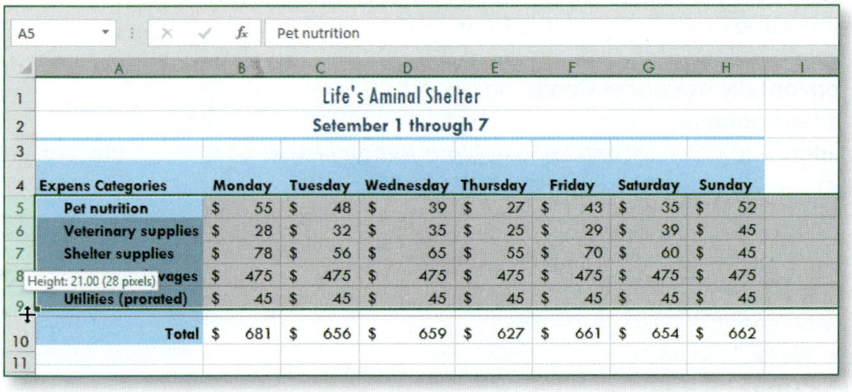

Figure 1-81 Change row heights for rows 5:9

14. Insert a row and change column width.
    a. Select cell **A9** and then right-click row heading **9**.
    b. Choose **Insert** from the context menu. The new row is located above the selected row; other rows shift down.
    c. Enter Cages and equipment in cell **A9**.
    d. Point to the border between columns **A** and **B** to display the resize arrow.
    e. Drag the pointer to a width of **22.50** (**185 pixels**) and release the pointer.

15. Enter the following data in row **9**. A zero (0) displays as a small dash.

	B	C	D	E	F	G	H
Cages and equipment	35	35	25	0	0	35	40

16. Insert borders and change the font size.
    a. Select cells **A4:H11**.
    b. Click the **Borders** button drop-down list and choose **All Borders**.
    c. Select cell **A2** and press **Ctrl+1** to open the *Format Cells* dialog box.
    d. Click the **Border** tab.
    e. Click the blue bottom border in the preview area to remove it.
    f. Click the **Color** drop-down arrow and select **Black, Text 1** (second column).
    g. Click to select the solid, thick line (second column, sixth style) in the *Style* group.

h. Click the bottom border in the preview area (Figure 1-82).
i. Click **OK**.
j. Select cell **A1** and change the font size to **24**.

17. Spell check a worksheet.
    a. Press **Ctrl+Home** to go to cell **A1**.
    b. Click the **Spelling** button [*Review* tab, *Proofing* group].
    c. Type Animal in the *Not in Dictionary* box and click **Change**.
    d. Choose "September" in the *Suggestions* list and click **Change**.
    e. Correct "Expens" when the error is located.
    f. Click **OK**.
    g. Press **Ctrl+Home**.

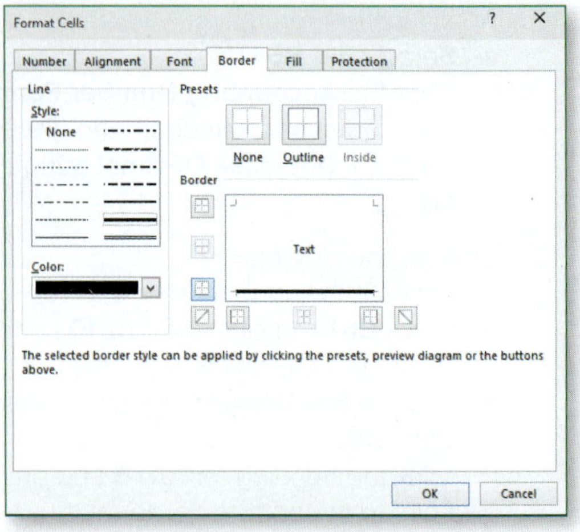

Figure 1-82 Create a custom border

18. Change page setup options.
    a. Click the **Page Layout** tab and click the **Page Setup** launcher.
    b. Select the **Landscape** radio button on the **Page** tab.
    c. Click the **Margins** tab.
    d. Select the **Horizontally** box under *Center on page*.
    e. Click the **Header/Footer** tab.
    f. Click the **Header** drop-down list and choose ***[your initials] Excel 1-1*** to insert the file name in the center section.
    g. Click **OK**.
    h. Press **Ctrl+F2** to preview the worksheet.
    i. Press **Esc** to close the *Backstage* view.

19. Copy and edit a worksheet.
    a. Right-click the **Week 1** tab name.
    b. Select **Move or Copy** from the menu.
    c. Select **(move to end)** in the *Before sheet* list.
    d. Select the **Create a copy** box and click **OK**.
    e. Select cells **B5:H10** on the copied worksheet, and delete the data.
    f. Double-click cell **A2** to start *Edit* mode.
    g. Change "September 1 through 7" to September 8 through 14.
    h. Double-click the **Week 1 (2)** tab name.
    i. Type Week 2 and press **Enter**.
    j. Right-click the **Week 2** tab name and choose **Tab Color**.
    k. Select **Green, Accent4, Darker 50%** (eighth column).

20. Click the **Week 1** sheet tab.

21. Preview a worksheet.
    a. Click the **File** tab and select **Print**.
    b. Press **Esc** to return to the worksheet.

22. Change the zoom size and freeze panes.
    a. Select cell **B5**.
    b. Click the **Zoom In** button in the *Status* bar five times.
    c. Click the **Freeze Panes** button [*View* tab, *Window* group].
    d. Choose **Freeze Panes**.
    e. Scroll the window on the right so that column **F** is immediately to the right of column **A** (Figure 1-83). (Increase or decrease the zoom size as needed.)
    f. Select cell **A1**.

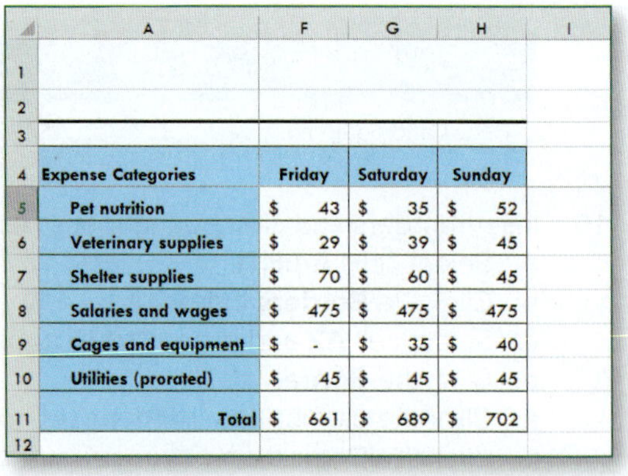

	A	F	G	H	I
1					
2					
3					
4	Expense Categories	Friday	Saturday	Sunday	
5	Pet nutrition	$ 43	$ 35	$ 52	
6	Veterinary supplies	$ 29	$ 39	$ 45	
7	Shelter supplies	$ 70	$ 60	$ 45	
8	Salaries and wages	$ 475	$ 475	$ 475	
9	Cages and equipment	$ -	$ 35	$ 40	
10	Utilities (prorated)	$ 45	$ 45	$ 45	
11	Total	$ 661	$ 689	$ 702	
12					

Figure 1-83 Panes frozen and positioned

23. Save and close the workbook (Figure 1-84).

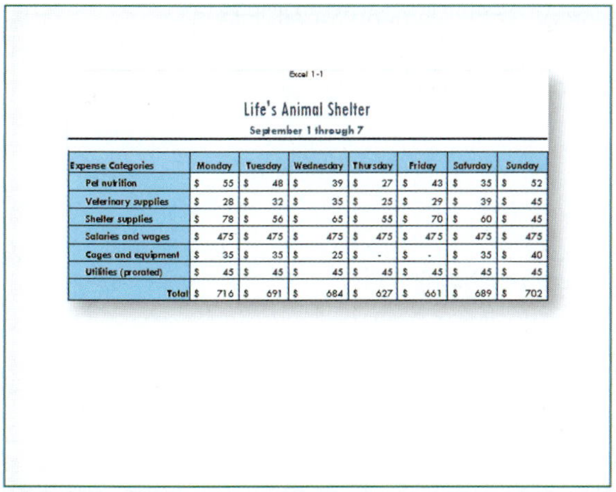

Excel 1-1

Life's Animal Shelter

September 1 through 7

Expense Categories	Monday	Tuesday	Wednesday	Thursday	Friday	Saturday	Sunday
Pet nutrition	$ 55	$ 48	$ 39	$ 27	$ 43	$ 35	$ 52
Veterinary supplies	$ 28	$ 32	$ 35	$ 25	$ 29	$ 39	$ 45
Shelter supplies	$ 78	$ 56	$ 65	$ 55	$ 70	$ 60	$ 45
Salaries and wages	$ 475	$ 475	$ 475	$ 475	$ 475	$ 475	$ 475
Cages and equipment	$ 35	$ 35	$ 25	$ -	$ -	$ 35	$ 40
Utilities (prorated)	$ 45	$ 45	$ 45	$ 45	$ 45	$ 45	$ 45
Total	$ 716	$ 691	$ 684	$ 627	$ 661	$ 689	$ 702

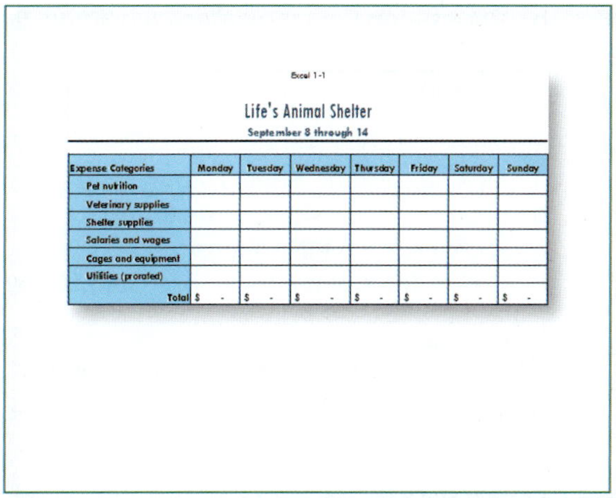

Excel 1-1

Life's Animal Shelter

September 8 through 14

Expense Categories	Monday	Tuesday	Wednesday	Thursday	Friday	Saturday	Sunday
Pet nutrition							
Veterinary supplies							
Shelter supplies							
Salaries and wages							
Cages and equipment							
Utilities (prorated)							
Total	$ -	$ -	$ -	$ -	$ -	$ -	$ -

Figure 1-84 Excel 1-1 completed

Guided Project 1-2

In this project, you edit a worksheet for Eller Software Services representative Adam White. He maintains client data with sales revenue and specific products or services. You plan to format the data, complete the calculation, and prepare the worksheet for sharing with management.
[Student Learning Outcomes 1.1, 1.2, 1.3, 1.4, 1.5, 1.6, 1.7, 1.8]

File Needed: ***EllerSoftwareServices-01.xlsx*** [*Student data files are available in the* Library *of your SIMnet account.*]
Completed Project File Name: ***[your initials] Excel 1-2.xlsx***

Skills Covered in This Project

- Open and save a workbook.
- Choose a workbook theme.
- Rename and apply color to sheet tabs.
- Enter and copy labels using the *Fill Handle*.
- Set font attributes and number formats.
- Use *SUM*.
- Center labels across a selection.
- Change page orientation and scale a worksheet for printing.
- Design borders.
- Insert a row.
- Adjust page setup options.

---

1. Open the workbook ***EllerSoftwareServices-01.xlsx*** from your student data files. If the workbook opens in *Protected View*, click **Enable Editing** in the security bar.
2. Save the workbook with a new file name.
   a. Press **F12** (**FN+F12**) to open the *Save As* dialog box.
   b. Navigate to the folder where your files are stored.
   c. Rename the file [your initials] Excel 1-2.
   d. Click **Save**.

3. Choose a workbook theme.
   a. Click the **Themes** button [*Page Layout* tab, *Themes* group].
   b. Choose **Ion** from the gallery. A different font, *Century Gothic*, is used for all data in the worksheet.
   c. Double-click the border between the column **C** and column **D** headings to *AutoFit* column **C**.

4. Rename and color a sheet tab.
   a. Double-click the **Sheet1** tab.
   b. Type MN Clients and press **Enter**.
   c. Right-click the **MN Clients** tab.
   d. Select **Tab Color** and choose **Gold, Accent3** (seventh column).

5. Enter and copy data.
   a. Select cell **F5**, type **MN**, and press **Enter**.
   b. Select cell **F5** and point to the *Fill Handle*.
   c. Click and drag the *Fill* pointer to cell **F13**.

6. Format data.
   a. Select cells **D5:D13**.
   b. Press **Ctrl+1** to open the *Format Cells* dialog box.
   c. Click the **Number** tab.
   d. Click **Special** in the *Category* list.
   e. Select **Phone Number** in the *Type* list and click **OK** (Figure 1-85).
   f. Select cells **I6:I13**.
   g. Click the **Comma Style** button [*Home* tab, *Number* group].
   h. Select cell **I5**.
   i. Click the **Accounting Number Format** button [*Home* tab, *Number* group]. A series of # symbols, when they appear, means the column is not wide enough to display the data (Figure 1-86).
   j. Double-click the border between the column **I** and column **J** headings to *AutoFit* column **I**.

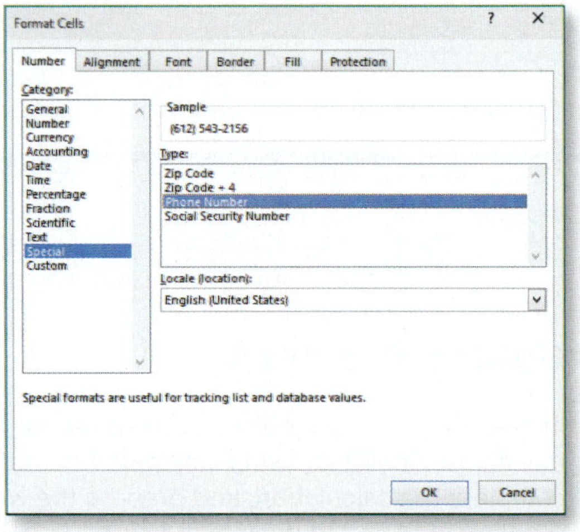

Figure 1-85 Special number format

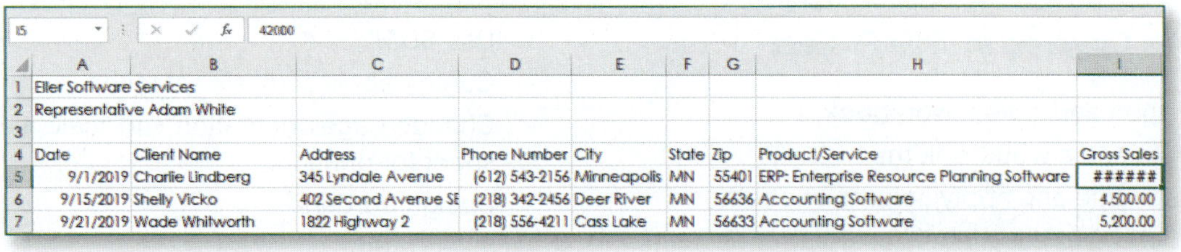

Figure 1-86 Column I is not wide enough

7. Enter and edit the reference range for the *SUM* function.
   a. Click cell **A15**, type Total, and press **Enter**.
   b. Select cell **I15**.
   c. Click the **AutoSum** button [*Home* tab, *Editing* group]. The suggested range includes an empty row.
   d. Click cell **I5** and drag to select cells **I5:I13**. Your selected range is highlighted and shown in the *Formula* bar and in the cell (Figure 1-87).
   e. Press **Enter** to accept the range. The *Accounting Number* format is applied.

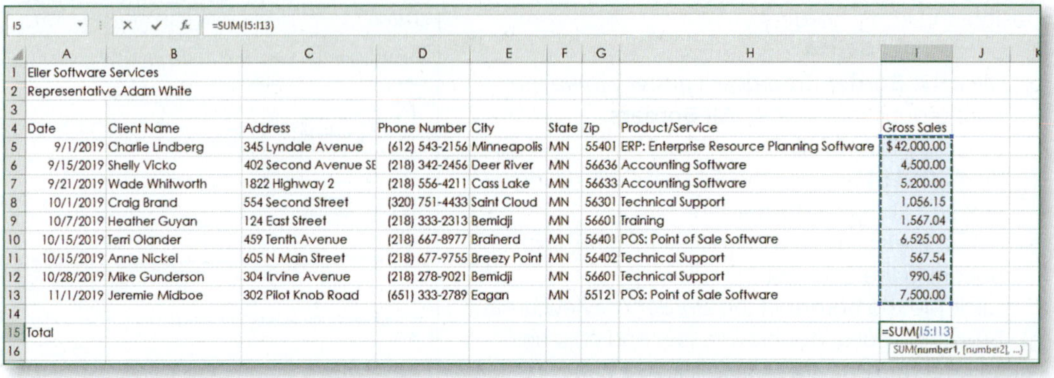

I5 =SUM(I5:I13)

	A	B	C	D	E	F	G	H	I	J
1	Eller Software Services									
2	Representative Adam White									
3										
4	Date	Client Name	Address	Phone Number	City	State	Zip	Product/Service	Gross Sales	
5	9/1/2019	Charlie Lindberg	345 Lyndale Avenue	(612) 543-2156	Minneapolis	MN	55401	ERP: Enterprise Resource Planning Software	$ 42,000.00	
6	9/15/2019	Shelly Vicko	402 Second Avenue SE	(218) 342-2456	Deer River	MN	56636	Accounting Software	4,500.00	
7	9/21/2019	Wade Whitworth	1822 Highway 2	(218) 556-4211	Cass Lake	MN	56633	Accounting Software	5,200.00	
8	10/1/2019	Craig Brand	554 Second Street	(320) 751-4433	Saint Cloud	MN	56301	Technical Support	1,056.15	
9	10/7/2019	Heather Guyan	124 East Street	(218) 333-2313	Bemidji	MN	56601	Training	1,567.04	
10	10/15/2019	Terri Olander	459 Tenth Avenue	(218) 667-8977	Brainerd	MN	56401	POS: Point of Sale Software	6,525.00	
11	10/15/2019	Anne Nickel	605 N Main Street	(218) 677-9755	Breezy Point	MN	56402	Technical Support	567.54	
12	10/28/2019	Mike Gunderson	304 Irvine Avenue	(218) 278-9021	Bemidji	MN	56601	Technical Support	990.45	
13	11/1/2019	Jeremie Midboe	302 Pilot Knob Road	(651) 333-2789	Eagan	MN	55121	POS: Point of Sale Software	7,500.00	
14										
15	Total								=SUM(I5:I13)	
16									SUM(number1, [number2], ...)	

Figure 1-87 New range selected for *SUM*

8. Center labels across a selection.
   a. Select cells **A1:I2** and click the **Alignment** launcher [*Home* tab, *Alignment* group].
   b. Click the *Horizontal* arrow and select **Center Across Selection**.
   c. Click **OK**.
9. Apply font attributes and cell styles.
   a. Select cell **A1**, click the **Font Size** drop-down list [*Home* tab, *Font* group], and select **24**.
   b. Select cell **A2** and change the font size to **18**.
   c. Select cells **A4:A15**, press **Ctrl**, and then select cells **B4:I4**.
   d. Click the **Cell Styles** button or the **More** button and select **Light Yellow, 40% - Accent3** (third column) in the *Themed Cell Styles* category.
   e. Click the **Bold** button [*Home* tab, *Font* group] while the cells are selected.
   f. Select cell **I15** and apply the **Total** cell style.
   g. Select cells **A4:I4**.
   h. Click the **Font Size** drop-down list [*Home* tab, *Font* group] and select **12**.
   i. Click the **Center** button [*Home* tab, *Alignment* group].
   j. *AutoFit* column **D**.
   k. Select cell **A15** and click the **Align Right** button [*Home* tab, *Alignment* group].
10. Edit a label.
    a. Double-click cell **H9** to start *Edit* mode.
    b. Press **Home** to position the insertion point before the word "Training."
    c. Type ERP and press **Spacebar**.
    d. Press **Enter**.
11. Insert a row.
    a. Right-click row heading **10**.
    b. Choose **Insert** from the context menu.
    c. In cell **A10**, type 10/10/19 and press **Tab**.
    d. Complete the data as shown here. For the phone number, do not type any spaces; it is automatically formatted when you press **Tab** to move to the next cell. For the city, state, and product/service columns, press **Tab** to accept the *AutoComplete* suggestion.

       B10 Hillary Marschke
       C10 245 West Third Avenue
       D10 3203555443 (press **Tab**)
       E10 sa (press **Tab**)
       F10 m (press **Tab**)
       G10 56301
       H10 t (press **Tab**)
       I10 750

12. Design and apply borders.
    a. Select cells **A4:I14**.
    b. Click the **Border** drop-down arrow [*Home* tab, *Font* group] and choose **All Borders**.
    c. Select cells **A16:I16**.
    d. Press **Ctrl+1** to open the *Format Cells* dialog box and click the **Border** tab.
    e. Select the solid, single line (first column, sixth option) in the *Style* list.
    f. Click the top border in the *Border* preview area.
    g. Select the solid, double line (second column, seventh option) in the *Style* list.
    h. Click the bottom border in the *Border* preview area (Figure 1-88).
    i. Click **OK**.
    j. Select cells **A15:I16**.
    k. Click the **Border** arrow [*Home* tab, *Font* group] and choose **Left Border**.
    l. Click the **Border** arrow [*Home* tab, *Font* group] and choose **Right Border**.

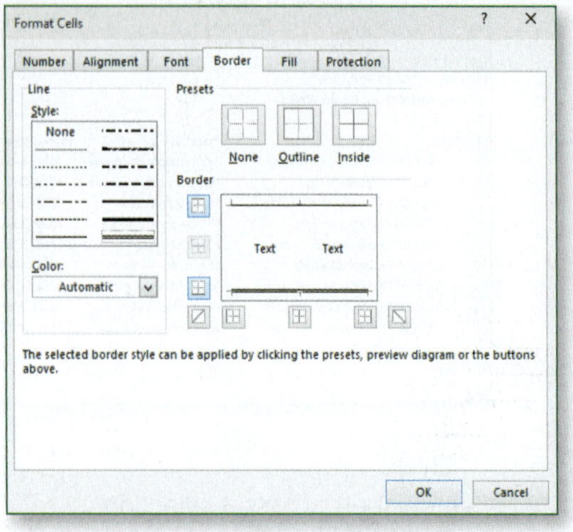

Figure 1-88 Design a double border

13. Hide a column.
    a. Right-click the column **E** heading.
    b. Select **Hide**.
    c. Press **Ctrl+Home**.
14. Change page setup options.
    a. Click the **Page Layout** tab.
    b. Click the **Orientation** button [*Page Setup* group] and choose **Landscape**.
    c. In the *Scale to Fit* group, click the **Width** arrow and choose **1 page**.
    d. Click the **Insert** tab.
    e. Click the **Header & Footer** button In the *Text* group. The view switches to *Page Layout* with the insertion point in the center header section. The *Header & Footer Tools Design* toolbar displays.
    f. Click the **Go to Footer** button in the *Navigation* group.
    g. Click the **Footer** button in the *Header & Footer* group (Figure 1-89).

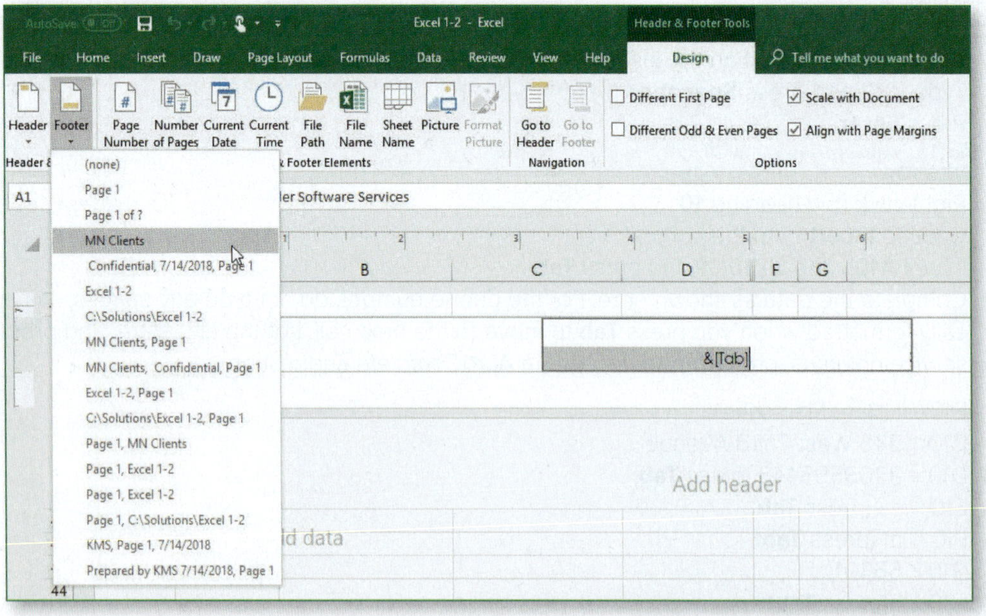

Figure 1-89 Select a built-in footer

h. Choose **MN Clients** to insert the sheet name in the footer. The *Header & Footer Tools Design* toolbar closes.

i. Click the **Normal** button in the *Status* bar. The footer is not visible in this view.

15. Preview and print the worksheet.
    a. Select **Print** from the *File* tab.
    b. Review the worksheet layout.
    c. Click **Print** or press **Esc** to return to the workbook.
16. Save and close the workbook (Figure 1-90).

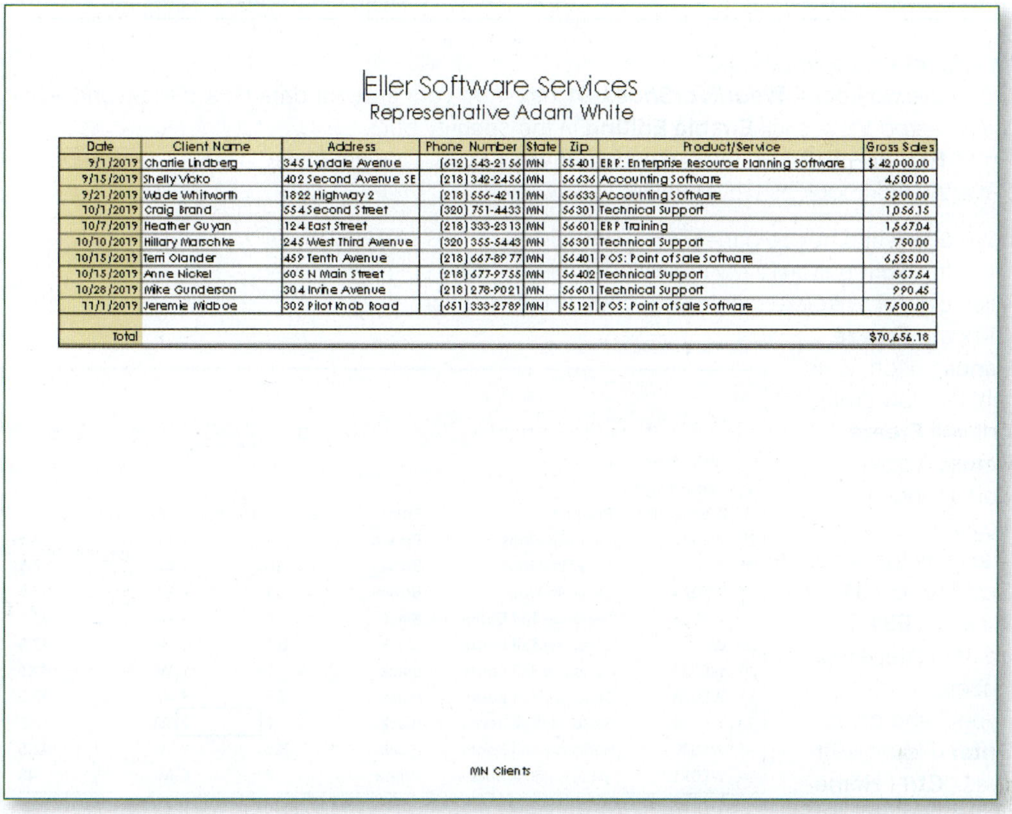

Eller Software Services
Representative Adam White

Date	Client Name	Address	Phone Number	State	Zip	Product/Service	Gross Sales
9/1/2019	Charlie Lindberg	345 Lyndale Avenue	(612) 543-2156	MN	55401	ERP: Enterprise Resource Planning Software	$ 42,000.00
9/15/2019	Shelly Vicko	402 Second Avenue SE	(218) 342-2456	MN	56636	Accounting Software	4,500.00
9/21/2019	Wade Whitworth	1822 Highway 2	(218) 556-4211	MN	56633	Accounting Software	5,200.00
10/1/2019	Craig Brand	554 Second Street	(320) 751-4433	MN	56301	Technical Support	1,056.15
10/7/2019	Heather Guyan	124 East Street	(218) 333-2313	MN	56601	ERP Training	1,567.04
10/10/2019	Hillary Marschke	245 West Third Avenue	(320) 355-5443	MN	56301	Technical Support	750.00
10/15/2019	Terri Olander	459 Tenth Avenue	(218) 667-8977	MN	56401	POS: Point of Sale Software	6,525.00
10/15/2019	Anne Nickel	605 N Main Street	(218) 677-9755	MN	56402	Technical Support	567.54
10/28/2019	Mike Gunderson	304 Irvine Avenue	(218) 278-9021	MN	56601	Technical Support	990.45
11/1/2019	Jeremie Midboe	302 Pilot Knob Road	(651) 333-2789	MN	55121	POS: Point of Sale Software	7,500.00
Total							$70,656.18

MN Clients

Figure 1-90 Excel 1-2 completed

Guided Project 1-3

In this project, you edit a worksheet for Wear-Ever Shoes that tracks their product inventory. You change the zoom size, reset the panes, and format data. You copy an existing formula to calculate the value of the current stock and insert a column for new data. After adjusting print options, you set a print area for a specific product line.
[Student Learning Outcomes 1.1, 1.2, 1.4, 1.5, 1.6, 1.7, 1.8]

File Needed: ***WearEverShoes-01.xlsx*** [*Student data files are available in the* Library *of your SIMnet account.*]
Completed Project File Name: ***[your initials] Excel 1-3.xlsx***

Skills Covered in This Project

- Open and save a workbook.
- Change zoom size and remove a split.
- Freeze panes.
- Format labels and values.
- Use the *Fill Handle* to copy a formula and fill a series.
- Check spelling.
- Apply a workbook theme, cell styles, and font attributes.
- Merge and center labels.
- Insert a column and adjust column widths and row heights.
- Adjust alignment, indents, and borders.
- Rename the sheet tab.
- Use *Page Layout* view to insert a footer.

---

1. Open and rename a workbook.
   a. Open the workbook ***WearEverShoes-01.xlsx*** from your student data files. If the workbook opens in *Protected View,* click **Enable Editing** in the security bar.
   b. Press **F12** (**FN+F12**) and locate the folder where your files are saved.
   c. Save the workbook as [your initials] Excel 1-3.
2. Remove a split and freeze panes.
   a. Click the **Split** button [*View* tab, *Window* group]. The split is removed.
   b. Click cell **A4** to freeze the column titles at this position.
   c. Click the **Freeze Panes** button [*View* tab, *Window* group].
   d. Choose **Freeze Panes**. A solid border appears between rows 3 and 4 to mark the pane.
   e. Scroll to row **31** and click cell **E31**. The column titles are frozen.
   f. Type 3 and press **Enter** (Figure 1-91).
   g. Press **Ctrl+Home**. The insertion point returns to cell **A4**.

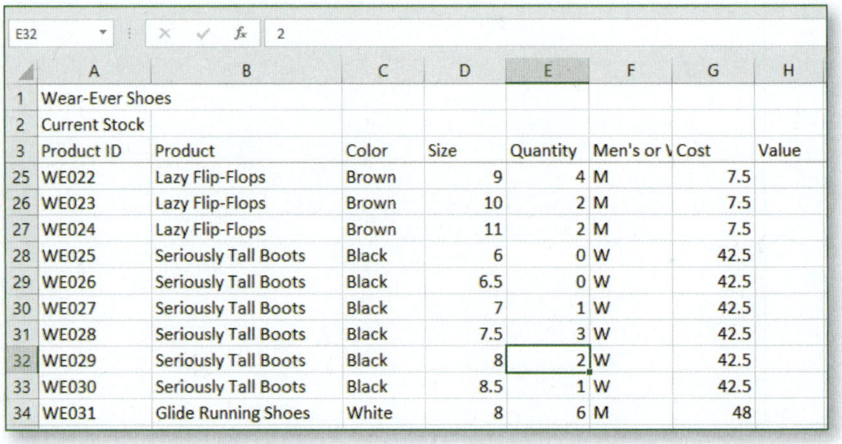

E32 | 2

	A	B	C	D	E	F	G	H
1	Wear-Ever Shoes							
2	Current Stock							
3	Product ID	Product	Color	Size	Quantity	Men's or \	Cost	Value
25	WE022	Lazy Flip-Flops	Brown	9	4	M	7.5	
26	WE023	Lazy Flip-Flops	Brown	10	2	M	7.5	
27	WE024	Lazy Flip-Flops	Brown	11	2	M	7.5	
28	WE025	Seriously Tall Boots	Black	6	0	W	42.5	
29	WE026	Seriously Tall Boots	Black	6.5	0	W	42.5	
30	WE027	Seriously Tall Boots	Black	7	1	W	42.5	
31	WE028	Seriously Tall Boots	Black	7.5	3	W	42.5	
32	WE029	Seriously Tall Boots	Black	8	2	W	42.5	
33	WE030	Seriously Tall Boots	Black	8.5	1	W	42.5	
34	WE031	Glide Running Shoes	White	8	6	M	48	

Figure 1-91 Panes frozen at cell A4

3. Change zoom size and unfreeze the pane.
   a. Click the **100%** button [*View* tab, *Zoom* group].
   b. Click the **Freeze Panes** button [*View* tab, *Window* group].
   c. Choose **Unfreeze Panes**.
   d. Click cell **A1**.
4. Check spelling in the worksheet.
   a. Click the **Spelling** button [*Review* tab, *Proofing* group]. The first occurrence of "Hikin" is found as misspelled.
   b. Select **Hiking** in the *Suggestions* list.
   c. Click **Change All** to correct all occurrences of the misspelled word (Figure 1-92).
   d. Click **OK**.
5. Use the *Fill Handle* to copy a formula.
   a. Click **H4**. The formula displays in the *Formula* bar. The formula multiplies the quantity by the cost to calculate the value of the current stock.

b. Point to the *Fill Handle* for cell **H4** (Figure 1-93).

c. Double-click the *Fill* pointer. The formula is copied down the entire column.

d. Press **Ctrl+Home**.

6. Click the **Themes** button [*Page Layout* tab, *Themes* group] and choose **Ion** from the gallery.

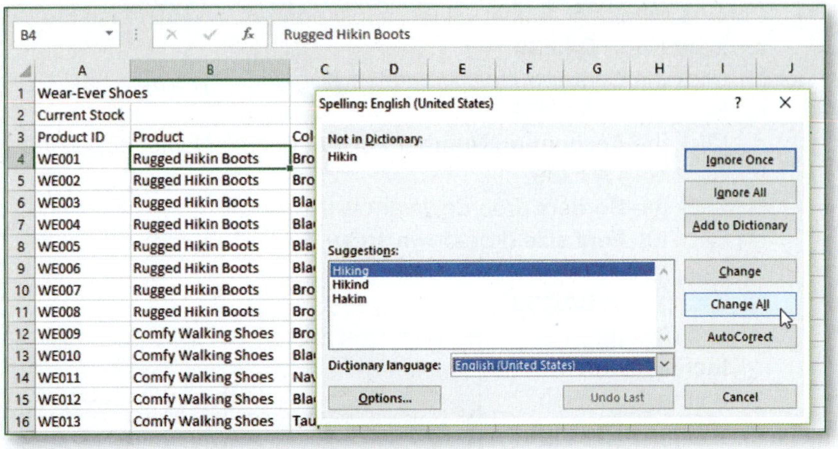

Figure 1-92 Change all occurrences of a misspelled word

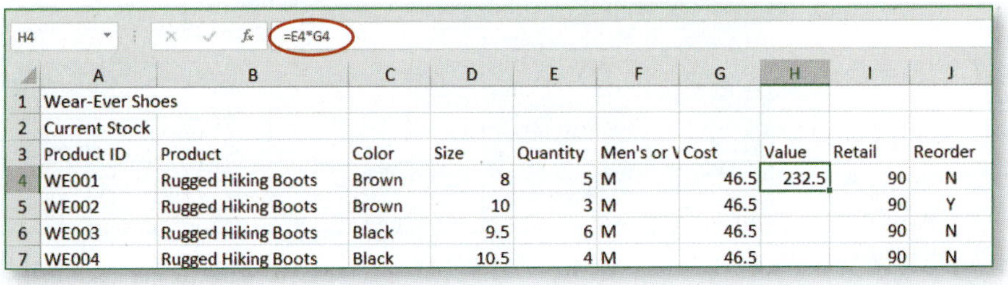

Figure 1-93 Formula to be copied

7. Merge and center the titles.
   a. Select cells **A1:J1** and click the **Merge & Center** button [*Home* tab, *Alignment* group].
   b. Merge and center cells **A2:J2**.

8. Apply cell styles and adjust row height.
   a. Select cell **A1**, click the **Cell Styles** button or the **More** button [*Home* tab, *Styles* group], and select **Title** in the *Titles and Headings* category.
   b. Select cell **A2** and apply the **Heading 4** style.
   c. Click the **Font Size** arrow [*Home* tab, *Font* group] and select **14 pt**. The font size change overwrites the font size of the cell style.
   d. Point to the row **1** heading and drag to select row headings **1:2**.
   e. Click the **Format** button [*Home* tab, *Cells* group] and choose **Row Height**.
   f. Type 22 as the new row height and press **Enter**.
   g. Select cells **A3:J3**.
   h. From the *Cell Styles* gallery [*Home* tab], select **Light Yellow, 40% - Accent3**.
   i. Apply **bold** to the selected cells.
   j. Click the row **3** heading.
   k. Point to the bottom border of the row heading to display the resize arrow.
   l. Drag the resize arrow to **21.00** (**28 pixels**) as the new row height and release the pointer (Figure 1-94).
   m. Click the **Zoom Out** button in the *Status* bar if necessary so that you can see all rows (1:39).

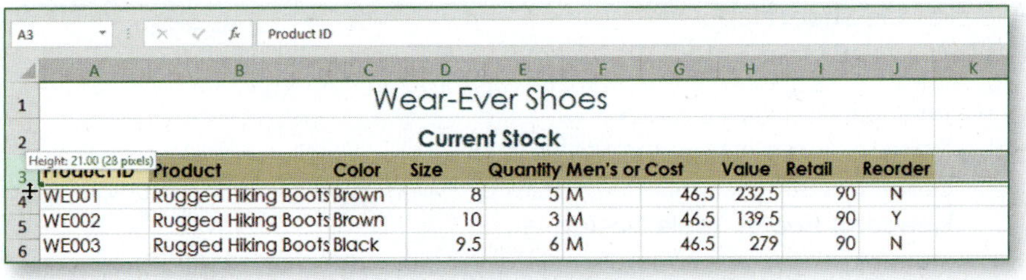

Figure 1-94 Adjust row height from the row heading

9. Change alignment, format values, apply borders, and increase the indent.
   a. Select cells **D4:F39**.
   b. Click the **Center** button [*Home* tab, *Alignment* group].
   c. Select cells **G4:H39**.
   d. Click the **Accounting Number Format** button [*Home* tab, *Alignment* group].
   e. Click cells **A3:J39**.
   f. Click the **Borders** drop-down arrow [*Home* tab, *Font* group] and select **All Borders**.
   g. Click the **Font size** drop-down arrow [*Home* tab, *Font* group] and choose **12** while the cells are selected.
   h. Select cells **B4:C39** and click the **Increase Indent** button [*Home* tab, *Alignment* group] one time. This moves the label away from the border for easier reading.
   i. Click and drag to select columns **A:J**.
   j. Double-click the border between columns J and K to *AutoFit* the selected columns (Figure 1-95).
   k. Select and **center** align the labels in row **3**.

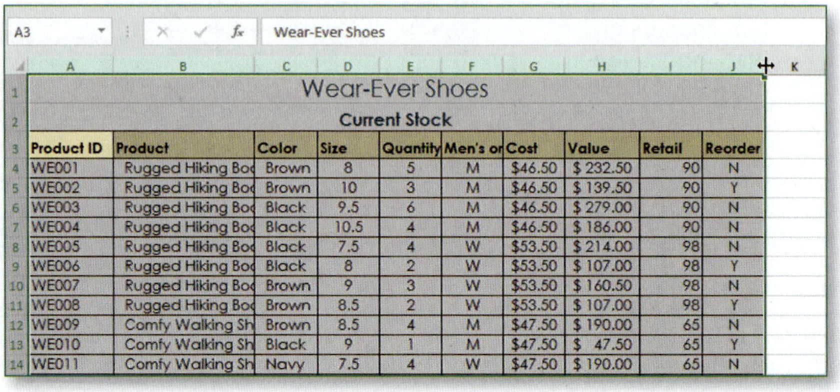

Figure 1-95 Select column headings to *AutoFit*

10. Insert a column and create a pattern to fill data.
   a. Right-click column heading **B**.
   b. Choose **Insert** from the context menu.
   c. In cell **B3**, type Disc? and press **Enter**.
   d. In cell **B4**, type No and press **Enter**.
   e. In cell **B5**, type No and press **Enter**.
   f. In cell **B6**, type Yes and press **Enter**. The pattern is two occurrences of *No* and one occurrence of *Yes*.
   g. Select cells **B4:B6** and increase the indent twice.
   h. Select cells **B4:B6** and double-click the *Fill* pointer (Figure 1-96).
   i. Select cells **A4:A39** and increase the indent one time.
   j. Press **Ctrl+Home**.

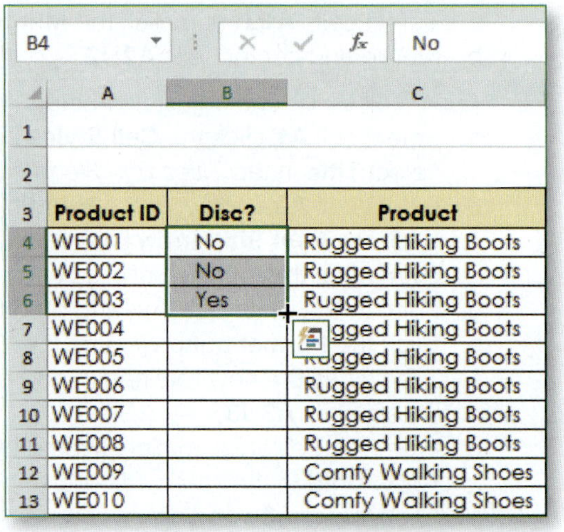

Figure 1-96 Double-click the *Fill* pointer to complete a series

11. Rename the sheet tab.
   a. Double-click the **Sheet1** tab.
   b. Type Inventory and press **Enter**.

12. Use *Page Layout* view to insert a footer.
   a. Click the **Page Layout** button in the *Status* bar.
   b. Click the center header section. The *Header & Footer Tools Design* tab displays.
   c. Click the **Header & Footer Tools Design** tab.

d. Click the **Go to Footer** button [*Header & Footer Tools Design* tab, *Navigation* group].
e. Click the middle section if necessary.
f. Click the **File Name** button in the *Header & Footer Elements* group. The code is *&[File]*.
g. Click a worksheet cell to see the file name.
h. Switch to *Normal* view and press **Ctrl+Home**.

13. Change page setup options.
    a. Click the **Page Layout** tab and click the **Page Setup** launcher.
    b. Display the *Page* tab and select the **Landscape** radio button under *Orientation*.
    c. Select the **Fit to** radio button and enter 1 page wide by 1 tall.
    d. Click **OK**.
14. Set a print area.
    a. Select cells **A1:K11**.
    b. Click the **Page Layout** tab.
    c. Click the **Print Area** button [*Page Setup* group] and select **Set Print Area**.
    d. Press **Ctrl+Home**.
    e. Click the **File** tab and select **Print** to preview the worksheet print area.
    f. Return to the worksheet.
15. Click the **Save** button in the *Quick Access* toolbar to save the workbook changes. The print area is saved.
16. Close the workbook (Figure 1-97).

Wear-Ever Shoes

Current Stock

Product ID	Disc?	Product	Color	Size	Quantity	Men's or Women's	Cost	Value	Retail	Reorder
WE001	No	Rugged Hiking Boots	Brown	8	5	M	$ 46.50	$ 232.50	90	N
WE002	No	Rugged Hiking Boots	Brown	10	3	M	$ 46.50	$ 139.50	90	Y
WE003	Yes	Rugged Hiking Boots	Black	9.5	6	M	$ 46.50	$ 279.00	90	N
WE004	No	Rugged Hiking Boots	Black	10.5	4	M	$ 46.50	$ 186.00	90	N
WE005	No	Rugged Hiking Boots	Black	7.5	4	W	$ 53.50	$ 214.00	98	N
WE006	Yes	Rugged Hiking Boots	Black	8	2	W	$ 53.50	$ 107.00	98	Y
WE007	No	Rugged Hiking Boots	Brown	9	3	W	$ 53.50	$ 160.50	98	N
WE008	No	Rugged Hiking Boots	Brown	8.5	2	W	$ 53.50	$ 107.00	98	Y
WE009	Yes	Comfy Walking Shoes	Brown	8.5	4	M	$ 47.50	$ 190.00	65	N
WE010	No	Comfy Walking Shoes	Black	9	1	M	$ 47.50	$ 47.50	65	Y
WE011	No	Comfy Walking Shoes	Navy	7.5	4	W	$ 47.50	$ 190.00	65	N
WE012	Yes	Comfy Walking Shoes	Black	8	1	W	$ 47.50	$ 47.50	65	Y
WE013	No	Comfy Walking Shoes	Taupe	7.5	2	W	$ 47.50	$ 95.00	65	N
WE014	No	Comfy Walking Shoes	Brown	8	3	W	$ 47.50	$ 142.50	65	Y
WE015	Yes	Lazy Flip-Flops	Pink	6	4	W	$ 7.50	$ 30.00	14	N
WE016	No	Lazy Flip-Flops	Pink	7	0	W	$ 7.50	$ -	14	N
WE017	No	Lazy Flip-Flops	Pink	8	2	W	$ 7.50	$ 15.00	14	Y
WE018	Yes	Lazy Flip-Flops	White	6	3	W	$ 7.50	$ 22.50	14	N
WE019	No	Lazy Flip-Flops	White	7	1	W	$ 7.50	$ 7.50	14	N
WE020	No	Lazy Flip-Flops	White	8	2	W	$ 7.50	$ 15.00	14	Y
WE021	Yes	Lazy Flip-Flops	Brown	8	2	M	$ 7.50	$ 15.00	14	Y
WE022	No	Lazy Flip-Flops	Brown	9	4	M	$ 7.50	$ 30.00	14	N
WE023	No	Lazy Flip-Flops	Brown	10	2	M	$ 7.50	$ 15.00	14	Y
WE024	Yes	Lazy Flip-Flops	Brown	11	2	M	$ 7.50	$ 15.00	14	Y
WE025	No	Seriously Tall Boots	Black	6	0	W	$ 42.50	$ -	80	Y
WE026	No	Seriously Tall Boots	Black	6.5	0	W	$ 42.50	$ -	80	Y
WE027	Yes	Seriously Tall Boots	Black	7	1	W	$ 42.50	$ 42.50	80	Y
WE028	No	Seriously Tall Boots	Black	7.5	3	W	$ 42.50	$ 127.50	80	Y
WE029	No	Seriously Tall Boots	Black	8	2	W	$ 42.50	$ 85.00	80	Y
WE030	Yes	Seriously Tall Boots	Black	8.5	1	W	$ 42.50	$ 42.50	80	Y
WE031	No	Glide Running Shoes	White	8	6	M	$ 48.00	$ 288.00	75	N
WE032	No	Glide Running Shoes	White	9	6	M	$ 48.00	$ 288.00	75	N
WE033	Yes	Glide Running Shoes	White	10	6	M	$ 48.00	$ 288.00	75	N
WE034	No	Glide Running Shoes	Black	8	2	M	$ 48.00	$ 96.00	75	N
WE035	No	Glide Running Shoes	Black	9	3	M	$ 48.00	$ 144.00	75	N
WE036	Yes	Glide Running Shoes	Black	10	1	M	$ 48.00	$ 48.00	75	Y

Excel 1-3

Figure 1-97 Excel 1-3 completed

Independent Project 1-4

As a staff member at Blue Lake Sports Company, you are expected to prepare the monthly sales worksheet. You edit and format data, complete calculations, and prepare the workbook for distribution. You also copy the sheet for next month's data.
[Student Learning Outcomes 1.1, 1.2, 1.3, 1.4, 1.5, 1.6, 1.8]

File Needed: ***BlueLakeSports-1.xlsx*** [*Student data files are available in the* Library *of your SIMnet account.*]
Completed Project File Name: ***[your initials] Excel 1-4.xlsx***

Skills Covered in This Project

- Open and save a workbook.
- Choose a workbook theme.
- Edit and format data.
- Center labels across a selection.
- Use *SUM* and the *Fill Handle*.
- Adjust column width and row height.
- Insert a header and a footer.
- Adjust page layout options.
- Copy and rename a worksheet.

---

1. Open ***BlueLakeSports-01.xlsx*** from your student data files. If the workbook opens in *Protected View*, click **Enable Editing** in the security bar.
2. Save the workbook as [your initials] Excel 1-4 in your usual location.
3. Apply the **Slice** theme to the worksheet.
4. Edit worksheet data.
   a. Edit the title in cell **A2** to display Monthly Sales by Department.
   b. Edit cell **D6** to 1950.
5. Select cells **A1:F2** and click the **Alignment** launcher [*Home* tab]. Click the *Horizontal* arrow, choose **Center Across Selection**, and click **OK**.
6. Select and delete row **8**.
7. Use the *Fill Handle* to complete a series.
   a. Select cell **B3**.
   b. Use the *Fill Handle* to complete the series to **Week 4** in column **E**.
   c. *AutoFit* columns **C:E** to display the complete label.
8. Use *SUM* and the *Fill Handle* to calculate totals.
   a. Use the **AutoSum** button to build a *SUM* function in cell **F4**.
   b. Use the *Fill Handle* to copy the formula in cell **F4** to cells **F5:F16**.
   c. Delete the contents of cell **F17** if you copied the formula to that cell.
   d. Select cells **B17:F17** and click the **AutoSum** button. The *SUM* formula is inserted, and a **Quick Analysis** options button appears (Figure 1-98).
   e. Press **Esc** to ignore the *Quick Analysis* options.

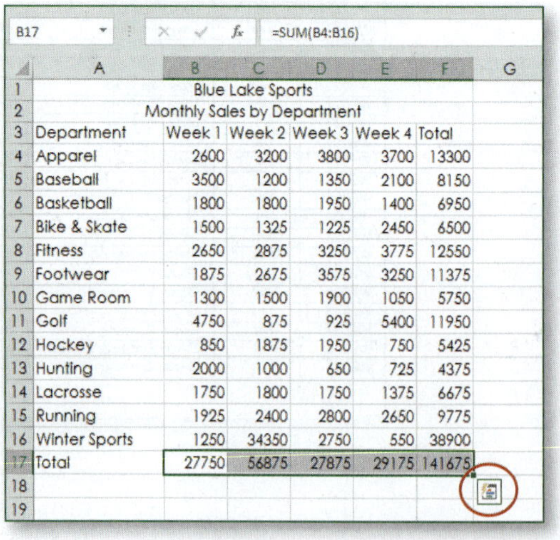

Figure 1-98 ***AutoSum*** **complete with** ***Quick Analysis*** **button**

9. Format labels and values.
   a. Select cells **A1:A2** and increase the font size to **18**.
   b. Increase the row height of rows **1:2** to **24 (32 pixels)**.
   c. Format cells **A3:F3** as **Bold** and increase the row height to **18 (24 pixels)**.
   d. Center the data in cells **B3:F3**.
   e. Format cells **B4:F16** with **Comma Style** and decrease the decimal two times.
   f. Select cells **B17:F17** and apply the **Accounting Number Format** with no decimal places.
   g. Apply the **All Borders** format to cells **A3:F17**.
   h. *AutoFit* columns **B:F**.

10. Finalize the worksheet.
    a. Click the **Insert** tab and click the **Header & Footer** button [*Text* group].
    b. In the right header section, insert the **Sheet Name** field.
    c. Go to the footer and click the right section.
    d. Type [your first and last name] (Figure 1-99).

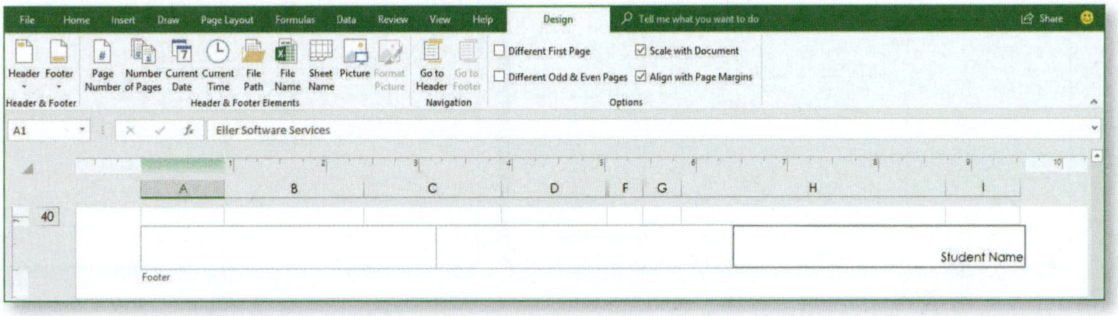

Figure 1-99 Add a footer in *Page Layout* view

   e. Click a cell in the worksheet and then return to *Normal* view.
   f. Center the worksheet horizontally on the page.

11. Copy and rename a worksheet.
    a. Right-click the *January* sheet tab and choose **Move or Copy**.
    b. Make a copy of the sheet at the end.
    c. Rename the copied sheet February.
    d. Format the *February* sheet tab color to **Dark Blue, Accent1** (fifth column).
    e. Delete the values in cells **B4:E16** and press **Ctrl+Home**.
    f. Return to the *January* sheet and press **Ctrl+Home**.

12. Preview the *January* sheet.

13. Save and close the workbook (Figure 1-100).

January

Blue Lake Sports
Monthly Sales by Department

Department	Week 1	Week 2	Week 3	Week 4	Total
Apparel	2,600	3,200	3,800	3,700	13,300
Baseball	3,500	1,200	1,350	2,100	8,150
Basketball	1,800	1,800	1,950	1,400	6,950
Bike & Skate	1,500	1,325	1,225	2,450	6,500
Fitness	2,650	2,875	3,250	3,775	12,550
Footwear	1,875	2,675	3,575	3,250	11,375
Game Room	1,300	1,500	1,900	1,050	5,750
Golf	4,750	875	925	5,400	11,950
Hockey	850	1,875	1,950	750	5,425
Hunting	2,000	1,000	650	725	4,375
Lacrosse	1,750	1,800	1,750	1,375	6,675
Running	1,925	2,400	2,800	2,650	9,775
Winter Sports	1,250	34,350	2,750	550	38,900
Total	$27,750	$56,875	$27,875	$29,175	$141,675

Student Name

February

Blue Lake Sports
Monthly Sales by Department

Department	Week 1	Week 2	Week 3	Week 4	Total
Apparel					-
Baseball					-
Basketball					-
Bike & Skate					-
Fitness					-
Footwear					-
Game Room					-
Golf					-
Hockey					-
Hunting					-
Lacrosse					-
Running					-
Winter Sports					-
Total	$ -	$ -	$ -	$ -	$ -

Student Name

Figure 1-100 Excel 1-4 completed

Independent Project 1-5

Clemenson Imaging employs certified staff to perform mobile medical imaging at several hospitals statewide. Your worksheet maintains a log of which hospitals were visited and what images were made. You need to format the data and finalize the worksheet.
[Student Learning Outcomes 1.1, 1.2, 1.3, 1.4, 1.5, 1.6, 1.7, 1.8]

File Needed: ***ClemensonImaging-01.xlsx*** [*Student data files are available in the* Library *of your SIMnet account.*]
Completed Project File Name: ***[your initials] Excel 1-5.xlsx***

Skills Covered in This Project

- Open and save a workbook.
- Use *SUM.*
- Unfreeze panes and change the zoom size.
- Format data.
- Merge and center labels.
- Adjust column width and row height.
- Apply borders.
- Copy a sheet and rename a tab.
- Add document properties.
- Change page layout options.

1. Open ***ClemensonImaging-01**.xlsx* from your student data files and save it as [your initials] Excel 1-5. If the workbook opens in *Protected View*, click **Enable Editing** in the security bar.

2. Edit the label in cell **A1** to insert LLC after "Clemenson Imaging." Edit the label in cell **A2** to show "Second Quarter . . ." instead of "First Quarter."

3. Merge and center the label in cell **A1** across the worksheet data and then do the same for the label in cell **A2**.

4. Scroll to and select cell **A41**. Type Total. Right-align this label and apply bold format.

5. Use *SUM* in cell **F41** to add the values in cells **F5:F40**.

6. Unfreeze the panes and set a zoom size to display rows 1:30.

7. *AutoFit* columns **D:G**.

8. Format data.
   a. Click cell **A1** and set the font size to **18**.
   b. Change the label in cell **A2** to a font size of **14**.
   c. Select cells **A4:H4** and apply bold and center alignment.
   d. Format cells **A4:H4** to use the **White, Background 1, Darker 15%** fill color (first column).
   e. Format the row height for row **4** to **21.00 (28 pixels)**.
   f. Select cells **A4:H41** and apply **All Borders**.
   g. Select cells **A41:H41** and apply the fill color **White, Background 1, Darker 15%** (first column).
   h. Bold the value in cell **F41**.

9. Set page layout options.
   a. Change the page orientation to **Landscape**.
   b. Center the worksheet horizontally.
   c. Scale the sheet to fit on a single page.
   d. Add a footer that displays the current date in the left section and your first and last name in the right section.

10. Add document properties.
    a. Click the **File** tab and select **Info**.
    b. Click the **Properties** drop-down arrow and select **Advanced Properties**.
    c. Click the **Summary** tab, click the **Title** box, and type Procedures.
    d. Click the **Author** box and type your first and last name (Figure 1-101).
    e. Click **OK** and return to the worksheet.

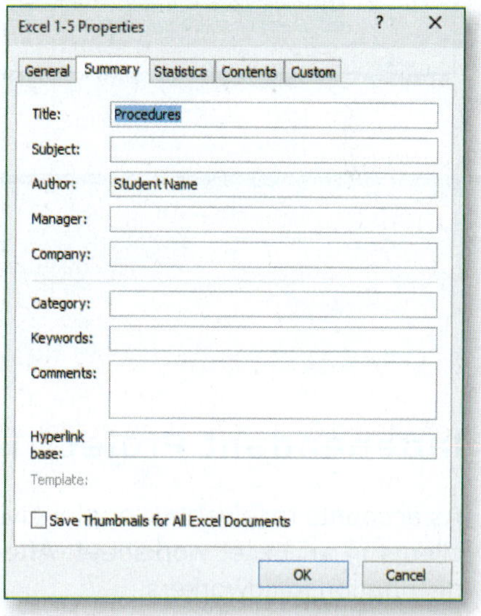

Figure 1-101 ***Properties* dialog box**

11. Rename *Sheet1* as Second Qtr.

12. Copy the *Second Qtr* sheet and place it at the end. Name the copy Third Qtr. Set this tab color to **Blue, Accent1, Darker 50%** (fifth column).

13. Select the *Third Qtr* sheet, and edit the label in cell **A2** to show "Third Quarter. . .".

14. Delete the contents of cells **A5:H40** on the *Third Qtr* sheet.

15. Select cell **A5** and return to the *Second Qtr* sheet.

16. Press **Ctrl+Home** and preview the entire workbook (Figure 1-102).

17. Save and close the workbook (Figure 1-103).

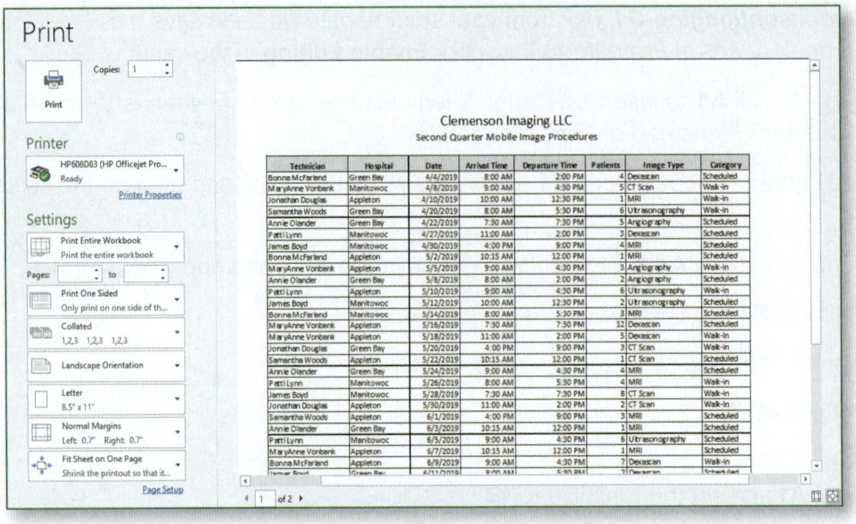

Figure 1-102 Entire workbook selected for preview and print

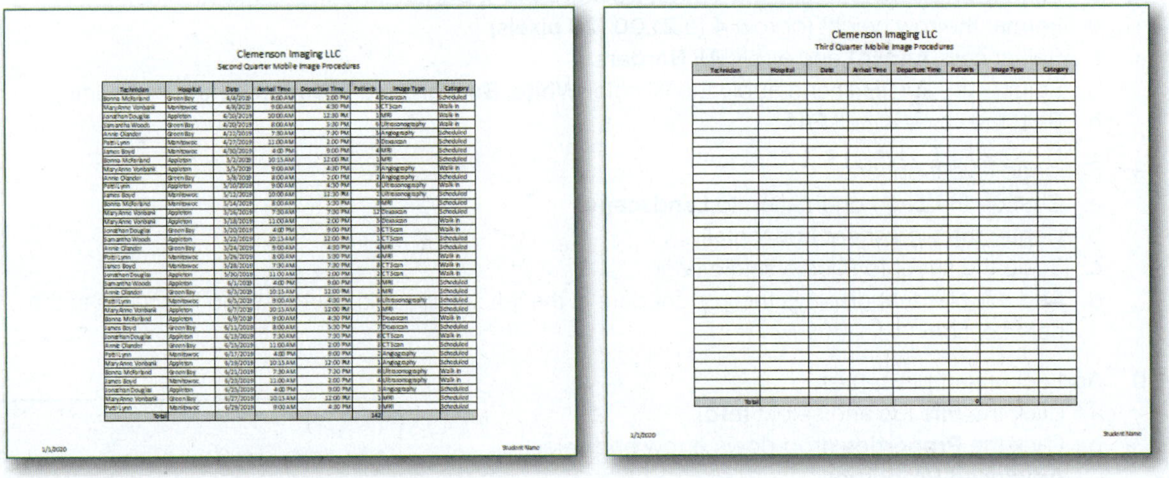

Figure 1-103 Excel 1-5 completed

Independent Project 1-6

As accounts receivable clerk for Livingood Income Tax and Accounting, you track daily payments from clients in an Excel worksheet. After entering the data, you format the worksheet and prepare it for distribution to coworkers.
[Student Learning Outcomes 1.1, 1.2, 1.4, 1.5, 1.6, 1.8]

File Needed: None
Completed Project File Name: ***[your initials] Excel 1-6.xlsx***

Skills Covered in This Project

- Create and save a workbook.
- Enter labels, dates, and values.
- Use the *Fill Handle* to build series.
- Change font size and attributes.
- Adjust column width and row height.
- Choose a theme and cell styles.
- Choose page layout options.
- Rename and apply color to sheet tabs.

---

1. Create a new workbook and save it as [your initials] Excel 1-6.
2. Apply the **Organic** theme for the workbook.
3. Type Livingood Income Tax and Accounting in cell **A1** and press **Enter**.
4. Type Accounts Receivable in cell **A2** and press **Enter**.
5. Type the labels in row **4** as shown here in Figure 1-104:

	A	B	C	D	E	F
1	Livingood Income Tax and Accounting					
2	Accounts Receivable					
3						
4	Date	Invoice	Client ID	Amount	Payment Date	Payment Type
5						

Figure 1-104 Data to be entered

6. *AutoFit* columns **E:F** to display each label in row 4.
7. Type 8/18/19 in cell **A5** to enter the date. In cell **A6**, type 8/20/19 to set a pattern for the dates.
8. Select cells **A5:A6** and use the *Fill Handle* to fill in dates to cell A15.
9. Select cell **B5** and type 1001 for the first invoice number. In cell **B6**, type 1002 to set a pattern for the invoice numbers.
10. Select cells **B5:B6** and use the *Fill Handle* to fill in invoice numbers to reach cell B15.
11. Type LITA001 in cell **C5** as the first client ID. In cell **C6**, type LITA002 to set a pattern.
12. Use the *Fill Handle* to complete the client ID numbers.
13. Type 425 in cell **D5**. In cell **D6**, type 450 to set the pattern and fill in the amounts.
14. Type the first two payment dates in column **E** and fill the cells (Figure 1-105).

	A	B	C	D	E	F
1	Livingood Income Tax and Accounting					
2	Accounts Receivable					
3						
4	Date	Invoice	Client ID	Amount	Payment Date	Payment Type
5	8/18/2019	1001	LITA001	425	8/28/2019	Check
6	8/20/2019	1002	LITA002	450	8/29/2019	EFT
7	8/22/2019	1003	LITA003	475	8/30/2019	Credit card
8	8/24/2019	1004	LITA004	500	8/31/2019	Check
9	8/26/2019	1005	LITA005	525	9/1/2019	EFT
10	8/28/2019	1006	LITA006	550	9/2/2019	Credit card
11	8/30/2019	1007	LITA007	575	9/3/2019	Check
12	9/1/2019	1008	LITA008	600	9/4/2019	EFT
13	9/3/2019	1009	LITA009	625	9/5/2019	Credit card
14	9/5/2019	1010	LITA010	650	9/6/2019	Check
15	9/7/2019	1011	LITA011	675	9/7/2019	EFT

Figure 1-105 All columns filled

15. Type the first three payment types in cells **F5:F7** and then use the *Fill Handle* to complete the cells in column F.
16. Format data.
    a. Select cells **C5:C15**, increase the indent one time, and *AutoFit* the column. Do the same for the payment type data.
    b. Format the values in column **D** as **Accounting Number Format**.
    c. Select cells **A1:F2** and click the **Alignment** launcher [*File* tab]. Click the *Horizontal* arrow, choose **Center Across Selection**, and click **OK**. Change the font size to **18**.
    d. Select the labels in row **4** and apply bold and center alignment.
    e. *AutoFit* columns that do not show all the data.
    f. Apply **All Borders** to cells **A4:F15**. Apply an **Outside Border** for cells **A1:F2**.
    g. Apply the **Green, Accent1, Lighter 60%** fill color (fifth column) to cells **A1:F2** and **A4:F4**.
    h. Apply the **Green, Accent1, Lighter 60%** fill color (fifth column) to cells **A6:F6**.
    i. Use the **Ctrl** key to select the data in rows **8**, **10**, **12**, and **14** and apply the same fill color.

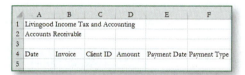

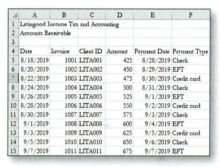

17. Rename *Sheet1* as AR and set the tab color to **Green, Accent1** (fifth column).
18. Define page layout and add document properties.
    a. Center the worksheet horizontally on the page.
    b. Create a header with the sheet name in the left section and your name in the right section.
    c. Delete an existing author name and key your first and last name as *Author* in the *Properties* dialog box.
    d. Type Receivables in the *Title* box (Figure 1-106).
    e. Preview your worksheet.
19. Save and close the workbook (Figure 1-107).

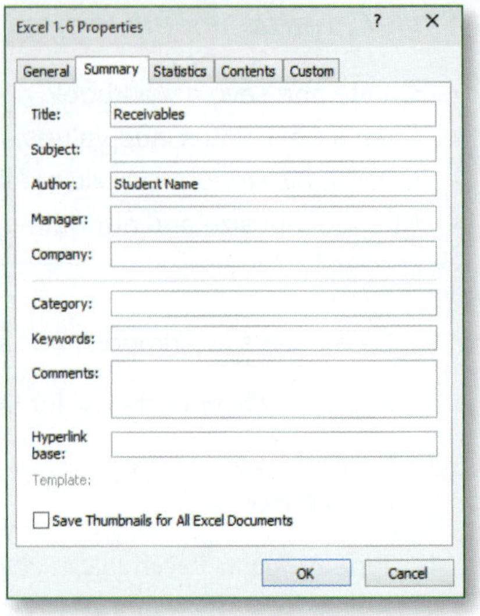

Figure 1-106 Properties entered in dialog box

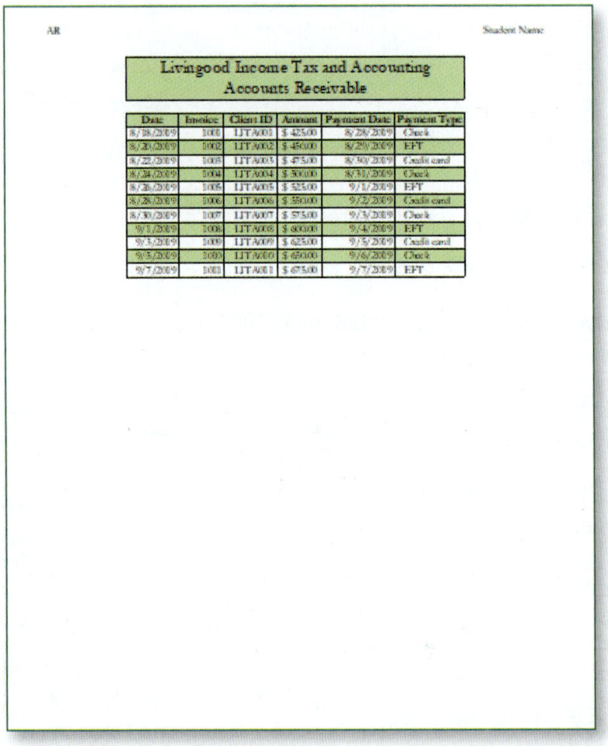

Figure 1-107 Excel 1-6 completed

Improve It Project 1-7

In this project, you complete a worksheet that maintains flight statistics for Boyd Air. The data has been imported from the reservation system, and you now need to add finishing touches.
[Student Learning Outcomes 1.1, 1.2, 1.3, 1.4, 1.5, 1.6, 1.7, 1.8]

File Needed: ***BoydAir-01.xlsx*** [*Student data files are available in the* Library *of your SIMnet account.*]
Completed Project File Name: ***[your initials] Excel 1-7.xlsx***

Skills Covered in This Project

- Open and save a workbook.
- Change the zoom level and remove a split.
- Enter and merge and center labels.
- Insert a row and set column width.
- Format data.
- Use *SUM.*
- Apply cell styles.
- Rename and color the sheet tab.
- Adjust page layout options.
- Add document properties.

---

1. Open the workbook ***BoydAir-01.xlsx*** from your student data files. If the workbook opens in *Protected View*, click **Enable Editing** in the security bar.
2. Save the workbook as [your initials] Excel 1-7.
3. Remove the split from the window.
4. Type Boyd Air in cell **A1** and Flight Statistics in cell **A2**.
5. Merge and center the labels in cells **A1** and **A2**. Change the font size for both labels to **16**.
6. Insert a row at row **3**.
7. Center and bold the labels in row **4**. *AutoFit* columns to show each label in row 4.
8. Change the zoom size to **100%**.
9. Select cells **B5:D18**, press **Ctrl**, and select cells **G5:G18**. Increase the indent one time.
10. Apply **All Borders** for cells **A4:H19**.
11. Calculate the total number of passengers in cell **H19**.
12. Apply the **Orange, Accent2** cell style to cells **A3:H3** and cells **A20:H20**.
13. Select cells **A3:H3** and **A20:H20** and apply **Outside Borders**.
14. Modify page layout options.
    a. Change the orientation to **Landscape**.
    b. Center the worksheet horizontally on the page.
    c. Show the file name in the left header section.
    d. Type your first and last name in the right header section.
15. Name the sheet tab Feb-Mar and format the tab color as **Orange, Accent2** (sixth column).
16. Set the document properties to show your first and last name as the *Author*. In the *Title* field, type Flight Stats.
17. Preview your worksheet.
18. Save and close the workbook (Figure 1-108).

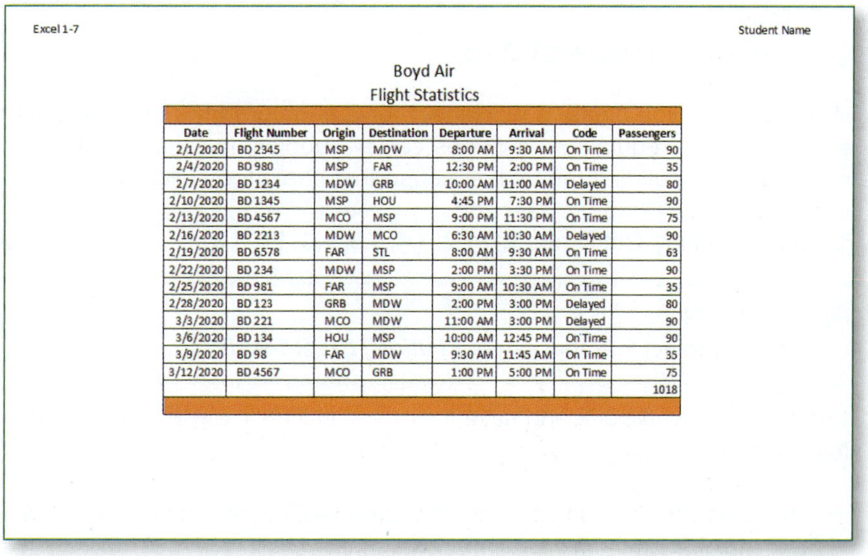
Excel 1-7 Student Name

Boyd Air
Flight Statistics

Date	Flight Number	Origin	Destination	Departure	Arrival	Code	Passengers
2/1/2020	BD 2345	MSP	MDW	8:00 AM	9:30 AM	On Time	90
2/4/2020	BD 980	MSP	FAR	12:30 PM	2:00 PM	On Time	35
2/7/2020	BD 1234	MDW	GRB	10:00 AM	11:00 AM	Delayed	80
2/10/2020	BD 1345	MSP	HOU	4:45 PM	7:30 PM	On Time	90
2/13/2020	BD 4567	MCO	MSP	9:00 PM	11:30 PM	On Time	75
2/16/2020	BD 2213	MDW	MCO	6:30 AM	10:30 AM	Delayed	90
2/19/2020	BD 6578	FAR	STL	8:00 AM	9:30 AM	On Time	63
2/22/2020	BD 234	MDW	MSP	2:00 PM	3:30 PM	On Time	90
2/25/2020	BD 981	FAR	MSP	9:00 AM	10:30 AM	On Time	35
2/28/2020	BD 123	GRB	MDW	2:00 PM	3:00 PM	Delayed	80
3/3/2020	BD 221	MCO	MDW	11:00 AM	3:00 PM	Delayed	90
3/6/2020	BD 134	HOU	MSP	10:00 AM	12:45 PM	On Time	90
3/9/2020	BD 98	FAR	MDW	9:30 AM	11:45 AM	On Time	35
3/12/2020	BD 4567	MCO	GRB	1:00 PM	5:00 PM	On Time	75
							1018

Figure 1-108 Excel 1-7 completed

Challenge Project 1-8

In this project, you create a workbook that lists and tracks candy and beverage sales at a gourmet chocolate store for selected holidays or special events. You enter and format the data and then finalize the workbook for distribution.
[Student Learning Outcomes 1.1, 1.2, 1.3, 1.4, 1.5, 1.6, 1.8]

File Needed: None
Completed Project File Name: ***[your initials] Excel 1-8.xlsx***

Create a new workbook and save it as [your initials] Excel 1-8. Modify your workbook according to the following guidelines:

- Choose a workbook theme.
- Determine and type a name for the store in cell **A1**. In cell **A2**, type Sales by Holiday.
- Starting in cell **B3**, type the names of four chocolate candies and one chocolate beverage (cells B3:F3).
- Type the names of five holidays, celebrations, or special events in cells **A4:A8**.
- Fill in values to reflect dollar or unit sales, and format these values appropriately.
- Calculate a total for each holiday and a total for each candy or beverage. Add labels for these totals.
- Use cell styles, borders, fill color, or other formatting to design your worksheet.
- *AutoFit* columns and adjust row heights as needed.
- Insert a footer that includes your name in one section and the date in another section.
- Use portrait orientation and fit the worksheet to a single page. Center it horizontally.
- Name the sheet tab and set a tab color.
- Enter the company name in the *Title* field in the document properties.

Challenge Project 1-9

In this project, you create a worksheet for a photography club that rents retail space for selling used equipment. The equipment includes camera bodies, lenses, tripods, cases, accessories, books, and more. You are building the worksheet so that expected selling prices can be entered each month for each item.
[Student Learning Outcomes 1.1, 1.2, 1.4, 1.5, 1.6, 1.7, 1.8]

File Needed: None
Completed Project File Name: ***[your initials] Excel 1-9.xlsx***

Create a new workbook and save it as [your initials] Excel 1-9. Modify your workbook according to the following guidelines:

- Create and type a name for the photography club as a main label. As a second label, type a label that specifies the purpose of the worksheet.
- Type Jan in cell **B3**. Fill the months to **Dec** in column **M**.

- In cells **A4:A13**, type the names of ten items related to any type of photography equipment. Research a web site that sells similar items.
- As the January price for the first item, type a realistic value as a resale price. For the February price, type a value that is a few dollars more than the January price. Select these two cells to identify a pattern and fill prices for the remaining months.
- Repeat the tasks in the previous step for each of the ten items to fill in values for all the items.
- Use cell styles, borders, fill color, or other formatting to design the worksheet.
- Adjust column widths and row heights.
- Insert a header that includes your name in the right section.
- Use landscape orientation and fit the worksheet to a single page.
- Enter the club's name in the *Author* field in the document properties pane.
- Name the worksheet tab and choose a tab color.
- Split the sheet at cell **G1**. Arrange the data so that you see cell **A1** in each window.

Challenge Project 1-10

In this project, you create a spreadsheet that details your expected monthly income and expenses. [Student Learning Outcomes 1.1, 1.2, 1.3, 1.4, 1.5, 1.6, 1.8]

File Needed: None
Completed Project File Name: ***[your initials] Excel 1-10.xlsx***

Create a new workbook and save it as [your initials] Excel 1-10. Modify your workbook according to the following guidelines:

- Type the main label Expected Monthly Income and Estimated Expenses. Type your name as a second label.
- Type Income in cell **A3**. In cells **A4:A7**, enter labels for four categories of income. For example, you may have regular wages from one or more jobs, interest from a certificate of deposit, rent from property that you own, income from internet sales, etc. Include descriptive labels, enter values in cells **B4:B7**, and include an income calculation using *SUM* in cell **B8**.
- Type Expenses in cell **D3**. In cells **D4:D9**, enter labels for six categories of expenses. These include rent, a mortgage payment, insurance, loan payments, food, clothing, entertainment, transportation, and so on. Complete labels, enter values in cells **E4:E9**, and use *SUM* to calculate total expenses in cell **E10**.
- Format the data with borders, fill color, font styles, and number formats. Adjust page layout options so that the sheet fits on a single portrait page.
- Spell check the sheet.
- Name the sheet Jan and choose a tab color.
- Copy the sheet and name the copy Feb. Choose a different tab color.
- Delete the expense amounts on the *Feb* sheet.
- Copy the *Feb* sheet to create a worksheet for March.
- Add document properties to identify the workbook.

Source of screenshots Microsoft Office 365 (2019): Word, Excel, Access, Powerpoint.

CHAPTER

2

Working with Formulas and Functions

CHAPTER OVERVIEW

With its capabilities in mathematical, scientific, engineering, and other calculations, Excel is a valuable tool for business, government, education, and you. Use Excel to create a simple addition formula or a sophisticated calculation with layers of arithmetic. In this chapter, you learn how to build a basic formula and how to use mathematical rules. You also explore Excel function categories.

STUDENT LEARNING OUTCOMES (SLOs)

After completing this chapter, you will be able to:

SLO 2.1 Build and edit basic formulas (p. E2-89).

SLO 2.2 Set the mathematical order of operations in a formula (p. E2-91).

SLO 2.3 Use absolute, mixed, relative, and 3D references in a formula (p. E2-93).

SLO 2.4 Use formula auditing tools in a worksheet (p. E2-99).

SLO 2.5 Work with *Statistical* and *Date & Time* functions (p. E2-106).

SLO 2.6 Work with functions from the *Financial*, *Logical*, and *Lookup & Reference* categories (p. E2-114).

SLO 2.7 Build functions from the *Math & Trig* category (p. E2-122).

CASE STUDY

In the Pause & Practice projects in this chapter, you work with a multi-sheet workbook for Paradise Lakes Resort (PLR), the northern Minnesota chain of resorts. You build formulas to complete a simple income statement, to calculate data for the boutique division, and to track information about the youth camp.

Pause & Practice 2-1: Build and audit formulas in a worksheet.

Pause & Practice 2-2: Insert *Statistical* and *Date & Time* functions in a workbook.

Pause & Practice 2-3: Use *Financial*, *Logical*, *Lookup*, and *Math & Trig* functions in a workbook.

EXCEL

SLO 2.1

Building and Editing a Formula

An Excel ***formula*** is an expression or statement that uses common arithmetic operations to perform a calculation. Basic arithmetic operations are addition, subtraction, multiplication, and division. The formula is entered in a cell and refers to other cells or ranges in the worksheet or workbook. The formula appears in the *Formula* bar, but the results appear in the cell.

You learned in Chapter 1 that a function is a built-in formula. Like a function, a formula begins with an equals sign (=). After the equals sign, you enter the address of the first cell, followed by the arithmetic operator, followed by the next cell in the calculation. An example of a simple addition formula is **=B5 +B6** which adds the values in cells B5 and B6.

Basic arithmetic operators are listed in Table 2-1. Enter arithmetic operators using the numeric keypad or the symbols on the number keys at the top of the keyboard.

In the multiplication formula **=C5*C6**, the value in cell C5 is multiplied by the value in cell C6. Use cell references in a formula or a value known as a ***constant***. In the formula **=D5*85%**, the constant is 85%.

Table 2-1: Arithmetic Operators

Character	Operation
+	Addition
–	Subtraction
*	Multiplication
/	Division

Type a Formula

For a simple formula, type it. Click the cell, type the equals sign, type the first cell address, type the operator, type the next cell address, and so on. Press any completion key when the formula is finished. Formulas are not case sensitive, so you can type cell addresses in lowercase letters. Excel automatically converts cell references to uppercase when the formula is completed. If you press **Esc** before completing a formula, it is canceled and nothing is entered in the cell.

As you type a cell address after the equals sign, ***Formula AutoComplete*** displays a list of functions and range names that match the character that you typed. You can ignore the list and continue typing. In addition, the ***Range Finder*** highlights and color codes each cell as you type its address.

HOW TO: Type a Formula

1. Click the cell for the formula.
2. Type an equals sign (=) to begin the formula.
3. Type the column letter for the first cell reference (Figure 2-1).
    - *Formula AutoComplete* displays a list of functions and range names.
    - You can type a lowercase or uppercase character.
4. Type the row number for the cell reference.
    - The *Range Finder* color codes the cell and its reference.
5. Type the arithmetic operator.
6. Type the cell address for the next reference.

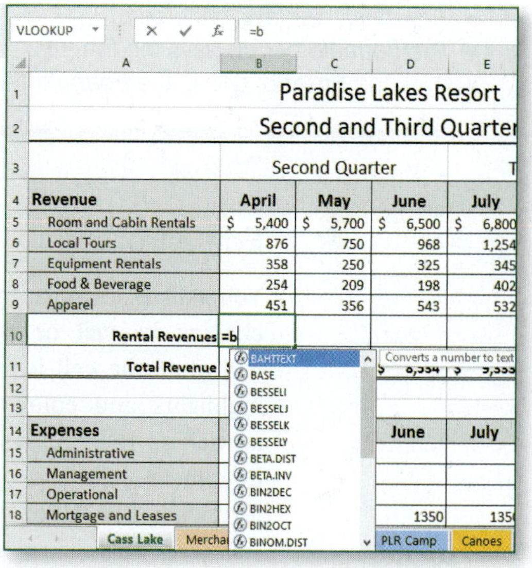

Figure 2-1 *Formula AutoComplete* while typing a formula

7. Press **Enter**.
   - The result displays in the cell where the formula is located (Figure 2-2).
   - The *Formula* bar displays the formula.
   - One way to complete a formula is to click the **Enter** button (the check mark) in the *Formula* bar.
   - Press **Ctrl+Enter** to complete a formula.

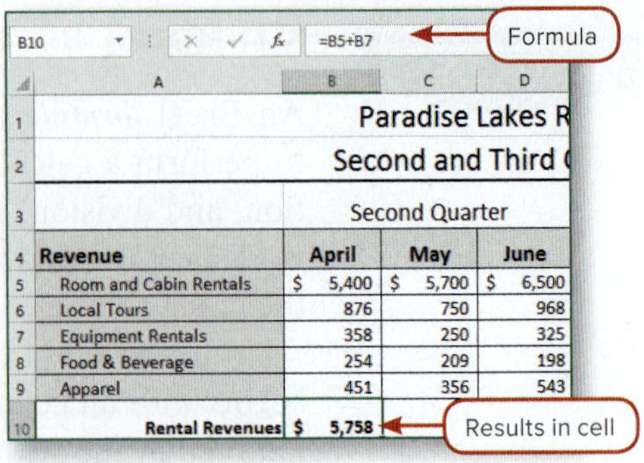

Figure 2-2 Formula and result

Point and Click to Build a Formula

Instead of typing a cell address, you can point to and click the cell to enter its address in a formula. This method guards against your typing the wrong address. You will not see a *Formula AutoComplete* list, but the *Range Finder* will highlight and color code the cells.

HOW TO: Point and Click to Build a Formula

1. Click the cell for the formula.
2. Type an equals sign (=) to start the formula.
3. Point to and click the first cell for the formula.
   - The reference is entered in the cell and in the *Formula* bar.
   - The *Range Finder* highlights and color codes the reference.
   - If you click the wrong cell, click the correct cell to replace the address.
4. Type the arithmetic operator.
5. Point to and click the next cell for the formula (Figure 2-3).
   - The reference is entered in the cell and in the *Formula* bar.
   - The *Range Finder* highlights and color codes the reference.
6. Press **Enter**.
   - The result displays in the cell.
   - The *Formula* bar displays the formula.
   - Click the **Enter** button in the *Formula* bar or press **Ctrl+Enter** to complete a formula.

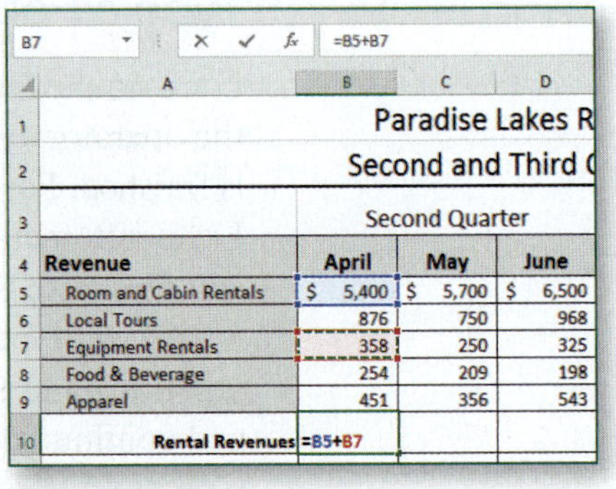

Figure 2-3 Point and click to build a formula

Edit a Formula

You edit a formula in *Edit* mode by double-clicking its cell or by clicking the *Formula* bar while the cell is active. The *Range Finder* highlights and color codes the formula cell as well as the cells used in the formula. Add or remove cells and operators to build a new formula in the cell or in the *Formula* bar.

ANOTHER WAY

Click the cell and press **F2 (FN+F2)** to start *Edit* mode.

HOW TO: Edit a Formula

1. Double-click the formula cell.
   - The *Range Finder* highlights and color codes the cells.
2. Edit the formula in the cell (Figure 2-4).
   - Edit the cell address or type a different operator.
   - Select a cell address and click a different cell to replace the reference.
   - Use the *Formula* bar to edit a formula.
3. Press **Enter**.
   - Click the **Enter** button in the *Formula* bar or press **Ctrl+Enter** to complete a formula.

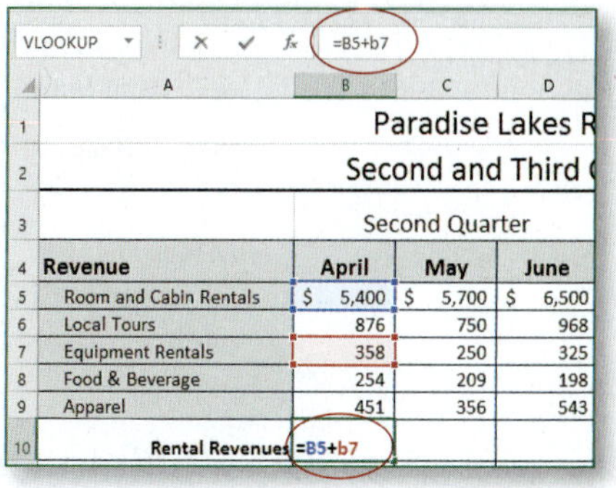

Figure 2-4 Edit a formula in the cell

SLO 2.2

Setting Mathematical Order of Operations

A formula can have more than one operator, such as a combination of addition and multiplication. Figure 2-5 illustrates two formulas a restaurant might use to calculate a bill for a couple who ordered the same items. The formula in cell B6 lists the additions first and multiplies by 2; the total of $24 is incorrect. The formula in cell B8 is the same except for the parentheses; the correct amount is $42.

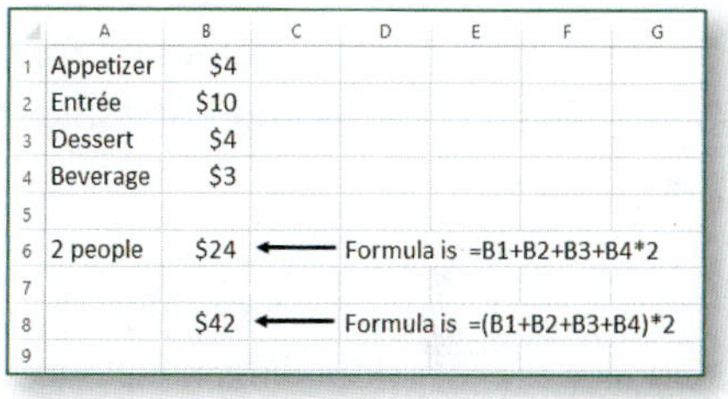

Figure 2-5 Formulas with multiple operators

Excel follows ***mathematical order of operations***, which is the sequence of arithmetic calculations. The order in which the mathematics in a formula is carried out depends on the operator, as well as left-to-right order. The basic sequence is left to right, but multiplication and division are done before addition and subtraction. This concept is also known as ***order of precedence*** or ***math hierarchy***.

You control the order of operations with parentheses. The formula in cell B8 (see Figure 2-5) uses parentheses to reorder the calculation. The parentheses group the addition ($4+$10+$4+$3 = 21) and multiply the result by 2 ($21*2 = $42).

In a formula with multiple operators, references enclosed in parentheses are calculated first. If a value with an exponent exists, it is calculated next. Multiplication and division follow, and finally addition and subtraction. When two operators have the same precedence, Excel calculates them from left to right.

Table 2-2: Mathematical Order of Precedence

Operator	Operation	Order of Precedence
()	Parentheses	First
^	Exponent	Second
*	Multiplication	Third
/	Division	Third
+	Addition	Fourth
–	Subtraction	Fourth

> **MORE INFO**
>
> Use a popular acronym to recall the arithmetic order of operations: **Please Excuse My Dear Aunt Sally.**

Exponents raise a number to a power. The formula **3^3** multiplies 3 * 3 * 3, 27. Use the caret symbol (**^**) to build a formula with an exponent.

Multiple Operators in a Formula

When different operators are used in a formula, you must determine how the calculation should be completed and if parentheses are necessary to set the proper order. Here are formulas with two operators. Because addition and subtraction are equal in priority, Excel calculates from left to right.

$$5 + 1 - 3 = 3 \qquad 5 - 1 + 3 = 7$$

Below are formulas with two operators with different priority. Excel calculates the multiplication first and then follows left to right order.

$$2 + 5 * 3 = 17 \qquad 2 * 5 + 3 = 13$$

Consider this formula with three different operators. Because multiplication and division are equal priority but are higher than addition, the multiplication is first, followed by the division (left to right). The result of those calculations is added to 5.

$$=2 * 5/2 + 5 = 10$$

▸HOW TO: Use Multiple Operators in a formula

1. Type = to start the formula.
2. Type ((left parenthesis) to start the calculation that should have priority.
   - The calculation in parentheses can occur anywhere in the formula.
3. Click the first cell for the calculation to be enclosed in parentheses.
4. Type the arithmetic operator.
5. Click the next cell for the calculation to be enclosed in parentheses.
6. Type) (right parenthesis) to end the calculation with priority (Figure 2-6).
   - You must have matching parentheses.
7. Complete the formula.
8. Press **Enter**.

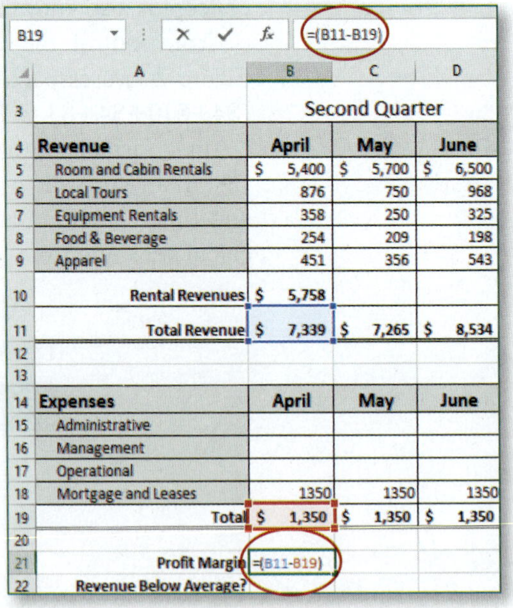
B19 =(B11-B19)

	A	B	C	D
3		Second Quarter		
4	Revenue	April	May	June
5	Room and Cabin Rentals	$ 5,400	$ 5,700	$ 6,500
6	Local Tours	876	750	968
7	Equipment Rentals	358	250	325
8	Food & Beverage	254	209	198
9	Apparel	451	356	543
10	Rental Revenues	$ 5,758		
11	Total Revenue	$ 7,339	$ 7,265	$ 8,534
12				
13				
14	Expenses	April	May	June
15	Administrative			
16	Management			
17	Operational			
18	Mortgage and Leases	1350	1350	1350
19	Total	$ 1,350	$ 1,350	$ 1,350
20				
21	Profit Margin	=(B11-B19)		
22	Revenue Below Average?			

Figure 2-6 Set the order of operations with parentheses

SLO 2.3

Using Absolute, Mixed, Relative, and 3D References

Cell references in a formula are identified in different ways. How a cell reference is identified affects how the formula is adjusted when it is copied.

- A ***relative cell reference*** is the location of a cell, such as cell **B2**. In column B, the formula is **=B5+B7**, but when copied to column C, it is **=C5+C7**. When you copy a formula with relative references, copied references are updated to the new locations.
- An ***absolute cell reference*** is indicated with dollar signs as in cell **$B$2**. When an absolute reference is copied, it does not change. In the formula **=$B$6–C7**, $B$6 would not change when copied anywhere in the workbook. C7, on the other hand, would reflect where the copy is located. You can type the dollar signs in an absolute reference, but it is easier to use the **F4** (**FN+F4**) function key. When building a formula, enter the cell address and then press **F4** (**FN+F4**).
- A ***mixed cell reference*** has one relative and one absolute reference. Cell **$B2** is a mixed reference. When it is copied, it always refers to column B, but the row number updates to the row where the copy is located. The formula **=$B5+C$6** has two mixed references. When copied, this formula will always show column B for the first address and row 6 for the second address.
- A ***3D cell reference*** is a cell located in another worksheet in the same workbook. It can be absolute, mixed, or relative. A 3D reference includes the name of the sheet as in **Sheet2!B2** or **Inventory!$B2**. The sheet name is followed by an exclamation point. When you point and click to build a 3D reference, the sheet name and the exclamation point are automatically entered. When the sheet name includes special characters (@, #, &, etc.), the name is enclosed in single quotes as in **'Inventory#'!$B2**. When you type a 3D reference, you must spell the sheet name correctly and include the exclamation point and single quotes.

Table 2-3 illustrates each cell reference type:

Table 2-3: Cell Reference Types

Cell Reference	Reference Type	Behavior When Copied
B2	Relative	Cell address updates to new location(s).
$B$2	Absolute	Cell address does not change.
$B2	Mixed	Column does not change; row updates to new location(s).
B$2	Mixed	Row does not change; column updates to new location(s).
Sheet2!B2	3D Relative	Cell address updates to new location(s).

MORE INFO

When used in a reference, the dollar sign ($) and the exclamation point (!) are identifiers. The dollar sign is not treated as a currency symbol, and the exclamation point is not considered punctuation.

Copy a Formula with a Relative Reference

When a formula with relative references is copied, the copied formulas use cell addresses that reflect their locations in the worksheet. In the Paradise Lakes worksheet shown in Figure 2-7, the formula to calculate rental revenue in cell B10 is **=B5+B7**. The formula for cell C10 is **=C5+C7**. The formula in cell B10 can be copied to cells C10:G10 and will automatically adjust for each column.

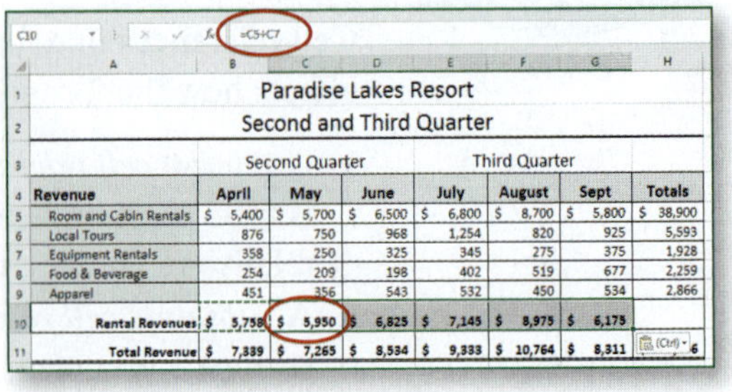

Figure 2-7 Copy a formula with a relative reference

▸HOW TO: Copy a Formula with a Relative Reference

1. Select the cell with the formula.
   - Select multiple adjacent cells.
2. Press **Ctrl+C** to copy the formula(s).
   - Click and drag the *Fill* pointer if the copies are adjacent to the original formula(s).
   - Use the **Copy** button on the *Home* tab if you prefer.
3. Select the destination cell or range.
   - Click the first cell in a destination range when pasting multiple cells.
4. Press **Ctrl+V** to paste the formula (see Figure 2-7).
   - The pasted formula reflects its location on the worksheet.
   - Ignore the **Paste Options** button.
   - Use the **Paste** button on the *Home* tab if you prefer.
5. Press **Esc** to cancel the **Paste** command.

Build and Copy a Formula with an Absolute Reference

An absolute reference in a formula maintains that address when copied. An example is a worksheet in which expenses are calculated as a percentage of revenue. You type the percentage once in a worksheet cell, use an absolute reference to that cell in the first occurrence of the formula, and copy the formula.

To change a cell address to an absolute reference, press the **F4 (FN+F4)** function key while keying or editing the formula. The first press of the key inserts dollar signs for the row and column reference. Another press of the **F4 (FN+F4)** key changes to a mixed reference, and each press of the key cycles to the next option.

▸HOW TO: Build and Copy a Formula with an Absolute Reference

1. Click the cell for the formula.
2. Type an equals sign (=) to begin the formula.
3. Click the cell to be referenced in the formula.
4. Press **F4** (**FN+F4**).
   - The reference becomes absolute (Figure 2-8).
5. Complete the formula and press **Enter**.

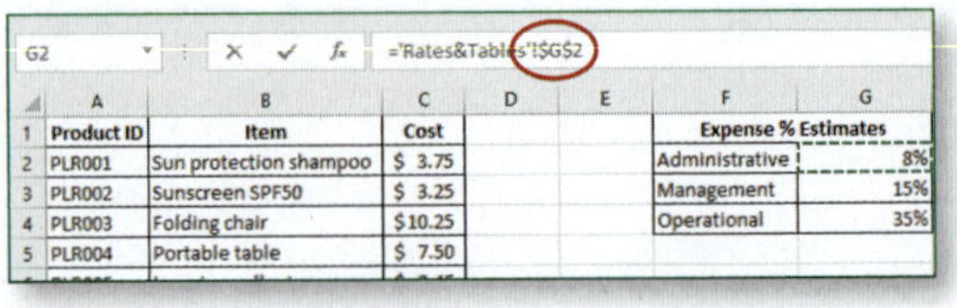

Figure 2-8 Make a reference absolute

6. Select the cell with the formula.
7. Press **Ctrl+C** to copy the formula(s).
    - Use the **Copy** button on the *Home* tab if you prefer.
    - Click and drag the *Fill* pointer if the copies are adjacent to the original formula.
8. Select the destination cell or range.
9. Press **Ctrl+V** to paste the formula.
    - The pasted formula uses the same cell reference as the original.
    - Use the **Paste** button on the *Home* tab if you prefer.
    - Ignore the **Paste Options** button.

MORE INFO

When you type a constant in a formula, such as **=B7*12**, the constant (12) is treated as an absolute value.

Build and Copy a Formula with a Mixed Reference

A mixed cell reference has one relative and one absolute reference in the cell address. Part of the copied formula is unchanged and part is updated. A mixed reference has one dollar sign. You still use the **F4 (FN+F4)** function key, because each press of the function key cycles through different combinations for displaying the dollar signs.

HOW TO: Build and Copy a Formula with a Mixed Reference

1. Click the cell for the formula.
2. Type an equals sign (**=**) to begin the formula.
3. Click the cell to be referenced in the formula.
4. Press **F4** (**FN+F4**).
    - The reference is absolute.
5. Press **F4** (**FN+F4**) again.
    - The column reference is relative and the row reference is absolute.
6. Press **F4** (**FN+F4**) again (Figure 2-9).
    - The row reference is relative and the column reference is absolute.
7. Complete the formula and press **Enter**.
8. Select the formula cell.
9. Press **Ctrl+C** to copy the formula(s).
    - You can use the **Copy** button on the *Home* tab.
    - Drag the *Fill* pointer if copies are adjacent to the original formula.
10. Click the destination cell or range.
11. Press **Ctrl+V** to paste the formula.
    - The pasted formula does not change the absolute part of the reference but updates the relative part.
    - Use the **Paste** button on the *Home* tab if you prefer.

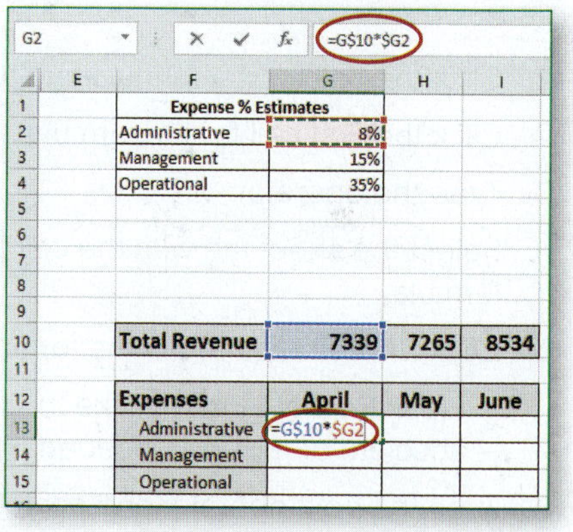

Figure 2-9 Formula with mixed references

Create a Formula with a 3D Reference

An important feature of an Excel workbook is being able to refer to data on any sheet in a formula. This type of formula is called a ***3D reference***, because it uses more than one sheet or surface to calculate a result.

A 3D reference includes the name of the worksheet and can be absolute, mixed, or relative.

Table 2-4: Sample 3D References

Cell on Sheet1	Formula on Sheet1	Results
B4	=B3+Sheet2!B3+Sheet3!B3	Adds the values in cell B3 on Sheet1, Sheet2, and Sheet3.
B7	=SUM(B4:B6)+Sheet2!A12	Adds the values in cells B4:B6 on Sheet1 to the value in cell A12 on Sheet2.
C8	=C7*Sheet2!$D$4	Multiplies the value in cell C7 by the value in cell D4 on Sheet2.
D10	=Sheet2!$B$2/Sheet3!B2	Divides the value in cell B2 on Sheet2 by the value in cell B2 on Sheet3.

MORE INFO

An external reference formula refers to a cell in another workbook. It can be absolute, mixed, or relative. An external reference includes the name of the workbook in square brackets as in **[PLRSales]Sheet!B$2**.

HOW TO: Create a Formula with a 3D Reference

1. Click the cell for the formula and type **=**.
2. Click the first cell for the formula.
3. Type the operator.
4. Select the sheet tab with the cell to be used in the formula.
5. Click the cell required in the formula.
   - Press **F4** (**FN+F4**) to make the reference absolute or mixed as needed (Figure 2-10).
6. Type the next operator and complete the formula as needed.
   - The next cell can be on the same or another sheet.
7. Press **Enter** or any completion key.

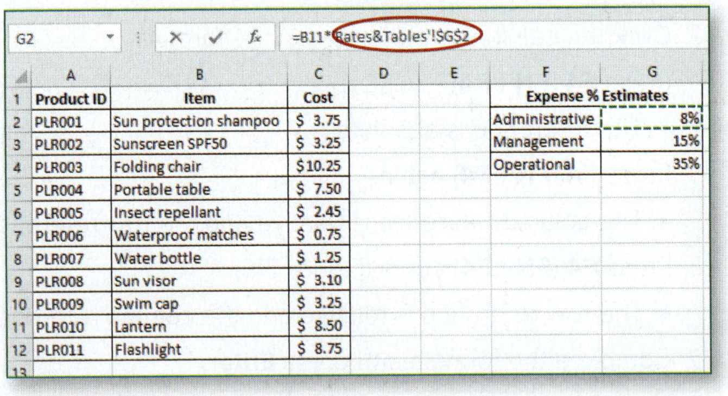
G2 =B11*Rates&Tables'!$G$2

	A	B	C	D	E	F	G
1	Product ID	Item	Cost			Expense % Estimates	
2	PLR001	Sun protection shampoo	$ 3.75			Administrative	8%
3	PLR002	Sunscreen SPF50	$ 3.25			Management	15%
4	PLR003	Folding chair	$10.25			Operational	35%
5	PLR004	Portable table	$ 7.50				
6	PLR005	Insect repellant	$ 2.45				
7	PLR006	Waterproof matches	$ 0.75				
8	PLR007	Water bottle	$ 1.25				
9	PLR008	Sun visor	$ 3.10				
10	PLR009	Swim cap	$ 3.25				
11	PLR010	Lantern	$ 8.50				
12	PLR011	Flashlight	$ 8.75				

Figure 2-10 3D cell reference

Range Names and Formula AutoComplete

A ***range name*** is a label assigned to a single cell or a group of cells. You can use range names instead of cell references in a formula. Instead of **=B11*10%**, name cell B11 as "Revenue" to build the formula **=Revenue*10%**. Descriptive range names help you interpret a formula.

In addition, named cell ranges appear in the *Formula AutoComplete* list for ease in building formulas. A named cell range is an absolute reference in a formula.

You create a range name using the *Name* box or from the *Defined Names* group on the *Formulas* tab. The *Name Manager* command in this group enables you to create, edit, and delete range names. If you alter a range name, Excel automatically updates formulas that use that range name. The *Apply Names* command (*Define Name* button) enables you to assign a name to existing formulas that refer to the cells identified in the range name.

Follow these basic rules for naming a cell range:

- Begin a range name with a letter.
- Use a short, descriptive name.
- Do not use spaces or special characters in a range name.
- Separate words in a range name with an underscore as in "First_Qtr," or use initial caps for each word such as "FirstQtr."
- Do not name a range with a single character such as "N."
- Do not name a range with a cell reference such as "B2."

To use the name in a formula, type the first character of the name to display the *Formula AutoComplete* list. You may need to type a second character to see the name in a workbook that includes many range names. Select the range name in the list and press **Tab**, or double-click the name to enter it in the formula. Range names are automatically substituted in formulas when you select the named cell range in the worksheet while building a formula.

▸HOW TO: Name a Range and Use Formula AutoComplete

1. Select the cell or range to be named.
2. Click the **Name** box at the left of the *Formula* bar.
3. Type the name and press **Enter** (Figure 2-11).
4. Click the cell for the formula.
5. Type = to start the formula.
6. Type the first one or two letters of the range name.
   - The *Formula AutoComplete* list shows range and function names.
   - The list is alphabetical, and function names are uppercase.
7. Find the range name and double-click it (Figure 2-12).
   - The name is inserted in the formula.
   - You can also click the name in the list to highlight it and press **Tab**.
8. Complete the formula.
9. Press **Enter** when the formula is complete.

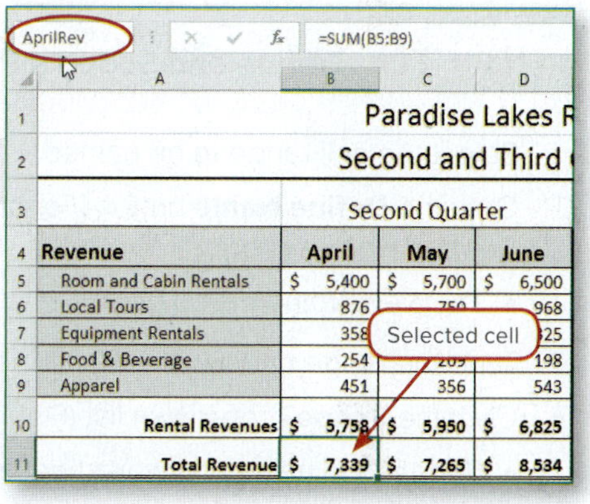

Figure 2-11 Name a range in the *Name* box

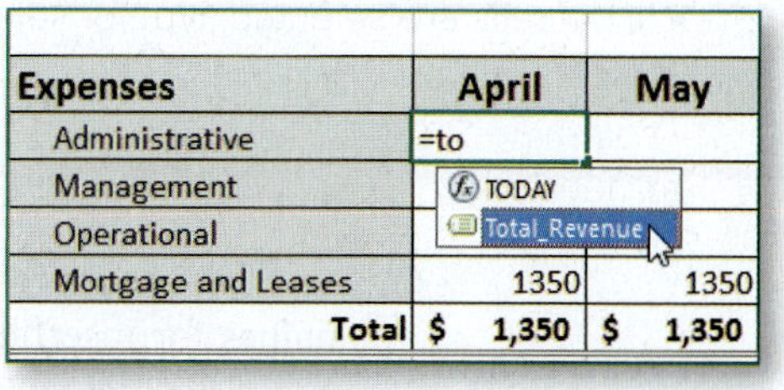

Figure 2-12 Use *Formula AutoComplete* with a range name

In addition to selecting cell ranges to name them, use row and column labels to create range names. The *Create from Selection* button on the *Formulas* tab automatically assigns range names based on labels in the top row, the left column, or both.

▸HOW TO: Create Names from a Selection

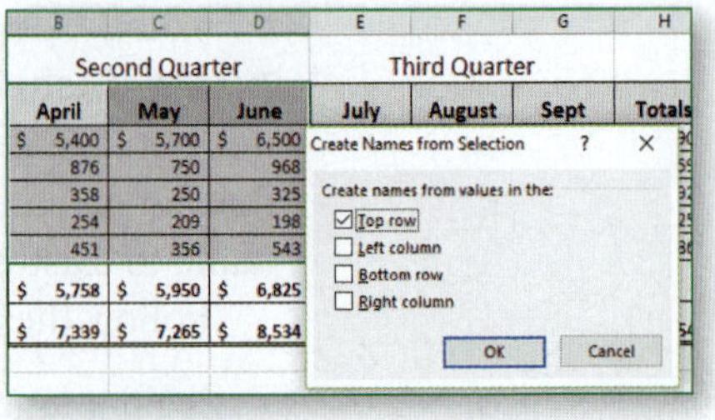

Figure 2-13 ***Create Names from Selection* dialog box**

1. Select the range including row or column labels (or both) (Figure 2-13).
   - Values and related labels must be adjacent.
2. Click the **Create from Selection** button [*Formulas* tab, *Defined Names* group].
   - The *Create Names from Selection* dialog box opens.
3. Select the **Top row** or **Left column** box.
   - Choose both options if appropriate for the data.
   - Other options include bottom row and right column.
4. Click **OK**.
5. Click the **Name box** arrow in the *Formula* bar.
   - All range names are listed.

The **Define Name** button [*Formulas* tab, *Defined Names* group] opens the *New Name* dialog box. Type the name, enter a comment, select the cells, and specify a ***scope***. The scope determines if the range applies to a particular sheet or to the entire workbook. By default, a range name applies to the workbook. If you use the name "JanSales" on Sheet1, you cannot use it again on Sheet2, unless you scope each name to a particular sheet. When you scope names to a worksheet, you can use the name multiple times in the workbook.

▸HOW TO: Define and Scope a Range Name

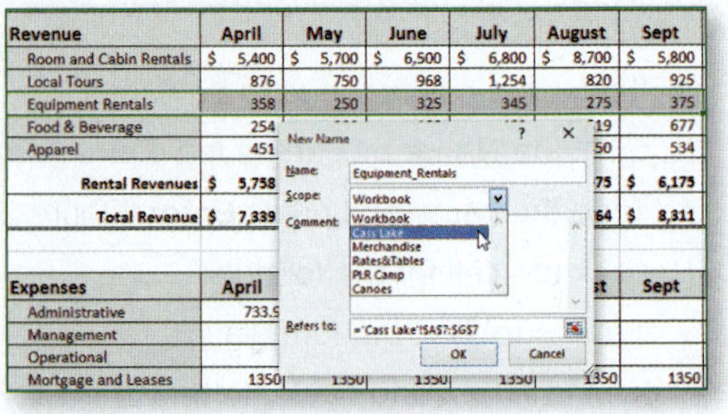

Figure 2-14 ***New Name* dialog box and the *Scope* list**

1. Select the cell range to be named.
2. Click the **Define Name** button [*Formulas* tab, *Defined Names* group].
   - The *New Name* dialog box opens.
3. Type the range name in the *Name* box.
4. Click the **Scope** drop-down list (Figure 2-14).
   - Choose the name of a worksheet as desired.
5. Select or edit the *Refers to* entry.
   - The selected cell range address displays.
   - If no cells are selected, type or select the range address.
6. Click **OK**.

The *Use in Formula* button [*Formulas* tab, *Defined Names* group] displays a list of range names for insertion in a formula. You can also display a list of range names using the *Paste Name* dialog box. Press the **F3** (**FN+F3**) function key to open the *Paste Name* dialog box.

▸HOW TO: Paste a Range Name in a Formula and Paste a List

1. Click the formula cell and type =.
2. Press **F3** (**FN+F3**) to open the *Paste Name* dialog box.
   - Range names appear in alphabetical order.

3. Find the range name and double-click it (Figure 2-15).
    - Select the range name and press **Enter** or click **OK**.
    - The range name displays in the formula.
    - The worksheet displays the highlighted range.
4. Complete the formula and press **Enter**.
5. Click a blank cell in an unused area of the worksheet.
    - Select a cell on another worksheet.
6. Click the **Use in Formula** button [*Formulas* tab, *Defined Names* group].
7. Select **Paste Names**.
    - The *Paste Name* dialog box opens.
8. Click **Paste List**.
    - A list of range names and cell references is pasted.
    - You can edit and format the list of range names.

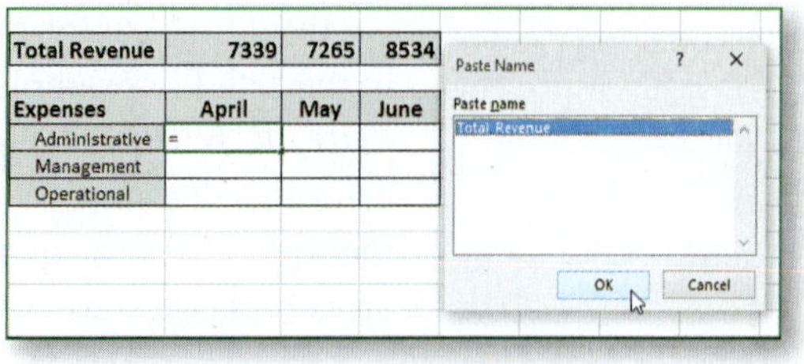

Figure 2-15 Choose a range name for the formula

SLO 2.4

Using Formula Auditing Tools

Formula auditing is the process of reviewing formulas for accuracy. Excel automatically audits formulas as you enter them and when you open a workbook based on its error checking rules [*File* tab, *Options*, *Formulas* pane]. Excel recognizes many errors, but not all of them. For example, if you type a formula that multiplies the values in two cells when it should add the values, you must find that error on your own. You may encounter circumstances when Excel identifies an error but the formula is correct.

MORE INFO

Open the Excel *Options* dialog box to set whether automatic error checking is enabled and to select which rules are used.

When Excel finds an error in a formula, it displays a small green error triangle in the top-left corner of the cell. Click the cell to see the *Trace Error* button and point to the button to see a *ScreenTip* about the error. The *Trace Error* button has a drop-down list with options for dealing with the error.

HOW TO: Trace an Error

1. Click the cell with the triangle error.
    - The *Trace Error* button appears.
2. Point to the **Trace Error** button to display a *ScreenTip*.
3. Click the **Trace Error** drop-down list (Figure 2-16).
    - Options for handling the error display.
4. Choose an option for the error.
    - The options depend on the type of error.
    - Select **Ignore Error** if the formula is correct.

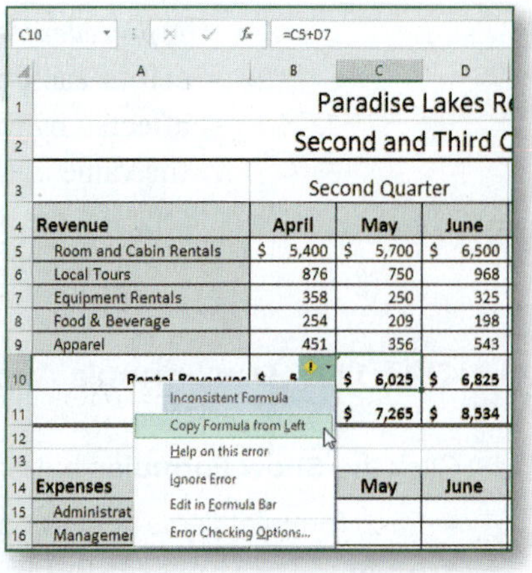

Figure 2-16 *Trace Error* button and its drop-down list

In addition to the green triangle error, Excel functions can result in a standard error message in the cell. For example, if you create a division formula that divides by a blank cell, the result is *#DIV/0!*. When you click the *Trace Error* button, it is identified as a division by zero error. Excel error messages occur for a syntax error, such as spelling a function name incorrectly, using an incorrect operator or symbol, having the wrong number of arguments, and so on. A standard error message starts with the number sign (**#**) and ends with an exclamation point (**!**).

> **MORE INFO**
>
> Use the *Go to Special* dialog box [*Find & Select* button, *Home* tab, *Editing* group] to highlight cells with formula errors, blank cells, and cells with precedents and dependents. This command helps identify potential problems in a workbook.

The Formula Auditing Group

The *Formula Auditing* group on the *Formulas* tab includes tools to check formulas for logic, consistency, and accuracy. These commands enable you to examine what contributes to a formula and to analyze if the formula is correct. The tools are helpful, but they do require that you correct the problem.

Table 2-5: Formula Auditing Buttons

Button	Description
Trace Precedents	Displays lines with arrows to identify all cells referenced in the formula in the active cell
Trace Dependents	Displays lines with arrows to all cells that use the active cell directly or indirectly in a formula
Remove Arrows	Removes all lines and arrows from the *Trace Precedents* or *Trace Dependents* buttons
Show Formulas	Displays formulas in the cells
Error Checking	Checks data against the error rules in Excel *Options*
Evaluate Formula	Steps through each part of a formula and displays an outcome for each part so that an error can be isolated
Watch Window	Opens a floating window that displays selected cells and values for monitoring

Trace Precedents and Dependents

A ***precedent*** is a cell that contributes to the formula results. Excel displays lines from the formula cell to each precedent cell for an easy way to audit your formula. A ***dependent*** is a cell that is affected by the active cell. Excel displays lines from the active cell to each cell that depends on the value in that cell. The lines may be blue or red, depending on the type of error identified, if any. If a precedent or dependent cell is located on a different worksheet, a black line and arrow point to a small worksheet icon, but this does not identify the actual error cell address.

HOW TO: Use Formula Auditing Tools

1. Click the **Show Formulas** button [*Formulas* tab, *Formula Auditing* group].
   - Each formula displays in its cell.
   - Show or hide formulas by pressing **Ctrl+`** (grave accent next to the 1 key at the top of the keyboard).
2. Select the formula cell.

3. Click the **Trace Precedents** button [*Formulas* tab, *Formula Auditing* group].
   - Lines and arrows identify cells that contribute to the formula results (Figure 2-17).
   - You can trace precedents and dependents with formulas shown or hidden.
4. Click the **Remove Arrows** button [*Formulas* tab, *Formula Auditing* group].
   - Clicking the button removes all arrows.
   - Click the **Remove Arrows** drop-down list to specify the type of arrow to remove.
5. Click a cell that is referenced in a formula.
   - The cell need not have a formula.
6. Click the **Trace Dependents** button [*Formulas* tab, *Formula Auditing* group].
   - Lines and arrows trace to cells that are affected by the active cell.
7. Click the **Remove Arrows** button [*Formulas* tab, *Formula Auditing* group].
8. Click the **Show Formulas** button [*Formulas* tab, *Formula Auditing* group].
   - Formulas are hidden.
   - Show or hide formulas by pressing **Ctrl+`**.

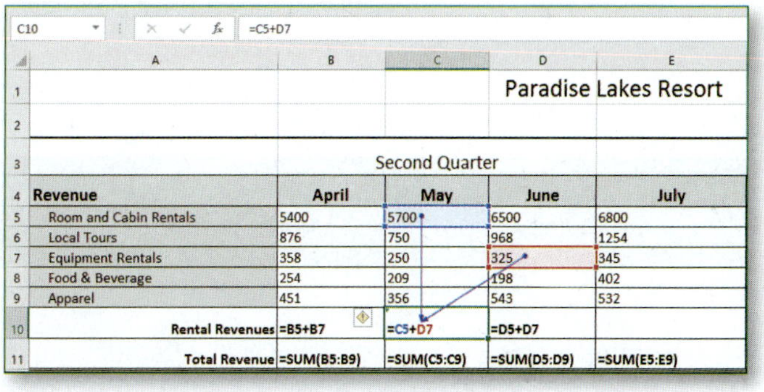

Figure 2-17 *Trace Precedents* **arrows with formulas shown**

> **MORE INFO**
>
> In a complex worksheet with sophisticated formulas, click the **Trace Precedents** button [*Formulas* tab, *Formula Auditing* group] once to trace the first layer of precedents. Then click the button again to trace the precedents of the precedents.

The Formula Correction Message Window

As you complete a formula with a minor error (for example, typing "5c" as a cell address), Excel displays a message box with information about the error (Figure 2-18). For many of these types of errors, review the suggested correction and select **Yes**. For an error that Excel finds but to which it cannot offer a solution, a message box opens with suggestions. However, you need to solve the problem on your own.

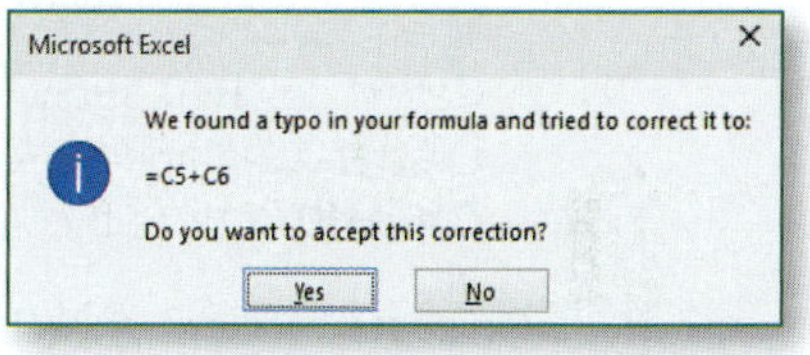

Figure 2-18 Formula correction message window

Circular Reference

A ***circular reference*** is an error that occurs when a formula includes the cell address of the formula. For example, if the formula in cell **B10** is **=B5+B10**, the reference is circular. When you try to complete such a formula, a message box opens as shown in Figure 2-19. The *Status* bar displays the location of circular references, but Excel does not correct this type of error. You can keep a circular reference in a worksheet, but the formula results are inaccurate.

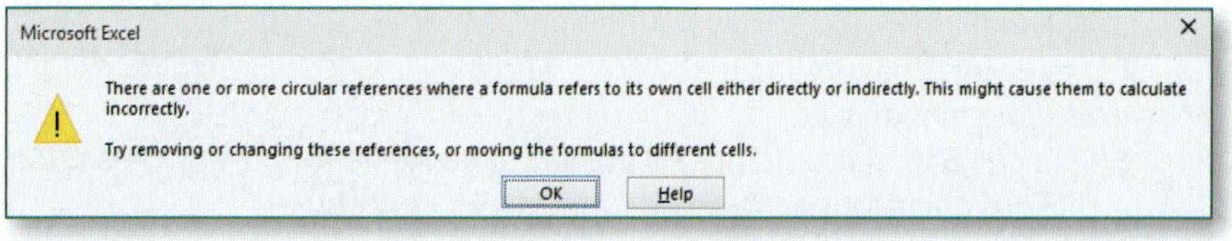

Figure 2-19 Circular reference and its message window

> **MORE INFO**
>
> A workbook can be saved with a circular reference. When you open it, you will see the message box, and the reference is noted in the *Status* bar.

PAUSE & PRACTICE: EXCEL 2-1

For this project, you build formulas in a Paradise Lakes Resort worksheet. You use mixed and absolute references, a 3D reference, and set an order of precedence. You also name cell ranges and use auditing tools.

File Needed: ***ParadiseLakes-02.xlsx*** *(Student data files are available in the* Library *of your SIMnet account.)*
Completed Project File Name: ***[your initials] PP E2-1.xlsx***

1. Open the ***ParadiseLakes-02.xlsx*** workbook from your student data files. (If the workbook opens in *Protected View*, click **Enable Editing**.)
2. Save the workbook as [your initials] PP E2-1.
3. Enter and copy an addition formula.
   a. Click cell **B10** on the **Cass Lake** sheet.
   b. Type **=** to start a formula.
   c. Click cell **B5** to insert the first rental item in the formula.
   d. Type **+** as the mathematical operator.
   e. Click cell **B7** to add the second rental item. The formula is **=B5+B7** (Figure 2-20).
   f. Press **Enter** or click the **Enter** button in the *Formula* bar. The result is $5,758.
   g. Select cell **B10** and point to the *Fill* handle.
   h. Drag the *Fill* pointer to copy the formula to cells **C10:H10**. Ignore the *Auto Fill Options* button.

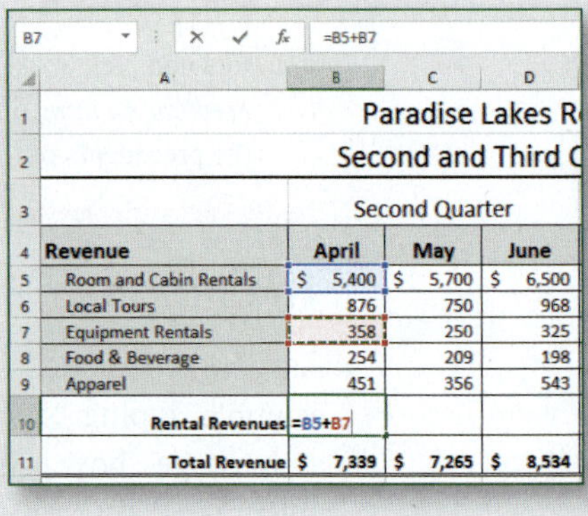

Figure 2-20 Point and click to build a formula

4. Create and copy a 3D formula with absolute cell references.
   a. Select cell **B15**. Administrative expense is calculated by multiplying the total revenue for the month by a set percentage.
   b. Type **=** to start the formula.
   c. Click cell **B11**, the total revenue for April.
   d. Type * to indicate multiplication.
   e. Click the **Rates&Tables** sheet tab. The sheet name is inserted in the *Formula* bar with single quotes and an exclamation point.
   f. Click cell **G2**, the percentage for administrative expenses. The cell address is added to the formula.
   g. Press **F4** (**FN+F4**) to make the reference absolute (Figure 2-21).
   h. Press **Enter**. The formula is complete and the *Cass Lake* sheet is active.
   i. Select cell **B15** and drag the *Fill* pointer to copy the formula to cells **C15:G15**. The reference to cell G2 remains for each copied formula (Figure 2-22).

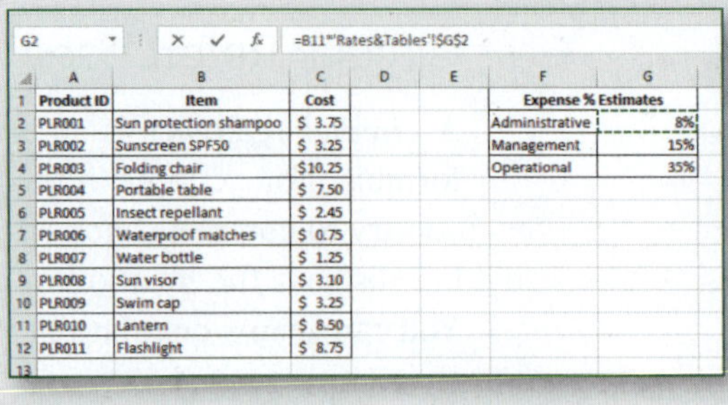

Figure 2-21 Absolute 3D reference in the formula

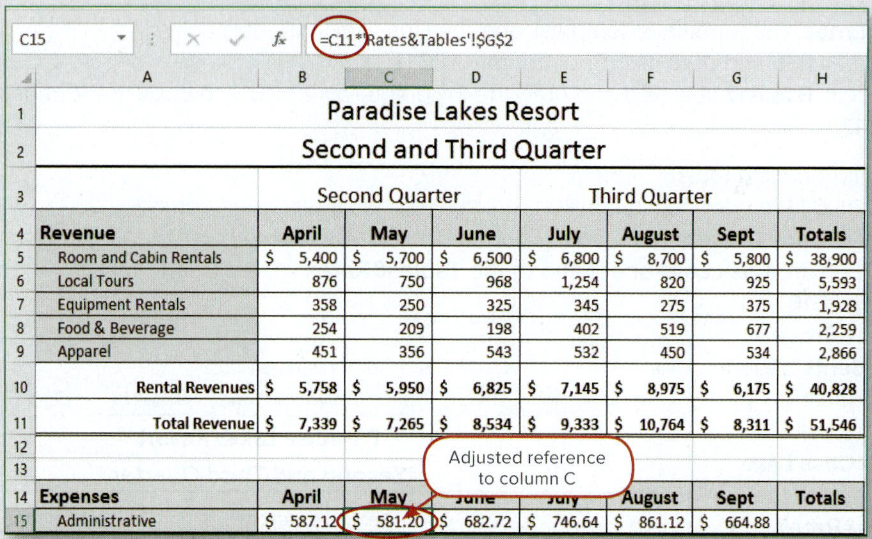

Figure 2-22 Copied formula with absolute reference

5. Create and copy a 3D formula with mixed references.
   a. Select cell **B16**. Management expense is calculated by multiplying the total revenue for the month by the set percentage.
   b. Type = to start the formula.
   c. Click cell **B11**, the total revenue for April.
   d. Press **F4** (**FN+F4**) to make the reference absolute ($B$11).
   e. Press **F4** (**FN+F4**) to make the reference mixed with the row reference absolute (B$11). When the formula is copied to row 17, it will remain B$11 (Figure 2-23). When copied to column C, the relative reference will be C$11.
   f. Type * for multiplication.
   g. Click the **Rates&Tables** sheet tab. The sheet name is inserted in the *Formula* bar.
   h. Click cell **G3**, the percentage for management expenses.
   i. Press **F4** (**FN+F4**) to make the reference absolute ($G$3).
   j. Press **F4** (**FN+F4**) to make the reference mixed with the row reference absolute (G$3).
   k. Press **F4** (**FN+F4**) to make the column reference absolute ($G3) (Figure 2-24). When copied to row 17 in the **Cass Lake** sheet, the relative reference will be $G4.

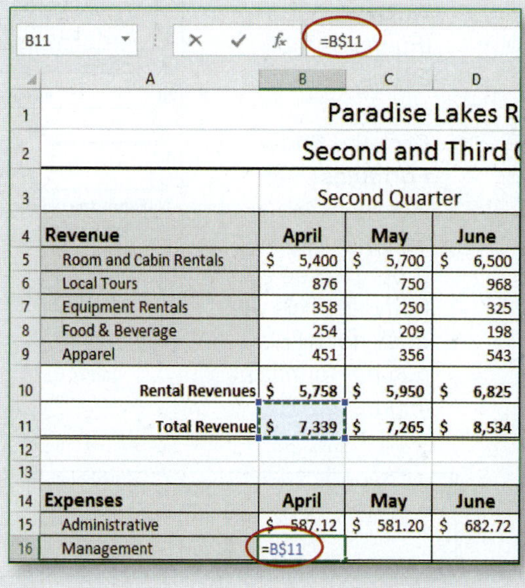

Figure 2-23 Mixed cell reference

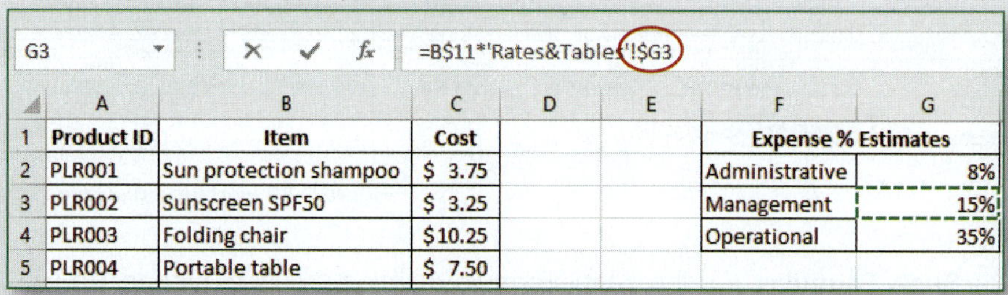

Figure 2-24 Absolute reference to column G

l. Press **Enter**. The formula is complete and the *Cass Lake* sheet is active.
m. Select cell **B16** and drag its *Fill* pointer to cell **B17**.
n. Keep cells **B16:B17** selected and drag the *Fill* pointer for cell B17 to copy the formulas to cells **C16:G17**.

6. Use *Formula Auditing* tools.
   a. Click cell **D17** to view how the mixed reference formula has been copied.
   b. Click the **Trace Precedents** button [*Formulas* tab, *Formula Auditing* group]. The formula refers to cell D11 on the **Cass Lake** sheet and to the **Tables&Rates** sheet.
   c. Click cell **E16** and click the **Trace Precedents** button. The formula refers to cell E11 on the **Cass Lake** sheet and to the **Tables&Rates** sheet (Figure 2-25).
   d. Click the **Remove Arrows** button [*Formulas* tab, *Formula Auditing* group].
   e. Click the **Show Formulas** [*Formulas* tab, *Formula Auditing* group] to see all formulas. This view does not display number formatting (Figure 2-26).

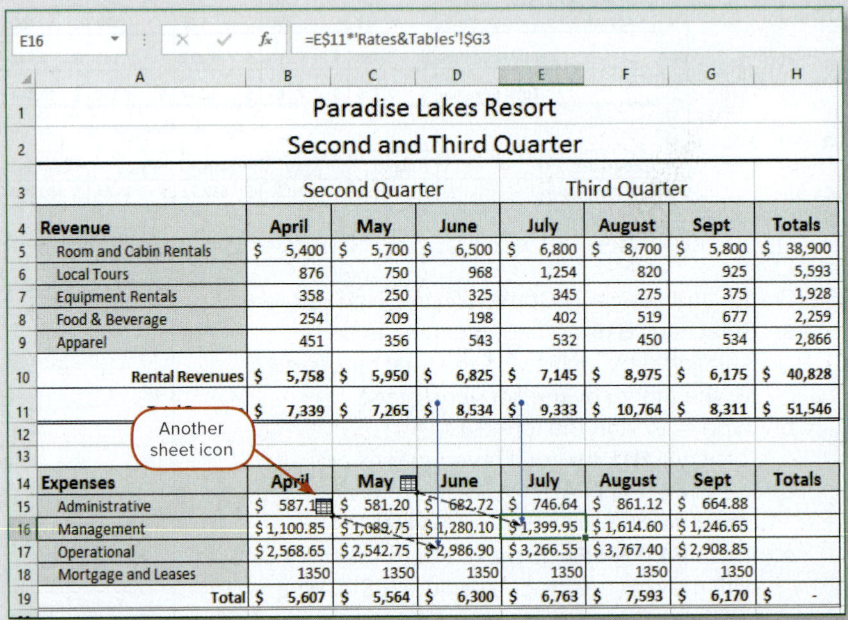

Figure 2-25 Formula precedents

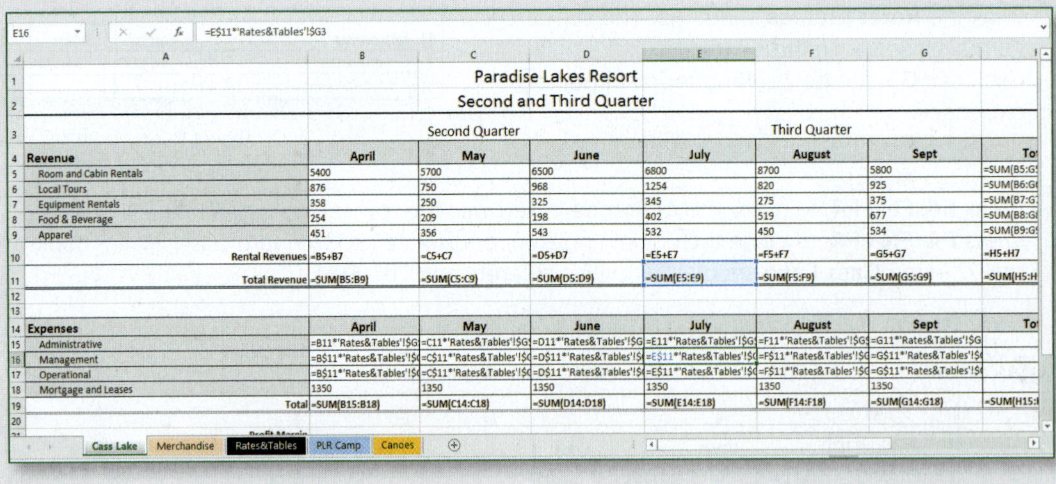

Figure 2-26 Formulas displayed in worksheet

   f. Click the **Show Formulas** [*Formulas* tab, *Formula Auditing* group] to hide the formulas.

7. Edit a formula and correct an error.
 a. Select cells **H15:H18** and click the **AutoSum** button [*Home* tab, *Editing* group]. The *SUM* function displays in each cell.
 b. Widen column **H** to display all data.
 c. Double-click cell **H16** to start *Edit* mode.
 d. Edit the cell range in the *SUM* formula to display **B15:G16** and press **Enter** to create a deliberate error. The green error triangle appears in the upper-left corner of the cell.
 e. Click cell **H16** to display the **Trace Error** button and then click the button. This formula is now inconsistent with others in the column (Figure 2-27).

| H16 | | × | ✓ | fx | =SUM(B15:G16) | | | |

	A	B	C	D	E	F	G	H
1	Paradise Lakes Resort							
2	Second and Third Quarter							
3		Second Quarter			Third Quarter			
4	Revenue	April	May	June	July	August	Sept	Totals
5	Room and Cabin Rentals	$ 5,400	$ 5,700	$ 6,500	$ 6,800	$ 8,700	$ 5,800	$ 38,900
6	Local Tours	876	750	968	1,254	820	925	5,593
7	Equipment Rentals	358	250	325	345	275	375	1,928
8	Food & Beverage	254	209	198	402	519	677	2,259
9	Apparel	451	356	543				2,866
10	Rental Revenues	$ 5,758	$ 5,950	$ 6,825	$			$ 40,828
11	Total Revenue	$ 7,339	$ 7,265	$ 8,534	$			$ 51,546
12								
13								
14	Expenses	April	May	June				Totals
15	Administrative	$ 587.12	$ 581.20	$ 682.72	$			$ 4,123.68
16	Management	$ 1,100.85	$ 1,089.75	$ 1,280.10	$ 1,399.95	$ 1,614.60	$ 1,24	$ 11,855.58
17	Operational	$ 2,568.65	$ 2,542.75	$ 2,986.90	$ 3,266.55	$ 3,767.40	$ 2,908.85	$ 18,041.10

Context menu shown:
- Inconsistent Formula
- Copy Formula from Above
- Help on this error
- Ignore Error
- Edit in Formula Bar
- Error Checking Options...

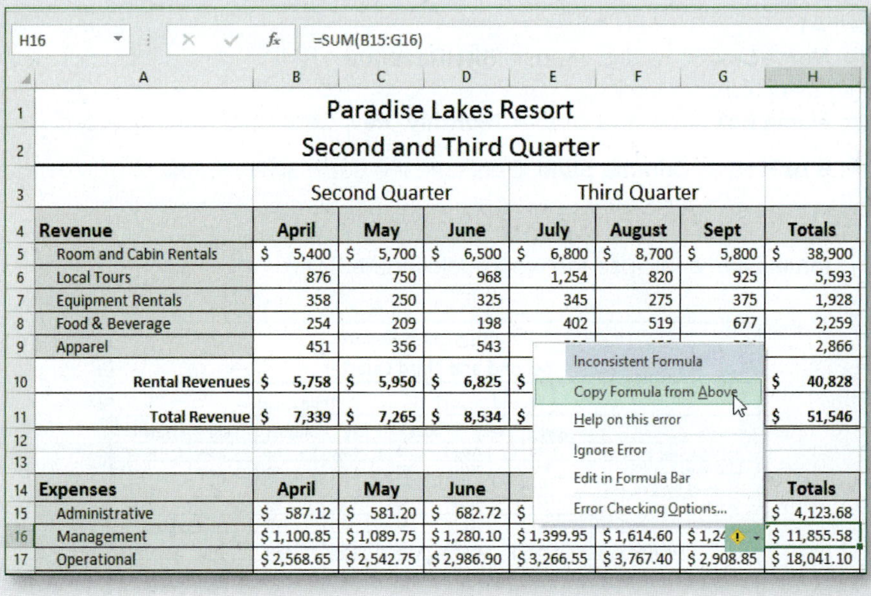

Figure 2-27 *Trace Error* button and options

 f. Select **Copy Formula from Above** to correct the error.
 g. Click cell **H16** and click the **Trace Precedents** button [*Formulas* tab, *Formula Auditing* group]. The formula refers to the correct cells in row 16.
 h. Click the **Remove Arrows** button [*Formulas* tab, *Formula Auditing* group].

8. Set mathematical order of operations.
 a. Select cell **B21**. Profit margin, as a percentage, is revenue minus expenses divided by revenue. The formula is **=(B11−B19)/B11**; the parentheses are necessary so that the subtraction is done before the division.
 b. Type **=(** to start the formula and insert the opening parenthesis.
 c. Click cell **B11**, the total revenue for April.
 d. Type **−** for subtraction.
 e. Click cell **B19**, total expenses for April.
 f. Type **)** to set the precedence with the closing parenthesis.
 g. Type **/** for division and click cell **B11** (Figure 2-28).
 h. Press **Enter**. The result is formatted as *Accounting Number* format to match the source cells.

| B11 | | × | ✓ | fx | =(B11-B19)/B11 | |

	A	B	C	D	E
2	Second and Third Quarter				
3	Second Quarter				Th
4	Revenue	April	May	June	July
5	Room and Cabin Rentals	$ 5,400	$ 5,700	$ 6,500	$ 6,800
6	Local Tours	876	750	968	1,254
7	Equipment Rentals	358	250	325	345
8	Food & Beverage	254	209	198	402
9	Apparel	451	356	543	532
10	Rental Revenues	$ 5,758	$ 5,950	$ 6,825	$ 7,145
11	Total Revenue	$ 7,339	$ 7,265	$ 8,534	$ 9,333
12					
13					
14	Expenses	April	May	June	July
15	Administrative	$ 587.12	$ 581.20	$ 682.72	$ 746.64
16	Management	$ 1,100.85	$ 1,089.75	$ 1,280.10	$ 1,399.95
17	Operational	$ 2,568.65	$ 2,542.75	$ 2,986.90	$ 3,266.55
18	Mortgage and Leases	1350	1350	1350	1350
19	Total	$ 5,607	$ 5,564	$ 6,300	$ 6,763
20					
21	Profit Margin	=(B11-B19)/B11			
22	Revenue Below Average?				

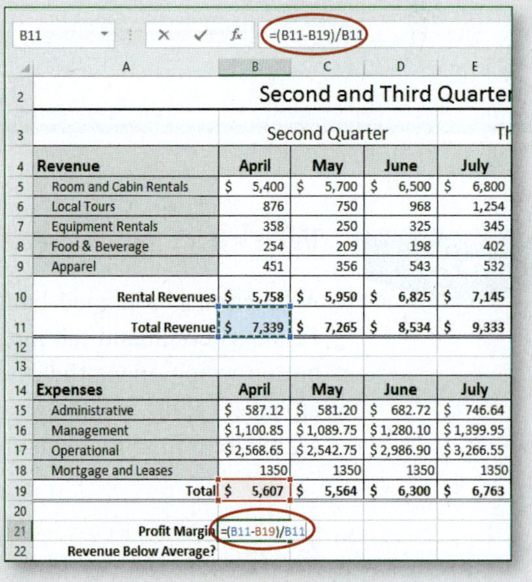

Figure 2-28 Set arithmetic order

i. Click cell **B21** and click the **Percent Style** button [*Home* tab, *Number* group].
j. Copy the formula in cell **B21** to cells **C21:G21**.

9. Name a cell range.
   a. Select cell **H11** and click the **Name** box.
   b. Type TotalRevenue in the *Name* box and press **Enter**.
   c. Select cells **B11:G11**.
   d. Click the **Define Name** button [*Formulas* tab, *Defined Names* group].
   e. Type Monthly_Rev in the *Name* box and click **OK** (Figure 2-29).
   f. Click cell **A1**.
   g. Click the **Name box** arrow and choose **TotalRevenue**. Cell H11 is selected.
   h. Click the **Name box** arrow and choose **Monthly_Rev**. Cells B11:G11 are selected.

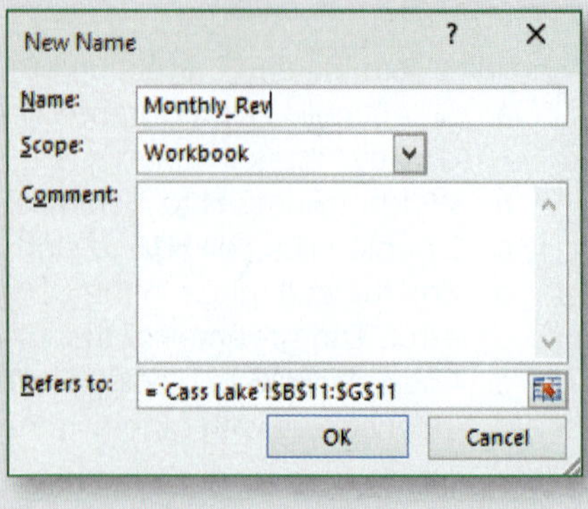

Figure 2-29 Use the *New Name* dialog box to name a range

10. Format cells **B16:H18** as **Comma Style**. Decrease the decimal two times.
11. Select cells **B15:H15** and decrease the decimal two times.
12. Press **Ctrl+Home**. Save and close the workbook (Figure 2-30).

Paradise Lakes Resort							
Second and Third Quarter							
	Second Quarter			Third Quarter			
Revenue	**April**	**May**	**June**	**July**	**August**	**Sept**	**Totals**
Room and Cabin Rentals	$ 5,400	$ 5,700	$ 6,500	$ 6,800	$ 8,700	$ 5,800	$ 38,900
Local Tours	876	750	968	1,254	820	925	5,593
Equipment Rentals	358	250	325	345	275	375	1,928
Food & Beverage	254	209	198	402	519	677	2,259
Apparel	451	356	543	532	450	534	2,866
Rental Revenues	**$ 5,758**	**$ 5,950**	**$ 6,825**	**$ 7,145**	**$ 8,975**	**$ 6,175**	**$ 40,828**
Total Revenue	**$ 7,339**	**$ 7,265**	**$ 8,534**	**$ 9,333**	**$ 10,764**	**$ 8,311**	**$ 51,546**
Expenses	**April**	**May**	**June**	**July**	**August**	**Sept**	**Totals**
Administrative	$ 587	$ 581	$ 683	$ 747	$ 861	$ 665	$ 4,124
Management	1,101	1,090	1,280	1,400	1,615	1,247	7,732
Operational	2,569	2,543	2,987	3,267	3,767	2,909	18,041
Mortgage and Leases	1,350	1,350	1,350	1,350	1,350	1,350	8,100
Total	**$ 5,607**	**$ 5,564**	**$ 6,300**	**$ 6,763**	**$ 7,593**	**$ 6,170**	**$ 37,997**
Profit Margin	24%	23%	26%	28%	29%	26%	
Revenue Below Average?							

Figure 2-30 PP E2-1 completed

SLO 2.5

Working with Statistical and Date & Time Functions

A function is a named built-in formula. Excel functions are grouped into categories on the *Formulas* command tab in the *Function Library* group. This group also has an *Insert Function* button which opens the *Insert Function* dialog box. From this dialog box, you can display an alphabetical list of all functions, a list by category, or a recently used list. Use this dialog box to search for a function by name.

MORE INFO

A formula such as **=B2+B3−B6** is usually not called a function because it has no function name.

The *Statistical* function category includes calculations that determine an average, a maximum, a minimum, and a count. These common functions are options on the *AutoSum* button on the *Home* tab. The *Formulas* tab also has an *AutoSum* button with the same options.

AVERAGE Function

The *AVERAGE* function calculates the arithmetic ***mean*** of a range of cells. The mean is determined by adding all the values and dividing the result by the number of values. The *AVERAGE* function ignores empty cells or cells that include labels. When calculating an average, do not include total values in the range to be averaged.

The *AVERAGE* function has one argument, *numberN*. A number argument can be a range such as B11:G11. You can average up to 255 numbers (or ranges). The proper syntax for an *AVERAGE* function is:

=AVERAGE(number1, [number2], [number3], . . .)

The *number1* argument is required and others are optional.

When you choose a function from the *AutoSum* button, you will see the function name, an assumed range within parentheses, and an ***Argument ScreenTip*** below the cell that displays the syntax. When you choose to type a function, the *ScreenTip* shows the next argument in bold type as a guideline.

▶HOW TO: Use the AVERAGE Function

1. Click the cell for the function.
2. Click the **AutoSum** button arrow [*Formulas* tab, *Function Library* group].
3. Select **Average**.
   - The function and an assumed argument range display in the *Formula* bar and in the cell.
4. Select the correct cell range (Figure 2-31).
   - You can type cell addresses rather than selecting cells.
   - When the selected cells have been named, the range name is substituted in the formula.

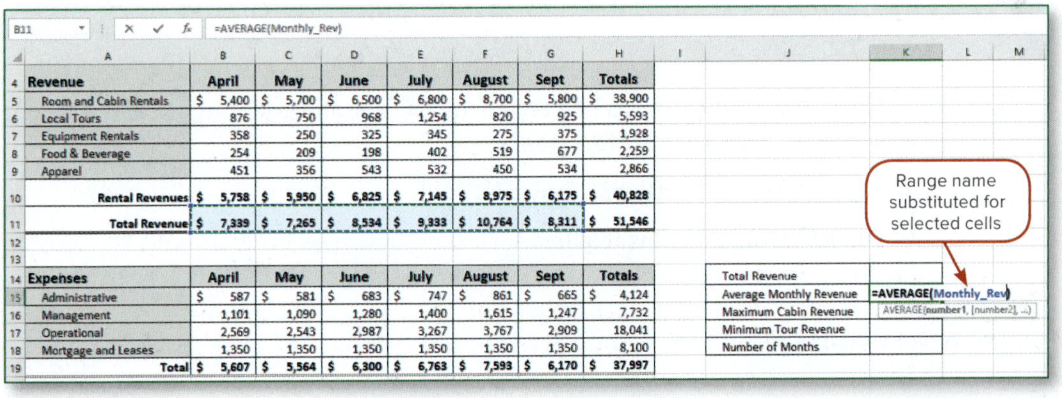

Figure 2-31 *AVERAGE* function

5. Press **Enter**.
   - Use any completion key.

MORE INFO

The *MEDIAN* function in the *Statistical* category determines the precise middle value in the range.

COUNT Functions

Five functions in the *Statistical* category are *COUNT* functions. Count functions tally the number of items in a range. The basic *COUNT* function is an option on the *AutoSum* button, but it appears in the list as *Count Numbers*. The *COUNT* function includes only cells with values in its result.

From the *Statistical* group, choose *COUNTA* to include cells with values and labels. The *COUNTBLANK* function counts cells that are empty. Table 2-6 describes the *Statistical COUNT* functions.

MORE INFO

The *Database* function category includes *DCOUNT* and *DCOUNTA* functions. This category is available from the *Insert Function* dialog box.

Table 2-6: Statistical COUNT Functions

Count Functions	Description	Example Syntax
COUNT (Count Numbers)	Counts the cells that contain values within a range	=COUNT(A1:A15)
COUNTA	Counts the cells that contain any data type within a range	=COUNTA(A1:A15)
COUNTBLANK	Counts empty cells in a range	=COUNTBLANK(A1:A15)
COUNTIF	Counts the cells that meet the criteria argument within a range	=COUNTIF(A1:A15, "Services")
COUNTIFS	Counts the cells in one or more criteria ranges that meet respective criteria arguments	=COUNTIFS(B2:B5,"=A", C2:C5,"=21")

The *COUNT* function has one argument, *valueN*, and counts up to 255 cells or ranges. The proper syntax for a *COUNT* function is:

=COUNT(value1, [value2], [value3], . . .)

The *Value1* argument is required.

HOW TO: Use the COUNT Function

1. Click the cell for the function.
2. Click the **AutoSum** button arrow [*Formulas* tab, *Function Library* group].
3. Select **Count Numbers**.
   - The *COUNT* function is inserted with an assumed range.
   - The function appears in the cell and in the *Formula* bar (Figure 2-32).

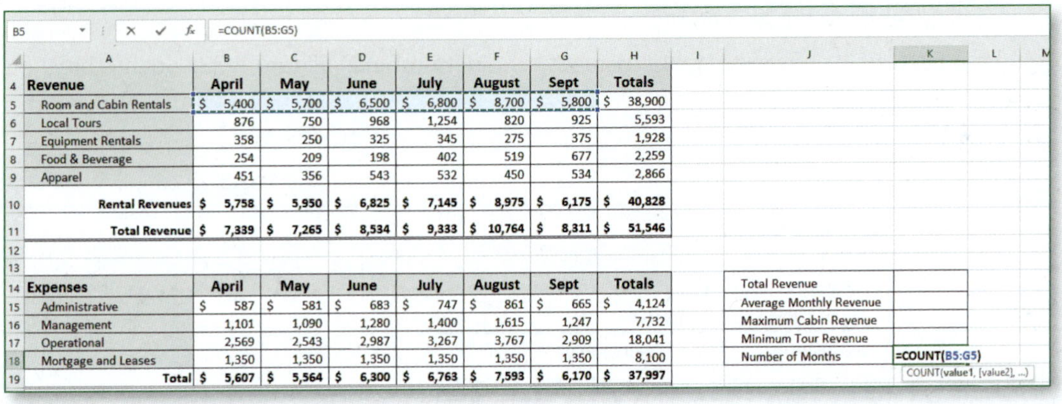

B5 =COUNT(B5:G5)

Revenue	April	May	June	July	August	Sept	Totals
Room and Cabin Rentals	$ 5,400	$ 5,700	$ 6,500	$ 6,800	$ 8,700	$ 5,800	$ 38,900
Local Tours	876	750	968	1,254	820	925	5,593
Equipment Rentals	358	250	325	345	275	375	1,928
Food & Beverage	254	209	198	402	519	677	2,259
Apparel	451	356	543	532	450	534	2,866
Rental Revenues	**$ 5,758**	**$ 5,950**	**$ 6,825**	**$ 7,145**	**$ 8,975**	**$ 6,175**	**$ 40,828**
Total Revenue	**$ 7,339**	**$ 7,265**	**$ 8,534**	**$ 9,333**	**$ 10,764**	**$ 8,311**	**$ 51,546**

Expenses	April	May	June	July	August	Sept	Totals
Administrative	$ 587	$ 581	$ 683	$ 747	$ 861	$ 665	$ 4,124
Management	1,101	1,090	1,280	1,400	1,615	1,247	7,732
Operational	2,569	2,543	2,987	3,267	3,767	2,909	18,041
Mortgage and Leases	1,350	1,350	1,350	1,350	1,350	1,350	8,100
Total	**$ 5,607**	**$ 5,564**	**$ 6,300**	**$ 6,763**	**$ 7,593**	**$ 6,170**	**$ 37,997**

Total Revenue	
Average Monthly Revenue	
Maximum Cabin Revenue	
Minimum Tour Revenue	
Number of Months	=COUNT(B5:G5)

COUNT(value1, [value2], ...)

Figure 2-32 ***COUNT* function**

4. Select the correct cell range.
   - Type cell addresses rather than selecting cells.
5. Press **Enter** or any completion key.

MORE INFO

If you use *COUNT* with a range of labels, the result is zero (0).

MAX and MIN Functions

The *MAX* function finds the largest value in a range, and the *MIN* function finds the smallest value. Both functions are options on the *AutoSum* button. Each has one argument: the cells to be evaluated.

The proper syntax for *MAX* and *MIN* functions is:

=MAX(number1, [number2], [number3], . . .)
=MIN(number1, [number2], [number3], . . .)

In many worksheets, an argument range is a group of adjacent cells such as B11:G11, but the cells need not be next to each other. You can select individual cells anywhere in the worksheet for an argument, and they are separated by commas as in =MAX(B11, B15, B18).

HOW TO: Use the MAX Function with Nonadjacent Cells

1. Click the cell for the function.
2. Click the **AutoSum** button arrow [*Formulas* tab, *Function Library* group].
3. Select **Max**.
   - The function displays in the cell and in the *Formula* bar.
   - The *Argument ScreenTip* shows the next argument in bold **number1**.
4. Click the first cell to be evaluated.

5. Type **,** (a comma) to separate the arguments.
   - The *Argument ScreenTip* shows the next argument in bold **[number2]** (Figure 2-33). Square brackets mean the argument is optional.

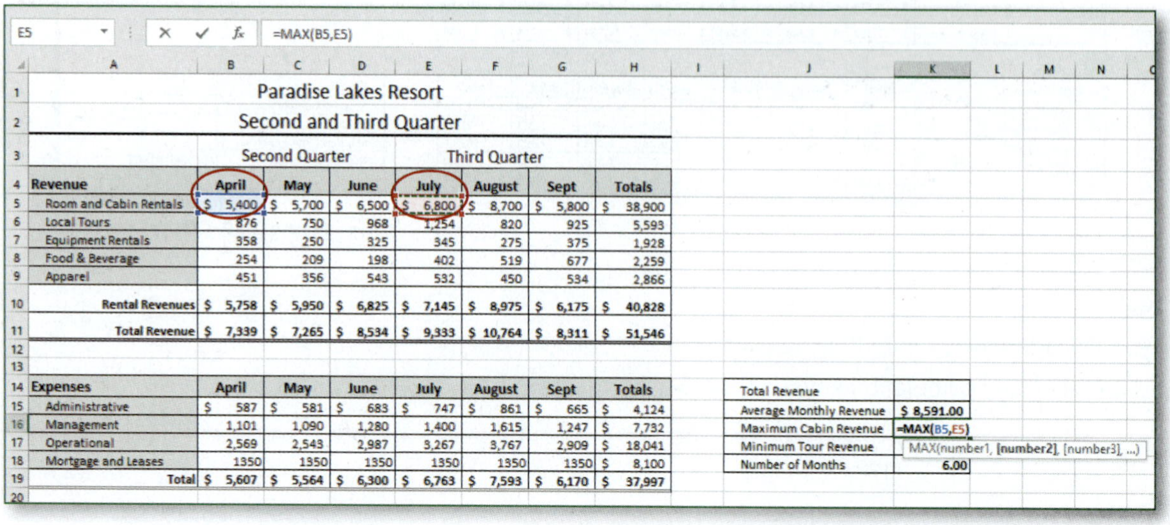

Figure 2-33 Use nonadjacent cells for *MAX*

6. Click the next cell to be evaluated.
7. Type a comma **,** to add additional cells to the argument.
8. Press **Enter** when all the cells are listed.

AutoCalculate

The ***AutoCalculate*** feature is located on the right side of the *Status* bar where statistical and mathematical results display for selected cells. The calculations are *Average, Count, Numerical Count, Maximum, Minimum,* and *Sum.* The *Count* calculation is the equivalent of *COUNTA,* and *Numerical Count* is the same as *COUNT. AutoCalculate* enables you to see results without inserting a function in the worksheet. You can see and change which calculations are visible by right-clicking the *Status* bar to open the *Customize Status Bar* menu.

▶HOW TO: Use AutoCalculate

1. Select the cell range or individual cells in the worksheet.
2. View the results on the *Status* bar.
   - Selected options appear on the *Status* bar when appropriate; no *SUM* displays when you select labels.
3. Right-click the right side of the *Status* bar (Figure 2-34).
   - The *Customize Status Bar* menu opens.
   - If a function name has a check mark to the left, it is active.

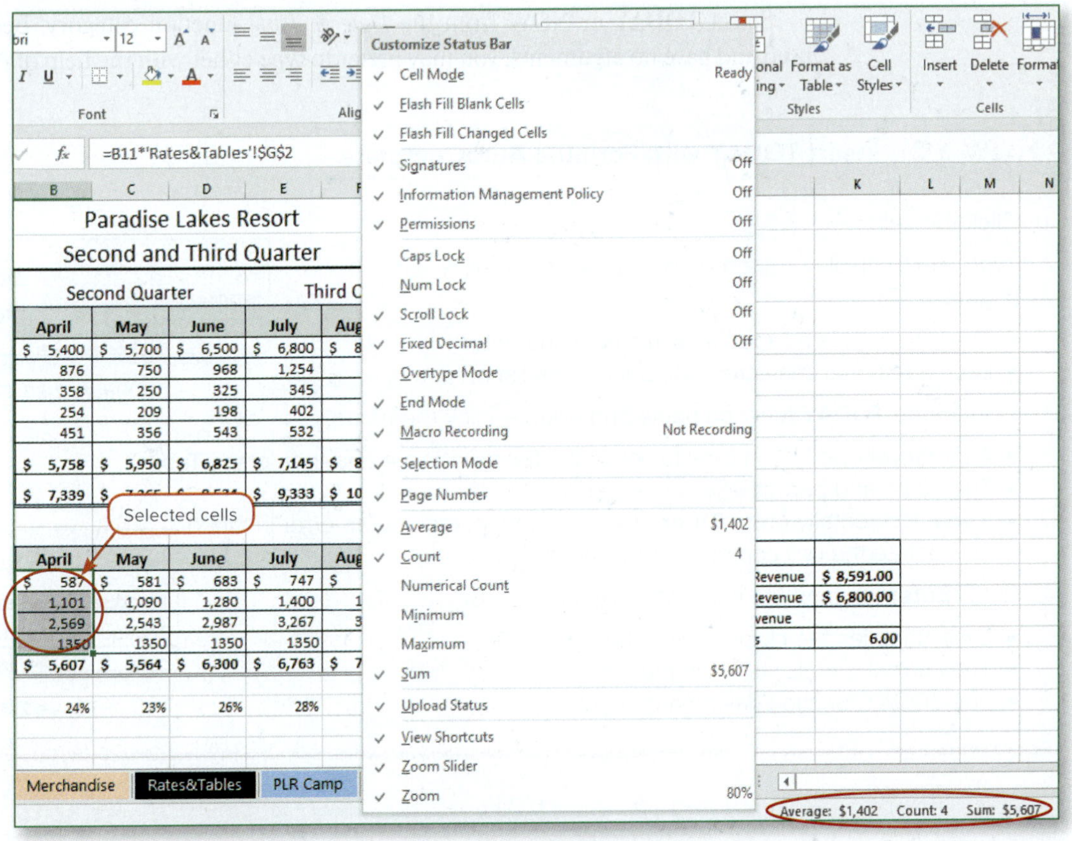

Figure 2-34 *AutoCalculate* results and other status bar options

4. Select a calculation name to activate it and show it on the *Status* bar.
5. Select a calculation name with a check mark to hide it from the *Status* bar.

TODAY and NOW Functions

The *Date & Time* category includes many functions for date and time arithmetic, for converting dates and times to values, and for controlling how dates and times display.

The *TODAY* function inserts the current date in the cell and updates each time the workbook opens. It uses the computer's clock, and the syntax is =TODAY(). The parentheses are necessary, but no arguments are required. The *NOW* function uses the syntax =NOW() and has no arguments. These two functions are ***volatile*** which means that the result depends on the current date, time, and computer.

After either function is inserted, you can format results to show both the date and the time. The *Format Cells* dialog box has a *Date* category and a *Time* category with many preset styles. Two date formats are available from the *Number Format* list [*Home* tab, *Number* group], *Short Date*, and *Long Date*.

Excel treats each date as a ***serial number***, a unique value assigned to each date. Excel starts by setting January 1, 1900, as number 1; January 2, 1900 is number 2, and so on. January 1, 2020, is number 43831. You can see the serial number for any date by applying the *General* format to the cell.

MORE INFO

Display the Excel *Options* dialog box [*File* tab] and select the *Advanced* pane to set a 1904 date system which matches the date system in the Macintosh operating system.

Select **TODAY** or **NOW** from the *Date & Time* function category. Because they are widely used and have no arguments, you may prefer to type either with the help of *Formula AutoComplete*.

▶HOW TO: Insert TODAY with Formula AutoComplete

1. Click the cell.
2. Type =to to display a filtered *Formula AutoComplete* list (Figure 2-35).
   - The list appears as soon as you type a character.
   - Each additional character further limits the list of names.

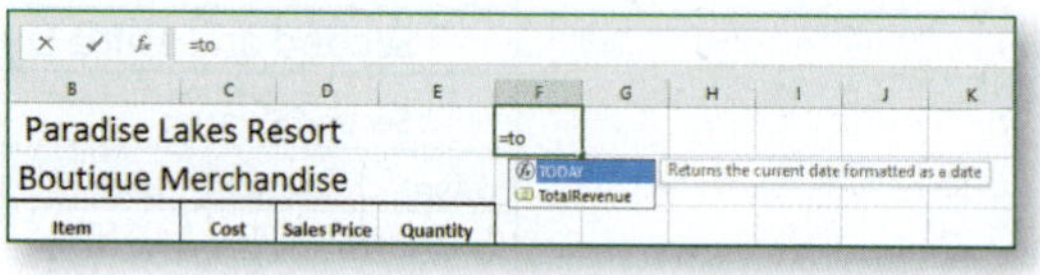

Figure 2-35 ***Formula Autocomplete*** **list**

3. Point to the **TODAY** function name and double-click the name.
   - Alternatively, point and click to select the function name and then press **Tab**.
   - The name and parentheses are inserted.
   - If you accidentally press **Enter** to select a name and see an error in the cell, delete the cell contents and try again.
4. Press **Enter** to complete the function (Figure 2-36).
   - Excel supplies the closing parenthesis.
   - The current date is shown in the cell.
   - The *TODAY* function has no arguments.

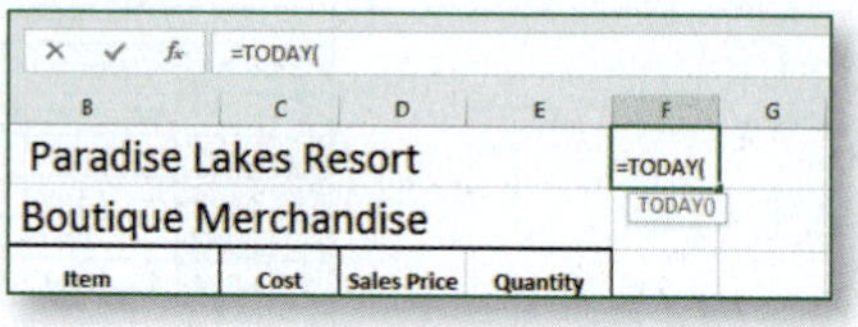

Figure 2-36 ***TODAY*** **inserted in cell**

PAUSE & PRACTICE: EXCEL 2-2

For this project, you open your Pause & Practice file and insert Excel functions to complete more of the worksheet. You insert functions from the *AutoSum* button and by typing. You also use *AutoCalculate* to check results.

File Needed: ***[your initials] PP E2-1.xlsx***
Completed Project File Name: ***[your initials] PP E2-2.xlsx***

1. Open the ***[your initials] PP E2-1.xlsx*** workbook completed in *Pause & Practice 2-1* and save it as [your initials] PP E2-2.
2. Enter functions using the *AutoSum* button.
   a. Click the **Cass Lake** worksheet tab and select cell **K14**.
   b. Click the **AutoSum** button arrow [*Formulas* tab, *Function Library* group].
   c. Choose **Sum**. The function name and parentheses are inserted, and a *Function ScreenTip* is visible.
   d. Select cells **B11:G11**. The range is highlighted on screen, and Excel has substituted the defined name that you set in *Pause & Practice 2-1* (Figure 2-37).
   e. Press **Enter**.
   f. Select cell **K15** and click the **AutoSum** button arrow [*Formulas* tab, *Function Library* group].
   g. Choose **Average**. The name and parentheses are inserted.
   h. Select cells **B11:G11**. The range is highlighted, but the range name is substituted.
   i. Press **Enter**. Average sales are $8,591.

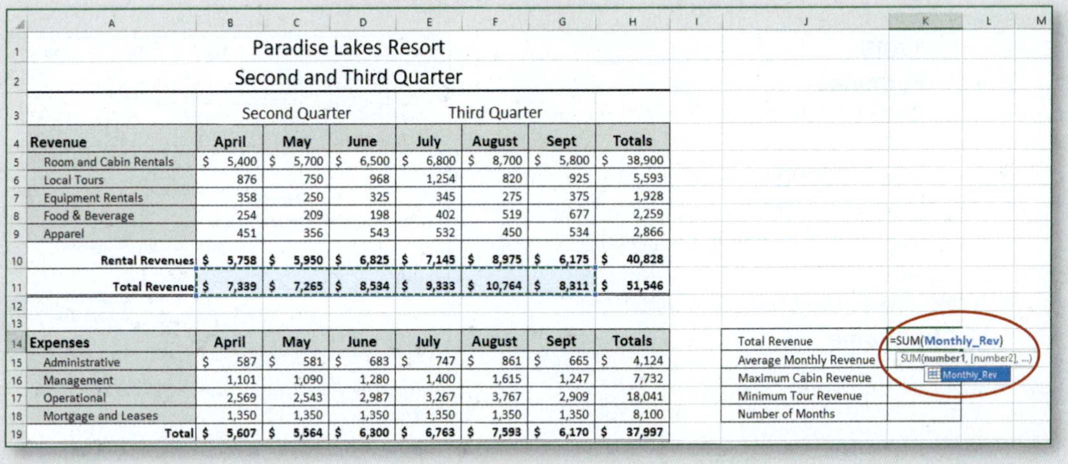

Figure 2-37 Range name substituted in formula

3. Enter the *MAX* function by typing.
   a. Select cell **K16**.
   b. Type =ma to display the *Formula AutoComplete* list. You only need type as many characters as necessary to see the function name.
   c. Point to **MAX** in the list, click to select it, and press **Tab** (Figure 2-38).
   d. Select cells **B5:G5** for the *number1* argument. This range is not named.
   e. Press **Enter**. Excel supplies the closing parenthesis.

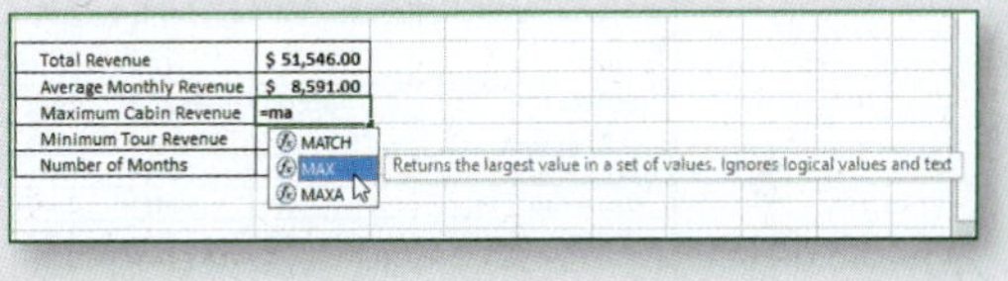

Figure 2-38 Choose *MAX* from *Formula AutoComplete* list

4. Copy and edit a function.
   a. Select cell **K16** and use the *Fill* pointer to copy the formula to cell **K17**.
   b. Double-click cell **K17**. Note that the argument cell range was updated because it was a relative reference.
   c. Replace the function name *MAX* in the cell with **min** (Figure 2-39).
   d. Press **Enter**. The minimum tour value is $750.

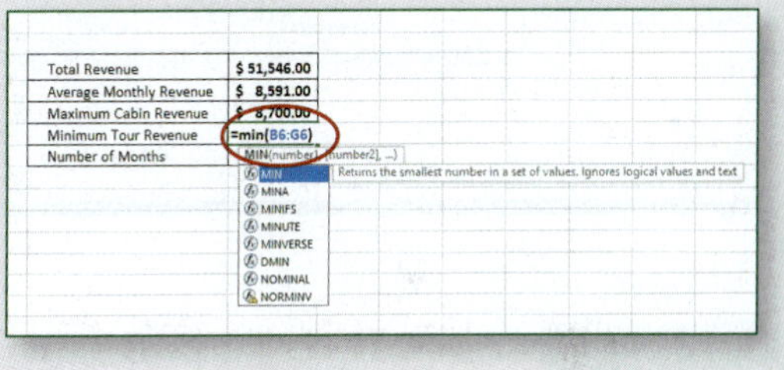

Figure 2-39 Edit a function name

5. Type the *COUNT* function.
   a. Select cell **K18**.
   b. Type =cou to display the *Formula AutoComplete* list.
   c. Double-click **COUNTA** in the list. This function counts cells with labels and values. The *ScreenTip* shows the first argument as *value1*.
   d. Select cells **B4:G4** to count the months. The formula is =COUNTA(B4:G4).
   e. Press **Enter**. The final parenthesis is supplied and the result is 6.00.
   f. Select cells **K14:K18** and decrease the decimal two times.
   g. Apply the **General** format to cell **K18** [*Home* tab, *Number* group, *Number Format* drop-down list].
6. Check results with *AutoCalculate*.
   a. Select cells **B11:G11**.
   b. Right-click near the middle of the *Status* bar to display the options.
   c. Verify that **Average**, **Count**, and **Sum** are checked.
   d. Left-click anywhere in the *Status* bar to close the menu.
   e. Compare the values shown in the *Status* bar with the results in column K.

7. Insert the *TODAY* function.
   a. Select cell **A25**.
   b. Click the **Formulas** tab.
   c. Click the **Date & Time** button [*Function Library* group].
   d. Find and select **TODAY**. A *Function Arguments* dialog box notes that this function does not have any arguments and that it is volatile (Figure 2-40).
   e. Click **OK**. The current date is inserted.
   f. Press **Ctrl+Home**.
8. Save and close the workbook (Figure 2-41).

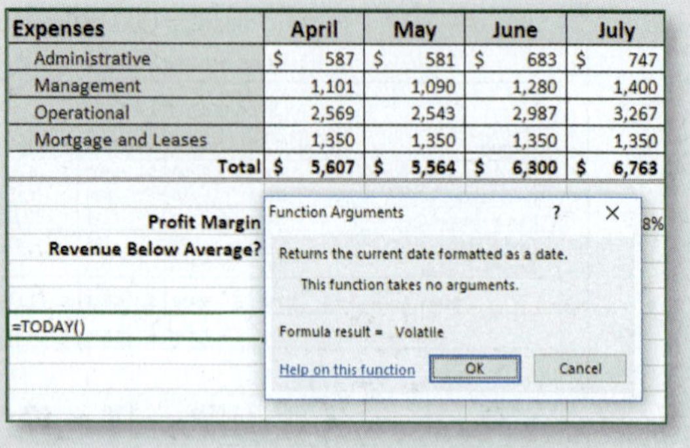

Expenses | April | May | June | July
Administrative | $ 587 | $ 581 | $ 683 | $ 747
Management | 1,101 | 1,090 | 1,280 | 1,400
Operational | 2,569 | 2,543 | 2,987 | 3,267
Mortgage and Leases | 1,350 | 1,350 | 1,350 | 1,350
Total | $ 5,607 | $ 5,564 | $ 6,300 | $ 6,763
Profit Margin
Revenue Below Average?
=TODAY()
Function Arguments
Returns the current date formatted as a date.
This function takes no arguments.
Formula result = Volatile
Help on this function
OK
Cancel

Figure 2-40 *Function Arguments* dialog box for *TODAY*

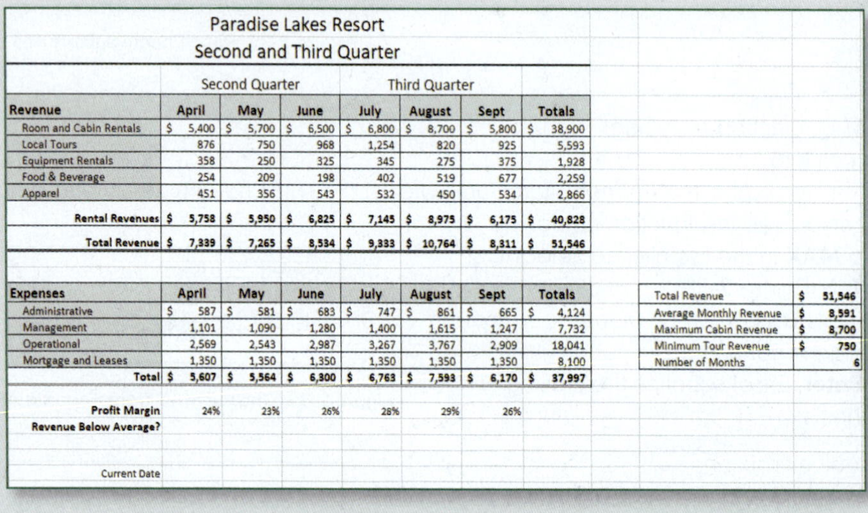

Paradise Lakes Resort
Second and Third Quarter

Revenue	April	May	June	July	August	Sept	Totals
	Second Quarter			Third Quarter			
Room and Cabin Rentals	$ 5,400	$ 5,700	$ 6,500	$ 6,800	$ 8,700	$ 5,800	$ 38,900
Local Tours	876	750	968	1,254	820	925	5,593
Equipment Rentals	358	250	325	345	275	375	1,928
Food & Beverage	254	209	198	402	519	677	2,259
Apparel	451	356	543	532	450	534	2,866
Rental Revenues	$ 5,758	$ 5,950	$ 6,825	$ 7,145	$ 8,975	$ 6,175	$ 40,828
Total Revenue	$ 7,339	$ 7,265	$ 8,534	$ 9,333	$ 10,764	$ 8,311	$ 51,546

Expenses	April	May	June	July	August	Sept	Totals
Administrative	$ 587	$ 581	$ 683	$ 747	$ 861	$ 665	$ 4,124
Management	1,101	1,090	1,280	1,400	1,615	1,247	7,732
Operational	2,569	2,543	2,987	3,267	3,767	2,909	18,041
Mortgage and Leases	1,350	1,350	1,350	1,350	1,350	1,350	8,100
Total	$ 5,607	$ 5,564	$ 6,300	$ 6,763	$ 7,593	$ 6,170	$ 37,997
Profit Margin	24%	23%	26%	28%	29%	26%	
Revenue Below Average?							
Current Date							

Total Revenue	$ 51,546
Average Monthly Revenue	$ 8,591
Maximum Cabin Revenue	$ 8,700
Minimum Tour Revenue	$ 750
Number of Months	6

Figure 2-41 PP E2-2 completed

SLO 2.6

Working with Financial, Logical, and Lookup Functions

The *Financial* category includes functions that determine loan payments, the amount of interest earned, the rate of return on an investment, and more. Most of the functions in the *Logical* category display TRUE or FALSE as the result, but the *IF* function in this group returns results that you specify. An *IF* function can test if monthly revenue is above or below average and display "Yes" or "No" in the cell. The *Lookup & Reference* category is used to find and display information from a list in the workbook. For example, you might use a *Lookup* function to insert a price from a price list.

The Function Arguments Dialog Box

Functions require arguments in a particular order. They are easy to learn and build when you use the *Function Arguments* dialog box. This dialog box opens when you choose a function name from a category on the *Formulas* tab or when you use the *Insert Function* dialog box.

The *Function Arguments* dialog box shows each argument with an entry box and an explanation (Figure 2-42). You can select cells to enter an address, or type directly in the entry box. In addition to doing the work for you, the *Function Arguments* dialog box helps you learn the proper syntax for a function.

Function arguments may be required or optional. Optional arguments generally add a level of refinement to the calculation. In the *Function Arguments* dialog box and the *ScreenTip*, a required argument name is shown in bold. When you use *Formula AutoComplete* to build a function, the *ScreenTip* shows optional arguments in square brackets (example: [type]).

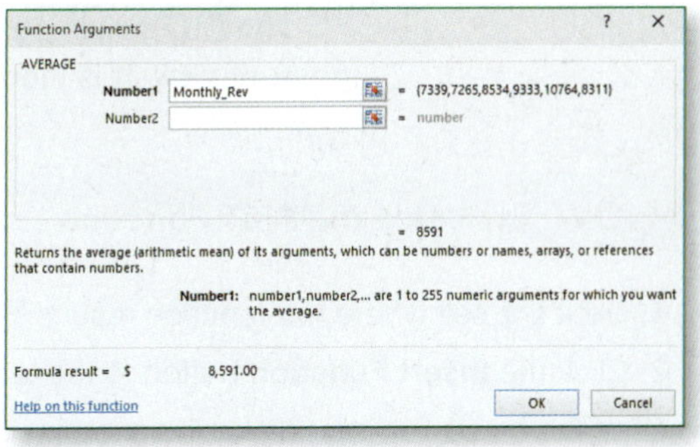

Figure 2-42 ***Function Arguments* dialog box for *AVERAGE***

When you are not sure about a function's name or category, search for it in the *Insert Function* dialog box. Open this dialog box by clicking the **Insert Function** button on the *Formulas* tab [*Function Library* group] or the same button to the left of the *Formula* bar. In the search area, type the name of the function or a brief description of what you want the function to do. For example, type "rate of return" to list *Financial* functions that calculate a rate of return for an investment.

> **ANOTHER WAY**
>
> **Shift+F3** opens the *Insert Function* dialog box.

PMT Function

The *PMT* function is in the *Financial* category. It calculates a constant loan payment amount for a period of time at a stated interest rate. When you borrow money for tuition or to buy a car, use the *PMT* function to determine your monthly payment for a selected payback time.

The *PMT* function has five arguments. Three of them are required: *rate*, *nper*, and *pv*. The other arguments are optional: *fv* and *type*. The proper syntax for a *PMT* formula is:

=PMT(rate, nper, pv, [fv], [type])

- ***Rate*** is the interest rate, a percentage of the amount borrowed. Most rates are set at a yearly rate. To determine monthly payments, you must divide the rate by 12.
- ***Nper*** is the total number of periods for repayment. If you make monthly payments for five years, the *nper* argument is 60.
- ***Pv*** is the present value, the amount borrowed.
- ***Fv*** is any future value after the last payment, an amount still owed at the end of the loan. When the *fv* argument is omitted, it means zero or that you have paid back the entire amount.
- ***Type*** indicates if payments are made at the beginning or the end of the period. Most loan payments are at the beginning of the period, because the interest amount is less. The number *1* is used to set payment at the beginning of the period.

Figure 2-43 shows a *PMT* function in cell B7 **=PMT(B6/12,B5*12,B4,,1)**. In the *Formula* bar, arguments are separated by commas. Where two commas display with nothing between them, an argument has been omitted. In this case, it is the *fv* argument.

B6/12 is the interest *rate* divided by 12 to determine a monthly payment.
B5*12 is the *nper* argument, the number of years times 12, to determine the total number of payments.
B4 is the *pv* argument, the amount of money borrowed.
1 is the *type* argument and indicates that payment occurs at the beginning of the period.

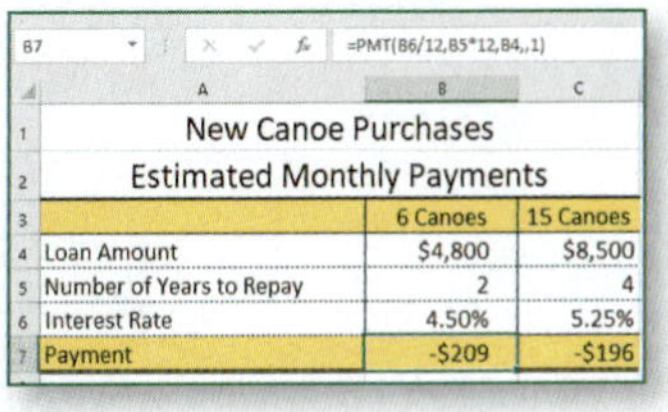

B7
=PMT(B6/12,B5*12,B4,,1)
New Canoe Purchases
Estimated Monthly Payments
6 Canoes
15 Canoes
Loan Amount
$4,800
$8,500
Number of Years to Repay
2
4
Interest Rate
4.50%
5.25%
Payment
-$209
-$196

Figure 2-43 ***PMT* function is in cell B7**

The *PMT* result is a negative number, because the function is calculated from the borrower's point of view. It is money paid out.

HOW TO: Use the PMT Function

1. Click the cell where the function results should display.
2. Click the **Insert Function** button to the left of the *Formula* bar.
   - The *Insert Function* dialog box opens.
3. Type payment in the *Search for a function* box.
4. Click **Go**.
   - A list of functions that include a type of payment displays (Figure 2-44).
5. Select **PMT** and click **OK**.
   - The *Function Arguments* dialog box opens.
   - The dialog box includes a description of the function.
6. Click the **Rate** box and click the cell with the interest rate.
   - You can type the rate in the entry box with the percent sign.
   - An explanation of the argument displays.
7. Type /12 immediately after the address in the *Rate* box.
   - Divide by 12 for monthly payments.
   - If payments are quarterly, divide by 4.
8. Click the **Nper** box and click the cell that contains the loan term.
9. Type *12 immediately after the address in the *Nper* box.
   - If the loan term is years and payments are quarterly, multiply by 4.
   - If the cell already displays the total number of payments, just click to enter the address.
10. Click the **Pv** box and click the cell that contains the amount of the loan.
11. Click the **Type** box.
    - The *Fv* argument is usually omitted, because loans require a zero balance at the end.
12. Type 1 in the *Type* box to set a payment at the beginning of the period (Figure 2-45).
    - Most loan payments are at the beginning, because the payment is less than if it were at the end of the period.
13. Click **OK**.

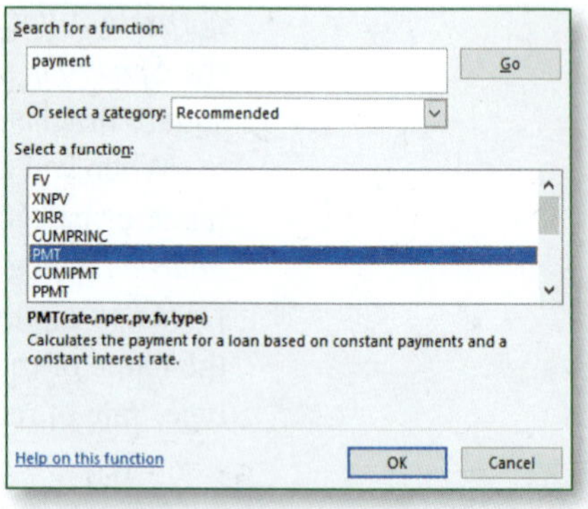

Figure 2-44 *Insert Function* **dialog box**

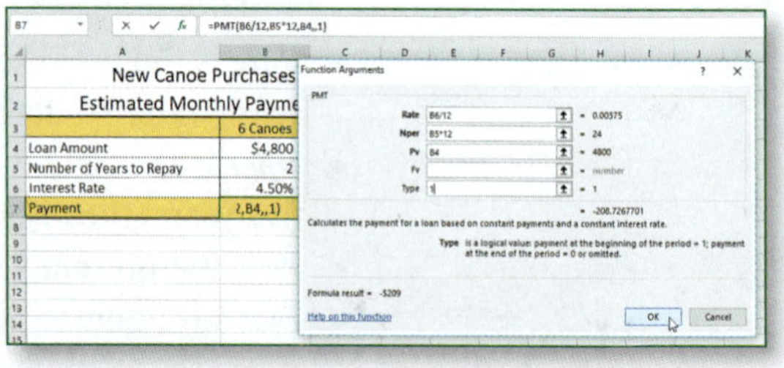

Figure 2-45 *Function Arguments* **dialog box for** *PMT*

MORE INFO

To show the payment as a positive value, type a minus sign (−) before the loan amount in the worksheet or before its cell address in the *Function Arguments* dialog box.

ANOTHER WAY

Choose the *PMT* function from the **Financial** button [*Formulas* tab, *Function Library* group].

IF Function

The *IF* function tests a condition or statement; if it is true, a specified result displays; if it is false, an alternative result displays. In the Paradise Lakes revenue worksheet, you can use an *IF* formula to determine if each month's revenue is above average. If it is, you can display "Yes," in the cell, and if it is not, you can display "No."

> **MORE INFO**
>
> An *IF* function is similar to an *IF* statement in many programming languages.

An *IF* function has three arguments, and its syntax is:

=IF (logical_test, value_if_true, value_if_false)

- The ***logical_test*** is the value or statement to be evaluated.
- The ***value_if_true*** is the result displayed in the cell when the *logical_test* is true. You can select a cell, enter text, or use a formula for this argument.
- The ***value_if_false*** is the result displayed in the cell when the *logical_test* is false. You can select a cell, enter text, or use a formula for this argument.

An *IF* function can use comparison or logical operators in its arguments. Table 2-7 describes the comparison operators:

Table 2-7: Comparison Operators

Operator	Description
=	Equal to
<>	Not equal to
>	Greater than
>=	Greater than or equal to
<	Less than
<=	Less than or equal to

Figure 2-46 has an *IF* function in cell D5 **=IF(B5>=4,18,20)**. When you use the *Function Arguments* dialog box to build a function, the commas to separate arguments are entered automatically.

B5>=4 is the *logical_test*. It determines if the value in cell B5 is equal to or greater than 4. Cell B5 is a relative reference so when the formula is copied, it will update to show the new row. The *value_if_true* argument is **18**. If the age is 4 or higher, the fee is $18. This value is a constant. It does not change when the formula is copied. The *value_if_false* argument is **20**, another constant. If the age is not 4 or higher, it must be lower and the fee is $20. The constant does not change when the formula is copied.

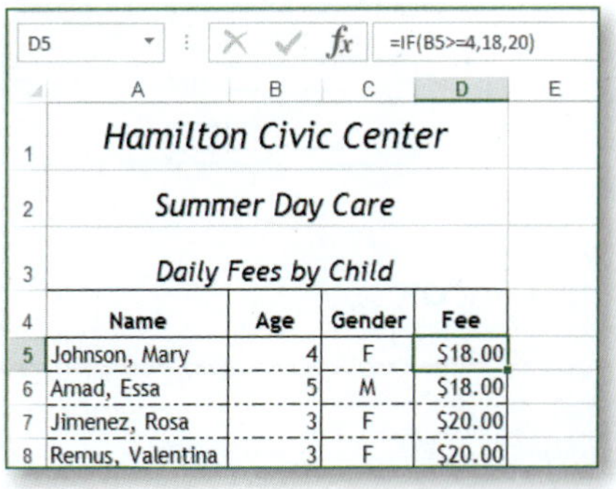

Figure 2-46 *IF* function in cell D5

Insert the *IF* function from the *Logical* category on the *Formulas* tab, from the *Insert Function* button, or by typing it. When you type an *IF* function, you must type the commas to separate arguments, and you must enclose text arguments within quotation marks.

▸HOW TO: Build an IF Function

1. Click the cell for the function.
2. Click the **Logical** button [*Formulas* tab, *Function Library* group].
   - The list of *Logical* functions opens.
3. Select **IF** in the list.
   - The *Function Arguments* dialog box for *IF* opens.
4. Click the **Logical_test** box.
5. Click the cell that will be evaluated.
   - Make the reference absolute if you know that the formula will be copied and that the reference should not change.
6. Type a comparison operator immediately after the cell address.
7. Type a value or click a cell to complete the expression to be tested.
   - Build a statement such as B11=K15 or B11<10000.
   - Make a cell reference absolute or mixed if necessary.
8. Click the **Value_if_true** box.
9. Type the label or click a cell that contains data that should display if the *logical_test* is true.
   - Type a value in the text box.
10. Click the **Value_if_false** box.
11. Type the label or click a cell that contains data that should display if the *logical_test* is false (Figure 2-47).
    - Results for the current cell display in the *Function Arguments* dialog box.
    - The *Function Arguments* dialog box provides quotation marks for text entries.

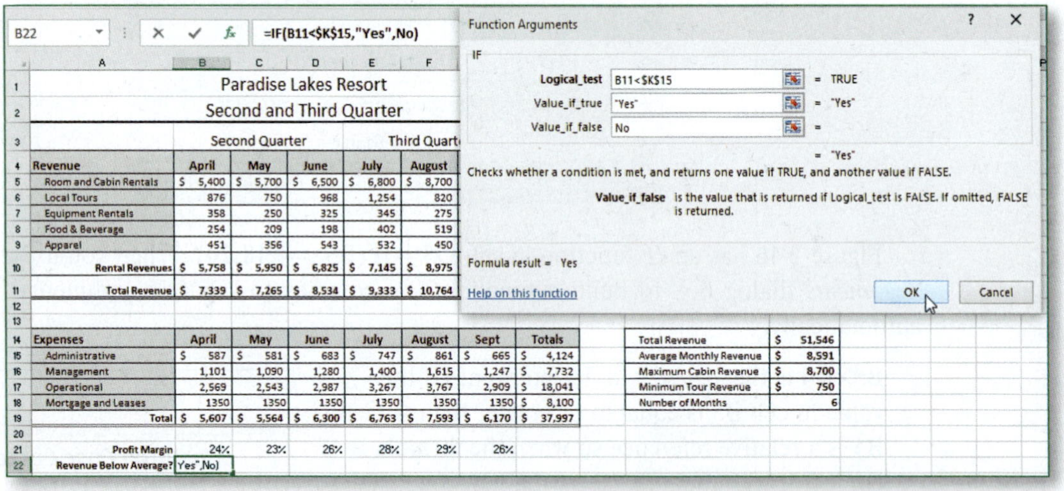

Figure 2-47 ***Function Arguments* dialog box for *IF***

12. Click **OK**.

MORE INFO

The *value_if_false* argument for the *logical_test* can be another *IF* function which enables you to test for more than one possibility.

Lookup Functions

A *Lookup* function displays a piece of data from a range of cells in another part of the workbook. Two *Lookup* functions, *VLOOKUP* (vertical) and *HLOOKUP* (horizontal), are available. These two functions have the same syntax and similar arguments. *VLOOKUP* uses a lookup table that is organized in columns, and *HLOOKUP* uses a lookup range that is arranged in rows.

A *VLOOKUP* function has four arguments, and the syntax is:

=VLOOKUP (lookup_value, table_array, col_index_num, [range_lookup])

- The ***lookup_value*** is the data to be found or matched. It is usually a cell address, but you can type a value or a text string. The function locates this *lookup_value* in the first column of the table array. It then displays data from the designated column in the same row as the *lookup_value*.
- The ***table_array*** is a range of cells, sorted in ascending order by the first column. The range can be located on a different worksheet or in a different workbook. It is good practice to name the range so that its reference is absolute.
- The ***col_index_num*** sets which column in the *table_array* contains the data to display in the result. The columns are counted from left to right.
- The ***[range lookup]*** argument is either TRUE or FALSE. TRUE means that Excel finds the closest match to the *lookup_value*, which can return unexpected results. If the data in the table array is sorted, however, TRUE will generally return the correct match. When you set this argument to FALSE, Excel finds an exact match and the data can be in any order.

Figure 2-48 shows a *VLOOKUP* function in cell D3 in the worksheet on the left. The result (250) is from the third column in row 6 in the table array in the worksheet on the right. Both sheets are in the same workbook.

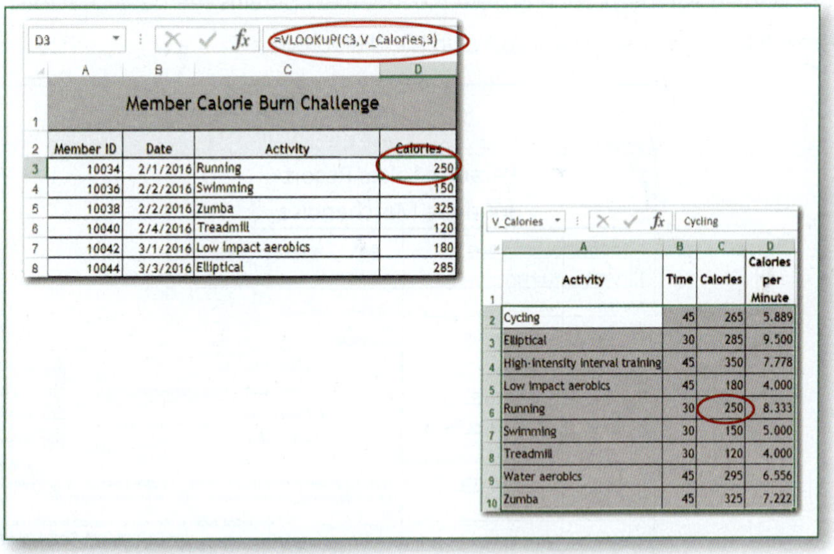

Figure 2-48 ***VLOOKUP*** **function in cell D3 on the left**

=VLOOKUP(C3,V_Calories,3)

- The *lookup_value* argument is cell C3 ("Running").
- The *table_array* argument is a named cell range, *V_Calories*. The "V" is a reminder that this range is a vertical lookup table. The *V_Calories* range is cells A2:D10 in the sheet on the right.
- The *col_index_num* argument is *3*, so the result is from the third column, the "Calories" column, in the *V_Calories* range.
- The *range_lookup* argument is omitted or TRUE. The data in the table array (on the right) is sorted so TRUE is acceptable for this argument.

Insert the *VLOOKUP* function from the *Lookup & Reference* category on the *Formulas* tab or by searching for it in the *Insert Function* dialog box. When you are experienced using the function, type it in the cell and use *Formula AutoComplete*.

▸HOW TO: Enter the VLOOKUP Function

1. Click the cell for the function.
2. Click the **Lookup & Reference** button [*Formulas* tab].
3. Select **VLOOKUP**.
   - The *Function Arguments* dialog box opens.
   - Move the dialog box if it covers data that you need to see or select.
4. Click the **Lookup_value** box.
5. Click the cell to be matched.
   - The *lookup_value* is typically a cell in the same row as the function.
   - This reference is usually relative.
6. Click the **Table_array** box.
7. Select the cell range with the lookup data.
   - When the lookup table is named, the range name is substituted.
   - The *Function Arguments* dialog box collapses while you select cells.
8. Press **F4** (**FN+F4**) to make the reference absolute if cell addresses are used.
   - When a range name has been substituted, you need not do this.
9. Click the **Col_index_num** box.
10. Type the column number, counting from the left, that contains the data to be displayed (Figure 2-49).
    - The result for the current cell displays in the dialog box.

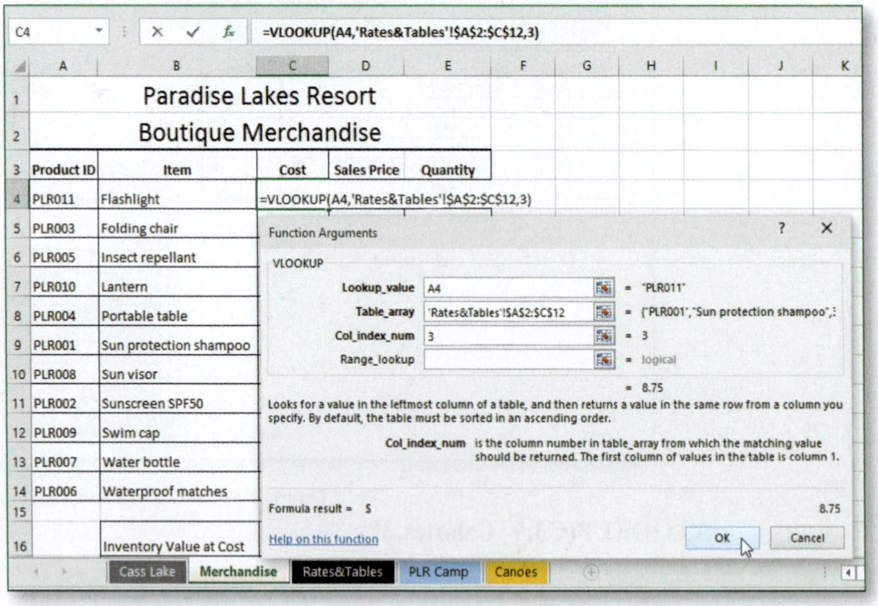

Figure 2-49 ***Function Arguments* dialog box for *VLOOKUP***

11. Leave the *Range_lookup* argument box empty if the data in the table array is sorted in ascending order.
    - Type FALSE in the entry box to find an exact match when the data is not sorted.
12. Click **OK**.

The *HLOOKUP* function has a *row_index_num* argument instead of the *col_index_num* argument. The *table_array* is set up horizontally as seen in Figure 2-50, and the first row is arranged in alphabetical order from left to right. The *HLOOKUP* function is in cell C6 in the sheet on the left. The lookup table is named *H_Fees*, shown in the sheet on the right.

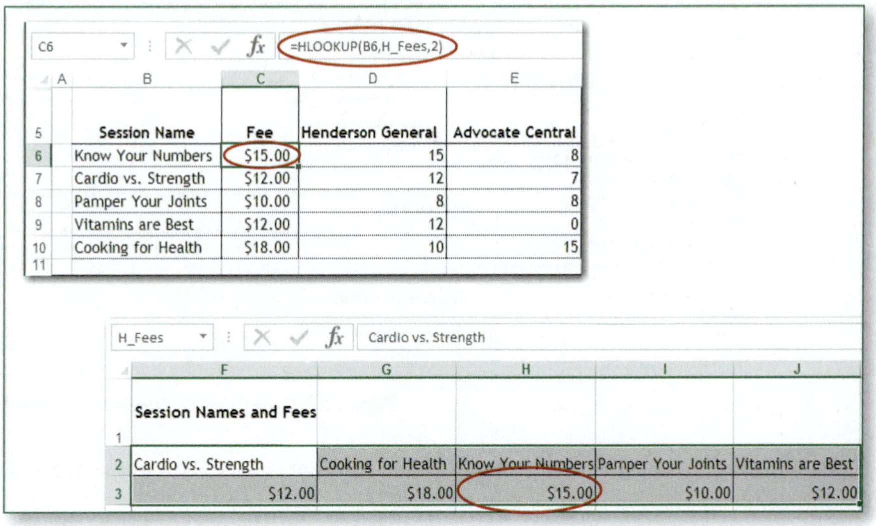

Figure 2-50 ***HLOOKUP*** **in cell C6**

=HLOOKUP(B6,H_Fees,2)

- The *lookup_value* argument is cell B6 ("Know Your Numbers").
- The *table_array* argument is a named cell range, *H_Fees*. The "H" is a visual cue for a horizontal lookup table. The *H_Fees* range is cells F2:J3 on the right.
- The *row_index_num* argument is *2*, so the data shown in cell C6 is from the second row of the *H_Fees* range.
- The *range_lookup* argument is omitted, because the first row in the data range is sorted alphabetically from left to right.

HOW TO: Use The HLOOKUP Function

1. Click the cell for the function.
2. Click the **Lookup & Reference** button [*Formulas* tab].
3. Select **HLOOKUP**.
   - The *Function Arguments* dialog box opens.
4. Click the **Lookup_value** box.
5. Click the cell to be matched.
   - The *lookup_value* is typically a cell in the same row as the function.
   - This reference is usually relative.
6. Click the **Table_array** box.
7. Select the cell range with the lookup data.
   - When the lookup table is named, the range name is substituted.
   - The *Function Arguments* dialog box collapses while you select cells.
8. Press **F4** (**FN+F4**) to make the reference absolute when cell addresses are used.
9. Click the **Row_index_num** box.

10. Type the row number, counting the first row of the *table_array* as 1 (Figure 2-51).
    - The result for the current cell displays in the dialog box.

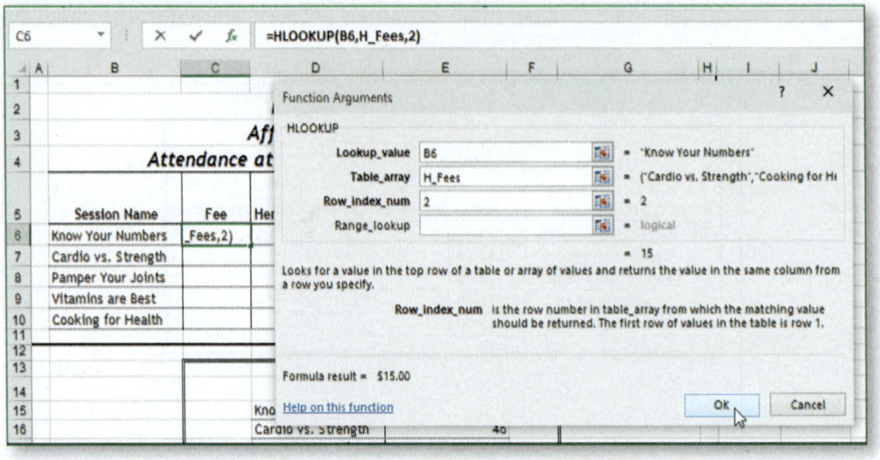

Figure 2-51 ***HLOOKUP Function Arguments*** **dialog box**

11. Leave the *Range_lookup* argument box empty if the first row of data in the table array is arranged alphabetically from left to right.
12. Click **OK**.

SLO 2.7

Using Math & Trig Functions

You have already used *SUM* from the *Math & Trig* function category. This category includes functions to display the absolute value of data, to calculate the cosine of an angle, or to return the power of a number. You might recognize the function *PI* or π from a math class. Three *Math & Trig* functions that are often used in business or personal calculations are *ROUND*, *SUMIF*, and *SUMPRODUCT*.

Round Function

Rounding means that a value is adjusted to display a specified number of decimal places or a whole number. You can round the numbers on your tax return in the United States, which means that you need not show any cents, just dollars.

The *ROUND* function has two arguments: *number* and *num_digits*.

=ROUND(number, num_digits)

- The ***number*** is the cell or the value to be adjusted.
- The ***num_digits*** sets the number of decimal places for rounding. When this argument is zero (0), the value displays as the nearest whole number. When the *num_digits* argument is greater than zero, the value is rounded to that number of decimal places. You can use a negative number for the *num_digits* argument, which rounds the value to the left of the decimal point. Make sure you understand the results when you round to the left of the decimal point.

When a value used in rounding is 5 or greater, results round up to the next digit. If you round 5.523 to show zero (0) decimal places, it rounds up to display as 6 because the value after the decimal point is 5. If you round 5.423 to two places, it rounds to 5.42 because the value used for rounding is 3. The *Increase Decimal* and *Decrease Decimal* buttons follow these rounding principles for displaying values in the cell, as do the *Accounting Number* and *Currency* formats. These formats, however, keep the full unrounded value in the cell and use that value in calculations.

> **MORE INFO**
>
> When a value is rounded, the rounded value is used in calculations, not the full unrounded number.

HOW TO: Use the ROUND Function

1. Click the cell for the function.
2. Type =rou and press **Tab**.
   - *Formula AutoComplete* inserts the function in the cell.
   - The *number* argument is bold in the *ScreenTip*.
3. Select the cell to be rounded.
   - The cell address appears in the cell and in the *Formula* bar.
   - You can type a value as the *number* argument.
4. Type , (a comma) to separate the arguments.
   - The *num_digits* argument is bold in the *ScreenTip*.
5. Type a number to set the number of decimal places (Figure 2-52).
6. Press **Enter**.

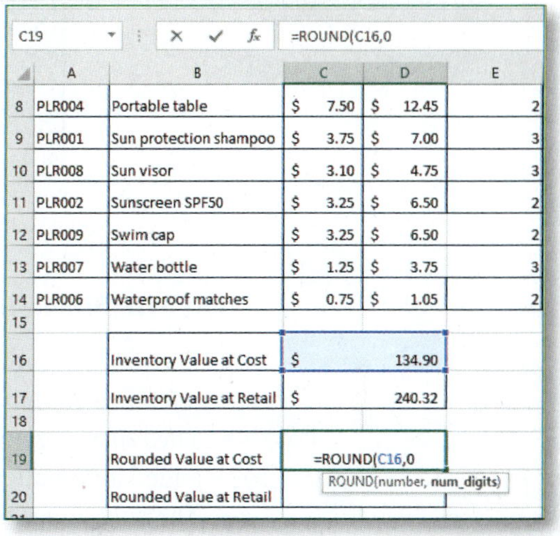

Figure 2-52 Type the *ROUND* function

> **MORE INFO**
>
> Excel has a *ROUNDDOWN* function that always rounds a number down or toward zero. The *ROUNDUP* function rounds a value up, away from zero.

SUMIF Function

The *SUMIF* function controls which data in a range are included in the total. It enables you to eliminate cells from the calculation by criteria that you set. ***Criteria*** are restrictions, conditions, or rules that must be met. In a *SUMIF* function, cell values are included in the sum only if they match the criteria.

The *SUMIF* function has three arguments.

=SUMIF (range, criteria, [sum_range])

- The ***range*** is the range of cells to be evaluated or searched, the values that are compared to the criteria.
- The ***criteria*** argument defines which cells from the range should be included in the sum. You can use comparison operators, cell references, a value, or text. When you use text or a comparison operator, the criteria must be enclosed in quotation marks.

- The *[sum_range]* is the cell range to be summed. This argument is optional, because it is omitted when the range to be summed is the same as the *range* argument.

Figure 2-53 illustrates a *SUMIF* function in cell I5 that totals sales for products that have a price greater than $10.

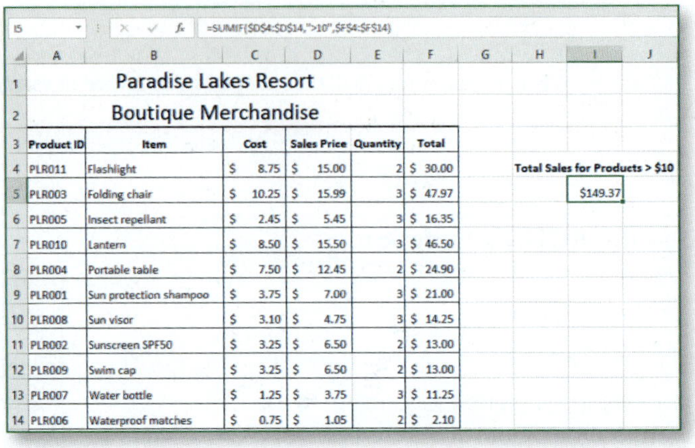

Figure 2-53 ***SUMIF*** **function in cell I5**

=SUMIF($D$4:$D$14,">10",$F$4:$F14)

- The *range* argument is the sales price column, cells $D$4:$D$14. It is an absolute reference so that the formula can be copied.
- The *criteria* argument is >10, shown in quotation marks. The quotation marks are added automatically when you use the *Function Arguments* dialog box.
- The *sum_range* argument is cells $F$4:$F$14, the cells to be added if the price is greater than 10.

MORE INFO

You can use wildcards (* or ?) in a criteria argument. For example, to sum sales for all items that begin with the letter S, use s* as the criteria. Criteria are not case-sensitive.

HOW TO: Build a SUMIF Function

1. Click the cell for the function.
2. Click the **Math & Trig** button [*Formulas* tab, *Function Library* group].
3. Select **SUMIF**.
4. Click the **Range** box.
5. Select the cell range to be compared against the criteria.
   - Make the reference absolute if the formula might be copied.
   - Press **F3** (**FN+F3**) to paste a range name rather than selecting the range.
6. Click the **Criteria** box.
   - Type text to be compared or a value to be matched.
   - Type an expression with operators to be evaluated.
   - Quotation marks are automatically supplied.

7. Click the **Sum_range** box (Figure 2-54).
    - Select the cells to be added.
    - If the cells to be added are the same as those in the *range* argument, leave the entry blank.

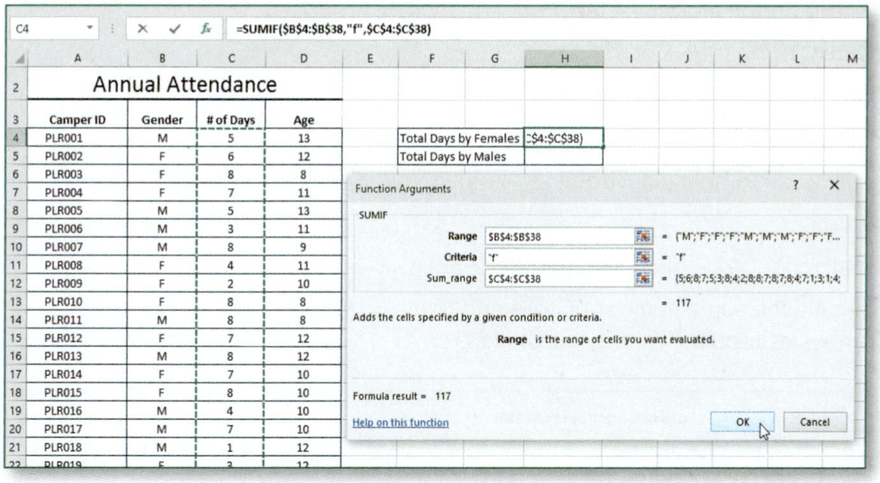

Figure 2-54 ***Function Arguments* dialog box for *SUMIF***

8. Click **OK**.

SUMPRODUCT Function

The *SUMPRODUCT* function calculates the sum of the product of several ranges. It multiplies the cells identified in its *array* arguments and then it totals those individual products. A ***product*** is the result of a multiplication problem; 4 is the product of 2 times 2. An ***array*** is a range of cells in a row or a column. An array has a ***dimension***, which is the number of columns or rows. The arrays A1:A5 and C1:C5 have the same dimension, five rows and one column.

The *SUMPRODUCT* function has the following syntax.

=SUMPRODUCT(array1, array2, [arrayN])

- The ***array1*** argument is the first range of cells for the multiplication.
- The ***array2*** argument is the range that is multiplied by the corresponding cells in the *array1* range. These two ranges must have the same number of cells, the same dimension.

It is possible to use more than two arrays so that you could have an *array3* argument or even more.

In Figure 2-55, the *SUMPRODUCT* function in cell C22 multiplies the first array C6:C20 by the corresponding values in cells F6:F20 and totals those products.

=SUMPRODUCT(C6:C20,F6:F20)

The value in cell C6 is multiplied by cell F6, cell C7 is multiplied by cell F7, and so on. Those individual products are summed, and the result is $249.15.

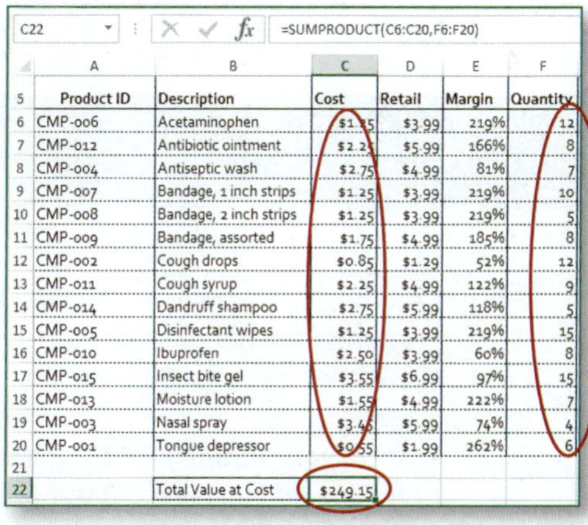

Figure 2-55 ***SUMPRODUCT* in cell C22**

▸ HOW TO: Build a SUMPRODUCT Function

1. Click the cell for the function.
2. Click the **Math & Trig** button [*Formulas* tab, *Function Library* group].
3. Select **SUMPRODUCT**.
   - The *Function Arguments* dialog box opens.
4. Click the **Array1** box.
5. Select the first cell range to be multiplied.
6. Click the **Array2** box.
7. Select the next cell range to be multiplied (Figure 2-56).
   - All arrays must have the same number of cells and rows.
   - Use as many arrays as required for the calculation.

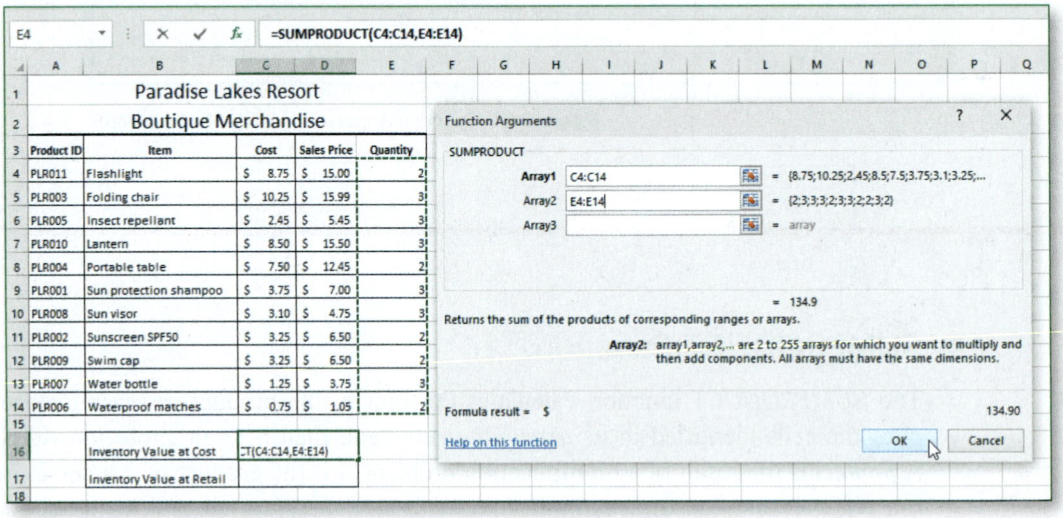

Figure 2-56 ***Function Arguments*** **dialog box for** ***SUMPRODUCT***

8. Click **OK**.

MORE INFO

If an array in a *SUMPRODUCT* formula includes an empty cell, Excel treats that value as 0, but the multiplication by zero does not affect the sum.

PAUSE & PRACTICE: EXCEL 2-3

For this project, you continue working on the workbook for Paradise Lakes. You calculate totals related to camp attendance and merchandise inventory using functions from the *Math & Trig*, *Financial*, *Logical*, *Lookup & Reference*, and *Date & Time* categories.

File Needed: ***[your initials] PP E2-2.xlsx***
Completed Project File Name: ***[your initials] PP E2-3.xlsx***

1. Open the ***[your initials] PP E2-2.xlsx*** workbook completed in *Pause & Practice 2-2* and save it as [your initials] PP E2-3.
2. Click the **Cass Lake** worksheet tab.
3. Enter an *IF* function to determine if a month's revenue was below average.
   a. Click cell **B22** and click the **Formulas** tab.
   b. Click the **Logical** button In the *Function Library* group and select **IF**. The *Function Arguments* dialog box opens.
   c. Click the **Logical_test** text box and click cell **B11**.
   d. Type < for a less than operator after "B11" in the *Logical_test* box.
   e. Click cell **K15** and press **F4** (**FN+F4**) to make this an absolute reference.
   f. Click the **Value_if_true** box and type Yes. You need not type quotation marks when you use the *Function Arguments* dialog box.
   g. Press **Tab** to move to the *Value_if_false* box. Excel supplies the quotation marks for "Yes."
   h. Type No (Figure 2-57).
   i. Click **OK**. For April, the result is *Yes*.
   j. Click cell **B22** and click the **Center** button [*Home* tab, *Alignment* group].
   k. Use the *Fill* pointer to copy the formula in cell **B22** to cells **C22:G22**.
   l. Press **Ctrl+Home**.

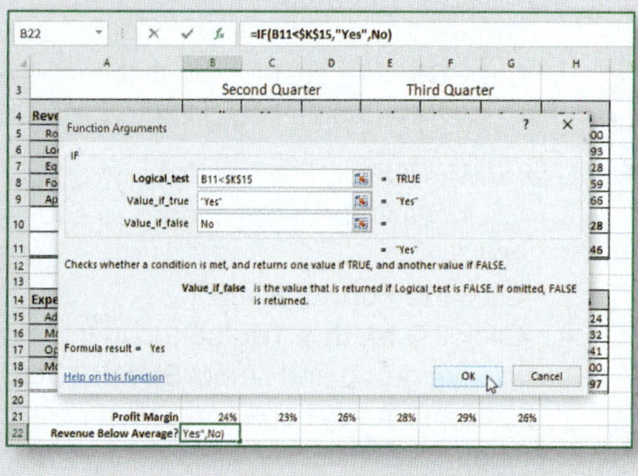

Figure 2-57 Build an *IF* function

4. Use *SUMIF* to calculate results.
   a. Click the **PLR Camp** worksheet tab. The number of attendees is tracked with the camper's ID, gender, and age.
   b. Select cell **H4** and click the **Formulas** tab.
   c. Click the **Math & Trig** button in the *Function Library* group and select **SUMIF**.
   d. Click the **Range** text box and select cells **B4:B38**.
   e. Press **F4** (**FN+F4**) to make the reference absolute.
   f. Press **Tab** and type f in the *Criteria* box. Criteria are not case-sensitive. The cells in column B will be checked to determine if they show "F."
   g. Click the **Sum_range** box, select cells **C4:C38**, and press **F4** (**FN+F4**). The values in this range will be summed for those rows in which the gender is F (Figure 2-58).
   h. Click **OK**. Female camp days are 117.
   i. Click cell **H4** and use the *Fill* pointer to copy the formula to cell **H5**.
   j. Edit the formula in cell **H5** to show m instead of "f."

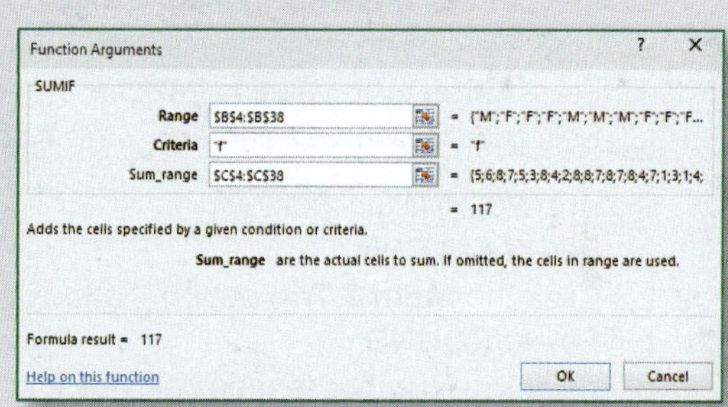

Figure 2-58 Build a *SUMIF* function

5. Use *VLOOKUP* to display costs.
   a. Click the **Merchandise** sheet tab and select cell **C4**. Individual costs are missing, but they are listed on the **Rates&Tables** sheet.
   b. Click the **Lookup & Reference** button [*Formulas* tab, *Function Library* group].
   c. Select **VLOOKUP**.
   d. Click the **Lookup_value** box and select cell **A4**.
   e. Click the **Table_array** box. The table with the costs is on the **Rates&Tables** sheet.
   f. Click the **Rates&Tables** worksheet tab and select cells **A2:C12**. This array or range includes the ID, the name, and the cost. The costs are in column C, the third column from the left.

g. Press **F4** (**FN+F4**) to make the array an absolute reference.
h. Click the **Col_index_num** box and type 3. The ID in cell A4 will be located in cells A2:C12 on the **Rates&Tables** sheet, and the cost in the third column will be displayed.
i. Click the **Range_lookup** box and type false (Figure 2-59).
j. Click **OK**. The cost for the first item is $8.75.
k. Copy the formula in cell **C4** to cells **C5:C14**.

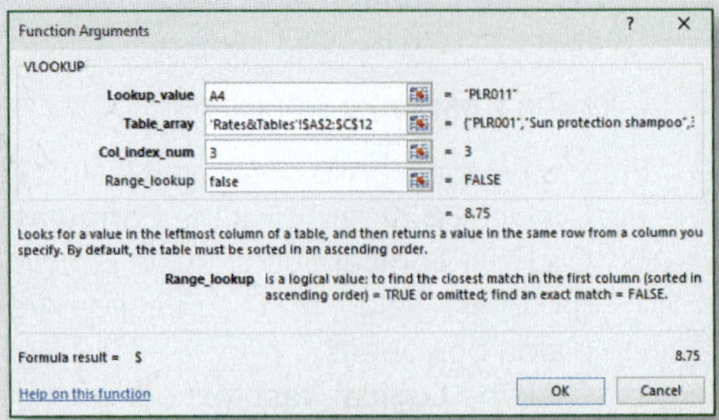

Figure 2-59 Build a *VLOOKUP* function

6. Use *SUMPRODUCT* to calculate inventory values.
a. Click cell **C16**. This is a merged and centered cell.
b. Click the **Formulas** tab.
c. Click the **Math & Trig** button in the *Function Library* group and select **SUMPRODUCT**.
d. Click the **Array1** box and select cells **C4:C14**. The range includes 11 values.
e. Click the **Array2** box and select cells **E4:E14**. The range includes 11 values, and each one will be multiplied by the corresponding value in the same row in column C.
f. Click **OK**. The value of the inventory at cost is 134.9.
g. Click cell **C17**, type =sump, and press **Tab**. The function is inserted and the *ScreenTip* shows the next argument, *array1*.
h. Select cells **D4:D14** and type , (a comma) to separate the first argument from the second.
i. Select cells **E4:E14** (Figure 2-60). You need not type the closing parenthesis.
j. Press **Enter**. The value is 240.32.
k. Select cells **C16:C17** and apply the **Accounting Number** format.

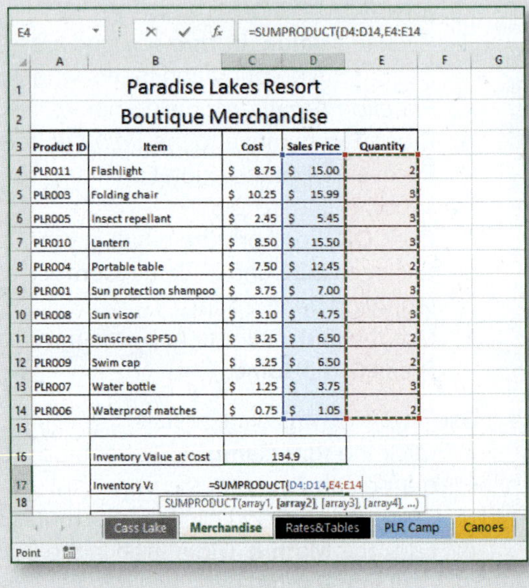

Figure 2-60 Type a *SUMPRODUCT* function

7. Use the *ROUND* function.
a. Select cell **C19**.
b. Click the **Math & Trig** button [*Formulas* tab, *Function Library* group].
c. Select **ROUND**.
d. Click the **Number** text box and click cell **C16**.
e. Type 0 in the *Num_digits* text box.
f. Press **Enter**. The value is rounded up to $135.00.
g. Copy the formula in cell **C19** to cell **C20**. The value from cell C17 is rounded down to $240.00.

8. Use the *PMT* function to determine payments for new canoe purchases.
a. Click the **Canoes** sheet tab and click cell **B7**.
b. Click the **Formulas** tab and the **Financial** button [*Function Library* group].
c. Select **PMT**.
d. Click the **Rate** box and click cell **B6**.
e. Type /12 immediately after "B6," to divide the rate by 12 for monthly payments.
f. Click the **Nper** box and click cell **B5**. Type *12 to multiply by 12 for 12 months per year.
g. Click the **Pv** box and click cell **B4**. This is the amount of the loan.
h. Click the **Fv** box. Leave this blank to indicate no balance due at the end of the loan term.

i. Click the **Type** box and type 1. The payment will be made at the beginning of the month (Figure 2-61).

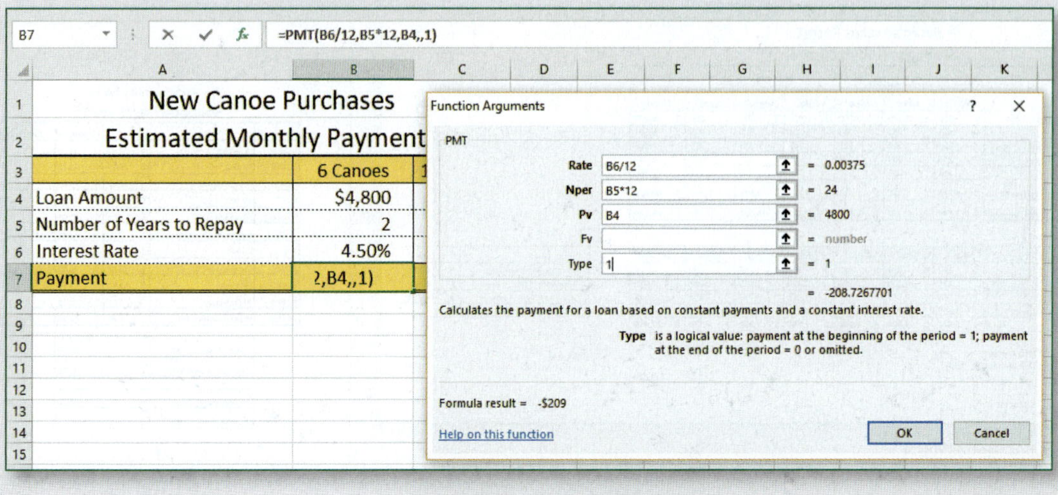

Figure 2-61 *PMT* function for payment at the beginning of the period

j. Click **OK**. The payment is −$209, a negative value because it is money paid out. This cell was formatted to show no decimal places.

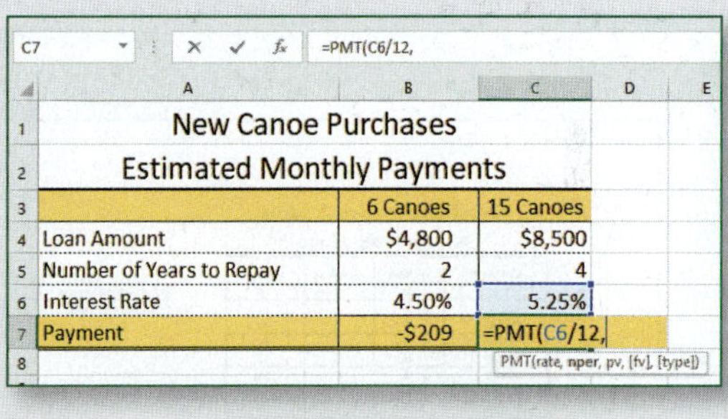

Figure 2-62 Type a *PMT* function

9. Type the *PMT* function.
   a. Click cell **C7**.
   b. Type =pm, and press **Tab**. The *ScreenTip* shows the first argument, *rate*.
   c. Click cell **C6** and type /12 and then type , (a comma). This divides the rate by 12 and enters a comma to separate the arguments (Figure 2-62).
   d. Click cell **C5** and type *12 and then type , (a comma) to multiply the number of years by 12 and move to the next argument.
   e. Click cell **C4** for the *pv* argument, the amount of the loan.
   f. Type , (a comma) to move to the *fv* argument.
   g. Type , (another comma) to move to the *type* argument. *Formula AutoComplete* lists two options for the argument (Figure 2-63).
   h. Double-click **1 - beginning of the period** in the *ScreenTip*.
   i. Press **Enter**. The payment is −$196.
   j. Press **Ctrl+Home**.

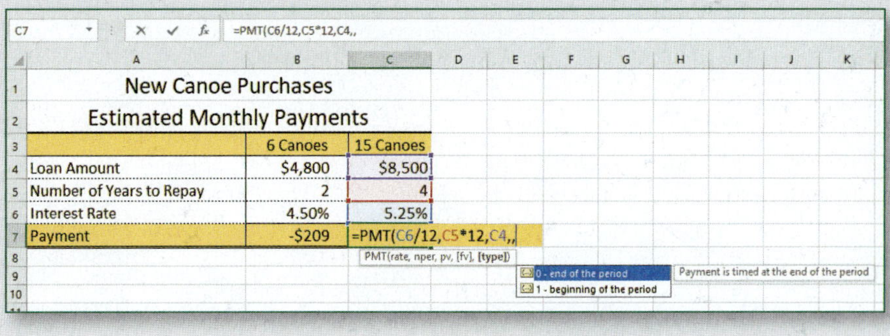

Figure 2-63 *Formula AutoComplete* for argument choices

10. Save and close the workbook (Figure 2-64).

Paradise Lakes Resort
Second and Third Quarter

Revenue		Second Quarter				Third Quarter			
	April	May	June	July	August	Sept	Totals
Room and Cabin Rentals	$ 5,400	$ 5,700	$ 6,500	$ 6,800	$ 8,700	$ 5,800	$ 38,900
Local Tours	876	750	968	1,254	820	925	5,593
Equipment Rentals	358	250	325	345	275	375	1,928
Food & Beverage	254	209	198	402	519	677	2,259
Apparel	451	356	543	532	450	534	2,866
Rental Revenues	$ 5,758	$ 5,950	$ 6,825	$ 7,145	$ 8,975	$ 6,175	$ 40,828
Total Revenue	$ 7,339	$ 7,265	$ 8,534	$ 9,333	$ 10,764	$ 8,311	$ 51,546

Expenses	April	May	June	July	August	Sept	Totals
Administrative	$ 587	$ 581	$ 683	$ 747	$ 861	$ 665	$ 4,124
Management	1,101	1,090	1,280	1,400	1,615	1,247	7,732
Operational	2,569	2,543	2,987	3,267	3,767	2,909	18,041
Mortgage and Leases	1,350	1,350	1,350	1,350	1,350	1,350	8,100
Total	$ 5,607	$ 5,564	$ 6,300	$ 6,763	$ 7,593	$ 6,170	$ 37,997

Profit Margin	24%	23%	26%	28%	29%	26%	
Revenue Below Average?	Yes	Yes	Yes	No	No	Yes	

Total Revenue	$ 51,546
Average Monthly Revenue	$ 8,591
Maximum Cabin Revenue	$ 8,700
Minimum Tour Revenue	$ 750
Number of Months	6

Current Date

Paradise Lakes Resort
Boutique Merchandise

Product ID	Item	Cost	Sales Price	Quantity
PLR011	Flashlight	$ 8.75	$ 15.00	2
PLR003	Folding chair	$ 10.25	$ 15.99	3
PLR005	Insect repellant	$ 2.45	$ 5.45	3
PLR010	Lantern	$ 8.50	$ 15.50	3
PLR004	Portable table	$ 7.50	$ 12.45	3
PLR005	Sun protection shampoo	$ 3.75	$ 7.00	3
PLR006	Sun visor	$ 3.10	$ 4.75	3
PLR002	Sunscreen SPF50	$ 3.25	$ 6.50	2
PLR009	Swim cap	$ 3.25	$ 6.50	2
PLR007	Water bottle	$ 1.25	$ 3.75	2
PLR008	Waterproof matches	$ 0.75	$ 1.05	2

Inventory Value at Cost	$ 134.95
Inventory Value at Retail	$ 240.32
Rounded Value at Cost	$ 135.00
Rounded Value at Retail	$ 240.00

Paradise Lakes Youth Camp
Annual Attendance

Camper ID	Gender	# of Days	Age
PLR001	M	5	13
PLR002	F	6	12
PLR003	F	8	8
PLR004	F	7	11
PLR005	M	5	13
PLR006	M	3	13
PLR007	M	3	9
PLR008	F	4	11
PLR009	F	2	10
PLR010	F	8	8
PLR011	M	8	8
PLR012	F	7	12
PLR013	M	8	12
PLR014	F	7	10
PLR015	F	8	10
PLR016	M	4	10
PLR017	M	7	10
PLR018	M	1	12
PLR019	F	3	12
PLR020	F	3	12
PLR021	F	4	13
PLR022	M	10	9
PLR023	M	5	11
PLR024	F	8	11
PLR025	F	10	13
PLR026	F	8	10
PLR027	M	6	8
PLR028	M	7	9
PLR029	F	4	11
PLR030	F	4	13
PLR031	F	10	11
PLR032	F	3	10
PLR033	F	3	10
PLR034	M	3	12
PLR035	F	4	8

Total Days by Females	157
Total Days by Males	79

New Canoe Purchases
Estimated Monthly Payments

	6 Canoes	15 Canoes
Loan Amount	$4,800	$8,500
Number of Years to Repay	2	4
Interest Rate	4.50%	5.25%
Payment	-$209	-$196

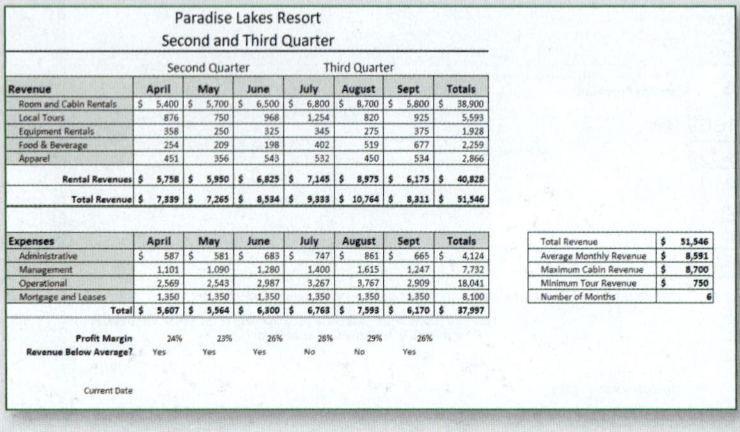

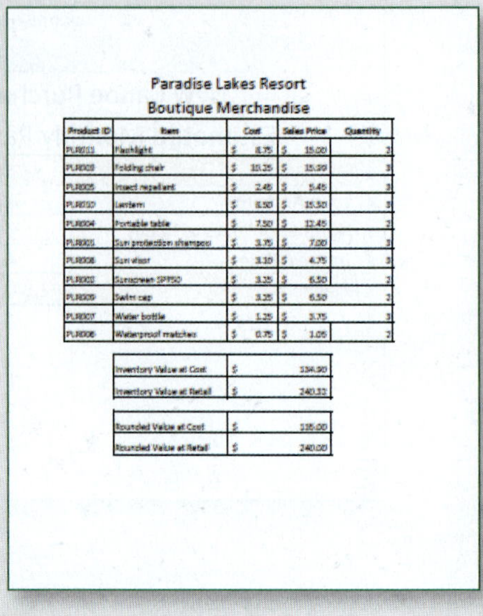

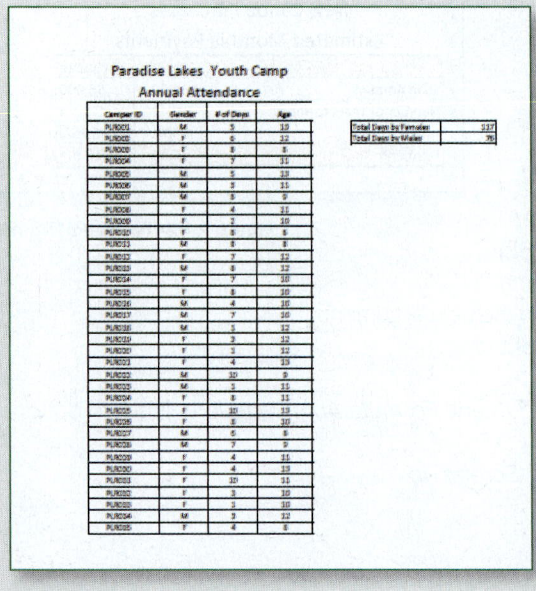

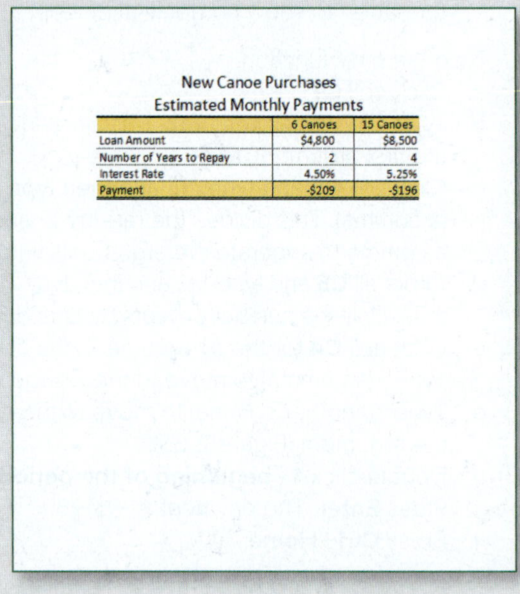

Figure 2-64 PP E2-3 completed

Chapter Summary

2.1 Build and edit basic formulas (p. E2-89).

- A ***formula*** is a calculation that uses arithmetic operators, worksheet cells, and constant values. Basic arithmetic operations are addition, subtraction, multiplication, and division.
- Type a formula in the cell or point and click to select cells.
- When you type a formula, ***Formula AutoComplete*** displays suggestions for completing the formula.
- Formulas are edited in the *Formula* bar or in the cell to change cell addresses, use a different operator, or add cells to the calculation.

2.2 Set mathematical order of operations in a formula (p. E2-91).

- Excel follows mathematics rules for the order in which operations are carried out when a formula has more than one operator.
- Control the sequence of calculations by placing operations that should be done first within parentheses.
- Use the following acronym to help remember the order of arithmetic operations: **P**lease **E**xcuse **M**y **D**ear **A**unt **S**ally (**P**arentheses, **E**xponentiation, **M**ultiplication, **D**ivision, **A**ddition, **S**ubtraction).

2.3 Use absolute, mixed, relative, and 3D references in a formula (p. E2-93).

- A ***relative cell reference*** in a formula is the cell address which, when copied, updates to the address of the copy.
- An ***absolute cell reference*** is the cell address with dollar signs, as in $A$5. This reference does not change when the formula is copied.
- A ***mixed cell reference*** contains one relative and one absolute address, as in $B5 or B$5. When copied, the absolute part of the reference does not change.
- A ***3D cell reference*** is a cell in another worksheet in the same workbook. It includes the name of the worksheet followed by an exclamation point, as in *Inventory!B2*.
- Name a single cell or a group of cells with a defined ***range name***.
- Use range names in formulas instead of cell addresses.
- *Formula AutoComplete* displays range names so that you can paste them in a formula.
- A named range is an absolute reference.

2.4 Use formula auditing tools in a worksheet (p. E2-99).

- Excel highlights several types of formula errors as you work, but you still need to review errors and make corrections.
- Excel automatically error-checks formulas based on its internal rules. A potential error is marked in the upper-left corner of the cell with a small triangle.
- ***Formula auditing*** tools include several commands to aid your review of workbook formulas and functions.
- The *Formula Auditing* group on the *Formulas* tab includes the *Trace Precedents* and *Trace Dependents* buttons.
- A ***circular reference*** is an error that occurs when a formula includes the address of the formula.
- Occasionally, errors are noted as you press a completion key and can be quickly corrected by accepting the suggested correction in the message window.

2.5 Work with *Statistical* and *Date & Time* functions (p. E2-106).

- The *AVERAGE* function calculates the arithmetic mean by adding values and dividing by the number of values.
- The *COUNT* function tallies the number of cells in a range. Different *COUNT* functions are available based on whether cell contents are labels, values, or blank.
- *MAX* and *MIN* functions find the largest and the smallest values, respectively, in a range.
- Commonly used statistical functions are options on the *AutoSum* button.
- The ***AutoCalculate*** feature displays numerical results such as *Sum*, *Average*, and *Count* on the *Status* bar for selected cells.
- The *Date & Time* category includes a *TODAY* function and a *NOW* function that display the current date and time.

2.6 Work with functions from the *Financial*, *Logical*, and *Lookup & Reference* categories (p. E2-114).

- Use the *Function Arguments* dialog box for help in completing an Excel function.

- The *Function Arguments* dialog box includes a description of the function and an explanation of each argument.
- The *PMT* function from the *Financial* category calculates a constant payment amount for a loan.
- The *Logical* function *IF* evaluates a statement or condition and displays a particular result when the statement is true and another result when the condition is false.
- A *Lookup* function displays data from a cell located in another part of the workbook.
- Two widely used *Lookup* functions are *VLOOKUP* (vertical) and *HLOOKUP* (horizontal).

2.7 Build functions from the *Math & Trig* category (p. E2-122).

- The *ROUND* function adjusts a value up or down based on the number of decimal places.
- The *SUMIF* function includes cells in a total only if they meet a set criteria or condition.
- The *SUMPRODUCT* function multiplies corresponding cells from an ***array*** and then totals the results of each multiplication.

Check for Understanding

The SIMbook for this text (within your SIMnet account) provides the following resources for concept review:

- Multiple-choice questions
- Short answer questions
- Matching exercises

Guided Project 2-1

Courtyard Medical Plaza (CMP) has doctor offices, a pharmacy, x-ray and lab services, insurance and billing support, optometry and dental facilities, and on-site dining. You will complete an inventory worksheet for the pharmacy as well as insurance and payment data for the optometry group.
[Student Learning Outcomes 2.1, 2.2, 2.3, 2.4, 2.5, 2.6, 2.7]

File Needed: ***CourtyardMedical-02.xlsx*** *(Student data files are available in the* Library *of your SIMnet account.)*
Completed Project File Name: ***[your initials] Excel 2-1.xlsx***

Skills Covered in This Project

- Build and copy formulas.
- Name cell ranges.
- Set the mathematical order of operations.
- Use relative, mixed, and absolute cell references in formulas.
- Use *AVERAGE*, *MAX*, and *MIN*.
- Use *SUMIF*.
- Check results with *AutoCalculate*.
- Use the *VLOOKUP* function.
- Use formula auditing tools.
- Use the *PMT* and *SUMPRODUCT* functions.
- Insert the *TODAY* function.

---

1. Open the ***CourtyardMedical-02.xlsx*** workbook from your student data files and save it as [your initials] Excel 2-1.
2. Enter and copy subtraction formulas.
   a. Click cell **E2** on the **Lookup_Data** worksheet. To calculate the dollar amount of the margin, subtract the cost from the retail price.
   b. Type an equals sign (=) to start the formula.
   c. Click cell **D2**, the retail price.
   d. Type a minus sign or hyphen (–) to subtract and click cell **C2**, the cost.
   e. Click the **Enter** button (check mark) in the *Formula* bar. The pointer stays in the formula cell. The margin for acetaminophen is $1.49.
   f. Drag the *Fill* pointer to copy the formula in cell **E2** to cells **E3:E16**. The *Auto Fill Options* button appears near cell E16.
   g. Click the **Auto Fill Options** button and choose **Fill Without Formatting** (Figure 2-65). This option copies the formula without the top border from cell E2.
   h. Format cells **E3:E16** as **Currency**.
   i. Click the **Optometry** sheet tab and select cell **G5**.
   j. Type = to start the formula to subtract the patient's share from the billed amount.
   k. Click cell **E5**, the billed amount.

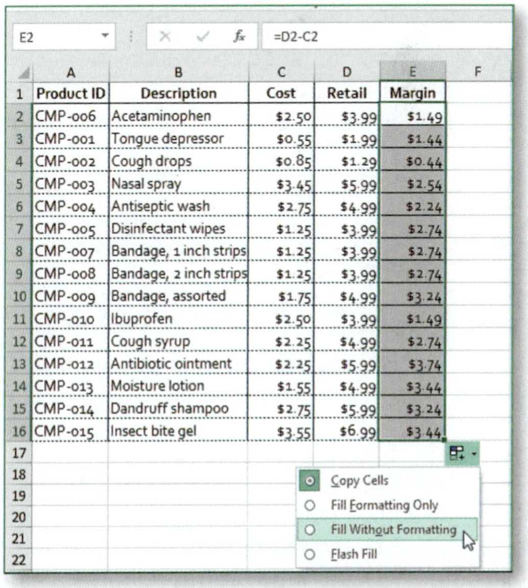

Figure 2-65 Copy without formatting to preserve borders

l. Type −, click cell **F5**, and press **Enter**.
m. Copy the formula in cell **G5** to cells **G6:G24** without formatting to maintain the fill color.

3. Name cell ranges.
   a. Select cells **E5:E24**. This named range will refer to the billable amounts.
   b. Click the **Name** box.
   c. Type Billables in the *Name* box and press **Enter**.
   d. Click the **Lookup_Data** worksheet tab.
   e. Select cells **A2:D16**. This named range will not include the calculated margin.
   f. Click the **Name** box.
   g. Type Costs in the *Name* box and press **Enter**.
   h. Select cells **H2:I5** and name the range Insurers.
   i. Click cell **A1** and click the **Name** box arrow to see the range names in the workbook (Figure 2-66).

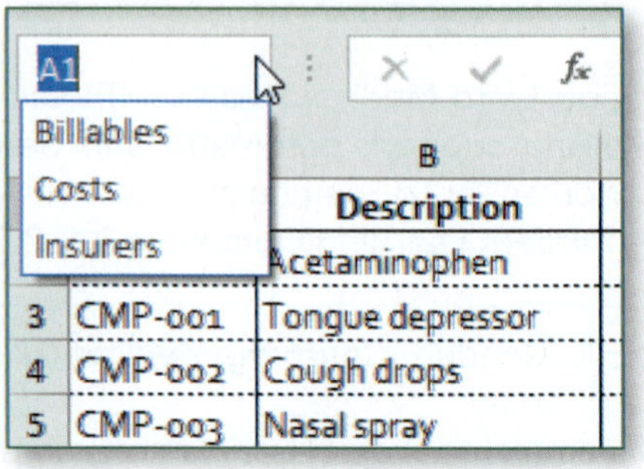

Figure 2-66 Range names in the worksheet

4. Use range names with *AVERAGE*, *MIN*, and *MAX*.
   a. Click the **Optometry** sheet tab and select cell **D27**.
   b. Type =aver and press **Tab**.
   c. Select cells **E5:E24** and press **Enter**. The range name is substituted in the formula when you select the cells in the worksheet.
   d. Select cell **D28**, click the **AutoSum** button arrow [*Home* tab, *Editing* group], and select **Max**.
   e. Select cells **E5:E24** and press **Enter**.
   f. Use *MIN* in cell **D29** with the same cell range.
   g. Apply the **Currency** format to cells **D27:D29**.

5. Unhide a column and set the order of operations in a formula.
   a. Click the **Insurance** sheet tab. Column D is hidden.
   b. Point to the column **C** heading and click and drag to select columns **C:E**.
   c. Right-click either column heading and choose **Unhide**. Column D has a *VLOOKUP* formula to display the service fee from the Insurers range on the **Lookup_Data** sheet.
   d. Select cell **E5**. The total with service charge is calculated by multiplying 1 plus the service fee times the billed amount.
   e. Type = and click cell **C5**.
   f. Type *(immediately after **C5**.
   g. Type 1+ immediately after the left parenthesis.
   h. Click cell **D5**. This part of the formula will be calculated first (Figure 2-67).
   i. Press **Enter**. Because the formula refers to a range name, the missing parenthesis is not automatically supplied (Figure 2-68).
   j. Click **Yes** to accept the suggested correction.
   k. Copy the formula to cells **E5:E24**.

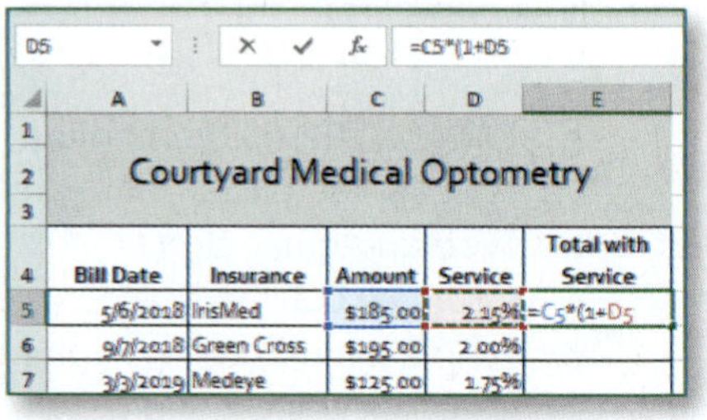

Figure 2-67 Set the order of the calculations in a formula

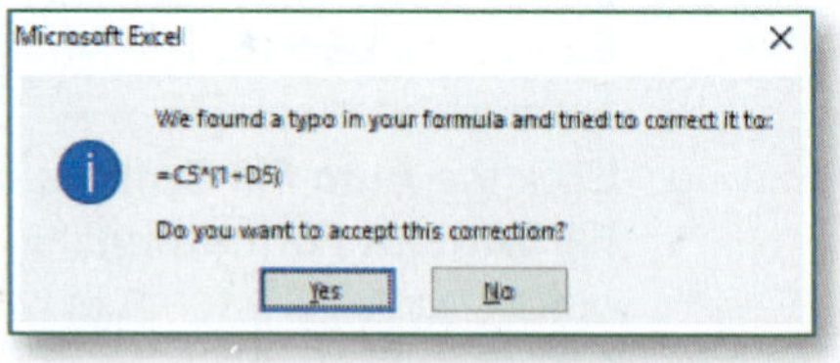

Figure 2-68 Formula correction message window

6. Format cells **E5:E24** as **Currency** from the *Number Format* drop-down list. The values are rounded to two decimal places (Figure 2-69).

7. Use the *SUMIF* function to calculate billable amounts by insurance company.
   a. Click the **Optometry** worksheet tab and select cell **D31**.
   b. Click the **Math & Trig** button [*Formulas* tab, *Function Library* group].
   c. Select **SUMIF**.
   d. Click the **Range** box, select cells **C5:C24**, and press **F4 (FN+F4)** to make the reference absolute.

e. Click the **Criteria** box and select cell **C31** to use a relative reference to the company name.
f. Click the **Sum_range** text box and select cells **E5:E24**. The range name is substituted and is an absolute reference (Figure 2-70).
g. Click **OK**. The result is 1030, the total amount billed to Green Cross.

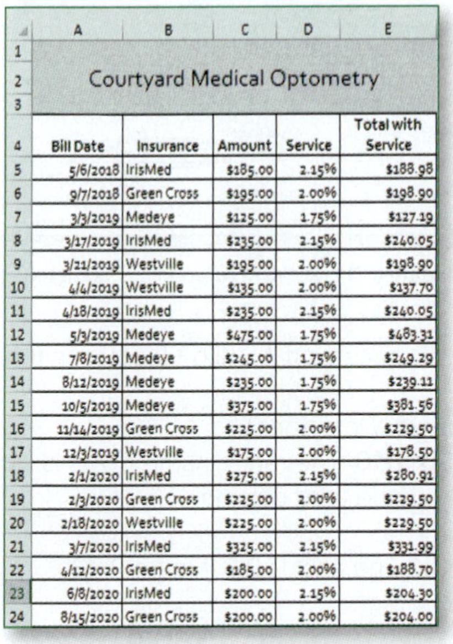

Figure 2-69 Results are rounded by the Currency format

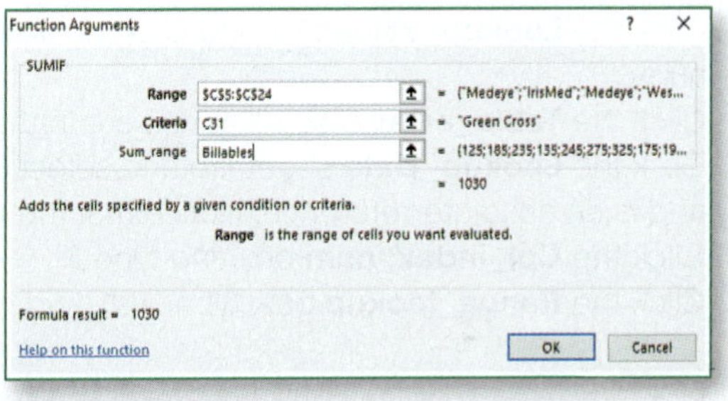

Figure 2-70 Absolute and relative reference arguments for *SUMIF*

8. Verify results with *AutoCalculate*.
   a. Select cells **E13:E15**.
   b. Press **Ctrl** and select cells **E20:E21**. These are the billable amounts for the Green Cross insurance company.
   c. Compare the *SUM* in the *Status* bar with the result in cell **D31** (Figure 2-71).

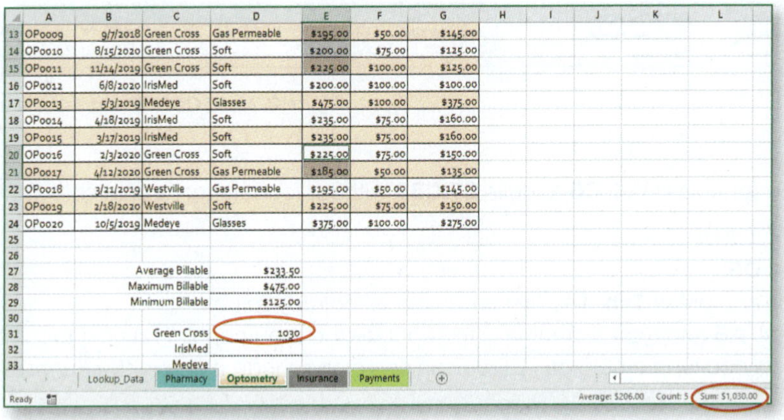

Figure 2-71 *AutoCalculate* results in *Status* bar

9. Copy the *SUMIF* function with a relative reference.
   a. Select cell **D31**.
   b. Drag the *Fill* pointer to copy the formula in cell **D31** to cells **D32:D34**. The *Auto Fill Options* button appears near cell D34.

c. Select cell **D32**. The reference to cell C31 in the original formula is updated to cell C32 in the copied formula (Figure 2-72).

10. Format cells **D31:D34** as **Currency** from the *Number Format* drop-down list. Press **Ctrl+Home**.

11. Use *VLOOKUP* with a range name to display costs.
    a. Click the **Pharmacy** worksheet tab and select cell **C6**. Cost and retail prices are missing.
    b. Click the **Lookup & Reference** button [*Formulas* tab, *Function Library* group] and select **VLOOKUP**.

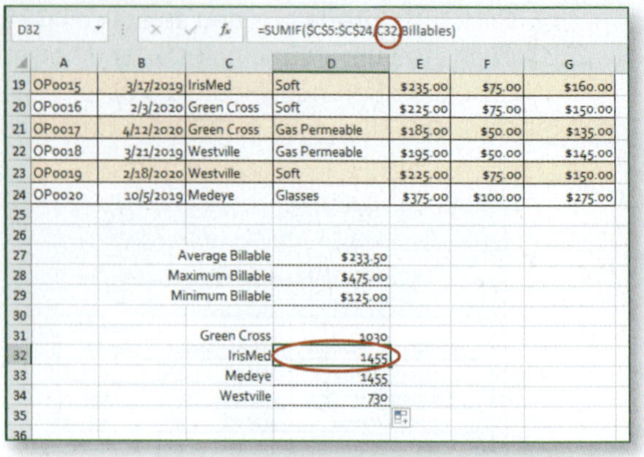

Figure 2-72 Relative reference is adjusted after copying

    c. Click the **Lookup_value** box and click cell **A6**. The ID in column A will be located in the table array.
    d. Click the **Table_array** box. All prices are in the *Lookup_Data* sheet.
    e. Click the **Lookup_Data** sheet tab and select cells **A2:D16**. The range name *Costs* is substituted and is an absolute reference. Notice that the cost is in the third column.
    f. Click the **Col_index_num** box and type 3.
    g. Click the **Range_lookup** box, type false, and click **OK**. The cost is 2.5 (Figure 2-73).

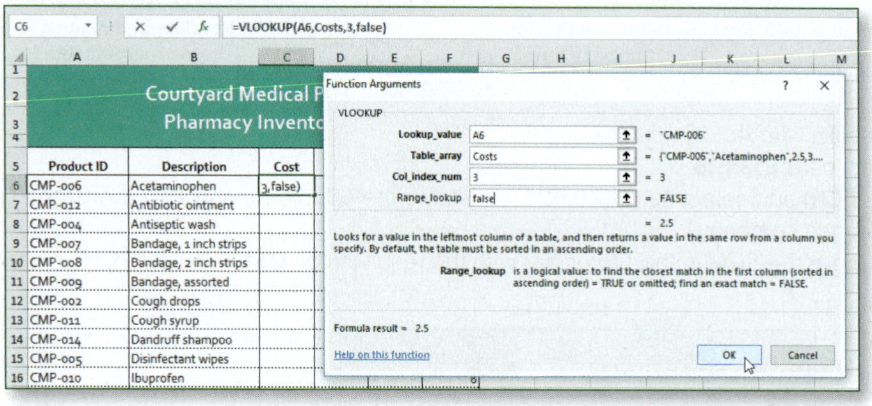

Figure 2-73 *VLOOKUP* and its arguments

    h. Copy the formula in cell **C6** to cells **C7:C20** without formatting. Format cells **C6:C20** as **Currency**.

12. Type the *VLOOKUP* function.
    a. Click cell **D6**.
    b. Type =vl and press **Tab**. The first argument is *lookup_value*.
    c. Select cell **A6** and type a comma (,) to separate the arguments. The next argument is *table_array*.
    d. Type costs and type a comma (,). (You can select the range name in the *Formula AutoComplete* list.)
    e. Type 4 for the *Col_index_num* argument and type a comma (,). The retail price is in the fourth column of the *Costs* range.
    f. Double-click **FALSE – Exact match** in the *ScreenTip* and press **Enter**. The closing parenthesis is supplied, and the retail price for acetaminophen is 3.99 (Figure 2-74).
    g. Copy the formula in cell **D6** to cells **D7:D20** without formatting to keep the borders and then format the cells as **Currency**.

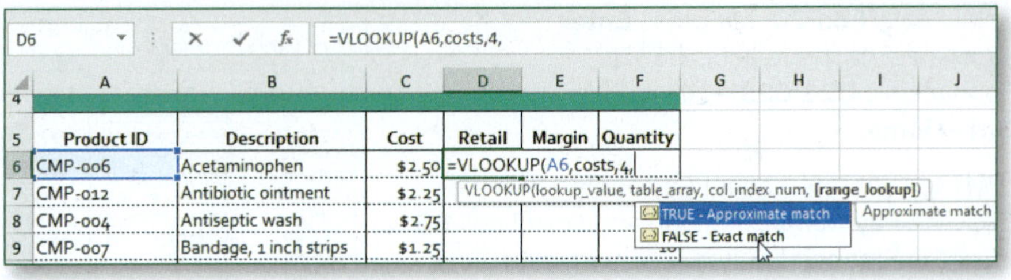

Figure 2-74 Double-click an option in the *ScreenTip*

13. Set the order of precedence in a formula.
    a. Click cell **E6**. The formula to calculate the margin subtracts the cost from the retail price and then divides by the cost. The margin is shown as a markup percentage.
    b. Type =(to start the formula and enter the opening parenthesis.
    c. Click cell **D6** for the retail price.
    d. Type – and click cell **C6** to subtract the cost from the retail price.
    e. Type) for the closing parenthesis. This forces the subtraction to be carried out first.
    f. Type / for division and click cell **C6** to divide the results by the cost (Figure 2-75).
    g. Press **Enter**. The results are formatted as currency.
    h. Apply **Percent Style** to cell **E6**. A margin of 60% means that the retail price is about 1.6 times the cost.
    i. Copy the formula in cell **E6** to cells **E7:E20** without formatting; then apply **Percent Style** to cells **E7:E20**.

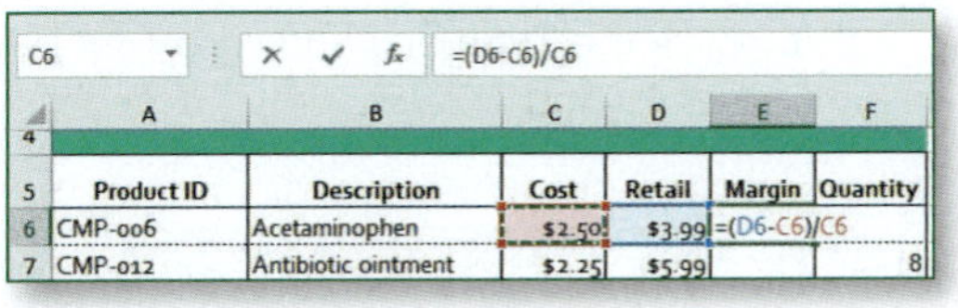

Figure 2-75 Formula to calculate profit margin

14. Trace precedents and dependents for formulas.
    a. Select cell **C6**.
    b. Click the **Trace Precedents** button [*Formulas* tab, *Formula Auditing* group]. The formula uses data from another worksheet and from cell **A6**.
    c. Select cell **E6** and click the **Trace Precedents** button.
    d. Select cell **D7** and click the **Trace Dependents** button. The arrow points to cell **E7**.
    e. Click the **Remove Arrows** button [*Formulas* tab, *Formula Auditing* group].

15. Enter a *SUMPRODUCT* function to calculate inventory values.
    a. Click cell **C22**.
    b. Click the **Math & Trig** button [*Formulas* tab, *Function Library* group] and select **SUMPRODUCT**.
    c. Click the **Array1** box and select cells **C6:C20**.
    d. Click the **Array2** box and select cells **F6:F20**. Both arrays have the same dimension (Figure 2-76).
    e. Click **OK**. The result in cell C22 is 264.15. Each value in column C is multiplied by its corresponding value in column E, and those results are summed.

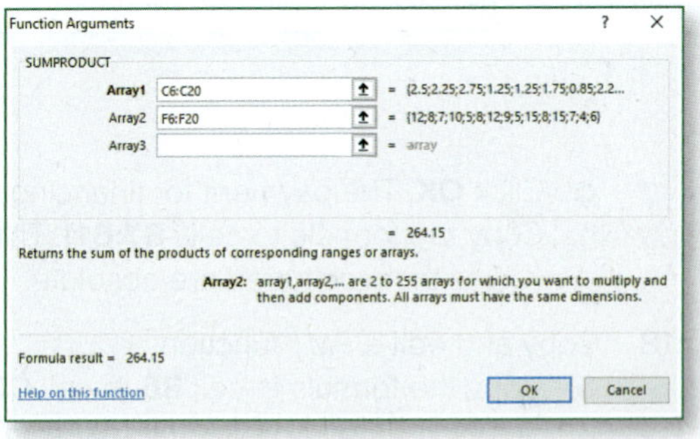

Figure 2-76 Two arrays for *SUMPRODUCT*

16. Type the *SUMPRODUCT* function.
    a. Click cell **C23**.
    b. Type =sump and press **Tab**. The first argument is *array1*.
    c. Select cells **D6:D20** and type a comma (,) to separate the arguments. The next argument is *array2*.

d. Select cells **F6:F20** and press **Enter** (Figure 2-77). The result is 588.29.

e. Format cells **C22:C23** as **Currency**. Press **Ctrl+Home**.

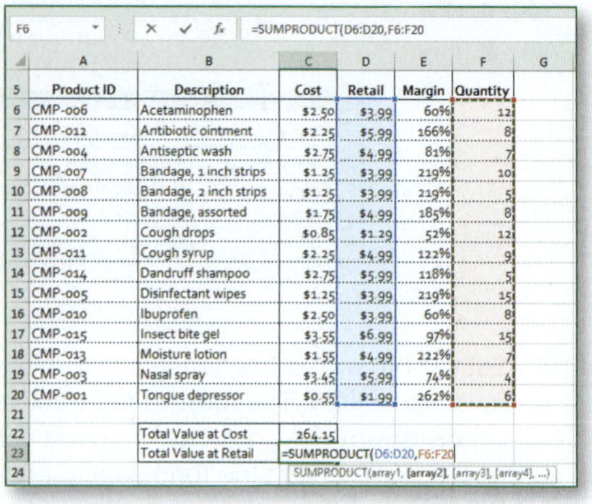

Figure 2-77 Both arrays have the same dimension

17. Use *PMT* to calculate patient payments.

a. Click the **Payments** sheet tab and select cell **B6**.

b. Click the **Financial** button [*Formulas* tab, *Function Library* group] and select **PMT**.

c. Click the **Rate** box and type 2.75%/12. You can type the rate when it is not shown in a cell. Yearly rates are divided by 12 for monthly payments.

d. Click the **Nper** box and type 24. The length of the loan is indicated in the label in cell A4. Two-year financing means 24 monthly payments.

e. Click the **Pv** box and click cell **A6**, the amount of a loan.

f. Click the **Type** box and type 1 for payment at the beginning of the month. The *Fv* argument is blank (Figure 2-78).

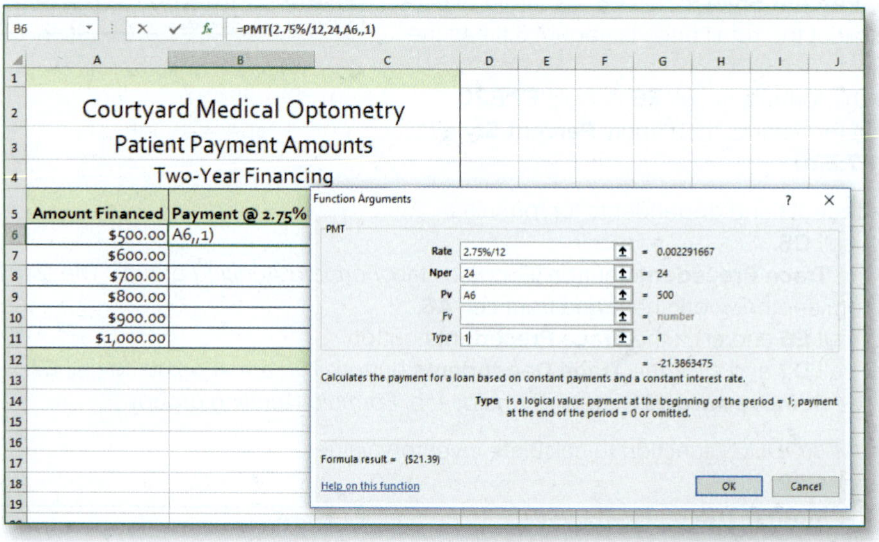

Figure 2-78 ***PMT*** **arguments**

g. Click **OK**. The payment for financing $500 is ($21.39).

h. Copy the formula to cells **B7:B11**. The reference to cell A6 is relative, and the *rate* and *nper* values that you typed are absolute.

18. Copy and edit a *PMT* function.

a. Copy the formula in cell **B6** to cell **C6**.

b. Select cell **C6** and click the **Insert Function** button in the *Formula* bar. The *Function Arguments* dialog box opens with the formula.

c. Click the **Rate** text box and edit the calculation to 3.25%/12.

d. Click the **Pv** box and set cell **A6** as the argument.

e. Click **OK**. The payment for financing $500 at 3.25% is ($21.49).

f. Copy the formula to cells **C7:C11**.

19. Enter the *TODAY* function.
    a. Select cell **A14**.
    b. Type =to, press **Tab**, and press **Enter**.
    c. Press **Ctrl+Home**.
20. Save and close the workbook (Figure 2-79).

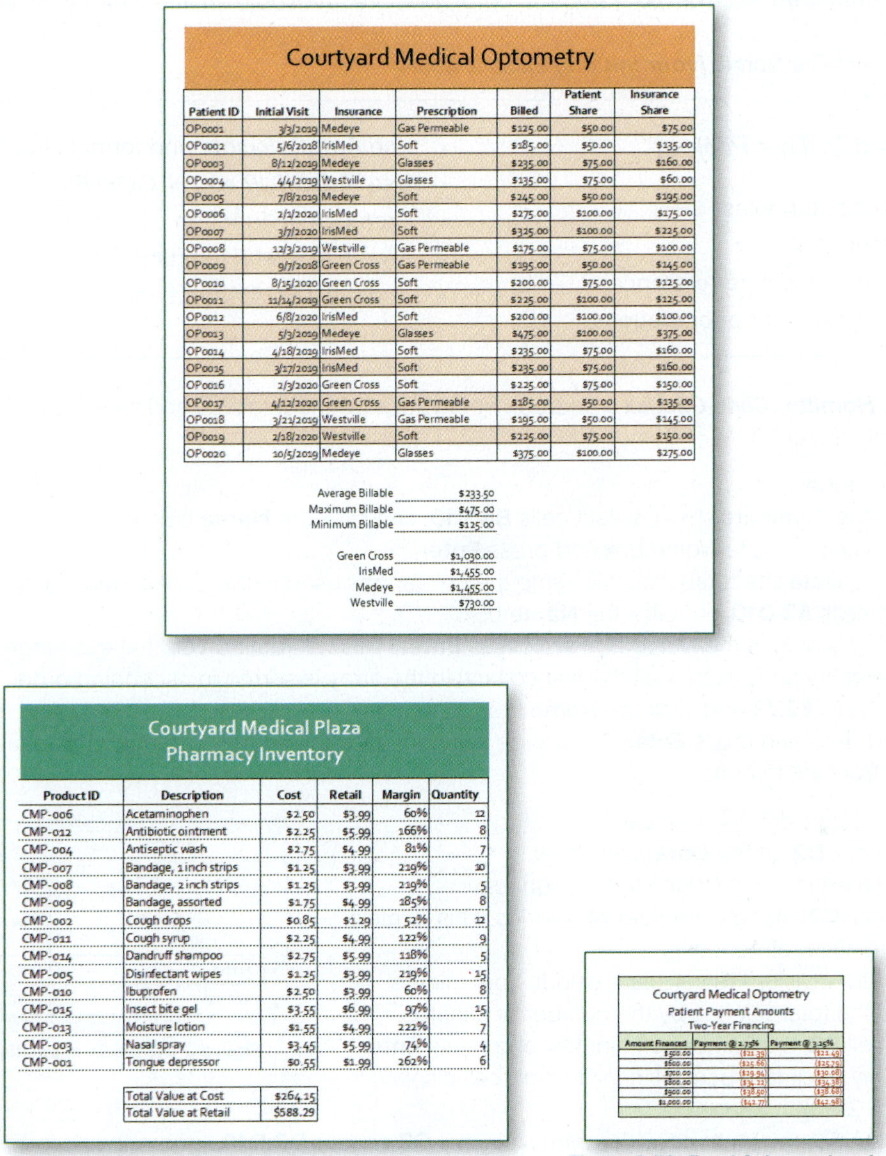

Courtyard Medical Optometry

Patient ID	Initial Visit	Insurance	Prescription	Billed	Patient Share	Insurance Share
OP0001	3/3/2019	Medeye	Gas Permeable	$125.00	$50.00	$75.00
OP0002	5/6/2018	IrisMed	Soft	$185.00	$50.00	$135.00
OP0003	8/12/2019	Medeye	Glasses	$235.00	$75.00	$160.00
OP0004	4/4/2019	Westville	Glasses	$135.00	$75.00	$60.00
OP0005	7/8/2019	Medeye	Soft	$245.00	$50.00	$195.00
OP0006	2/1/2020	IrisMed	Soft	$275.00	$100.00	$175.00
OP0007	3/7/2020	IrisMed	Soft	$325.00	$100.00	$225.00
OP0008	12/3/2019	Westville	Gas Permeable	$175.00	$75.00	$100.00
OP0009	9/7/2018	Green Cross	Gas Permeable	$195.00	$50.00	$145.00
OP0010	8/15/2020	Green Cross	Soft	$200.00	$75.00	$125.00
OP0011	11/14/2019	Green Cross	Soft	$225.00	$100.00	$125.00
OP0012	6/8/2020	IrisMed	Soft	$200.00	$100.00	$100.00
OP0013	5/3/2019	Medeye	Glasses	$475.00	$100.00	$375.00
OP0014	4/18/2019	IrisMed	Soft	$235.00	$75.00	$160.00
OP0015	3/17/2019	IrisMed	Soft	$235.00	$75.00	$160.00
OP0016	2/3/2020	Green Cross	Soft	$225.00	$75.00	$150.00
OP0017	4/12/2020	Green Cross	Gas Permeable	$185.00	$50.00	$135.00
OP0018	3/21/2019	Westville	Gas Permeable	$195.00	$50.00	$145.00
OP0019	2/18/2020	Westville	Soft	$225.00	$75.00	$150.00
OP0020	10/5/2019	Medeye	Glasses	$375.00	$100.00	$275.00

Average Billable	$233.50
Maximum Billable	$475.00
Minimum Billable	$125.00
Green Cross	$1,030.00
IrisMed	$1,455.00
Medeye	$1,455.00
Westville	$730.00

Courtyard Medical Plaza
Pharmacy Inventory

Product ID	Description	Cost	Retail	Margin	Quantity
CMP-006	Acetaminophen	$2.50	$3.99	60%	12
CMP-012	Antibiotic ointment	$2.25	$5.99	166%	8
CMP-004	Antiseptic wash	$2.75	$4.99	81%	7
CMP-007	Bandage, 1 inch strips	$1.25	$3.99	219%	10
CMP-008	Bandage, 2 inch strips	$1.25	$3.99	219%	5
CMP-009	Bandage, assorted	$1.75	$4.99	185%	8
CMP-002	Cough drops	$0.85	$1.29	52%	12
CMP-011	Cough syrup	$2.25	$4.99	122%	9
CMP-014	Dandruff shampoo	$2.75	$5.99	118%	5
CMP-005	Disinfectant wipes	$1.25	$3.99	219%	15
CMP-010	Ibuprofen	$2.50	$3.99	60%	8
CMP-015	Insect bite gel	$3.55	$6.99	97%	15
CMP-013	Moisture lotion	$1.55	$4.99	222%	7
CMP-003	Nasal spray	$3.45	$5.99	74%	4
CMP-001	Tongue depressor	$0.55	$1.99	262%	6

Total Value at Cost	$264.15
Total Value at Retail	$588.29

Courtyard Medical Optometry
Patient Payment Amounts
Two-Year Financing

Amount Financed	Payment @ 2.75%	Payment @ 3.25%
$500.00	($21.39)	($21.49)
$600.00	($25.66)	($25.79)
$700.00	($29.94)	($30.08)
$800.00	($34.22)	($34.38)
$900.00	($38.50)	($38.68)
$1,000.00	($42.77)	($42.98)

Figure 2-79 Excel 2-1 completed

Guided Project 2-2

Hamilton Civic Center (HCC) is a nonprofit community fitness center with an indoor pool, sauna, indoor track, project room, racquetball courts, meeting rooms, and a boutique. In this workbook, you complete tasks related to health seminars, a member challenge, and the daycare program.
[Student Learning Outcomes 2.1, 2.2, 2.3, 2.4, 2.5, 2.6, 2.7]

File Needed: ***HamiltonCivic-02.xlsx*** *(Student data files are available in the* Library *of your SIMnet account.)*
Completed Project File Name: ***[your initials] Excel 2-2.xlsx***

Skills Covered in This Project

- Create and copy formulas.
- Name cell ranges.
- Use relative and absolute references.
- Set mathematical order of operations.
- Use *AutoCalculate* and formula auditing tools.
- Use *VLOOKUP* and *HLOOKUP*.
- Create an *IF* function.
- Create a *SUMIF* function.
- Use the *TODAY* function.

---

1. Open the ***HamiltonCivic-02.xlsx*** workbook from your student data files and save it as [your initials] Excel 2-2.
2. Name cell ranges.
   a. Select the **Seminars** sheet, select cells **B6:B10**, and click the **Name** box.
   b. Type Seminars in the *Name* box and press **Enter**.
   c. Click the **Data** sheet tab. You will name the cell ranges used in the *Lookup* functions.
   d. Select cells **A2:D10** and click the **Name** box.
   e. Type V_Calories in the *Name* box and press **Enter**. This will remind you that this range is a vertical table array. Note that the first column in the array is sorted in ascending order.
   f. Select cells **F2:J3** and click the **Name** box.
   g. Type H_Fees and press **Enter**. This range is a horizontal table array, arranged in alphabetical order from left to right.
3. Enter and copy a division formula.
   a. Select cell **D2** on the **Data** worksheet.
   b. Type an equals sign (=) to start the formula.
   c. Click cell **C2**, the total number of calories. This formula uses relative references.
   d. Type / for division. To calculate calories per minute, divide the total calories by the number of minutes.
   e. Click cell **B2**, the number of minutes, and press **Enter**. As many decimal places as can fit in the cell display (Figure 2-80).

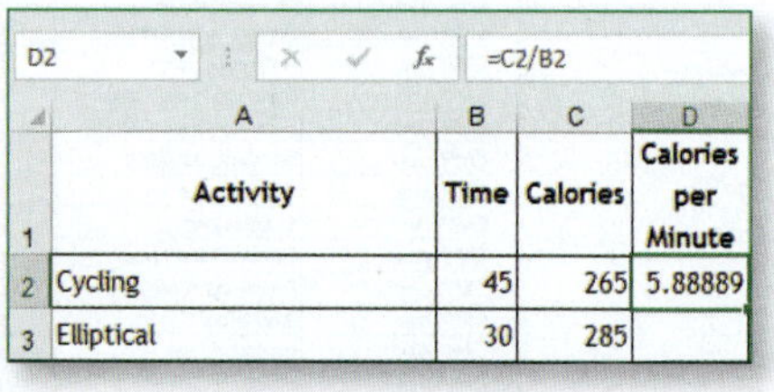

Figure 2-80 Decimal positions fill the cell

   f. Drag the *Fill* pointer to copy the formula in cell **D2** to cells **D3:D10**. Ignore the *Auto Fill Options* button.
   g. Select cells **D2:D10** if necessary, and click the **Decrease Decimal** button [*Home* tab, *Number* group] two times. This applies the same number of decimal positions for all results.
4. Use *HLOOKUP* with a range name to display fees.
   a. Click the **Seminars** worksheet tab and select cell **C6**. Fees are in the *H_Fees* range.
   b. Click the **Lookup & Reference** button [*Formulas* tab, *Function Library* group] and select **HLOOKUP**.
   c. Click the **Lookup_value** box and click cell **B6**.

   d. Click the **Table_array** box.
   e. Type h_fees the name of the range. It is not case sensitive, and quotation marks are not necessary.
   f. Click the **Row_index_num** box and type 2 because the fees are in the second row of the *H_Fees* range. The **Range_lookup** box is empty (Figure 2-81).
   g. Click **OK**. The fee is $15.00.
   h. Copy the formula in cell **C6** to cells **C7:C10**.

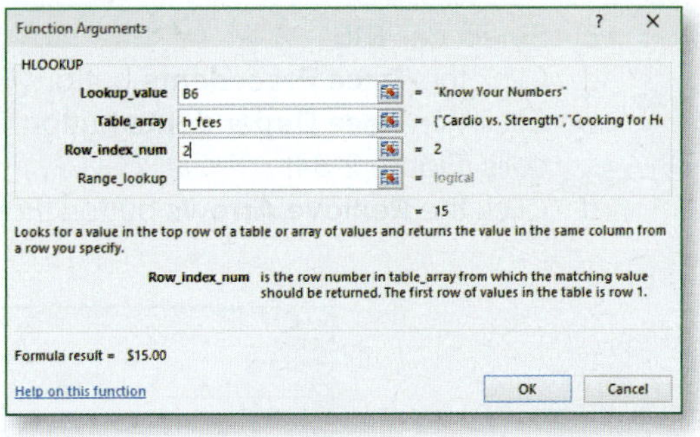

Figure 2-81 Arguments for *HLOOKUP*

5. Enter and copy an addition formula.
   a. Click cell **E15** and type an equals sign (=) to start the formula.
   b. Click cell **D6**, the number of attendees for the seminar in Hendersonville.
   c. Type + for addition.
   d. Click cell **E6** to add the number of attendees for Advocate Central.
   e. Type +, click cell **F6**, type +, and click cell **G6** (Figure 2-82).
   f. Press **Enter**.
   g. Drag the *Fill* pointer to copy the formula in cell **E15** to cells **E16:E19**. Ignore the *Auto Fill Options* button.
   h. Click cell **E20**, click the **AutoSum** button [*Home* tab, *Editing* group], and press **Enter**. The total is 209 attendees.

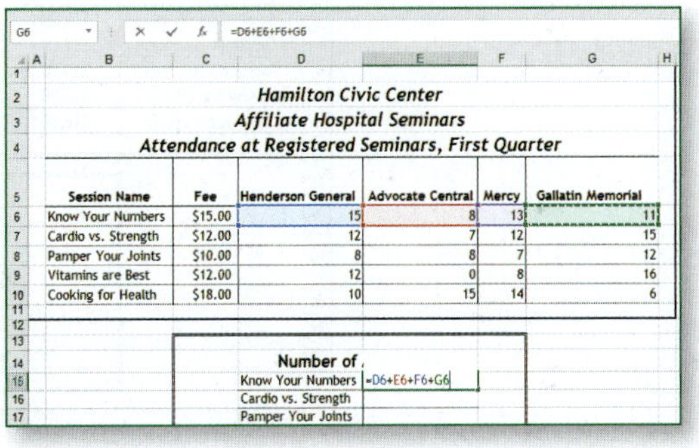

Figure 2-82 Simple addition formula

6. Set the order of operations in a formula.
   a. Select cell **E24**.
   b. Type = to start the formula and click cell **C6**.
   c. Type * to multiply. The fee is multiplied by the sum of the attendees at each hospital.
   d. Type (for the opening parenthesis. This forces the addition to be carried out first.
   e. Click cell **D6**, type +, click cell **E6**, type +, click cell **F6**, type +, and click cell **G6**. Cells D6:G6 must be added first and that result is multiplied by cell C6.
   f. Type) for the closing parenthesis (Figure 2-83).
   g. Press **Enter**. The result is 705.
   h. Format cell **E24** as **Currency** and copy the formula to cells **E25:E28**.
   i. Click cell **E29**, click the **AutoSum** button [*Home* tab, *Editing* group], and press **Enter**.

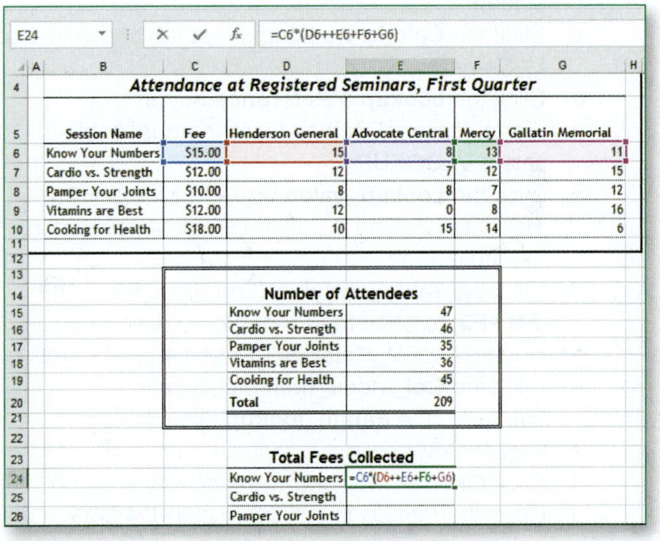

Figure 2-83 Addition done before multiplication

7. Use *AutoCalculate* and formula auditing tools.
   a. Select cells **E24:E28**.
   b. Compare the *SUM* in the *Status* bar with the result in cell E29.

c. Select cell **E15**.
d. Click the **Trace Precedents** button [*Formulas* tab, *Formula Auditing* group].
e. Click the **Trace Dependents** button. The formula in cell E15 has both precedent and dependent cells (Figure 2-84).
f. Click the **Remove Arrows** button [*Formulas* tab, *Formula Auditing* group].

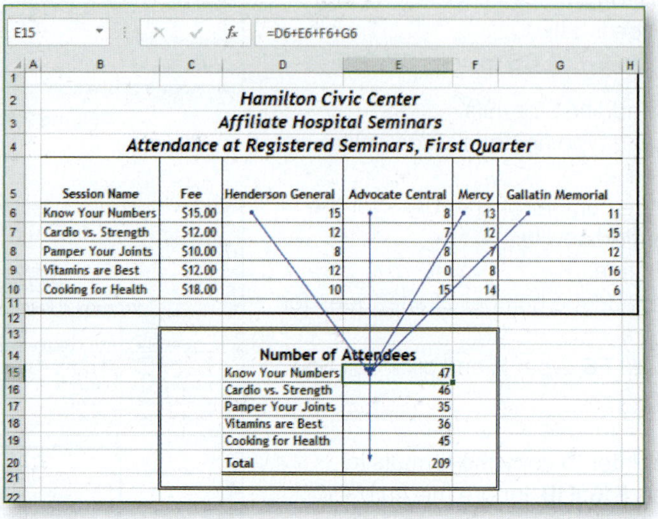

Figure 2-84 Precedent and dependent cells

8. Use *VLOOKUP* with a range name to display calories expended.
   a. Click the **Data** sheet tab.
   b. Click the **Name** box arrow and select **V_Calories**. Notice that total calories are in the third column.
   c. Click the **Calorie Tracking** sheet tab and select cell **D3**. Calories by activity are within the range *V_Calories*.
   d. Click the **Lookup & Reference** button [*Formulas* tab, *Function Library* group] and select **VLOOKUP**.
   e. Click the **Lookup_value** box and click cell **C3**. The activity name in column C will be located in the table array.
   f. Click the **Table_array** box and press **F3** (**FN+F3**) to open the *Paste Name* dialog box.
   g. Double-click **V_Calories** to insert it.
   h. Click the **Col_index_num** box, type 3, and leave the **Range_lookup** box empty (Figure 2-85).
   i. Click **OK**. Calories for the first activity are 250.
   j. Copy the formula in cell **D3** to cells **D4:D23**.

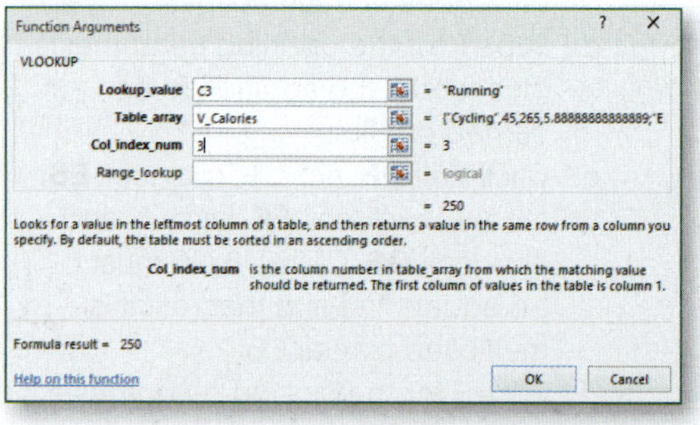

Figure 2-85 Arguments for the *VLOOKUP* function

9. Build a *SUMIF* formula with absolute and relative references.
   a. Select cell **D28** on the **Calorie Tracking** sheet.
   b. Click the **Recently Used** button [*Formulas* tab, *Function Library* group].
   c. Look for and choose **SUMIF**. (If you do not see *SUMIF* in the list, click the **Math & Trig** button to find and select **SUMIF**.)
   d. Click the **Range** box and select cells **C3:C23**, the range that will be evaluated.
   e. Press **F4** (**FN+F4**) to make the cell references absolute.

f. Click the **Criteria** box and select cell **C28** to find rows with "cycling" as the activity. This is a relative reference.
g. Click the **Sum_range** box and select cells **D3:D23**, the values to be summed if the activity is cycling.
h. Press **F4** (**FN+F4**) to make the references absolute (Figure 2-86).
i. Click **OK**. The result is 795 calories.

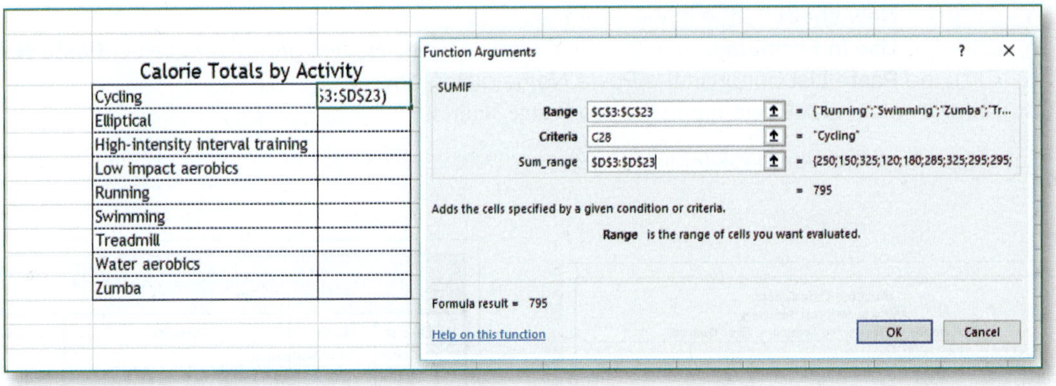

Figure 2-86 *SUMIF* function for cycling

10. Copy the formula in cell **D28** to cells **D29:D36** without formatting (Figure 2-87).
11. Create an *IF* function to calculate a fee based on age.
    a. Click the **Day Care** sheet tab and select cell **D5**.
    b. Click the **Logical** button [*Formulas* tab, *Function Library* group] and select **IF**.
    c. Click the **Logical_test** box and click cell **B5**.
    d. Type >=4 to test if the child is 4 years old or greater.
    e. Click the **Value_if_true** box and click cell **I9**. The fee for a child 4 years old or greater is $18.
    f. Press **F4** (**FN+F4**) to make the reference absolute.
    g. Click the **Value_if_false** box and click cell **I8**. If the child is not 4 years old or greater, the higher fee applies.
    h. Press **F4** (**FN+F4**) to make the reference absolute (Figure 2-88).
    i. Click **OK**. The fee for Mary is 18.
    j. Format the result as **Currency**.
    k. Copy the formula in cell **D5** to cells **D6:D14** without formatting to preserve the borders.

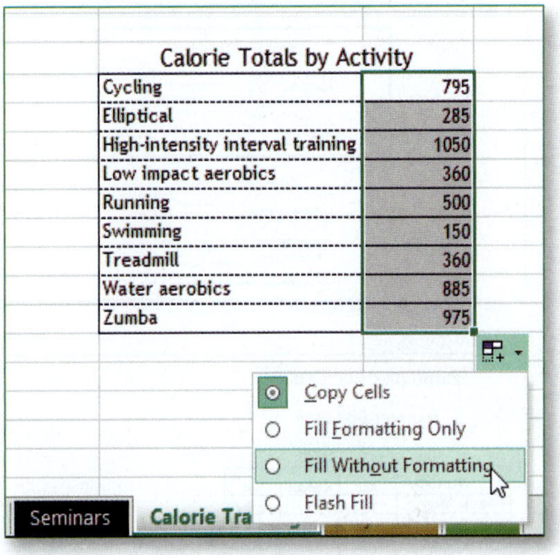

Figure 2-87 Copy the formula without formatting

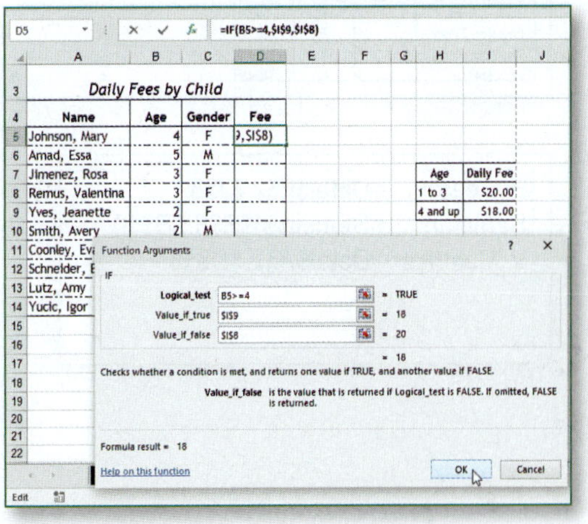

Figure 2-88 *IF* function to determine the fee

12. Insert the current date as a function.
    a. Click the **Data** sheet tab and click cell **A12**.
    b. Type =to and press **Tab** to select the function.
    c. Press **Enter**.
    d. Press **Ctrl+Home**.

13. Paste range names.
    a. Click the **New sheet** button in the sheet tab area.
    b. Click the **Use in Formula** button [*Formulas* tab, *Defined Names* group] and select **Paste Names**.
    c. Click the **Paste List** button in the *Paste Name* dialog box.
    d. *AutoFit* columns **A:B** and name the tab Range Names.

14. Save and close the workbook (Figure 2-89).

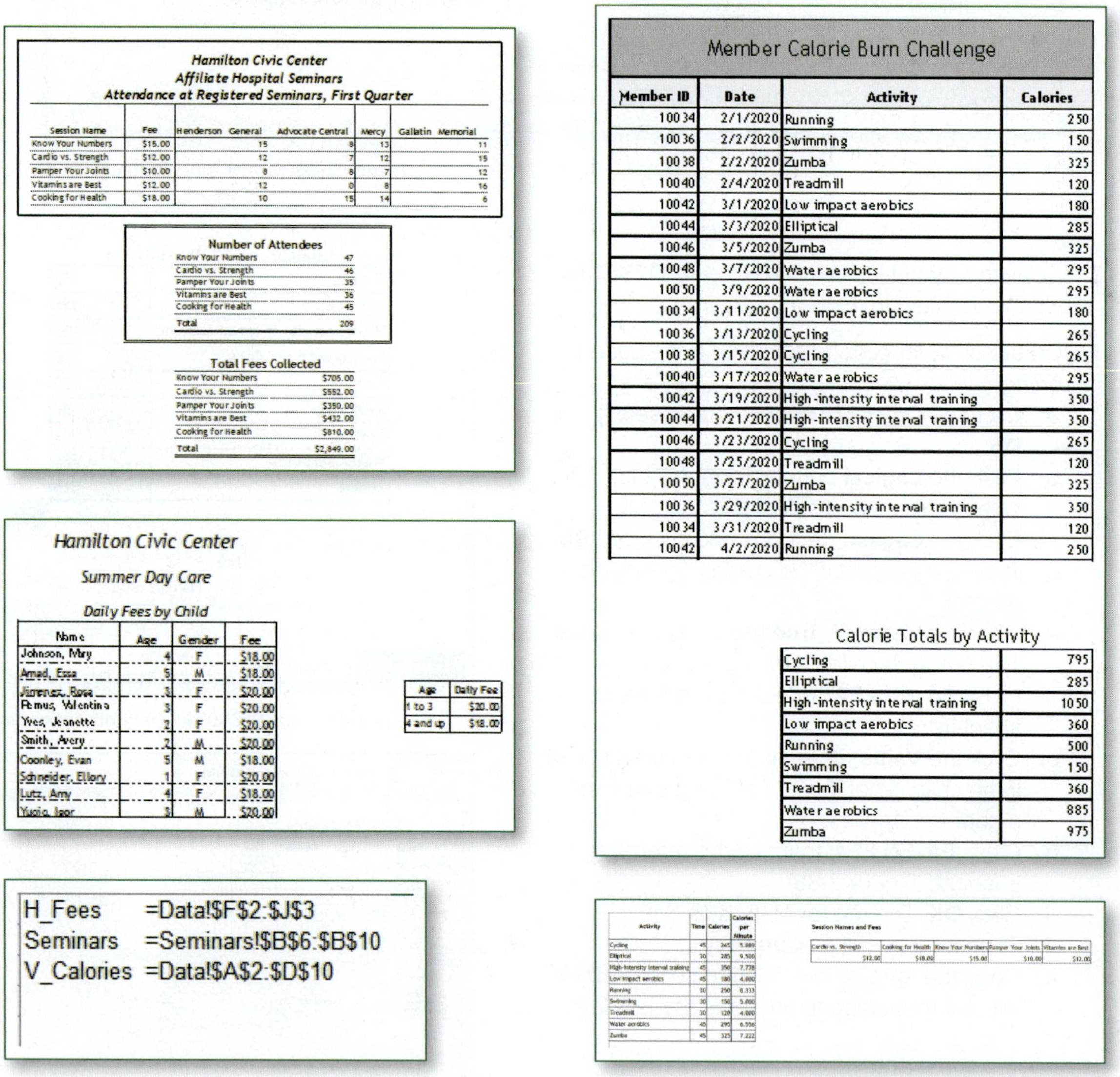

Hamilton Civic Center
Affiliate Hospital Seminars
Attendance at Registered Seminars, First Quarter

Session Name	Fee	Henderson General	Advocate Central	Mercy	Gallatin Memorial
Know Your Numbers	$15.00	15	8	13	11
Cardio vs. Strength	$12.00	12	7	12	15
Pamper Your Joints	$10.00	8	8	7	12
Vitamins are Best	$12.00	12	0	8	16
Cooking for Health	$18.00	10	15	14	6

Number of Attendees	
Know Your Numbers	47
Cardio vs. Strength	46
Pamper Your Joints	35
Vitamins are Best	36
Cooking for Health	45
Total	209

Total Fees Collected	
Know Your Numbers	$705.00
Cardio vs. Strength	$552.00
Pamper Your Joints	$350.00
Vitamins are Best	$432.00
Cooking for Health	$810.00
Total	$2,849.00

Hamilton Civic Center

Summer Day Care

Daily Fees by Child

Name	Age	Gender	Fee
Johnson, Mary	4	F	$18.00
Amad, Essa	5	M	$18.00
Jimenez, Rosa	3	F	$20.00
Remus, Valentina	3	F	$20.00
Yves, Jeanette	2	F	$20.00
Smith, Avery	2	M	$20.00
Coonley, Evan	5	M	$18.00
Schneider, Ellory	1	F	$20.00
Lutz, Amy	4	F	$18.00
Yugio, Igor	3	M	$20.00

Age	Daily Fee
1 to 3	$20.00
4 and up	$18.00

H_Fees	=Data!$F$2:$J$3
Seminars	=Seminars!$B$6:$B$10
V_Calories	=Data!$A$2:$D$10

Member Calorie Burn Challenge

Member ID	Date	Activity	Calories
10034	2/1/2020	Running	250
10036	2/2/2020	Swimming	150
10038	2/2/2020	Zumba	325
10040	2/4/2020	Treadmill	120
10042	3/1/2020	Low impact aerobics	180
10044	3/3/2020	Elliptical	285
10046	3/5/2020	Zumba	325
10048	3/7/2020	Water aerobics	295
10050	3/9/2020	Water aerobics	295
10034	3/11/2020	Low impact aerobics	180
10036	3/13/2020	Cycling	265
10038	3/15/2020	Cycling	265
10040	3/17/2020	Water aerobics	295
10042	3/19/2020	High-intensity interval training	350
10044	3/21/2020	High-intensity interval training	350
10046	3/23/2020	Cycling	265
10048	3/25/2020	Treadmill	120
10050	3/27/2020	Zumba	325
10036	3/29/2020	High-intensity interval training	350
10034	3/31/2020	Treadmill	120
10042	4/2/2020	Running	250

Calorie Totals by Activity

Cycling	795
Elliptical	285
High-intensity interval training	1050
Low impact aerobics	360
Running	500
Swimming	150
Treadmill	360
Water aerobics	885
Zumba	975

Activity	Time	Calories	Calories per Minute
Cycling	45	265	5.889
Elliptical	30	285	9.500
High-intensity interval training	45	350	7.778
Low impact aerobics	45	180	4.000
Running	30	250	8.333
Swimming	30	150	5.000
Treadmill	30	120	4.000
Water aerobics	45	295	6.556
Zumba	45	325	7.222

Session Names and Fees

Cardio vs. Strength	Cooking for Health	Know Your Numbers	Pamper Your Joints	Vitamins are Best
$12.00	$18.00	$15.00	$10.00	$12.00

Figure 2-89 Excel 2-2 completed

Guided Project 2-3

Sierra Pacific Community College District (SPCCD) consists of four individual community colleges. The workbook for this project includes an amortization schedule for student loans and a fee and credit hour summary for several departments.
[Student Learning Outcomes 2.1, 2.2, 2.3, 2.4, 2.5, 2.6, 2.7]

File Needed: ***SierraPacific-02.xlsx*** *(Student data files are available in the* Library *of your SIMnet account.)*
Completed Project File Name: ***[your initials] Excel 2-3.xlsx***

Skills Covered in This Project

- Name cell ranges.
- Create and copy formulas.
- Set mathematical order of operations.
- Use absolute references in formulas.
- Insert the current date as a function.
- Use the *PMT* function.
- Audit formulas.
- Use *SUMIF* and *SUMPRODUCT*.

1. Open the ***SierraPacific-02.xlsx*** workbook from your student data files and save it as [your initials] Excel 2-3.
2. Set range names for the workbook.
   a. Select the **Student Loan** sheet and select cells **B5:C8**.
   b. Click the **Create from Selection** button [*Formulas* tab, *Defined Names* group].
   c. Verify that the **Left column** box in the *Create Names from Selection* dialog box is selected.
   d. Deselect the **Top row** box if it is checked and click **OK**.
   e. Select cells **E5:F7**. Repeat steps a–d to create range names.
   f. Click the **Name Manager** button [*Formulas* tab, *Defined Names* group] to view the names in the *Name Manager* dialog box (Figure 2-90). Notice that the cell references are absolute.
   g. Click **Close**.

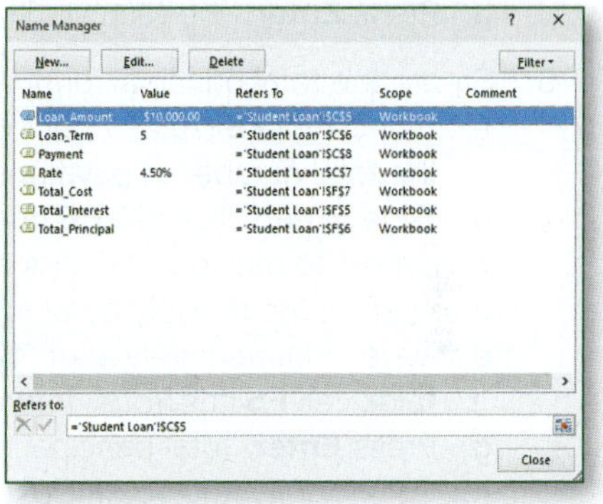

Figure 2-90 ***Name Manager*** **dialog box**

3. Enter a *PMT* function.
   a. Select **C8**.
   b. Click the **Financial** button [*Formulas* tab, *Function Library* group] and select **PMT**.
   c. Click the **Rate** box and click cell **C7**. The range name *Rate* is substituted and is an absolute reference.
   d. Type /12 immediately after **Rate** to divide by 12 for monthly payments.
   e. Click the **Nper** box and click cell **C6**. The substituted range name is *Loan_Term*.
   f. Type *12 after **Loan_Term** to multiply by 12.
   g. Click the **Pv** box and type a minus sign (–) to set the argument as a negative amount.
   h. Click cell **C5** (*Loan_Amount*) for the *pv* argument. A negative loan amount reflects the lender's perspective, because the money is paid out now (Figure 2-91).
   i. Leave the *Fv* and *Type* boxes empty.

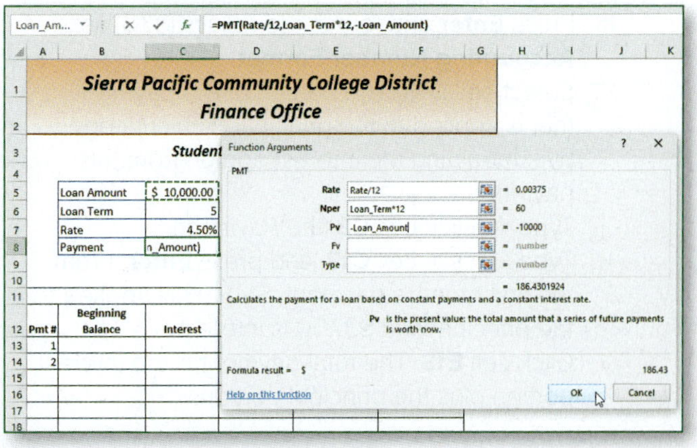

Figure 2-91 ***Pv*** **argument is negative in the** ***PMT*** **function**

j. Click **OK**. The payment for a loan at this rate is $186.43, shown as a positive value.
k. Verify or format cell **C8** as **Accounting Number Format** to match cell **C5**.

4. Create a total interest formula.
   a. Click cell **F5** (*Total_Interest*). This value is calculated by multiplying the monthly payment by the total number of payments to determine total outlay. From this amount, you subtract the loan amount.
   b. Type = and click cell **C8** (the *Payment*).
   c. Type * to multiply and click cell **C6** (*Loan_Term*).
   d. Type *12 to multiply by 12 for monthly payments. Values typed in a formula are constants and are absolute references.
   e. Type – immediately after ***12** to subtract.
   f. Click cell **C5** (the *Loan_Amount*). The formula is *Payment * Loan_Term * 12 – Loan_Amount*. Parentheses are not required, because the multiplications are done from left to right, followed by the subtraction (Figure 2-92).
   g. Press **Enter**. The result is $1,185.81.

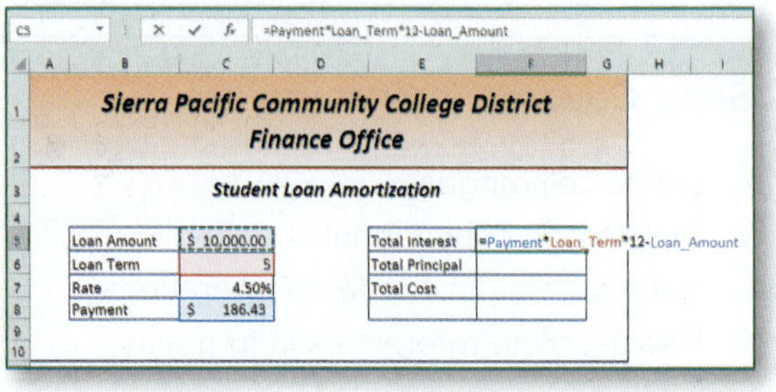

Figure 2-92 Left-to-right operations

5. Create the total principal formula and the total loan cost.
   a. Select cell **F6** (*Total_Principal*). This value is calculated by multiplying the monthly payment by the total number of payments. From this amount, subtract the total interest.
   b. Type = and click cell **C8** (the *Payment*).
   c. Type * to multiply and click cell **C6** (*Loan_Term*).
   d. Type *12 to multiply by 12 for monthly payments.
   e. Type – immediately after ***12** to subtract.
   f. Click cell **F5** (the *Total_Interest*). The formula is *Payment * Loan_Term * 12 – Total_Interest*.
   g. Press **Enter**. Total principal is the amount of the loan.
   h. Click cell **F7**, the *Total_Cost* of the loan. This is the total principal plus the total interest.
   i. Type =, click cell **F5**, type +, click cell **F6**, and then press **Enter**.

6. Set order of mathematical operations to build an amortization schedule.
   a. Click cell **B13**. The beginning balance is the loan amount.
   b. Type =, click cell **C5**, and press **Enter**.
   c. Format the value as **Accounting Number Format**.
   d. Select cell **C13**. The interest for each payment is calculated by multiplying the balance in column B by the rate divided by 12.
   e. Type = and click cell **B13**.
   f. Type *(and click cell **C7**.
   g. Type /12). Parentheses are necessary so that the division is done first (Figure 2-93).
   h. Press **Enter** and format the results (37.5) as **Accounting Number Format**.
   i. Select cell **D13**. The portion of the payment that is applied to the principal is calculated by subtracting the interest portion from the payment.
   j. Type =, click cell **C8** (the *Payment*).
   k. Type –, click cell **C13**, and press **Enter**. From the first month's payment, $148.93 is applied to the principal and $37.50 is interest.
   l. Click cell **E13**. The total payment is the interest portion plus the principal portion.

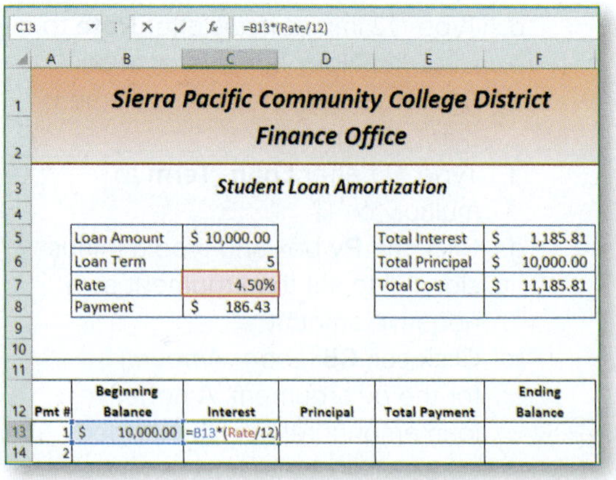

Figure 2-93 The interest formula

m. Type =, click cell **C13**, type +, click cell **D13**, and then press **Enter**. The value matches the amount in cell **C8**.
n. Select cell **F13**. The ending balance is the beginning balance minus the principal payment. The interest is part of the cost of the loan.
o. Type =, click cell **B13**, type–, click cell **D13**, and then press **Enter**. The ending balance is $9,851.07.

B13	=Loan_Amount
C13	=B13*(Rate/12)
D13	=Payment–C13
E13	=C13+D13
F13	=B13–D13

7. Fill data and copy formulas.
   a. Select cells **A13:A14**. This is a series with an increment of 1.
   b. Drag the *Fill* pointer to reach cell **A72**. This sets 60 payments for a five-year loan term.
   c. Select cell **B14**. The beginning balance for the second payment is the ending balance for the first payment.
   d. Type =, click cell **F13**, and press **Enter**.
   e. Double-click the *Fill* pointer for cell **B14** to fill the formula down to row **72**. The results are zero (displayed as a hyphen in Accounting Number Format) until the rest of the schedule is complete.
   f. Select cells **C13:F13**.
   g. Double-click the *Fill* pointer at cell **F13**. All of the formulas are filled (copied) to row **72** (Figure 2-94).
   h. Scroll to see the values in row **72**. The loan balance reaches 0.
   i. Press **Ctrl+Home**.

12	Pmt #	Beginning Balance	Interest	Principal	Total Payment	Ending Balance
13	1	$ 10,000.00	$ 37.50	$ 148.93	$ 186.43	$ 9,851.07
14	2	$ 9,851.07	$ 36.94	$ 149.49	$ 186.43	$ 9,701.58
15	3	$ 9,701.58	$ 36.38	$ 150.05	$ 186.43	$ 9,551.53
16	4	$ 9,551.53	$ 35.82	$ 150.61	$ 186.43	$ 9,400.92
17	5	$ 9,400.92	$ 35.25	$ 151.18	$ 186.43	$ 9,249.74
18	6	$ 9,249.74	$ 34.69	$ 151.74	$ 186.43	$ 9,098.00
19	7	$ 9,098.00	$ 34.12	$ 152.31	$ 186.43	$ 8,945.69
20	8	$ 8,945.69	$ 33.55	$ 152.88	$ 186.43	$ 8,792.80
21	9	$ 8,792.80	$ 32.97	$ 153.46	$ 186.43	$ 8,639.35
22	10	$ 8,639.35	$ 32.40	$ 154.03	$ 186.43	$ 8,485.31
23	11	$ 8,485.31	$ 31.82	$ 154.61	$ 186.43	$ 8,330.70
24	12	$ 8,330.70	$ 31.24	$ 155.19	$ 186.43	$ 8,175.51
25	13	$ 8,175.51	$ 30.66	$ 155.77	$ 186.43	$ 8,019.74
26	14	$ 8,019.74	$ 30.07	$ 156.36	$ 186.43	$ 7,863.38
27	15	$ 7,863.38	$ 29.49	$ 156.94	$ 186.43	$ 7,706.44
28	16	$ 7,706.44	$ 28.90	$ 157.53	$ 186.43	$ 7,548.91
60	48	$ 2,361.15	$ 8.85	$ 177.58	$ 186.43	$ 2,183.57
61	49	$ 2,183.57	$ 8.19	$ 178.24	$ 186.43	$ 2,005.33
62	50	$ 2,005.33	$ 7.52	$ 178.91	$ 186.43	$ 1,826.42
63	51	$ 1,826.42	$ 6.85	$ 179.58	$ 186.43	$ 1,646.84
64	52	$ 1,646.84	$ 6.18	$ 180.25	$ 186.43	$ 1,466.58
65	53	$ 1,466.58	$ 5.50	$ 180.93	$ 186.43	$ 1,285.65
66	54	$ 1,285.65	$ 4.82	$ 181.61	$ 186.43	$ 1,104.05
67	55	$ 1,104.05	$ 4.14	$ 182.29	$ 186.43	$ 921.76
68	56	$ 921.76	$ 3.46	$ 182.97	$ 186.43	$ 738.78
69	57	$ 738.78	$ 2.77	$ 183.66	$ 186.43	$ 555.12
70	58	$ 555.12	$ 2.08	$ 184.35	$ 186.43	$ 370.77
71	59	$ 370.77	$ 1.39	$ 185.04	$ 186.43	$ 185.73
72	60	$ 185.73	$ 0.70	$ 185.73	$ 186.43	$ 0.00

Figure 2-94 Formulas copied down columns

8. Build a multiplication formula.
   a. Click the **Fees & Credit** sheet tab and select cell **F7**. Credit hours times number of sections times the fee calculates the total fees from a course.
   b. Type =, click cell **C7**, type *, click cell **D7**, type *, click cell **E7**, and then press **Enter**. No parentheses are necessary because multiplication is done in left to right order (Figure 2-95).
   c. Double-click the *Fill* pointer for cell **F7** to copy the formula.
   d. Verify that cells **F7:F18** are **Currency** format. Set a single bottom border for cell **F18**.

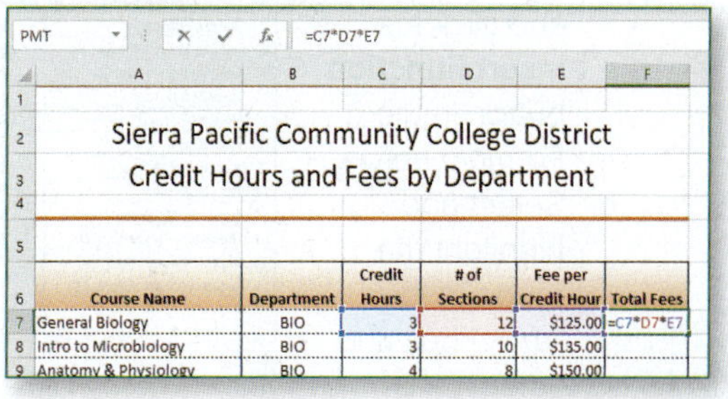

Figure 2-95 Formula to calculate total fees per course

9. Use *SUMIF* to calculate fees by department.
   a. Select cell **C26**.
   b. Click the **Math & Trig** button [*Formulas* tab, *Function Library* group] and select **SUMIF**.
   c. Click the **Range** box and select cells **B7:B18**. This range will be matched against the criteria.
   d. Press **F4** (**FN+F4**) to make the reference absolute.
   e. Click the **Criteria** box and select cell **B26**.
   f. Click the **Sum_range** box, select cells **F7:F18**, and press **F4** (**FN+F4**).
   g. Click **OK**. Total fees for the Biology department are 13350 (Figure 2-96).

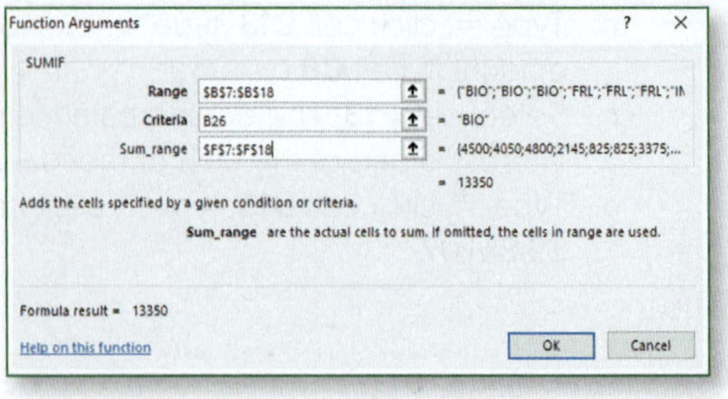

Figure 2-96 ***Function Arguments* dialog box for *SUMIF***

10. Copy a *SUMIF* function.
    a. Click cell **C26** and drag its *Fill* pointer to copy the formula to cells **C27:C29** without formatting to preserve the borders (Figure 2-97).
    b. Format cells **C26:C29** as **Currency**.

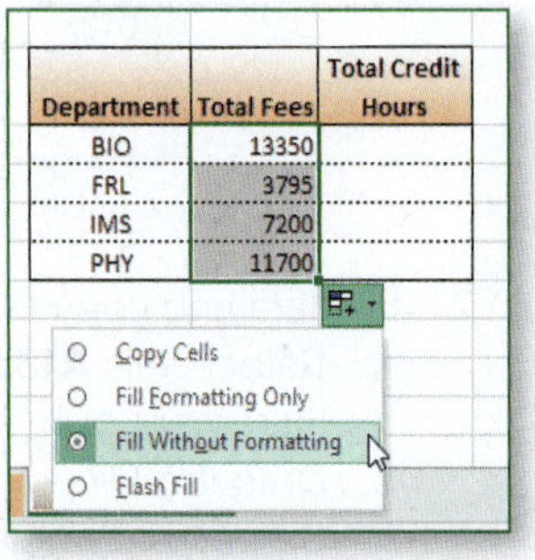

Figure 2-97 Formula is copied without formatting

11. Use *SUMPRODUCT* and trace an error.
    a. Select cell **D26** and click the **Formulas** tab.
    b. Click the **Math & Trig** button in the *Function Library* group and select **SUMPRODUCT**.
    c. Click the **Array1** box and select cells **C7:C9**, credit hours for courses in the Biology Department.
    d. Click the **Array2** box and select cells **D7:D9**, the number of sections for the Biology Department.
    e. Click **OK**. The Biology Department offered 98 total credit hours.
    f. Click cell **D26** and point to its **Trace Error** button. The formula omits adjacent cells in the worksheet but it is correct.
    g. Click the **Trace Error** button and select **Ignore Error**.

12. Copy and edit *SUMPRODUCT*.
    a. Click cell **D26** and drag its *Fill* pointer to copy the formula to cells **D27:D29** without formatting to preserve the borders.
    b. Click cell **D27** and click the **Insert Function** button in the *Formula* bar.
    c. Select and highlight the range in the *Array1* box and select cells **C10:C12**. The range you select replaces the range in the dialog box (Figure 2-98).

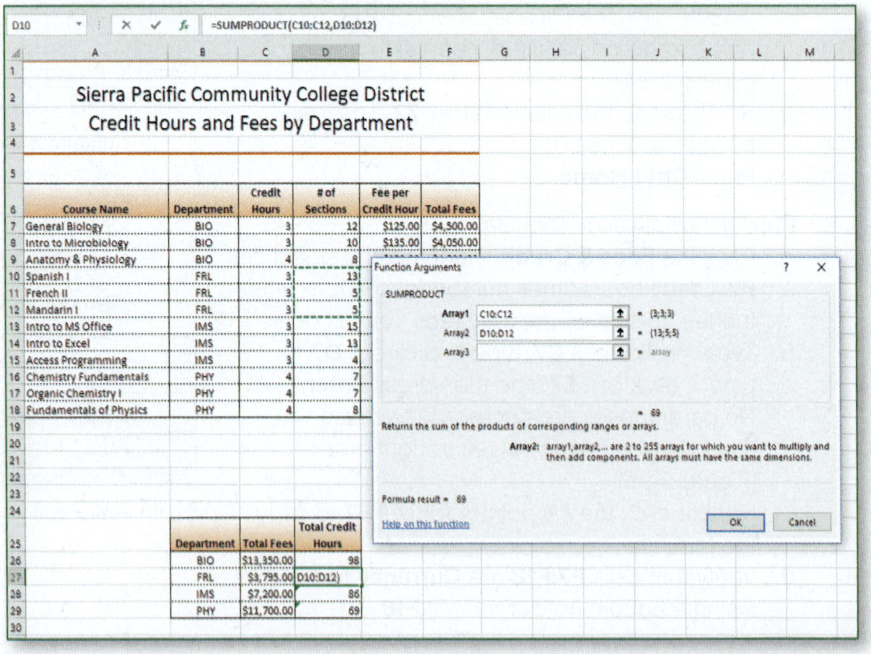

Figure 2-98 Replace the *ArrayN* arguments

d. Select the range in the *Array2* box and select cells **D10:D12**.
e. Click **OK**.
f. Edit and complete the formulas in cells **D28:D29** and ignore errors.

13. Insert the current date as a function.
    a. Select cell **F20**.
    b. Type =to and press **Tab** to select the function.
    c. Press **Enter**.
    d. Press **Ctrl+Home**.

14. Paste range names.
    a. Click the **New sheet** button in the sheet tab area.
    b. Name the new sheet **Range Names**.
    c. Press **F3** (**FN+F3**) to open the *Paste Name* dialog box.
    d. Click the **Paste List** button.
    e. *AutoFit* columns **A:B**.

15. Save and close the workbook (Figure 2-99).

Sierra Pacific Community College District
Credit Hours and Fees by Department

Course Name	Department	Credit Hours	# of Sections	Fee per Credit Hour	Total Fees
General Biology	BIO	3	12	$125.00	$4,500.00
Intro to Microbiology	BIO	3	10	$135.00	$4,050.00
Anatomy & Physiology	BIO	4	8	$150.00	$4,800.00
Spanish I	FRL	3	13	$55.00	$2,145.00
French II	FRL	3	5	$55.00	$825.00
Mandarin I	FRL	3	5	$55.00	$825.00
Intro to MS Office	IMS	3	15	$75.00	$3,375.00
Intro to Excel	IMS	3	13	$75.00	$2,925.00
Access Programming	IMS	3	4	$75.00	$900.00
Chemistry Fundamentals	PHY	4	7	$125.00	$3,500.00
Organic Chemistry I	PHY	4	7	$150.00	$4,200.00
Fundamentals of Physics	PHY	4	8	$125.00	$4,000.00

Today

Department	Total Fees	Total Credit Hours
BIO	$13,350.00	98
FRL	$3,795.00	69
IMS	$7,200.00	96
PHY	$11,700.00	88

Loan_Amount	='Student Loan'!$C$5
Loan_Term	='Student Loan'!$C$6
Payment	='Student Loan'!$C$8
Rate	='Student Loan'!$C$7
Total_Cost	='Student Loan'!$F$7
Total_Interest	='Student Loan'!$F$5
Total_Principal	='Student Loan'!$F$6

Sierra Pacific Community College District
Finance Office

Student Loan Amortization

Loan Amount	$ 10,000.00	Total Interest	$ 1,185.81
Loan Term	5	Total Principal	$ 10,000.00
Rate	4.50%	Total Cost	$ 11,185.81
Payment	$ 186.43		

Pmt #	Beginning Balance	Interest	Principal	Total Payment	Ending Balance
1	$ 10,000.00	$ 37.50	$ 148.93	$ 186.43	$ 9,851.07
2	$ 9,851.07	$ 36.94	$ 149.49	$ 186.43	$ 9,701.58
3	$ 9,701.58	$ 36.38	$ 150.05	$ 186.43	$ 9,551.53
4	$ 9,551.53	$ 35.82	$ 150.61	$ 186.43	$ 9,400.92
5	$ 9,400.92	$ 35.25	$ 151.18	$ 186.43	$ 9,249.74
6	$ 9,249.74	$ 34.69	$ 151.74	$ 186.43	$ 9,098.00
7	$ 9,098.00	$ 34.12	$ 152.31	$ 186.43	$ 8,945.69
8	$ 8,945.69	$ 33.55	$ 152.88	$ 186.43	$ 8,792.80
9	$ 8,792.80	$ 32.97	$ 153.46	$ 186.43	$ 8,639.35
10	$ 8,639.35	$ 32.40	$ 154.03	$ 186.43	$ 8,485.31
11	$ 8,485.31	$ 31.82	$ 154.61	$ 186.43	$ 8,330.70
12	$ 8,330.70	$ 31.24	$ 155.19	$ 186.43	$ 8,175.51
13	$ 8,175.51	$ 30.66	$ 155.77	$ 186.43	$ 8,019.74
14	$ 8,019.74	$ 30.07	$ 156.36	$ 186.43	$ 7,863.38
15	$ 7,863.38	$ 29.49	$ 156.94	$ 186.43	$ 7,706.44
16	$ 7,706.44	$ 28.90	$ 157.53	$ 186.43	$ 7,548.91
17	$ 7,548.91	$ 28.31	$ 158.12	$ 186.43	$ 7,390.79
18	$ 7,390.79	$ 27.72	$ 158.71	$ 186.43	$ 7,232.07
19	$ 7,232.07	$ 27.12	$ 159.31	$ 186.43	$ 7,072.76
20	$ 7,072.76	$ 26.52	$ 159.91	$ 186.43	$ 6,912.86
21	$ 6,912.86	$ 25.92	$ 160.51	$ 186.43	$ 6,752.35
22	$ 6,752.35	$ 25.32	$ 161.11	$ 186.43	$ 6,591.24
23	$ 6,591.24	$ 24.72	$ 161.71	$ 186.43	$ 6,429.53
24	$ 6,429.53	$ 24.11	$ 162.32	$ 186.43	$ 6,267.21
25	$ 6,267.21	$ 23.50	$ 162.93	$ 186.43	$ 6,104.28
26	$ 6,104.28	$ 22.89	$ 163.54	$ 186.43	$ 5,940.74
27	$ 5,940.74	$ 22.28	$ 164.15	$ 186.43	$ 5,776.59
28	$ 5,776.59	$ 21.66	$ 164.77	$ 186.43	$ 5,611.82
29	$ 5,611.82	$ 21.04	$ 165.39	$ 186.43	$ 5,446.44
30	$ 5,446.44	$ 20.42	$ 166.01	$ 186.43	$ 5,280.43
31	$ 5,280.43	$ 19.80	$ 166.63	$ 186.43	$ 5,113.80
32	$ 5,113.80	$ 19.18	$ 167.25	$ 186.43	$ 4,946.55
33	$ 4,946.55	$ 18.55	$ 167.88	$ 186.43	$ 4,778.67
34	$ 4,778.67	$ 17.92	$ 168.51	$ 186.43	$ 4,610.16
35	$ 4,610.16	$ 17.29	$ 169.14	$ 186.43	$ 4,441.01
36	$ 4,441.01	$ 16.65	$ 169.78	$ 186.43	$ 4,271.24
37	$ 4,271.24	$ 16.02	$ 170.41	$ 186.43	$ 4,100.82
38	$ 4,100.82	$ 15.38	$ 171.05	$ 186.43	$ 3,929.77
39	$ 3,929.77	$ 14.74	$ 171.69	$ 186.43	$ 3,758.08
40	$ 3,758.08	$ 14.09	$ 172.34	$ 186.43	$ 3,585.74
41	$ 3,585.74	$ 13.45	$ 172.98	$ 186.43	$ 3,412.76
42	$ 3,412.76	$ 12.80	$ 173.63	$ 186.43	$ 3,239.13
43	$ 3,239.13	$ 12.15	$ 174.28	$ 186.43	$ 3,064.84
44	$ 3,064.84	$ 11.49	$ 174.94	$ 186.43	$ 2,889.91
45	$ 2,889.91	$ 10.84	$ 175.59	$ 186.43	$ 2,714.31
46	$ 2,714.31	$ 10.18	$ 176.25	$ 186.43	$ 2,538.06
47	$ 2,538.06	$ 9.52	$ 176.91	$ 186.43	$ 2,361.15
48	$ 2,361.15	$ 8.85	$ 177.58	$ 186.43	$ 2,183.57
49	$ 2,183.57	$ 8.19	$ 178.24	$ 186.43	$ 2,005.33
50	$ 2,005.33	$ 7.52	$ 178.91	$ 186.43	$ 1,826.42
51	$ 1,826.42	$ 6.85	$ 179.58	$ 186.43	$ 1,646.84
52	$ 1,646.84	$ 6.18	$ 180.25	$ 186.43	$ 1,466.58
53	$ 1,466.58	$ 5.50	$ 180.93	$ 186.43	$ 1,285.65
54	$ 1,285.65	$ 4.82	$ 181.61	$ 186.43	$ 1,104.05
55	$ 1,104.05	$ 4.14	$ 182.29	$ 186.43	$ 921.76
56	$ 921.76	$ 3.46	$ 182.97	$ 186.43	$ 738.78
57	$ 738.78	$ 2.77	$ 183.66	$ 186.43	$ 555.12
58	$ 555.12	$ 2.08	$ 184.35	$ 186.43	$ 370.77
59	$ 370.77	$ 1.39	$ 185.04	$ 186.43	$ 185.73
60	$ 185.73	$ 0.70	$ 185.73	$ 186.43	$ 0.00

Figure 2-99 Excel 2-3 completed

Independent Project 2-4

Central Sierra Insurance (CSI) sets bonus percentages based on commissions earned by each agent and calculates totals by branch office. This workbook also tracks fundraising efforts of employees for a community event.
[Student Learning Outcomes 2.1, 2.2, 2.3, 2.5, 2.6, 2.7]

File Needed: ***CentralSierra-02.xlsx*** *(Student data files are available in the* Library *of your SIMnet account.)*
Completed Project File Name: ***[your initials] Excel 2-4.xlsx***

Skills Covered in This Project

- Create, copy, and edit formulas.
- Name cell ranges.
- Set mathematical order of operations.
- Set cell references to be absolute.
- Use the *NOW* function.
- Use *HLOOKUP* and *VLOOKUP* functions.
- Use the *SUMIF* function.
- Build an *IF* function.

1. Open the ***CentralSierra-02.xlsx*** workbook from your student data files and save it as [your initials] Excel 2-4. Review the data on each sheet.
2. Select the **Tables** sheet, select cells **A6:B10**, and create range names using the **Create from Selection** button [*Formulas* tab, *Defined Names* group].
3. Select cells **B1:F2** and click the **Name** box. Name the selection H_Rates. Note that the first row is arranged in ascending order.
4. Create an *HLOOKUP* function to display the bonus rate.
   a. Click the **Commissions** sheet tab and select cell **F5**.
   b. Start the *HLOOKUP* function and use cell **E5** as the *lookup_value*.
   c. For the *table_array* argument, use the **H_Rates** range.
   d. Use the second row for the *row_index_num* argument (Figure 2-100).

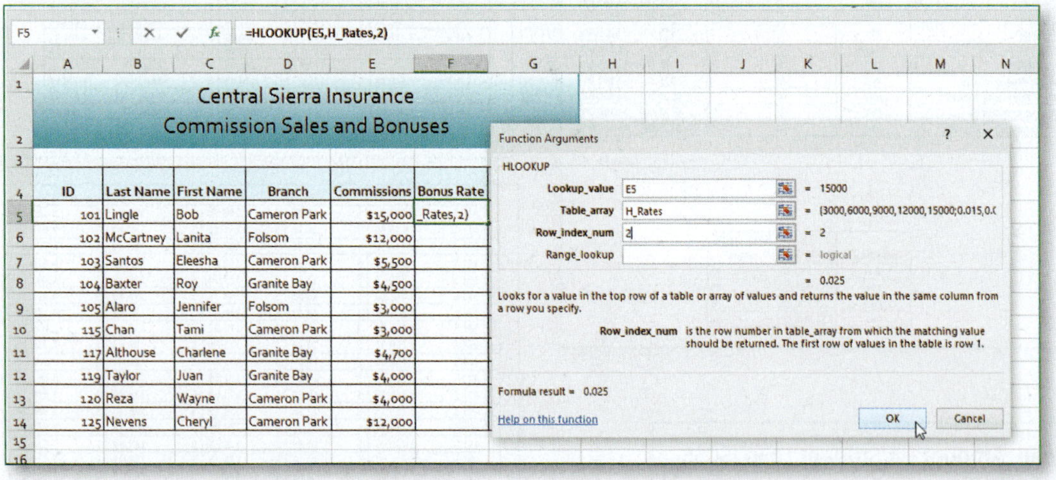

Figure 2-100 ***HLOOKUP* function to display bonus rate**

5. Format the results as **Percent Style** with two decimal places.
6. Copy the formula in cell **F5** to cells **F6:F14**.
7. Set order of operations to calculate total earnings.
   a. Select cell **G5**.
   b. Build a formula to add the commissions amount (E5) to the commissions amount times the rate (F5*E5).
   c. Copy the formula in cell **G5** to cells **G6:G14**.

8. Create and copy a *SUMIF* function to calculate total earnings by branch office.
   a. Select cell **E18**.
   b. Start the *SUMIF* function with cells **$D$5:$D$14** as the *Range* argument.
   c. Set the *Criteria* argument as a relative reference to cell **C18**.
   d. Select cells **G5:G14** for the *Sum_range* argument and make the references absolute.
   e. Copy the formula in cell **E18** to cells **E19:E20** without formatting to preserve borders.
   f. Format cells **E18:E21** as **Currency**.
9. Total the earnings in cell **E21**.
10. Create and format the current date.
    a. Select cell **G23** and insert the *NOW* function.
    b. Select cell **G23** and click the **Number** group launcher [*Home* tab]. On the *Number* tab, select the **Date** category.
    c. Scroll the *Type* list to find the date that displays the month spelled out, the date, a comma, and a four-digit year (Figure 2-101).
    d. Click **OK**. Press **Ctrl+Home**.

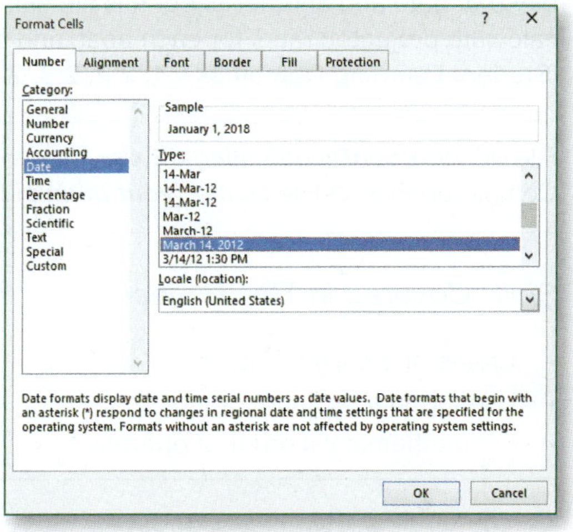

Figure 2-101 Date format selected

11. Create and copy a *VLOOKUP* function to display goals for each funding source.
    a. Click the **Family Day** sheet tab and select cell **F6**.
    b. Start the *VLOOKUP* function and use cell **E6** as the *lookup_value*.
    c. Click the **Tables** sheet tab for the *table_array* argument and use cells **$A$6:$B$10**. The data is sorted by the first column in ascending order.
    d. Use the second column as the *col_index_num* argument. The *range_lookup* argument is empty.
    e. Copy the formula in cell **F6** to cells **F7:F20** without formatting to preserve the fill color.
    f. Format cells **F6:F20** as **Currency** with no decimal places.
12. Create and copy an *IF* function.
    a. Select cell **H6** and start an *IF* function.
    b. Type a *logical_argument* to determine if cell **G6** is greater than or equal to (**>=**) cell **F6**.
    c. Type Yes as the *Value_if_true* argument and No as the *Value_if_false* argument.
    d. Copy the formula in cell **H6** to cells **H7:H20** without formatting to maintain the fill color.
    e. Center align cells **H6:H20**.
    f. Press **Ctrl+Home**.
13. Insert a new sheet at the end of the tab names and paste the range names starting in cell A1. *AutoFit* columns **A:B** and name the worksheet as Range Names.
14. Save and close the workbook (Figure 2-102).

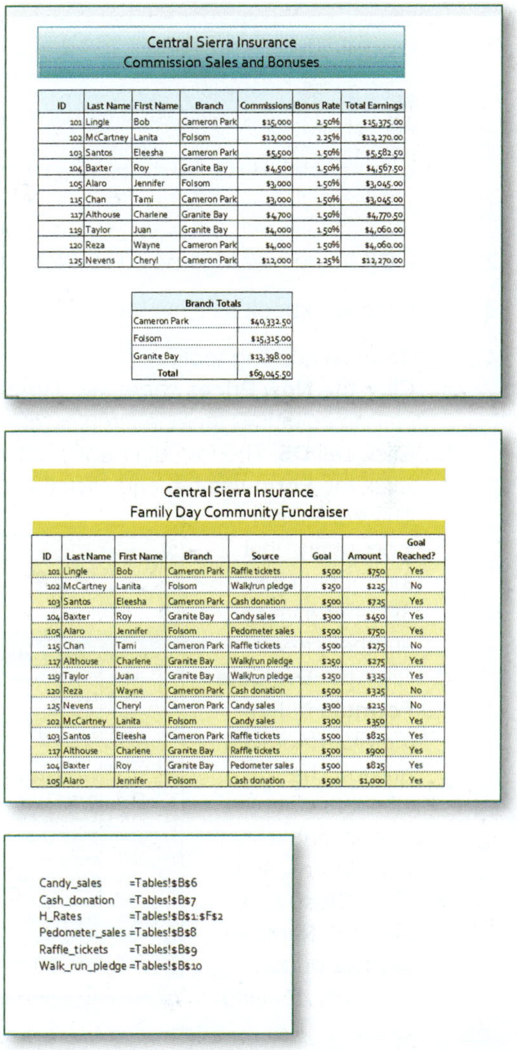

Central Sierra Insurance
Commission Sales and Bonuses

ID	Last Name	First Name	Branch	Commissions	Bonus Rate	Total Earnings
101	Lingle	Bob	Cameron Park	$15,000	2.50%	$15,375.00
102	McCartney	Lanita	Folsom	$12,000	2.25%	$12,270.00
103	Santos	Eleesha	Cameron Park	$5,500	1.50%	$5,582.50
104	Baxter	Roy	Granite Bay	$4,500	1.50%	$4,567.50
105	Alaro	Jennifer	Folsom	$3,000	1.50%	$3,045.00
115	Chan	Tami	Cameron Park	$3,000	1.50%	$3,045.00
117	Althouse	Charlene	Granite Bay	$4,700	1.50%	$4,770.50
119	Taylor	Juan	Granite Bay	$4,000	1.50%	$4,060.00
120	Reza	Wayne	Cameron Park	$4,000	1.50%	$4,060.00
125	Nevens	Cheryl	Cameron Park	$12,000	2.25%	$12,270.00

Branch Totals	
Cameron Park	$40,332.50
Folsom	$15,315.00
Granite Bay	$13,398.00
Total	$69,045.50

Central Sierra Insurance
Family Day Community Fundraiser

ID	Last Name	First Name	Branch	Source	Goal	Amount	Goal Reached?
101	Lingle	Bob	Cameron Park	Raffle tickets	$500	$750	Yes
102	McCartney	Lanita	Folsom	Walk/run pledge	$250	$225	No
103	Santos	Eleesha	Cameron Park	Cash donation	$500	$725	Yes
104	Baxter	Roy	Granite Bay	Candy sales	$300	$450	Yes
105	Alaro	Jennifer	Folsom	Pedometer sales	$500	$750	Yes
115	Chan	Tami	Cameron Park	Raffle tickets	$500	$275	No
117	Althouse	Charlene	Granite Bay	Walk/run pledge	$250	$275	Yes
119	Taylor	Juan	Granite Bay	Walk/run pledge	$250	$325	Yes
120	Reza	Wayne	Cameron Park	Cash donation	$500	$325	No
125	Nevens	Cheryl	Cameron Park	Candy sales	$300	$215	No
102	McCartney	Lanita	Folsom	Candy sales	$300	$350	Yes
103	Santos	Eleesha	Cameron Park	Raffle tickets	$500	$825	Yes
117	Althouse	Charlene	Granite Bay	Raffle tickets	$500	$900	Yes
104	Baxter	Roy	Granite Bay	Pedometer sales	$500	$825	Yes
105	Alaro	Jennifer	Folsom	Cash donation	$500	$1,000	Yes

Candy_sales	=Tables!$B$6
Cash_donation	=Tables!$B$7
H_Rates	=Tables!$B$1:$F$2
Pedometer_sales	=Tables!$B$8
Raffle_tickets	=Tables!$B$9
Walk_run_pledge	=Tables!$B$10

Figure 2-102 Excel 2-4 completed

Independent Project 2-5

San Diego Sailing keeps data about its fleet of rental and charter boats. One of the sheets is missing a piece of data and another sheet has circular reference errors. You will complete work on these sheets, calculate projected rates for each boat, and build basic statistics about past rentals.
[Student Learning Outcomes 2.1, 2.2, 2.3, 2.4, 2.5, 2.6, 2.7]

File Needed: ***SanDiegoSailing-02.xlsx*** *(Student data files are available in the* Library *of your SIMnet account.)*
Completed Project File Name: ***[your initials] Excel 2-5.xlsx***

Skills Covered in This Project

- Create and copy formulas.
- Use formula auditing tools.
- Set mathematical order of operations.
- Use relative, mixed, and 3D cell references.
- Use *COUNTIF* and *SUMIF* functions.
- Build an *IF* formula.
- Insert the *TODAY* function.

---

1. Open the ***SanDiegoSailing-02.xlsx*** workbook from your student data files. When a workbook has a circular reference, a message box appears immediately as you open it (Figure 2-103).

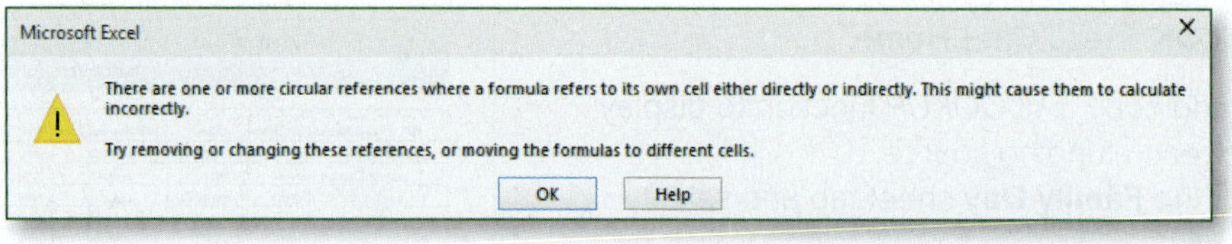

Figure 2-103 Circular reference message

2. Click **OK** in the message box. The *Status* bar indicates the workbook contains *Circular References*.
3. Save the workbook as [your initials] Excel 2-5. Review the data on each sheet.
4. Use formula auditing tools.
   a. Click the **New Prices** sheet tab. The *Status* bar identifies a cell that has a circular reference. The cells in column D include circular references.
   b. Click cell **D5**. The formula begins with 1 plus the value in cell D5, the circular reference.
   c. Click the **Formulas** tab and click the **Trace Precedents** button in the *Formula Auditing* group. The worksheet icon means that the formula has a 3D reference to another sheet.
   d. Click the **Evaluate Formula** button [*Formula Auditing* group]. The circular reference is identified as cell D5 (Figure 2-104).
   e. Click **Close** and click the **Remove Arrows** button [*Formula Auditing* group].

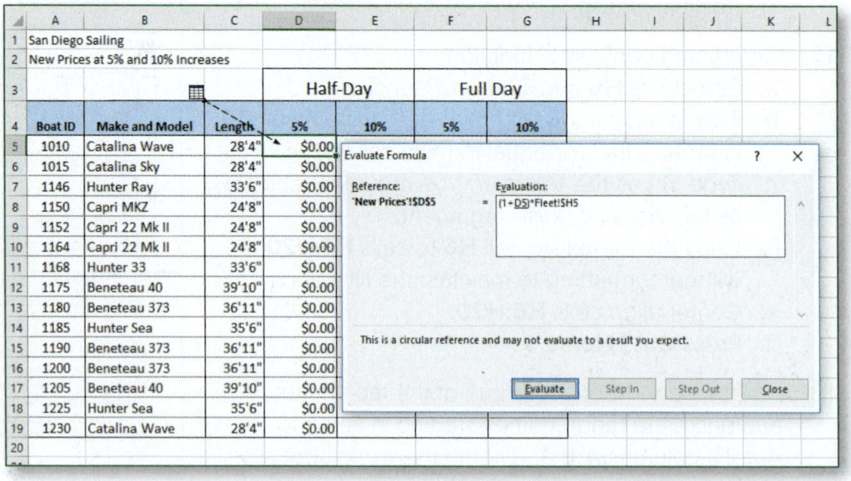

Figure 2-104 *Evaluate Formula* dialog box

5. Edit and copy a formula with mixed references.
   a. Edit the formula in cell **D5** to show D$4 instead of "D5." The formula should multiply one plus the percentage value in cell D4 by the current rate on the **Fleet** sheet ($H5). With an absolute reference to row 4 and column H on the **Fleet** sheet, you can copy the formula down the column (Figure 2-105).

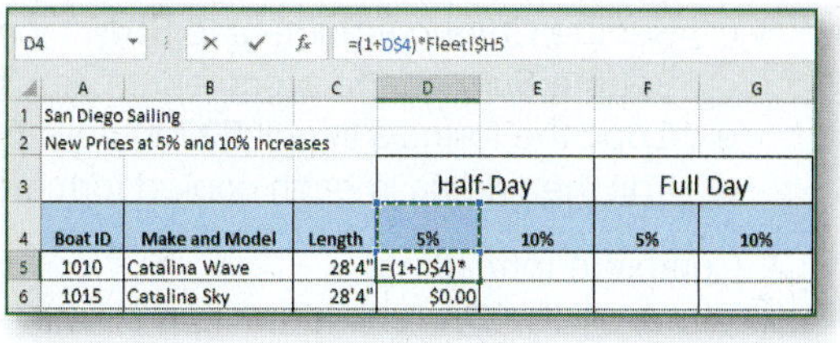

Figure 2-105 Mixed reference in the edited formula

   b. Copy the formula in cell **D5** to cells **D6:D19** without formatting to preserve the border. When the circular reference message box opens, click **OK**.
   c. Select cells **D5:D19** and drag the *Fill* pointer to copy the formulas to cells **E5:E19**.
   d. Click cell **E6**. The formula is adjusted to use the percentage value in cell E4 in place of cell D4. Note also that the reference on the **Fleet** sheet ($H6) is adjusted to show the correct row.

6. Build a formula with mixed references.
   a. Click cell **F5** and type =(1+ to start the formula.
   b. Select cell **F4** and make it an absolute reference to the row but not the column.
   c. Type)* for the closing parenthesis and multiplication.
   d. Click cell **I5** on the **Fleet** sheet, and make the reference absolute for the column but not the row (Figure 2-106).

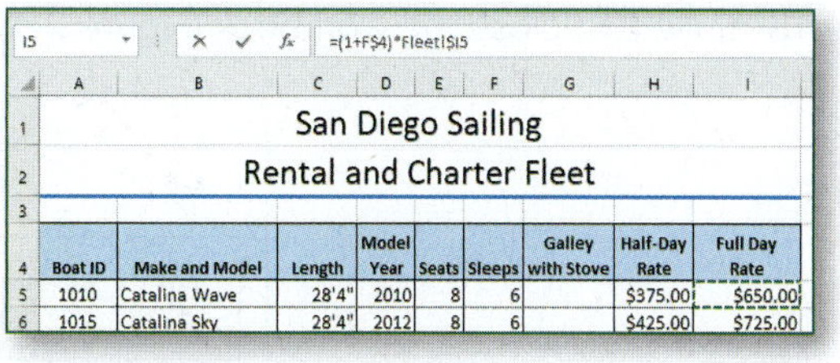

Figure 2-106 Mixed references in the new formula

   e. Copy the formula down column **F** without formatting to preserve the border.
   f. Format cells **F5:F19** as **Currency** and then copy cells **F5:F19** to cells **G5:G19**.

7. Build an *IF* function formula.
   a. Click the **Fleet** sheet tab and select cell **G5**. Rental boats with a stove in the galley must seat 8 or more people.
   b. Create an *IF* function in which the *logical_test* argument determines if there are 8 or more seats.
   c. Use Yes for the *value_if_true* argument. Use No for the *value_if_false* argument. (If you type the formula, enclose the text arguments within quotation marks.)
   d. Copy the formula to cells **G6:G19** without formatting and then center the data in column G.

8. Insert the *TODAY* function in cell **B21**. Format the date to show the month spelled out, the date, and four digits for the year (January 1, 2020).

9. Create a division formula.
   a. Click the **Bookings** sheet tab and select cell **F5**. Calculate average revenue per passenger by dividing the fee by the number of passengers.
   b. Build the division formula.
   c. Copy the formula in cell **F5** to cells **F6:F19**.

10. Create and copy a *COUNTIF* function to count bookings by boat manufacturer.
   a. Select cell **D27**.
   b. Start the *COUNTIF* function from the *Statistical* category by clicking the **More Functions** button in the *Function Library* group.
   c. Use cells **$C$5:$C$19** as the *Range* argument.
   d. Set a *Criteria* argument that will select all boats in the "Beneteau" group. The criteria is **ben***. If you type the formula, include quotation marks.
   e. Copy the formula in cell **D27** to cells **D28:D30**.
   f. Edit the criteria in each copied formula in cells **D28:D30** to reflect the boat make.

11. Create and copy a *SUMIF* function to calculate total revenue by boat make.
   a. Select cell **E27**.
   b. Start the *SUMIF* function with cells **$C$5:$C$19** as the *Range*.

c. Set the *Criteria* argument to ben*.
d. Set the *Sum_range* argument to cells **$E$5:$E$19**.
e. Copy the formula in cell **E27** to cells **E28:E30**.
f. Edit the criteria in each copied formula in cells **E28:E30** as needed.

12. Complete formatting.
   a. Apply the **Currency** format to all values that represent money.
   b. Format the labels in cells **A1:A2** as **18** point.
   c. Select cells **A1:F2** and click the **Alignment** launcher [*Home* tab, *Alignment* group]. Center the labels across the selection.
   d. Merge and center the label in cell **C25** over cells **C25:E25** and format it at **16** points.
   e. Bold and center the labels in rows **4** and **26**.
   f. Select cells **A4:F19** and apply **All Borders**. Do the same for cells **C25:E30**.
   g. Center the page horizontally.

13. Save and close the workbook (Figure 2-107).

San Diego Sailing Bookings
Revenue per Passenger

Date	Boat ID	Make anad Model	# of Passengers	Total Fees	Revenue per Passenger
4/5/2020	1010	Catalina Wave	4	$525.00	$131.25
4/8/2020	1015	Catalina Sky	6	$850.00	$141.67
4/11/2020	1146	Hunter Ray	6	$500.00	$83.33
4/14/2020	1150	Capri MKZ	6	$525.00	$87.50
4/17/2020	1152	Capri 22 Mk II	4	$325.00	$81.25
4/20/2020	1164	Capri 22 Mk II	3	$475.00	$158.33
4/23/2020	1168	Hunter 33	6	$725.00	$120.83
4/26/2020	1175	Beneteau 40	10	$850.00	$85.00
4/29/2020	1180	Beneteau 373	8	$350.00	$43.75
5/2/2020	1185	Hunter Sea	8	$650.00	$81.25
5/5/2020	1190	Beneteau 373	10	$625.00	$62.50
5/8/2020	1200	Beneteau 373	8	$725.00	$90.63
5/11/2020	1205	Beneteau 40	12	$850.00	$70.83
5/14/2020	1225	Hunter Sea	8	$725.00	$90.63
5/17/2020	1230	Catalina Wave	6	$675.00	$112.50

Bookings by Make		
	Count	Total Revenue
Beneteau	5	$3,400.00
Capri	3	$1,325.00
Catalina	3	$2,050.00
Hunter	4	$2,600.00

San Diego Sailing
Rental and Charter Fleet

Boat ID	Make and Model	Length	Model Year	Seats	Sleeps	Galley with Stove	Half-Day Rate	Full Day Rate
1010	Catalina Wave	28'4"	2010	8	6	Yes	$375.00	$650.00
1015	Catalina Sky	28'4"	2012	8	6	Yes	$425.00	$725.00
1146	Hunter Ray	33'6"	2014	10	6	Yes	$350.00	$500.00
1150	Capri MKZ	24'8"	2011	6	4	No	$325.00	$500.00
1152	Capri 22 Mk II	24'8"	2016	6	4	No	$325.00	$500.00
1164	Capri 22 Mk II	24'8"	2016	6	4	No	$325.00	$500.00
1168	Hunter 33	33'6"	2018	10	6	Yes	$425.00	$725.00
1175	Beneteau 40	39'10"	2018	12	6	Yes	$489.00	$750.00
1180	Beneteau 373	36'11"	2017	10	6	Yes	$369.00	$725.00
1185	Hunter Sea	35'6"	2009	10	6	Yes	$349.00	$550.00
1190	Beneteau 373	36'11"	2017	10	6	Yes	$369.00	$625.00
1200	Beneteau 373	36'11"	2017	10	6	Yes	$369.00	$625.00
1205	Beneteau 40	39'10"	2018	12	6	Yes	$489.00	$750.00
1225	Hunter Sea	35'6"	2012	10	6	Yes	$349.00	$725.00
1230	Catalina Wave	28'4"	2019	8	6	Yes	$439.00	$675.00

January 1, 2020

San Diego Sailing
New Prices at 5% and 10% Increases

			Half-Day		Full Day	
Boat ID	Make and Model	Length	5%	10%	5%	10%
1010	Catalina Wave	28'4"	$393.75	$412.50	$682.50	$715.00
1015	Catalina Sky	28'4"	$446.25	$467.50	$761.25	$797.50
1146	Hunter Ray	33'6"	$367.50	$385.00	$525.00	$550.00
1150	Capri MKZ	24'8"	$341.25	$357.50	$525.00	$550.00
1152	Capri 22 Mk II	24'8"	$341.25	$357.50	$525.00	$550.00
1164	Capri 22 Mk II	24'8"	$341.25	$357.50	$525.00	$550.00
1168	Hunter 33	33'6"	$446.25	$467.50	$761.25	$797.50
1175	Beneteau 40	39'10"	$513.45	$537.90	$787.50	$825.00
1180	Beneteau 373	36'11"	$387.45	$405.90	$761.25	$797.50
1185	Hunter Sea	35'6"	$366.45	$383.90	$577.50	$605.00
1190	Beneteau 373	36'11"	$387.45	$405.90	$656.25	$687.50
1200	Beneteau 373	36'11"	$387.45	$405.90	$656.25	$687.50
1205	Beneteau 40	39'10"	$513.45	$537.90	$787.50	$825.00
1225	Hunter Sea	35'6"	$366.45	$383.90	$761.25	$797.50
1230	Catalina Wave	28'4"	$460.95	$482.90	$708.75	$742.50

Figure 2-107 Excel 2-5 completed

Independent Project 2-6

Placer Hills Real Estate has regional offices throughout central California, and each office tracks its listings and sales data. In the workbook, you need to insert agent names, calculate market days, and determine sale price as a percentage of list price. You also calculate summary statistics. **[Student Learning Outcomes 2.1, 2.3, 2.5, 2.6]**

File Needed: ***PlacerHills-02.xlsx*** *[Student data files are available in the* Library *of your SIMnet account.]*
Completed Project File Name: ***[your initials] Excel 2-6.xlsx***

Skills Covered in This Project

- Use the *VLOOKUP* function.
- Create and copy formulas.
- Use dates in a subtraction formula.
- Name cell ranges.
- Use relative and 3D cell references in formulas.
- Use *AVERAGE*, *MAX*, *MIN*, and *COUNT*.
- Use *COUNTIF*.

1. Open the ***PlacerHills-02.xlsx*** workbook from your student data files and save it as [your initials] Excel 2-6. Review the data on each sheet.
2. Use the *VLOOKUP* function to insert the agent's last name in a new column on the **Listings** sheet.
   a. Insert a column at column **D**.
   b. Type Name in cell **D3** and click cell **D4**.
   c. Start a *VLOOKUP* function and set the agent ID (C4) as the *lookup_value* argument.
   d. Use an absolute reference to cells A2:B7 on the **Agents** sheet for the *table_array* argument. Do not include column titles in a table array, and note that the array is sorted in ascending order by the first column.
   e. Enter 2 for the *col_index_num* argument to display the agent's last name and leave the *range_lookup* argument blank.
   f. Copy the formula without formatting to preserve borders and display each agent's name. *AutoFit* column **D**.
3. Build a subtraction formula with dates.
   a. Select cell **O4** on the **Listings** sheet. Subtract the older date from the later date to determine the number of days on the market.
   b. Type = and click cell **N4**, the sold date.
   c. Type – for subtraction and click cell **B4**, the listing date.
   d. Press **Enter**. The result is formatted as a date (Figure 2-108).

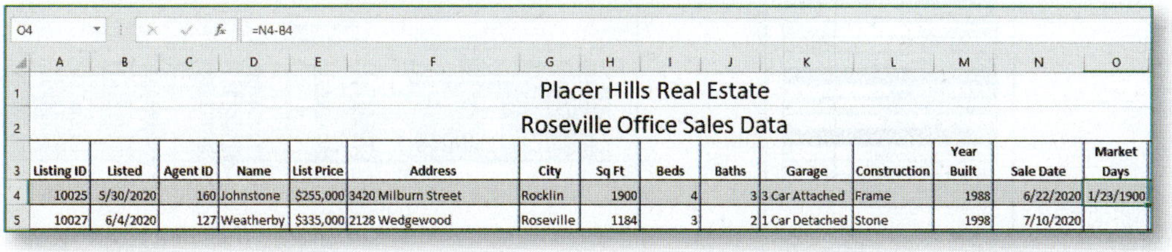
O4 =N4-B4

	A	B	C	D	E	F	G	H	I	J	K	L	M	N	O
1	Placer Hills Real Estate														
2	Roseville Office Sales Data														
3	Listing ID	Listed	Agent ID	Name	List Price	Address	City	Sq Ft	Beds	Baths	Garage	Construction	Year Built	Sale Date	Market Days
4	10025	5/30/2020	160	Johnstone	$255,000	3420 Milburn Street	Rocklin	1900	4	3	3 Car Attached	Frame	1988	6/22/2020	1/23/1900
5	10027	6/4/2020	127	Weatherby	$335,000	2128 Wedgewood	Roseville	1184	3	2	1 Car Detached	Stone	1998	7/10/2020	

Figure 2-108 Result is formatted as a date

   e. Copy the formula in cell **O4** to cells **O5:O12** without formatting to preserve the fill color.
   f. Format cells **O4:O12** as **General**.
4. Calculate the sold price as a percentage of the list price.
   a. Select cell **Q4** and type =.
   b. Build a formula to divide the selling price by the list price.
   c. Copy the formula without formatting to preserve fill and format the column as **Percent Style** with **two** decimal places.

5. Name cell ranges.
   a. Select cells **E3:E12**.
   b. Press **Ctrl** and select cells **G3:G12**, **L3:L12**, and **P3:P12**.
   c. Click the **Create from Selection** button [*Formulas* tab, *Defined Names* group] and use the **Top row** to create range names.
   d. Press **Ctrl+Home**.
   e. Format this sheet to fit one page, landscape orientation.
   f. Insert a footer that displays the file name in the right section.

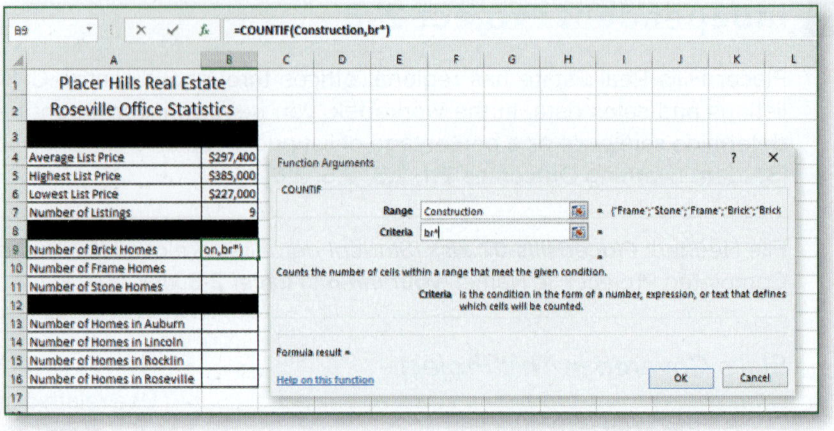

Figure 2-109 Arguments for *COUNTIF*

6. Calculate statistics for the agency.
   a. Click the **Statistics** sheet tab and select cell **B4**.
   b. Click the **AutoSum** button arrow and choose *Average*. No assumed range displays.
   c. Press **F3** (**FN+F3**) to open the *Paste Name* dialog box.
   d. Choose **List_Price** and click **OK**. Press **Enter**.
   e. Continue on this sheet to calculate the highest and lowest list prices as well as the number of listings. Be careful to select the correct range name, and remove **Currency** format as needed.
7. Use *COUNTIF* to calculate statistics.
   a. Select cell **B9**.
   b. Click the **More Functions** button in the *Function Library* group, choose **Statistical**, and select **COUNTIF**.
   c. Use the range name **Construction** for the *Range* argument (Figure 2-109).
   d. Type **br*** for the *Criteria* and click **OK**.
   e. Copy the formula and edit the criteria for cells **B10:B11**.
   f. Start a new *COUNTIF* function in cell **B13** with the **City** range name and wildcard criteria to locate Auburn. Then copy and edit the formula for cells **B14:B16**. Be sure to use criteria that will distinguish between city names that begin with "ro."
8. Center the sheet horizontally. Add a footer with the file name in the center section.
9. Save and close the workbook (Figure 2-110).

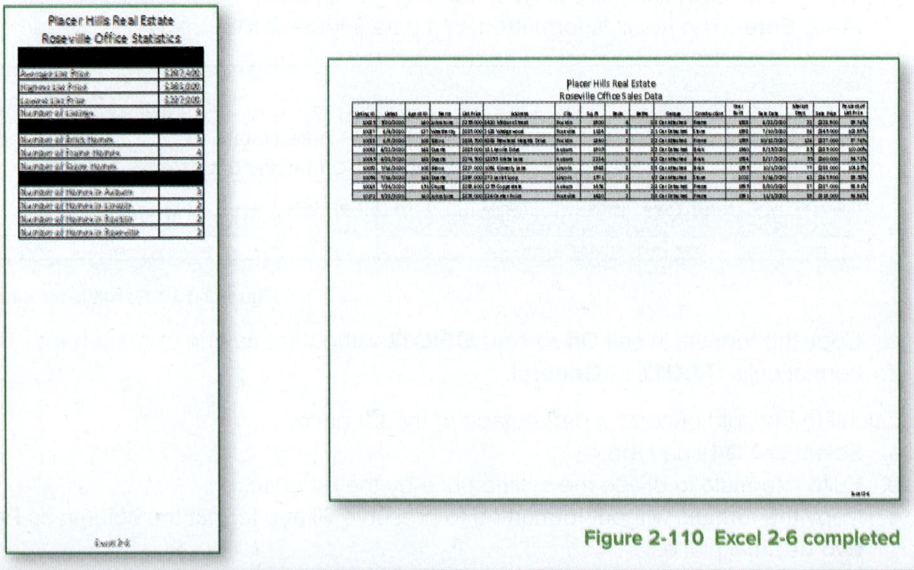

Figure 2-110 Excel 2-6 completed

Improve It Project 2-7

Mary's Rentals serves the light-to-heavy equipment rental needs of contractors, as well as the general public. Data has been imported from an Access database and needs to be handled for better management in Excel. Once that is done, you can calculate several statistics for the company.
[Student Learning Outcomes 2.1, 2.3, 2.4, 2.5, 2.7]

File Needed: ***MarysRentals-02.xlsx*** *(Student data files are available in the* Library *of your SIMnet account.)*
Completed Project File Name: ***[your initials] Excel 2-7.xlsx***

Skills Covered in This Project

- Use formula auditing tools.
- Name cell ranges.
- Create, copy, and edit formulas.
- Use relative references and range names in formulas.
- Use *Statistical* functions.
- Use functions from the *Math & Trig* category.

1. Open the ***MarysRentals-02.xlsx*** workbook from your student data files and save it as [your initials] Excel 2-7. The *Equipment* sheet is an inventory of equipment available for rental.

2. Correct errors on the *Rentals* sheet.
   a. Click the **Rentals** tab. This data was imported from an Access database, and error triangles display in many cells.
   b. Select cells **A2:A47** and click the **Trace Error** button near cell A2 (Figure 2-111). This data was imported as text (labels) but should be set as values.
   c. Select **Convert to Number**. The data are formatted as values and are right-aligned.
   d. Repeat for cells **B2:C47**.
   e. Center align cells **E2:E47**. This column specifies whether the rental was daily, weekly, or monthly.
   f. Press **Ctrl+Home**.

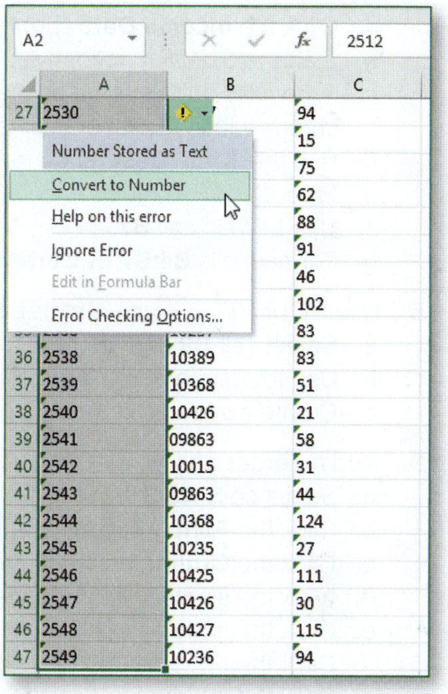

Figure 2-111 ***Trace Error*** **button for a selected range**

3. Name cell ranges.
   a. Select cells **B1:B47**, press **Ctrl**, and select cells **E1:E47** and cells **I1:I47**.
   b. Create names from the selection [*Formulas* tab, *Defined Names* group].
   c. Press **Ctrl+Home**.

4. Create and copy a *SUMIF* function with a relative reference.
   a. Click the **Generators** sheet tab and select cell **C5**.
   b. Start the *SUMIF* function with *Equipment_ID* as the *Range* argument.
   c. The *Criteria* argument is cell **A5**.
   d. The *Sum_range* argument is the *Total_Cost* range.
   e. Copy the formula in cell **C5** to cells **C6:C7**. The relative cell reference to cell A5 is adjusted.
   f. Format cells **C5:C7** as **Currency** with no decimal places.

5. Build a custom border.
   a. Select cells **A4:C7**.
   b. Press **Ctrl+1** to open the *Format Cells* dialog box and click the **Border** tab.
   c. Click the **Outline** button in the *Presets* section.
   d. Click the dotted line style (second option, first column, just below *None*) in the *Style* section.

e. Click the middle horizontal position in the *Border* preview area.
f. Click the single solid line style (last option, first column) in the *Style* section.
g. Click the middle vertical position in the *Border* preview area (Figure 2-112).
h. Click **OK**.

6. Complete formatting.
   a. Apply bold and centering to cells **A4:C4**.
   b. Format cells **A1:A2** to **16** points.
   c. Select cells **A1:C2** and use **Center Across Selection**.
   d. Center the sheet horizontally.
   e. Insert a header with the file name in the right section.

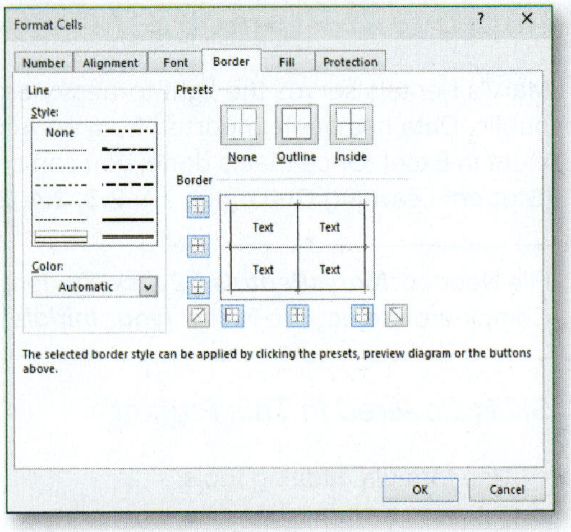

Figure 2-112 Build a custom border in the *Format Cells* dialog box

7. Use *SUMIF* to calculate daily, weekly, and monthly income rentals.
   a. Click the **Income Data** sheet tab and select cell **B4**.
   b. Start the *SUMIF* function with **Type** as the *Range* argument.
   c. Type d for daily income as the *Criteria* argument. If you type the formula, remember to enclose the criteria within quotation marks.
   d. Use the **Total_Cost** range for the *Sum_range* argument.
   e. Enter *SUMIF* formulas in cells **B5:B6**, or copy and edit the formula in cell B4.
   f. Use *SUM* in cell **B7**.
   g. Format cells **B4:B7** as **Currency** with no decimal places.

8. Use *COUNTIF* to count rentals by type.
   a. Select cell **B9** and start the *COUNTIF* function from the *Statistical* category.
   b. Use the range name **Type** as the *Range* argument. The *Criteria* is d.
   c. Create a separate formula in cells **B10:B11**, or copy and edit the formula in cell B9.

9. Add a border and fill.
   a. Select cells **A3:B12**.
   b. Click the **Font** group launcher [*Home* tab] and click the **Border** tab.
   c. Click the **Outline** button in the *Presets* section.
   d. Click the single solid line style (last option, first column) in the *Style* section.
   e. Click the middle vertical position in the *Border* preview area.
   f. Click the dotted line style (second option, first column) in the *Style* section.
   g. Click the middle horizontal position in the *Border* preview area.
   h. Click **OK**.
   i. Select cells **A3:B3**, **A8:B8**, and **A12:B12**.
   j. Click the arrow with the **Fill Color** button and choose **Black, Text 1, Lighter 50%** (second column).
   k. Select cells **A1:B2** and use **Center Across Selection**.
   l. Increase the font size for cells **A1:B2** to **16**.
   m. Center the sheet horizontally.
   n. Insert a footer with the file name in the right section.

10. Save and close the workbook (Figure 2-113).

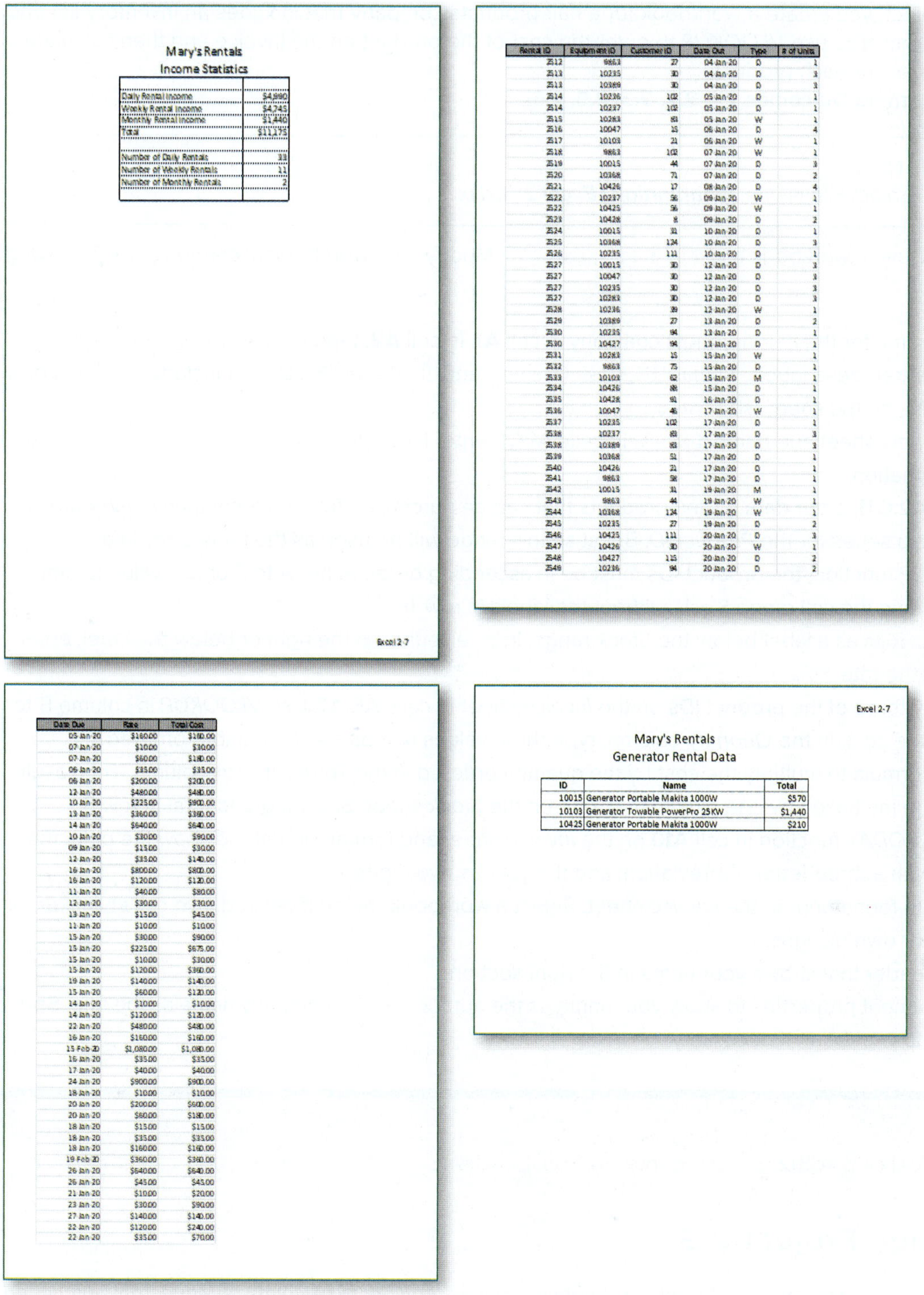

Mary's Rentals
Income Statistics

Daily Rental Income	$4,990
Weekly Rental Income	$4,745
Monthly Rental Income	$1,440
Total	$11,175
Number of Daily Rentals	33
Number of Weekly Rentals	11
Number of Monthly Rentals	2

Excel 2-7

Rental ID	Equipment ID	Customer ID	Date Out	Type	# of Units
2512	9863	27	04 Jan 20	D	1
2513	10235	30	04 Jan 20	D	3
2513	10389	30	04 Jan 20	D	3
2514	10236	102	05 Jan 20	D	1
2514	10237	102	05 Jan 20	D	1
2515	10283	83	05 Jan 20	W	1
2516	10047	15	06 Jan 20	D	4
2517	10103	21	06 Jan 20	W	1
2518	9863	102	07 Jan 20	W	1
2519	10015	44	07 Jan 20	D	3
2520	10368	71	07 Jan 20	D	2
2521	10426	17	08 Jan 20	D	4
2522	10237	56	09 Jan 20	W	1
2522	10425	56	09 Jan 20	W	1
2523	10428	8	09 Jan 20	D	2
2524	10015	31	10 Jan 20	D	1
2525	10368	124	10 Jan 20	D	3
2526	10235	111	10 Jan 20	D	1
2527	10015	30	12 Jan 20	D	3
2527	10047	30	12 Jan 20	D	3
2527	10235	30	12 Jan 20	D	3
2527	10283	30	12 Jan 20	D	3
2528	10236	39	12 Jan 20	W	1
2529	10389	27	13 Jan 20	D	2
2530	10235	94	13 Jan 20	D	1
2530	10427	94	13 Jan 20	D	1
2531	10283	15	15 Jan 20	W	1
2532	9863	75	15 Jan 20	D	1
2533	10103	62	15 Jan 20	M	1
2534	10426	88	15 Jan 20	D	1
2535	10428	91	16 Jan 20	D	1
2536	10047	46	17 Jan 20	W	1
2537	10235	102	17 Jan 20	D	1
2538	10237	83	17 Jan 20	D	3
2538	10389	83	17 Jan 20	D	3
2539	10368	51	17 Jan 20	D	1
2540	10426	21	17 Jan 20	D	1
2541	9863	58	17 Jan 20	D	1
2542	10015	31	19 Jan 20	M	1
2543	9863	44	19 Jan 20	W	1
2544	10368	124	19 Jan 20	W	1
2545	10235	27	19 Jan 20	D	2
2546	10425	111	20 Jan 20	D	3
2547	10426	30	20 Jan 20	W	1
2548	10427	115	20 Jan 20	D	2
2549	10236	94	20 Jan 20	D	2

Date Due	Rate	Total Cost
05 Jan 20	$160.00	$160.00
07 Jan 20	$10.00	$30.00
07 Jan 20	$60.00	$180.00
06 Jan 20	$35.00	$35.00
06 Jan 20	$200.00	$200.00
12 Jan 20	$480.00	$480.00
10 Jan 20	$225.00	$900.00
13 Jan 20	$360.00	$360.00
14 Jan 20	$640.00	$640.00
10 Jan 20	$30.00	$90.00
09 Jan 20	$15.00	$30.00
12 Jan 20	$35.00	$140.00
16 Jan 20	$800.00	$800.00
16 Jan 20	$120.00	$120.00
11 Jan 20	$40.00	$80.00
12 Jan 20	$30.00	$30.00
13 Jan 20	$15.00	$45.00
11 Jan 20	$10.00	$10.00
15 Jan 20	$30.00	$90.00
15 Jan 20	$225.00	$675.00
15 Jan 20	$10.00	$30.00
15 Jan 20	$120.00	$360.00
19 Jan 20	$140.00	$140.00
15 Jan 20	$60.00	$120.00
14 Jan 20	$10.00	$10.00
14 Jan 20	$120.00	$120.00
22 Jan 20	$480.00	$480.00
16 Jan 20	$160.00	$160.00
15 Feb 20	$1,080.00	$1,080.00
16 Jan 20	$35.00	$35.00
17 Jan 20	$40.00	$40.00
24 Jan 20	$900.00	$900.00
18 Jan 20	$10.00	$10.00
20 Jan 20	$200.00	$600.00
20 Jan 20	$60.00	$180.00
18 Jan 20	$15.00	$15.00
18 Jan 20	$35.00	$35.00
18 Jan 20	$160.00	$160.00
19 Feb 20	$360.00	$360.00
26 Jan 20	$640.00	$640.00
26 Jan 20	$45.00	$45.00
21 Jan 20	$10.00	$20.00
23 Jan 20	$30.00	$90.00
27 Jan 20	$140.00	$140.00
22 Jan 20	$120.00	$240.00
22 Jan 20	$35.00	$70.00

Excel 2-7

Mary's Rentals
Generator Rental Data

ID	Name	Total
10015	Generator Portable Makita 1000W	$570
10103	Generator Towable PowerPro 25KW	$1,440
10425	Generator Portable Makita 1000W	$210

Figure 2-113 Excel 2-7 completed

Challenge Project 2-8

For this project, you create a workbook for a hair products company that includes an inventory list and an invoice form. You use *VLOOKUP* to enter the cost of the product on the invoice and then calculate a total with taxes for each product.
[Student Learning Outcomes 2.1, 2.2, 2.3, 2.5, 2.6]

File Needed: None
Completed Project File Name: ***[your initials] Excel 2-8.xlsx***

Create and save a workbook as [your initials] Excel 2-8. Modify your workbook according to the following guidelines:

- Type a name for the hair products company in cell **A1**. In cell **A2**, type Customer Invoice. In cells **A4:D4**, enter these labels: Product ID, Cost, Quantity, and Total with Tax. Do not include a comma or a period. Name the sheet tab Invoice.
- Insert a new sheet and name it Stock. In cells **A1:C1**, enter labels for Product ID, Name, and Cost with no punctuation.
- In cells **A2:C11**, enter data for ten products that can be purchased from your company. Use *AutoFill* to create a series for the *Product ID*. Because this range will be used as the table array in a *VLOOKUP* function, the product IDs must be in ascending order, either A to Z or low value to high value. Name the cell range Stock (without the labels in row 1).
- Enter Tax Rate as a label below the *Stock* range. In a cell either to the right or below the label, enter 3.75% as the rate.
- Type any three of the product IDs on the *Invoice* sheet in cells **A5:A7**. Use *VLOOKUP* in column B to display the cost. In the *Quantity* column, type three values to indicate the number ordered.
- Build a formula to multiply the cost by the quantity ordered in the *Total with Tax* column. This result should be multiplied by one plus the tax rate on the *Stock* sheet. Show a grand total in row 8.
- Use the *TODAY* function in cell **A10** on the *Invoice* sheet and format the date to show the date, the month with a three-letter abbreviation, and the year as two digits.
- Complete formatting on the *Invoice* sheet. Select a workbook theme if desired, use cell styles, or build your own designs.
- Add a header that shows your name in the right section.
- Set document properties to show your name as the author and the company name as the title. Spell check the workbook if necessary.

Challenge Project 2-9

For this project, you create a workbook for a mobile services provider to calculate revenue from purchased mobile apps. You enter and format data and use *SUMPRODUCT* to determine revenue by category.
[Student Learning Outcomes 2.1, 2.3, 2.5, 2.7]

File Needed: None
Completed Project File Name: ***[your initials] Excel 2-9.xlsx***

Create and save a workbook as [your initials] Excel 2-9. Modify your workbook according to the following guidelines:

- Enter a name for your mobile services company in cell **A1**.
- Type Last Month's Activity in cell **A2**.
- Enter the labels App Name, Times Downloaded, and Cost in cells **B3**:**D3**.
- Type Books as the first category in cell **A4**. In cells **A7**, **A10**, and **A13**, type the names of three other categories of mobile applications. Examples might be "Travel," "Entertainment," "Games," "Health," "Sports," and so on.
- Complete data for two apps in the *Books* category in cells **B5:D6**. Then do the same for the other categories.
- Create a section that calculates revenue from each app category using the *SUMPRODUCT* function starting in row **18**.
- Use the *TODAY* function in a cell below the data and format the date to show a short date.
- Select a workbook theme if desired, use cell styles, or set your own formatting.
- Add a footer that shows the current date in the left section and your name in the right section.
- Set document properties to show your name as the author and a title of your choice. Spell check the workbook if necessary.

Challenge Project 2-10

In this project, you create a workbook that calculates monthly payments for a major purchase at four possible interest rates and different payback times.
[Student Learning Outcomes 2.1, 2.3, 2.5, 2.6]

File Needed: None
Completed Project File Name: ***[your initials] Excel 2-10.xlsx***

Create and save a workbook as [your initials] Excel 2-10. Modify your workbook according to the following guidelines:

- Enter main labels that identify the worksheet and your proposed purchase.
- Build the first section for a *PMT* formula with the labels Loan, Rate, Term, and Payment. Because you plan to copy the section to show other possibilities, do not use range names.
- Fill in values for the loan amount, an interest rate, and the term. Include the percent sign when you type the interest rate. For the term, use the number of years or the number of months.
- Use *PMT* to calculate the payment made at the beginning of the month (*Type* argument). If you set months for the term, do not multiply the *Nper* argument by 12.
- Copy the entire section once below the current location with a blank row or two between. Then copy these two groupings one or two columns to the right. You should have four possible payment scenarios on the sheet.
- Edit the interest rate and term for each of the copied sections. Be consistent in how you indicate the term of the loan (years or months). Assume that the loan amount is the same.
- Use the *TODAY* function in a row below the data, and format the date to show a short date.
- Apply formatting choices to build an easy-to-read report.
- Add a footer with your name in the right section.
- Set document properties to show your name as the author, and spell check the workbook if necessary.

Source of screenshots Microsoft Office 365 (2019): Word, Excel, Access, Powerpoint.

CHAPTER

3

Creating and Editing Charts

CHAPTER OVERVIEW

In addition to building formulas and functions in a worksheet, use Excel to graph or chart data. After selecting values and labels, you can quickly create a professional looking chart with a few clicks of the mouse. This chapter introduces you to the basics of creating, editing, and formatting Excel charts.

STUDENT LEARNING OUTCOMES (SLOs)

After completing this chapter, you will be able to:

SLO 3.1 Create Excel chart objects and chart sheets (p. E3-163).

SLO 3.2 Use quick layouts and chart styles to design a chart (p. E3-167).

SLO 3.3 Edit chart elements including titles, data labels, and source data (p. E3-172).

SLO 3.4 Format chart elements with shape styles, fills, outlines, and special effects (p. E3-179).

SLO 3.5 Use pictures, shapes, and *WordArt* in a chart (p. E3-183).

SLO 3.6 Build pie charts and combination charts (p. E3-188).

SLO 3.7 Create sunburst and waterfall charts (p. E3-191).

SLO 3.8 Insert and format sparklines in a worksheet (p. E3-194).

CASE STUDY

In the Pause & Practice projects in this chapter, you use data in a Paradise Lakes Resort workbook to build charts that compare revenue categories for two quarters. You build column and pie charts as objects and separate sheets. You also add trendlines and sparklines to illustrate aspects of the data.

Pause & Practice 3-1: Create and edit column and bar charts.

Pause & Practice 3-2: Edit and format charts and chart elements.

Pause & Practice 3-3: Create and format pie, combo, and sunburst charts and insert sparklines.

EXCEL

SLO 3.1

Creating a Chart Object and a Chart Sheet

An Excel ***chart*** is a visual representation of numeric data in a worksheet. A chart helps you identify trends, make comparisons, and recognize patterns in the numbers. Charts are dynamic and linked to the data, so when values in the worksheet change, the chart is automatically redrawn. You can display a chart in the worksheet with its data, or place a chart on its own sheet.

Excel includes different kinds of charts and can recommend the best chart type based on your selected data. It is essential, however, that you select appropriate data for a chart, because it is possible to build charts that illustrate nothing of any consequence. With experience and practice, you will learn how to create charts for your work that have meaning.

Create a Chart Object

A ***chart object*** is a distinct item surrounded by a square border that is separate from worksheet data. A chart object contains chart elements such as titles, axes, and gridlines that can be selected for editing. You can size and position a chart object in a worksheet, as well as size and position each chart element on the chart.

Source data are the cells that contain values and labels to be graphed in a chart. When you select data for a chart, you usually do not include sums, averages, or similar calculations. In Figure 3-1, the source data include the series names in column A, the category names in row 4,

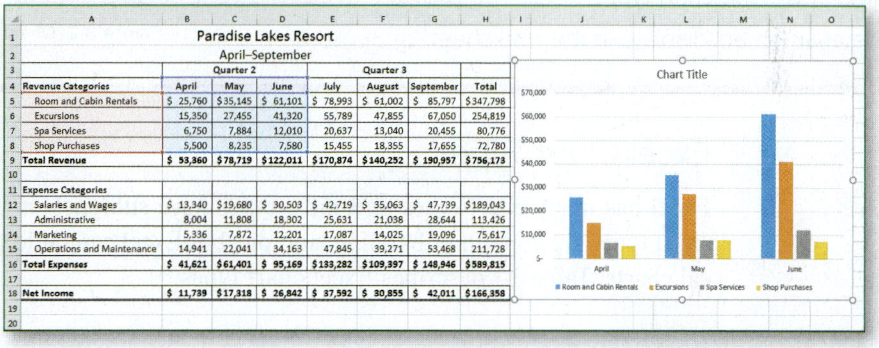

Figure 3-1 Chart object and its source data

and four values for each of three months. Each of the values is a ***data point***, a cell containing a value. Each group of data points or values is a ***data series***. This example includes four data series, one for each revenue category. Each data series has a name or label.

The text label that describes a data series is a ***category label***. In Figure 3.1, the category labels are the month names.

> **ANOTHER WAY**
>
> Create a default chart object by selecting the data and pressing **Alt+F1**.

Data for a chart is best arranged with labels and values in adjacent cells and no empty rows. If you do not include labels for the source data, the chart does not include labels to describe the data. An empty row within the source data is graphed as a data point with a value of zero (0) and will distort the chart's ability to illustrate a comparison or trend.

When you select contiguous source data (all cells are next to each other), the ***Quick Analysis*** button appears in the lower-right corner of the selection. The *Quick Analysis* tool lists command groups you would be likely to use for the selected data, such as *Formatting*, *Charts*, or *Totals*. When you select the *Charts* command, Excel shows recommended chart types. As you point to each type, you see a preview of the chart. Click the preferred type to create the chart object in the worksheet.

▸HOW TO: Create a Chart Object from the Quick Analysis Tool

1. Select the source data range with labels and values.
   - The *Quick Analysis* button appears in the lower-right corner of the range.
2. Click the **Quick Analysis** button.
   - A dialog box with command categories opens (Figure 3-2).
3. Select **Charts**.
   - Possible chart types are listed.
4. Point to a chart type.
   - A preview of the chart object displays.
5. Click to select the chart type.
   - The chart object displays in the worksheet.

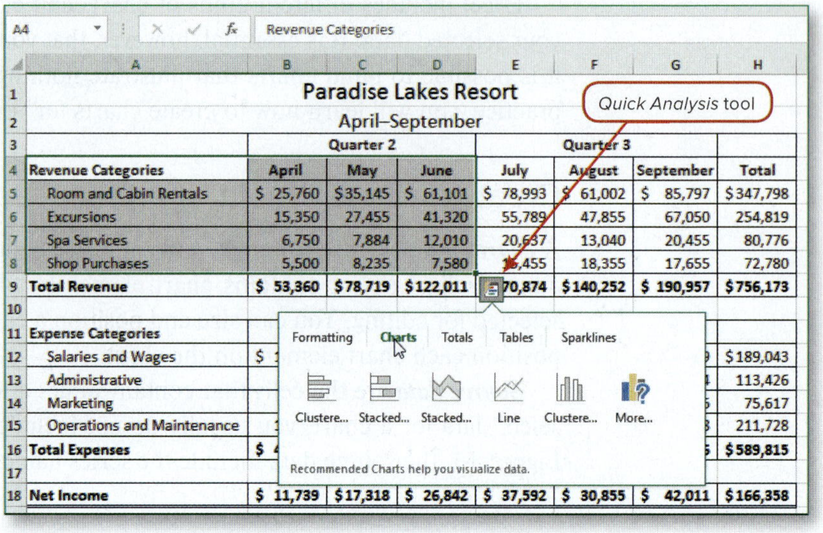

Figure 3-2 Chart preview from *Quick Analysis* choice

Excel Chart Types

Excel has many chart types and most types have subtypes or variations. The most common chart types are column or bar, line, and pie, but Excel can build powerful scientific and statistical charts. Table 3-1 describes Excel chart types:

Table 3-1: Excel Chart Types

Chart Type	Purpose	Data Example	Categories (Labels)	Values (Numbers)
Column	Illustrates data changes over a period of time or shows comparisons among items	Monthly sales data for three automobile models	Horizontal axis	Vertical axis
Bar	Displays comparisons among individual items or values at a specific period of time	Number of pairs sold for eight shoe styles	Vertical axis	Horizontal axis
Pie	Uses one data series to display each value as a percentage of the whole	Expenses or revenue by department for one quarter		One data series shown by slice size
Line	Displays trends in data over time, emphasizing the rate of change	Number of weekly web site views over a ten-week period	Horizontal axis	Vertical axis
Area	Displays the magnitude of change over time and shows the rate of change	Yearly consumption of apples, bananas, and pears over a ten-year period	Horizontal axis	Vertical axis
XY (Scatter) or Bubble	Displays relationships among numeric values in two or more data series; these charts do not have a category	Number of times a patient visits a doctor, amount billed to insurance, and cost billed to patient	Horizontal axis (value 1-x)	Vertical axis (value 2-y)

Continued

Chart Type	Purpose	Data Example	Categories (Labels)	Values (Numbers)
Stock	Displays three series of data to show fluctuations in stock prices from high to low to close	Opening, closing, and high price for Microsoft stock each day for 30 days	Horizontal axis	Vertical axis
Surface	Displays results for combinations of two sets of values on a surface	Windchill factor based on wind speed and outdoor temperature	NA	NA
Radar	Displays the frequency of multiple data series relative to a center point. There is an axis for each category	Style, comfort, and value ratings for three snow boot styles	NA	NA
TreeMap	Displays a hierarchical view of data with different sized and colored rectangles and sub-rectangles to compare the sizes of groups	Soda sales by product name, continent, country, and city	NA	NA
Sunburst	Displays a hierarchical view of data with concentric rings. The top hierarchy is the inner ring and each outer ring is related to its adjacent inner ring	Tablet sales by screen size, continent, country, and city	NA	NA
Histogram	Column-style chart that shows frequencies within a distribution	Number of students in each of five grade categories for an exam	Horizontal axis	Vertical axis
Box & Whisker	Displays the distribution of data with minimum, mean, maximum, and outlier values	Sales prices of homes in five suburbs during a three-week period	Horizontal axis	Vertical axis
Waterfall	Plots each element in a running total and displays negative and positive effects of each on the totals	Banking or savings account register	Horizontal axis	Vertical axis
Funnel	Plots values that progressively decrease from one stage or process to the next	Job applications received, applications selected, online interviews, team interviews	Vertical axis	Horizontal axis
Combo Chart	Uses two types of charts to graph values that are widely different	Line chart for number of monthly web site visits and a column chart for monthly sales of a selected product	Either	Either
Map Chart	Compares and plots values across geographical regions such as countries, states, counties, or postal codes	Tax revenue from all counties in a state or province	Either	Either

Size and Position a Chart Object

When you select a chart object, it is active and surrounded by eight selection handles. A ***selection handle*** is a small circle shape on each corner and in the middle of each side. To select the chart object, point to its border and click. When you select a chart object, the *Range Finder* highlights the source data in the worksheet. When you point to a selection handle, you will see a two-pointed resize arrow. Drag a corner handle to size the height and width proportionally.

To move a chart object, point to the chart border to display a four-pointed move pointer. Then drag the chart object to the desired location.

When a chart is active or selected, the contextual *Chart Tools Design* and *Format* tabs are available in the *Ribbon* and three *Quick Chart Tools* are available in the top-right corner of the object: *Chart Elements*, *Chart Styles*, and *Chart Filters*.

> **MORE INFO**
>
> You can select individual elements or parts of the chart, and each element has its own selection handles.

▶ HOW TO: Move and Size a Chart Object

1. Select the chart object.
   - Point to the border of the chart and click.
2. Point to the outside border of the chart to display a move pointer.
   - Point anywhere along the border.
3. Drag the chart object to a new location and release the pointer button (Figure 3-3).
4. Point to a corner selection handle to display a resize arrow.
5. Drag the pointer to resize the chart proportionally.

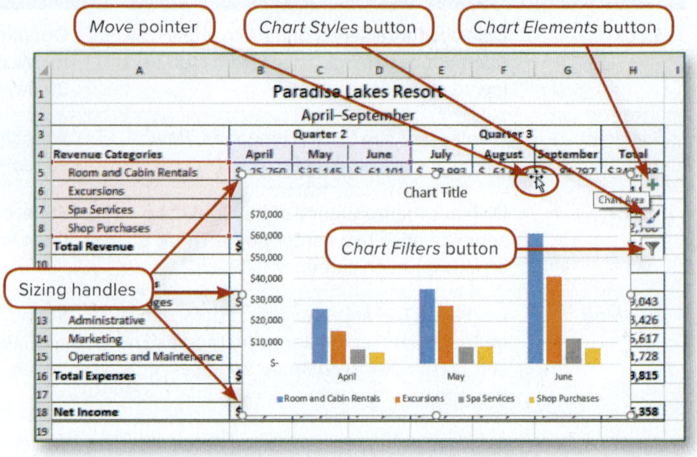

Figure 3-3 Selected chart object and move pointer

Create a Chart Sheet

A ***chart sheet*** is an Excel chart that displays on its own sheet in the workbook. A chart sheet does not have rows, columns, and cells, but the chart is linked to its data on the source worksheet.

From the *Quick Analysis* tool or the *Insert* tab, Excel creates a chart object. You must move the chart object to its own sheet with the *Move Chart* button on the *Chart Tools Design* tab. Excel uses default sheet names *Chart1*, *Chart2*, and so on, but you can type a descriptive name in the *Move Chart* dialog box. You can also rename the sheet at any time.

Create an automatic column chart sheet by selecting the data and pressing the **F11** (**FN+F11**) function key.

> **MORE INFO**
>
> When the *Recommended Charts* button does not recommend a chart type, select the source data again in a left-to-right order. If no suggestions display, click the **All Charts** tab and choose a type.

Source data for a chart need not be contiguous. The *Quick Analysis* tool does not appear for noncontiguous data, but you can click the **Recommended Charts** button in the *Charts* group on the *Insert* tab. The *Insert Chart* dialog box opens and recommends chart types.

▶ HOW TO: Create a Chart Sheet for Noncontiguous Cells

1. Select the values and labels for the chart.
   - Select the first range, press the **Ctrl** key, and select each range (Figure 3-4).
2. Click the **Recommended Charts** button [*Insert* tab, *Charts* group].
   - The *Insert Chart* dialog box opens.
   - Click the **All Charts** tab to select any chart type.
3. Click the thumbnail for a chart type to preview the results.

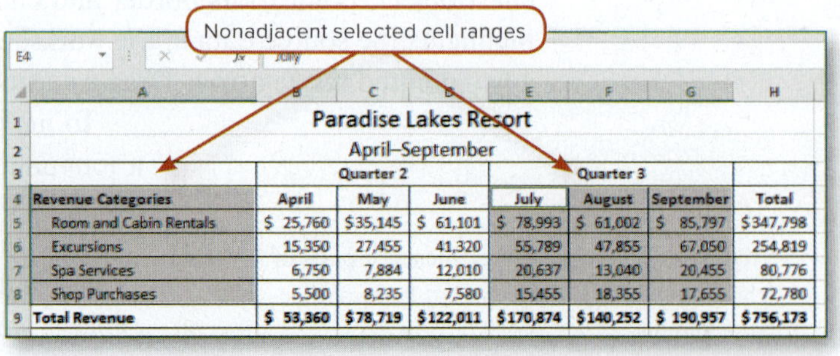

Figure 3-4 Source data ranges that are not next to each other

4. Click the preferred chart type and click **OK**.
   - The chart object is active.
   - The *Chart Tools* tabs are available.
5. Click the **Move Chart** button [*Chart Tools Design* tab, *Location* group].
6. Click the **New sheet** radio button (Figure 3-5).
7. Type a descriptive name for the chart sheet.
8. Click **OK**.

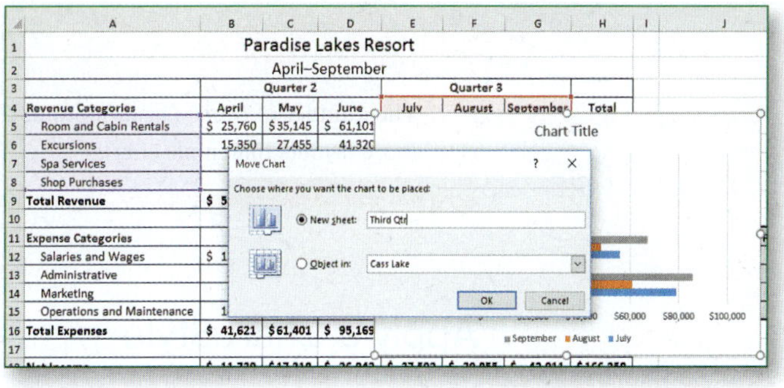

Figure 3-5 *Move Chart* dialog box

SLO 3.2

Using Quick Layouts and Chart Styles

A newly created chart has a default layout, color, and style. Excel has various tools to help you enhance the appearance of your chart for originality, readability, and appeal. The *Chart Tools Design* tab includes commands for selecting a chart layout, choosing a chart style, or changing the color scheme.

Apply a Quick Layout

A *chart layout* is a set of elements and the location of those elements. Elements are individual parts of a chart such as a main title, a legend, and axes titles. The *Quick Layout* button [*Chart Tools Design* tab, *Chart Layouts* group] opens a gallery of predefined layouts (Figure 3-6). As you point to an option in the gallery, *Live Preview* redraws the chart. When a chart layout adds an element such as a title, the element displays a generic label like "Chart Title." You can add or remove individual elements, as well as edit placeholder text.

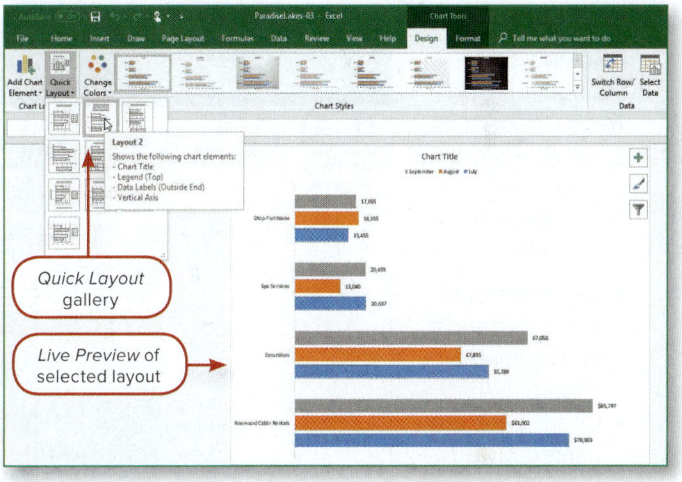

Figure 3-6 *Quick Layout* gallery

HOW TO: Apply a Quick Layout to a Chart

1. Select the chart object or the chart sheet tab.
2. Click the **Quick Layout** button [*Chart Tools Design* tab, *Chart Layouts* group].
   - The gallery displays a list of elements for each layout when you point to a thumbnail image.
   - Quick layouts are named *Layout 1* through the last number.
3. Point to a layout thumbnail to preview it in the chart.
4. Click a thumbnail to select it.
   - The chart is reformatted with the *Quick Layout* elements.

MORE INFO

The number of *Quick Layout* options depends on the chart type. For example, a column chart has more layouts than a pie chart.

Apply a Chart Style

A ***chart style*** is a preset combination of colors and effects for a chart, its background, and its elements. The chart styles available for a chart are based on the current workbook theme. If you change the theme, the chart style colors are updated, and your chart reflects the new color palette. You can find chart styles in the *Chart Styles* group on the *Chart Tools Design* tab. Like a chart layout, you can preview the effects of a chart style as you point to each style in the gallery.

HOW TO: Apply a Chart Style

1. Select the chart object or the chart sheet tab.
2. Point to a *Style* thumbnail [*Chart Tools Design* tab, *Chart Styles* group] or click the *Chart Styles* **More** button to open the gallery.
   - The number of styles depends on the chart type (Figure 3-7).
   - Chart styles are named *Style 1* through the last number.
3. Point to a style thumbnail to see a *Live Preview* in the chart.
4. Click to select a style.
   - The chart is redrawn with the selected style.

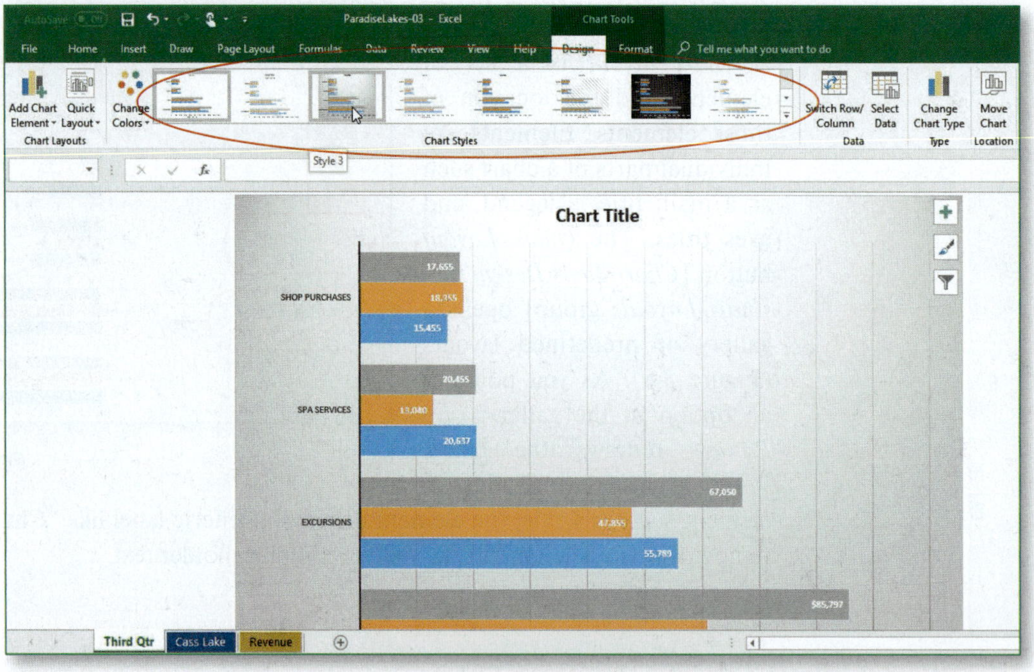

Figure 3-7 *Chart Styles* gallery and preview of selected style

MORE INFO

Chart styles may affect the chart layout. For example, a style may reposition or resize the legend or a main title to display special effects.

Change Chart Colors

The workbook theme and the chart style form the basis for a chart's color scheme. The *Chart Styles* group [*Chart Tools Design* tab] includes a *Change Colors* button with optional color palettes. These palettes are divided into *Colorful* and *Monochromatic* groups.

▸HOW TO: Change Chart Colors

1. Select the chart object or the chart sheet tab.
2. Click the **Change Colors** button [*Chart Tools Design* tab, *Chart Styles* group].
   - A gallery of color palettes opens (Figure 3-8).
   - Color schemes are named with the category (*Colorful* or *Monochromatic*) and a number.
3. Point to a palette to see a *Live Preview* in the chart.
4. Click to select a palette.
   - The chart is formatted with new colors.

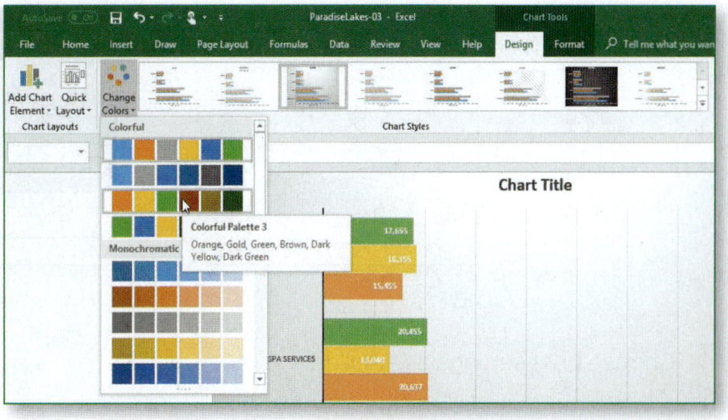

Figure 3-8 ***Change Colors*** **gallery**

Print a Chart

A chart object can be printed on the page with worksheet data, or it can be printed separately. To print a chart with the data, deselect the chart object by clicking a worksheet cell. Size and position the chart and scale the sheet to fit a printed page. Then use regular *Page Setup* commands to complete the print task, such as choosing the orientation or inserting headers or footers.

> **MORE INFO**
>
> When you insert a header or footer in a selected chart object, that header or footer is not inserted on the worksheet.

To print only the chart object on its own sheet, select it and use regular *Print* and *Page Setup* options. A selected chart object, by default, prints scaled to fit a landscape page. A chart sheet also prints in landscape orientation and fits the page.

▸HOW TO: Print a Chart with Its Source Data

1. Click any cell in the worksheet.
   - Size and position the chart object as needed.
2. Click the **File** tab to open the *Backstage* view (Figure 3-9).
3. Select **Print**.

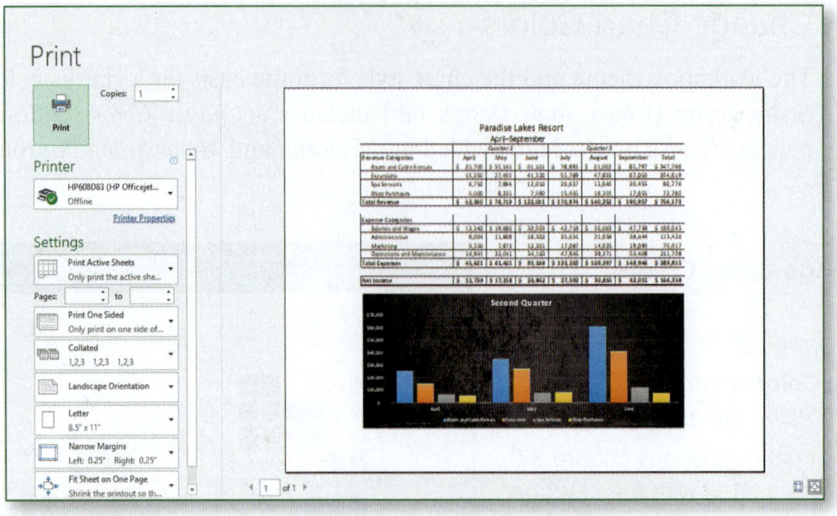

Figure 3-9 Print a chart with the data

4. Choose print settings as needed.
   - Set margins and scale the sheet to fit.
5. Click **Print**.

PAUSE & PRACTICE: EXCEL 3-1

In this project, you insert a clustered column chart object in a worksheet that tracks revenue and expenses for Paradise Lakes Resort. You also insert a clustered bar chart sheet to highlight second quarter results.

File Needed: ***ParadiseLakes-03.xlsx*** *(Student data files are available in the* Library *of your SIMnet account.)*
Completed Project File Name: ***[your initials] PP E3-1.xlsx***

1. Open the ***ParadiseLakes-03*** workbook from your student data files and save it as [your initials] PP E3-1.
2. Create a chart object.
   a. Select cells **A4:D8** on the **Cass Lake** sheet. The cells include labels and values for the chart.
   b. Click the **Quick Analysis** button and select **Charts**.
   c. Click the **Clustered Column** icon.
3. Position and size the chart object.
   a. Click the chart object if it is not selected.
   b. Point to the chart border to display a move pointer.
   c. Drag the chart object so that its top-left corner is at cell **A20**.
   d. Point to the lower-right selection handle to display a resize arrow.
   e. Drag the pointer to reach cell **H35**.
4. Choose a quick layout.
   a. Select the chart object if necessary.
   b. Click the **Quick Layout** button [*Chart Tools Design* tab, *Chart Layouts* group].
   c. Click **Layout 3** (Figure 3-10).

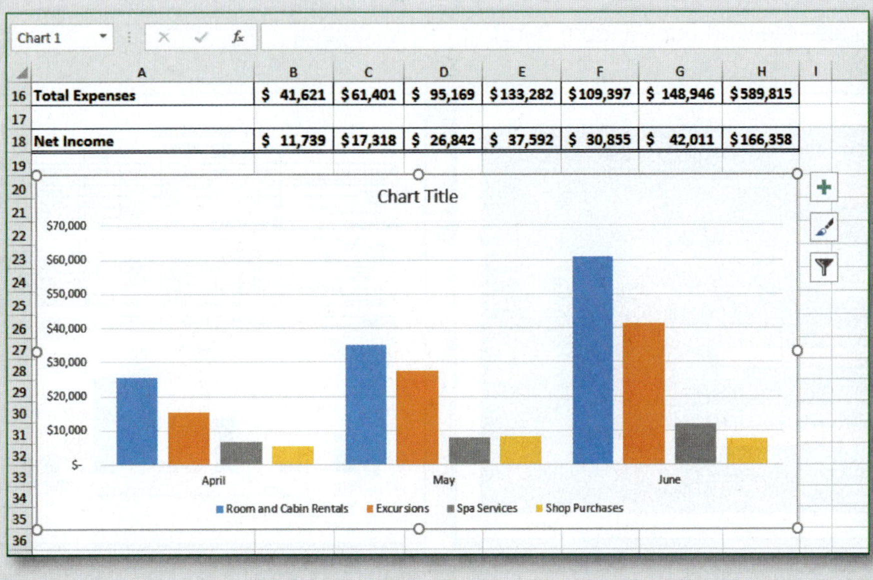

Figure 3-10 Chart object sized and positioned

5. Create a chart sheet.
   a. Select cells **A4:A8**.
   b. Press **Ctrl** and select cells **E4:G8**.
   c. Click the **Recommended Charts** button [*Insert* tab, *Charts* group].
   d. Select **Clustered Bar**.
   e. Click **OK**. The chart object is inserted and selected.
   f. Click the **Move Chart** button [*Chart Tools Design* tab, *Location* group].
   g. Click the **New sheet** radio button.
   h. Type Third Qtr as the sheet name.
   i. Click **OK**. The chart sheet tab is active.
6. Choose a chart style.
   a. Click the **More** button to open the *Chart Styles* gallery [*Chart Tools Design* tab, *Chart Styles* group].
   b. Select **Style 7**.
7. Preview the charts.
   a. Select the **Third Qtr** sheet if necessary.
   b. Click the **File** tab to open the *Backstage* view.
   c. Choose **Print** to preview the chart sheet (Figure 3-11).
   d. Click the **Back** arrow to return to the worksheet.
   e. Click the **Cass Lake** worksheet tab and select cell **A1**.
   f. Click the **File** tab and select **Print**. The worksheet and chart are previewed on a single page.
   g. Click the **Back** arrow to return to the worksheet.

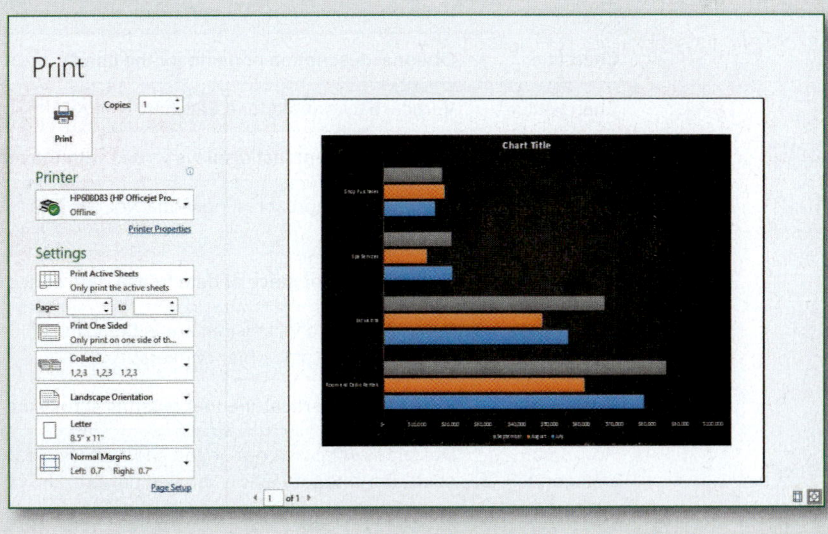

Figure 3-11 Print preview for chart sheet

8. Save and close the workbook (Figure 3-12).

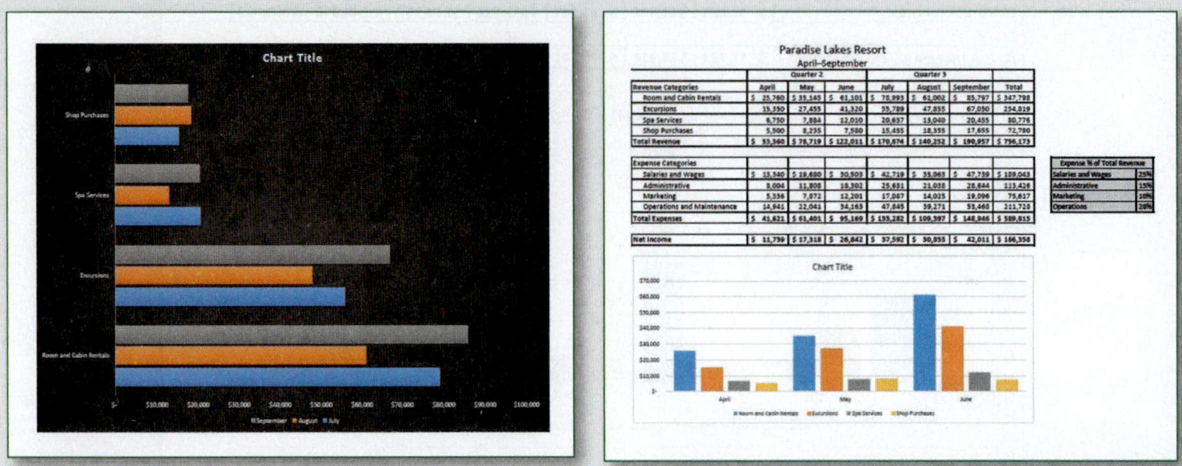

Figure 3-12 PP E3-1 completed chart object and chart sheet

SLO 3.3

Editing Chart Elements and Data

A ***chart element*** is a separate object. The chart layout and style affect which elements are initially displayed, but you can add, remove, format, size, and position elements as you design a chart. Table 3-2 describes common chart elements:

Table 3-2: Excel Chart Elements

Element	Description
Axis	Horizontal or vertical boundary that identifies what is plotted.
Axis title	Optional description for the categories or values.
Chart area	Background for the chart; can be filled with a color, gradient, or pattern.
Chart floor	Base or bottom for a 3D chart.
Chart title	Optional description or name for the chart.
Chart wall	Vertical background for a 3D chart.
Data label	Optional element that displays values with the marker for each data series.
Data marker	Element that represents individual values. The marker is a bar, a column, a slice, or a point on a line.
Data point	A single value or piece of data from a data series.
Data series	Group of related values that are in the same column or row and translate into the columns, lines, pie slices, and other markers.
Gridline	Horizontal or vertical line that extends across the plot area to help identify values.
Horizontal (category) axis	Describes what is shown in the chart and is created from row or column headings. In a bar chart, the category axis is the vertical axis; the category axis is the horizontal axis in a column chart.

Continued

Element	Description
Legend	Element that explains symbols, textures, or colors used to differentiate data series.
Plot area	Rectangular area bounded by the horizontal and vertical axes.
Tick mark	Small line or marker on an axis to guide in reading values
Trendline	Line or curve that displays averages in the data and can be used to forecast future averages.
Vertical (value) axis	Shows the numbers on the chart. In a bar chart, the vertical axis is along the bottom; in a column chart, the vertical axis is along the side.

MORE INFO

Not all charts have all elements. For example, a pie chart does not have any axes or axes titles.

Add and Remove Chart Elements

When you point to a chart element, a *ScreenTip* describes it. When you click the element, it is active and surrounded by selection handles, as shown for the legend in Figure 3-13. In addition to clicking, you can select an element from the *Chart Elements* drop-down list on the *Chart Tools Format* tab. The name of the selected element appears in the *Chart Elements* box.

Show or hide chart elements using the *Chart Elements* button in the top-right corner of a chart. When you click the button, the *Chart Elements* pane opens with a list of available elements for the chart type. In this pane, select or deselect the box to show or remove an element. To hide the pane, click the **Chart Elements** button again.

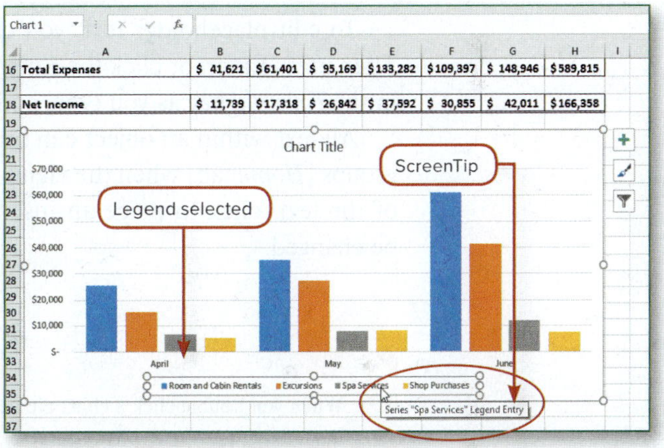

Figure 3-13 Selected legend and *ScreenTip* for a data series

ANOTHER WAY

Click the **Add Chart Element** button [*Chart Tools Design* tab, *Chart Layouts* group] to show a chart element.

Chart and Axes Titles

Chart layouts may include placeholders for a main chart title and for axes titles. If the quick layout does not include titles, you can add them. In either case, you must edit the placeholder text.

A main chart title is usually positioned above the chart, but within the chart area. Once you insert a title text box, you can select it and move it anywhere on the chart. You might use an axis title to clarify the categories or values represented in the chart. If the chart graphs the data well, axes titles are often not necessary.

▸HOW TO: Insert a Chart Title

1. Click the chart object or the chart sheet tab.
2. Click the **Chart Elements** button in the top-right corner of the chart.
3. Select the **Chart Title** box.
   - The *Chart Title* placeholder displays above the chart.
4. Click the **Chart Title** arrow in the *Chart Elements* pane to select a position for the title.
5. Select the *Chart Title* placeholder text (Figure 3-14).
   - The mini toolbar opens.
   - Triple-click the placeholder text or drag to select it.
6. Type a title to replace the placeholder text.
7. Click the chart border.
   - The title object is deselected.
   - If you press **Enter** while typing in the text box, you insert a new line in the title. Press **Backspace** to remove it, and then click the chart border.

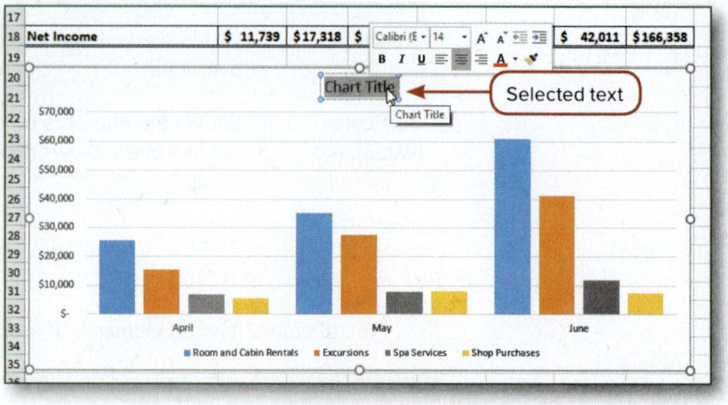

Figure 3-14 Placeholder text to be edited

To edit placeholder text, you can also select the object and type text in the *Formula* bar. Then press **Enter**, or click the **Enter** button in the *Formula* bar to complete it. The label appears in the *Formula* bar as you type, and you will not see it on the chart until you press **Enter**.

All text within an object can be formatted with font attributes from the *Font* and *Alignment* groups [*Home* tab] when the element is selected. When you want to apply a format to a portion of the text, click to place an insertion point inside the element and select the characters to be changed.

> **MORE INFO**
>
> When you double-click a chart element, the *Format* pane opens with format and design choices for that element.

Removing a chart element creates more room for the actual chart. In Figure 3-15, for example, the vertical axis title "Dollars" is probably not necessary. By removing it, the chart resizes to fit the chart area. You can always show the element again if you change your mind.

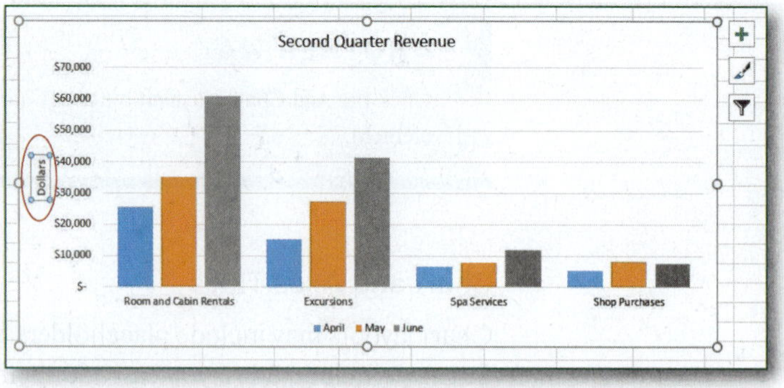

Figure 3-15 Delete an axis title to make more room for the chart

To delete a chart element, select it and press **Delete**. You can confirm which element is selected in the *Chart Elements* box on the *Chart Tools Format* tab [*Current Selection* group].

▶HOW TO: Delete a Chart Element

1. Click the chart element.
   - The element displays selection handles.
   - Confirm which element is selected in the *Chart Elements* list box [*Chart Tools Format* tab, *Current Selection* group].
2. Press **Delete**.
   - The chart resizes to fit the area.
   - Right-click the chart element and choose **Delete**.

> **ANOTHER WAY**
>
> To remove an element, click the **Chart Elements** button in the top-right corner of the chart and deselect the box for that element.

Data Labels

Data labels display the number represented by a column, bar, pie slice, or other marker on the chart. Because the value axis uses a scale, it cannot show a precise value, but a data label can display that number. Data labels should be used when the chart does not have too many data series because they can clutter a chart. Or you can select just one or two of the data points (the individual bars or columns) and show labels for only that data.

Display data labels using the *Chart Elements* button on the chart or from the same button on the *Chart Tools Design* tab [*Chart Layouts* group].

▶HOW TO: Add Data Labels

1. Select the chart object or the chart sheet tab.
2. Click the **Chart Elements** button in the top-right corner of the chart.
3. Select the **Data Labels** box.
   - *Live Preview* shows data labels for each data point in the data series.
4. Point to **Data Labels** in the pane and point to its arrow (Figure 3-16).
   - Position choices for the labels are listed.
   - *Live Preview* updates as you point to each option.
5. Choose a location for the data labels.

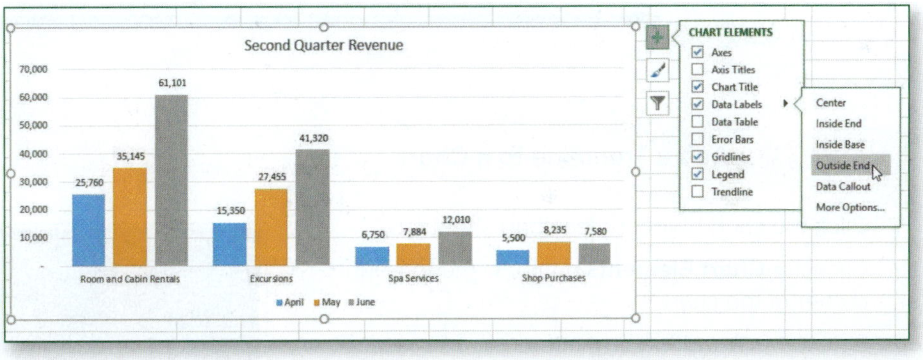

Figure 3-16 Data labels shown outside column markers

Data Table

A chart ***data table*** is a columnar display of the values for each data series in a chart, located just below the chart. When your readers do not have access to the source data for a chart, a data table can supply valuable information.

To include a data table below your chart, you can use the *Add Chart Element* button on the *Chart Tools Design* tab in the *Chart Layouts* group or the *Chart Elements* button on the chart.

You can show a data table with or without legend markers, a mini legend to the left of the table (Figure 3-17).

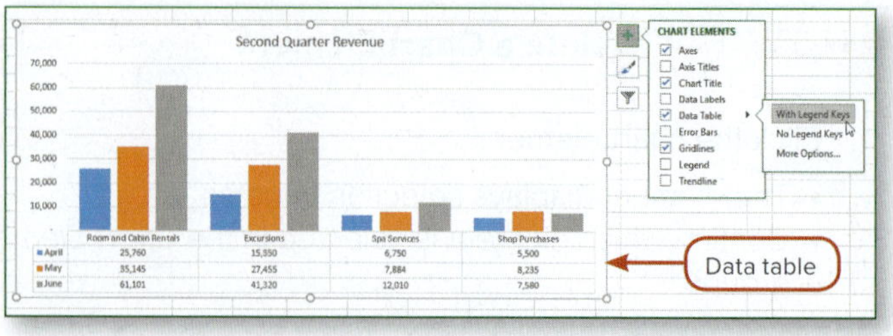

Figure 3-17 Data table element for a chart

Trendlines

A ***trendline*** is a chart element that plots patterns using a moving average of the current data. It uses a straight or curved line and can extend past the data to predict future averages. Not all chart types are suitable for trendlines, such as a pie or a treemap chart. A basic linear trendline is appropriate for values that tend to increase or decrease as time passes. A trendline traces data for one data series, as seen in Figure 3-18. If you have multiple data series, as in a typical column chart, add a trendline for each series.

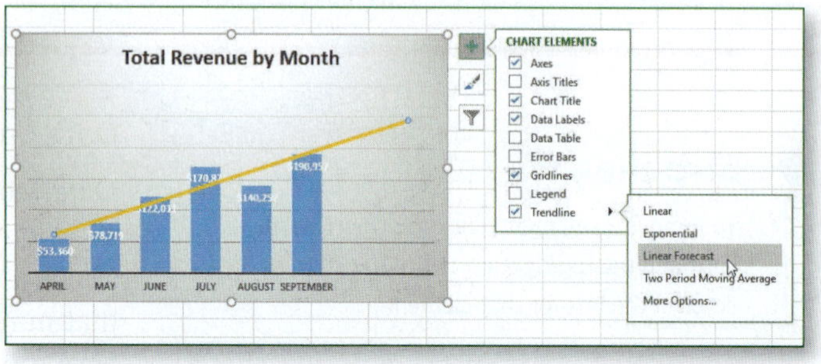

Figure 3-18 Column chart with "Total Revenue" linear trendline

ANOTHER WAY

Right-click a data series marker (its column) and choose **Add Trendline** to open the *Format Trendline* task pane and build a trendline.

HOW TO: Add a Trendline to a Chart

1. Click the chart object or the chart sheet tab.
2. Click the **Chart Elements** button in the top-right corner of the chart.
3. Select the **Trendline** box in the *Chart Elements* pane.
   - The *Add Trendline* dialog box lists the names of the data series.
   - When the chart has only one data series, the trendline is added to the chart.
4. Choose a data series for the trendline and click **OK** (Figure 3-19).
5. Point to the **Trendline** arrow in the *Chart Elements* pane.
   - Choose **Linear** to show a line for existing data.
   - Choose **Linear Forecast** to build a line for current and future data.

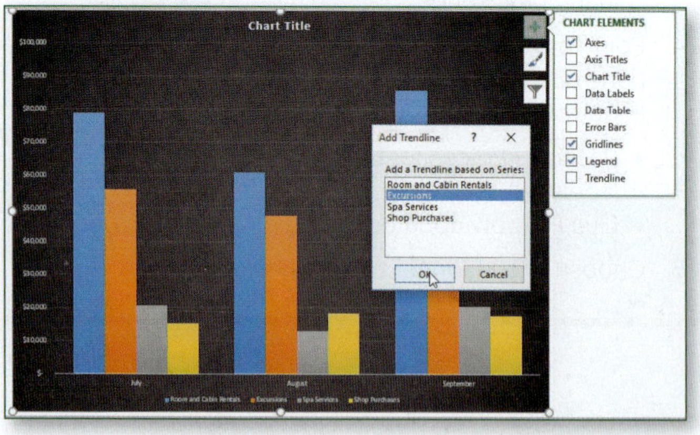

Figure 3-19 ***Add Trendline*** **dialog box for chart with multiple data series**

> **MORE INFO**
>
> Excel uses logarithmic and other statistical concepts as it builds a trendline. Explore these options in the *Trendline Format* task pane if your work often requires trendlines.

Switch Row and Column Data

Excel plots the data series based on the number of rows and columns selected in the worksheet and the chart type. Based on your choices, Excel determines if the labels are along the bottom or the side of the chart. When necessary, you can change which data series is plotted on the x-axis and which is plotted on the y-axis. In a column chart, the x-axis is along the bottom of the chart; the y-axis is along the left.

HOW TO: Switch Row and Column Data

1. Click the chart object or the chart sheet tab.
2. Click the **Switch Row/Column** button [*Chart Tools Design* tab, *Data* group] (Figure 3-20).
   - The data series becomes the categories.
   - Switch between how columns and rows are plotted as desired.

> **ANOTHER WAY**
>
> Click the **Chart Filters** button in the top-right corner of the chart and choose **Select Data** at the bottom of the pane to open the *Select Data Source* dialog box and click the **Switch Row/Column** button.

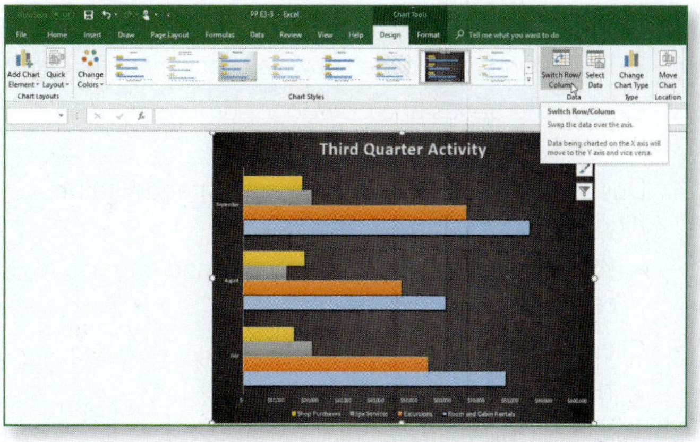

Figure 3-20 Column and row data switched

Change the Chart Type

When a chart does not depict what you intended, or you need a variety of chart types for a project, or you simply prefer a different chart, change the chart type. Changing the chart type assumes that the source data are the same and that they can be graphed in the new chart. You should not, for example, change a column chart with three data series into a pie chart, because a pie chart has only one series. The resulting chart would not represent the data as expected.

The **Change Chart Type** button is on the *Chart Tools Design* tab in the *Type* group. For a selected chart object or sheet, you can also right-click and choose **Change Chart Type** from the context menu. The *Change Chart Type* dialog box includes *Recommended Charts* and *All Charts* tabs like the *Insert Chart* dialog box.

HOW TO: Change the Chart Type

1. Click the chart object or chart sheet.
2. Click the **Change Chart Type** button [*Chart Tools Design* tab, *Type* group].
   - The *Change Chart Type* dialog box opens.
3. Click the **Recommended Charts** tab.
   - Click the **All Charts** tab if the recommended charts are not adequate.

4. Click a thumbnail image to preview the chart in the dialog box.
5. Select a chart type and click **OK**.

Filter Source Data

A chart displays all the categories and all the data series for the selected cells. You can, however, filter or refine which data displays by hiding categories or series. A ***filter*** is a requirement or condition that identifies which data are shown and which data are hidden. Chart filters do not change the underlying cell range for a chart, but they enable you to focus on particular data.

Filter chart data from the *Chart Filters* button in the top-right corner of the chart or in the *Select Data Source* dialog box [*Chart Tools Design* tab, *Data* group].

HOW TO: Filter Source Data

1. Select the chart object or chart sheet tab.
2. Click the **Chart Filters** button in the top-right corner.
   - The *Chart Filters* pane shows a check mark for selected series and categories.
3. Expand the *Series* and *Categories* groups if needed.
4. Deselect the box for each series or category to be hidden.
   - You must select at least one series and one category.
5. Click **Apply** (Figure 3-21).
   - The chart is redrawn.
6. Click the **Chart Filters** button to close the pane.
   - Display the *Chart Filter* pane to show the hidden data when desired.

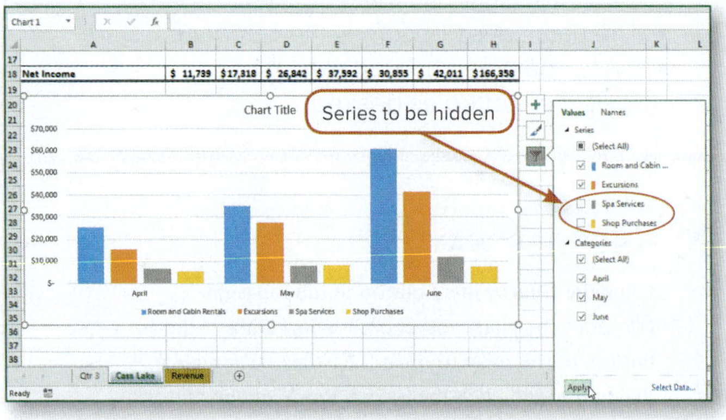

Figure 3-21 ***Chart Filters*** **pane**

Edit Source Data

The cells used to build a chart are its source data. Edit this data to change, add, or remove cells. In a column chart, for example, you can add a data series, or another column. To add or delete a data series in a chart object, select the chart and drag the sizing arrow in the lower-right corner of the highlighted cell range to expand or shrink the data range, as shown in Figure 3-22. Removing cells from the data range deletes that data series from the chart.

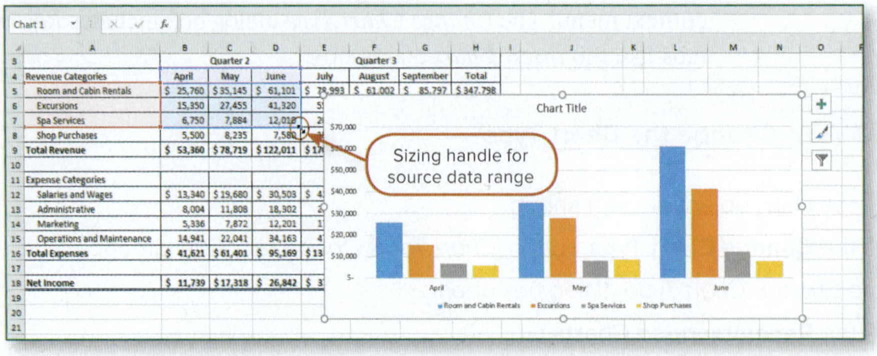

Figure 3-22 The "Shop Purchases" column will be removed from the chart

To edit the source data for a chart sheet, click the **Select Data** button on the *Chart Tools Design* tab [*Data* group] to open the *Select Data Source* dialog box.

▸HOW TO: Add a Data Series in a Chart Sheet

1. Click the chart sheet tab.
2. Click the **Select Data** button [*Chart Tools Design* tab, *Data* group].
   - The *Select Data Source* dialog box opens.
   - The worksheet is active, and the source cells are highlighted.
3. Select the new cell range in the worksheet (Figure 3-23).
   - If the cell ranges are not adjacent, select the first one, type a comma, and select the next range.
   - You can type cell addresses in the *Chart data range* box rather than selecting cells.
4. Click **OK**.
   - The chart sheet is active and redrawn with the edited source data range.

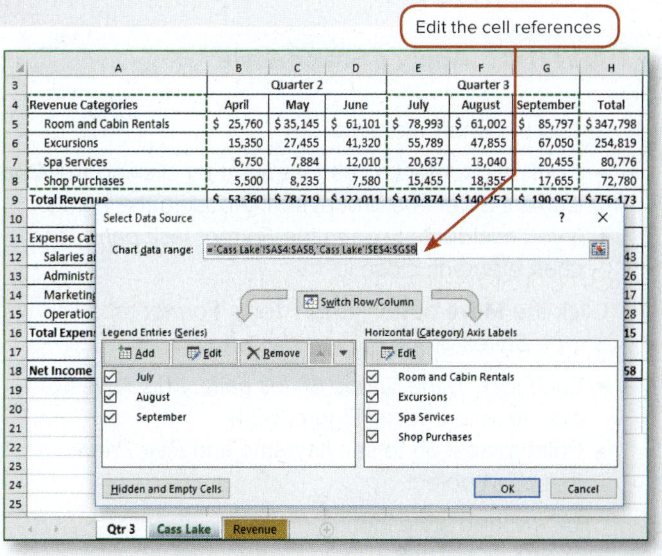

Figure 3-23 *Select Data Source* dialog box for a chart sheet

ANOTHER WAY

Open the *Select Data Source* dialog box by clicking **Select Data** at the bottom of the *Chart Filters* pane. Define filters from this dialog box by selecting or deselecting a series or category name box.

SLO 3.4

Formatting Chart Elements

Quick Layout and *Chart Styles* apply formatting, but you can change most attributes to personalize your work. Applying your own format choices enables you to distinguish your charts from those of other Excel users. You can also use company, association, or school colors and images to further differentiate your charts.

Chart elements may consist of a group of related elements. A data series, for example, is the group of values for a particular item. Each data series includes data points. You can format the entire data series or an individual data point.

When you select a chart element, certain options on the *Chart Tools Design* tab apply to only that element. When the chart area (background) is selected, for example, you can change only its fill or border color.

Apply a Shape Style

A ***shape style*** is a predesigned set of borders, fill colors, and effects for a chart element. ***Shape fill*** is the background color, and ***shape outline*** is the border around the element. ***Shape effects*** include shadows, glows, bevels, or soft edges. All of these commands are available in the *Shape Styles* group on the *Chart Tools Format* tab.

> **MORE INFO**
>
> Click the **Undo** button to remove a format choice in a chart.

Shape styles are shown in a gallery and are grouped as *Theme Styles* or *Presets*. Point to an icon to see a *ScreenTip* with a descriptive name and click an icon to apply it to the selected element. *Live Preview* is available for a chart object but not for a chart sheet.

HOW TO: Apply a Shape Style

1. Select the chart element.
    - Confirm or select a chart element by clicking the **Chart Elements** drop-down arrow [*Chart Tools Format* tab, *Current Selection* group] and choosing the name.
    - If you accidentally open the *Format* task pane for a chart element, close it.
2. Click the **More** button [*Chart Tools Format* tab, *Shape Styles* group].
    - Each icon in the *Shape Styles* gallery displays fill, outline, and effects (Figure 3-24).
    - Point to an icon to see its name and *Live Preview* in a chart object.
3. Click a shape style icon.
    - The chart element is reformatted.

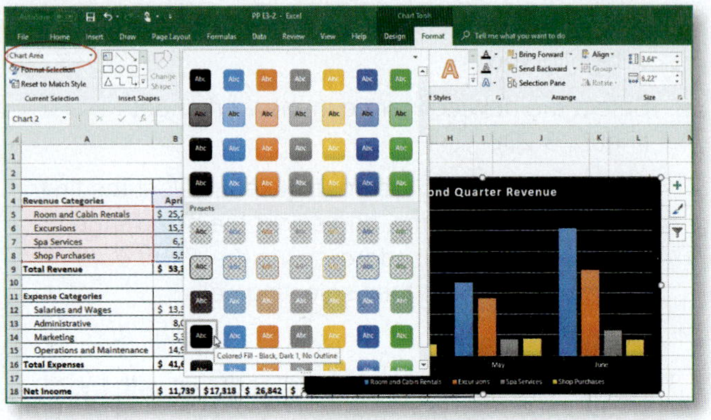

Figure 3-24 ***Shape Style*** **gallery for the chart area**

Apply Shape Fill, Outline, and Effects

Fill color, outline width and color, and special effects are available separately, and your choices override shape style settings already applied.

For fill color, you choose from the gallery, standard colors, or a custom color. After you choose a color, you can format it to use a gradient, a variegated blend of the color.

HOW TO: Apply Gradient Fill to a Chart Element

1. Select the chart element.
    - Confirm or select a chart element from the **Chart Elements** list [*Chart Tools Format* tab, *Current Selection* group].
2. Click the **Shape Fill** button [*Chart Tools Format* tab, *Shape Styles* group].
    - The gallery and menu options display.
3. Point to a color tile to see its name in a *ScreenTip*.
    - *Live Preview* applies the color to an element in a chart object.
4. Select a color tile to apply the color.
5. Click the **Shape Fill** [*Chart Tools Format* tab, *Shape Styles* group].
6. Choose **Gradient** to open the gallery (Figure 3-25).
7. Point to a tile to see its description.
8. Click the preferred gradient.

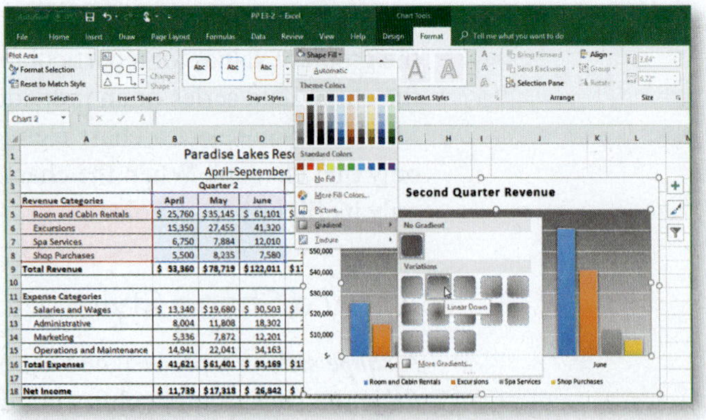

Figure 3-25 ***Shape Fill*** **and** ***Gradient*** **galleries**

ANOTHER WAY

Apply most formats from the *Home* tab for a selected chart element.

The outline for a shape is a border that surrounds or encircles the element. Not all chart elements are suited to an outline, but elements such as the chart or plot area often benefit from the use of an outline. When you add an outline to a chart element, you can select a weight or thickness for the line, as well as a color. The thickness of an outline is measured in points, like fonts. Excel provides a gallery of weights to help you visualize the width. After you apply an outline, it is easier to see the effect if you deselect the chart object.

HOW TO: Apply an Outline to a Chart Element

1. Select the chart element.
2. Click the **Shape Outline** button [*Chart Tools Format* tab, *Shape Styles* group].
   - The gallery and menu options display.
3. Choose a color.
4. Click the **Shape Outline** button [*Chart Tools Format* tab, *Shape Styles* group].
5. Click **Weight** to open its gallery.
6. Choose a width for the outline (Figure 3-26).
7. Click a worksheet cell or another chart element to see the outline.

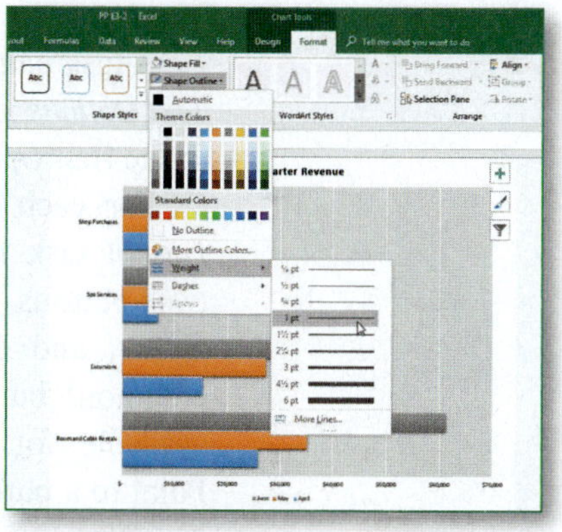

Figure 3-26 ***Outline color* and *Weight* galleries**

MORE INFO

To remove shape fill or outline, select the object, click the command button, and choose **No Fill** or **No Outline**.

Special effects commonly used are bevels and shadows, because they create a realistic, three-dimensional look. These effects are best used on larger elements, such as the chart area, because they can overwhelm smaller elements.

To remove an effect, select the element and click the **Shape Effects** button. Choose the effect group to select the first option such as *No Shadow* or *No Bevel*.

HOW TO: Apply an Effect to a Chart Element

1. Select the chart element.
2. Click the **Shape Effects** button [*Chart Tools Format* tab, *Shape Styles* group].
   - The gallery lists effect groups and then variations for each group.
3. Select a group for the effect (Figure 3-27).
   - If a group name is grayed out, it is not available for the selected element.
4. Point to an icon to see its name.
5. Click to choose an effect.
6. Click a worksheet cell or another chart element to see the effect.

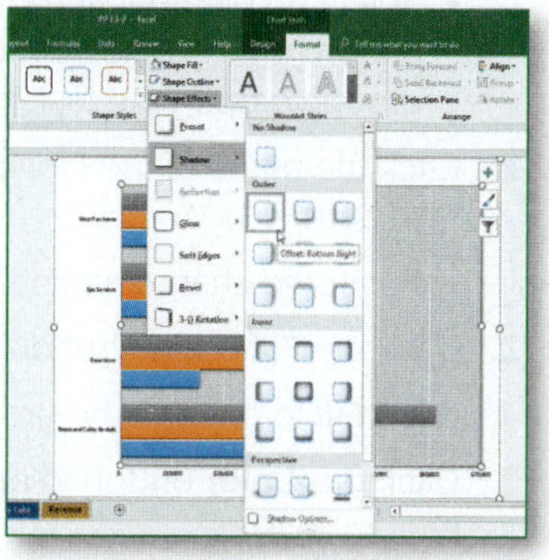

Figure 3-27 ***Shape Effects* gallery for the plot area**

The Format Task Pane

Every chart element has a *Format* task pane that consolidates shape, fill, and color options and provides custom commands for the element. To open the *Format* pane for a chart element, double-click the element or right-click it and choose *Format [Element Name]* from the menu. The *Format* pane opens to the right of the workbook window and automatically updates to reflect the selected element.

> **ANOTHER WAY**
>
> Open a *Format* task pane for a selected object by clicking the **Format Selection** button [*Chart Tools Format* tab, *Selection* group].

A task pane lists command options at the top of the pane. In Figure 3-28, *Title Options* and *Text Options* are available because the selected element is a chart title. The small triangle next to the first *Options* name enables you to choose a different chart element.

For each options group, the *Format* task panes have at least two buttons. The *Fill & Line*, *Effects*, and *Options* buttons are common, but other buttons are available for selected elements. Point to a button to see its *ScreenTip*. When you click a button, the pane displays relevant commands.

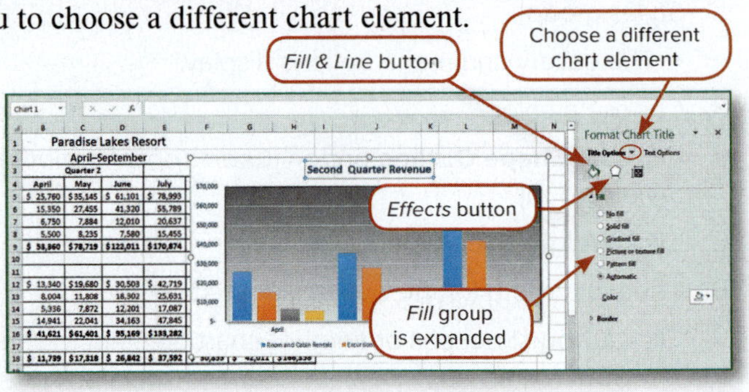

Figure 3-28 ***Format Chart Title* pane**

> **MORE INFO**
>
> Expand or collapse a command group in the *Format* task pane by clicking the command name.

HOW TO: Use the Format Task Pane to Change Shape Fill

1. Double-click the chart element.
   - The *Format* task pane for the element opens on the right.
   - Select another element in the chart to see its task pane.
   - Select an element and click the **Format Selection** button [*Chart Tools Format* tab, *Current Selection* group] to open the task pane.
2. Click the name of the *Options* group at the top of the task pane.
   - For some chart elements, only one group displays.
3. Click the **Fill & Line** button in the *Format* task pane.
4. Click **Fill** to expand the group.
5. Click the **Color** button to open the gallery (Figure 3-29).
6. Choose the desired color.

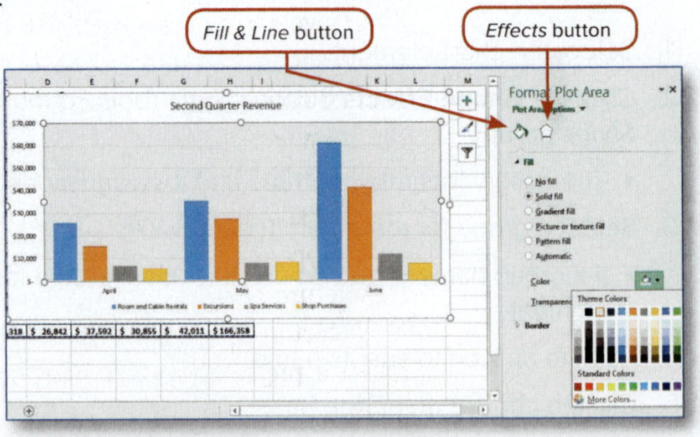

Figure 3-29 ***Fill & Line* command in the *Format Plot Area* task pane**

While the *Fill & Line* and *Effects* buttons offer similar commands for all elements, the *Options* button in a *Format* task pane is specific to the element. For a data series in a column chart, for example, these commands determine whether numbers are shown to the right or left of the chart (secondary or primary axis), or whether the columns overlap. A pie chart, on the other hand, has options that enable you to rotate the pie or explode slices.

▸HOW TO: Use the Format Task Pane to Format Data Labels

1. Double-click a data label element in the chart.
   - Right-click an element and choose **Format Data Labels**.
   - All data labels for one series are selected.
2. Choose **Label Options** at the top of the task pane.
   - Point to a button to see a *ScreenTip*.
   - *Text Options* are also available.
3. Click **Label Options** or **Number** to expand the command group.
4. Select format options for the labels (Figure 3-30).
   - Formats are applied as you select them.
5. Close the task pane.

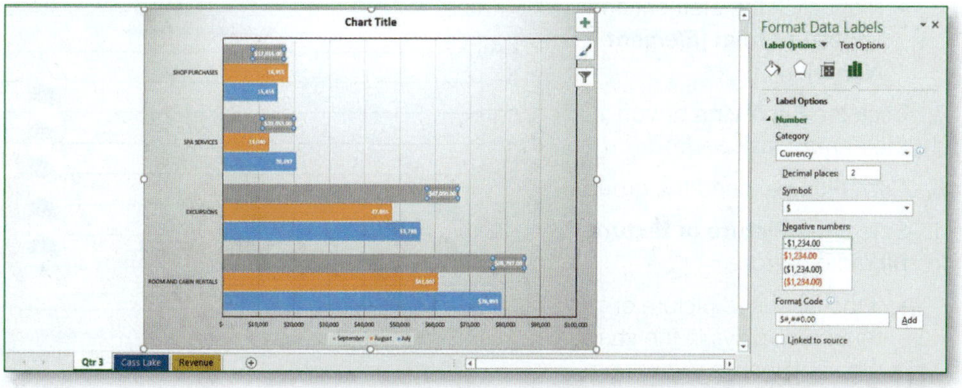

Figure 3-30 *Format Data Labels* pane with *Number* group expanded

SLO 3.5

Using Pictures, Shapes, and WordArt in a Chart

Enhance a chart with pictures, shapes, or *WordArt*. Insert pictures as separate design objects on the chart, or use them as fill for a chart element. You can draw a shape such as an arrow or a lightning bolt to highlight a particular data point on a chart. *WordArt* is often applied to a chart title for a distinctive look.

Use a Picture as Shape Fill

An image can be used to fill the chart area, the plot area, or a marker, especially bars, columns, or pie slices. You have probably seen bar charts with stick figures to illustrate population numbers or column charts with tiny automobile images to show auto sales. You can use an image file from your computer, from external media, or from an online source. Always verify that you have permission to use an image in your work.

The size and design of the picture is important, and you should guard against making the chart appear busy. You may be able to edit attributes of a picture in Excel, but this depends on the picture format.

Insert a picture using the ***Fill*** command on the *Format* task pane for the element. After you insert a picture, the task pane displays ***Stretch*** and ***Stack*** options. *Stretch* enlarges and elongates a single copy of a picture to fill the element. The *Stack* choice sizes and repeats the image to fill the area. Use the ***Stack and Scale*** setting for precise matching of the number of images used per unit of value.

> **MORE INFO**
>
> When you select the *Picture or texture fill* command for a chart element, it displays the most recently used image, if any, in the element.

▶HOW TO: Use a Picture as Fill

1. Double-click the chart element for the fill.
   - The *Format* task pane opens.
   - Right-click the element and choose **Format [*Element Name*]**.
2. Click the **Fill & Line** button in the *Format* task pane.
3. Click **Fill** to expand the group.
4. Select the **Picture or texture fill** radio button.
   - If the last-used picture or texture displays in the chart element, ignore it. It will be replaced.

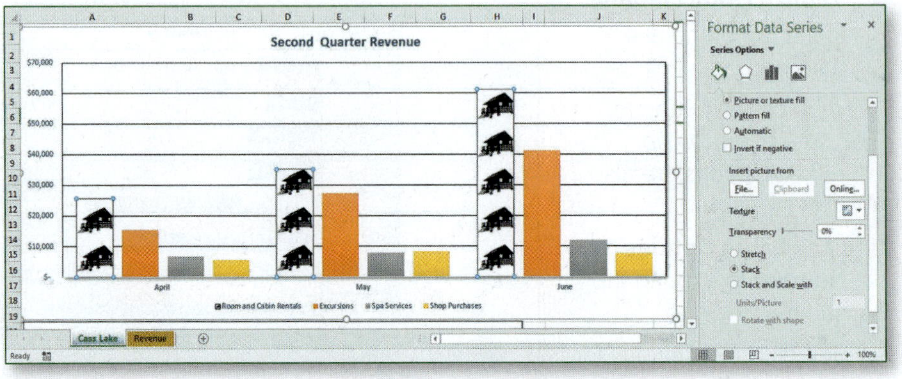

Figure 3-31 Image used as fill for data series

5. Click **Online** to search for an image or click **File** to choose a stored image.
6. Find and insert the image.
   - The picture fills the chart element.
7. Click the **Stack** button in the task pane (Figure 3-31).
   - Copies of the picture fill the element.

> **MORE INFO**
>
> Insert an image as a separate design element on a chart from the *Insert* tab and edit it from the *Picture Format* tab.

Insert Shapes

The *Shapes* gallery is located in the *Insert Shapes* group on the *Chart Tools Format* tab. These predefined shapes include arrows, lines, circles, and other basic figures. Shapes can be used to highlight or emphasize a point in the chart. They can be drawn anywhere on the chart, but are usually placed on the background or the plot area so they do not obscure any data. A shape, once drawn, is an object. When it is selected, the *Picture Tools Format* tab is available with commands for altering the appearance of the shape, as well as the *Format Shape* task pane.

▶HOW TO: Insert a Shape in a Chart

1. Select the chart object or the chart sheet tab.
2. Click the **More** button [*Chart Tools Format* tab, *Insert Shapes* group].
3. Select a shape.

4. Click and drag to draw the shape on the chart.
   - The shape is selected.
5. Type text for the shape (Figure 3-32).
   - Text is optional.
   - Not all shapes can display text.
6. Click the **Drawing Tools Format** tab to format the shape.
   - Apply formatting from the *Format Shape* task pane.
7. Click a worksheet cell or another chart element to deselect the shape.

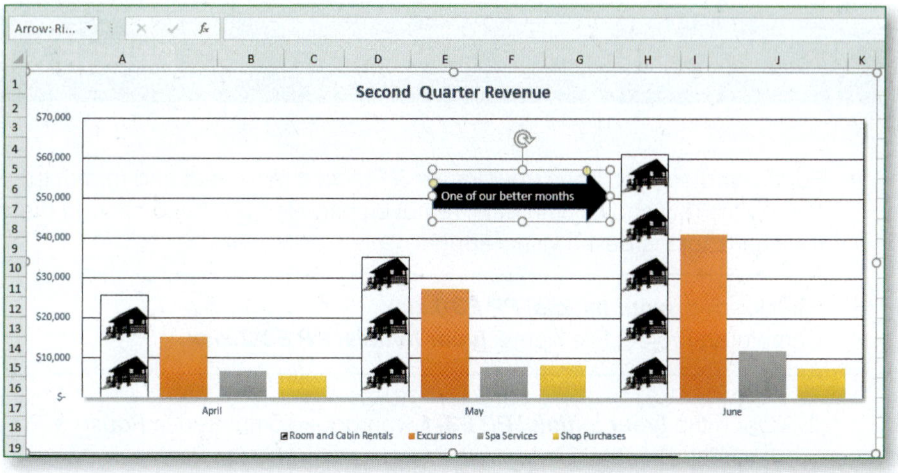

Figure 3-32 Shape inserted in chart

ANOTHER WAY

Insert a shape from the *Shapes* button on the *Insert* tab [*Illustrations* group].

Use WordArt in a Chart

WordArt is a text box with preset font style, fill, and effects. *WordArt* is best used for main titles, because smaller elements may be unreadable. You apply a *WordArt* style from the *Chart Tools Format* tab, *WordArt Styles* group. Format a *WordArt* style by individually changing its fill, outline, and effects.

MORE INFO

Insert a *WordArt* text box from the *Insert* tab [*Text* group] and position it on the chart.

HOW TO: Use WordArt in a Chart

1. Select the chart title object.
   - You can also apply *WordArt* to an axis title, a data label, or the legend.
2. Click the **More** button to open the *WordArt Styles* gallery [*Chart Tools Format* tab, *WordArt Styles* group].
3. Point to a style icon to see a *ScreenTip* with a description.
   - The styles use colors and effects from the workbook theme.
   - *Live Preview* works in a chart object but not on a chart sheet.
4. Click the preferred style (Figure 3-33).

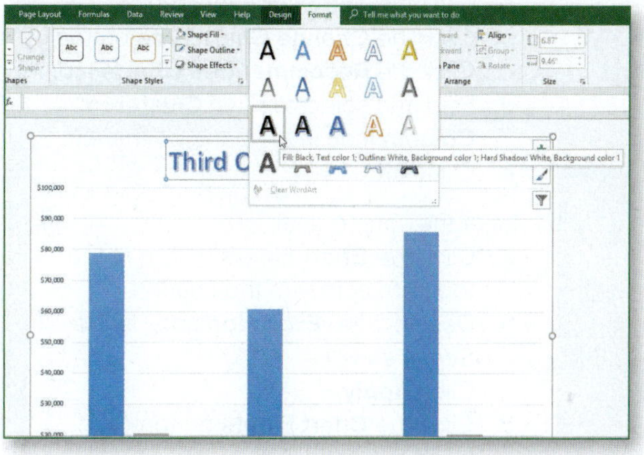

Figure 3-33 *WordArt Style* gallery for selected chart title

PAUSE & PRACTICE: EXCEL 3-2

For this project, you open your Pause & Practice file to edit and format the Paradise Lakes Resort charts. You switch row and column data, remove chart elements, and change the chart type. Finally, you format the charts for increased visual appeal.

File Needed: ***[your initials] PP E3-1.xlsx***
Completed Project File Name: ***[your initials] PP E3-2.xlsx***

1. Open the ***[your initials] PP E3-1*** workbook completed in *Pause & Practice 3-1* and save it as [your initials] PP E3-2.
2. Switch the row and column data in the chart object.
   a. Click the **Cass Lake** worksheet tab.
   b. Point to the border or edge of the chart object and click to select it.
   c. Click the **Switch/Row Column** button [*Chart Tools Design* tab, *Data* group].
3. Edit, add, and remove chart elements.
   a. Click to select the chart title box.
   b. Point to the placeholder text and triple-click to select all of it.
   c. Type Second Quarter Activity.
   d. Click the chart border to deselect the title.
   e. Click the **Chart Elements** button in the top-right corner of the chart.
   f. Select the **Axis Titles** box.
   g. Select the horizontal *Axis Title* placeholder below the columns and press **Delete**.
   h. Select the vertical *Axis Title* placeholder.
   i. Click the *Formula* bar, type Monthly Revenue, and press **Enter** (Figure 3-34).
   j. Click a worksheet cell to deselect the chart object.

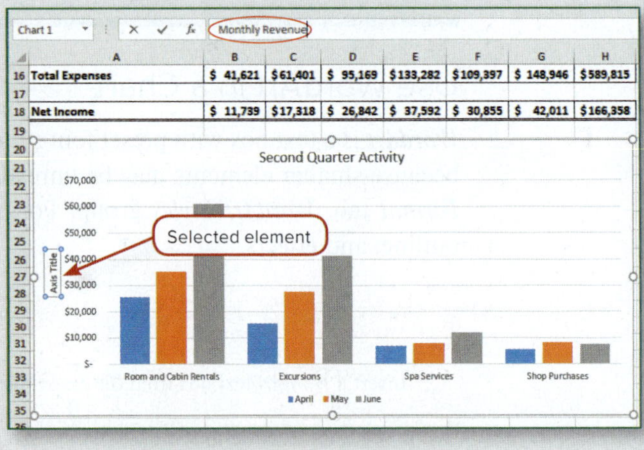

Figure 3-34 Edit placeholder text in the *Formula* bar

4. Change the chart type.
   a. Click the **Third Qtr** sheet tab.
   b. Click the **Change Chart Type** button [*Chart Tools Design* tab, *Type* group].
   c. Click the **Recommended Charts** tab.
   d. Find and select the first **Clustered Column** icon in the pane on the left.
   e. Click **OK**.
5. Filter the source data.
   a. Click the **Chart Filters** button at the top-right corner of the chart.
   b. Deselect the **Excursions** box in the *Series* area.
   c. Click **Apply**.
   d. Click the **Chart Filters** button to close the pane (Figure 3-35).

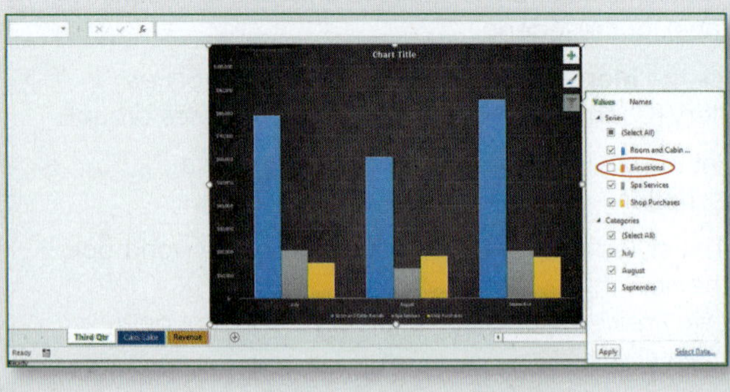

Figure 3-35 Filtered data in chart

6. Apply shape styles and outlines to chart elements.
   a. Click the **Cass Lake** tab and select the chart object.
   b. Click the **Chart Tools Format** tab and then click the **Chart Elements** drop-down arrow [*Current Selection* group].
   c. Choose **Plot Area** to select the plot area of the chart.
   d. Click the **More** button [*Chart Tools Format* tab, *Shape Styles* group].
   e. Click **Subtle Effect – Gold, Accent 4** in the fourth row in the *Theme Styles* group.
   f. Click the drop-down arrow for the **Shape Outline** button [*Chart Tools Format* tab, *Shape Styles* group].
   g. Choose **Black**, **Text 1** in the top row of the *Theme Colors*.
   h. Click the **Chart Elements** drop-down arrow [*Chart Tools Format* tab, *Current Selection* group].
   i. Choose **Vertical (Value) Axis Major Gridlines** to select the major gridlines in the plot area.
   j. Click the icon with the **Shape Outline** button [*Chart Tools Format* tab, *Shape Styles* group] to apply the last-used color (**Black, Text 1**).
   k. Click the **Chart Elements** drop-down arrow [*Chart Tools Format* tab, *Current Selection* group] and choose **Chart Area**.
   l. Apply **Black, Text 1** for the outline (Figure 3-36).
   m. Click a worksheet cell to deselect the chart object.

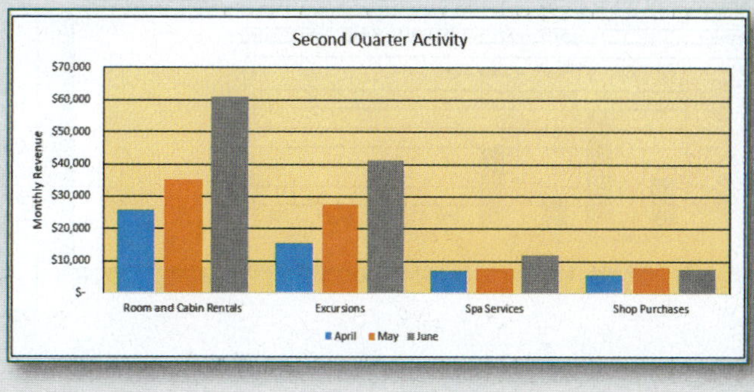

Figure 3-36 Plot area formatted

7. Use a picture as fill.
   a. Click the **Third Qtr** tab.
   b. Double-click one of the "Room and Cabin Rentals" columns to open the *Format Data Series* task pane.
   c. Click the **Fill & Line** button.
   d. Click **Fill** to expand the command group.
   e. Select the **Picture or texture fill** button.
   f. Click **Online**, type log cabin in the search box, and press **Enter**.
   g. Choose an image and insert it (Figure 3-37). If you choose an image that cannot be used as fill, a message appears in the columns; just select a different picture.
   h. Select the **Stack** radio button in the *Format Data Series* task pane.
   i. Click **Fill** to collapse the command group and click **Border** to expand its group.
   j. Select the **Solid line** radio button.
   k. Click the **Color** button and choose **Black, Text 1**.
   l. Close the task pane.

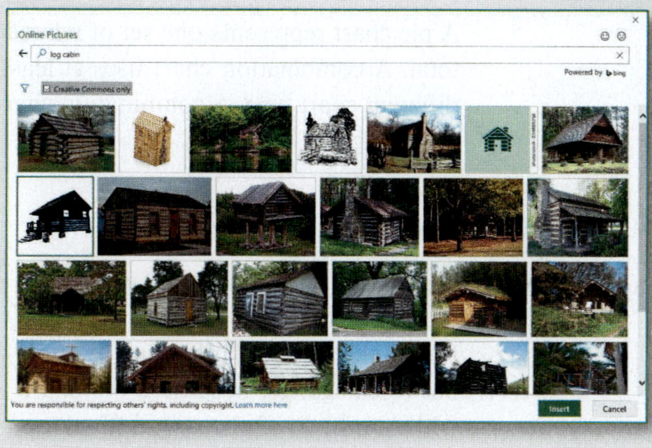

Figure 3-37 Online search for a picture as fill

8. Use *WordArt* in a chart.
   a. Triple-click the **Chart Title** placeholder text to select the text.
   b. Type Third Quarter Activity.
   c. Triple-click the new label and change the font size to **32 pt**.
   d. Click the border area of the chart title to display the selection handles for the text box.
   e. Click the **More** button [*Chart Tools Format* tab, *WordArt Styles* group].
   f. Choose **Fill: Light Gray, Background color 2; Inner Shadow** (third row).

9. Format the legend.
    a. Click to select the legend.
    b. Click the **Home** tab and change the font size to **12 pt**.
    c. Click the chart border to deselect the legend.
10. Save and close the workbook (Figure 3-38).

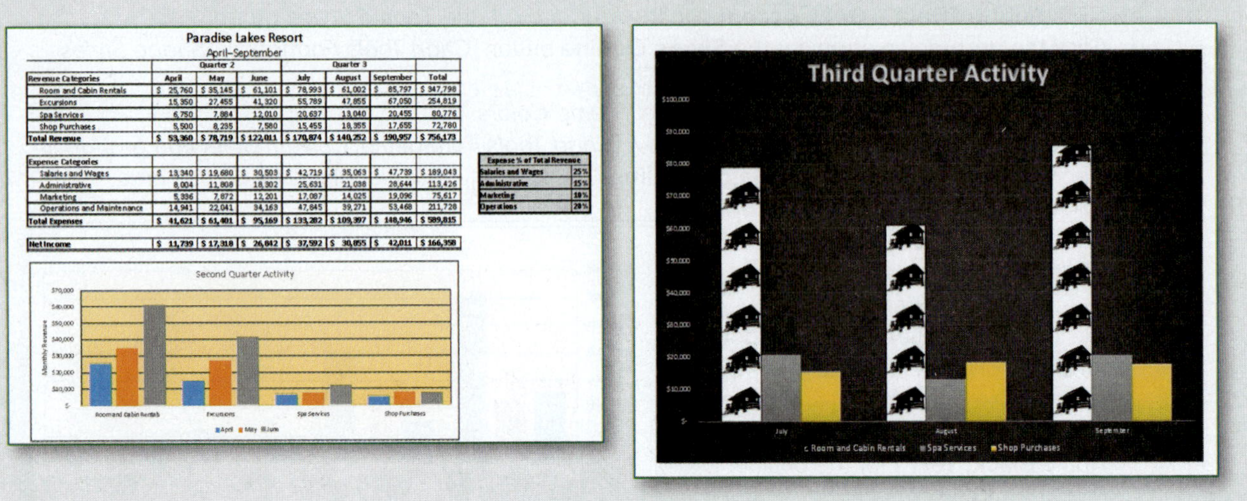

Figure 3-38 PP E3-2 completed worksheet and chart sheet

SLO 3.6

Building Pie and Combination Charts

A pie chart represents one set of related values and shows the proportion of each value to the total. A combination chart uses at least two sets of values and plots each data series with a different chart type. A combination chart can also have two value axes, one on the left and one on the right.

Create a 3-D Pie Chart

A pie chart graphs one data series and illustrates how each number relates to the whole. Be cautious about the number of categories, because a pie chart with hundreds of slices is difficult to interpret and does not depict the relationship among the values.

From the *Insert Pie or Doughnut Chart* button on the *Insert* tab, you can select from a gallery of 2-D or 3-D pie types, as well as a doughnut shape (Figure 3-39). You can also select options for a pie chart with a bar or another pie chart. As you point to each subtype, *Live Preview* previews the chart.

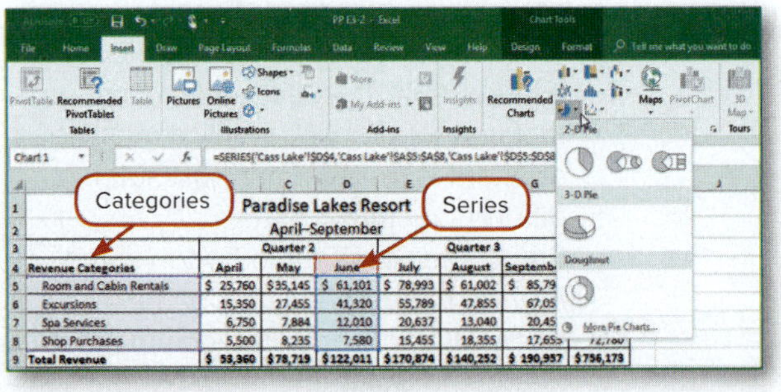

Figure 3-39 Selected data series and categories for a pie chart

▸HOW TO: Create a 3-D Pie Chart Sheet

1. Select the cells that include the values and the category labels.
    - The labels and values need not be adjacent.

2. Click the **Insert Pie or Doughnut Chart** button [*Insert* tab, *Charts* group].
3. Choose **3-D Pie**.
   - A pie chart object displays in the worksheet.
4. Click the **Move Chart** button [*Chart Tools Design* tab, *Location* group].
5. Click the **New sheet** button.
6. Type a name for the chart sheet.
7. Click **OK**.

Pie Chart Elements and Options

In a pie chart, the data series is represented by the whole pie. A data point is a slice of the pie. You can format the data series as a whole or as individual slices.

A pie chart can display a legend and a title. It does not, however, have axes and does not use axes titles. Use data labels in place of a legend, because they show the same information.

Custom commands for a pie chart are the angle of the first slice and the percent of explosion. These commands are available on the *Format* task pane for the data series (the whole pie) or for a selected data point (one slice). The angle of the first slice enables you to rotate the pie. The first slice starts at the top of the chart at 0° (zero degrees). As you increase that value, the slice arcs to the right. *Live Preview* displays the results, too.

Exploding a pie slice emphasizes that slice, because it moves the slice away from the rest of the pie. This uses more white space in the chart, and the pie gets smaller. You set explosion as a percentage.

HOW TO: Rotate a Pie Chart and Explode a Slice

1. Double-click the pie shape.
   - The *Format Data Series* task pane opens.
   - Right-click the pie shape and choose **Format Data Series**.
2. Click the **Series Options** button.
3. Drag the vertical slider to set the *Angle of first slice*.
   - The percentage is shown in the entry box.
   - Type a percentage or use the spinner arrows to set a value.
4. Click the data point (slice) to explode.
   - The *Format Data Point* task pane opens.
5. Drag the vertical slider to set the *Pie Explosion* (Figure 3-40).
   - The percentage is shown in the entry box.
   - The larger the percentage, the farther the slice is from the rest of the pie.
   - Type a percentage or use the spinner arrows to set a value.

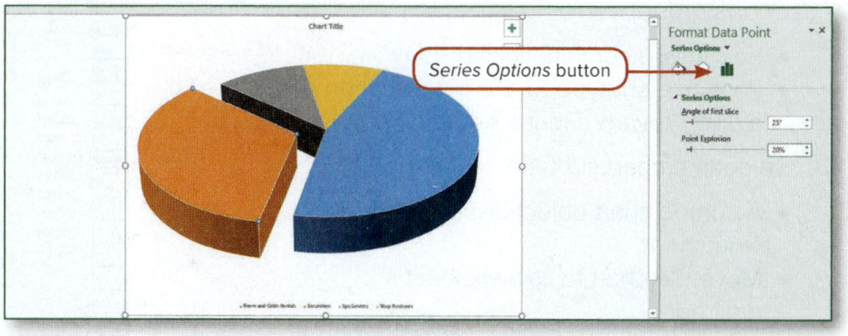

Figure 3-40 Exploded pie slice with angle of first slice changed

> **MORE INFO**
>
> Explode all the slices in a pie chart by selecting the data series, not a data point.

Create a Combination Chart

A combination chart includes at least two chart types such as a line chart and a column chart. Paradise Lakes Resort can use a combination chart to compare revenue from cabin and room rentals to total revenue. These two values require a wide range of numbers, so showing one series as a line and the other as a column focuses the comparison (Figure 3-41).

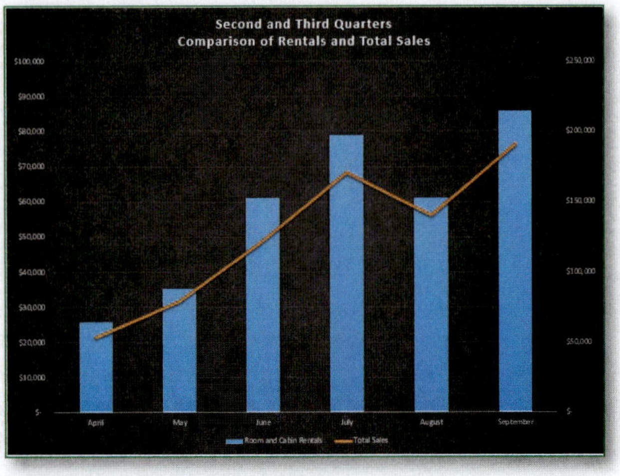

Figure 3-41 Line-Column combination chart

> **MORE INFO**
>
> A line and column combination chart resembles a column chart with a trendline, but the combination chart uses actual values. The trendline predicts values.

> **MORE INFO**
>
> Not all chart types can be combined. If you try to build an unacceptable combination, Excel opens a message box to inform you.

The most common combination of chart types is line and column, but you can also use a line and area combination. Excel offers an option to create a custom combination, but it is best to use this only after you have experience charting your data.

Create a combination chart from the *Insert Combo Chart* button in the *Charts* group on the *Insert* tab, as well as from the *All Charts* tab in the *Insert Chart* dialog box.

HOW TO: Create a Combination Chart

1. Select the cell ranges for the chart.
   - The cell ranges need not be contiguous.
2. Click the **Insert Combo Chart** button [*Insert* tab, *Charts* group].
   - Suggested combinations display.
   - Point to a subtype to see a description and a *Live Preview* (Figure 3-42).
3. Select the chart subtype.
   - A combo chart object displays in the worksheet.
   - Move the chart to its own sheet if desired.

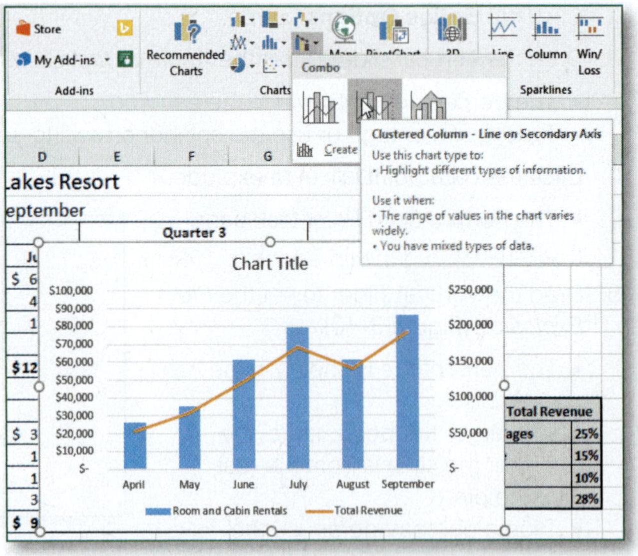

Figure 3-42 *Insert Combo Chart* button options

Combination Chart Elements and Options

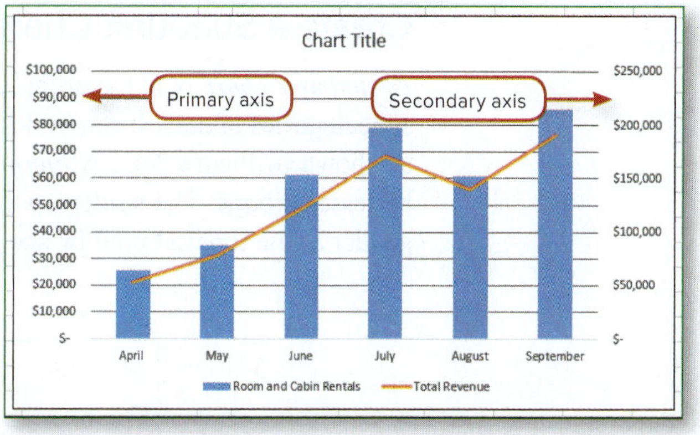

Figure 3-43 Secondary axis for a combo chart

A combination chart has at least two data series, each graphed in its own chart type. Keep this type of chart relatively simple, because its purpose is to compare unlike items and too many data series complicate what viewers see.

In a combination chart, you can display values on two vertical axes. The axis on the left is the primary axis; the one on the right is secondary (Figure 3-43). This option is best when the values are very different or use a different scale.

For the secondary axis, Excel builds the number scale based on the data. Select the data series to be plotted on the secondary axis and choose the option from the *Series Options* command group in the *Format* task pane. You can also define a secondary axis in the *Insert Chart* or the *Change Chart Type* dialog boxes.

A combination chart has the same elements and commands as a regular column or line chart. Apply chart styles and layouts, as well as shape fill, outline, effects, pictures, shapes, and *WordArt*.

▸HOW TO: Display a Secondary Axis on a Combination Chart

1. Select the chart object or the chart sheet tab.
2. Select the data series to be shown on the secondary axis.
   - Select the line or any column in a line-column combo chart.
   - You can also choose the data series from the *Chart Elements* box [*Chart Tools Format* tab, *Current Selection* group].
3. Click the **Format Selection** button [*Chart Tools Format* tab, *Current Selection* group].
4. Click the **Series Options** button in the task pane (Figure 3-44).
5. Click the **Secondary Axis** radio button.
   - Additional options for the axis depend on the chart type.
6. Close the *Format Data Series* task pane.

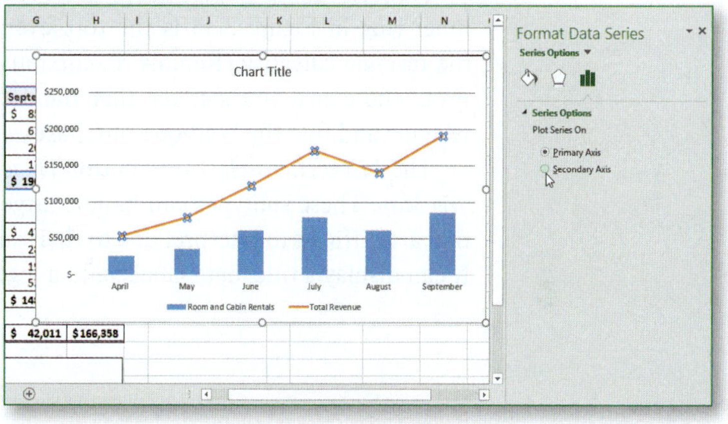

Figure 3-44 *Format Data Series* task pane to define a secondary axis

SLO 3.7

Creating Sunburst and Waterfall Charts

Specialty chart types in Excel visualize data in ways that previously required engineering, mapping, or other expert software. The *Charts* group on the *Insert* tab includes buttons for *Hierarchy*, *Statistic*, and *Map* charts. These charts have characteristics of standard Excel charts, as well as their own requirements or limitations. For example, to create a map chart, you must have high-detail geographical data and access to the *Bing Map* service.

Create a Sunburst Chart

A ***sunburst chart*** is a hierarchy chart that illustrates the relationship among categories and subcategories of data. It resembles a doughnut chart with concentric rings for each layer of data, as shown in Figure 3-45. A ***hierarchy*** is a division of data that identifies a top group followed by lesser groups. The student population at your college can be illustrated in a hierarchy with gender at the top, followed by age group, then home city, followed by area of study, and so on.

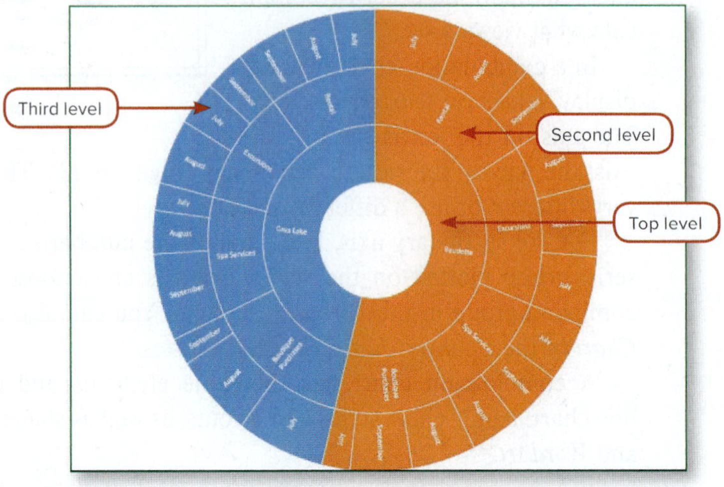

Figure 3-45 Sunburst chart for third quarter revenue for two locations

Paradise Lakes Resort keeps a record of revenue by location, category, and month. The inner ring in Figure 3-45 is the top level of the hierarchy, the location. The second level is the revenue category (Rentals, Excursions, etc.), and the outside ring is the month's revenue. From the chart, you can see that Baudette contributed slightly more than half of the total revenue and that the boutique purchases at Cass Lake were high.

The *Insert Hierarchy Chart* button [*Insert* tab, *Charts* group] has two subtypes, *Sunburst* and *TreeMap*. These subtypes can handle large amounts of data, but be careful not to build charts that are difficult to interpret due to their size. A sunburst chart has one data series and no axes. It can display a title, data labels, and a legend.

> **MORE INFO**
>
> A *TreeMap* chart illustrates hierarchical data using rectangles of various sizes and colors to represent the divisions and subdivisions.

HOW TO: Create a Sunburst Chart

1. Select the source data with labels and values.
2. Click the **Insert Hierarchy Chart** button [*Insert* tab, *Charts* group].
   - A menu lists the subtypes.
   - From the *Quick Analysis* button, select **Charts**, **More**, and then click the **All Charts** tab.

3. Point to **Sunburst** to see a *Live Preview.*
4. Click **Sunburst** to select it.
   - A chart object displays in the worksheet.
5. Click the **Move Chart** button [*Chart Tools Design* tab, *Location* group].
6. Select **New sheet**.
7. Type a name for the chart sheet and click **OK**.
   - The *Chart Tools Design* and *Format* tabs are available.
8. Click the sunburst shape to select the circle.
9. Point to a category name in the inner ring and click to select the data point.
   - The category and its related items are selected (Figure 3-46).

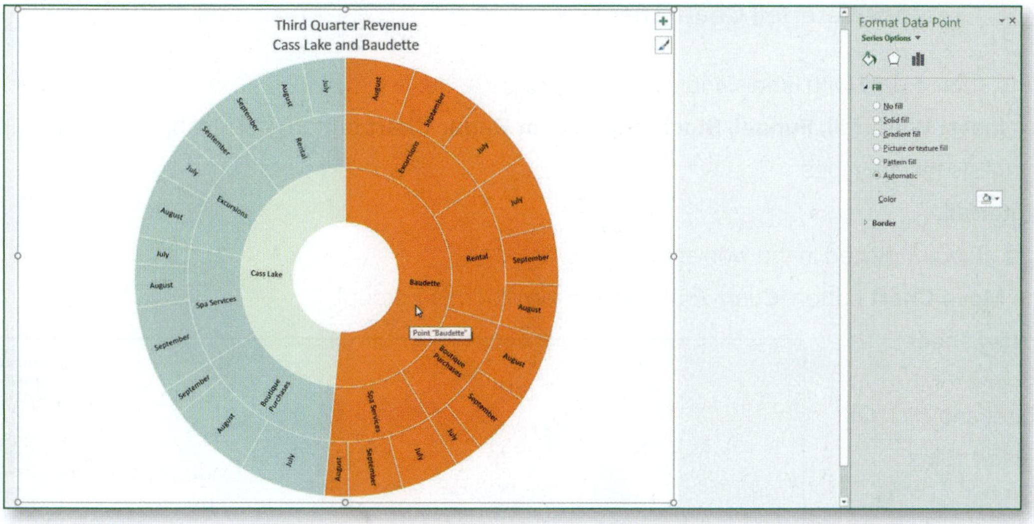

Figure 3-46 Sunburst chart sheet with selected data point

10. Format the data point as desired.
    - If the *Format Data Point* task pane is not open, click the **Format Selection** button [*Chart Tools Format* tab, *Current Selection* group].
11. Click outside the chart background to deselect the chart.

Create a Waterfall Chart

A ***waterfall chart*** is a financial chart that displays a moving total for positive and negative values. A waterfall chart graphs how each expense or outlay affects the account. You might, for example, build a waterfall chart to visualize your monthly income sources (inflows) and expenditures (outlays) to watch how you spend your resources.

In Figure 3-47, it is obvious that payroll consumes most of the cash account for Paradise Lakes Resort. In a waterfall chart, the depth or height of the marker indicates the value. In the figure, the beginning balance and ending total markers rest on the bottom axis. The other amounts are described as floating.

A waterfall chart plots one data series and has a legend that clarifies the increase, decrease, and total colors. A waterfall chart also includes axes, titles, gridlines, and data labels.

The *Insert Waterfall or Stock Chart* button is in the *Chart* group on the *Insert* tab.

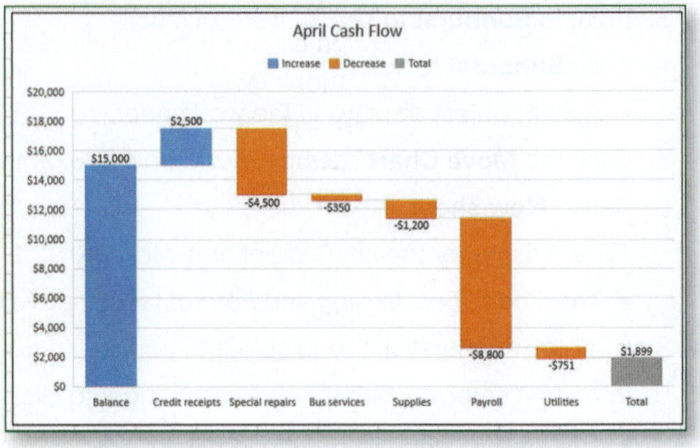

Figure 3-47 Waterfall chart for cash flow

▸HOW TO: Create a Waterfall Chart Sheet

1. Select the source data with labels and values.
2. Click the **Insert Waterfall, Funnel, Stock, Surface, or Radar Chart** button [*Insert* tab, *Charts* group].
   - A menu lists the subtypes.
3. Click **Waterfall**.
   - A chart object is placed in the worksheet.
4. Click the **Move Chart** button [*Chart Tools Design* tab, *Location* group].
5. Select **New sheet**.
6. Type a name for the chart sheet and click **OK**.
   - The *Chart Tools Design* and *Format* tabs are available.
7. Click a column marker to select the data series.
8. Click the ending marker to select only that marker.
9. Click the **Format Selection** button [*Chart Tools Format* tab, *Current Selection* group].
10. Click the **Series Options** button in the task pane.
11. Expand the *Series Options* group.
12. Select the **Set as total** box (Figure 3-48).
    - The marker rests on the bottom axis and is no longer floating.
13. Close the task pane and click outside the chart to deselect it.

Figure 3-48 Set a marker as a total

SLO 3.8

Inserting and Formatting Sparklines

Sparklines are miniature charts in a cell or cell range. Sparklines illustrate trends and patterns without adding a separate chart object or sheet. They do not have the same characteristics as an Excel chart.

Sparklines are created from a selected data range and placed in a location range, usually next to the data (Figure 3-49). They are embedded in the cell, almost like a background. If you enter a label or value in a cell with a sparkline, that data appears on top of the sparkline.

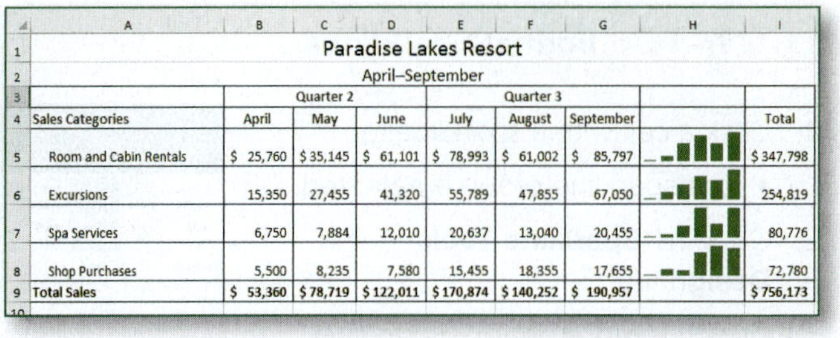

Figure 3-49 Column sparklines in a worksheet

Insert Sparklines

Three sparkline types are available: ***Line***, ***Column***, and ***Win/Loss***. The *Sparklines* commands are located on the *Insert* tab of the worksheet. The *Data Range* is the range of cells to be graphed, and the *Location Range* is the cell or range for the sparklines. The ***Sparkline Tools Design*** tab opens when you select the sparkline group.

▸HOW TO: Insert Column Sparklines in a Worksheet

1. Select the cell range of data to be graphed.
2. Click the **Column Sparkline** button [*Insert* tab, *Sparklines* group].
   - The selected range address is shown in the *Data Range* entry box.
   - Select or edit the data range.
3. Click the *Location Range* box.
4. Select the cell or range for the sparklines (Figure 3-50).
   - The range address displays as an absolute reference.
5. Click **OK**.

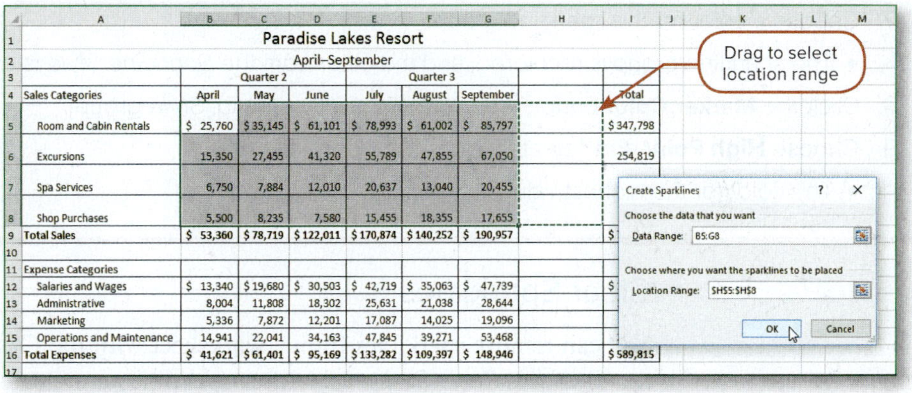

Figure 3-50 *Create Sparklines* dialog box

Sparkline Design Tools

When sparklines are selected, the *Sparkline Tools Design* tab opens. This contextual tab includes several options for changing the appearance of the sparklines. A *Sparkline Style* option changes the color scheme for the sparkline group, but you can also change colors with the *Sparkline Color* command. The *Marker Color* command enables you to choose a different color for identified values. A ***marker*** for a sparkline represents a data point value. You can use different colors to highlight the high, low, first, or last value, as well as negative values.

When you define a location range for sparklines, they are embedded as a group. If you select any cell in the sparkline range, the entire group is selected. Subsequent commands affect all sparklines in the group. From the *Group* section on the *Sparkline Tools Design* tab, you can ungroup the sparklines to format them individually.

From the *Sparkline Tools Design* tab, change the type of sparkline, such as making a column sparkline into a line sparkline. The *Show* group lists marker values that can be highlighted. When you select an option in the *Show* group, that individual marker is formatted with a different color.

▸HOW TO: Format Sparklines

1. Click a cell with a sparkline.
   - The sparkline group is selected.
2. Click the **Sparkline Tools Design** tab.
3. Click the **More** button [*Sparkline Tools Design* tab, *Style* group].
4. Choose a sparkline style.
   - The sparkline group is recolored.
5. Select the **High Point** box in the *Show* group (Figure 3-51).
   - A default color based on the sparkline style is applied to the highest value in the sparkline for each row.
6. Click the **Sparkline Color** button [*Sparkline Tools Design* tab, *Style* group].
7. Choose a color for the sparkline group.
   - The sparkline group is recolored, and the color from the *Sparkline Style* is overridden.
8. Click the **Marker Color** button [*Sparkline Tools Design* tab, *Style* group].
9. Choose **High Point** and select a color.
   - The color for the highest value is reset.

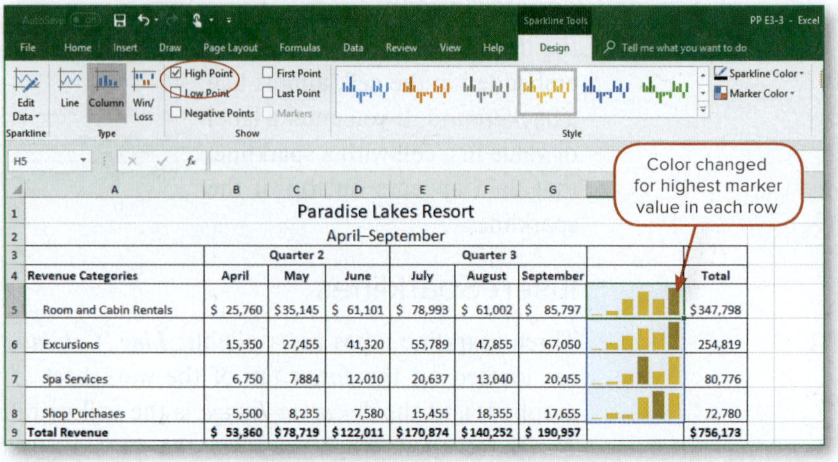

Figure 3-51 *High Point* marker selected for sparklines

Clear Sparklines

You can remove sparklines from a worksheet with the *Clear* command in the *Group* group on the *Sparkline Tools Design* tab. After sparklines are cleared, you may also need to delete the column where they were located or reset row heights and column widths.

▸HOW TO: Clear Sparklines

1. Select any cell in the sparklines range.
2. Click the arrow with the **Clear Selected Sparklines** button [*Sparkline Tools Design* tab, *Group* group].
   - If you click the button and not its arrow, the selected sparkline cell is cleared.
3. Choose **Clear Selected Sparklines Groups**.

MORE INFO

Ungroup sparklines to create individual sparklines in each cell.

PAUSE & PRACTICE: EXCEL 3-3

For this project, you complete Paradise Lakes' revenue report by inserting a pie chart that shows the proportion of each revenue category. You also insert a combination chart sheet to compare rentals with total revenue and a sunburst chart to analyze third quarter revenue. Finally, you insert sparklines in the worksheet.

File Needed: ***[your initials] PP E3-2.xlsx***
Completed Project File Name: ***[your initials] PP E3-3.xlsx***

1. Open the ***[your initials] PP E3-2*** workbook completed in *Pause & Practice 3-2* and save it as [your initials] PP E3-3.

2. Create a pie chart for total sales revenue.
   a. Select the **Cass Lake** tab.
   b. Select cells **A5:A8** as the category.
   c. Press **Ctrl** and select cells **H5:H8** as the data series.
   d. Click the **Insert Pie or Doughnut Chart** button [*Insert* tab, *Charts* group].
   e. Choose **3-D Pie**.
   f. Click the **Move Chart** button [*Chart Tools Design* tab, *Location* group].
   g. Click the **New sheet** button and type Pie Chart as the sheet name.
   h. Click **OK**.

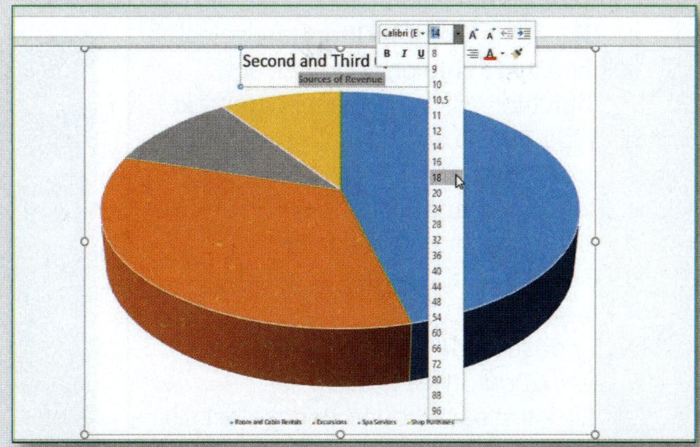

Figure 3-52 Chart titles typed and font size changed

3. Format a pie chart.
   a. Select the **Pie Chart** tab.
   b. Click the **Chart Title** placeholder to select it and then triple-click the **Chart Title** placeholder text.
   c. Type Second and Third Quarters and press **Enter**.
   d. Type Sources of Revenue on the second line.
   e. Drag to select the first line of the title.
   f. Use the mini toolbar to change the font size to **24 pt**.
   g. Drag to select the second line of the title.
   h. Use the mini toolbar to change the font size to **18 pt** (Figure 3-52).
   i. Click the chart border to deselect the title.
   j. Double-click the pie to open the *Format Data Series* task pane.
   k. Click the **Series Options** button in the *Format Data Series* task pane.
   l. Double-click the **Room and Cabin Rentals** slice to change to the *Format Data Point* task pane.
   m. Set the pie explosion percentage at **10%**.
   n. Close the task pane.
   o. Select the legend at the bottom of the chart to display selection handles.
   p. Click the **Home** tab and change the font size to **14 pt** (Figure 3-53).

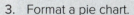

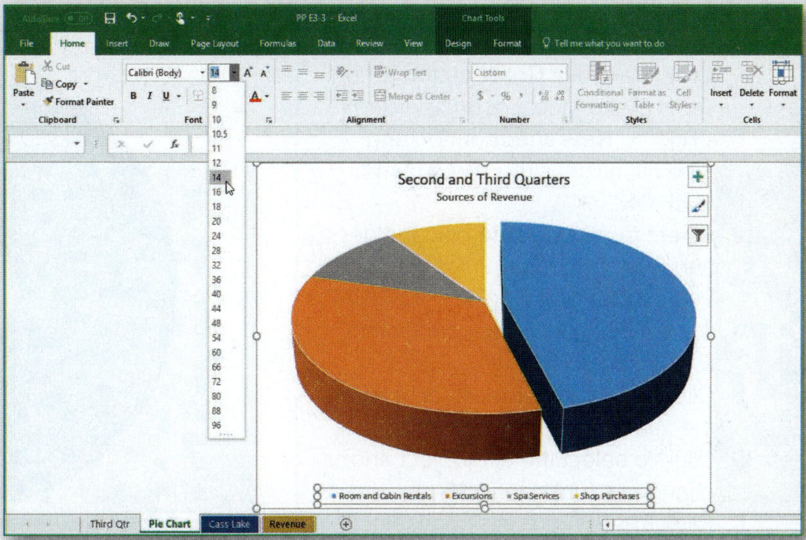

Figure 3-53 Change the font size from the *Home* tab

4. Create a combination chart for total sales revenue and room and cabin rentals.
   a. Select the **Cass Lake** tab.
   b. Select cells **A4:G5** as one data series and category.

c. Press **Ctrl** and select cells **A9:G9** as another data series and category.
d. Click the **Insert Combo Chart** button [*Insert* tab, *Charts* group].
e. Choose **Clustered Column – Line on Secondary Axis**.
f. Click the **Move Chart** button [*Chart Tools Design* tab, *Location* group].
g. Click the **New sheet** button and type Combo Chart as the sheet name.
h. Click **OK**.

5. Format a combination chart.
   a. Select the **Combo Chart** tab, select the **Chart Title** placeholder, and then triple-click the placeholder text.
   b. Type Second and Third Quarters and press **Enter**.
   c. Type Comparison of Rentals and Total Revenue on the second line.
   d. Click the chart border to deselect the chart title.
   e. Choose **Style 6** [*Chart Tools Design* tab, *Chart Styles* group].
   f. Click the background to deselect the chart (Figure 3-54).

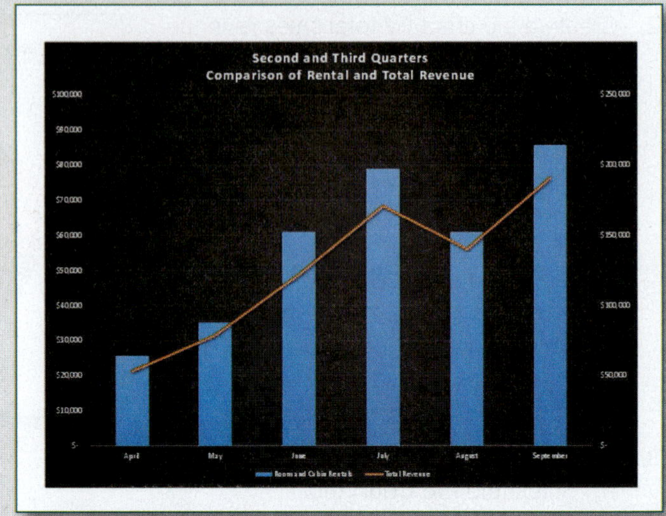

Figure 3-54 Combo chart with Style 6

6. Create a sunburst chart for third quarter revenue analysis.
   a. Select the **Revenue** tab.
   b. Select cells **A5:D28** as the data series and categories. This chart will illustrate revenue for Cass Lake and Baudette.
   c. Click the **Insert Hierarchy Chart** button [*Insert* tab, *Charts* group].
   d. Choose **Sunburst**.
   e. Click the **Move Chart** button [*Chart Tools Design* tab, *Location* group].
   f. Click the **New sheet** button and type Sunburst as the sheet name.
   g. Click **OK**.
   h. Select the **Chart Title** placeholder and type Third Quarter Revenue.
   i. Press **Enter** and type Cass Lake and Baudette on the second line (Figure 3-55).
   j. Click the chart border to deselect the title object.
   k. Click to select the title object and change its font size to **16 pt**.
   l. Click the background to deselect the chart.

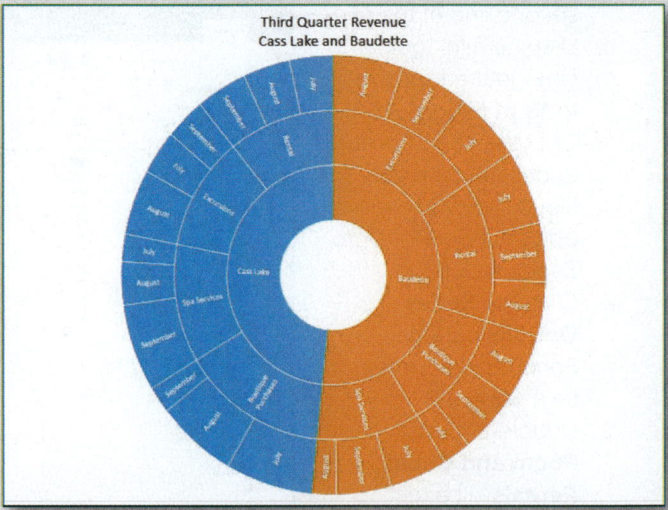

Figure 3-55 Sunburst chart with edited title

7. Insert sparklines in a worksheet.
   a. Select the **Cass Lake** tab.
   b. Right-click the column **H** heading and choose **Insert** to insert a new column.
   c. Select the cell range **B5:G8** as the data to be charted with sparklines.
   d. Click the **Column Sparkline** button [*Insert* tab, *Sparklines* group].
   e. Click the **Location Range** box and select cells **H5:H8**.
   f. Click **OK**.

8. Format sparklines.
   a. Click the **Sparkline Color** button [*Sparkline Tools Design* tab, *Style* group] and select **Green, Accent 6, Darker 25%** (last column).
   b. Select the sparkline group if necessary, click the **Format** button [*Home* tab, *Cells* group], and change the **Row Height** to **30 (40 pixels)**.
   c. Format column **H** to a width of **16.00 (117 pixels)**.
   d. Press **Ctrl+Home**.
9. Save and close the workbook (Figure 3-56).

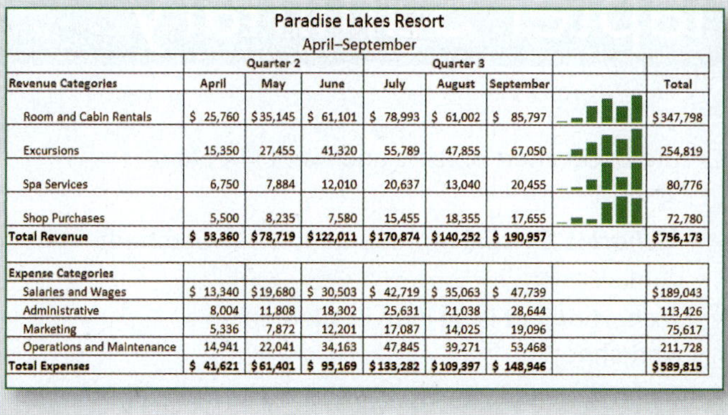

Paradise Lakes Resort
April–September

	Quarter 2			Quarter 3				
Revenue Categories	**April**	**May**	**June**	**July**	**August**	**September**		**Total**
Room and Cabin Rentals	$ 25,760	$35,145	$ 61,101	$ 78,993	$ 61,002	$ 85,797		$347,798
Excursions	15,350	27,455	41,320	55,789	47,855	67,050		254,819
Spa Services	6,750	7,884	12,010	20,637	13,040	20,455		80,776
Shop Purchases	5,500	8,235	7,580	15,455	18,355	17,655		72,780
Total Revenue	**$ 53,360**	**$78,719**	**$122,011**	**$170,874**	**$140,252**	**$ 190,957**		**$756,173**
Expense Categories								
Salaries and Wages	$ 13,340	$19,680	$ 30,503	$ 42,719	$ 35,063	$ 47,739		$189,043
Administrative	8,004	11,808	18,302	25,631	21,038	28,644		113,426
Marketing	5,336	7,872	12,201	17,087	14,025	19,096		75,617
Operations and Maintenance	14,941	22,041	34,163	47,845	39,271	53,468		211,728
Total Expenses	**$ 41,621**	**$61,401**	**$ 95,169**	**$133,282**	**$109,397**	**$ 148,946**		**$589,815**

Figure 3-56 PP E3-3 completed worksheet

Chapter Summary

3.1 Create Excel chart objects and chart sheets (p. E3-163).

- A ***chart*** is a visual representation of worksheet data.
- A ***chart object*** is an item or element in a worksheet.
- A ***chart sheet*** is an Excel chart on its own tab in the workbook.
- The cells with values and labels used to build a chart are its ***source data***.
- Chart objects and sheets are linked to their source data and contain chart elements such as data labels or a chart title.
- Commonly used chart types are *Column*, *Line*, *Pie*, and *Bar*, and Excel can build statistical, financial, geographical, and scientific charts.
- Size and position a chart object in a worksheet, or move it to its own sheet using the *Move Chart* button in the *Location* group on the *Chart Tools Design* tab.
- The *Quick Analysis* tool includes a command group for charts, and it appears when the selected source data are contiguous.

3.2 Use quick layouts and chart styles to design a chart (p. E3-167).

- A ***chart layout*** is a set of elements and their locations in a chart.
- The *Quick Layout* button [*Chart Tools Design* tab, *Chart Layouts* group] includes predefined layouts for the current chart type.
- A ***chart style*** is a predefined combination of colors and effects for chart elements.
- Chart styles are based on the current workbook theme.
- The *Change Colors* command [*Chart Tools Design* tab, *Chart Styles* group] provides color palettes for customizing a chart.
- Print a chart object with its worksheet data or on its own sheet.
- A chart sheet prints on its own page in landscape orientation.

3.3 Edit chart elements including titles, data labels, and source data (p. E3-172).

- Select a ***chart element*** for editing.
- Chart elements include chart and axes titles, data labels, legends, gridlines, and more, depending on the type of chart.
- Excel plots data based on the number of rows and columns selected and the chart type, but row and column data can be switched.
- Use the *Change Chart Type* button on the *Chart Tools Design* tab to change selected chart types into another type.
- Filter chart data to hide and display values or categories without changing the source data.
- Edit source data for a chart to use a different cell range or to add or remove a data series.

3.4 Format chart elements with shape styles, fill, outlines, and special effects (p. E3-179).

- A ***shape style*** is a predesigned set of fill colors, borders, and effects.
- Apply ***shape***, ***fill***, ***outline***, and ***effects*** to a chart element from the *Chart Tools Format* tab.
- A chart element has a *Format* task pane that includes fill, outline, and effects commands, as well as specific options for the element.
- Most formats can also be applied to a selected chart element from the *Home* tab.

3.5 Use pictures, shapes, and *WordArt* in a chart (p. E3-183).

- For chart shapes that have a fill color, you can use a picture as fill.
- Images used as fill can be from your own or online sources, but not all pictures work well as fill.
- Shapes are predefined outline drawings available from the *Insert Shapes* group on the *Chart Tools Format* tab or from the *Illustrations* group on the *Insert* tab.
- Place shapes on a chart to highlight or draw attention to a particular element.
- ***WordArt*** is a text box with a preset design, often used to format a chart title.

3.6 Build pie charts and combination charts (p. E3-188).

- A pie chart has one data series and shows each data point as a slice of the pie.
- A pie chart does not have axes, but it does have options to rotate or explode slices.

- A combination chart uses at least two chart types to highlight, compare, or contrast differences in data or values.
- Format a combination chart to show a secondary axis when values are widely different or use different scales.

3.7 Create sunburst and waterfall charts (p. E3-191).

- A ***sunburst chart*** has one data series that is grouped in a ***hierarchy***.
- A sunburst chart illustrates the relationship among the hierarchies in a pie-like chart with concentric rings.
- A ***waterfall chart*** depicts a running total for positive and negative values.
- A waterfall chart is used for financial or other data that shows inflows and outlays of resources.
- A waterfall chart resembles a column chart and has category and value axes.
- Place a sunburst chart or a waterfall chart as an object or on a separate sheet.

3.8 Insert and format sparklines in a worksheet (p. E3-194).

- A ***sparkline*** is a miniature chart in a cell or range of cells in the worksheet.
- Three sparkline types are available: ***Line***, ***Column***, and ***Win/Loss***.
- When inserted in a range of cells, sparklines are grouped and can be ungrouped.
- The *Sparkline Tools Design* tab is visible when a sparkline is selected and includes formatting options such as setting the color or identifying high and low values.

Check for Understanding

The SIMbook for this text (within your SIMnet account) provides the following resources for concept review:

- Multiple-choice questions
- Short answer questions
- Matching exercises

Guided Project 3-1

Life's Animal Shelter (LAS) is an animal care and adoption agency that accepts unwanted and abandoned domestic animals. For this project, you create expense charts and insert sparklines to help the agency track expenses for the first six months of the year. You also build a waterfall chart to graph cash flow for a month.
[Student Learning Outcomes 3.1, 3.2, 3.3, 3.4, 3.5, 3.6, 3.7, 3.8]

File Needed: ***LAS-03.xlsx*** *(Student data files are available in the* Library *of your SIMnet account.)*
Completed Project File Name: ***[your initials] Excel 3-1.xlsx***

Skills Covered in This Project

- Create a chart object.
- Create a chart sheet.
- Apply *Quick Layout* and chart styles.
- Add and format chart elements.
- Change the chart type.
- Filter the data series.
- Insert a shape in a chart.
- Create and format a combination chart.
- Insert and format sparklines in a worksheet.
- Create and format a waterfall chart.

---

1. Open the ***LAS-03*** workbook from your student data files and save it as [your initials] Excel 3-1.
2. Create a pie chart object.
   a. Select the **Jan-June** sheet and select cells **A5:A10**. Press **Ctrl** and select cells **I5:I10**.
   b. Click the **Insert Pie or Doughnut Chart** button [*Insert* tab, *Charts* group].
   c. Select the **2D-Pie** chart subtype.
3. Create a chart sheet.
   a. Select the pie chart object.
   b. Click the **Move Chart** button [*Chart Tools Design* tab, *Location* group].
   c. Click the **New sheet** button.
   d. Type Pie Chart in the text box.
   e. Click **OK**.
4. Apply a chart style.
   a. Click the **More** button [*Chart Tools Design* tab, *Chart Styles* group].
   b. Select **Style 12**.
5. Edit and format chart elements.
   a. Click the chart title element.
   b. Click the *Formula* bar, type January through June Expenses, and press **Enter**.
   c. Triple-click the new label in the chart and change the font size to **28 pt**.
   d. Click the legend element to select it and to deselect the title element.
   e. Click the **Font Size** arrow [*Home* tab, *Font* group] and change the legend size to **12 pt**.
   f. Select the chart area. (You can confirm the selected chart object on the *Chart Tools Format* tab, *Current Selection* group.)
   g. Click the **Shape Outline** button [*Chart Tools Format* tab, *Shape Styles* group].
   h. Choose **Black, Text 1** (second column) as the color.
   i. Click the **Shape Outline** button again.

j. Choose **Weight** and select **1 pt**.
k. Click outside the chart background to see the outline (Figure 3-57).

6. Create a bar chart object.
   a. Click the **Jan-June** sheet tab.
   b. Select cells **A4:G9** as source data, omitting the *Rent* expense.
   c. Click the **Quick Analysis** button and select **Charts**.
   d. Select the clustered bar icon (fifth tile in *Quick Analysis* group).
   e. Point to the chart border to display a move pointer.
   f. Drag the chart object so that its top-left corner is at cell **A13**.
   g. Point to the bottom-right selection handle to display a resize arrow.
   h. Drag the pointer to reach cell **I30** (Figure 3-58).
7. Change the chart type.
   a. Click the bar chart object.
   b. Click the **Change Chart Type** button [*Chart Tools Design* tab, *Type* group].
   c. Click the **Recommended Charts** tab.
   d. Find and choose the **Clustered Column** icon in the left pane that displays the months on the horizontal axis.
   e. Click **OK**.
8. Filter the source data.
   a. Click the column chart object.
   b. Click the **Chart Filters** button in the top-right corner of the chart.
   c. Deselect the **January**, **February**, and **March** boxes.
   d. Click **Apply** in the *Chart Filters* pane (Figure 3-59).
   e. Click the **Chart Filters** button to close the pane.
9. Edit, format, and add chart elements.
   a. Click the chart title object.
   b. Click the *Formula* bar.
   c. Type Second Quarter Variable Expenses and press **Enter**.
   d. Click the **Chart Elements** arrow [*Chart Tools Format* tab, *Current Selection* group] and choose **Chart Area**.
   e. Click the **Shape Outline** button [*Chart Tools Format* tab, *Shape Styles* group].
   f. Choose **Black, Text 1** (second column) as the color.
   g. Click the **Shape Outline** button again and choose **Weight** and **1 pt**.

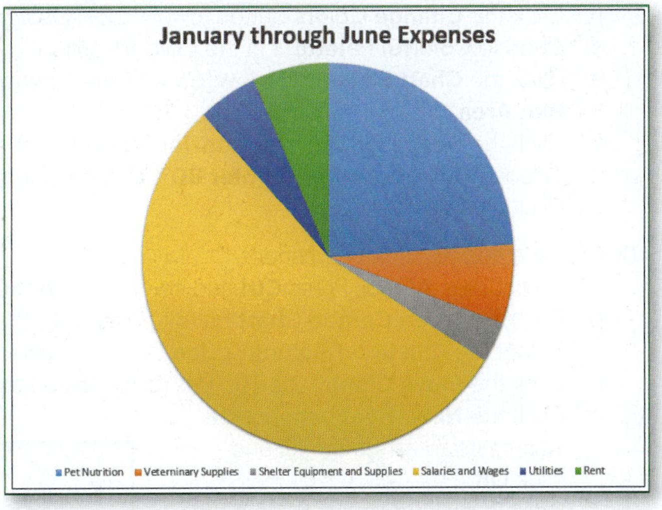

Figure 3-57 Pie chart sheet with format changes

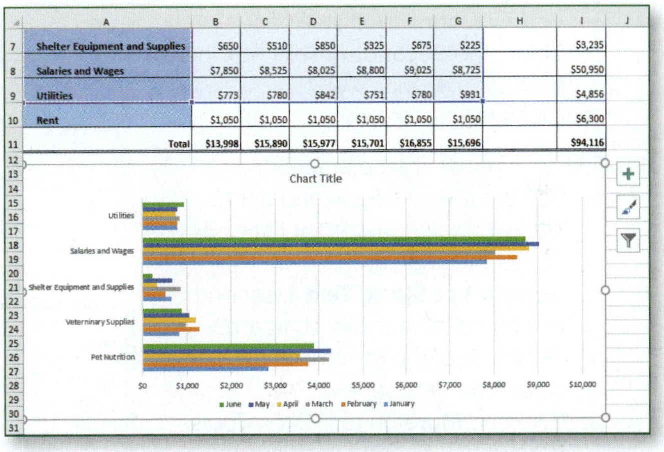

Figure 3-58 Bar chart object sized and positioned

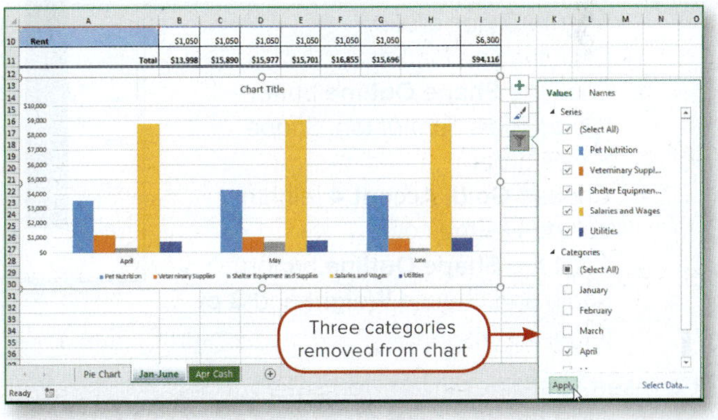

Figure 3-59 Chart filters applied

h. Click the **Change Colors** button [*Chart Tools Design* tab, *Chart Styles* group].
i. Choose **Colorful Palette 3** in the *Colorful* group.
j. Click the **Chart Elements** arrow [*Chart Tools Format* tab, *Current Selection* group] and choose **Plot Area**.
k. Click the **Shape Fill** button [*Chart Tools Format* tab, *Shape Styles* group].
l. Choose **Gold, Accent 4, Lighter 80%** (eighth column) as the color.
m. Click a worksheet cell.

10. Create a combination chart sheet.
a. Select cells **A9:G9**. Press **Ctrl** and select cells **A11:G11**.
b. Click the **Insert Combo Chart** button [*Insert* tab, *Charts* group].
c. Select the **Clustered Column - Line** chart subtype.
d. Click the **Move Chart** button [*Chart Tools Design* tab, *Location* group].
e. Click the **New sheet** button, type Combo Chart as the name, and click **OK**.
f. Double-click the line marker in the chart.
g. Click the **Series Options** button in the *Format Data Series* task pane.
h. Select the **Secondary Axis** box in the task pane (Figure 3-60).
i. Close the task pane.

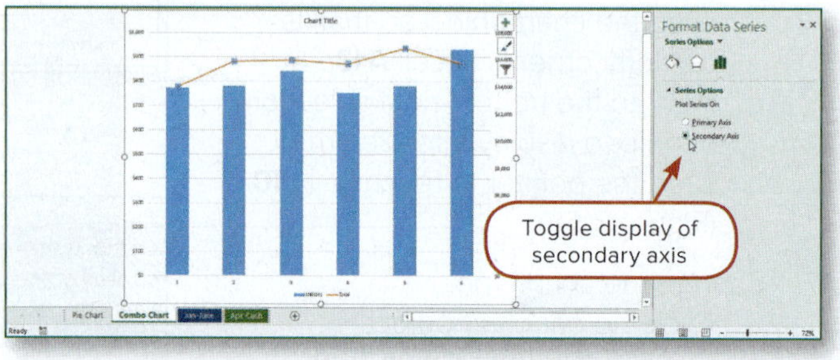

Figure 3-60 Combo chart and a secondary axis

11. Edit and format chart elements.
a. Edit the chart title placeholder to Utilities Expense and Total Expenses.
b. Select the chart area.
c. Apply a **1 pt Black, Text 1** (second column) outline to the chart area.
d. Click one of the column markers to select the data series.
e. Click the **More** button [*Chart Tools Format* tab, *Shape Styles* group].
f. Select **Moderate Effect – Black, Dark 1** (first column, fifth row) in the *Theme Styles* group.
g. Click the line marker.
h. Click the **Shape Outline** button [*Chart Tools Format* tab, *Shape Styles* group].
i. Choose **Gold, Accent 4** (eighth column) as the color.
j. Click the **Shape Outline** button again and choose **Weight** and **3 pt** (Figure 3-61).

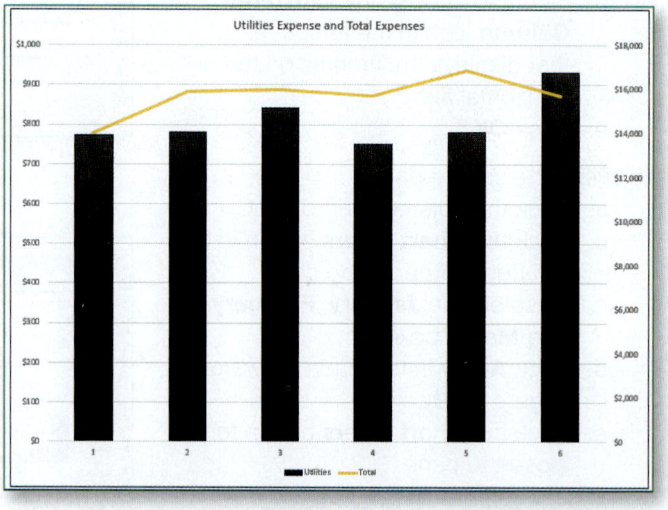

Figure 3-61 Line and column formatted in combo chart

12. Insert sparklines in the worksheet.
a. Click the **Jan-June** sheet tab.
b. Select cells **B5:G9** as the data range.
c. Click the **Column Sparkline** button [*Insert* tab, *Sparklines* group].
d. Select cells **H5:H9** for the *Location Range* and click **OK**.
e. Click the **Sparkline Color** button [*Sparkline Tools Design* tab, *Style* group].
f. Choose **White, Background 1, Darker 50%** (first column).

13. Insert a shape in a chart.
    a. Select the column chart object.
    b. Click the **More** button [*Chart Tools Format* tab, *Insert Shapes* group].
    c. Select the **Text Box** shape [*Basic Shapes* group].
    d. Draw a text box like the one shown in Figure 3-62.
    e. Type Utilities are to be removed from an updated chart per management request.
    f. Drag a selection handle to size the text box shape if necessary.
    g. Point to a border of the *Text Box* shape to display a four-pointed arrow and position it if needed.

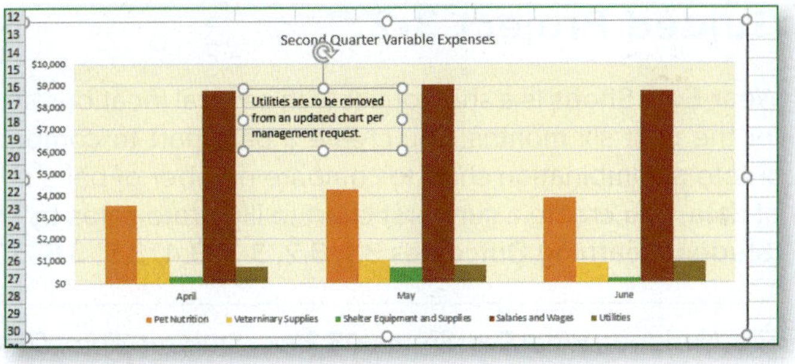

Figure 3-62 Text box shape inserted in chart

14. Click a worksheet cell and press **Ctrl+Home**.

15. Create a waterfall chart object.
    a. Select the **Apr Cash** sheet tab.
    b. Select cells **A5:B14**. These data represent cash coming in and going out for April.
    c. Click the **Insert Waterfall**, **Funnel**, **Stock**, **Surface**, **or Radar Chart** button [*Insert* tab, *Charts* group].
    d. Select **Waterfall**.

16. Size and position a chart object.
    a. Point to the chart border to display the move pointer.
    b. Drag the chart object so that its top-left corner is at cell **D1**.
    c. Point to the bottom-right selection handle to display the resize arrow.
    d. Drag the pointer to cell **M20**.

17. Format chart elements.
    a. Double-click the **Net Cash** column marker and then click the marker again to open the *Format Data Point* pane.
    b. Click the **Series Options** button in the task pane and expand the *Series Options* group.
    c. Select the **Set as total** box.
    d. Select the chart title placeholder, triple-click to select the text, and type April Cash Flow.
    e. Select the chart area and apply a **1 pt Text, Black 1** (second column) outline.
    f. Click a worksheet cell and press **Ctrl+Home**.

18. Save and close the workbook (Figure 3-63).

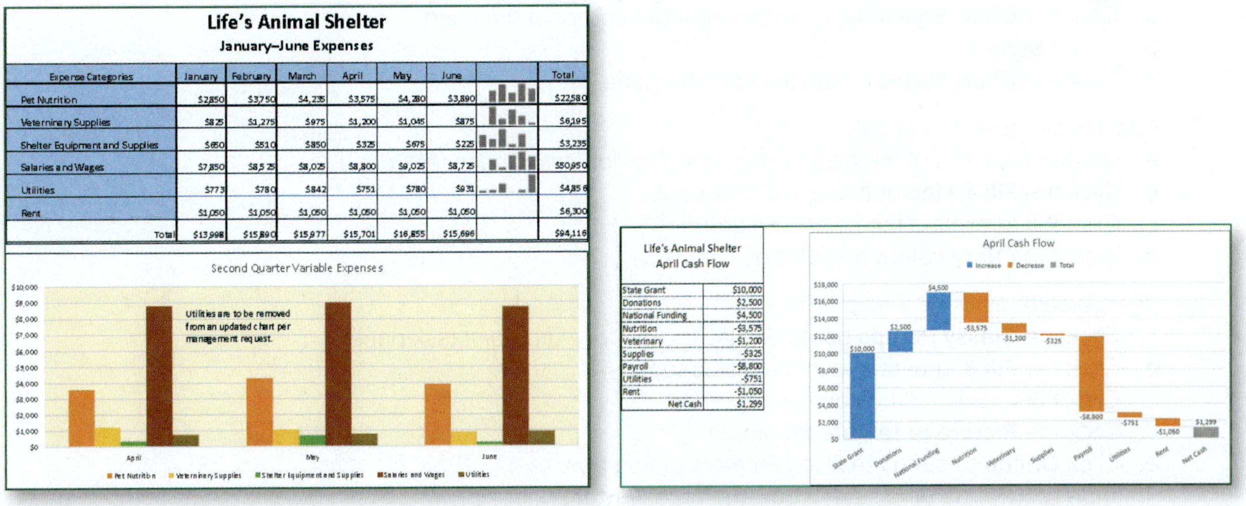

Expense Categories	January	February	March	April	May	June		Total
Pet Nutrition	$2,850	$3,750	$4,235	$3,575	$4,280	$3,890		$22,580
Veterinary Supplies	$825	$1,275	$975	$1,200	$1,045	$875		$6,195
Shelter Equipment and Supplies	$650	$510	$850	$325	$675	$225		$3,235
Salaries and Wages	$7,850	$8,525	$8,025	$8,800	$9,025	$8,725		$50,950
Utilities	$773	$780	$842	$751	$780	$931		$4,856
Rent	$1,050	$1,050	$1,050	$1,050	$1,050	$1,050		$6,300
Total	$13,998	$15,890	$15,977	$15,701	$16,855	$15,696		$94,116

State Grant	$10,000
Donations	$2,500
National Funding	$4,500
Nutrition	-$3,575
Veterinary	-$1,200
Supplies	-$325
Payroll	-$8,800
Utilities	-$751
Rent	-$1,050
Net Cash	$1,299

Figure 3-63 Excel 3-1 completed worksheets and charts

Guided Project 3-2

Wear-Ever Shoes is a shoe outlet with several locations. In a worksheet that tracks sales of popular items for the past six months, you create a bar chart to compare the number of pairs sold by style. You also create a combination chart to compare number of pairs sold and unit cost for each style. For another set of data, you create a sunburst chart to illustrate sales by shoe style, gender, and color.
[Student Learning Outcomes 3.1, 3.2, 3.3, 3.4, 3.5, 3.6, 3.7]

File Needed: ***WearEverShoes-03.xlsx*** *(Student data files are available in the* Library *of your SIMnet account.)*
Completed Project File Name: ***[your initials] Excel 3-2.xlsx***

Skills Covered in This Project

- Create a chart sheet.
- Change the chart type.
- Apply a chart style.
- Add and format chart elements.
- Use a picture as fill.
- Create and format a combination chart.
- Use *WordArt* in a chart.
- Create and format a sunburst chart.

1. Open the ***WearEverShoes-03*** workbook from your student data files and save it as [your initials] Excel 3-2.
2. Create a column chart sheet.
   a. Select cells **A5:B16** on the **Unit Sales** sheet.
   b. Click the **Quick Analysis** button and choose **Charts**.
   c. Click the **Clustered Column** icon.
   d. Click the **Move Chart** button [*Chart Tools Design* tab, *Location* group].
   e. Click the **New sheet** button.
   f. Type Sales Chart and click **OK**.
3. Change the chart type.
   a. Click the **Sales Chart** sheet tab if necessary.
   b. Click the **Change Chart Type** button [*Chart Tools Design* tab, *Type* group].
   c. Click the **Recommended Charts** tab.
   d. Choose **Clustered Bar** in the left pane and click **OK**.
4. Apply a chart style.
   a. Click the **Chart Styles** button in the top-right corner of the chart.
   b. Select **Style 7**.
   c. Click the **Chart Styles** button to close the pane.
5. Add fill color to a data series.
   a. Double-click one of the bars to open the *Format Data Series* task pane.
   b. Click the **Fill & Line** button in the task pane.
   c. Click **Fill** to expand the command group.
   d. Select the **Vary colors by point** box.
6. Use a picture as fill for a data point.
   a. Click the **Classy Pumps** bar to display its *Format Data Point* task pane.
   b. Click the **Fill & Line** button in the task pane.
   c. Click **Fill** to expand the command group.
   d. Click the **Picture or texture fill** button.
   e. Click **Online** to open the *Insert Pictures* dialog box.
   f. Type heels in the *Bing* search box and press **Enter** (Figure 3-64).

g. Select an image and click **Insert**.
h. Click the **Stack** radio button in the task pane.
i. Close the task pane and click the chart border.

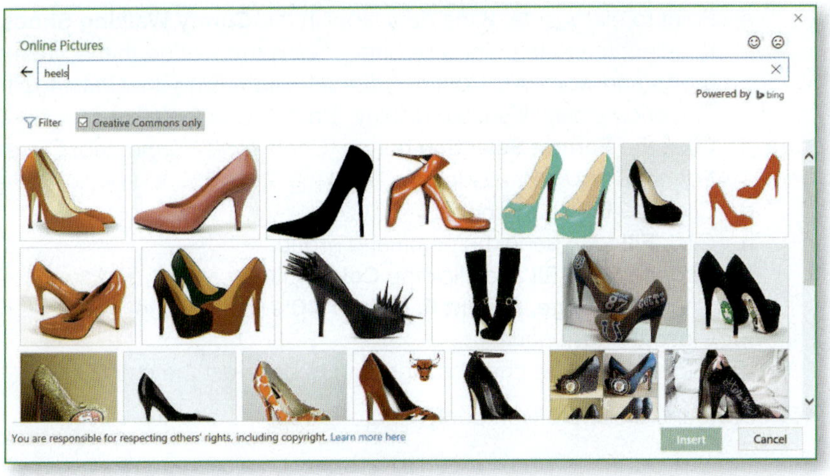

Figure 3-64 Online image search for fill in a data point

7. Create a combination chart sheet.
   a. Click the **Unit Sales** sheet tab.
   b. Select cells **A5:A16**. Press **Ctrl** and select cells **E5:F16**.
   c. Click the **Insert Combo Chart** button [*Insert* tab, *Charts* group].
   d. Select the **Clustered Column - Line on Secondary Axis** chart subtype.
   e. Click the **Move Chart** button [*Chart Tools Design* tab, *Location* group].
   f. Click the **New sheet** button.
   g. Type Cost&Retail and click **OK**.
8. Edit chart elements.
   a. Click the chart title placeholder.
   b. Type Cost and Selling Price Comparison in the *Formula* bar and press **Enter**.
   c. Select the chart title box.
   d. Click the **Home** tab and change the font size to **20 pt**.
   e. Select the chart area and apply a **1 pt Black, Text 1** outline.
   f. Click one of the column shapes to select the *Cost* series.
   g. Click the **More** button [*Chart Tools Format* tab, *Shapes Styles* group].
   h. Choose **Intense Effect - Blue, Accent 1** in the bottom row of the *Theme Styles* gallery.
   i. Select the line marker to select the *Retail Price* series.
   j. Click the **Shape Outline** button [*Chart Tools Format* tab, *Shape Styles* group] and choose **Black, Text 1** as the color.
   k. Change the weight of the line to **3 pt**.
9. Use *WordArt* in a chart.
   a. Click the chart title.
   b. Click the **More** button [*Chart Tools Format* tab, *WordArt Styles* group].
   c. Choose **Fill: Black, Text color 1; Shadow** in the first row of the gallery.
   d. Click the chart border to deselect the title.
10. Create a sunburst chart.
    a. Click the **Grouped Sales** sheet tab.
    b. Select cells **A5:D24**.
    c. Click the **Insert Hierarchy Chart** button [*Insert* tab, *Charts* group].
    d. Click **Sunburst** to select it.
    e. Click the **Move Chart** button [*Chart Tools Design* tab, *Location* group].
    f. Select **New sheet**, type Sunburst, and click **OK**.
11. Format a sunburst chart.
    a. Click the chart title element.
    b. Triple-click the placeholder text to select it.
    c. Type Sales by Style, Color, and Gender.
    d. Click the sunburst shape to select the circle and confirm that "Series" is the active element in the *Current Selection* group [*Chart Tools Format* tab].

e. Point to either side of the data label in the **Comfy Walking Shoes** arc in the inner ring and click to select the data point. The data point is the wedge that represents two colors of the style, men's and women's. Confirm your selection using the *Chart Tools Format* tab in the *Current Selection* group. It should display "Branch Comfy Walking."

f. Click the **Format Selection** button [*Chart Tools Format* tab, *Current Selection* group] to open the *Format Data Point* task pane.

g. Click the **Fill & Line** button.

h. Click **Fill** to expand the command group.

i. Choose **Solid fill** and click the **Color** button.

j. Choose **Orange, Accent 6, Lighter 40%** (last column)

k. Close the task pane.

l. Click outside the chart background to deselect the chart.

12. Save and close the workbook (Figure 3-65).

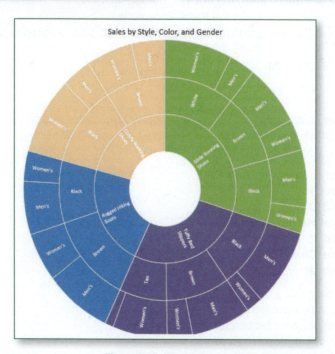

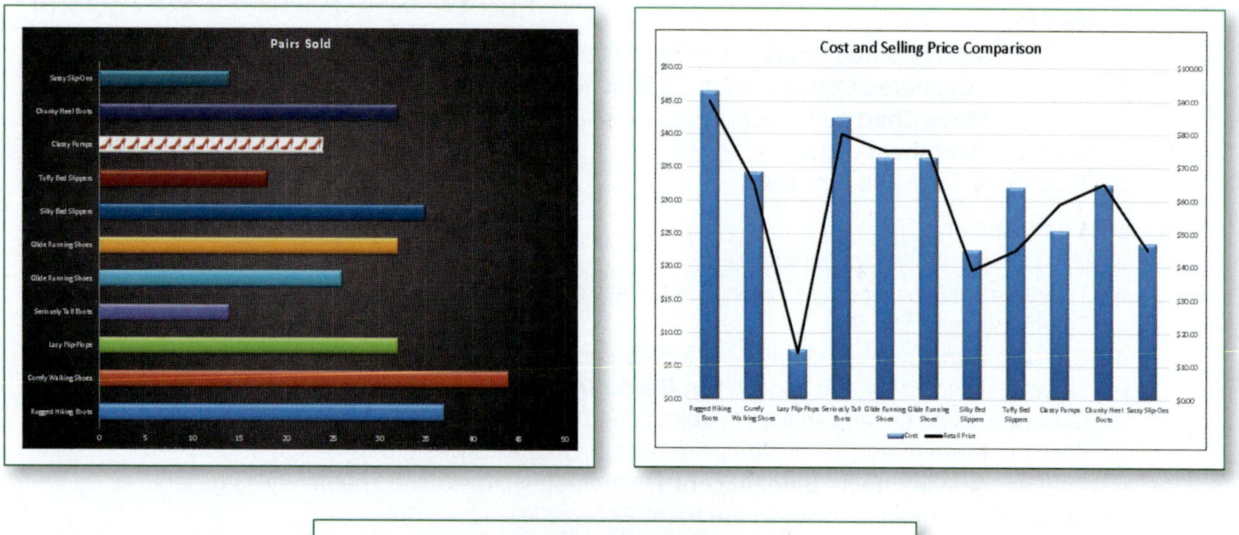

Figure 3-65 Excel 3-2 completed chart sheets

Guided Project 3-3

Blue Lake Sports has locations in several major cities and tracks sales by department in each store. For this project, you create a pie chart that shows each store's share of golf-related sales for the first quarter. You also create a line chart to illustrate week-to-week sales for specific departments in one of the stores and insert sparklines in the data.
[Student Learning Outcomes 3.1, 3.2, 3.3, 3.4, 3.6, 3.8]

File Needed: ***BlueLakeSports-03.xlsx*** *(Student data files are available in the* Library *of your SIMnet account.)*
Completed Project File Name: ***[your initials] Excel 3-3.xlsx***

Skills Covered in This Project

- Create, size, and position a pie chart object.
- Apply a chart style.
- Change the chart type.
- Add and format chart elements.
- Create a line chart sheet.
- Apply a chart layout.
- Insert and format sparklines in a worksheet.

1. Open the ***BlueLakeSports-03*** workbook from your student data files and save it as [your initials] Excel 3-3.
2. Create a pie chart object.
   a. Select the **Revenue by Department** sheet, select cells **A4:F4**, press **Ctrl**, and select cells **A13:F13**.
   b. Click the **Recommended Charts** button [*Insert* tab, *Charts* group].
   c. Choose **Pie** and click **OK**.
3. Apply a chart style.
   a. Select the chart object.
   b. Click the **More** button [*Chart Tools Design* tab, *Chart Styles* group].
   c. Select **Style 12**.
4. Size and position a chart object.
   a. Point to the chart object border to display the move pointer.
   b. Drag the chart object so its top-left corner is at cell **A21**.
   c. Point to the bottom-right selection handle to display the resize arrow.
   d. Drag the pointer to cell **G36**.
5. Change the chart type.
   a. Select the pie chart object and click the **Change Chart Type** button [*Chart Tools Design* tab, *Type* group].
   b. Select the **All Charts** tab and choose **Pie** in the left pane.
   c. Choose **3-D Pie** and click **OK**.
6. Format pie chart elements.
   a. Double-click the pie to open its *Format Data Series* task pane.
   b. Click the **Atlanta** slice to update the pane to the *Format Data Point* task pane. (Rest the pointer on a slice to see its identifying *ScreenTip*.)
   c. Click the **Series Options** button in the *Format Data Series* task pane.
   d. Set the pie explosion percentage at **10%**.
   e. Close the task pane.
   f. Click the chart object border to deselect the **Atlanta** slice.
7. Add and format chart elements in a pie chart.
   a. Click the **Chart Elements** button in the top-right corner of the chart.
   b. Select the **Data Labels** box.

c. Click the **Data Labels** arrow to open its submenu and choose **More Options**.
d. Click the **Label Options** button In the *Format Data Labels* pane.
e. Click **Label Options** to expand the group.
f. Select the **Percentage** box.

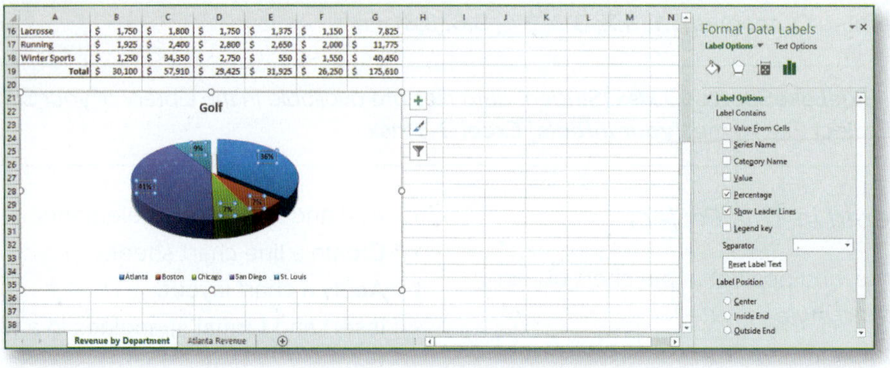

Figure 3-66 *Format Data* task pane for data labels

g. Deselect the **Value** box (Figure 3-66).
h. Press **Ctrl+B** to apply bold.
i. Change the font size to **12 pt** [*Home* tab, *Font* group].
j. Click the chart object border to select it.
k. Click the **Shape Outline** button *[Chart Tools Format* tab, *Shape Styles* group] and choose **Purple, Accent 4, Darker 50%** (eighth column).
l. Click the **Shape Outline** button and choose **Weight** and **1 pt**.
m. Click a worksheet cell.

8. Create a line chart sheet.
   a. Select the **Atlanta Revenue** sheet tab.
   b. Select cells **A4:E7**.
   c. Click the **Quick Analysis** button and choose **Charts**.
   d. Select **Line**.
   e. Click the **Move Chart** button [*Chart Tools Design* tab, *Location* group].
   f. Click the **New sheet** button.
   g. Type Promo Depts and click **OK**.
9. Apply a chart layout.
   a. Click the **Quick Layout** button [*Chart Tools Design* tab, *Chart Layouts* group].
   b. Select **Layout 5** to add a data table to the chart sheet (Figure 3-67).

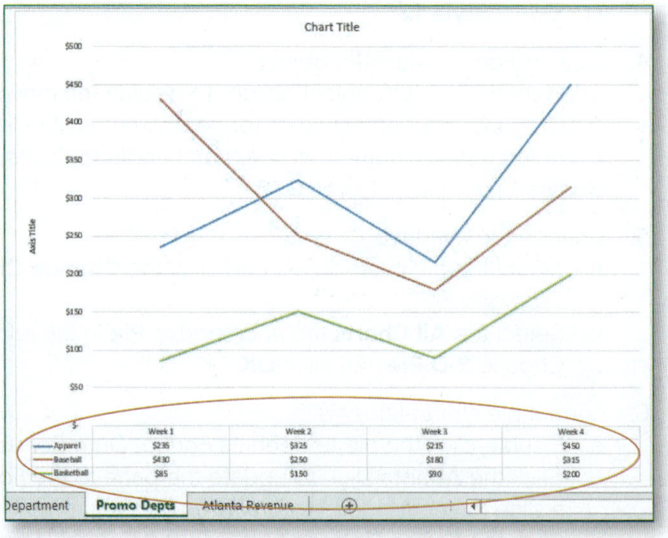

Figure 3-67 Data table added by *Quick Layout*

10. Change the chart type.
    a. Click the **Change Chart Type** button [*Chart Tools Design* tab, *Type* group].
    b. Select the **All Charts** tab and choose **Line with Markers** in the *Line* category.
    c. Click **OK**.

11. Edit chart elements in a line chart.
    a. Click the chart title placeholder.
    b. Type **Special Promotion Departments** in the *Formula* bar and press **Enter**.
    c. Click the vertical axis title placeholder.
    d. Type **Dollar Sales** in the *Formula* bar and press **Enter**.
    e. Click the **Chart Elements** drop-down arrow [*Chart Tools Format* tab, *Current Selection* group].
    f. Choose **Series "Apparel"** to select the line in the chart.

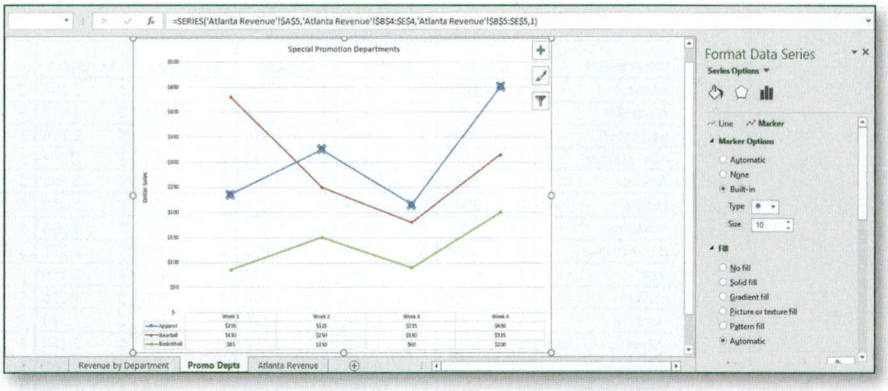

Figure 3-68 Marker options for the data series

    g. Click the **Format Selection** button [*Chart Tools Format* tab, *Current Selection* group].
    h. Click the **Fill & Line** button in the *Format Data Series* task pane.
    i. Click **Marker** and then click **Marker Options** to expand the group (Figure 3-68).
    j. Choose **Built-in** and set the **Size** to **10**.
    k. Click the *Series Options* triangle at the top of the task pane and choose **Series "Baseball"** (Figure 3-69).
    l. Apply the same marker changes for the baseball series.
    m. Select the **Basketball** series and apply the same marker changes.
    n. Close the task pane and click outside the chart.

12. Insert sparklines in the worksheet.
    a. Click the **Atlanta Revenue** tab.
    b. Right-click the column **F** heading and choose **Insert**.
    c. Select cells **B5:E18** as the data range.
    d. Click the **Line Sparkline** button [*Insert* tab, *Sparklines* group].
    e. Select cells **F5:F18** in the *Location Range* box.
    f. Click **OK**.

13. Format sparklines in worksheet.
    a. Click the **Format** button [*Home* tab, *Cells* group] and change the **Row Height** to **24**.
    b. Click the **Format** button [*Home* tab, *Cells* group] and set the **Column Width** to **35**.

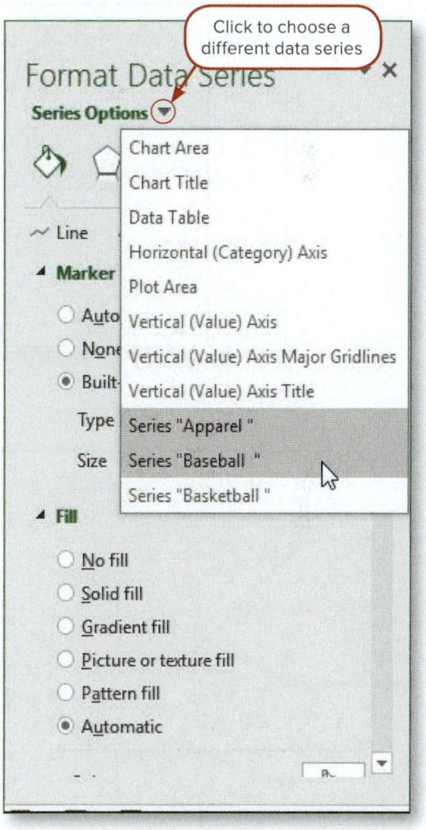

Figure 3-69 New data series selected

    c. Select the **Markers** box in the *Show* group in the *Sparkline Tools Design* tab.
    d. Click the **Sparkline Color** button [*Sparkline Tools Design* tab, *Style* group].
    e. Choose **Black, Text 1** (second column) for the line color.
    f. Click cell **A1**.

14. Change the page orientation to landscape.
15. Save and close the workbook (Figure 3-70).

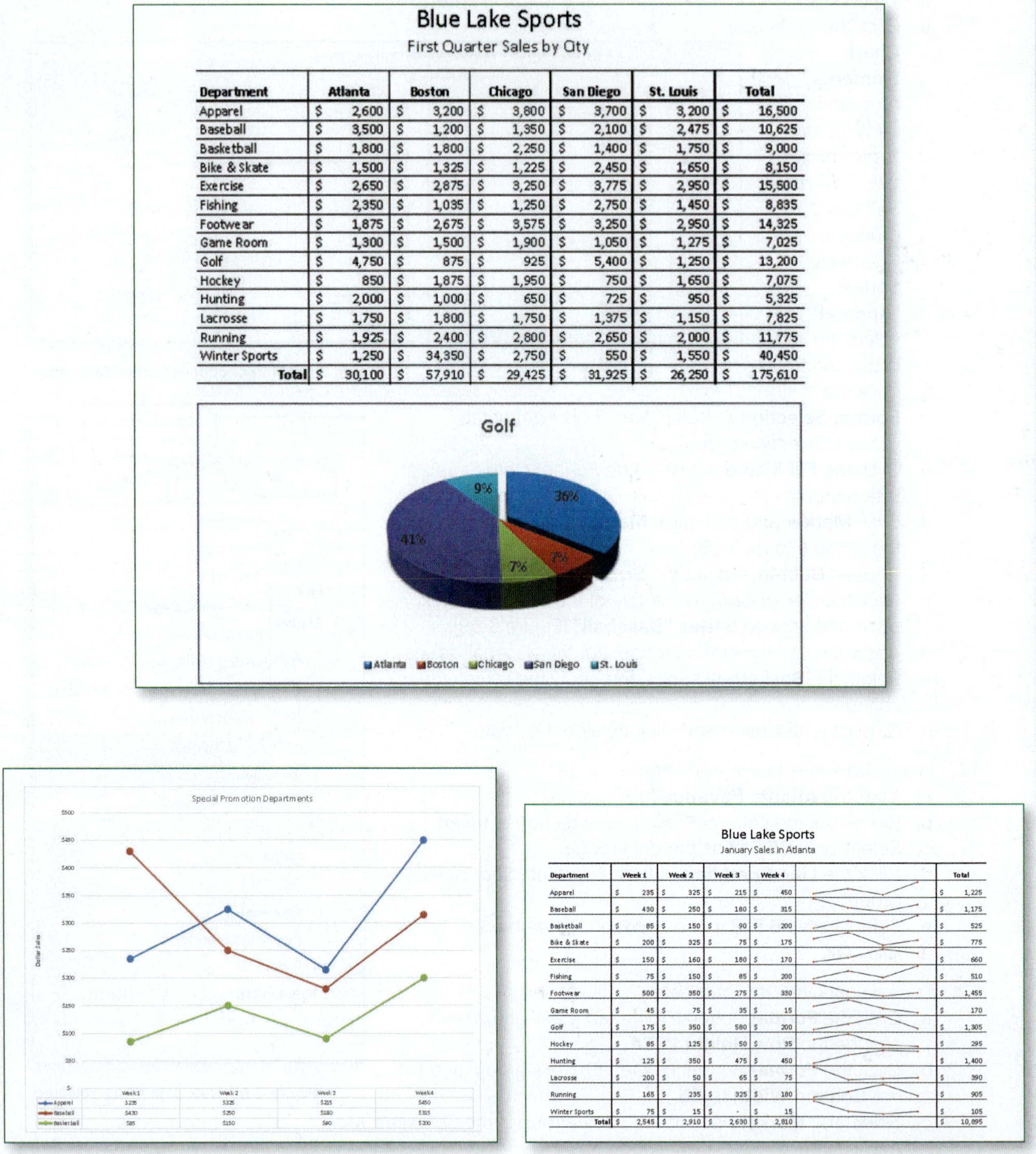

Blue Lake Sports

First Quarter Sales by City

Department	Atlanta	Boston	Chicago	San Diego	St. Louis	Total
Apparel	$ 2,600	$ 3,200	$ 3,800	$ 3,700	$ 3,200	$ 16,500
Baseball	$ 3,500	$ 1,200	$ 1,350	$ 2,100	$ 2,475	$ 10,625
Basketball	$ 1,800	$ 1,800	$ 2,250	$ 1,400	$ 1,750	$ 9,000
Bike & Skate	$ 1,500	$ 1,325	$ 1,225	$ 2,450	$ 1,650	$ 8,150
Exercise	$ 2,650	$ 2,875	$ 3,250	$ 3,775	$ 2,950	$ 15,500
Fishing	$ 2,350	$ 1,035	$ 1,250	$ 2,750	$ 1,450	$ 8,835
Footwear	$ 1,875	$ 2,675	$ 3,575	$ 3,250	$ 2,950	$ 14,325
Game Room	$ 1,300	$ 1,500	$ 1,900	$ 1,050	$ 1,275	$ 7,025
Golf	$ 4,750	$ 875	$ 925	$ 5,400	$ 1,250	$ 13,200
Hockey	$ 850	$ 1,875	$ 1,950	$ 750	$ 1,650	$ 7,075
Hunting	$ 2,000	$ 1,000	$ 650	$ 725	$ 950	$ 5,325
Lacrosse	$ 1,750	$ 1,800	$ 1,750	$ 1,375	$ 1,150	$ 7,825
Running	$ 1,925	$ 2,400	$ 2,800	$ 2,650	$ 2,000	$ 11,775
Winter Sports	$ 1,250	$ 34,350	$ 2,750	$ 550	$ 1,550	$ 40,450
Total	$ 30,100	$ 57,910	$ 29,425	$ 31,925	$ 26,250	$ 175,610

Blue Lake Sports

January Sales in Atlanta

Department	Week 1	Week 2	Week 3	Week 4		Total
Apparel	$ 235	$ 325	$ 215	$ 450		$ 1,225
Baseball	$ 430	$ 250	$ 180	$ 315		$ 1,175
Basketball	$ 85	$ 150	$ 90	$ 200		$ 525
Bike & Skate	$ 200	$ 325	$ 75	$ 175		$ 775
Exercise	$ 150	$ 160	$ 180	$ 170		$ 660
Fishing	$ 75	$ 150	$ 85	$ 200		$ 510
Footwear	$ 500	$ 350	$ 275	$ 330		$ 1,455
Game Room	$ 45	$ 75	$ 35	$ 15		$ 170
Golf	$ 175	$ 350	$ 580	$ 200		$ 1,305
Hockey	$ 85	$ 125	$ 50	$ 35		$ 295
Hunting	$ 125	$ 350	$ 475	$ 450		$ 1,400
Lacrosse	$ 200	$ 50	$ 65	$ 75		$ 390
Running	$ 165	$ 235	$ 325	$ 180		$ 905
Winter Sports	$ 75	$ 15	$ -	$ 15		$ 105
Total	$ 2,545	$ 2,910	$ 2,630	$ 2,810		$ 10,895

Figure 3-70 Excel 3-3 completed worksheet and charts

Independent Project 3-4

For this project, you create a column chart to illustrate April–September revenue for Classic Gardens and Landscapes. You also build a pie chart sheet to graph the proportion that each category contributes to total revenue.
[Student Learning Outcomes 3.1, 3.2, 3.3, 3.4, 3.5, 3.6]

File Needed: ***ClassicGardens-03.xlsx*** *(Student data files are available in the* Library *of your SIMnet account.)*
Completed Project File Name: ***[your initials] Excel 3-4.xlsx***

Skills Covered in This Project

- Create a chart object.
- Size and position a chart object.
- Edit and format chart elements.
- Edit the source data for a chart.
- Build a pie chart sheet.
- Use texture as fill.
- Add and format data labels in a chart.

---

1. Open the ***ClassicGardens-03*** workbook from your student data files and save it as [your initials] Excel 3-4.
2. Create a **Clustered Column** chart object for cells **A4:G9**.
3. Move the chart object so that its top-left corner is at cell **A12**. Size the bottom of the chart to reach cell **H30**.
4. Edit the chart title to display CGL Major Sales Revenue and press **Enter**. On the second line, type Second and Third Quarters. (In the *Formula* bar, press **Alt+Enter** to start a new line.)
5. Apply chart **Style 14** to the chart.
6. Format the first line of the chart title to a font size of **20 pt**. Format the second title line as **18 pt**.
7. Apply a **1 pt Black, Text 1** (second column) outline to the chart area.
8. Verify that the chart is still selected. In the highlighted range in the worksheet, drag the resize pointer to remove the *Design Consulting* data series from the chart (Figure 3-71).

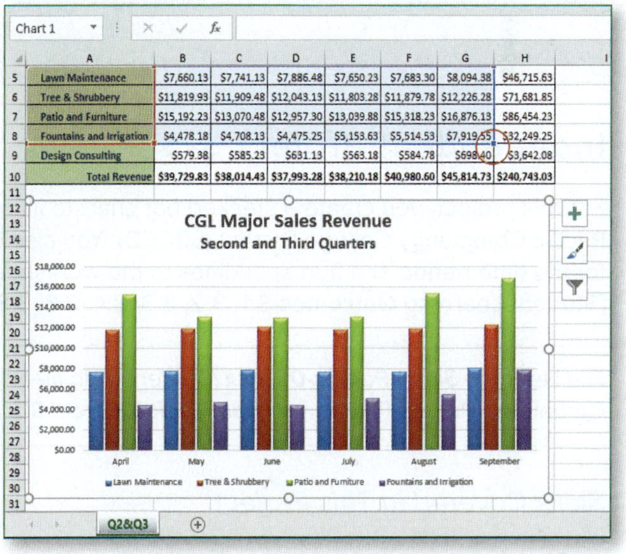

Figure 3-71 Resize the chart by dragging the resize pointer

9. Create a *3-D Pie* chart sheet for cells **A4:A9** and cells **H4:H9**. Move the chart to its own sheet named Revenue Breakdown.
10. Edit the chart title to display Revenue by Category. Change the font size to **32**.
11. Select the legend and change the font size to **12**.
12. Apply the **Woven mat** texture fill (first row, fourth column) to the *Patio and Furniture* slice.
13. Select the pie shape and add data labels to display in the center of each slice.
    a. Display the *Format Data Labels* task pane, choose the **Accounting** format [*Label Options* button, *Number* group], and set **0** decimal places.
    b. Change the data label font size to **14 pt** and apply **bold** [*Home* tab, *Font* group].

14. Deselect the chart.

15. Save and close the workbook (Figure 3-72).

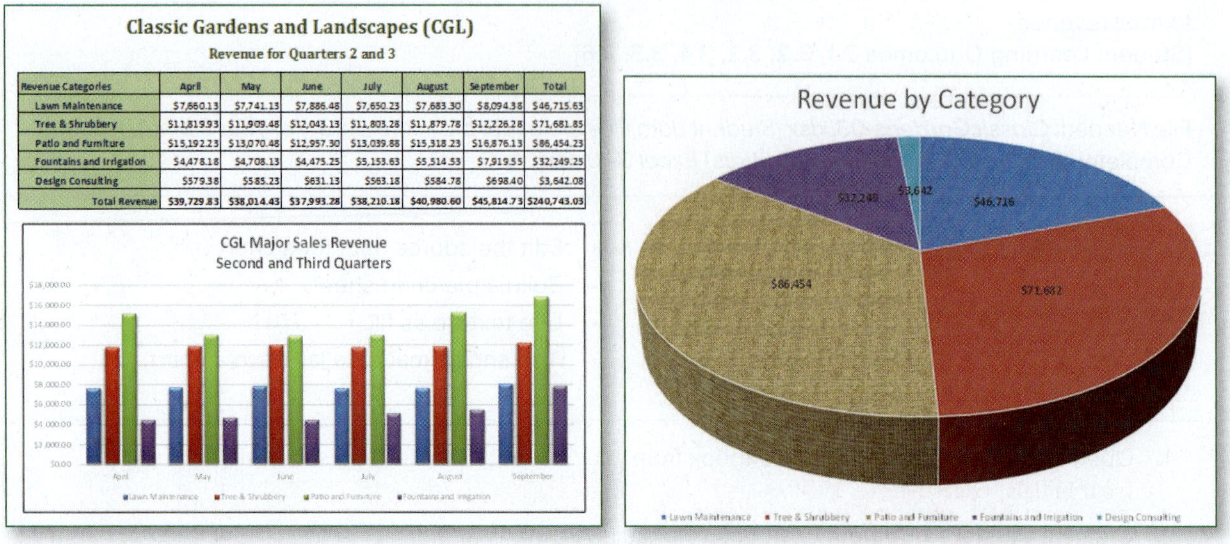

Figure 3-72 Excel 3-4 completed worksheet and chart

Independent Project 3-5

For this project, you create a stacked bar chart to illustrate projected tuition and fee amounts for Sierra Pacific Community College District (SPCCD). You also create a pie chart to show total projected revenue for the time period and add sparklines to the worksheet.
[Student Learning Outcomes 3.1, 3.2, 3.3, 3.4, 3.6, 3.8]

File Needed: ***SierraPacific-03.xlsx*** *(Student data files are available in the* Library *of your SIMnet account.)*
Completed Project File Name: ***[your initials] Excel 3-5.xlsx***

Skills Covered in This Project

- Create a chart object.
- Size and position a chart object.
- Apply a chart style.
- Switch row and column data.
- Edit chart source data.
- Create a pie chart sheet.
- Edit and format chart elements.
- Insert and format sparklines in a sheet.

1. Open the ***SierraPacific-03*** workbook from your student data files and save it as [your initials] Excel 3-5.
2. Select cells **A3:E7** and use the *Quick Analysis* tool to create a stacked bar chart object.
3. Size and position the chart below the worksheet data in cells **A10:G28**.
4. Apply **Style 6**.
5. Edit the chart title to display Tuition Revenue Projection.

6. Apply a ½ pt **Dark Blue, Text 2** outline (fourth column) to the chart object.
7. Edit the source data to remove the *Utilization and Facilities* fees from the chart.
8. Switch the row and column data for the chart so that semester names are shown on the vertical axis.
9. Create a 3-D pie chart sheet for cells **A4:A7** and cells **F4:F7**. Move the chart to a new sheet named Total Revenue.
10. Apply **Style 3** and a **Black, Text 1** (second column) ½ **pt** outline.
11. Edit the chart title to Projected Revenue Sources.
12. Format the legend font size to **12 pt**.
13. Select the **Tuition & Fees** sheet, and create a column sparkline with cell **G8** as the location range for cells **B8:E8**. Format cell **G8** with **Outside Borders** [*Home* tab, *Font* group].
14. Save and close the workbook (Figure 3-73).

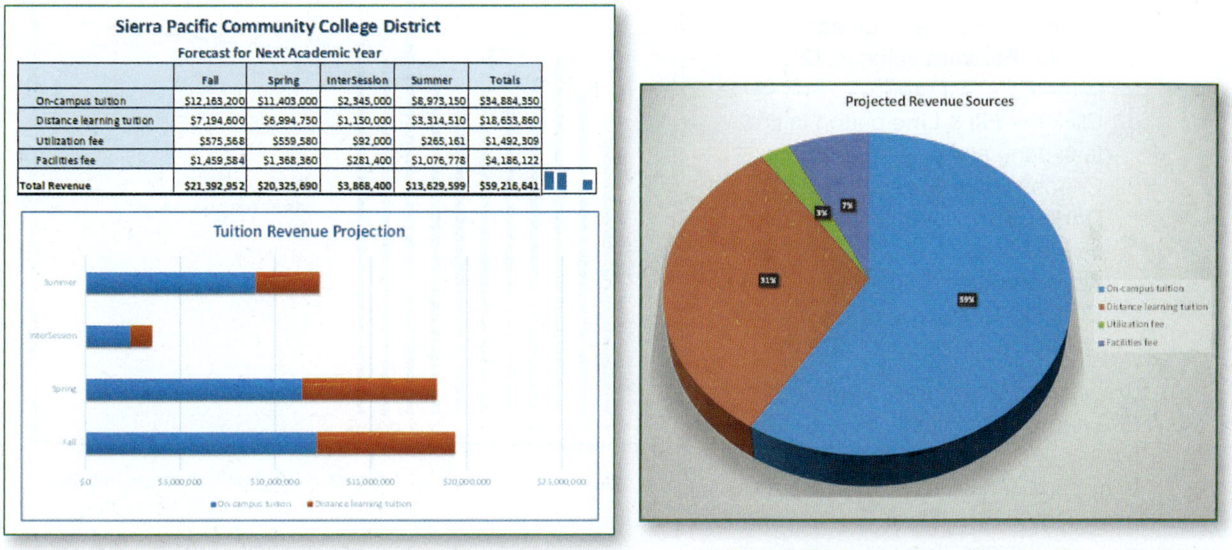

Figure 3-73 Excel 3-5 completed worksheet and chart

Independent Project 3-6

For this project, you create charts to illustrate data about the number of procedures performed at Courtyard Medical Plaza (CMP), as well as how patients came to the facility. You also prepare a waterfall chart for the operations account.
[Student Learning Outcomes 3.1, 3.2, 3.3, 3.4, 3.5, 3.7]

File Needed: ***CourtyardMedical-03.xlsx*** *(Student data files are available in the* Library *of your SIMnet account.)*
Completed Project File Name: ***[your initials] Excel 3-6.xlsx***

Skills Covered in This Project

- Create a column chart sheet.
- Add and edit chart elements.
- Add and format a trendline in a chart.
- Insert a text box shape in a chart.
- Display gridlines in a chart.
- Create a waterfall chart.

---

1. Open the ***CourtyardMedical-03*** workbook from your student data files and save it as [your initials] Excel 3-6.
2. Select the **Patient Arrivals** worksheet. Create a clustered column chart for cells **A5:M5** and cells **A7:M7**. Move the chart to its own sheet named Immed Care.
3. Edit the chart title to display Immediate Care Patient Count.
4. Click the **Chart Elements** button and select **Trendline**.
5. Click the options arrow next to **Trendline** and select **More Options** to open the *Format Trendline* task pane.
   a. Verify that the line is **Linear**.
   b. Set the **Forward** value to **12** in the *Forecast* group.
   c. Click the **Fill & Line** button in the task pane and select **Solid line**.
   d. Choose **Olive Green, Accent 3, Darker 50%** (seventh column) for the line color.
   e. Set the **Width** of the trendline to **4 pt**.
   f. Click the **Dash type** arrow and select the fourth option, **Dash**.
6. Draw a *Text Box* shape between the 300 and 400 gridlines and type The number of patients who come in for Immediate Care services will continue to grow. (Figure 3-74).

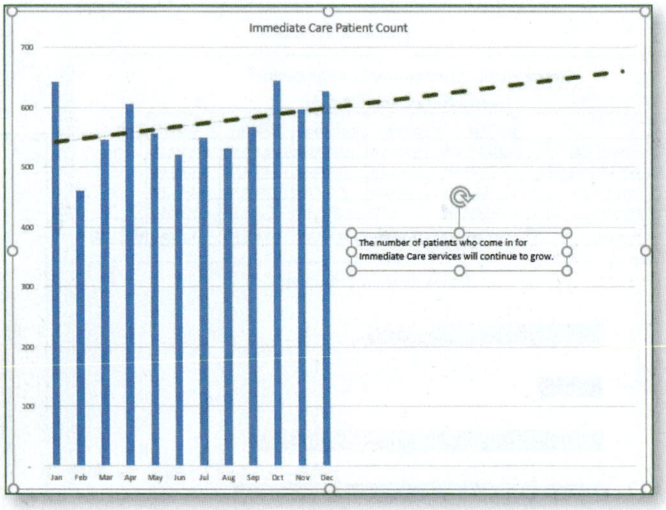

Figure 3-74 Text box shape in a chart

7. Select the **Procedures Count** worksheet and use the *Quick Analysis* tool to create a clustered column chart for cells **A5:D16**. Move the chart to its own sheet named Procedures Chart.
8. Edit the chart title to Number of Procedures on the first line and Three-Month Period on the second line.
9. Change the chart type to a clustered bar chart.
10. Click the **Chart Elements** button. Show **Primary Major Vertical**, **Primary Major Horizontal**, and **Primary Minor Vertical** gridlines.
11. Use the *Format* task pane to format each gridline group to use **Black, Text 1, Lighter 50%** (second column) as the line color.
12. Select the *Plot Area* and use the **Shape Fill** button to apply **Tan, Background 2** (third column).
13. Select the **Operations** sheet tab and create a waterfall chart object for cells **A3:B9**.
14. Position the waterfall chart object so that its top-left corner is at cell **A11**. Size the object to reach cell **I28**.
15. Select the ending balance marker and set it as a total.
16. Edit the chart title placeholder to CMP Operations Account.
17. Select the chart area and apply a **1 pt Black, Text 1** (second column) outline.
18. Click a worksheet cell and press **Ctrl+Home**.
19. Save and close the workbook (Figure 3-75).

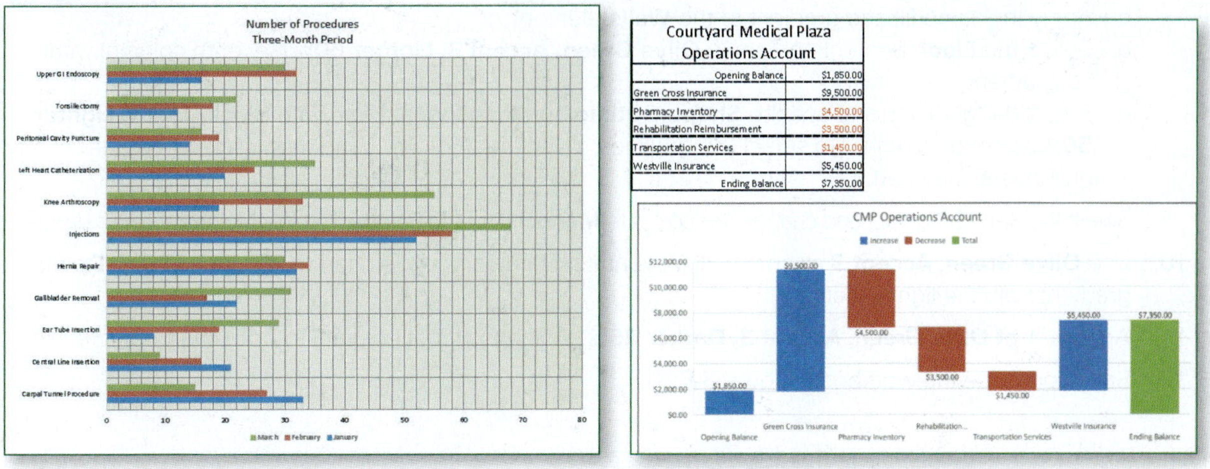

Figure 3-75 Excel 3-6 completed worksheet and charts

Improve It Project 3-7

Central Sierra Insurance is a multi-office company that handles commercial and personal insurance products. In this project, you add missing data and verify that the charts are updated.
[Student Learning Outcomes 3.2, 3.3, 3.4]

File Needed: ***CentralSierra-03.xlsx*** *(Student data files are available in the* Library *of your SIMnet account.)*
Completed Project File Name: ***[your initials] Excel 3-7.xlsx***

Skills Covered in This Project

- Edit source data.
- Switch row and column data.
- Change chart colors.
- Apply a chart style.
- Add and format elements in a chart.
- Use gradient fill for a chart object.
- Change the chart type.

1. Open the ***CentralSierra-03*** workbook from your student data files and save it as [your initials] Excel 3-7. Two chart objects display on the worksheet.
2. Insert a new row at row 8.
3. Type Motorcycle in cell **A8**. In cells **B8:D8**, type these values: 15, 82, and 24.
4. Change the pie chart object to a **3-D Pie** and apply **Style 3**. Notice that a data series for "Motorcycle" has been added.
5. Switch the row and column data for the column chart. The data series for "Motorcycle" is not included.
6. Click the **Select Data** button [*Chart Tools Design* tab, *Data* group] and reset the source data to show cells **A5:D10**.
7. Change the column chart color scheme to **Monochromatic Palette 7** in the *Monochromatic* list.
8. Format chart elements.
   a. Select the **Side Wall** of the column chart and apply **Olive Green, Accent 3** shape fill (seventh column).
   b. Use the **Shape Fill** button to apply the **Linear Down** gradient in the *Light Variations* group to the side wall.

c. Apply the same fill and gradient to the **Walls** element.
d. Select the **Floor** element and apply **Olive Green, Accent 3, Lighter 60%** (seventh column) with no gradient.
e. Select the gridlines and use the **Shape Outline** button to format them with **Black, Text 1, Lighter 50%** (second column). (To select the gridlines, select the *Plot Area* and then click one of the gridlines in the chart.)

9. Select the pie chart object and change the colors to **Monochromatic Palette 7** in the *Monochromatic* group.
10. Use **Olive Green, Accent 3** as shape fill (seventh column) for the pie chart area with a **Linear Down** gradient from the light variations.
11. Apply a **1 pt Olive Green, Accent 3, Darker 25%** outline (seventh column) to both chart objects.
12. Save and close the workbook (Figure 3-76).

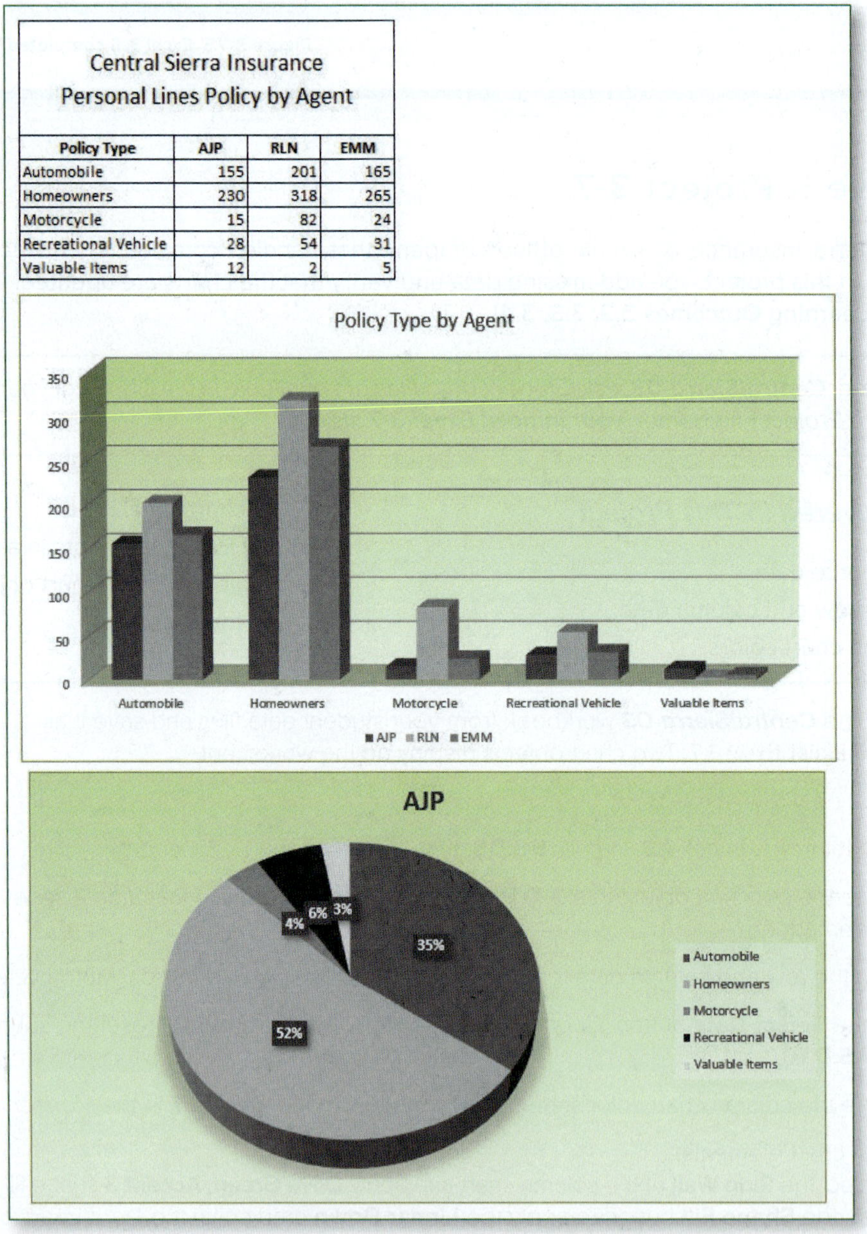

Central Sierra Insurance
Personal Lines Policy by Agent

Policy Type	AJP	RLN	EMM
Automobile	155	201	165
Homeowners	230	318	265
Motorcycle	15	82	24
Recreational Vehicle	28	54	31
Valuable Items	12	2	5

Figure 3-76 Excel 3-7 completed worksheet with charts

Challenge Project 3-8

For this project, you build a worksheet that displays data from three departments in a supermarket. Each department has one or more subgroups, and each subgroup lists one or more items. From this hierarchical data, you create a TreeMap chart.
[Student Learning Outcomes 3.1, 3.2, 3.3, 3.4, 3.7]

File Needed: None
Completed Project File Name: ***[your initials] Excel 3-8.xlsx***

Create a new workbook and save it as [your initials] Excel 3-8. Modify your workbook according to the following guidelines:

- Type Grocery in cell **A2** as a general category in the supermarket. In cell **B2**, type Coffee as a product subgroup. In cells **C2:C3**, type Ground and Whole Bean as further divisions of the coffee subgroup.
- Type Pasta in cell **B4**. In cells **C4:C5**, type the names of two types of pasta (spaghetti, rotini, vermicelli, bucatini, rigatoni, etc.).
- Type the name of another category of items in the supermarket in cell **B6**. Then in cells **C6:C7**, type the names of two products in the category.
- Select cell **A8** and type Produce. In cell **B8**, type Apples. In cells **C8:C9**, type the names of two varieties of apples.
- Complete another subgroup for the *Produce* category in cells **B10:C11**.
- Type a value for each item in column **D** that represents the number of items or dollars.
- Select the data and create a *TreeMap* hierarchy chart on its own sheet.
- Edit the chart title and apply a chart style.
- Insert two rows at row **8** and create a "Dairy" grouping for the supermarket and note how the *TreeMap* is adjusted.

Challenge Project 3-9

For this project, you create a worksheet and accompanying charts to track daily usage of your smartphone, tablet, or other device.
[Student Learning Outcomes 3.1, 3.2, 3.3, 3.4, 3.5]

File Needed: None
Completed Project File Name: ***[your initials] Excel 3-9.xlsx***

Create a new workbook and save it as [your initials] Excel 3-9. Modify your workbook according to the following guidelines:

- Enter the days of the week as column headings, starting in cell **B2**.
- Create row headings starting in cell **A3** by typing the names of five daily tasks or activities for your device. Examples are "Send text," "Receive phone call," "Use GPS," "View video," or similar tasks.
- Enter a value for the number of times you perform each task on each day.

- Type a main title for your data in row 1. Format your data.
- Create a column chart object that compares the number of times for each task on Monday.
- Size and position the chart object below the worksheet data.
- Change the layout or apply a chart style.
- Edit the chart title placeholder to display an appropriate title.
- Format chart elements to create an attractive, easy-to-understand chart of your data.
- Determine the task with the greatest Monday value, and create another column chart that displays daily numbers for that one task.
- Size and position this chart object below the first chart.
- Format the second chart to complement the first chart.

Challenge Project 3-10

For this project, you create a worksheet with a column/line combo chart that compares air temperature and humidity level in your city or town for 10 days. You also insert a single sparkline in the data.
[Student Learning Outcomes 3.1, 3.2, 3.3, 3.4, 3.6, 3.8]

File Needed: None
Completed Project File Name: ***[your initials] Excel 3-10.xlsx***

Create a new workbook and save it as [your initials] Excel 3-10. Modify your workbook according to the following guidelines:

- Enter dates in cells **A4:A13** for each of the last 10 days or each of the next 10 days.
- Enter a recorded or predicted temperature in degrees for each date at 12 noon in column **B**. Use an online weather reference or a weather app.
- Enter corresponding humidity levels as percentages in column **C**. Use the same weather reference or make an estimate.
- Type a main title for the data, as well as column labels.
- Create a clustered column/line combo chart with a secondary axis for the percentages. Move the chart to its own sheet.
- Change the layout or apply a chart style.
- Edit and format the chart elements as needed.
- Select the range of temperature values in the worksheet as the data range for a line sparkline. As the location range, select cell **D14**. Format column **D** as **32.00 (229 pixels)** wide.
- Format the sparkline and adjust row heights to better display the data and the sparkline.

CHAPTER 4

Formatting, Organizing, and Getting Data

CHAPTER OVERVIEW

Excel can use data from many sources, as well as provide data to other programs. When data are shared among applications, the data are usually in a list or table layout similar to a database. This chapter covers how to format data as an Excel table, how to sort and filter data, how to import data from other sources, and how to build a *PivotTable*.

STUDENT LEARNING OUTCOMES (SLOs)

After completing this chapter, you will be able to:

SLO 4.1 Create and format a list as an Excel table (p. E4-222).

SLO 4.2 Apply *Conditional Formatting* rules, as well as *Color Scales*, *Icon Sets*, and *Data Bars* (p. E4-228).

SLO 4.3 Sort data by one or more columns or by attribute (p. E4-235).

SLO 4.4 Filter data by using *AutoFilters* and by creating an *Advanced Filter* (p. E4-238).

SLO 4.5 Use subtotals, groups, and outlines for tabular data in a worksheet (p. E4-242).

SLO 4.6 Import data into an Excel worksheet from a text file, a database file, and other sources (p. E4-248).

SLO 4.7 Export Excel data as a text file and into a Word document (p. E4-254).

SLO 4.8 Build and format a *PivotTable* (p. E4-259).

CASE STUDY

For the Pause & Practice projects in this chapter, you create worksheets for Paradise Lakes Resort. To complete the work, you format a list as an Excel table, sort and filter data, import and clean data, and create a PivotTable.

Pause & Practice 4-1: Format data as an Excel table and set conditional formatting.

Pause & Practice 4-2: Sort, filter, and subtotal data.

Pause & Practice 4-3: Import and *Flash Fill* data in a workbook.

Pause & Practice 4-4: Create and format a *PivotTable* and a *PivotChart*.

EXCEL

SLO 4.1

Creating and Formatting an Excel Table

An Excel ***table*** is a list of related pieces of information that is formatted with a title row followed by rows of data (Figure 4-1). When data are in a table format, you can organize, sort, filter, and calculate results easily and quickly, much like a database.

The ***header row*** is the first row of a table with descriptive titles or labels. Each row of data is a ***record*** and each column is a ***field***. The label in the header row is sometimes referred to as the ***field name***. When you format Excel data as a table, follow these guidelines to optimize your tables for use of Excel commands:

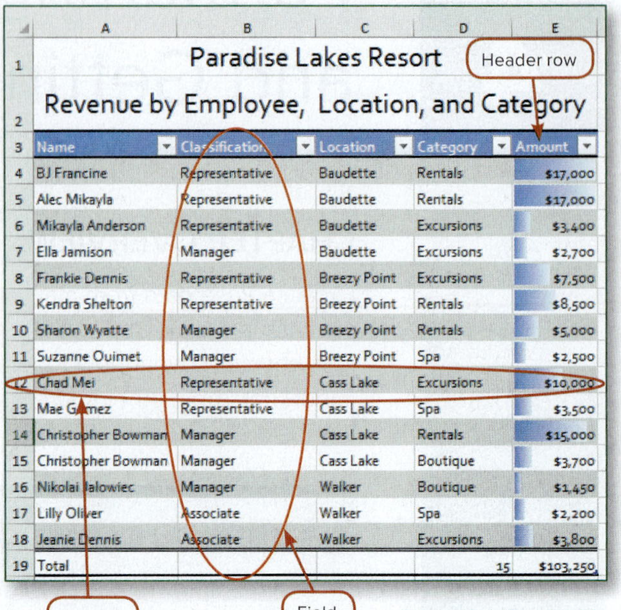

Figure 4-1 Excel table

- Type descriptive labels in the first row and begin each label with a letter, not a number.
- Assign each header a unique label; do not repeat any of the descriptive labels.
- Keep the same type of data within each column (text or values).
- Do not leave blank rows within the data.
- Keep the table separate from other data on the worksheet.

Create an Excel Table

When data are arranged as a list and conform to the guidelines just described, a simple format command creates an Excel table. Select the data and click the **Format as Table** button in the *Styles* group on the *Home* tab to open the *Table Styles* gallery. Choose a style and click **OK** in the *Format as Table* dialog box. A second way to create an Excel table is to select the data and click the **Table** button in the *Tables* group on the *Insert* tab. The *Format as Table* dialog box opens and creates the table with a default style.

After your data are formatted as a table, each label in the header row displays an ***AutoFilter*** arrow, and the contextual *Table Tools Design* tab opens with command groups for modifying the table. Recall from chapter 3 that a filter is criteria that determine which data are shown and which are hidden. From *AutoFilter* arrows, you can show records for employees in a particular location or display revenue from certain months.

> **MORE INFO**
>
> *AutoFilter* arrows replace the worksheet column headings (A, B, C, and so on) when you scroll down in a table with many records. *AutoFilter* arrows do not print.

HOW TO: Create an Excel Table

1. Select the cells to be formatted as a table.
   - Include the header row with column titles.
2. Click the **Format as Table** button [*Home* tab, *Styles* group] to open the table gallery.
   - Table styles are organized in light, medium, and dark categories.

3. Click a table style.
   - Apply a different style after the table is created (Figure 4-2).

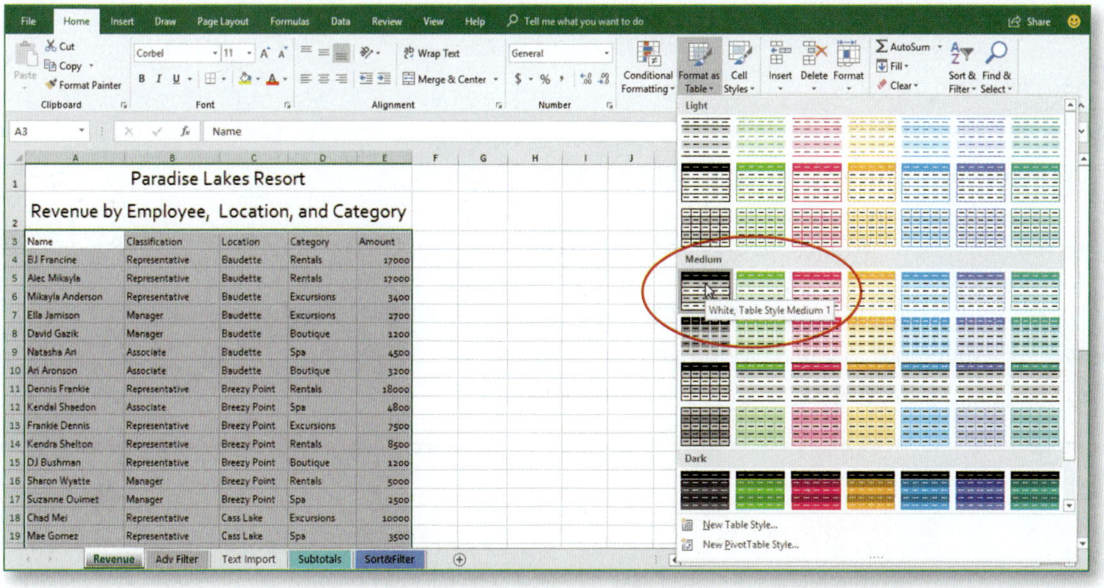

Figure 4-2 *Table Styles* gallery and selected data

4. Confirm the cell range in the *Format As Table* dialog box.
   - Drag to select a different range if necessary.
5. Select the **My table has headers** box in the *Format As Table* dialog box.
   - When the selected range does not have column titles, Excel inserts a row above the data with the labels *Column1*, *Column2*, and so on. You can edit these names.
6. Click **OK**.
   - When the selected range includes data from an outside source, you will see a message box asking to remove the data connection. Click **Yes** to create the table (Figure 4-3).

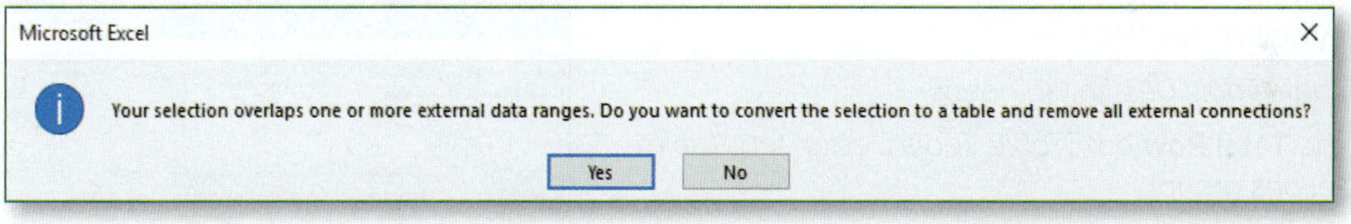

Figure 4-3 Message box for data from an outside source

ANOTHER WAY

Select the header and data rows, click the **Quick Analysis** tool, and choose **Tables**. Then, click the **Table** button to format the data in a default table style. This method is not available for data from an outside source.

Table Styles and Options

A ***table style*** is a predesigned set of format settings with a color scheme, alternating fill for rows and columns, vertical and horizontal borders, and more. You select a style when you create a table from the **Format as Table** button, or apply a different style at any time. Predefined table styles are classified as *Light*, *Medium*, and *Dark* and use colors based on the workbook theme. Remove a style by selecting *None* in the *Light* group.

HOW TO: Apply a Table Style

1. Click any cell within the table.
    - The *Table Tools Design* tab displays.
2. Click the **More** button [*Table Tools Design* tab, *Table Styles* group].
    - The *Table Styles* gallery opens.
    - Styles are named *ColorName, Table Style Light 1*; *ColorName*, *Table Style Medium 4*; *ColorName, Table Style Dark 8*, and so on.
    - The *None* style is the first icon in the *Light* group when an existing style is already applied.
3. Point to a style thumbnail to see a *Live Preview* in the table.
4. Click to select and apply a style.

MORE INFO

Create and save a custom table style by clicking the **More** button in the *Table Styles* group [*Table Tools Design* tab] and choosing **New Table Style**.

The *Table Style Options* group on the *Table Tools Design* tab includes commands for showing or hiding various parts of the table such as the header row or a total row. When you select a total row, a blank row inserts as the last row, and you can choose which calculation displays in each column. Other options are banded columns or rows, which alternate fills or borders. A command to apply bold to data in the first or last column or both is available. You can also hide the *AutoFilter* arrows.

HOW TO: Display a Total Row in a Table

1. Click any cell within the table.
    - The *Table Tools Design* tab opens.
2. Select the **Total Row** box [*Table Tools Design* tab, *Table Style Options* group].
    - The total row displays as the last row in the table.
3. Click a cell in the total row and click its arrow to open the calculation list.
    - The default calculation is *Sum* for numeric data.
4. Choose the calculation for the column (Figure 4-4).
    - Use *Count* for alphanumeric columns.

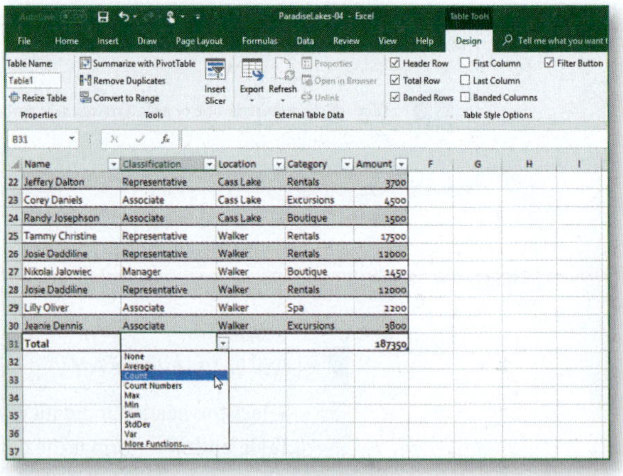

Figure 4-4 Table with total row

MORE INFO

Custom Views [*View* tab, *Workbook Views* group] are not available in an Excel table.

The Table Tools and Properties Groups

The *Tools* group on the *Table Tools Design* tab includes commands to remove duplicate records and to convert the table to a regular cell range. The *Insert Slicer* command opens a filter window for hiding or showing records in the table. The *Properties* group includes the table name and a command to resize the table.

A ***duplicate row*** is a record in a table that has exactly the same information in one or more columns. The *Remove Duplicates* command scans a table to locate and delete rows with repeated data in the specified columns. In the *Remove Duplicates* dialog box, you set which columns might have duplicate data. If you check all the columns, a row must have the same data in every column as another row.

HOW TO: Remove Duplicates

1. Click any cell within the table.
2. Click the **Remove Duplicates** button [*Table Tools Design* tab, *Tools* group] (Figure 4-5).
3. Select the box for each column that might have duplicate data.
   - Click **Unselect All** to remove all checkmarks and select a single label.
   - Excel recognizes headers and does not scan them for duplicate content.
4. Click **OK**.
   - A message box indicates how many duplicate values were removed and how many unique values remain.
5. Click **OK**.
   - The rows are removed from the table.
   - The command does not preview which rows are deleted.
   - **Undo** this command if needed.

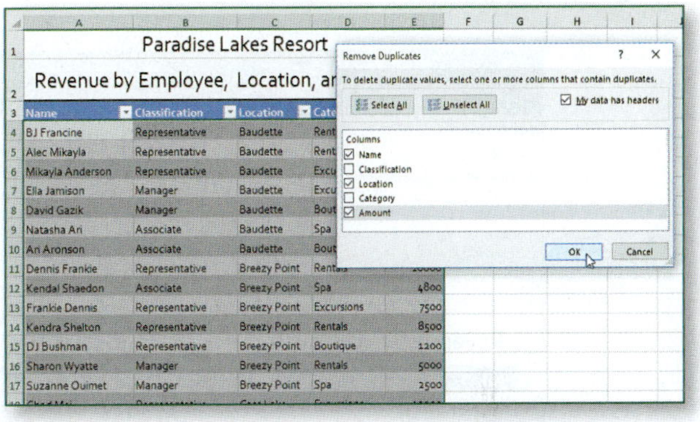

Figure 4-5 *Remove Duplicates* dialog box

The *Insert Slicer* command opens a floating window that is used as a visual filter, enabling you to work with smaller pieces of large datasets. If a table has 10,000 records but you are concerned with one location or category, insert a slicer to control which records display in the table. A *Slicer* window is an object that can be sized and positioned, and it displays selection handles like other objects. The contextual *Slicer Tools Options* tab is available when a slicer object is active with settings to customize the floating window.

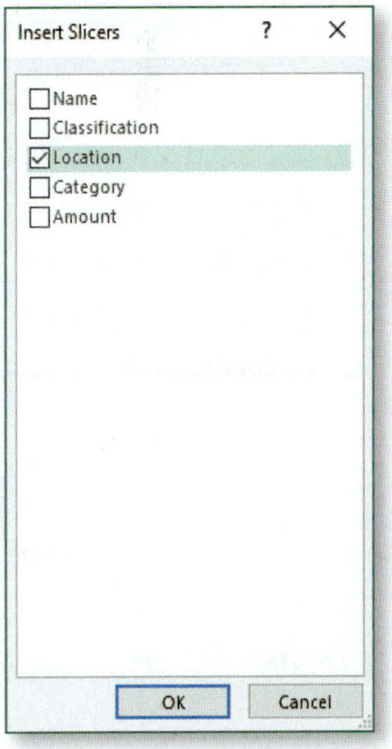

Figure 4-6 *Insert Slicers* dialog box

HOW TO: Insert a Slicer

1. Click any cell within the table.
2. Click the **Insert Slicer** button [*Table Tools Design* tab, *Tools* group].
   - The *Insert Slicers* dialog box lists all field names in the table.
3. Select the box for the field to be used for filtering (Figure 4-6).
   - You can select more than one field to open multiple slicers.

4. Click **OK**.
   - The *Slicer* window is a graphic object and can be selected.
   - All records display in the table.
5. Click an item name to filter the data.
   - The records are filtered.
   - You can press **Ctrl** and click another item to apply more than one filter.
   - You can toggle the **Multi-Select** button in the *Slicer* title bar and then click to turn off multiple items for filtering.
6. Click the **Clear Filter** button in the *Slicer* title bar.
   - All the records display.
7. Click the **More** button [*Slicer Tools Options* tab, *Slicer Styles* group].
8. Select a style for the *Slicer*.
9. Click the **Columns** spinner button [*Slicer Tools Options* tab, *Buttons* group] to set the number of columns in the *Slicer* (Figure 4-7).

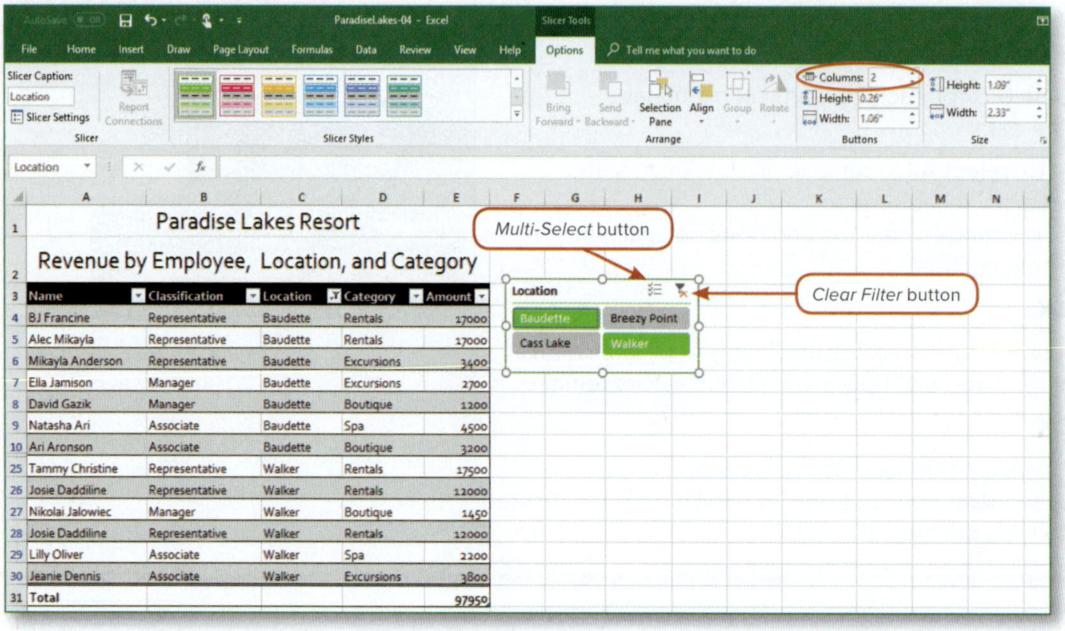

Figure 4-7 ***Slicer*** **window for a table**

10. Click and drag a corner selection handle to resize the *Slicer*.
    - Set a specific size in the *Size* group [*Slicer Tools Options* tab].
11. Press **Delete** to remove the *Slicer* window.
    - The *Slicer* window must be selected to be deleted.

The *Convert to Range* command removes table formatting and options except for font style and fill colors. You may need to convert a table to a range when combining data from different sources or when sharing data with applications that require unformatted data.

HOW TO: Convert a Table to a Range

1. Click any cell within the table.
2. Click the **Convert to Range** button [*Table Tools Design* tab, *Tools* group] (Figure 4-8).

3. Click **Yes** in the message box.
   - The data display as a regular range of cells.
   - Font size, font style, and colors remain.
   - Format the data as needed.

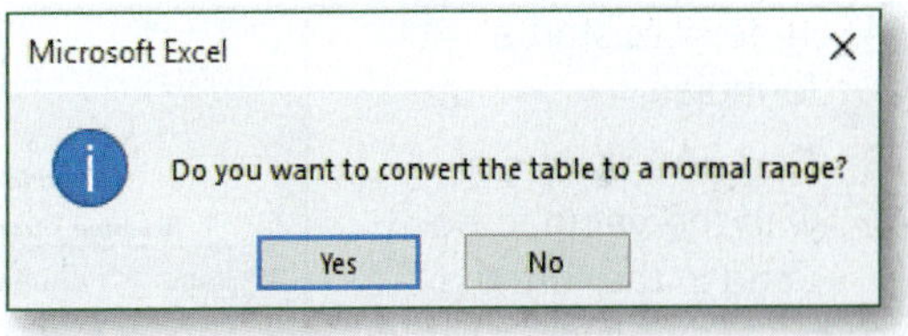

Figure 4-8 ***Convert to Normal Range*** **message box**

MORE INFO

If a normal data range has a header row, show *AutoFilter* arrows by clicking the **Filter** button on the *Data* tab.

Tables are named automatically as *TableN* where *N* is a number. To change the name to a more descriptive label, click the *Table Name* box in the *Properties* group on the *Table Tools Design* tab and type the name. Do not use spaces in a table name, and table names in a workbook must be unique. From the *Properties* group, you can also open the *Resize Table* dialog box to select an expanded or reduced cell range for the table. A table also has a resize arrow in its bottom right cell that you drag to grow or shrink the table. Tables grow automatically when you press **Tab** after the last item in the last row to start a new record.

Structured References and Table Formulas

In addition to the table name, each column is assigned a name using the label in its header row. The column name with its table name is known as a ***structured reference***. An example is *Table1[Category]* as the reference for the category column in *Table1*. Column names are enclosed in square brackets. In addition to column names, specific table item names are *#All*, *#Data*, *#Headers*, *#This Row*, and *#Totals*, each preceded by the # symbol as an identifier.

Structured references are supplied automatically in formulas, making it easy to identify what is being calculated. When you point to build a formula, you will see [*@ColumnName*] as the reference, with @ inserted as an identifier (Figure 4-9). The table name and structured reference names appear in *Formula AutoComplete* lists, and you can refer to those ranges in formulas outside the table. As you work with structured references, expand the *Formula* bar to better see a lengthy formula. The *Expand/Collapse Formula Bar* button is on the right edge of the *Formula* bar.

MORE INFO

To enter cell references in a table formula instead of structured references, disable **Use table names in formulas** in Excel *Options* [*File* tab, *Options*, *Formulas* pane].

Tables are automatically expanded to include a new column when you type a label adjacent to the last row heading. As part of its *Table AutoExpansion* feature, Excel copies a formula to complete a column with a calculation.

HOW TO: Add a Calculation Column in a Table

1. Select the cell to the right of the last column heading in the table.
   - The data must be formatted as an Excel table.
2. Type the new column label and press **Enter**.
   - A column is added to the table.
3. Select the cell below the new label.

4. Type = to start a formula.
5. Click the table cell with the value to be used in the formula.
   - The column name in square brackets preceded by an @ symbol is inserted.
6. Complete the formula (Figure 4-9).
   - You can refer to non-table cells in the worksheet or type a constant.
7. Press **Enter**.
   - The formula is copied down the entire column.
   - Enter the formula in any row in the column for it to be copied.

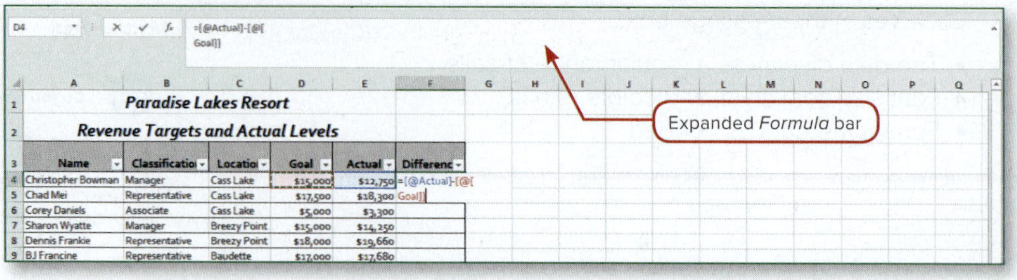

=[@Actual]-[@[Goal]]
Paradise Lakes Resort
Revenue Targets and Actual Levels
Name
Classification
Location
Goal
Actual
Difference
Christopher Bowman
Manager
Cass Lake
$15,000
$12,750
=[@Actual]-[@[Goal]]
Chad Mei
Representative
Cass Lake
$17,500
$18,300
Corey Daniels
Associate
Cass Lake
$5,000
$3,300
Sharon Wyatte
Manager
Breezy Point
$15,000
$14,250
Dennis Frankie
Representative
Breezy Point
$18,000
$19,660
BJ Francine
Representative
Baudette
$17,000
$17,680
Expanded Formula bar

Figure 4-9 Structured references in a table

MORE INFO

Disable automatic copying of table formulas in the *AutoCorrect Options, AutoFormat As You Type* tab [*File* tab, *Options*, *Proofing* pane].

SLO 4.2

Applying Conditional Formatting

Conditional formatting commands apply formats to cells only when the cells meet the criteria. For example, use conditional formatting to display revenue amounts below a certain level in a bold red font. Conditional formatting is dynamic; the formatting adapts if the data change.

Basic conditional formatting commands are *Highlight Cells Rules* and *Top/Bottom Rules*. For these commands, you set the rule or criteria in a dialog box and choose the format. Another type of conditional formatting is ***data visualization***, in which the cell displays a fill color, a horizontal bar, or an icon.

Highlight Cells Rules

Highlight Cells Rules use relational or comparison operators to determine if the value or label should be formatted. *Highlight Cells Rules* include common operators such as *Equal To* and *Greater Than*. You can also create your own rule using other operators or a formula.

Access all of the conditional formatting options from the *Conditional Formatting* button in the *Styles* group on the *Home* tab (Figure 4-10). You can also choose a default conditional formatting rule from the *Quick Analysis* tool options.

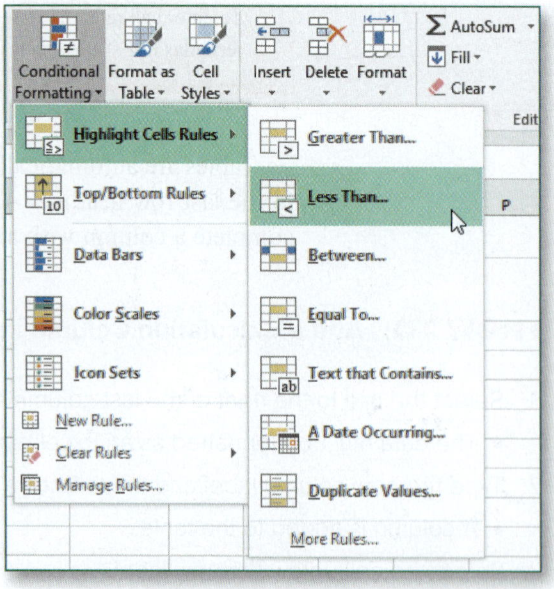

Figure 4-10 *Highlight Cells Rules* menu

▶HOW TO: Create a "Less Than" Highlight Cells Rule

1. Select the cell range.
2. Click the **Conditional Formatting** button [*Home* tab, *Styles* group].
3. Select **Highlight Cells Rules** and select **Less Than**.
   - The *Less Than* dialog box opens.
4. Type a value in the *Format cells that are LESS THAN* box.
   - *Live Preview* applies the default format to cells that meet the criteria.
5. Click the arrow for the *with* box.
   - A list of preset formats displays.
6. Choose a format (Figure 4-11).
   - Choose *Custom Format* to open the *Format Cells* dialog box and build a format.
7. Click **OK**.
   - Formatting is applied to cells that meet the criteria.
   - Click a cell away from the range to better see the formatting.

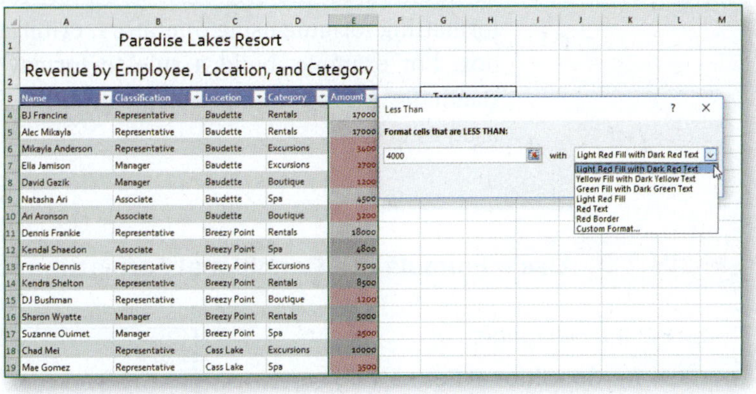

Figure 4-11 ***Less Than* dialog box**

Top/Bottom Rules

Top/Bottom Rules use ranking to format the highest (top) or lowest (bottom) items, either by number or percentage. You set the number or percentage in the dialog box as well as the format. You can also set a rule to format values that are above or below average (Figure 4-12).

For a selected range, the *Formatting* group in the *Quick Analysis* tool provides the most likely conditional formatting choices.

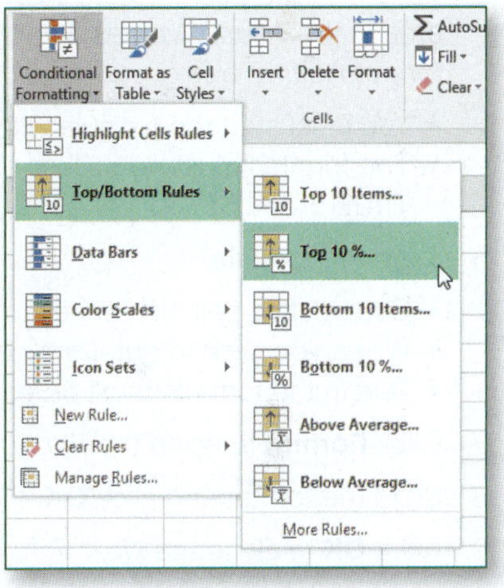

Figure 4-12 ***Top/Bottom Rules***

▶HOW TO: Create a Top 10% Rule

1. Select the cell range.
   - The *Quick Analysis* button appears in the bottom right cell of the range.
2. Click the **Quick Analysis** button.
3. Choose **Formatting**.
   - Commonly used conditional format choices are listed.
4. Choose **Top 10%** (Figure 4-13).
   - The number of cells equal to the *Top 10%* of the number of cells in the column are formatted with a default format.
   - Edit the format to use different attributes.

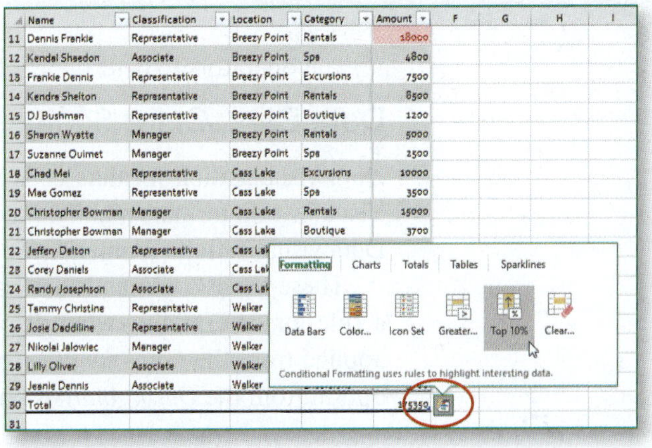

Figure 4-13 ***Quick Analysis* options for conditional formatting**

Use a Formula for a Rule

In addition to the *Highlight Cells* or *Top/Bottom* rules, you can create a conditional formatting formula using operators, criteria, and settings in the *New Formatting Rule* dialog box. For example, build a rule to format cells in the amount column if the location is Baudette. A formula must result in either TRUE or FALSE (a Yes or No question) to be used as criteria.

HOW TO: Use a Formula in a Conditional Formatting Rule

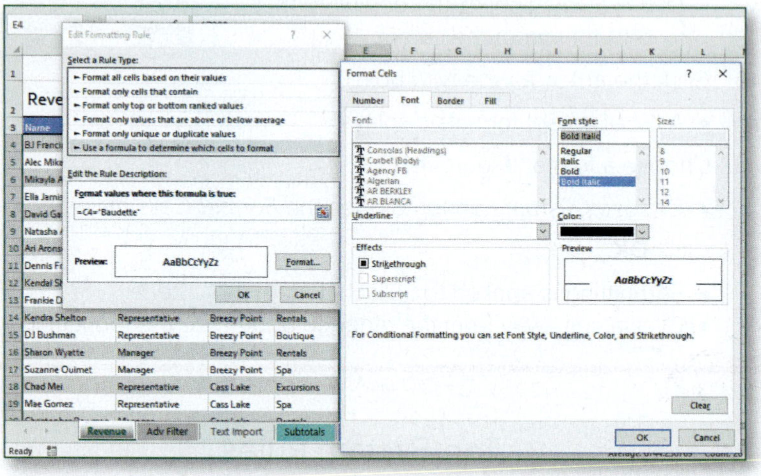

Figure 4-14 *New Formatting Rule* and *Format Cells* dialog boxes

1. Select the cell range.
2. Click the **Conditional Formatting** button [*Home* tab, *Styles* group].
3. Select **New Rule**.
   - The *New Formatting Rule* dialog box opens.
   - The choices in the dialog box update based on the rule type.
4. Choose **Use a formula to determine which cells to format** in the *Select a Rule Type* list.
5. Type = in the *Edit the Rule Description* area in the *Format values where this formula is true* box.
   - You must start the formula with an equals sign (=).
   - The formula must be built so that the result is either TRUE or FALSE.
6. Type the formula.
   - Use relative cell references to the first row of data (Figure 4-14).
   - When you click to enter the cell reference, it is absolute; press **F4 (FN+F4)** to change it to relative.
   - Text in the formula must be enclosed in quotation marks.
7. Click **Format** to open the *Format Cells* dialog box.
8. Build the format and click **OK**.
9. Click **OK** to close the *New Formatting Rule* dialog box.
   - Cells that meet the formula condition are formatted.

Data Bars, Color Scales, and Icon Sets

Data visualization formats cells with icons, fill color, or shaded bars to distinguish values. Visualization formats highlight low, middle, or top values or compare the values to each other. Data visualization commands are *Data Bars*, *Color Scales*, and *Icon Sets*.

These three commands are part of the conditional formatting group, because they apply a rule for determining what displays in the cell. You can choose which colors or icons are applied from the *Conditional Formatting* button [*Home* tab, *Styles* group]. When you select an option from the *Quick Analysis* button, however, a default choice is applied.

▶HOW TO: Format Data with Data Bars

1. Select the cell range.
2. Click the **Quick Analysis** button.
3. Choose **Formatting**.
   - *Data Bars* compare the value in each cell to the other values in the range by the length of the bar.
   - *Color Scales* use a variation of two or three colors to indicate low, middle, and high values.
   - *Icon Sets* insert icons that represent the upper, middle, or lower values of the cell range.
4. Choose **Data Bars** (Figure 4-15).
   - A default data bar style and color is applied.

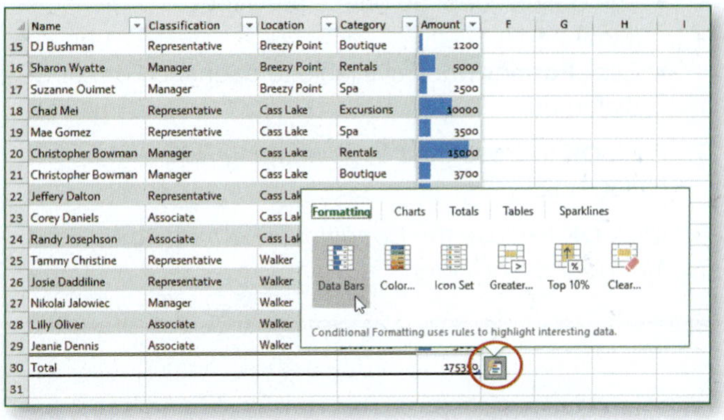

Figure 4-15 Setting *Data Bars* from the *Quick Analysis* button

Manage Conditional Formatting Rules

You can edit any conditional formatting rule, including data visualization commands, from the *Conditional Formatting Rules Manager* dialog box. From this dialog box, you can reset the range to be formatted, change the actual format, change the rule, or delete the rule.

If you select the formatted range before you start the *Manage Rules* command, the rule for that selection displays in the *Conditional Formatting Rules Manager* dialog box. You can also show all the rules in the current sheet or another one (Figure 4-16).

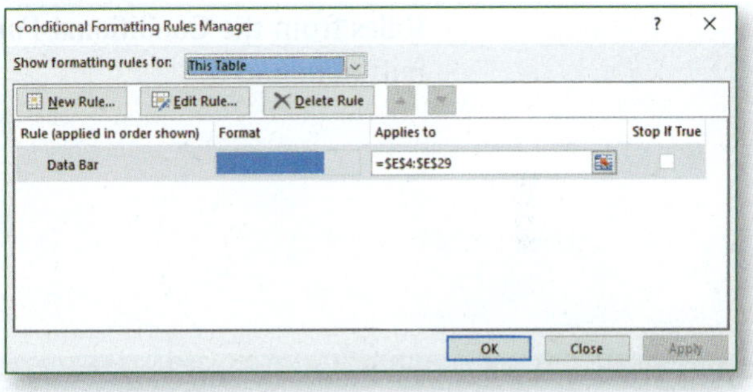

Figure 4-16 *Conditional Formatting Rules Manager* dialog box

When you click **Edit Rule**, the *Edit Formatting Rule* dialog box opens. This dialog box is similar to the *New Formatting Rule* dialog box, and you set options the same way.

▶HOW TO: Manage Conditional Formatting Rules

1. Select the formatted cell range.
2. Click the **Conditional Formatting** button [*Home* tab, *Styles* group].
3. Choose **Manage Rules**.
   - *Current Selection* is listed in the *Show formatting rules for* box.
   - Choose **This Worksheet** to list all rules in the worksheet.
4. Select the rule name to be modified.
5. Select **Edit Rule**.
   - The *Edit Formatting Rule* dialog box opens.
   - The current *Rule Description* displays.
   - You can select another rule type in the top half of the dialog box.

6. Select options to change the rule in the *Edit the Rule Description* area.
   - The options depend on the rule type (Figure 4-17).
   - Click **Format** when available to open the *Format Cells* dialog box.
7. Click **OK** to close the *Edit Formatting Rule* dialog box.
8. Click **OK** to close the *Conditional Formatting Rules Manager* dialog box.

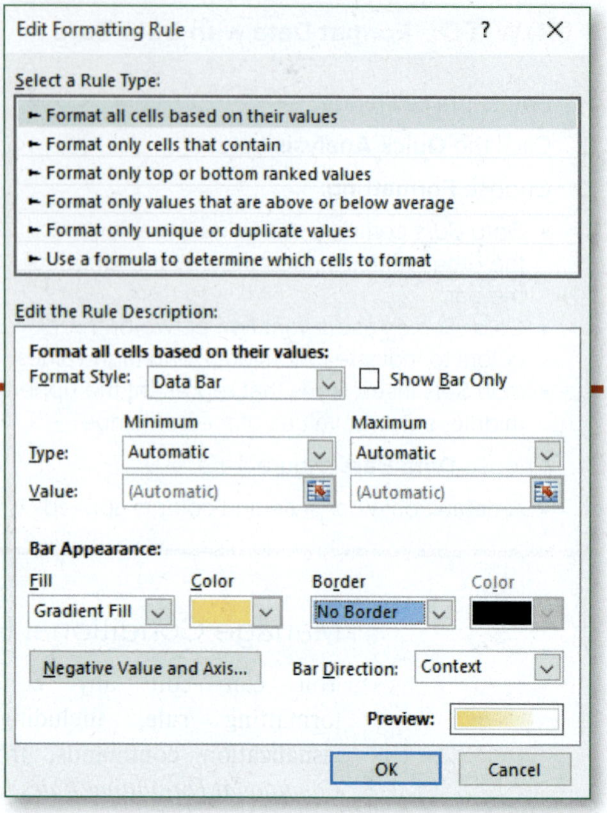

Figure 4-17 ***Edit Formatting Rule*** **dialog box for data bars**

You can clear conditional formatting from a selected range or from the entire sheet. For a selected range, click the **Quick Analysis** button and choose **Clear...** You can also choose **Clear Rules** from the **Conditional Formatting** button menu.

PAUSE & PRACTICE: EXCEL 4-1

For this project, you format data as a table, add a total row, and remove duplicate records. As you complete formulas on the sheet, you see structured references. You also set conditional formatting with data bars.

File Needed: ***ParadiseLakes-04.xlsx*** *(Student data files are available in the* Library *of your SIMnet account.)*
Completed Project File Name: ***[your initials] PP E4-1.xlsx***

1. Open the ***ParadiseLakes-04*** workbook from your student data files and save it as [your initials] PP E4-1.
2. Click the **Revenue** sheet tab.
3. Format data as an Excel table.
   a. Select cells **A3:E30**.
   b. Click the **Format as Table** button [*Home* tab, *Styles* group].
   c. Select **Periwinkle, Table Style Medium 20** from the gallery (third row in the group).
   d. Verify that the **My table has headers** box is selected in the *Format As Table* dialog box.
   e. Click **OK**.

4. Add a total row to a table.
   a. Click a cell within the table.
   b. Select the **Total Row** box [*Table Tools Design* tab, *Table Style Options* group].
   c. Click cell **D31** and choose **Count** from the drop-down list.
   d. Select the amounts in cells **E4:E31** and format them as **Currency**. Decrease the decimal two times to show zero decimal places (Figure 4-18).

5. Remove duplicate rows in a table.
   a. Click a cell within the table.
   b. Click the **Remove Duplicates** button [*Table Tools Design* tab, *Tools* group].
   c. Click **Unselect All** to deselect all the boxes.
   d. Select the **Name** box and the **Amount** box. When you look for duplicate data in specific columns, you can speed up search activities.
   e. Click **OK** in the *Remove Duplicates* dialog box. One record will be removed, the one for Josie Daddiline. The records for Christopher Bowman are not duplicated in the selected columns.
   f. Click **OK** in the message box.

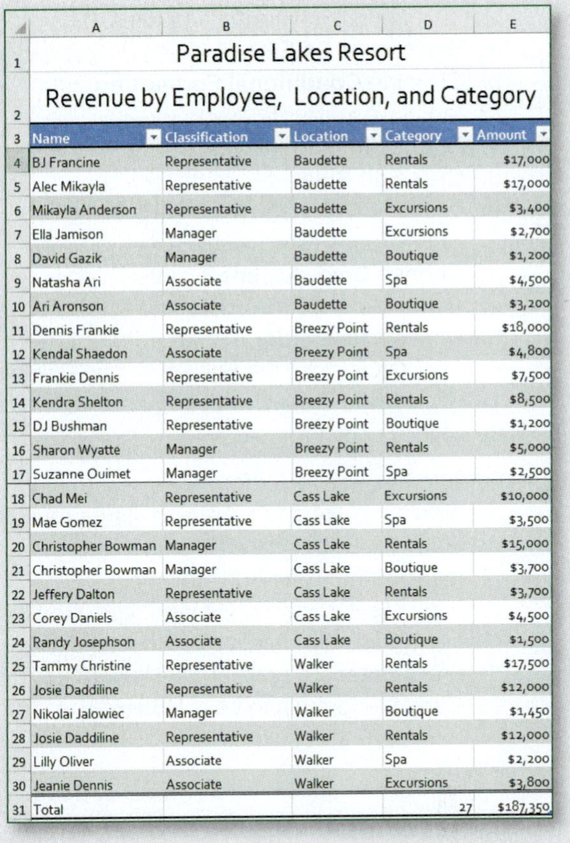

	A	B	C	D	E
1	Paradise Lakes Resort				
2	Revenue by Employee, Location, and Category				
3	Name	Classification	Location	Category	Amount
4	BJ Francine	Representative	Baudette	Rentals	$17,000
5	Alec Mikayla	Representative	Baudette	Rentals	$17,000
6	Mikayla Anderson	Representative	Baudette	Excursions	$3,400
7	Ella Jamison	Manager	Baudette	Excursions	$2,700
8	David Gazik	Manager	Baudette	Boutique	$1,200
9	Natasha Ari	Associate	Baudette	Spa	$4,500
10	Ari Aronson	Associate	Baudette	Boutique	$3,200
11	Dennis Frankie	Representative	Breezy Point	Rentals	$18,000
12	Kendal Shaedon	Associate	Breezy Point	Spa	$4,800
13	Frankie Dennis	Representative	Breezy Point	Excursions	$7,500
14	Kendra Shelton	Representative	Breezy Point	Rentals	$8,500
15	DJ Bushman	Representative	Breezy Point	Boutique	$1,200
16	Sharon Wyatte	Manager	Breezy Point	Rentals	$5,000
17	Suzanne Ouimet	Manager	Breezy Point	Spa	$2,500
18	Chad Mei	Representative	Cass Lake	Excursions	$10,000
19	Mae Gomez	Representative	Cass Lake	Spa	$3,500
20	Christopher Bowman	Manager	Cass Lake	Rentals	$15,000
21	Christopher Bowman	Manager	Cass Lake	Boutique	$3,700
22	Jeffery Dalton	Representative	Cass Lake	Rentals	$3,700
23	Corey Daniels	Associate	Cass Lake	Excursions	$4,500
24	Randy Josephson	Associate	Cass Lake	Boutique	$1,500
25	Tammy Christine	Representative	Walker	Rentals	$17,500
26	Josie Daddiline	Representative	Walker	Rentals	$12,000
27	Nikolai Jalowiec	Manager	Walker	Boutique	$1,450
28	Josie Daddiline	Representative	Walker	Rentals	$12,000
29	Lilly Oliver	Associate	Walker	Spa	$2,200
30	Jeanie Dennis	Associate	Walker	Excursions	$3,800
31	Total			27	$187,350

Figure 4-18 Data formatted as a table

6. Apply conditional formatting using data bars.
   a. Select cells **E4:E29**.
   b. Click the **Conditional Formatting** button [*Home* tab, *Styles* group].
   c. Point to **Data Bars** to see its menu.
   d. Select **Blue Data Bar** in the *Gradient Fill* group (Figure 4-19).

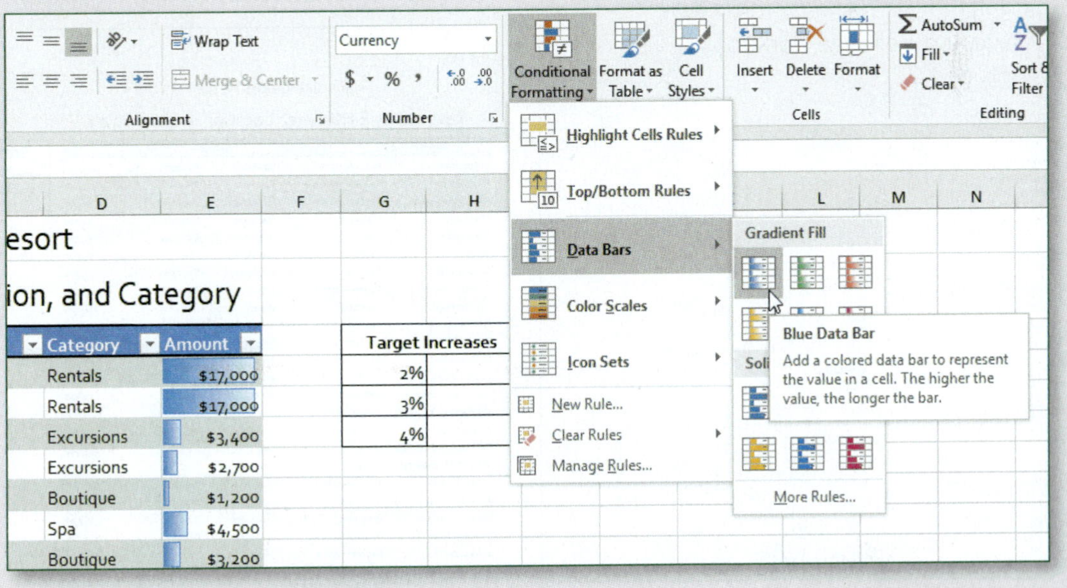

Figure 4-19 Choose a gradient fill for data bars

7. Manage conditional formatting rules.
   a. Select cells **E4:E29**.
   b. Click the **Conditional Formatting** button [*Home* tab, *Styles* group].
   c. Choose **Manage Rules**.
   d. Click **Edit Rule**.
   e. Click the **Color** arrow for **Fill** in the *Bar Appearance* area.
   f. Choose **Gold, Accent 3** (seventh column).
   g. Click the arrow for **Border** in the *Bar Appearance* area.
   h. Choose **No Border** (Figure 4-20).
   i. Click **OK** to close the *Edit Formatting Rule* dialog box.
   j. Click **OK** to close the *Conditional Formatting Rules Manager* dialog box.

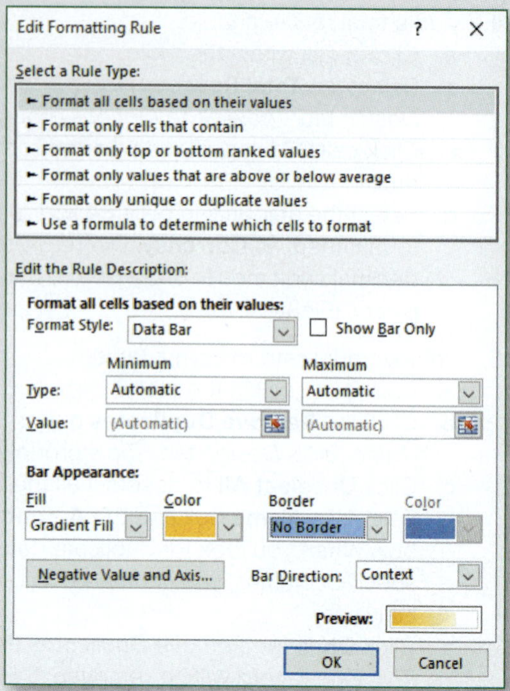

Figure 4-20 Edit the rule for data bars

8. Refer to a structured reference in a formula.
   a. Select cell **H4** and type = to start a formula.
   b. Click cell **E30** to insert a structured reference to the total in the Amount column.
   c. Type *(1+, click cell **G4**, and type) to calculate a new total that reflects a 2% increase (Figure 4-21).
   d. Press **Enter**. The target total is $178,857.
   e. Copy the formula to cells **H5:H6**. The structured reference is absolute.

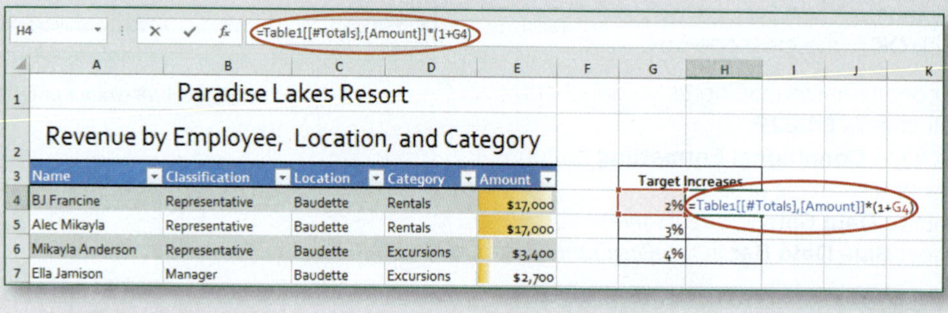

Figure 4-21 Structured reference in a formula

9. Save and close the workbook (Figure 4-22).

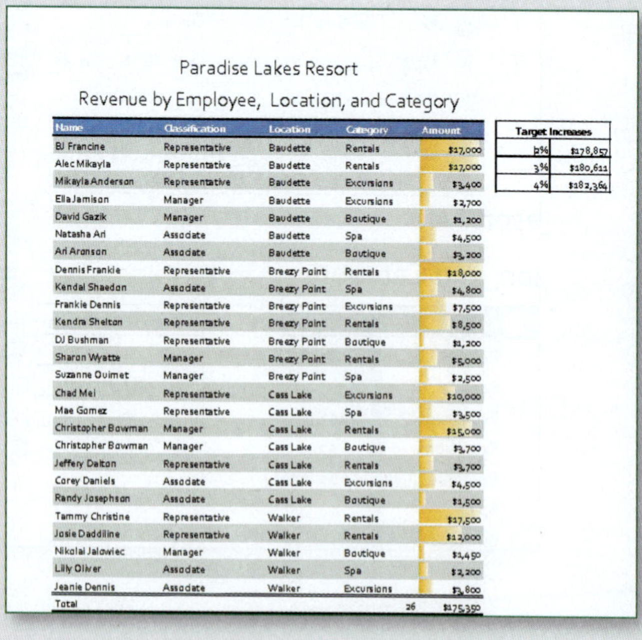

Paradise Lakes Resort

Revenue by Employee, Location, and Category

Name	Classification	Location	Category	Amount
BJ Francine	Representative	Baudette	Rentals	$17,000
Alec Mikayla	Representative	Baudette	Rentals	$17,000
Mikayla Anderson	Representative	Baudette	Excursions	$3,400
Ella Jamison	Manager	Baudette	Excursions	$2,700
David Gazik	Manager	Baudette	Boutique	$1,200
Natasha Ari	Associate	Baudette	Spa	$4,500
Ari Aronson	Associate	Baudette	Boutique	$3,200
Dennis Frankie	Representative	Breezy Point	Rentals	$18,000
Kendal Shaedon	Associate	Breezy Point	Spa	$4,800
Frankie Dennis	Representative	Breezy Point	Excursions	$7,500
Kendra Shelton	Representative	Breezy Point	Rentals	$8,500
DJ Bushman	Representative	Breezy Point	Boutique	$1,200
Sharon Wyatte	Manager	Breezy Point	Rentals	$5,000
Suzanne Ouimet	Manager	Breezy Point	Spa	$2,500
Chad Mei	Representative	Cass Lake	Excursions	$10,000
Mae Gomez	Representative	Cass Lake	Spa	$3,500
Christopher Bowman	Manager	Cass Lake	Rentals	$15,000
Christopher Bowman	Manager	Cass Lake	Boutique	$3,700
Jeffery Dalton	Representative	Cass Lake	Rentals	$3,700
Corey Daniels	Associate	Cass Lake	Excursions	$4,500
Randy Josephson	Associate	Cass Lake	Boutique	$1,500
Tammy Christine	Representative	Walker	Rentals	$17,500
Josie Daddiline	Representative	Walker	Rentals	$12,000
Nikolai Jalowiec	Manager	Walker	Boutique	$1,450
Lilly Oliver	Associate	Walker	Spa	$2,200
Jeanie Dennis	Associate	Walker	Excursions	$3,800
Total			26	$175,350

Target Increases	
2%	$178,857
3%	$180,611
4%	$182,364

Figure 4-22 PP E4-1 completed

Sorting Data

Sorting is the process of arranging rows of data in an identified order. For Paradise Lakes Resort, you can arrange the revenue table by classification to compare results for a particular job title or by highest to lowest amount.

Ascending order sorts data alphabetically from A to Z or numerically from the smallest to the largest value. In a ***descending*** sort, data are arranged alphabetically Z to A or numerically from the largest to the smallest value.

Sort Options

To be sorted, data must be organized in rows and columns like an Excel table, but it need not be formatted as a table. In addition to text or number sorting, you can sort data by fill color, font color, or cell icon from *Conditional Formatting*.

The *Sort & Filter* button on the *Home* tab in the *Editing* group lists *A to Z* sort, *Z to A* sort, and *Custom Sort* (multiple columns) commands. The same commands are available in the *Sort & Filter* group on the *Data* tab as separate buttons.

Sort Data by One Column

When data have a header row followed by rows of data with at least one empty row above and below the data, click any cell in the column you want to sort and choose a sort command. Excel recognizes and sorts the entire dataset.

Data to be sorted include text, numbers, or dates. Dates are treated as values. An ascending sort (smallest to largest) arranges dates so that the earliest date is first. A descending date sort organizes the data so that the most current date is first.

Undo a sort task by clicking the **Undo** button [*Quick Access* toolbar]. You can also sort data many times to arrange it in your preferred order.

▸HOW TO: Sort Data by a Single Column

1. Select a cell in the column to be used for sorting.
   - Click a cell with data, not the column header.
2. Click the **Sort A to Z** button [*Data* tab, *Sort & Filter* group] (Figure 4-23).
   - The records are arranged in alphabetical or smallest-to-largest order based on the first character in each cell in the column.
   - If the first character in an alphanumeric column is a value or special character, that record is sorted at the top.
3. Click the **Sort Z to A** button [*Data* tab, *Sort & Filter* group].
   - The records are arranged in reverse alphabetical or largest-to-smallest order based on the first character.
   - If the first character in an alphanumeric column is a value or special character, that record is sorted at the bottom.

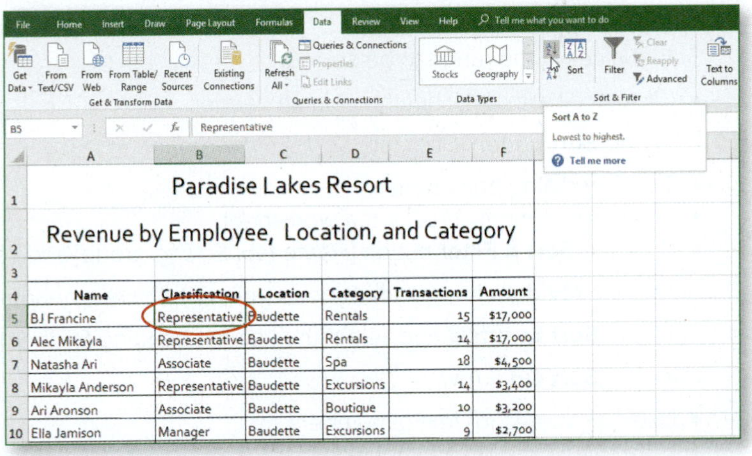

Figure 4-23 Cell B5 selected to sort by classification

ANOTHER WAY

To sort by a single column, right-click a cell in the column, choose **Sort**, and then choose the type of sort.

Sort Data by Multiple Columns

You can sort data by more than one column. An example of data that are often sorted by two columns is a list with cities in one column and states or provinces in another. Data can be sorted by state so that Alabama is before Arizona, and within Arizona, Phoenix is before Tuscon. When you use the *Sort & Filter* button [*Home* tab, *Editing* group] or a sort button on the *Data* tab, you sort first by the least important field. The least important field in a city and state sort is the city. Use the *Sort* dialog box which opens when you click the **Sort** button [*Data* tab, *Sort & Filter* group] or when you choose **Custom Sort** from the *Sort & Filter* button options.

The data in Figure 4-24 are sorted by two columns: classification and amount. *Classification* is the top or first sort level and *Amount* is second. When you use the *Sort* dialog box, sort by *Classification* first and then by *Amount*. When you use the *Sort & Filter* button, sort first by *Amount* and then by *Classification*.

	A	B	C	D	E	F
2	Revenue by Employee, Location, and Category					
3						
4	Name	Classification	Location	Category	Transactions	Amount
5	Randy Josephson	Associate	Cass Lake	Boutique	12	$1,500
6	Lilly Oliver	Associate	Walker	Spa	10	$2,200
7	Ari Aronson	Associate	Baudette	Boutique	10	$3,200
8	Jeanie Dennis	Associate	Walker	Excursions	8	$3,800
9	Natasha Ari	Associate	Baudette	Spa	18	$4,500
10	Corey Daniels	Associate	Cass Lake	Excursions	22	$4,500
11	Kendal Shaedon	Associate	Breezy Point	Spa	20	$4,800
12	David Gazik	Manager	Baudette	Boutique	6	$1,200
13	Nikolai Jalowiec	Manager	Walker	Boutique	6	$1,450
14	Suzanne Ouimet	Manager	Breezy Point	Spa	4	$2,500
15	Ella Jamison	Manager	Baudette	Excursions	9	$2,700
16	Christopher Bowman	Manager	Cass Lake	Boutique	15	$3,700
17	Sharon Wyatte	Manager	Breezy Point	Rentals	7	$5,000
18	Christopher Bowman	Manager	Cass Lake	Rentals	14	$15,000
19	DJ Bushman	Representative	Breezy Point	Boutique	5	$1,200
20	Mikayla Anderson	Representative	Baudette	Excursions	14	$3,400
21	Mae Gomez	Representative	Cass Lake	Spa	12	$3,500
22	Jeffery Dalton	Representative	Cass Lake	Rentals	5	$3,700
23	Frankie Dennis	Representative	Breezy Point	Excursions	16	$7,500
24	Kendra Shelton	Representative	Breezy Point	Rentals	10	$8,500

Figure 4-24 Data sorted by "Classification" and "Amount"

HOW TO: Sort Data by Multiple Columns

1. Select a cell in the range to be sorted.
   - Click a cell with data, not the column header.
2. Click the **Sort** button [*Data* tab, *Sort & Filter* group].
   - The *Sort* dialog box opens.
   - The range is highlighted in the worksheet.
   - Click the **Sort & Filter** button [*Home* tab, *Editing* group] and select **Custom Sort**.
3. Select the **My data has headers** box if your data have a header row.
4. Click the **Sort by** arrow and select the column heading for the first sort level.
5. Click the **Sort On** arrow.
   - Use *Cell Values* for text or numbers.
   - If the data have a cell attribute such as a font color, select the name of the attribute.
6. Click the **Order** arrow and choose a sort option.
   - For columns with numbers or dates, the options are *Smallest to Largest* and *Largest to Smallest*.
   - The *Custom List* option provides special sorting orders for days of the week and months of the year so that data are sorted chronologically.

7. Click **Add Level** to add a second sort column.
8. Click the **Then by** arrow and select the second column heading.
9. Click the **Sort On** arrow and choose **Cell Values** or an attribute.
10. Click the **Order** arrow and choose a sort order (Figure 4-25).
    - Click the **Options** button in the *Sort* dialog box to specify case-sensitive sorting or to change the orientation of ascending and descending sorts.
11. Click **OK**.

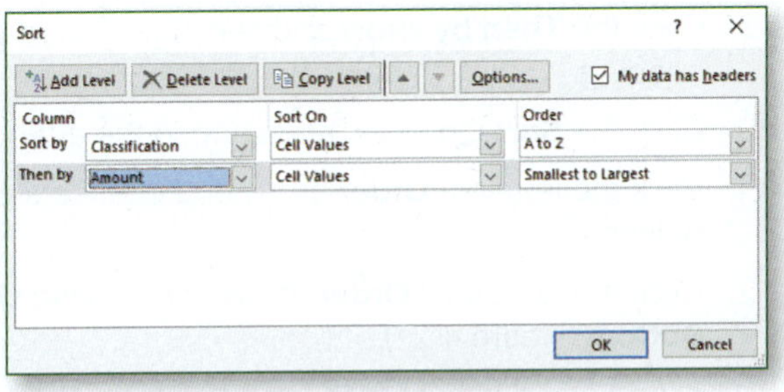

Figure 4-25 ***Sort* dialog box**

Sort Data by Cell Attribute

An ***attribute*** is a setting or property. Cell attributes used for sorting are font color, cell fill color, and the conditional formatting icon. These choices are options for the *Sort On* choice in the *Sort* dialog box, and they are available when you choose **Sort** from a cell's context menu.

When you sort by font or fill color, the *Order* choices are the colors used in the column. You choose a color and set its position in the sorted column. Column E in Figure 4-26 is sorted by the icon set with the green checkmark icon on the top.

	A	B	C	D	E	F
4	Name	Classification	Location	Category	Transactions	Amount
5	Christopher Bowman	Manager	Cass Lake	Rentals	14	✔ $15,000
6	Chad Mei	Representative	Cass Lake	Excursions	24	✔ $10,000
7	Josie Daddiline	Representative	Walker	Rentals	10	✔ $12,000
8	Josie Daddiline	Representative	Walker	Rentals	12	✔ $12,000
9	BJ Francine	Representative	Baudette	Rentals	15	✔ $17,000
10	Alec Mikayla	Representative	Baudette	Rentals	14	✔ $17,000
11	Tammy Christine	Representative	Walker	Rentals	16	✔ $17,500
12	Dennis Frankie	Representative	Breezy Point	Rentals	16	✔ $18,000
13	Sharon Wyatte	Manager	Breezy Point	Rentals	7	! $5,000
14	Frankie Dennis	Representative	Breezy Point	Excursions	16	! $7,500
15	Kendra Shelton	Representative	Breezy Point	Rentals	10	! $8,500
16	Randy Josephson	Associate	Cass Lake	Boutique	12	✖ $1,500
17	Lilly Oliver	Associate	Walker	Spa	10	✖ $2,200
18	Ari Aronson	Associate	Baudette	Boutique	10	✖ $3,200
19	Jeanie Dennis	Associate	Walker	Excursions	8	✖ $3,800
20	Natasha Ari	Associate	Baudette	Spa	18	✖ $4,500
21	Corey Daniels	Associate	Cass Lake	Excursions	22	✖ $4,500
22	Kendal Shaedon	Associate	Breezy Point	Spa	20	✖ $4,800
23	David Gazik	Manager	Baudette	Boutique	6	✖ $1,200

Figure 4-26 Data sorted by icon in "Amount" column

HOW TO: Sort Data by Cell Attribute

1. Select a cell in the column to sort.
2. Click the **Sort** button [*Data* tab, *Sort & Filter* group].
    - The *Sort* dialog box opens.
    - Click the **Sort & Filter** button [*Home* tab, *Editing* group] and select **Custom Sort**.
3. Select the **My data has headers** box if the data have a header row.
4. Click the **Sort by** arrow and select the column heading.
5. Click the **Sort On** arrow and choose the attribute.
    - The column must have data with different font colors, cells with different fill colors, or conditional formatting icons.
6. Click the leftmost **Order** arrow and choose a color or icon.
7. Click the rightmost **Order** arrow and choose **On Top** or **On Bottom**.
8. Click **Add Level**.

9. Click the **Then by** arrow and select the same column heading.
10. Click the **Sort On** arrow and choose the attribute.
11. Click the leftmost **Order** arrow and choose a color or icon.
12. Click the rightmost **Order** arrow and choose **On Top** or **On Bottom** (Figure 4-27).
    - Add and define as many sort levels as needed.
13. Click **OK**.

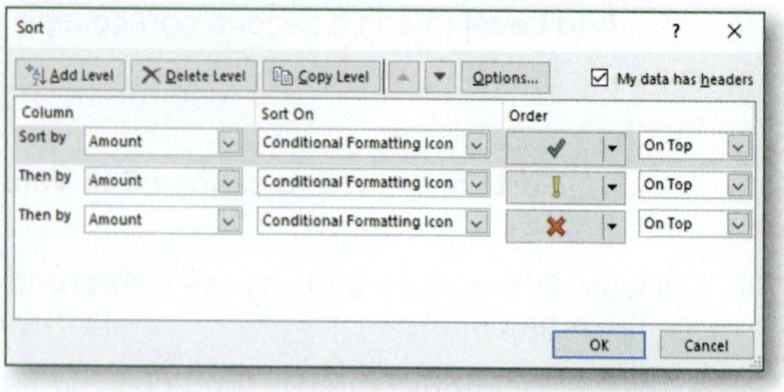

Figure 4-27 Conditional formatting icon order in the *Sort* dialog box

> **MORE INFO**
>
> To sort by icon sets, right-click a cell with the icon that you want first and select **Sort** and then **Put Selected Formatting Icon on Top**.

Sort Data in an Excel Table

When data are formatted as a table, you can sort from the *AutoFilter* arrows with each label in the header row. Sort choices are listed at the top of the pane that opens when you click an *AutoFilter* arrow.

HOW TO: Sort Data in an Excel Table

1. Click the **AutoFilter** arrow for the column heading that represents the lowest sort level.
    - The *AutoFilter* pane lists sort choices at the top.
2. Choose **Sort A to Z** or **Sort Smallest to Largest** (Figure 4-28).
    - The table is sorted by the column.
    - *Sort Smallest to Largest* appears for numeric data.
3. Click the **AutoFilter** arrow for the column heading that represents the top sort level.
4. Choose **Sort A to Z** or **Sort Smallest to Largest**.
    - The table maintains the sort order from the first selected column within the sorted data for the top-level column.

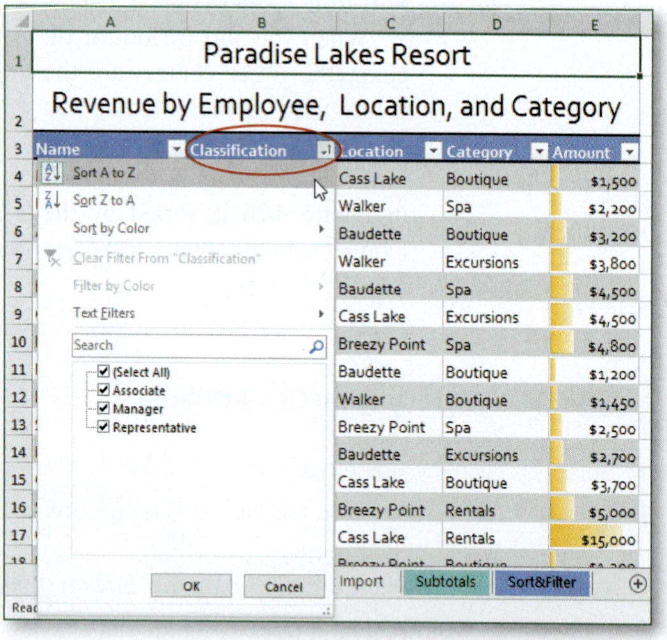

Figure 4-28 *AutoFilter* arrow sort choices

SLO 4.4 Filtering Data

You can usually work more efficiently when you filter large amounts of data to show only rows of importance to your task. For example, filter data to show records for the year, the month, the individual, the product, or a similar grouping. When you filter data, information that does not meet the requirements is temporarily hidden. A filter specifies which data are shown and which are hidden.

AutoFilters

In list-type data or an Excel table, the *Filter* button [*Data* tab, *Sort & Filter* group] displays or hides the *AutoFilter* arrow for each label in the header row. When you click an *AutoFilter* arrow, a pane displays sort options, filter types based on the data type, and check boxes for every piece of data. You can select boxes to mark which records display, or build a filter.

HOW TO: Display and Use AutoFilters

1. Select a cell in the list.
2. Click the **Filter** button [*Data* tab, *Sort & Filter* group].
   - *AutoFilter* arrows appear in the header row with each label.
   - *AutoFilter* arrows display by default in an Excel table.
3. Click the **AutoFilter** arrow for the column used for filtering.
   - All items are selected and displayed in the data.
   - Filter options depend on the type of data in the column.
4. Click the **(Select All)** box to remove all checkmarks.
5. Select the box for each item to be shown (Figure 4-29).
6. Click **OK**.
   - Records that meet the criteria display with row headings in blue.
   - Records that do not meet the criteria and their row numbers are hidden.
   - A filter symbol appears with the column *AutoFilter* arrow.

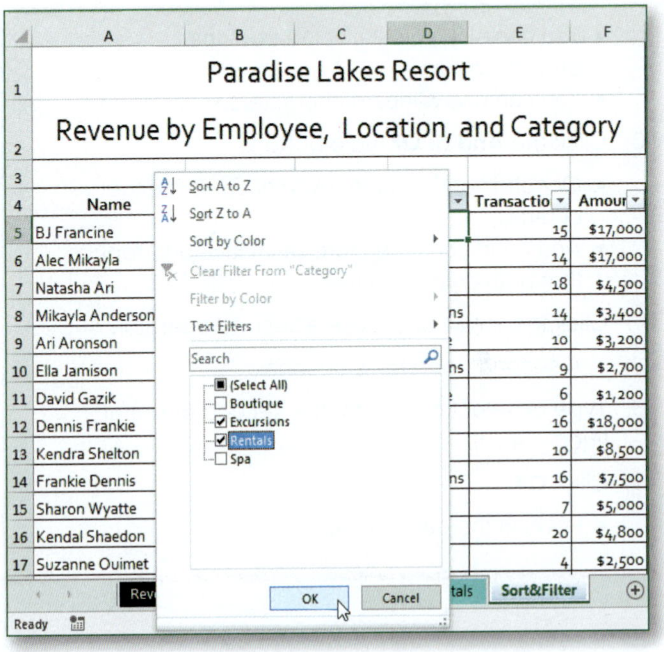

Figure 4-29 *AutoFilter* for "Category" column

To remove a filter and display the complete list, click the **AutoFilter** arrow for the column and choose **Clear Filter From (ColumnName)**. You can also click the **Clear** button in the *Sort & Filter* group on the *Data* tab.

ANOTHER WAY

An *AutoFilter* arrow and a *Slicer* window display the same results.

Custom AutoFilter

A ***custom AutoFilter*** is criteria that you build in a dialog box. A custom *AutoFilter* provides more options for how rows display, because you can use multiple criteria with *AND* and *OR*. For a column with alphanumeric data, *Text Filters* are available, or use *Number Filters* and *Date Filters* for columns with those types of data. Operators use common words such as *Equals*, *Begins With*, or *Contains* (Figure 4-30).

▸HOW TO: Create a Custom Text AutoFilter

1. Select a cell in the data to filter.
2. Click the **Filter** button [*Data* tab, *Sort & Filter* group] to display *AutoFilter* arrows for the header row.
3. Click the **AutoFilter** arrow for the column used for filtering.
4. Select **Text Filters** and choose an operator.
   - The *Custom AutoFilter* dialog box opens.
5. Type criteria for the first operator in the box on the right.
   - You can also select a value from the drop-down list.
   - You can use wildcard characters.
6. Click the **And** or **Or** radio button.
   - *Or* conditions include rows that match either criteria.
   - *And* conditions are more restrictive and require that both criteria be met.
7. Click the arrow to choose a second operator.
   - A second operator is optional.
8. Type or select criteria for the second operator (Figure 4-31).
9. Click **OK**.
   - Rows in the data are filtered.

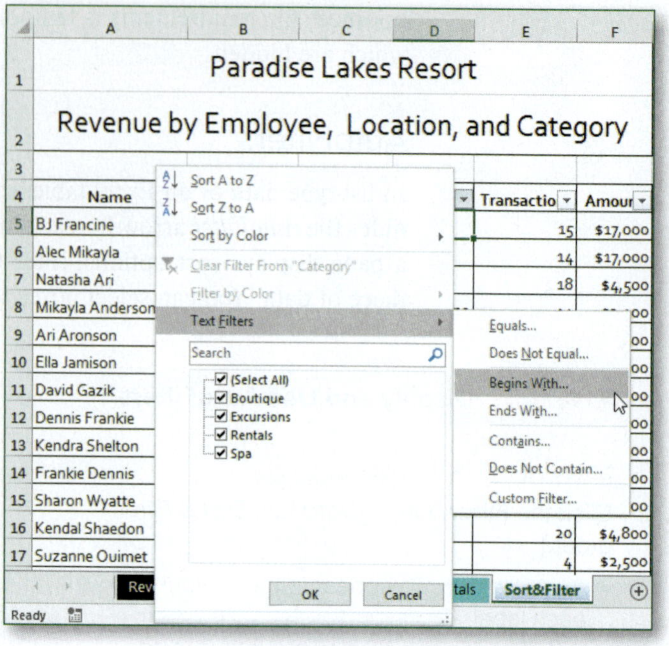

Figure 4-30 Text filters for a custom *AutoFilter*

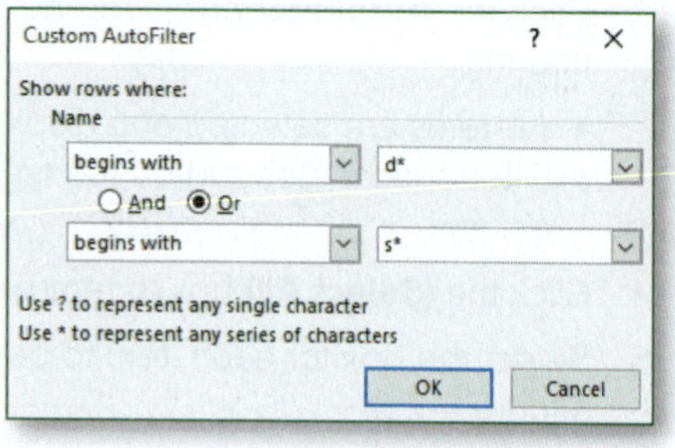

Figure 4-31 *Custom AutoFilter* dialog box

Advanced Filter

For an *Advanced Filter*, you build a criteria range separate from the data and type the conditions within that range. You can show the results in the data range, or you can display filtered data in another location on the sheet. Using another location for results enables you to create separate reports with filtered rows while the main list displays all data. An *Advanced Filter* requires more setup work, but it enables you to apply more complex filters. You can even use a formula in the criteria.

A ***criteria range*** is at least two rows in which the first row must use the same column names as the data; the second row is where criteria are entered. You need not use all column names, and you can use more than one row for criteria. Create a criteria range in empty rows anywhere on the worksheet or on another sheet. In Figure 4-32, the criteria range is cells G5:K6.

Multiple rows below the header row in the criteria range set *AND* or *OR* conditions. If you enter criteria on the same row, they are treated as *AND* conditions. In Figure 4-32, "assoc*" in cell H6 and ">2500" in cell K6 are criteria. Both criteria must be met for a record to be displayed. For an *OR* condition, use a second (or third) row in the criteria range. An *OR* filter displays a record if any one of the requirements is met.

To show filtered results in another location, create an ***output*** or ***extract range***. You specify one row for this range, and it should include the same column headings as the data.

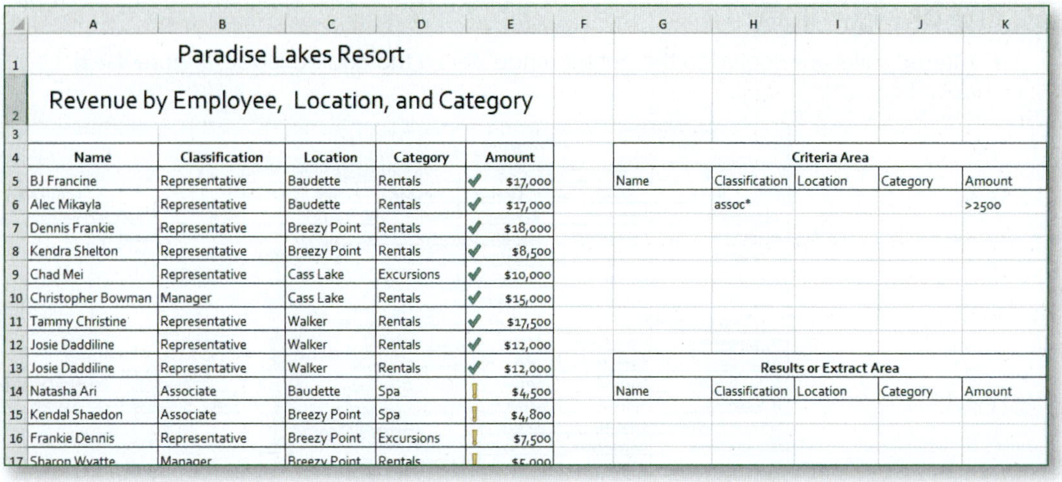

Figure 4-32 *Advanced Filter* **setup**

In Figure 4-32, the extract range is cells G14:K14. Filtered rows are copied below these headings and take up as many rows as necessary. The output range must be on the same worksheet as the data, but you can copy the results to another sheet or another workbook.

HOW TO: Create an Advanced Filter

1. Select labels in the header row for fields that will be used for filtering.
   - Copy all the labels in the header row if preferred.
2. Copy the labels to a *Criteria* area.
   - The criteria area can be on the same sheet or another sheet in the workbook.
   - If the criteria range is above the data, leave at least one blank row between it and the data.
3. Copy the labels again to an *Extract* area.
   - The output or extract area must be on the same sheet as the data.
   - Leave blank rows below the labels for the filtered results.
4. Type criteria in the criteria range.
   - Criteria is not case sensitive.
   - Use wildcard characters in the criteria.
5. Click a cell in the data range.
6. Click the **Advanced** button [*Data* tab, *Sort & Filter* group].
   - The *Advanced Filter* dialog box opens.
7. Select **Copy to another location** In the *Action* group.
8. Verify or select the range (including the header row) in the *List range* box.
   - If the data range is named, press **F3 (FN+F3)** and select the name.
9. Select the criteria cell range with its header row in the *Criteria range* box.
   - If the criteria range is named, press **F3 (FN+F3)** and select the name.
   - Type cell references to identify the criteria range.
10. Select the extract range in the *Copy to* box.
    - This range is the row of labels.

11. Click **OK** (Figure 4-33).
   - Filtered rows are copied to the output range below the copied labels (Figure 4-34).

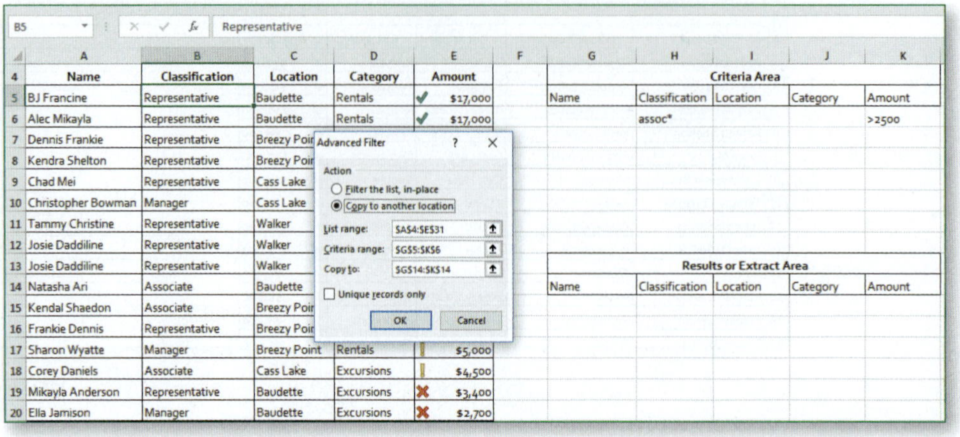

Figure 4-33 ***Advanced Filter*** **dialog box**

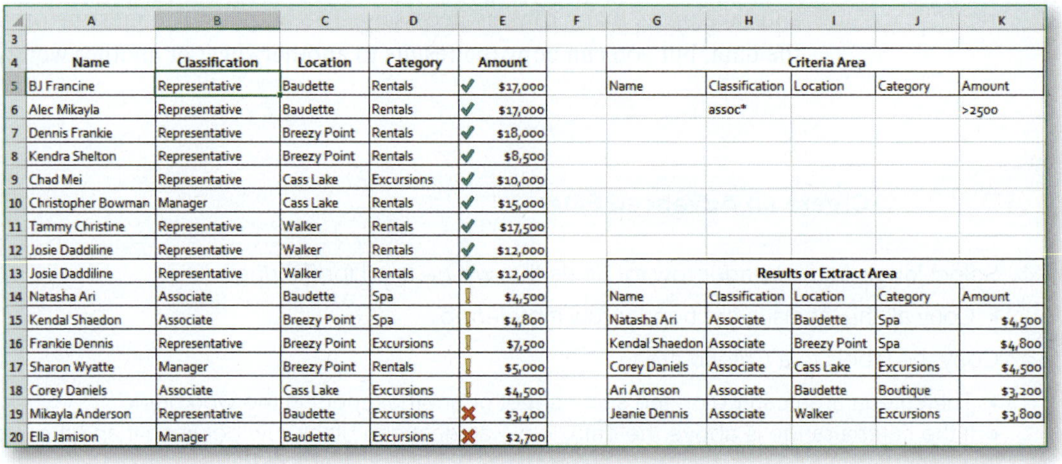

Figure 4-34 ***Advanced Filter*** **results copied to another location**

> **MORE INFO**
>
> Enter < > as criteria to display records that have any entry in the column. Enter = as criteria to show rows that have no entry in the column.

SLO 4.5

Using Subtotals, Groups, and Outlines

A ***subtotal*** is a summary row for data that are grouped. A ***group*** is a set of data that have the same entry in one or more columns. Figure 4-35 shows groups by "Location" with subtotals in the "Transactions" and "Amount" columns. An ***outline*** is a summary that groups records so that individual groups can be displayed or hidden from view. Use these three features to organize and calculate results for worksheets with large sets of data.

The Subtotal Command

The ***Subtotal*** command in the *Outline* group on the *Data* tab inserts summary rows for a sorted list and formats the data as an *outline*. The *Subtotal* command is available for a normal range of cells, not an Excel table. The *Subtotal* command includes *SUM*, *AVERAGE*, *MAX*, or *MIN*, as well as other *Statistical* functions.

To use the *Subtotal* command, the data should have a header row with data rows following, and you must sort the rows by the main field (column) to be summarized or totaled. To display revenue numbers by location, for example, sort the data by location. The *Subtotal* command groups the rows by this field but can show subtotals for any column.

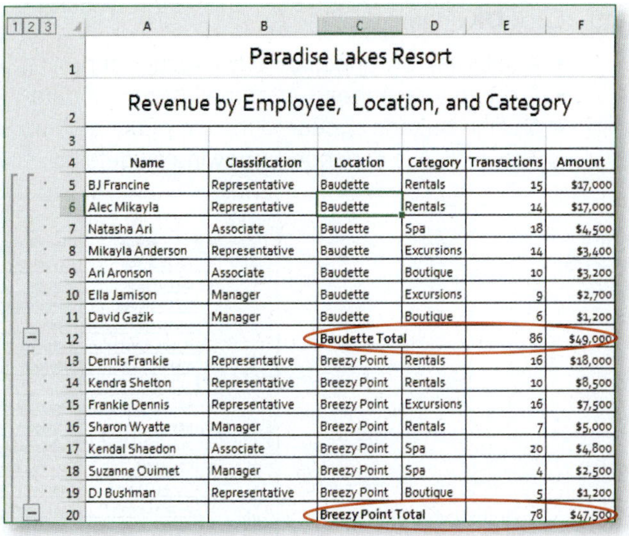

	A	B	C	D	E	F
1	Paradise Lakes Resort					
2	Revenue by Employee, Location, and Category					
3						
4	Name	Classification	Location	Category	Transactions	Amount
5	BJ Francine	Representative	Baudette	Rentals	15	$17,000
6	Alec Mikayla	Representative	Baudette	Rentals	14	$17,000
7	Natasha Ari	Associate	Baudette	Spa	18	$4,500
8	Mikayla Anderson	Representative	Baudette	Excursions	14	$3,400
9	Ari Aronson	Associate	Baudette	Boutique	10	$3,200
10	Ella Jamison	Manager	Baudette	Excursions	9	$2,700
11	David Gazik	Manager	Baudette	Boutique	6	$1,200
12			Baudette Total		86	$49,000
13	Dennis Frankie	Representative	Breezy Point	Rentals	16	$18,000
14	Kendra Shelton	Representative	Breezy Point	Rentals	10	$8,500
15	Frankie Dennis	Representative	Breezy Point	Excursions	16	$7,500
16	Sharon Wyatte	Manager	Breezy Point	Rentals	7	$5,000
17	Kendal Shaedon	Associate	Breezy Point	Spa	20	$4,800
18	Suzanne Ouimet	Manager	Breezy Point	Spa	4	$2,500
19	DJ Bushman	Representative	Breezy Point	Boutique	5	$1,200
20			Breezy Point Total		78	$47,500

Figure 4-35 Grouped rows with subtotals in two columns

> **MORE INFO**
>
> If data are formatted as an Excel table, convert it to a normal cell range [*Table Tools Design* tab, *Tools* group] to use the *Subtotal* command.

▶HOW TO: Display Subtotals

1. Sort the data by the column for which subtotals will be calculated.
2. Click a cell in the data range.
3. Click the **Subtotal** button [*Data* tab, *Outline* group].
   - When data have a header row followed by data rows, the range is selected.
4. Click the **At each change in** arrow.
5. Choose the column heading name that was used for sorting.
   - Subtotals need not be shown for this column.
6. Click the **Use function** arrow and select the function.
7. Select each field that should display a subtotal in the **Add subtotal to** list.
   - Verify the function applies to the column data type; for example, do not use *Sum* for a text column.
8. Choose **Replace current subtotals**.
   - If the range already has subtotals, they are replaced.
9. Choose **Summary below data** (Figure 4-36).
   - The "Summary" row can be placed above the data if you prefer.
   - Choose the option to split a group across pages.
   - Use this dialog box to remove subtotals.

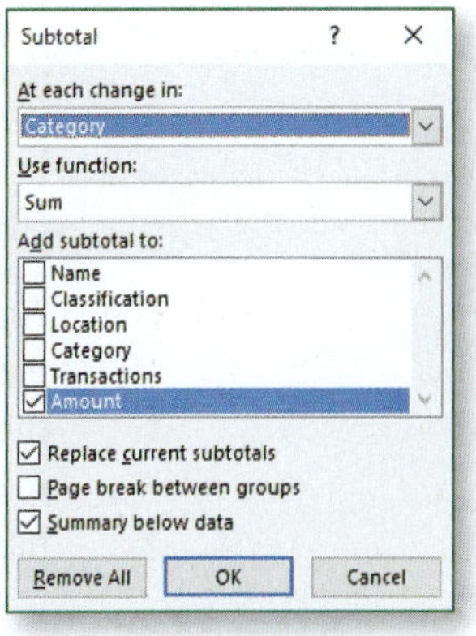

Figure 4-36 *Subtotal* dialog box

10. Click **OK** (Figure 4-37).
    - A subtotal row appears below each group.
    - A grand total appears after the last row of data.
    - Outline buttons appear to the left of the column and row headings.
    - The outline is expanded, showing all details.

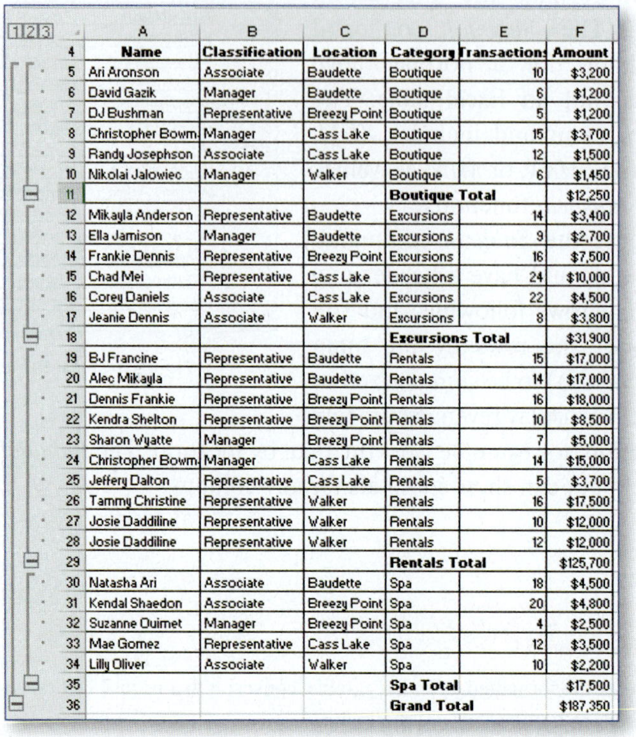

	A	B	C	D	E	F
4	Name	Classification	Location	Category	Transactions	Amount
5	Ari Aronson	Associate	Baudette	Boutique	10	$3,200
6	David Gazik	Manager	Baudette	Boutique	6	$1,200
7	DJ Bushman	Representative	Breezy Point	Boutique	5	$1,200
8	Christopher Bowm	Manager	Cass Lake	Boutique	15	$3,700
9	Randy Josephson	Associate	Cass Lake	Boutique	12	$1,500
10	Nikolai Jalowiec	Manager	Walker	Boutique	6	$1,450
11				Boutique Total		$12,250
12	Mikayla Anderson	Representative	Baudette	Excursions	14	$3,400
13	Ella Jamison	Manager	Baudette	Excursions	9	$2,700
14	Frankie Dennis	Representative	Breezy Point	Excursions	16	$7,500
15	Chad Mei	Representative	Cass Lake	Excursions	24	$10,000
16	Corey Daniels	Associate	Cass Lake	Excursions	22	$4,500
17	Jeanie Dennis	Associate	Walker	Excursions	8	$3,800
18				Excursions Total		$31,900
19	BJ Francine	Representative	Baudette	Rentals	15	$17,000
20	Alec Mikayla	Representative	Baudette	Rentals	14	$17,000
21	Dennis Frankie	Representative	Breezy Point	Rentals	16	$18,000
22	Kendra Shelton	Representative	Breezy Point	Rentals	10	$8,500
23	Sharon Wyatte	Manager	Breezy Point	Rentals	7	$5,000
24	Christopher Bowm	Manager	Cass Lake	Rentals	14	$15,000
25	Jeffery Dalton	Representative	Cass Lake	Rentals	5	$3,700
26	Tammy Christine	Representative	Walker	Rentals	16	$17,500
27	Josie Daddiline	Representative	Walker	Rentals	10	$12,000
28	Josie Daddiline	Representative	Walker	Rentals	12	$12,000
29				Rentals Total		$125,700
30	Natasha Ari	Associate	Baudette	Spa	18	$4,500
31	Kendal Shaedon	Associate	Breezy Point	Spa	20	$4,800
32	Suzanne Ouimet	Manager	Breezy Point	Spa	4	$2,500
33	Mae Gomez	Representative	Cass Lake	Spa	12	$3,500
34	Lilly Oliver	Associate	Walker	Spa	10	$2,200
35				Spa Total		$17,500
36				Grand Total		$187,350

Figure 4-37 "Amount" subtotals for each category

The *Subtotal* command inserts the *SUBTOTAL* function in each cell with a result. Its arguments are *Function_num*, and *RefN*. *Function_num* is a number from 1 through 11 that specifies which calculation was selected in the *Subtotal* dialog box. *Ref1* is the range to be summed. If you chose *Sum*, for example, the function is =SUBTOTAL(9,F5:F11) in which "9" represents the *SUM* function, and the range is cells F5:F11.

MORE INFO

The *Function_num* arguments are in alphabetical order, so that *AVERAGE* is 1, *COUNT* is 2, and so on. See the argument list in Excel *Help* for this function.

Outline Buttons

An outline groups and summarizes data. A worksheet can have only one outline; the outline includes all of the worksheet data or a portion of the data. Outlines have levels, indicated by the numbered buttons to the left of the column headings. Each *Outline Level* button shows an increasing level of detail. An outline can have up to eight levels. The worksheet in Figure 4-37 has three levels: a grand total (1), a category total for each group (2), and all the rows (3).

Each group has an *Expand/Collapse* button, shown to the left of the row headings. This button is a toggle and shows a minus sign (−) or a plus sign (+). When an individual group is collapsed, you do not see details for that group, only the subtotal.

▸HOW TO: Use Outline Buttons

1. Click a collapse button (−) to hide details for a group.
   - Only the subtotal row displays.
2. Click an expand button (+) to display details for a group.
3. Click the **Level 1** button (1) to reveal the grand total.
4. Click the **Level 2** button (2) to see the second outline level details (Figure 4-38).
5. Click the **Level 3** button (3) to display all details.

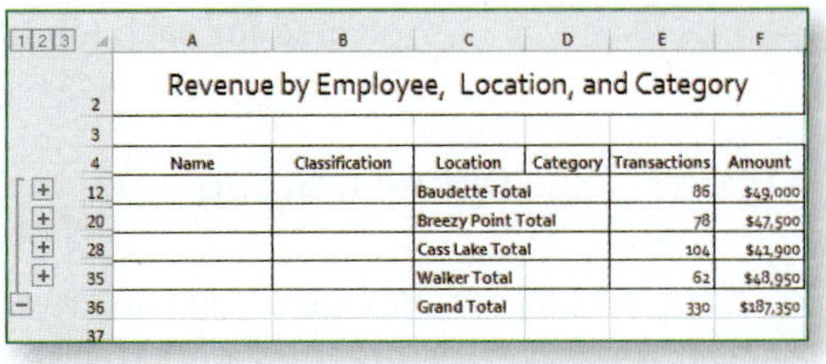

Figure 4-38 Level 2 outline results

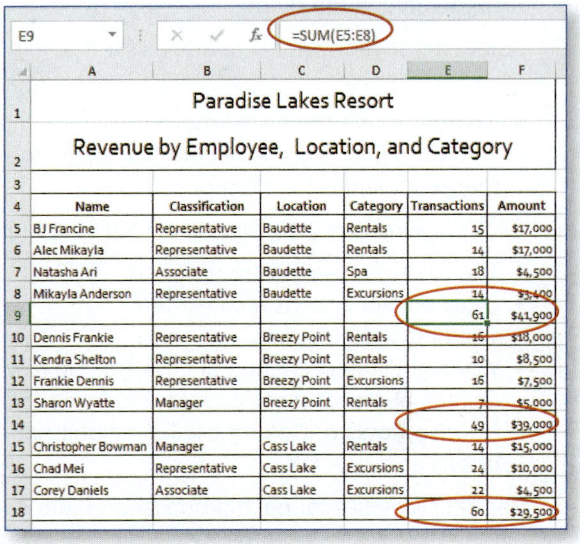

Figure 4-39 Data sorted by location with formulas for each group

Create an Auto Outline

An ***Auto Outline*** inserts groups based on where formulas are located. Consistent data and formulas that follow a pattern are necessary. The data in Figure 4-39 are grouped by location, and *SUM* formulas display after each group in columns E and F.

If data are not properly formatted, Excel displays a message that an *Auto Outline* cannot be created.

▸HOW TO: Create an Auto Outline

1. Click a cell within the data range.
2. Click the **Group** button arrow [*Data* tab, *Outline* group].
3. Select **Auto Outline**.
   - Outline level buttons are inserted.
   - The outline is expanded.
4. Click each collapse button to hide details (Figure 4-40).

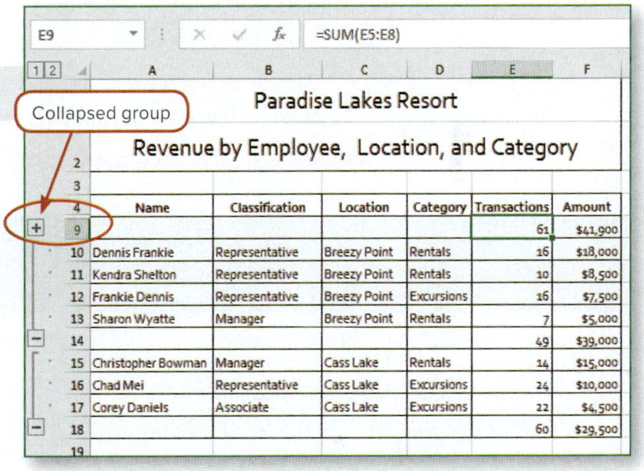

Figure 4-40 *Auto Outline* with two levels; "Baudette" group is collapsed

Define Groups

You can create a group, by rows or columns, for data that does not have totals or formulas. This can be a time-consuming task for a large set of records, but you can use groups to hide irrelevant records and concentrate on groups that require editing.

To define groups, data must be sorted or arranged so that you can select a range of cells to indicate the group. In addition, you must insert a blank summary row either above or below the group (or a blank column to the left or right of the group). Use blank rows to enter subtitles for the data before or after grouping.

The data in Figure 4-41 are sorted by the "Classification" column, so that groups can be created for each job title. Note that a blank row has been inserted after each group.

▸HOW TO: Define a Group

1. Sort the data (or arrange columns) based on the preferred grouping.
2. Insert a blank row at the end of each sort group (or at the start of each group).
   - Insert the blank row above the group if you want to label each group.
   - For column data, the summary column is usually to the right of the group.
3. Select the row or column headings for the first group.
   - Do not include the blank row or column.
   - You can select a range of cells that spans the rows or columns for the group.
4. Click the **Group** button [*Data* tab, *Outline* group].
   - The rows or columns are grouped.
   - Outline level buttons are inserted.
   - The data are expanded.
   - When you select a range of cells, not the row or column headings, the *Group* dialog box opens. Choose **Rows** or **Columns** if the dialog box opens and click **OK**.
5. Repeat steps 1–4 for each group (see Figure 4-41).

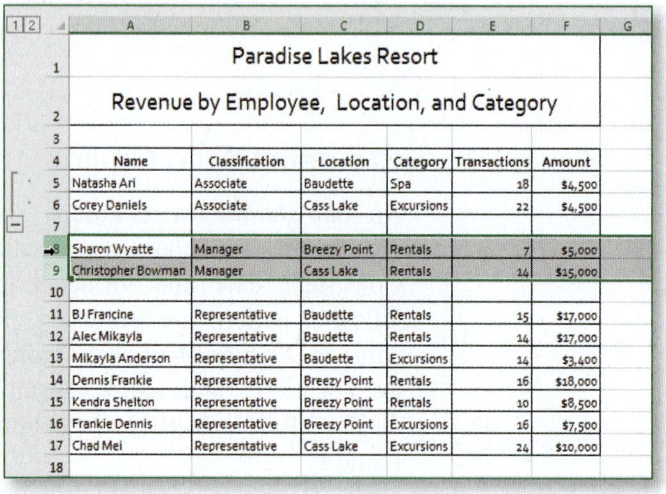

Figure 4-41 Data sorted by "Classification"; blank rows inserted after each title

MORE INFO

To clear an *Auto Outline* or remove all groups, click a cell within the group. Then, click the **Ungroup** button arrow [*Data* tab, *Outline* group] and select **Clear Outline**.

PAUSE & PRACTICE: EXCEL 4-2

For this project, you sort and filter data for Paradise Lakes Resort based on location. You use a *Number Filter* to display records within a range of values, build an advanced filter, and include subtotals in the workbook.

File Needed: ***[your initials] PP E4-1.xlsx***
Completed Project File Name: ***[your initials] PP E4-2.xlsx***

1. Open the ***[your initials] PP E4-1*** workbook completed in *Pause & Practice 4-1* and save it as [your initials] PP E4-2.
2. Click the **Sort&Filter** sheet tab.

3. Sort data in a worksheet.
   a. Click cell **A5**.
   b. Click the **Sort** button [*Data* tab, *Sort & Filter* group].
   c. Select the **My data has headers** box if necessary.
   d. Click the **Sort by** arrow and select **Location**.
   e. Choose **Cell Values** for *Sort On* and **A to Z** for *Order*.
   f. Click **Add Level**.
   g. Click the **Then by** arrow and select **Amount**.
   h. Choose **Cell Values** for *Sort On* and **Largest to Smallest** for *Order* (Figure 4-42).
   i. Click **OK**. The data sort alphabetically by location and then by amount in descending order.

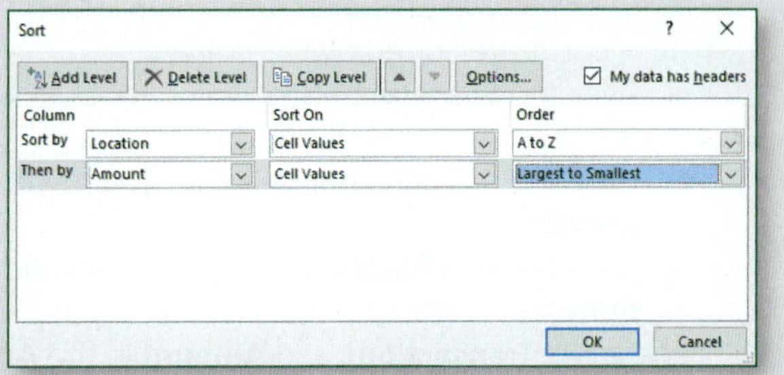

Figure 4-42 Multiple column sort with text and numeric data

4. Use a *Number AutoFilter*.
   a. Click cell **A5**.
   b. Click the **Filter** button [*Data* tab, *Sort & Filter* group] to display *AutoFilter* arrows.
   c. Click the *AutoFilter* arrow for "Amount."
   d. Point to **Number Filters** and select **Between**.
   e. Type 5000 in the **is greater than or equal to** box.
   f. Type 10000 in the **is less than or equal to** box (Figure 4-43).
   g. Click **OK**.

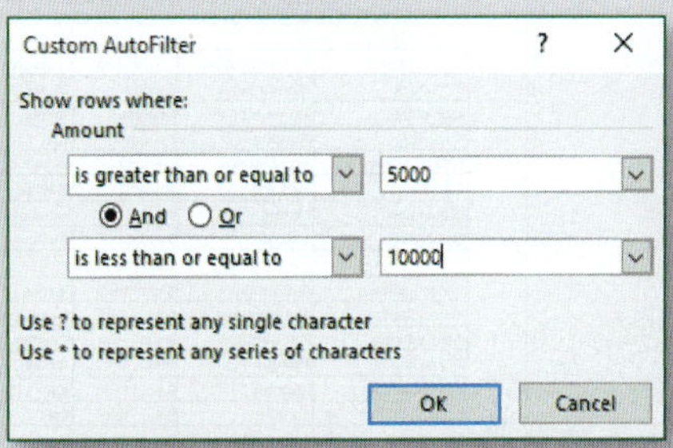

Figure 4-43 *Custom AutoFilter* dialog box for "Amount" between $5,000 and $10,000

5. Click the **Adv Filter** sheet tab.

6. Set a criteria range.
   a. Type assoc* in cell **H6**.
   b. Type >1500 in cell **K6**.

7. Run an *Advanced Filter*.
   a. Click cell **A5**.
   b. Click the **Advanced** button [*Data* tab, *Sort & Filter* group].
   c. Select the **Copy to another location** radio button.
   d. Verify that cells **$A$4:$E$31** are identified in the **List range** box.
   e. Click the **Criteria range** box and select cells **G5:K6**.
   f. Click the **Copy to** box and select cells **G14:K14** (Figure 4-44).
   g. Click **OK**. Six records are extracted and displayed.
   h. Widen column **G** to display the names.

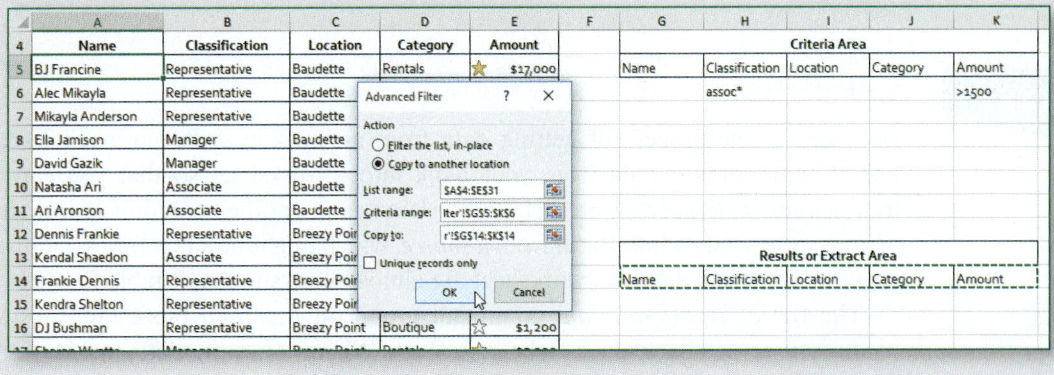

Figure 4-44 Criteria and extract ranges; *Advanced Filter* dialog box

8. Click the **Subtotals** sheet tab.
9. Show subtotals in a list.
    a. Click a cell in the **Location** column. The records are sorted by this column.
    b. Click the **Subtotal** button [*Data* tab, *Outline* group].
    c. Click the **At each change in** arrow and choose **Location**.
    d. Click the **Use function** arrow and choose **Sum**.
    e. Select **Transactions** and **Amount** in the **Add subtotal to list** box.
    f. Click **OK** (Figure 4-45).

Criteria Area

Name	Classification	Location	Category	Amount
	assoc*			>1500

Results or Extract Area

Name	Classification	Location	Category	Amount
Natasha Ari	Associate	Baudette	Spa	$4,500
Ari Aronson	Associate	Baudette	Boutique	$3,200
Kendal Shaedon	Associate	Breezy Point	Spa	$4,800
Corey Daniels	Associate	Cass Lake	Excursions	$4,500
Lilly Oliver	Associate	Walker	Spa	$2,200
Jeanie Dennis	Associate	Walker	Excursions	$3,800

Paradise Lakes Resort

Revenue by Employee, Location, and Category

Name	Classification	Location	Category	Transactions	Amount
BJ Francine	Representative	Baudette	Rentals	15	$17,000
Alec Mikayla	Representative	Baudette	Rentals	14	$17,000
Natasha Ari	Associate	Baudette	Spa	18	$4,500
Mikayla Anderson	Representative	Baudette	Excursions	14	$3,400
Ari Aronson	Associate	Baudette	Boutique	10	$3,200
Ella Jamison	Manager	Baudette	Excursions	9	$2,700
David Gazik	Manager	Baudette	Boutique	6	$1,300
		Baudette Total		86	$49,000
Dennis Frankie	Representative	Breezy Point	Rentals	16	$18,000
Kendra Shelton	Representative	Breezy Point	Rentals	10	$8,500
Frankie Dennis	Representative	Breezy Point	Excursions	16	$7,500
Sharon Wyatte	Manager	Breezy Point	Rentals	7	$5,000
Kendal Shaedon	Associate	Breezy Point	Spa	10	$4,800
Suzanne Ouimet	Manager	Breezy Point	Spa	4	$2,500
DJ Bushman	Representative	Breezy Point	Boutique	5	$1,300
		Breezy Point Total		78	$47,500
Christopher Bowman	Manager	Cass Lake	Rentals	14	$15,000
Chad Mei	Representative	Cass Lake	Excursions	24	$10,000
Corey Daniels	Associate	Cass Lake	Excursions	11	$4,500
Christopher Bowman	Manager	Cass Lake	Boutique	15	$3,700
Jeffery Dalton	Representative	Cass Lake	Rentals	5	$3,700
Mae Gomez	Representative	Cass Lake	Spa	11	$3,500
Randy Josephson	Associate	Cass Lake	Boutique	11	$1,500
		Cass Lake Total		104	$41,900
Tammy Christine	Representative	Walker	Rentals	16	$17,500
Josie Daddline	Representative	Walker	Rentals	10	$12,000
Josie Daddline	Representative	Walker	Rentals	11	$12,000
Jeanie Dennis	Associate	Walker	Excursions	8	$3,800
Lilly Oliver	Associate	Walker	Spa	10	$2,200
Nikolai Jalowiec	Manager	Walker	Boutique	6	$1,450
		Walker Total		61	$48,950
		Grand Total		330	$187,350

Paradise Lakes Resort

Revenue by Employee, Location, and Category

Name	Classification	Location	Category	Transactions	Amount
Kendra Shelton	Representative	Breezy Point	Rentals	10	$8,500
Frankie Dennis	Representative	Breezy Point	Excursions	16	$7,500
Sharon Wyatte	Manager	Breezy Point	Rentals	7	$5,000
Chad Mei	Representative	Cass Lake	Excursions	24	$10,000

Figure 4-45 PP E4-2 completed

10. Save and close the workbook.

SLO 4.6

Importing Data

Importing is the process of getting data from an outside source into an Excel worksheet. For example, import data from your bank into a worksheet so that you can analyze your transactions. ***External data*** are data that originated in another program or format. You import or copy external data into Excel from a ***source***, which might be a text file, a database, or a cloud location. Imported data in a worksheet are almost always in list or table format.

The *Get & Transform Data* command group on the *Data* tab establishes a connection to the source so that data can be refreshed. When you copy data into a worksheet using *Copy* and *Paste* command, no connection to the source is established. Data connections are discussed later in this section.

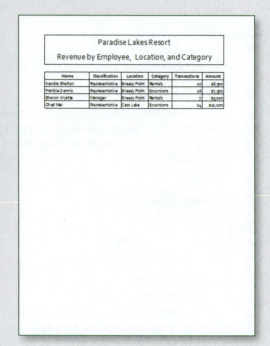

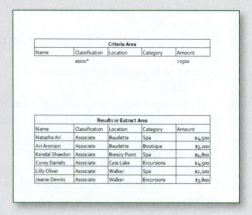

Text Files

A ***text file*** is a document that includes raw data with no formatting. Text files are .txt (text) documents such as those created in NotePad or WordPad. Another widely used text format is .csv (comma separated values); you might see this type of file when you download a bank statement.

Text files separate data into ***fields***. In one method, a character such as a comma or a tab separates the fields, and the file is described as ***delimited*** (tab-delimited file). A ***delimiter*** is the character used to separate the data. Common delimiters are the tab, space, and comma characters.

A second way to separate fields in a text file is by ***fixed width***. Each field is a specified number of characters followed by a space. If the first name field is set at 25 characters, the name "Tom," is imported as 3 characters plus 22 spaces. The second field always starts at position 26.

When you click the **From Text/CSV** button in the *Get & Transform Data* group on the *Data* tab, the *Import Data* dialog box opens (Figure 4-46). The data preview with the recognized delimiter and data types and display in the worksheet. Text files are imported through a query. A ***query*** is a combination of definitions and filters that connects to and extracts the data. Manage imported text data as an Excel table, or use Excel's *Query Editor*.

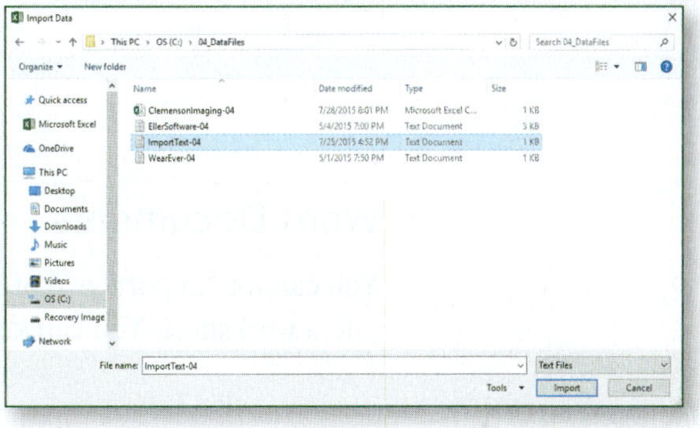

Figure 4-46 ***Import Data* dialog box**

> **MORE INFO**
>
> Many legacy or mainframe computer systems use fixed width files for data.

▸HOW TO: Import a Tab-Delimited Text File into a Worksheet

1. Select the cell in which imported data should begin.
2. Click the **From Text/CSV** button [*Data* tab, *Get & Transform Data* group].
3. Navigate to and select the text file name in the *Import Data* dialog box.
4. Click **Import**.
   - A simple query dialog box shows how the data will be separated into columns.
   - The delimiter character is identified.
   - The data type is identified based on the first rows of data.
5. Click the **Load** arrow and select **Load To** so that you can specify where the text displays (Figure 4-47).
   - A second *Import Data* dialog box opens.
6. Select **Existing worksheet**.
   - The active cell displays as the location.
   - Select another cell as needed.

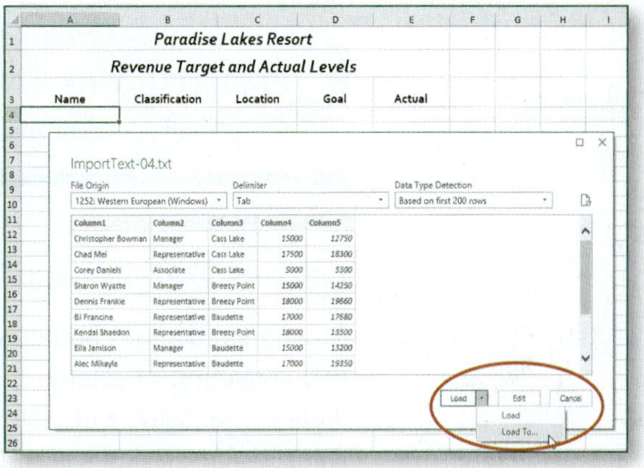

Figure 4-47 Query preview for imported text file

7. Click **OK**.
   - The data are available in the worksheet in an Excel table.
   - The *Queries & Connections* pane displays at the right and can be dragged to another location.
   - The *Table Tools* and *Query Tools* command tabs display (Figure 4-48).
8. Close the *Queries & Connections* pane.
   - Open the *Queries & Connections* pane from the *Data* tab.
   - Refresh data from the *Data* tab or the *Query Tools* tab.

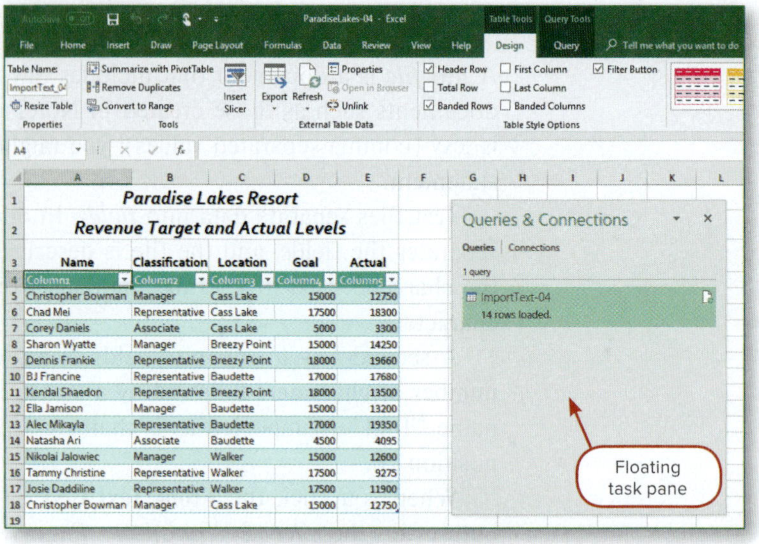

Figure 4-48 Imported text file

Word Documents

You cannot "import" a Word document into Excel, but you can copy and paste data from Word into a worksheet. You can keep the Word formatting, or choose the current worksheet format.

HOW TO: Copy Data from a Word Document

1. Select the cell in which imported data should begin.
2. Start Word and open the document.
3. Select the data to be copied.
4. Click the **Copy** button [*Home* tab, *Clipboard* group].
5. Switch to the Excel worksheet.
6. Click the arrow with the **Paste** button [*Home* tab, *Clipboard* group].
7. Choose **Match Destination Formatting** from the *Paste* gallery.
   - The data are pasted in the worksheet.
   - If you click the **Paste** button, data are pasted with the Word formatting.

ANOTHER WAY

Save a Word document as a text file (.txt) and import the text file into Excel.

Access Database Files

Most organizations and enterprises maintain large amounts of data in a database. A ***database*** is a collection of related tables, queries, forms, and reports. ***Microsoft Access*** is a relational database management system that is part of the Office suite. You can import a table or a query from an Access database into an Excel worksheet. In Access, a table is a data list, and a query is a subset of the list.

Because a database includes many tables and queries, the *Navigator* dialog box opens so that you can choose the table or query to import. Access data are imported as an Excel table, a *PivotTable*, or a *PivotChart*.

> **MORE INFO**
>
> Load imported data directly into the *Query Editor* for further management before loading into the worksheet.

HOW TO: Import an Access Table into a Worksheet

1. Select the cell in which imported data should begin.
2. Click the **Get Data** button [*Data* tab, *Get & Transform Data* group].
3. Select **From Database** and then choose **From Microsoft Access Database**.
4. Navigate to and select the database name in the *Import Data* dialog box.
5. Click **Import**.
   - The *Navigator* window displays the names of queries and tables in the database.
6. Select the name of the table or query.
   - The data display in the preview window (Figure 4-49).

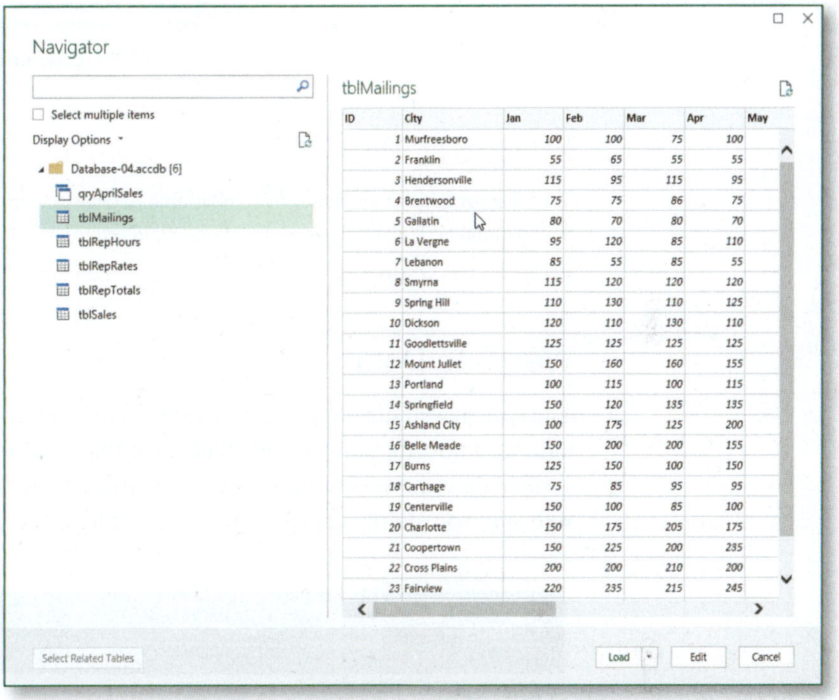

Figure 4-49 ***Navigator* preview for table to be imported**

7. Click the **Load** arrow and select **Load To**.
   - The *Import Data* dialog box opens.
   - You can import data as a *PivotTable*, a *PivotChart*, or as a connection for later use.
8. Select **Existing worksheet**.
   - The active cell displays as the location.
   - You can select another cell.
9. Click **OK**.
   - The data are available in the worksheet in an Excel table.
   - The *Queries & Connections* pane displays at the right.
   - Field names from the Access table or query are column headings in the Excel table.
10. Click the *Table Tools Design* tab.
11. Click the **Properties** button [*External Table Data* group].
    - The *External Data Properties* dialog box opens.
    - Adjust formatting and refresh options.

12. Click the **Query Properties** button (to the right of the *Name* box).
    - The *Query Properties* dialog box opens (Figure 4-50).
    - Type a description for the query.
    - Set how the data are refreshed or updated.
    - The *Definition* tab identifies the source of the imported data.
13. Click **Cancel** to close the *Query Properties* dialog box.
14. Click **Cancel** to close the *External Data Properties* dialog box.

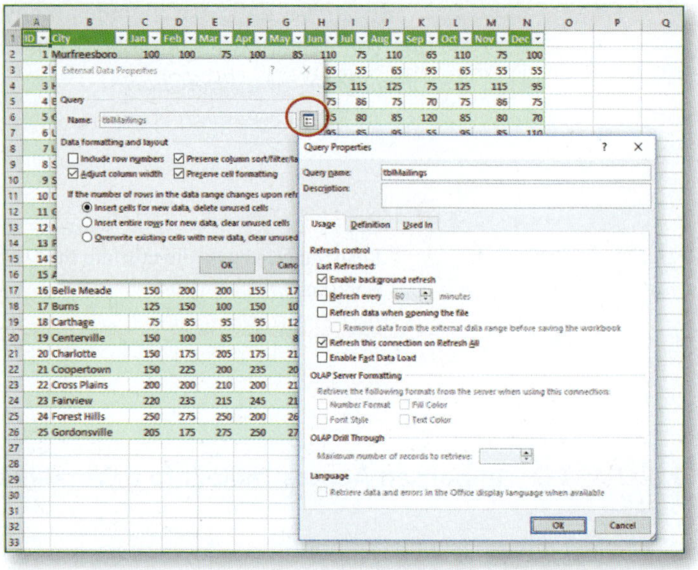

Figure 4-50 ***External Data Properties*** **and** ***Query Properties*** **dialog boxes**

> **MORE INFO**
>
> Import tables and queries from relational databases with the *Get Data* button, *From Other Sources* command [*Data* tab, *Get & Transform Data* group].

Web Site Data

The typical web site has protected multimedia content with images, video, and audio, not list-type data for importing into Excel. Web sites that deal with research, statistics, demographics, and similar data, however, usually have downloadable text or Excel files (Figure 4-51). From the web site, you simply click the link to download the data.

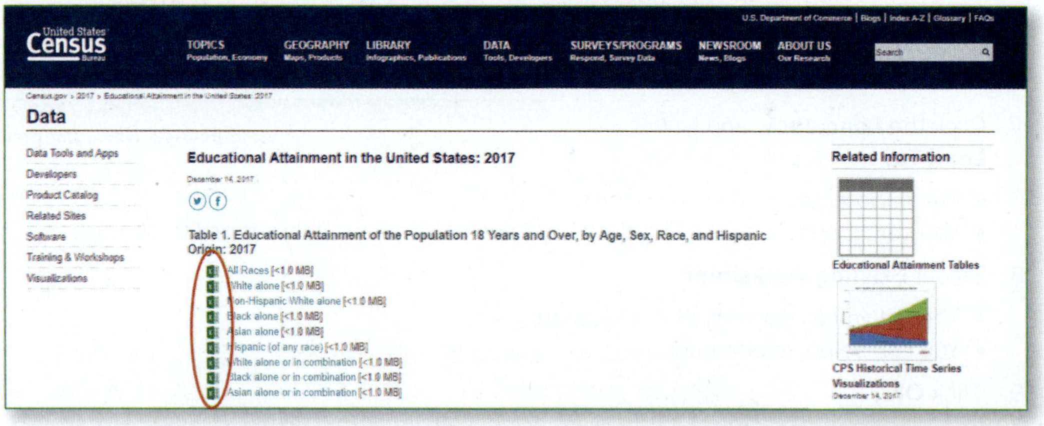

Figure 4-51 Web page with data in Excel format

Use the *From web* command on the *Data* tab to import data that are formatted as an HTML table. You navigate to the page with data, copy the URL for the web page, and paste the URL into the *From web* dialog box. This command builds an underlying query to display the data in the worksheet and uses the *Navigator* window to preview the data.

Workbook Queries and Connections

When you use the *Get & Transform Data* group on the *Data* tab, Excel builds a query that you can edit, refresh, name, or remove. The query includes a ***connection***, an identifier and a link for data that originates outside the workbook.

When you open a workbook that has data connections, you will usually see a security warning bar at the top of the worksheet. When you are sure that the connection is safe, click **Enable Content** to work with the data.

HOW TO: Manage External Data

1. Click a cell within the imported data.
2. Click the **Properties** button [*Data* tab, *Queries & Connections* group].
   - The *External Data Properties* dialog box displays.
   - The dialog box lists format and refresh options for imported data.
3. Close the *External Data Properties* dialog box.
4. Click the **Queries & Connections** button [*Data* tab, *Queries & Connections* group] to display or hide the *Queries & Connections* pane.
   - The button toggles the display of the pane.
   - Existing queries and connections are listed.
5. Point to a table or query name in the *Queries & Connections* pane.
   - A pop-up window displays with information about the data.
6. Click the ellipsis (. . .) near the bottom of the window and select **Properties** (Figure 4-52).
   - The *Query Properties* dialog box opens.
   - Rename the query or table, add a description, or set how data are refreshed.
   - Click the *Definition* tab to edit a query in the *Query Editor*.
7. Click **Cancel** to close the *Query Properties* dialog box.

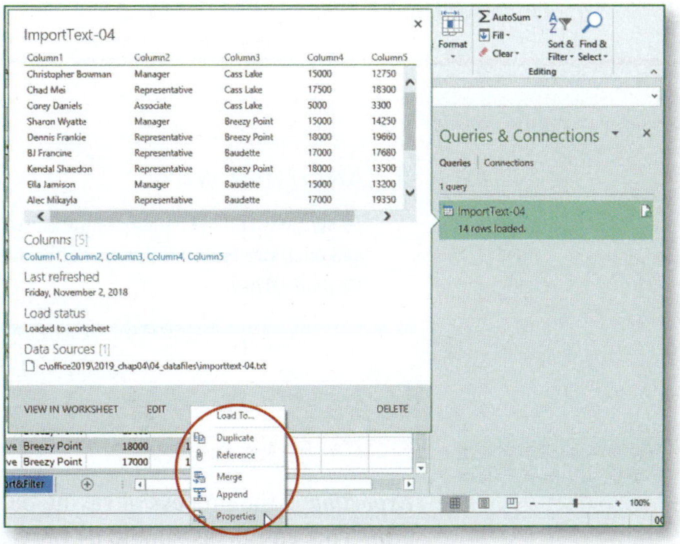

Figure 4-52 Pop-up window for imported data

Flash Fill

Imported data often need to be "cleaned" because they may not be in the correct sort order, they may have missing or incorrect data, and so on. ***Flash Fill*** is a feature that recognizes a pattern in the first cell and suggests data for the remaining rows in a column. For example, imagine that imported data lists first and last names in a single column, but you want first and last names in separate columns. Type the first person's name in an empty column next to the original column. As you start to type a second name below the first one, *Flash Fill* previews the completed column. Just press **Enter** to complete the column. The *Flash Fill Options* button appears after you press **Enter** so that you can undo the fill if necessary or accept all the suggestions.

▸HOW TO: Flash Fill Data in a Worksheet

1. Click the first cell in an empty column next to the original data.
   - The first *Flash Fill* column must be adjacent to the original data.
   - Use an empty column or insert a column.
2. Type the data as you want it to appear.
3. Press **Enter** and type data in the cell below the first cell.
   - The suggested list is previewed.
   - If the suggestion list does not appear, try typing a third item in the column (Figure 4-53).
   - The data must be consistent and follow a recognizable pattern.
4. Press **Enter** to complete the *Flash Fill*.
   - If no *Flash Fill* suggestion list displays, click the **Flash Fill** button [*Data* tab, *Data Tools* group] with the insertion point in the column.

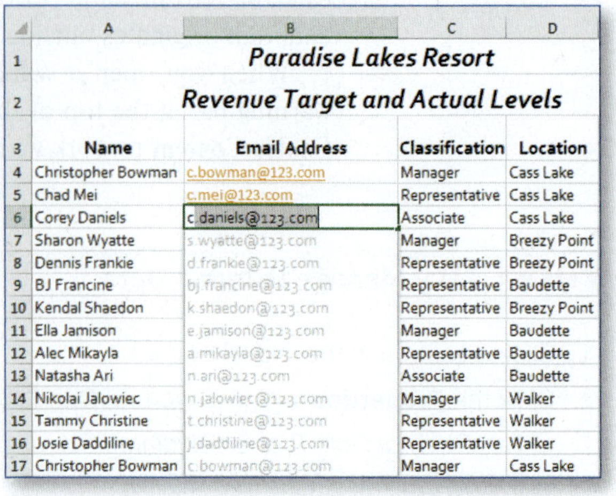

	A	B	C	D
1	Paradise Lakes Resort			
2	Revenue Target and Actual Levels			
3	Name	Email Address	Classification	Location
4	Christopher Bowman	c.bowman@123.com	Manager	Cass Lake
5	Chad Mei	c.mei@123.com	Representative	Cass Lake
6	Corey Daniels	c.daniels@123.com	Associate	Cass Lake
7	Sharon Wyatte	s.wyatte@123.com	Manager	Breezy Point
8	Dennis Frankie	d.frankie@123.com	Representative	Breezy Point
9	BJ Francine	bj.francine@123.com	Representative	Baudette
10	Kendal Shaedon	k.shaedon@123.com	Representative	Breezy Point
11	Ella Jamison	e.jamison@123.com	Manager	Baudette
12	Alec Mikayla	a.mikayla@123.com	Representative	Baudette
13	Natasha Ari	n.ari@123.com	Associate	Baudette
14	Nikolai Jalowiec	n.jalowiec@123.com	Manager	Walker
15	Tammy Christine	t.christine@123.com	Representative	Walker
16	Josie Daddiline	j.daddiline@123.com	Representative	Walker
17	Christopher Bowman	c.bowman@123.com	Manager	Cass Lake

Figure 4-53 ***Flash Fill* suggestion list**

ANOTHER WAY

To split data into separate columns, insert blank columns to the right. Select the column to be split and click the **Text to Columns** button [*Data* tab, *Data Tools* group]. Complete the *Convert Text to Columns Wizard.*

SLO 4.7

Exporting Data

Exporting is the process of saving data in a format to be used by another program or application. This can be as simple as providing a PDF file for viewing, copying data into Word, or saving worksheet data as a text file.

Export Data as a Text File

Most software applications can read a text file, a common way to transfer or share data. You can save Excel data as a tab-delimited, space-delimited, or comma-delimited file. When you save worksheet data as a text file, Excel renames the sheet with the same file name that you type for the text file. You can save only one worksheet in a text file. If a workbook has multiple sheets, a message box will alert you that only the current sheet will be saved.

▸HOW TO: Save Excel Data as a Tab-Delimited File

1. Click the worksheet tab with data to export.
   - The insertion point can be in any cell.
2. Click the **File** tab and select **Export**.
3. Select **Change File Type**.

4. Select **Text (Tab delimited)** as the file type (Figure 4-54).

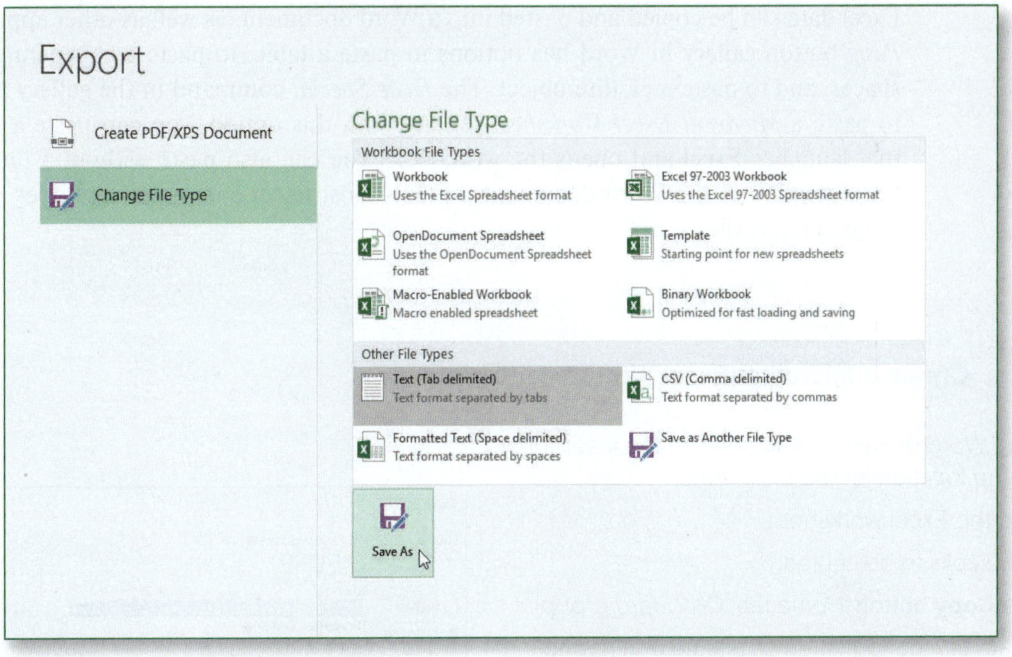

Figure 4-54 *Export* command in *Backstage* view

5. Click **Save As**.
   - The *Save As* dialog box opens with *Text (Tab-delimited)* as the *Save as type*.
6. Navigate to the location for the exported data.
7. Type a file name for the text file in the *File name* box.
8. Click **Save**.
   - If a workbook has more than one sheet, a message box reminds you that only one sheet can be exported. Click **OK** in this message box.
9. Click **Yes** to acknowledge that Excel features may be lost if the message box appears.
   - The worksheet tab has the same name as the exported file.
10. Rename the sheet tab as desired.
11. Click the **File** tab and choose **Save As**.
12. Select **Excel Workbook** as the *Save as type* in the *Save As* dialog box.
13. Navigate to the folder for saved work.
14. Select or type the original workbook file name and click **Save**.
15. Click **Yes** to replace the file.
16. Close the workbook.
   - The exported text file is available in the folder selected for saving.
   - The original workbook is unchanged and resaved.

MORE INFO

To use Excel data in an Access table, export the data as a text file. You can then import the text file into an Access table.

Export Data via the Clipboard

Excel data can be copied and pasted into a Word document, as well as other applications. The *Paste* button gallery in Word has options to paste a table, to paste text separated by tabs or spaces, and to paste a picture object. The *Paste Special* command in the gallery has an option to paste a *Microsoft Excel Worksheet Object*. With this option, you can paste a link in Word that launches Excel and opens the workbook. You can also paste without a link to open an Excel window in the Word document that has most Excel commands but does not affect the original Excel file.

▸HOW TO: Create a Microsoft Excel Worksheet Object

1. Open the Word document and position the insertion point at the location for the Excel data.
2. Switch to the Excel worksheet.
3. Select the cells to be copied.
4. Click the **Copy** button [*Home* tab, *Clipboard* group].
   - The data can be formatted as a table or a normal range.
   - You can also press **Ctrl+C** to copy.
5. Switch to the Word document.
6. Click the arrow with the **Paste** button [*Home* tab, *Clipboard* group] and choose **Paste Special**.
7. Select **Microsoft Excel Worksheet Object** in the *Paste Special* dialog box.
8. Select **Paste link** in the *Paste Special* dialog box (Figure 4-55).
9. Click **OK**.
   - The data are pasted as a worksheet object.
10. Complete work in the Word document.
    - Use horizontal alignment commands to position the object if necessary.
    - Double-click anywhere in the object to launch Excel and open the source workbook.

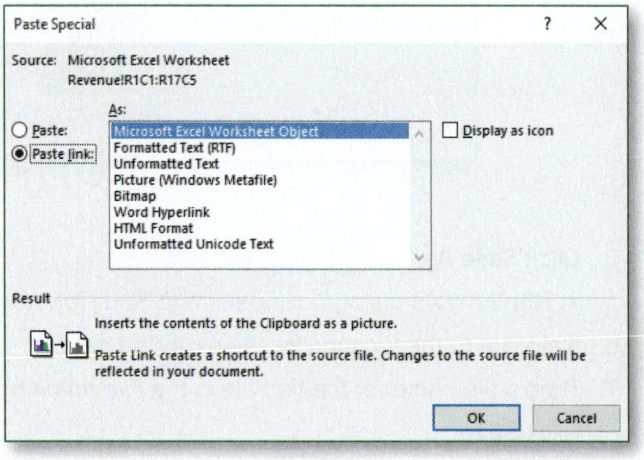

Figure 4-55 ***Paste Special*** **dialog box**

SharePoint Lists

SharePoint Server and ***SharePoint Online*** are a family of products that enables collaboration and simultaneous work by co-workers and team members. You can export data in an Excel table to a *SharePoint* list so that others in your work circle have access to the data. The *Export* button is in the *External Table Data* group on the *Table Tools Design* tab, and it launches the *Export Table to SharePoint List Wizard*. To work with *SharePoint*, you must have access and permission from the service administrator.

PAUSE & PRACTICE: EXCEL 4-3

For this project, you import data from a text file into an Excel worksheet, format the data as an Excel table, copy data from a Word document, and use *Flash Fill* to complete the worksheet for Paradise Lakes Resort.

Files Needed: ***[your initials] PP E4-2.xlsx***, ***ImportText-04.txt***, and ***CopyWord-04.docx*** *(Student data files are available in the* Library *of your SIMnet account.)*
Completed Project File Name: ***[your initials] PP E4-3.xlsx***

1. Open the ***[your initials] PP E4-2*** workbook completed in *Pause & Practice 4-2* and save it as [your initials] PP E4-3.
2. Import data from a text file.
   a. Select cell **A4** on the **Text Import** tab.
   b. Click the **From Text/CVS** button [*Data* tab, *Get & Transform Data* group].
   c. Navigate to and select ***ImportText-04.txt*** from your student data files in the *Import Data* dialog box.
   d. Click **Import**.
   e. Click the **Load** arrow and select **Load To**.
   f. Select **Existing worksheet**.
   g. Confirm or select cell **A4** as the location.
   h. Click **OK** in the *Import Data* dialog box.
   i. Close the *Queries & Connections* pane.
   j. Select cells **A3:E3** and drag and drop (or cut and paste) the cells to cells **A4:E4** and replace the column labels.
3. Copy data from a Word document.
   a. Select cell **A19**.
   b. Open Microsoft Word and open the ***CopyWord-04*** document from your student data files. Enable editing if necessary.
   c. Select all the data and click the **Copy** button [*Home* tab, *Clipboard* group].
   d. Switch to the Excel window.
   e. Click the arrow on the **Paste** button [*Home* tab, *Clipboard* group] and choose **Match Destination Formatting** (Figure 4-56).
   f. Select cells **D5:E28** and apply the **Currency** number format with zero decimals.
   g. Adjust the widths of columns **C:E** to **11.43 (85 pixels)**.

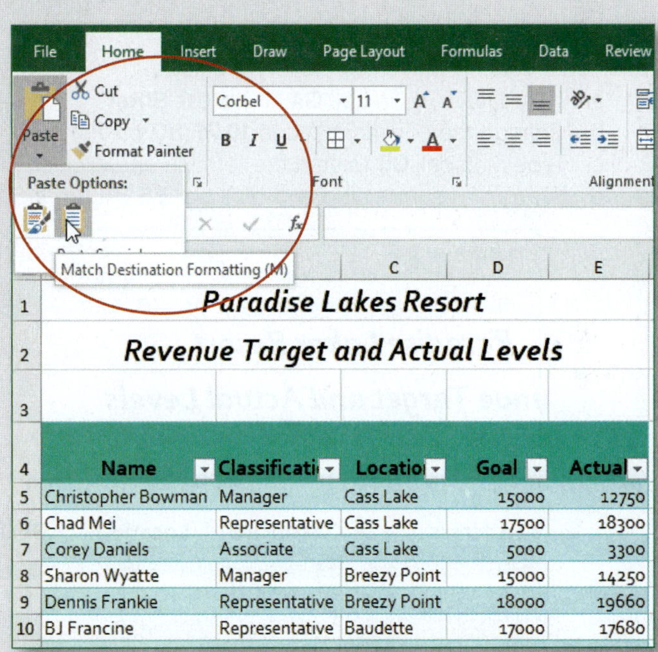

Figure 4-56 ***Paste Options*** **for copied data**

4. Use *Flash Fill* to create an email address column.
   a. Insert a column between columns **A** and **B**.
   b. Type Email Address in cell **B4**.

c. Increase the width of the "Email Address" column to **31.00 (222 pixels)**.

d. In cell **B5**, type c.bowman@somewhere.com and press **Enter**.

e. Select cell **B6** and type c.m to start the second address and display the *Flash Fill* suggested list.

f. Press **Enter**. If the *Flash Fill* suggestion list did not appear, click the **Flash Fill** button [*Data* tab, *Data Tools* group].

5. Format data as an Excel table.

a. Select cells **A4:F28**. Because the data were imported from different sources, you must select the range.

b. Click the **Format as Table** button [*Home* tab, *Styles* group].

c. Choose **White, Table Style Light 1** (first row in the group) (Figure 4-57).

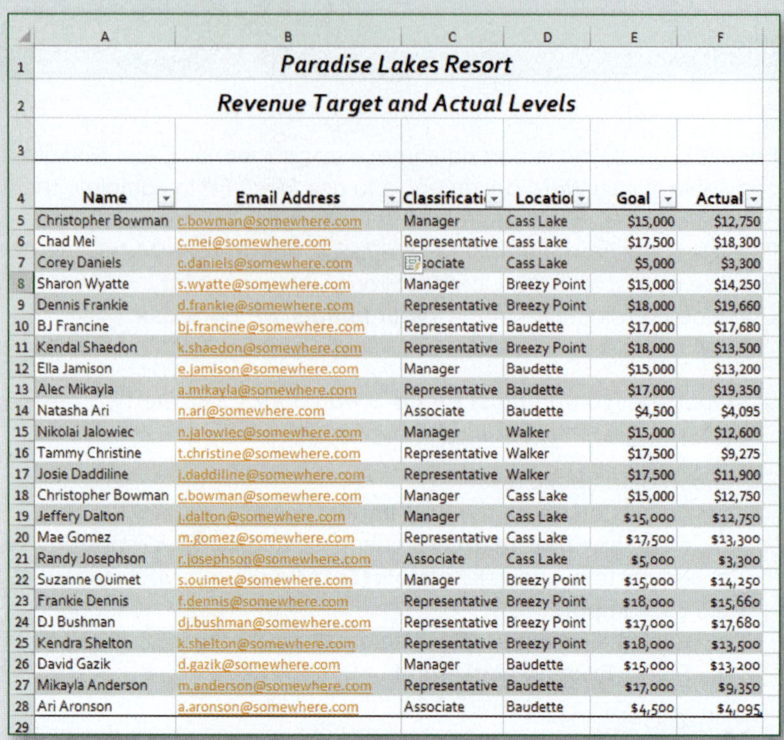

	A	B	C	D	E	F
1		Paradise Lakes Resort				
2		Revenue Target and Actual Levels				
3						
4	Name	Email Address	Classificati	Locatio	Goal	Actual
5	Christopher Bowman	c.bowman@somewhere.com	Manager	Cass Lake	$15,000	$12,750
6	Chad Mei	c.mei@somewhere.com	Representative	Cass Lake	$17,500	$18,300
7	Corey Daniels	c.daniels@somewhere.com	sociate	Cass Lake	$5,000	$3,300
8	Sharon Wyatte	s.wyatte@somewhere.com	Manager	Breezy Point	$15,000	$14,250
9	Dennis Frankie	d.frankie@somewhere.com	Representative	Breezy Point	$18,000	$19,660
10	BJ Francine	bj.francine@somewhere.com	Representative	Baudette	$17,000	$17,680
11	Kendal Shaedon	k.shaedon@somewhere.com	Representative	Breezy Point	$18,000	$13,500
12	Ella Jamison	e.jamison@somewhere.com	Manager	Baudette	$15,000	$13,200
13	Alec Mikayla	a.mikayla@somewhere.com	Representative	Baudette	$17,000	$19,350
14	Natasha Ari	n.ari@somewhere.com	Associate	Baudette	$4,500	$4,095
15	Nikolai Jalowiec	n.jalowiec@somewhere.com	Manager	Walker	$15,000	$12,600
16	Tammy Christine	t.christine@somewhere.com	Representative	Walker	$17,500	$9,275
17	Josie Daddiline	j.daddiline@somewhere.com	Representative	Walker	$17,500	$11,900
18	Christopher Bowman	c.bowman@somewhere.com	Manager	Cass Lake	$15,000	$12,750
19	Jeffery Dalton	j.dalton@somewhere.com	Manager	Cass Lake	$15,000	$12,750
20	Mae Gomez	m.gomez@somewhere.com	Representative	Cass Lake	$17,500	$13,300
21	Randy Josephson	r.josephson@somewhere.com	Associate	Cass Lake	$5,000	$3,300
22	Suzanne Ouimet	s.ouimet@somewhere.com	Manager	Breezy Point	$15,000	$14,250
23	Frankie Dennis	f.dennis@somewhere.com	Representative	Breezy Point	$18,000	$15,660
24	DJ Bushman	dj.bushman@somewhere.com	Representative	Breezy Point	$17,000	$17,680
25	Kendra Shelton	k.shelton@somewhere.com	Representative	Breezy Point	$18,000	$13,500
26	David Gazik	d.gazik@somewhere.com	Manager	Baudette	$15,000	$13,200
27	Mikayla Anderson	m.anderson@somewhere.com	Representative	Baudette	$17,000	$9,350
28	Ari Aronson	a.aronson@somewhere.com	Associate	Baudette	$4,500	$4,095
29						

Figure 4-57 Imported data formatted with new table style

6. Add a column with a calculation to a table.

a. Type Difference in cell **G4** and press **Enter**.

b. Change the column width to **10.71 (80 pixels)** and set a black bottom border for cell **G4**.

c. Type = in cell **G5** to start the formula and click cell **F5**.

d. Type – for subtraction and click cell **E5** (Figure 4-58).

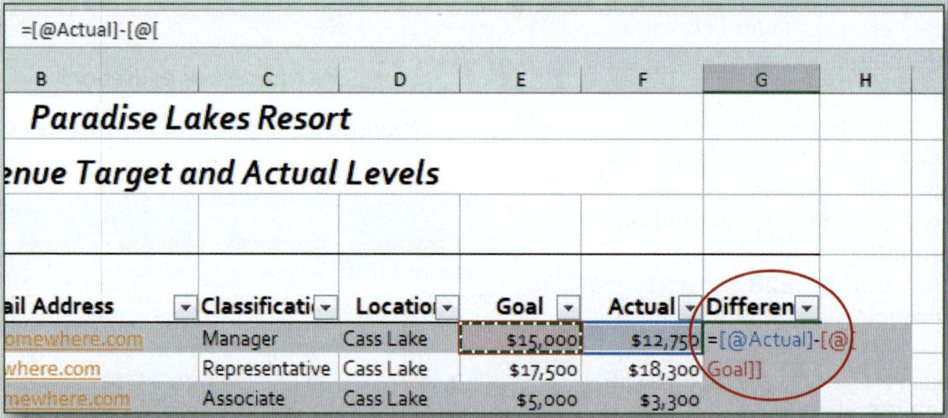

Figure 4-58 Structured references in a table formula

e. Press **Enter** to copy the formula in the column.

f. Select cells **G5:G28** and press **Ctrl+1** to open the *Format Cells* dialog box.

g. Select the *Number* tab, choose **Currency** with zero decimal places and negative numbers in red (no parentheses), and close the dialog box.

h. Select cell **G4** and apply a black **Bottom Border**.

i. Select cells **A1:G1** and click the **Merge & Center** button [*Home* tab, *Alignment* group] to remove the centering. Then, click the **Merge & Center** button again to re-center the cells over the new range.

j. Unmerge and then re-merge and center cells **A2:G2**.
k. Format row **3** with a height of **15.00 (20 pixels)** and row **4** at **22.50 (30 pixels)**.
l. Change the page orientation to **Landscape**.

7. Save and close the workbook. Close the Word document (Figure 4-59).

Paradise Lakes Resort

Revenue Target and Actual Levels

Name	Email Address	Classification	Location	Goal	Actual	Difference
Christopher Bowman	c.bowman@somewhere.com	Manager	Cass Lake	$15,000	$12,750	$2,250
Chad Mei	c.mei@somewhere.com	Representative	Cass Lake	$17,500	$18,300	$800
Corey Daniels	c.daniels@somewhere.com	Associate	Cass Lake	$5,000	$3,300	$1,700
Sharon Wyatte	s.wyatte@somewhere.com	Manager	Breezy Point	$15,000	$14,250	$750
Dennis Frankie	d.frankie@somewhere.com	Representative	Breezy Point	$18,000	$19,660	$1,660
BJ Francine	bj.francine@somewhere.com	Representative	Baudette	$17,000	$17,680	$680
Kendal Shaedon	k.shaedon@somewhere.com	Representative	Breezy Point	$18,000	$13,500	$4,500
Ella Jamison	e.jamison@somewhere.com	Manager	Baudette	$15,000	$13,200	$1,800
Alec Mikayla	a.mikayla@somewhere.com	Representative	Baudette	$17,000	$19,350	$2,350
Natasha Ari	n.ari@somewhere.com	Associate	Baudette	$4,500	$4,095	$405
Nikolai Jalowiec	n.jalowiec@somewhere.com	Manager	Walker	$15,000	$12,600	$2,400
Tammy Christine	t.christine@somewhere.com	Representative	Walker	$17,500	$9,275	$8,225
Josie Daddiline	j.daddiline@somewhere.com	Representative	Walker	$17,500	$11,900	$5,600
Christopher Bowman	c.bowman@somewhere.com	Manager	Cass Lake	$15,000	$12,750	$2,250
Jeffery Dalton	j.dalton@somewhere.com	Manager	Cass Lake	$15,000	$12,750	$2,250
Mae Gomez	m.gomez@somewhere.com	Representative	Cass Lake	$17,500	$13,300	$4,200
Randy Josephson	r.josephson@somewhere.com	Associate	Cass Lake	$5,000	$3,300	$1,700
Suzanne Ouimet	s.ouimet@somewhere.com	Manager	Breezy Point	$15,000	$14,250	$750
Frankie Dennis	f.dennis@somewhere.com	Representative	Breezy Point	$18,000	$15,660	$2,340
DJ Bushman	dj.bushman@somewhere.com	Representative	Breezy Point	$17,000	$17,680	$680
Kendra Shelton	k.shelton@somewhere.com	Representative	Breezy Point	$18,000	$13,500	$4,500
David Gazik	d.gazik@somewhere.com	Manager	Baudette	$15,000	$13,200	$1,800
Mikayla Anderson	m.anderson@somewhere.com	Representative	Baudette	$17,000	$9,350	$7,650
Ari Aronson	a.aronson@somewhere.com	Associate	Baudette	$4,500	$4,095	$405

Figure 4-59 PP E4-3 completed

Building and Formatting PivotTables

SLO 4.8

A ***PivotTable*** is a cross tabulation report based on list-type data. It is a separate worksheet in which you sort, filter, and calculate large amounts of data. *PivotTables* are analysis tools, an important part of ***Business Intelligence (BI)***. Business intelligence is a combination of applications and processes that enable you to "drill-down" into data and assess various types of results or changes. In a table or list with thousands of records, build a *PivotTable* to quickly show average revenue by state, by city, or other criteria, and, just as quickly, return to the entire list (Figure 4-60).

	A	B	C	D	E	F	G
1							
2							
3	Sum of Amount	Column Labels					
4	Row Labels	Boutique	Excursions	Rentals	Spa	Grand Total	
5	Baudette	$4,400	$6,100	$34,000	$4,500	$49,000	
6	Breezy Point	$1,200	$7,500	$31,500	$7,300	$47,500	
7	Cass Lake	$5,200	$14,500	$18,700	$3,500	$41,900	
8	Walker	$1,450	$3,800	$29,500	$2,200	$36,950	
9	Grand Total	$12,250	$31,900	$113,700	$17,500	$175,350	
10							
11							

Figure 4-60 An Excel *PivotTable*

PivotTables are interactive, because you rearrange the report for analysis by clicking or dragging. Rearranging data is *pivoting* the data so that you look at it from a different perspective. It takes time and practice to create and understand all the features of a *PivotTable*, but it is easy to experiment with placing fields, sorting data, or filtering results.

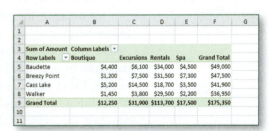

Create a PivotTable

Data for a *PivotTable* should follow the same guidelines as those recommended for an Excel table in the beginning of this chapter. Data can be formatted as a table or as a list. A *PivotTable* is placed on its own sheet in the workbook.

The *Tables* group on the *Insert* tab includes the *PivotTable* button, as well as the *Recommended PivotTables* button. When you are first learning about *PivotTables*, the *Recommended PivotTables* button may help you gain experience building these reports.

After you create a *PivotTable*, the contextual *PivotTable Tools Analyze* and *Design* tabs are available for additional format choices and data commands.

HOW TO: Create a PivotTable

1. Click a cell in the data range.
   - The data range must have a header row.
2. Click the **Recommended PivotTables** button [*Insert* tab, *Tables* group] (Figure 4-61).
   - A data range is assumed and highlighted in the worksheet.
3. Point to a preview tile on the left to see a *ScreenTip* for the proposed *PivotTable*.
4. Select the preferred *PivotTable* and click **OK**.
   - The *PivotTable* report is created on a separate sheet.

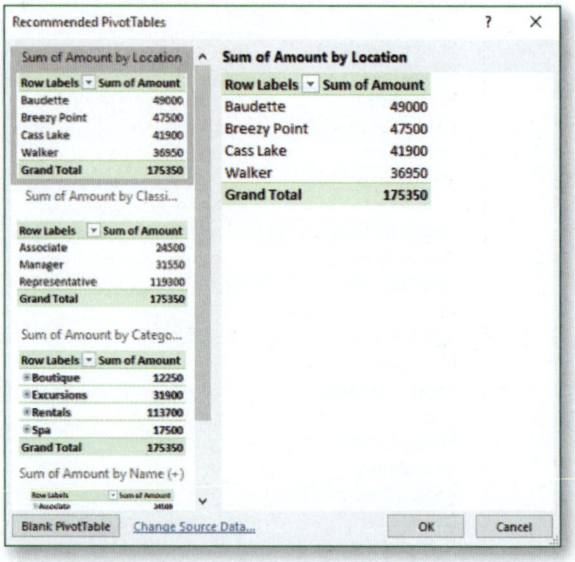

Figure 4-61 ***Recommended PivotTables* for a data range**

The PivotTable Fields Pane

A *PivotTable* is created on a new sheet in the workbook, and the *PivotTable Fields* pane opens at the right. From this pane, add and remove fields from the report and drag field names into different areas in the pane to reset how the data are organized (Figure 4-62).

Filters, *Columns*, *Rows*, and *Values* areas display in the pane. Each item from a field in the *Rows* area appears in its own row in the *PivotTable*. Each item in a field in the *Columns* area displays as a column. Columns and rows are usually the categories of data, not the actual values. Fields in the *Values* area are the ones that are summed, averaged, counted, or otherwise used in a calculation. *Filters* are fields placed as separate buttons above the *PivotTable* which act like *AutoFilter* arrows. Row and column labels include a filter arrow in the body of the *PivotTable*, and row data have collapse/expand buttons for certain field layouts. You can filter data from the filter arrows with a field, or insert a *Slicer* window.

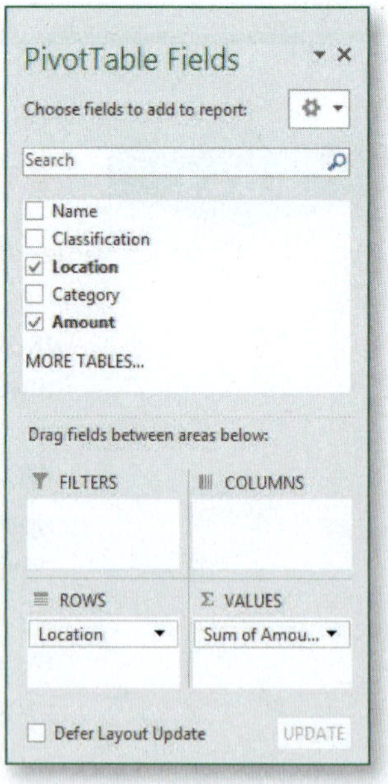

Figure 4-62 ***PivotTable Fields* pane**

Float the *PivotTable Fields* pane by pointing to its title bar and dragging it into the worksheet area.

▸HOW TO: Adjust Fields in a PivotTable

1. Click a cell in the body of the *PivotTable*.
2. Drag a field name from the *Choose fields to add to report* area into the *Columns* area in the *PivotTable Fields* pane and release the pointer button.
   - Columns for the field items are added to the report.
   - A grand total column is added.
3. Drag a field name into the *Filters* area and release the pointer button (Figure 4-63).
   - The field is added as a filter button in row 1 of the *PivotTable*.
   - No filter is applied.

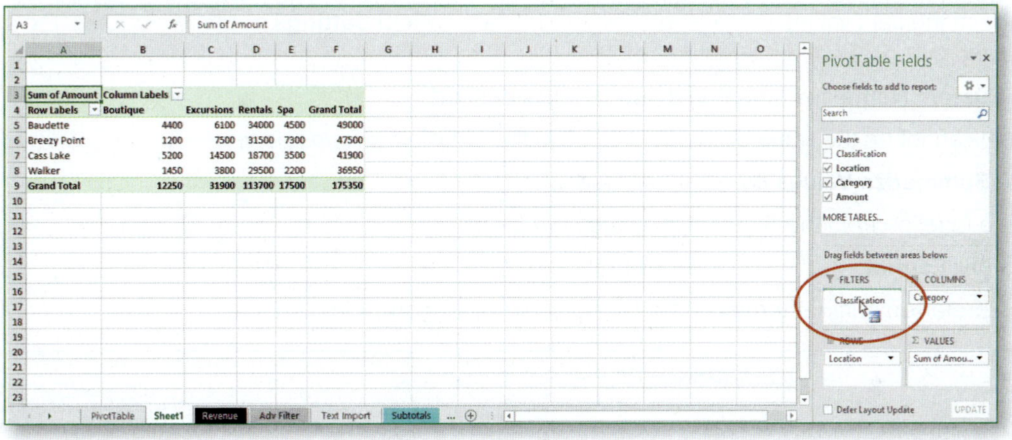

Figure 4-63 Drag fields in the *PivotTable Fields* pane

4. Drag a field name from the *Rows* area to the left and into the worksheet area.
   - The field is removed from the *PivotTable*.
5. Drag a field name from one area in the *PivotTable Fields* pane to another area.
   - The *PivotTable* is updated after each change.

Field Settings

Fields in a *PivotTable* include settings or attributes that depend on the type of data. ***Field Settings*** for a text field include layout and print options, as well as subtotal and filter choices. The *Layout* group on the *PivotTable Tools Design* tab includes many of the same commands as the *Field Settings* dialog box.

The ***Value Field Settings*** for a *PivotTable Values* field determine how data are summarized. The default function is *SUM*, but you can change the function or select a custom percentage, difference, or ranking. From the *Value Field Settings* dialog box, edit the label that appears in the *PivotTable*, choose a function, and set how numbers are formatted. To select a field in a *PivotTable*, click the field name in the *Row Labels* row or any cell in the column.

ANOTHER WAY

Right-click a field in the *PivotTable* and select **Field Settings** or **Value Field Settings** to open the dialog box.

MORE INFO

Show a field more than once in a *PivotTable* and choose different settings for each occurrence.

HOW TO: Change Value Field Settings in a PivotTable

1. Click the arrow for *Sum of [Field Name]* in the *Values* area in the *PivotTable Fields* pane.
2. Select **Value Field Settings** from the menu.
   - The *Value Field Settings* dialog box opens.
   - Click one of the field values in the *PivotTable*, and click the **Field Settings** button [*PivotTable Tools Analyze* tab, *Active Field* group] to open the dialog box.
3. Click the **Custom Name** box and type a new label as desired.
   - The label cannot be the same as the field name in the *PivotTable Fields* pane.
4. Select the **Summarize Values By** tab if necessary.
5. Choose the function from the *Summarize value field by* list.
6. Click **Number Format**.
7. Select the preferred number format in the *Format Cells* dialog box (Figure 4-64).

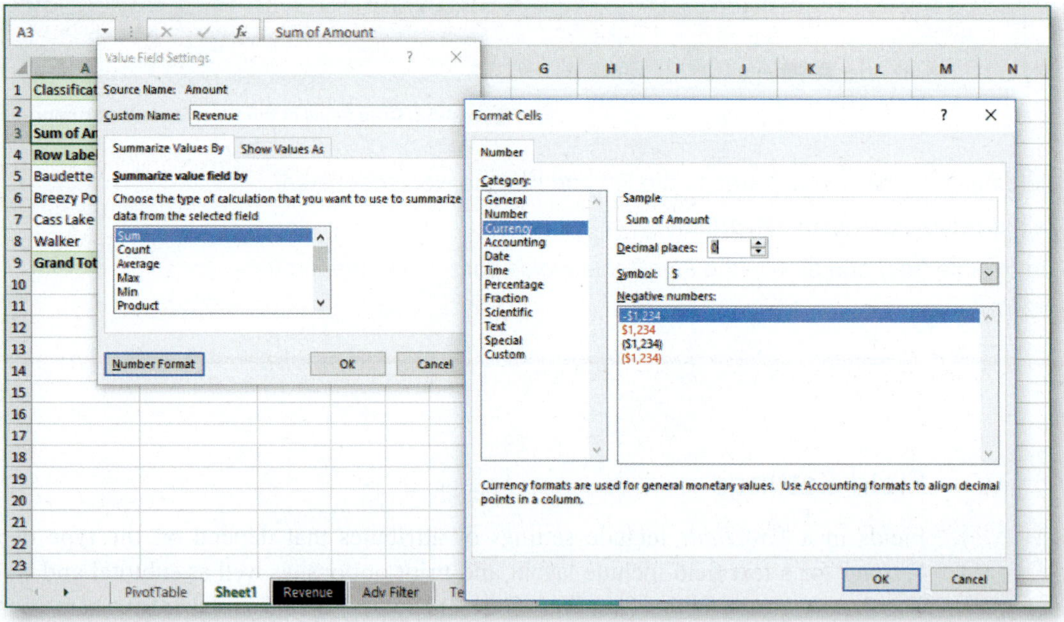

Figure 4-64 ***Value Field Settings*** **dialog box and** ***Number Format*** **options**

8. Click **OK** to close the *Format Cells* dialog box.
9. Click **OK** to close the *Value Field Settings* dialog box.
   - A new label, if entered, displays in the *PivotTable* and in the task pane.
   - The entire field is formatted.

Format a PivotTable

A *PivotTable* is formatted from the *PivotTable Tools Design* tab or from the *Home* tab. The *PivotTable Tools Design* contextual tab includes *PivotTable* styles which are similar to Excel table styles. Changes made from the *PivotTable Tools Design* tab affect the entire table.

From the *PivotTable Style Options* group, choose whether row and column headings are bold and filled and whether columns and rows are banded with fill or borders. These options depend on the *PivotTable* style. From the *Home* tab, change the font size and style, set alignment, and more. When you apply changes from the *Home* tab, the format is applied to the selected cell or cells.

HOW TO: Format a PivotTable

1. Click a cell in the *PivotTable*.
2. Click the **More** button for the *PivotTable Styles* group [*PivotTable Tools Design* tab].
   - The style gallery is categorized by light, medium, and dark colors.
3. Point to a style thumbnail to see a *Live Preview*.
   - The styles are named *(Color), Pivot Style Light 1, (Color), Pivot Style Light 2,* and so on.
   - You can design your own style.
4. Click to select a style.
5. Select the box for **Banded Rows** in the *PivotTable Styles Options* group [*PivotTable Tools Design* tab].
   - The rows are filled or a border is applied, based on the selected *PivotTable* style.
6. Select the box for **Banded Columns** in the *PivotTable Styles Options* group [*PivotTable Tools Design* tab].
   - The columns are filled or a border is applied.

PivotTable Layout

The *Layout* group commands on the *PivotTable Tools Design* tab alter the appearance of a *PivotTable*. You can hide or display subtotals and grand totals, insert a blank row after items, or repeat row labels. The *Report Layout* command offers choices for the report design and selections for repeated labels.

HOW TO: Adjust Layout and PivotTable Options

1. Click a cell in the *PivotTable*.
2. Click the **Subtotals** button [*PivotTable Tools Design* tab, *Layout* group].
   - Subtotals can be hidden or shown.
   - Subtotals can be placed at the top or the bottom of each item.
3. Select an option for subtotals.
4. Click the **Grand Totals** button [*PivotTable Tools Design* tab, *Layout* group].
   - Grand totals display at the right for columns and at the bottom for rows.
5. Choose an option for grand totals (Figure 4-65).
6. Click the **Report Layout** button [*PivotTable Tools Design* tab, *Layout* group].
   - A *Compact* format places row data in one column and occupies the least amount of horizontal space.
   - An *Outline* form places row data in separate columns (Figure 4-66).

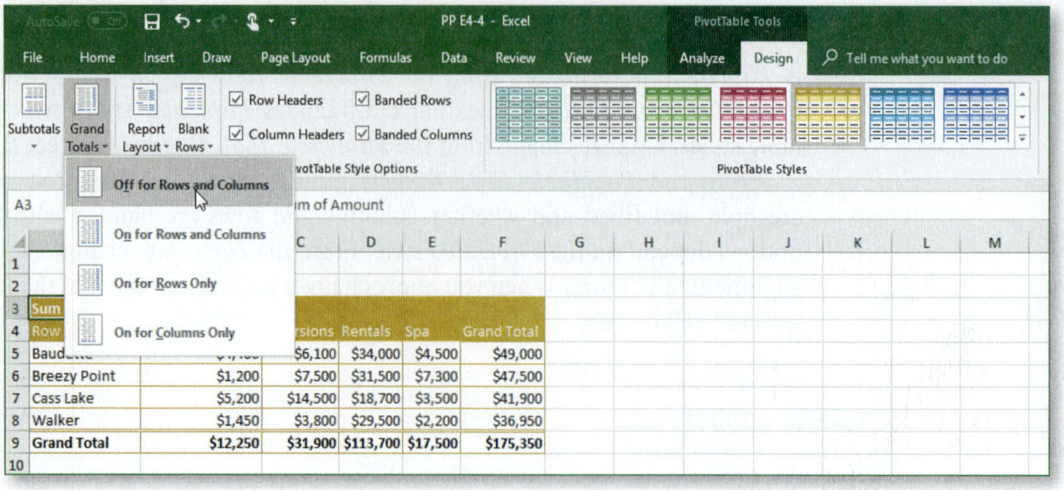

Figure 4-65 Display or hide total column and row

- *Tabular* form starts row data in the same row but in separate columns.
- *Repeat Item Labels* displays the row data in each row like an Excel table.

7. Click the **Blank Rows** button [*PivotTable Tools Design* tab, *Layout* group].
   - You can display a blank row before or after each item.
8. Click the **Options** button [*PivotTable Tools Analyze* tab, *PivotTable* group] (Figure 4-67).
   - The *PivotTable Options* dialog box has six tabs.
   - Some options are also available in the *Layout* group on the *PivotTable Tools Design* tab.

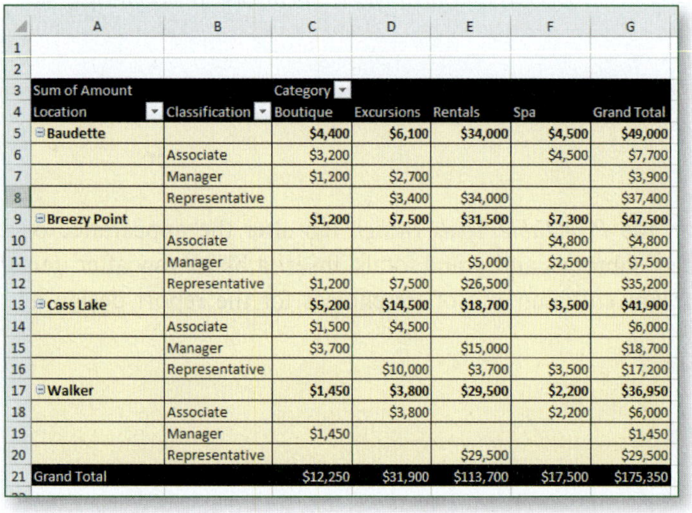

	A	B	C	D	E	F	G
3	Sum of Amount		Category				
4	Location	Classification	Boutique	Excursions	Rentals	Spa	Grand Total
5	Baudette		$4,400	$6,100	$34,000	$4,500	$49,000
6		Associate	$3,200			$4,500	$7,700
7		Manager	$1,200	$2,700			$3,900
8		Representative		$3,400	$34,000		$37,400
9	Breezy Point		$1,200	$7,500	$31,500	$7,300	$47,500
10		Associate				$4,800	$4,800
11		Manager			$5,000	$2,500	$7,500
12		Representative	$1,200	$7,500	$26,500		$35,200
13	Cass Lake		$5,200	$14,500	$18,700	$3,500	$41,900
14		Associate	$1,500	$4,500			$6,000
15		Manager	$3,700		$15,000		$18,700
16		Representative		$10,000	$3,700	$3,500	$17,200
17	Walker		$1,450	$3,800	$29,500	$2,200	$36,950
18		Associate		$3,800		$2,200	$6,000
19		Manager	$1,450				$1,450
20		Representative			$29,500		$29,500
21	Grand Total		$12,250	$31,900	$113,700	$17,500	$175,350

Figure 4-66 ***Outline* report layout**

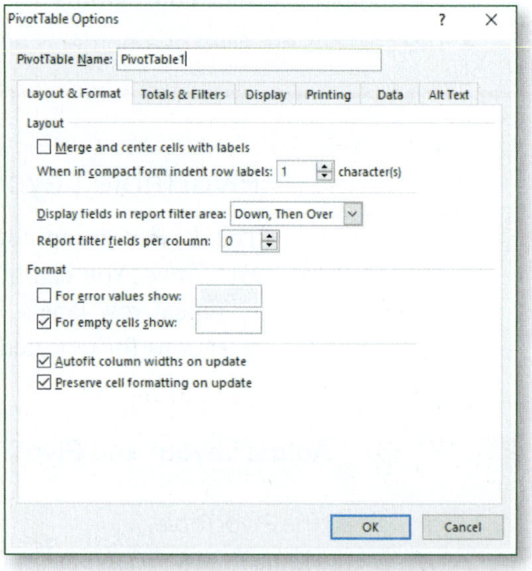

Figure 4-67 ***PivotTable Options* dialog box**

Refresh a PivotTable

Although a *PivotTable* is based on worksheet data, the *PivotTable* is not automatically updated when data are edited. This is a security measure because a *PivotTable* can be associated with data in a different workbook or an external source such as a database. Use the context-sensitive menu for any cell in the *PivotTable* and choose **Refresh**, or click the **Refresh** button in the *Data* group on the *PivotTable Tools Analyze* tab.

MORE INFO

A *PivotTable* option automatically refreshes the data each time the workbook is opened. Click the **Options** button [*PivotTable Tools Analyze* tab, *PivotTable* group] and select the **Data** tab.

HOW TO: Refresh Data in a PivotTable

1. Click any cell in the *PivotTable*.
2. Click the **Refresh** button [*PivotTable Tools Analyze* tab, *Data* group].
   - *PivotTable* data updates.
   - Refresh all data connections in the workbook by clicking the arrow for the **Refresh** button and selecting **Refresh All**.

Calculated Fields

A ***calculated field*** is a field in the *PivotTable* that is not a field in the source data. A calculated field uses a value field from the *PivotTable*'s underlying data in a formula. When you insert a calculated field, it displays as the rightmost field in the *PivotTable*, but you can move it and edit its *Value Field Settings*.

HOW TO: Insert a Calculated Field

1. Click a cell in the *PivotTable*.
2. Click the **Fields, Items, and Sets** button [*PivotTable Tools Analyze* tab, *Calculations* group].
3. Select **Calculated Field**.
4. Click the **Name** box in the *Insert Calculated Field* dialog box.
5. Type a name for the calculated field.
   - The name must be unique.
6. Click the **Formula** box and delete the zero and the space after the equals sign.
7. Enter the formula (Figure 4-68).
   - Double-click a field name in the *Fields* list to insert it in the formula.
   - Select a field name and click **Insert Field**.
   - Type an operator or a constant value to build the formula.
8. Click **OK**.
   - The calculated field is added at the right in the *PivotTable* (Figure 4-69).
   - The field name is included in the *PivotTable Fields* pane.
   - An associated *PivotChart* is updated to include the new field.

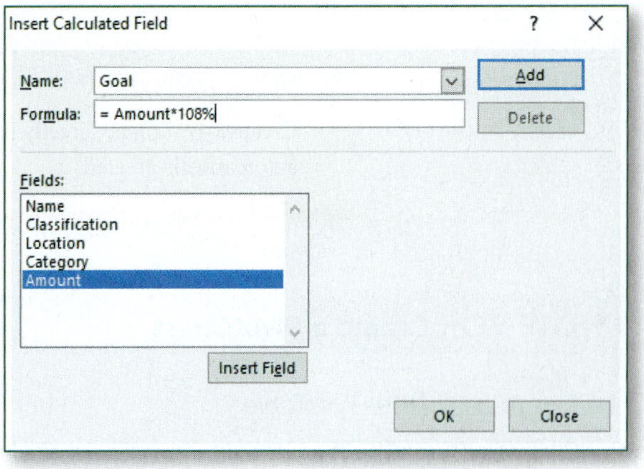

Figure 4-68 A calculated field uses a *PivotTable* field in a formula

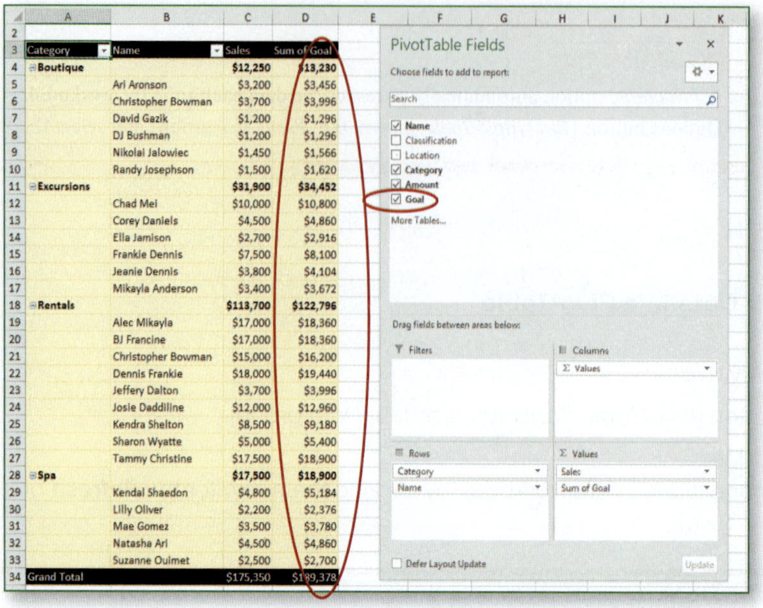

Figure 4-69 Calculated field inserted in the *PivotTable*

MORE INFO

Delete a calculated field by right-clicking a cell in the column and choosing *Remove "Field Name."*

Create a PivotChart

A ***PivotChart*** contains charted data that updates with the *PivotTable* and has the same field buttons and filter options. The *PivotChart* button is on the *PivotTable Tools Analyze* tab.

Format a *PivotChart* like an Excel chart from its *PivotChart Tools Design* and *Format* tabs. Select a style, switch row and column data, change the chart type, and so on. When the chart object is selected, you will see the *PivotChart Tools Analyze* tab with the same commands as the *PivotTable Tools Analyze* tab and the *PivotChart Fields* task pane. A *PivotChart* and its *PivotTable* are linked, and you make changes from command tabs for the table or the chart.

MORE INFO

Create a *PivotChart* directly from a list in the worksheet; its underlying *PivotTable* is automatically created.

HOW TO: Create a PivotChart

1. Click a cell in the *PivotTable*.
2. Click the **PivotChart** button [*PivotTable Tools Analyze* tab, *Tools* group].
   - The *Insert Chart* dialog box opens.
3. Select a chart type from the list on the left.

4. Select a subtype for the chart.
5. Click **OK** (Figure 4-70).
   - The chart displays as a chart object.
   - The *PivotChart Tools Analyze, Design,* and *Format* tabs are available.
   - The *PivotChart Fields* pane is similar to the *PivotTable Fields* pane.

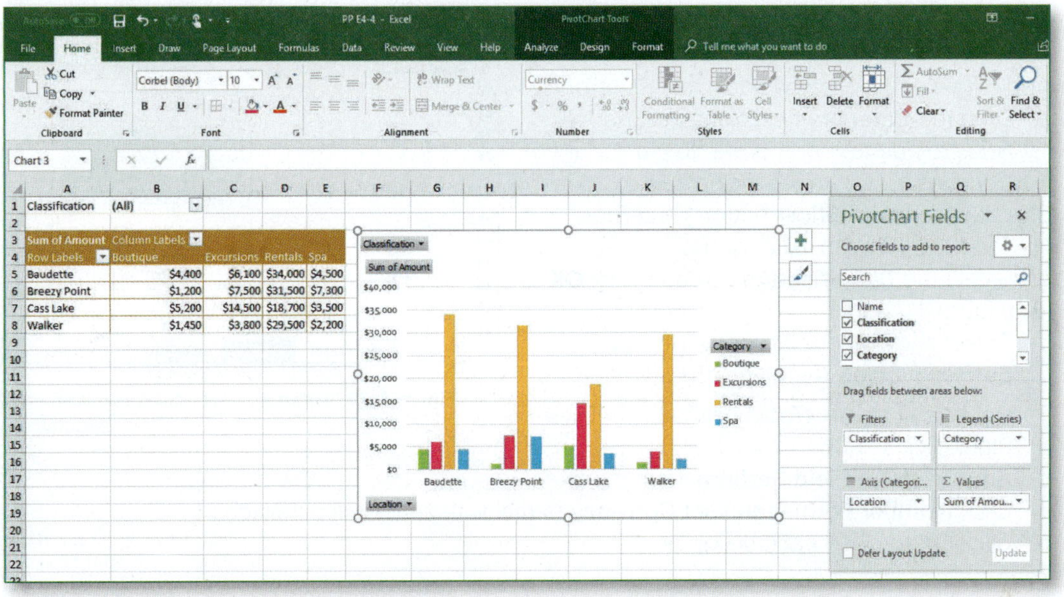

Figure 4-70 ***PivotChart*** **inserted as object**

PAUSE & PRACTICE: EXCEL 4-4

For this project, you create a *PivotTable* for Paradise Lakes Resort using the Excel table as its source. You also create a *PivotChart* and add a slicer to the worksheet. Your workbook now has data connections, so you may see a security warning when you open the file, depending on the settings on your computer.

File Needed: ***[your initials] PP E4-3.xlsx***
Completed Project File Name: ***[your initials] PP E4-4.xlsx***

1. Open the ***[your initials] PP E4-3*** workbook completed in *Pause & Practice 4-3*. The security bar informs you that the data connections have been disabled (Figure 4-71).
2. Click **Enable Content**. (If you did not see the security bar, continue to step 3.)
3. Save the workbook as [your initials] PP E4-4.

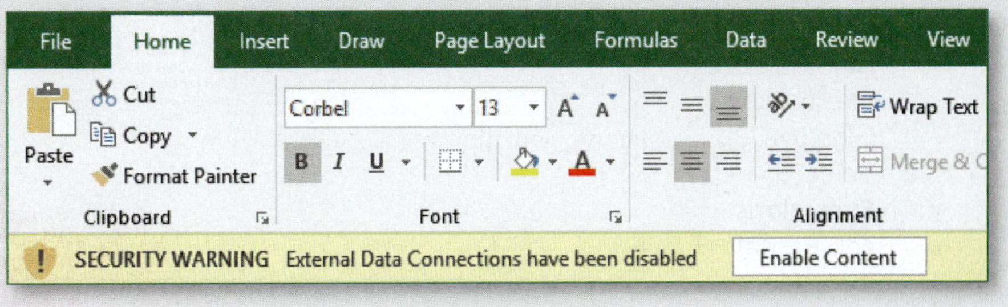

Figure 4-71 Security warning for a workbook with data connections

4. Create a *PivotTable*.
   a. Click cell **A4** on the **Revenue** sheet tab.
   b. Click the **Recommended PivotTables** button [*Insert* tab, *Tables* group].
   c. Locate and click the **Sum of Amount by Location** preview tile.
   d. Click **OK**.
   e. Name the worksheet tab PivotTable.
5. Add a field and a *Slicer* window in a *PivotTable*.
   a. Drag the **Category** field from the *Choose fields to add to report* group to the *Columns* area in the *PivotTable Fields* pane.
   b. Click the **Insert Slicer** button [*PivotTable Tools Analyze* tab, *Filter* group].
   c. Select the **Classification** box and click **OK** (Figure 4-72).
   d. Select and drag the *Slicer* window to position it below the *PivotTable*.

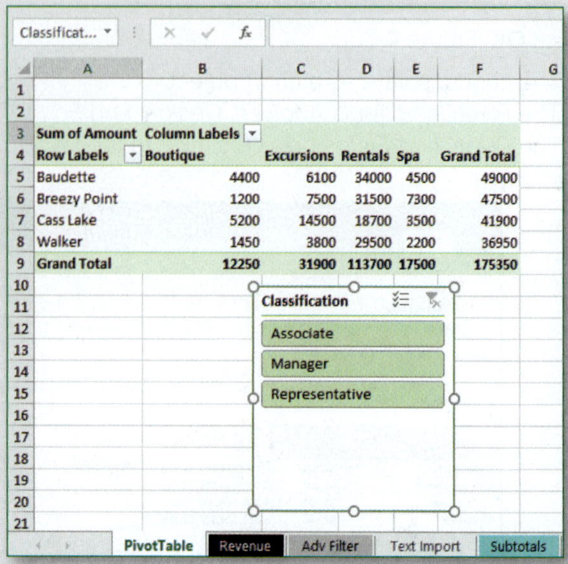

Figure 4-72 *Category* field added as column and *Slicer* window displayed

6. Format fields in a *PivotTable*.
   a. Right-click cell **B5**.
   b. Choose **Value Field Settings** from the menu.
   c. Click **Number Format** and set **Currency** format with zero decimal places.
   d. Click **OK** to close each dialog box.
7. Create a *PivotChart*.
   a. Click the **PivotChart** button [*PivotTable Tools Analyze* tab, *Tools* group].
   b. Select **Clustered Column** from the *Column* group and click **OK**.
   c. Click the **Quick Layout** button [*PivotChart Tools Design* tab, *Chart Layouts* group].
   d. Select **Layout 3**.
   e. Click to select the **Chart Title** placeholder.
   f. Click the *Formula* bar, type Revenue by Category, and press **Enter**.
   g. Position the chart object so that its top-left corner is at cell **H3**.
8. Adjust fields in a *PivotTable* and *PivotChart*.
   a. Click **Representative** in the *Slicer* window. The data are filtered in the *PivotTable* and in the *PivotChart*.
   b. Click the **Category** button in the chart.
   c. Deselect **(Select All)** to remove all the checkmarks (Figure 4-73).
   d. Select the **Excursions** and **Rentals** boxes and click **OK**.

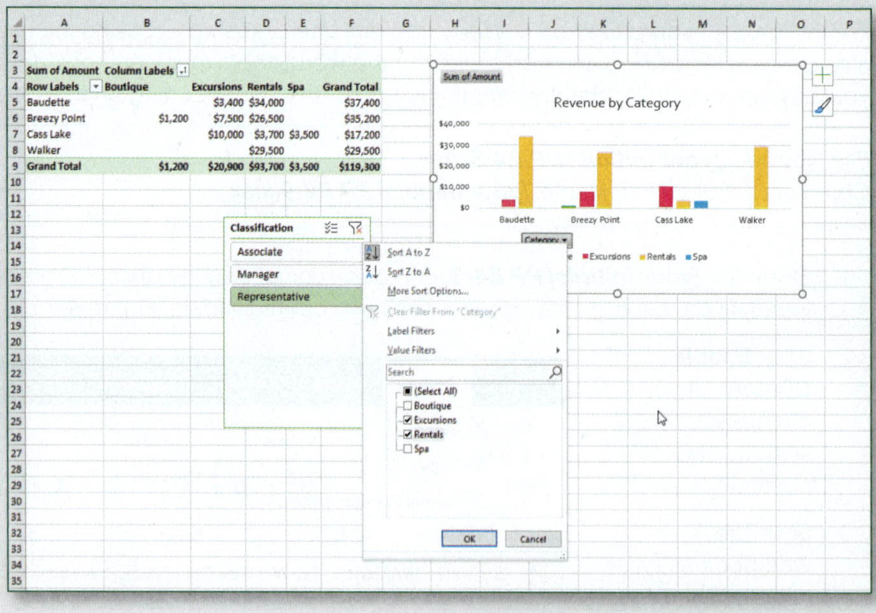

Figure 4-73 Data will be filtered in the chart and the table

9. Click cell **A1**.

10. Save and close the workbook (Figure 4-74).

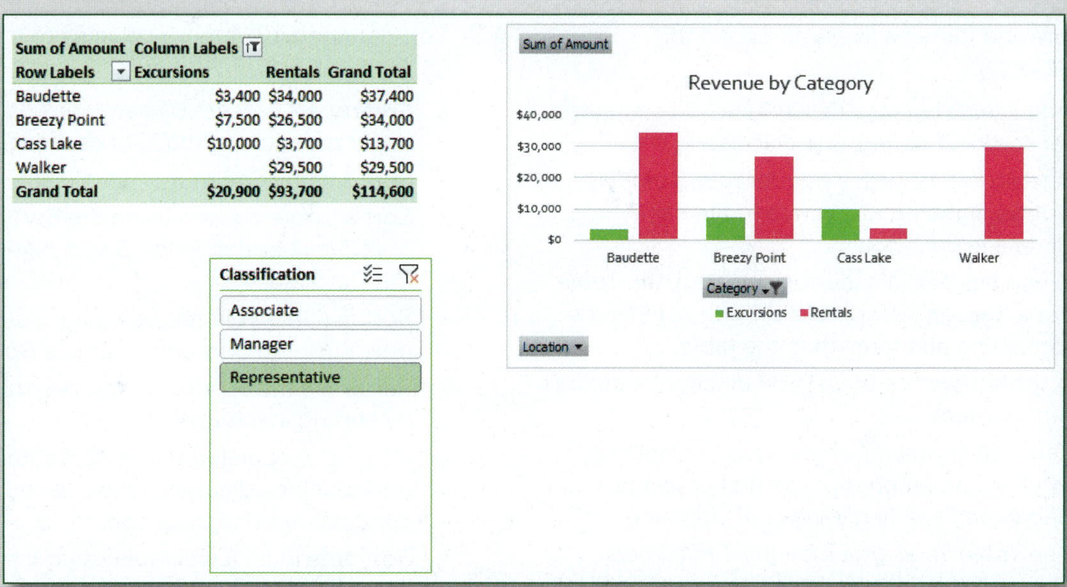

Figure 4-74 PP E4-4 completed

Chapter Summary

4.1 Create and format a list as an Excel table (p. E4–222).

- An Excel ***table*** provides enhanced commands for sorting, filtering, and calculating data.
- A table is a list with a ***header row***, *AutoFilter* arrows in the header row, and the same type of data in each column.
- When any cell in a table is selected, the *Table Tools Design* tab is available with commands for editing and formatting the table.
- A ***table style*** is a preset combination of colors and borders.
- Table style options enable you to display a total row, to emphasize the first or last column, and to add shading to rows or columns.
- The *Table Tools* group on the *Table Tools Design* tab has commands to remove duplicate rows, to convert a table to a normal cell range, or to insert a *slicer* window for filtering the data.
- The automatic name for a table and several of its parts are ***structured references***.
- Structured references appear in *Formula AutoComplete* lists and are substituted automatically in formulas that refer to certain cell ranges in the table.

4.2 Apply *Conditional Formatting* rules as well as *Color Scales, Icon Sets,* and *Data Bars* (p. E4–228).

- ***Conditional formatting*** formats only cells that meet specified criteria.
- *Highlight Cells Rules* use relational or comparison operators such as *Greater Than* or *Equals* to determine which cells are formatted.
- *Top/Bottom Rules* use ranking or averages to format cells.
- Use the *New Rule* dialog box to create a rule that uses a formula to determine which cells are formatted.
- ***Data visualization*** uses rules to format cells with *Icon Sets, Color Scales,* or *Data Bars*.
- Edit any conditional formatting rule with the *Manage Rules* command.
- Remove conditional formatting from a selected cell range or from the entire sheet with the *Clear Rules* command.

4.3 Sort data by one or more columns or by attribute (p. E4–235).

- ***Sorting*** is a process that arranges data in order, either ***ascending*** (A to Z) or ***descending*** (Z to A).
- Sort data by one or by multiple columns.
- Sort a single column using the *Sort A to Z* or *Sort Z to A* button in the *Sort & Filter* group on the *Data* tab.
- Sort multiple columns using the *Sort* dialog box. Click the *Sort* button on the *Data* tab.
- Perform a multiple column sort within the data by sorting in lowest to highest sort priority.
- Use the *Sort* dialog box to sort data by cell attribute including font color, cell fill color, or conditional formatting icon.
- Sort data in an Excel table using the *AutoFilter* arrows in the header row.

4.4 Filter data by using *AutoFilters* and by creating an *Advanced Filter* (p. E4–238).

- The *Filter* button [*Data* tab, *Sort & Filter* group] displays an *AutoFilter* arrow for each column heading in list-type data.
- Use an *AutoFilter* arrow to select records to be shown or hidden or to build a custom filter.
- A custom *AutoFilter* uses operators such as *Equals* or *Greater Than*, as well as AND and OR conditions.
- An ***Advanced Filter*** provides filter options such as using a formula in the filter definition.
- An *Advanced Filter* requires a criteria range in the same workbook and can display filtered results separate from the data.

4.5 Use subtotals, groups, and outlines for tabular data in a worksheet (p. E4–242).

- The ***Subtotal*** command inserts summary rows for sorted data using *SUM* or a statistical function.
- The *Subtotal* command formats the data as an ***outline***, which groups records to be displayed or hidden.
- Outline buttons appear next to row and column headings and determine the level of detail shown in the data.
- An ***Auto Outline*** creates groups based on formulas that are located in a consistent pattern in a list.

- Define groups by sorting data, inserting blank rows, and using the *Group* button in the *Outline* group on the *Data* tab.

4.6 Import data into an Excel worksheet from a text file, a database file, and other sources (p. E4–248).

- ***Import*** text files into a worksheet to save time and increase accuracy.
- Common text file formats include .txt (text) and .csv (comma separated values).
- Data in a text file is ***delimited*** or ***fixed width***.
- Text data are imported through a query and display in an Excel table.
- Copy data from a Word document into a worksheet.
- Import a table or a query into a worksheet from a ***Microsoft Access database***.
- Many web sites offer data in Excel or text format for downloading into a worksheet.
- Data imported from a command in the *Get & Transform Data* group establishes a data connection so that the data can be refreshed.
- The ***Flash Fill*** command recognizes and copies typing actions from one or more cells and suggests data for the remaining rows in the same column.

4.7 Export Excel data as a text file and into a Word document (p. E4–254).

- Export data in a worksheet for use in another program or application.
- Export Excel data as a text file.
- Text file formats can be tab-, space-, or comma-delimited.
- Use the Windows or Office *Clipboard* to copy data from Excel into Word and other programs.

4.8 Build and format a *PivotTable* (p. E4–259).

- A ***PivotTable*** is a cross-tabulated summary report on its own worksheet.
- When a *PivotTable* is active, the *PivotTable Tools Analyze* and *Design* tabs are available.
- The *PivotTable Fields* pane displays on the right and is turned on and off from the *Show* group [*PivotTable Tools Analyze* tab].
- The *PivotTable Fields* pane includes a list of available fields and areas in the report where the fields can be positioned.
- Drag field names in the *PivotTable Fields* pane to reposition them and analyze data from a different perspective.
- Modify and format fields in a *PivotTable* using the *Field Settings* dialog box.
- Format *PivotTables* using the *PivotTable Tools Design* tab. Format selected cells using the *Home* tab.
- *PivotTable* layout options include subtotals and grand totals, repeated labels, and display formats.
- Refresh a *PivotTable* after editing the source data by clicking the *Refresh* button [*PivotTable Tools Analyze* tab, *Data* group].
- Click the *Fields, Items, & Sets* button [*PivotTable Tools Analyze* tab, *Calculations* group] to insert a calculated field in a *PivotTable*.
- A ***PivotChart*** is a chart based on a *PivotTable* and has similar features as the *PivotTable*.

Check for Understanding

The SIMbook for this text (within your SIMnet account) provides the following resources for concept review:

- Multiple-choice questions
- Short answer questions
- Matching exercises

Guided Project 4-1

For this project, you import a text file to complete the inventory worksheet for Wear-Ever Shoes. You use *Flash Fill* to enter product codes and sort the data by supplier and code. You use *AutoFilter* for several tasks, format data as an Excel table, prepare subtotals, build a *PivotTable,* and export data as a text file. [Student Learning Outcomes 4.1, 4.2, 4.3, 4.4, 4.5, 4.6, 4.7, 4.8]

Files Needed: ***WearEver-04.xlsx*** and ***WearEverText-04.txt*** *(Student data files are available in the* Library *of your SIMnet account.)*
Completed Project File Names: ***[your initials] Excel 4-1.xlsx*** and ***[your initials] Excel 4-1Export.txt***

Skills Covered in This Project

- Import a text file.
- Sort data.
- Use *Flash Fill* to complete data.
- Use an *AutoFilter.*
- Set conditional formatting.
- Create an Excel table.
- Use the *Subtotal* command.
- Create and format a *PivotTable.*
- Export data as a tab-delimited file.

---

1. Open the ***WearEver-04*** workbook from your student data files and save it as [your initials] Excel 4-1.
2. Import a text file.
   a. Select cell **I3**. The text file includes headings that will display in row 4 after importing.
   b. Click the **From Text/CSV** button [*Data* tab, *Get & Transform Data* group].
   c. Find and select the ***WearEverText-04.txt*** file from your student data files in the *Import Data* window.
   d. Click **Import**.
   e. Click the **Delimiter** arrow in the *Navigator* window and choose **Tab** (Figure 4-75).
   f. Click the **Load** arrow and select **Load To**.
   g. Select **Existing worksheet**.
   h. Verify that cell **$I$3** displays as the location and click **OK**. The supplier name and phone number are imported and added to the list.
3. Select cells **I3:J40** and click the **Convert to Range** button [*Table Design* tab, *Tools* group] (Figure 4-76).

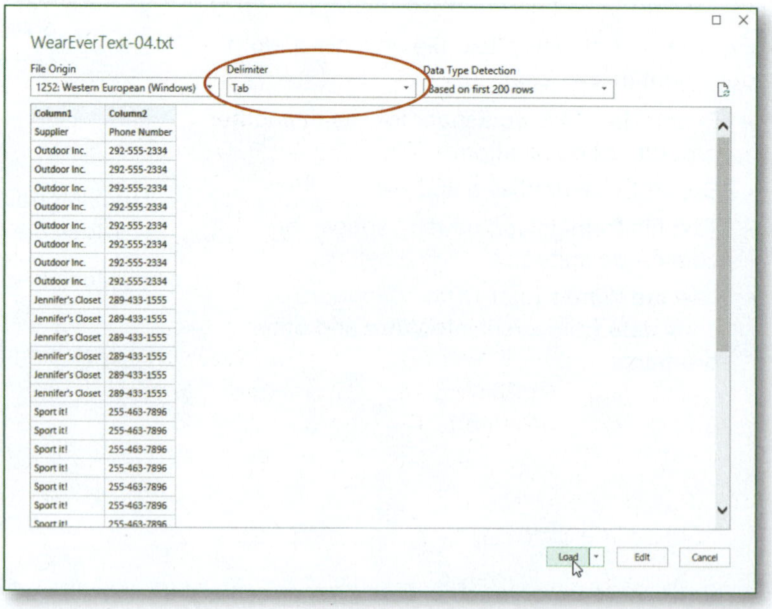

Figure 4-75 Delimiter character selected in the *Navigator* window

4. Click **OK** to remove the query definition, and close the *Queries & Connections* pane.

5. Use the **Format Painter** button to copy formatting from cell **H4** to cells **I4:J4**.

6. Select cells **I5:J40** and clear formats [*Home* tab, *Editing* group]. Format cells **I5:J40** with **Trebuchet MS** from the *Theme Fonts*.

7. Select cells **I3:J3** and clear all [*Home* tab, *Editing* group].

8. *AutoFit* columns **I:J**.

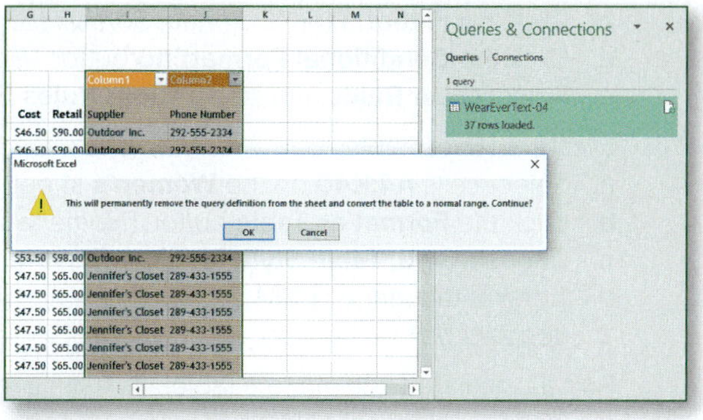

Figure 4-76 Data connection will be removed to create the table

9. Select cells **A1:J2** and click the **Launcher** in the *Alignment* group [*Home* tab]. From the *Horizontal* list, choose **Center Across Selection** and click **OK**.

10. Sort data in multiple columns.
    a. Select cell **A5** and click the **Sort** button [*Data* tab, *Sort & Filter* group].
    b. Select the **My data has headers** box if necessary.
    c. Click the **Sort by** arrow and choose **Supplier**.
    d. Verify that **Cell Values** is selected for *Sort On*.
    e. Choose **A to Z** for *Order*.
    f. Click **Add Level**.
    g. Click the **Then by** arrow and choose **Product**.
    h. Verify that **Cell Values** is selected for *Sort On* and that **A to Z** is selected for *Order*.
    i. Click **OK**. The data are in order by supplier name and then by product name.

11. Use *Flash Fill* to insert product codes.
    a. Insert a column between columns **B** and **C**.
    b. Type Code in cell **C4**.
    c. Type CWS in cell **C5** and press **Enter**.
    d. Type c in cell **C6** and press **Enter**. Regular *AutoComplete* completes the entries based on what is already in the column. The *Flash Fill* suggestion list does not appear because no recognizable pattern was identified.
    e. Click the **Fill** button [*Home* tab, *Editing* group] in cell **C7** and choose **Flash Fill**.
    f. *AutoFit* column **C**.

12. Apply conditional formatting.
    a. Select cells **F5:F40**, the quantity in stock.
    b. Click the **Conditional Formatting** button [*Home* tab, *Style* group].
    c. Click **Highlight Cells Rules** and select **Less Than**.
    d. Type 2 in the *Format cells that are LESS THAN* box.
    e. Click **OK** to accept the *Light Red Fill with Dark Red Text* format.

13. Use an *AutoFilter*.
    a. Select cell **A5** and click the **Filter** button [*Data* tab, *Sort & Filter* group].
    b. Click the *AutoFilter* arrow for the **Supplier** column.
    c. Deselect the **(Select All)** box to remove all the checkmarks.
    d. Select the **Jennifer's Closet** box.
    e. Click **OK**. The data are filtered to show only records from one supplier.

14. Copy the **Inventory** worksheet to the end and name the copy Women's. Set the tab color to **Gold, Accent 4** (eighth column).

15. Clear a filter and conditional formatting.
    a. Select the **Women's** sheet and click the *AutoFilter* arrow for the **Supplier** column.
    b. Select **Clear Filter from "Supplier"**.

c. Click the **Filter** button [*Data* tab, *Sort & Filter* group] to hide the *AutoFilter* arrows.
d. Click the **Conditional Formatting** button [*Home* tab, *Style* group].
e. Select **Clear Rules** and select **Clear Rules From Entire Sheet**.

16. Create an Excel table.
   a. Select cells **A4:K40** on the **Women's** sheet.
   b. Click the **Format as Table** button [*Home* tab, *Styles* group].
   c. Choose **Gold, Table Style Medium 5** in the *Table Styles* gallery.
   d. Confirm the range ($A$4:$K$40) in the *Format as Table* dialog box, that the *My table has headers* box is checked, and click **OK**.

17. Add a calculated column to a table.
   a. Insert a column at column **J**.
   b. Type Markup in cell **J4** and press **Enter**.
   c. Type = in cell **J5** and click cell **I5**.
   d. Type – for subtraction and click cell **H5** (Figure 4-77).
   e. Press **Enter** to copy the formula.

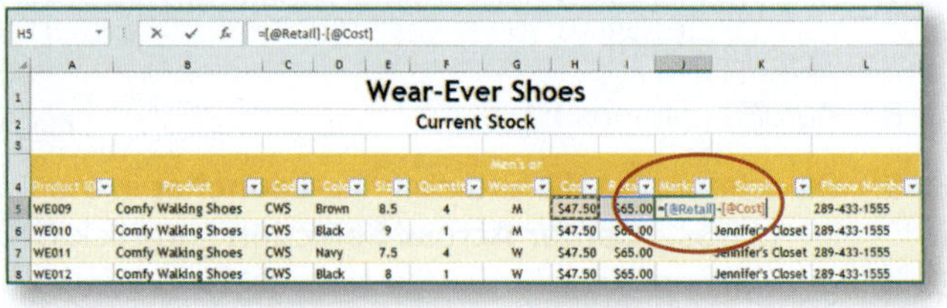
Figure 4-77 Add a calculated column to the table

18. Filter data in a table.
   a. Click the *AutoFilter* arrow for the **Men's or Women's** column.
   b. Deselect the **(Select All)** box to remove all the checkmarks.
   c. Select the **W** box and click **OK**.
   d. Press **Ctrl+Home**.

19. Copy the **Inventory** worksheet to the end and name the copy Subtotals. Set the tab color to **Black, Text 1** (second column).

20. Clear a filter and conditional formatting.
   a. Select the **Subtotals** sheet and clear the filter for the **Supplier**.
   b. Click the **Filter** button [*Data* tab, *Sort & Filter* group] to hide the *AutoFilter* arrows.
   c. Click the **Conditional Formatting** button [*Home* tab, *Style* group] and clear rules from the sheet.

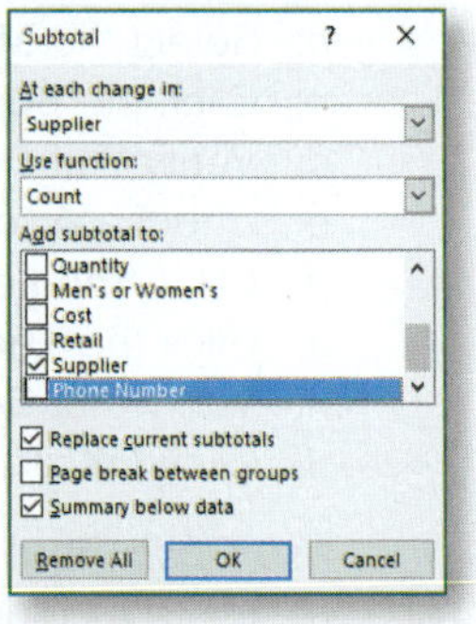
Figure 4-78 *Subtotal* dialog box to count number of products by supplier

21. Use the *Subtotal* command.
   a. Select cell **J5** on the **Subtotals** sheet. The records are sorted by the "Supplier" column.
   b. Click the **Subtotal** button [*Data* tab, *Outline* group].
   c. Click the **At each change in** arrow and choose **Supplier**.
   d. Click the **Use function** arrow and choose **Count**.
   e. Check the **Supplier** box in the *Add subtotal to* area.
   f. Deselect any other selected fields in the *Add subtotal to* list (Figure 4-78).
   g. Click **OK**. A subtotal row displays at the bottom of each group and shows how many products are available from each supplier.
   h. Format the label in cell **I17** as **right-aligned**.
   i. **Right-align** the remaining subtotal labels in column **I** (Figure 4-79).

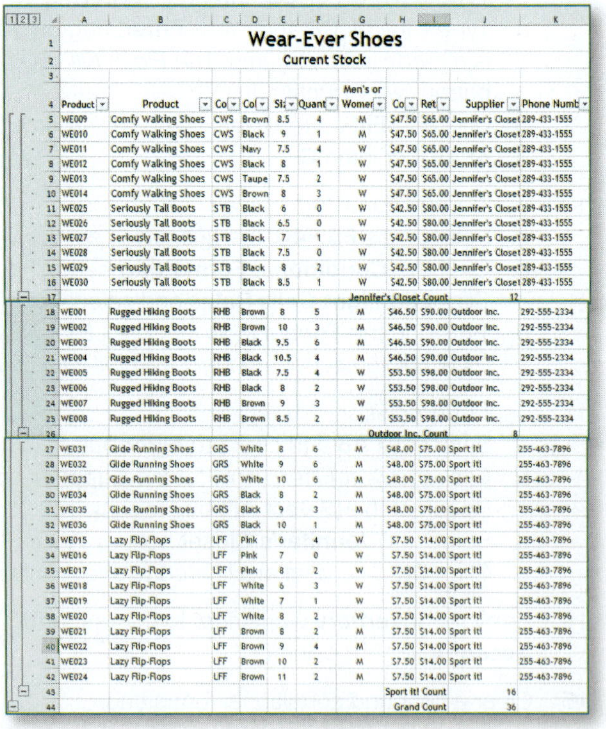
Figure 4-79 Subtotals inserted for each group

22. Create a *PivotTable*.
 a. Click the **Inventory** sheet tab and select cell **A5**.
 b. Click the **PivotTable** button [*Insert* tab, *Tables* group].
 c. Verify that the *Table/Range* is **A4:K40** in the *Create PivotTable* dialog box and that the *New Worksheet* button is selected.

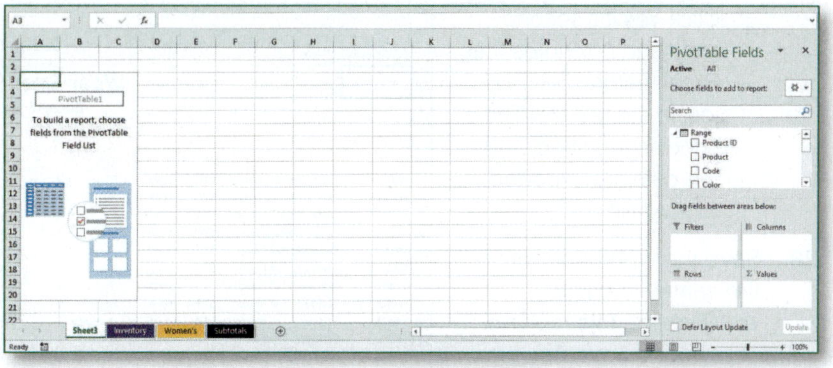

Figure 4-80 Blank *PivotTable* layout

 d. Click **OK**. A blank *PivotTable* layout displays on a new sheet (Figure 4-80).
 e. Name the sheet PivotTable.

23. Add fields in a *PivotTable*.
 a. Select the **Product** box in the *PivotTable Fields* pane to place it in the *Rows* area.
 b. Select the **Quantity** box to place it in the *Values* area.
 c. Drag the **Supplier** field name into the *Columns* area.

24. Format a *PivotTable*.
 a. Click the **More** button in the *PivotTable Styles* group [*PivotTable Tools Design* tab].
 b. Select **Light Orange, Pivot Style Medium 7**.
 c. Select the **Banded Rows** box [*PivotTable Tools Design* tab, *PivotTable Style Options* group].
 d. Select the **Banded Columns** box [*PivotTable Tools Design* tab, *PivotTable Style Options* group] (Figure 4-81).

A	B	C	D	E
1					
2					
3	Sum of Quantity	Column Labels ▼			
4	Row Labels ▼	Jennifer's Closet	Outdoor Inc.	Sport it!	Grand Total
5	Comfy Walking Shoes	15			15
6	Glide Running Shoes			24	24
7	Lazy Flip-Flops			22	22
8	Rugged Hiking Boots		29		29
9	Seriously Tall Boots	4			4
10	Grand Total	19	29	46	94

Figure 4-81 Formatted *PivotTable*

25. Copy the **Inventory** worksheet to the end and do not rename it.

26. Select the copied sheet, clear the filter from the **Supplier** column, and remove the *AutoFilter* arrows. Conditional formatting need not be cleared.

27. Export data as a tab-delimited file.
 a. Click cell **A1** in the copied sheet.
 b. Click the **File** tab and select **Export**.
 c. Select **Change File Type**.
 d. Select **Text (Tab delimited)** as the file type.
 e. Click **Save As**.
 f. Navigate to the save location for the exported data in the *Save as type* dialog box.
 g. Type [your initials]Excel 4-1Export as the file name.
 h. Click **Save**.
 i. Click **OK** in the message box to save only the current sheet (Figure 4-82).

Microsoft Excel ✕

The selected file type does not support workbooks that contain multiple sheets.

• To save only the active sheet, click OK.
• To save all sheets, save them individually using a different file name for each, or choose a file type that supports multiple sheets.

[OK] [Cancel]

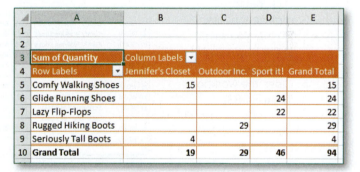

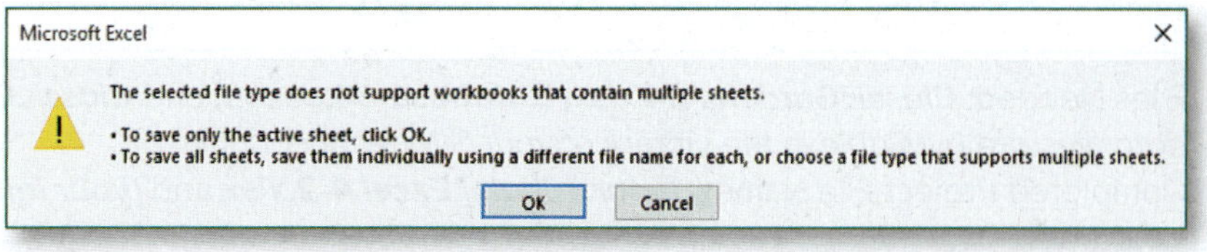

Figure 4-82 Only the current sheet is saved as a text file

j. Click **Yes** if a second message box notes that Excel features may be lost in the text file. The sheet is renamed, and the data are exported to a *.txt* file.

28. Save the workbook with the same file name.
    a. Click the **File** tab and choose **Save As**.
    b. Navigate to the folder for saved work.
    c. Select **Excel Workbook** as the *Save as type* in the *Save As* dialog box.
    d. Select ***[your initials] Excel 4-1*** or retype that file name.
    e. Click **Save** and click **Yes** to replace the .xlsx file that you saved at the beginning of this project.
    f. Close the workbook (Figure 4-83).

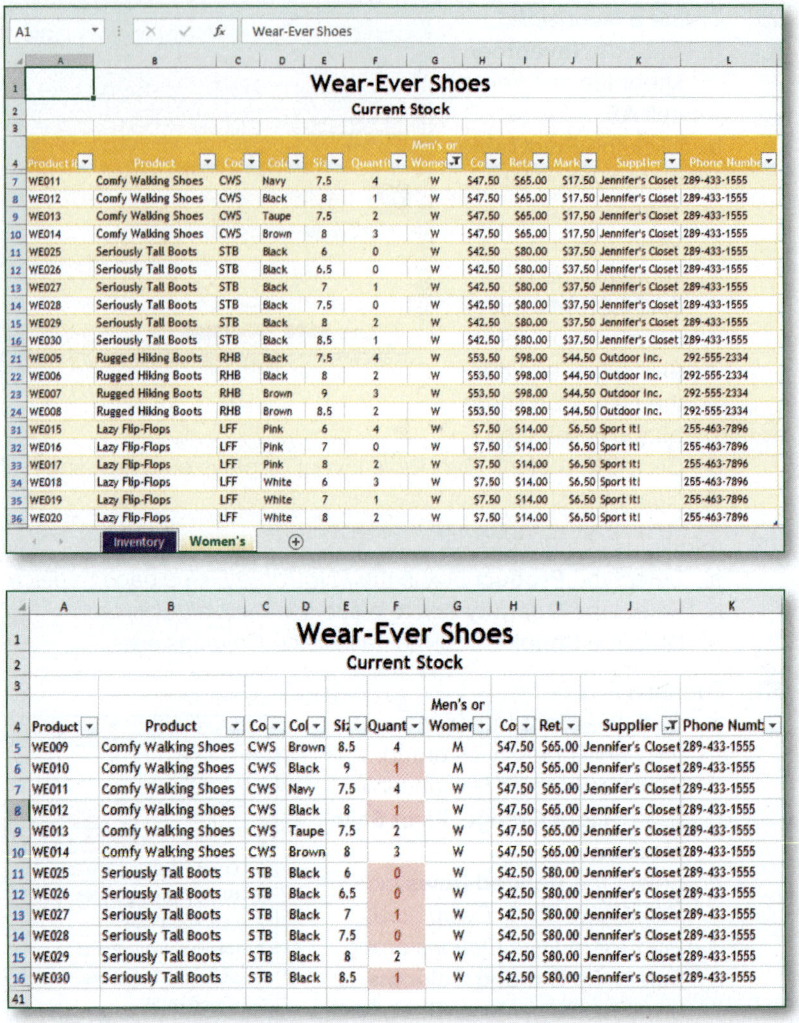

Figure 4-83 Excel 4-1 completed

Guided Project 4-2

Classic Gardens and Landscapes is building a workbook with data about revenue and promotion campaigns. You copy data from Word and import data from an Access database. You set conditional formatting, format an Excel table, sort and filter data, and build a *PivotTable* and *PivotChart*.
[Student Learning Outcomes 4.1, 4.2, 4.3, 4.4, 4.5, 4.6, 4.7, 4.8]

Files Needed: ***ClassicGardens-04.xlsx, Database-04.accdb,*** and ***ClassicGardensWord-04.docx*** *(Student data files are available in the* Library *of your SIMnet account.)*
Completed Project File Names: ***[your initials] Excel 4-2.xlsx*** and ***[your initials] Excel 4-2Text.csv***

Skills Covered in This Project

- Copy data from Word.
- Use conditional formatting with an icon set.
- Prepare data for an *Auto Outline*.
- Import a table from a database file.
- Apply a table style and show a total row.
- Sort and filter data in a table.
- Build and format a *PivotTable*.
- Build a *PivotChart*.
- Filter data in a *PivotChart*.
- Export data as a comma-separated text file.

---

1. Open the ***ClassicGardens-04*** workbook from your student data files and save it as [your initials] Excel 4-2.
2. Select the **Quarterly** sheet; insert six columns between columns **G** and **H**.
3. Copy data from Word.
   a. Open the Word document ***ClassicGardensWord-04.docx*** from your student data files.
   b. Select all the data in Word and copy it.
   c. Select cell **H4** in the Excel workbook.
   d. Click the **Paste** button arrow [*Home* tab, *Clipboard* group] and choose **Match Destination Formatting**.
   e. Select cell **N5** and click the **AutoSum** button [*Home* tab, *Editing* group].
   f. Verify or select the range **B5:M5** and press **Enter**.
   g. Copy the formula to cells **N6:N9**.
   h. Select cells **H10:M10** and click the **AutoSum** button [*Home* tab, *Editing* group].
4. Apply conditional formatting.
   a. Select cells **N5:N9**.
   b. Click the **Quick Analysis** button.
   c. Verify that **Formatting** is selected.
   d. Choose **Icon Set** (Figure 4-84). The cells display a default icon to represent the upper, middle, or lower values of the range.

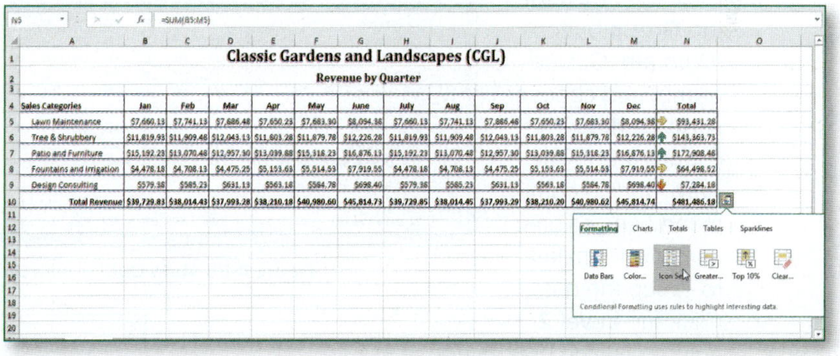

Figure 4-84 Icon set conditional formatting

5. *AutoFit* the columns and verify all data are visible.
6. Click the **AutoOutline** sheet tab.
7. Use *AutoSum* to calculate subtotals and totals.
   a. Select cells **E5:E18**, press **Ctrl** and select cells **I5:I18**, **M5:M18**, and **Q5:Q18** (Figure 4-85).
   b. Click the **AutoSum** button [*Home* tab, *Editing* group].

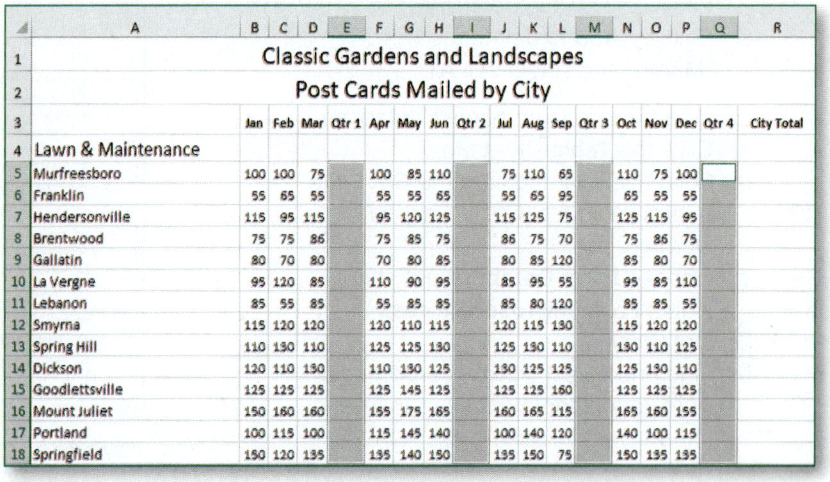

Classic Gardens and Landscapes
Post Cards Mailed by City
Jan
Feb
Mar
Qtr 1
Apr
May
Jun
Qtr 2
Jul
Aug
Sep
Qtr 3
Oct
Nov
Dec
Qtr 4
City Total
Lawn & Maintenance
Murfreesboro
Franklin
Hendersonville
Brentwood
Gallatin
La Vergne
Lebanon
Smyrna
Spring Hill
Dickson
Goodlettsville
Mount Juliet
Portland
Springfield

Figure 4-85 *SUM* function in a consistent pattern

c. Select cells **R5:R18** and click the **AutoSum** button [*Home* tab, *Editing* group]. Excel sums the *Qtr 1, Qtr 2, Qtr 3,* and *Qtr 4* columns (Q5, M5, I5, E5).
d. Select cells **B19:R19** and click the **AutoSum** button [*Home* tab, *Editing* group].
e. *AutoFit* columns to display all the data.
f. Select cells **E21:E25**, press **Ctrl** and select cells **I21:I25**, **M21:M25**, and **Q21:Q25**.
g. Click the **AutoSum** button [*Home* tab, *Editing* group].
h. Use *AutoSum* in cells **R21:R25** and verify that the *SUM* function refers to columns Q, M, I, and E.
i. Select cells **B26:R26** and click the **AutoSum** button [*Home* tab, *Editing* group].
j. Select cells **E28:E33**, **I28:I33**, **M28:M33**, **Q28:Q33** and use *AutoSum*.
k. Complete the *SUM* function for cells **R28:R33** and then for cells **B34:R34**.
l. *AutoFit* the columns.

8. Insert formulas to calculate monthly totals.
   a. Type **=** in cell **B35** to start a formula.
   b. Click cell **B19**, type **+**, click cell **B26**, type **+**, click cell **B34**, and press **Enter**. The formula is **=B19 + B26 + B34**.
   c. Copy the formula in cell **B35** to cells **C35:R35**.
   d. *AutoFit* columns to display all the data.

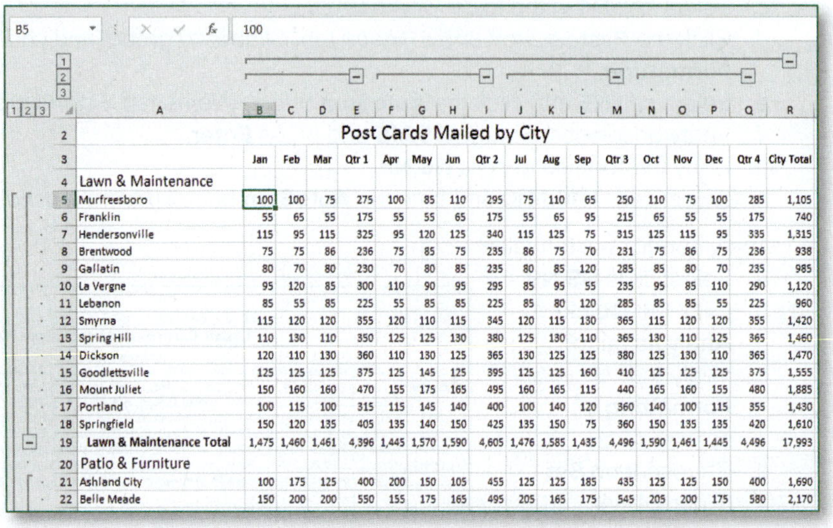

Figure 4-86 *Auto Outline* with three row levels and three column levels

9. Create an *Auto Outline*.
   a. Click cell **B5**.
   b. Click the arrow for the **Group** button [*Data* tab, *Outline* group] and choose **Auto Outline** (Figure 4-86). The *Auto Outline* command uses column and row formulas to group the data.
   c. Click the **Level 2** column outline button (above the column headings). Only the quarter totals display (Figure 4-87).
   d. Edit cell **A35** to delete the word "Month" and select cell **A1**.

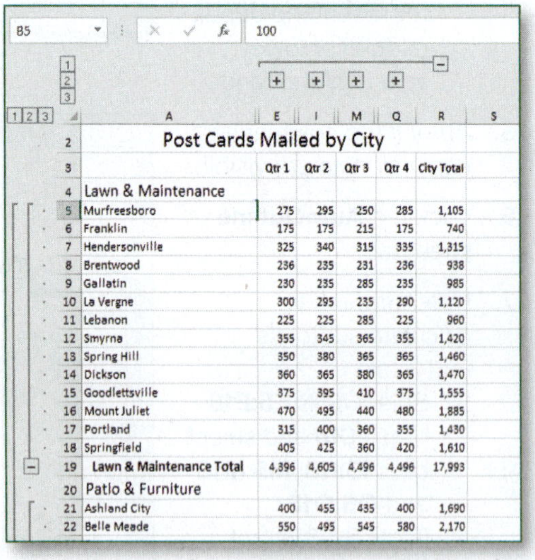

Figure 4-87 Outline collapsed at Level 2 column group

10. Import a table from an Access database.
    a. Click the **Table** sheet tab.
    b. Select cell **A4** and click the **Get Data** button [*Data* tab, *Get & Transform Data* group].
    c. Choose **From Database** and then select **From Microsoft Access Database**.
    d. Find and select ***Database-04.accdb*** from your student data files in the *Import Data* window.

e. Click **Import**.
f. Click **tblMailings** in the *Navigator* dialog box (Figure 4-88).
g. Click the **Load** arrow and choose **Load To**.
h. Select **Existing worksheet**, verify that cell **A4** is the destination cell, and click **OK**.

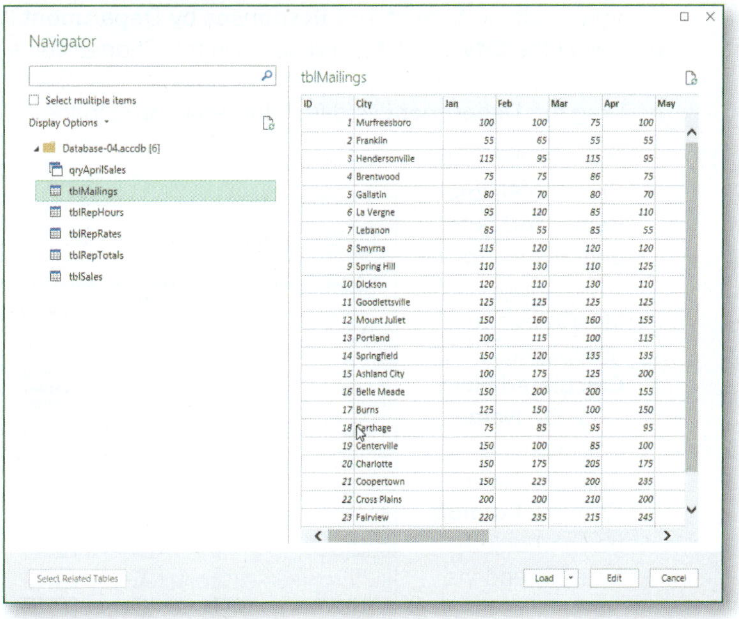

ID	City	Jan	Feb	Mar	Apr	May
1	Murfreesboro	100	100	75	100	
2	Franklin	55	65	55	55	
3	Hendersonville	115	95	115	95	
4	Brentwood	75	75	86	75	
5	Gallatin	80	70	80	70	
6	La Vergne	95	120	85	110	
7	Lebanon	85	55	85	55	
8	Smyrna	115	120	120	120	
9	Spring Hill	110	130	110	125	
10	Dickson	120	110	130	110	
11	Goodlettsville	125	125	125	125	
12	Mount Juliet	150	160	160	155	
13	Portland	100	115	100	115	
14	Springfield	150	120	135	135	
15	Ashland City	100	175	125	200	
16	Belle Meade	150	200	200	155	
17	Burns	125	150	100	150	
18	Carthage	75	85	95	95	
19	Centerville	150	100	85	100	
20	Charlotte	150	175	205	175	
21	Coopertown	150	225	200	235	
22	Cross Plains	200	200	210	200	
23	Fairview	220	235	215	245	

Figure 4-88 ***Navigator*** **dialog box for an Access database**

11. Apply a table style and show a total row.
    a. Click cell **B5** in the table.
    b. Click the **More** button [*Table Tools Design* tab, *Table Styles* group].
    c. Choose **White, Table Style Medium 15**.
    d. Select the **Total Row** box [*Table Tools Design* tab, *Table Style Options* group].
    e. Click cell **C30** (January total) and choose **Sum**. Then copy the formula to cells **D30:M30**.

12. Sort and filter data in an Excel table.
    a. Click the *AutoFilter* arrow for **City**.
    b. Choose **Sort A to Z**.
    c. Click the *AutoFilter* arrow for **City**.
    d. Select **Text Filters** and **Equals**.
    e. Type **c*** in the first criteria box to select cities that begin with "C."
    f. Select the **Or** radio button.
    g. Select **equals** as the second operator.
    h. Type **m*** in the second criteria box to select cities that begin with "M" (Figure 4-89).
    i. Click **OK**.

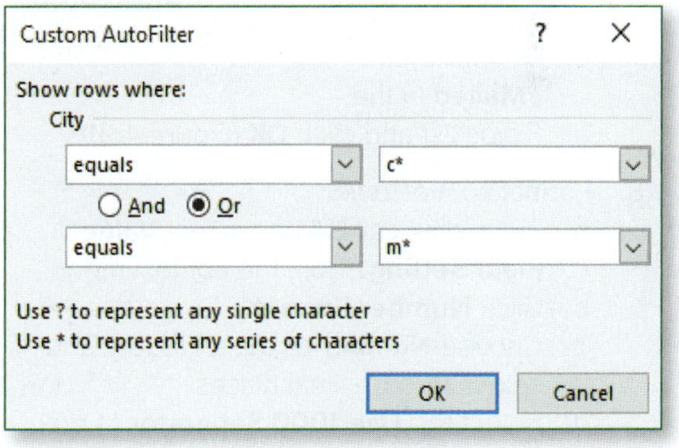

Figure 4-89 ***Custom AutoFilter*** **for cities that begin with "C" or "M"**

13. Select cells **A1:N1**, merge and center the labels, and change the font size to **18 pt**. (Figure 4-90).

14. Repeat these steps for cells **A2:N2** (Figure 4-90).

15. Close the *Queries & Connections* pane and select the **Pivot Source** sheet tab.

16. Create a *PivotTable*.
    a. Select cell **A5**.
    b. Click the **Recommended PivotTables** button [*Insert* tab, *Tables* group].

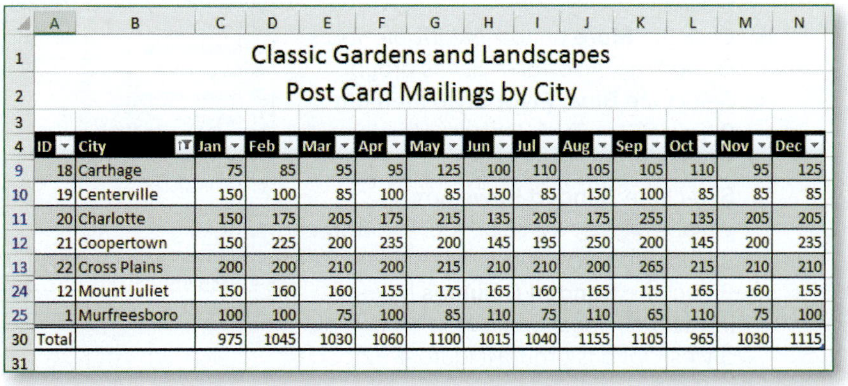

Classic Gardens and Landscapes

Post Card Mailings by City

ID	City	Jan	Feb	Mar	Apr	May	Jun	Jul	Aug	Sep	Oct	Nov	Dec
18	Carthage	75	85	95	95	125	100	110	105	105	110	95	125
19	Centerville	150	100	85	100	85	150	85	150	100	85	85	85
20	Charlotte	150	175	205	175	215	135	205	175	255	135	205	205
21	Coopertown	150	225	200	235	200	145	195	250	200	145	200	235
22	Cross Plains	200	200	210	200	215	210	210	200	265	215	210	210
12	Mount Juliet	150	160	160	155	175	165	160	165	115	165	160	155
1	Murfreesboro	100	100	75	100	85	110	75	110	65	110	75	100
Total		975	1045	1030	1060	1100	1015	1040	1155	1105	965	1030	1115

Figure 4-90 Imported data sorted and filtered

c. Verify that the **Sum of # of Responses by Department** thumbnail is selected and click **OK**.
d. Select the **City** and **# Mailed** boxes in the *Choose fields to add to report* area to add them to the report.
e. Drag the **Department** field from the *Rows* area to the *Filters* area in the *PivotTable Fields* pane.

17. Insert a calculated field in a *PivotTable*.
   a. Click the **Fields, Items, and Sets** button [*PivotTable Tools Analyze* tab, *Calculations* group] and select **Calculated Field**.
   b. Click the **Name** box and type Response Ratio.
   c. Click the **Formula** box and delete the zero and the space after the equals sign.
   d. Double-click **# Responses** in the *Fields* list and type / for division.
   e. Double-click **#Mailed** in the *Fields* list and click **OK** (Figure 4-91).

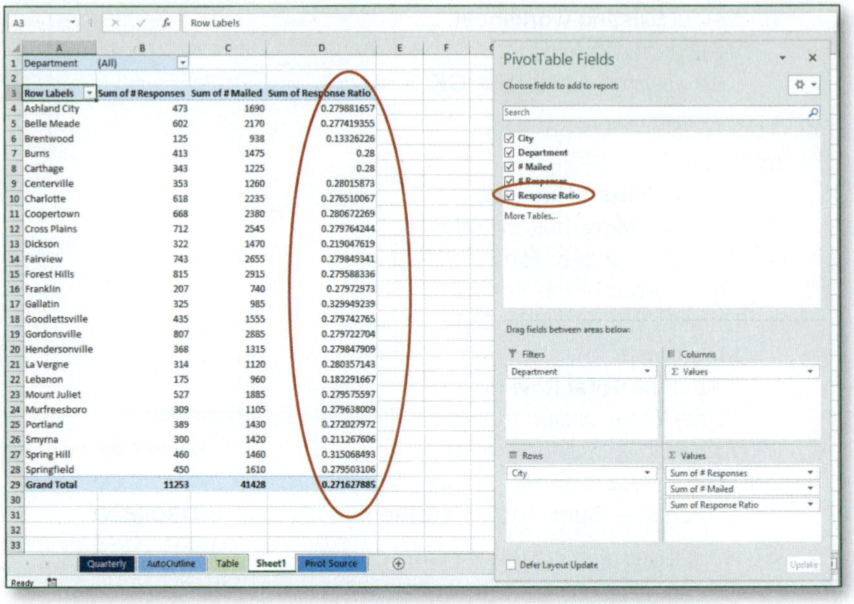

Figure 4-91 ***PivotTable*** **with calculated field**

18. Format a *PivotTable*.
   a. Right-click cell **B4** and select **Value Field Settings** from the context menu.
   b. Click **Number Format**.
   c. Choose **Number** as the *Category* and select zero decimal places.
   d. Select the **Use 1000 Separator (,)** box.
   e. Click **OK** to close each dialog box.
   f. Apply the same number format for "Sum of # Mailed" field.
   g. Select cell **D4** and format the field to use **Percentage** with 2 decimal places.
   h. Click the **More** button [*PivotTable Tools Design* tab, *PivotTable Styles* group].
   i. Select **Ice Blue, Pivot Style Medium 9** [*PivotTable Tools Design* tab, *PivotTable Styles* group].
   j. Select the **Banded Rows** box [*PivotTable Tools Design* tab, *PivotTable Styles Options* group].
   k. Select the **Banded Columns** box [*PivotTable Tools Design* tab, *PivotTable Styles Options* group] (Figure 4-92).

	A	B	C	D
1	Department	(All)		
2				
3	Row Labels	Sum of # Responses	Sum of # Mailed	Sum of Response Ratio
4	Ashland City	473	1,690	27.99%
5	Belle Meade	602	2,170	27.74%
6	Brentwood	125	938	13.33%
7	Burns	413	1,475	28.00%
8	Carthage	343	1,225	28.00%
9	Centerville	353	1,260	28.02%
10	Charlotte	618	2,235	27.65%
11	Coopertown	668	2,380	28.07%
12	Cross Plains	712	2,545	27.98%
13	Dickson	322	1,470	21.90%
14	Fairview	743	2,655	27.98%
15	Forest Hills	815	2,915	27.96%
16	Franklin	207	740	27.97%
17	Gallatin	325	985	32.99%
18	Goodlettsville	435	1,555	27.97%
19	Gordonsville	807	2,885	27.97%
20	Hendersonville	368	1,315	27.98%
21	La Vergne	314	1,120	28.04%
22	Lebanon	175	960	18.23%
23	Mount Juliet	527	1,885	27.96%
24	Murfreesboro	309	1,105	27.96%
25	Portland	389	1,430	27.20%
26	Smyrna	300	1,420	21.13%
27	Spring Hill	460	1,460	31.51%
28	Springfield	450	1,610	27.95%
29	Grand Total	11,253	41,428	27.16%

Figure 4-92 Formatted ***PivotTable***

19. Create and format a *PivotChart*.
   a. Click the **PivotChart** button [*PivotTable Tools Analyze* tab, *Tools* group].
   b. Select **Bar** as the chart type and **Clustered Bar** as the subtype.
   c. Click **OK**.
   d. Position the chart object so that its top-left corner is at cell **F3**.
   e. Drag the bottom-right selection handle to reach cell **P24**.
   f. Click the **More** button [*PivotChart Tools Design* tab, *Chart Styles* group] and choose **Style 5**.
   g. Click the **Shape Outline** button [*PivotChart Tools Format* tab, *Shape Styles* group] and select **Blue, Accent 1** (fifth column).

20. Filter data in a *PivotChart*.
   a. Click the **Department** filter button in the chart.
   b. Select the **Select Multiple Items** box.
   c. Deselect the **(All)** box.
   d. Select the **Landscape Design** box and click **OK**.
   e. Select cell **A13** to deselect the *PivotTable* and *PivotChart* (Figure 4-93).
   f. Name the sheet PivotTable.

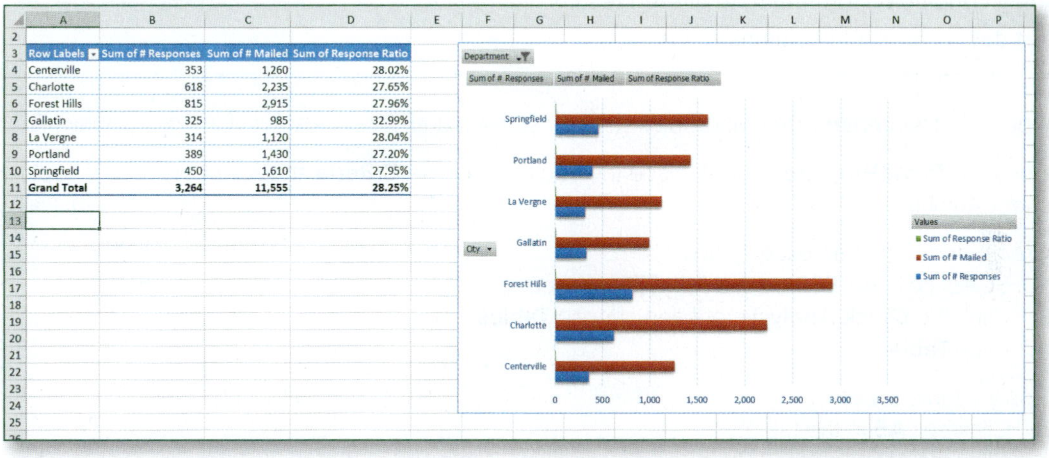

Figure 4-93 Filtered data in *PivotChart* and *PivotTable*

21. Export data as a comma-separated file.
   a. Click the **Quarterly** sheet tab.
   b. Click the **File** tab and select **Export**.
   c. Select **Change File Type**.
   d. Select **CSV (Comma delimited)** as the file type.
   e. Click **Save As**.
   f. Navigate to the save location for the exported data in the *Save as type* dialog box.
   g. Type [your initials]Excel 4-2Text as the file name.
   h. Click **Save**.
   i. Click **OK** in the message box to save the current sheet. The sheet is renamed, and the data are exported to a *.csv* file.
   j. Close the *Possible Data Loss* message bar if it opens.
   k. Rename the sheet as Quarterly.

22. Resave the workbook with the same file name.
   a. Click the **File** tab and choose **Save As**.
   b. Navigate to the folder for saved work.
   c. Select **Excel Workbook** as the *Save as type*.
   d. Select ***[your initials] Excel 4-2*** or retype the file name.
   e. Click **Save** and click **OK** to replace the file.

23. Save and close the workbook. Close Word.

Guided Project 4-3

Clemenson Imaging analyzes expense reports from field representatives as well as patient and image data. To complete the worksheets, you format data as a table and build an advanced filter. You import a comma-separated text file (.csv) and use the *Subtotal* command. Finally, you display data in a *PivotTable*.
[Student Learning Outcomes 4.1, 4.2, 4.3, 4.4, 4.5, 4.6, 4.7, 4.8]

Files Needed: ***Clemenson-04.xlsx, ClemensonText-04.csv***, and ***ClemensonWord.docx*** *(Student data files are available in the* Library *of your SIMnet account.)*
Completed Project File Names: ***[your initials] Excel 4-3.xlsx*** and ***[your initials] Excel 4-3Word.docx***

Skills Covered in This Project

- Format data as an Excel table.
- Build an *Advanced Filter*.
- Apply conditional formatting to filtered results.
- Sort data by multiple columns.
- Import a comma-separated text file.
- Use the *Subtotal* command.
- Export data via the *Clipboard*.
- Create a *PivotTable*.

---

1. Open the ***Clemenson-04*** workbook from your student data files and save it as [your initials] Excel 4-3.
2. Copy the **Past&Projected** sheet, place the copy before the **Criteria** sheet, and name the copied sheet Adv Filter.
3. Create and format an Excel table.
   a. Select cells **A4:E60** on the **Adv Filter** sheet.
   b. Click the **Quick Analysis** tool and choose **Tables**.
   c. Click **Table**.
4. Apply a table style.
   a. Click cell **A5** in the table.
   b. Click the **More** button [*Table Tools Design* tab, *Table Styles* group].
   c. Select **White, Table Style Medium 15**.
5. Create an output range for an *Advanced Filter*.
   a. Select cells **A4:E4** and copy and paste them to cell **G4**.
   b. Type Extract Range in cell **G3** and set the font to **Cambria 16 pt**.
   c. Adjust column widths for columns **G:K** to show the labels.
   d. Adjust row **4** to a height of **33.75 (45 pixels)**.
6. Create an *Advanced Filter*.
   a. Click the **Criteria** sheet tab.
   b. Type >12/31/18 in cell **A3** to find records after 2018.
   c. Type mri in cell **B3**.
   d. Type >12/31/19 in cell **A4**, to find records after 2019.
   e. Type ct scan in cell **B4**. This criteria will find records dated 2019 or later for MRIs *and* records for CT scans dated 2020 or later (Figure 4-94).
   f. Click cell **A5** on the **Adv Filter** sheet.
   g. Click the **Advanced** button [*Data* tab, *Sort & Filter* group].
   h. Select the **Copy to another location** radio button.

	A	B	C	D	E
1	Criteria Range				
2	Month	Image	Patients	Total Hours	# of Employees
3	>12/31/18	mri			
4	>12/31/19	ct scan			

Figure 4-94 Criteria for *Advanced Filter*

i. Verify that the **List range** is cells **$A$4:$E$60**. If the range is incorrect, click and drag to select the range including the header row.
j. Click the **Criteria range** box and select cells **A2:B4** on the **Criteria** sheet.
k. Click the **Copy to** box and select cells **G4:K4** on the **Adv Filter** sheet.
l. Click **OK** in the *Advanced Filter* dialog box.

7. Sort data in the output range.
   a. Select cell **G5** and click the **Sort** button [*Data* tab, *Sort & Filter* group].
   b. Click the **Sort by** arrow and choose **Image** for the first level.
   c. Verify that the **Sort On** selection is **Cell Values** and the **Order** is **A to Z**.
   d. Click **Add Level** and choose **Month** as the **Then by** selection.
   e. Verify or select **Cell Values** and **Oldest to Newest** for the second level.
   f. Click **OK**.

8. Apply conditional formatting and borders.
   a. Select the cells with values in column I.
   b. Click the **Conditional Formatting** button [*Home* tab, *Styles* group].
   c. Choose **Highlight Cells Rules** and **Greater Than**.
   d. Type 750 and choose **Green Fill with Dark Green Text**.
   e. Click **OK**.
   f. Select the extract range starting at cell **G5** and apply **All Borders** (Figure 4-95). (Your results may be different from Figure 4-95 depending on the current date.)
   g. Press **Ctrl+Home**.

Extract Range

Month	Image	Patients	Total Hours	# of Employees
Apr 2020	CT Scan	500	2400	3
Aug 2020	CT Scan	750	2400	3
Dec 2020	CT Scan	500	1800	4
Apr 2021	CT Scan	750	2400	2
Aug 2021	CT Scan	500	2400	3
Jan 2019	MRI	500	2400	3
May 2019	MRI	750	3000	5
Sep 2019	MRI	750	1800	4
Jan 2020	MRI	750	3000	3
May 2020	MRI	750	2400	2
Sep 2020	MRI	750	2400	4
Jan 2021	MRI	1000	1800	3
May 2021	MRI	750	3000	4

Figure 4-95 ***Advanced Filter*** **results**

9. Import a comma-separated values text file.
   a. Click the **Expense Info** sheet tab.
   b. Select cell **A4**.
   c. Click the **From Text/CSV** button [*Data* tab, *Get & Transform Data* group].
   d. Find and select the ***ClemensonText-04.csv*** file from your student data files in the *Import Data* window.
   e. Click **Import**.
   f. Verify that **Comma** is selected as the **Delimiter** in the *Navigator* window.
   g. Click the **Load** arrow and select **Load To**. Select **Existing worksheet**.
   h. Verify that cell **A4** displays as the destination and that **Table** is how the data will be imported.
   i. Click **OK** to import the text data (Figure 4-96).
   j. Cut and paste (or drag and drop) the labels in row **3** to replace the labels in row **4**.
   k. Select cell **A5** and click the **Convert to Range** button [*Table Design* tab, *Tools* group]. Click **OK** to remove the query definition.
   l. Select cells **A4:D31** and clear the formats [*Home* tab, *Editing* group].
   m. Select cells **A4:D31**, if necessary, and change the font size to **11 pt**.
   n. Select the labels in row **4** and center align them.
   o. Format the dates in column **C** with the **Short Date** format.
   p. Select columns **A:D** and size each column to **12.14 (90 pixels)** wide. Deselect the columns.

A4 | fx | Column1

	A	B	C	D
1	Clemenson Imaging			
2	Expense Report Information			
3	Last Name	First Name	Date	Amount
4	Column1	Column2	Column3	Column4
5	Allen	Mary Jo	1/1/2019	450
6	Gabrys	Elizabeth	1/1/2019	555
7	Bashir	Atef	1/1/2019	635
8	Gomez	Paola	1/1/2019	845
9	McAllister	Lex	1/1/2019	925
10	Allen	Mary Jo	2/1/2019	750
11	Gabrys	Elizabeth	2/1/2019	635
12	Bashir	Atef	2/1/2019	575

Figure 4-96 CSV file imported as a table

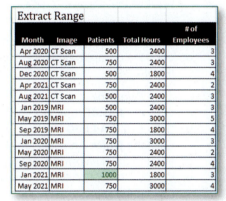

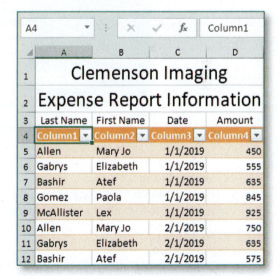

10. Use the *Subtotal* command.
    a. Close the *Queries & Connections* pane and click cell **A5**.
    b. Click the **Sort A to Z** button [*Data* tab, *Sort & Filter* group] to sort by last name.
    c. Click the **Subtotal** button [*Data* tab, *Outline* group].
    d. Verify or choose **Last Name** for the **At each change in** box.
    e. Click the **Use function** arrow and choose **Average**.
    f. Check the **Amount** box in the *Add subtotal to* area.
    g. Click **OK**.
    h. Format the values in column **D** as **Currency** with zero decimal places.

11. Collapse outline groups.
    a. Click the collapse symbol (—) for Allen in row **8**.
    b. Click the collapse symbol (—) for McAllister (Figure 4-97).

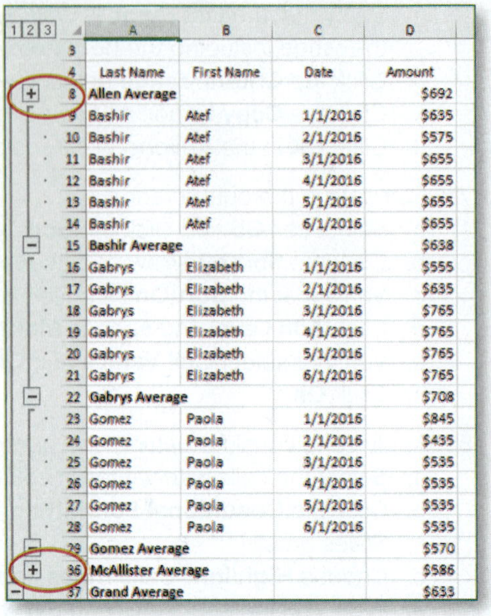

Figure 4-97 Subtotals added and outline collapsed for two groups

12. Create a *PivotTable*.
    a. Click the **Past&Projected** sheet tab.
    b. Select cells **A4:E60**.
    c. Click the **Quick Analysis** tool and choose **Tables**.
    d. Point to each *PivotTable* option to see the *Live Preview*.
    e. Choose the option that shows a sum of the employees, the total hours, and the patients by image (Figure 4-98).

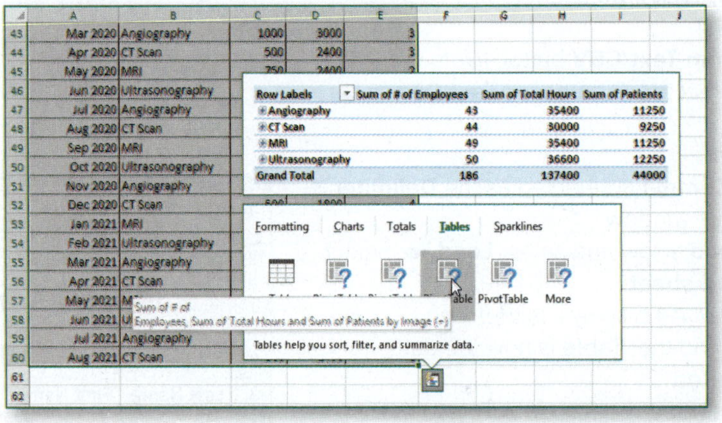

Figure 4-98 Suggested *PivotTable* choices from the *Quick Analysis* tool

    f. Rename the sheet PivotTable.
    g. Drag the **Month** field in the *Rows* area in the *PivotTable Fields* pane out of the pane and into the worksheet to remove the field from the *PivotTable*.

13. Format a *PivotTable*.
    a. Click cell **C4**.
    b. Click the **Field Settings** button [*PivotTable Tools Analyze* tab, *Active Field* group].
    c. Click **Number Format**.
    d. Choose **Number** as the *Category*.
    e. Select the **Use 1000 Separator (,)** box and set zero decimal places.
    f. Click **OK** to close each dialog box.
    g. Apply the same number format for the "Sum of Patients" field.

h. Click the **More** button [*PivotTable Tools Design* tab, *PivotTable Styles* group].
i. Select **Dark Gray, Pivot Style Dark 9** [*PivotTable Tools Design* tab, *PivotTable Styles* group].
j. Select the **Banded Rows** box [*PivotTable Tools Design* tab, *PivotTable Styles Options* group].
k. Select the **Banded Columns** box [*PivotTable Tools Design* tab, *PivotTable Styles Options* group] (Figure 4-99).

	A	B	C	D
1				
2				
3	Row Labels	Sum of # of	Sum of Total Hours	Sum of Patients
4	Angiography	43	35,400	11,250
5	CT Scan	44	30,000	9,250
6	MRI	49	35,400	11,250
7	Ultrasonography	50	36,600	12,250
8	Grand Total	186	137,400	44,000

Figure 4-99 ***PivotTable* with new settings**

14. Create and format a *PivotChart*.
   a. Click the **PivotChart** button [*PivotTable Tools Analyze* tab, *Tools* group].
   b. Select **Bar** as the chart type and **Stacked Bar** as the subtype.
   c. Click **OK**.
   d. Position the chart object so that its top-left corner is at cell **A12**.
   e. Drag the bottom-right selection handle to reach cell **J30**.
   f. Click the **More** button [*PivotChart Tools Design* tab, *Chart Styles* group] and choose **Style 8**.
   g. Click the **Change Colors** button [*PivotChart Tools Design* tab, *Chart Styles* group].
   h. Select **Monochromatic Palette 1** in the *Monochromatic* group.
   i. Deselect the **# of Employees** box in the *PivotChart Fields* pane (Figure 4-100).
   j. Click cell **A1**.

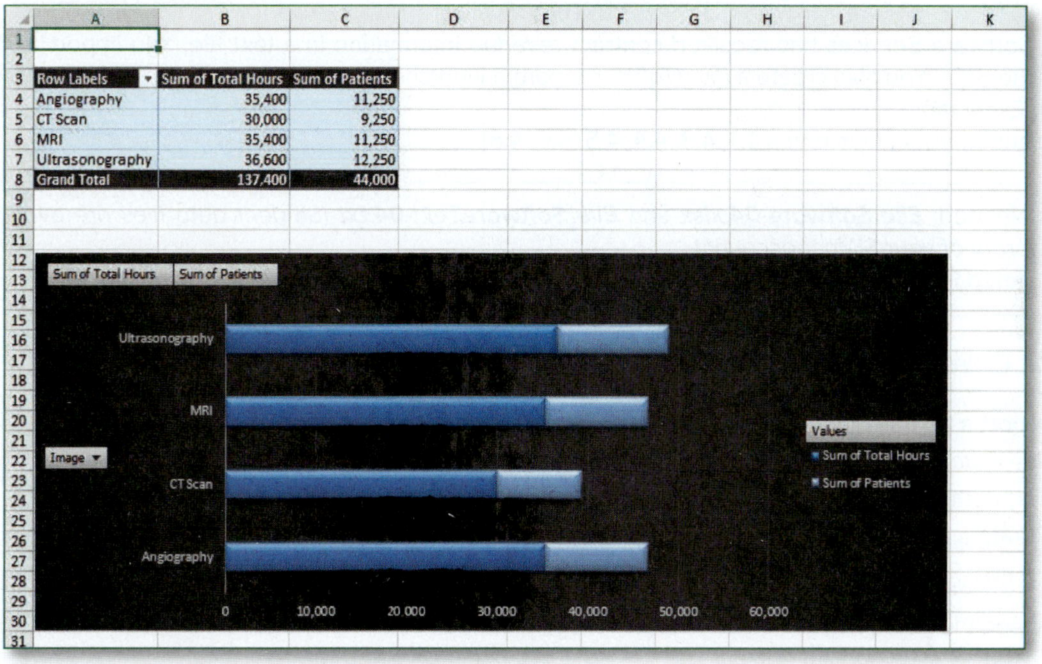

Figure 4-100 ***PivotChart* object**

15. Export data using the *Clipboard*.
   a. Click the **Adv Filter** sheet tab.
   b. Starting at cell **G4**, select the cells in the *Extract Range* and click the **Copy** button [*Home* tab, *Clipboard* group].
   c. Open the **ClemensonWord-04** Word document from your student data files. Enable editing if prompted.

d. Press **Ctrl+End** to position the insertion point.

e. Click the arrow with the **Paste** button [*Home* tab, *Clipboard* group] and choose **Paste Special**.

f. Select **Microsoft Excel Worksheet Object** in the *Paste Special* dialog box.

g. Select the **Paste link** radio button in the *Paste Special* dialog box and click **OK**. (The Excel data in your document may be different from the figure.)

h. Click the **Center** button [*Home* tab, *Paragraph* group].

i. Save the Word document as ***[your initials] Excel 4-3Word*** in your usual folder (Figure 4-101).

j. Close Word.

16. Save and close the Excel workbook.

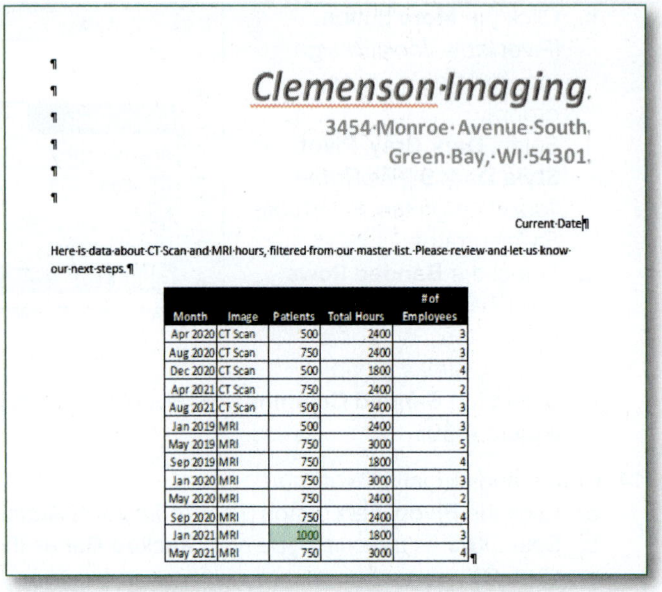
Clemenson·Imaging
3454·Monroe·Avenue·South
Green·Bay,·WI·54301
Current·Date¶
Here·is·data·about·CT·Scan·and·MRI·hours,·filtered·from·our·master·list.·Please·review·and·let·us·know·our·next·steps.¶

Month	Image	Patients	Total Hours	# of Employees
Apr 2020	CT Scan	500	2400	3
Aug 2020	CT Scan	750	2400	3
Dec 2020	CT Scan	500	1800	4
Apr 2021	CT Scan	750	2400	2
Aug 2021	CT Scan	500	2400	3
Jan 2019	MRI	500	2400	3
May 2019	MRI	750	3000	5
Sep 2019	MRI	750	1800	4
Jan 2020	MRI	750	3000	3
May 2020	MRI	750	2400	2
Sep 2020	MRI	750	2400	4
Jan 2021	MRI	1000	1800	3
May 2021	MRI	750	3000	4

Figure 4-101 Word document with pasted Excel object

Independent Project 4-4

Eller Software Services has received contract revenue information in a text file. You import, sort, and filter the data. You also create a *PivotTable,* prepare a worksheet with subtotals, and format related data as an Excel table.
[Student Learning Outcomes 4.1, 4.3, 4.4, 4.5, 4.6, 4.8]

Files Needed: ***EllerSoftware-04.xlsx*** and ***EllerSoftwareText-04.txt*** *(Student data files are available in the Library of your SIMnet account.)*
Completed Project File Name: ***[your initials] Excel 4-4.xlsx***

Skills Covered in This Project

- Import a text file.
- Use *AutoFilters.*
- Sort data by multiple columns.
- Create a *PivotTable.*
- Format fields in a *PivotTable.*
- Use the *Subtotal* command.
- Format data in an Excel table.
- Sort data in an Excel table.

---

1. Open the ***EllerSoftware-04*** workbook from your student data files and save it as [your initials] Excel 4-4.
2. Import the ***EllerSoftwareText-04.txt*** file from your student data files and load it to begin in cell **A4**. The text file is tab-delimited.
3. Format the values in column **H** as **Currency** with zero decimal places.
4. Click cell **G4** and use the *AutoFilter* arrow to sort by date oldest to newest.
5. Click cell **F4** and use the *AutoFilter* arrow to sort by product/service name in ascending order.

6. Filter the *Date* column to show only contracts for **September** using the **All Dates in the Period** option.
7. Edit the label in cell **A2** to display Contract Amounts for September.
8. Select cells **A1:H2** and press **Ctrl+1** to open the *Format Cells* dialog box. On the *Alignment* tab, choose **Center Across Selection**.
9. Change the font size for cells **A1:H2** to **20 pt**. (Figure 4-102) and close the *Queries & Connections* pane.

	A	B	C	D	E	F	G	H
1	Eller Software Services							
2	Contract Amounts for September							
3								
4	Client Name	Address	Phone Number	City	Zip	Product/Service	Date	Contract
5	Glenn Ladewig	1600 Highway 2	218-555-4211	Cass Lake	56633	Accounting Software	9/1/2019	$4,500
6	Karen Talon	1600 Highway 3	218-555-4287	Cass Lake	56633	Accounting Software	9/1/2019	$4,000
7	Shelly Vlcko	402 2nd Avenue SE	218-555-2456	Deer River	56636	Accounting Software	9/15/2019	$4,500
8	Arnold Robert	500 2nd Avenue SW	218-555-2556	Deer River	56636	Accounting Software	9/15/2019	$3,000
9	Wade Whitworth	1822 Highway 2	218-555-4211	Cass Lake	56633	Accounting Software	9/21/2019	$5,200
11	Charlie Lindberg	345 Lyndale Avenue	612-555-2156	Minneapolis	55401	ERP: Enterprise Resource Planning	9/1/2019	$12,000
12	Robert Gneiss	245 Western Avenue	612-555-2356	Minneapolis	55401	ERP: Enterprise Resource Planning	9/1/2019	$10,000
14	Jerri Salzman	800 Lake Avenue	218-555-8927	Brainerd	56401	POS: Point of Sale Software	9/15/2019	$7,000
20	Robert Lawlor	245 Western Avenue	612-555-2376	Minneapolis	55401	Technical	9/1/2019	$1,400

Figure 4-102 Imported data sorted and filtered

10. Copy the **Contracts** sheet to the end and name the copy Data.
11. Clear the date filter.
12. Select cell **A5** and click the **PivotTable** button [*Insert* tab, *Tables* group]. The range is identified as the *EllerSoftwareText* file.
13. Verify that **New Worksheet** is selected, deselect the **Add this data to the Data Model** button, and click **OK**.
14. Name the sheet PivotTable.
15. Show the **Product/Service** and **Contract** fields in the *PivotTable*.
16. Drag the **Contract** field from the *Choose fields to add to report* area below the **Sum of Contract** field in the *Values* area so that it appears twice in the report layout and the pane (Figure 4-103).

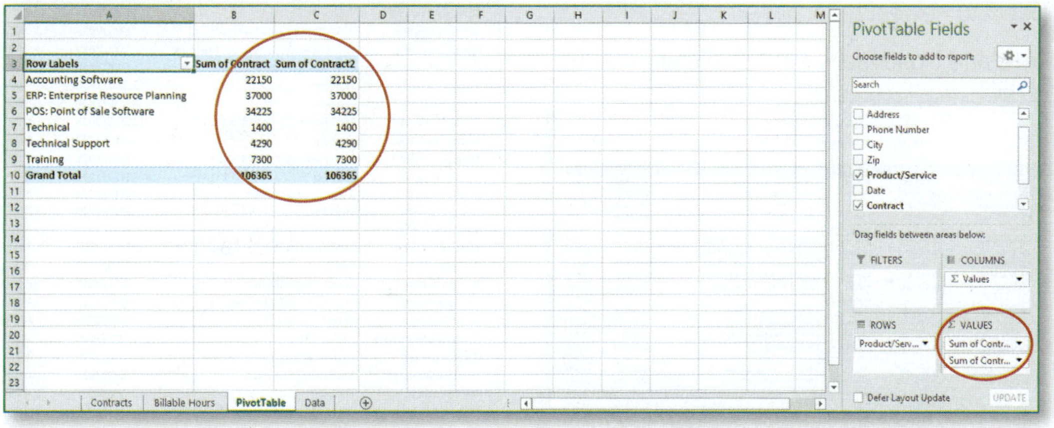

Figure 4-103 "Contract" field appears twice in the report

17. Select cell **C4** and click the **Field Settings** button [*PivotTable Tools Analyze* tab, *Active Field* group]. Type Average Contract as the *Custom Name*, choose **Average** as the calculation, and set the *Number Format* to **Currency** with zero decimal places.
18. Select cell **B4** and set its *Custom Name* to Total Contracts and the number format to **Currency** with zero decimal places.

19. Apply **Brown, Pivot Style Dark 3**.
20. Select the **Data** sheet tab and copy cells **A1:A2**. Paste them in cell **A1** on the **PivotTable** sheet.
21. Select **Align Left** for cells **A1:A2** and **16 pt**. as the font size. Edit the label in cell **A2** to display Contract Amounts, September through December (Figure 4-104).
22. Copy the **Data** sheet to the end and name the copy Subtotals.
23. Select cell **D5** and sort by **City** in **A to Z** order.
24. Select cell **A5** and convert the table to a range. Select cells **A5:H31** and apply **No Fill** [*Home* tab, *Font* group].
25. Use the *Subtotal* command to show a **SUM** for the contract amounts for each city.
26. Edit the label in cell **A2** to display Contract Amounts by City.
27. Format the sheet to **Landscape** orientation, center the page horizontally, and scale it to fit one page.
28. Click the **Billable Hours** sheet tab and select cell **A4**.
29. Click the **Format as Table** button [*Home* tab, *Styles* group], use **Orange, Table Style Medium 10**, and remove the data connections.
30. Type 5% Add On in cell **E4** and press **Enter**.
31. Build a formula in cell **E5** to multiply cell **D5** by **105%** and press **Enter** to copy the formula.
32. Select cells **A1:A2** and left align them. Then select cells **A1:E2**, click the **Launcher** for the *Alignment* group [*Home* tab], and select **Center Across Selection** from the *Horizontal* list.
33. Use the *AutoFilter* arrows to sort by date in oldest to newest order.
34. Save and close the workbook (Figure 4-105).

	A	B	C
1	Eller Software Services		
2	Contract Amounts, September through December		
3	Row Labels	Total Contracts	Average Contract
4	Accounting Software	$22,150	$3,692
5	ERP: Enterprise Resource Planning	$37,000	$12,333
6	POS: Point of Sale Software	$34,225	$5,704
7	Technical	$1,400	$1,400
8	Technical Support	$4,290	$858
9	Training	$7,300	$1,217
10	Grand Total	$106,365	$3,939

Figure 4-104 Completed *PivotTable*

Eller Software Services
Contract Amounts by City

Client Name	Address	Phone Number	City	Zip	Product/Service	Date	Contract
Martin Green	127 Oak Street	218-555-2353	Bemidji	56601	Accounting Software	12/15/2019	$850
Mike Gunderson	304 Irvine Avenue	218-555-9021	Bemidji	56601	Technical Support	10/28/2019	$990
Heather Guyan	124 East Street	218-555-2313	Bemidji	56601	Training	10/7/2019	$1,500
Paula Valentine	127 Oak Street	218-555-2313	Bemidji	56601	Training	10/15/2019	$950
			Bemidji Total				$4,390
Jerri Salzman	800 Lake Avenue	218-555-8927	Brainerd	56401	POS: Point of Sale Software	9/15/2019	$7,000
Terri Olander	459 10th Avenue	218-555-8977	Brainerd	56401	POS: Point of Sale Software	10/15/2019	$6,525
Christine Barton	902 Clinton Street	218-555-8977	Brainerd	56401	POS: Point of Sale Software	11/15/2019	$5,500
Michelle Cronin	800 Lake Avenue	218-555-8977	Brainerd	56401	POS: Point of Sale Software	12/15/2019	$4,500
Patricia Glunz	902 Gunter Street	218-555-8900	Brainerd	56401	POS: Point of Sale Software	12/15/2019	$3,200
			Brainerd Total				$26,725
Glenn Ladewig	1600 Highway 2	218-555-4211	Cass Lake	56633	Accounting Software	9/1/2019	$4,500
Karen Talon	1600 Highway 3	218-555-4287	Cass Lake	56633	Accounting Software	9/1/2019	$4,000
Wade Whitworth	1822 Highway 2	218-555-4211	Cass Lake	56633	Accounting Software	9/21/2019	$5,200
Thomas Larson	1044 Highway 2	218-555-1234	Cass Lake	56633	Training	10/15/2019	$2,500
			Cass Lake Total				$16,200
Shelly Vicko	402 2nd Avenue SE	218-555-2456	Deer River	56636	Accounting Software	9/15/2019	$4,500
Arnold Robert	500 2nd Avenue SW	218-555-2556	Deer River	56636	Accounting Software	9/15/2019	$3,000
			Deer River Total				$7,500
Jeremie Midboe	Pilot Knob Road	651-555-2789	Eagan	55121	POS: Point of Sale Software	11/1/2019	$7,500
			Eagan Total				$7,500
Charlie Lindberg	345 Lyndale Avenue	612-555-2156	Minneapolis	55401	ERP: Enterprise Resource Planning	9/1/2019	$12,000
Robert Gneiss	245 Western Avenue	612-555-2356	Minneapolis	55401	ERP: Enterprise Resource Planning	9/1/2019	$10,000
Susan Charlotte	507 Lyndale Avenue	612-555-2177	Minneapolis	55401	ERP: Enterprise Resource Planning	11/1/2019	$15,000
Robert Lawlor	245 Western Avenue	612-555-2376	Minneapolis	55401	Technical	9/1/2019	$1,400
			Minneapolis Total				$38,400
Craig Brand	554 2nd Street	320-555-4433	Saint Cloud	56301	Technical Support	10/1/2019	$1,050
Arthur Weston	554 3rd Street	320-555-4433	Saint Cloud	56301	Technical Support	10/1/2019	$750
Richard Malinowski	309 Fifth Street	320-555-4433	Saint Cloud	56301	Technical Support	10/1/2019	$750
Elizabeth Jones	450 Fifth Street	320-555-4422	Saint Cloud	56301	Technical Support	10/1/2019	$750
Hilary Marschke	245 West 3rd Avenue	320-555-5443	Saint Cloud	56301	Training	11/15/2019	$750
Juan Garcia	400 South Avenue	320-555-5448	Saint Cloud	56301	Training	11/15/2019	$800
Amir Atef	300 South Avenue	320-555-5443	Saint Cloud	56301	Training	12/15/2019	$800
			Saint Cloud Total				$5,850
			Grand Total				$106,365

Eller Software Services
Billable Hours

Client Name	Product/Service	Date	Billable	5% Add On
Robert Gneiss	ERP: Enterprise Resource Planning	9/1/2019	6.00	6.3
Glenn Ladewig	Accounting Software	9/1/2019	5.00	5.25
Karen Talon	Accounting Software	9/1/2019	3.50	3.675
Charlie Lindberg	ERP: Enterprise Resource Planning	9/1/2019	4.00	4.2
Shelly Vicko	Accounting Software	9/15/2019	5.00	5.25
Arnold Robert	Accounting Software	9/15/2019	5.00	5.25
Karen Talon	Accounting Software	10/1/2019	5.50	5.775
Craig Brand	Technical Support	10/1/2019	8.00	8.4
Arthur Weston	Technical Support	10/1/2019	3.00	3.15
Richard Malinowski	Technical Support	10/1/2019	4.50	4.725
Elizabeth Jones	Technical Support	10/1/2019	3.50	3.675
Heather Guyan	Training	10/7/2019	3.25	3.4125
Terri Olander	POS: Point of Sale Software	10/15/2019	6.50	6.825
Paula Valentine	Training	10/15/2019	4.00	4.2
Paula Valentine	Training	10/15/2019	4.00	4.2
Mike Gunderson	Technical Support	10/28/2019	4.75	4.9875
Jeremie Midboe	POS: Point of Sale Software	11/1/2019	3.50	3.675
Susan Charlotte	ERP: Enterprise Resource Planning	11/1/2019	6.00	6.3
Wade Whitworth	Accounting Software	11/14/2019	5.00	5.25
Paula Valentine	Training	11/15/2019	4.00	4.2
Hilary Marschke	Training	11/15/2019	5.00	5.25
Christine Barton	POS: Point of Sale Software	11/15/2019	4.00	4.2
Hilary Marschke	Training	11/15/2019	5.00	5.25
Christine Barton	POS: Point of Sale Software	11/15/2019	2.00	2.1
Juan Garcia	Training	11/15/2019	4.00	4.2
Shelly Vicko	Accounting Software	11/16/2019	5.00	5.25
Thomas Larson	Training	12/5/2019	5.00	5.25
Michelle Cronin	POS: Point of Sale Software	12/15/2019	4.00	4.2
Michelle Cronin	POS: Point of Sale Software	12/15/2019	4.00	4.2
Amir Atef	Training	12/15/2019	4.00	4.2
Martin Green	Accounting Software	12/15/2019	5.00	5.25
Patricia Glunz	POS: Point of Sale Software	12/15/2019	3.25	3.4125
Mike Gunderson	Technical Support	12/18/2019	4.50	4.725
Richard Malinowski	Technical Support	1/5/2020	3.00	3.15
Robert Lawlor	Technical Support	1/8/2020	2.75	2.8875
Wade Whitworth	Accounting Software	2/2/2020	6.00	6.3
Heather Guyan	Training	2/3/2020	4.50	4.725
Robert Gneiss	ERP: Enterprise Resource Planning	2/5/2020	7.00	7.35
Susan Charlotte	ERP: Enterprise Resource Planning	3/5/2020	8.00	8.4
Martin Green	Accounting Software	3/7/2020	4.00	4.2
Hilary Marschke	Training	3/8/2020	5.00	5.25
Jerri Salzman	POS: Point of Sale Software	3/9/2020	4.50	4.725
Thomas Larson	Training	3/18/2020	4.00	4.2
Paula Valentine	Training	4/5/2020	4.00	4.2
Charlie Lindberg	ERP: Enterprise Resource Planning	4/5/2020	6.00	6.3
Arthur Weston	Technical Support	5/5/2020	6.00	6.3
Wade Whitworth	Accounting Software	5/17/2020	5.00	5.25

Figure 4-105 Excel 4-4 completed

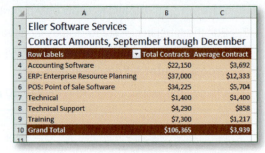

Independent Project 4-5

Boyd Air is monitoring flight arrival status, as well as capacities. Before formatting the data as an Excel table, you will export it as a text file for use in the reservation software. You will filter the data in the table, build a *PivotTable,* and create a *PivotChart.*
[Student Learning Outcomes 4.1, 4.2, 4.3, 4.4, 4.7, 4.8]

File Needed: ***BoydAir-04.xlsx*** *(Student data files are available in the* Library *of your SIMnet account.)*
Completed Project File Names: ***[your initials] Excel 4-5.xlsx*** and ***[your initials] Excel 4-5Export.txt***

Skills Covered in This Project

- Export data as a text file.
- Format data as an Excel table.
- Use a number filter in a table.
- Set conditional formatting with an icon set.
- Filter data by cell icon.
- Create and format a *PivotTable.*
- Create and format a *PivotChart.*

1. Open the ***BoydAir-04*** workbook from your student data files and save it as [your initials] Excel 4-5.
2. Export the data to a tab-delimited text file named ***[your initials] Excel 4-5Export*** in your usual location for saving work. The sheet is renamed after the data are exported.
3. Rename the sheet tab Stats.
4. Use the *Save As* command to save and replace ***[your initials] Excel 4-5*** as an **Excel Workbook**.

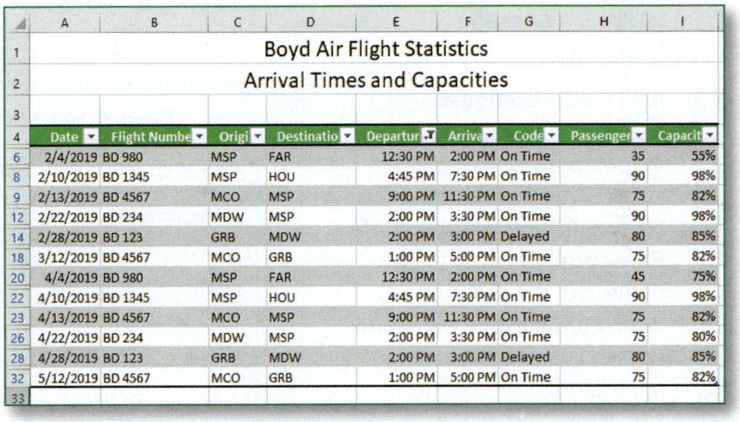

Boyd Air Flight Statistics
Arrival Times and Capacities

	Date	Flight Numbe	Origi	Destinatio	Departur	Arriva	Code	Passenger	Capacit
6	2/4/2019	BD 980	MSP	FAR	12:30 PM	2:00 PM	On Time	35	55%
8	2/10/2019	BD 1345	MSP	HOU	4:45 PM	7:30 PM	On Time	90	98%
9	2/13/2019	BD 4567	MCO	MSP	9:00 PM	11:30 PM	On Time	75	82%
12	2/22/2019	BD 234	MDW	MSP	2:00 PM	3:30 PM	On Time	90	98%
14	2/28/2019	BD 123	GRB	MDW	2:00 PM	3:00 PM	Delayed	80	85%
18	3/12/2019	BD 4567	MCO	GRB	1:00 PM	5:00 PM	On Time	75	82%
20	4/4/2019	BD 980	MSP	FAR	12:30 PM	2:00 PM	On Time	45	75%
22	4/10/2019	BD 1345	MSP	HOU	4:45 PM	7:30 PM	On Time	90	98%
23	4/13/2019	BD 4567	MCO	MSP	9:00 PM	11:30 PM	On Time	75	82%
26	4/22/2019	BD 234	MDW	MSP	2:00 PM	3:30 PM	On Time	75	80%
28	4/28/2019	BD 123	GRB	MDW	2:00 PM	3:00 PM	Delayed	80	85%
32	5/12/2019	BD 4567	MCO	GRB	1:00 PM	5:00 PM	On Time	75	82%

Figure 4-106 Filter results for *Departure Time* field

5. Select cell **A4** and format the data as an Excel table using **Green, Table Style Medium 21**.
6. Copy the **Stats** sheet to the end and name the copy PM Flights.
7. Select the **PM Flights** sheet, and use a *Greater Than* filter to display flights with a departure time after 12:00 PM (Figure 4-106).
8. Select the **Stats** worksheet, select cells **I5:I32**, and set conditional formatting to use **3 Flags** from the *Icon Sets*.
9. Build a two-level *Custom Sort* for the *Capacity* column to sort by icon. Show the green flag at the top, followed by the yellow flag. The red flag will default to the bottom (Figure 4-107).

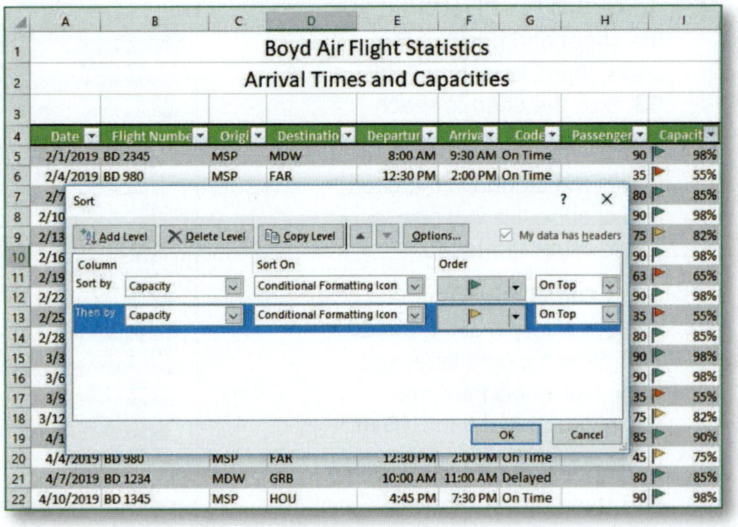

Figure 4-107 Custom sort for the *3 Flags* icon set

10. Select the **Stats** worksheet, select cells **A4:I32**, and use the *Quick Analysis* tool to create a *PivotTable* to display average of capacity by origin (Figure 4-108).
11. Rename the sheet PivotTable&Chart.
12. Select cell **B3** in the *PivotTable* and use **Field Settings** to set a **Number Format** of **Percentage** with two decimal places. Edit the *Custom Name* to display **Average Capacity**.
13. Add the **Passengers** field to the *PivotTable Values* area with a sum calculation. Edit the field settings to display **# of Passengers** as the custom name. Set the number format to **Number** with zero decimals and a thousand's separator.
14. Use **White, Pivot Style Light 8** for the *PivotTable* and show banded rows and columns.
15. Add a **3-D Pie PivotChart** to the sheet and position the chart object to start in cell **E3**. Size the chart to reach cell **N22**.
16. Select the legend in the chart and change the font size to **11** from the *Home* tab.
17. Show **Data Labels** on the chart positioned at the **Inside End**. Select a data label and format all labels from the *Home* tab as **bold** and **10 pt**.
18. Select cell **A1** and save and close the workbook (Figure 4-109).

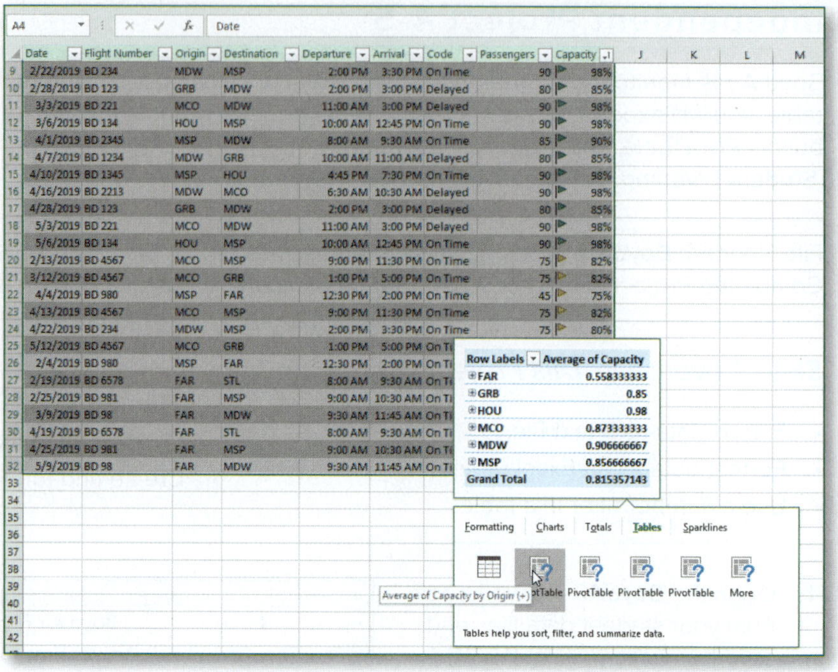

Figure 4-108 *PivotTable* suggestions from the *Quick Analysis* tool

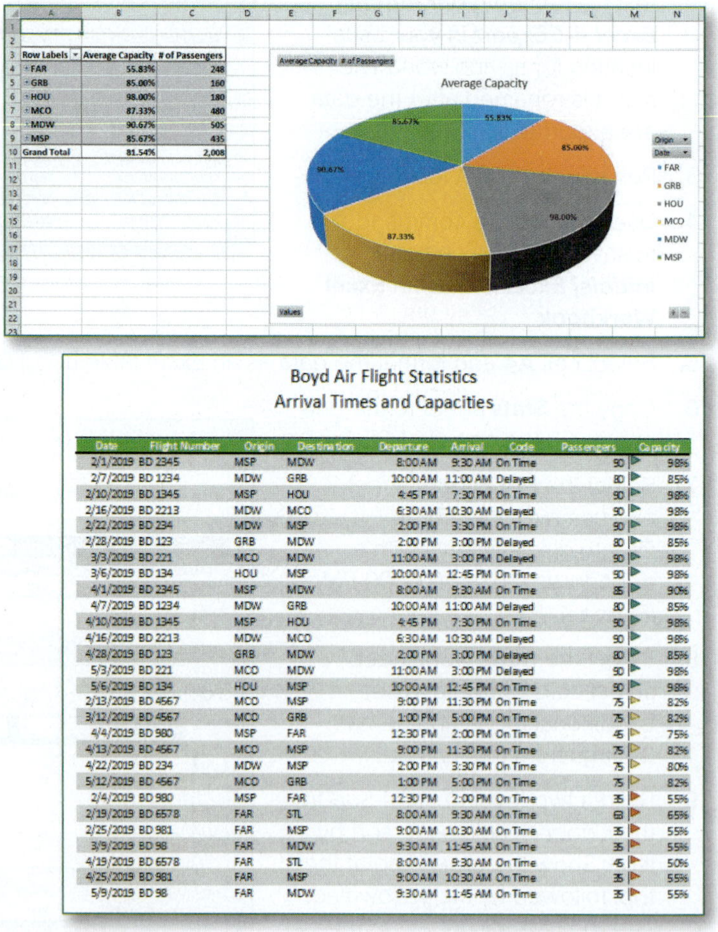

Figure 4-109 Excel 4-5 completed

Independent Project 4-6

Life's Animal Shelter has a list of suppliers in a worksheet to be copied to Word. You will also build an advanced filter to show suppliers for specific product categories and define groups based on supplier name. Your final task is to create an Excel table for sorting and filtering.
[Student Learning Outcomes 4.1, 4.3, 4.4, 4.5, 4.7]

File Needed: ***LAShelter-04.xlsx*** *(Student data files are available in the* Library *of your SIMnet account.)*
Completed Project File Names: ***[your initials] Excel 4-6.xlsx*** and ***[your initials] Excel 4-6Word.docx***

Skills Covered in This Project

- Copy Excel data to Word.
- Create an advanced filter.
- Use *Flash Fill* to complete a column.
- Format data as a table.
- Filter data.
- Define groups in a worksheet.

---

1. Open the ***LAShelter-04*** workbook from your student data files and save it as [your initials] Excel 4-6.
2. Select the **LAS Suppliers** sheet, select cells **A4:D32**, and copy them to the Windows *Clipboard*.
3. Open Word and create a new document.
4. Paste the data into Word with the **Use Destination Styles** option (Figure 4-110).
5. Save the Word document as [your initials] Excel 4-6Word.docx.
6. Close the Word document and exit Word.
7. Press **Esc** to remove the moving border, and click the **Criteria** sheet tab.

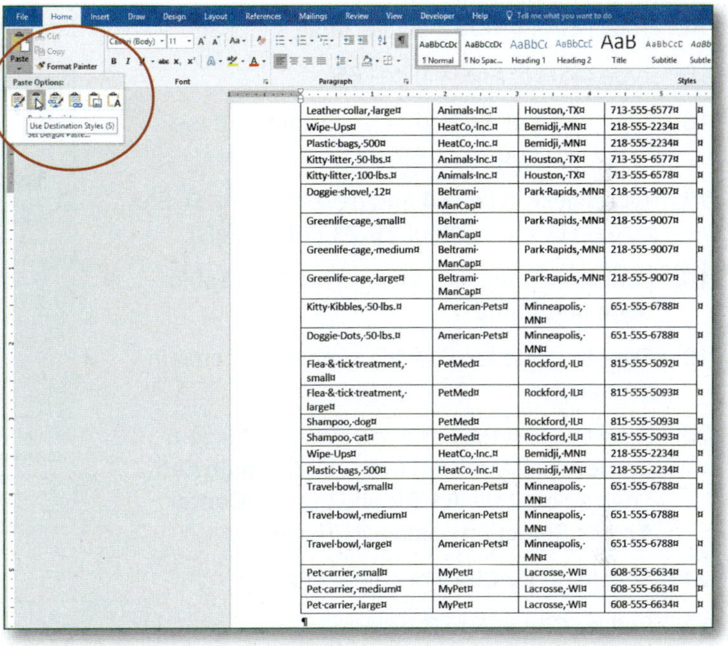

Figure 4-110 Word *Paste Options* for Excel data

8. Type *cage* in cell **A2** and type *carrier* in cell **A3**. This is *OR* criteria that will find products that include either the word "cage" or the word "carrier."
9. Select the **LAS Suppliers** sheet and format the labels in row **4** as **bold** and **centered** to distinguish the header row from other data.
10. Click cell **A5** on the **LAS Suppliers** sheet.
11. Build an advanced filter that uses the data on the **LAS Suppliers** sheet, the criteria range on the **Criteria** sheet, and cells **F6:G6** as the output range. In the *Advanced Filter* dialog box, select the **Unique records only** box (Figure 4-111).

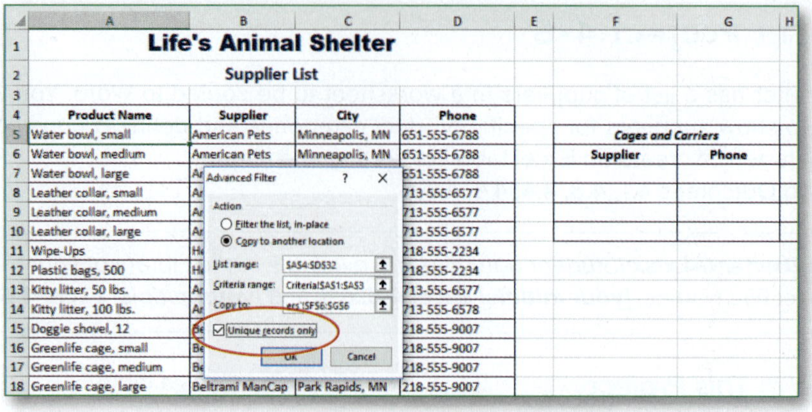

Figure 4-111 Advanced filter to select unique records

12. Replace the criteria on the **Criteria** sheet with *bowl* and *collar* to build a second advanced filter and show the filtered results where indicated on the **LAS Suppliers** sheet.
13. Select cells **A4:D32** on the **LAS Suppliers** sheet and copy them to cell **A4** on the **Table** sheet. Remove all borders.
14. Select cells **A5:D32** on the **Table** sheet and sort the data by product name in ascending order.
15. Type (651) 555-6788 in cell **E5**.
16. Type (2 in cell **E6** and press **Enter** when the *Flash Fill* suggestion appears.
17. Type Phone in cell **E4** and delete column **D**. Set column **D** to a width of **15.71 (115 pixels)**.
18. Format the data as a table using **Blue, Table Style Medium 2**.
19. Filter the data to show the suppliers located in Minnesota.
20. Select cells **A1:A2** and remove the **Merge & Center** command. Set both cells to **Align Left**. Then select cells **A1:D2** and use the **Center Across Selection** command (Figure 4-112).
21. Select the **By City** worksheet tab.
22. Sort by **City** in **A to Z** order.
23. Insert a row at row **5** and type Bemidji in cell **A5**. Left align the label.
24. Insert a row at row **10** and type Houston in cell **A10. Bold** the label.
25. Insert blank rows and type labels for the remaining cities.
26. Select the row headings for rows **6:9** and click the **Group** button [*Data* tab, *Outline* group]. Do not include the row with the city name in the group.
27. Repeat the command to group the rows for each city (Figure 4-113).

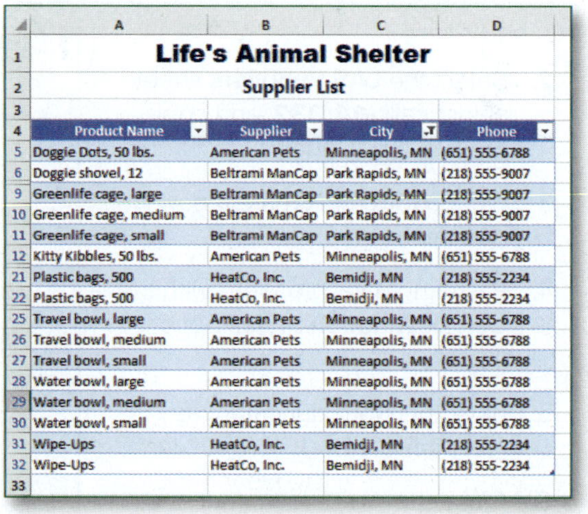

Figure 4-112 Completed table

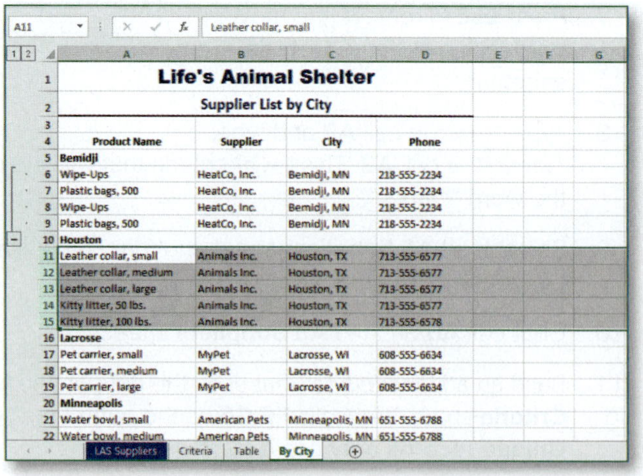

Figure 4-113 Data manually defined in groups

28. Select and delete column **C**.

29. Collapse the *Houston* and *Minneapolis* groups (Figure 4-114).

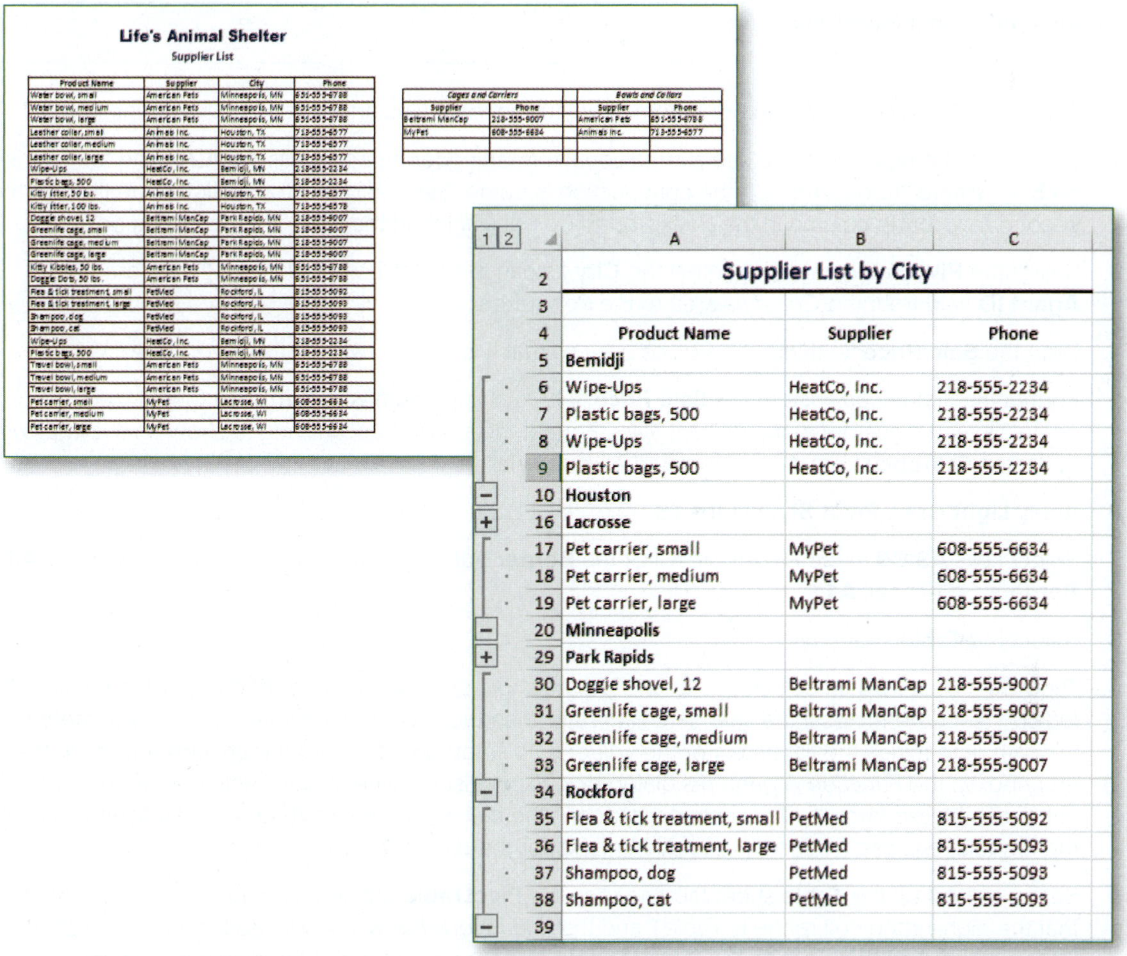

Life's Animal Shelter

Supplier List

Product Name	Supplier	City	Phone
Water bowl, small	American Pets	Minneapolis, MN	651-555-6788
Water bowl, medium	American Pets	Minneapolis, MN	651-555-6788
Water bowl, large	American Pets	Minneapolis, MN	651-555-6788
Leather collar, small	Animals Inc.	Houston, TX	713-555-6577
Leather collar, medium	Animals Inc.	Houston, TX	713-555-6577
Leather collar, large	Animals Inc.	Houston, TX	713-555-6577
Wipe-Ups	HeatCo, Inc.	Bemidji, MN	218-555-2234
Plastic bags, 500	HeatCo, Inc.	Bemidji, MN	218-555-2234
Kitty litter, 50 lbs.	Animals Inc.	Houston, TX	713-555-6577
Kitty litter, 100 lbs.	Animals Inc.	Houston, TX	713-555-6578
Doggie shovel, 12	Beltrami ManCap	Park Rapids, MN	218-555-9007
Greenlife cage, small	Beltrami ManCap	Park Rapids, MN	218-555-9007
Greenlife cage, medium	Beltrami ManCap	Park Rapids, MN	218-555-9007
Greenlife cage, large	Beltrami ManCap	Park Rapids, MN	218-555-9007
Kitty Kibbles, 50 lbs.	American Pets	Minneapolis, MN	651-555-6788
Doggie Dots, 50 lbs.	American Pets	Minneapolis, MN	651-555-6788
Flea & tick treatment, small	PetMed	Rockford, IL	815-555-5092
Flea & tick treatment, large	PetMed	Rockford, IL	815-555-5093
Shampoo, dog	PetMed	Rockford, IL	815-555-5093
Shampoo, cat	PetMed	Rockford, IL	815-555-5093
Wipe-Ups	HeatCo, Inc.	Bemidji, MN	218-555-2234
Plastic bags, 500	HeatCo, Inc.	Bemidji, MN	218-555-2234
Travel bowl, small	American Pets	Minneapolis, MN	651-555-6788
Travel bowl, medium	American Pets	Minneapolis, MN	651-555-6788
Travel bowl, large	American Pets	Minneapolis, MN	651-555-6788
Pet carrier, small	MyPet	Lacrosse, WI	608-555-6634
Pet carrier, medium	MyPet	Lacrosse, WI	608-555-6634
Pet carrier, large	MyPet	Lacrosse, WI	608-555-6634

Cages and Carriers			*Bowls and Collars*	
Supplier	Phone		Supplier	Phone
Beltrami ManCap	218-555-9007		American Pets	651-555-6788
MyPet	608-555-6634		Animals Inc.	713-555-6577

	A	B	C
2	**Supplier List by City**		
3			
4	**Product Name**	**Supplier**	**Phone**
5	**Bemidji**		
6	Wipe-Ups	HeatCo, Inc.	218-555-2234
7	Plastic bags, 500	HeatCo, Inc.	218-555-2234
8	Wipe-Ups	HeatCo, Inc.	218-555-2234
9	Plastic bags, 500	HeatCo, Inc.	218-555-2234
10	**Houston**		
16	**Lacrosse**		
17	Pet carrier, small	MyPet	608-555-6634
18	Pet carrier, medium	MyPet	608-555-6634
19	Pet carrier, large	MyPet	608-555-6634
20	**Minneapolis**		
29	**Park Rapids**		
30	Doggie shovel, 12	Beltrami ManCap	218-555-9007
31	Greenlife cage, small	Beltrami ManCap	218-555-9007
32	Greenlife cage, medium	Beltrami ManCap	218-555-9007
33	Greenlife cage, large	Beltrami ManCap	218-555-9007
34	**Rockford**		
35	Flea & tick treatment, small	PetMed	815-555-5092
36	Flea & tick treatment, large	PetMed	815-555-5093
37	Shampoo, dog	PetMed	815-555-5093
38	Shampoo, cat	PetMed	815-555-5093
39			

Figure 4-114 Excel 4-6 completed

30. Save and close the workbook.

Improve It Project 4-7

Placer Hills Real Estate wants its latest *PivotTable* to show sales by agent listing. In the source data, you highlight certain listings for insurance purposes. In a separate table, you create a calculation column to determine the number of market days.
[Student Learning Outcomes 4.1, 4.2, 4.8]

File Needed: ***PlacerHills-04.xlsx*** *(Student data files are available in the* Library *of your SIMnet account.)*
Completed Project File Name: ***[your initials] Excel 4-7.xlsx***

Skills Covered in This Project

- Pivot fields in a *PivotTable.*
- Format fields in a *PivotTable.*
- Add a field to a table.
- Set conditional formatting with a formula.

1. Open the ***PlacerHills-04*** workbook from your student data files and save it as [your initials] Excel 4-7.
2. Select the **Listings** sheet and use a conditional formatting formula for cells **A5:A26**. The formula is **=k5 = "frame"** to determine if the construction is frame. Set the format to use light blue fill from the second row, fourth column in the *Background Colors* (*Fill* tab in the *Format Cells* dialog box.).
3. Select the **PivotTable** sheet, deselect the **City** field in the *PivotTable Fields* pane, and drag the **Agent ID** field from the *Columns* area to the *Rows* area.
4. Drag the **Sale Price** field into the *Values* area so that it is shown twice in the *PivotTable*.
5. Format the first occurrence of the **Sale Price** field to show a sum with **Currency** format, zero decimals, and a custom name of Total Sales. Format the second occurrence to show an average with the same **Currency** format and the name Average Sale.
6. Apply **Light Gray, Pivot Style Light 15**.
7. Select cells **A3:C9** in the *PivotTable*. Click the **Border** button [*Home* tab, *Font* group] and apply **All Borders**. Select cell **A1**.
8. Select the **Table** sheet tab.
9. Type Days in cell **O4**. In cell **O5**, build an *IF* formula to display the number of days on the market. The *logical_test* determines if the sale date is greater than the list date. The *value_if_true* argument is the sale date minus the list date. For the *value_if_false* argument, press the **spacebar** once in the entry box in the *Function Arguments* dialog box; Excel displays the space within quotation marks " " in the completed formula. This inserts a space in the cell when no sale date is available. (If you type the formula, enclose a space in quotation marks for the *value_if_false* argument.)
10. Select cell **A4** on the **Table** sheet tab and click the **PivotTable** button [*Insert* tab, *Tables* group]. Verify that the highlighted cell range is *Table1* and that the *PivotTable* will be placed in a new worksheet. Deselect the **Add this data to the Data Model** box near the bottom of the dialog box. (If you select this box, you will not be able to create a calculated field in step 13.) Name the sheet PivotTable 2.
11. Place the **Listing ID** field in the *Rows* area and the **List Price** and **Sale Price** fields in the *Values* area. Format the values as **Currency** with no decimals.
12. Edit the labels in row 3 to Listing, List, Sale.
13. Insert a calculated field named Difference and build a formula that subtracts the sale price from the list price. Change the display label in the *PivotTable* for the calculated field to Variance and *AutoFit* the column.
14. Select all the cells in the *PivotTable* and apply **All Borders**.
15. Save and close the workbook (Figure 4-115).

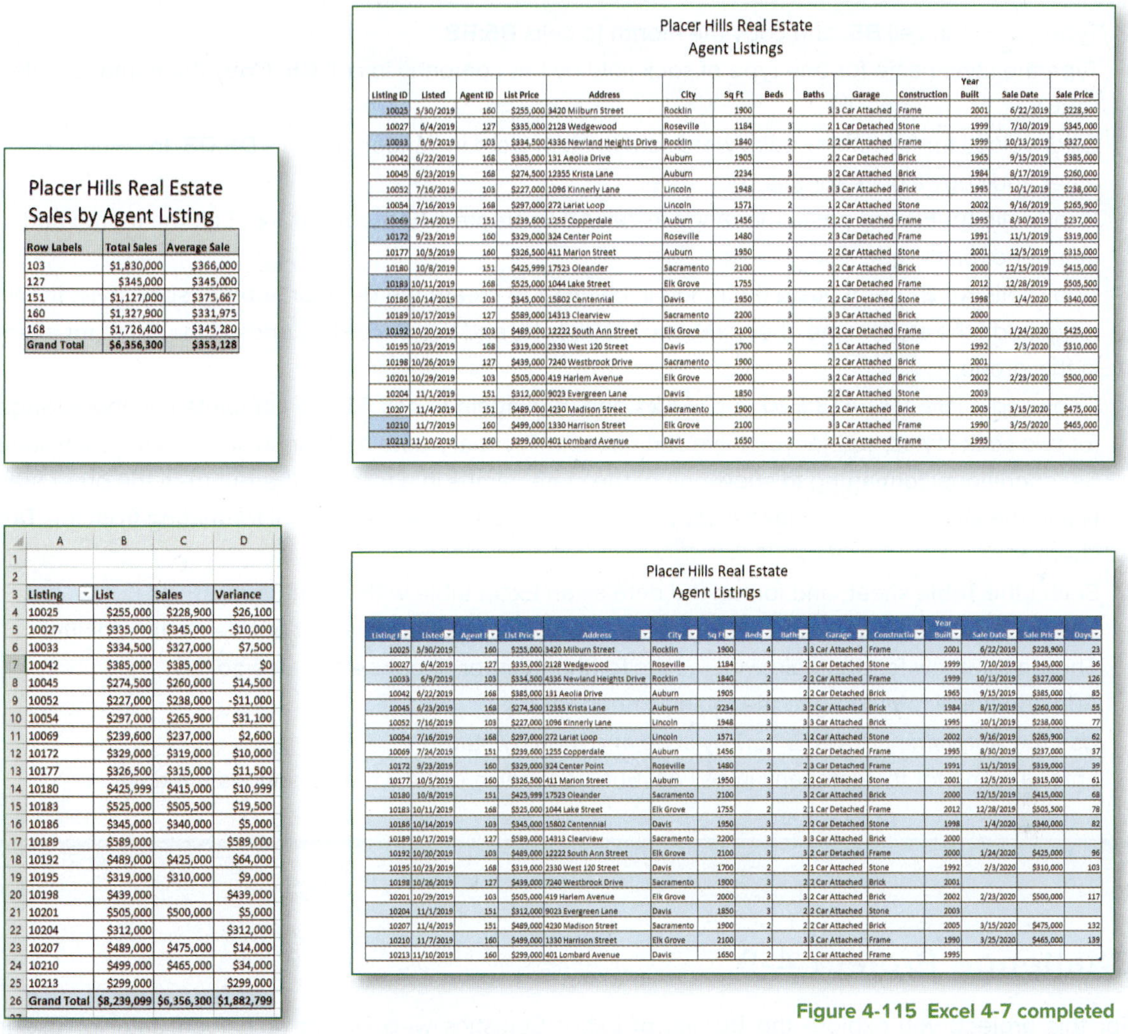

Placer Hills Real Estate
Sales by Agent Listing

Row Labels	Total Sales	Average Sale
103	$1,830,000	$366,000
127	$345,000	$345,000
151	$1,127,000	$375,667
160	$1,327,900	$331,975
168	$1,726,400	$345,280
Grand Total	$6,356,300	$353,128

Placer Hills Real Estate
Agent Listings

Listing ID	Listed	Agent ID	List Price	Address	City	Sq Ft	Beds	Baths	Garage	Construction	Year Built	Sale Date	Sale Price
10025	5/30/2019	160	$255,000	3420 Milburn Street	Rocklin	1900	4	3	3 Car Attached	Frame	2001	6/22/2019	$228,900
10027	6/4/2019	127	$335,000	2128 Wedgewood	Roseville	1184	3	2	1 Car Detached	Stone	1999	7/10/2019	$345,000
10033	6/9/2019	103	$334,500	4336 Newland Heights Drive	Rocklin	1840	2	2	2 Car Attached	Frame	1999	10/13/2019	$327,000
10042	6/22/2019	168	$385,000	131 Aeolia Drive	Auburn	1905	3	2	2 Car Detached	Brick	1965	9/15/2019	$385,000
10045	6/23/2019	168	$274,500	12355 Krista Lane	Auburn	2234	3	3	2 Car Attached	Brick	1984	8/17/2019	$260,000
10052	7/16/2019	103	$227,000	1096 Kinnerly Lane	Lincoln	1948	3	3	3 Car Attached	Brick	1995	10/1/2019	$238,000
10054	7/16/2019	168	$297,000	272 Lariat Loop	Lincoln	1571	2	1	2 Car Attached	Stone	2002	9/16/2019	$265,900
10069	7/24/2019	151	$239,600	1255 Copperdale	Auburn	1456	3	2	2 Car Detached	Frame	1995	8/30/2019	$237,000
10172	9/23/2019	160	$329,000	324 Center Point	Roseville	1480	2	2	3 Car Detached	Frame	1991	11/1/2019	$319,000
10177	10/5/2019	160	$326,500	411 Marion Street	Auburn	1950	3	2	2 Car Attached	Stone	2001	12/5/2019	$315,000
10180	10/8/2019	151	$425,999	17523 Oleander	Sacramento	2100	3	3	2 Car Attached	Brick	2000	12/15/2019	$415,000
10183	10/11/2019	168	$525,000	1044 Lake Street	Elk Grove	1755	2	2	1 Car Detached	Frame	2012	12/28/2019	$505,500
10186	10/14/2019	103	$345,000	15802 Centennial	Davis	1950	3	2	2 Car Detached	Stone	1998	1/4/2020	$340,000
10189	10/17/2019	127	$589,000	14313 Clearview	Sacramento	2200	3	3	3 Car Attached	Brick	2000		
10192	10/20/2019	103	$489,000	12222 South Ann Street	Elk Grove	2100	3	3	2 Car Detached	Frame	2000	1/24/2020	$425,000
10195	10/23/2019	168	$319,000	2330 West 120 Street	Davis	1700	2	2	1 Car Attached	Stone	1992	2/3/2020	$310,000
10198	10/26/2019	127	$439,000	7240 Westbrook Drive	Sacramento	1900	3	2	2 Car Attached	Brick	2001		
10201	10/29/2019	103	$505,000	419 Harlem Avenue	Elk Grove	2000	3	3	2 Car Attached	Brick	2002	2/23/2020	$500,000
10204	11/1/2019	151	$312,000	9023 Evergreen Lane	Davis	1850	3	2	2 Car Attached	Stone	2003		
10207	11/4/2019	151	$489,000	4230 Madison Street	Sacramento	1900	2	2	2 Car Attached	Brick	2005	3/15/2020	$475,000
10210	11/7/2019	160	$499,000	1330 Harrison Street	Elk Grove	2100	3	3	3 Car Attached	Frame	1990	3/25/2020	$465,000
10213	11/10/2019	160	$299,000	401 Lombard Avenue	Davis	1650	2	2	1 Car Attached	Frame	1995		

	A	B	C	D
1				
2				
3	Listing	List	Sales	Variance
4	10025	$255,000	$228,900	$26,100
5	10027	$335,000	$345,000	-$10,000
6	10033	$334,500	$327,000	$7,500
7	10042	$385,000	$385,000	$0
8	10045	$274,500	$260,000	$14,500
9	10052	$227,000	$238,000	-$11,000
10	10054	$297,000	$265,900	$31,100
11	10069	$239,600	$237,000	$2,600
12	10172	$329,000	$319,000	$10,000
13	10177	$326,500	$315,000	$11,500
14	10180	$425,999	$415,000	$10,999
15	10183	$525,000	$505,500	$19,500
16	10186	$345,000	$340,000	$5,000
17	10189	$589,000		$589,000
18	10192	$489,000	$425,000	$64,000
19	10195	$319,000	$310,000	$9,000
20	10198	$439,000		$439,000
21	10201	$505,000	$500,000	$5,000
22	10204	$312,000		$312,000
23	10207	$489,000	$475,000	$14,000
24	10210	$499,000	$465,000	$34,000
25	10213	$299,000		$299,000
26	Grand Total	$8,239,099	$6,356,300	$1,882,799

Placer Hills Real Estate
Agent Listings

Listing I	Listed	Agent I	List Pric	Address	City	Sq Ft	Beds	Baths	Garage	Constructio	Year Built	Sale Date	Sale Pric	Days
10025	5/30/2019	160	$255,000	3420 Milburn Street	Rocklin	1900	4	3	3 Car Attached	Frame	2001	6/22/2019	$228,900	23
10027	6/4/2019	127	$335,000	2128 Wedgewood	Roseville	1184	3	2	1 Car Detached	Stone	1999	7/10/2019	$345,000	36
10033	6/9/2019	103	$334,500	4336 Newland Heights Drive	Rocklin	1840	2	2	2 Car Attached	Frame	1999	10/13/2019	$327,000	126
10042	6/22/2019	168	$385,000	131 Aeolia Drive	Auburn	1905	3	2	2 Car Detached	Brick	1965	9/15/2019	$385,000	85
10045	6/23/2019	168	$274,500	12355 Krista Lane	Auburn	2234	3	3	2 Car Attached	Brick	1984	8/17/2019	$260,000	55
10052	7/16/2019	103	$227,000	1096 Kinnerly Lane	Lincoln	1948	3	3	3 Car Attached	Brick	1995	10/1/2019	$238,000	77
10054	7/16/2019	168	$297,000	272 Lariat Loop	Lincoln	1571	2	1	2 Car Attached	Stone	2002	9/16/2019	$265,900	62
10069	7/24/2019	151	$239,600	1255 Copperdale	Auburn	1456	3	2	2 Car Detached	Frame	1995	8/30/2019	$237,000	37
10172	9/23/2019	160	$329,000	324 Center Point	Roseville	1480	2	2	3 Car Detached	Frame	1991	11/1/2019	$319,000	39
10177	10/5/2019	160	$326,500	411 Marion Street	Auburn	1950	3	2	2 Car Attached	Stone	2001	12/5/2019	$315,000	61
10180	10/8/2019	151	$425,999	17523 Oleander	Sacramento	2100	3	3	2 Car Attached	Brick	2000	12/15/2019	$415,000	68
10183	10/11/2019	168	$525,000	1044 Lake Street	Elk Grove	1755	2	2	1 Car Detached	Frame	2012	12/28/2019	$505,500	78
10186	10/14/2019	103	$345,000	15802 Centennial	Davis	1950	3	2	2 Car Detached	Stone	1998	1/4/2020	$340,000	82
10189	10/17/2019	127	$589,000	14313 Clearview	Sacramento	2200	3	3	3 Car Attached	Brick	2000			
10192	10/20/2019	103	$489,000	12222 South Ann Street	Elk Grove	2100	3	3	2 Car Detached	Frame	2000	1/24/2020	$425,000	96
10195	10/23/2019	168	$319,000	2330 West 120 Street	Davis	1700	2	2	1 Car Attached	Stone	1992	2/3/2020	$310,000	103
10198	10/26/2019	127	$439,000	7240 Westbrook Drive	Sacramento	1900	3	2	2 Car Attached	Brick	2001			
10201	10/29/2019	103	$505,000	419 Harlem Avenue	Elk Grove	2000	3	3	2 Car Attached	Brick	2002	2/23/2020	$500,000	117
10204	11/1/2019	151	$312,000	9023 Evergreen Lane	Davis	1850	3	2	2 Car Attached	Stone	2003			
10207	11/4/2019	151	$489,000	4230 Madison Street	Sacramento	1900	2	2	2 Car Attached	Brick	2005	3/15/2020	$475,000	132
10210	11/7/2019	160	$499,000	1330 Harrison Street	Elk Grove	2100	3	3	3 Car Attached	Frame	1990	3/25/2020	$465,000	139
10213	11/10/2019	160	$299,000	401 Lombard Avenue	Davis	1650	2	2	1 Car Attached	Frame	1995			

Figure 4-115 Excel 4-7 completed

Challenge Project 4-8

For this project, you build a worksheet for a company that sells four varieties of socks in four eastern states. When the data are complete, format the data as an Excel table.
[Student Learning Outcomes 4.1, 4.2, 4.3]

File Needed: None
Completed Project File Name: ***[your initials] Excel 4-8.xlsx***

Create a new workbook and save it as [your initials] Excel 4-8. Modify your workbook according to the following guidelines:

- Type the labels State, Month, Style, Pairs, and Price in cells **A4:E4**.
- Type Connecticut, Maine, New Hampshire, and Vermont in cells **A5:A8**.

- Type January in cell **B5**, and copy the month to cells **B6:B8**.
- Type the style name for one type of sock sold by the company in cell **C5**. Copy the name to cells **C6:C8**.
- Enter values for how many pairs were sold in each state in January in cells **D5:D8**. In column E, enter and copy a price for this sock style.
- Copy cells **A5:E8** and paste the range in cell **A9** to create a February group. Edit the month and the number of pairs sold.
- Copy cells **A5:E12** and paste the range in cell **A13** to create the data for another sock style. In this range, edit the style name, the number of pairs sold, and the price. The price is the same for all rows in this group.
- Copy and paste cells **A13:E20** to cell **A21** and then again to cell **A29** to complete two more ranges for two sock styles, so that you have January and February data for four sock styles for each state.
- Set conditional formatting to show one of the state names in a format different from the other states.
- Name the sheet Data and make a copy named Table. Clear the conditional formatting from the **Table** sheet.
- Select the **Table** sheet, and format the data as an Excel table with a light table style.
- Type Total in cell **F4** and create a formula to calculate the dollar amount of sales in the column. Show a total row for the table with results for the number of pairs and sales dollars.
- Add additional formatting to the table as needed.
- Use the *AutoFilter* arrows to sort by style and then by state.
- Enter a name for the company in cell **A1**. Enter a label in cell **A2** that describes the data.

Challenge Project 4-9

For this project, you explore the Bureau of Labor Statistics web site to download data for use in a worksheet. After you have arranged and formatted the data, you copy it to a Word document.
[Student Learning Outcomes 4.1, 4.2, 4.6, 4.7]

File Needed: None
Completed Project File Names: ***[your initials] Excel 4-9.xlsx*** and ***[your initials] Excel 4-9Word.docx***

Create a new workbook and save it as [your initials] Excel 4-9. Modify your workbook according to the following guidelines:

- Go to www.bls.gov/data.
- Review the subject areas and choose one to explore. Find a topic and subtopic which provides an .xlsx file for download.
- Download or copy the data into your worksheet.
- Format the data as an Excel table (if it is not already formatted) or apply a different table style.
- Determine and apply conditional formatting for an aspect of the data.
- Determine and set a different sort order.
- Add a main title to your worksheet and set other format attributes to effectively display your information.
- Copy all or a logical portion of the data to a new Word document and save the Word document as [your initials] Excel 4-9Word.docx.

Challenge Project 4-10

For this project, you create a worksheet that lists names, birth dates, and hair color for 20 people. You format the list as a table for sorting and filtering. You convert the table to a range and use the *Subtotal* command.
[Student Learning Outcomes 4.1, 4.3, 4.4, 4.5]

File Needed: None
Completed Project File Name: ***[your initials] Excel 4-10.xlsx***

Create a new workbook and save it as [your initials] Excel 4-10. Modify your workbook according to the following guidelines:

- Type your first name, your last name, your birthdate, and your hair color in a row using one column for each item.
- Type data for 19 more people, using fictitious or real data. Use birthdates that are the same year as yours, as well as four other years, so that your list has only five different years. Use at least three hair colors in your list, such as brown, blond, red.
- Format the data as a table and apply a table style.
- Sort the date by birthdate with the youngest people listed first. Then, filter the data to show only those records from the first year listed in the data.
- Make a copy of the sheet and convert the table to a normal range. Use the *Subtotal* command to count the number of persons with each hair color.

CHAPTER 5

Consolidating and Linking Data and Inserting Objects

CHAPTER OVERVIEW

When multiple worksheets have identical layouts and labels, you can summarize data with the *Consolidate* command. You can also link to data in a different workbook to build a formula or display information. In this chapter, you will learn how to consolidate data from multiple sheets in the same workbook and how to link multiple workbooks with an external reference formula. You will also insert *SmartArt* graphics, illustrations, and hyperlinks in a worksheet.

STUDENT LEARNING OUTCOMES (SLOs)

After completing this chapter, you will be able to:

CASE STUDY

In the Pause & Practice projects in this chapter, you build consolidated worksheets and link workbooks for Paradise Lakes Resort. You create an illustration to accompany the data and add basic security to the workbook.

Pause & Practice 5-1: Create static and dynamic data consolidations and format grouped sheets.

Pause & Practice 5-2: Link workbooks.

Pause & Practice 5-3: Insert *SmartArt*, hyperlinks, a screenshot, and an icon in a workbook; mark a workbook as final.

EXCEL

SLO 5.1

Creating a Static Data Consolidation

A ***consolidated worksheet*** summarizes data from multiple sheets with a mathematical or statistical function. The *Consolidate* command on the *Data* tab calculates totals, averages, or other functions for data from multiple worksheets. Worksheets must have common data in the same rows and columns on each sheet for consolidation *by position*.

Each location for Paradise Lakes Resort follows the same layout for its net income worksheet, but the values are different. Figure 5-1 shows worksheets for two locations, and revenue items and values are in cells A5:D8 on each sheet. When worksheets use the same pattern, the *Consolidate* command gathers data from each sheet to calculate a total, an average, or similar function.

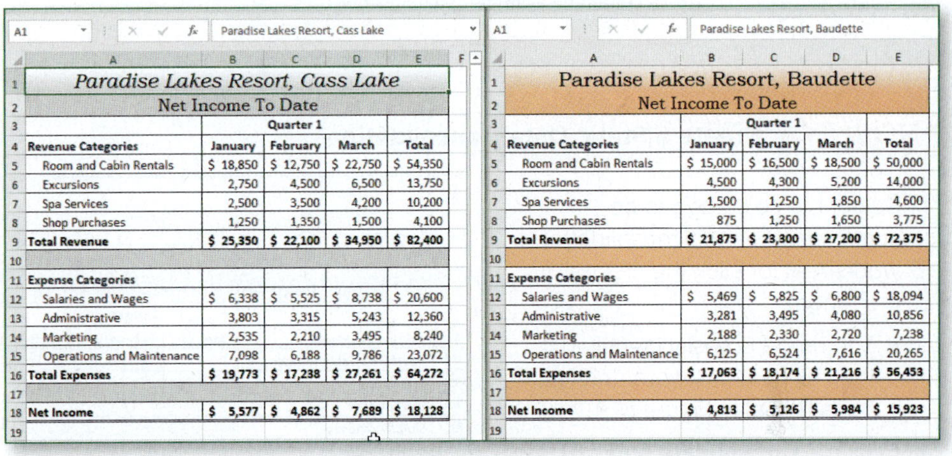

A1 | Paradise Lakes Resort, Cass Lake

	A	B	C	D	E
1	Paradise Lakes Resort, Cass Lake				
2	Net Income To Date				
3		Quarter 1			
4	Revenue Categories	January	February	March	Total
5	Room and Cabin Rentals	$ 18,850	$ 12,750	$ 22,750	$ 54,350
6	Excursions	2,750	4,500	6,500	13,750
7	Spa Services	2,500	3,500	4,200	10,200
8	Shop Purchases	1,250	1,350	1,500	4,100
9	Total Revenue	$ 25,350	$ 22,100	$ 34,950	$ 82,400
10					
11	Expense Categories				
12	Salaries and Wages	$ 6,338	$ 5,525	$ 8,738	$ 20,600
13	Administrative	3,803	3,315	5,243	12,360
14	Marketing	2,535	2,210	3,495	8,240
15	Operations and Maintenance	7,098	6,188	9,786	23,072
16	Total Expenses	$ 19,773	$ 17,238	$ 27,261	$ 64,272
17					
18	Net Income	$ 5,577	$ 4,862	$ 7,689	$ 18,128
19					

A1 | Paradise Lakes Resort, Baudette

	A	B	C	D	E
1	Paradise Lakes Resort, Baudette				
2	Net Income To Date				
3		Quarter 1			
4	Revenue Categories	January	February	March	Total
5	Room and Cabin Rentals	$ 15,000	$ 16,500	$ 18,500	$ 50,000
6	Excursions	4,500	4,300	5,200	14,000
7	Spa Services	1,500	1,250	1,850	4,600
8	Shop Purchases	875	1,250	1,650	3,775
9	Total Revenue	$ 21,875	$ 23,300	$ 27,200	$ 72,375
10					
11	Expense Categories				
12	Salaries and Wages	$ 5,469	$ 5,825	$ 6,800	$ 18,094
13	Administrative	3,281	3,495	4,080	10,856
14	Marketing	2,188	2,330	2,720	7,238
15	Operations and Maintenance	6,125	6,524	7,616	20,265
16	Total Expenses	$ 17,063	$ 18,174	$ 21,216	$ 56,453
17					
18	Net Income	$ 4,813	$ 5,126	$ 5,984	$ 15,923
19					

Figure 5-1 Two sheets prepared for consolidation by position

A ***consolidation worksheet*** is a separate summary sheet in the workbook. You create a consolidation sheet by copying one of the ***source worksheets***. On the consolidation sheet, it is common practice to delete the contents of cells to be consolidated. Create the consolidation worksheet before you start the *Consolidate* command.

▸HOW TO: Prepare a Consolidation Sheet

1. Copy one of the source worksheets in the workbook.
2. Rename the copied sheet as desired.
3. Delete the contents of cells to be consolidated (Figure 5-2).
   - Do not delete formulas that will be used on the consolidation sheet.
   - If cell contents are not deleted, the data is replaced with consolidation results.

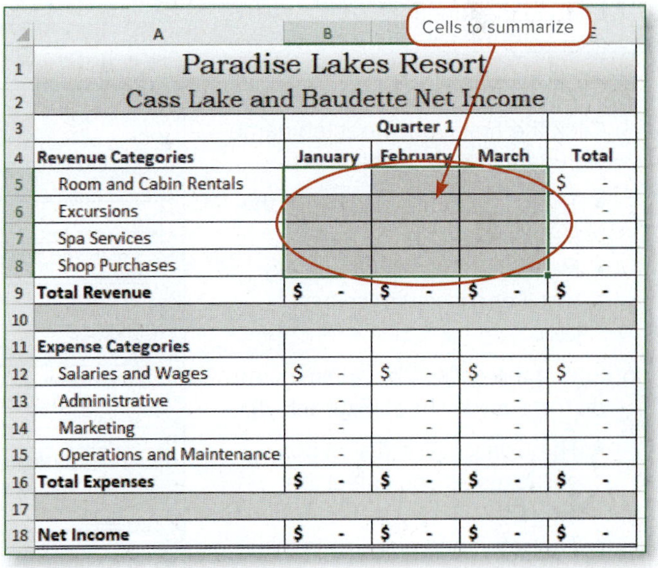

	A	B	C	D	E
1	Paradise Lakes Resort				
2	Cass Lake and Baudette Net Income				
3		Quarter 1			
4	Revenue Categories	January	February	March	Total
5	Room and Cabin Rentals				$ -
6	Excursions				-
7	Spa Services				-
8	Shop Purchases				-
9	Total Revenue	$ -	$ -	$ -	$ -
10					
11	Expense Categories				
12	Salaries and Wages	$ -	$ -	$ -	$ -
13	Administrative	-	-	-	-
14	Marketing	-	-	-	-
15	Operations and Maintenance	-	-	-	-
16	Total Expenses	$ -	$ -	$ -	$ -
17					
18	Net Income	$ -	$ -	$ -	$ -

Figure 5-2 Copied worksheet ready for consolidation

Static Data Consolidation

A ***static data consolidation*** summarizes the data and displays a result on the consolidated sheet. The result does not change when a value on any source worksheet is edited. A static data consolidation for the data in Figure 5-1 displays 2,125 in cell B8 (1,250 + 875) on the consolidation sheet. If cell B8 on either sheet is changed after consolidation, cell B8 on the consolidation sheet does not recalculate. When you know that source data is final and will not be edited, use a static data consolidation.

> **MORE INFO**
>
> If values are edited in source worksheets used in a static data consolidation, run the *Consolidate* command again to update results.

HOW TO: Create a Static Data Consolidation

1. Select the cell range to be summarized on the consolidation worksheet (or click the first cell in the range).
   - The range is easily identified if the cell contents were deleted (cells B5:D8 in Figure 5-3).
2. Click the **Consolidate** button [*Data* tab, *Data Tools* group].
   - The *Consolidate* dialog box opens.
   - If recently used cell ranges are listed in the *All references* box, select each reference and click **Delete** in the dialog box.
3. Click the **Function** arrow and choose the function (Figure 5-3).
4. Click the **Reference** box.
5. Click the first worksheet tab name with data to be consolidated.
   - The sheet name displays in the *Reference* box.
   - Move the *Consolidate* dialog box if necessary to select cells.
6. Select the cells to be summarized on the source sheet (Figure 5-4).
   - The *Consolidate* dialog box collapses as you select the range.
   - The reference appears in the *Reference* box.

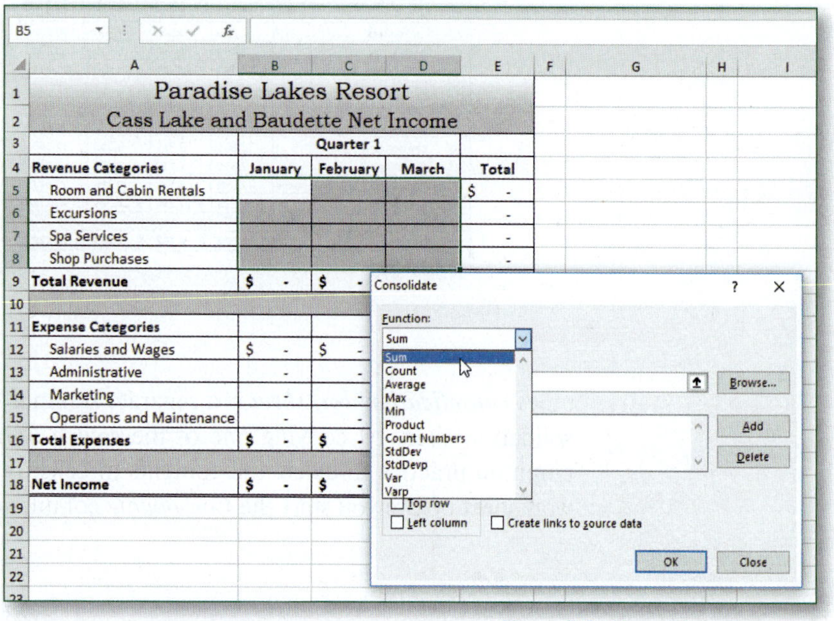

Figure 5-3 *Consolidate* dialog box

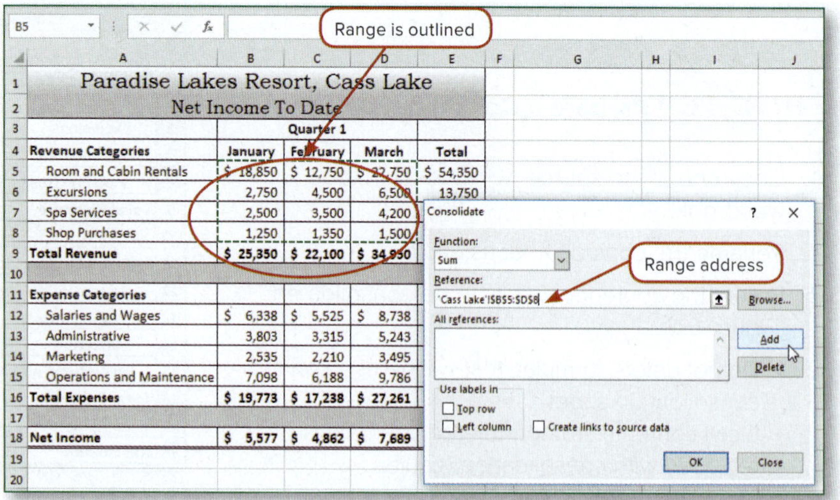

Figure 5-4 Range selected on first sheet

7. Click **Add** in the *Consolidate* dialog box.
   - The first reference displays in the *All references* list.
   - The first selected sheet tab is active with the range selected.
8. Click the next worksheet tab name with data to be consolidated.
   - The same cell range is selected.
9. Click **Add**.
   - The reference is placed in the *All references* list.
10. Repeat steps 8 and 9 for each worksheet to include in the consolidation (Figure 5-5).
11. Click **OK**.
   - The data is summarized.
   - The consolidated sheet displays a result in each cell (Figure 5-6).

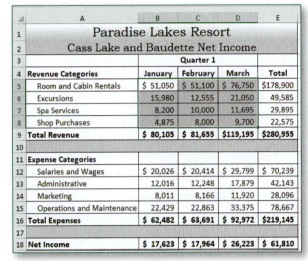

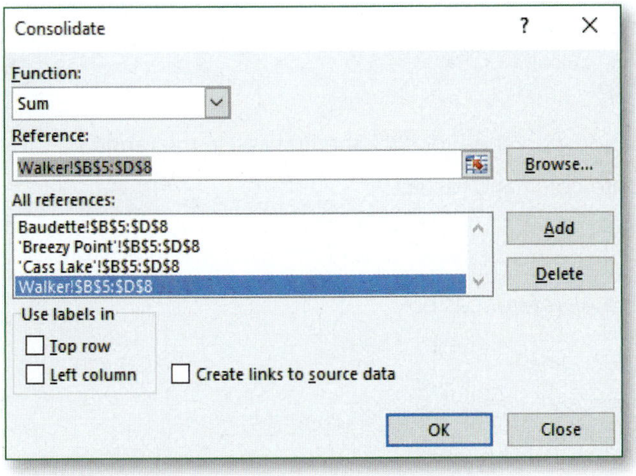

Figure 5-5 Data to be consolidated by *SUM* on four worksheets

	A	B	C	D	E
1	Paradise Lakes Resort				
2	Cass Lake and Baudette Net Income				
3		Quarter 1			
4	**Revenue Categories**	**January**	**February**	**March**	**Total**
5	Room and Cabin Rentals	$ 51,050	$ 51,100	$ 76,750	$178,900
6	Excursions	15,980	12,555	21,050	49,585
7	Spa Services	8,200	10,000	11,695	29,895
8	Shop Purchases	4,875	8,000	9,700	22,575
9	**Total Revenue**	**$ 80,105**	**$ 81,655**	**$119,195**	**$280,955**
10					
11	**Expense Categories**				
12	Salaries and Wages	$ 20,026	$ 20,414	$ 29,799	$ 70,239
13	Administrative	12,016	12,248	17,879	42,143
14	Marketing	8,011	8,166	11,920	28,096
15	Operations and Maintenance	22,429	22,863	33,375	78,667
16	**Total Expenses**	**$ 62,482**	**$ 63,691**	**$ 92,972**	**$219,145**
17					
18	**Net Income**	**$ 17,623**	**$ 17,964**	**$ 26,223**	**$ 61,810**

Figure 5-6 Consolidated results

SLO 5.2

Creating a Dynamic Data Consolidation

A ***dynamic data consolidation*** places formulas on the consolidated sheet in an outline. When data on a source worksheet is edited, the formula recalculates. Use dynamic data consolidation when data on source worksheets might be edited after you have created the consolidation worksheet.

MORE INFO

An Excel outline can show or hide details as discussed in *SLO 4.5: Using Subtotals, Groups, and Outlines*.

Dynamic Data Consolidation

Build a dynamic data consolidation sheet the same way that you build a static data consolidation sheet. In the *Consolidate* dialog box, however, choose the option to create links to the source data. The resulting outline in the consolidation sheet uses 3D reference formulas (Figure 5-7). The formulas identify the sheet name and cell used for consolidation. In a dynamic data consolidation, expand outline items to display individual values that are summarized.

ANOTHER WAY

Use 3D references in your own formulas to dynamically consolidate data.

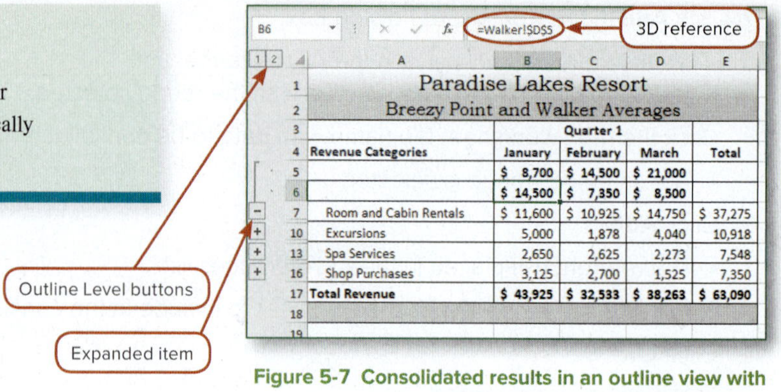

Figure 5-7 Consolidated results in an outline view with 3D reference

▸HOW TO: Create a Dynamic Data Consolidation

1. Select the cell range to be summarized on the consolidation worksheet or click the first cell in the range.
   - Existing cell contents will be replaced by the *Consolidate* command results.
2. Click the **Consolidate** button [*Data* tab, *Data Tools* group].
   - The *Consolidate* dialog box opens.
   - Select and delete recently used reference ranges in the *All references* box.
3. Click the **Function** arrow and choose the function.
4. Click the **Reference** box.
5. Click the first worksheet tab name with data to be consolidated.
   - The sheet name displays in the *Reference* box.
   - Move the *Consolidate* dialog box if necessary to select cells.
6. Select the cells to be summarized.
   - The *Consolidate* dialog box collapses as you select the range.
   - The reference appears in the *Reference* box.
7. Click **Add** in the *Consolidate* dialog box.
   - The first reference is listed in the *All references* box.
   - The first selected sheet tab is active with the range selected.
8. Click the next worksheet tab name with data to be consolidated.
   - The same cell range is selected.
9. Click **Add**.
   - The second reference is listed in the *All references* box.
10. Repeat steps 8 and 9 for each worksheet to include in the consolidation.
11. Select the **Create links to source data** box (Figure 5-8).
12. Click **OK** (Figure 5-9).
    - The data is consolidated in outline format.
    - Each item is collapsed.
    - The consolidated sheet displays a 3D reference in each cell above the result cell when the outline is expanded.

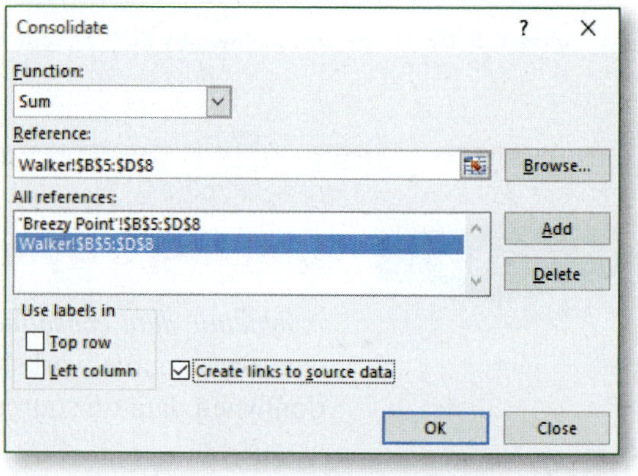

Figure 5-8 Data to be consolidated by *SUM* with links

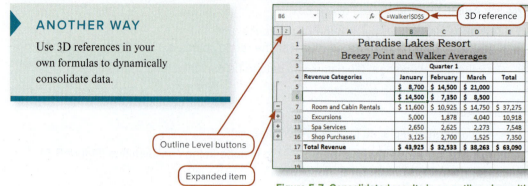

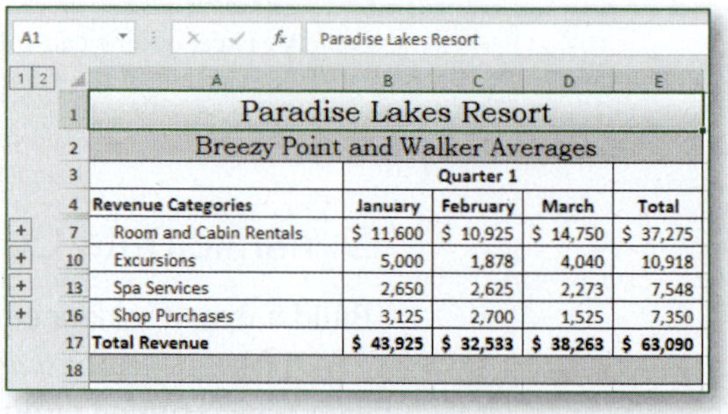

Figure 5-9 Dynamic data consolidation results

Consolidating Data by Category

When data in multiple worksheets is arranged differently but has the same row and column labels, you can build a consolidation *by category*. Category refers to the row or column labels. Consolidation by category can be static or dynamic.

Data Consolidation by Category

The worksheets shown in Figure 5-10 have data for January, February, and March. The month names are not arranged in the same way, but they are spelled alike on both sheets.

To consolidate data by category, copy one of the source worksheets. On the consolidation sheet, delete the contents of cells to be consolidated including the labels, cells B4:D8 in Figure 5-10. When you select the range on each source sheet, select the same range (B4:D8). In the *Consolidate* dialog box, activate the option to use the top row or left column labels or both.

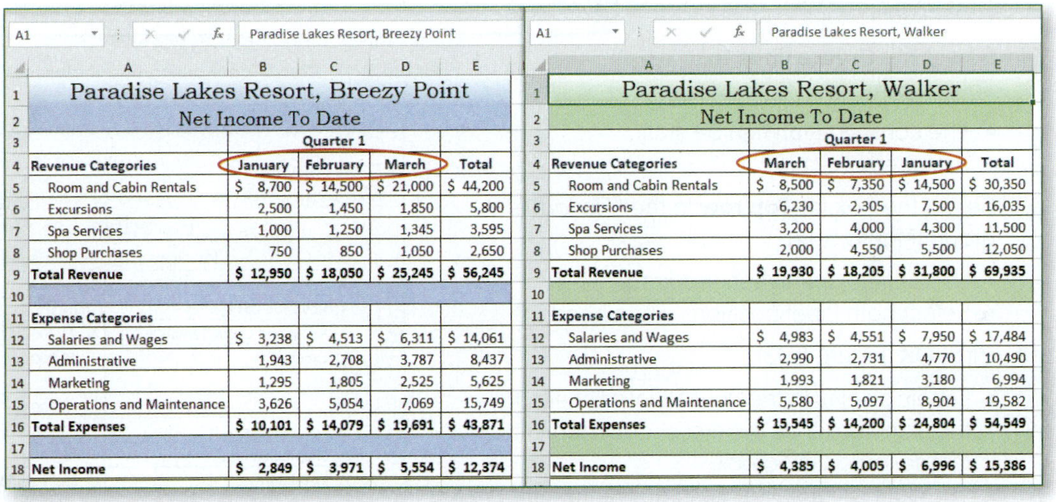

A1 — Paradise Lakes Resort, Breezy Point

	A	B	C	D	E
1	Paradise Lakes Resort, Breezy Point				
2	Net Income To Date				
3		Quarter 1			
4	Revenue Categories	January	February	March	Total
5	Room and Cabin Rentals	$ 8,700	$ 14,500	$ 21,000	$ 44,200
6	Excursions	2,500	1,450	1,850	5,800
7	Spa Services	1,000	1,250	1,345	3,595
8	Shop Purchases	750	850	1,050	2,650
9	Total Revenue	$ 12,950	$ 18,050	$ 25,245	$ 56,245
10					
11	Expense Categories				
12	Salaries and Wages	$ 3,238	$ 4,513	$ 6,311	$ 14,061
13	Administrative	1,943	2,708	3,787	8,437
14	Marketing	1,295	1,805	2,525	5,625
15	Operations and Maintenance	3,626	5,054	7,069	15,749
16	Total Expenses	$ 10,101	$ 14,079	$ 19,691	$ 43,871
17					
18	Net Income	$ 2,849	$ 3,971	$ 5,554	$ 12,374

A1 — Paradise Lakes Resort, Walker

	A	B	C	D	E
1	Paradise Lakes Resort, Walker				
2	Net Income To Date				
3		Quarter 1			
4	Revenue Categories	March	February	January	Total
5	Room and Cabin Rentals	$ 8,500	$ 7,350	$ 14,500	$ 30,350
6	Excursions	6,230	2,305	7,500	16,035
7	Spa Services	3,200	4,000	4,300	11,500
8	Shop Purchases	2,000	4,550	5,500	12,050
9	Total Revenue	$ 19,930	$ 18,205	$ 31,800	$ 69,935
10					
11	Expense Categories				
12	Salaries and Wages	$ 4,983	$ 4,551	$ 7,950	$ 17,484
13	Administrative	2,990	2,731	4,770	10,490
14	Marketing	1,993	1,821	3,180	6,994
15	Operations and Maintenance	5,580	5,097	8,904	19,582
16	Total Expenses	$ 15,545	$ 14,200	$ 24,804	$ 54,549
17					
18	Net Income	$ 4,385	$ 4,005	$ 6,996	$ 15,386

Figure 5-10 Data has same labels in different order

▸HOW TO: Create a Dynamic Data Consolidation by Category

1. Delete the contents of the cells to be summarized including labels on the consolidation sheet.
2. Select the range of cells to be summarized including label cells (Figure 5-11).
3. Click the **Consolidate** button [*Data* tab, *Data Tools* group].
   - The *Consolidate* dialog box opens.
   - Select and delete references in the *All references* box.
4. Click the **Function** arrow and choose the function.
5. Click the first sheet tab name with data to be consolidated.
   - The sheet name displays in the *Reference* box.

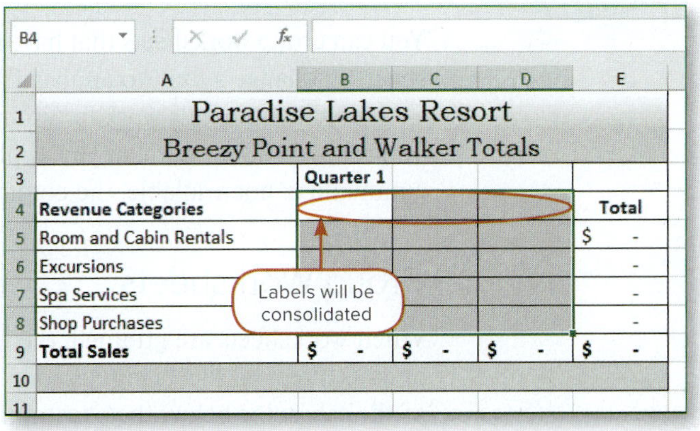

B4

	A	B	C	D	E
1	Paradise Lakes Resort				
2	Breezy Point and Walker Totals				
3		Quarter 1			
4	Revenue Categories				Total
5	Room and Cabin Rentals				$ -
6	Excursions				-
7	Spa Services				-
8	Shop Purchases				-
9	Total Sales	$ -	$ -	$ -	$ -
10					

Figure 5-11 Consolidation sheet with labels and data deleted

6. Select data and label cells to be summarized.
7. Click **Add** in the *Consolidate* dialog box.
   - The first reference appears in the *All references* list.
8. Click the next worksheet tab name.
   - The same cell range is selected.
9. Click **Add**.
   - The second reference appears in the *All references* list.
10. Repeat steps 8 and 9 for each worksheet to include in the consolidation.
11. Select the **Create links to source data** box.
   - The consolidation can be static if desired.
12. Select the box for **Top row** in the *Use labels in* group (Figure 5-12).
   - Use *Left column* when required.
   - Select both label positions when needed.
13. Click **OK** (Figure 5-13).
   - Labels display in the consolidated sheet in the same order as the first sheet listed in the *Consolidate* dialog box.
   - The data is consolidated in outline format.
   - The 3D references indicate the cells used for each result on the consolidation sheet.

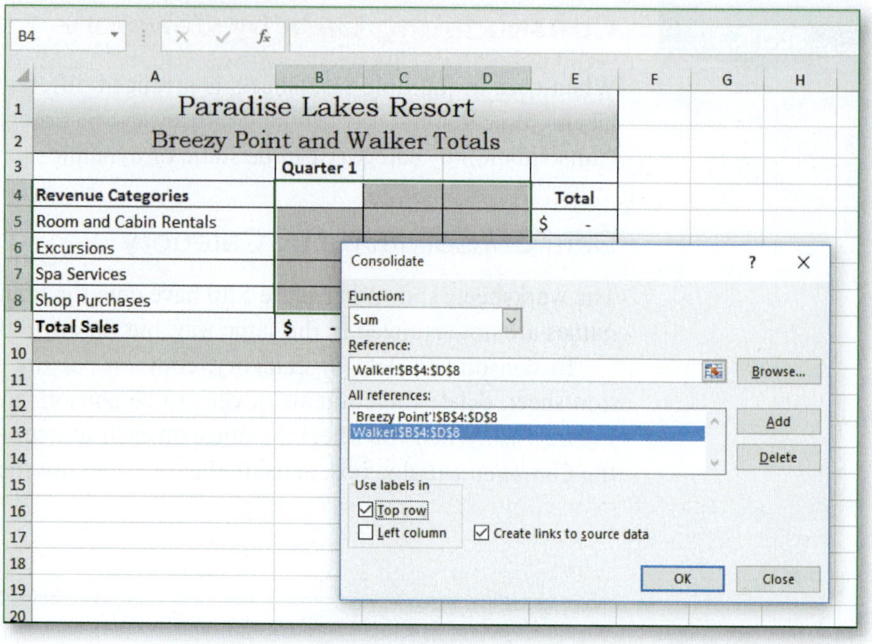

Figure 5-12 *Consolidate* **dialog box choices for consolidation by category**

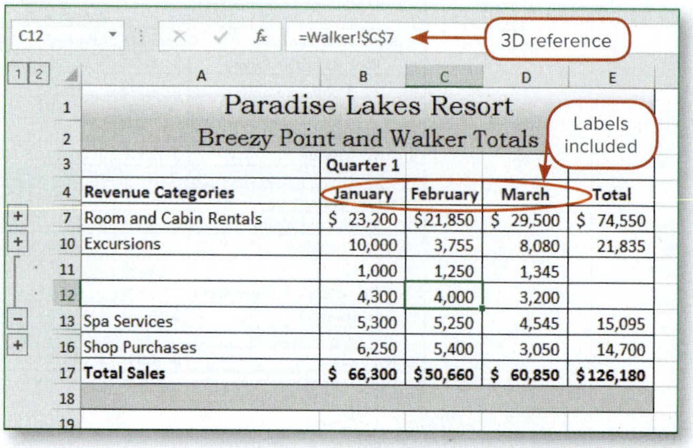

Figure 5-13 Consolidation results

SLO 5.4

Working with Grouped Worksheets

You can group worksheets that have identical layouts for common editing or formatting. Group sheets to change a font, to apply a fill color, to set alignment, to edit data, and more.

Not all commands work for grouped worksheets. For example, you cannot insert a graphic on grouped sheets, nor can you apply conditional formatting. When sheets are grouped and a command is not available, the command button or option is grayed out on the *Ribbon*.

Group Worksheets

When worksheets are grouped, the title bar shows *[Group]* after the file name, and commands or edits affect all sheets in the group. The tabs for grouped worksheets appear white with a hint of the tab color below the sheet name. When grouping sheets, you may find it helpful to set different tab colors so that it is easier to recognize grouped sheets.

To group worksheets, press **Ctrl** or **Shift** to select multiple tab names. Select all sheets in a workbook from the context menu for any tab. To ungroup sheets, click any tab name that is not part of the group. When all sheets are grouped, right-click any tab name and choose **Ungroup Sheets**.

HOW TO: Group Worksheets

1. Click the first sheet tab to be included in the group.
2. Press **Shift** and click the last tab name for the group to select adjacent sheets.
   - The first sheet remains visible.
3. Right-click any sheet tab and choose **Ungroup Sheets**.
4. Press **Ctrl** and click each tab name to select nonadjacent sheets (Figure 5-14).
5. Right-click any tab and choose **Ungroup Sheets**.
6. Right-click any sheet tab and choose **Select All Sheets** to group all sheets in a workbook.

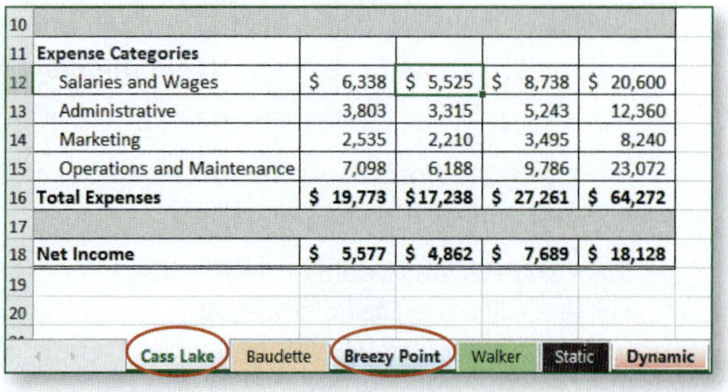

10					
11	Expense Categories				
12	Salaries and Wages	$ 6,338	$ 5,525	$ 8,738	$ 20,600
13	Administrative	3,803	3,315	5,243	12,360
14	Marketing	2,535	2,210	3,495	8,240
15	Operations and Maintenance	7,098	6,188	9,786	23,072
16	Total Expenses	$ 19,773	$17,238	$ 27,261	$ 64,272
17					
18	Net Income	$ 5,577	$ 4,862	$ 7,689	$ 18,128
19					
20					

Figure 5-14 Nonadjacent grouped worksheets, Cass Lake and Breezy Point

> **MORE INFO**
>
> If you save a workbook while sheets are grouped, the workbook opens with grouped sheets.

Edit and Format Grouped Worksheets

All worksheets in a group are affected by a command, so worksheets should be identical in layout. If they are not, you might apply changes that are not appropriate for every sheet in the group.

One command that you *can* apply to grouped sheets that are not identical is a header or footer command. You can also change page orientation for multiple sheets that are not identical in format and content.

HOW TO: Edit and Format Grouped Sheets

1. Group the worksheets.
2. Click a cell to be edited.
   - Any sheet in the group can be active or visible.
3. Enter data and press **Enter**.
   - The edit is made on all sheets in the group.
4. Select cells to be formatted.
5. Apply the format.
   - The format displays on all sheets in the group.
6. Ungroup the sheets.

For this project, you create a static data consolidation for Paradise Lakes Resort to sum income data. You also create a dynamic data consolidation to average income data and group sheets for formatting.

File Needed: ***ParadiseLakes-05.xlsx*** *(Student data files are available in the* Library *of your SIMnet account.)*
Completed Project File Name: ***[your initials] PP E5-1.xlsx***

1. Open the ***ParadiseLakes-05*** workbook from your student data files and save it as [your initials] PP E5-1.
2. Create a static data consolidation.
   a. Click the **Static** sheet tab.
   b. Select cells **B5:D8** and press **Delete**. The formulas calculate to zero, which displays as a hyphen in this worksheet.
   c. Click the **Consolidate** button [*Data* tab, *Data Tools* group].
   d. Verify that the *SUM* function is selected.
   e. Select and delete recently used reference ranges in the *All references* box if any are listed.
   f. Click the **Reference** box and click the **Cass Lake** sheet tab.
   g. Select cells **B5:D8**.
   h. Click **Add** in the *Consolidate* dialog box.
   i. Click the **Baudette** sheet tab. Verify that the same cell range (B5:D8) is selected. If it is not selected, select it.
   j. Click **Add** (Figure 5-15).
   k. Click **OK**.

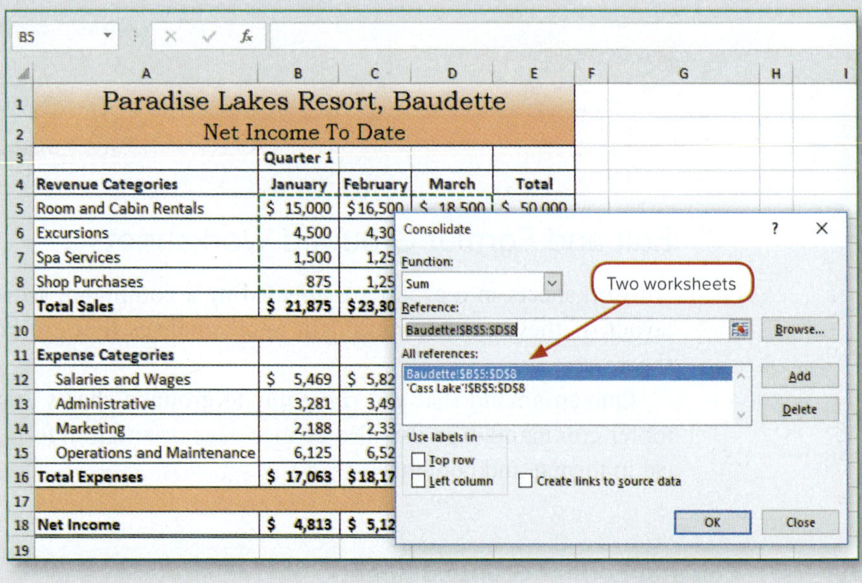

Figure 5-15 *Consolidate* dialog box for two worksheets in a static data consolidation

3. Create a dynamic data consolidation by category.
   a. Click the **Dynamic** sheet tab.
   b. Select cells **B4:D8** and delete them. The labels in row 4 will be consolidated.
   c. Click the **Consolidate** button [*Data* tab, *Data Tools* group].
   d. Click the **Function** drop-down list and choose **AVERAGE**.
   e. Select and delete each reference displayed in the *All references* box, if any.
   f. Click the **Reference** box and click the **Breezy Point** sheet tab.
   g. Select cells **B4:D8** and click **Add** in the *Consolidate* dialog box.

h. Click the **Walker** sheet tab. Note that the month names are in different order.
i. Click **Add**.
j. Select the **Top row** box in the *Consolidate* dialog box.
k. Select the **Create links to source data** box (Figure 5-16).
l. Click **OK**. The labels are consolidated in the same order as the **Breezy Point** sheet.

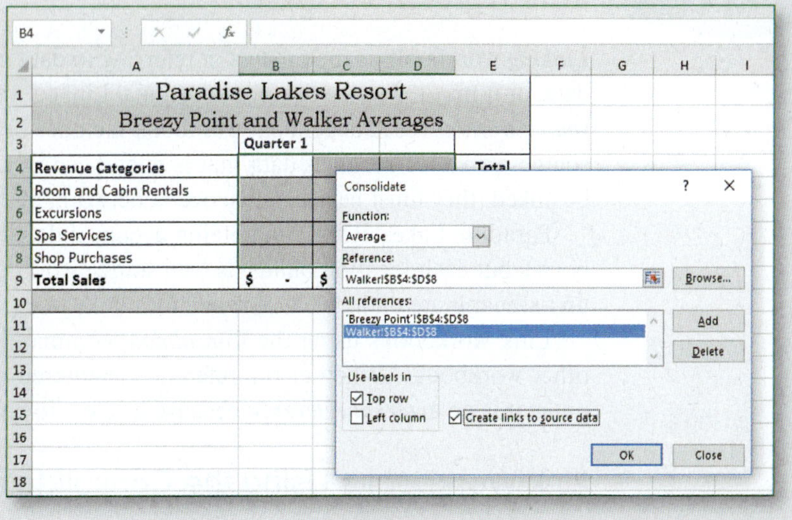

Figure 5-16 *Consolidate* dialog box for a dynamic data consolidation by category

4. Group, format, and edit sheets.
   a. Click the **Cass Lake** sheet tab.
   b. Press **Shift** and click the **Dynamic** sheet tab to group all sheets.
   c. Select cells **A5:A8**.
   d. Click the **Increase Indent** button [*Home* tab, *Alignment* group] two times.
   e. Select cells **B3:D3**.
   f. Click the **Merge & Center** button [*Home* tab, *Alignment* group].
   g. Select cell **A9** and edit the label to show Total Revenue.
   h. Format columns **B:E** to be **10.00 (75 pixels)** wide.
   i. Press **Ctrl+Home**.
   j. Right-click the **Cass Lake** sheet tab and choose **Ungroup Sheets**.
   k. Select the **Dynamic** sheet. The labels on this sheet are not indented because the outline format uses different row numbers.
   l. Select cell **A10**. Press **Ctrl** and select cell **A13** and then cell **A16**. Increase the indent two times.
   m. Edit the label in cell **A17** to display Total Revenue.
   n. Press **Ctrl+Home**.
5. Save and close the workbook (Figure 5-17).

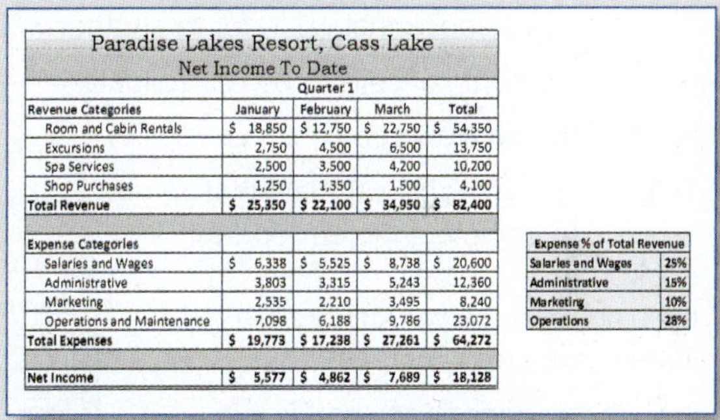

Paradise Lakes Resort, Cass Lake
Net Income To Date

	Quarter 1			
Revenue Categories	January	February	March	Total
Room and Cabin Rentals	$ 18,850	$ 12,750	$ 22,750	$ 54,350
Excursions	2,750	4,500	6,500	13,750
Spa Services	2,500	3,500	4,200	10,200
Shop Purchases	1,250	1,350	1,500	4,100
Total Revenue	$ 25,350	$ 22,100	$ 34,950	$ 82,400
Expense Categories				
Salaries and Wages	$ 6,338	$ 5,525	$ 8,738	$ 20,600
Administrative	3,803	3,315	5,243	12,360
Marketing	2,535	2,210	3,495	8,240
Operations and Maintenance	7,098	6,188	9,786	23,072
Total Expenses	$ 19,773	$ 17,238	$ 27,261	$ 64,272
Net Income	$ 5,577	$ 4,862	$ 7,689	$ 18,128

Expense % of Total Revenue	
Salaries and Wages	25%
Administrative	15%
Marketing	10%
Operations	28%

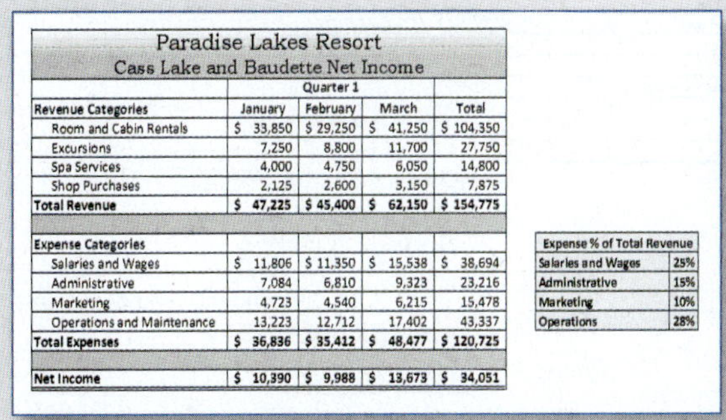

Paradise Lakes Resort
Cass Lake and Baudette Net Income

	Quarter 1			
Revenue Categories	January	February	March	Total
Room and Cabin Rentals	$ 33,850	$ 29,250	$ 41,250	$ 104,350
Excursions	7,250	8,800	11,700	27,750
Spa Services	4,000	4,750	6,050	14,800
Shop Purchases	2,125	2,600	3,150	7,875
Total Revenue	$ 47,225	$ 45,400	$ 62,150	$ 154,775
Expense Categories				
Salaries and Wages	$ 11,806	$ 11,350	$ 15,538	$ 38,694
Administrative	7,084	6,810	9,323	23,216
Marketing	4,723	4,540	6,215	15,478
Operations and Maintenance	13,223	12,712	17,402	43,337
Total Expenses	$ 36,836	$ 35,412	$ 48,477	$ 120,725
Net Income	$ 10,390	$ 9,988	$ 13,673	$ 34,051

Expense % of Total Revenue	
Salaries and Wages	25%
Administrative	15%
Marketing	10%
Operations	28%

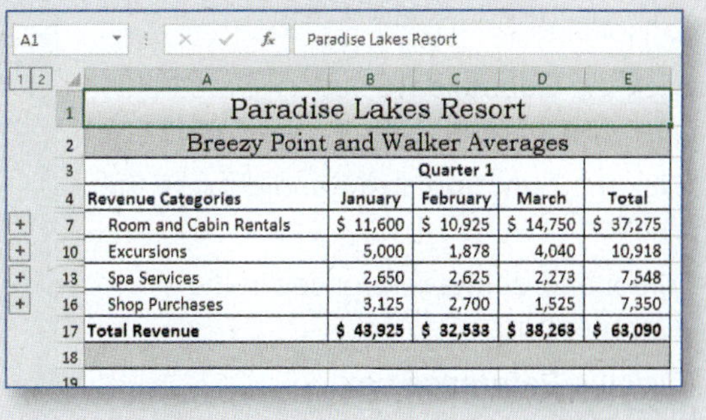

Paradise Lakes Resort
Breezy Point and Walker Averages

Row		Quarter 1			
4	Revenue Categories	January	February	March	Total
7	Room and Cabin Rentals	$ 11,600	$ 10,925	$ 14,750	$ 37,275
10	Excursions	5,000	1,878	4,040	10,918
13	Spa Services	2,650	2,625	2,273	7,548
16	Shop Purchases	3,125	2,700	1,525	7,350
17	Total Revenue	$ 43,925	$ 32,533	$ 38,263	$ 63,090

Figure 5-17 Completed PP E5-1 worksheets

SLO 5.5

Linking Workbooks

Linking workbooks is the process of referring to data in another workbook. Linking may display data, or it may reference data for a formula. Linked workbooks are referred to as ***dependent*** and ***source workbooks***. A dependent workbook includes or refers to data from another workbook. A source workbook includes data that is referenced in a dependent workbook. For workbooks to be linked, they must be accessible over a network, on the same computer, or in the cloud.

Paradise Lakes Resort maintains a consolidated income workbook (a dependent workbook), but each location builds its own source workbook. The consolidated workbook displays up-to-the-minute data, because it includes links to each of the individual workbooks.

Link workbooks using the *Consolidate* command, or build formulas that refer to cells in other workbooks. Whether the reference is entered in the *Consolidate* dialog box or in a formula, it is an ***external reference*** because it refers to cells in another workbook.

Link Workbooks Using the Consolidate Command

An external reference includes the name of the workbook in square brackets, the sheet name, cell address(es), and ***identifiers***. An identifier is a character such as an exclamation point that marks or signifies a component of the reference. When the name of the workbook or worksheet includes a nonalphabetic character (a space, a hyphen, a symbol), the name is enclosed in single quotation marks. The complete syntax for an external reference is:

='[Workbook Name]Worksheet Name'!CellRange

All workbooks must be open when you use the *Consolidate* command.

HOW TO: Link Workbooks with a Dynamic Data Consolidation

1. Open the dependent workbook.
   - This is the workbook that will refer to another workbook.
2. Delete the contents of cells to be consolidated.
3. Open the source workbook.
   - This is the workbook with data that is needed to complete the dependent workbook.
   - If multiple source workbooks are to be linked, open each of them.
4. Return to the dependent workbook.
5. Select the range of cells to be consolidated.
6. Click the **Consolidate** button [*Data* tab, *Data Tools* group].
7. Click the **Function** arrow and choose the function.
8. Select and delete references in the *All references* list.
9. Click the **Reference** box.
10. Click the workbook icon on the Windows taskbar for the first source workbook (Figure 5-18).
    - Alternatively, press **Ctrl+F6** to switch to the next open workbook.

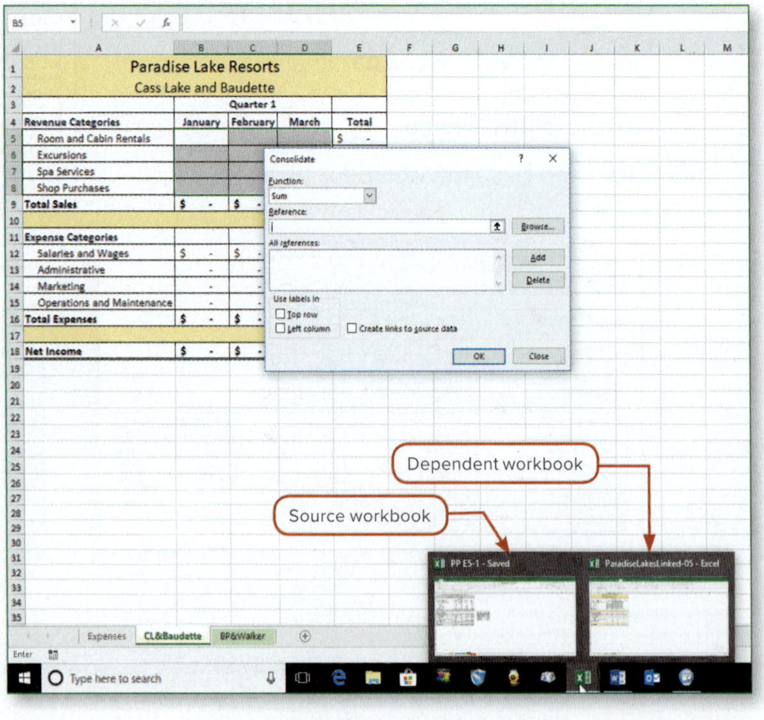

Figure 5-18 Open workbooks icons on the Windows taskbar

11. Select the sheet tab with data to be consolidated.
12. Select the cell range and click **Add**.
    - The reference includes the workbook and sheet names.
13. Click the next tab name and click **Add**.
    - If multiple workbooks are used, click the **Reference** box and click the icon for the next source workbook on the Windows taskbar.
    - Repeat this step for each sheet or workbook to be used as a source in the consolidation.
14. Select the **Create links to source data** box (Figure 5-19).

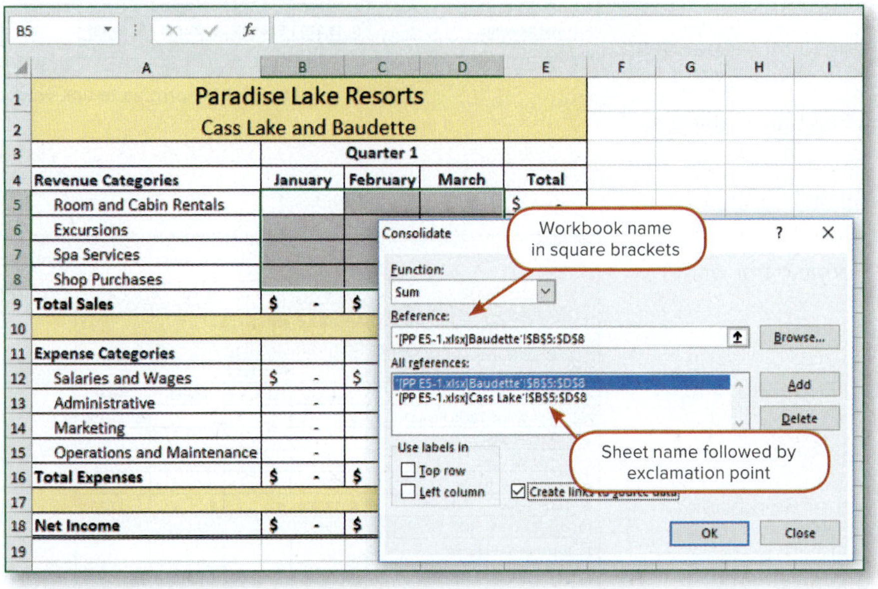

Figure 5-19 References with identifiers to another workbook

15. Click **OK**.
16. Switch to the dependent workbook.
    - The outline is collapsed.
    - External references are placed above the result cell.
    - External references include the name of the workbook, the sheet name, and the cell address or range (Figure 5-20).

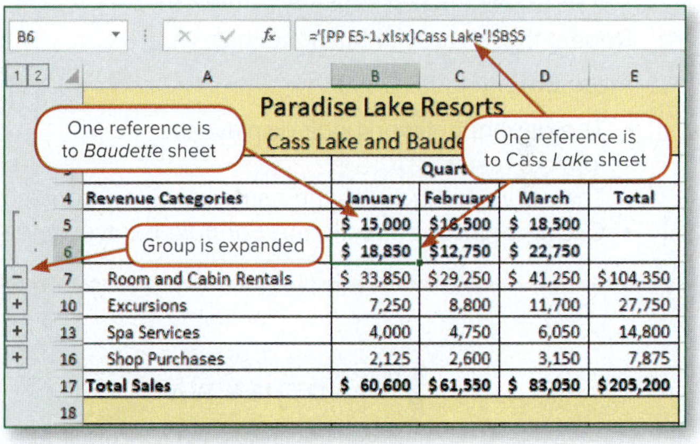

Figure 5-20 Dynamic data consolidation with another workbook

Link Workbooks Using a Formula

The *Consolidate* command includes a limited list of functions and requires that the same cell range be referenced in all worksheets. These limitations do not apply in an external reference or linking formula.

An external reference formula refers to cells in another workbook and establishes a link to the source workbook. When the source workbook is open, you can point to build the formula. The source workbook need not be open to build an external reference formula, but you must type the formula with proper syntax and all identifiers.

When you point to create an external reference, it is built with absolute references. Edit the references to be relative or mixed when you plan to copy the formula.

HOW TO: Link Workbooks with an Addition Formula

1. Open the dependent workbook.
   - This is the workbook that will include a formula with references to another workbook.
2. Open all source workbooks.
3. Return to the dependent workbook.
4. Click the cell for the formula.
5. Type = to start the formula.
   - You can enter an Excel function in the dependent workbook when needed.
6. Click the icon on the Windows taskbar for the first source workbook.
7. Click the sheet tab and click the cell for the first argument.
   - The formula displays in the *Formula* bar with identifiers.
8. Type + for addition.
   - Use the required mathematical operator in a formula.
9. Click the next sheet tab.
   - If the next reference is in another workbook, click its icon on the taskbar.
10. Click the cell for the next formula argument (Figure 5-21).
    - The cell address need not be the same cell address as the first sheet or workbook.
11. Repeat these steps to build the formula.
12. Press **Enter** (Figure 5-22).
    - The dependent workbook displays the formula result.
    - The reference includes the name of the workbook, the sheet name, and absolute cell references.
    - Click the **Enter** button in the *Formula* bar to complete the formula and return to the dependent workbook.

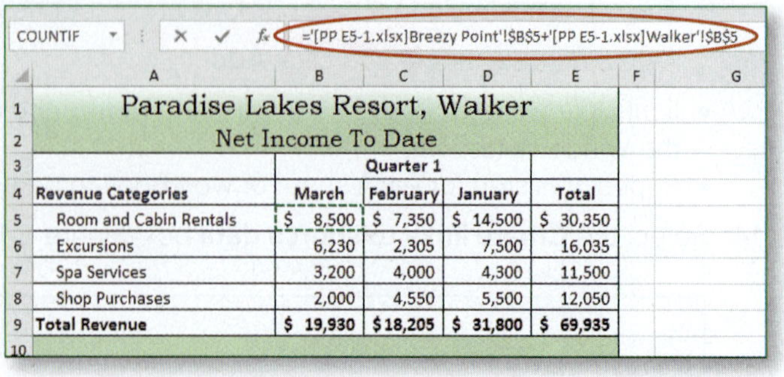

	A	B	C	D	E
1	Paradise Lakes Resort, Walker				
2	Net Income To Date				
3		Quarter 1			
4	Revenue Categories	March	February	January	Total
5	Room and Cabin Rentals	$ 8,500	$ 7,350	$ 14,500	$ 30,350
6	Excursions	6,230	2,305	7,500	16,035
7	Spa Services	3,200	4,000	4,300	11,500
8	Shop Purchases	2,000	4,550	5,500	12,050
9	Total Revenue	$ 19,930	$ 18,205	$ 31,800	$ 69,935
10					

Figure 5-21 Formula to link workbooks

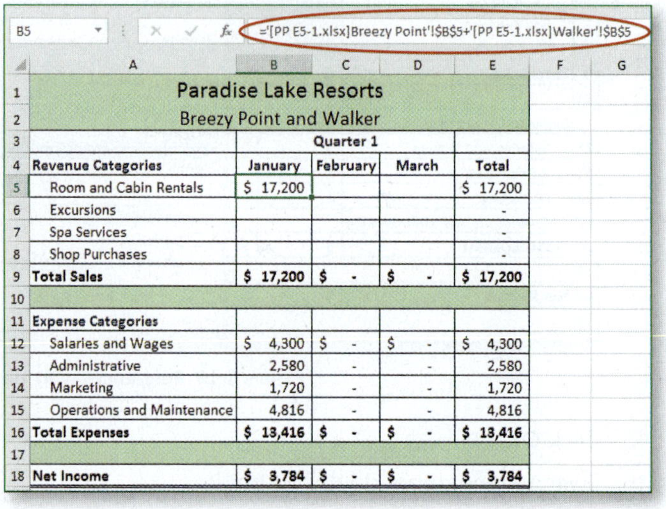

	A	B	C	D	E
1	Paradise Lake Resorts				
2	Breezy Point and Walker				
3		Quarter 1			
4	Revenue Categories	January	February	March	Total
5	Room and Cabin Rentals	$ 17,200			$ 17,200
6	Excursions				-
7	Spa Services				-
8	Shop Purchases				-
9	Total Sales	$ 17,200	$ -	$ -	$ 17,200
10					
11	Expense Categories				
12	Salaries and Wages	$ 4,300	$ -	$ -	$ 4,300
13	Administrative	2,580	-	-	2,580
14	Marketing	1,720	-	-	1,720
15	Operations and Maintenance	4,816	-	-	4,816
16	Total Expenses	$ 13,416	$ -	$ -	$ 13,416
17					
18	Net Income	$ 3,784	$ -	$ -	$ 3,784

Figure 5-22 An external reference formula in the dependent workbook

ANOTHER WAY

Arrange open workbooks side by side or horizontally tiled and switch between them by pointing and clicking.

Examine and Edit Links

An external reference formula creates a ***link*** to the source workbook, a data connection. The link specifies the file name and location at the time the formula was created. You can choose how links are handled when a workbook is opened from the *Trust Center Settings* for *External Content* (Excel *Options*) (Figure 5-23).

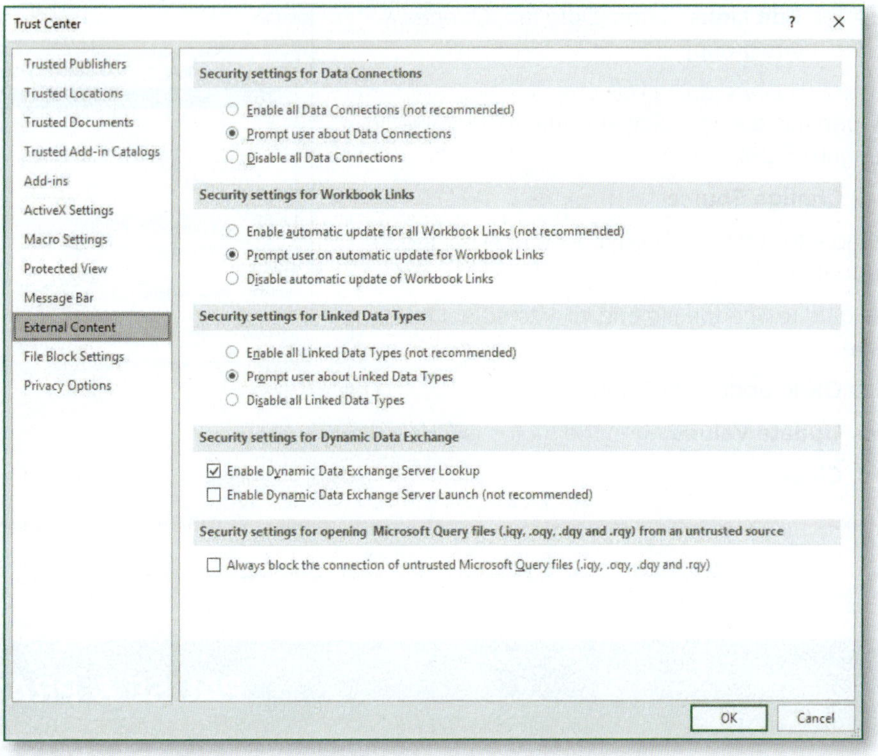

Figure 5-23 *Trust Center Settings for External Content*

Links can be updated when the source workbook is accessible. If a source workbook was renamed or moved to another location, the link should be edited to show a current result. You can open a workbook without updating a link, but the formula result may not be accurate.

You can break a link to remove the data connection but keep formula results as values in a dependent workbook.

HOW TO: Update Links in a Workbook

1. Open the dependent workbook.
   - This workbook has a formula that refers to another workbook.
   - The source workbook need not be open.
2. Click **Enable Content** in the security message bar if it opens.
   - A link may be automatically updated during a work session.
3. Click **Update** in the message box (Figure 5-24) when the link is not automatically refreshed.
   - If the source workbook is accessible, the data is refreshed.
   - If the source workbook is not accessible, a message box displays options to continue without editing or to edit the links.
4. Click **Continue** to open the workbook with the existing values (Figure 5-25).

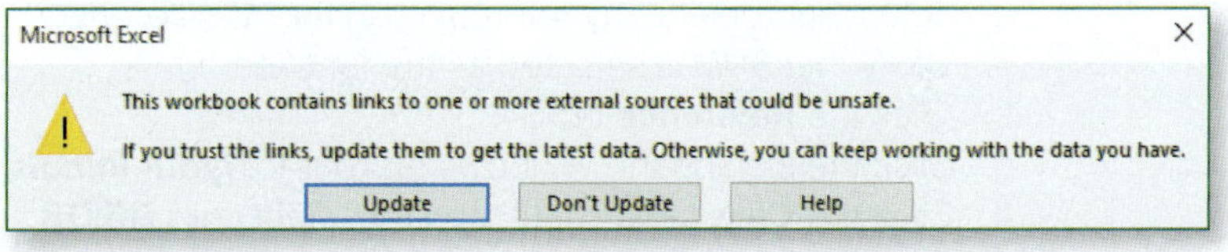

Figure 5-24 Message box when opening linked workbooks

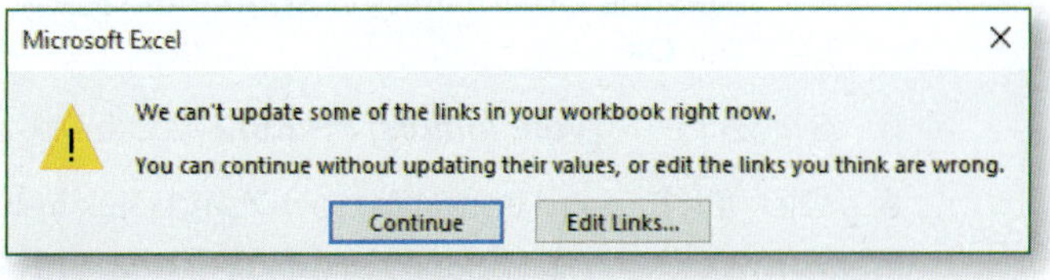

Figure 5-25 Message box when links are not accessible

5. Click the **Edit Links** button [*Data* tab, *Queries & Connections* group].
   - The *Edit Links* dialog box opens.
   - Open this dialog box at any time to examine links (Figure 5-26).
6. Click **Change Source**.
   - Find a file that has been moved or renamed to update its *Status*.
7. Navigate to find the file and click to select its name.
8. Click **OK** to update the source.
9. Click **Update Values** when the *Status* is *OK*.
10. Click **Close**.

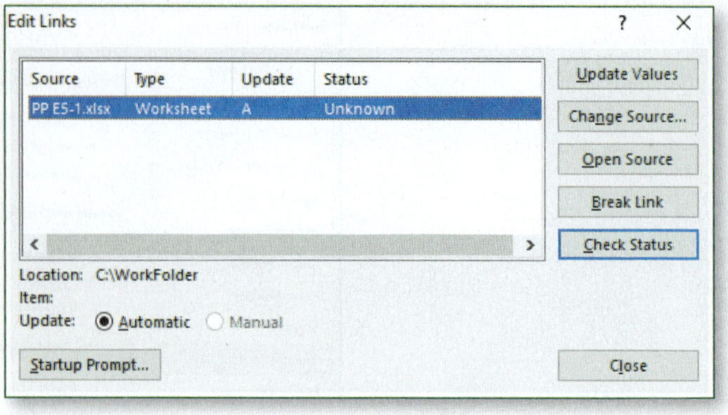

Figure 5-26 ***Edit Links*** **dialog box**

PAUSE & PRACTICE: EXCEL 5-2

For this project, you create a dynamic data consolidation with links to another workbook. You also create and copy an external reference formula.

Files Needed: ***[your initials] PP E5-1.xlsx*** and ***ParadiseLakesLinked-05.xlsx*** *(Student data files are available in the* Library *of your SIMnet account.)*
Completed Project File Name: ***[your initials] PP E5-2.xlsx***

1. Open the ***ParadiseLakesLinked-05*** workbook from your student data files.
2. Save the workbook as [your initials] PP E5-2. This is the dependent workbook.
3. Open the ***[your initials] PP E5-1*** workbook completed in *Pause & Practice 5-1*. This is the source workbook.
4. Use the *Consolidate* command to link workbooks.
   a. Return to the ***[your initials] PP E5-2*** workbook and click the **CL&Baudette** sheet tab.
   b. Select cells **B5:D8**.
   c. Click the **Consolidate** button [*Data* tab, *Data Tools* group].
   d. Select and delete any references in the *All references* list.
   e. Verify that *SUM* is selected as the function.
   f. Click the **Reference** box.
   g. Click the icon on the Windows taskbar for ***[your initials] PP E5-1***.
   h. Click the **Cass Lake** sheet tab and select cells **B5:D8**.
   i. Click **Add**.
   j. Click the **Baudette** sheet tab and click **Add**.
   k. Select the **Create links to source data** box.
   l. Click **OK**.
5. Switch to the ***[your initials] PP E5-2*** workbook and format columns **B:E** to be **10.00 (75 pixels)** wide.
6. Click the **Expand** button for row **7** and click cell **B6** (Figure 5-27).

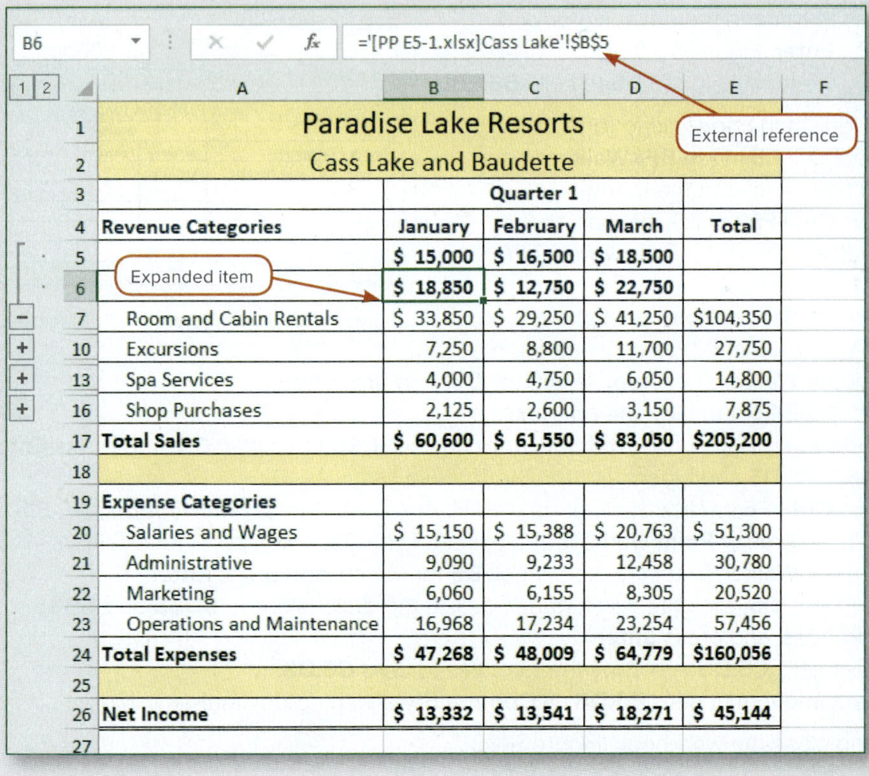

	A	B	C	D	E
1	Paradise Lake Resorts				
2	Cass Lake and Baudette				
3		Quarter 1			
4	Revenue Categories	January	February	March	Total
5		$ 15,000	$ 16,500	$ 18,500	
6		$ 18,850	$ 12,750	$ 22,750	
7	Room and Cabin Rentals	$ 33,850	$ 29,250	$ 41,250	$104,350
10	Excursions	7,250	8,800	11,700	27,750
13	Spa Services	4,000	4,750	6,050	14,800
16	Shop Purchases	2,125	2,600	3,150	7,875
17	Total Sales	$ 60,600	$ 61,550	$ 83,050	$205,200
18					
19	Expense Categories				
20	Salaries and Wages	$ 15,150	$ 15,388	$ 20,763	$ 51,300
21	Administrative	9,090	9,233	12,458	30,780
22	Marketing	6,060	6,155	8,305	20,520
23	Operations and Maintenance	16,968	17,234	23,254	57,456
24	Total Expenses	$ 47,268	$ 48,009	$ 64,779	$160,056
25					
26	Net Income	$ 13,332	$ 13,541	$ 18,271	$ 45,144

Figure 5-27 Dynamic data consolidation

7. Link workbooks using a formula.
   a. Click the **BP&Walker** sheet tab in ***[your initials] PP E5-2***.
   b. Click cell **B5**.
   c. Type = to start the formula.
   d. Press **Ctrl+F6** or click the icon on the Windows taskbar for ***[your initials] PP E5-1***.
   e. Click the **Breezy Point** worksheet tab.
   f. Select cell **B5** and type + for addition.
   g. Click the **Walker** sheet tab (Figure 5-28).
   h. Select cell **D5** for the January amount and press **Enter**.
8. Edit and copy the formula.
   a. Select cell **B5** in the **BP&Walker** sheet.
   b. Click the *Formula* bar and click within the absolute reference **$B$5**.
   c. Press **F4 (FN+F4)** three times to remove the dollar signs in **$B$5** and display **B5**.
   d. In the *Formula* bar, click within the **$D$5** address, press **F4 (FN+F4)** three

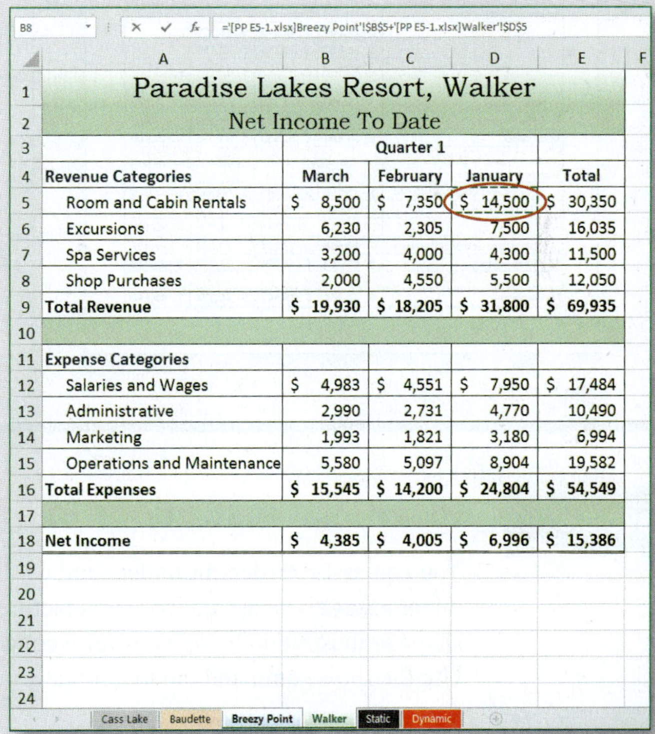

	A	B	C	D	E
1	Paradise Lakes Resort, Walker				
2	Net Income To Date				
3		Quarter 1			
4	Revenue Categories	March	February	January	Total
5	Room and Cabin Rentals	$ 8,500	$ 7,350	$ 14,500	$ 30,350
6	Excursions	6,230	2,305	7,500	16,035
7	Spa Services	3,200	4,000	4,300	11,500
8	Shop Purchases	2,000	4,550	5,500	12,050
9	Total Revenue	$ 19,930	$ 18,205	$ 31,800	$ 69,935
10					
11	Expense Categories				
12	Salaries and Wages	$ 4,983	$ 4,551	$ 7,950	$ 17,484
13	Administrative	2,990	2,731	4,770	10,490
14	Marketing	1,993	1,821	3,180	6,994
15	Operations and Maintenance	5,580	5,097	8,904	19,582
16	Total Expenses	$ 15,545	$ 14,200	$ 24,804	$ 54,549
17					
18	Net Income	$ 4,385	$ 4,005	$ 6,996	$ 15,386

Figure 5-28 Point to build an external reference formula

times to remove the dollar signs, and press **Enter** (Figure 5-29).

e. Copy the formula in cell **B5** to cells **B6:B8**.

9. Create, edit, and copy linking formulas.

a. Select cell **C5** in the **BP&Walker** sheet and type = to start the formula.

b. Press **Ctrl+F6** or click the icon on the Windows taskbar for ***[your initials] PP E5-1***.

c. Click the **Breezy Point** worksheet tab, select cell **C5** and type + for addition.

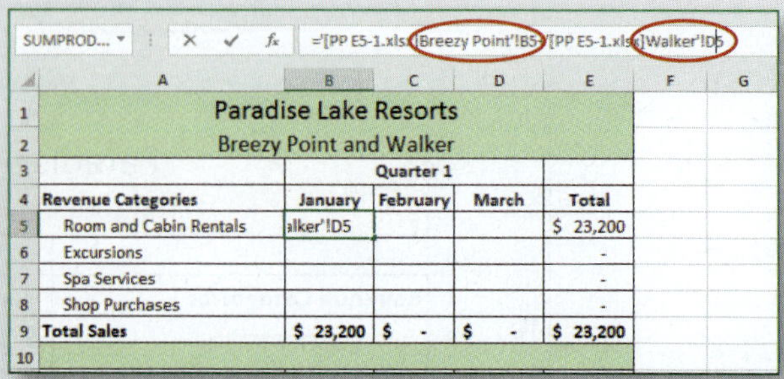

Figure 5-29 Linking formula edited to use relative references

d. Click the **Walker** sheet tab, select cell **C5**, and press **Enter**.

e. Select cell **C5** and click the *Formula* bar.

f. Delete the dollar signs in both occurrences of **$C$5** to display **C5**, and press **Enter**.

g. Select cell **D5** and type = to start the formula.

h. Press **Ctrl+F6** or click the icon on the Windows taskbar for ***[your initials] PP E5-1***.

i. Click the **Breezy Point** worksheet tab, select cell **D5**, and type + for addition.

j. Click the **Walker** sheet tab, select cell **B5** for March, and press **Enter**.

k. Select cell **D5**, click the *Formula* bar, delete the dollar signs in **$D$5** and **$B$5** to create relative references, and press **Enter**.

l. Select cells **C5:D5** and copy the formulas to cells **C6:D8**.

m. Select and format cells **B6:D8** as **Comma Style** with no decimals.

10. Save and close the workbook (Figure 5-30).

11. Close ***[your initials] PP E5-1*** without saving it.

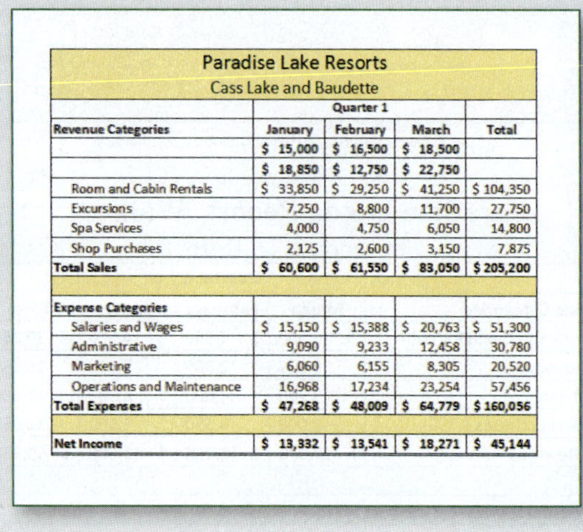

Paradise Lake Resorts Cass Lake and Baudette				
	Quarter 1			
Revenue Categories	January	February	March	Total
	$ 15,000	$ 16,500	$ 18,500	
	$ 18,850	$ 12,750	$ 22,750	
Room and Cabin Rentals	$ 33,850	$ 29,250	$ 41,250	$ 104,350
Excursions	7,250	8,800	11,700	27,750
Spa Services	4,000	4,750	6,050	14,800
Shop Purchases	2,125	2,600	3,150	7,875
Total Sales	$ 60,600	$ 61,550	$ 83,050	$ 205,200
Expense Categories				
Salaries and Wages	$ 15,150	$ 15,388	$ 20,763	$ 51,300
Administrative	9,090	9,233	12,458	30,780
Marketing	6,060	6,155	8,305	20,520
Operations and Maintenance	16,968	17,234	23,254	57,456
Total Expenses	$ 47,268	$ 48,009	$ 64,779	$ 160,056
Net Income	$ 13,332	$ 13,541	$ 18,271	$ 45,144

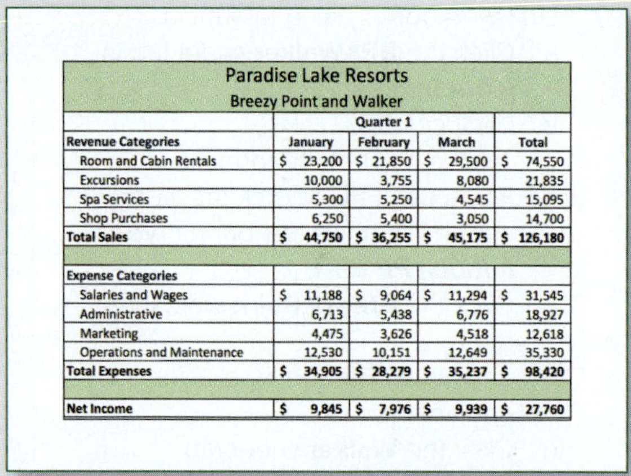

Paradise Lake Resorts Breezy Point and Walker				
	Quarter 1			
Revenue Categories	January	February	March	Total
Room and Cabin Rentals	$ 23,200	$ 21,850	$ 29,500	$ 74,550
Excursions	10,000	3,755	8,080	21,835
Spa Services	5,300	5,250	4,545	15,095
Shop Purchases	6,250	5,400	3,050	14,700
Total Sales	$ 44,750	$ 36,255	$ 45,175	$ 126,180
Expense Categories				
Salaries and Wages	$ 11,188	$ 9,064	$ 11,294	$ 31,545
Administrative	6,713	5,438	6,776	18,927
Marketing	4,475	3,626	4,518	12,618
Operations and Maintenance	12,530	10,151	12,649	35,330
Total Expenses	$ 34,905	$ 28,279	$ 35,237	$ 98,420
Net Income	$ 9,845	$ 7,976	$ 9,939	$ 27,760

Figure 5-30 Completed PP E5-2 worksheets

SLO 5.6

Inserting Illustrations in a Worksheet

You can assist readers in understanding and navigating through your work in many ways. You might insert an image, an icon, or a picture to create interest on the worksheet. You can create a shape or illustration to help convey a concept or add a link to direct users to another worksheet. Use the *Draw* command tab to annotate a worksheet using the pointer or your touch screen.

SmartArt Graphics

A ***SmartArt*** graphic is a text-focused illustration and is not linked to worksheet data. Examples of *SmartArt* are organization charts, matrices, pyramids, bulleted lists, and similar diagrams.

SmartArt graphics may include pictures from a file or from online sources as well as icons. Figure 5-31 is a *SmartArt* graphic with text, pictures, and icons.

A *SmartArt* graphic has a pane for entering text, or you can type directly inside a component shape. The text pane appears on the left or right side of the graphic depending where the graphic is positioned. As you type an entry, the text and its shape are sized to fit the content.

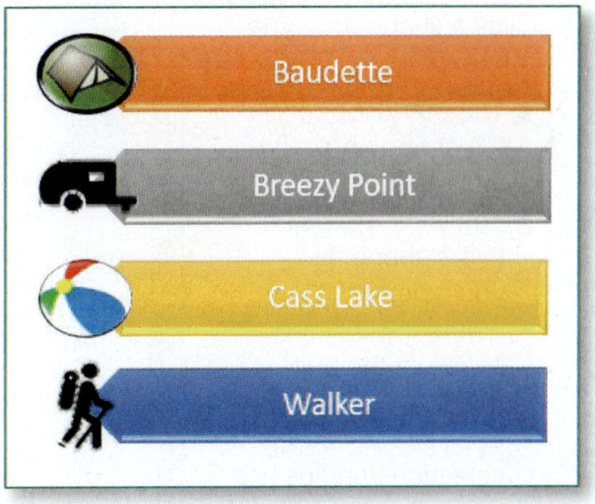

Figure 5-31 ***SmartArt*** **graphic with text, pictures, and icons**

▸HOW TO: Insert a SmartArt Graphic

1. Click the worksheet tab for the *SmartArt*.
2. Click the **Insert a SmartArt Graphic** button [*Insert* tab, *Illustrations* group].
   - The *Choose a SmartArt Graphic* dialog box opens (Figure 5-32).
3. Choose a category from the list on the left.
   - The *All* category displays all available designs.
   - Click a thumbnail image to see a preview and a description on the right.

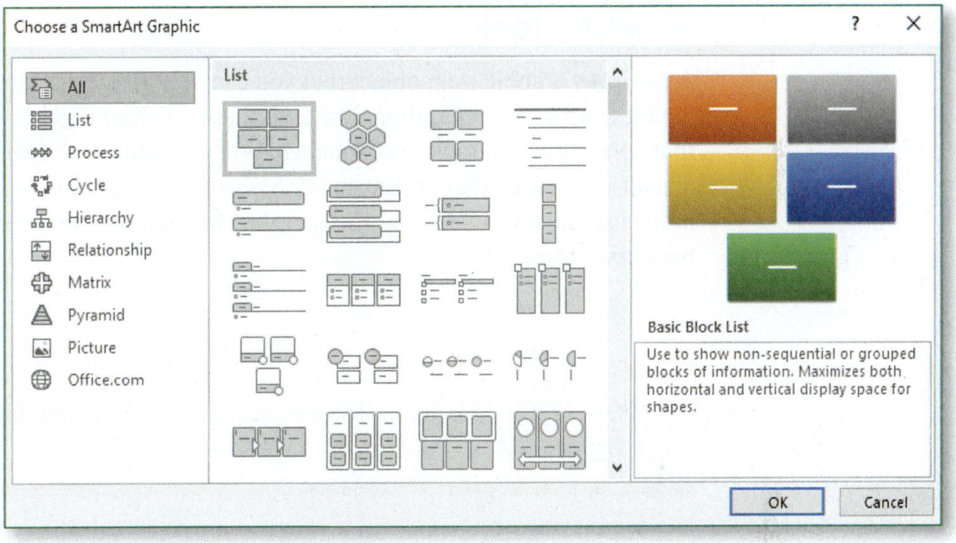

Figure 5-32 ***Choose a SmartArt Graphic*** **dialog box**

4. Select the *SmartArt* graphic and click **OK** (Figure 5-33).
   - A default object is placed at a default size in the worksheet.
   - The *Name* box displays *Diagram N*, where "N" is a number.
   - Display or hide the text pane by clicking the control at the left or right edge of the graphic frame or by clicking the **Text Pane** button [*SmartArt Tools Design* tab, *Create Graphic* group].

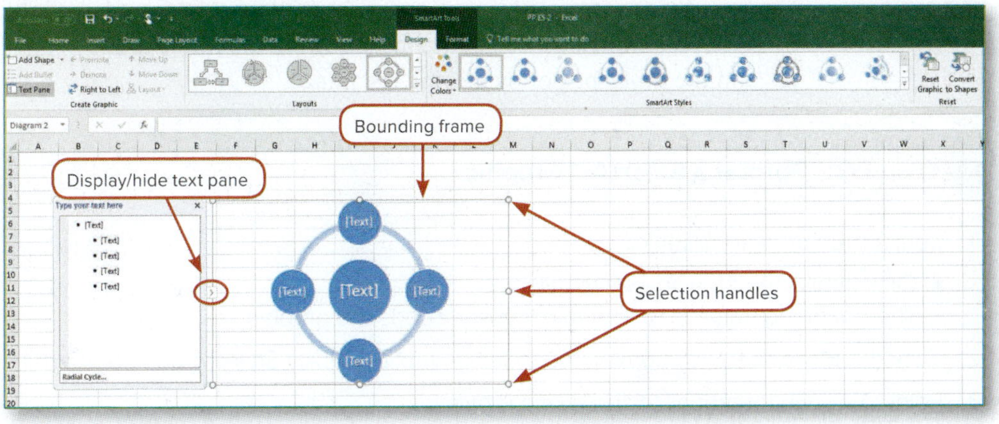

Figure 5-33 ***SmartArt*** **graphic with text frame**

5. Click a shape and type the text (Figure 5-34).
   - The entry appears in the shape and in the text pane.
   - The label is sized to fit the shape as you type.
   - Edit text within the shape or the text pane.
   - Each shape has its own selection handles and frame.
6. Click another shape or click the frame of the *SmartArt* object.

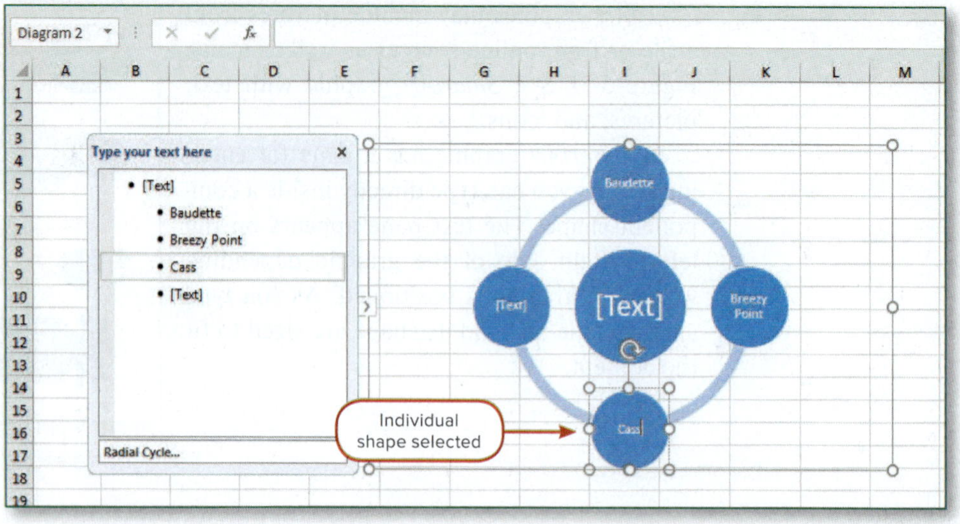

Figure 5-34 Text entered in *SmartArt* graphic

SmartArt Tools

A *SmartArt* graphic is an object that you can select, size, and format. It has selection and sizing handles as well as a bounding frame, similar to a chart object. A *SmartArt* graphic is one object that consists of several smaller shapes. When you insert a *SmartArt* image, it is placed with the default number of shapes. For many *SmartArt* diagrams, you can add or remove shapes. Each individual shape in a *SmartArt* object has its own selection handles, a rotation handle, and a bounding frame.

MORE INFO

A few *SmartArt* shapes are limited in the number of smaller shapes they contain due to the layout and purpose of the diagram.

When a *SmartArt* object is selected, the *SmartArt Tools Design* and *Format* contextual tabs are available. From these tabs, change the image, choose a style, add a shape, reposition shapes, and add fill, outline, and effects.

A *SmartArt* graphic rests on an invisible, transparent layer in the worksheet, covering cells. Select a worksheet cell that appears within the frame of the *SmartArt* by typing the cell address in the *Name* box or by moving the image.

HOW TO: Format a SmartArt Graphic

1. Select the *SmartArt* graphic.
   - Click near one of the shapes to select the diagram.
   - The bounding frame is a rectangle that surrounds the graphic.
2. Click the **More** button [*SmartArt Tools Design* tab, *SmartArt Styles* group] to open the gallery.
3. Point to a style thumbnail to see a *Live Preview*.
4. Click a style icon to apply it.

5. Click the **Change Colors** button [*SmartArt Tools Design* tab, *SmartArt Styles* group].
6. Point to a color thumbnail to see a *Live Preview.*
7. Click a color scheme to apply it.
8. Click an individual shape in the graphic.
9. Click the arrow with the **Shape Fill** button [*SmartArt Tools Format* tab, *Shape Styles* group].
10. Choose a color from the gallery (Figure 5-35).
11. Point to a corner sizing handle on the *SmartArt* frame.
    - The pointer displays a resize arrow.
12. Drag the resize arrow to increase or decrease the size of the graphic.
13. Point to the *SmartArt* frame.
    - The pointer displays a move arrow.
14. Drag the graphic to the desired location.
15. Click a worksheet cell to deselect the *SmartArt* graphic.

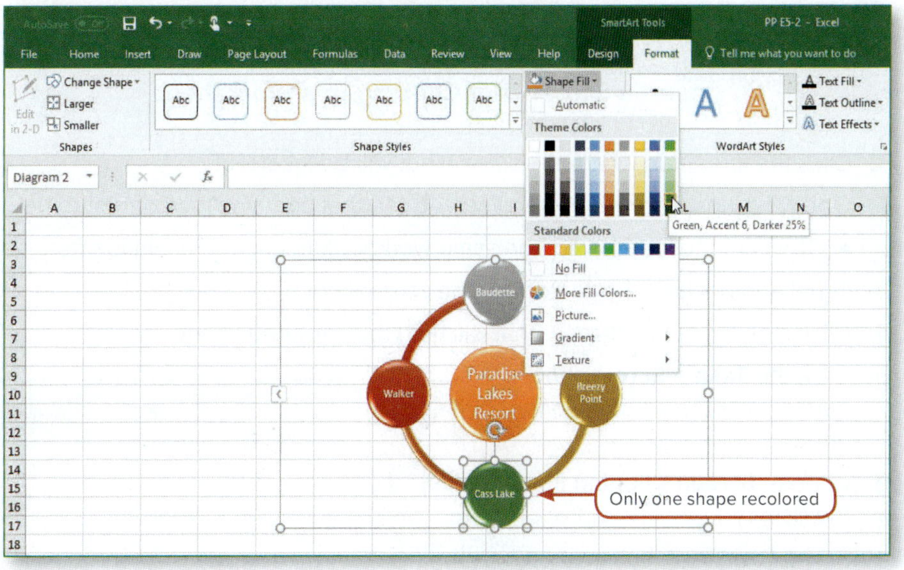

Figure 5-35 ***Shape Fill*** **color gallery for a *SmartArt* shape**

Screenshots

A ***screenshot*** is a picture of a full or partial computer screen inserted as an object in a worksheet. When capturing screenshots of online data or another person's work, you should have permission from the author or owner to use the image.

The *Take a Screenshot* button is located on the *Insert* tab in the *Illustrations* group. When you click the button, you see a gallery of open application windows (Figure 5-36). If you select a window thumbnail, a capture of the full screen is placed in your worksheet. To select part of a window, choose **Screen Clipping** from the gallery.

Once you place a screenshot in the worksheet, it is a picture object that you can format, position, and size.

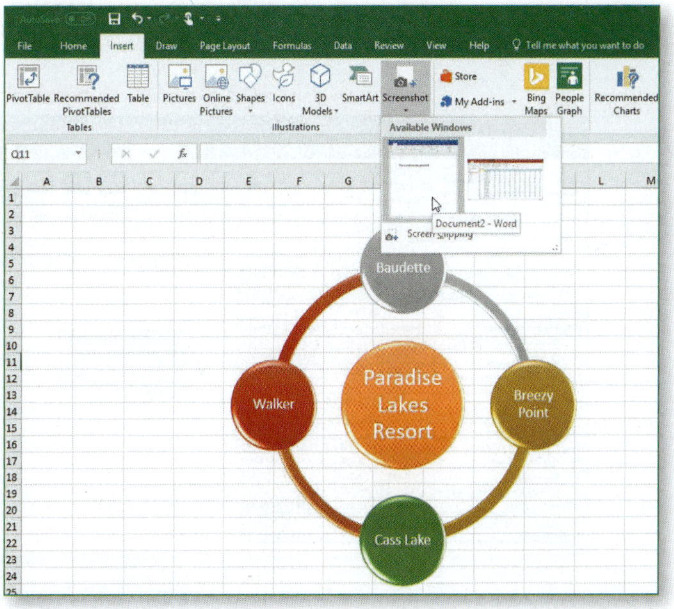

Figure 5-36 ***Screenshot*** **gallery with two available windows**

> **MORE INFO**
>
> When you take a screen clipping, open only two windows to streamline the task. One window holds the screenshot and the other provides the image.

HOW TO: Insert a Screenshot Clipping in a Worksheet

1. Click the sheet tab where the screenshot will be inserted.
2. Open the workbook, document, or web site that contains the content to be captured.
   - Open another window for the same workbook to capture an image from another worksheet.
3. Scroll and position the content for the screenshot.
4. Click a cell in the worksheet that will hold the captured image.
5. Click the **Take a Screenshot** button [*Insert* tab, *Illustrations* group].
6. Choose **Screen Clipping** from the gallery.
   - The focus switches to the next open window.
   - The entire screen dims in a few seconds.
7. Draw a rectangle around the content to be captured with the pointer (Figure 5-37).
   - The selected area is no longer dim.
8. Release the pointer button (Figure 5-38).
   - The focus returns to the worksheet.
   - The screenshot displays at a default size and position.
   - The *Picture Tools Format* tab displays.

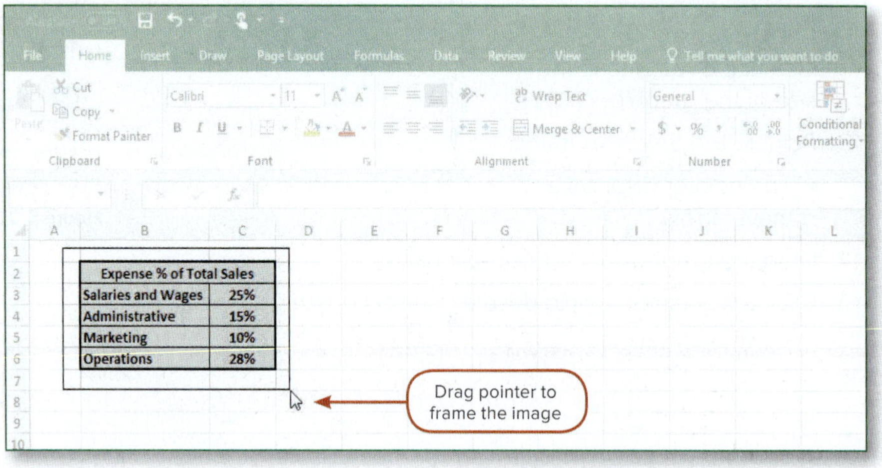

Figure 5-37 Dimmed screen for screenshot

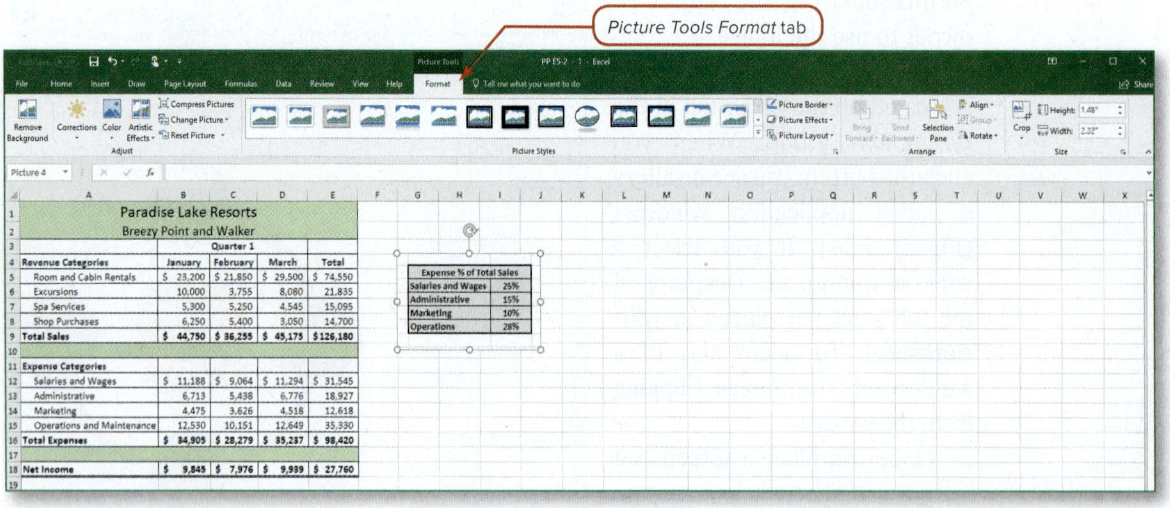

Figure 5-38 Screenshot image placed in worksheet and *Picture Tools Format* tab

Picture Tools

A screenshot is a picture object with selection and sizing handles, a rotation handle, and a bounding frame. When the object is selected, the *Picture Tools Format* tab displays with command groups for altering the appearance of the image.

Like a *SmartArt* graphic, a screenshot image is placed on the invisible, transparent layer of the worksheet.

▸HOW TO: Work with Picture Tools

1. Select the screenshot or picture object.
   - The bounding frame is rectangular.
   - Selection and sizing handles appear on the bounding frame.
2. Click the **More** button [*Picture Tools Format* tab, *Picture Styles* group].
   - The gallery includes preset combinations of border, fill, and rotation settings.
3. Point to a thumbnail to see a *Live Preview.*
4. Click an icon to apply the style (Figure 5-39).

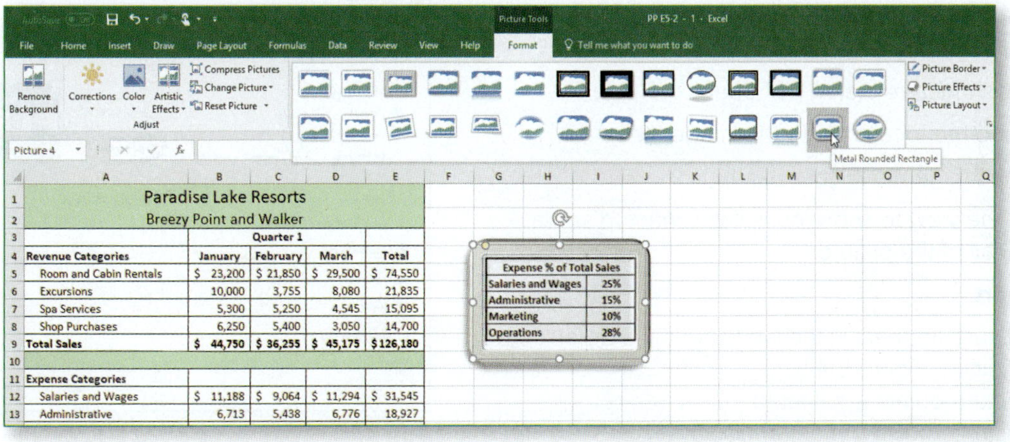

Figure 5-39 Style applied to a screenshot

5. Click the **Artistic Effects** button [*Picture Tools Format* tab, *Adjust* group].
6. Point to a thumbnail to see a *Live Preview.*
   - Many effects may not be appropriate for worksheet images.
7. Click an icon to apply an effect.
8. Click the **Rotate** button [*Picture Tools Format* tab, *Arrange* group].
9. Point to a menu choice to see a *Live Preview.*
10. Click a rotation option to apply the setting.
11. Point to a corner sizing handle on the picture border to display a resize arrow.
    - Use a corner handle to size proportionally.
12. Drag the resize arrow to increase or decrease the picture size.
13. Point to the picture border.
    - The pointer displays a move arrow.
14. Drag the picture to the desired location.
15. Click a worksheet cell to deselect the picture object.

Pictures, Shapes, Icons, and 3D Models

From the *Illustrations* group on the *Insert* command tab, you can insert pictures, line art shapes, icons, and even 3D models. Use illustrations in an Excel worksheet for clarification, emphasis, or visual appeal, and always investigate copyright issues when you use work from outside sources.

The *Pictures* and *Online Pictures* commands insert images from your network, your computer, or cloud sources. The *Shapes* button offers several categories of simple line art illustrations such as arrows, callouts, and banners. From the *Icons* command, insert recognizable symbols from popular categories. Insert three-dimensional drawings and images from the *3D Models* button. Each illustration type has a contextual tab for modifying the object, too.

> **MORE INFO**
>
> Do not use too many illustrations in a worksheet so that you do not draw attention away from the data.

HOW TO: Insert a Picture from a File

1. Click a blank cell in the worksheet.
2. Click the **Pictures From File** button [*Insert* tab, *Illustrations* group].
   - The *Insert Picture* dialog box opens.
3. Navigate to the location with the image file.
4. Select the image file (Figure 5-40).
   - Adjust the view to show icons if you want to see a thumbnail of the picture.
5. Click **Insert**.
   - The picture appears in the worksheet at a default size and position (Figure 5-41).
   - The picture object is selected.
   - The *Picture Tools Format* tab displays.
6. Point to a corner selection handle to display a resize arrow and drag the pointer to shrink or enlarge the image.
7. Point to the image frame to display a move pointer and drag the picture to the desired location in the sheet.

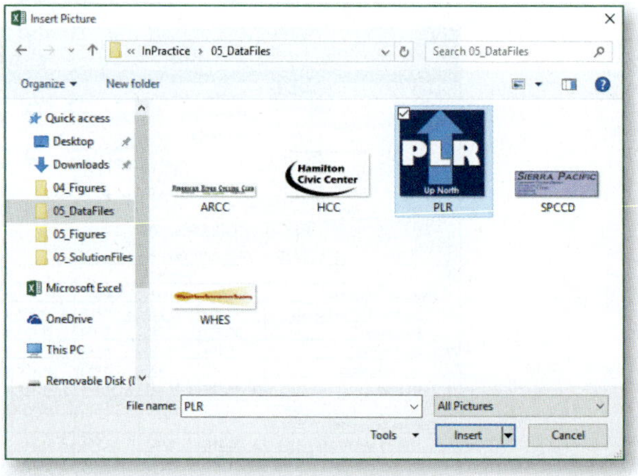

Figure 5-40 Select a picture from a file

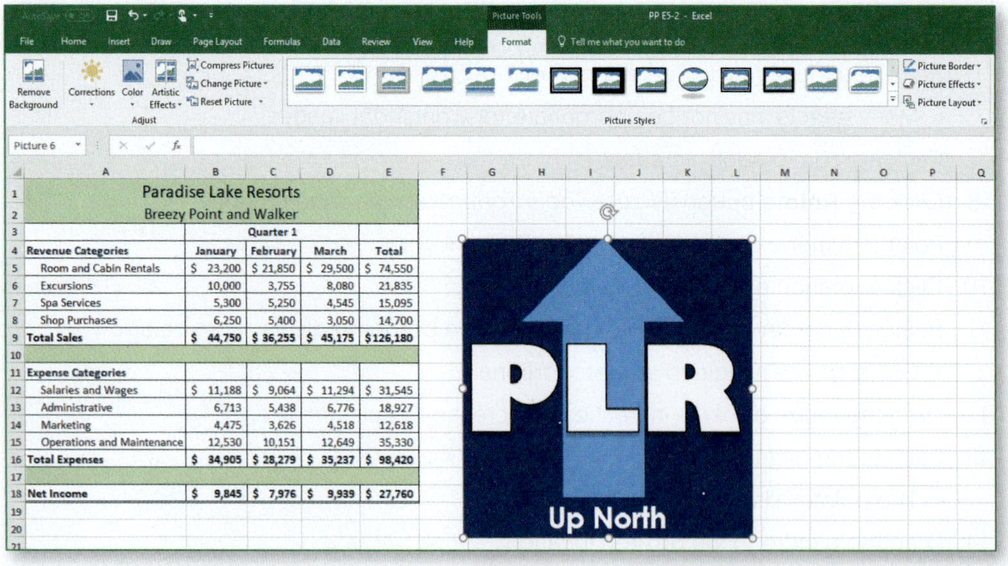

Figure 5-41 Picture placed at default size and position

SLO 5.7

Inserting Hyperlinks in a Worksheet

A ***hyperlink*** is a text string or object that moves the pointer to another location after it is clicked. You might use a hyperlink to open a source workbook, to switch to another worksheet, or to navigate to a *SmartArt* image.

Cell Hyperlinks

A cell hyperlink is a text shortcut or jump term in a cell. It appears as underlined text in the color set in the document theme for hyperlinks. After a hyperlink is created, change the font color, font name, and font size from the mini toolbar or from the *Font* group on the *Home* tab.

> **ANOTHER WAY**
>
> The keyboard shortcut to insert a hyperlink is **Ctrl+K**.

The *Link* button is located on the *Insert* command tab, or insert a hyperlink from the shortcut menu for a cell.

> **MORE INFO**
>
> Choose the hyperlink text color by clicking the **Colors** button on the *Page Layout* tab and selecting **Customize Colors**.

HOW TO: Create a Cell Hyperlink

1. Click the cell where the hyperlink text should appear.
2. Click the **Link** button [*Insert* tab, *Links* group].
   - The *Insert Hyperlink* dialog box opens.
3. Select **Place in This Document** in the *Link to* list on the left.
   - The *Or select a place in this document* box displays locations in the workbook.
   - The names of existing sheets are listed in the *Cell Reference* group.
   - The *Defined Names* group displays range names in the workbook.
   - The *Cell Reference* and *Defined Names* groups have expand and collapse buttons.
4. Select a worksheet name to jump to that sheet.
   - Choose the name of the current sheet if the hyperlink will move to a location on this sheet.
5. Click the **Type the cell reference** box.
6. Type the cell address that should be selected when the hyperlink is clicked.
   - The default is cell **A1**.
7. Click the **Text to display** box and enter text for the hyperlink cell.
   - Select and delete default text.
8. Click the **ScreenTip** button (Figure 5-42).
   - The *Set Hyperlink ScreenTip* dialog box opens.

9. Type an optional *ScreenTip*.
   - The default *ScreenTip* identifies the file and provides basic instructions for a hyperlink.
10. Click **OK** to close the *Set Hyperlink ScreenTip* dialog box.
11. Click **OK** to close the *Insert Hyperlink* dialog box (Figure 5-43).
    - The underlined hyperlink text appears in the cell.
    - When you point to the link, the *ScreenTip* displays.
12. Click the hyperlink to navigate to the location.

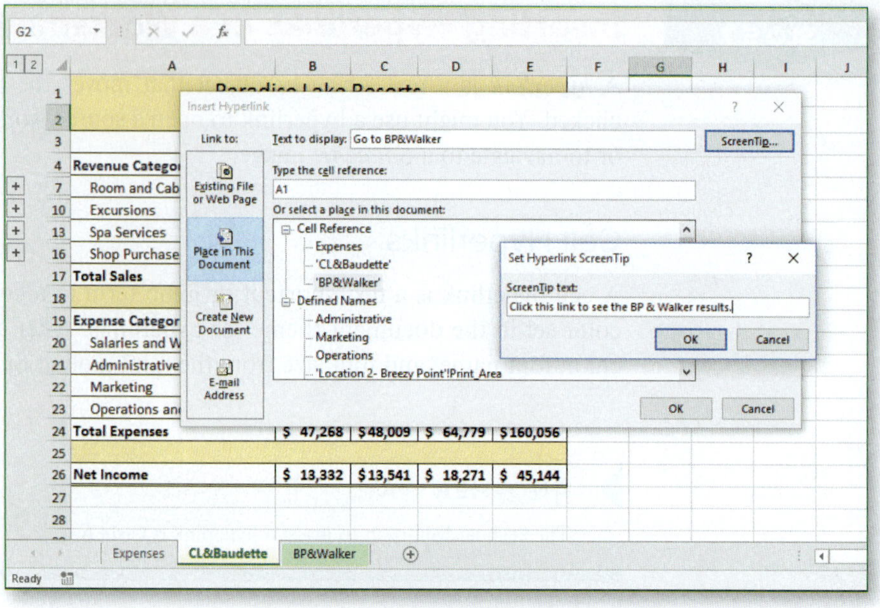

Figure 5-42 ***Hyperlink*** **and custom** ***ScreenTip*** **dialog boxes**

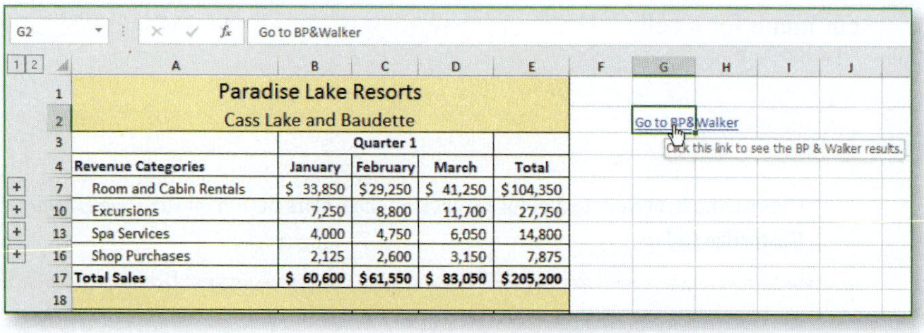

Figure 5-43 ***Hyperlink*** **text and its** ***ScreenTip***

When you choose *Existing File or Web Page* in the *Insert Hyperlink* dialog box, you browse to the location for the file or the web page. The path to the file or the URL for the web address appears in the *Address* box.

Object Hyperlinks

An object hyperlink is a shortcut assigned to an object such as a *SmartArt* graphic, a chart, or an icon. An object hyperlink does not include underlined text, but you can use the hyperlink *ScreenTip* to provide information.

HOW TO: Create a Hyperlink to Open a File

1. Select the image or object.
   - The selection handles should be visible.
2. Click the **Link** button [*Insert* tab, *Links* group].
   - The *Insert Hyperlink* dialog box opens.

3. Select **Existing File or Web Page** in the *Link to* list on the left.
   - The *Look in* box displays the name of the current folder.
   - The names of workbooks in the current folder are listed.
   - You can navigate to other folders in this dialog box.
4. Select a workbook name.
   - The file name is entered in the *Address* box (Figure 5-44).
5. Click the **ScreenTip** button.
6. Type text for a *ScreenTip* to describe the action.
7. Click **OK** to close the *Set Hyperlink ScreenTip* dialog box.
8. Click **OK** to close the *Insert Hyperlink* dialog box (Figure 5-45).
9. Click a worksheet cell to deselect the object.
10. Point to the object to see the *ScreenTip*.
11. Click the object to open the file.
    - The file opens with the active sheet and cell based on its last save command.

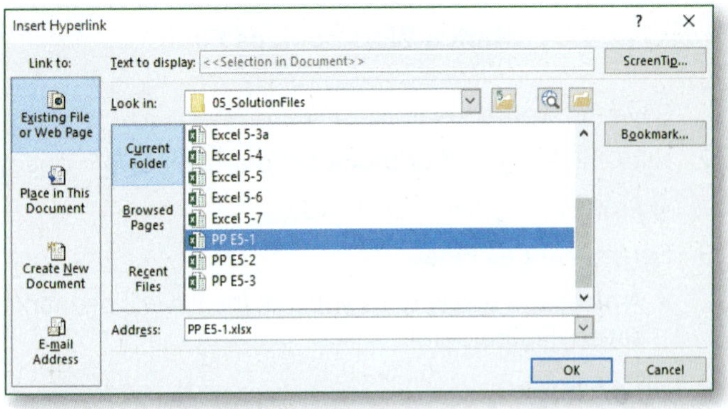

Figure 5-44 Workbook name selected for hyperlink

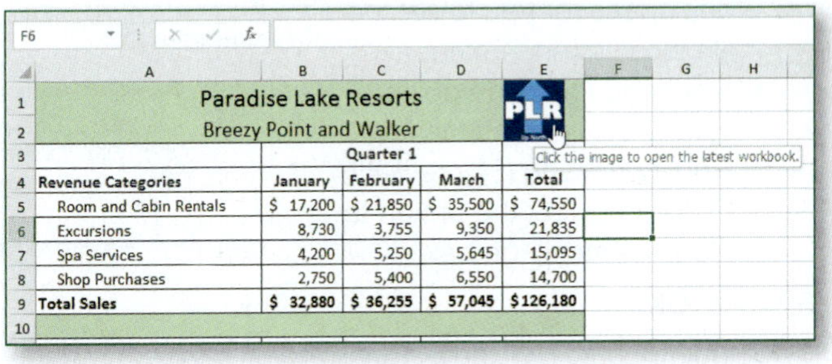

Figure 5-45 Object hyperlink in worksheet

To remove a hyperlink from a cell or from an object, right-click the cell or the object and choose **Remove Hyperlink**. You can also edit a hyperlink from the shortcut menu to change the *ScreenTip*, reset the file, or change a URL address.

SLO 5.8

Safeguarding a Workbook

Excel has two commands that provide a simple level of security to protect your work from unwanted changes. One command is a courtesy message or warning and one command is the assignment of a password.

Mark a Workbook as Final

To let others know that your work is complete and should not be edited, use the ***Mark as Final*** command to set a read-only file property. When the workbook opens, you will see a security message bar, an icon in the *Status* bar, and a *[Read-Only]* label in the title bar. You and others can remove the property by clicking the *Edit Anyway* button in the security message bar.

ANOTHER WAY

Remove the *Mark as Final* property by clicking the **Protect Workbook** button [*File* tab, *Info* option] and choosing **Mark as Final**.

▸HOW TO: Mark a Workbook as Final

1. Save the workbook.
2. Click the **Protect Workbook** button [*File* tab, *Info* option].
   - Protection commands display.
3. Select **Mark as Final**.
   - A message box informs you that the file will be marked and saved (Figure 5-46).
4. Click **OK**.
   - The workbook is resaved with the same file name.
   - If the workbook has not yet been saved, the *Save As* dialog box opens for you to set the file location and name.
   - A second message box provides details about the *Mark as Final* command (Figure 5-47). (You can select the option to hide this message box.)
5. Click **OK**.
   - The security bar shows the property (Figure 5-48).
   - The icon on the *Status* bar indicates that the workbook is final.

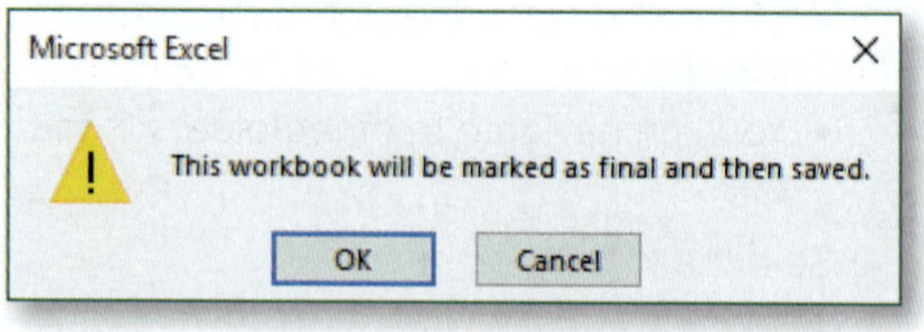

Figure 5-46 Message box that workbook will be saved and marked as final

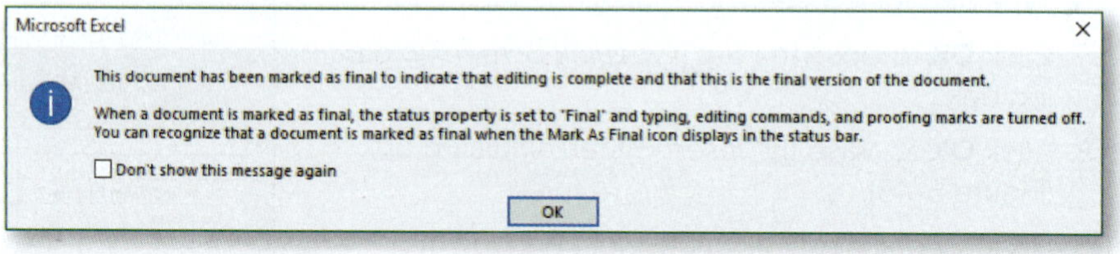

Figure 5-47 Details about the *Mark as Final* property

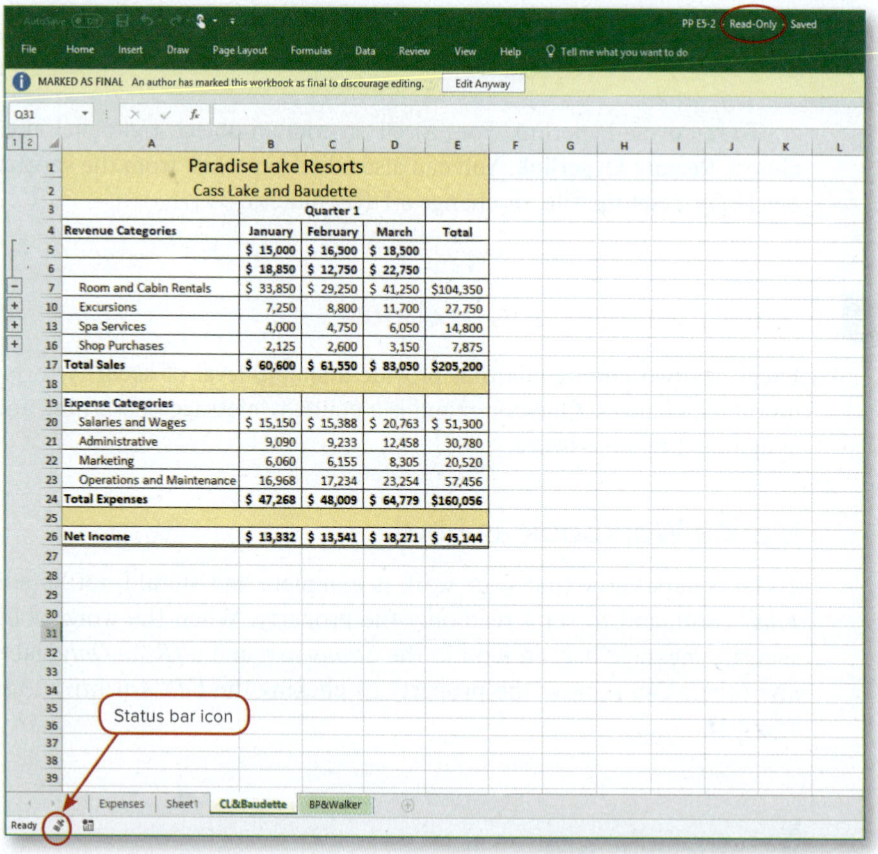

Figure 5-48 Workbook that is marked as final

Encrypt a Workbook with a Password

Password protection requires that you type the password as you open the workbook. After you set a password, the *Protect Workbook* button [*File* tab, *Info* pane] indicates that the workbook requires a password as shown in Figure 5-49.

To remove a password, you must open the workbook and enter the password. Then click the **Protect Workbook** button, select **Encrypt with Password**, delete the password, leave the *Password* box empty, and resave the workbook.

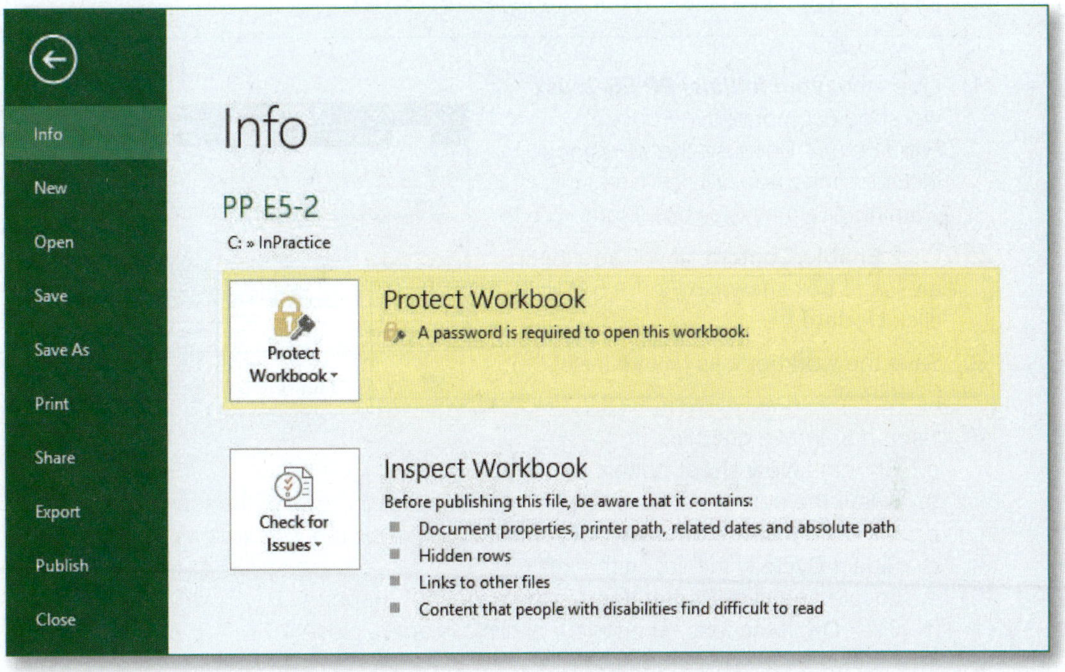

Figure 5-49 *Info* pane for a workbook with a password

HOW TO: Password Protect a Workbook

1. Click the **Protect Workbook** button [*File* tab, *Info* pane].
2. Select **Encrypt with Password**.
   - The *Encrypt Document* dialog box opens.
3. Type a password in the *Password* box (Figure 5-50).
   - Passwords are hidden as you type them.
   - Passwords are case sensitive.
4. Click **OK**.
   - The *Confirm Password* dialog box requires that you retype the same password.
5. Retype the password and click **OK**.
6. Click **Close** in the command list and then click **Save**.

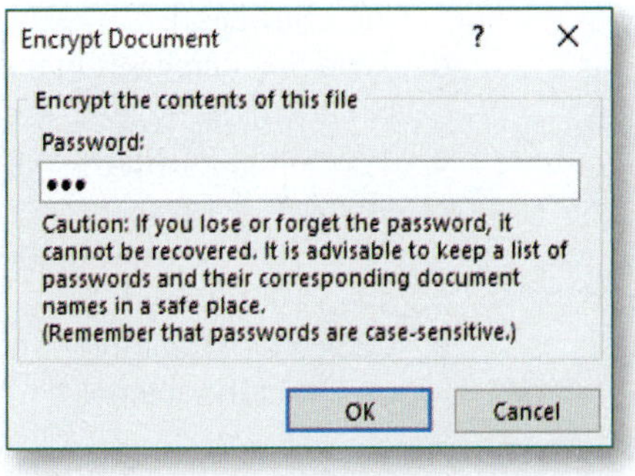

Figure 5-50 Passwords are case sensitive and are hidden as you type them.

PAUSE & PRACTICE: EXCEL 5-3

For this project, you insert a *SmartArt* graphic to illustrate how revenue results are consolidated for Paradise Lakes Resort. You insert a hyperlink to the *SmartArt*, add the company logo to a sheet, and mark your work as final.

Files Needed: ***[your initials] PP E5-2.xlsx*** and ***PLR.png*** *(Student data files are available in the* Library *of your SIMnet account.)*
Completed Project File Name: ***[your initials] PP E5-3.xlsx***

1. Open the ***[your initials] PP E5-2.xlsx*** workbook completed in *Pause & Practice 5-2*. Because the workbook includes links, you will see a security warning or a message box (Figure 5-51).

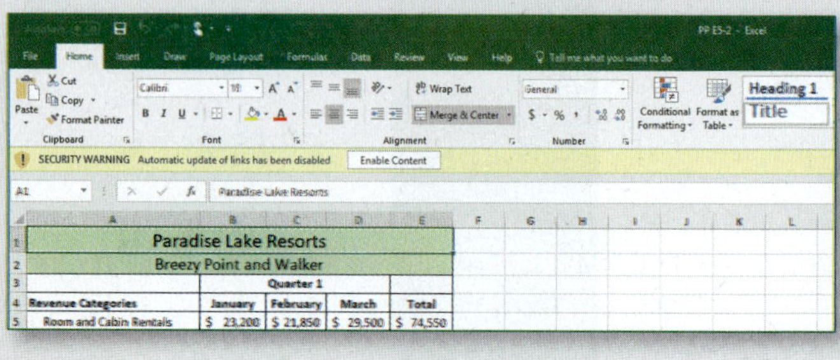

Figure 5-51 Security messages for workbook with links

2. Click **Enable Content**. (If you see the message box shown in Figure 5-24, click **Update**.)
3. Save the workbook as [your initials] PP E5-3.
4. Insert a *SmartArt* graphic.
   a. Click the **New sheet** button.
   b. Name the new sheet SmartArt and position it at the end of the tab names.
   c. Click the **Insert a SmartArt Graphic** button [*Insert* tab, *Illustrations* group].
   d. Select **Cycle** in the list on the left.
   e. Locate and click **Radial Venn** in the gallery of graphics.
   f. Click **OK**. If the text pane for the graphic is open, close it.
5. Add text to a *SmartArt* graphic.
   a. Select the top circle shape.
   b. Type Room and Cabin Rentals. Do not press **Enter**; if you did, press **Backspace**.
   c. Select the leftmost circle shape and type Excursions. If you make an error, click again in the shape and make the correction.
   d. Type Spa Purchases in the bottom circle shape.
   e. Type Shop Purchases in the rightmost shape.
   f. Type Total Revenue in the center shape (Figure 5-52).
   g. Click a cell near the center circle to deselect the shape.

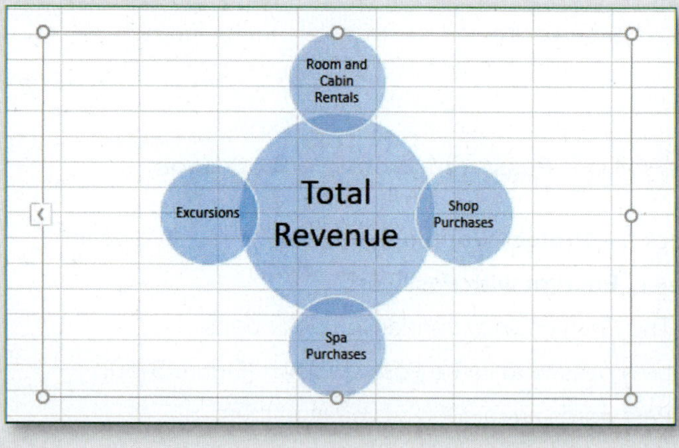

Figure 5-52 Text entered in shapes in *SmartArt* graphic

6. Format, position, and size a *SmartArt* graphic.
   a. Click the frame of the *SmartArt* graphic to select it.
   b. Click the **More** button [*SmartArt Tools Design* tab, *SmartArt Styles* group].
   c. Choose **Inset** in the *3-D* group.
   d. Click the **Change Colors** button [*SmartArt Tools Design* tab, *SmartArt Styles* group].

e. Choose **Colorful – Accent Colors**, the first icon in the group.
f. Point to the *SmartArt* frame to display a move pointer.
g. Drag the graphic to position the top left selection handle in cell **A1**. When a *SmartArt* graphic is selected, you can also use a keyboard directional arrow key to nudge the object into position.
h. Point to the bottom right selection handle to display a resize arrow.
i. Drag the frame to reach cell **I22** (Figure 5-53).
j. Click cell **K1** to deselect the *SmartArt*.

7. Insert a hyperlink.
   a. Click the **BP&Walker** sheet tab.
   b. Select cell **G2**.
   c. Click the **Link** button [*Insert* tab, *Links* group].
   d. Select **Place in This Document**.
   e. Select the sheet name **SmartArt** in the *Or select a place in this document* list.
   f. Select the default text in the *Text to display* box and type View Illustration without a period..
   g. Click the **ScreenTip** button and type Click this link to view the graphic. including the period. (Figure 5-54).
   h. Click **OK** in the *Set Hyperlink ScreenTip* dialog box.
   i. Click **OK** in the *Insert Hyperlink* dialog box.
   j. Click cell **G3**.
   k. Click the link to test it.

8. Insert a picture.
   a. Click the **CL&Baudette** sheet tab and collapse any outline group that is expanded.
   b. Click the **Pictures From File** button [*Insert* tab, *Illustrations* group].
   c. Navigate to the folder with your student data files.
   d. Choose **PLR** and click **Insert**.
   e. Click the **Height** box [*Picture Tools Format* tab, *Size* group].
   f. Replace the default height with .55 and press **Enter**.
   g. Click the **Color** button [*Picture Tools Format* tab, *Adjust* group].

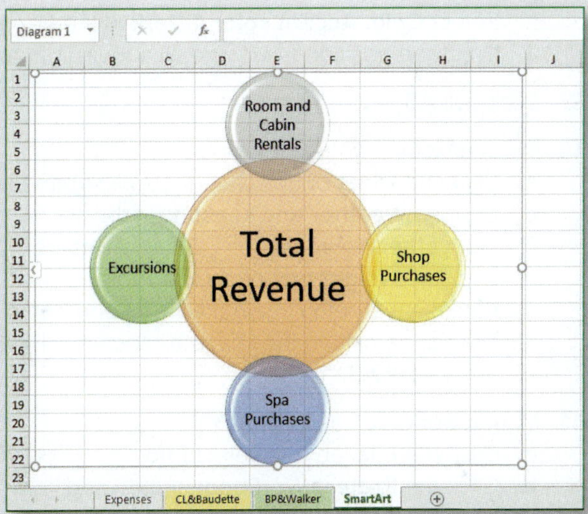

Figure 5-53 Styled and positioned *SmartArt*

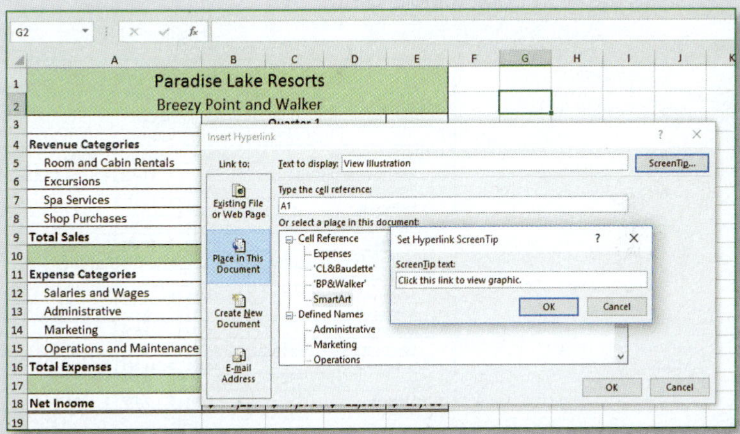

Figure 5-54 Hyperlink text and *ScreenTip*

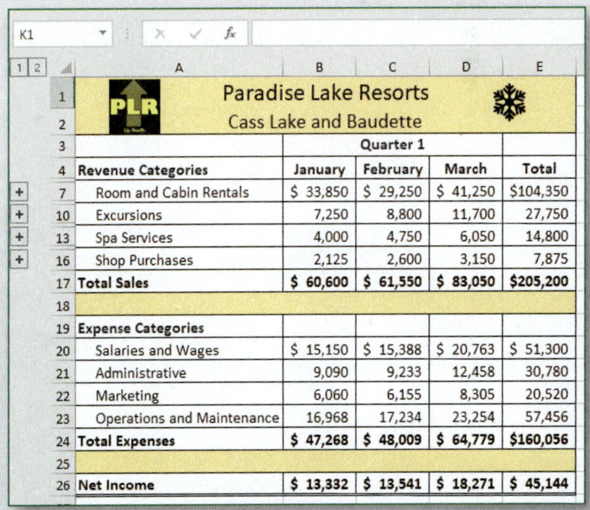

Figure 5-55 Image and icon inserted in worksheet

   h. Select **Gold, Accent color 4 Dark** in the *Recolor* group (second row).
   i. Drag and position the image as shown in Figure 5-55.

9. Click cell **A3**.

10. Insert an icon.
   a. Click the **Icons** button [*Insert* tab, *Illustrations* group].
   b. Choose **Weather and seasons** in the list.
   c. Select the **snowflake** icon and click **Insert**.
   d. Click the **Height** box [*Graphics Tools Format* tab, *Size* group].
   e. Replace the default height with .55 and press **Enter**.
   f. Drag and position the image as shown in Figure 5-55.
   g. Select cell **A3**.

11. Mark a workbook as final.
   a. Click the **File** tab and select **Info**.
   b. Click the **Protect Workbook** button and select **Mark as Final**.
   c. Click **OK** to resave the file.
   d. Click **OK** to close the message box.

12. Close the workbook (Figure 5-56).

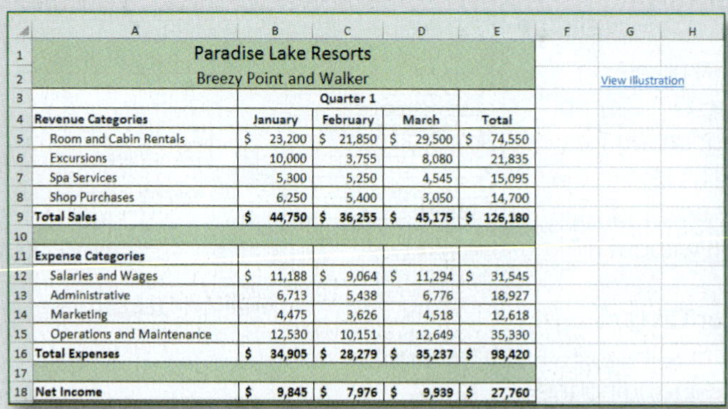

	A	B	C	D	E	F	G	H
1	Paradise Lake Resorts							
2	Breezy Point and Walker						View Illustration	
3		Quarter 1						
4	**Revenue Categories**	**January**	**February**	**March**	**Total**			
5	Room and Cabin Rentals	$ 23,200	$ 21,850	$ 29,500	$ 74,550			
6	Excursions	10,000	3,755	8,080	21,835			
7	Spa Services	5,300	5,250	4,545	15,095			
8	Shop Purchases	6,250	5,400	3,050	14,700			
9	**Total Sales**	**$ 44,750**	**$ 36,255**	**$ 45,175**	**$ 126,180**			
10								
11	**Expense Categories**							
12	Salaries and Wages	$ 11,188	$ 9,064	$ 11,294	$ 31,545			
13	Administrative	6,713	5,438	6,776	18,927			
14	Marketing	4,475	3,626	4,518	12,618			
15	Operations and Maintenance	12,530	10,151	12,649	35,330			
16	**Total Expenses**	**$ 34,905**	**$ 28,279**	**$ 35,237**	**$ 98,420**			
17								
18	**Net Income**	**$ 9,845**	**$ 7,976**	**$ 9,939**	**$ 27,760**			

Figure 5-56 Completed worksheet for PP E5-3

Chapter Summary

5.1 Create a static data consolidation (p. E5-299).

- A ***consolidated worksheet*** combines data from multiple worksheets using a mathematical or statistical function.
- When labels and values are in the same position on all worksheets, the consolidation is by position.
- A ***static data consolidation*** places a non-changing result in the consolidation sheet. If the source data is edited, the consolidated sheet is not updated.
- The **Consolidate** button is located on the *Data* tab in the *Data Tools* group.

5.2 Create a dynamic data consolidation (p. E5-301).

- A ***dynamic data consolidation*** places formulas in the consolidation worksheet. If the source data is edited, the consolidated sheet is automatically updated.
- A dynamic data consolidation formats the results as an Excel outline.
- To build a dynamic data consolidation, choose the *Create links to source data* option in the *Consolidate* dialog box.

5.3 Consolidate data by category (p. E5-303).

- When labels and values are not in the same position on all worksheets, you may be able to consolidate data by category.
- A category is a row or column label.
- A consolidate by category command includes the label cells on the source worksheets.
- The consolidated sheet displays labels in the same order as the first sheet listed in the *Consolidate* dialog box.
- Consolidation by category can be static or dynamic.

5.4 Group worksheets for editing and formatting (p. E5-304).

- When worksheets are grouped, editing and format commands affect all sheets in the group.
- Apply formats, enter formulas, or enter data in grouped sheets.
- Not all commands are available in grouped sheets.
- When a command is not available, it is grayed out on the *Ribbon*.
- Press **Shift** or **Ctrl** to group contiguous or non-contiguous sheets.
- Ungroup sheets when finished editing to guard against applying a command in error to the group.

5.5 Link workbooks to consolidate data (p. E5-308).

- ***Linking*** workbooks is the process of referring to data in another workbook.
- A ***dependent workbook*** refers to data in another workbook.
- A ***source workbook*** supplies data to another workbook.
- An ***external reference*** formula is in a dependent workbook and refers to cells in a source workbook.
- An external reference includes the name of the workbook, the sheet name, cell addresses, and ***identifiers***.
- Link workbooks by using the *Consolidate* command on the *Data* tab when all source workbooks are open.
- Link workbooks by building a formula that refers to another workbook.
- If the source workbook is open, point to build an external reference formula.
- If the source workbook is not open, build an external reference formula by typing the complete path and file name, the sheet name, cell addresses, and all identifiers.
- The *Excel Trust Center* includes security options for workbooks with links.

5.6 Insert illustrations in a worksheet (p. E5-314).

- A ***SmartArt*** graphic is an illustration such as a matrix, a cycle diagram, an organization chart, or a process chart.
- *SmartArt* graphics are not linked to worksheet data; they contain descriptive text.
- When a *SmartArt* graphic is selected, the *SmartArt Tools Design* and *Format* tabs are available.
- A *SmartArt* graphic consists of several smaller shapes, each of which can be formatted separately.
- A ***screenshot*** is an image of data on the screen inserted as a picture object in a worksheet.

- Pictures are inserted in a worksheet from a file or from online sources.
- When a picture object is selected, the *Picture Tools Format* tab displays with commands for changing the appearance of the image.
- The *Icons* button displays thumbnails of common symbols for use in a worksheet.
- Insert 3D models in a worksheet from the *Illustrations* group on the *Insert* tab.
- Each illustration object, when selected, opens a related contextual tools tab.

5.7 Insert hyperlinks in a worksheet (p. E5-321).

- A hyperlink acts as a jump term or a shortcut to another location in the workbook, on the computer, or in the cloud.
- A ***hyperlink*** is a line of text in a cell or an object in a worksheet.
- A cell hyperlink is underlined text in the color specified by the document theme.
- An object hyperlink is a shortcut assigned to an image, a *SmartArt* graphic, or another object.
- The *Link* button is located in the *Links* group on the *Insert* tab.

5.8 Safeguard work by marking it as final or by setting a password (p. E5-323).

- Assign a simple level of security to a workbook by marking it as final.
- The *Mark as Final* command is a reminder that the work is complete and should not be edited.
- Remove the *Mark as Final* setting by clicking **Enable Editing** in the security message bar.
- The *Encrypt with Password* command enables you to assign a password to a workbook.
- You must type the password before the workbook can be opened.
- The *Mark as Final* and *Encrypt with Password* commands are available from the *Protect Workbook* button [*File* tab, *Info* pane].

Check for Understanding

The SIMbook for this text (within your SIMnet account) provides the following resources for concept review:

- Multiple-choice questions
- Short answer questions
- Matching exercises

Guided Project 5-1

Blue Lake Sports maintains sales data for specialty departments. For this project, you reformat worksheets as a group, insert the *SUM* function, build static and dynamic data consolidation sheets, insert a *SmartArt* graphic, and create a hyperlink.
[Student Learning Outcomes 5.1, 5.4, 5.5, 5.6, 5.7, 5.8]

Files Needed: ***BlueLakeSports-05.xlsx*** and ***BlueLakeSportsLinked-05.xlsx*** *(Student data files are available in the* Library *of your SIMnet account.)*
Completed Project File Names: ***[your initials] Excel 5-1.xlsx*** and ***[your initials] Excel 5-1a.xlsx***

Skills Covered in This Project

- Group and format worksheets.
- Edit grouped worksheets.
- Enter a *SUM* function in grouped worksheets.
- Create a static data consolidation.
- Link workbooks using an external reference.
- Encrypt a workbook with a password.
- Insert and format a *SmartArt* graphic.
- Insert and format a hyperlink.

---

1. Open the ***BlueLakeSports-05*** workbook from your student data files and save it as [your initials] Excel 5-1.
2. Group and format worksheets.
   a. Right-click the **First Qtr** tab and choose **Select All Sheets**.
   b. Select cell **A2** and change the font to **Calibri**.
   c. Select cells **A4:E8** and apply **All Borders**.
   d. Select cells **A8:E8** and apply a **Top and Double Bottom Border**.
   e. Click the **Launcher** in the *Page Setup* group on the *Page Layout* tab.
   f. Select the **Horizontally** box on the *Margins* tab to center the data on the page.
   g. Click the **Header/Footer** tab.
   h. Click the **Footer** drop-down arrow and select ***[your initials] Excel 5-1***.
   i. Click **OK**.
3. Enter a formula for grouped sheets.
   a. Click cell **E5** and enter a *SUM* function to add cells **B5:D5**.
   b. Select cell **E5** and copy the formula to cells **E6:E7**.
   c. Select cells **B5:E5** and cells **B8:E8**.
   d. Click the **Accounting Number Format** button [*Home* tab, *Number* group].
   e. Click the **Decrease Decimal** button twice [*Home* tab, *Number* group].
   f. Select cells **B6:E7** and click the **Decrease Decimal** button twice [*Home* tab, *Number* group].
   g. Press **Ctrl+Home** (Figure 5-57).
   h. Right-click the **Static** tab and choose **Ungroup Sheets**.
4. Create a static data consolidation.
   a. Select cell **B5** on the **Static** sheet.
   b. Click the **Consolidate** button [*Data* tab, *Data Tools* group].
   c. Choose the **SUM** function.
   d. Select each reference, if any, in the *All references* box and click **Delete**.

e. Click the **Reference** box and click the **First Qtr** worksheet tab.
f. Select cells **B5:D7**.
g. Click **Add** in the *Consolidate* dialog box.
h. Click the **Second Qtr** tab. Verify that cells B5:D7 are selected.
i. Click **Add** in the *Consolidate* dialog box.
j. Add cells **B5:D7** from the **Third Qtr** and **Fourth Qtr** worksheets to the *All references* list in the *Consolidate* dialog box.
k. Click **OK**. (Figure 5-58).

5. Select cell **A1**.

6. Open the ***BlueLakeSportsLinked-05.xlsx*** workbook from your student data files and save it as [your initials] Excel 5-1a.

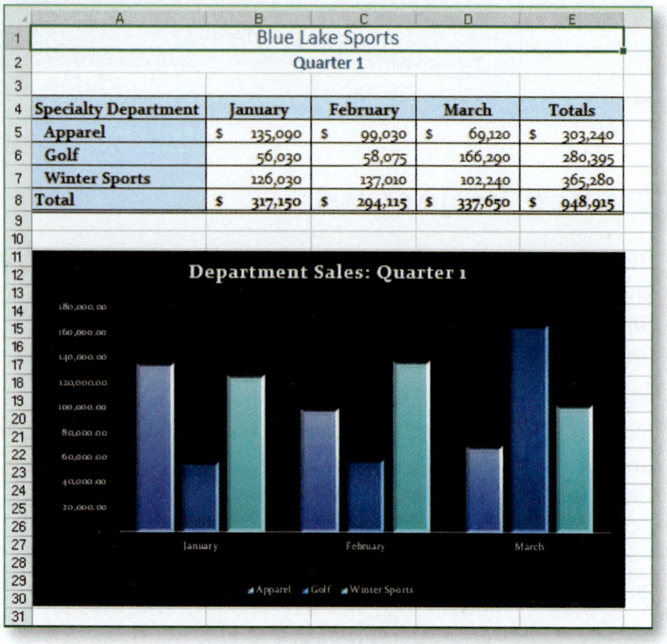

Figure 5-57 Completed *First Qtr* sheet; other sheets are the same

7. Tile the windows.
a. Click the **Arrange All** button [*View* tab, *Window* group].
b. Choose **Vertical** and click **OK**.
c. Verify that the **Static** sheet is active in ***[your initials] Excel 5-1***.

8. Link workbooks with an external reference formula.
a. Click cell **B5** in ***[your initials] Excel 5-1a***.
b. Type = to start the external reference.
c. Double-click cell **E5** in ***[your initials] Excel 5-1***. The first click activates the window, and the second click selects the cell (Figure 5-59).
d. Press **Enter**. The result is formatted to show two decimal places.
e. Select cell **B5** and press **F2 (FN+F2)** to start *Edit* mode.
f. Delete both dollar signs (**$**) to make the reference relative (**E5**) and press **Enter**.
g. Select cell **B5** and click the **Decrease Decimal** button twice [*Home* tab, *Number* group].
h. Copy the formula in cell **B5** to cells **B6:B8**.
i. Select cell **B8** and apply a **Bottom Double Border** if the border was removed by your copy command.

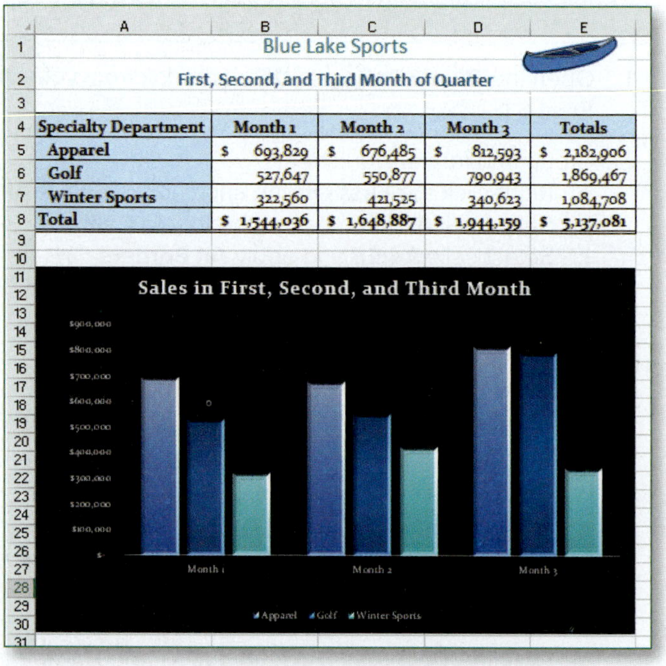

Figure 5-58 Consolidated results

9. Insert a *SmartArt* graphic.
a. Click cell **D2** on the **Dynamic** sheet. Maximize the window.
b. Click the **Insert a SmartArt Graphic** button [*Insert* tab, *Illustrations* group].

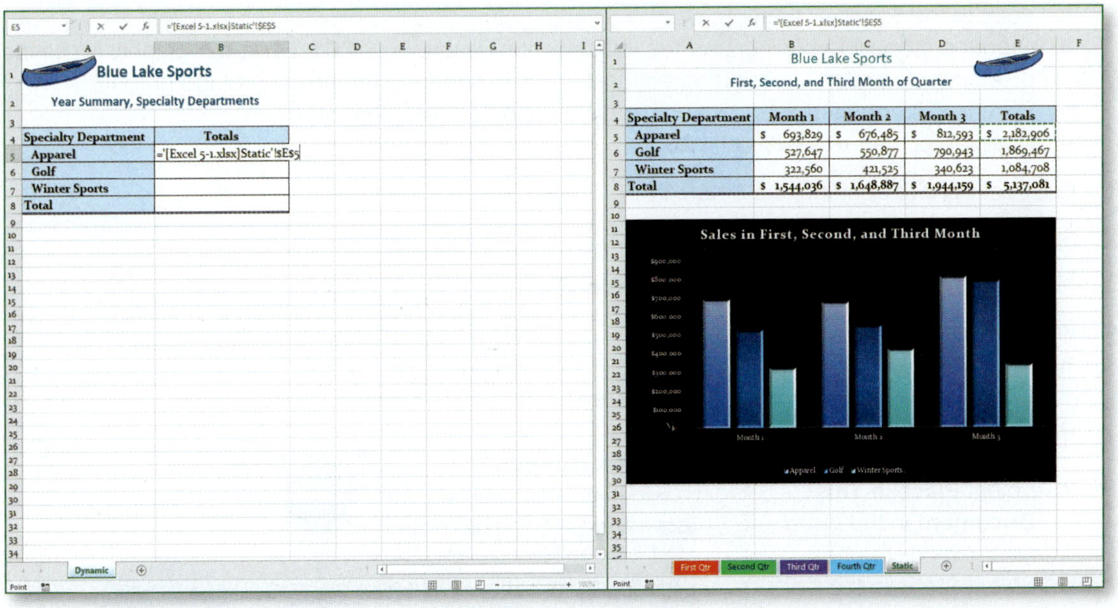

Figure 5-59 External reference formula for *Apparel*

c. Click **Process** in the list at the left.
d. Find and click **Vertical Equation** in the gallery of graphics.
e. Click **OK** to insert the *SmartArt* graphic. Close the text pane if necessary.
f. Click the top left circle shape and type Apparel. Do not press **Enter**; if you did, press **Backspace**.
g. Click the shape below *Apparel* and type Golf.
h. Click the **Add Shape** button [*SmartArt Tools Design* tab, *Create Graphic* group] (Figure 5-60).

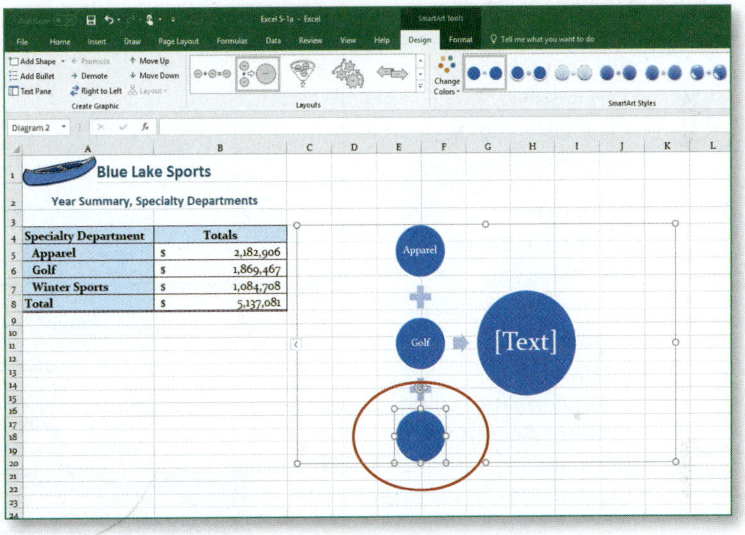

Figure 5-60 Shape added to *SmartArt* graphic

i. Type Winter Sports in the bottom shape.
j. Click the large circle shape on the right and type Specialty Departments.

10. Format, position, and size a *SmartArt* graphic.
    a. Click the frame of the *SmartArt* graphic to select it.
    b. Click the **More** button [*SmartArt Tools Design* tab, *SmartArt Styles* group].
    c. Choose **Polished** in the *3-D* group.
    d. Click the **Change Colors** button [*SmartArt Tools Design* tab, *SmartArt Styles* group].
    e. Choose **Colored Fill – Accent 1** in the *Accent 1* group (second icon).
    f. Click the **Shape Fill** button [*SmartArt Tools Format* tab, *Shapes Styles* group].
    g. Choose **White, Background 1, Darker 15%** (first column)
    h. Click the **Shape Outline** button [*SmartArt Tools Format* tab, *Shapes Styles* group].
    i. Choose **Weight** and select **½ pt**.
    j. Click the **Shape Outline** button again and choose **Blue, Accent 1** (fifth column).

k. Point to the *SmartArt* frame to display a move pointer.
l. Drag the graphic to position the top left selection handle in cell **C1**. While the graphic is selected, press the *Up* or *Left* keyboard directional arrow to fine-tune the position of the graphic.
m. Point to the bottom right selection handle to display a resize pointer.
n. Drag the pointer to reach cell **L20**.

11. Click cell **A10** to deselect the *SmartArt*.
12. Save and close the workbook (Figure 5-61).
13. Maximize the window for ***[your initials] Excel 5-1***.
14. Insert a hyperlink.
    a. Click the **Fourth Qtr** sheet tab and select cell **F9**.
    b. Click the **Link** button [*Insert* tab, *Links* group].
    c. Select **Place in This Document** in the *Insert Hyperlink* dialog box.
    d. Select **Static** in the *Cell Reference* group in the *Or select a place in this document* list.
    e. Select the default text in the *Text to display* box and type See Totals.
    f. Click **OK** in the *Insert Hyperlink* dialog box.
15. Format a hyperlink.
    a. Right-click the cell hyperlink.
    b. Format the font size to **16 pt** from the mini toolbar.
    c. Format the font color to **Blue, Accent 1** (fifth column).
    d. Click cell **G1** (Figure 5-62).
16. Click the hyperlink to test it.
17. Encrypt a workbook with a password.
    a. Click the **Protect Workbook** button [*File* tab, *Info* pane].
    b. Select **Encrypt with Password**.
    c. Type 123 in the *Password* box.
    d. Click **OK**.
    e. Retype 123 to confirm the password and click **OK**.
    f. Click **Close**.
    g. Click **Save**.

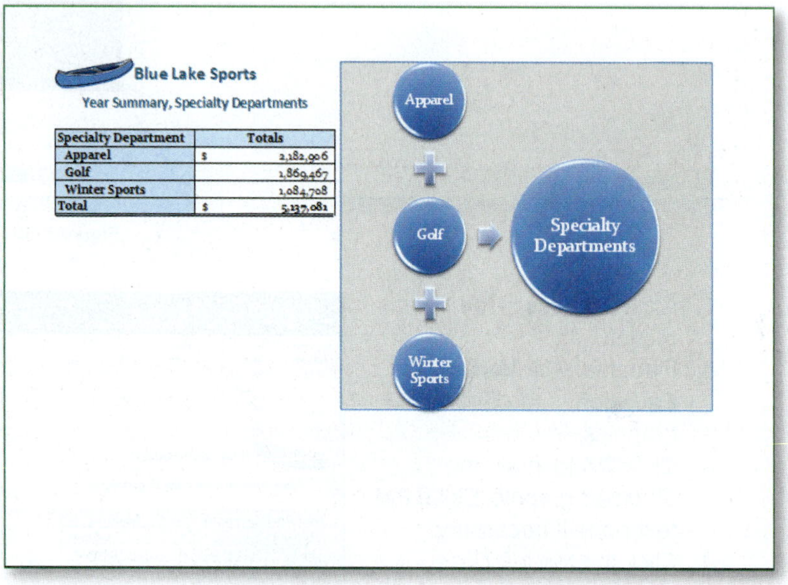

Figure 5-61 Completed *SmartArt* graphic and worksheet

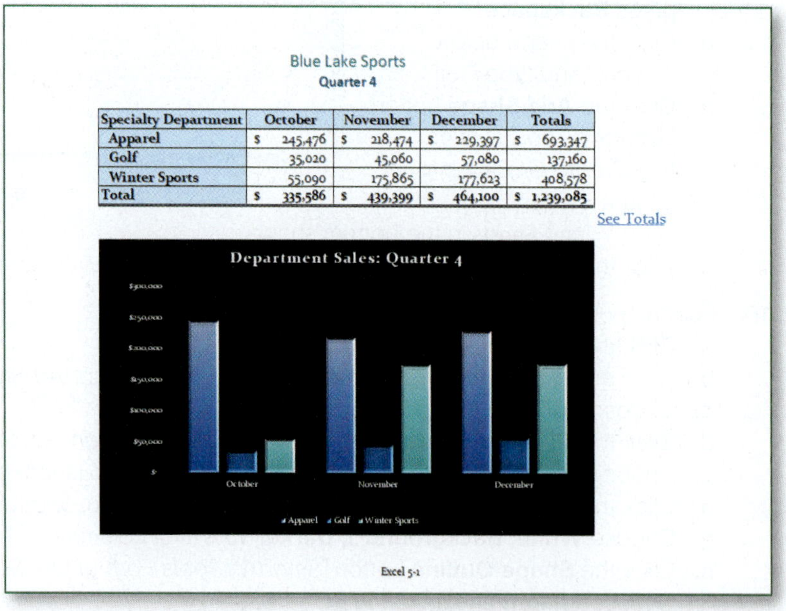

Figure 5-62 Completed worksheet for Excel 5-1

Guided Project 5-2

Eller Software Services collects monthly data for products and services. In this project, you consolidate and link data to create management reports and format grouped sheets.
[Student Learning Outcomes 5.1, 5.2, 5.3, 5.4, 5.5, 5.6, 5.7, 5.8]

Files Needed: ***EllerSoftware-05.xlsx*** and ***EllerSoftwareLinked-05.xlsx*** *(Student data files are available in the* Library *of your SIMnet account.)*
Completed Project File Names: **[*your initials*] *Excel 5-2.xlsx*** and **[*your initials*] *Excel 5-2a.xlsx***

Skills Covered in This Project

- Group and format worksheets.
- Build a static data consolidation by category.
- Build a dynamic data consolidation by category.
- Link workbooks with a formula.
- Insert a screenshot in a worksheet.
- Size and format a screenshot.
- Insert an object hyperlink.
- Mark a workbook as final.

---

1. Open ***EllerSoftware-05.xlsx*** from your student data files and save it as [your initials] Excel 5-2.
2. Group and format worksheets.
   a. Right-click the **2018** sheet tab and choose **Select All Sheets**.
   b. Select cells **B4:F4** and **B9:F9**.
   c. Click the **Accounting Number Format** button [*Home* tab, *Number* group].
   d. Click the **Decrease Decimal** button [*Home* tab, *Number* group] two times.
   e. Select cells **B5:F8** and apply **Comma Style** with no decimals.
   f. Select cells **B9:F9** and click the **AutoSum** button [*Home* tab, *Editing* group].
   g. Select cell **A9** and **right-align** it.
   h. Select cell **A1**.
   i. Right-click the **2018** tab and choose **Ungroup Sheets**.
3. Click the **2020** sheet tab. The product and service labels are in a different order on this sheet.
4. Make a copy of the **2020** sheet at the end of the tabs and name the copy as Static.
5. Create a static data consolidation by category.
   a. Select cells **A4:E8** on the **Static** sheet and press **Delete**.
   b. Click the **Consolidate** button [*Data* tab, *Data Tools* group].
   c. Select and delete references in the *All references* box, if any.
   d. Verify that *SUM* is the selected function.
   e. Click the **Reference** box and select the **2018** sheet tab.
   f. Select cells **A4:E8** on the **2018** sheet.
   g. Click **Add** in the *Consolidate* dialog box.
   h. Click the **2019** tab name and add the same range to the *All references* list.
   i. Repeat for the **2020** sheet.
   j. Select the **Left column** box in the *Use labels in* group (Figure 5-63).
   k. Click **OK**. The labels are consolidated in the same order as the labels on the first sheet used in the consolidation (2018).
   l. Press **Ctrl+Home**.
6. Make a copy of the **2020** sheet at the end and name the copy as Dynamic.
7. Create a dynamic data consolidation by category.
   a. Select cells **A4:E8** on the **Dynamic** sheet and press **Delete**.
   b. Click the **Consolidate** button [*Data* tab, *Data Tools* group].

c. Click the **Function** arrow and choose **Average**.
d. Click the **Reference** box and select the same cells as those used in step 5 (cells **A4:E8** on the **2018**, **2019**, and **2020** sheets).
e. Select the **Left column** box.
f. Select the **Create links to source data** box and click **OK** (Figure 5-64).

8. Edit the label in cell **A2** to insert the word Average before “Billings.”
9. Right-click the column **G** heading and delete the column. Right click the row **24** heading and delete the row.
10. Set the width of column **A** to **28.57 (205 pixels)** and expand row **7** in the outline. A new column B identifies the source data file (Figure 5-65).
11. Hide column **B** and collapse row **7**. Press **Ctrl+Home**.
12. Open ***EllerSoftware Linked-05.xlsx*** from your student data files and save it as [your initials] Excel 5-2a.
13. Click the **Arrange All** button [*View* tab, *Window* group]. Choose **Vertical** and click **OK**. It does not matter which workbook is in the left pane.

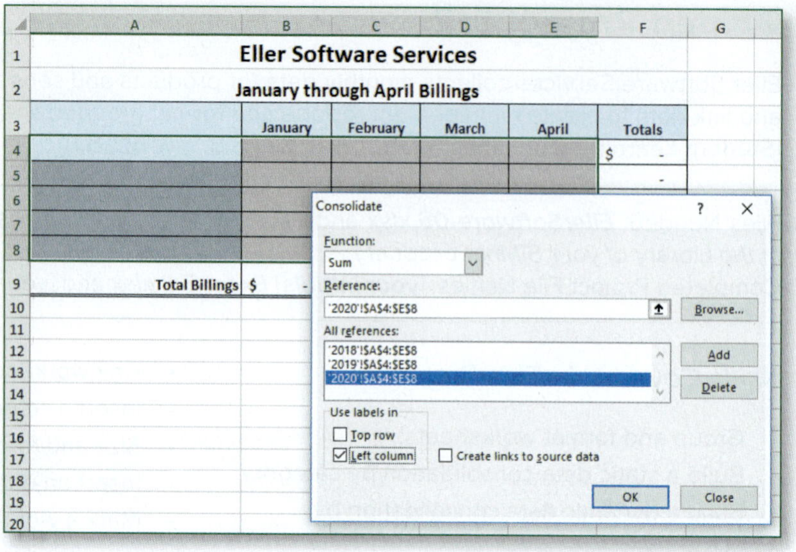

Figure 5-63 Consolidating by category

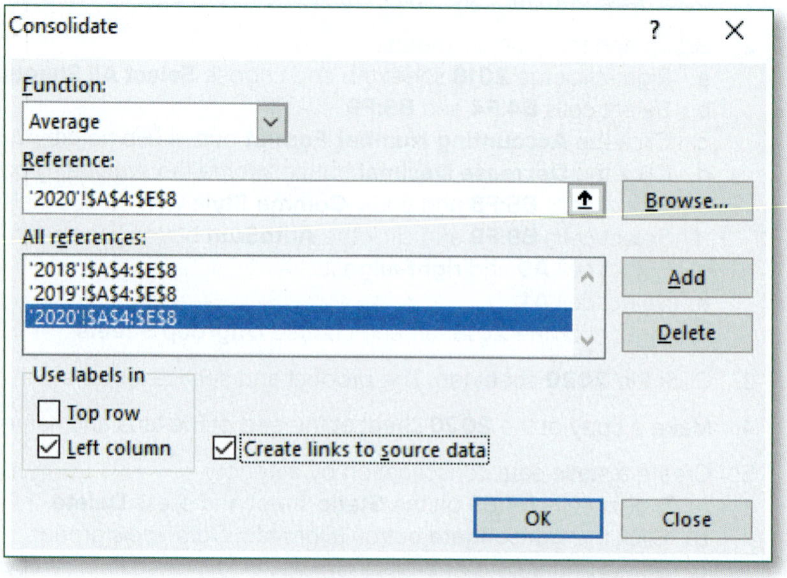

Figure 5-64 Dynamic data consolidation by category

14. Link workbooks with a formula.
    a. Select cell **B5** in the ***[your initials] Excel 5-2a*** workbook and type =.
    b. Double-click the **Static** sheet tab in ***[your initials] Excel 5-2*** to activate it and select cell **E4** (Figure 5-66).
    c. Press **Enter**. The reference is placed with an absolute reference.

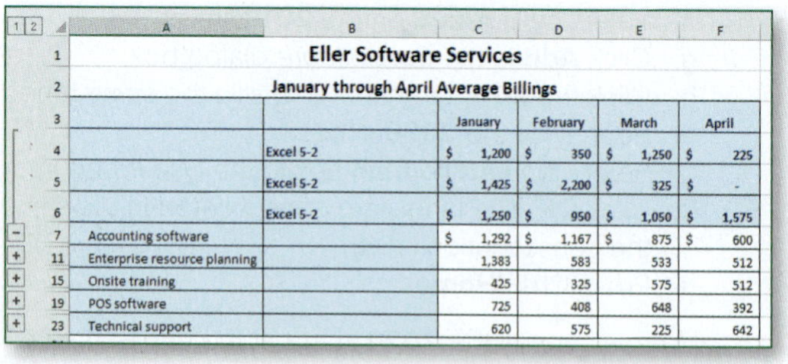

Figure 5-65 Completed *Dynamic* sheet with column B shown

15. Copy and edit a linked formula.
    a. Select cell **B5** in ***[your initials] Excel 5-2a***.
    b. Click the *Formula* bar and delete both dollar signs. Click after **E4**, type *125% to multiply by 125%, and press **Enter** (Figure 5-67).

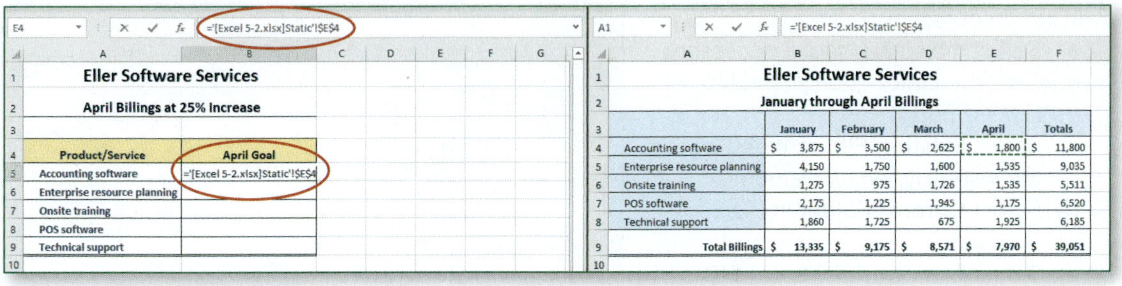

Figure 5-66 External reference with absolute reference

c. Copy the formula in cell **B5** to cells **B6:B9** without formatting to preserve the borders.
d. Format cells **B5:B9** as **Currency** with zero decimal places.
e. Maximize the ***[your initials] Excel 5-2a*** window.

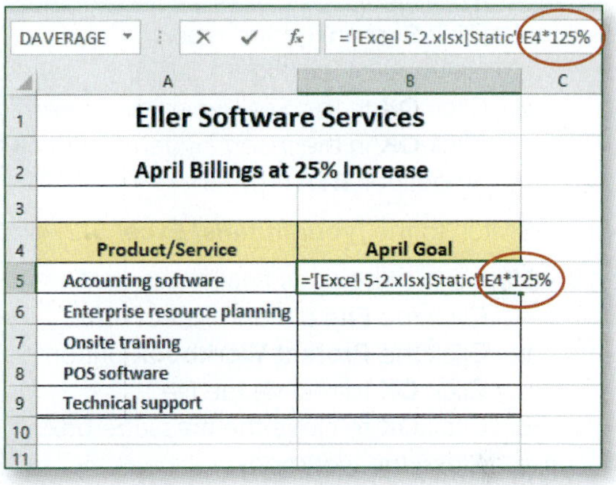

Figure 5-67 Edit the formula

16. Insert and format a screenshot in a workbook.
 a. Switch to the ***[your initials] Excel 5-2*** workbook and maximize the window.
 b. Select the **Static** sheet tab.
 c. Deselect the **Gridlines** box [*View* tab, *Show* group].
 d. Switch to ***[your initials] Excel 5-2a*** and select cell **A11**. (It is easier to take screenshots when only the two windows of interest are open, so if you have other programs running, close them and return to ***[your initials] Excel 5-2a***.)
 e. Click the **Take a Screenshot** button [*Insert* tab, *Illustrations* group].
 f. Choose **Screen Clipping** from the gallery. The focus switches to ***[your initials] Excel 5-2*** and the screen dims after a few seconds.
 g. Draw a rectangle with the crosshair pointer to frame the data in cells **A1:F9** without row or column headings and release the pointer.
 h. Click the **More** button [*Picture Tools Format* tab, *Picture Styles* group].
 i. Find and select **Center Shadow Rectangle** (Figure 5-68).

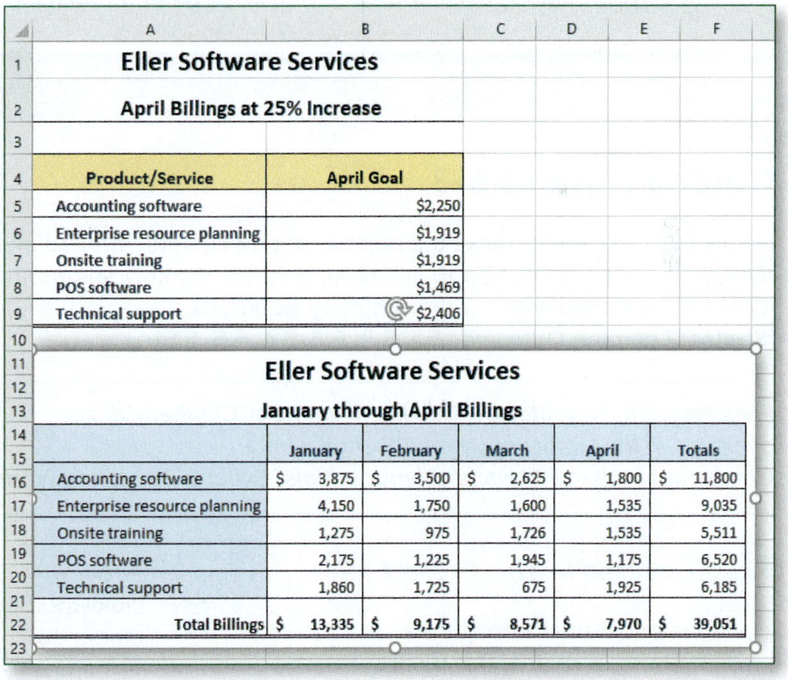

Figure 5-68 Screenshot placed in worksheet

17. Insert an object hyperlink.
    a. Select the screenshot if necessary.
    b. Click the **Link** button [*Insert* tab, *Links* group].
    c. Select **Existing File or Web Page** in the *Insert Hyperlink* dialog box.
    d. Select **Current Folder** in the *Look in* group.
    e. Select ***[your initials] Excel 5-2*** in the file name list. If your file is not listed, navigate to the correct folder to locate it.
    f. Click **ScreenTip** and type Click to open source file (Figure 5-69).
    g. Click **OK** in the *Set Hyperlink ScreenTip* dialog box.
    h. Click **OK** in the *Insert Hyperlink* dialog box.
    i. Select cell **A1**.

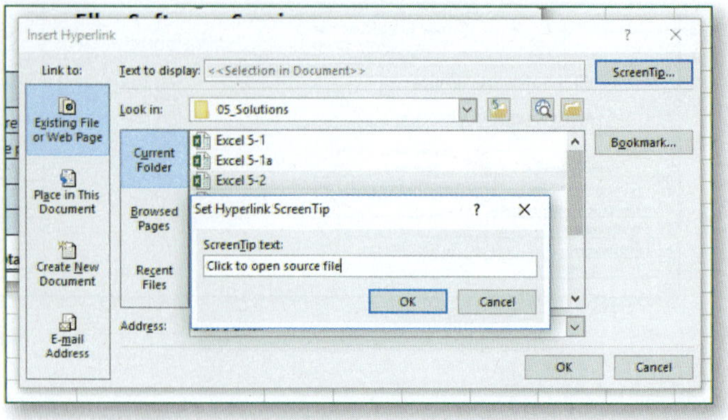

Figure 5-69 Hyperlink to open another workbook

18. Switch to the ***[your initials] Excel 5-2*** window.
19. Mark a workbook as final.
    a. Click the **File** tab and select **Info**.
    b. Click the **Protect Workbook** button and select **Mark as Final**.
    c. Click **OK** to resave the file.
    d. Click **OK** to close the message box.
    e. Close the workbook.
20. Click the hyperlink (the screenshot) in ***[your initials] Excel 5-2a*** to test it. The ***[your initials] Excel 5-2*** workbook opens in *Read-Only* mode because it is marked as final.
21. Close ***[your initials] Excel 5-2***. Save and close ***[your initials] Excel 5-2a***.

Guided Project 5-3

Hamilton Civic Center tracks the number of participants enrolled in classes and seminars. You create a dynamic data consolidation to link data, prepare monthly sheets for consolidation, copy the company logo, and complete work for the summary workbook.
[Student Learning Outcomes 5.1, 5.2, 5.3, 5.4, 5.5, 5.6]

Files Needed: ***HamiltonCC-05.xlsx***, ***HamiltonCCLinked-05.xlsx***, and ***HCC.png*** *(Student data files are available in the* Library *of your SIMnet account.)*
Completed Project File Names: ***[your initials] Excel 5-3.xlsx*** and ***[your initials] Excel 5-3a.xlsx***

Skills Covered in This Project

- Group and format worksheets.
- Create a static data consolidation by category.
- Sort consolidated data.
- Copy a picture.
- Break links in a workbook.
- Link workbooks in the *Consolidate* dialog box.
- Create a dynamic data consolidation.
- Insert, size, and position a picture.

---

1. Open the ***HamiltonCC-05*** workbook from your student data files and save it as [your initials] Excel 5-3.
2. Group the worksheets.
   a. Click the **January** worksheet tab.
   b. Press **Shift** and click the **March** tab.
3. Format grouped worksheets.
   a. Select cells **A5:F12**.
   b. Click the arrow with the **Borders** button [*Home* tab, *Font* group] and select **More Borders**.
   c. Click the **Color** arrow and choose **Black, Text 1** (second column).
   d. Click the thin solid line **Style** (bottom choice in the first column of styles).
   e. Click the **vertical middle** of the preview box. If you place a border in the wrong location, click the line in the preview to remove it.
   f. Click the second line **Style** in the first column (two below **None**).
   g. Click the **horizontal middle** of the preview box. This border will appear between rows.
   h. Click the bottom line **Style** in the second column (a double border).
   i. Click the **bottom** of the preview area to place a bottom horizontal border (Figure 5-70).
   j. Click **OK**.

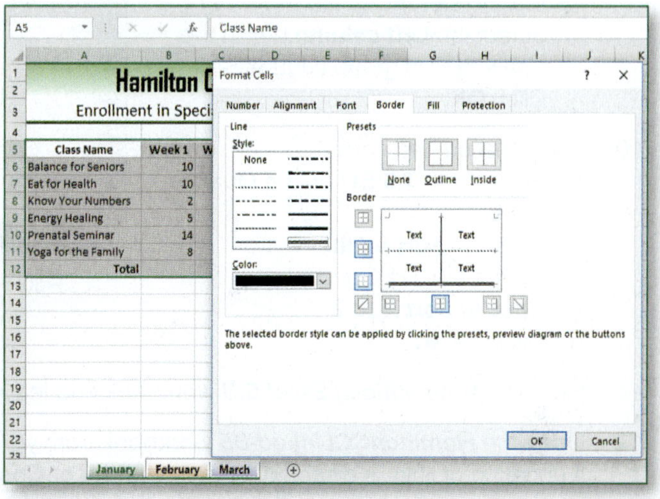

Figure 5-70 ***Border*** **tab in** ***Format Cells*** **dialog box**

4. Enter *SUM* in grouped worksheets.
   a. Select cells **F6:F11**.
   b. Click the **AutoSum** button [*Home* tab, *Editing* group].
   c. Use **SUM** in cells **B12:F12**.
   d. Click cell **A1**.
   e. Right-click the **February** sheet tab and choose **Ungroup Sheets**.
5. Copy a picture.
   a. Click to select the organization logo on the **February** sheet.
   b. Press **Ctrl+C** to copy the picture.
   c. Click the **January** sheet tab.
   d. Press **Ctrl+V** to paste the picture.
   e. Point to the picture frame to display a move pointer.
   f. Drag the picture to fine-tune its location so that it appears in column A to the left of "Hamilton Civic Center." Nudge the image with any keyboard directional arrow key.
   g. Click cell **B1**.
6. Copy the **March** sheet to the end and name it Quarter 1.
7. Set the tab color to **Black, Text 1** (second column)
8. Edit cell **A3** to read First Quarter Enrollment.
9. Create a static data consolidation by category.
   a. Delete the contents of cells **A6:E11** on the **Quarter 1** sheet. The labels in column A are not in the same order on the quarterly sheets.
   b. Click the **Consolidate** button [*Data* tab, *Data Tools* group].

c. Choose the **SUM** function.
d. Select and delete references in the *All references* box.
e. Click the **Reference** box and click the **January** tab.
f. Select cells **A6:E11** and click **Add** in the *Consolidate* dialog box.
g. Click the **February** tab, verify that cells **A6:E11** are selected, and click **Add**.
h. Add the **March** worksheet data to the *All references* list.
i. Select the **Left column** box in the *Use labels in* group (Figure 5-71).
j. Click **OK**.

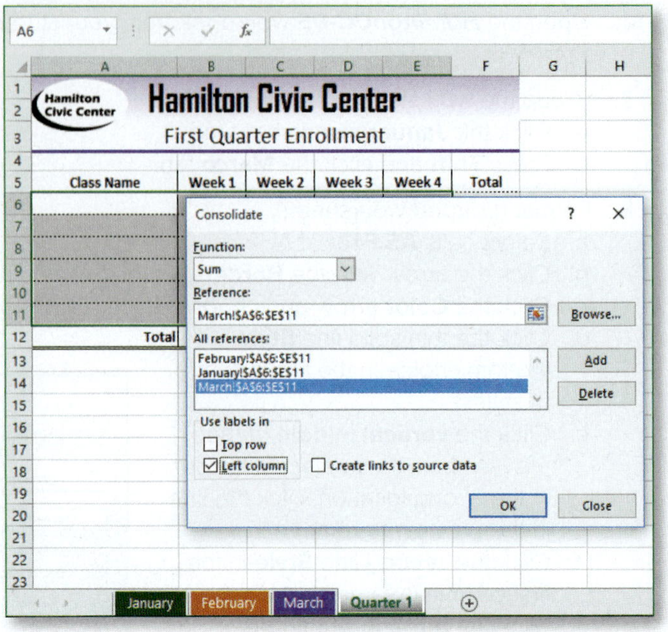

Figure 5-71 ***Consolidate*** **dialog box to consolidate by category**

10. Sort consolidated data.
    a. Select cells **A6:E11** on the **Quarter 1** sheet.
    b. Click the **Sort & Filter** button [*Home* tab, *Editing* group].
    c. Choose **Sort A to Z**.
    d. Click cell **B1**.
11. Save the ***[your initials] Excel 5-3*** workbook and leave it open.
12. Open the ***HamiltonCCLinked-05*** workbook from your student data files. Click **Enable Content** if updating of links is disabled, or click **Update** or **Continue** without updating. The message box depends on file management procedures on your computer.
13. Save the workbook as [your initials] Excel 5-3a.
14. View and break links in the workbook.
    a. Click cell **D7**. The link is incorrect; it should refer to the **Quarter 1** sheet in ***[your initials] Excel 5-3***.
    b. Click the **Edit Links** button [*Data* tab, *Queries & Connections* group].
    c. Click **Break Link**. When you break a link, formulas are replaced with values and the command cannot be undone (Figure 5-72).

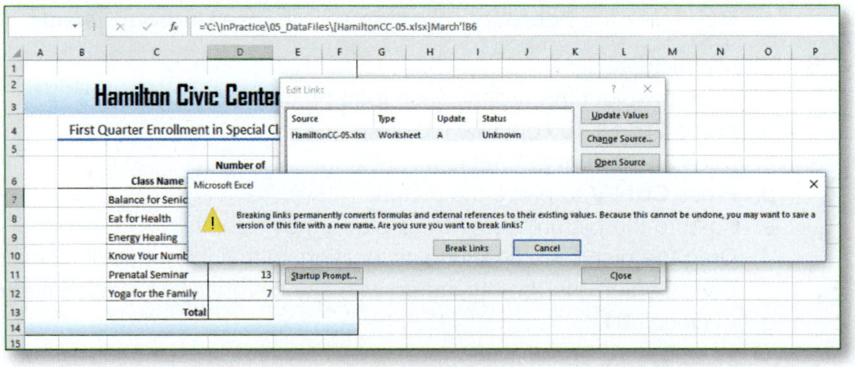

Figure 5-72 ***Edit Links*** **dialog box and** ***Break Links*** **message box**

    d. Click **Break Links**.
    Formulas are removed, but the cells display the values.
    e. Click **Close**.

15. Create a dynamic data consolidation to link workbooks.
    a. Select cells **D7:D12** on the **FirstQuarter** sheet.
    b. Click the **Consolidate** button [*Data* tab, *Data Tools* group].
    c. Choose the **SUM** function.
    d. Select and delete references in the *All references* box.
    e. Click the **Reference** box and press **Ctrl+F6** to switch to the ***[your initials] Excel 5-3*** workbook.
    f. Click the **Quarter 1** sheet tab if necessary.
    g. Select cells **F6:F11**.
    h. Select the **Create links to source data** box (Figure 5-73).
    i. Click **OK**. When you have only one reference, you don't need to click *Add*.
    j. Switch to the ***[your initials] Excel 5-3a*** workbook if necessary.
    k. Select cell **D19**, click the **AutoSum** button [*Home* tab, *Editing* group], and press **Enter**.

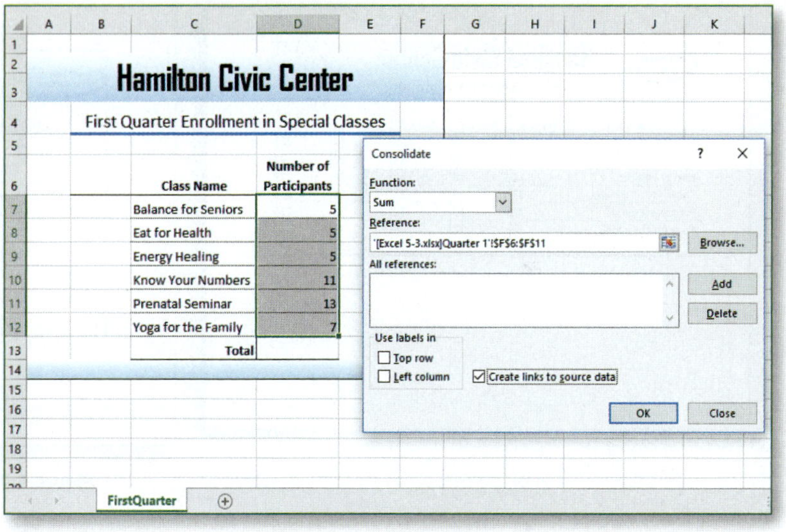

Figure 5-73 ***Consolidate*** **dialog box to link workbooks**

16. Insert a picture from a file.
    a. Click cell **G2** on the **FirstQuarter** sheet.
    b. Click the **Pictures** button [*Insert* tab, *Illustrations* group].
    c. Find and select **HCC** from your student data files (Figure 5-74).
    d. Click **Insert**. The picture is placed at a default size.
    e. Click the **Height** box [*Picture Tools Format* tab, *Size* group].
    f. Type .5 to replace the default height and press **Enter**. The image is proportionally resized.
    g. Point to the logo frame to display a move pointer.
    h. Drag the image to cover cells **A1:B3**.
    i. Click cell **C1**.

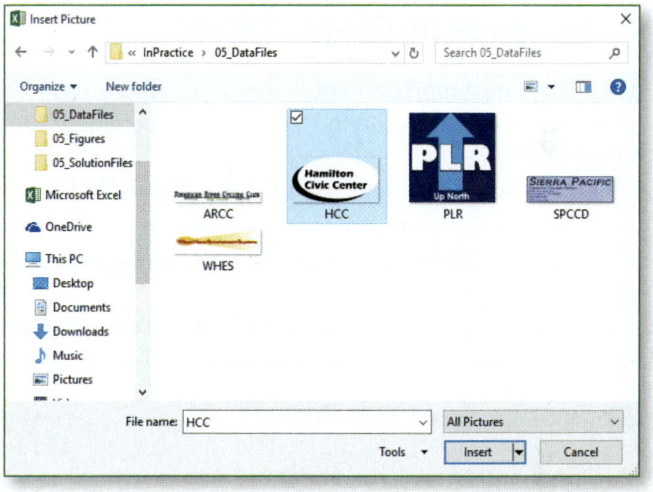

Figure 5-74 ***Insert Picture*** **dialog box**

17. Save and close the ***[your initials] Excel 5-3a*** workbook. Save and close the ***[your initials] Excel 5-3*** workbook (Figure 5-75).

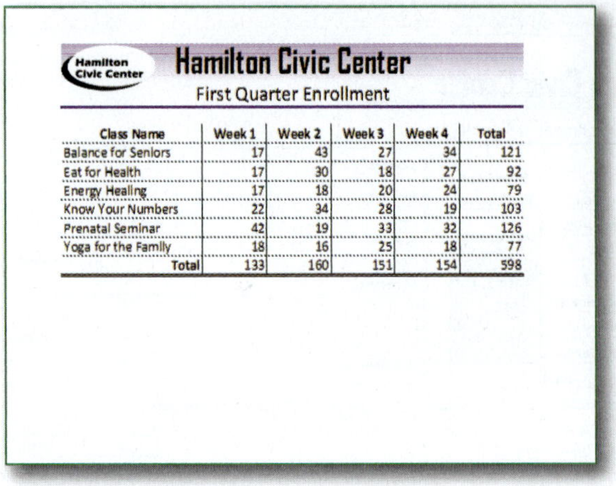

Hamilton Civic Center

Hamilton Civic Center

First Quarter Enrollment

Class Name	Week 1	Week 2	Week 3	Week 4	Total
Balance for Seniors	17	43	27	34	121
Eat for Health	17	30	18	27	92
Energy Healing	17	18	20	24	79
Know Your Numbers	22	34	28	19	103
Prenatal Seminar	42	19	33	32	126
Yoga for the Family	18	16	25	18	77
Total	133	160	151	154	598

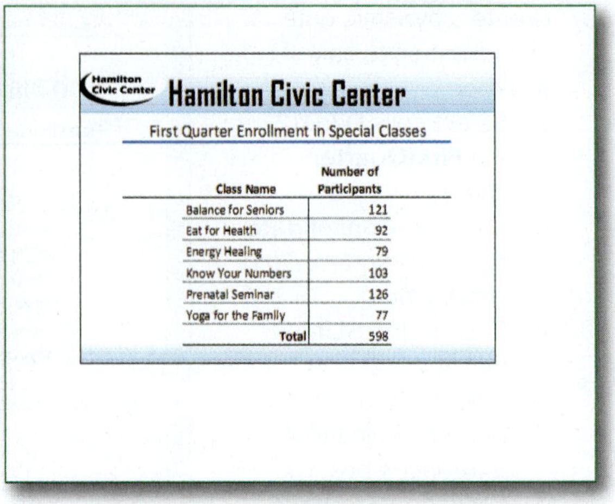

Hamilton Civic Center

Hamilton Civic Center

First Quarter Enrollment in Special Classes

Class Name	Number of Participants
Balance for Seniors	121
Eat for Health	92
Energy Healing	79
Know Your Numbers	103
Prenatal Seminar	126
Yoga for the Family	77
Total	598

Figure 5-75 Completed worksheets for Excel 5-3a

Independent Project 5-4

Wilson Home Entertainment Systems monitors cash flow at their individual locations separately and consolidates data. After the summary is complete, you insert hyperlinks to each of the supporting worksheets.

[Student Learning Outcomes 5.1, 5.4, 5.6, 5.7, 5.8]

Files Needed: ***WilsonHome-05.xlsx*** and ***WHES.png*** *(Student data files are available in the* Library *of your SIMnet account.)*

Completed Project File Name: ***[your initials] Excel 5-4.xlsx***

Skills Covered in This Project

- Group and format worksheets.
- Create a static data consolidation with *SUM*.
- Insert a picture from a file.
- Insert a hyperlink.
- Copy a hyperlink.
- Encrypt a workbook with a password.

---

1. Open the ***WilsonHome-05*** workbook from your student data files and save it as [your initials] Excel 5-4.
2. Group all the worksheets.
3. Edit and format grouped sheets.
   a. Select cells **A1:B2** and click the **Launcher** in the *Alignment* group [*Home* tab]. Choose **Center Across Selection** from the *Horizontal* list and click **OK**.
   b. Click the **Launcher** in the *Page Setup* group [*Page Layout* tab] and click the **Margins** tab.
   c. Choose **Horizontally** from the *Center on page* list and click **OK**.
   d. Edit the contents of cell **A10** to read Cash paid for marketing.
   e. Select cell **A1** and ungroup the sheets.
4. Select the **CashFlow** sheet.

5. Build a static data consolidation for the *Cash flow from operations* section.
   a. Select cells **B4:B12**.
   b. Use **SUM** to consolidate the data from the three location sheets without links. (Figure 5-76).

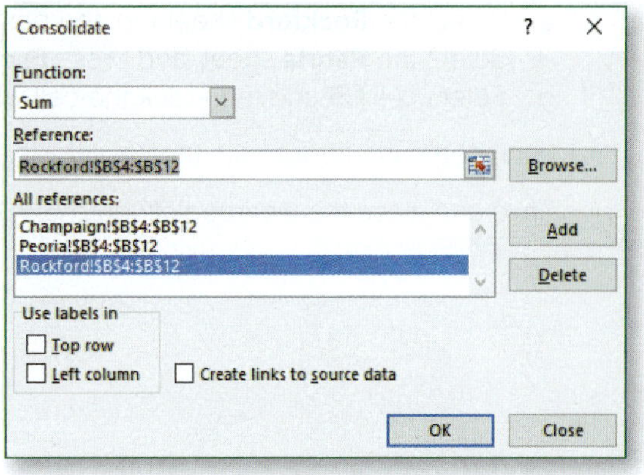

Figure 5-76 ***Consolidate*** **dialog box for cash flow**

6. Build a static data consolidation for the *Cash flow from banking and investment* section in cells **B15:B21**. Delete the references in the *Consolidate* dialog box and use **SUM** as the function.

7. Build a static data consolidation for the *Cash balance at the beginning of the quarter* amounts in cell **B24** with **SUM** as the function.

8. Insert a picture from a file.
   a. Delete the contents of cell **A1** on the **CashFlow** sheet.
   b. Click cell **D2**.
   c. Click the **Pictures** button [*Insert* tab, *Illustrations* group].
   d. Find and select **WHES** from your student data files.
   e. Click **Insert**. The picture is placed at a default size.
   f. Click the **Height** box [*Picture Tools Format* tab, *Size* group].
   g. Type 1.2 to replace the default height and press **Enter**.
   h. Format the height of row **1** to **86.25 (115 pixels)**.
   i. Point to the logo frame to display a move pointer.
   j. Drag the image to appear in cell **A1** as a main label for the worksheet (Figure 5-77).
   k. Click cell **D2** to deselect the image.

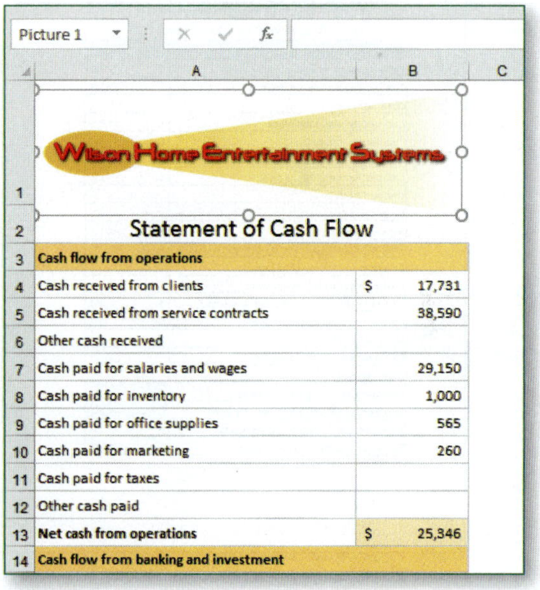

Figure 5-77 Image positioned as title

9. Insert and copy a hyperlink.
   a. Click cell **C3** on the **Peoria** worksheet.
   b. Create a hyperlink that displays Total Cash Flow and switches to cell **A1** on the **Cash Flow** worksheet (Figure 5-78).
   c. Right-click cell **C3** and choose **Copy** from the menu.
   d. Select the **Champaign** sheet tab and paste the hyperlink in cell **C3**.

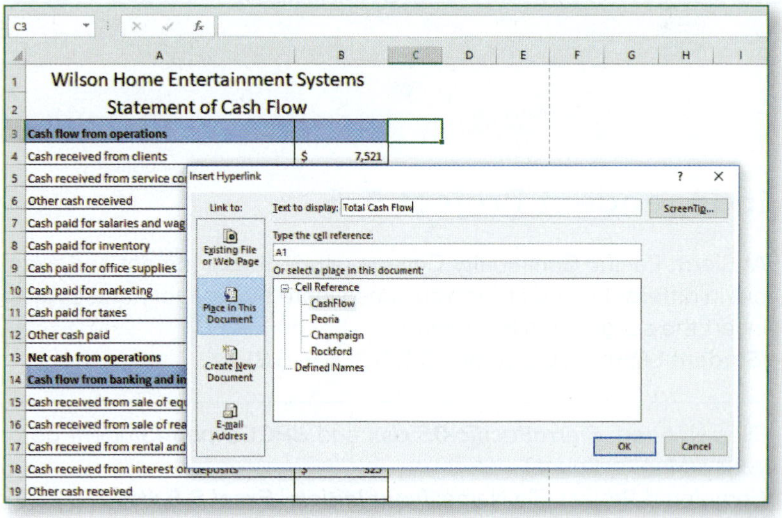

Figure 5-78 Hyperlink text to switch to ***Cash Flow*** **sheet**

e. Select the **Rockford** sheet tab and paste the hyperlink in cell **C3**.
f. Select the **Peoria** sheet, and press **Esc** to remove the copy marquee if it is still visible.
g. Select cell **C5** and then click the cell with the hyperlink to test it.

10. Encrypt the workbook with the password abc.
11. Save and close the workbook (Figure 5-79).

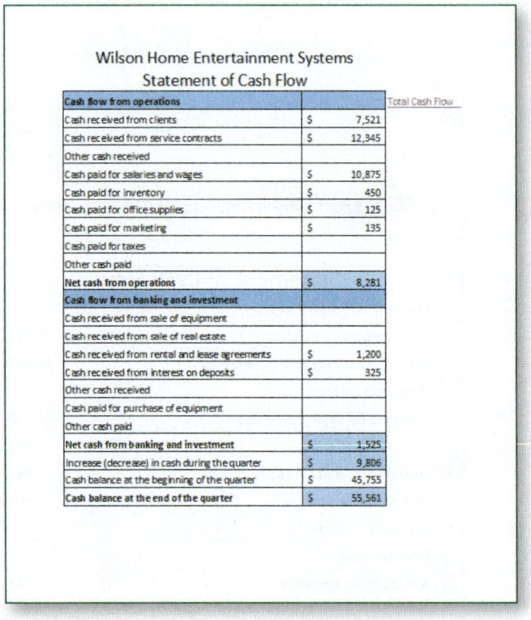

Wilson Home Entertainment Systems
Statement of Cash Flow

Cash flow from operations			Total Cash Flow
Cash received from clients	$	7,521	
Cash received from service contracts	$	12,345	
Other cash received			
Cash paid for salaries and wages	$	10,875	
Cash paid for inventory	$	450	
Cash paid for office supplies	$	125	
Cash paid for marketing	$	135	
Cash paid for taxes			
Other cash paid			
Net cash from operations	$	8,281	
Cash flow from banking and investment			
Cash received from sale of equipment			
Cash received from sale of real estate			
Cash received from rental and lease agreements	$	1,200	
Cash received from interest on deposits	$	325	
Other cash received			
Cash paid for purchase of equipment			
Other cash paid			
Net cash from banking and investment	$	1,525	
Increase (decrease) in cash during the quarter	$	9,806	
Cash balance at the beginning of the quarter	$	45,755	
Cash balance at the end of the quarter	$	55,561	

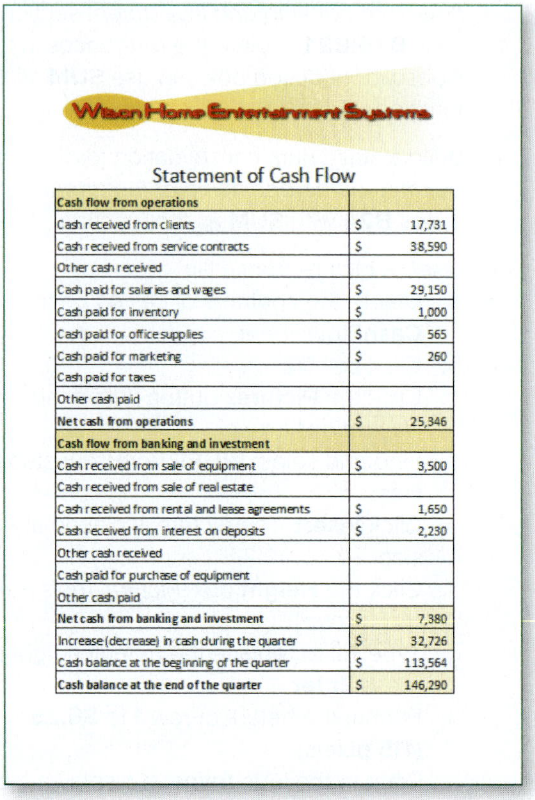

Statement of Cash Flow

Cash flow from operations		
Cash received from clients	$	17,731
Cash received from service contracts	$	38,590
Other cash received		
Cash paid for salaries and wages	$	29,150
Cash paid for inventory	$	1,000
Cash paid for office supplies	$	565
Cash paid for marketing	$	260
Cash paid for taxes		
Other cash paid		
Net cash from operations	$	25,346
Cash flow from banking and investment		
Cash received from sale of equipment	$	3,500
Cash received from sale of real estate		
Cash received from rental and lease agreements	$	1,650
Cash received from interest on deposits	$	2,230
Other cash received		
Cash paid for purchase of equipment		
Other cash paid		
Net cash from banking and investment	$	7,380
Increase (decrease) in cash during the quarter	$	32,726
Cash balance at the beginning of the quarter	$	113,564
Cash balance at the end of the quarter	$	146,290

Figure 5-79 ***Peoria*** **worksheet with hyperlink and completed** ***CashFlow*** **sheet for Excel 5-4**

Independent Project 5-5

At Sierra Pacific Community College, student assignment and exam points are listed on a single sheet but in different name order. You consolidate by category and copy the results to another sheet. You also insert the school logo in a header.
[Student Learning Outcomes 5.1, 5.3, 5.6, 5.8]

Files Needed: ***SierraPacific-05.xlsx*** and ***SPCCD.png*** *(Student data files are available in the Library of your SIMnet account.)*
Completed Project File Name: ***[your initials] Excel 5-5.xlsx***

Skills Covered in This Project

- Remove the *Mark as Final* property.
- Create a static data consolidation.
- Consolidate data by category.
- Insert a picture from a file in a header.
- Size a picture.
- Change the color of a picture.

---

1. Open the ***SierraPacific-05*** workbook and click **Edit Anyway** to remove the *Read-Only* property from the *Mark as Final* command.
2. Save the workbook as [your initials] Excel 5-5. On the **PPT&Access** sheet, student names are not listed in the same order.
3. Consolidate points by category.
   a. Select cells **I4:K25** on the **PPT&Access** sheet. Consolidated data will be placed in this range.
   b. Open the *Consolidate* dialog box.
   c. Select and delete any references in the *All references* list.
   d. Choose **SUM** as the function.
   e. Click the **Reference** box, select cells **A4:C25**, and click **Add**.
   f. Select cells **E4:G25** and click **Add**.
   g. Select the **Left column** box (Figure 5-80).
   h. Do not use links.
   i. Click **OK**. The columns are consolidated, and the names are in the same order as the PowerPoint list, alphabetical order.

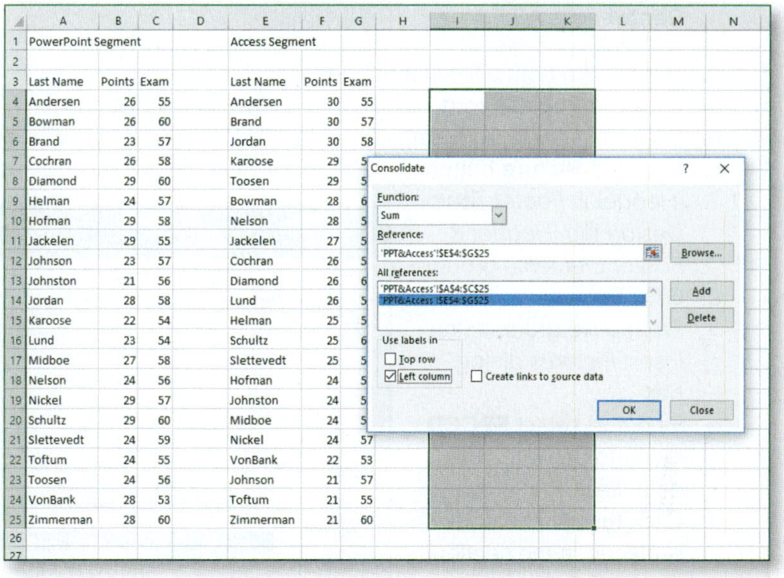

Figure 5-80 Consolidating by label

4. Copy and format consolidation results.
   a. Select cells **J4:K25** and click the **Copy** button [*Home* tab, *Clipboard* group] (Figure 5-81).
   b. Click the **Total** sheet tab. Student names are already entered in alphabetical order.
   c. Click cell **C4** and click the **Paste** button [*Home* tab, *Clipboard* group].

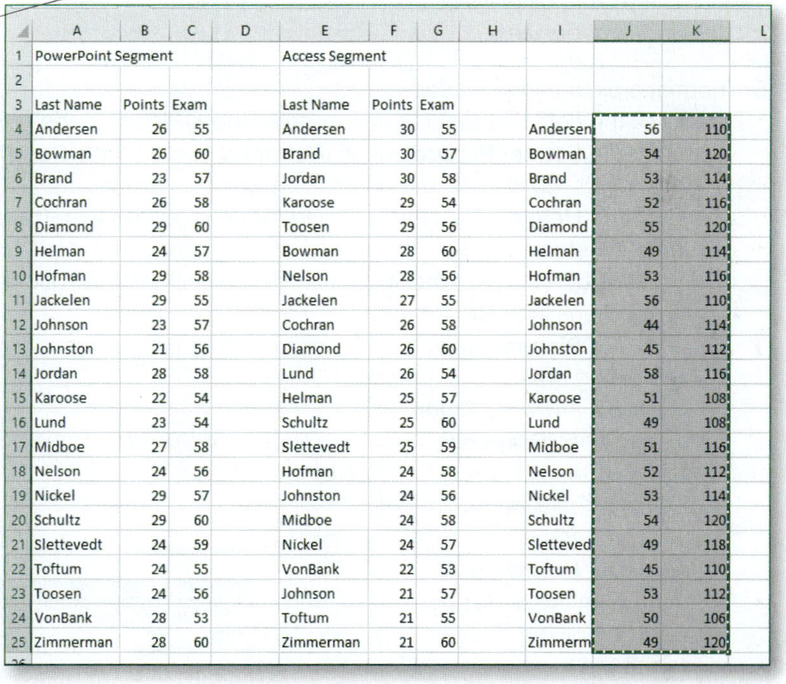

Figure 5-81 Copy consolidated values to another sheet

d. Select cell **A4** and click the **Format as Table** button [*Home* tab, *Styles* group].
e. Use **Blue, Table Style Medium 16**.
f. Show the **Total Row** with **Average** as the function in the **Points** and **Exam** columns.
g. Type Average in cell **A26** and format it bold and right-aligned.
h. Type Total in cell **E3**.
i. Enter a formula in cell **E4** to add cells **C4** and **D4**.
j. Show **Average** in the **Total Row** for column **E**.
k. Format cells **C26:E26** to display two decimal places.
l. Format cell **A1** with a **16 pt** font size.
m. Format row **1** as **22.50 (30 pixels)** high.
n. **Center** cells **A3:E3**.

5. Insert a picture from a file in a header.
   a. Click the **Page Layout** view button on the *Status* bar.
   b. Click the right header section.
   c. Click the **Picture** button [*Header & Footer Tools Design* tab, *Header & Footer Elements* group].
   d. Click **Browse** for the *From a file* group in the *Insert Pictures* dialog box.
   e. Find and select **SPCCD** in the folder with your data files.
   f. Click **Insert**. The code is placed in the section (Figure 5-82).
   g. Click a worksheet cell. The picture displays in *Page Layout* view.

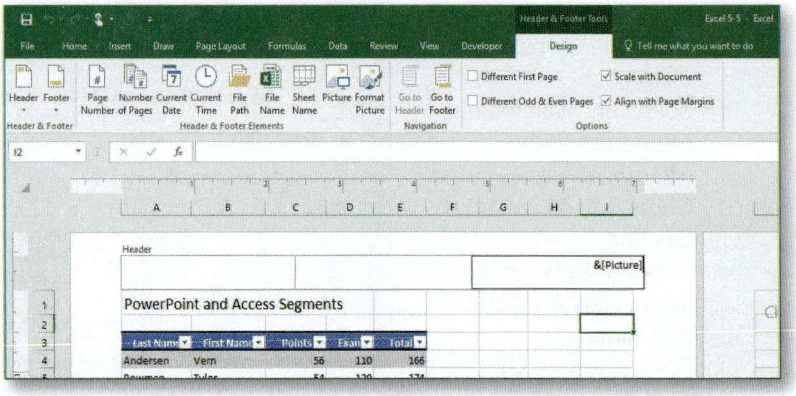

Figure 5-82 Picture code in header

6. Format a picture in a header.
   a. Click the right header section to display the *&[Picture]* code.
   b. Click the **Format Picture** button [*Header & Footer Tools Design* tab, *Header & Footer Elements* group].
   c. Click the **Height** box in the *Size and rotate* group on the *Size* tab and type .50 to replace the default height.
   d. Press **Tab** to move to the *Width* box. When *Lock aspect ratio* is active, the image is automatically proportionally sized.
   e. Click the **Picture** tab in the dialog box.
   f. Click the arrow for **Color** and choose **Grayscale**.
   g. Click **OK** and click a worksheet cell (Figure 5-83).
   h. Click the **Normal** view button on the *Status* bar. You do not see headers in this view.
   i. Press **Ctrl+Home**.

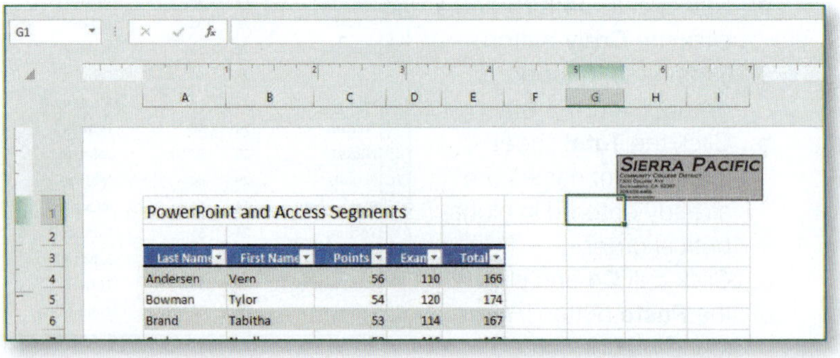

Figure 5-83 Reformatted picture

7. Save and close the workbook (Figure 5-84).

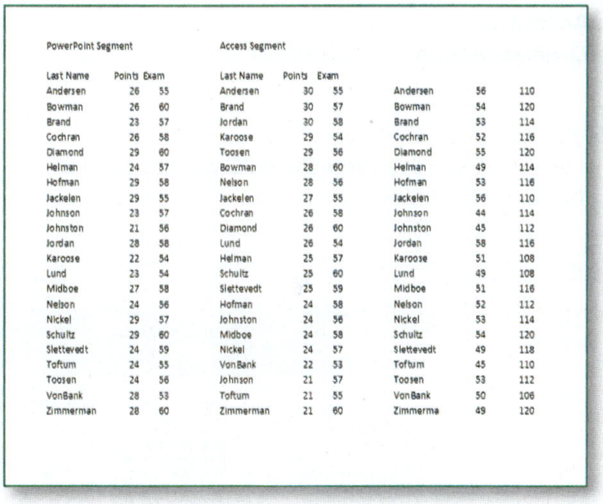

PowerPoint Segment / Access Segment

Last Name	Points	Exam	Last Name	Points	Exam			
Andersen	26	55	Andersen	30	55	Andersen	56	110
Bowman	26	60	Brand	30	57	Bowman	54	120
Brand	23	57	Jordan	30	58	Brand	53	114
Cochran	26	58	Karoose	29	54	Cochran	52	116
Diamond	29	60	Toosen	29	56	Diamond	55	120
Helman	24	57	Bowman	28	60	Helman	49	114
Hofman	29	58	Nelson	28	56	Hofman	53	116
Jackelen	29	55	Jackelen	27	55	Jackelen	56	110
Johnson	23	57	Cochran	26	58	Johnson	44	114
Johnston	21	56	Diamond	26	60	Johnston	45	112
Jordan	28	58	Lund	26	54	Jordan	58	116
Karoose	22	54	Helman	25	57	Karoose	51	108
Lund	23	54	Schultz	25	60	Lund	49	108
Midboe	27	58	Slettevedt	25	59	Midboe	51	116
Nelson	24	56	Hofman	24	58	Nelson	52	112
Nickel	29	57	Johnston	24	56	Nickel	53	114
Schultz	29	60	Midboe	24	58	Schultz	54	120
Slettevedt	24	59	Nickel	24	57	Slettevedt	49	118
Toftum	24	55	VonBank	22	53	Toftum	45	110
Toosen	24	56	Johnson	21	57	Toosen	53	112
VonBank	28	53	Toftum	21	55	VonBank	50	106
Zimmerman	28	60	Zimmerman	21	60	Zimmerma	49	120

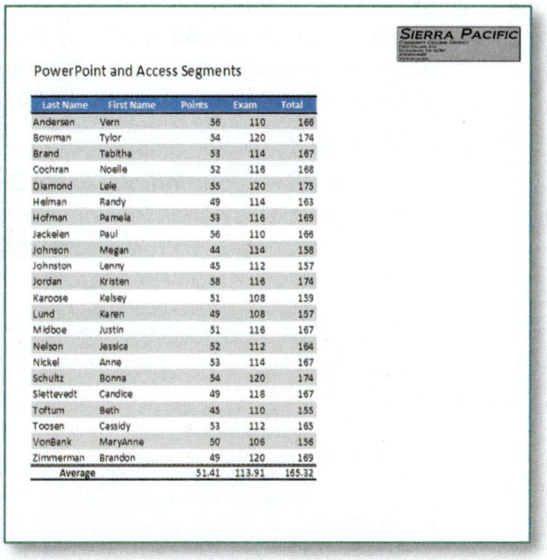

PowerPoint and Access Segments

Last Name	First Name	Points	Exam	Total
Andersen	Vern	56	110	166
Bowman	Tylor	54	120	174
Brand	Tabitha	53	114	167
Cochran	Noelle	52	116	168
Diamond	Lele	55	120	175
Helman	Randy	49	114	163
Hofman	Pamela	53	116	169
Jackelen	Paul	56	110	166
Johnson	Megan	44	114	158
Johnston	Lenny	45	112	157
Jordan	Kristen	58	116	174
Karoose	Kelsey	51	108	159
Lund	Karen	49	108	157
Midboe	Justin	51	116	167
Nelson	Jessica	52	112	164
Nickel	Anne	53	114	167
Schultz	Bonna	54	120	174
Slettevedt	Candice	49	118	167
Toftum	Beth	45	110	155
Toosen	Cassidy	53	112	165
VonBank	MaryAnne	50	106	156
Zimmerman	Brandon	49	120	169
Average		51.41	113.91	165.32

Figure 5-84 Completed worksheets for Excel 5-5

Independent Project 5-6

Wear-Ever Shoes plans to link workbooks with best-seller data. The linking formula uses addition, and you insert a hyperlink to open the source workbook. You illustrate the process to build an external reference formula in a *SmartArt* graphic, too.
[Student Learning Outcomes 5.5, 5.6, 5.7]

File Needed: ***WearEver-05.xlsx*** *(Student data files are available in the* Library *of your SIMnet account.)*
Completed Project File Name: ***[your initials] Excel 5-6.xlsx***

Skills Covered in This Project

- Link workbooks with an addition formula.
- Edit and copy an external reference formula.
- Insert a hyperlink.
- Insert a *SmartArt* graphic.
- Add text to *SmartArt*.
- Format a *SmartArt* graphic.

1. Create a new workbook and save it as [your initials] Excel 5-6.
2. Open the ***WearEver-05*** workbook from your student data files.
3. Arrange the two workbooks to be vertically tiled.
4. Copy the **North** worksheet in the ***WearEver-05*** workbook to ***[your initials] Excel 5-6*** by selecting your workbook name from the *To book* list in the *Move or Copy* dialog box. The fill color for the copied sheet is different.
5. Select the ***[your initials] Excel 5-6*** workbook, rename the copied sheet as Totals, and delete **Sheet1**.

6. Prepare the linked workbook.
   a. In ***[your initials] Excel 5-6***, delete the contents of cells **B6:B16**.
   b. Select and delete columns **C:D**.
   c. Edit the label in cell **A3** to display Best Sellers All Regions.
   d. Change the sheet tab color to **Orange, Accent 2** (sixth column).
   e. Change the **Fill Color** for cells **A1:F4** to **Orange, Accent 2, Lighter 60%** (sixth column).
7. Link workbooks with an addition formula.
   a. Click cell **B6** in ***[your initials] Excel 5-6*** and type = to start the formula.
   b. Add the contents of cell **B6** from each of the sheets in the ***WearEver-05*** workbook in the formula (Figure 5-85). Press **Enter** after the last cell reference.

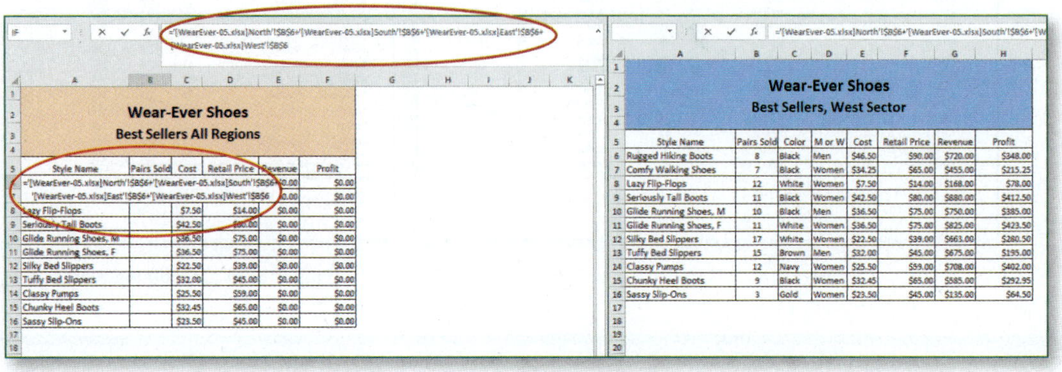

Figure 5-85 External reference formula to link workbooks

8. Close the ***WearEver-05*** workbook without saving and maximize your workbook window.
9. Edit and copy an external reference formula.
   a. Click cell **B6** in ***[your initials] Excel 5-6***.
   b. Edit the formula to change each absolute reference to a relative reference. Note that the external reference shows the complete path for the source workbook because it is no longer open (Figure 5-86).
   c. Copy the formula to complete the column.

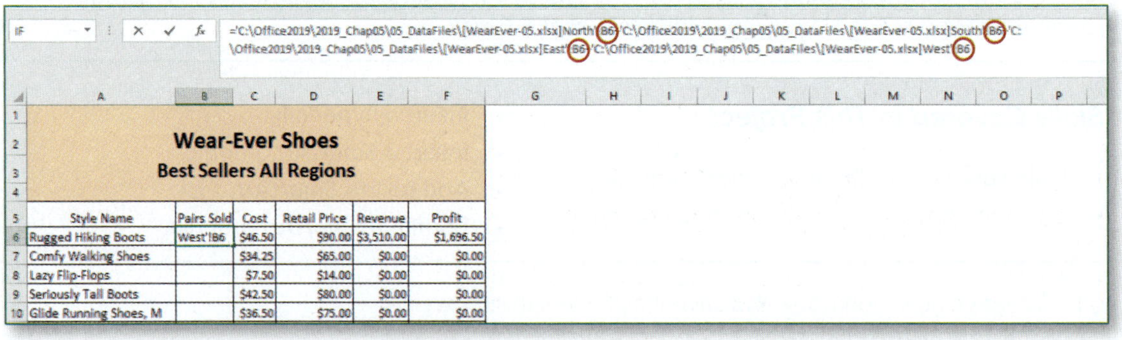

Figure 5-86 Formula edited for copying

10. Insert a hyperlink to open the source workbook ***WearEver-05***.
    a. Click cell **G3**.
    b. Create a cell hyperlink and edit the display text to read Open source data.
    c. Click the **Look in** arrow and navigate to the folder with the ***WearEver-05*** workbook. Select the filename and click **OK**.
    d. Right-click the hyperlink and format its text color to **Orange, Accent 2** (sixth column).

e. Right-click the hyperlink again and make it bold.
f. Test the hyperlink and close the source workbook without saving.

11. Insert a *SmartArt* graphic.
   a. Click cell **B20** on the **Totals** sheet, and insert a **Basic Process** graphic.
   b. Type Create new workbook in the leftmost text box. Do not press *Enter* after typing the label.
   c. Type Open source file in the middle box.
   d. Type Copy sheet and delete data in the rightmost box.
   e. Click the **Add Shape** button [*SmartArt Tools Design* tab, *Create Graphic* group] (Figure 5-87).
   f. Type Build formula in the new shape.

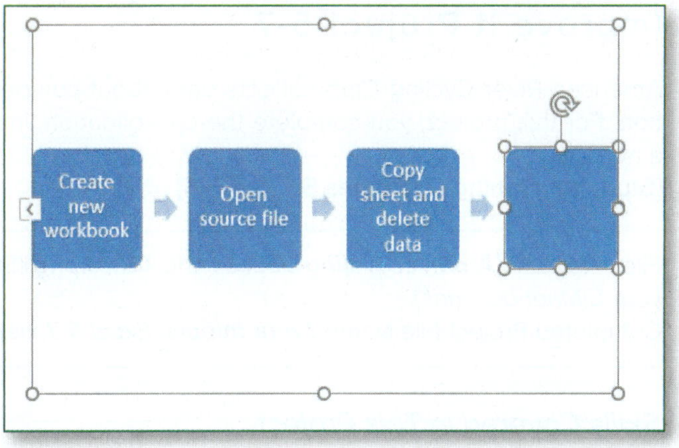

Figure 5-87 Fourth shape added to *SmartArt*

12. Format a *SmartArt* graphic.
   a. Click the frame of the *SmartArt* graphic to select it.
   b. Click the **More** button [*SmartArt Tools Design* tab, *SmartArt Styles* group].
   c. Choose **Brick Scene** in the *3-D* group.
   d. Click the **Change Colors** button [*SmartArt Tools Design* tab, *SmartArt Styles* group].
   e. Choose **Colorful Range – Accent Colors 3 to 4** in the *Colorful* group.
   f. Format the *SmartArt* frame with a **½ pt black** outline.
   g. Point to the *SmartArt* frame and drag the graphic to position the top left selection handle in cell **A18**.
   h. Point to the bottom right selection handle and resize the frame to reach cell **F35**.
   i. Select cell **A1**.

13. Save and close the workbook (Figure 5-88).

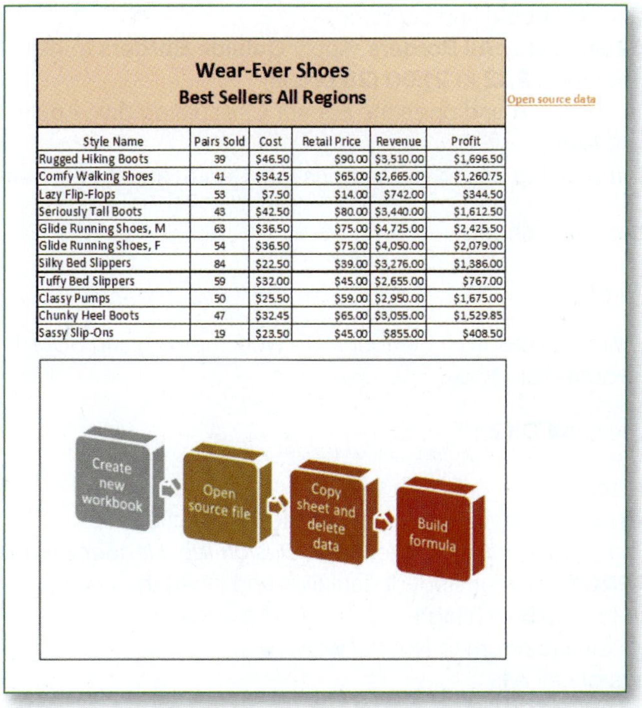

Wear-Ever Shoes
Best Sellers All Regions

Open source data

Style Name	Pairs Sold	Cost	Retail Price	Revenue	Profit
Rugged Hiking Boots	39	$46.50	$90.00	$3,510.00	$1,696.50
Comfy Walking Shoes	41	$34.25	$65.00	$2,665.00	$1,260.75
Lazy Flip-Flops	53	$7.50	$14.00	$742.00	$344.50
Seriously Tall Boots	43	$42.50	$80.00	$3,440.00	$1,612.50
Glide Running Shoes, M	63	$36.50	$75.00	$4,725.00	$2,425.50
Glide Running Shoes, F	54	$36.50	$75.00	$4,050.00	$2,079.00
Silky Bed Slippers	84	$22.50	$39.00	$3,276.00	$1,386.00
Tuffy Bed Slippers	59	$32.00	$45.00	$2,655.00	$767.00
Classy Pumps	50	$25.50	$59.00	$2,950.00	$1,675.00
Chunky Heel Boots	47	$32.45	$65.00	$3,055.00	$1,529.85
Sassy Slip-Ons	19	$23.50	$45.00	$855.00	$408.50

Figure 5-88 Completed worksheet for Excel 5-6

Improve It Project 5-7

American River Cycling Club collects data about competitions from April through June for consolidation. For this project, you complete the consolidation, improve formatting, and insert the club's logo in a header.
[Student Learning Outcomes 5.1, 5.4, 5.6]

Files Needed: ***AmRiverCycling-05.xlsx*** and ***ARRC.png*** (*Student data files are available in the* Library *of your SIMnet account.)*
Completed Project File Name: ***[your initials] Excel 5-7.xlsx***

Skills Covered in This Project

- Group and format worksheets.
- Create a static data consolidation.
- Insert a picture in a header.

1. Open the ***AmRiverCycling-05*** workbook from your student data files and save it as [your initials] Excel 5-7.
2. Group and format worksheets.
   a. Group the four sheets with a state name as the tab name.
   b. Select and delete columns **C:D** in the grouped sheets.
   c. Type American River Cycling Club in cell **A1** on the grouped sheets. Format the font size as **20 pt**.
   d. Type April-June Race Participation in cell **A2** and format the font size as **18 pt**.
   e. Select cells **A1:E2** and open the *Format Cells* dialog box. Find and select the **Center Across Selection** command.
   f. *AutoFit* columns **A:C**.
   g. Format the labels in row **3** bold and centered.
   h. Select cells **A3:E12** and apply **All Borders**. Apply **Outside Borders** to cells **A1:E2**.
   i. Format the **Height** of rows **3:12** to **21.00 (28 pixels)**.
   j. Select the dates in column **A** and open the *Format Cells* dialog box. Apply a **Date** format that displays the date as *1-Apr*.
   k. Open the *Page Setup* dialog box to the *Margins* tab. Center the sheets horizontally on the page.
3. Click cell **A1** and ungroup the sheets.
4. Click the **Static** sheet tab.
5. Consolidate the data without links from the four state worksheets using *SUM*. Make necessary changes in the *Consolidate* dialog box.
6. Apply **All Borders** to cells **A4:D12**.
7. Insert a picture in a header.
   a. Switch to *Page Layout* view and click the center header section.
   b. Click the **Picture** button [*Header & Footer Tools Design tab, Header & Footer Elements* group].
   c. Find and select **ARRC** from your student data files and insert the image.
   d. Format the picture to be **.75** inch high.
   e. Click a worksheet cell and return to *Normal* view.
   f. Delete the contents of cell **A1**.

8. Save and close the workbook (Figure 5-89).

American River Cycling Club
April-June Race Participation

Date	City	# of Riders	Male	Female
1-Apr	Algonquin	35	18	17
4-Apr	Blue Island	27	14	13
14-Apr	Cicero	28	12	16
23-Apr	Midlothian	28	12	16
1-May	Peoria	32	16	16
8-May	Rockford	39	20	19
21-May	Salem	35	15	20
1-Jun	Springfield	39	18	21
5-Jun	Urbana	33	18	15

American River Cycling Club
April-June Race Participation

Date	City	# of Riders	Male	Female
1-Apr	Bainbridge Island	21	15	6
4-Apr	Bellevue	30	16	14
14-Apr	Bothell	26	18	8
23-Apr	Kirkland	28	15	13
1-May	Lynnwood	40	21	19
8-May	Parkland	34	18	16
21-May	Poulsbo	30	18	12
1-Jun	Redmond	29	15	14
5-Jun	Tacoma	27	16	11

American River Cycling Club
April-June Race Participation

Date	City	# of Riders	Male	Female
1-Apr	Arlington	40	24	16
4-Apr	Brookline	37	20	17
14-Apr	Cambridge	28	19	9
23-Apr	Chestnut Hill	38	18	20
1-May	Everett	35	20	15
8-May	Framingham	29	19	10
21-May	Foxboro	29	18	11
1-Jun	Revere	35	21	14
5-Jun	Watertown	39	22	17

American River Cycling Club
www.arcc.org Cycling...a way of life info@arcc.org

Race Participation Totals

Date	# of Riders	Male	Female
April 1	117	68	49
April 4	115	59	56
April 14	114	69	45
April 23	121	59	62
May 1	134	72	62
May 8	135	75	60
May 21	121	72	49
June 1	132	69	63
June 5	121	67	54

American River Cycling Club
April-June Race Participation

Date	City	# of Riders	Male	Female
1-Apr	Addison	21	11	10
4-Apr	Arlington	21	9	12
14-Apr	Denton	32	20	12
23-Apr	Fort Worth	27	14	13
1-May	Grand Prairie	27	15	12
8-May	Irving	33	18	15
21-May	Plano	27	21	6
1-Jun	River Oaks	29	15	14
5-Jun	San Antonio	22	11	11

Figure 5-89 Completed worksheets for Excel 5-7

Challenge Project 5-8

For this project, you work with a classmate (or on your own) to develop source and dependent workbooks. The source workbook includes details about time spent each weekday on each of five activities for four weeks. The dependent workbook uses external reference formulas to summarize the week's activities.

[Student Learning Outcomes 5.4, 5.5, 5.7]

File needed: None
Completed Project File Names: ***[your initials] Excel 5-8.xlsx*** and ***[your initials] Excel 5-8a.xlsx***

Create a new workbook and save it as [your initials] Excel 5-8. Modify your workbook according to the following guidelines:

- Type the names of the five weekdays as column labels, starting in cell B3. Type Total in cell G3.
- Type the names of five tasks or activities as row labels, starting in cell A4. Choose activities such as Prepare meals, Work on class assignments,Exercise or workout, and other daily tasks.
- Name the sheet Week 1 and enter number of minutes per day for each activity.
- Copy the sheet to create separate sheets for weeks 2, 3, and 4.
- Group the sheets and enter main labels in rows 1:2 to describe the data. Use a *SUM* formula to total each activity for the week in column G.
- Format the grouped sheets in an attractive, easy-to-view style.
- Ungroup the sheets and edit three values on each of the worksheets for weeks 2, 3, and 4.
- Create a new workbook named [your initials] Excel 5-8a.
- Copy one of the sheets from ***[your initials] Excel 5-8*** into this workbook and name the sheet Month.
- Create an external reference formula to add the first task minutes for Monday using ***[your initials] Excel 5-8*** as the source workbook.
- Edit and copy the formula to complete the data.
- Insert a hyperlink in the dependent workbook to open the source workbook.

Challenge Project 5-9

For this project, you build worksheets with data about an activity or concept from your neighborhood or your workplace. You group sheets for formatting, copy a sheet from one workbook to the other, and insert a *SmartArt* graphic.
[Student Learning Outcomes 5.2, 5.4, 5.5, 5.6, 5.7]

File Needed: None
Completed Project File Names: ***[your initials] Excel 5-9.xlsx*** and ***Excel 5-9a.xlsx***

Create a new source workbook and save it as [your initials] Excel 5-9. Modify your workbook according to the following guidelines:

- Key labels and values to illustrate a concept of interest to you. For example, build a worksheet to track the average number of automobiles owned by street in your community, the number of workers by department at your office, travel distances to campus by your classmates, and so on.
- Copy the sheet and change one value in each column in the copied sheet.
- Group the sheets and apply formatting that suits both sheets.
- Review the *SmartArt* categories to find a graphic to illustrate a concept related to your data. Place the *SmartArt* on its own sheet. If necessary, add or remove shapes from the graphic.
- Format the *SmartArt* graphic with a style, change the colors, or add fill or a border. Size and position the graphic.

- Insert a hyperlink on each worksheet to link to the *SmartArt* sheet.
- Save the workbook and leave it open.
- Create a second workbook and save it as [your initials] Excel 5-9a.
- Copy either sheet from ***[your initials] Excel 5-9*** to ***[your initials] Excel 5-9a***.
- Name the copied sheet in ***[your initials] Excel 5-9a*** to indicate that it is a consolidation worksheet.
- Dynamically consolidate data from the two sheets in ***[your initials] Excel 5-9*** or build an external reference formula.
- Save and close both workbooks.

Challenge Project 5-10

For this project, you create a timesheet workbook for five employees. After four weeks, you consolidate data to create a worksheet that displays average number of hours worked on a given day by each employee.
[Student Learning Outcomes 5.1, 5.4, 5.6, 5.8]

File Needed: None
Completed Project File Name: ***[your initials] Excel 5-10.xlsx***

Create a new workbook and save it as [your initials] Excel 5-10. Modify your workbook according to the following guidelines:

- Insert worksheets so that you have five worksheets in the workbook.
- Name the sheets Week 1, Week 2, Week 3, Week 4, and Averages.
- Group all the sheets and type the names of five employees in cells A4:A8. Enter the names of the weekdays in row 3, starting at cell B3.
- Type a main title to indicate a company name.
- While the sheets are grouped, enter number of hours worked for each day. Include values that are decimals, such as 5.5 or 6.25, and enter zero (0) for days an employee did not work.
- While the sheets are grouped, total weekly hours by employee in column I. Calculate total hours worked by day in row 9.
- Apply formatting to the grouped sheets.
- Ungroup the sheets and prepare the *Averages* sheet for consolidation. Do not use links. Edit labels as needed, and delete any total column or row.
- Insert an icon, a 3D model, or a picture from an online source on the *Averages* sheet to complement your company name. Size and format the image to enhance the overall appearance of the worksheet.
- Mark the workbook as final.

CHAPTER 6

Exploring the Function Library

CHAPTER OVERVIEW

The Excel *Function Library* includes functions that perform complex and sophisticated calculations for use in business, government, education, and research. In this chapter, you learn about functions in the *Database, Logical, Date & Time, Financial*, and *Text* categories. You also nest functions and build time, date, and statistical calculations.

STUDENT LEARNING OUTCOMES (SLOs)

After completing this chapter, you will be able to:

SLO 6.1 Use *Database* functions such as *DSUM* and *DAVERAGE* (p. E6-355).

SLO 6.2 Build *Logical* functions including *AND, OR*, and *IFS* functions (p. E6-357).

SLO 6.3 Explore the *Lookup & Reference* category with *INDEX, MATCH*, and *TRANSPOSE* (p. E6-370).

SLO 6.4 Build date, time, and statistical calculations (p. E6-375).

SLO 6.5 Use *Financial* functions such as *PV, FV*, and *NPV* (p. E6-386).

SLO 6.6 Work with *Text* functions including *TEXTJOIN, CONCAT, EXACT*, and *REPLACE* (p. E6-389).

SLO 6.7 Use multiple criteria in *SUMIFS, AVERAGEIFS*, and *COUNTIFS* functions (p. E6-396).

SLO 6.8 Monitor and edit functions with the *Watch Window* and *Find and Replace* (p. E6-399).

CASE STUDY

In the Pause & Practice projects in this chapter, you work on revenue, inventory and forecasting, financial planning, and human resources worksheets for Paradise Lakes Resort (PLR) using Excel functions.

Pause & Practice 6-1: Use *Database* and *Logical* functions.

Pause & Practice 6-2: Work with date and time calculations and *Lookup & Reference* functions.

Pause & Practice 6-3: Build *Financial* and *Text* functions.

Pause & Practice 6-4: Use multiple criteria, the *Watch Window*, and *Find and Replace*.

EXCEL

Working with Database Functions

A ***database function*** performs a mathematical or statistical calculation for data that meet criteria. In a worksheet with revenue numbers for Paradise Lakes Resort, for example, use a database function to total results only for Cass Lake.

Database Function Syntax

The term ***database*** refers to a range of cells that includes a header row and rows of data, like a list or a table. Each row in a database is a ***record*** and includes the same information for each entity. A column is a ***field***.

Database functions use the following syntax:

FunctionName(database, field, criteria)

The first argument, *database*, is the range of cells to be analyzed which can be a named range or cell addresses. In Figure 6-1, the *database* argument is the named range *List*.

> **MORE INFO**
>
> Press **F3 (FN+F3)** to paste a range name as an argument.

The *field* argument refers to the column used for the calculation. Type the label or the position number of the column in the list. The first column is 1, the second is 2, and so on.

The third argument is *criteria*, a cell range on the same or another sheet where you type specifications. The *criteria* argument includes labels in one row and conditions in the row below. In Figure 6-1, the criteria range is cells B2:B3. Labels in the range must be spelled exactly like those in the database. In Figure 6-1, the *DMAX* function in cell D21 calculates the highest value in the "Goal" column for cells that show "Cass Lake" in the "Location" column.

You can specify *AND* criteria in the same row, build *OR* criteria in separate rows, and use wildcard characters in the criteria.

Table 6.1 explains popular *Database* functions.

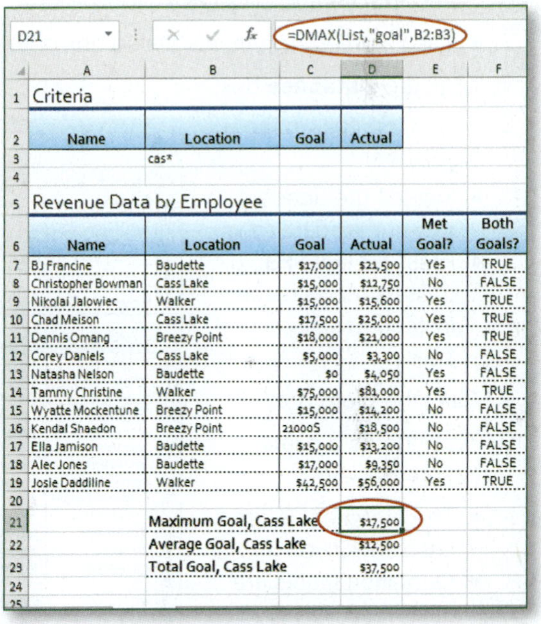

Figure 6-1 ***DMAX*** **function for tabular data**

Table 6-1: Database Functions

Function Name	Explanation
DAVERAGE	Averages the values of cells in the field (column) that meet the criteria
DCOUNT	Counts cells with values in the field (column) that meet the criteria
DCOUNTA	Counts cells in the field (column) that are not empty that meet the criteria

Function Name	Explanation
DMAX	Displays the largest value in the field (column) that meets the criteria
DMIN	Displays the smallest value in the field (column) that meets the criteria
DSUM	Sums the values of cells in the field (column) that meet the criteria

The *Database* function category is listed in the *Insert Function* dialog box. If you type = and a few characters of the function name, you can also choose the function from the *Formula AutoComplete* list.

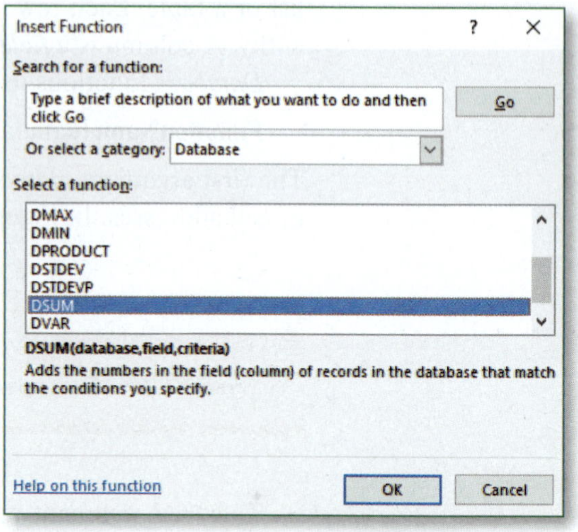

Figure 6-2 *Insert Function* dialog box and the *Database* category

HOW TO: Build a DSUM Function

1. Copy the labels that are used to specify criteria.
2. Enter criteria below the label in the criteria range.
3. Click the cell for *DSUM* results.
4. Click the **Insert Function** button [*Formulas* tab, *Function Library* group].
5. Choose **Database** in the *Or select a category* list (Figure 6-2).
   - Click a function name in the list to display its description and syntax.
6. Select **DSUM** and click **OK**.
   - The *Function Arguments* dialog box opens.
7. Click the **Database** box.
8. Select the cells in the worksheet.
   - Include the header row and all data rows.
   - Press **F3** (**FN+F3**) to paste a range name instead of selecting cells.
9. Click the **Field** box.
10. Type the field name (column label).
    - The argument is not case sensitive.
    - Quotation marks are automatically supplied when you use the *Function Arguments* dialog box.
    - Type a number to indicate the column's position in the database instead of typing the label.
11. Click the **Criteria** box.
12. Select the criteria range (Figure 6-3).
    - The criteria range can be located on a different worksheet.
    - Key the range address if you prefer.
13. Click **OK** or press **Enter** to close the dialog box.
    - Results appear in the cell.

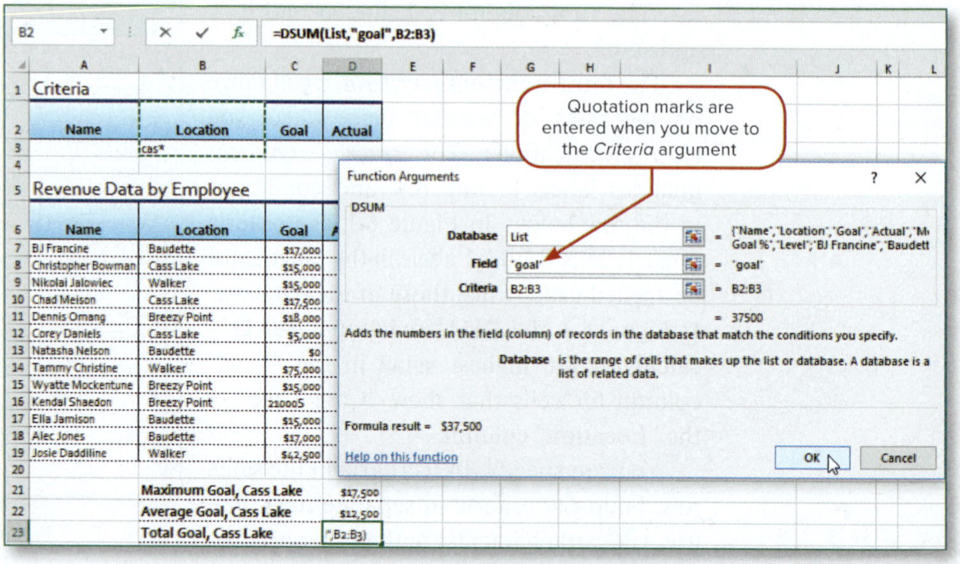

Figure 6-3 *Function Arguments* dialog box for *DSUM*

SLO 6.2

Building Logical Functions

Functions in the *Logical* group determine if one or all conditions are met and display TRUE or FALSE as the result. The *IFS* function displays TRUE or FALSE, text, or calculated results.

The AND Function

The *AND* function defines multiple conditions that must be met for a TRUE result. Paradise Lakes Resort uses an *AND* function to determine if an employee met an individual sales goal and a department goal.

The syntax for an *AND* function is:

= AND(LogicalN)

An *AND* function has one argument named *LogicalN*. *N* is a number; arguments are named *Logical1*, *Logical2*, *Logical3*, up to *Logical255*. In each *LogicalN* argument, build a simple statement. An argument such as *D7<C7* means that the value in cell D7 must be less than the value in cell C7 for the result to be TRUE. If you build five *LogicalN* arguments, every statement must be true for the result to display TRUE. If one of those five statements is not true, the result in the cell is FALSE.

> **MORE INFO**
>
> *AND* functions with many arguments are restrictive or limiting.

HOW TO: Build an AND Function

1. Click the cell for the result.
2. Click the **Logical** button [*Formulas* tab, *Function Library* group].
3. Choose **AND**.
    - Two *LogicalN* argument boxes display in the dialog box.
    - Additional arguments become available as you complete the previous argument.
4. Click the **Logical1** box.
5. Build the first statement to be evaluated.
    - Type the statement.
    - Select cells in the worksheet or use range names.
    - If the statement includes text, enclose the text in quotation marks.
6. Click the **Logical2** box.
    - A third argument box opens.
7. Build the second statement to be evaluated (Figure 6-4).
8. Build additional *LogicalN* arguments as needed.
9. Click **OK** or press **Enter**.
    - If all statements are true, the word TRUE appears in the cell.
    - If one of the statements is false, the word FALSE displays in the cell.

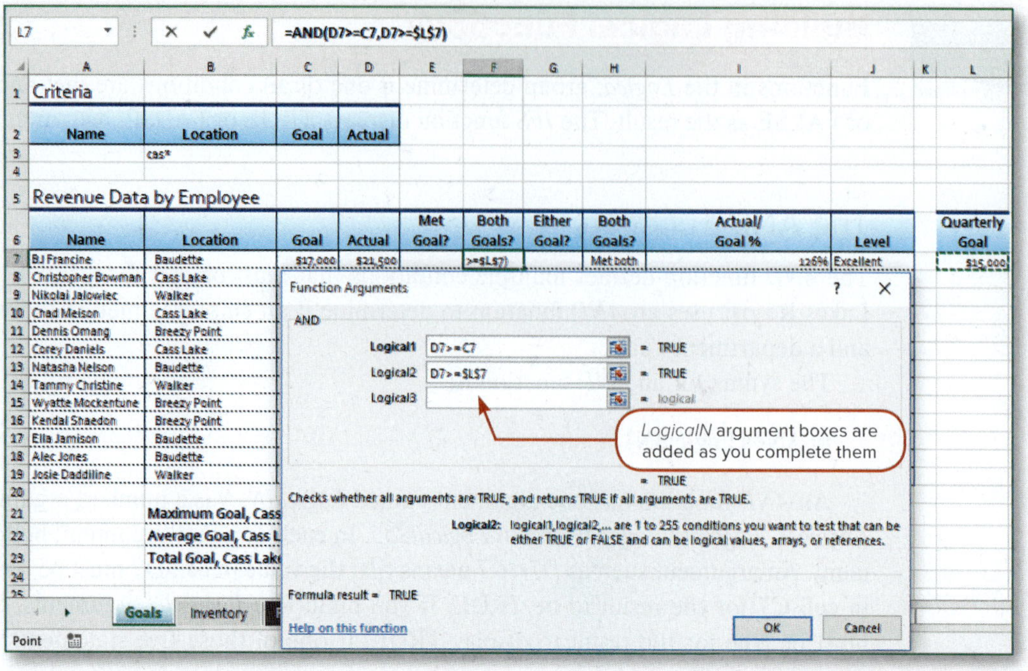

Figure 6-4 *AND* function in the *Function Arguments* dialog box

The OR Function

An *OR* function is less restrictive than an *AND* statement. In an *OR* function, if one of the arguments is true, the result is TRUE. All arguments must be false for FALSE to display as the result. An *OR* function has up to 255 *LogicalN* arguments.

The syntax for an *OR* function is:

= OR(LogicalN)

> **MORE INFO**
>
> Use absolute or relative cell references in *AND* or *OR* functions as required if the formula will be copied.

HOW TO: Type an OR Function

1. Click the cell for the result.
2. Type =or and press **Tab**.
   - **=OR(** displays in the cell.
   - The first argument *logical1* is bold in the *ScreenTip*.
3. Build the first statement to be evaluated.
   - Type the statement or select cells.
   - Press **F3 (FN+F3)** to paste a range name.
   - If the statement includes text, enclose the text in quotation marks.
4. Type a comma , to separate the arguments.
   - The next argument *logical2* appears bold in the *ScreenTip*.

5. Build the second statement to be evaluated (Figure 6-5).

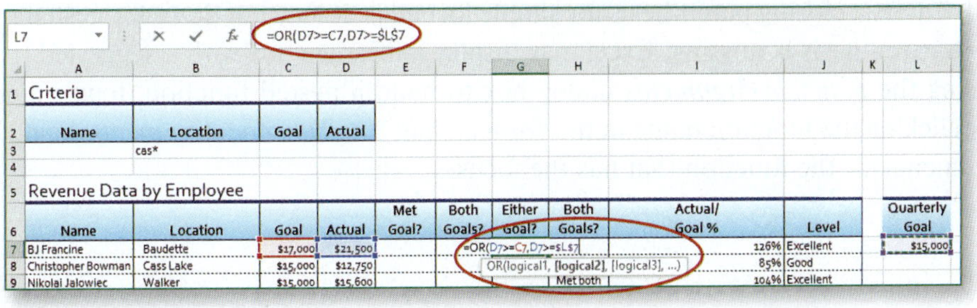

Figure 6-5 *OR* function with two arguments

6. Type a comma **,** to add another *logicalN* argument.
7. Press **Enter** when all arguments are typed.
   - If one statement is true, the word TRUE displays in the cell.
   - If no statement is true, the word FALSE appears in the cell.

The IF Function with AND and OR

A ***nested function*** is a function within a function. Logical functions are commonly nested. For example, use *AND* and *OR* with an *IF* function to build a statement that specifies multiple requirements. The *Value_if_true* and *Value_if_false* arguments in the *IF* function determine and display the results.

Table 6.2 illustrates examples of nesting *AND* or *OR* within an *IF* function in cell D4.

Table 6-2: Sample Nested Functions

Function	Arguments	Explanation
=IF(C4>15000, 5000,0)	Logical_test = C4>15000 Value_if_true = 5000 Value_if_false = 0	If the value in cell C4 is greater than 15,000, cell D4 displays 5,000. If the value in cell C4 is less than 15,000, cell D4 displays 0.
=IF(AND(C4>15000,C7>12500), 5000,0)	Logical_test = C4>15000 and C7>12500 Value_if_true = 5000 Value_if_false = 0	If the value in cell C4 is greater than 15,000 **and** if the value in cell C7 is greater than 12,500, cell D4 displays 5,000. If either of these conditions is false, cell D4 displays 0.
=IF(OR(C4>15000,C7>12500), 5000,0)	Logical_test = C4>15000 or C7>12500 Value_if_true = 5000 Value_if_false = 0	If the value in cell C4 is greater than 15,000 **or** if the value in cell C7 is greater than 12,500, cell D4 displays 5,000. Cell D4 displays 0 when the value in cell C4 is equal to or less than 15,000 **and** the value in cell C7 is equal to or less than 12,500.

MORE INFO

Do not type commas as thousand separators in formulas, because Excel mistakes the comma for an argument separator.

In the *Function Arguments* dialog box for a nested function, Excel supplies separators and parentheses. Parentheses are color-coded to help you follow formula syntax. Although Excel automatically enters a closing parenthesis for simple formulas, it may not do so for nested functions. When a parenthesis is missing, Excel may display a message box with a suggested fix.

When using the *Function Arguments* dialog box to build a nested function, toggle among functions by clicking the function name in the *Formula* bar. The *Function Arguments* dialog box displays arguments for the function that has the focus.

MORE INFO

Always use opening and closing parentheses in pairs.

HOW TO: Nest AND and IF Functions

1. Click the cell for the result.
2. Type =if(to display the *ScreenTip*.
   - The *logical_test* argument appears bold.
   - The *logical_test* argument is the *AND* function.
3. Type and and press **Tab**.
   - The *ScreenTip* displays arguments for the *AND* function.
4. Type the first *logicalN* statement and type a comma , (Figure 6-6).

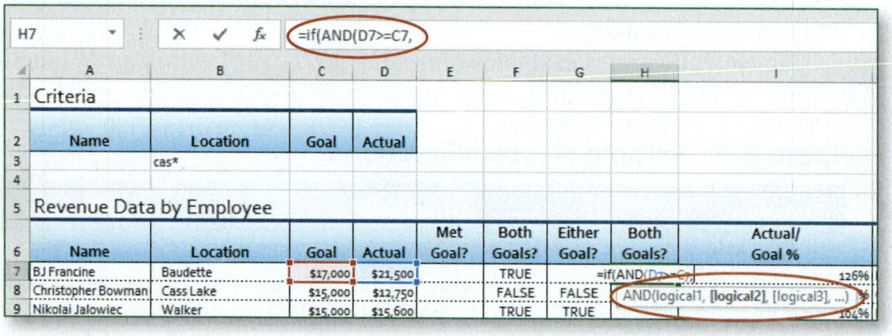

Figure 6-6 *AND* function is *logical_test* argument

   - Select a worksheet cell rather than type the reference.
   - Use absolute or relative references as required.
5. Enter each *logicalN* argument followed by a comma.
6. Type the closing parenthesis and a comma), after the last argument for the *AND* function (Figure 6-7).
   - The focus returns to the *IF* function.

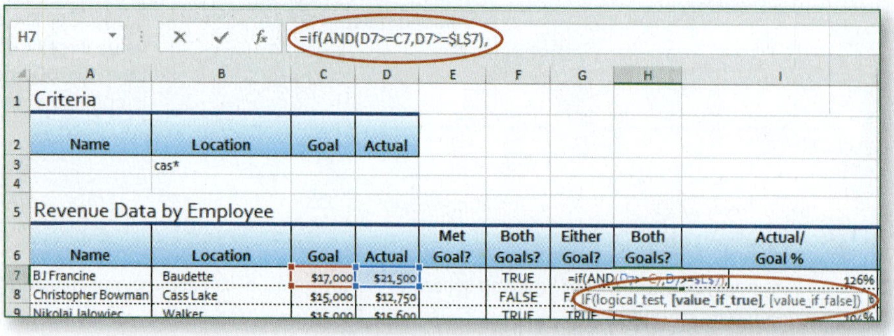

Figure 6-7 Closing parenthesis returns focus to *IF* function

7. Enter the *value_if_true* argument.
   - If the argument is text, enclose it in quotation marks.
   - Select a cell or type its address with absolute or relative references as required.
8. Type a comma , to move to the *value_if_false* argument.
9. Enter the *value_if_false* argument.
10. Type the closing parenthesis) (Figure 6-8).

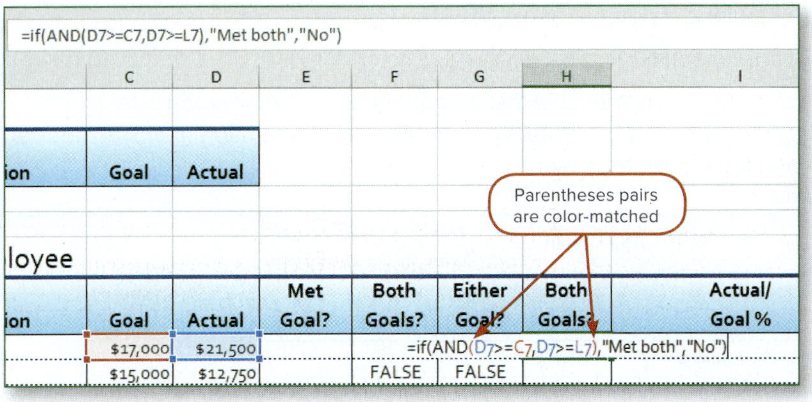

Figure 6-8 ***AND*** **function nested within** ***IF***

11. Press **Enter**.

The IFS Function

An *IFS* function has one or more logical tests with corresponding results for each test. The result that displays in the cell represents the first logical test that evaluates to TRUE. Here is an *IFS* function to display a letter grade:

=IFS(D2>=92,"A",D2>=84,"B",D2>=76,"C",D2<76,"D")

If you receive 92 or more points, the first logical test is TRUE, you receive an A grade, and the *IFS* function ends. When that is not true, the next logical test runs to determine if your score is 84 or higher (but not 92 points or higher). When that is true, the *IFS* function ends, and the result cell displays a B. The third logical test uses 76 points or higher (but not 84 points or higher), and the last test uses fewer than 76 points.

The syntax for an *IFS* function is:

=IFS(logical_test1, value_if_true1, [logical_test2, value_if_true2], ...)

Each *logical_testN* argument must have a *value_if_trueN* argument with up to 127 logical tests.

IFS functions are usually built from high value to low value.

MORE INFO

In earlier versions of Excel, a nested *IF* formula checked multiple logical tests. In a nested *IF* formula, the number of outcomes minus 1 is the number of logical tests required.

▸ HOW TO: Create an IFS Function

1. Click the cell for the *IFS* function.
2. Click the **Logical** button [*Formulas* tab, *Function Library* group].
3. Choose **IFS** to open the *Function Arguments* dialog box.
4. Enter the *Logical_test1* argument.
   - Click a cell or type its address.
   - Use an operator to build a statement or expression.
5. Enter the *Value_if_true1* result (Figure 6-9).
   - If the *Logical_test1* argument is true, this result appears and no more logical tests run.
   - The *Function Arguments* dialog box enters parentheses and quotation marks as needed.
   - Use uppercase and lowercase as preferred for results.

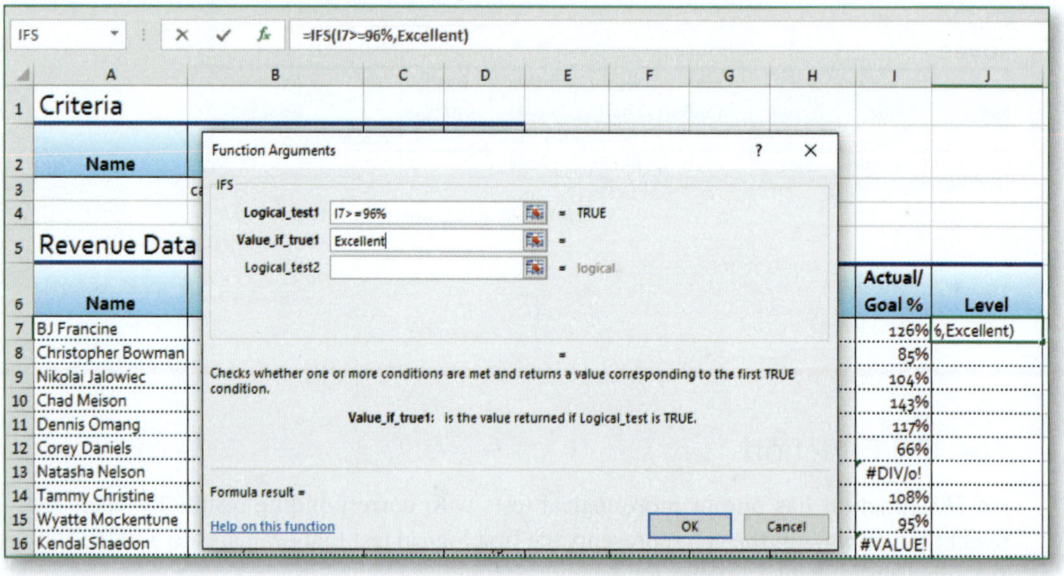

Figure 6-9 First logical test in an *IFS* formula

6. Enter the *Logical_test2* argument.
   - If the *Logical_test1* argument is false, the second test runs.
7. Enter the *Value_if_true2* result.
   - If the *Logical_test2* argument is true, this result appears and the function ends.
8. Enter *Logical_testN* arguments as needed.
9. Enter *Value_if_trueN* results for each *Logical_testN* argument (Figure 6-10).
10. Click **OK**.
    - The *Value_if_true* argument for the first *Logical_test* that is TRUE displays in the cell.

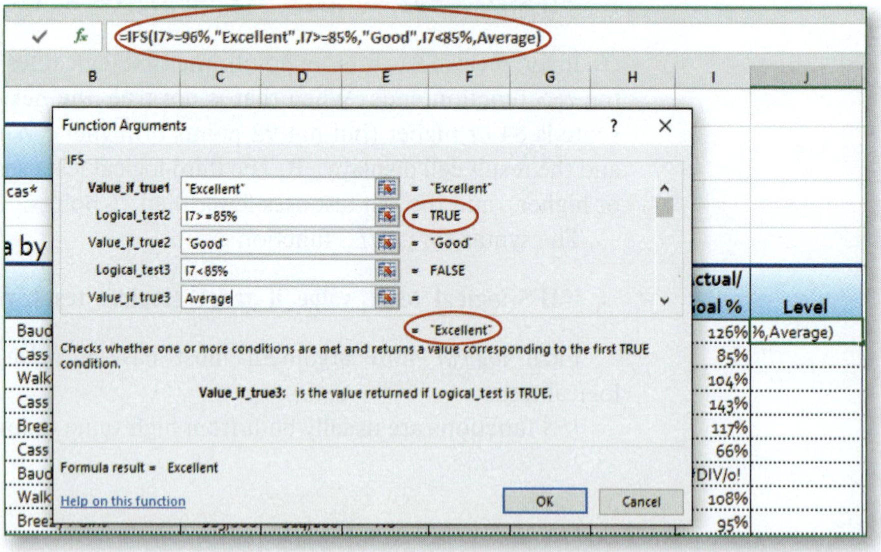

Figure 6-10 Three logical tests and results for an *IFS* formula

The SWITCH Function

The *SWITCH* function compares a value to a list and displays the result for the first match in the list. It "switches" a value to a result. The syntax for a *SWITCH* function is:

=SWITCH(expression, value1, result1, [default_or_value2, result2,]...)

The *expression* is the value, cell reference, or formula that is replaced or switched. The *value* and *result* arguments form a comparison list and corresponding results. The *expression* can be matched against 127 pairs of *values* and *results*. In Figure 6-11, the *SWITCH* function is:

=SWITCH(B3,"bd","Baudette","bp","Breezy Point","cl","Cass Lake","wk","Walker", "No Match")

It displays "Baudette" when the value in column B is "BD," "Breezy Point" when the value is "BP," "Cass Lake," when the value is "CL," and "Walker" when the value is "WK." When the value in column B is anything else, the *SWITCH* function displays "No Match."

MORE INFO

An *IFS* function to display the same results requires that the reference to cell B3 be repeated for each *logical_test*.

Although the *SWITCH* function can have 127 pairs of values and results, it is best to use the function with fewer than eight pairs.

ANOTHER WAY

Use cell references instead of typing *value* and *result* arguments in a *SWITCH* function.

HOW TO: Create a SWITCH Function

1. Click the cell for the *SWITCH* function.
2. Click the **Logical** button [*Formulas* tab, *Function Library* group].
3. Choose **SWITCH** to open the *Function Arguments* dialog box.
4. Enter the *Expression* argument.
   - Click a cell or type the cell address of the value to be changed.
   - Use an operator to build a statement or expression.
5. Enter the *Value1* argument.
   - Each *ValueN* argument is an expression to be matched with a result.
6. Press **Tab** to move to the *Result1* argument.
   - The *Result1* argument displays when the expression matches the *Value1* argument.
7. Press **Tab** to move to the *Default_or_value2* argument.

8. Enter the *Value2* argument.
   - Each *ValueN* argument is a possible value for the expression.
9. Press **Tab** to move to the *Result2* argument.
   - The *Result2* argument is the replacement when the expression matches the *value2* argument.
10. Complete *Default_or_valueN* arguments as needed (Figure 6-11).
    - Enter an optional *Default_or_valueN* argument without a matching *ResultN* argument for expressions that do not have corresponding results.
11. Click **OK**.

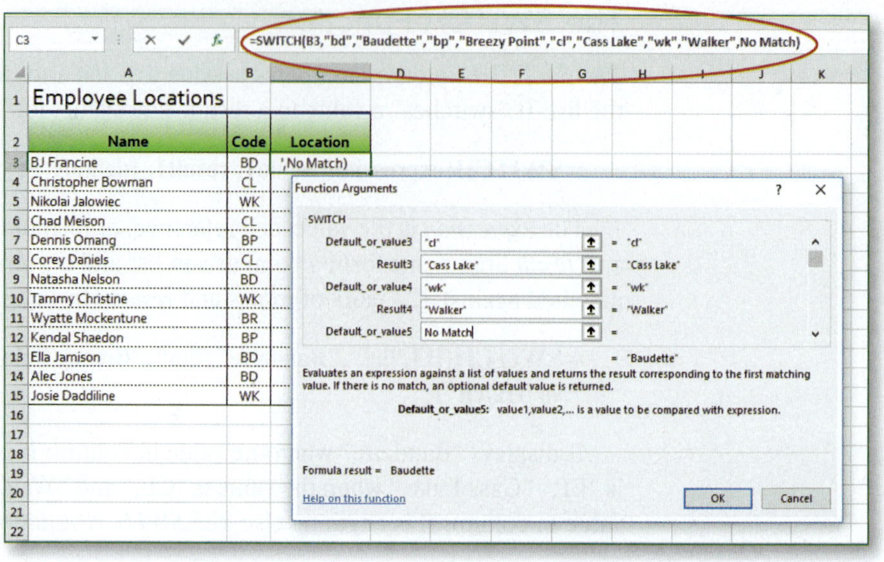

Figure 6-11 ***SWITCH* function and arguments**

The IFERROR Function

A formula syntax error displays an Excel error value message in the cell. Common syntax errors include typing the letter "o" instead of a zero (0) or typing a letter as part of a value as shown in row 16 in Figure 6-12. Excel displays #VALUE! in the formula cell. When you anticipate an error that you or someone else might make, use the *IFERROR* function to display a custom error message such as "Check that all entries are numbers."

5	Revenue Data by Employee									
6	Name	Location	Goal	Actual	Met Goal?	Both Goals?	Either Goal?	Both Goals?	Actual/ Goal %	Level
7	BJ Francine	Baudette	$17,000	$21,500		TRUE	TRUE	Met Both	126%	Excellent
8	Christopher Bowman	Cass Lake	$15,000	$12,750		FALSE	FALSE		85%	Good
9	Nikolai Jalowiec	Walker	$15,000	$15,600		TRUE	TRUE		104%	Excellent
10	Chad Meison	Cass Lake	$17,500	$25,000		TRUE	TRUE		143%	Excellent
11	Dennis Omang	Breezy Point	$18,000	$21,000		TRUE	TRUE		117%	Excellent
12	Corey Daniels	Cass Lake	$5,000	$3,300		FALSE	FALSE		66%	Average
13	Natasha Nelson	Baudette	$0	$4,050		FALSE	TRUE		#DIV/0!	#DIV/0!
14	Tammy Christine	Walker	$75,000	$81,000		TRUE	TRUE		108%	Excellent
15	Wyatte Mockentune	Breezy Point	$15,000	$14,200		FALSE	FALSE		95%	Good
16	Kendal Shaedon	Breezy Point	21000S	$18,500		FALSE	TRUE		#VALUE!	#VALUE!
17	Ella Jamison	Baudette	$15,000	$13,200		FALSE	FALSE		88%	Good
18	Alec Jones	Baudette	$17,000	$9,350		FALSE	FALSE		55%	Average
19	Josie Daddiline	Walker	$42,500	$56,000		TRUE	TRUE		132%	Excellent

Figure 6-12 Standard, default error messages

The *IFERROR* function works only for formulas that can return a standard Excel error value message. When a formula uses incorrect mathematics or the wrong cell address, an error may not be identified or may result in an error triangle, and *IFERROR* is not relevant. Table 6-3 lists error values and descriptions.

Table 6-3: Excel Error Messages

Error Value	Description
#N/A	A value or an argument is missing.
#VALUE!	An incorrect data type is used (for example, a label is used instead of a value).
#REF!	A cell reference is empty, usually because cells were deleted.
#DIV/0!	The formula divides by zero (0) or an empty cell.
#NUM!	The formula uses an invalid numeric entry (for example, it could be a wrong data type or a negative number instead of a required positive value).
#NAME?	The formula uses unrecognized text such as a misspelled function, sheet, or range name.
#NULL!	The formula refers to an intersection of two cell ranges that do not intersect, or uses an incorrect range separator (for example, a semicolon or comma instead of a colon).

An *IFERROR* function has two arguments. The *value* argument is the formula that might display an error message. The *value_if_error* argument is the text that should appear in place of the default Excel error message.

=IFERROR(value, value_if_error)

=IFERROR(A7/A9, "Check the values in column A.")

▶HOW TO: Create an IFERROR Function

1. Click the cell for the result.
   - This is a formula cell that may result in a standard error message.
2. Delete the cell contents if the formula is already entered in the cell.
3. Click the **Logical** button [*Formulas* tab, *Function Library* group].
4. Choose **IFERROR**.
5. Enter the *Value* argument.
   - Key the formula using lowercase letters or select cells in the worksheet.
   - You don't need to key an equals sign when you use the *Function Arguments* dialog box.
6. Enter the *Value_if_error* argument (Figure 6-13).
   - Use uppercase, lowercase, and punctuation as you want it to appear in your message.
   - Quotation marks are supplied when you use the *Function Arguments* dialog box.

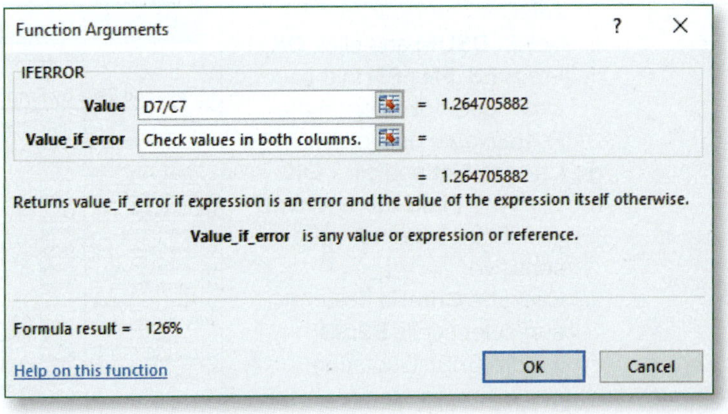

Figure 6-13 *IFERROR* with both arguments complete

7. Click **OK**.
   - The error message appears only when an error would have resulted in a standard error message (Figure 6-14).

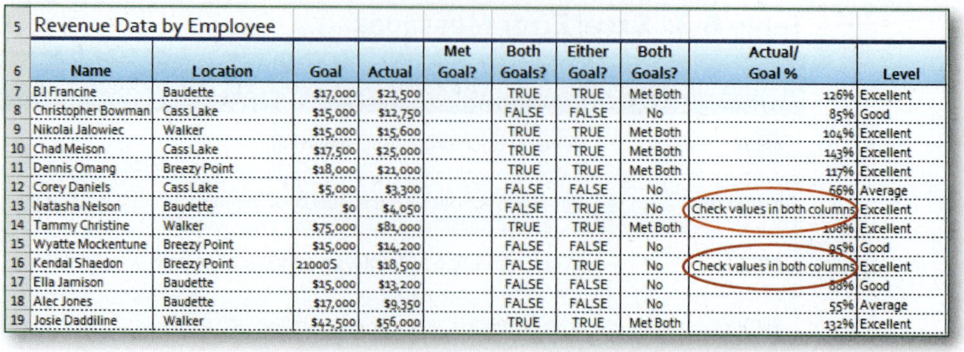

5	Revenue Data by Employee									
6	Name	Location	Goal	Actual	Met Goal?	Both Goals?	Either Goal?	Both Goals?	Actual/ Goal %	Level
7	BJ Francine	Baudette	$17,000	$21,500		TRUE	TRUE	Met Both	126%	Excellent
8	Christopher Bowman	Cass Lake	$15,000	$12,750		FALSE	FALSE	No	85%	Good
9	Nikolai Jalowiec	Walker	$15,000	$15,600		TRUE	TRUE	Met Both	104%	Excellent
10	Chad Meison	Cass Lake	$17,500	$25,000		TRUE	TRUE	Met Both	143%	Excellent
11	Dennis Omang	Breezy Point	$18,000	$21,000		TRUE	TRUE	Met Both	117%	Excellent
12	Corey Daniels	Cass Lake	$5,000	$3,300		FALSE	FALSE	No	66%	Average
13	Natasha Nelson	Baudette	$0	$4,050		FALSE	TRUE	No	Check values in both columns	Excellent
14	Tammy Christine	Walker	$75,000	$81,000		TRUE	TRUE	Met Both	108%	Excellent
15	Wyatte Mockentune	Breezy Point	$15,000	$14,200		FALSE	FALSE	No	95%	Good
16	Kendal Shaedon	Breezy Point	21000S	$18,500		FALSE	TRUE	No	Check values in both columns	Excellent
17	Ella Jamison	Baudette	$15,000	$13,200		FALSE	FALSE	No	88%	Good
18	Alec Jones	Baudette	$17,000	$9,350		FALSE	FALSE	No	55%	Average
19	Josie Daddiline	Walker	$42,500	$56,000		TRUE	TRUE	Met Both	132%	Excellent

Figure 6-14 Custom error message appears in place of Excel default message

PAUSE & PRACTICE: EXCEL 6-1

In this project, you complete calculations for Paradise Lakes Resort using *Database* and *Logical* functions.

File Needed: ***ParadiseLakes-06.xlsx*** *(Student data files are available in the* Library *of your SIMnet account.)*
Completed Project File Name: ***[your initials] PP E6-1.xlsx***

1. Open ***ParadiseLakes-06.xlsx*** from your student data files and save it as [your initials] PP E6-1.
2. Build a *DSUM* function using the *Function Arguments* dialog box.
   a. Click the **Goals** sheet tab and select cell **B3**.
   b. Type cas*. Criteria is not case sensitive, and wildcard characters are acceptable.
   c. Click cell **C23** and click the **Insert Function** button in the *Formula* bar.
   d. Choose **Database** in the *Or select a category* list.
   e. Select **DSUM** and click **OK**.
   f. Press **F3** (**FN+F3**) in the *Database* box to open the *Paste Name* dialog box.
   g. Choose **List** and click **OK**.
   h. Click the **Field** box and type goal. Entries are not case sensitive.
   i. Click the **Criteria** box and select cells **B2:B3** (Figure 6-15). Quotation marks are entered for the *Field* argument.
   j. Click **OK**. The total for Cass Lake is $37,500.

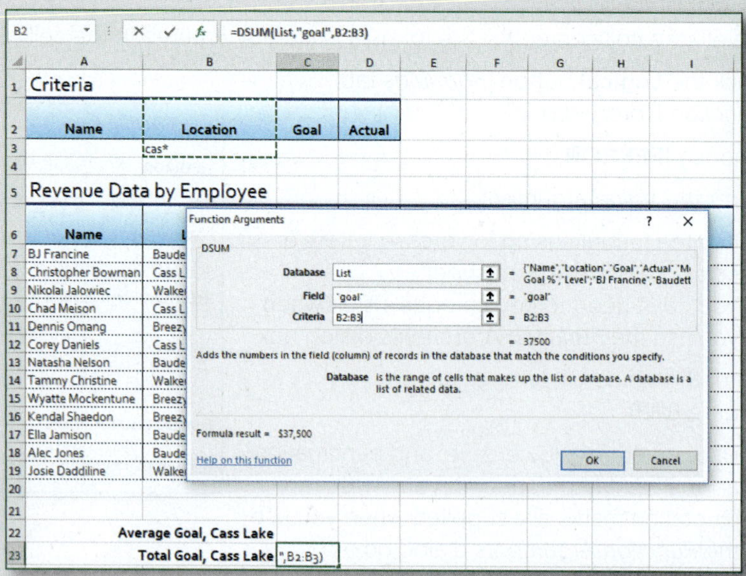

Figure 6-15 *DSUM* and its arguments

3. Type a *DAVERAGE* function.
   a. Click cell **C22**.
   b. Type =dav to display the *Formula AutoComplete* list and press **Tab** to move to the *database* argument.
   c. Type a lowercase L (l) to open *Formula AutoComplete* again.
   d. Double-click **List** (Figure 6-16).

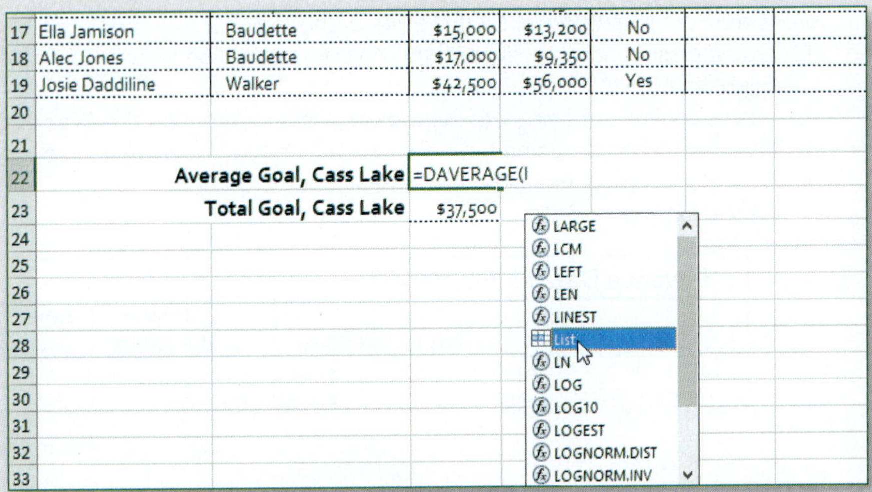

Figure 6-16 ***DAVERAGE*** **and** ***Formula AutoComplete***

   e. Type a comma , to move to the *field* argument.
   f. Type "goal" including the quotation marks.
   g. Type a comma , to move to the *criteria* argument.
   h. Select cells **B2:B3** and press **Enter**. The closing parenthesis is supplied. The average for Cass Lake is $12,500.

4. Type an *OR* function.
   a. Select cell **F7**.
   b. Type =or and press **Tab**.
   c. Type d7>=c7 for the *logical1* argument.
   d. Type a comma , to move to the *logical2* argument.
   e. Type d7>=, select cell **K7**, and press **F4** (**FN+F4**) (Figure 6-17).

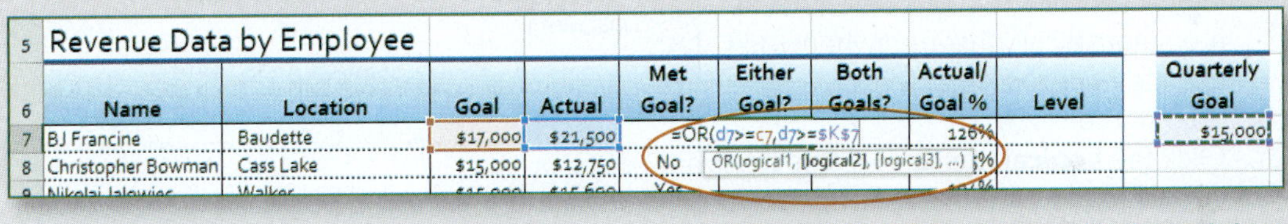

Figure 6-17 ***OR*** **function typed in the worksheet**

   f. Press **Enter**. The result for cell F7 is TRUE.
   g. Copy the formula in cell **F7** to cells **F8:F19**.

5. Nest *AND* and *IF* functions.
   a. Select cell **G7**.
   b. Type =if(an and press **Tab** (Figure 6-18). The focus is on the *AND* formula as is the *ScreenTip*.

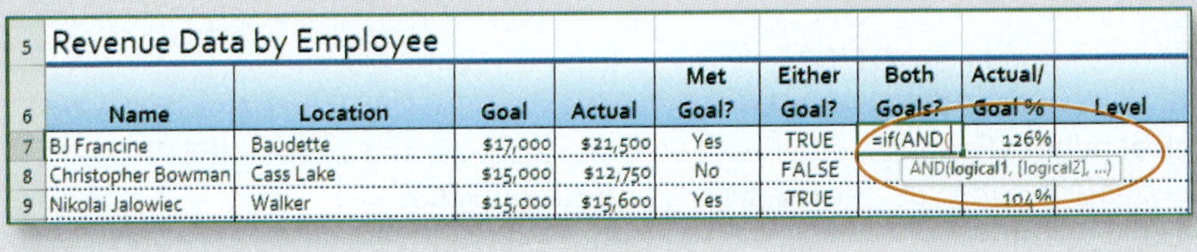

Figure 6-18 ***AND*** **function as logical test for** ***IF*** **function**

   c. Type d7>=c7 for the *logical1* argument.
   d. Type a comma , to move to the *logical2* argument.

e. Type d7>=k7 and press **F4** (**FN+F4**) for the *logical2* argument.
f. Type a closing parenthesis) for the *AND* function. The focus and *ScreenTip* return to the *IF* function.
g. Type a comma , to complete the *logical_test* argument for the *IF* function.
h. Type "Met both" including the quotation marks for the *value_if_true* argument.
i. Type a comma , to move to the *value_if_false* argument.
j. Type "No" (Figure 6-19).

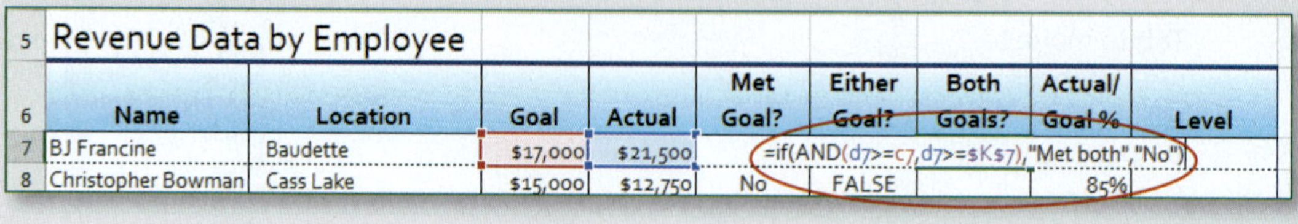

Figure 6-19 Arguments for the *IF* function

k. Type a closing parenthesis) for the *IF* function and press **Enter**.
l. Copy the formula in cell **G7** to cells **G8:G19**.

6. Create an *IFS* function. (Use the nested *IF* function **=IF(H7>=96%,"Excellent", IF(H7>=85%,"Good","Average"))** if your version of Excel does not include *IFS*.)
   a. Select cell **I7**, click the **Logical** button [*Formulas* tab, *Function Library* group], and choose **IFS**.
   b. Select cell **H7** and type >=96% in the *Logical_test1* box.
   c. Click the **Value_if_true1** box and type Excellent. If the percentage in cell H7 is 96% or higher, the formula displays *Excellent* and no additional logical tests are run.
   d. Click the **Logical_test2** box, select cell **H7**, and type >=85%.
   e. Click the **Value_if_true2** box and type Good. If the percentage in cell H7 is 85% or higher up to 96%, the formula displays *Good* and no more logical tests are run. Quotation marks are automatically inserted when you use the *Function Arguments* dialog box (Figure 6-20).
   f. Click the **Logical_test3** box, select cell **H7**, and type <85%.
   g. Click the **Value_if_true3** box and type Average. If the percentage in cell H7 is less than 85%, the formula displays *Average*.
   h. Click **OK**.
   i. Increase the indent one time for cell **I7**.
   j. Copy the formula in cell **I7** to cells **I8:I19**. (Figure 6-21).

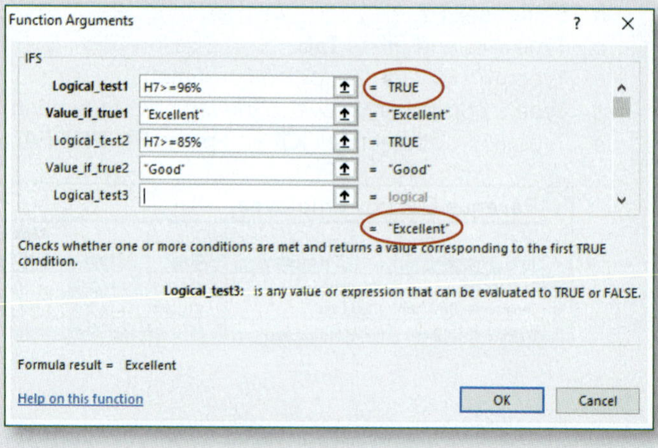

Figure 6-20 First *Logical_test* returns TRUE so result is "Excellent"

7. Create an *IFERROR* function.
   a. Select cell **H7**. The formula is **=D7/C7**.
   b. Delete the contents of cell **H7**.
   c. Click the **Logical** button [*Formulas* tab, *Function Library* group] and choose **IFERROR**.
   d. In the *Value* argument box, click cell **D7**, type /, and click cell **C7**.
   e. Click the **Value_if_error** box.
   f. Type Verify all values. including the period. If the formula results in an error, your message displays instead of a standard error value message.
   g. Click **OK**.
   h. Copy the formula in cell **H7** to cells **H8:H19**.

4									
5	Revenue Data by Employee								
6	Name	Location	Goal	Actual	Met Goal?	Either Goal?	Both Goals?	Actual/ Goal %	Level
7	BJ Francine	Baudette	$17,000	$21,500	Yes	TRUE	Met both	126%	Excellent
8	Christopher Bowman	Cass Lake	$15,000	$12,750	No	FALSE	No	85%	Good
9	Nikolai Jalowiec	Walker	$15,000	$15,600	Yes	TRUE	Met both	104%	Excellent
10	Chad Meison	Cass Lake	$17,500	$25,000	Yes	TRUE	Met both	143%	Excellent
11	Dennis Omang	Breezy Point	$18,000	$21,000	Yes	TRUE	Met both	117%	Excellent
12	Corey Daniels	Cass Lake	$5,000	$3,300	No	FALSE	No	66%	Average
13	Natasha Nelson	Baudette	$0	$4,050	Yes	TRUE	No	#DIV/0!	#DIV/0!
14	Tammy Christine	Walker	$75,000	$81,000	Yes	TRUE	Met both	108%	Excellent
15	Wyatte Mockentune	Breezy Point	$15,000	$14,200	No	FALSE	No	95%	Good
16	Kendal Shaedon	Breezy Point	21000S	$18,500	No	TRUE	No	#VALUE!	#VALUE!
17	Ella Jamison	Baudette	$15,000	$13,200	No	FALSE	No	88%	Good
18	Alec Jones	Baudette	$17,000	$9,350	No	FALSE	No	55%	Average
19	Josie Daddiline	Walker	$42,500	$56,000	Yes	TRUE	Met both	132%	Excellent

Figure 6-21 *IFS* **function results in "Level" column**

i. *AutoFit* column **H** (Figure 6-22).

	A	B	C	D	E	F	G	H	I	J	K
1	Criteria										
2	Name	Location	Goal	Actual							
3		cas*									
4											
5	Revenue Data by Employee										
6	Name	Location	Goal	Actual	Met Goal?	Either Goal?	Both Goals?	Actual/ Goal %	Level		Quarterly Goal
7	BJ Francine	Baudette	$17,000	$21,500	Yes	TRUE	Met both	126%	Excellent		$15,000
8	Christopher Bowman	Cass Lake	$15,000	$12,750	No	FALSE	No	85%	Good		
9	Nikolai Jalowiec	Walker	$15,000	$15,600	Yes	TRUE	Met both	104%	Excellent		
10	Chad Meison	Cass Lake	$17,500	$25,000	Yes	TRUE	Met both	143%	Excellent		
11	Dennis Omang	Breezy Point	$18,000	$21,000	Yes	TRUE	Met both	117%	Excellent		
12	Corey Daniels	Cass Lake	$5,000	$3,300	No	FALSE	No	66%	Average		
13	Natasha Nelson	Baudette	$0	$4,050	Yes	TRUE	No	Verify all values.	Excellent		
14	Tammy Christine	Walker	$75,000	$81,000	Yes	TRUE	Met both	108%	Excellent		
15	Wyatte Mockentune	Breezy Point	$15,000	$14,200	No	FALSE	No	95%	Good		
16	Kendal Shaedon	Breezy Point	21000S	$18,500	No	TRUE	No	Verify all values.	Excellent		
17	Ella Jamison	Baudette	$15,000	$13,200	No	FALSE	No	88%	Good		
18	Alec Jones	Baudette	$17,000	$9,350	No	FALSE	No	55%	Average		
19	Josie Daddiline	Walker	$42,500	$56,000	Yes	TRUE	Met both	132%	Excellent		
20											
21											
22		Average Goal, Cass Lake	$12,500								
23		Total Goal, Cass Lake	$37,500								
24											

Figure 6-22 Completed ***Goals*** **worksheet**

j. Press **Ctrl+Home**.

8. Create a *SWITCH* function. (Use the nested *IF* function **=IF(B3="bd","Baudette",IF(B3="cl","Cass Lake",IF(B3="bp","Breezy Point",IF(B3="wk","Walker","No Match"))))** if your version of Excel does not include *SWITCH*.)
   a. Click the **Locations** sheet tab and select cell **C3**.
   b. Click the **Logical** button [*Formulas* tab, *Function Library* group] and choose **SWITCH**.
   c. Click cell **B3** for the *Expression* argument.
   d. Click the **Value1** box and type bd.
   e. Click the **Result1** box and type Baudette. If cell B3 displays "BD", "Baudette" displays in cell C3.
   f. Click the **Default_or_value2** box and type bp (Figure 6-23).

g. Click the **Result2** box and type Breezy Point.
h. Complete the arguments as shown here:

Default_or_value3	cl
Result3	Cass Lake
Default_or_value4	wk
Result4	Walker
Default_or_value5	No Match

i. Click **OK** when the arguments are complete.
j. Copy the formula in cell **C3** to cells **C4:C15**.
k. Format cell **C15** with a solid bottom border (Figure 6-24).

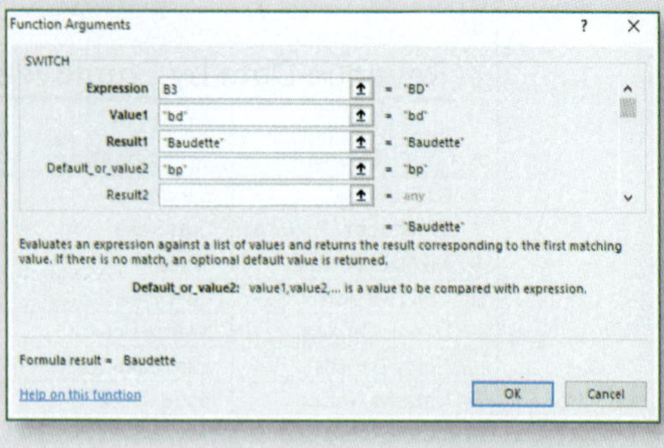

Figure 6-23 *SWITCH* function

9. Save and close the workbook.

	A	B	C
1	Employee Locations		
2	Name	Code	Location
3	BJ Francine	BD	Baudette
4	Christopher Bowman	CL	Cass Lake
5	Nikolai Jalowiec	WK	Walker
6	Chad Meison	CL	Cass Lake
7	Dennis Omang	BP	Breezy Point
8	Corey Daniels	CL	Cass Lake
9	Natasha Nelson	BD	Baudette
10	Tammy Christine	WK	Walker
11	Wyatte Mockentune	BR	No Match
12	Kendal Shaedon	BP	Breezy Point
13	Ella Jamison	BD	Baudette
14	Alec Jones	BD	Baudette
15	Josie Daddiline	WK	Walker
16			

Figure 6-24 Completed *Locations* worksheet

SLO 6.3

Exploring the Lookup & Reference Category

The functions in the *Lookup & Reference* group are used to find, refer to, or manipulate data. These functions do not perform a calculation; they enable you to work with large datasets that might otherwise be unmanageable.

The INDEX Function

The *INDEX* function displays the contents of the cell at the intersection of a specified column and row. In a large inventory sheet, use *INDEX* to determine the product name in the third row, fourth column, at any given time. The *INDEX* function is rarely used alone and is usually nested with the *MATCH* function.

The *INDEX* function has two arguments lists. The first list is the array form of the function and includes an array or range of cells, the row number, and the column number. The syntax for an INDEX function (array form) is:

=INDEX(array, row_num, column_num)

The *array* argument is a cell range to be searched. Select cells or enter a range name. The *row_num* argument is a row number in the array. The *column_num* argument identifies the column location, counting left to right. When the array consists of one column, a *column_num* argument is not necessary.

The second argument list for *INDEX* is referred to as the reference form, because it has a reference argument to identify multiple cell ranges. The syntax for an INDEX function (reference form) is:

=INDEX(reference, row_num, [column_num], [area_num])

▸HOW TO: Create an INDEX (Array Form) Function

1. Select the cell for the result.
2. Click the **Lookup & Reference** button [*Formulas* tab, *Function Library* group].
3. Choose **INDEX**.
   - The *Select Arguments* dialog box shows two argument lists (Figure 6-25).
4. Select **array, row_num, column_num** and click **OK**.
5. Select the cell range in the worksheet for the *Array* argument.
   - Press **F3** (**FN+F3**) to paste a range name.
6. Click the **Row_num** box and type the row number.
7. Click the **Column_num** box and type the column number (Figure 6-26).
8. Click **OK**.
   - The result displays the contents of the cell identified by the *Row_num* and *Column_num* arguments.

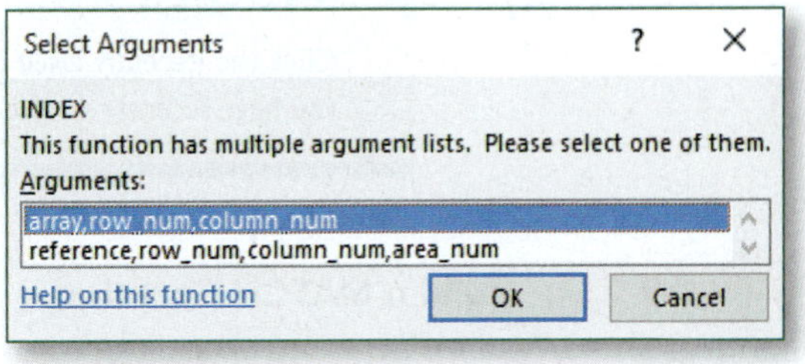

Figure 6-25 ***Select Arguments* dialog box for *INDEX***

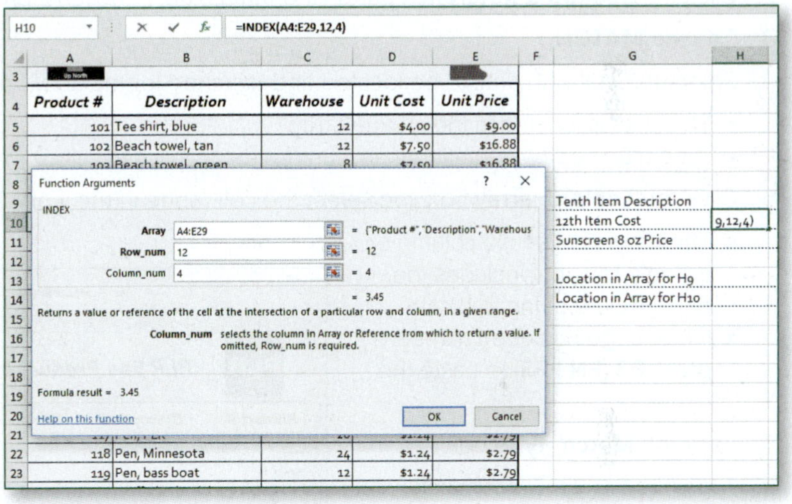

Figure 6-26 ***Function Arguments* dialog box for *INDEX***

The MATCH Function

The *MATCH* function looks for data that matches your specifications and displays the location of the data within a list. It is similar to *VLOOKUP*, but *MATCH* shows a row or column identifier, not the data. The syntax for a *MATCH* function is:

=MATCH(lookup_value, lookup_array, [match_type])

The *lookup_value* argument is the text or value that you want to locate. You can enter a cell address that contains the data or type a label or value. *Lookup_array* is a range, either a single row or a single column. Select the range or use a defined name. These two arguments are required.

The *match_type* argument establishes how the *lookup_value* is compared to values in the *lookup_array*. The *match_type* argument is optional, but use 0 as the *match_type* for an exact match. Table 6-4 explains options for the *match_type* argument.

Table 6-4: Match_Type Arguments

Argument	Result
1 or omitted	The function finds the largest value that is less than or equal to the *lookup_value*. The *lookup_array* must be sorted in ascending order.
0	The function finds the first value that exactly matches the *lookup_value*. The *lookup_array* can be in any order.
−1	The function finds the smallest value that is greater than or equal to the *lookup_value*. The *lookup_array* must be sorted in descending order.

ANOTHER WAY

Click the **Recently Used** button in the *Function Library* group [*Formulas* tab] to choose a function that you have recently selected.

HOW TO: Build a MATCH Function

1. Select the cell for the result.
2. Click the **Lookup & Reference** button [*Formulas* tab, *Function Library* group].
3. Choose **MATCH**.
4. Select the cell with data to be located and matched for the *Lookup_value* argument.
   - This data is located in the lookup array.
   - Type a text entry; quotation marks are entered automatically.
5. Click the **Lookup_array** box and select the cell range in the worksheet.
   - The range is a single column or a single row that includes the data you are trying to locate.
   - If the range has been named, press **F3** (**FN+F3**) to paste the name.
6. Click the **Match_type** box.
7. Type 0 to find an exact match (Figure 6-27).
   - Type 1 or leave the text box empty when the array is sorted in ascending order and you want to find the closest match that is greater than the lookup value.
8. Click **OK**. The relative position of the *lookup_value* in the *lookup_array* displays in the cell.

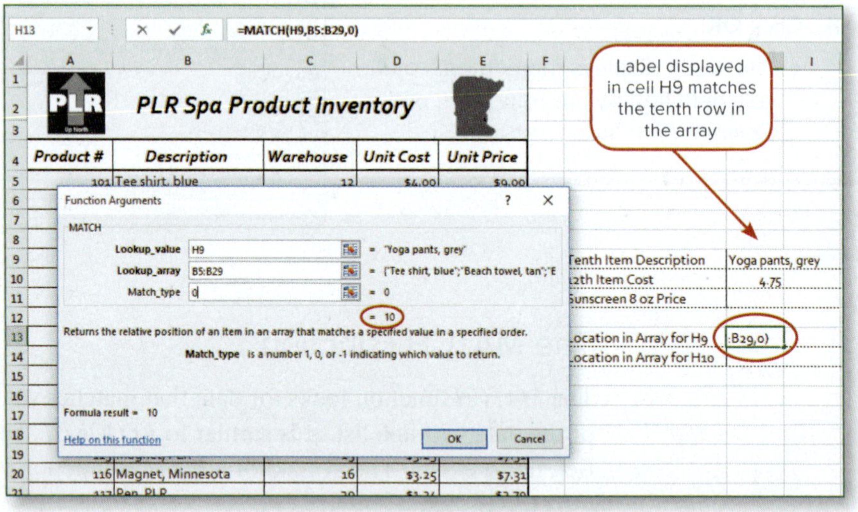

Figure 6-27 ***Function Arguments*** **dialog box for** ***MATCH***

MATCH Nested in INDEX

The *INDEX* and *MATCH* functions, when used together, work quickly on large sets of data. Although you can often accomplish the same task by sorting, filtering, or using a *LOOKUP* function, these methods can take a long time in a worksheet with millions of records.

Below is an *INDEX* function that nests *MATCH* for the *row_num* and *column_num* arguments. The *INDEX array* argument is the named range "Inventory." The *INDEX row_num* argument is a *MATCH* function that finds and exactly matches the data in cell B15 in cells B5:B29. The *INDEX column_num* argument is a second *MATCH* function that finds and matches the data in cell E4 in cells A4:E4.

=INDEX(Inventory,MATCH(B15,B5:B29,0),MATCH(E4,A4:E4,0))

▸HOW TO: Nest MATCH in INDEX

1. Select the cell for the result.
2. Click the **Lookup & Reference** button [*Formulas* tab, *Function Library* group].
3. Choose **INDEX**.
4. Select the first argument list **array, row_num, column_num** and click **OK**.
5. Select the cells in the worksheet for the *Array* argument.
   - This range is the entire list.
   - Press **F3** (**FN+F3**) to paste a range name.
6. Click the **Row_num** box, click the **Name** box arrow, and choose **MATCH**.
   - Click **More Functions** if necessary to find and select **MATCH**.
7. Select the cell with data to be located and matched as the *Lookup_value* argument for *MATCH*.
   - You can type a text entry.
8. Click the **Lookup_array** box and select the cell range in the worksheet.
   - The range is a single column or a single row that includes the *Lookup_value*.
   - If the range has been named, press **F3** (**FN+F3**) to paste the name.
9. Click the **Match_type** box and type 0 (Figure 6-28).
10. Click the name **INDEX** in the *Formula* bar.
    - The *Function Arguments* dialog box presents the *INDEX* function again.
    - Ignore the *Select Arguments* list dialog box if it opens.
11. Click the **Column_num** box, click the **Name** box arrow, and choose **MATCH**.
12. Select the cell with data to be located and matched for the *Lookup_value* argument.
    - You can type a text entry.
13. Click the **Lookup_array** box and select the cell range.
    - The range is the single row or column that includes the *Lookup_value* argument.

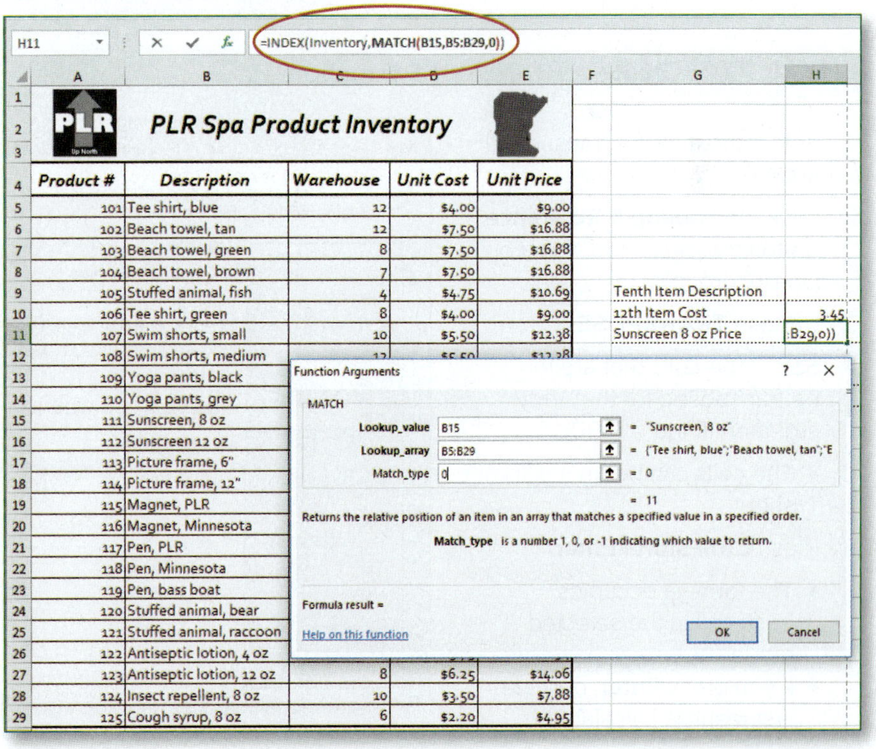

Figure 6-28 Complete arguments for the first nested *MATCH*

14. Click the **Match_type** box and type 0.
15. Click the name **INDEX** in the *Formula* bar and click **OK** (Figure 6-29).

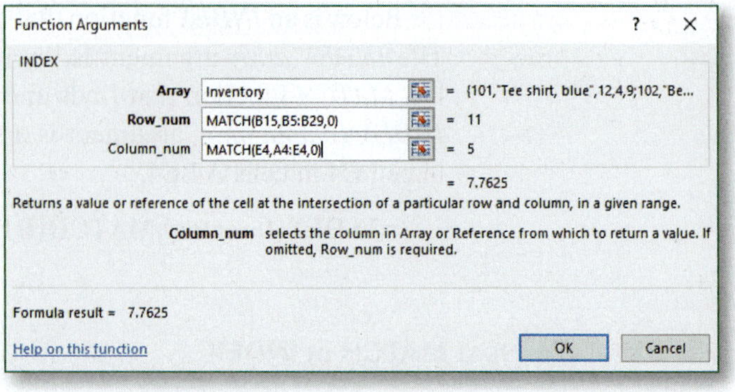

Figure 6-29 *MATCH* nested as *Column_num* argument

The TRANSPOSE Function

The *TRANSPOSE* function displays columnar data in rows and vice versa, and results display in multiple cells. An ***array formula*** is a formula that calculates results across a range of cells. Many Excel functions can be executed as array formulas by pressing **Ctrl+Shift+Enter** as completion keys. These types of formulas are referred to as **CSE** formulas.

An array formula appears in each cell of the results range. The formula includes an equals sign, the name of the function, and the argument in parentheses. The entire function is enclosed in curly braces to indicate that it is an array formula.

{=TRANSPOSE(SheetName!B1:S1)}

The *TRANSPOSE* function has one argument, *array*, which are the cells to be rearranged. To use *TRANSPOSE*, first select the range that will hold the transposed data. If the array occupies 15 columns in a single row, select 15 cells in a column to transpose the data.

> ANOTHER WAY
>
> The *Paste Special* dialog box includes an option to transpose copied data.

HOW TO: Create a TRANSPOSE Function

1. Select the cells for transposed results.
2. Click the **Lookup & Reference** button [*Formulas* tab, *Function Library* group].
3. Choose **TRANSPOSE**.
4. Select the cells that are to be transposed for the *Array* argument (Figure 6-30).
   - The cells can be on a different sheet.
5. Press **Ctrl+Shift+Enter**.
   - The formula occupies each cell in the selected range.
   - If you press **Enter**, only the first result is calculated.

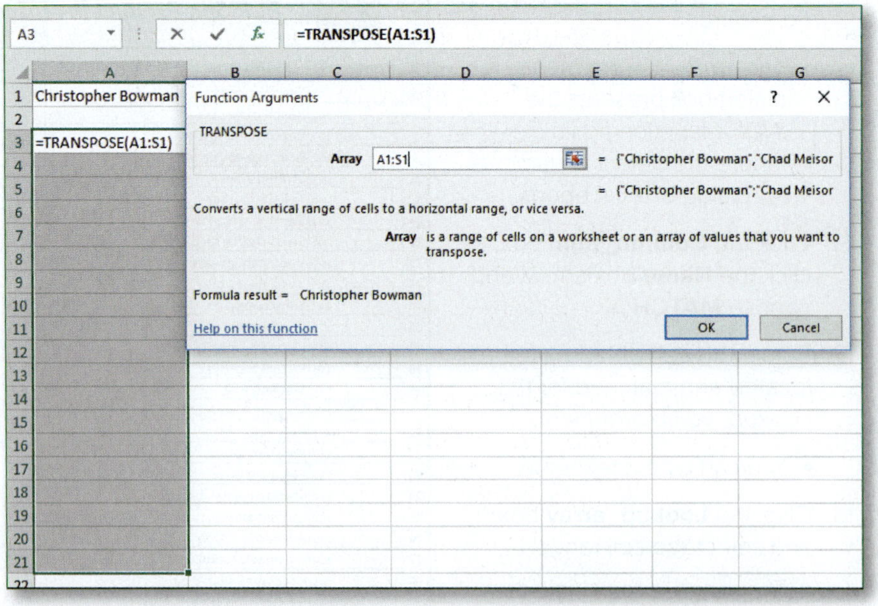

Figure 6-30 *TRANSPOSE* dialog box

SLO 6.4

Building Date, Time, and Statistical Calculations

Date and time calculations enable you to determine arrival dates, to age accounts receivable, or to figure hours worked. If you depend on market research for your work, concepts such as a mean absolute deviation or a standard deviation are important numbers. These types of tasks can be handled by an Excel formula.

Date and Time Formats

For ease in building date and time calculations, you must understand how dates and times are entered, formatted, and recognized. Excel uses serial numbers for dates which set January 1, 1900, as 1; January 2, 1900, as 2; and so on. For years between 1900 and 1929, you must key "19" to identify the twentieth century; otherwise Excel assumes the twenty-first century.

Dates are often entered in *mm/dd/yy* format in the United States. Excel recognizes a date typed in this style and applies the *Short Date* format. Depending on how you key a date, however, the onscreen format might be different because Excel applies the closest format from its list of preset formats.

> **MORE INFO**
>
> International and military dates are often entered in *dd/mm/yy* or *yy/mm/dd* format.

Excel uses a 24-hour day in time calculations but can display results using a 12-hour or a 24-hour clock. If you key 14:30 in a cell, Excel displays 2:30 PM in the *Formula* bar. If you key 1:30, the *Formula* bar shows 1:30 AM.

The *Date*, *Time*, and *Custom* categories in the *Format Cells* dialog box provide preset and special display formats for dates and times. From the *Custom* category, scroll a list of formats, choose one that is close to what you prefer, and edit the codes in the *Type* box. When time or date calculations display unexpected results, always check and reset the format as needed.

HOW TO: Create Custom Date and Time Formats

1. Type the date and press **Enter**.
   - The date is formatted if it is recognized as a date.
2. Select the cell with the date.
3. Click the **Launcher** for the *Number* group [*Home* tab].
4. Choose **Custom** in the *Category* list.
   - Choose **Date** in the list to select a preset format.
5. Scroll the *Type* list and choose a format.
   - The codes for a date are *d*, *y*, and *m* for day, year, and month.
   - The *Sample* box previews the formatted date.
6. Click the **Type** box above the list and edit the format codes as desired (Figure 6-31).
   - You can enter special characters in the *Type* box such as a hyphen or a comma.

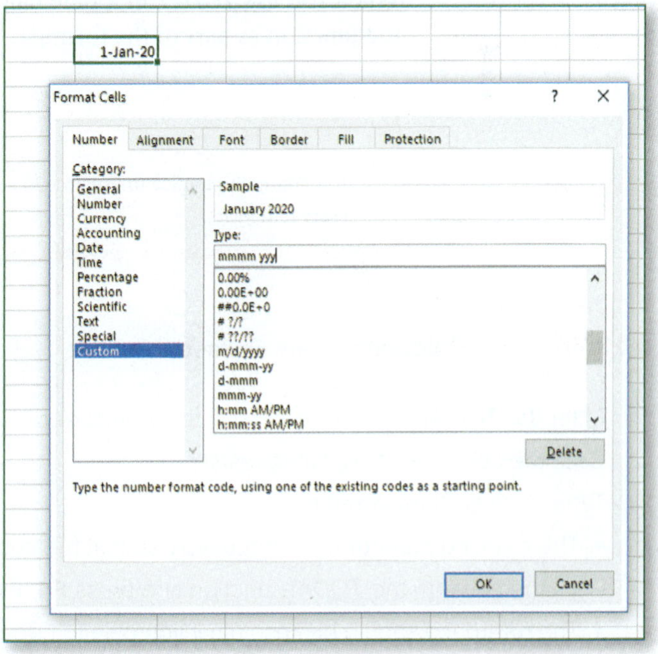

Figure 6-31 Build a custom date format

7. Press **Enter** or click **OK**.
8. Type the time and press **Enter**.
    - Include **AM** or **PM** to use a 12-hour clock.
    - A colon is required for times not on the hour such as 1:30.
9. Select the cell with the time.
10. Click the **Launcher** for the *Number* group [*Home* tab].
11. Choose **Custom** in the *Category* list.
    - Choose **Time** in the list to select a preset format instead.
12. Scroll the *Type* list and choose a format.
    - The *Sample* box previews the formatted time.
13. Click the **Type** box and edit the format codes as desired.
    - The codes for a time are *h*, *m*, and *s* for hour, minute, and second (Figure 6-32).
14. Press **Enter** or click **OK**.

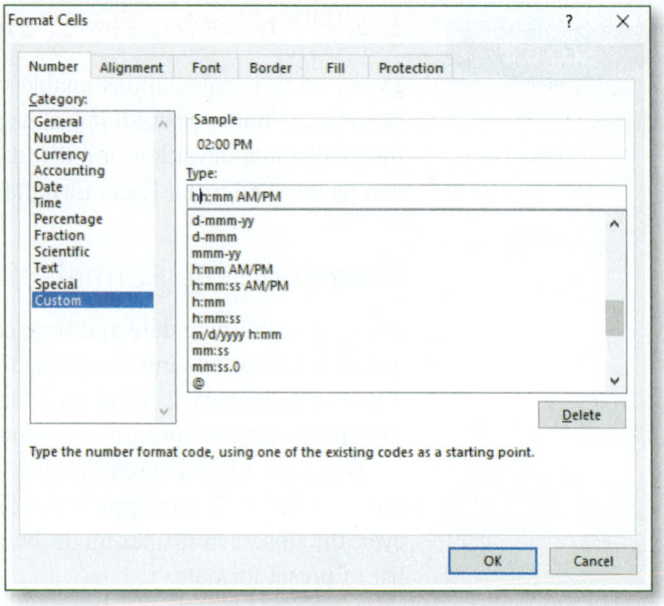

Figure 6-32 Build a custom time format

Date Calculations

Date calculations include determining your age, counting the days until your next holiday, or estimating expiration dates. Formula results calculate the number of days, but you can convert days into years (or months). Be careful about mathematical order of preference in date calculations, because formulas typically include multiple operators.

Many date formulas use the *TODAY* function to calculate how much time has passed. To determine your age, for example, subtract your birth date from *TODAY* and divide by 365.25. When you use *TODAY* in a date calculation, you can refer to a cell with the function or enter the function as part of the formula.

MORE INFO

It is common practice to use 365.25 as the number of days in a year which accounts for a leap year every four years.

HOW TO: Calculate Years Passed

1. Enter the *TODAY* function in a cell in the worksheet.
2. Click the cell for the calculated results.
3. Type =(to start the formula.
    - The opening parenthesis is necessary so that the subtraction is done first.
4. Click the cell with the *TODAY* function and press **F4** (**FN+F4**).
    - The reference should be absolute if you plan to copy the formula.
5. Type – to subtract the next date.

6. Select the cell with the starting date.
 - *TODAY* minus the start date is the subtraction.
 - You can also type the starting date in *mm/dd/yy* format.
7. Type)/ for the closing parenthesis and division.
8. Type 365.25 to convert the result to years (Figure 6-33).
 - Without the division, the result displays the number of days.
9. Press **Enter**.
 - The result displays as many decimals as will fit in the cell.
 - Format the results with decimal places as desired.

D3	▼	:	× ✓ fx	=(F1-C3)/365.25		
◢	A	B	C	D	E	F
1	\multicolumn{3}{l}{PLR Employee Hire Dates}				1/1/2020	
2	First Name	Last Name	Hire Date	Years		
3	BJ	Francine	3/15/2016	=(F1-C3)/365.25		
4	Alec	Jones	9/18/2016			
5	Mikayla	Anderson	7/15/2017			
6	Ella	Jamison	5/11/2017			

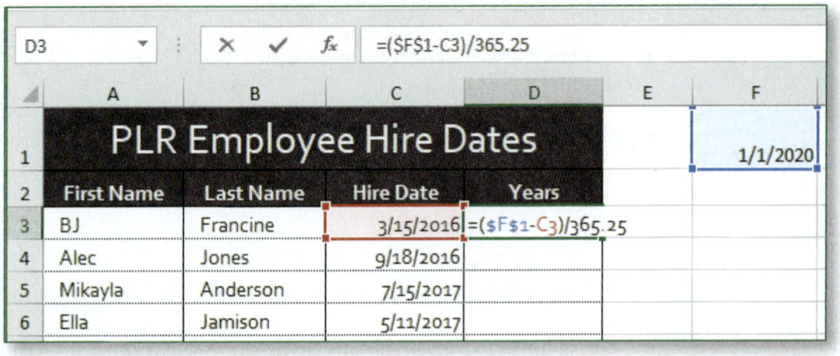

Figure 6-33 Build a date calculation

> **MORE INFO**
>
> The *DATEVALUE* and *TIMEVALUE* functions convert text data into date or time values for use in date/time arithmetic.

Time Calculations

Time calculations include calculating hours worked, upload or delivery times, or processing time. As long as you have a start time and end time, you can determine how many hours have passed. Excel shows time results as a fraction of a 24-hour day. Multiply time results by 24 to convert to hours.

▶**HOW TO:** Calculate Time Passed

1. Click the cell for the result.
2. Type =(to start the formula and enter the opening parenthesis.
 - The parentheses set the subtraction as the first operation.
3. Click the cell with the ending time.
4. Type − to subtract.
5. Select the cell with the beginning time.
6. Type)* for the closing parenthesis and multiplication.
7. Type 24 to convert the result to hours by multiplying by 24 (Figure 6-34).
8. Press **Enter**.
 - The result may be formatted as a time.

◢	A	B	C	D	E	F
1	PLR	\multicolumn{2}{l}{*Fishing Derby*}				
2	First Name	Last Name	Start	First Catch	Hours	
3	Greenfield	Timothy	9:00 AM	10:15 AM	=(D3-C3)*24	
4	Adams	Adeline	9:00 AM	9:35 AM		

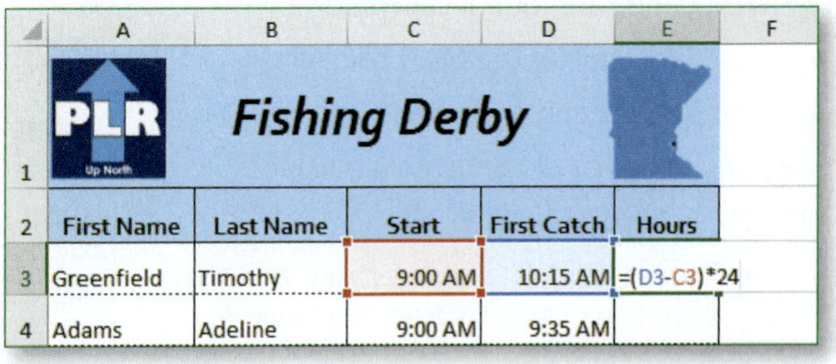

Figure 6-34 Build a time calculation

9. Select the cell and apply the **General** format [*Home* tab, *Number* group, *Number Format* drop-down list].
 - The time passed is shown with as many decimals as will fit in the cell.
 - Format the results with decimal places as desired.

> **MORE INFO**
>
> Convert time displayed in hours into minutes by multiplying by 60 or format time with fractions instead of decimals.

Forecast Errors and MAD Calculations

A ***forecast error*** is the difference between an actual amount and a predicted value, an important analysis tool for business and research. A forecast error is a ***deviation***, a simple subtraction formula. Paradise Lakes Resort compares the number of products sold with predicted sales to manage inventory. A small forecast error or deviation means good inventory procedures while a large error signifies better control is needed.

A popular measure of how spread out a set of values is from the average (the mean) is the ***mean absolute deviation***. Its acronym is ***MAD***, and it is a calculation that uses two Excel functions, *ABS* and *AVERAGE*.

When analyzing deviations, it generally is not important whether the value is positive or negative. The *ABS* function displays the numeric value of a number–the value without any sign, the *absolute* value. A MAD formula calculates the absolute difference for each cell and then averages those values.

HOW TO: Calculate MAD

1. Click the cell for the first absolute result.
2. Type =ab and press **Tab**.
   - The *ScreenTip* shows the *number* argument.
3. Click the cell with the forecasted or planned value.
4. Type – and click the cell with the actual value (Figure 6-35).
5. Press **Enter**.
6. Copy the *ABS* formula as needed.
7. Click the cell for the MAD calculation.
8. Type =aver and press **Tab**.
9. Select the cells with absolute values.
10. Press **Enter** (Figure 6-36).
    - The result is, on average, how far each deviation or error is from the mean of those errors.

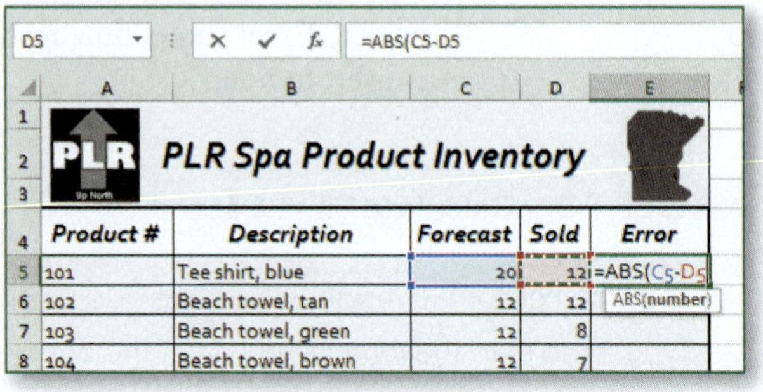

Figure 6-35 ***ABS*** **function and argument**

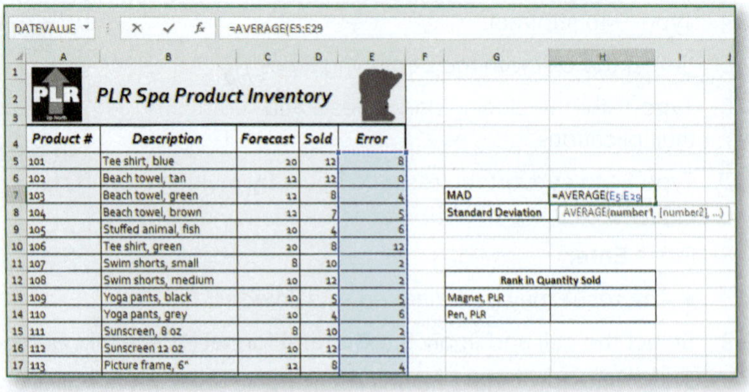

Figure 6-36 Calculate the mean absolute deviation

ANOTHER WAY

The *AVEDEV* function in the *Statistical* category calculates the average deviation of the absolute values in a range.

Standard Deviation

A ***standard deviation*** measures how broadly values differ from the mean or average value in a range of numbers, a popular statistical calculation. The *STDEV.S* function applies to sample populations and ignores text and logical values. A ***sample*** is a subset of a population; a ***population*** is all the data. To calculate the standard deviation for an entire population, use the function ***STDEV.P***.

MORE INFO

The mean square error (MSE) is a popular measure of variability that uses *SUMSQ* and *COUNT* to sum the squares of the values and divide by the number of values in the range.

The syntax for a *STDEV.S* function is:

=STDEV.S(number1,[number2],...)

The required argument is *number1*, the first value or range. When values to be analyzed are not adjacent, use additional *number* arguments to include each cell in the formula.

▶HOW TO: Use the STDEV.S Function

1. Click the cell for the result.
2. Click the **More Functions** button [*Formulas* tab, *Function Library* group] and choose **Statistical**.
3. Find and choose **STDEV.S**.
4. Select the cells to be analyzed for the *Number1* argument (Figure 6-37).
5. Click **OK**.

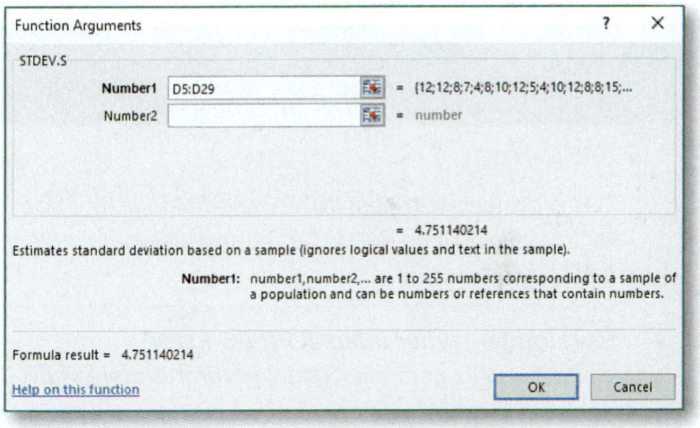

Figure 6-37 ***STDEV.S Function Arguments* dialog box**

The RANK.EQ Function

In a large set of data, use *RANK.EQ* to calculate where a particular value falls relative to all the other values. The syntax for a *RANK.EQ* function is:

=RANK.EQ(number, ref,[order])

The *number* is the cell that you want to rank. *Ref* is the range of values in which the *number* lies. *Order* identifies whether you want the values to be considered in ascending or descending order. Values in descending order place the highest value as rank 1. When duplicate values exist in the range, *RANK.EQ* shows the lower rank.

▶HOW TO: Use the RANK.EQ Function

1. Click the cell for the rank result.
2. Click the **More Functions** button [*Formulas* tab, *Function Library* group] and choose **Statistical**.
3. Find and choose **RANK.EQ**.
4. Click the **Number** box and select the cell to be ranked.
5. Click the **Ref** box and select the cells with related values (Figure 6-38).
   - This is the range in which the cell to be ranked is located.
6. Leave the **Order** box empty to indicate descending order (top rank is 1).
7. Click **OK**.
   - The value's position in relation to the other values is indicated.

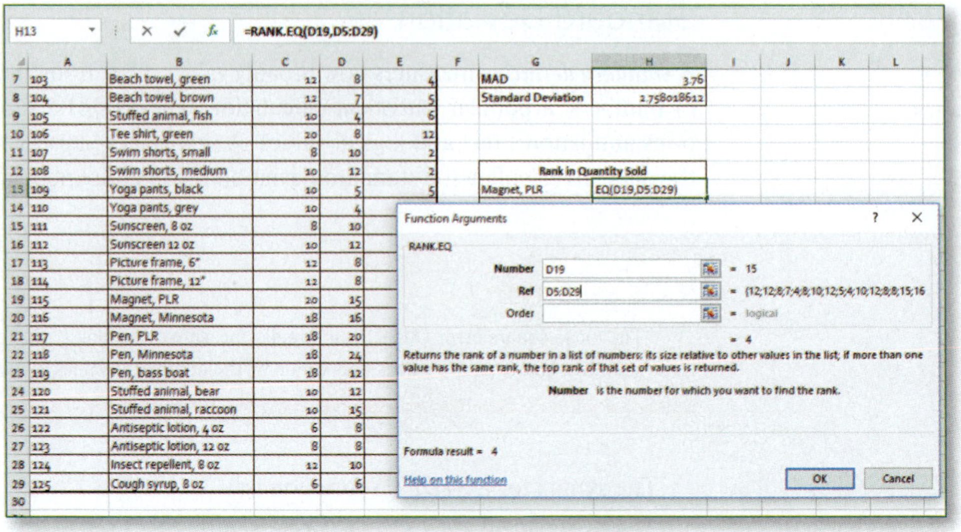

Figure 6-38 *RANQ.EQ Function Arguments* dialog box

PAUSE & PRACTICE: EXCEL 6-2

In this project, you nest *INDEX* and *MATCH* functions to display information on the inventory worksheet for Paradise Lakes Resort. You transpose data, calculate statistics for inventory, and prepare time and date calculations.

File Needed: ***[your initials] PP E6-1.xlsx***
Completed Project File Name: ***[your initials] PP E6-2.xlsx***

1. Open ***[your initials] PP E6-1.xlsx*** completed in *Pause & Practice 6-1* and save it as [your initials] PP E6-2.
2. Click the **Inventory** worksheet tab.
3. Use the *INDEX* function with one column of data.
   a. Select cell **H9**.
   b. Click the **Lookup & Reference** button [*Formulas* tab, *Function Library* group] and choose **INDEX**.
   c. Select the first argument list **array, row_num, column_num** and click **OK**.
   d. Select cells **B5:B29** for the *Array* argument.
   e. Click the **Row_num** box and type 10 to show data from the tenth row in the range. When using a single column as the array, there is no *Column_num* argument (Figure 6-39).
   f. Click **OK**. "Yoga pants, grey" is the description.

4. Use the *INDEX* function with a range name.
   a. Select cell **H10**.
   b. Click the **Recently Used** button [*Formulas* tab, *Function Library* group] and choose **INDEX**.
   c. Select the first argument list and click **OK**.
   d. Press **F3** (**FN+F3**) to open the *Paste Name* dialog box in the *Array* argument box.
   e. Choose **Inventory** and click **OK**.
   f. Click the **Row_num** box and type 12 to show data from the twelfth row.
   g. Click the **Column_num** box and type 4 to display data from the "Unit Cost" column, the fourth column in the "Inventory" range (Figure 6-40).
   h. Click **OK** and format cell **H10** as **Currency**. The cost of the twelfth item (12 oz. sunscreen) is $4.75.

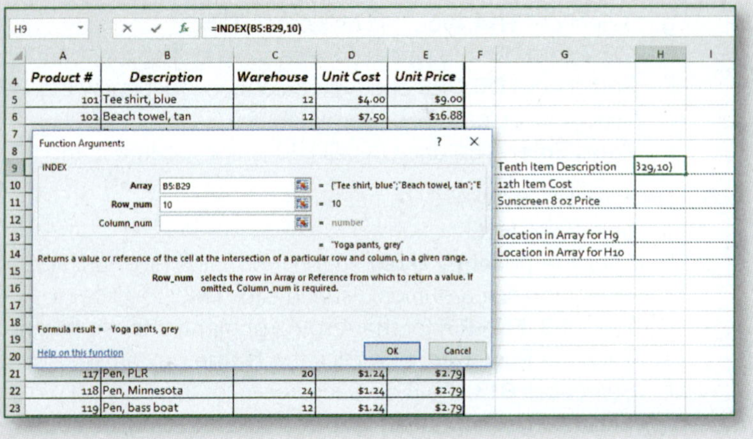

Figure 6-39 *INDEX* function to show data from tenth row

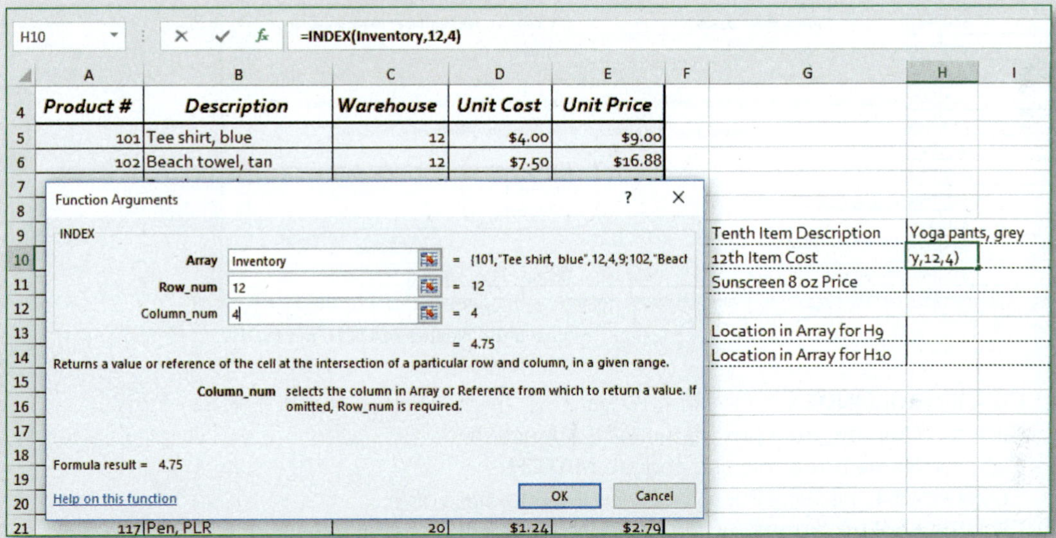

Figure 6-40 *INDEX* function to show data from twelfth row, fourth column

5. Use the *MATCH* function.
   a. Select cell **H13**.
   b. Click the **Lookup & Reference** button [*Formulas* tab, *Function Library* group] and choose **MATCH**.
   c. Select cell **H9** for the *Lookup_value* argument.
   d. Click the **Look_up array** box and select cells **B5:B29**. These two arguments will find a match in cells B5:B29 for the data in cell H9.
   e. Click the **Match_type** argument and type 0 to look for an exact match (Figure 6-41).
   f. Click **OK**. The data in cell H9 is located in the tenth row in the array.

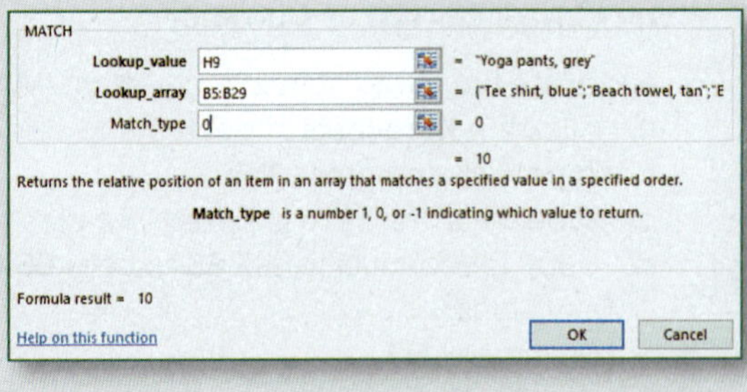

Figure 6-41 *MATCH* function for an exact match

g. Select cell **H14**, type =m and press **Tab**.
h. Click cell **H10** and type a comma , to move to the *look_up array* argument.
i. Select cells **D5:D29** and type a comma , to display the *Formula AutoComplete* list.
j. Type 0 to look for an exact match.
k. Press **Enter**. The price in cell H10 is first located in the fifth row.

6. Nest *INDEX* and *MATCH* functions.
   a. Select cell **H11**.
   b. Click the **Recently Used** button [*Formulas* tab, *Function Library* group] and choose **INDEX**.
   c. Select the first argument list and click **OK**.
   d. Press **F3** (**FN+F3**) for the *Array* argument, choose **Inventory**, and click **OK**.
   e. Click the **Row_num** box, click the **Name** box arrow, and choose **MATCH**.
   f. Select cell **B15**, the 8 oz. sunscreen, for the *Lookup_value*.
   g. Click the **Lookup_array** box and select cells **B5:B29**.
   h. Click the **Match_type** box and type 0. This completes the nested *MATCH* function for the *Row_num* argument (Figure 6-42).

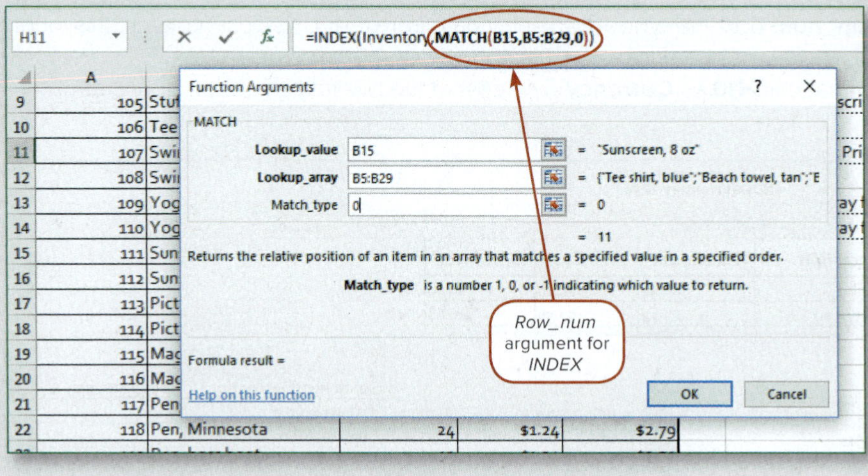

Figure 6-42 Nested *MATCH* and *INDEX*

   i. Click the word **INDEX** in the *Formula* bar.
   j. Click the **Column_num** box for the *INDEX* function.
   k. Click the **Name** box arrow and choose **MATCH**.
   l. Select cell **E4**, the "Unit Price" label, for the *Lookup_value*.
   m. Click the **Lookup_array** box and select cells **A4:E4**, the label row.
   n. Click the **Match_type** box and tpe 0. This is the nested *MATCH* function for the *Column_num* argument.
   o. Click the word **INDEX** in the *Formula* bar (Figure 6-43). (The formula is **=INDEX(Inventory, MATCH(B15,B5:B29,0),MATCH(E4,A4:E4,0))**.
   p. Click **OK**. The price for the 8 oz. sunscreen displays unrounded as 7.7625.
   q. Format cell **H11** as **Currency**.

7. Calculate the mean absolute deviation (MAD) for forecast errors.
   a. Click the **Forecasts** sheet tab and select cell **E5**.
   b. Type =ab and press **Tab**.
   c. Type c5-d5 and press **Enter**. The closing parenthesis is provided.
   d. Copy the formula in cell **E5** to cells **E6:E29** without formatting. Absolute values do not show any signs.
   e. Select cell **H7**.
   f. Use the *AVERAGE* function with cells **E5:E29** as the argument.

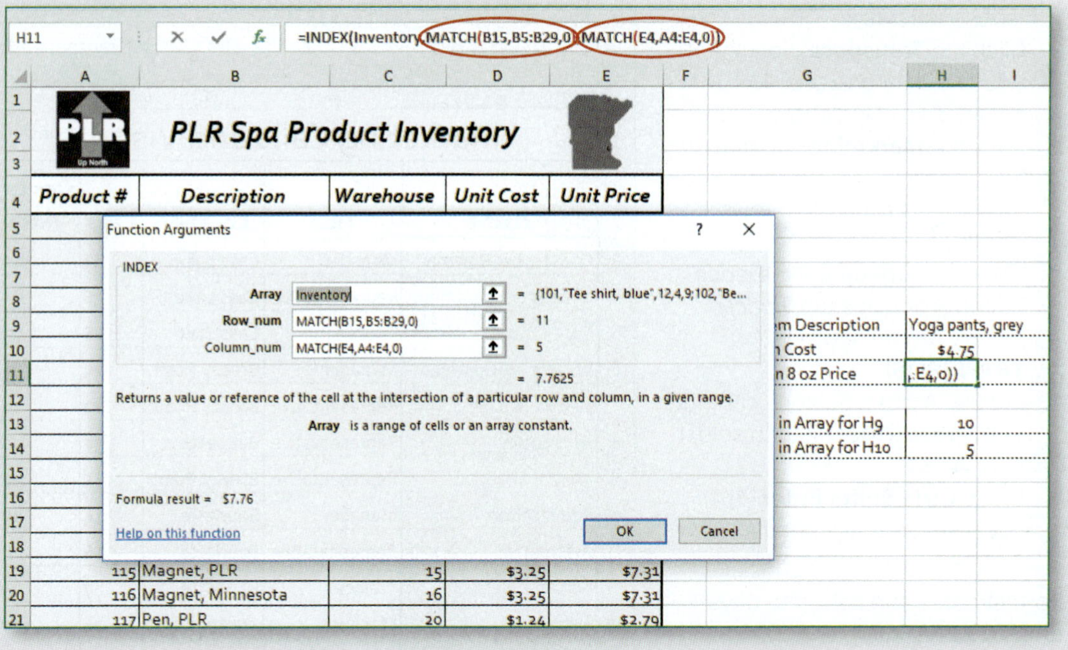

Figure 6-43 *MATCH* functions are *Row_num* and *Column_num* arguments

8. Calculate a standard deviation for number sold.
   a. Select cell **H8**.
   b. Type =std, select **STDEV.S** from the list, and press **Tab**.
   c. Select cells **D5:D29** and press **Enter**.
9. Rank products by quantity sold.
   a. Select cell **H13**.
   b. Click the **More Functions** button [*Formulas* tab, *Function Library* group] and choose **Statistical**.
   c. Select **RANK.EQ**.
   d. Select cell **D19**, the number of magnets sold, for the *Number* argument.
   e. Click the **Ref** box and select cells **D5:D29** (Figure 6-44).
   f. Click **OK**.
   g. Select cell **H14** and use *RANK.EQ* to rank the quantity sold for the pen.

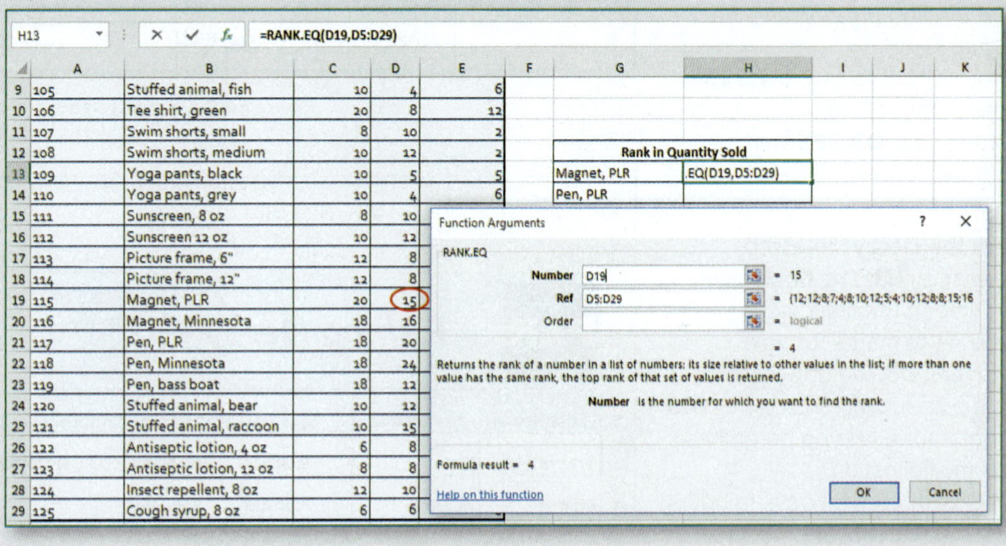

Figure 6-44 Rank a value in the list

10. Transpose data using *TRANSPOSE*.
    a. Click the **Transpose** worksheet tab. The data occupies 19 columns in a single row.
    b. Click the **Marketing** worksheet tab.
    c. Select cells **A3:A21**, 19 rows in a single column.
    d. Click the **Lookup & Reference** button [*Formulas* tab, *Function Library* group] and select **TRANSPOSE**.
    e. For the *Array* argument, click the **Transpose** sheet tab and select cells **A1:S1**.
    f. Press **Ctrl+Shift+Enter** to create an array formula (Figure 6-45).

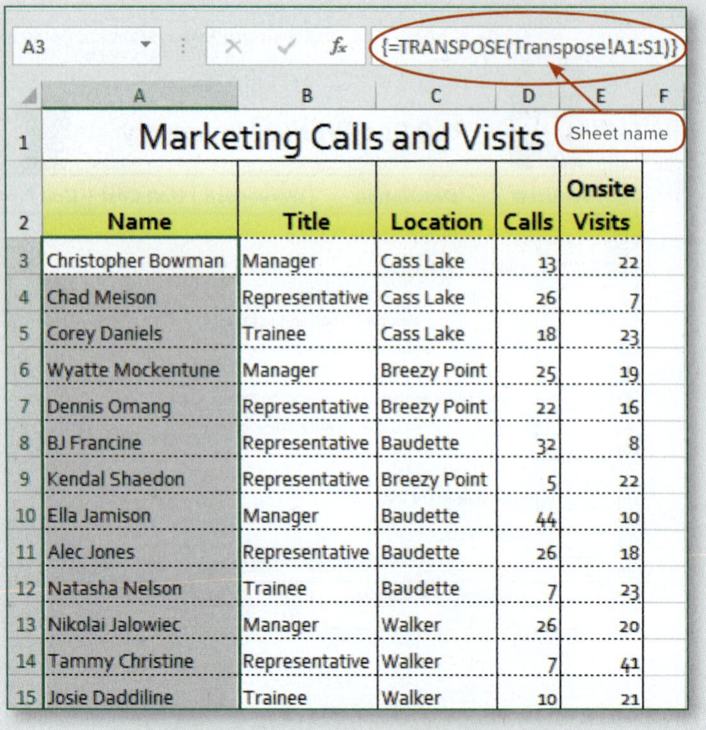

	A	B	C	D	E
1	Marketing Calls and Visits				
2	Name	Title	Location	Calls	Onsite Visits
3	Christopher Bowman	Manager	Cass Lake	13	22
4	Chad Meison	Representative	Cass Lake	26	7
5	Corey Daniels	Trainee	Cass Lake	18	23
6	Wyatte Mockentune	Manager	Breezy Point	25	19
7	Dennis Omang	Representative	Breezy Point	22	16
8	BJ Francine	Representative	Baudette	32	8
9	Kendal Shaedon	Representative	Breezy Point	5	22
10	Ella Jamison	Manager	Baudette	44	10
11	Alec Jones	Representative	Baudette	26	18
12	Natasha Nelson	Trainee	Baudette	7	23
13	Nikolai Jalowiec	Manager	Walker	26	20
14	Tammy Christine	Representative	Walker	7	41
15	Josie Daddiline	Trainee	Walker	10	21

Figure 6-45 *TRANSPOSE* in an array formula

11. Format dates and calculate days employed.
    a. Click the **Hire Dates** sheet tab.
    b. Select cells **C3:C25**. These are serial numbers that represent hire dates.
    c. Click the **Launcher** in the *Number* group [*Home* tab] and select the **Date** category.
    d. Select the format that shows a leading zero **03/14/12** and click **OK**.
    e. Enter the *TODAY* function in cell **A27**.
    f. Select cell **D3**.
    g. Type =(to start a formula.
    h. Click cell **A27** and press **F4** (**FN+F4**) to make it absolute.
    i. Type – to subtract and click cell **C3**.
    j. Type)/ for a closing parenthesis and division.
    k. Type 365.25 to convert results to years and press **Enter** (Figure 6-46).
    l. Copy cell **D3** to cells **D4:D25** without formatting.
    m. Format cells **D3:D25** with the **Number** format.

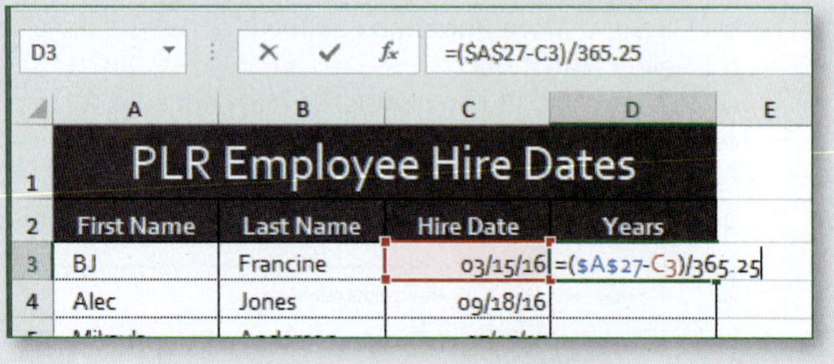

	A	B	C	D
1	PLR Employee Hire Dates			
2	First Name	Last Name	Hire Date	Years
3	BJ	Francine	03/15/16	=($A$27-C3)/365.25
4	Alec	Jones	09/18/16	

Figure 6-46 Calculate years employed

12. Calculate time.
    a. Click the **Derby** sheet tab.
    b. Select cell **E3**. The ending time is the time of the first catch.
    c. Type =(to start a formula.
    d. Click cell **D3**, the end time.
    e. Type – to subtract and click cell **C3**.
    f. Type)* for a closing parenthesis and multiplication.
    g. Type 24 to convert days to hours.
    h. Type *60 to convert hours to minutes (Figure 6-47).

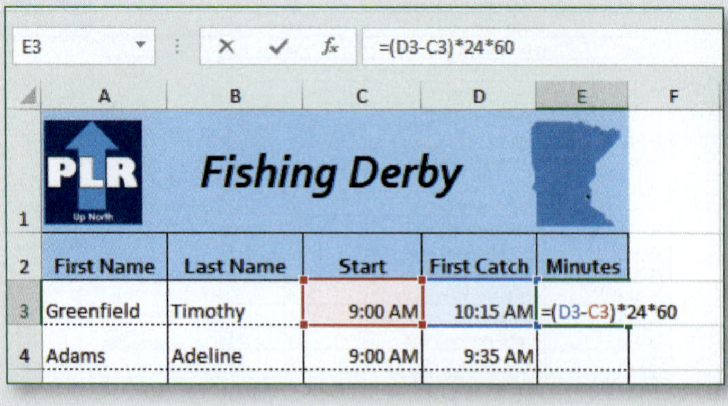

	A	B	C	D	E
2	First Name	Last Name	Start	First Catch	Minutes
3	Greenfield	Timothy	9:00 AM	10:15 AM	=(D3-C3)*24*60
4	Adams	Adeline	9:00 AM	9:35 AM	

Figure 6-47 Calculate time as minutes

i. Press **Enter**. The results displays as 12:00 AM.
j. Copy cell **E3** to cells **E4:E8** without formatting.
k. Format the results as **General** from the *Number Format* list [*Home* tab, *Number* group].

13. Save and close the workbook (Figure 6-48).

G	H
Tenth Item Description	Yoga pants, grey
12th Item Cost	$4.75
Sunscreen 8 oz Price	$7.76
Location in Array for H9	10
Location in Array for H10	5

t Inventory

Forecast	Sold	Error
20	12	8
12	12	0
12	8	4
12	7	5
10	4	6
20	8	12
8	10	2
10	12	2
10	5	5
10	4	6
8	10	2
10	12	2
12	8	4
12	8	4
20	15	5
18	16	2
18	20	2
18	24	6
18	12	6
10	12	2
10	15	5
6	8	2
8	8	0
12	10	2
6	6	0

MAD	3.76
Standard Deviation	4.751140214

Rank in Quantity Sold	
Magnet, PLR	4
Pen, PLR	2

Marketing Calls and Visits

	Name	Title	Location	Calls	Onsite Visits
3	Christopher Bowman	Manager	Cass Lake	13	22
4	Chad Meison	Representative	Cass Lake	26	7
5	Corey Daniels	Trainee	Cass Lake	18	23
6	Wyatte Mockentune	Manager	Breezy Point	25	19
7	Dennis Omang	Representative	Breezy Point	22	16
8	BJ Francine	Representative	Baudette	32	8
9	Kendal Shaedon	Representative	Breezy Point	5	22
10	Ella Jamison	Manager	Baudette	44	10
11	Alec Jones	Representative	Baudette	26	18
12	Natasha Nelson	Trainee	Baudette	7	23
13	Nikolai Jalowiec	Manager	Walker	26	20
14	Tammy Christine	Representative	Walker	7	41
15	Josie Daddiline	Trainee	Walker	10	21
16	Tara Miller	Trainee	Breezy Point	32	17
17	Robert Andrew	Representative	Walker	15	10
18	Coryn Gomez	Representative	Baudette	35	5
19	Elizabeth Gabrys	Trainee	Cass Lake	43	9
20	Rita Larson	Trainee	Walker	6	36
21	Michael Gentile	Representative	Baudette	38	9

PLR Employee Hire Dates

	First Name	Last Name	Hire Date	Years
3	BJ	Francine	03/15/16	3.85
4	Alec	Jones	09/18/16	3.34
5	Mikayla	Anderson	07/15/17	2.52
6	Ella	Jamison	05/11/17	2.69
7	David	Gazik	11/14/17	2.18
8	Natasha	Nelson	10/24/17	2.24
9	Ari	Aronson	05/10/18	1.70
10	Dennis	Omang	04/15/18	1.77
11	Kendal	Shaedon	06/14/16	3.60
12	Frankie	Dennis	08/18/16	3.42
13	Kendra	Shelton	01/15/16	4.01
14	DJ	Bushman	04/30/17	2.72
15	Wyatte	Mockentune	06/30/19	0.56
16	Suzanne	Ouimet	07/16/17	2.51
17	Chad	Meison	10/23/17	2.24
18	Mae	Gomez	12/07/16	3.12
19	Christopher	Bowman	05/15/19	0.68
20	Jeffery	Dalton	08/18/16	3.42
21	Corey	Daniels	01/21/16	4.00
22	Randy	Josephson	08/09/17	2.45
23	Tammy	Christine	09/13/17	2.35
24	Josie	Daddiline	10/08/17	2.28
25	Nikolai	Jalowiec	11/07/17	2.20
26				
27	1/20/2020			

PLR Fishing Derby

First Name	Last Name	Start	First Catch	Minutes
Greenfield	Timothy	9:00 AM	10:15 AM	75
Adams	Adeline	9:00 AM	9:35 AM	35
Larson	Joseph	9:30 AM	10:45 AM	75
Elaim	Esom	9:30 AM	10:15 AM	45
Gonalez	José	10:00 AM	11:15 AM	75
Martin	Josiah	10:00 AM	11:30 AM	90

Figure 6-48 Completed data for PP E6-2 worksheets

SLO 6.5

Using Financial Functions

Functions in the *Financial* category analyze money transactions and use the *rate*, *pmt*, and *nper* arguments. ***Rate*** is an interest rate for the time period. ***Nper*** is the total number of payments over the life of the transaction. The ***pmt*** argument is the amount saved or invested each period.

> **MORE INFO**
>
> Financial functions use the concept of an ***annuity***, a series of payments (or receipts) for a specified period of time.

The PV Function

The *PV* function calculates *present value* or the cost now to reach a target value at some time in the future. If you want to have $200,000 cash in ten years, can add $10,000 a year, and expect to earn 5% a year, use the *PV* function to calculate a required starting amount to reach your goal.

The syntax for a *PV* function is:

=PV(rate,nper,pmt,[fv],[type])

The *rate*, *nper*, and *pmt* arguments are required. *Rate* and *nper* arguments must use the same time division such as months or years. If you make monthly payments but the interest rate is annual, the rate must be divided by 12. The *fv* argument, future value, is a cash balance or target amount at the end of the last period. When the *fv* argument is zero, the *PV* function displays what the payments will be worth at the rate and time period specified. The *type* argument indicates if the payment is made at the beginning or the end of the period. When you earn interest, the beginning of the period is preferable.

HOW TO: Use the PV Function

1. Click the cell for the result.
2. Click the **Financial** button [*Formulas* tab, *Function Library* group] and choose **PV**.
3. Select the cell that contains the interest rate for the *Rate* box.
   - If the interest rate is an annual rate and payments are monthly, type /12 after the cell address.
   - If the interest rate is an annual rate and payments are quarterly, type /4 after the cell address.
   - Type the interest rate in the entry box as a percent or its decimal equivalent.
4. Click the **Nper** box and select the cell that contains the number of years.
   - If the term is shown in years and payments are monthly, type *12 after the cell address.
   - If the term is shown in years and payments are quarterly, type *4 after the cell address.
   - Type the total number of payments.
5. Click the **Pmt** box and select the cell that contains the payment amount.
6. Click the **Fv** box and select the cell with the target amount.
   - Type a value in the entry box instead of selecting a cell.
   - Type a zero (0) or leave the entry blank to indicate no cash balance.

7. Click the **Type** box and type 1 for payment at the beginning of the period (Figure 6-49).
   - Type 0 or leave the entry blank to indicate payment at the end of the period.

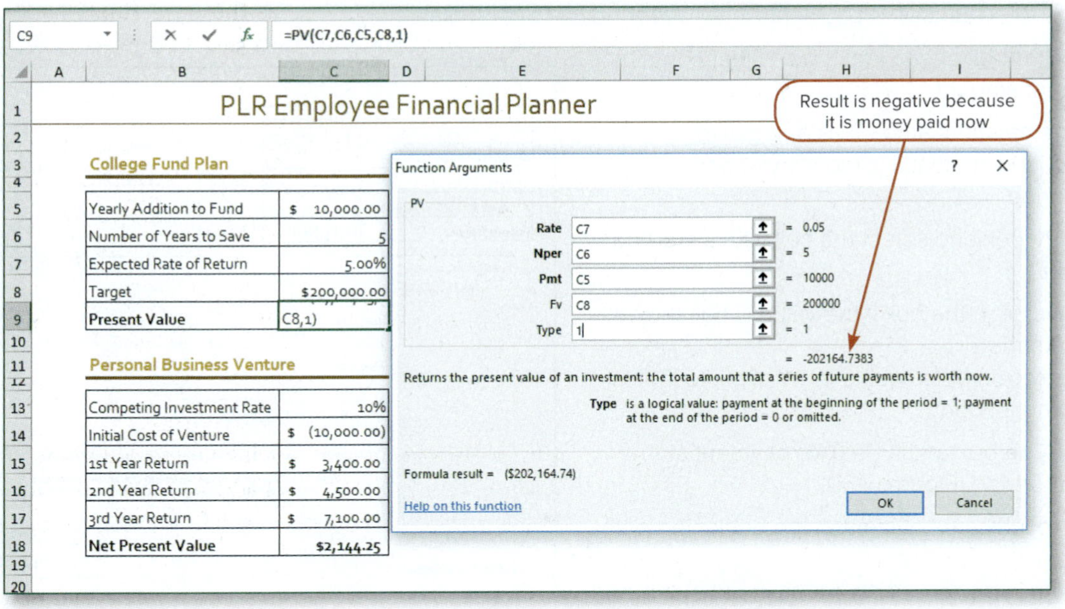

Figure 6-49 *Function Arguments* **dialog box for** *PV*

8. Click **OK**.
   - The result is a negative number when the *pmt* argument is a positive value.

The FV Function

The *FV* function determines the *future value* of a series of payments at the same interest rate for a specified period of time. Use this function to calculate results for a savings plan in which you deposit a specific amount each period.

The syntax for an *FV* function is:

=FV(rate,nper,pmt,[pv],[type])

Rate, *nper*, and *pmt* are required; *pv* and *type* are optional. The *pv* argument, the present value, might be a required initial investment or an amount already in the account. The *type* argument is either 1 or 0 (or omitted) to indicate if payment is made at the beginning or the end of the period. For a retirement savings account, payment is often made at the end of the time period.

HOW TO: Use the FV Function

1. Click the cell for the result.
2. Click the **Financial** button [*Formulas* tab, *Function Library* group] and choose **FV**.
3. Select the cell that contains the interest rate for the *Rate* box.
   - If the interest rate is an annual rate and payments are monthly, type /12 after the cell address.
   - If the interest rate is an annual rate and payments are quarterly, type /4 after the cell address.
   - Type the interest rate in the *Rate* box instead of selecting a cell.

4. Click the **Nper** argument box and select the cell that contains the number of years.
    - If the term is years and payments are monthly, type *12 after the cell address.
    - If the term is years and payments are quarterly, type *4 after the cell address.
    - Type the total number of payments in the *Nper* box.
5. Click the **Pmt** box and select the cell that contains the payment amount.
    - Enter the payment amount as a negative value to indicate that it is money you pay each period.
6. Click the **Pv** box and select the cell with a starting amount, if any.
    - Type a value in the box if the value is not shown in the worksheet.
    - Type a zero (0) or leave the entry blank to indicate no starting amount.
7. Click the **Type** box and type 0 for payment at the end of the period (Figure 6-50).
    - Type 1 to indicate payment at the beginning of the period.
    - Leave the *Type* box empty for payment at the end of the period.
8. Click **OK**.

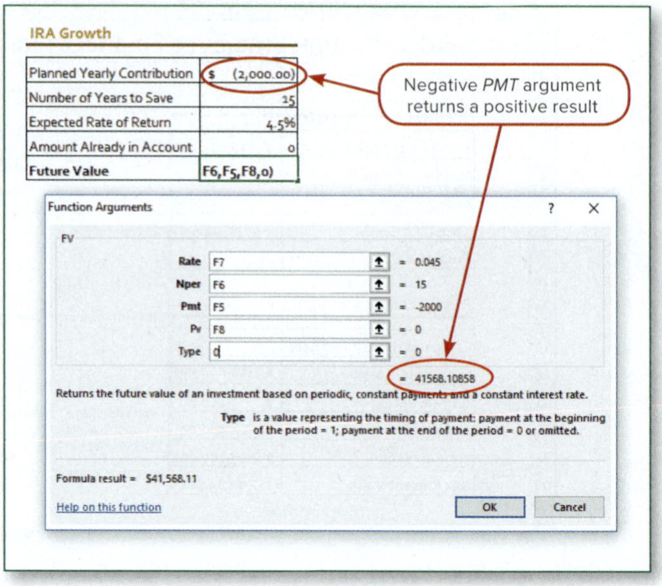

Figure 6-50 ***Function Arguments*** **dialog box for** ***FV***

The NPV Function

The *NPV* function calculates the *net present value* of an investment using a discount rate and a series of payments and receipts. A ***discount rate*** represents the cost of financing or the rate of return possible with a competing investment. In the *NPV* function, the series of payments and receipts can vary.

The syntax for an *NPV* function is:

=NPV(rate,value1,value2,...)

Rate is the discount rate, an interest rate. The *valueN* arguments are positive and negative ***cash flows***, payments or receipts. *Value* arguments are listed in the order in which they occur. For example, if you earn $3,400 in the first period, that amount is the *value1* argument. The *value2* argument is the next payment or receipt, and so on. A separate initial payment or cost is not a *value* argument but is added to the result of the *NPV* function as a negative amount.

MORE INFO

The *NPV* function assumes that cash flows occur at the end of each period.

HOW TO: Use the NPV Function

1. Click the cell for the result.
2. Click the **Financial** button [*Formulas* tab, *Function Library* group] and choose **NPV**.

3. Click the cell that contains the discount interest rate for the *Rate* box.
   - Use a percentage (10%) or its decimal equivalent (.1).
   - Type a value instead of selecting a cell.
4. Click the **Value1** box and select the cell that contains the amount of cash flow at the end of the first period.
   - Cash flow amounts can be negative or positive values.
5. Click the **Value2** argument box and select the cell that contains the amount of cash flow at the end of the second period.
6. Click each additional **Value** box and select the cell (Figure 6-51).
   - For a year with no cash flow, type a zero (0) as the *ValueN* argument to prevent the sequence of cash flows from moving forward one year.

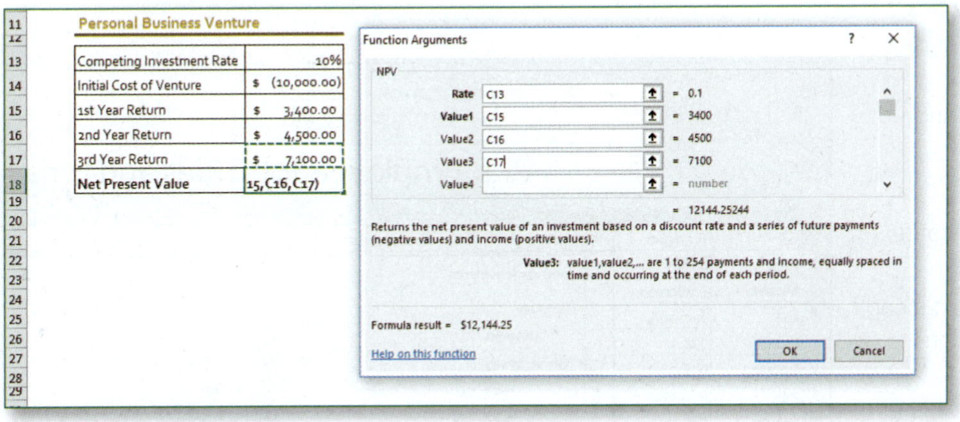

Figure 6-51 ***Function Arguments*** **dialog box for** ***NPV***

7. Click **OK**.
8. Click the *Formula* bar to edit the formula to include an initial payment.
   - The initial payment should be formatted as a negative value.
9. Press **End** to position the insertion point after the closing parentheses and type +.
10. Click the cell with the initial payment and press **Enter** (Figure 6-52).

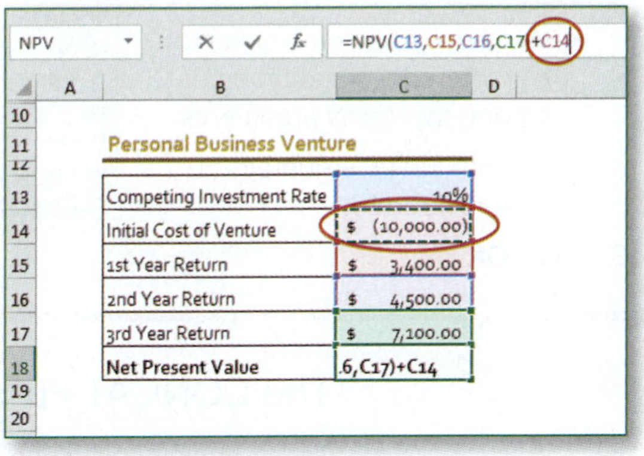

Figure 6-52 **Edited** ***NPV*** **function to include initial cost**

SLO 6.6

Working with Text Functions

Text functions split, join, or convert labels and values. With a *Text* function, you can format a value as a label to control alignment or display labels in uppercase or lowercase letters.

The TEXTJOIN Function

The *TEXTJOIN* function combines strings of text, values, or characters. A common use of *TEXTJOIN* is to display a person's full name in a single cell by joining two or more cells.

The syntax for a *TEXTJOIN* function is:

=TEXTJOIN(delimiter, ignore_empty, text1, [text2], ...)

The *delimiter* argument specifies the character used to separate the *textN* arguments. You can have up to 252 *textN* arguments but only one delimiter. A *text* argument is a cell reference or data that you type.

When you combine text strings, such as first and last names or city, state, and ZIP code, the delimiter is a space character. *TEXTJOIN* results are usually placed in a separate column or row to preserve the original data.

▸HOW TO: Use the TEXTJOIN Function

1. Click the cell for the result.
2. Click the **Text** button [*Formulas* tab, *Function Library* group] and choose **TEXTJOIN**.
   - Press **Spacebar** to insert a space character in the *Delimiter* box.
   - The *Delimiter* space character displays with quotation marks.
3. Click the **Ignore_empty** box.
   - Leave this box empty for the default TRUE option.
   - A cell with no data is ignored in the function results.
4. Click the **Text1** argument box.
5. Select the cell with the first text string to be joined.
   - Alternatively, type a text string, a value, or a punctuation character.
6. Click the **Text2** box and select the cell or type data to be joined (Figure 6-53).
   - You can use a combination of cell references and typed data among the *TextN* arguments.
7. Complete *TextN* argument boxes as needed.
8. Click **OK**.

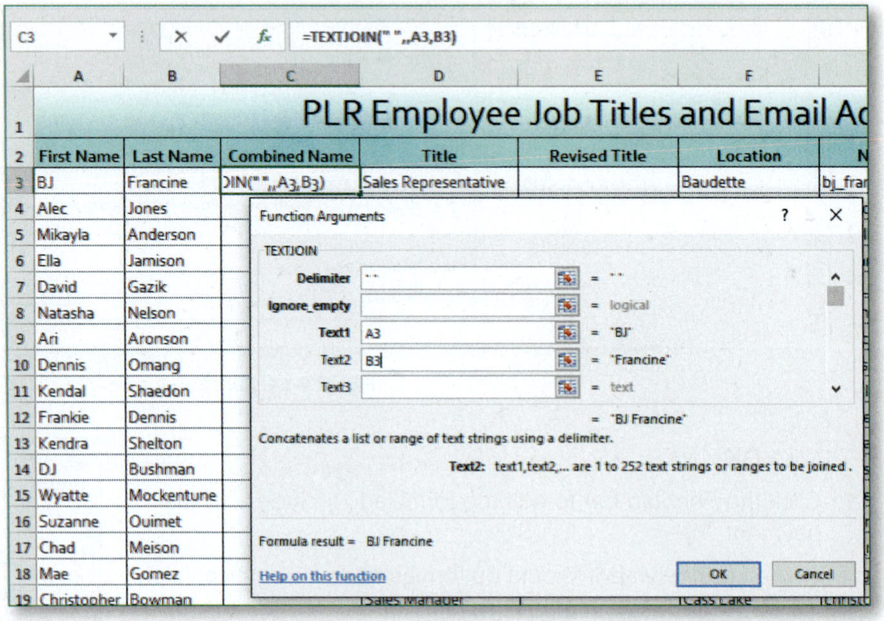

Figure 6-53 ***Function Arguments*** **dialog box for *TEXTJOIN***

The CONCAT Function

To ***concatenate*** means to link or join; the *TEXTJOIN* function concatenates text strings. Excel has another *Text* function *CONCAT* that joins or combines data strings. The *CONCAT* function does not have a *delimiter* argument which enables you to specify a different delimiter between each two *textN* arguments in the formula.

The syntax for a *CONCAT* function is:

=CONCAT(text1, [text2], ...)

The *CONCAT* function has one argument *textN*, where *N* is a number from 1 to 255. The *text* argument is a cell reference, data that you type, or a delimiter character.

> **ANOTHER WAY**
>
> Join data in a formula by using the & operator. The formula **=A1&B1** returns the same result as **=CONCAT(A1,B1)**.

When you concatenate text strings, such as first and last names, you must include space characters to separate words or values. Concatenated results are placed in a separate column or row to preserve original data.

In previous versions of Excel, *CONCAT* was named *CONCATENATE*.

▸HOW TO: Use the CONCAT Function

1. Click the cell for the result.
2. Click the **Text** button [*Formulas* tab, *Function Library* group] and choose **CONCAT**.
3. Select the cell with the first text string for the *Text1* argument.
   - Type a text string rather than selecting a cell.
   - You do not need to include quotation marks when you use the *Function Arguments* dialog box.
4. Click the **Text2** box and enter the next string to be concatenated.
   - Type a delimiter such as a space, a period, or a comma.
   - Click a cell with the second text string.
5. Click the **Text3** box and select or type the next text string (Figure 6-54).

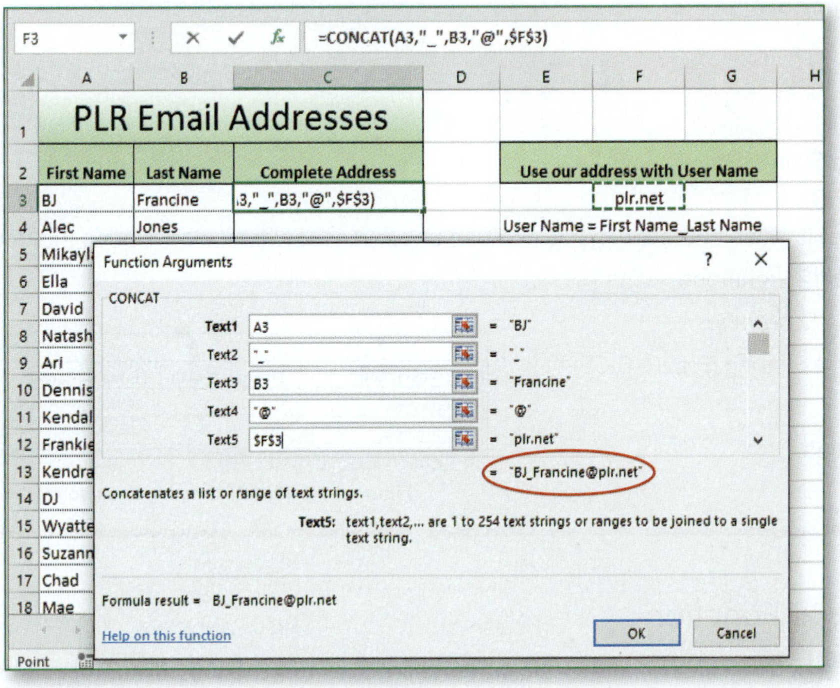

Figure 6-54 ***Function Arguments*** **dialog box for** ***CONCAT***

6. Complete *TextN* argument boxes as needed.
7. Click **OK**.

ANOTHER WAY

Include a space or punctuation character immediately after a cell reference in a *TextN* argument box.

> **MORE INFO**
>
> Use *TEXTJOIN* when the same delimiter is necessary for all *TextN* arguments. Use *CONCAT* to build a unique combination of *TextN* arguments and delimiters.

The EXACT Function

The *EXACT* function compares two text strings, values, or characters to determine if they are identical. For example, if you import email names, you can compare imported names to your current list.

The syntax for an *EXACT* function is:

=EXACT(text1, text2)

The *EXACT* function has two required arguments, *text1* and *text2*. *Text1* is the first text string, and *text2* is the second text string. The arguments are case sensitive, but the function does not check formatting. The result for an *EXACT* function is TRUE or FALSE.

HOW TO: Use the EXACT Function

1. Click the cell for the result.
2. Type =ex and press **Tab**.
   - The *text1* argument is bold in the *ScreenTip*.
3. Select the cell or type the text string.
   - If you type the text string, enclose it within quotation marks and use upper- and lowercase as used in the data.
4. Type a comma (,) to move to the *text2* argument.
   - The *text2* argument is bold in the *ScreenTip*.
5. Select the cell or type the second text string (Figure 6-55).
6. Press **Enter**.
   - The closing parenthesis is supplied.
   - The result is TRUE or FALSE.

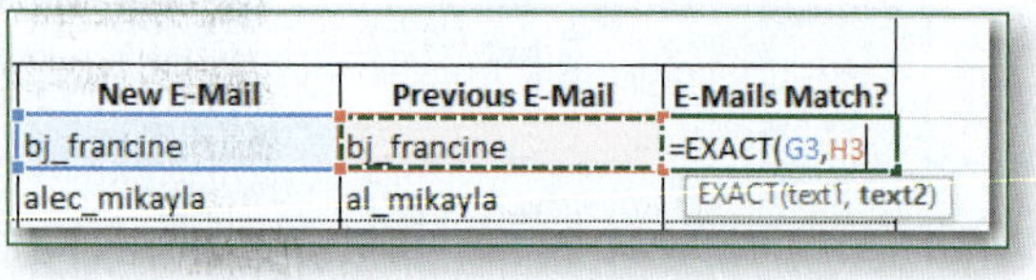

Figure 6-55 ***EXACT* function has two arguments**

The REPLACE Function

The *REPLACE* function enables you to substitute characters for a specified number of characters in existing data. This command is helpful when data in a column follows a pattern. For example, if Paradise Lakes Resort products have an ID that starts with PAR, use the *REPLACE* function to change each occurrence of PAR to PLR.

> **ANOTHER WAY**
>
> Use the *SUBSTITUTE* function in the *Text* category to replace specified text within a cell.

The syntax for a *REPLACE* function is:

=REPLACE(old_text, start_num, num_chars, new_text)

The *old_text* argument is the cell with data that you want to change. The *start_num* argument is the position in the cell of the first character to be replaced. If you want to replace the first three characters, the *start_num* is 1. However, if you want to replace characters in the second word in the cell, count each character position, including spaces, to determine the number.

The *num_chars* argument determines how many characters from the *start_num* position are replaced, and the *new_text* argument is the replacement text.

▸HOW TO: Use the REPLACE Function

1. Click the cell for the result.
2. Click the **Text** button [*Formulas* tab, *Function Library* group] and choose **REPLACE**.
3. Select the cell with data to be replaced for the *Old_text* argument.
4. Click the **Start_num** box.
   - Count character positions from the first character on the left.
5. Type a number to indicate the position at which replacement should begin.
6. Click the **Num_chars** box.
   - Count how many characters are to be replaced.
7. Type the number of replacement characters.
8. Click the **New_text** box.
9. Type the replacement text (Figure 6-56).
   - The new text can have more or fewer characters than the *Num_chars* argument.
   - Quotation marks are not necessary when you use the *Function Arguments* dialog box.
   - Use upper- and lowercase as required.
10. Press **Enter** or click **OK**.
    - The new text displays in the cell.

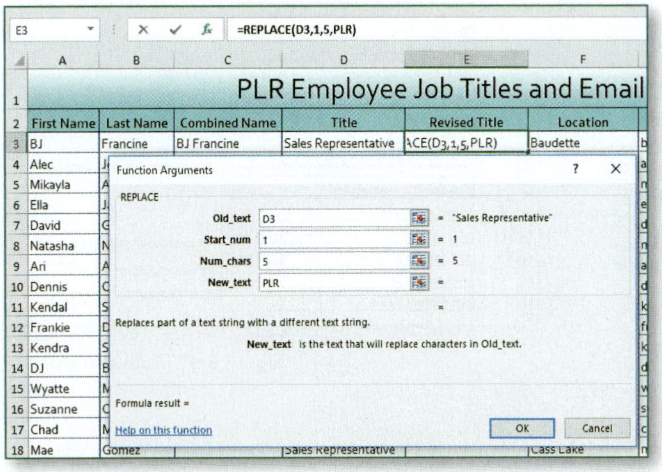

Figure 6-56 ***REPLACE*** **function has four arguments**

PAUSE & PRACTICE: EXCEL 6-3

In this project, you complete a financial planning worksheet for Paradise Lakes Resort staff. You also update the employee data sheet using *Text* functions.

File Needed: ***[your initials] PP E6-2.xlsx***
Completed Project File Name: ***[your initials] PP E6-3.xlsx***

1. Open ***[your initials] PP E6-2.xlsx*** completed in *Pause & Practice 6-2* and save it as [your initials] PP E6-3.
2. Click the **Financial Planner** sheet tab.

3. Use the *PV* function.
   a. Select cell **C9**.
   b. Click the **Financial** button [*Formulas* tab, *Function Library* group] and choose **PV**.
   c. Select cell **C7** for the *Rate* argument and type /12 after **C7**, because additions to the fund are monthly.
   d. Click the **Nper** argument box and select cell **C6**.
   e. Type *12 after **C6** to convert the number of years to months. The *Rate* and *Nper* arguments must use the same time aspect.
   f. Click the **Pmt** box and select cell **C5**.
   g. Click the **Fv** box and select cell **C8**. This value is the future goal.
   h. Press **Tab** to move to the *Type* box.
   i. Type 1 to indicate that payments are made at the beginning of the period (Figure 6-57).
   j. Click **OK**. The college fund will be slightly more than $55,000 short of the $200,000 goal at the terms shown.

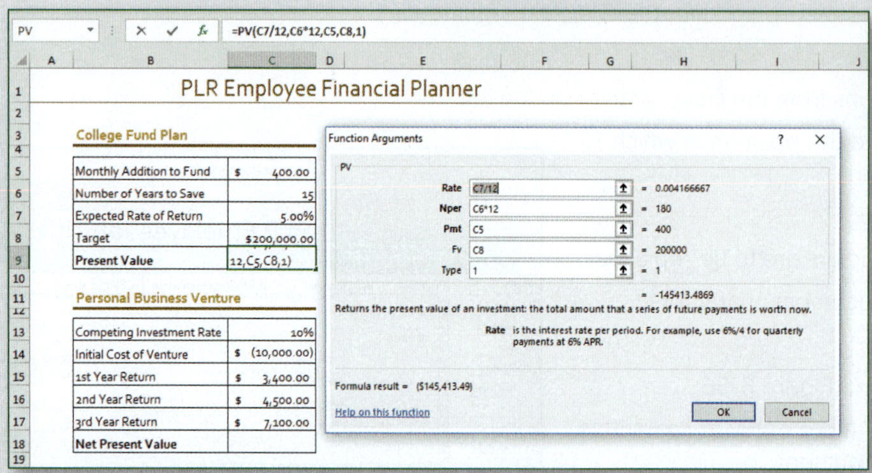

Figure 6-57 *Rate* **and** *Nper* **arguments are monthly, and payment is made at the beginning of period**

4. Use the *FV* function.
   a. Select cell **F9**.
   b. Click the **Financial** button [*Formulas* tab, *Function Library* group] and choose **FV**.
   c. Click cell **F7** for the *Rate* argument. The payment is once a year and the rate is annual.
   d. Click the **Nper** argument box and select cell **F6** for one payment per year.
   e. Click the **Pmt** box and select cell **F5**. The amount is negative, because you must pay it each year.
   f. Press **Tab** two times to skip the *Pv* box and move to the *Type* box.
   g. Type 0 in the *Type* box. Retirement contributions are typically made at the end of the year (Figure 6-58).
   h. Click **OK**. If you invest $2,000 a year in an IRA account that earns 4.5% per year, you will have over $40,000 at the end of 15 years.

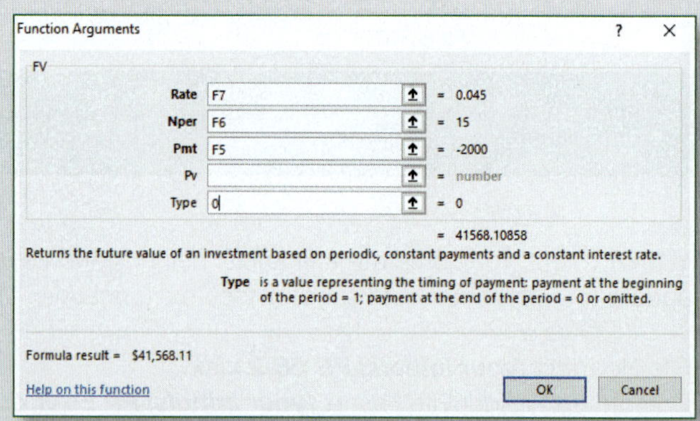

Figure 6-58 Rate and payment are yearly

5. Use the *NPV* function.
   a. Select cell **C18**.
   b. Click the **Financial** button [*Formulas* tab, *Function Library* group] and choose **NPV**.

c. Select cell **C13** for the *Rate* argument. The rate represents other opportunities for the money.
d. Click the **Value1** box and select cell **C15**.
e. Click the **Value2** box and select cell **C16**.
f. Click the **Value3** box and select cell **C17** (Figure 6-59).

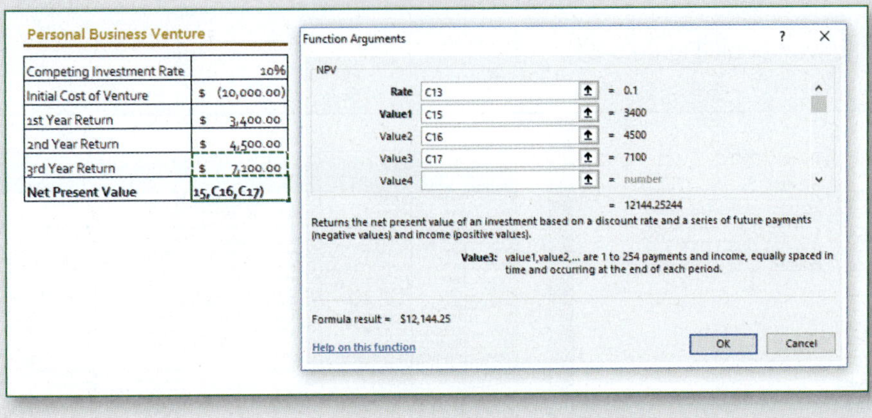

Figure 6-59 Initial cost (cell C14) is not a *value* argument

g. Click **OK**.
h. Click the *Formula* bar and press **End** to position the insertion point after **C17)**.
i. Type + and select cell **C14** to add the cost of the venture.
j. Press **Enter**. Based on projected cash flows, the investment has a present value of $2,144.25.

6. Use the *TEXTJOIN* function.
   a. Click the **Title&EMail** sheet tab and select cell **C3**.
   b. Click the **Text** button [*Formulas* tab, *Function Library* group] and choose **TEXTJOIN**.
   c. Press **Spacebar** for the *Delimiter* argument.
   d. Click the **Text1** box and select cell **A3**. The *Ignore_empty* argument is blank which means empty cells are ignored.
   e. Click the **Text2** box and select cell **B3**.
   f. Click **OK**.
   g. Copy the *TEXTJOIN* formula in cell **C3** to cells **C4:C25** without formatting.
   h. Format column **C** to be **19.29 (140 pixels)** wide (Figure 6-60).

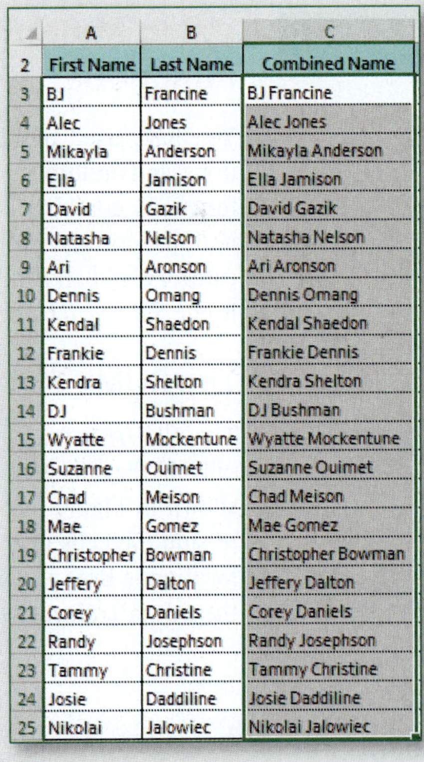

	A	B	C
2	First Name	Last Name	Combined Name
3	BJ	Francine	BJ Francine
4	Alec	Jones	Alec Jones
5	Mikayla	Anderson	Mikayla Anderson
6	Ella	Jamison	Ella Jamison
7	David	Gazik	David Gazik
8	Natasha	Nelson	Natasha Nelson
9	Ari	Aronson	Ari Aronson
10	Dennis	Omang	Dennis Omang
11	Kendal	Shaedon	Kendal Shaedon
12	Frankie	Dennis	Frankie Dennis
13	Kendra	Shelton	Kendra Shelton
14	DJ	Bushman	DJ Bushman
15	Wyatte	Mockentune	Wyatte Mockentune
16	Suzanne	Ouimet	Suzanne Ouimet
17	Chad	Meison	Chad Meison
18	Mae	Gomez	Mae Gomez
19	Christopher	Bowman	Christopher Bowman
20	Jeffery	Dalton	Jeffery Dalton
21	Corey	Daniels	Corey Daniels
22	Randy	Josephson	Randy Josephson
23	Tammy	Christine	Tammy Christine
24	Josie	Daddiline	Josie Daddiline
25	Nikolai	Jalowiec	Nikolai Jalowiec

Figure 6-60 *TEXTJOIN* formula shows results in a single cell

7. Use the *REPLACE* function.
   a. Select cell **E3**.
   b. Click the **Text** button [*Formulas* tab, *Function Library* group] and choose **REPLACE**.
   c. Click cell **D3** for the *Old_text* argument.
   d. Click the **Start_num** box and type 1.
   e. Click the **Num_chars** box and type 5 to count five characters starting at the "S" "Sales" and preserve the space after the word.
   f. Click the **New_text** box.
   g. Type PLR. The replacement string is case sensitive.
   h. Press **Enter** or click **OK**.
   i. Copy the *REPLACE* formula in cell **E3** to cells **E4:E25** without formatting.
   j. Hide column **D** and *AutoFit* columns **E**, **F**, and **H**.

8. Use the *EXACT* function.
   a. Select cell **I3**.
   b. Type =ex and press **Tab** to select **EXACT**.

c. Select cell **G3** for the *text1* argument and type a comma **,** to move to the *text2* argument.
d. Select cell **H3** and press **Enter**.
e. Copy the *EXACT* formula in cell **I3** to cells **I4:I25** without formatting.
f. Apply a *Highlight Cells* rule to cells **I3:I25** to show FALSE values in **Light Red Fill with Dark Red Text**.

9. Save and close the workbook (Figure 6-61).

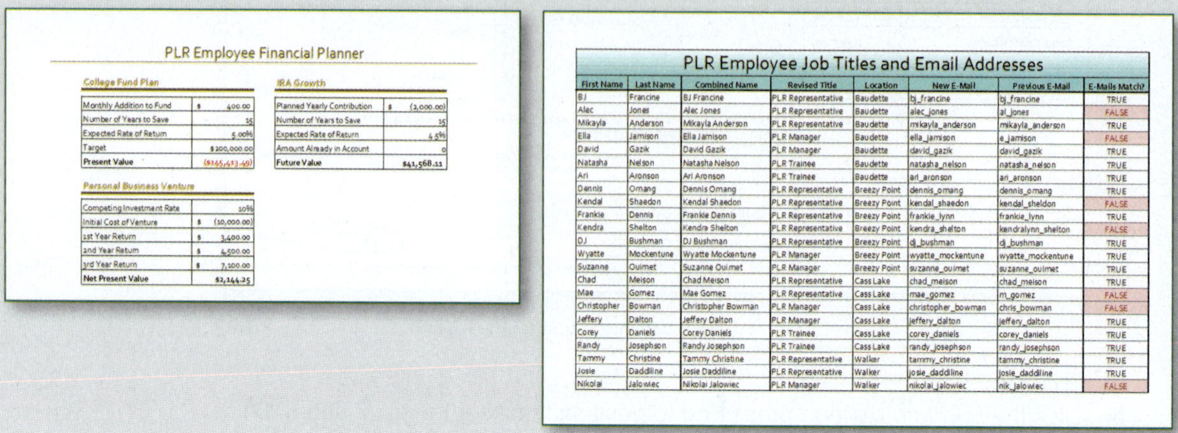

Figure 6-61 Completed worksheets for PP E6-3

SLO 6.7

Using Multiple Criteria in Functions

You have used multiple arguments in functions and multiple criteria in filters. Three functions combine multiple arguments with multiple criteria: *SUMIFS* in the *Math & Trig* category and *AVERAGEIFS* and *COUNTIFS* in the *Statistical* category.

The SUMIFS Function

The *SUMIFS* function adds or totals cells only if they meet the criteria. In the data shown in Figure 6-62, *SUMIFS* can be used to sum the cells in the "Calls" column if the location is Breezy Point (first criteria) and if the title is Trainee (second criteria).

Marketing Calls and Visits

Name	Title	Location	Calls	Onsite Visits
Christopher Bowman	Manager	Cass Lake	13	22
Chad Meison	Representative	Cass Lake	26	7
Corey Daniels	Trainee	Cass Lake	18	23
Wyatte Mockentune	Manager	Breezy Point	25	19
Dennis Omang	Representative	Breezy Point	22	16
BJ Francine	Representative	Baudette	32	8
Kendal Shaedon	Representative	Breezy Point	5	22
Ella Jamison	Manager	Baudette	44	10
Alec Jones	Representative	Baudette	26	18
Natasha Nelson	Trainee	Baudette	7	23
Nikolai Jalowiec	Manager	Walker	26	20
Tammy Christine	Representative	Walker	7	41
Josie Daddiline	Trainee	Walker	10	21
Tara Miller	Trainee	Breezy Point	32	17
Robert Andrew	Representative	Walker	15	10
Coryn Gomez	Representative	Baudette	35	5
Elizabeth Gabrys	Trainee	Cass Lake	43	9
Rita Larson	Trainee	Walker	6	36
Michael Gentile	Representative	Baudette	38	9

Figure 6-62 Criteria from more than one column can be used in *SUMIFS*, *AVERAGEIFS*, or *COUNTIFS*

MORE INFO

The *SUMIFS* function is best used in large lists for which it would be time-consuming to calculate these types of results.

The syntax for a *SUMIFS* function is:

=SUMIFS(sum_range, criteria_range1, criteria1, [criteria_range2, criteria2], ...)

The three required arguments are *sum_range*, *criteria_range1*, and *criteria1*. The *sum_range* is the cell range to be added. *Criteria_rangeN* is the range of cells that holds the criteria; it must have the same number of rows and columns as the *sum_range*. The *criteriaN* argument is a cell or typed data that must be matched for the cells to be included in the total.

A *SUMIFS* formula includes one *sum_range* and up to 127 *criteria_rangeN* arguments, each with a corresponding *criteriaN* argument.

HOW TO: Use SUMIFS

1. Click the cell for the result.
2. Click the **Math & Trig** button [*Formulas* tab, *Function Library* group] and choose **SUMIFS**.
3. Select the cells with data to be totaled for the *Sum_range* argument.
   - You can type cell references instead of selecting them.
4. Click the **Criteria_range1** argument box.
5. Select the range of cells with the first set of data to be matched with criteria.
   - This range must be the same size as the *Sum_range*.
6. Click the **Criteria1** argument box.
7. Type the data to be used as a condition.
   - If the criteria are located in a cell on the worksheet, select the cell.
   - Text criteria are not case sensitive.
   - Use wildcard characters in typed criteria.
8. Click the **Criteria_range2** argument box.
9. Select the range with the next set of data to be matched.
   - This range must be the same size as the *Sum_range*.
10. Click the **Criteria2** argument box.
11. Type the second requirement or condition (Figure 6-63).

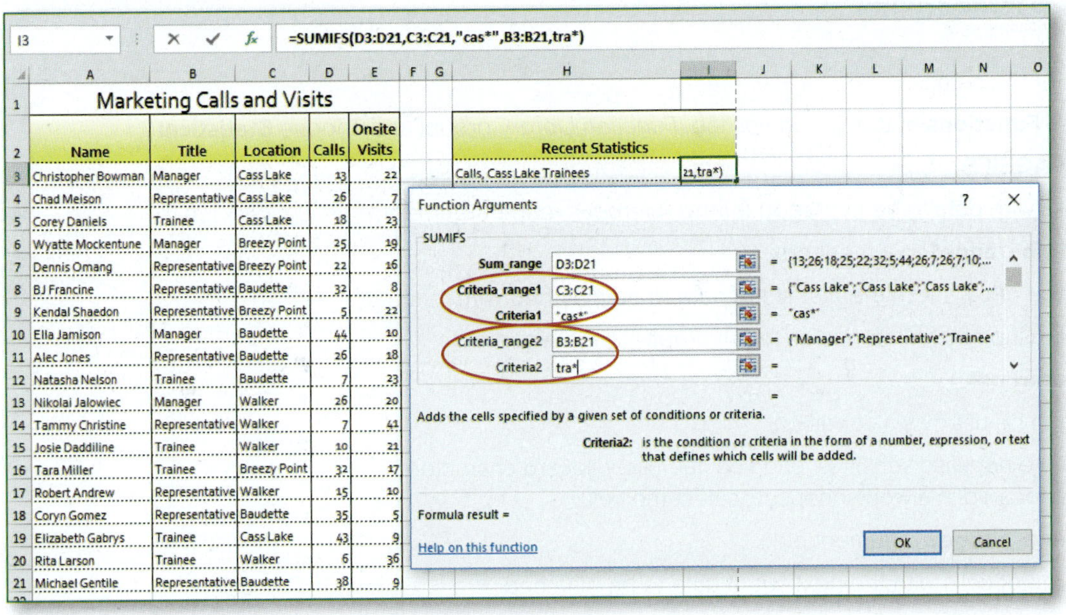

Figure 6-63 Data is included in sum only if it meets both criteria

12. Add *Criteria_range* and *Criteria* arguments as needed.
    - The size of each *Criteria_range* must match the size of the *Sum_range*.
    - Each *Criteria_range* argument must have a corresponding *Criteria* argument.
13. Click **OK**.

The AVERAGEIFS and COUNTIFS Functions

AVERAGEIFS and *COUNTIFS* perform their computations only when the data meets multiple criteria, like the *SUMIFS* function. For the data in Figure 6-64, use *AVERAGEIFS* to calculate the average number of onsite visits made by Walker representatives.

ANOTHER WAY

Results calculated by *SUMIFS, AVERAGEIFS,* or *COUNTIFS* can also be determined by filtering and sorting data in an Excel table.

The syntax for the *AVERAGEIFS* function is:

=AVERAGEIFS(average_range, criteria_range1, criteria1, [criteria_range2, criteria2]...)

The three arguments in an *AVERAGEIFS* calculation are *average_range, criteria_rangeN,* and *criteriaN.* There is one *average_range*, and the *criteria_range* arguments must be the same size as the *average_range*. You can use up to 127 criteria ranges, and each one must have corresponding criteria.

The *COUNTIFS* function has multiple *criteria_range* arguments, which are the cell ranges with data to be counted. There is a corresponding *criteria* argument for each *criteria_range* argument, up to 127.

The syntax for the *COUNTIFS* function is:

=COUNTIFS(criteria_range1, criteria1, [criteria_range2, criteria2]...)

HOW TO: Use AVERAGEIFS

1. Click the cell for the result.
2. Click the **More Functions** button [*Formulas* tab, *Function Library* group] and choose **Statistical**.
3. Choose **AVERAGEIFS**.
4. Select the cells with data to be averaged for the *Average_range* argument.
5. Click the **Criteria_range1** argument box.
6. Select the range of cells with the first set of data to be matched with criteria.
    - This range must be the same size as the *Average_range* argument.
7. Click the **Criteria1** box.
8. Type the data to be used as a condition.
    - Text criteria are not case sensitive, and you can use wildcard characters.
    - If criteria are located in a worksheet cell, select the cell.
9. Click the **Criteria_range2** argument box.
10. Select the range of cells with the next set of data to be matched.
    - This range must be the same size as the *Average_range* argument.

11. Click the **Criteria2** box.
12. Type the second requirement or condition (Figure 6-64).

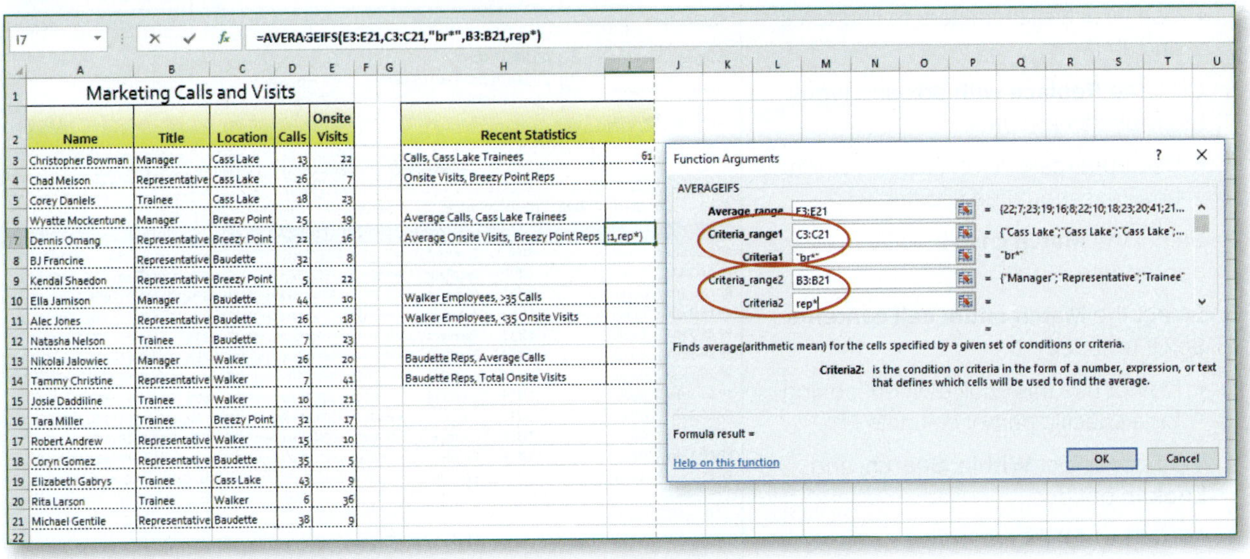

Figure 6-64 Data is included in average only if it meets both criteria

13. Add *Criteria_range* and *Criteria* arguments as needed.
    - The size of each *Criteria_range* must match the size of the *Average_range*.
    - Each *Criteria_range* argument must have a corresponding *Criteria* argument.
14. Click **OK**.

SLO 6.8

Editing and Monitoring Functions

With the *Find and Replace* command, you can make batch changes to functions or formulas. You can monitor results in different parts of a large worksheet or in a multi-sheet workbook from the *Watch Window*.

Find and Replace

Use *Find and Replace* to change a function or an argument throughout a worksheet. For example, edit an incorrect *value_if_true* argument in a nested *IF* function in thousands of rows with *Find and Replace*.

HOW TO: Replace a Function Argument

1. Select the cell range with data to be replaced.
2. Click the **Find & Select** button [*Home* tab, *Editing* group] and choose **Replace**.
3. Click **Options>>** to expand the *Find and Replace* options.
4. Click the **Find what** box.
    - Delete existing search strings.
    - If necessary, click the **Format** arrow and clear the find format.

5. Type the data to be replaced.
   - Use uppercase if it will be necessary to match case.
   - Use wildcard characters to shorten a find string.
6. Click the **Replace with** box and type the replacement data.
   - Use uppercase for characters when new text should be capitalized.
7. Select the **Match case** box if appropriate.
8. Select the **Match entire cell contents** box if required.
   - Do not use this choice when looking for a specific part of cell data.
9. Verify or select **Within**, **Search**, and **Look In** options.
10. Click **Find All** (Figure 6-65).
    - Size the *Find and Replace* dialog box to view the results.
11. Click **Replace All**.
    - Replace occurrences one at a time if preferred.
12. Click **OK** in the message box.
13. Close the *Find and Replace* dialog box.
    - Undo a *Find and Replace* task by pressing **Ctrl+Z** or by clicking the **Undo** button on the *Quick Access* toolbar.

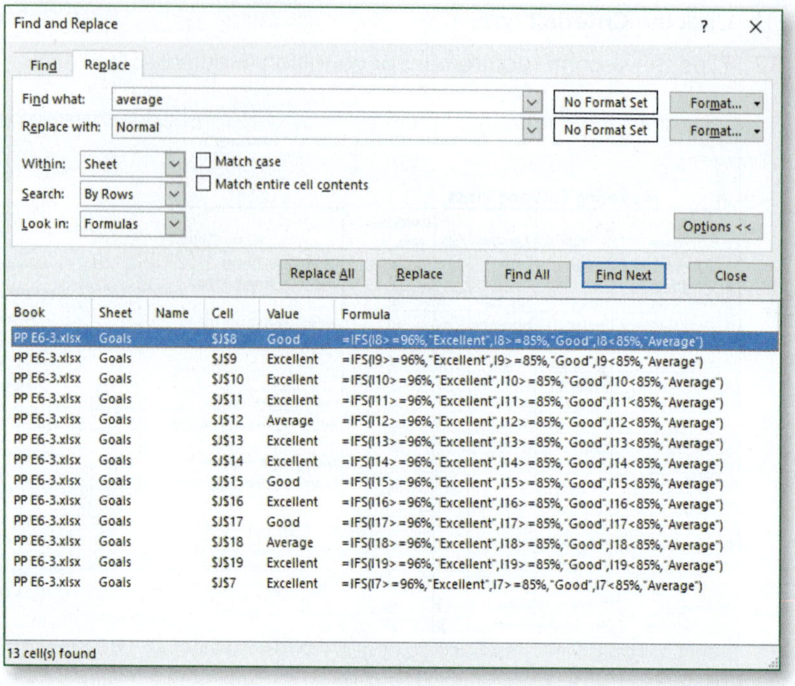

Figure 6-65 All occurrences that will be replaced

ANOTHER WAY

Use the *Find and Replace* command to replace formats such as font name, fill color, or border style.

The Watch Window

Use the *Watch Window* to observe the effects of changes without having to scroll through a large sheet or switch between multiple sheets. A ***Watch Window*** is a floating dialog box with identifying data from selected cells. You can position and size a *Watch Window* like any dialog box. In addition, when you click a cell address in the *Watch Window*, the insertion point moves to that location, like a bookmark.

HOW TO: Monitor Changes in the Watch Window

1. Click the **Watch Window** button [*Formulas* tab, *Formula Auditing* group].
   - The *Watch Window* opens.
2. Select the first cell or range to monitor and click **Add Watch** in the floating window.
3. Click **Add** in the *Add Watch* dialog box.

4. Repeat steps 2–3 to add cells or ranges to the *Watch Window*.
   - Size the *Watch Window* and its columns to see the contents (Figure 6-66).
   - Position the window as desired.
5. Edit data in the workbook as needed.
   - Switch to another worksheet if necessary.
6. Select a watch in the *Watch Window* and click **Delete Watch** in the floating window.
   - Use regular selection methods to select more than one watch.
7. Close the *Watch Window*.

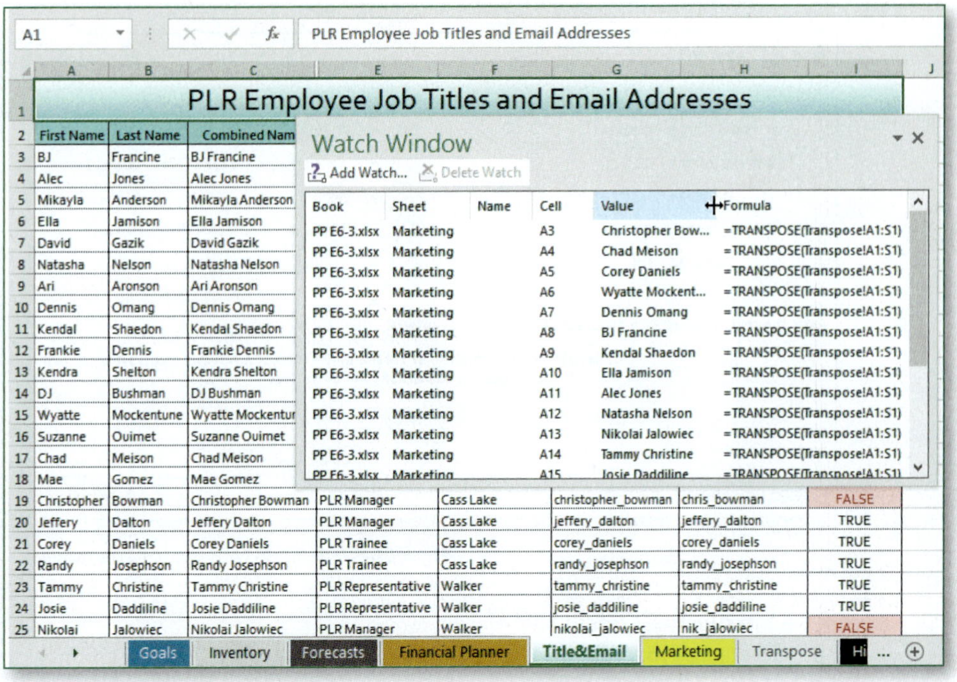

Figure 6-66 ***Watch Window* for *Marketing* sheet while working on *Title&Email* sheet**

PAUSE & PRACTICE: EXCEL 6-4

In this project, you use functions from the *Math & Trig* and *Statistical* categories with multiple criteria ranges to analyze Paradise Lakes Resort marketing data. You update an argument in an *IFS* function and watch changes in transposed data.

File Needed: ***[your initials] PP E6-3.xlsx***
Completed Project File Name: ***[your initials] PP E6-4.xlsx***

1. Open ***[your initials] PP E6-3.xlsx*** completed in *Pause & Practice 6-3* and save it as [your initials] PP E6-4.
2. Click the **Marketing** sheet tab.
3. Use the *SUMIFS* function.
   a. Select cell **I3**.
   b. Click the **Math & Trig** button [*Formulas* tab, *Function Library* group] and choose **SUMIFS**.
   c. Select cells **D3:D21** for the *Sum_range* argument, the number of calls.
   d. Click the **Criteria_range1** box and select cells **C3:C21**, the "Location" column.
   e. Click the **Criteria1** box and type cas* to include cells with data for Cass Lake.
   f. Click the **Criteria_range2** box and select cells **B3:B21**, the "Title" column.
   g. Click the **Criteria2** box and type tr* to include trainee data (Figure 6-67).
   h. Click **OK**. The number of calls made by Cass Lake trainees is 61.
   i. Select cell **I4** and use *SUMIFS* to total the number of onsite visits made by Breezy Point representatives.

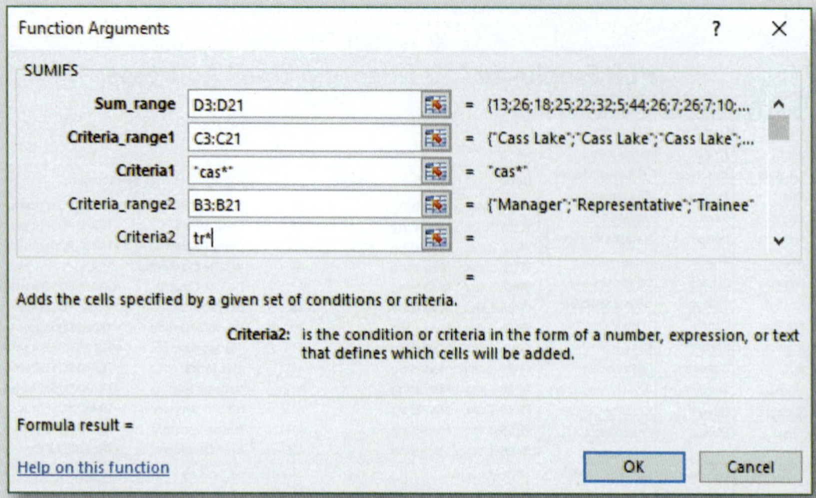

Figure 6-67 *SUMIFS* with two criteria ranges

4. Use the *AVERAGEIFS* function.
   a. Select cell **I6**.
   b. Click the **More Functions** button [*Formulas* tab, *Function Library* group] and choose **Statistical**.
   c. Choose **AVERAGEIFS**.
   d. Select cells **D3:D21** for the *Average_range* argument.
   e. Click the **Criteria_range1** box and select cells **C3:C21** for the location.
   f. Click the **Criteria1** box and type cas* for Cass Lake as the location.
   g. Click the **Criteria_range2** box and select cells **B3:B21** for the job title.
   h. Click the **Criteria2** box and type tr* (Figure 6-68).

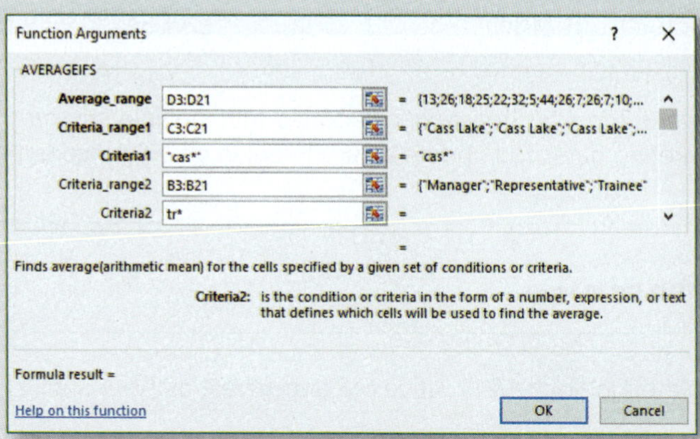

Figure 6-68 *AVERAGEIFS* with two criteria ranges

   i. Click **OK**. The average number of calls made by Cass Lake trainees is 30.5.
   j. Click cell **I7** and use *AVERAGEIFS* to find the average number of onsite visits made by Breezy Point representatives.
5. Use *COUNTIFS*.
   a. Select cell **I10**.
   b. Click the **More Functions** button [*Formulas* tab, *Function Library* group], **Statistical**, and select **COUNTIFS**.
   c. Select cells **C3:C21** for the *Criteria_range1* argument.
   d. Click the **Criteria1** box and type wa* to count Walker data.
   e. Click the **Criteria_range2** box and select cells **D3:D21**.

f. Click the **Criteria2** box and type >35. The function will count the number of cells in which the location is Walker and the number of calls is greater than 35 (Figure 6-69).

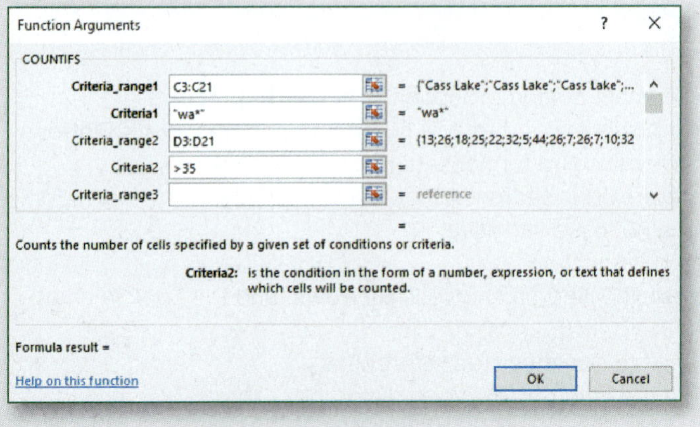

Figure 6-69 ***COUNTIFS*** **with two criteria ranges**

g. Click **OK**. No Walker representatives made more than 35 calls.

h. Click cell **I11** and use *COUNTIFS* to count the number of Walker representatives who made fewer than 35 onsite visits.

6. Click cell **I13** and use *AVERAGEIFS* based on the data in cell **H13**.

7. Click cell **I14** and use *SUMIFS*.

8. Watch edits in the *Watch Window*.
   a. Select cells **A3:A21** on the **Marketing** sheet.
   b. Click the **Watch Window** button [*Formulas* tab, *Formula Auditing* group].
   c. Select and delete any previous watches.
   d. Click **Add Watch**, verify the selection, and click **Add**.
   e. Size the *Watch Window* to see more rows and more data in each column.
   f. Click the **Transpose** sheet tab.
   g. Click cell **B1**, change the name to Barton Miles, and press **Enter** (Figure 6-70). The name is updated on the **Marketing** sheet as shown in the *Watch Window*.

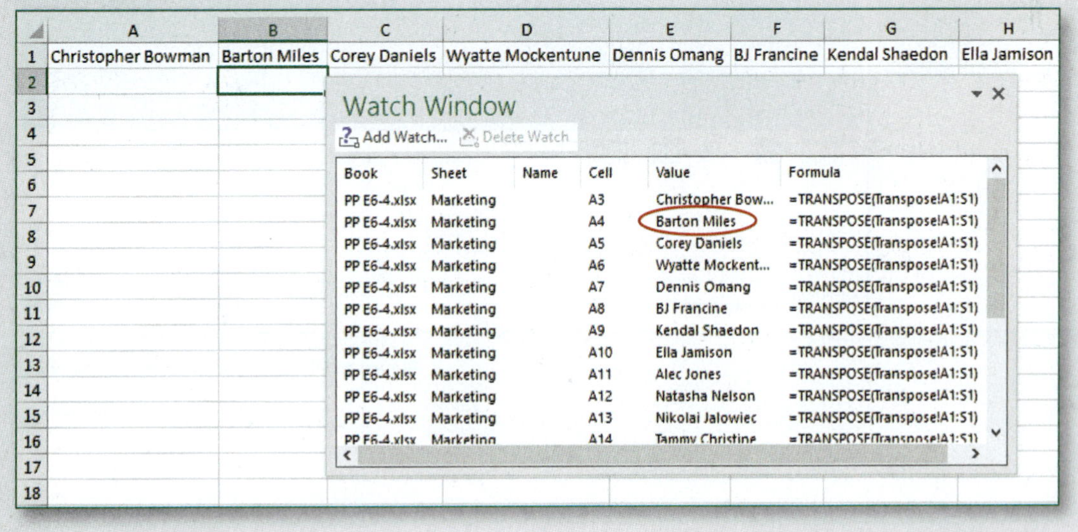

Figure 6-70 Name is changed on ***Marketing*** **sheet**

h. Select the first watch in the *Watch Window*.
i. Press **Shift** and select the last watch.
j. Click **Delete Watch** and close the *Watch Window*.

9. Use *Find and Replace*.
   a. Click the **Goals** sheet tab.
   b. Click the **Find & Select** button [*Home* tab, *Editing* group] and choose **Replace**.
   c. Click **Options>>**. When the dialog box is expanded, this command appears as **<<Options**.
   d. Click the **Format** arrow and clear previous find format settings if necessary.
   e. Click the **Find what** box and delete previous search strings.
   f. Type average. The *Find what* string is not case sensitive.
   g. Click the **Replace with** box and type Normal.
   h. Verify that the *Within* choice is **Sheet**, the *Search* choice is **By Rows**, and the *Look In* choice is **Formulas**.
   i. Click **Find All** and size the dialog box to see the listed references.
   j. Select the reference for cell **$I$7** in the *Find and Replace* dialog box.
   k. Scroll the list, press **Shift**, and select the reference for cell **$I$19**. The selection excludes the use of "average" in cells B22 and C22 (Figure 6-71).
   l. Click **Replace All** and then click **OK**.
   m. Close the *Find and Replace* dialog box.

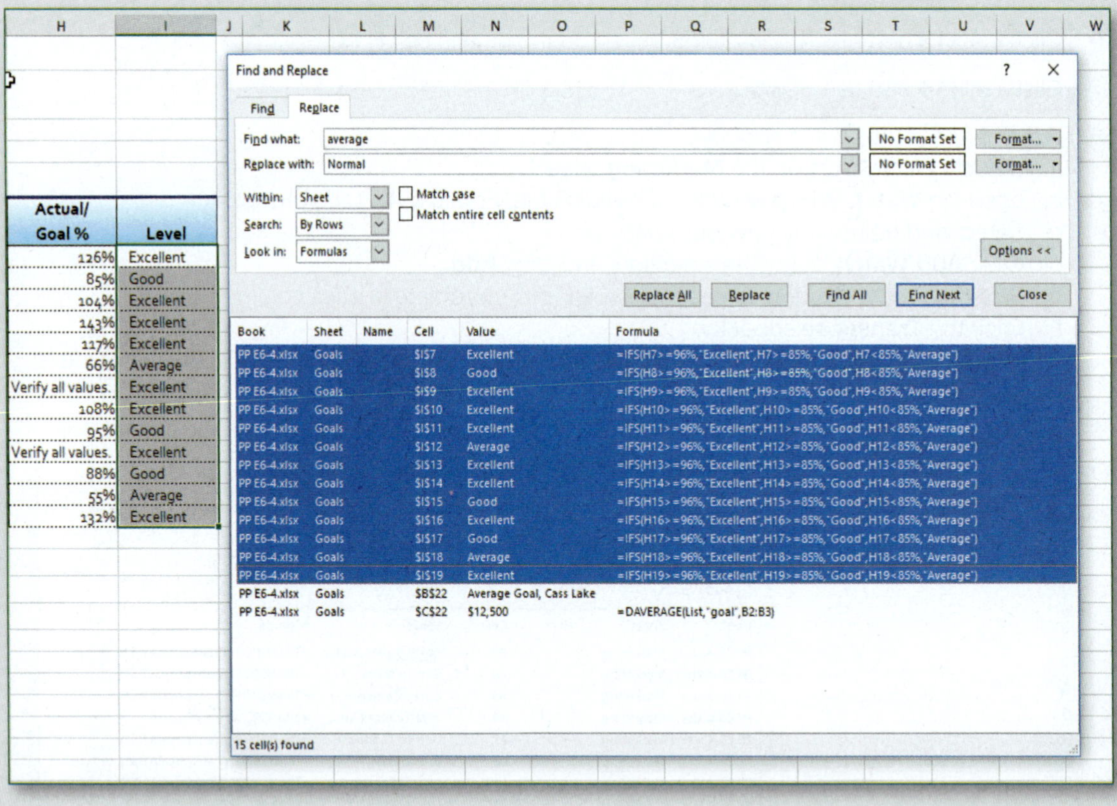

Figure 6-71 Select occurrences to be replaced

10. Save and close the workbook (Figure 6-72).

Marketing Calls and Visits

Name	Title	Location	Calls	Onsite Visits
Christopher Bowman	Manager	Cass Lake	13	22
Barton Miles	Representative	Cass Lake	26	7
Corey Daniels	Trainee	Cass Lake	18	23
Wyatte Mockentune	Manager	Breezy Point	25	19
Dennis Omang	Representative	Breezy Point	22	16
BJ Francine	Representative	Baudette	32	8
Kendal Shaedon	Representative	Breezy Point	5	22
Ella Jamison	Manager	Baudette	44	10
Alec Jones	Representative	Baudette	26	18
Natasha Nelson	Trainee	Baudette	7	23
Nikolai Jalowiec	Manager	Walker	26	20
Tammy Christine	Representative	Walker	7	41
Josie Daddiline	Trainee	Walker	10	21
Tara Miller	Trainee	Breezy Point	32	17
Robert Andrew	Representative	Walker	15	10
Coryn Gomez	Representative	Baudette	35	5
Elizabeth Gabrys	Trainee	Cass Lake	43	9
Rita Larson	Trainee	Walker	6	36
Michael Gentile	Representative	Baudette	38	9

Recent Statistics	
Calls, Cass Lake Trainees	61
Onsite Visits, Breezy Point Reps	38
Average Calls, Cass Lake Trainees	30.5
Average Onsite Visits, Breezy Point Reps	19
Walker Employees, >35 Calls	0
Walker Employees, <35 Onsite Visits	3
Baudette Reps, Average Calls	32.75
Baudette Reps, Total Onsite Visits	40

Revenue Data by Employee

Name	Location	Goal	Actual	Met Goal?	Either Goal?	Both Goals?	Actual/ Goal %	Level
BJ Francine	Baudette	$17,000	$21,500	Yes	TRUE	Met both	126%	Excellent
Christopher Bowman	Cass Lake	$15,000	$12,750	No	FALSE	No	85%	Good
Nikolai Jalowiec	Walker	$15,000	$15,600	Yes	TRUE	Met both	104%	Excellent
Chad Meison	Cass Lake	$17,500	$25,000	Yes	TRUE	Met both	143%	Excellent
Dennis Omang	Breezy Point	$18,000	$21,000	Yes	TRUE	Met both	117%	Excellent
Corey Daniels	Cass Lake	$5,000	$3,300	No	FALSE	No	66%	Normal
Natasha Nelson	Baudette	$0	$4,050	Yes	TRUE	No	Verify all values.	Excellent
Tammy Christine	Walker	$75,000	$81,000	Yes	TRUE	Met both	108%	Excellent
Wyatte Mockentune	Breezy Point	$15,000	$14,200	No	FALSE	No	95%	Good
Kendal Shaedon	Breezy Point	21000S	$18,500	No	TRUE	No	Verify all values.	Excellent
Ella Jamison	Baudette	$15,000	$13,200	No	FALSE	No	88%	Good
Alec Jones	Baudette	$17,000	$9,350	No	FALSE	No	55%	Normal
Josie Daddiline	Walker	$42,500	$56,000	Yes	TRUE	Met both	132%	Excellent

Average Goal, Cass Lake	$12,500
Total Goal, Cass Lake	$37,500

Figure 6-72 Completed worksheets for PP E6-4

Chapter Summary

6.1 Use *Database* functions such as *DSUM* and *DAVERAGE* (p. E6-355).

- Functions in the *Database* category perform a calculation only when data meet the criteria.
- ***Database functions*** are used with list or table-type data.
- The syntax for a *Database* function is *FunctionName (database, field, criteria).*
- The *criteria* argument is a range of cells with labels in one row and criteria below the label row on the same or another sheet.
- The criteria range recognizes *AND* conditions in the same row or *OR* criteria in separate rows.

6.2 Build *Logical* functions including *AND*, *OR*, and *IFS* functions (p. E6-357).

- *AND* and *OR* functions return TRUE or FALSE as a result.
- An *AND* function tests multiple conditions and shows TRUE only when all conditions are met.
- An *OR* function tests multiple conditions and shows TRUE if one condition is met and shows FALSE only when all statements are false.
- *AND* and *OR* functions have one argument, *logicalN*, but can have up to 255 *logicalN* statements.
- A ***nested function*** is a function within another function.
- *AND* or *OR* are nested within *IF* to check for multiple conditions by using an *AND* or *OR* function as the *logical_test* argument.
- An *IFS* function can use multiple *logical_test* arguments with a corresponding *value_if_true* argument for each test.
- The *SWITCH* function compares an expression to a list and displays the matching result.
- A formula syntax error results in a default error message in the cell such as #N/A or #VALUE!
- For formulas that may result in a default error message, use the *IFERROR* function to display a custom message.

6.3 Explore the *Lookup & Reference* category with *INDEX*, *MATCH*, and *TRANSPOSE* (p. E6-370).

- An *INDEX* function displays the contents of the cell at the intersection of a specified column and row.
- The *MATCH* function returns the relative location of data in a list.
- *MATCH* and *INDEX* are nested to accomplish the same tasks as a *VLOOKUP* formula but at a faster speed.
- Nested *MATCH* and *INDEX* formulas are well-suited to datasets with millions of rows.
- The *TRANSPOSE* function displays columnar data in rows and vice versa.

6.4 Build date, time, and statistical calculations (p. E6-375).

- Date arithmetic is possible because Excel uses a serial numbering system for dates.
- Date and time calculations are straightforward, but an unsuitable format can disguise the results.
- The *Date & Time* function category includes functions that convert text into dates, determine workdays in a range of dates, or display the day of the week for a date.
- Use Excel functions to build common statistical forecasting calculations.
- A ***forecast error*** is the deviation or difference between actual values and predicted or forecasted values.
- The ***mean absolute deviation*** (***MAD***) is a statistical measure of how spread out a group of values is from the average.
- A ***standard deviation*** measures how broadly values vary from the mean (average) value, a common statistical calculation.

6.5 Use *Financial* functions such as *PV*, *FV*, and *NPV* (p. E6-386).

- Financial functions analyze money transactions.
- Many functions in the *Financial* category include ***rate***, ***pmt***, and ***nper*** arguments.
- The *PV* function calculates the current value of regular payments at a set interest rate for a specified period of time.
- The *FV* function calculates the future value of regular payments or deposits invested at a constant interest rate for a specified period of time.
- The *NPV* function calculates the net present value of an investment using a ***rate*** and a series of ***cash flows*** which can be receipts or payments.

6.6 Work with *Text* functions including *TEXTJOIN, CONCAT, EXACT,* and *REPLACE* (p. E6-389).

- Text functions join, convert, and split labels and values in a worksheet.
- The *TEXTJOIN* function combines up to 252 strings of text, values, or characters in a single cell and uses a delimiter to separate the strings.
- The *CONCAT* function combines up to 255 strings of text, values, or characters in a single cell, and delimiters must be included in the arguments.
- The *EXACT* function compares two text, value, or character strings and displays TRUE if they are identical.
- The *REPLACE* function removes characters in a data string and replaces them with new characters.

6.7 Use multiple criteria in *SUMIFS*, *AVERAGEIFS*, and *COUNTIFS* functions (p. E6-396).

- The *SUMIFS* function is in the *Math & Trig* category and sums values for cells that meet up to 127 criteria.
- *AVERAGEIFS* and *COUNTIFs* are both in the *Statistical* category.
- *AVERAGIFS* averages values for cells that meet the criteria and *COUNTIFS* counts them.

6.8 Monitor and edit functions with the *Watch Window* and *Find and Replace* (p. E6-399).

- Use the *Find and Replace* command to locate and replace function arguments as well as function names in a workbook.
- The ***Watch Window*** is a floating dialog box, sized and positioned to show as much data as necessary.
- Add cell references to the *Watch Window* to observe changes in another part of the worksheet or workbook.

Check for Understanding

The SIMbook for this text (within your SIMnet account) provides the following resources for concept review:

- Multiple-choice questions
- Short answer questions
- Matching exercises

Guided Project 6-1

In this project, you use *Database* functions to calculate results for the Boyd Air flight schedule. You build a worksheet that tracks flight hours for staff and work with *Text* and *Financial* functions.
[Student Learning Outcomes 6.1, 6.2, 6.3, 6.4, 6.5, 6.6, 6.7, 6.8]

File Needed: ***BoydAir-06.xlsx*** *(Student data files are available in the* Library *of your SIMnet account.)*
Completed Project File Name: ***[your initials] Excel 6-1.xlsx***

Skills Covered in This Project

- Use *Database* functions *DAVERAGE*, *DCOUNTA*, and *DMIN*.
- Use *COUNTIFS* and *SUMIFS*.
- Nest *MATCH* and *INDEX* functions.
- Build time and deviation calculations.
- Build *Logical* functions with *OR*.
- Create an *IFERROR* formula.
- Build an *IFS* formula.
- Use and nest *Text* functions.
- Create formulas with *Financial* functions.
- Find and replace data on multiple worksheets.

1. Open the ***BoydAir-06*** workbook from your student data files and save it as [your initials] Excel 6-1.
2. Use *DCOUNTA* to determine the number of flights originating in Chicago.
    a. Click the **Flight Stats** sheet tab.
    b. Select cells **A4:H18** and name the range Flights. The range includes the labels in row 4.
    c. Click the **Criteria** sheet tab.
    d. Click cell **C2** and type mdw for Midway airport in Chicago.
    e. Click the **Flight Stats** sheet, select cell **E22**, and click the **Insert Function** button on the *Formula* bar.
    f. Choose **Database** in the *Or select a category* list.
    g. Select **DCOUNTA** and click **OK**.
    h. Press **F3** (**FN+F3**) for the *Database* argument to open the *Paste Name* dialog box.
    i. Choose **Flights** and click **OK**.
    j. Click the **Field** argument box and type origin.
    k. Click the **Criteria** argument box and select cells **C1:C2** on the **Criteria** sheet. (Figure 6-73).
    l. Click **OK**. The result is 3.
3. Use *DCOUNTA* to determine the number of flights terminating in Minneapolis.
    a. Click the **Criteria** sheet tab.
    b. Click cell **D2** and type msp for the Minneapolis-St. Paul airport.
    c. Click the **Flight Stats** sheet tab and select cell **E23**.
    d. Click the **Recently Used** button [*Formulas* tab, *Function Library* group] and select **DCOUNTA**.
    e. Press **F3** (**FN+F3**) for the *Database* argument, choose **Flights**, and click **OK**.
    f. Click the **Field** argument box and type 4 for the fourth column from the left in the range, the destination.
    g. Click the **Criteria** box, click the **Criteria** sheet tab, and select cells **D1:D2**.
    h. Click **OK**. The result is 4.

4. Copy cells **A1:H2** on the **Criteria** sheet to cells **A4:H5**. Delete the contents of cells **C5:D5**.

5. Select cell **D5** and type grb for the Green Bay airport.

6. Click the **Flight Stats** sheet and select cell **E24**. Start a *DAVERAGE* formula, select the **Flights** range name, and use the "passengers" column. The criteria is located in cells **D4:D5** on the **Criteria** sheet; the result is 77.5.

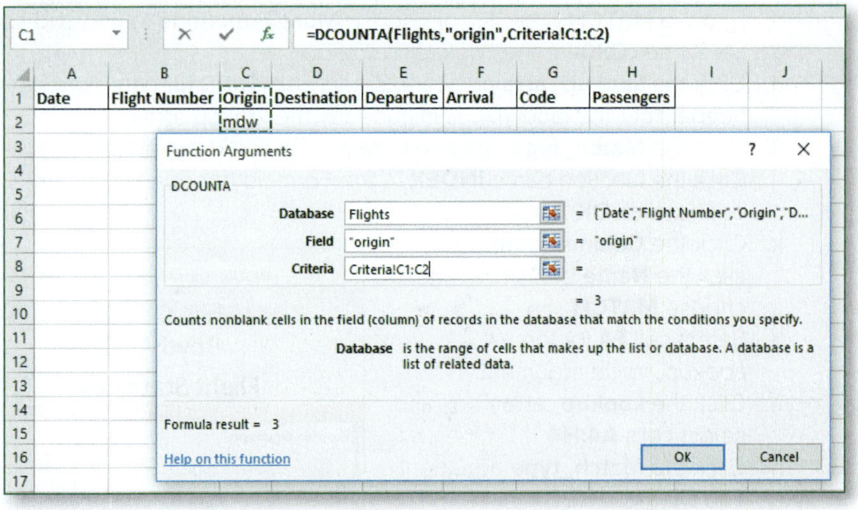

Figure 6-73 ***DCOUNTA*** **function to count flights that originated at MDW**

7. Use *COUNTIFS* to count flights delayed into Chicago.
   a. Select cell **E25** on the **Flight Stats** sheet.
   b. Click the **More Functions** button [*Formulas* tab, *Function Library* group] and choose **Statistical**.
   c. Choose **COUNTIFS**.
   d. Select cells **D5:D18** for the *Criteria_range1* argument.
   e. Click the **Criteria1** box and type mdw for Midway airport.
   f. Click the **Criteria_range2** box and select cells **G5:G18**.
   g. Click the **Criteria2** box and type del* for "Delayed" (Figure 6-74).
   h. Click **OK**. The result is 2.

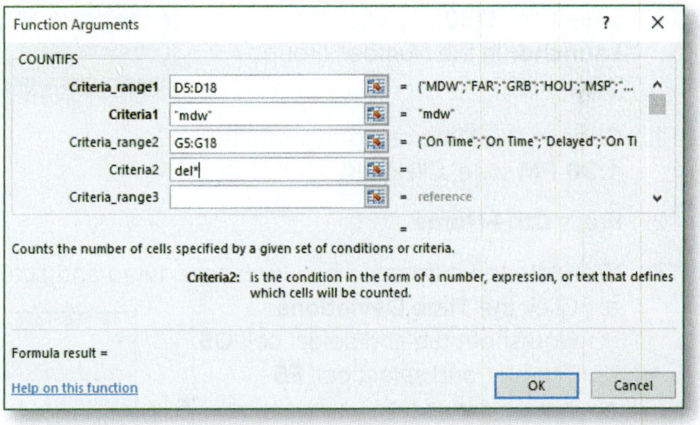

Figure 6-74 ***COUNTIFS*** **with two criteria**

8. Use *SUMIFS* to count total passengers delayed into Chicago.
   a. Select cell **E26**.
   b. Click the **Math & Trig** button [*Formulas* tab, *Function Library* group] and choose **SUMIFS**.
   c. Select cells **H5:H18** for the *Sum_range* argument.
   d. Click the **Criteria_range1** box and select cells **D5:D18**, the destination field.
   e. Click the **Criteria1** box and type mdw.
   f. Click the **Criteria_range2** box and select cells **G5:G18**, the code field.
   g. Click the **Criteria2** box and type del*.
   h. Click **OK**. The count is 170 passengers.

9. Nest *MATCH* with *INDEX* function to display an arrival time.
   a. Select cell **D30**.
   b. Click the **Lookup & Reference** button [*Formulas* tab, *Function Library* group] and choose **INDEX**.
   c. Select the first argument list **array, row_num, column_num** and click **OK**.
   d. Paste the **Flights** range name for the *Array* argument.
   e. Click the **Row_num** box and click the **Name** box arrow.

f. Choose **MATCH** in the list or choose **More Functions** to find and select **MATCH**.
g. Select cell **C30** for the *Lookup_value* box.
h. Click the **Lookup_array** box and select cells **D4:D18**. When the named range includes the header row, the label row is included in the lookup array.
i. Click the **Match_type** box and type 0 to use an exact match.
j. Click the function name **INDEX** in the *Formula* bar. (If an argument lists box opens, click **OK**).
k. Click the **Column_num** box, click the **Name** box arrow, and choose **MATCH**.
l. Select **F4** for the *Lookup_value* argument.
m. Click the **Lookup_array** box and select cells **A4:H4**.
n. Click the **Match_type** argument and type 0.
o. Click **INDEX** in the *Formula* bar to see the complete nested formula (Figure 6-75).
p. Click **OK**. The result is formatted as a number.

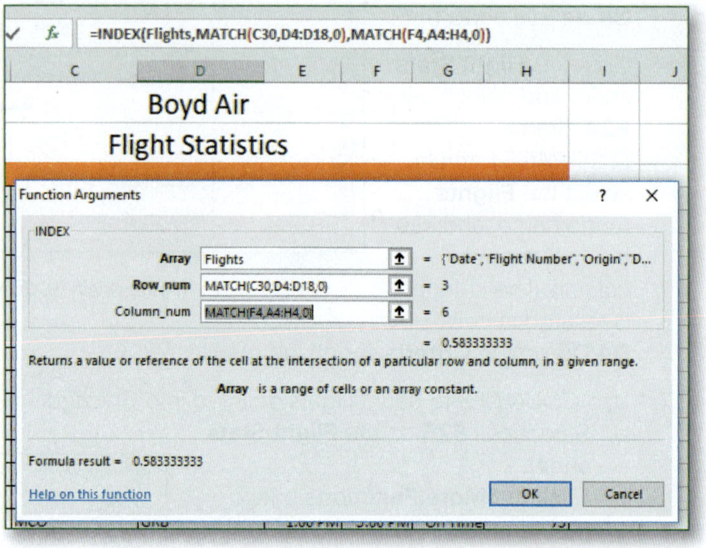

Figure 6-75 *MATCH* nested for both *INDEX* arguments

10. Select cell **D30** and click the **Launcher** in the *Number* group [*Home* tab].
11. Choose the **Time** category and the **1:30 PM** style. Click **OK**.
12. Press **Ctrl+Home**.
13. Calculate the difference between scheduled and actual arrival time.
    a. Click the **Time Deviations** worksheet tab and select cell **G5**.
    b. Type =(and select cell **F5**.
    c. Type a minus sign –, select cell **E5**, and type the closing parenthesis).
    d. Type *24*60 to convert the result to days and then to minutes (Figure 6-76).
    e. Press **Enter**. A series of ### symbols means the column is not wide enough.
    f. Copy the formula in cell **G5** to cells **G6:G24**.
    g. Select cells **G5:G24** and apply the **General** format. A negative number of minutes means the flight was early.

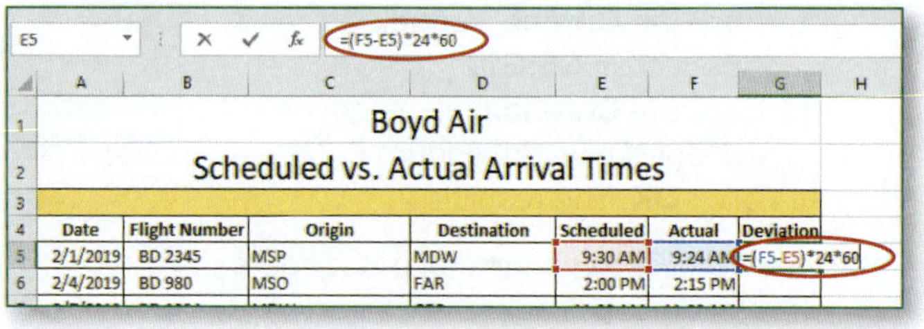

Figure 6-76 Time difference is converted to minutes

14. Calculate the mean absolute deviation (MAD) for arrival times.
    a. Select cell **I5**.
    b. Click the **Math & Trig** button [*Formulas* tab, *Function Library* group] and choose **ABS**.
    c. Select cell **G5** for the *Number* argument and click **OK**.
    d. Copy the formula in cell **I5** to cells **I6:I24**.
    e. Select cell **D27**.
    f. Use the *AVERAGE* function to calculate the mean (or average) for cells **I5:I24**. The result is 10.35.
    g. Right-click the column **I** heading and choose **Hide**.

15. Calculate the standard deviation for arrival times.
    a. Select cell **D28**.
    b. Click the **More Functions** button [*Formulas* tab, *Function Library* group], choose **Statistical**, and choose **STDEV.S**.
    c. Select cells **G5:G24** for the *Number1* argument and press **Enter**. The result is 13.3111548.
    d. Press **Ctrl+Home**.

16. Use the *Function Arguments* dialog box to enter an *OR* function.
    a. Click the **Flight Hours** tab and select cell **F4**.
    b. Click the **Logical** button [*Formulas* tab, *Function Library* group] and choose **OR**.
    c. Click the **Logical1** argument box, select cell **D4**, and type >20.
    d. Click the **Logical2** box, select cell **E4**, and type >20 (Figure 6-77).

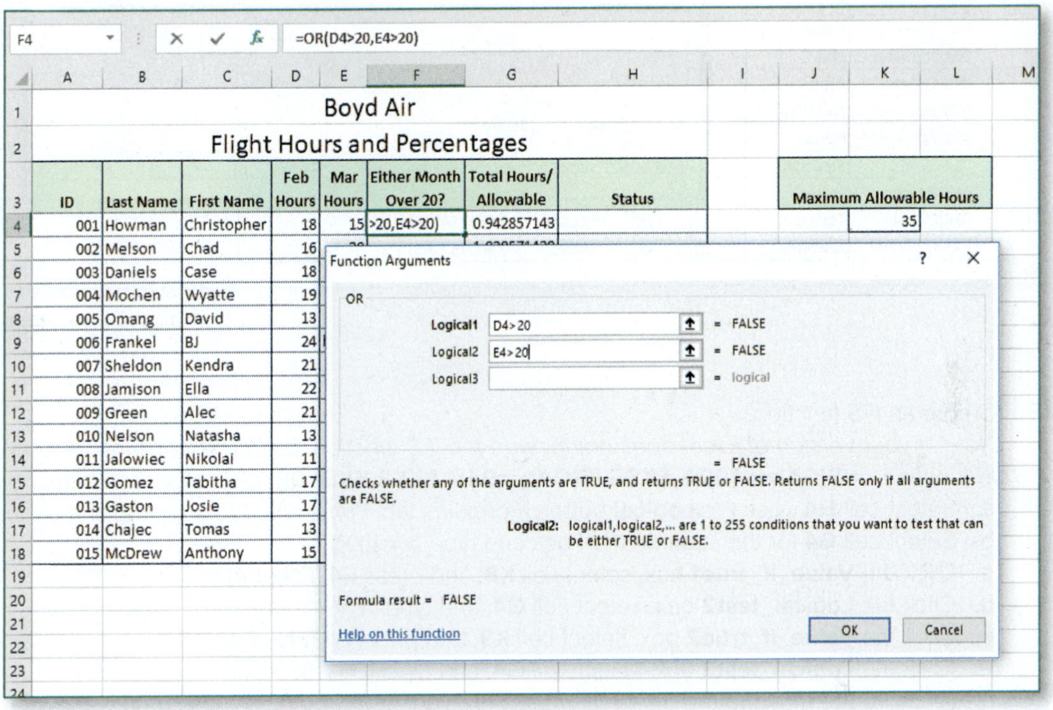

Figure 6-77 *OR* **formula**

    e. Click **OK**. The first result is FALSE.
    f. Copy the formula in cell **F4** to cells **F5:F18** without formatting.

17. Use *IFERROR* to display a custom message.
    a. Select cell **G4**. The formula adds the hours for February and March and then divides by the allowable hours in cell K4. A standard Excel error message displays in cell **G9** because the data in cell E9 is text.
    b. Delete the formula in cell **G4**.
    c. Click the **Logical** button [*Formulas* tab, *Function Library* group] and choose **IFERROR**.
    d. Type a left parenthesis (in the *Value* argument box, select cell **D4**, type +, and select cell **E4.**
    e. Type a right parenthesis and a forward slash for division)/, click cell **K4**, and press **F4** (**FN+F4**) to make it absolute.
    f. Click the **Value_if_error** box and type Check values. (Figure 6-78).
    g. Click **OK.**
    h. Copy the formula in cell **G4** to cells **G5:G18** without formatting. Widen the column to display the complete message.
    i. Format cells **G4:G18** with **Percent Style** and two decimal places.

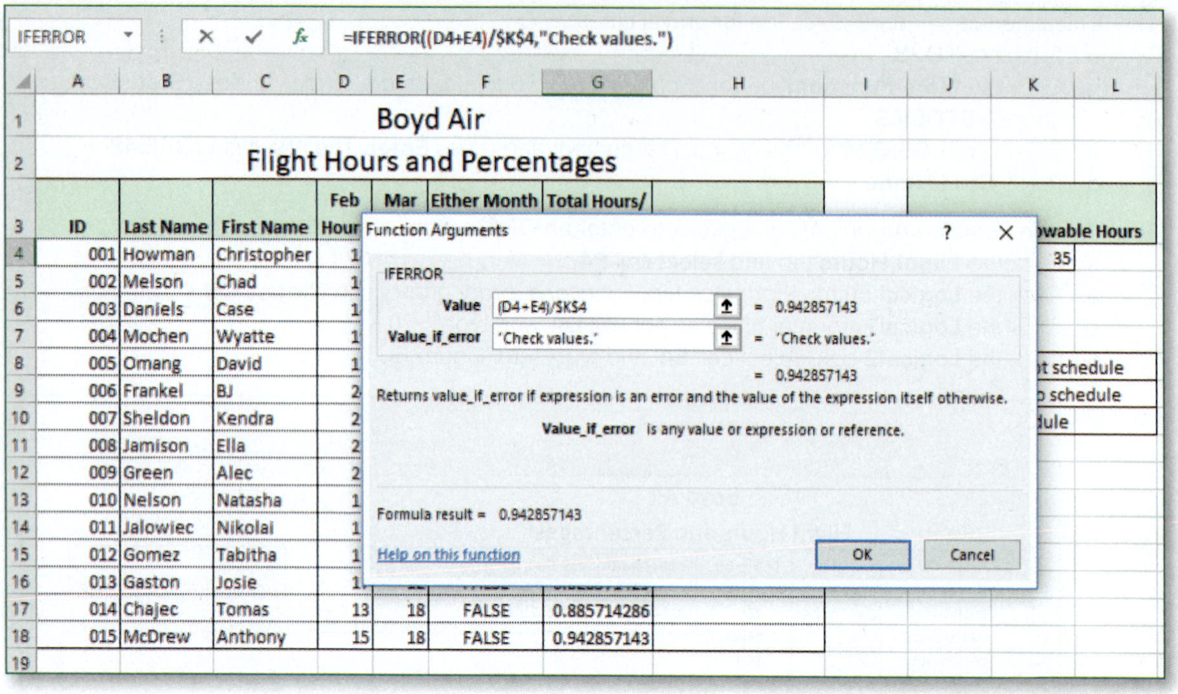

Figure 6-78 *IFERROR* formula

18. Create an *IFS* function.
    Note: If your version of Excel does not include the IFS function, build the following nested IF function: **=IF(G4>=100%,$K$8,IF(G4>=91%,$K$9,$K$10))** *to display the status.*
    a. Select cell **H4**, click the **Logical** button [*Formulas* tab, *Function Library* group] and choose **IFS**.
    b. Select cell **G4** for the *Logical_test1* box and type >=100%.
    c. Click the **Value_if_true1** box, select cell **K8**, and press **F4** (**FN+F4**).
    d. Click the **Logical_test2** box, select cell **G4**, and type >=91%.
    e. Click the **Value_if_true2** box, select cell **K9**, and press **F4** (**FN+F4**).
    f. Click the **Logical_test3** box, select cell **G4**, and type <=91%.
    g. Press **Tab** to move to the *Value_if_true3* box, select cell **K10**, and press **F4** (**FN+F4**) (Figure 6-79).
    h. Click **OK**.
    i. Copy the formula in cell **H4** to cells **H5:H18** without formatting.
    j. Increase the indent one time for the data in column **H**.
    k. Press **Ctrl+Home**.

19. Create a nested *Text* function with *UPPER* and *CONCAT*.
    a. Click the **Flight Staff** sheet tab and select cell **D4**. Data in this column is exported to another application and must display first and last names in uppercase characters.
    b. Click the **Text** button [*Formulas* tab, *Function Library* group] and choose **UPPER**. The argument is the *Text* to be shown in uppercase letters.
    c. Click the **Name** box arrow, and choose **More Functions** for the *Text* argument.
    d. Choose **Text** as the category, select **CONCAT**, and click **OK**. The *Function Arguments* dialog box shows arguments for the *CONCAT* function. (Use *CONCATENATE* If your version of Excel does not include *CONCAT*.)
    e. Select cell **C4** for the *Text1* argument.
    f. Click the **Text2** argument box and press **Spacebar**.
    g. Click the **Text3** argument box and select cell **B4** (Figure 6-80).
    h. Click **OK**.

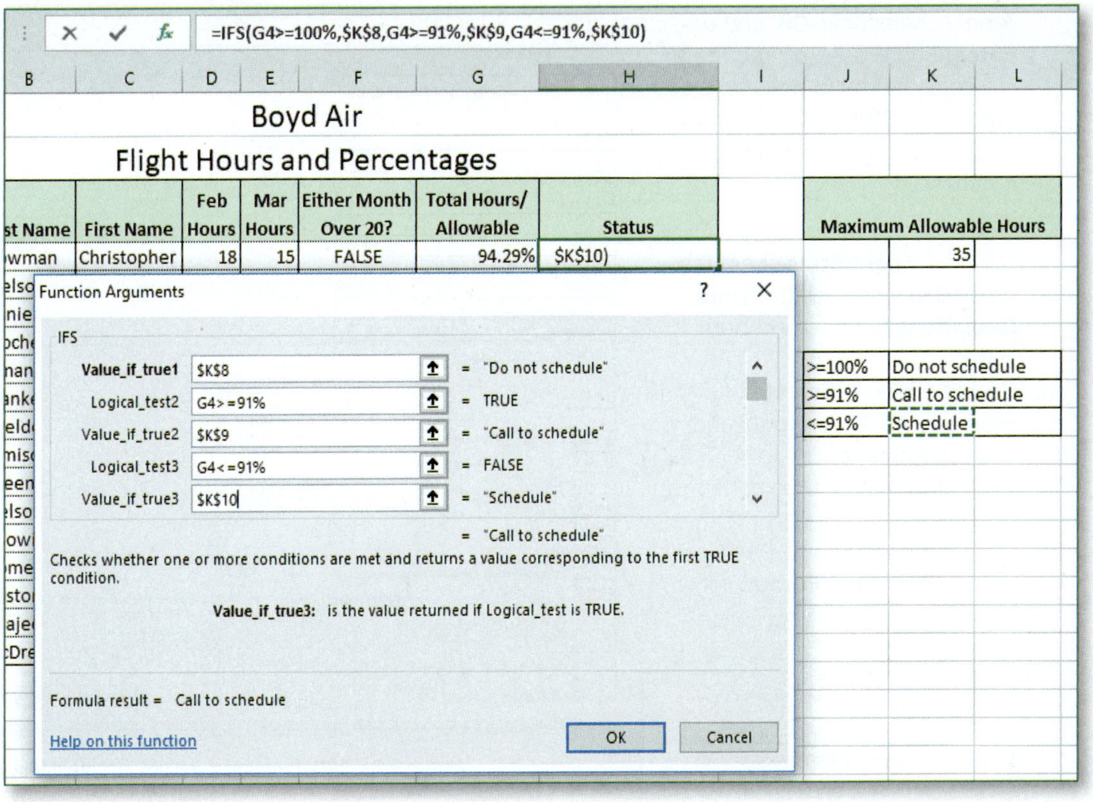

Figure 6-79 *IFS* function

i. Copy the formula in cell **D4** to cells **D5:D18** without formatting.
j. Press **Ctrl+Home**.

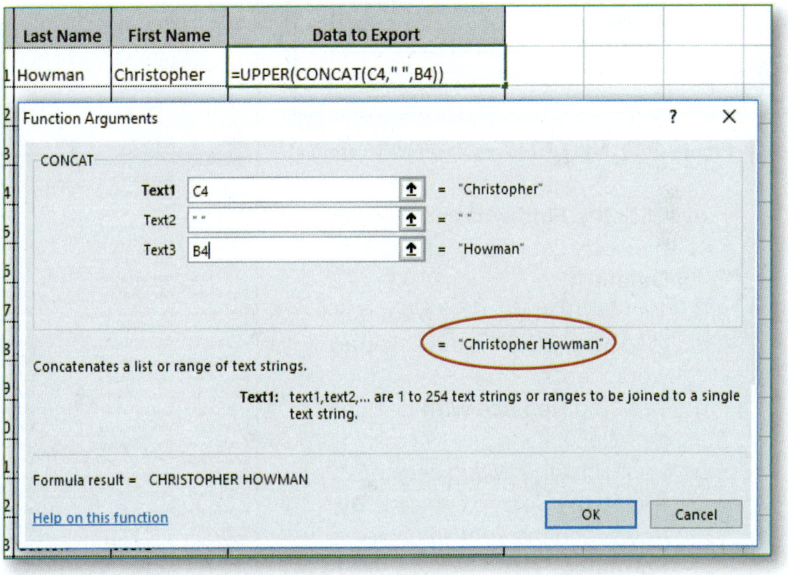

Figure 6-80 *CONCAT* and *UPPER* functions

20. Determine the net present value of new equipment purchases.
   a. Click the **Equipment Eval** sheet tab and select cell **C12**.
   b. Click the **Financial** button [*Formulas* tab, *Function Library* group] and choose **NPV**.
   c. Select cell **C5** for the *Rate* argument.
   d. Click the **Value1** box and select cell **C8**, the expected savings in the first year.
   e. Click the **Value2** box and select cell **C9**, expected savings in the second year.
   f. For the **Value3** argument, select cell **C10** (Figure 6-81).
   g. Click **OK**.
   h. Click the *Formula* bar and press **End** to position the insertion point after the right parenthesis.

i. Type +, select cell **C6**, and press **Enter** (Figure 6-82) to add the initial cost to the formula results.

j. Select cell **C24** and build an *NPV* calculation for a competing purchase.

21. Use *Find and Replace*.

a. Click the **Flight Stats** sheet tab, press **Ctrl**, and click the **Time Deviations** tab to select both sheets.

b. Click the **Find & Select** button [*Home* tab, *Editing* group] and choose **Replace**.

c. Click **Options>>** to expand the options.

d. Click the **Format** arrow and select **Clear Find Format** if it is available.

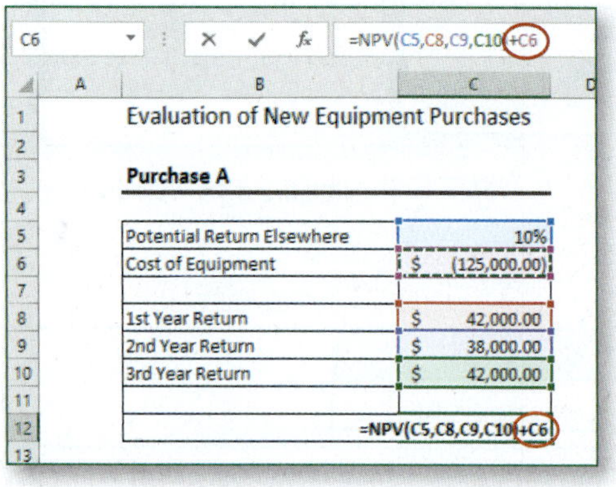

Figure 6-82 Add cost to results of *NPV* formula

e. Click the **Find what** box, select previous data if any, and press **Delete**.

f. Type 2019 in the *Find what* box to locate "2019" in the selected worksheets.

g. Click the **Replace with** box and type 2020.

h. Verify that the *Within* choice is **Sheet**, the *Search* choice is **By Rows**, and the *Look In* choice is **Formulas**.

i. Click **Find All**. Thirty-four cells are found (Figure 6-83).

j. Click **Replace All** and click **OK**. Close the *Find and Replace* dialog box.

k. Right-click the **Flight Stats** sheet and ungroup the sheets.

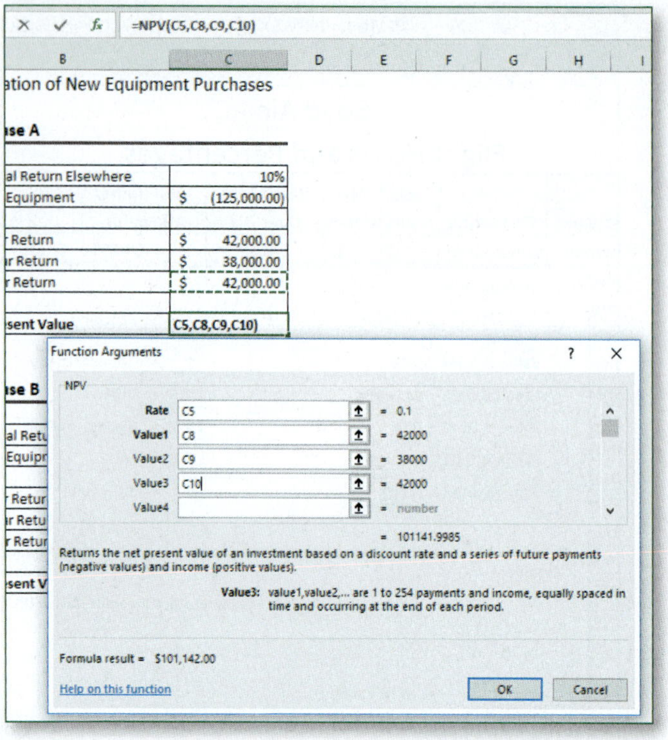

Figure 6-81 *NPV* function does not include initial cost

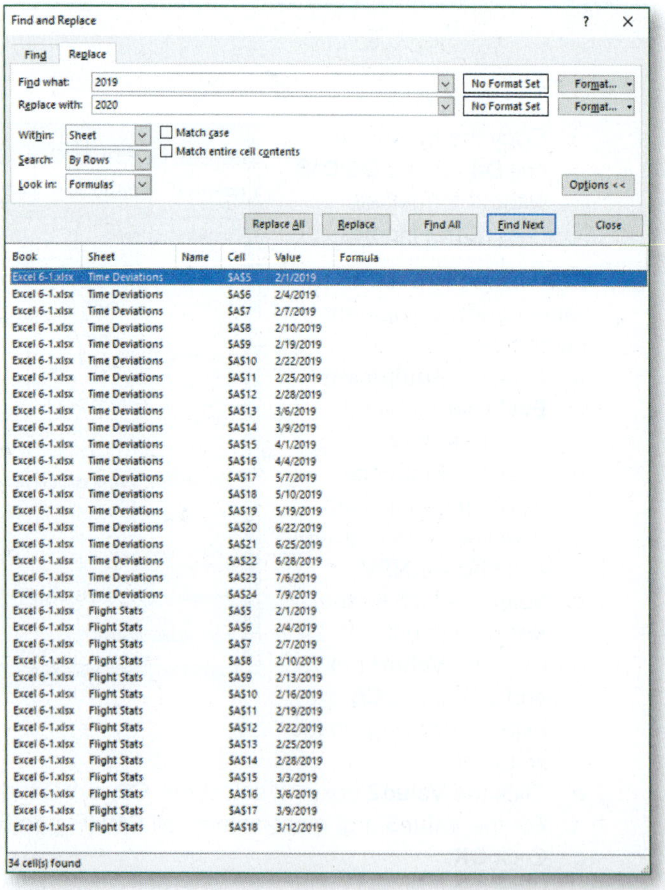

Figure 6-83 Cells with data to be replaced

22. Save and close the workbook (Figure 6-84).

Boyd Air
Flight Statistics

Date	Flight Number	Origin	Destination	Departure	Arrival	Code	Passengers
2/1/2020	BD 2345	MSP	MDW	8:00 AM	9:30 AM	On Time	90
2/4/2020	BD 980	MSP	FAR	12:30 PM	2:00 PM	On Time	35
2/7/2020	BD 1234	MDW	GRB	10:00 AM	11:00 AM	Delayed	80
2/10/2020	BD 1345	MSP	HOU	4:45 PM	7:30 PM	On Time	90
2/13/2020	BD 4567	MCO	MSP	9:00 PM	11:30 PM	On Time	75
2/16/2020	BD 2213	MDW	MCO	6:30 AM	10:30 AM	Delayed	90
2/19/2020	BD 6578	FAR	STL	8:00 AM	9:30 AM	On Time	63
2/22/2020	BD 234	MDW	MSP	2:00 PM	3:30 PM	On Time	90
2/25/2020	BD 981	FAR	MSP	9:00 AM	10:30 AM	On Time	35
2/28/2020	BD 123	GRB	MDW	2:00 PM	3:00 PM	Delayed	80
3/3/2020	BD 221	MCO	MDW	11:00 AM	3:00 PM	Delayed	90
3/6/2020	BD 134	HOU	MSP	10:00 AM	12:45 PM	On Time	90
3/9/2020	BD 98	FAR	MDW	9:30 AM	11:45 AM	On Time	35
3/12/2020	BD 4567	MCO	GRB	1:00 PM	5:00 PM	On Time	75

Number of flights originating in MDW	3
Number of flights arriving in MSP	4
Average number of passengers to GRB	77.5
Total flights delayed into MDW	2
Total passengers delayed into MDW	170

City	Arrival Time
FAR	2:00 PM

Boyd Air
Flight Staff

ID	Last Name	First Name	Data to Export
001	Howman	Christopher	CHRISTOPHER HOWMAN
002	Melson	Chad	CHAD MELSON
003	Daniels	Case	CASE DANIELS
004	Mochen	Wyatte	WYATTE MOCHEN
005	Omang	David	DAVID OMANG
006	Frankel	BJ	BJ FRANKEL
007	Sheldon	Kendra	KENDRA SHELDON
008	Jamison	Ella	ELLA JAMISON
009	Green	Alec	ALEC GREEN
010	Nelson	Natasha	NATASHA NELSON
011	Jalowiec	Nikolai	NIKOLAI JALOWIEC
012	Gomez	Tabitha	TABITHA GOMEZ
013	Gaston	Josie	JOSIE GASTON
014	Chajec	Tomas	TOMAS CHAJEC
015	McDrew	Anthony	ANTHONY MCDREW

Evaluation of New Equipment Purchases

Purchase A

Potential Return Elsewhere	10%
Cost of Equipment	$ (125,000.00)
1st Year Return	$ 42,000.00
2nd Year Return	$ 38,000.00
3rd Year Return	$ 42,000.00
Net Present Value	($23,858.00)

Purchase B

Potential Return Elsewhere	8%
Cost of Equipment	$ (79,000.00)
1st Year Return	$ 42,000.00
2nd Year Return	$ 38,000.00
3rd Year Return	$ 42,000.00
Net Present Value	**$25,808.72**

Boyd Air
Scheduled vs. Actual Arrival Times

Date	Flight Number	Origin	Destination	Scheduled	Actual	Deviation
2/1/2020	BD 2345	MSP	MDW	9:30 AM	9:24 AM	-6
2/4/2020	BD 980	MSO	FAR	2:00 PM	2:15 PM	15
2/7/2020	BD 1234	MDW	GRB	11:00 AM	11:02 AM	2
2/10/2020	BD 1345	MSP	HOU	7:30 PM	7:56 PM	26
2/19/2020	BD 6578	FAR	STL	9:30 AM	9:14 AM	-16
2/22/2020	BD 234	MDW	MSP	3:30 PM	3:20 PM	-10
2/25/2020	BD 981	FAR	MSP	10:30 AM	10:15 AM	-15
2/28/2020	BD 123	GRB	MDW	3:00 PM	3:24 PM	24
3/6/2020	BD 134	HOU	MSP	12:45 PM	1:15 PM	30
3/9/2020	BD 98	FAR	MDW	11:45 AM	11:52 AM	7
4/1/2020	BD 2345	MSP	MDW	9:30 AM	9:32 AM	2
4/4/2020	BD 980	MSP	FAR	2:00 PM	2:14 PM	14
5/7/2020	BD 1234	MDW	GRB	11:00 AM	10:48 AM	-12
5/10/2020	BD 1345	MSP	HOU	7:30 PM	7:41 PM	11
5/19/2020	BD 6578	FAR	STL	9:30 AM	9:27 AM	-3
6/22/2020	BD 234	MDW	MSP	3:30 PM	3:30 PM	0
6/25/2020	BD 981	FAR	MSP	10:30 AM	10:30 AM	0
6/28/2020	BD 123	GRB	MDW	3:00 PM	2:55 PM	-5
7/6/2020	BD 134	HOU	MSP	12:45 PM	12:42 PM	-3
7/9/2020	BD 98	FAR	MDW	11:45 AM	11:51 AM	6

MAD	10.35
Standard Deviation	13.3111548

Boyd Air
Flight Hours and Percentages

ID	Last Name	First Name	Feb Hours	Mar Hours	Either Month Over 20?	Total Hours/ Allowable	Status
001	Howman	Christopher	18	15	FALSE	94.29%	Call to schedule
002	Melson	Chad	16	20	FALSE	102.86%	Do not schedule
003	Daniels	Case	18	10	FALSE	80.00%	Schedule
004	Mochen	Wyatte	19	18	FALSE	105.71%	Do not schedule
005	Omang	David	13	19	FALSE	91.43%	Call to schedule
006	Frankel	BJ	24	ll	TRUE	Check values.	Do not schedule
007	Sheldon	Kendra	21	22	TRUE	122.86%	Do not schedule
008	Jamison	Ella	22	15	TRUE	105.71%	Do not schedule
009	Green	Alec	21	23	TRUE	125.71%	Do not schedule
010	Nelson	Natasha	13	14	FALSE	77.14%	Schedule
011	Jalowiec	Nikolai	11	16	FALSE	77.14%	Schedule
012	Gomez	Tabitha	17	14	FALSE	88.57%	Schedule
013	Gaston	Josie	17	12	FALSE	82.86%	Schedule
014	Chajec	Tomas	13	18	FALSE	88.57%	Schedule
015	McDrew	Anthony	15	18	FALSE	94.29%	Call to schedule

Maximum Allowable Hours
35

>=100%	Do not schedule
>=91%	Call to schedule
<=90%	Schedule

Figure 6-84 Completed worksheets for Excel 6-1

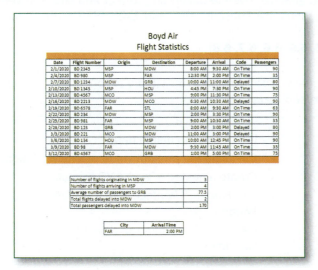

Guided Project 6-2

In a workbook for Eller Software Services, you analyze revenue based on product and city. You verify phone numbers, calculate present value for software subscriptions, and determine representative assignments.
[Student Learning Outcomes 6.1, 6.2, 6.3, 6.4, 6.5, 6.6, 6.7, 6.8]

File Needed: ***EllerSoftware-06.xlsx*** *(Student data files are available in the* Library *of your SIMnet account.)*
Completed Project File Name: ***[your initials] Excel 6-2.xlsx***

Skills Covered in This Project

- Calculate the mean absolute deviation (MAD).
- Use the *STDEV.S* function.
- Nest *MATCH* and *INDEX* functions.
- Build *SUMIFS* formulas.
- Use functions from the *Database* category.
- Use *EXACT* to match data.
- Calculate the present value of a subscription.
- Create a nested *IF* and *AND* formula.
- Use *Find and Replace* with the *Watch Window*.
- Calculate the number of days between two dates.

---

1. Open the ***EllerSoftware-06*** workbook from your student data files and save it as [your initials] Excel 6-2.
2. Calculate the mean absolute deviation (MAD) for the difference between estimated and actual sales.
   a. Click the **Revenue** sheet and select cell **I5**.
   b. Type =ab and press **Tab** to select *ABS*.
   c. Select cell **H5** for the *number* argument, type – to subtract, select cell **G5**, and press **Enter**.
   d. Copy the formula to cells **I6:I17** without formatting to preserve the fill color.
   e. Select cell **D20** and use the *AVERAGE* function with the cell range **I5:I17**.
   f. Format the results as **Number** from the *Number Format* drop-down list [*Home* tab, *Number* group]. The result is 2340.73.
3. Calculate the standard deviation for actual sales.
   a. Select cell **D21**.
   b. Type =std and double-click **STDEV.S** in the list.
   c. Select cells **G5:G17** for the *number1* argument and press **Enter**. The closing parenthesis is supplied, and the result is 12871.23785.
4. Create a nested function using *INDEX* and *MATCH* to display a phone number.
   a. Select cell **D24** and type Jeremie Midboe.
   b. Select cell **D25**. Click the **Lookup & Reference** button [*Formulas* tab, *Function Library* group] and choose **INDEX**.
   c. Select the first argument list **array, row_num, column_num** and click **OK**.
   d. Press **F3** (**FN+F3**) and select **Clients** for the *Array* argument.
   e. Click the **Row_num** box, click the **Name** box arrow, and choose **More Functions**.
   f. Choose **Lookup & Reference** as the category, select **MATCH**, and press **Enter**. The *Function Arguments* dialog box shows *MATCH* arguments.
   g. Select cell **D24** for the *Lookup_value* argument.
   h. Click the **Lookup_array** box and select cells **A5:A17**. The *MATCH* function finds the value in column A that matches cell D24.
   i. Click the **Match_type** box and type 0.
   j. Click the name **INDEX** in the *Formula* bar. If the *Select Arguments* dialog box opens, click **OK**.
   k. Click the **Column_num** box, click the **Name** box arrow, and choose **MATCH**.
   l. Type phone number in the *Lookup_value* box.
   m. Click the **Lookup_array** box and select cells **A4:I4**. This *MATCH* function locates data in the "Phone Number" column for the result of the first *MATCH* function (Figure 6-85).

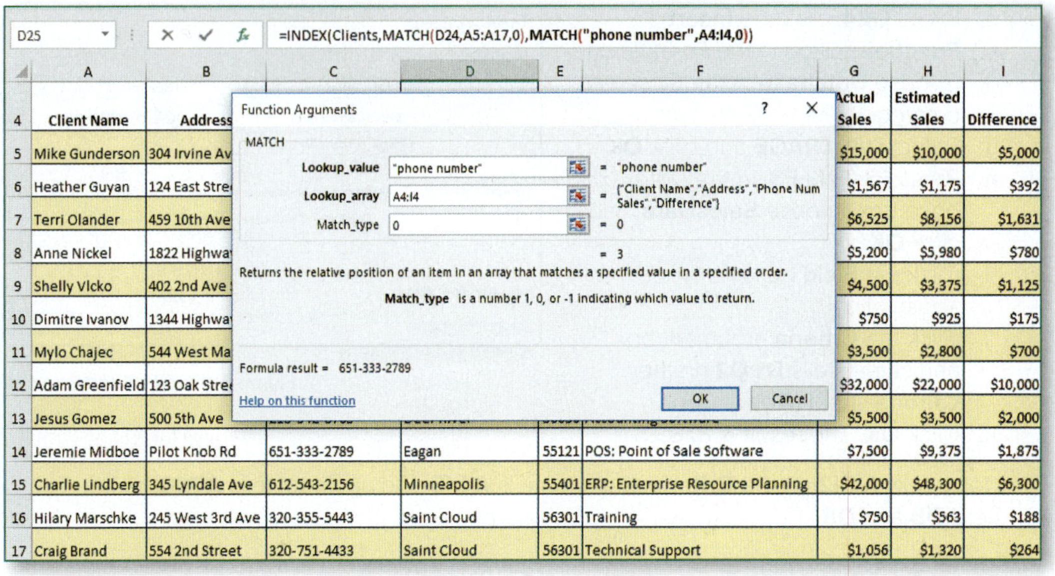

Figure 6-85 Nested *MATCH* and *INDEX* functions

n. Click the **Match_type** box and type 0. The formula is **=INDEX(Clients,MATCH(D24,A5:A17,0),MATCH("phone number",A4:I4,0))**.
o. Click **OK**.
p. Select cell **D24**, type Anne Nickel, and press **Enter**. The phone number changes.

5. Use *SUMIFS* to total revenue by category and city.
   a. Select cell **G20**.
   b. Click the **Math & Trig** button [*Formulas* tab, *Function Library* group] and choose **SUMIFS**.
   c. Select cells **G5:G17** for the *Sum_range* argument and press **F4** (**FN+F4**) to make it absolute.
   d. Click the **Criteria_range1** box, select cells **D5:D17**, the "City" field, and press **F4** (**FN+F4**).
   e. Click the **Criteria1** box and type eag*.
   f. Click the **Criteria_range2** box, select cells **F5:F17**, and press **F4** (**FN+F4**).
   g. Click the **Criteria2** box, type pos* (Figure 6-86).
   h. Click **OK**. The total POS sales for Eagan are 11000.
   i. Copy the *SUMIFS* function in cell **G20** to cell **G21**. Edit the formula criteria to calculate the ERP total for Minneapolis.
   j. Format cells **G20:G21** as **Currency** with no decimal places.

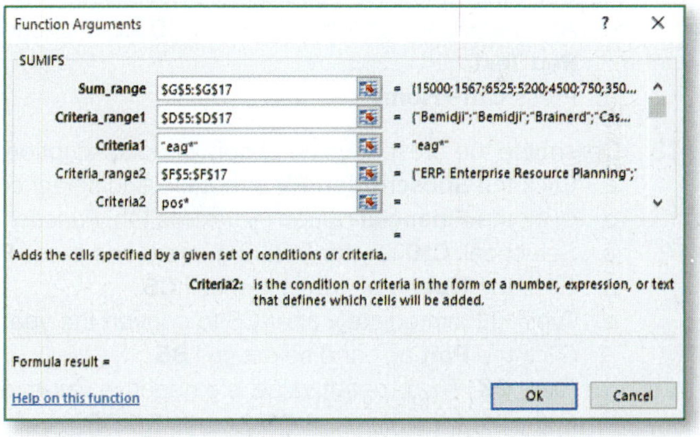

Figure 6-86 *SUMIFS* with its arguments

6. Use *DAVERAGE* to calculate average sales in Bemidji.
   a. Select cells **A4:I17** and name the range SalesData. The range includes column labels.
   b. Select cell **G24** and note the label in cell **F24**.
   c. Click the **Criteria** sheet tab and type be* for Bemidji in cell **D2**.
   d. Click the **Revenue** sheet tab.

e. In cell **G24**, click the **Insert Function** button in the *Formula* bar.
f. Choose **Database** in the *Or select a category* list.
g. Select **DAVERAGE** and click **OK**.
h. Press **F3** (**FN+F3**) in the *Database* box, choose **SalesData**, and click **OK**.
i. Click the **Field** box and type actual sales.
j. Click the **Criteria** argument box and select cells **D1:D2** on the **Criteria** sheet (Figure 6-87).
k. Click **OK**. The result is 8283.5.

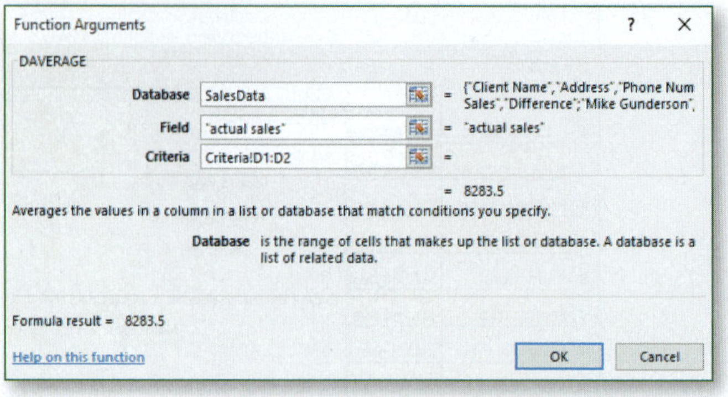

Figure 6-87 ***DAVERAGE*** **and its arguments**

7. Copy cells **A1:I2** on the **Criteria** sheet to cells **A4:I5** and again to cells **A7:I8**. Delete the contents of cells **D5** and **D8**.

8. Select cell **D5** and type min*. Select cell **D8** and type de*.

9. Click the **Revenue** sheet tab. Select cell **G25** and use *DMAX* to display the top sale in Minneapolis.

10. Select cell **G26** and use *DMIN*.

11. Format cells **G24:G26** as **Currency** with no decimal places and press **Ctrl+Home**.

12. Create a *Text* function with *EXACT*.
    a. Click the **Phone Numbers** sheet tab and select cell **D5**. The phone numbers on this sheet will be compared to those on the **Revenue** sheet.
    b. Click the **Text** button [*Formulas* tab, *Function Library* group] and choose **EXACT**.
    c. Select cell **C5** for the *Text1* argument.
    d. Click the **Text2** argument, click the **Revenue** sheet tab, and select cell **C5**.
    e. Click **OK**. If the phone number is an exact match, the result is TRUE.
    f. Copy the formula in cell **D5** to cells **D6:D17**.
    g. Apply a *Highlight Cells* rule to cells **D5:D17** to show FALSE in **Light Red Fill with Dark Red Text**.
    h. Press **Ctrl+Home**.

13. Determine the present value of software subscription plans.
    a. Click the **Subscription PV** sheet tab and select cell **D5**.
    b. Click the **Financial** button [*Formulas* tab, *Function Library* group] and choose **PV**.
    c. Select cell **C10** for the *Rate* argument and press **F4(FN+F4)**.
    d. Click the **Nper** box and select cell **C5**.
    e. Type *12 immediately after C5 to convert the yearly rate to monthly.
    f. Click the **Pmt** box and select cell **B5**.
    g. Click **OK**. The present value is a negative value ($17,545.18).
    h. Copy the formula in cell **D5** to cells **D6:D8**.
    i. Press **Ctrl+Home**.

14. Create a nested *IF* function with *AND* functions as the logical tests.
    a. Click the **Rep Assignments** sheet tab and select cell **F6**.
    b. Click the **Logical** button [*Formulas* tab, *Function Library* group] and choose **IF**.
    c. For the *Logical_test* box, click the **Name** box arrow and choose **AND** from the list, or choose **More Functions** to find and select **AND**.
    d. Click the **Logical1** argument box, select cell **B6** and type ="yes". Quotations marks are required, but the argument is not case sensitive.

e. Click the **Logical2** box, select cell **D6**, and type ="yes". The *AND* formula determines if both cells B6 and D6 show "Yes."

f. Click the word **IF** in the *Formula* bar to return to the *IF Function Arguments* dialog box (Figure 6-88).

g. Click the **Value_if_true** box, select cell **I5**, and press **F4** (**FN+F4**). If cells B6 and D6 show "Yes," the rep's name in cell I5 displays.

h. Click the **Value_if_false** box. If the *Logical_test* is false, a second *IF* statement runs.

i. Click **IF** in the *Name* box or choose **More Functions** to find and select **IF**.

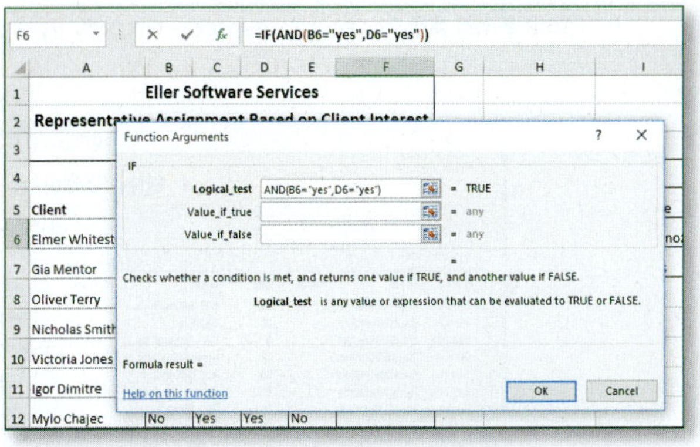

Figure 6-88 First *IF* function and its *Logical_test* argument

j. Click the **Name** box arrow and choose **AND** for the *Logical_test* for the second *IF* statement.

k. Click the **Logical1** box, select cell **C6**, and type ="yes".

l. Click the **Logical2** box, click cell **D6**, and type ="yes". This *AND* formula determines if both cells C6 and D6 show "Yes."

m. In the *Formula* bar, click the second occurrence of **IF** to return to the nested *IF Function Arguments* dialog box

n. Click the **Value_if_true** box, select cell **I6**, and press **F4** (**FN+F4**). If cells C6 and D6 show "Yes," the rep's name in cell I6 displays.

o. Click the **Value_if_false** box, select cell **I7**, and press **F4** (**FN+F4**). If neither *IF* logical test is true, the rep's name in cell I7 displays (Figure 6-89).

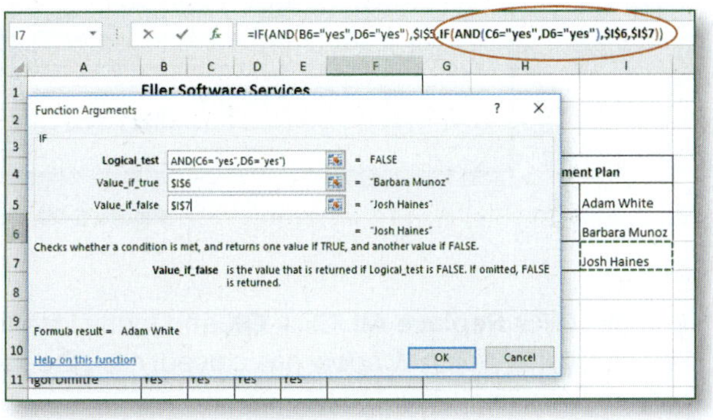

Figure 6-89 The second *IF* function in the nested formula

p. Click **OK** and copy the formula in cell **F6** to cells **F7:F18** without formatting.

15. Use the *Watch Window* and *Find and Replace*.
   a. Click the **Project Duration** sheet tab and select cells **B5:B17**.
   b. Click the **Watch Window** button [*Formulas* tab, *Formula Auditing* group].
   c. Click **Add Watch** and click **Add**.
   d. Click the **Subscription PV** sheet tab, select cell **A8**, click **Add Watch**, and then click **Add**.
   e. Click the **Revenue** sheet tab.
   f. Click the **Find & Select** button [*Home* tab, *Editing* group] and choose **Replace**.
   g. Click **Options>>** to expand the options. If necessary, click the **Format** arrow and clear previous find format settings.
   h. Delete previous search strings in the *Find what* and *Replace with* boxes.
   i. Click the **Find what** box and type acc*.
   j. Click the **Replace with** box and type AR/AP for accounts receivable and accounts payable.
   k. Click the **Within** arrow and choose **Workbook**.

l. Click **Find All**. Nine occurrences display in the *Find and Replace* dialog box (Figure 6-90).

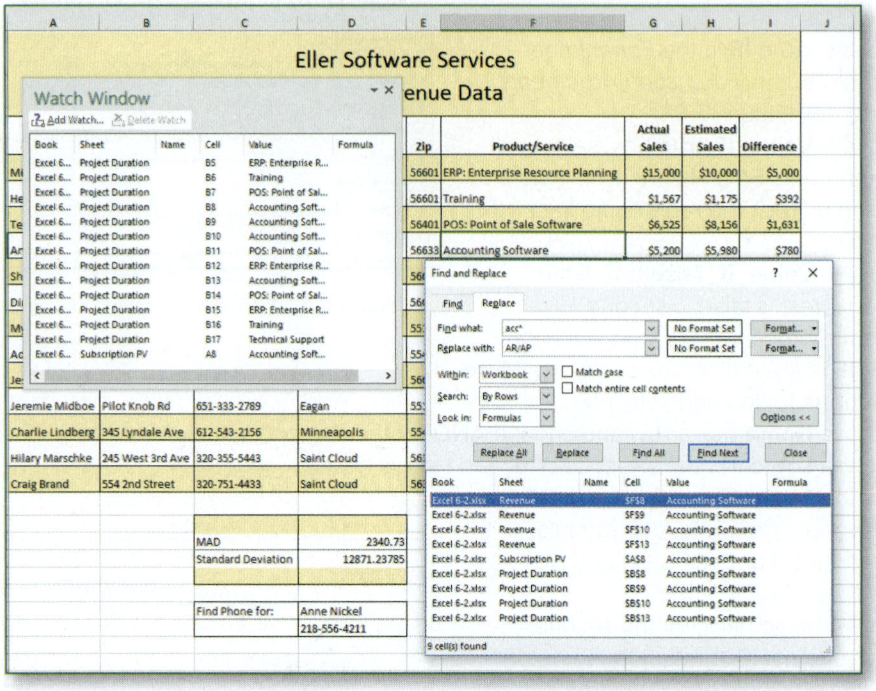

Figure 6-90 ***Find and Replace* dialog box and *Watch Window***

m. Click **Replace All**. Click **OK** and then close the *Find and Replace* dialog box.
n. If the *Watch Window* has closed, click the **Watch Window** button [*Formulas* tab, *Formula Auditing* group] to open it.
o. Select the first reference in the *Watch Window*, press **Shift**, and click the last reference.
p. Click **Delete Watch** and close the *Watch Window*.
q. Press **Ctrl+Home**.

16. Calculate project duration in days.
    a. Click the **Project Duration** sheet tab and select cell **E5**.
    b. Type = and click cell **D5**, the ending date.
    c. Type – to subtract and click cell **C5**, the starting date.
    d. Press **Enter**. The result is formatted as a date.
    e. Copy the formula in cell **E5** to cells **E6:E17** without formatting to preserve the fill color.
    f. Format cells **E5:E17** with the **General** format [*Number Format* drop-down list, *Home* tab].
    g. Press **Ctrl+Home**.

17. Save and close the workbook (Figure 6-91).

Eller Software Services
Client Revenue Data

Client Name	Address	Phone Number	City	Zip	Product/Service	Actual Sales	Estimated Sales	Difference
Mike Gunderson	304 Irvine Ave	218-278-9021	Bemidji	56601	ERP: Enterprise Resource Planning	$15,000	$10,000	$5,000
Heather Guyan	124 East Street	218-333-2313	Bemidji	56601	Training	$1,567	$1,175	$392
Terri Olander	459 10th Avenue	218-667-8977	Brainerd	56401	POS: Point of Sale Software	$6,525	$8,156	$1,631
Anne Nickel	1822 Highway 2	218-556-4211	Cass Lake	56633	AR/AP	$5,200	$5,980	$780
Shelly Vicko	402 2nd Ave SE	218-342-2456	Deer River	56636	AR/AP	$4,500	$3,375	$1,125
Dimitre Ivanov	1344 Highway 3	218-556-3009	Cass Lake	56633	AR/AP	$750	$925	$175
Mylo Chajec	544 West Main	651-345-9071	Eagan	55121	POS: Point of Sale Software	$3,500	$2,800	$700
Adam Greenfield	123 Oak Street	612-543-0090	Minneapolis	55402	ERP: Enterprise Resource Planning	$32,000	$22,000	$10,000
Jesus Gomez	500 5th Ave	218-342-8765	Deer River	56636	AR/AP	$5,500	$3,500	$2,000
Jeremie Midboe	Pilot Knob Rd	651-333-2789	Eagan	55121	POS: Point of Sale Software	$7,500	$9,375	$1,875
Charlie Lindberg	345 Lyndale Ave	612-543-2156	Minneapolis	55402	ERP: Enterprise Resource Planning	$42,000	$48,300	$6,300
Hilary Marschke	245 West 3rd Ave	320-355-5443	Saint Cloud	56301	Training	$750	$563	$188
Craig Brand	554 2nd Street	320-751-4433	Saint Cloud	56301	Technical Support	$1,056	$1,320	$264

MAD	2540.73
Standard Deviation	12871.23785

POS Sales, Eagan	$11,000
ERP, Minneapolis	$74,000

Find Phone for:	Anne Nickel
	218-556-4211

Average Sale, Bemidji	$8,284
Highest Sale, Minneapolis	$42,000
Lowest Sale, Deer River	$4,500

Eller Software Services
Present Value of Software Subscription

Software Application	Subscription (Monthly)	Duration (Years)	Present Value
ERP: Enterprise Resource Planning	$1,200	3	($17,545.18)
Training	$225	2	($2,823.83)
POS: Point of Sale Software	$1,450	4	($22,692.54)
AR/AP	$950	5	($15,353.36)

Competitive Rate of Return (ROR) 6%

Eller Software Services
Updated Phone List

Client Name	Address	Phone Number	OK?
Mike Gunderson	304 Irvine Ave	218-278-9021	TRUE
Heather Guyan	124 East Street	218-333-2312	FALSE
Terri Olander	459 10th Avenue	218-667-8977	TRUE
Anne Nickel	1822 Highway 2	218-556-4211	TRUE
Shelly Vlcko	402 2nd Ave SE	218-342-2456	TRUE
Dimitre Ivanov	1344 Highway 3	218-556-3009	TRUE
Mylo Chajec	544 West Main	651-345-9000	FALSE
Adam Greenfield	123 Oak Street	612-543-0090	TRUE
Jesus Gomez	500 5th Ave	218-342-8765	TRUE
Jeremie Midboe	Pilot Knob Rd	651-333-2789	TRUE
Charlie Lindberg	345 Lyndale Ave	612-543-3290	FALSE
Hilary Marschke	245 West 3rd Ave	320-355-5443	TRUE
Craig Brand	554 2nd Street	320-751-4433	TRUE

Eller Software Services
Project Duration

Project ID	Product/Service	Start	End	Time
ESS014	ERP: Enterprise Resource Planning	5/1/19	6/2/19	32
ESS016	Training	6/3/19	8/5/19	63
ESS018	POS: Point of Sale Software	7/7/19	7/10/19	3
ESS020	AR/AP	9/7/19	11/7/19	61
ESS022	AR/AP	10/2/19	12/21/19	80
ESS024	AR/AP	2/3/20	5/8/20	95
ESS026	POS: Point of Sale Software	4/2/20	4/5/20	3
ESS028	ERP: Enterprise Resource Planning	5/1/20	8/13/20	104
ESS030	AR/AP	5/5/20	8/12/20	99
ESS032	POS: Point of Sale Software	6/6/20	6/10/20	4
ESS034	ERP: Enterprise Resource Planning	7/1/20	8/30/20	60
ESS036	Training	8/5/20	8/15/20	10
ESS038	Technical Support	10/1/20	10/10/20	9

Eller Software Services
Representative Assignment Based on Client Interest

	Product Group				
Client	ERP	HR	POS	AR/AP	Assigned Rep
Elmer Whitestead	Yes	No	Yes	No	Adam White
Gia Mentor	No	No	Yes	No	Josh Haines
Oliver Terry	Yes	Yes	No	Yes	Josh Haines
Nicholas Smith	Yes	Yes	Yes	No	Adam White
Victoria Jones	No	Yes	Yes	No	Barbara Munoz
Igor Dimitre	Yes	Yes	Yes	Yes	Adam White
Mylo Chajec	No	Yes	Yes	No	Barbara Munoz
Lester Simmons	No	Yes	No	Yes	Josh Haines
Kelly MacNeil	Yes	No	Yes	No	Adam White
Jerome Decker	No	No	Yes	No	Josh Haines
Charlie Strom	No	Yes	No	No	Josh Haines
Clinton Olmstead	Yes	No	Yes	Yes	Adam White
Michael Conover	Yes	Ys	Yes	No	Adam White

Assignment Plan	
ERP and POS	Adam White
HR and POS	Barbara Munoz
Others	Josh Haines

Figure 6-91 Completed worksheets for Excel 6-2

Guided Project 6-3

The Wear-Ever Shoes company maintains inventory data and customer survey results in your workbook. You use *Lookup & Reference*, *Database*, and *Logical* functions to complete the data. You also use a *Financial* function to calculate depreciation and a *Text* function to enter email addresses.
[Student Learning Outcomes 6.1, 6.2, 6.3, 6.5, 6.6, 6.7]

File Needed: ***WearEverShoes-06.xlsx*** *(Student data files are available in the* Library *of your SIMnet account.)*
Completed Project File Name: ***[your initials] Excel 6-3.xlsx***

Skills Covered in This Project

- Nest *INDEX* and *MATCH* functions.
- Use *SUMIFS* from the *Math & Trig* category.
- Use *DAVERAGE*.
- Create an *IFS* formula.
- Use a *Text* function to concatenate text strings.
- Calculate depreciation with the *DB* function.

---

1. Open the ***WearEverShoes-06*** workbook from your student data files and save it as [your initials] Excel 6-3.
2. Click the **Inventory** sheet tab.
3. Select cells **A3:I39**, click the **Name** box, type Inventory as the range name, and press **Enter**.
4. Select cell **L5** and type WE006.
5. Create a nested function with *INDEX* and *MATCH* to display inventory for a product.
   a. Select cell **L6**.
   b. Click the **Lookup & Reference** button [*Formulas* tab, *Function Library* group] and choose **INDEX**. Select the first argument list **array, row_num, column_num** and click **OK**.
   c. For the *Array* argument, press **F3** (**FN+F3**) and select **Inventory**.
   d. Click the **Row_num** box and click the **Name** box arrow. Choose **MATCH** in the list or choose **More Functions** to find and select **MATCH**. The *INDEX* function uses this *MATCH* statement to find the row.
   e. Click cell **L5** for the *Lookup_value* argument.
   f. Click the **Lookup_array** box and select cells **A3:A39**. This *MATCH* function finds the row that matches cell L5 in column A.
   g. Click the **Match_type** argument and type 0.
   h. Click **INDEX** in the *Formula* bar. (Click **OK** if the argument list opens.)
   i. Click the **Column_num** argument, click the **Name** box arrow, and choose **MATCH** (Figure 6-92).
   j. Type quantity in the *Lookup_value* box.
   k. Click the **Lookup_array** box and select cells **A3:I3**. This *MATCH* function finds the cell in the "Quantity" column after the row is located by the first *MATCH* function.
   l. Click the **Match_type** box and type 0. The formula is **=INDEX(Inventory,MATCH(L5,A3:A39,0), MATCH("quantity",A3:I3,0))**.
   m. Click **OK**. The result is 2.
   n. Click cell **L5**, type WE015, and press **Enter**. The quantity is updated.
6. Use *SUMIFS* to calculate total pairs in stock by specific criteria.
   a. Select cell **M13**.
   b. Click the **Math & Trig** button [*Formulas* tab, *Function Library* group] and choose **SUMIFS**.
   c. Select cells **E4:E39** for the *Sum_range* argument and press **F4** (**FN+F4**) to make the references absolute.

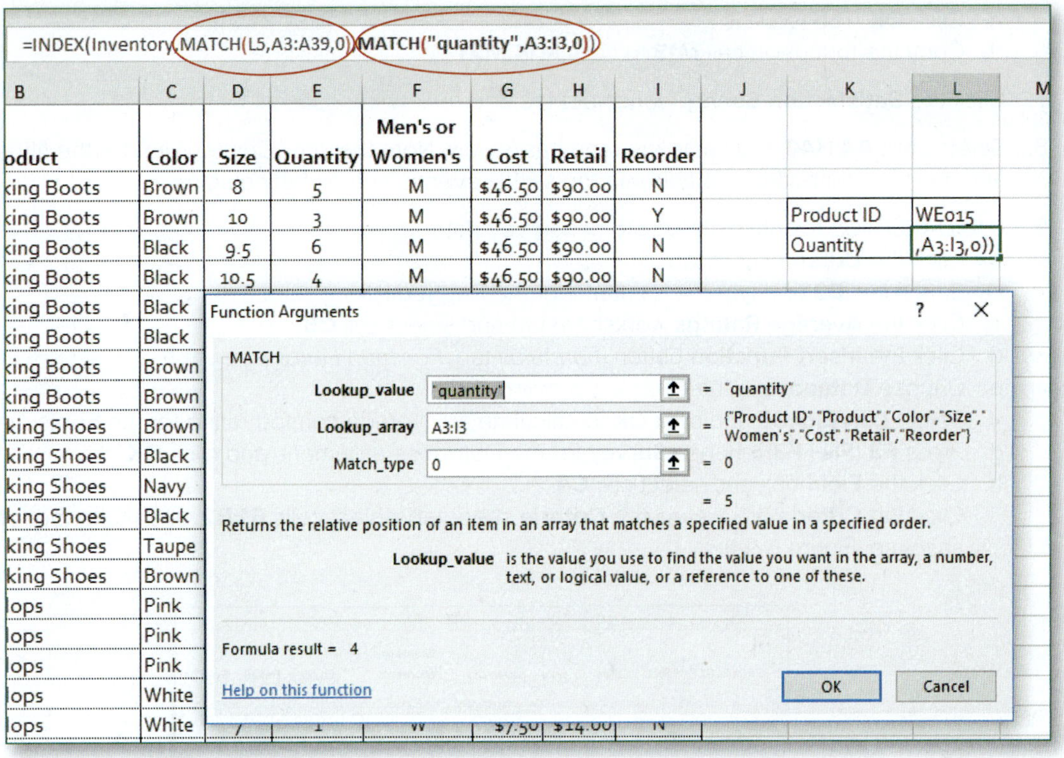

Figure 6-92 *MATCH* is nested twice

d. Click the **Criteria_range1** box, select cells **C4:C39**, the "Color" field, and press **F4** (**FN+F4**).
e. Click the **Criteria1** box and select cell **K13**. Leave this as a relative reference.
f. Click the **Criteria_range2** box, select cells **D4:D39**, and make the references absolute.
g. Click the **Criteria2** box and select cell **L13**. The criteria specifies the number of black pairs, size 8 (Figure 6-93).

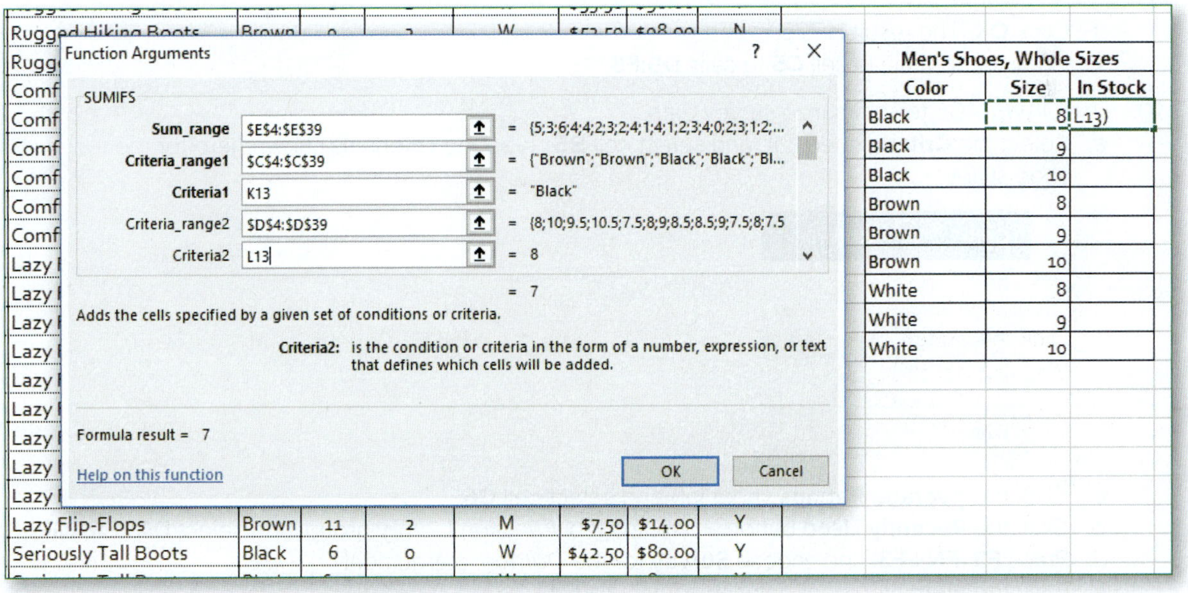

Figure 6-93 *SUMIFS* to calculate number by color and size

h. Click **OK**. The result is 7.
i. Copy the formula in cell **M13** to cells **M14:M21**.

7. Click the **Satisfaction Survey** worksheet tab and review the data.

8. Select cells **A4:H40** and name the range as Survey. Note that the "Comfort" field is the fifth column and that the other attributes follow in the sixth, seventh, and eighth columns.

9. Use *DAVERAGE* to summarize customer survey data.
   a. Click the **Criteria** sheet tab.
   b. Select cell **B2** and type rug*, criteria for the Rugged Hiking Boots.
   c. Click the **Average Ratings** worksheet tab and select cell **C5**.
   d. Click the **Insert Function** button [*Formulas* tab, *Function Library* group].
   e. Choose **Database** in the *Or select a category* list.
   f. Select **DAVERAGE** and click **OK** to calculate an average comfort rating for the boots.
   g. Press **F3** (**FN+F3**), choose **Survey** for the *Database* argument, and click **OK**.
   h. Click the **Field** box and select cell **C4**.
   i. Click the **Criteria** box, select the **Criteria** sheet tab, select cells **B1:B2**, and make the references absolute (Figure 6-94).

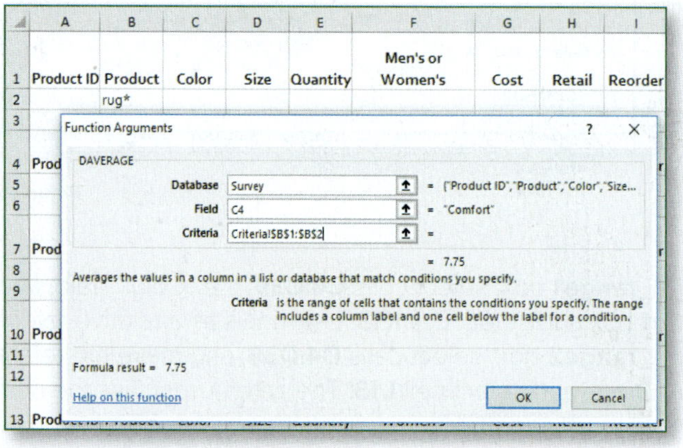

Figure 6-94 ***DAVERAGE*** **for comfort rating**

   j. Click **OK**. The result is 7.75.
   k. Copy the formula in cell **C5** to cells **D5:F5**.

10. Use *DAVERAGE* to summarize survey data.
   a. Select the **Criteria** sheet tab and select cell **B5**. Type the criteria as shown here for the shoe styles.

Cell	Criteria
B5	com*
B8	laz*
B11	ser*
B14	gli*

   b. Click the **Average Ratings** sheet tab and select cell **C6**.
   c. Click the **Recently Used** button [*Formulas* tab, *Function Library* group] and select **DAVERAGE**.
   d. Press **F3** (**FN+F3**) and choose **Survey** for the *Database* argument.
   e. Click the **Field** argument box and select cell **C4**.

f. Click the **Criteria** box, select cells **B4:B5** on the **Criteria** sheet, and press **F4** (**FN+F4**).
g. Click **OK**. The result is 7.5.
h. Copy the formula in cell **C6** to cells **D6:F6**.

11. Build *DAVERAGE* functions for the remaining shoe styles on the **Average Ratings** sheet.

12. Select cells **G5:G9** on the **Average Ratings** sheet, click the **AutoSum** arrow [*Home* tab, *Editing* group], and choose **Average**.

13. Create an *IFS* function.

Note: If your version of Excel does not include the IFS function, build the following nested IF function **=IF(G5>=9,$J$5,IF(G5>=8,$J$6,IF(G5>=5,$J$7,$J$8)))** *to show the ratings.*

a. Select cell **H5**, click the **Logical** button [*Formulas* tab, *Function Library* group], and choose **IFS**.
b. Click the **Logical_test1** argument, select cell **G5**, and type >=9.
c. Click the **Value_if_true1** box, click cell **J5**, and press **F4** (**FN+F4**) to make the reference absolute.
d. Click the **Logical_test2** box, click cell **G5**, and type >=8.
e. Click the **Value_if_true2** box, click cell **J6**, and press **F4** (**FN+F4**).
f. Click the **Logical_test3** box, click cell **G5**, and type >=5.
g. Click the down scroll arrow to reveal the *Value_if_true3* box, click cell **J7**, and press **F4** (**FN+F4**).
h. Click the down scroll arrow to reveal the *Logical_test4* box, click cell **G5**, and type <5.
i. Click the down scroll arrow to reveal the *Value_if_true4* box, click cell **J8**, and press **F4** (**FN+F4**) (Figure 6-95). The complete formula is:

=IFS(G5>=9,$J$5,G5>=8,$J$6,G5>=5,$J$7,G5<5,$J$8)

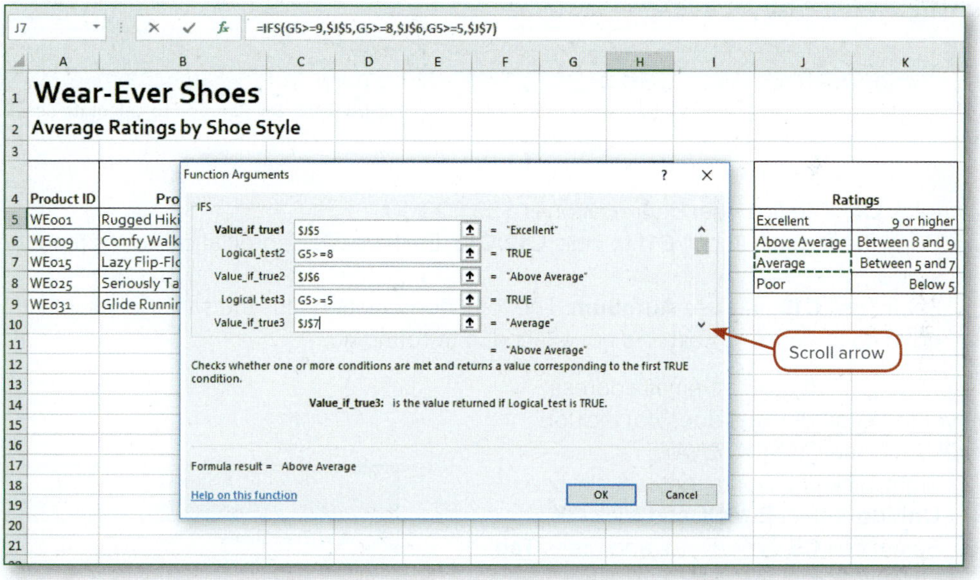

Figure 6-95 ***IFS*** **function with multiple logical tests**

j. Click **OK** and copy the formula to cells **H6:H9**.
k. Format column **H** to be **13.57 (100 pixels)** wide.

14. Calculate depreciation for an asset using a *Financial* function.
a. Click the **Depreciation** sheet tab and select cell **C11**. Depreciation is the decrease in the value of an asset as it ages. The **DB** function calculates the loss in value over a specified period of time at a fixed rate.
b. Click the **Financial** button [*Formulas* tab, *Function Library* group] and choose **DB**.

c. Select cell **C6** for the *Cost* argument, and press **F4** (**FN+F4**) to make the reference absolute. This is the initial cost of the equipment.
d. Click the **Salvage** box, select cell **C7**, and press **F4** (**FN+F4**). This is the expected value of the equipment at the end of its life.
e. Click the **Life** box, select cell **C8**, and press **F4** (**FN+F4**). This is how long the equipment is expected to last.
f. Click the **Period** box and select cell **B11**. The first formula calculates depreciation for the first year (Figure 6-96).

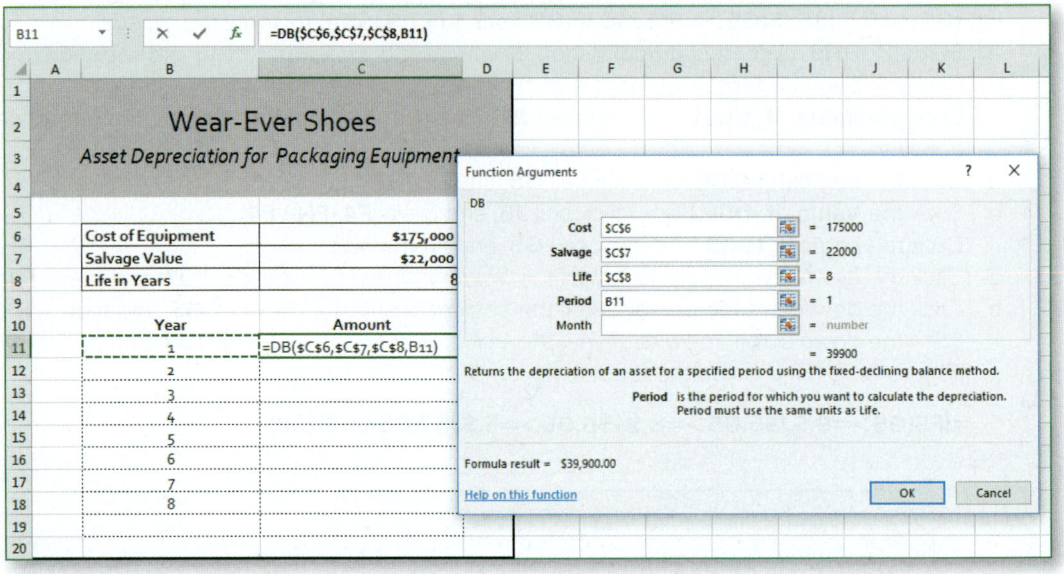

Figure 6-96 ***DB*** **function to calculate asset depreciation**

g. Click **OK**. The first year depreciation is $39,900.00.
h. Copy the formula in cell **C11** to cells **C12:C18**. Each year's depreciation is less than the previous year's.
i. Select cell **C19** and use **AutoSum**. The total depreciation plus the salvage value is approximately equal to the original cost. It is not exact due to rounding.

15. Use *CONCAT* to build an email address. (If your version of Excel does not include *CONCAT*, use *CONCATENATE*.)
    a. Right-click any worksheet tab, choose **Unhide**, select **E-Mail**, and click **OK**.
    b. Select cell **C5**, type =con, and press **Tab**. The *text1* argument is first.
    c. Select cell **A5** and type a comma (,) to move to the *text2* argument.
    d. Select cell **B5** and type a comma (,) to move to the *text3* argument.
    e. Type "@weshoes.org" including the quotation marks (Figure 6-97).
    f. Type the closing parenthesis ()) and press **Enter**.
    g. Copy the formula in cell **C5** to cells **C6:C8**.

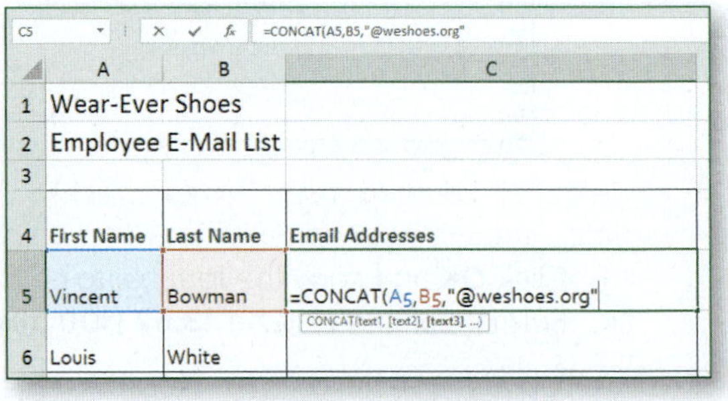

Figure 6-97 ***CONCAT*** **references and typed data**

16. Save and close the workbook (Figure 6-98).

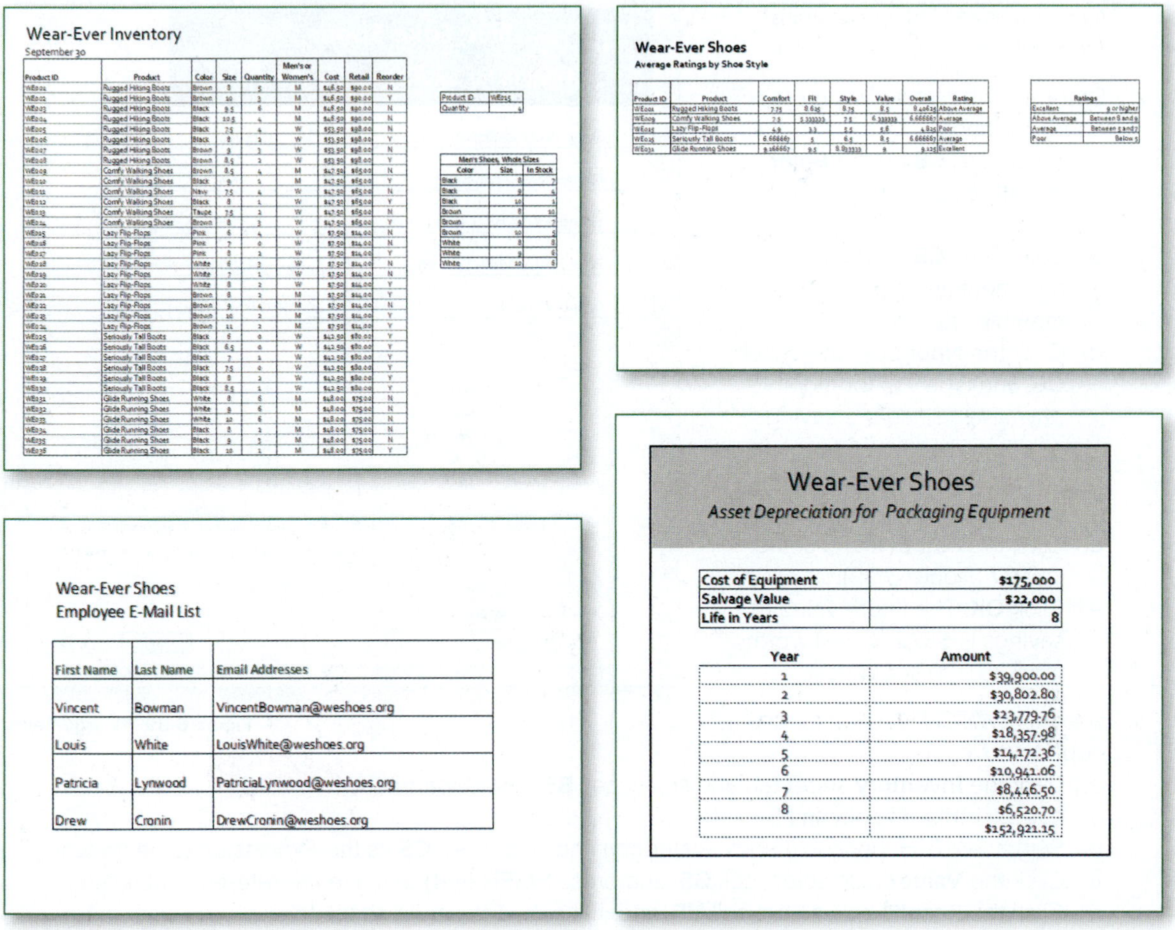

Wear-Ever Inventory
September 30

Product ID	Product	Color	Size	Quantity	Men's or Women's	Cost	Retail	Reorder
WE001	Rugged Hiking Boots	Brown	8	5	M	$46.50	$90.00	N
WE002	Rugged Hiking Boots	Brown	10	3	M	$46.50	$90.00	Y
WE003	Rugged Hiking Boots	Black	9.5	6	M	$46.50	$90.00	N
WE004	Rugged Hiking Boots	Black	10.5	4	M	$46.50	$90.00	N
WE005	Rugged Hiking Boots	Black	7.5	4	W	$53.50	$98.00	N
WE006	Rugged Hiking Boots	Black	8	2	W	$53.50	$98.00	Y
WE007	Rugged Hiking Boots	Brown	9	3	W	$53.50	$98.00	N
WE008	Rugged Hiking Boots	Brown	8.5	2	W	$53.50	$98.00	Y
WE009	Comfy Walking Shoes	Brown	8.5	4	M	$47.50	$65.00	N
WE010	Comfy Walking Shoes	Black	9	1	M	$47.50	$65.00	Y
WE011	Comfy Walking Shoes	Navy	7.5	4	W	$47.50	$65.00	N
WE012	Comfy Walking Shoes	Black	8	1	W	$47.50	$65.00	Y
WE013	Comfy Walking Shoes	Taupe	7.5	2	W	$47.50	$65.00	N
WE014	Comfy Walking Shoes	Brown	8	3	W	$47.50	$65.00	Y
WE015	Lazy Flip-Flops	Pink	6	4	W	$7.50	$14.00	N
WE016	Lazy Flip-Flops	Pink	7	0	W	$7.50	$14.00	N
WE017	Lazy Flip-Flops	Pink	8	2	W	$7.50	$14.00	Y
WE018	Lazy Flip-Flops	White	6	3	W	$7.50	$14.00	N
WE019	Lazy Flip-Flops	White	7	1	W	$7.50	$14.00	N
WE020	Lazy Flip-Flops	White	8	2	W	$7.50	$14.00	Y
WE021	Lazy Flip-Flops	Brown	8	2	M	$7.50	$14.00	Y
WE022	Lazy Flip-Flops	Brown	9	4	M	$7.50	$14.00	N
WE023	Lazy Flip-Flops	Brown	10	2	M	$7.50	$14.00	Y
WE024	Lazy Flip-Flops	Brown	11	2	M	$7.50	$14.00	Y
WE025	Seriously Tall Boots	Black	6	0	W	$42.50	$80.00	Y
WE026	Seriously Tall Boots	Black	6.5	0	W	$42.50	$80.00	Y
WE027	Seriously Tall Boots	Black	7	1	W	$42.50	$80.00	Y
WE028	Seriously Tall Boots	Black	7.5	0	W	$42.50	$80.00	Y
WE029	Seriously Tall Boots	Black	8	2	W	$42.50	$80.00	Y
WE030	Seriously Tall Boots	Black	8.5	1	W	$42.50	$80.00	Y
WE031	Glide Running Shoes	White	8	6	M	$48.00	$75.00	N
WE032	Glide Running Shoes	White	9	6	M	$48.00	$75.00	N
WE033	Glide Running Shoes	White	10	6	M	$48.00	$75.00	N
WE034	Glide Running Shoes	Black	8	2	M	$48.00	$75.00	N
WE035	Glide Running Shoes	Black	9	3	M	$48.00	$75.00	N
WE036	Glide Running Shoes	Black	10	1	M	$48.00	$75.00	Y

Product ID	WE015
Quantity	4

Men's Shoes, Whole Sizes		
Color	Size	In Stock
Black	8	7
Black	9	4
Black	10	1
Brown	8	10
Brown	9	7
Brown	10	5
White	8	8
White	9	6
White	10	6

Wear-Ever Shoes
Average Ratings by Shoe Style

Product ID	Product	Comfort	Fit	Style	Value	Overall	Rating
WE001	Rugged Hiking Boots	7.75	8.625	8.75	8.5	8.40625	Above Average
WE009	Comfy Walking Shoes	7.5	5.333333	7.5	6.333333	6.666667	Average
WE015	Lazy Flip-Flops	4.9	3.3	5.5	5.6	4.825	Poor
WE025	Seriously Tall Boots	6.666667	5	6.5	8.5	6.666667	Average
WE031	Glide Running Shoes	9.166667	9.5	8.833333	9	9.125	Excellent

Ratings	
Excellent	9 or higher
Above Average	Between 8 and 9
Average	Between 5 and 7
Poor	Below 5

Wear-Ever Shoes
Employee E-Mail List

First Name	Last Name	Email Addresses
Vincent	Bowman	VincentBowman@weshoes.org
Louis	White	LouisWhite@weshoes.org
Patricia	Lynwood	PatriciaLynwood@weshoes.org
Drew	Cronin	DrewCronin@weshoes.org

Wear-Ever Shoes
Asset Depreciation for Packaging Equipment

Cost of Equipment	$175,000
Salvage Value	$22,000
Life in Years	8

Year	Amount
1	$39,900.00
2	$30,802.80
3	$23,779.76
4	$18,357.98
5	$14,172.36
6	$10,941.06
7	$8,446.50
8	$6,520.70
	$152,921.15

Figure 6-98 Completed worksheets for Excel 6-3

Independent Project 6-4

Blue Lake Sports is analyzing the future value of energy savings from solar panels. They also plan to calculate statistics related to inventory using *Database* and other functions.
[Student Learning Outcomes 6.1, 6.2, 6.4, 6.5]

File Needed: ***BlueLakeSports-06.xlsx*** *(Student data files are available in the* Library *of your SIMnet account.)*
Completed Project File Name: ***[your initials] Excel 6-4.xlsx***

Skills Covered in This Project

- Calculate the future value of savings.
- Use the *SWITCH* function.
- Build a MAD calculation.
- Use *RANK.EQ* to rank sales for a product.
- Use *DAVERAGE* to summarize data.
- Create an *IFS* function.

1. Open the ***BlueLakeSports-06*** workbook from your student data files and save it as [your initials] Excel 6-4.
2. Determine the future value of energy savings.
   a. Select cell **C8** on the **Solar Install** sheet and start an *FV* formula.
   b. Select cell **C5** for the *Rate* argument and type /12 to use a monthly rate.
   c. Click the **Nper** box, select cell **C6**, and type *12 for monthly payments. Since the savings are estimated for a month, the *Rate* and *Nper* arguments are converted to monthly values.
   d. Click the **Pmt** box and select cell **C7** (Figure 6-99).
   e. Click **OK**. The future value of savings is $87,213, well worth the $25,000 setup cost.

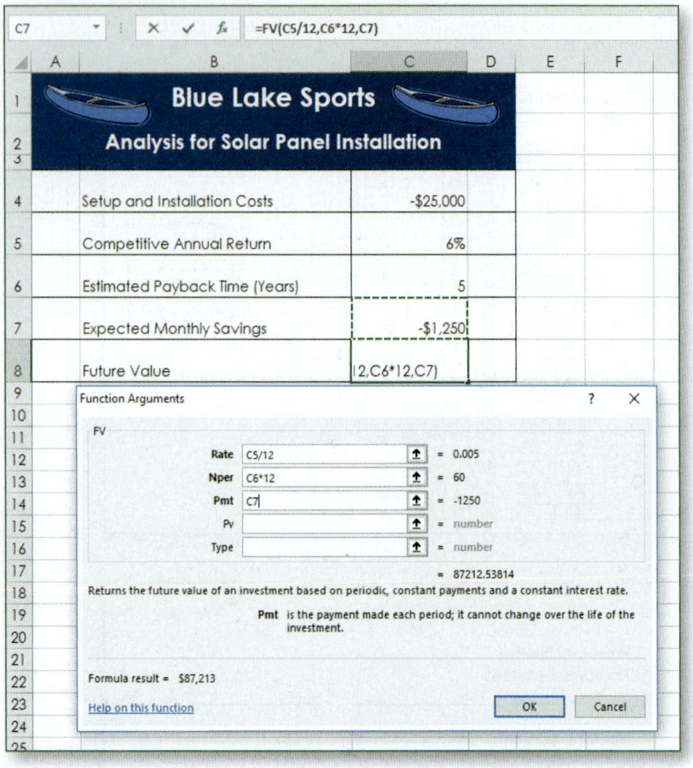

Figure 6-99 ***FV* arguments**

3. Use the *SWITCH* function to display department codes.
   a. Click the **Inventory** sheet tab and select cell **B5**. The department codes display in column H.
   b. Start a *SWITCH* function (*Logical* category) and select cell **C5** as the *Expression* to be switched.
   c. Click the **Value1** box, select cell **G5**, and press **F4(FN+F4)** to make the reference absolute.
   d. Click the **Result1** box, select cell **H5**, and make the reference absolute.
   e. Click the **Default_or_value2** box, select cell **G6**, and make the reference absolute.
   f. Click the **Result2** box, select cell **H6**, and make the reference absolute (Figure 6-100).
   g. Complete the arguments for the remaining two departments.
   h. Copy the formula and preserve the borders.
   i. Select cells **B5:B19** and increase the indent three times.
   j. Select and hide column **C** (Figure 6-101).

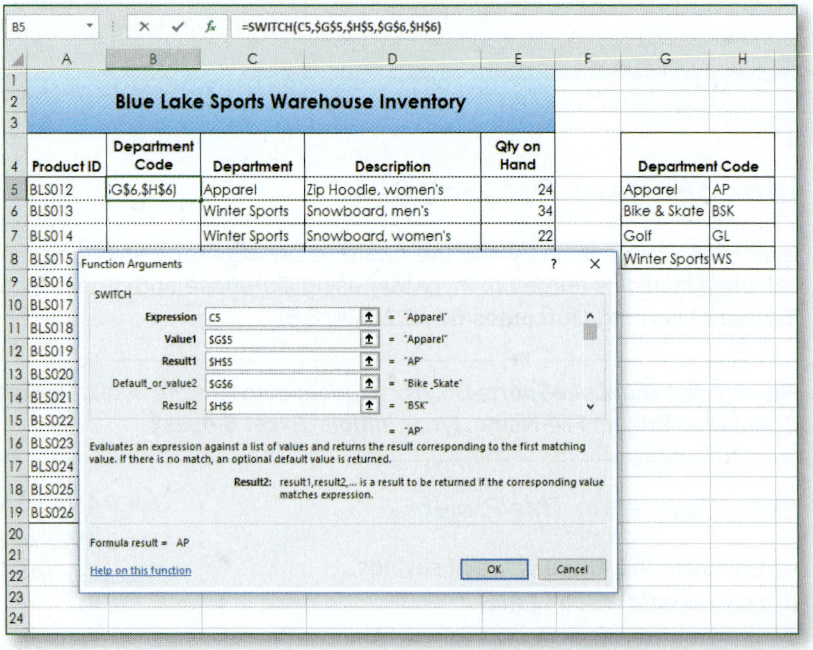

Figure 6-100 ***SWITCH* function with first two arguments**

4. Calculate the mean absolute deviation (MAD) for differences and the standard deviation for actual sales.
   a. Click the **Unit Sales** sheet tab and select cell **G6**.
   b. Start an *ABS* function to calculate the absolute value of the difference between the estimated and actual sales.
   c. Copy the formula in cell **G6** to cells **G7:G20**.
   d. Click cell **G22** and calculate the mean absolute deviation (MAD).
   e. Format the results in cell **G22** to display three decimal positions.
   f. Click cell **G23** and use *STDEV.S* to calculate the standard deviation for the actual sales amounts.
5. Click cell **G25** and use *RANK.EQ* to determine the rank in actual sales for the titanium driver (Figure 6-102).

Blue Lake Sports Warehouse Inventory

Product ID	Department Code	Description	Qty on Hand
BLS012	AP	Zip Hoodie, women's	24
BLS013	WS	Snowboard, men's	34
BLS014	WS	Snowboard, women's	22
BLS015	GL	Full Set, Ladies	8
BLS016	GL	Titanium Driver, Men's	12
BLS017	AP	Rain Jacket, girls	20
BLS018	BSK	Biking helmet, women's	25
BLS019	BSK	Biking helmet, child's	35
BLS020	BSK	Bicycle Trailer, single	15
BLS021	AP	Fleece Sweatshirt, men's	25
BLS022	GL	Rangefinder	18
BLS023	WS	Snow Tube, 44"	13
BLS024	BSK	Bike Rack, double	9
BLS025	AP	Soft Shell Jacket, boy's	14
BLS026	WS	Hockey Facemask, men's	16

Department Code	
Apparel	AP
Bike & Skate	BSK
Golf	GL
Winter Sports	WS

Figure 6-101 Department codes switched and column C hidden

Mean Absolute Deviation (MAD), Difference	8.600
Standard Deviation, Actual Sales	23.511294
Rank in Sales for Titanium Driver	8

Figure 6-102 Deviations and rank

6. Use *DAVERAGE* to summarize survey data.
   a. Click the **Product Evaluation** tab and name cells **A4:E19** as Data. Notice that the "Overall Rating" column is the fourth column in the range.
   b. Click the **Criteria** sheet and type ap* in cell **B2** to reference data from the "Apparel" department.
   c. Click the **Statistics** tab and select cell **B5**.
   d. Use *DAVERAGE* to calculate an overall average for product satisfaction by department. Use the named range **Data** for the *Database* argument. For the *Field* argument, type 4 to use the fourth column. The *Criteria* argument is cells **B1:B2** on the **Criteria** sheet.
   e. Click the **Criteria** sheet. Enter criteria in cells **B5**, **B8**, and **B11** for each of the three remaining departments on the **Statistics** sheet.
   f. Click the **Statistics** sheet tab and select cell **B6**. Use *DAVERAGE* and your criteria ranges to complete cells **B6:B8**.
7. On the **Statistics** sheet, set columns **A:B** each to **16 (133 pixels)** wide.
8. Select cells **A1:B3** and open the *Format Cells* dialog box. Choose **Center Across Selection** on the *Alignment* tab.
9. Center align the labels in row **4** and apply **All Borders** to cells **A4:B8** (Figure 6-103).
10. Create an *IFS* function.
    a. Click the **Product Evaluation** sheet tab and select cell **E5**. Evaluation criteria and ratings display in rows 21:24.

Blue Lake Sports
Third Quarter Summary Satistics
Satisfaction Rating by Department

Department	Average
Apparel	4.0625
Bike & Skate	3.875
Golf	4.45
Winter Sports	4.475

Figure 6-103 Completed *Statistics* worksheet

Note: If your version of Excel does not include the IFS *function, build the following nested* IF *function* **=IF(D5>=4.85,$D$21,IF(D5>=4.35,$D$22,IF(D5>=3.5,$D$23,$D$24)))** *to show the evaluation.*

b. Start an *IFS* function in cell **E5**, select cell **D5** for the *Logical_test1* box, and type >=4.85.

c. Click the **Value_if_true1** box, click cell **D21**, and press **F4** (**FN+F4**).

d. Click the **Logical_test2** box, click cell **D5** and type >=4.35.

e. Click the **Value_if_true2** box, click cell **D22**, and make the reference absolute.

f. Click the **Logical_test3** box. Complete the statement and its corresponding *Value_if_true* argument.

g. Complete the fourth logical test and *Value_if_true* argument (Figure 6-104) and click **OK**.

h. Copy the formula in cell **E5** to cells **E6:E19**.

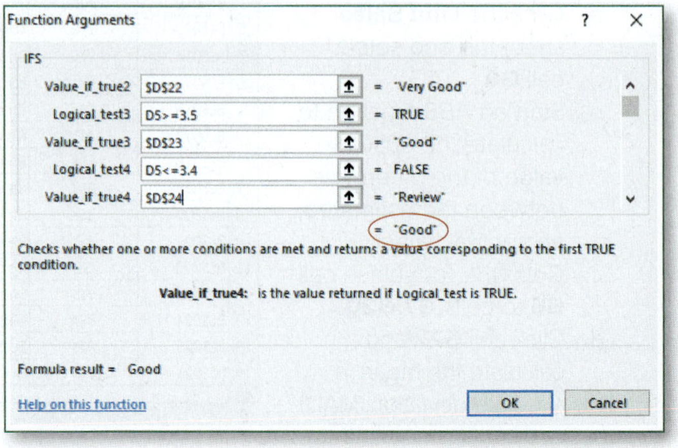

Figure 6-104 ***IFS* function displays the evaluation**

11. Apply **All Borders** to cells **A4:E19** and to cells **C21:D24**.

12. Use **Center Across Selection** for the labels in rows **1:3** and set the font size to **20 pt**.

13. *AutoFit* columns that do not show all the data.

14. Save and close the workbook (Figure 6-105).

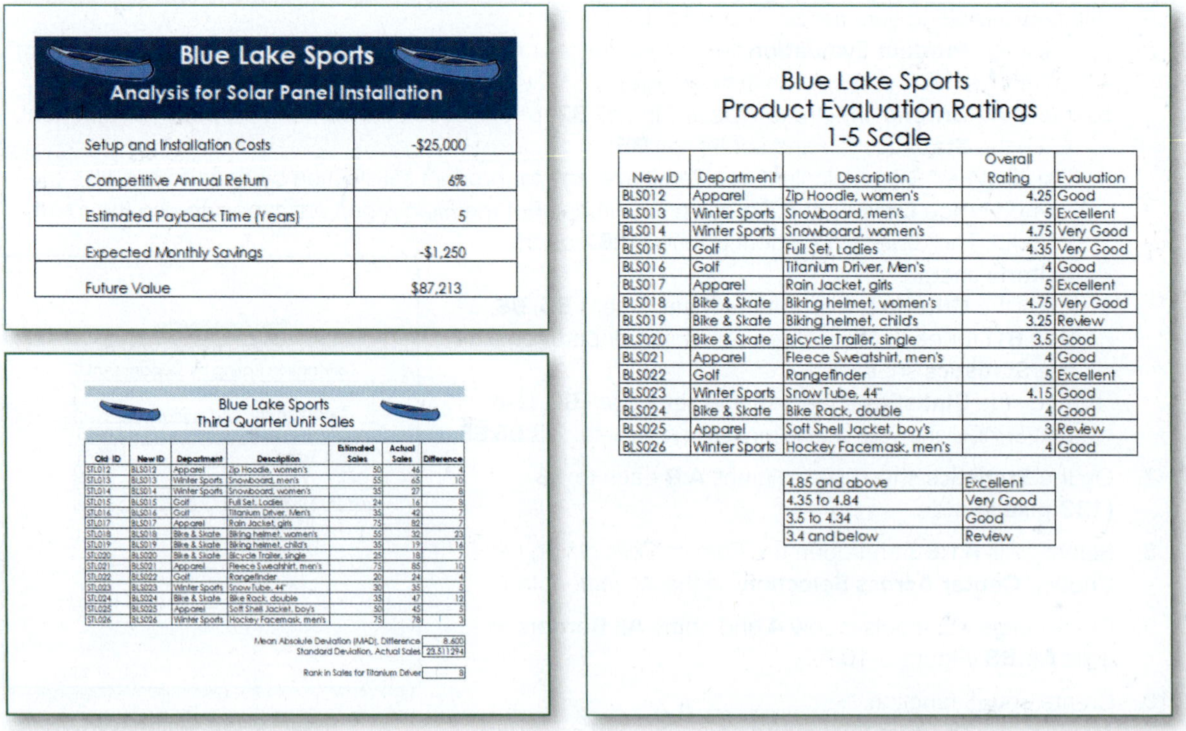

Figure 6-105 Completed worksheets for Excel 6-4

Independent Project 6-5

Classic Gardens and Landscapes counts responses to specialty promotions to determine effectiveness. You use *SUMIFS* and an *IFS* formula to complete the summary. You also calculate insurance statistics and display full names in one cell.
[Student Learning Outcomes 6.1, 6.2, 6.3, 6.6, 6.7]

File Needed: ***ClassicGardens-06.xlsx*** *(Student data files are available in the* Library *of your SIMnet account.)*
Completed Project File Name: ***[your initials] Excel 6-5.xlsx***

Skills Covered in This Project

- Nest *MATCH* and *INDEX* functions.
- Create *DSUM* formulas.
- Build an *IFS* function.
- Build *SUMIFS* formulas.
- Use *TEXTJOIN* to join labels.

---

1. Open the ***ClassicGardens-06*** workbook from your student data files and save it as [your initials] Excel 6-5.
2. Create a nested *INDEX* and *MATCH* function to display the number of responses from a city.
   a. Click the **Mailings** sheet tab and select and name cells **A3:D28** as Responses.
   b. Click the **Mailing Stats** sheet tab.
   c. Click cell **B21** and type Carthage.
   d. Click cell **C21**, start an **INDEX** function, and select the first argument list option.
   e. Choose or type the **Responses** range name for the *Array* argument.
   f. Click the **Row_num** box and nest a **MATCH** function. Select cell **B21** for the *Lookup_value* and cells **A3:A28** on the **Mailings** sheet for the *Lookup_array*. Click the **Match_type** argument box and type 0.
   g. Click **INDEX** in the *Formula* bar. Click the **Column_num** box and nest a second **MATCH** function to look up cell **D3** on the **Mailings** sheet in the lookup array **A3:D3**.
   h. Click the **Match_type** box and type 0 (Figure 6-106) and click **OK**. The result displays as 343.00.
   i. Format the results to show zero decimal places.
   j. Type Smyrna in cell **B21**.

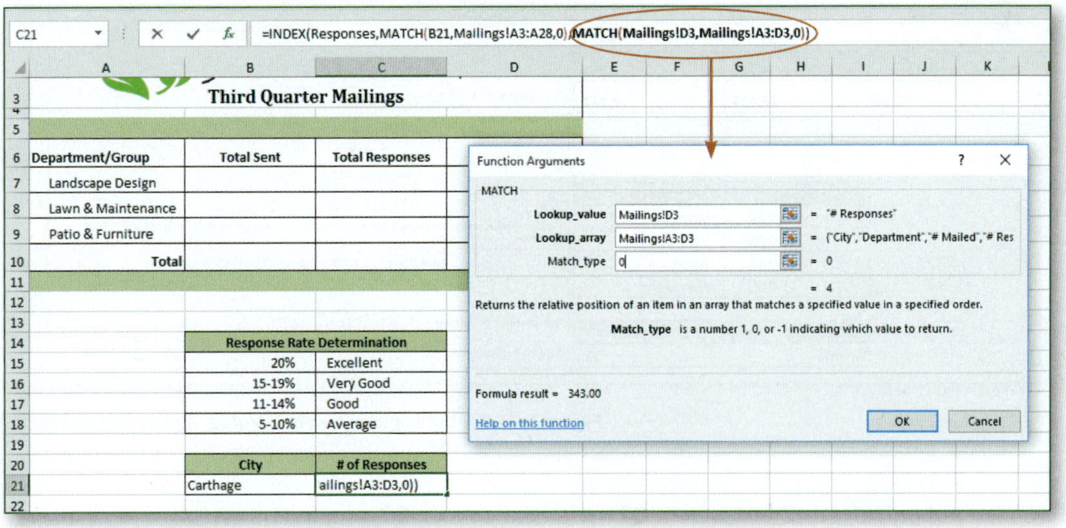

Figure 6-106 Nested *MATCH* and *INDEX* functions

3. Use *DSUM* to summarize mailing data.
   a. Select the **Mailings** sheet and note that number mailed is located in the third column and response data is in the fourth column.
   b. Click the **Criteria** sheet tab. Select cell **B2** and type lan* to select data for the Landscape Design department.
   c. Type law* in cell **B5** for the Lawn & Maintenance department.
   d. Type pat* in cell **B8** for the Patio & Furniture department.
   e. Click the **Mailing Stats** sheet tab and select cell **B7**.
   f. Use **DSUM** with the range name **Responses** as the *Database* argument. Type 3 for the *Field* argument (# Mailed column), and enter an absolute reference to cells **B1:B2** on the **Criteria** sheet as the *Criteria* argument.
   g. Copy the formula to cell **C7** and edit the *Field* argument to use the fourth column (# Responses).
   h. Use *DSUM* in cells **B8:C9** to calculate results for the two remaining departments.

4. Use *SUM* in cells **B10:C10**.

5. Format all values as **Comma Style** with no decimal places.

6. Create an *IFS* function to display a response rating. *Note: If your version of Excel does not include the* IFS *function, build the following nested* IF *function* **=IF(C7/B7>=20%,$C$15, IF(C7/B7>=15%,$C$16,IF(C7/B7>=11%,$C$17,$C$18)))** *to display the rating.*
   a. Click cell **D7**. The response rate and ratings are shown in rows 14:18.
   b. Start an *IFS* function and select **C7** for the *Logical_test1* argument. Type / for division and select cell **B7**. Type >=20% to complete the test.
   c. Click the **Value_if_true1** box, select **C15**, and press **F4 (FN+F4)** (Figure 6-107).

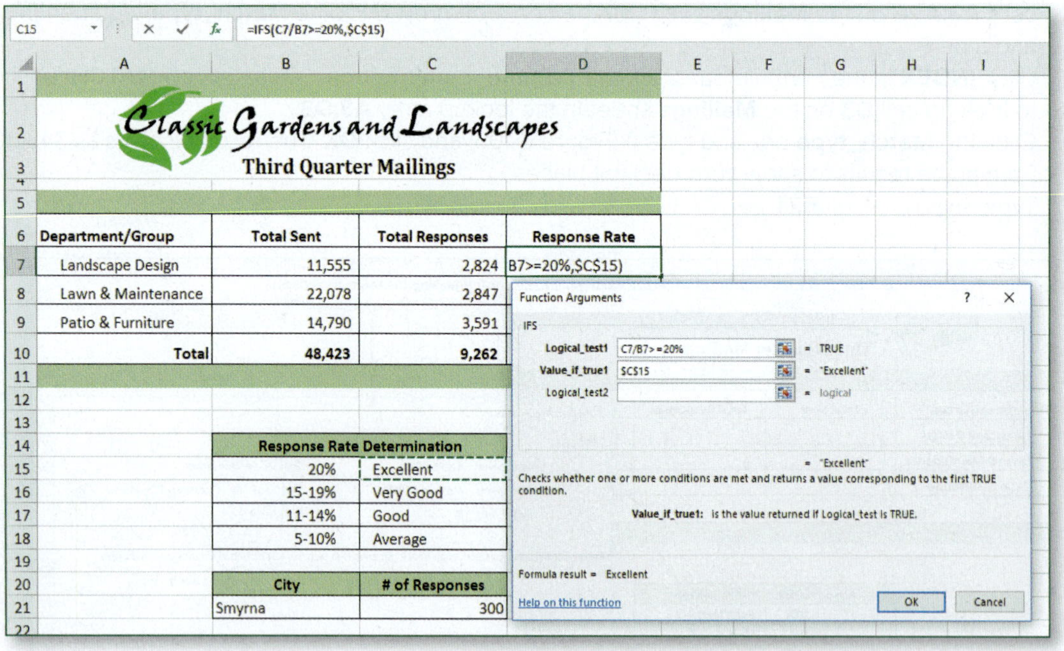

Figure 6-107 First *Logical_test* and *Value_if_true* arguments

   d. Click the **Logical_test2** box, select **C7**, type /, select cell **B7**, and type >=15%.
   e. Click the **Value_if_true2** box, click cell **C16**, and press **F4** (**FN+F4**).

f. Complete the third and fourth logical tests and *Value_if_true* arguments (Figure 6-108).
g. Copy the formula in cell **D7** to cells **D8:D10**.

7. Use *SUMIFS* to total insurance claims and dependents by city and department.
   a. Click the **Employee Insurance** sheet tab and select cell **E25**.
   b. Use *SUMIFS* with an absolute reference to cells **F4:F23** as the *Sum_range* argument.
      - The *Criteria_range1* argument is an absolute reference to cells **E4:E23**. The *Criteria1* argument is bre* to select the city of Brentwood.
      - The *Criteria_range2* argument is an absolute reference to cells **D4:D23**, the department column, with criteria of lan* to select the Landscape Design department.
      - Click **OK**. The result for cell **E25** is 10.
   c. Complete *SUMIFS* formulas for cells **E26:E28** using three-character criteria arguments to select each city.
   d. Format borders to remove inconsistencies, if any, and adjust column widths to display data.

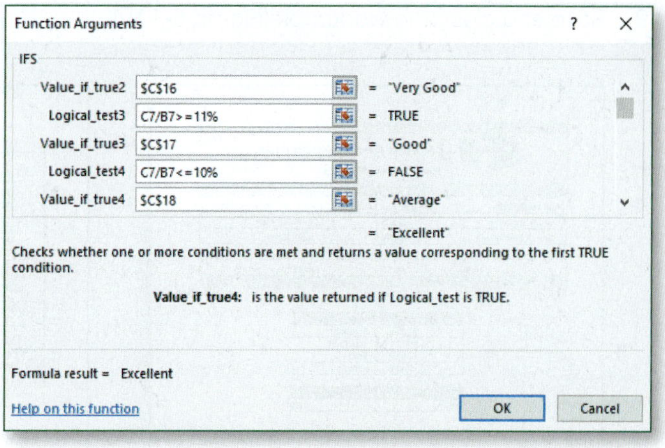

Figure 6-108 Completed *IFS* function arguments

8. Use *TEXTJOIN* to display names.
   a. Click the **Full Names** sheet tab and select cell **E4**.
   b. Start a *TEXTJOIN* function and press **Spacebar** for the *Delimiter* argument.
   c. Click the *Text1* box and select cell **C4**.
   d. Complete the *Text2* and *Text3* arguments to show middle and last names and click **OK** (Figure 6-109).
   e. Copy the formula to display full names in column E.

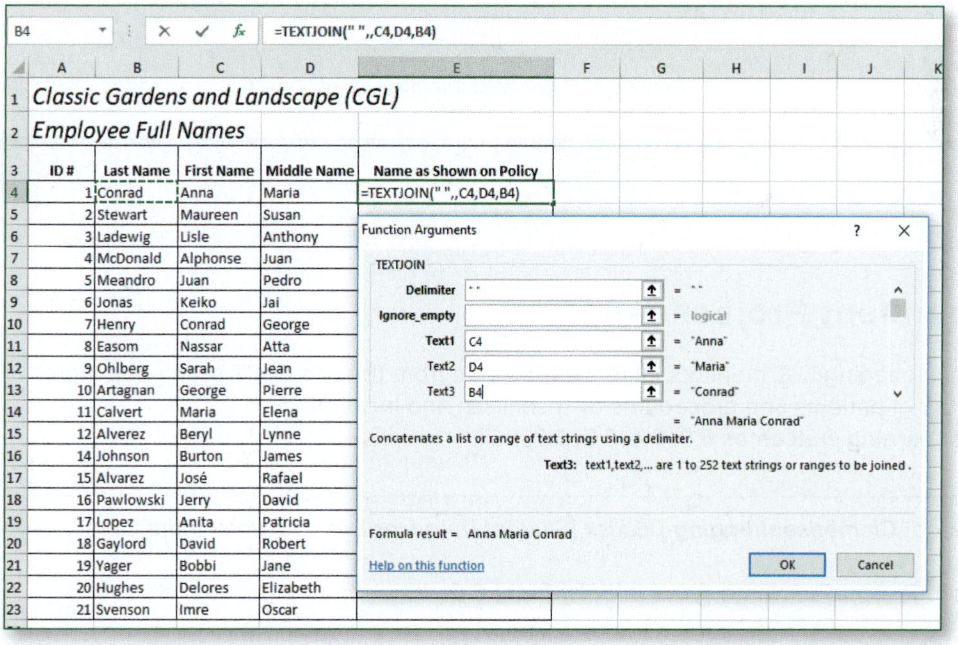

Figure 6-109 Delimiter is a space

9. Save and close the workbook (Figure 6-110).

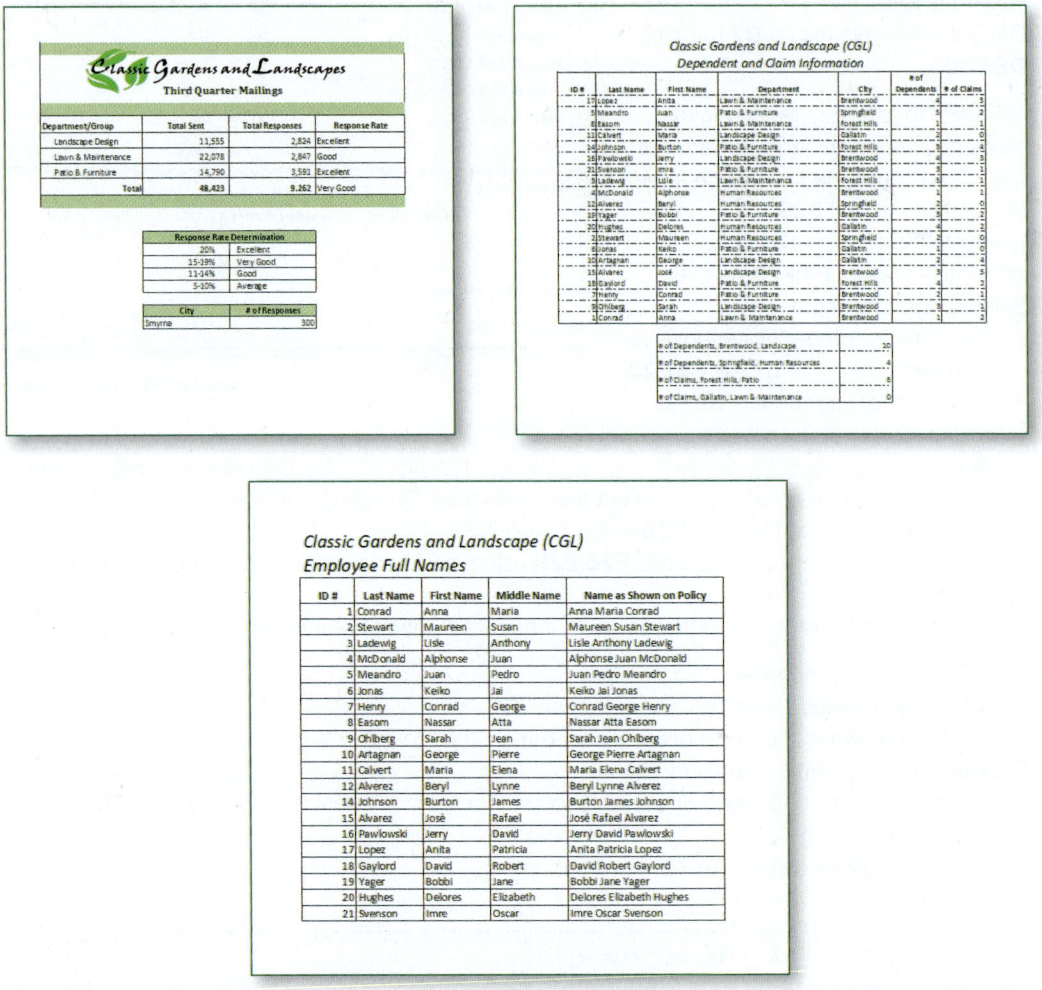

Classic Gardens and Landscapes

Third Quarter Mailings

Department/Group	Total Sent	Total Responses	Response Rate
Landscape Design	11,555	2,824	Excellent
Lawn & Maintenance	22,078	2,847	Good
Patio & Furniture	14,790	3,591	Excellent
Total	48,423	9,262	Very Good

Response Rate Determination	
20%	Excellent
15-19%	Very Good
11-14%	Good
5-10%	Average

City	# of Responses
Smyrna	300

Classic Gardens and Landscape (CGL)

Dependent and Claim Information

ID #	Last Name	First Name	Department	City	# of Dependents	# of Claims
17	Lopez	Anita	Lawn & Maintenance	Brentwood	4	3
5	Meandro	Juan	Patio & Furniture	Springfield	5	2
8	Easom	Nassar	Lawn & Maintenance	Forest Hills	1	1
11	Calvert	Maria	Landscape Design	Gallatin	2	0
14	Johnson	Burton	Patio & Furniture	Forest Hills	3	4
16	Pawlowski	Jerry	Landscape Design	Brentwood	4	3
21	Svenson	Imre	Patio & Furniture	Brentwood	3	1
3	Ladewig	Lisle	Lawn & Maintenance	Forest Hills	5	1
4	McDonald	Alphonse	Human Resources	Brentwood	1	1
12	Alverez	Beryl	Human Resources	Springfield	2	0
19	Yager	Bobbi	Patio & Furniture	Brentwood	3	2
20	Hughes	Delores	Human Resources	Gallatin	4	2
2	Stewart	Maureen	Human Resources	Springfield	2	0
6	Jonas	Keiko	Patio & Furniture	Gallatin	1	0
10	Artagnan	George	Landscape Design	Gallatin	2	4
15	Alvarez	José	Landscape Design	Brentwood	3	5
18	Gaylord	David	Patio & Furniture	Forest Hills	4	2
7	Henry	Conrad	Patio & Furniture	Brentwood	2	1
9	Ohlberg	Sarah	Landscape Design	Brentwood	3	1
1	Conrad	Anna	Lawn & Maintenance	Brentwood	1	2

# of Dependents, Brentwood, Landscape	10
# of Dependents, Springfield, Human Resources	4
# of Claims, Forest Hills, Patio	6
# of Claims, Gallatin, Lawn & Maintenance	0

Classic Gardens and Landscape (CGL)

Employee Full Names

ID #	Last Name	First Name	Middle Name	Name as Shown on Policy
1	Conrad	Anna	Maria	Anna Maria Conrad
2	Stewart	Maureen	Susan	Maureen Susan Stewart
3	Ladewig	Lisle	Anthony	Lisle Anthony Ladewig
4	McDonald	Alphonse	Juan	Alphonse Juan McDonald
5	Meandro	Juan	Pedro	Juan Pedro Meandro
6	Jonas	Keiko	Jai	Keiko Jai Jonas
7	Henry	Conrad	George	Conrad George Henry
8	Easom	Nassar	Atta	Nassar Atta Easom
9	Ohlberg	Sarah	Jean	Sarah Jean Ohlberg
10	Artagnan	George	Pierre	George Pierre Artagnan
11	Calvert	Maria	Elena	Maria Elena Calvert
12	Alverez	Beryl	Lynne	Beryl Lynne Alverez
14	Johnson	Burton	James	Burton James Johnson
15	Alvarez	José	Rafael	José Rafael Alvarez
16	Pawlowski	Jerry	David	Jerry David Pawlowski
17	Lopez	Anita	Patricia	Anita Patricia Lopez
18	Gaylord	David	Robert	David Robert Gaylord
19	Yager	Bobbi	Jane	Bobbi Jane Yager
20	Hughes	Delores	Elizabeth	Delores Elizabeth Hughes
21	Svenson	Imre	Oscar	Imre Oscar Svenson

Figure 6-110 Completed worksheets for Excel 6-5

Independent Project 6-6

Clemenson Imaging LLC monitors increased revenue from the use of CT scan equipment. You analyze the number of patients and procedures by technician and location.
[Student Learning Outcomes 6.3, 6.4, 6.5, 6.6, 6.7]

File Needed: ***ClemensonImaging-06.xlsx*** *(Student data files are available in the* Library *of your SIMnet account.)*
Completed Project File Name: ***[your initials] Excel 6-6.xlsx***

Skills Covered in This Project

- Calculate the net present value of a purchase.
- Use *TRANSPOSE* to rearrange labels into a column.
- Concatenate cells to display full names.
- Use *SUMIFS* to summarize data.
- Calculate procedure times.
- Format times with fractions.

---

1. Open the ***ClemensonImaging-06*** workbook from your student data files and save it as [your initials] Excel 6-6.
2. Determine the net present value of a new equipment purchase.
   a. Click the **Financials** sheet tab and select cell **H5**.
   b. Use **NPV** with a *Rate* argument of **4.25%**.
   c. Select cells **D7:D13** for the *Value1* argument and click **OK**. This is the same as entering each value argument separately.
   d. Edit the formula to add both costs (cells **D4** and **D5**) at the end of the formula. The net present value is $268,921.79.
3. Use *TRANSPOSE* and *CONCAT* to display technician names.
   a. Click the **Technicians** sheet tab. The names are in rows.
   b. Select cells **A4:A10**, seven rows in one column.
   c. Select **TRANSPOSE** from the *Lookup & Reference* category and select cells **A1:G1** for the *Array* argument.
   d. Press **Ctrl+Shift+Enter** to complete the array formula.
   e. Repeat the *TRANSPOSE* task for the first names in cells **B4:B10**.
   f. Select cell **D4** and create a *CONCAT* formula to display the name in first name, last name order (Figure 6-111).
   g. Copy the formula in cell **D4** to cells **D5:D10**.

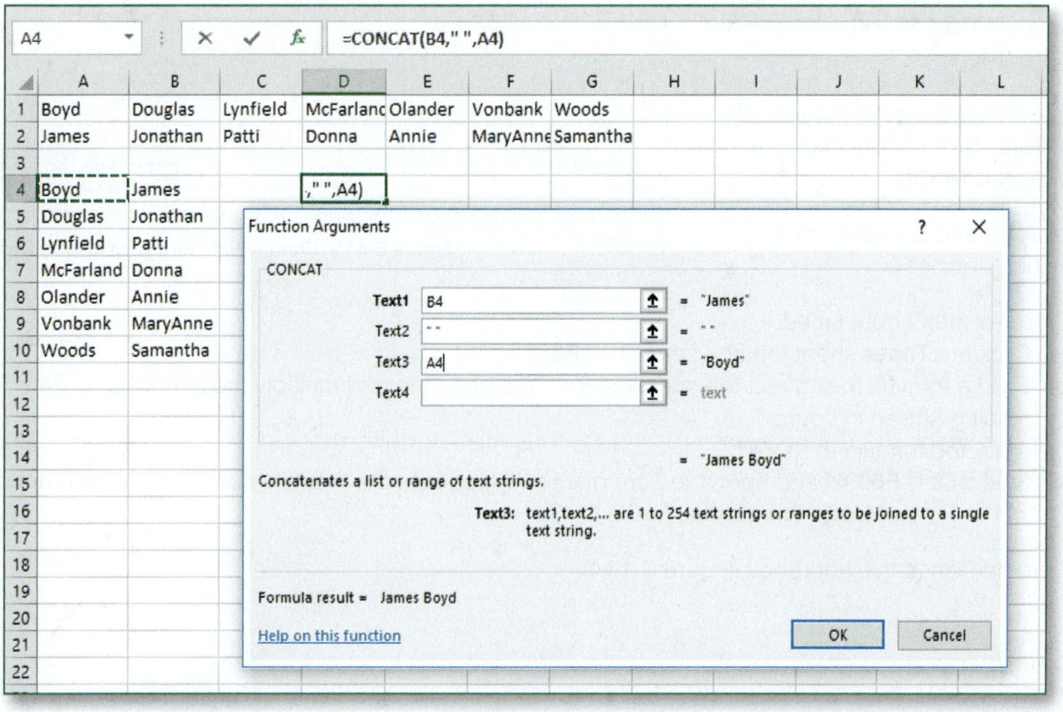

Figure 6-111 ***CONCAT* formula to display names**

h. Click the **Summary** sheet tab, select cell **A5**, and create a 3D reference to cell **D4** on the **Technicians** sheet.
i. Copy the formula and preserve the borders.

4. Use *SUMIFS* to total number of patients by procedure and technician.
   a. Click the **Summary** sheet tab and select cell **C5**.
   b. Use the *SUMIFS* function with an absolute reference to cells **$D$5:$D$41** on the **Procedures** sheet as the *Sum_range* argument.
      - The *Criteria_range1* argument is an absolute reference to the image type column on the **Procedures** sheet, cells **$E$5:$E$41**.
      - The *Criteria1* argument is a relative reference to cell **B5** on the **Summary** sheet.
      - The *Criteria_range2* argument is an absolute reference to the technician names column on the **Procedures** sheet.
   c. Select cell **A5** for the *Criteria2* argument (Figure 6-112).
   d. Copy the formula in cell **C5** to cells **C6:C11** and preserve the borders.

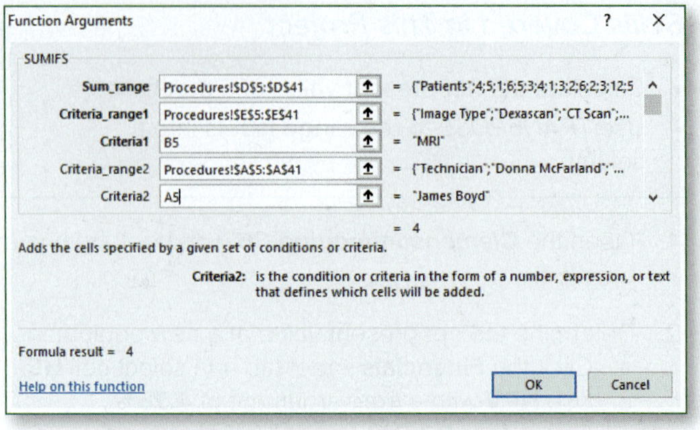

Figure 6-112 ***SUMIFS*** **with absolute and relative references**

5. Use *SUMIFS* to total number of patients by category and location in cells **C14:C15**.

6. Look for and correct format inconsistencies.

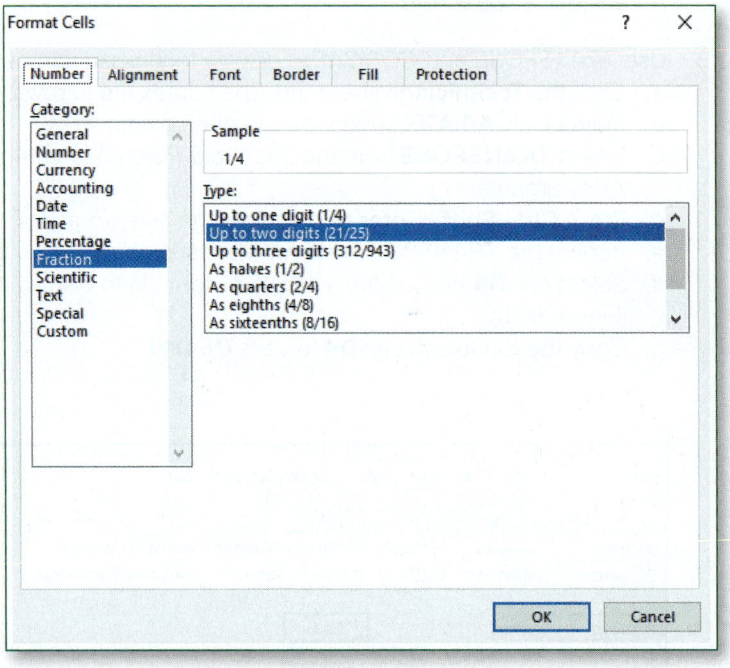

Figure 6-113 Change time format to display fractions

7. Calculate procedure times.
   a. Click the **Times** sheet tab and select cell **F6**.
   b. Build a formula to subtract the start time from the end time and multiply those results by 24. The result is shown in hours.
   c. Copy the formula to row **41**.
   d. Select cells **F6:F41** and open the *Format Cells* dialog box. On the *Number* tab, choose **Fraction** with a *Type* of **Up to two digits** (Figure 6-113).

8. Save and close the workbook (Figure 6-114).

Clemenson Imaging
Second Quarter Summary

Technician	Procedure	# of Patients
James Boyd	MRI	4
Jonathan Douglas	CT Scan	13
Patti Lynfield	Angiography	2
Donna McFarland	Angiography	0
Annie Olander	MRI	5
MaryAnne Vonbank	MRI	2
Samantha Woods	CT Scan	1

Patient Category	Location	# of Patients
Scheduled	Appleton	22
Walk-In	Green Bay	17

Clemenson Imaging, LLC
Purchase and Training Cost Analysis

Cost of CT Scan Equipment	-$1,500,000		
Cost of Staff Training	-$35,000	Net Present Value	$268,921.79
Additional Revenue Year 1	$150,000		
Additional Revenue Year 2	$150,000		
Additional Revenue Year 3	$250,000		
Additional Revenue Year 4	$300,000		
Additional Revenue Year 5	$350,000		
Additional Revenue Year 6	$500,000		
Additional Revenue Year 7	$500,000		

Clemenson Imaging
Time Duration for Procedures in Hours

Patient ID	Location	Image Type	Start	End	Duration
CL024	Green Bay	Dexascan	9:15 AM	9:30 AM	1/4
CL027	Manitowoc	CT Scan	1:00 PM	1:45 PM	3/4
CL030	Appleton	MRI	10:15 AM	11:30 AM	1 1/4
CL033	Green Bay	Ultrasonography	9:00 AM	10:00 AM	1
CL036	Green Bay	Angiography	2:30 PM	4:15 PM	1 3/4
CL039	Manitowoc	Dexascan	10:30	11:00 AM	1/2
CL042	Manitowoc	MRI	2:45 PM	4:15 PM	1 1/2
CL045	Appleton	MRI	8:00 AM	10:30 AM	2 1/2
CL048	Appleton	Angiography	1:30 PM	3:45 PM	2 1/4
CL051	Green Bay	Angiography	3:00 PM	4:45 PM	1 3/4
CL054	Appleton	Ultrasonography	1:00 PM	1:45 PM	3/4
CL057	Manitowoc	Ultrasonography	11:30 AM	1:45 PM	2 1/4
CL060	Manitowoc	MRI	10:15 AM	11:30 AM	1 1/4
CL063	Appleton	Dexascan	10:30	11:00 AM	1/2
CL066	Appleton	Dexascan	11:00 AM	11:20 AM	1/3
CL069	Green Bay	CT Scan	2:15 PM	3:30 PM	1 1/4
CL072	Appleton	CT Scan	3:30 PM	5:00 PM	1 1/2
CL075	Green Bay	MRI	8:00 AM	11:00 AM	3
CL078	Manitowoc	MRI	9:00 AM	11:30 AM	2 1/2
CL081	Manitowoc	CT Scan	4:00 PM	5:30 PM	1 1/2
CL084	Appleton	CT Scan	8:00 AM	9:45 AM	1 3/4
CL087	Appleton	MRI	12:00 PM	2:30 PM	2 1/2
CL090	Green Bay	MRI	2:15 PM	4:45 PM	2 1/2
CL093	Manitowoc	Ultrasonography	1:00 PM	1:45 PM	3/4
CL096	Appleton	MRI	10:15 AM	11:30 AM	1 1/4
CL099	Appleton	Dexascan	11:00 AM	11:20 AM	1/3
CL102	Green Bay	Dexascan	8:00 AM	8:20 AM	1/3
CL105	Appleton	CT Scan	2:00 PM	3:30 PM	1 1/2
CL108	Green Bay	CT Scan	3:00 PM	3:45 PM	3/4
CL111	Manitowoc	Angiography	4:00 PM	4:45 PM	3/4
CL114	Appleton	Angiography	3:45 PM	5:00 PM	1 1/4
CL117	Green Bay	Ultrasonography	11:00 AM	11:20 AM	1/3
CL120	Manitowoc	Ultrasonography	12:00 PM	1:30 PM	1 1/2
CL123	Appleton	Angiography	4:00 PM	4:45 PM	3/4
CL126	Green Bay	MRI	10:15 AM	11:30 AM	1 1/4
CL129	Manitowoc	MRI	9:00 AM	11:15 AM	2 1/4

Figure 6-114 Completed worksheets for Excel 6-6

Improve It Project 6-7

In the Livingood Income Tax and Accounting workbook, you use *IFERROR* to replace a standard error with a custom message. You correct the spelling of a client name throughout the worksheet, incorporate the *TODAY()* function in a concatenated statement, and calculate data about overdue accounts. **[Student Learning Outcomes 6.2, 6.4, 6.6, 6.7, 6.8]**

File Needed: ***Livingood-06.xlsx*** *(Student data files are available in the* Library *of your SIMnet account.)*
Completed Project File Name: ***[your initials] Excel 6-7.xlsx***

Skills Covered in This Project

- Use *IFERROR* to display a custom message.
- Add cell references to the *Watch Window*.
- Monitor *Find and Replace* in the *Watch Window*.
- Create a *SUMIFS* formula.
- Build a *COUNTIFS* formula.
- Concatenate *TODAY()* with text.
- Use date format codes in a function.

1. Open the ***Livingood-06*** workbook from your student data files and save it as [your initials] Excel 6-7.
2. Select cell **E6** on the **Accounts Aging** sheet and review the formula. The formula subtracts the invoice date from today's date in cell G1.
3. Use an *IFERROR* formula in cell **E6** that displays Re-enter date instead of a standard error message.
4. Copy the *IFERROR* formula to cells **E7:E20** and *AutoFit* the column.
5. Select cells **C6:C20** and add them as a watch to the *Watch Window*.
6. Click the **Aging Detail** sheet tab. Build a *Find and Replace* command to replace all occurrences of "accoustaff" with AccounStaff throughout the workbook. The search and replace strings maintain the comma and the word "Inc."
7. Select and delete the watches. Close the *Watch Window*.
8. Use *SUMIFS* to calculate totals that are late by 30 days or more.
   a. Click the **Aging Detail** sheet tab.
   b. Name cells **A5:E20** as Detail.
   c. Use *SUMIFS* in cell **H6** to calculate the total due from *AccounStaff* that is 30 or more days late.
   d. Copy the *SUMIFS* formula for *Custom Tax* in cell **H7**. If necessary, edit the copied formula.
   e. Format cells **H6:H7** as **Currency**.
9. Use *COUNTIFS* to calculate how many invoices are late by 30 days or more.
   a. Use *COUNTIFS* in cell **I6** to calculate the number of *AccounStaff* invoices that are 30 or more days overdue.
   b. Copy or enter a *COUNTIFS* formula for *Custom Tax* in cell **I7**.
10. Use *CONCAT* to display a sentence about the current date.
    a. Click cell **A22** and start a *CONCAT* formula.
    b. Type Today is with a space after the word "is" for the *Text1* argument.
    c. Click the **Text2** box and nest the **TEXT** function from the *Text* category.
    d. Type today() for the *Value* argument. The equals sign is not necessary when the function is used as an argument.
    e. Click the **Format_text** box and type mmmm d, yyy with a space after the comma. This format spells out the month, shows the date without leading zeros, and displays four digits for the year (Figure 6-115).
    f. Click **OK**.
11. Save and close the workbook (Figure 6-116). (Your results display dates based on today and will not match dates shown in Figure 6-116.)

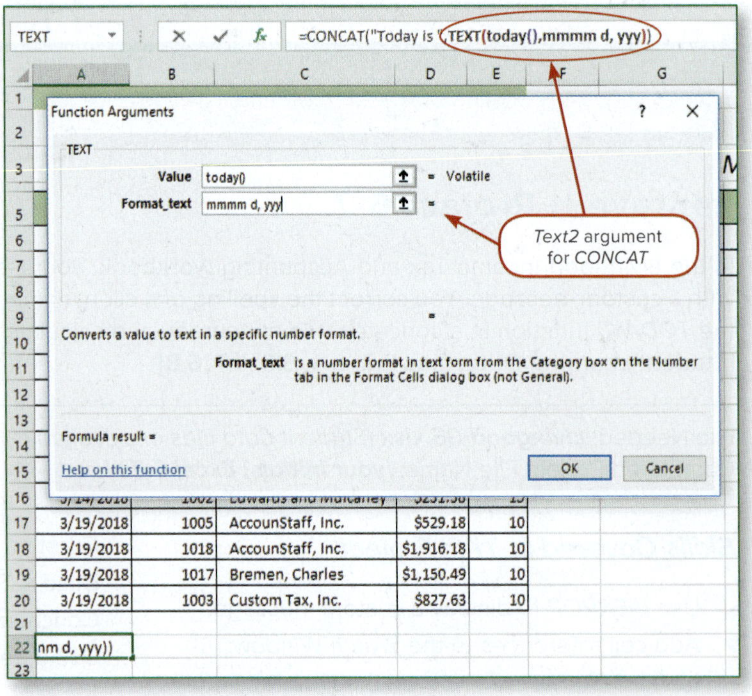

Figure 6-115 Nested *TEXT* function with custom date format

Livingood Income Tax & Accounting
Accounts Payable Aging Report

Invoice	Date	Client	Due	Age
1001	3/14/2018	Custom Tax, Inc.	$1,630.23	15
1002	3/14/2018	Edwards and Mulcahey	$231.38	15
1003	3/19/2018	Custom Tax, Inc.	$827.63	10
1004	3/14/2018	Bremen, Charles	$1,348.38	15
1005	3/19/2018	AccounStaff, Inc.	$529.18	10
1007	2/15/2018	AccounStaff, Inc.	$393.79	42
1010	2/26/2018	AccounStaff, Inc.	$233.86	31
1012	9/1/2016	Friedman, Gerald	$1,942.03	Re-enter date
1014	2/15/2018	Custom Tax, Inc.	$619.32	42
1015	2/26/2018	Custom Tax, Inc.	$716.74	31
1015	2/15/2018	Halvorsen, Susan	$1,014.52	42
1017	3/19/2018	Bremen, Charles	$1,150.49	10
1018	10/2/2016	AccounStaff, Inc.	$1,916.18	Re-enter date
1020	3/14/2018	Dunhill & Berks	$1,163.41	15
1020	2/15/2018	Goodings, Robert	$1,576.28	42

Livingood Income Tax & Accounting
Accounts Payable Aging Details

Date	Invoice	Client	Due	Age
2/15/2018	1007	AccounStaff, Inc.	$393.79	42
2/15/2018	1014	Custom Tax, Inc.	$619.32	42
2/15/2018	1020	Goodings, Robert	$1,576.28	42
2/15/2018	1015	Halvorsen, Susan	$1,014.52	42
2/26/2018	1010	AccounStaff, Inc.	$233.86	31
2/26/2018	1015	Custom Tax, Inc.	$716.74	31
2/26/2018	1012	Friedman, Gerald	$1,942.03	31
3/14/2018	1004	Bremen, Charles	$1,348.38	15
3/14/2018	1001	Custom Tax, Inc.	$1,630.23	15
3/14/2018	1020	Dunhill & Berks	$1,163.41	15
3/14/2018	1002	Edwards and Mulcahey	$231.38	15
3/19/2018	1005	AccounStaff, Inc.	$529.18	10
3/19/2018	1018	AccounStaff, Inc.	$1,916.18	10
3/19/2018	1017	Bremen, Charles	$1,150.49	10
3/19/2018	1003	Custom Tax, Inc.	$827.63	10

Today is January 1, 2020

30 Days or More Past Due

Client	Total	# of Invoices
AccounStaff, Inc.	$627.65	2
Custom Tax, Inc.	$1,336.06	2

Figure 6-116 Completed worksheets for Excel 6-7

Challenge Project 6-8

In this project, you build a list of names and use *Text* functions to create email addresses. You also use the *SUBSTITUTE* function to update the email address list to display a revised name.
[Student Learning Outcome 6.6]

File Needed: None
Completed Project File Name: ***[your initials] Excel 6-8.xlsx***

Create and save a workbook as [your initials] Excel 6-8. Modify your workbook according to the following guidelines:

- In cells **A3:B8**, type first and last names for six persons, first names in column A, last names in column B. Names can be friends, relatives, or colleagues.
- In cells **C3:C8**, use *CONCAT* to display an email address for each individual that consists of the first name, an underscore, the last name, and @ with a domain name. Use the same domain name for all, such as "abc.com" or "CompanyA.com."
- In cells **D3:D8**, use *SUBSTITUTE* to change the **Text** in column **C** to a different domain name. For example, change "CompanyA.com" to "CompanyB.com."
- Type labels and apply formatting to complete the worksheet.
- Insert a footer that displays the current date in the left section and your name in the right section.
- Set document properties to show your name as the author and a title of your choice. Spell check the workbook if necessary.

Challenge Project 6-9

In this project, you calculate net present value and modified rate of return for an electric car purchase. You include the increased cost of this type of automobile, a tax credit from your state government, and gasoline cost savings for five years of ownership.
[Student Learning Outcome 6.5]

File Needed: None
Completed Project File Name: ***[your initials] Excel 6-9.xlsx***

Create and save a workbook as [your initials] Excel 6-9. Modify your workbook according to the following guidelines:

- Enter the following labels in column A in separate rows: Price Premium, Tax Credit, and Year 1 Fuel Savings. Copy and edit the fuel savings label for years 2–5.
- In column B, enter a negative value as the price premium for an electric car. This value represents how much more an electric car costs than a gasoline-powered car.
- Enter a value for a tax credit that is 10 percent of the premium value; this is a positive value because it is a savings for you.
- For fuel savings, estimate yearly values based on driving an electric car rather than a gasoline-powered car. You can estimate the same or varying amounts for each year
- Enter labels in column A below the data for Net Present Value and Modified Rate of Return.
- Use *NPV* to calculate the net present value of the purchase in column B. For the discount rate, enter a percentage that is close to the percentage you might earn for a moderately safe investment.
- Research and explore the *MIRR* function in the *Financial* category. Investigate Microsoft and third-party help sites to learn how to use this function. Then use it to determine a rate of return in column B.
- Edit and enter new values to reach acceptable results for your investment.
- Insert main labels to identify the purpose of the sheet and apply formatting.
- Insert a header that shows the current date in the center section and your name in the right section.
- Edit document properties to show your name as the author.

Challenge Project 6-10

In this project, you create a worksheet that compares year-to-year usage for text messages, tweets, or blog posts. You calculate the percentage change and use *IFERROR* to identify incomplete data.
[Student Learning Outcome 6.2]

File Needed: None
Completed Project File Name: ***[your initials] Excel 6-10.xlsx***

Create and save a workbook as [your initials] Excel 6-10. Modify your workbook according to the following guidelines:

- Type January in cell **A3**, and fill the names of the months to December in the column.
- In cells **B2:D2**, enter labels for Year 1, Year 2, and % Change.

- Enter values for January through September for both years. These values can represent the number of tweets, text messages, or other posts of interest to you. Do not enter values for October through December.
- In column D, enter the formula to calculate the percentage change, year 2's value minus year 1's value divided by year 1's value. Remember that subtraction must be calculated before division. Format the results as **Percent Style** with two decimal places.
- Copy the formula for all months, including October through December, to display the standard error message *#DIV/0!* In the rows without values.
- Edit or replace the formulas in column D with an *IFERROR* formula to display Missing Data instead of the standard error.
- Insert main labels to identify the purpose of the sheet and complete formatting.
- Insert a header with your name in the right section.
- Edit document properties to show your name as the author.

CHAPTER 7

Working with Templates and Co-Authoring

CHAPTER OVERVIEW

Excel templates are model workbooks. When you create a new workbook, you use a default template with basic settings, including a document theme, a font name and size, and default margins. When you co-author a workbook, you and colleagues collaborate on a shared file.

STUDENT LEARNING OUTCOMES (SLOs)

After completing this chapter, you will be able to:

- **SLO 7.1** Use a template to create a workbook and save a workbook as a template (p. E7-443).
- **SLO 7.2** Set data validation, input messages, and error alerts (p. E7-445).
- **SLO 7.3** Use *Form Controls* in a workbook (p. E7-452).
- **SLO 7.4** Set worksheet and workbook protection to manage editing (p. E7-456).
- **SLO 7.5** Co-author a workbook (p. E7-462).
- **SLO 7.6** Finalize a workbook for distribution by inspecting it for personal information, accessibility, and compatibility (p. E7-466).

CASE STUDY

In the Pause & Practice projects in this chapter, you work with inventory and guest worksheets for Paradise Lakes Resort (PLR). You save the workbook as a template, add data validation and an option button, and check the workbook for distribution issues.

Pause & Practice 7-1: Create an Excel template and add data validation settings to a worksheet.

Pause & Practice 7-2: Create a workbook from a template, add a form control, and set worksheet and workbook protection.

Pause & Practice 7-3: Co-author a workbook and prepare a workbook for distribution.

EXCEL

SLO 7.1

Using Excel Templates

A ***template*** is a prototype or sample workbook. A template can include formulas, formatting, charts, images, controls, and more. Templates are best for work that requires the same layout, the same design, and the same data pattern each time you prepare a workbook.

Create a Workbook from a Template

The *Backstage* view for the *New* command displays recently developed and popular templates in its *Featured* group. Excel has thousands of templates, and *Backstage* view lists suggested search categories. When you create a workbook from a template, a copy of the template opens as an Excel workbook with the same name as the template followed by a number.

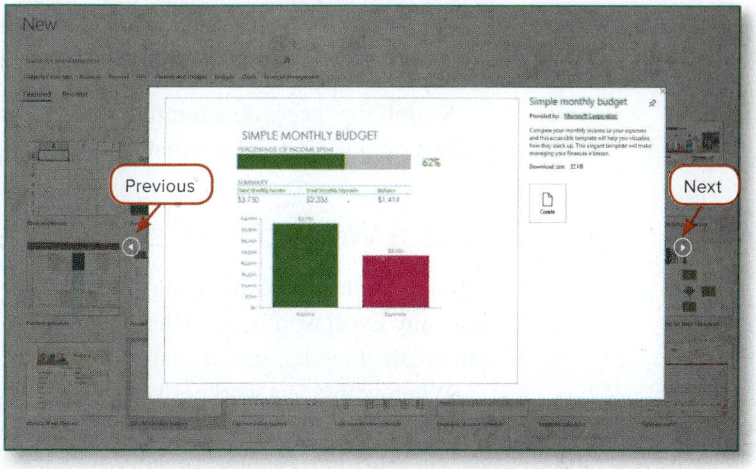

Figure 7-1 Preview of selected template in *Backstage* view

▸HOW TO: Create a Workbook from a Template

1. Click the **New** button [*File* tab].
   - The *New* command displays a thumbnail and name for each currently *Featured* template.
   - The *Blank workbook* template creates a new workbook.
   - Select a group from the *Suggested searches* to display additional online templates for the category.
   - Select **Personal** to use a template that you created.
2. Click the thumbnail for the template you want to use.
   - A preview window describes the template.
   - Click the **Previous** or **Next** arrows to see a different template preview (Figure 7-1).
3. Click **Create**.
   - A workbook with the same name as the template followed by a number opens.
   - Most online templates include sample data and multiple sheets.
   - Templates may also include input messages to guide a user in completing the worksheet (Figure 7-2).
4. Save the workbook in your usual location with a descriptive name.

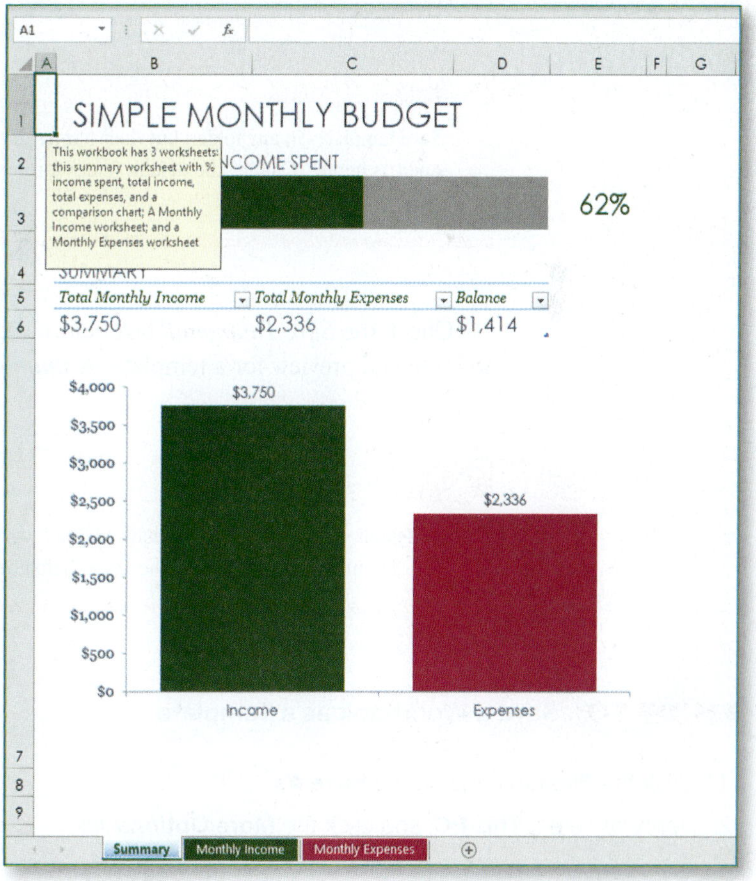

Figure 7-2 Workbook created from a template with an input message in cell A1

Accessible Templates

A template is accessible when it includes features and design elements that aid persons with visual, literacy, and other impairments to complete the worksheet. Office applications are engineered to work with screen readers, keyboards, and other assistive technology. You can further enhance the accessibility of your work by following these suggestions as you create a workbook or a template.

- Choose contrasting colors to distinguish areas and items in the worksheet.
- Utilize white space to identify explanatory text and images.
- Use larger fonts for easy reading.
- Provide descriptive labels and worksheet tab names.
- Include input messages, notes, or comments.

Search for "accessible templates" from the *New* command in the *Backstage* view to explore professionally designed templates that incorporate accessibility features.

Save a Workbook as a Template

Online templates provide a starting point for a new workbook, but you can create a template from any Excel workbook. When you use the same design, formulas, and objects for a task, you can create a model, save it as a template, and build new workbooks from the template.

When you save a workbook as an Excel template, it is saved in the *Custom Office Templates* folder in the *Documents* folder for the current user at your computer. Your saved templates are available in the *Personal* category in *Backstage* view for the *New* command [*File* tab]. Excel templates are saved with the .xltx file name extension.

MORE INFO

Save templates in any folder, but their names do not appear in the *Personal* category, and they do not open as copies. Change the default folder for personal templates in the *Excel Options* dialog box in the *Save* pane.

Check the *Save Thumbnail* box before you choose the *Save as type* in the *Save As* dialog box to include a preview for a template. A ***thumbnail*** is a tiny image of the active sheet.

MORE INFO

A default setting to save thumbnails with all workbooks is in the *Properties* dialog box on the *Summary* tab. Thumbnails are visible in the *Open* dialog box when you set view options to show icons.

HOW TO: Save a Workbook as a Template

1. Click the **File** tab and choose **Save As**.
2. Verify or select **This PC**, and click the **More Options** link.
   - The *Save As* dialog box opens.
   - The default name in the *File name* box is highlighted.

3. Type the template name.
4. Select the **Save Thumbnail** box (Figure 7-3).
5. Click the **Save as type** arrow and select **Excel Template**.
   - Excel displays the default *Custom Office Templates* folder name and its path.
   - You can navigate to another folder, but your template will not appear in the *Personal* category for the *New* command.
6. Click **Save**.
   - Select **No** if a message box about external data opens.
7. Close the template.

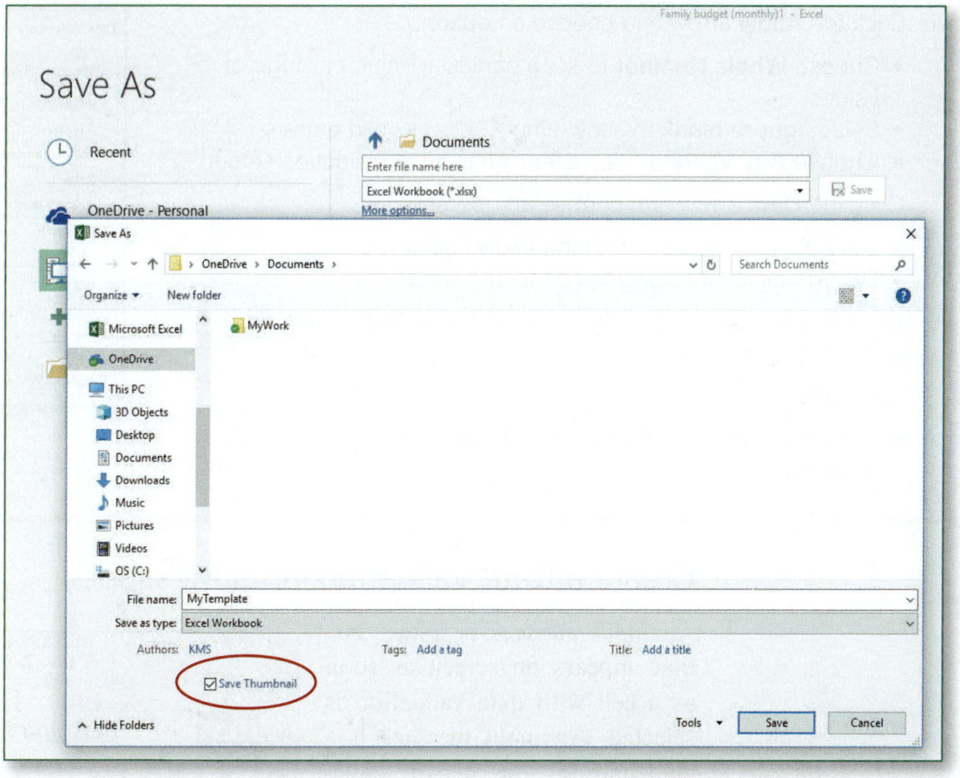

Figure 7-3 Save a thumbnail for a template

SLO 7.2

Setting Data Validation

Data validation is a process in which Excel checks data as it is entered to verify that it matches established requirements. In an inventory worksheet, Paradise Lakes Resort can set a data validation rule that requires the stock quantity to be a positive number. If a user enters a negative number, a pop-up message reminds the person about the error.

Validation Settings

Validation settings are rules applied to data as it is entered. Build a simple condition using relational operators, such as requiring that the data be a whole number within a range of values or that data be greater than or less than a value. You can allow or prohibit decimal values, specify date or time limits, or limit the length of a text entry. It is also possible to use a list or a formula in a data validation setting.

You usually set data validation for a range of cells before any data is entered. If you set validation after data is entered, data that does not meet the rule is not automatically identified.

HOW TO: Set Data Validation with an Operator

1. Select the cell or the cell range where data validation settings are required.
2. Click the **Data Validation** button [*Data* tab, *Data Tools* group].
   - The *Data Validation* dialog box includes three tabs.
3. Click the **Settings** tab.

4. Click the **Allow** arrow and choose an option.
    - Choose **Whole Number** to set a particular value or range of values.
    - Select **Ignore blank** to allow empty cells as valid entries.
    - Choose **Any Value** or click **Clear All** to clear validation settings.
5. Click the **Data** arrow and choose an operator.
    - *Data* options are based on the *Allow* choice.
    - Dialog box choices depend on the operator.
6. Enter a value or select a cell to complete the *Data Validation* settings (Figure 7-4).
7. Click **OK**.
    - Cells with existing data that do not match the criteria are not identified.

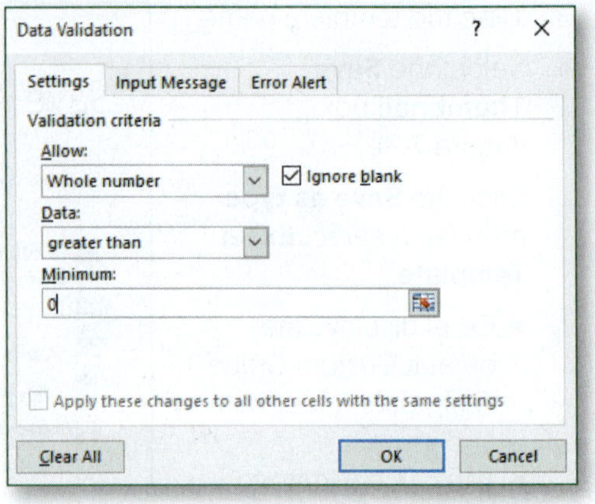

Figure 7-4 Data validation settings

Create a Data Validation Input Message

An ***input message*** is a text box that appears on screen as soon as a cell with data validation is selected. An input message is a guideline for the person entering data. It might display "Type a value between 1 and 10," or "Choose a name from this list." Figure 7-5 shows an input message before data is entered.

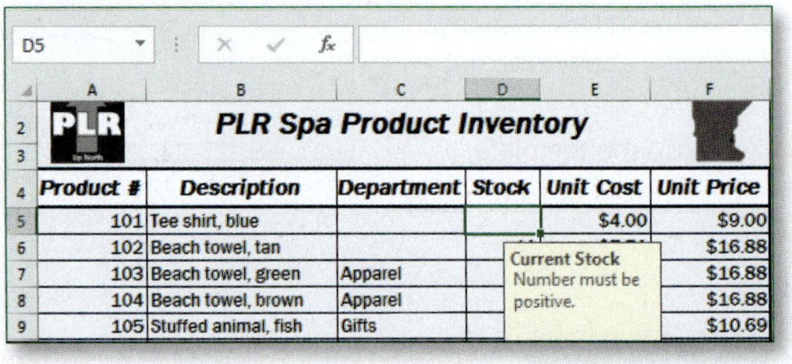

Figure 7-5 Input message when the cell is selected

▸HOW TO: Create an Input Message

1. Select the cell or the range with data validation settings.
2. Click the **Data Validation** button [*Data* tab, *Data Tools* group].
3. Click the **Input Message** tab.
4. Verify that the *Show input message when cell is selected* box is selected.
5. Click the **Title** box and type a name or title for the message box.
    - A title is optional.
6. Click the **Input message** box and type the message to appear on screen (Figure 7-6).
    - Use capitalization and punctuation as desired.
    - Be brief to keep the input box small.
7. Click **OK**.

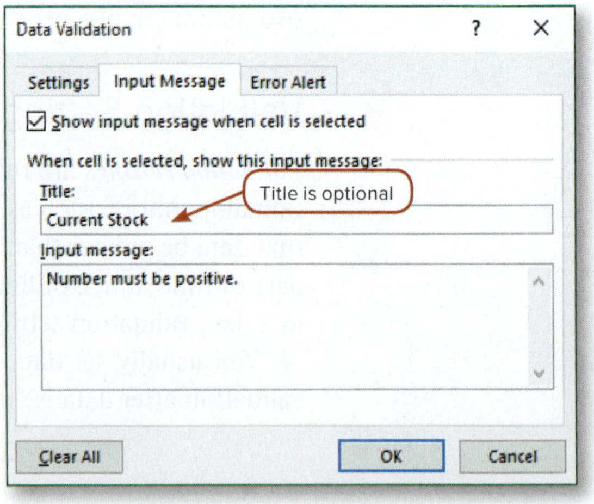

Figure 7-6 Input message for data validation

> **MORE INFO**
>
> Display a custom *ScreenTip* by creating an input message without a data validation setting.

Create a Data Validation Error Alert

An ***error alert*** is a pop-up message that appears after invalid data is entered, as shown in Figure 7-7. Each data validation setting can include an error alert as well as an input message.

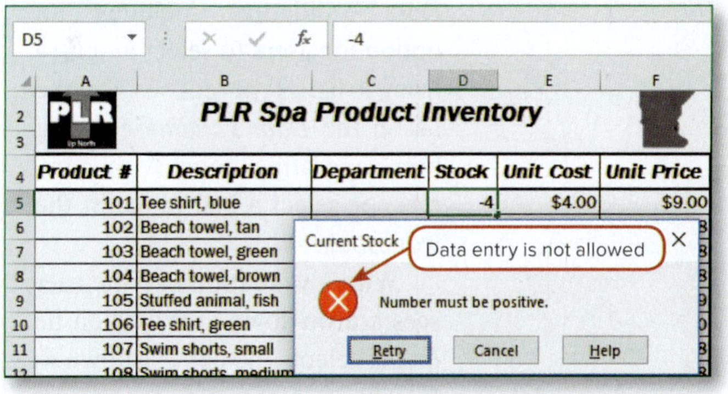

Figure 7-7 *Stop* style error alert

In an error alert, you specify the type of warning box. With a *Stop* warning, the user is prohibited from making an entry and can cancel the task or retry. A *Stop* warning displays a white **X** in a red circle. If you select a *Warning* alert, the message box shows an exclamation point (**!**) in a yellow triangle. With this type of warning, the entry is allowed or can be edited or canceled. The third warning style is *Information* which allows the entry to be made. This message box includes a lowercase **i** in a blue circle.

> **MORE INFO**
>
> If you allow invalid entries, set conditional formatting to highlight invalid entries for review.

After you set the type of warning, type an optional title for the message box. The *Error message* is text that appears on screen. The message should clearly and briefly explain what the user should do to create a valid entry.

HOW TO: Create an Error Alert

1. Select the cell or the range with data validation settings.
2. Click the **Data Validation** button [*Data* tab, *Data Tools* group].
3. Click the **Error Alert** tab.
4. Verify that the *Show error alert after invalid data is entered* box is selected.
5. Click the **Style** arrow and choose a warning type.
   - Use a *Stop* style if the entry should not be allowed.
   - Use a *Warning* or *Information* style if the entry is permissible.
6. Click the **Title** box and type a label for the message box.
   - The title is optional.
7. Click the **Error message** box and type the message to appear in the warning box (Figure 7-8).
   - Use capitalization and punctuation as you want it to appear on screen.
   - Check spelling and grammar carefully.
8. Click **OK**.

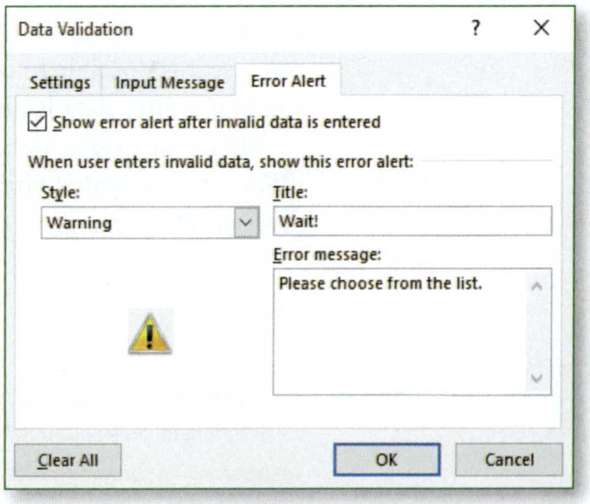

Figure 7-8 Warning style error alert

Validation Lists

Data validation includes an option for users to select an entry from a list. Type entries for the list in the *Data Validation* dialog box, separating items with commas, or select a cell range in the workbook.

With a validation list, the user sees a drop-down arrow when he or she selects the cell as shown in Figure 7-9. Enter data for the list in alphabetical or other logical order so that it is easy for the user to find his or her choice.

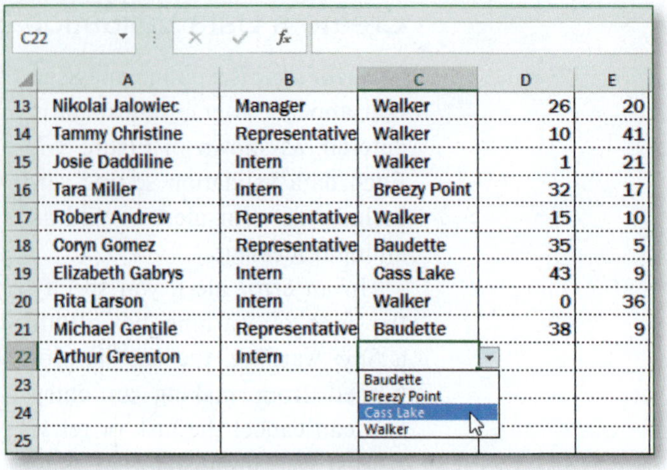

C22
A
B
C
D
E
13 Nikolai Jalowiec Manager Walker 26 20
14 Tammy Christine Representative Walker 10 41
15 Josie Daddiline Intern Walker 1 21
16 Tara Miller Intern Breezy Point 32 17
17 Robert Andrew Representative Walker 15 10
18 Coryn Gomez Representative Baudette 35 5
19 Elizabeth Gabrys Intern Cass Lake 43 9
20 Rita Larson Intern Walker 0 36
21 Michael Gentile Representative Baudette 38 9
22 Arthur Greenton Intern
23
24
25
Baudette
Breezy Point
Cass Lake
Walker

Figure 7-9 A data validation list

▸HOW TO: Set a Data Validation List

1. Select the cell or range for data validation.
2. Click the **Data Validation** button [*Data* tab, *Data Tools* group].
3. Click the **Settings** tab.
4. Click the **Allow** arrow and choose **List**.
5. Click the **Source** entry box and do one of the following:
   - Select the range of cells with the list.
   - Press **F3** (**FN+F3**) to open the *Paste Name* dialog box, choose the name, and click **OK** (Figure 7-10).
   - Type each entry for the list, followed by a comma.
6. Click **OK**.

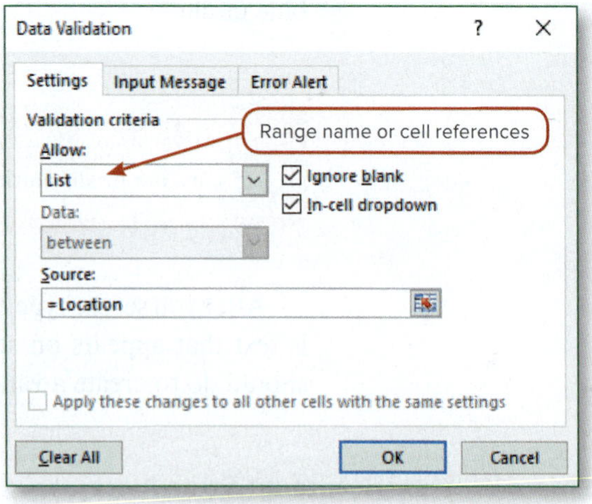

Figure 7-10 Validation settings for a list

Circle Invalid Data

Invalid data is a value or label that does not conform to validation criteria. Invalid data occurs because it is possible to copy data into a range with validation settings and because you can set validation after data is already entered.

Highlight invalid data with the *Circle Invalid Data* command. This command places a red ***ellipse*** (an elongated circle) around each cell in which the data does not match the validation criteria. The *Circle Invalid Data* command highlights cells. It does not edit or correct the data.

> **MORE INFO**
>
> Use the *Find & Select* command, *Go To Special* [*Home* tab, *Editing* group] and select *Data validation* to highlight cells with data validation settings.

▸ HOW TO: Circle Invalid Data

1. Select the cell or range with validation settings.
2. Click the arrow for the **Data Validation** button [*Data* tab, *Data Tools* group].
3. Select **Circle Invalid Data**.
   - A red ellipse highlights each cell with invalid data (Figure 7-11).
4. Type or select valid data for each invalid entry.
   - The ellipse is removed after valid data is entered.
5. Click the **Data Validation** button [*Data* tab, *Data Tools* group].
6. Select **Clear Validation Circles** to remove ellipses if necessary.

PLR Spa Product Inventory

Product #	Description	Department	Stock	Unit Cost	Unit Price
101	Tee shirt, blue		12	$4.00	$9.00
102	Beach towel, tan		12	$7.50	$16.88
103	Beach towel, green	Apparel	-8	$7.50	$16.88
104	Beach towel, brown	Apparel	7	$7.50	$16.88
105	Stuffed animal, fish	Gifts	4	$4.75	$10.69
106	Tee shirt, green	Apparel	8	$4.00	$9.00
107	Swim shorts, small	Apparel	10	$5.50	$12.38
108	Swim shorts, medium	Apparel	12	$5.50	$12.38
109	Yoga pants, black	Apparel	5	$12.50	$28.13
110	Yoga pants, grey	Apparel	4	$12.50	$28.13
111	Sunscreen, 8 oz	Health Aids	10	$3.45	$7.76
112	Sunscreen 12 oz	Health Aids	12	$4.75	$10.69
113	Picture frame, 6"	Gifts	8	$5.50	$12.38
114	Picture frame, 12"	Gifts	8	$6.50	$14.63
115	Magnet, PLR	Gifts	15	$3.25	$7.31
116	Magnet, Minnesota		-16	$3.25	$7.31
117	Pen, PLR		20	$1.24	$2.79
118	Pen, Minnesota	Gifts	24	$1.24	$2.79

Figure 7-11 Invalid data is circled

PAUSE & PRACTICE: EXCEL 7-1

In this project, you save a workbook as a template, set data validation rules with input and error messages, circle invalid data, and remove invalidation circles.

File Needed: ***ParadiseLakes-07.xlsx*** *(Student data files are available in the* Library *of your SIMnet account.)*
Completed Project File Name: ***[your initials] PP E7-1Template.xltx***

1. Open the ***ParadisesLakes-07*** workbook from your student data files.
2. Save a workbook as a template.
   a. Click the **File** tab and choose **Save As**.
   b. Select **This PC** and click the **More Options** link to open the *Save As* dialog box.
   c. Type [your initials] PP E7-1Template in the *File name* box.
   d. Select the **Save Thumbnail** box.
   e. Click the **Save as type** arrow and choose **Excel Template** (Figure 7-12). The default folder for templates is opened.
   f. Click **Save**.

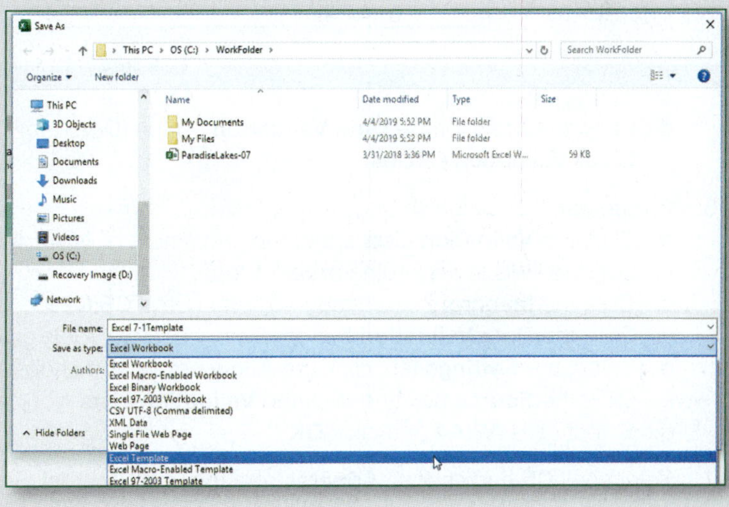

Figure 7-12 ***Save as type*** **sets the default templates folder**

3. Create data validation settings with an operator to require a positive value.
   a. Select cells **D5:D29** on the **Inventory** sheet.
   b. Click the **Data Validation** button [*Data* tab, *Data Tools* group].
   c. Click the **Allow** arrow and choose **Whole Number**.
   d. Click the **Data** arrow and choose **greater than**.
   e. Click the **Minimum** box and type 0.
   f. Do not click **OK**.

4. Create an input message for data validation settings.
   a. Click the **Input Message** tab.
   b. Verify that the *Show input message when cell is selected* box is selected.
   c. Click the **Title** box and type Current Stock.
   d. Click the **Input message** box and type Number must be positive. including the period.
   e. Click **OK**. The input message appears because the range is selected.
   f. Select cell **E5** to remove the input message.

5. Circle and delete invalid data.
   a. Click the arrow for the **Data Validation** button [*Data* tab, *Data Tools* group].
   b. Choose **Circle Invalid Data**.
   c. Select each cell with invalid data and press **Delete**. The validation setting requires a value greater than zero, so the circles are not removed (Figure 7-13).

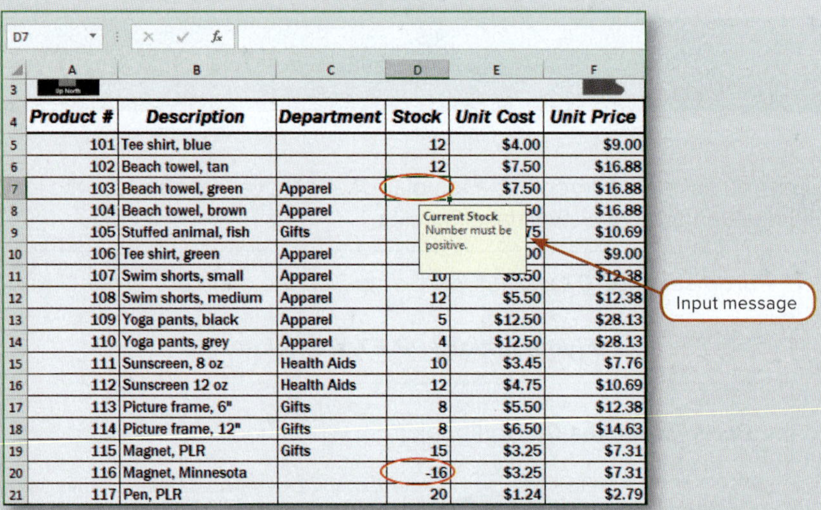

	A	B	C	D	E	F
4	Product #	Description	Department	Stock	Unit Cost	Unit Price
5	101	Tee shirt, blue		12	$4.00	$9.00
6	102	Beach towel, tan		12	$7.50	$16.88
7	103	Beach towel, green	Apparel		$7.50	$16.88
8	104	Beach towel, brown	Apparel	[illegible]	[illegible]	$16.88
9	105	Stuffed animal, fish	Gifts	[illegible]	[illegible]	$10.69
10	106	Tee shirt, green	Apparel	[illegible]	[illegible]	$9.00
11	107	Swim shorts, small	Apparel	[illegible]	[illegible]	$12.38
12	108	Swim shorts, medium	Apparel	12	$5.50	$12.38
13	109	Yoga pants, black	Apparel	5	$12.50	$28.13
14	110	Yoga pants, grey	Apparel	4	$12.50	$28.13
15	111	Sunscreen, 8 oz	Health Aids	10	$3.45	$7.76
16	112	Sunscreen 12 oz	Health Aids	12	$4.75	$10.69
17	113	Picture frame, 6"	Gifts	8	$5.50	$12.38
18	114	Picture frame, 12"	Gifts	8	$6.50	$14.63
19	115	Magnet, PLR	Gifts	15	$3.25	$7.31
20	116	Magnet, Minnesota		-16	$3.25	$7.31
21	117	Pen, PLR		20	$1.24	$2.79

Figure 7-13 Invalid data is circled

   d. Click the arrow for the **Data Validation** button [*Data* tab, *Data Tools* group] and choose **Clear Validation Circles**.

6. Create data validation settings with a list.
   a. Click the **Validation Lists** sheet tab and select cells **A2:A4**.
   b. Sort the cells in ascending order (*A to Z*).
   c. Click the **Inventory** sheet tab and select cells **C5:C29**.
   d. Click the **Data Validation** button [*Data* tab, *Data Tools* group].
   e. Select the **Settings** tab, click the **Allow** arrow, and choose **List**.
   f. Click the **Source** box and click the **Validation Lists** worksheet tab.
   g. Select cells **A2:A4** and click **OK**.

7. Select cell **C5** and choose **Apparel** from the validation list. Select cell **C6** and choose **Apparel**.

8. Select cell **C20** and choose **Gifts** from the validation list.

9. Choose **Gifts** for cells **C21** and **C23**.

10. Choose **Health Aids** for cells **C28:C29**.

11. Type the list for validation settings and add an error alert.
    a. Select the **Contacts** sheet tab and select cells **B3:B39**.
    b. Click the **Data Validation** button [*Data* tab, *Data Tools* group].
    c. Click the **Allow** arrow and choose **List**.
    d. Click the **Source** box.
    e. Type Intern,Manager,Representative with no space after each comma (Figure 7-14).
    f. Click the **Error Alert** tab.
    g. Verify that the *Show error alert after invalid data is entered* box is selected.
    h. Click the **Style** arrow and choose **Warning**. This style will allow an invalid entry to be made.
    i. Click the **Title** box and type Wait!.
    j. Click the **Error message** box and type Please choose from the list. including the period.
    k. Click **OK**.

12. Select cell **B4** and choose **Intern**.

13. Select cell **B5**, type Staff, and press **Enter** to display the error alert (Figure 7-15).

14. Choose **Yes** to allow the entry.

15. Choose **Manager** in cell **B6**.

16. Press **Ctrl+Home**. Click the **Save** button on the *Quick Access* toolbar to save the template with the same name.

17. Close the workbook (Figure 7-16).

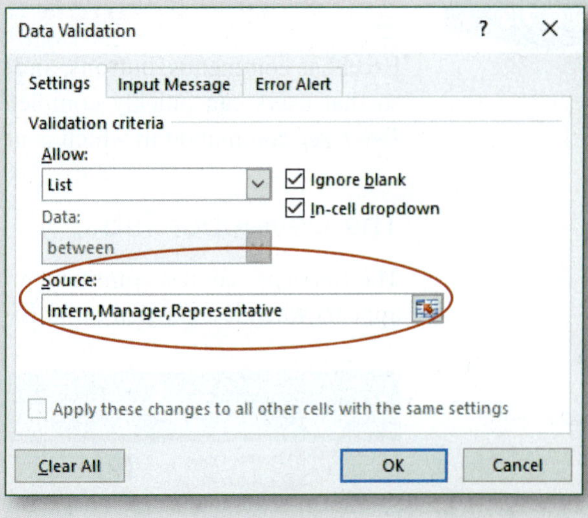

Figure 7-14 Typed validation list

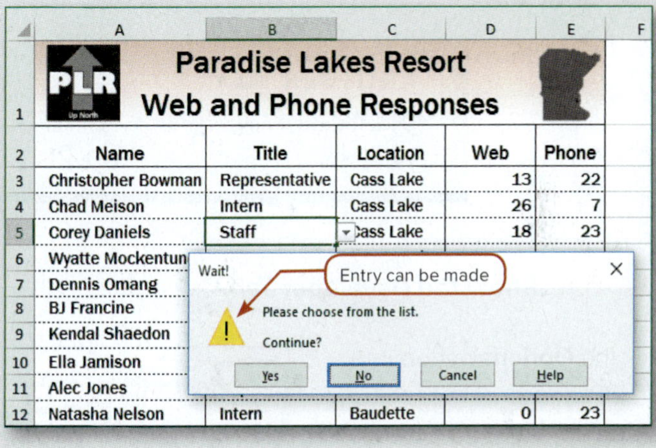

Figure 7-15 Error alert after invalid entry

PLR Spa Product Inventory

Product #	Description	Department	Stock	Unit Cost	Unit Price
101	Tee shirt, blue	Apparel	12	$4.00	$9.00
102	Beach towel, tan	Apparel	12	$7.50	$16.88
103	Beach towel, green	Apparel		$7.50	$16.88
104	Beach towel, brown	Apparel	7	$7.50	$16.88
105	Stuffed animal, fish	Gifts	4	$4.75	$10.69
106	Tee shirt, green	Apparel	8	$4.00	$9.00
107	Swim shorts, small	Apparel	10	$5.50	$12.38
108	Swim shorts, medium	Apparel	12	$5.50	$12.38
109	Yoga pants, black	Apparel	5	$12.50	$28.13
110	Yoga pants, grey	Apparel	4	$12.50	$28.13
111	Sunscreen, 8 oz	Health Aids	10	$3.45	$7.76
112	Sunscreen 12 oz	Health Aids	12	$4.75	$10.69
113	Picture frame, 6"	Gifts	8	$5.50	$12.38
114	Picture frame, 12"	Gifts	8	$6.50	$14.63
115	Magnet, PLR	Gifts	15	$3.25	$7.31
116	Magnet, Minnesota	Gifts		$3.25	$7.31
117	Pen, PLR	Gifts	20	$1.24	$2.79
118	Pen, Minnesota	Gifts	24	$1.24	$2.79
119	Pen, bass boat	Gifts	12	$1.24	$2.79
120	Stuffed animal, bear	Gifts	12	$4.75	$10.69
121	Stuffed animal, raccoon	Gifts	15	$4.75	$10.69
122	Antiseptic lotion, 4 oz	Health Aids	8	$5.75	$12.94
123	Antiseptic lotion, 12 oz	Health Aids	8	$6.25	$14.06
124	Insect repellent, 8 oz	Health Aids	10	$3.50	$7.88
125	Cough syrup, 8 oz	Health Aids	6	$2.20	$4.95

Paradise Lakes Resort
Web and Phone Responses

Name	Title	Location	Web	Phone
Christopher Bowman	Representative	Cass Lake	13	22
Chad Meison	Intern	Cass Lake	26	7
Corey Daniels	Staff	Cass Lake	18	23
Wyatte Mockentune	Manager	Breezy Point	25	19
Dennis Omang	Representative	Breezy Point	22	16
BJ Francine	Representative	Baudette	32	8
Kendal Shaedon	Representative	Breezy Point	5	22
Ella Jamison	Manager	Baudette	44	10
Alec Jones	Representative	Baudette	26	18
Natasha Nelson	Intern	Baudette	0	23
Nikolai Jalowiec	Manager	Walker	26	20
Tammy Christine	Representative	Walker	10	41
Josie Daddiline	Intern	Walker	1	21
Tara Miller	Intern	Breezy Point	32	17
Robert Andrew	Representative	Walker	15	10
Coryn Gomez	Representative	Baudette	35	5
Elizabeth Gabrys	Intern	Cass Lake	43	9
Rita Larson	Intern	Walker	0	36
Michael Gentile	Representative	Baudette	38	9

Figure 7-16 Completed worksheets for PP E7-1

SLO 7.3

Using Form Controls

Excel has commands, buttons, and tools that enable you to streamline data entry in a template so that users can quickly complete their work. Many of these tools are available from the *Developer* command tab which is not displayed on the *Ribbon* by default.

The Developer Tab

The *Developer* tab has command groups for working with macros, controls, and add-ins, and it appears when it is toggled on in Excel *Options* (Figure 7-17).

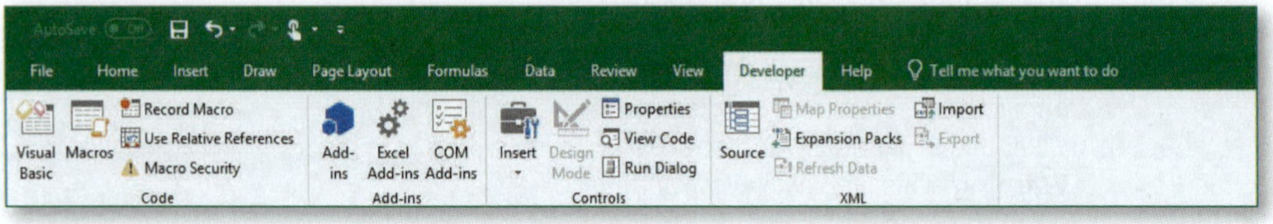

Figure 7-17 ***Developer* tab on the *Ribbon***

ANOTHER WAY

Click the arrow on the *Quick Access* toolbar and choose **More Commands** to open the *Excel Options* dialog box.

HOW TO: Show the Developer Tab

1. Click the **Options** button [*File* tab].
2. Select **Customize Ribbon** in the left pane.
3. Select the **Developer** box in the *Main Tabs* group (Figure 7-18).
4. Click **OK**.
   - The *Developer* tab displays at the right end of the *Ribbon*.

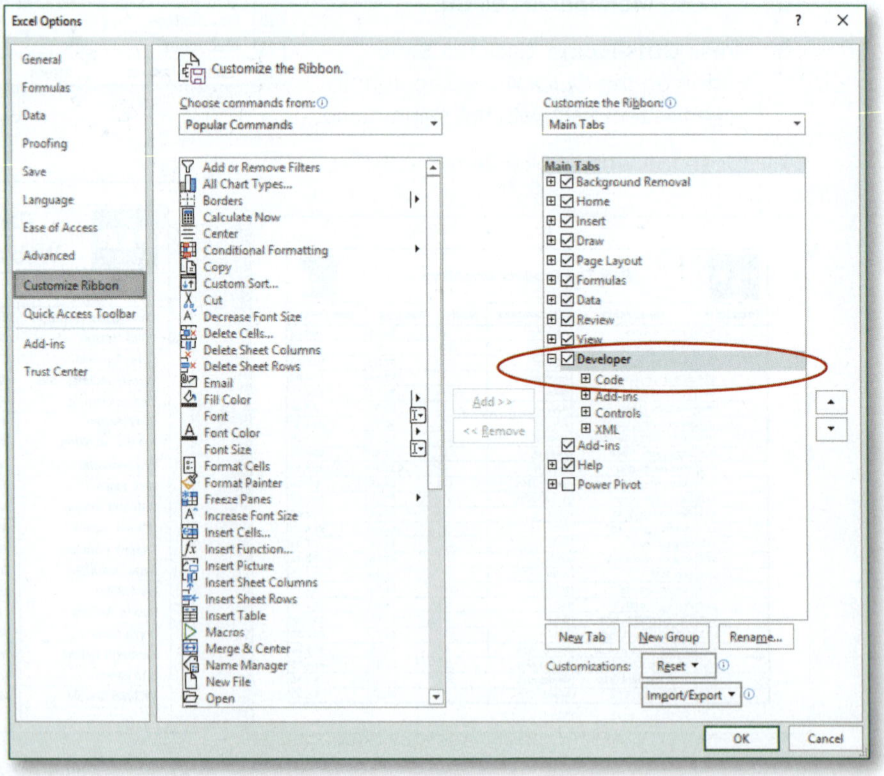

Figure 7-18 Excel *Options* dialog box to display the *Developer* tab

Form Controls

A ***form control*** is an object used to display a choice, to run a command, or to perform an action in a worksheet. Data entry is easier with form controls, and form controls improve the appearance of your work. Use form controls to select from a drop-down list, choose an option button, or click a check box.

Two categories, *Form Controls* and *ActiveX Controls*, are available from the ***Insert Controls*** button in the *Controls* group on the *Developer* tab. *ActiveX Controls* require that you write code in ***VBA (Visual Basic for Applications)***, a programming language for enhanced commands and features in Excel. *Form Controls* accomplish similar tasks without programming but with fewer refinements.

A selected form control has handles for sizing, a move arrow for positioning, and a context menu. The *Format Control* dialog box includes properties and settings specific to each type of control. When a form control is selected, the *Drawing Tools Format* tab is available, too.

> **MORE INFO**
>
> If a control's context menu shows *Assign Macro*, it is a *Form* control. If the context menu includes *Properties*, it is an *ActiveX* control.

Option Button Control

An ***Option Button*** control is a radio button that enables the user to select one choice from a set of possibilities. The default label for an option button control is "Option Button N" in which "n" is a number. Edit the label to specify the option names. Option button controls are usually organized in a ***Group Box*** control or a rectangular shape.

HOW TO: Insert an Option Button Form Control

1. Click the **Insert Controls** button [*Developer* tab, *Controls* group].
2. Click the **Option Button (Form Control)** button in the *Form Controls* group (Figure 7-19).
   - The pointer is a thin cross or plus sign.

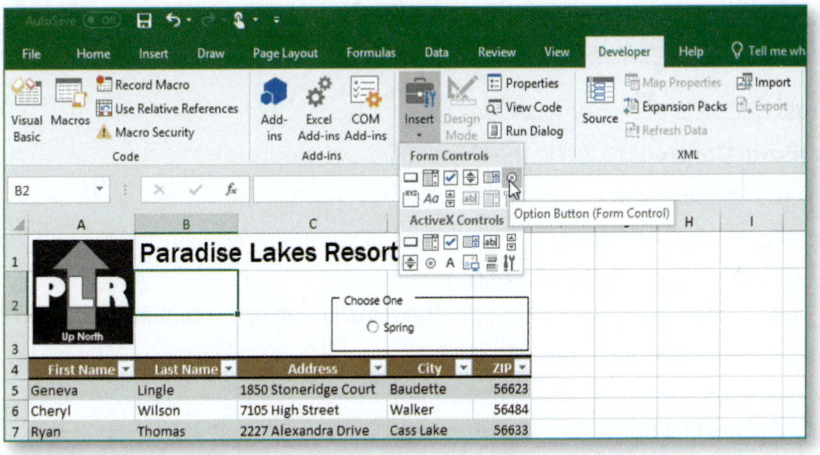

Figure 7-19 *Form Controls* gallery

3. Click and drag the pointer to draw the control.
   - The control is selected immediately after it is created.
   - An option button control includes a default label with a number.
   - To select a control, point to display the link select pointer (small hand with pointing finger) and right-click.
4. Click the **Properties** button [*Developer* tab, *Controls* group].
   - The *Format Control* dialog box opens.
   - Right-click the control and select **Format Control**.
5. Verify that the *Control* tab is selected.
6. Select the **Unchecked** button for *Value*.
   - Options depend on the type of control.
7. Select the **3-D shading** box (Figure 7-20).
8. Click **OK**.
9. Point to the control and right-click.
10. Select **Edit Text**.
    - The insertion point displays next to the default label.
11. Delete the default label.
12. Type a new label for the option button (Figure 7-21).
13. Select a worksheet cell to deselect the control.
    - Drag the control to the desired position on the sheet.
    - Size the control by dragging a selection handle.
    - Use *Drawing Tools* to align multiple controls.

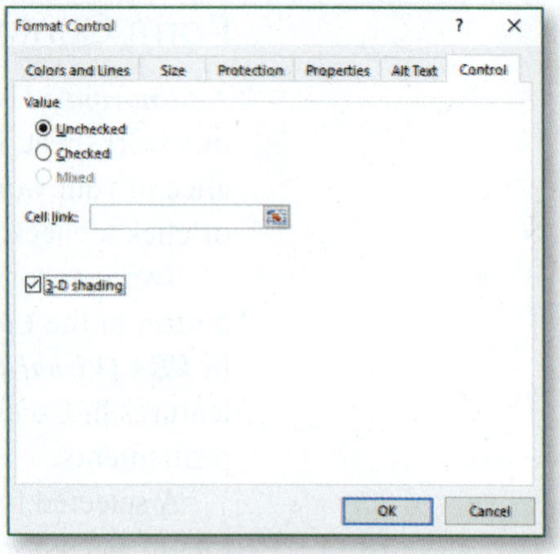

Figure 7-20 ***Format Control* dialog box**

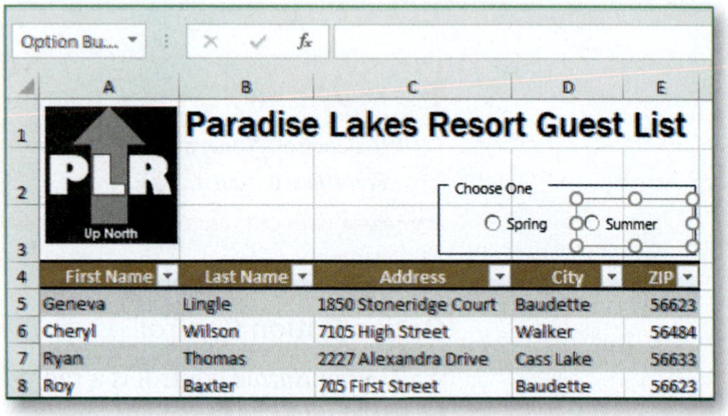

Figure 7-21 Option button control in worksheet

Combo Box Control

A ***Combo Box*** control creates a drop-down list from which you make a choice. The options in the list are from a cell range in the workbook. You link the control to a cell that displays a number that represents the position of your choice in the list. Display the actual choice instead of the number by using an *INDEX* command.

▶HOW TO: Use a Combo Box Form Control with INDEX

1. Click the **Insert Controls** button [*Developer* tab, *Controls* group].
2. Click the **Combo Box (Form Control)** button in the *Form Controls* group.
   - The pointer is a thin cross or plus sign.
3. Click and drag the pointer to draw the control.
   - The control is selected immediately after it is created.
   - To select a control, point to display the link select pointer (small hand with pointing finger) and right-click.
4. Right-click the control and select **Format Control**.
   - The *Format Control* dialog box opens.
   - Alternatively, click the **Properties** button in the *Controls* group [*Developer* tab].
5. Verify that the *Control* tab is selected.

6. Click the **Input range** box and select the cells with data for the combo box drop-down list.
    - You can type a range name, but you cannot paste a range name.
7. Click the **Cell link** box.
8. Click the worksheet cell where the choice made in the combo box will display.
    - Type a cell address if you prefer.
    - Hide the linked cell later by positioning the control over it.
9. Click the **Drop down lines** box and enter the number of lines to display in the combo box when the arrow is clicked.
    - When the number of drop-down lines is fewer than the number of items, the combo box displays scroll arrows.
10. Select the **3-D shading** check box (Figure 7-22).
11. Click **OK**.
12. Select the cell for the *INDEX* function.
    - Select a cell other than the *Cell link* cell.
    - This cell will display the actual data from the input range instead of the number.

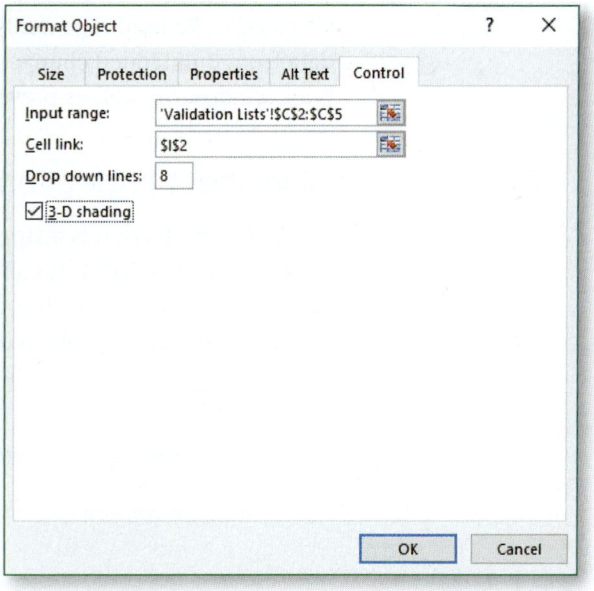

Figure 7-22 ***Format Object*** **dialog box for a combo box**

13. Start an *INDEX* function and select the **array, row_number, column_ num** argument list.
14. Select the same cell range used as the input range in the combo box for the *Array* argument.
    - You can type or paste a range name.
15. Click the **Row_num** box.
16. Select the same cell used as the *Cell link* in the control.
    - You can type the cell address.
17. Click **OK** to complete the *INDEX* formula.
18. Click the combo box arrow and make a choice.
    - The number indicating the position of your choice displays in the linked cell.
    - The *INDEX* formula returns the text of the choice (Figure 7-23).

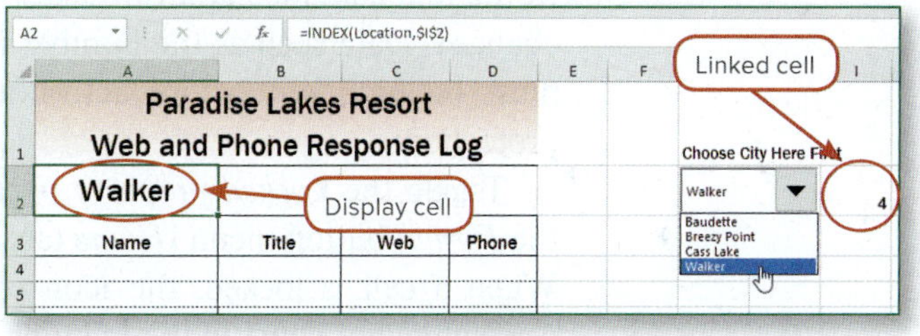

Figure 7-23 Combo box selection and ***INDEX*** **result**

Hide the Developer Tab

You can hide the *Developer* tab to return the *Ribbon* to its previous settings.

HOW TO: Hide the Form Button and the Developer Tab

1. Click the **File** tab and select **Options**.
2. Click **Customize Ribbon** in the left pane.
3. Deselect the **Developer** box in the *Main Tabs* group.
4. Click **OK**.
    - The *Developer* tab is removed from the *Ribbon*.

SLO 7.4

Setting Worksheet and Workbook Protection

Worksheet protection enables you to choose which cells can be edited. Because a template is designed to be used repeatedly and by others, worksheet protection safeguards the design and data from unintended changes. You can also prohibit changes to the size and position of workbook windows as well as prevent the addition or deletion of worksheets.

Worksheet Protection

Worksheet protection is a simple way to prevent changes to your work. When the *Protect Sheet* command is enabled, you can select a cell but you cannot edit it. If you attempt to edit a cell, you see an error message box as shown in Figure 7-24. Many *Ribbon* commands are grayed out when a worksheet is protected.

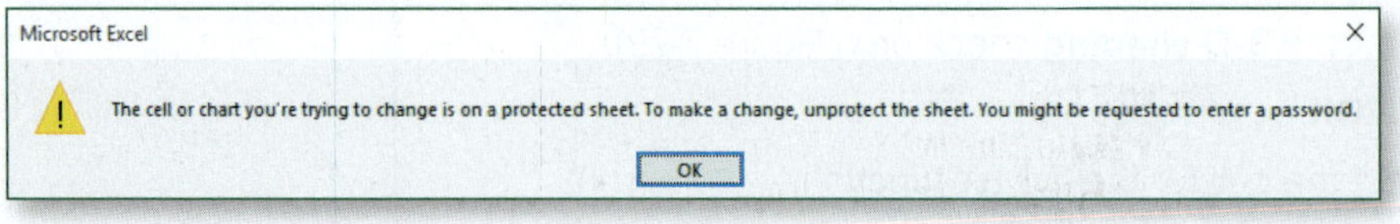

Figure 7-24 Message box when cells cannot be edited

The *Protect Sheet* command works in conjunction with the ***Locked*** cell property which is active for all cells and objects by default. Before setting worksheet protection, determine which cells and objects should be unlocked for editing.

Unlock Worksheet Cells

In the template for Paradise Lakes, you may not want prices, product IDs, or formulas to be changed. Data such as the number in stock, however, may be edited. Cells that can be edited must be unlocked before activating worksheet protection.

Toggle the *Locked* property on and off from the *Format* button menu [*Home* tab, *Cells* group]. When a cell is locked, the icon with the *Lock Cell* command name in the menu is outlined and shaded. The *Locked* property is also available on the *Protection* tab in the *Format Cells* dialog box.

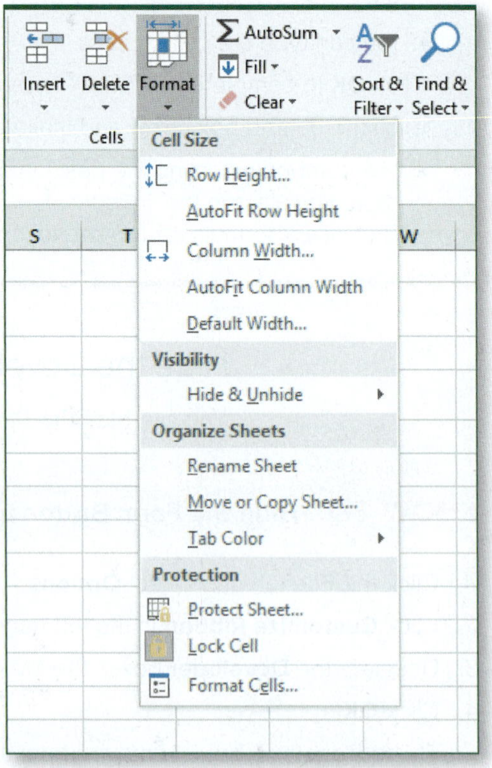

Figure 7-25 All cells are locked by default

HOW TO: Unlock Cells for Editing

1. Select the cell(s) to be unlocked.
   - Select ranges or noncontiguous cells.
2. Click the **Format** button [*Home* tab, *Cells* group].
   - The icon for *Lock Cell* is outlined and shaded to indicate that cells are locked (Figure 7-25).
   - All cells are locked by default.
3. Choose **Lock Cell**.
   - The selected cells are unlocked for editing.
4. Click the **Format** button [*Home* tab, *Cells* group].
   - The icon for *Lock Cell* is not shaded.
5. Click a cell to close the menu.

> **MORE INFO**
>
> The *Locked* property should be enabled for formula cells in a protected sheet so that formulas are not accidentally changed or deleted.

Allow Edit Ranges

The *Protect* group on the *Review* tab includes the *Allow Edit Ranges* command. With this command, you can password protect cells or ranges on the worksheet for editing by specific users. You identify those users from a trusted location and give them permission to edit the ranges (Figure 7-26). You can identify multiple ranges, assign each a unique password, and give permission to different user groups as needed.

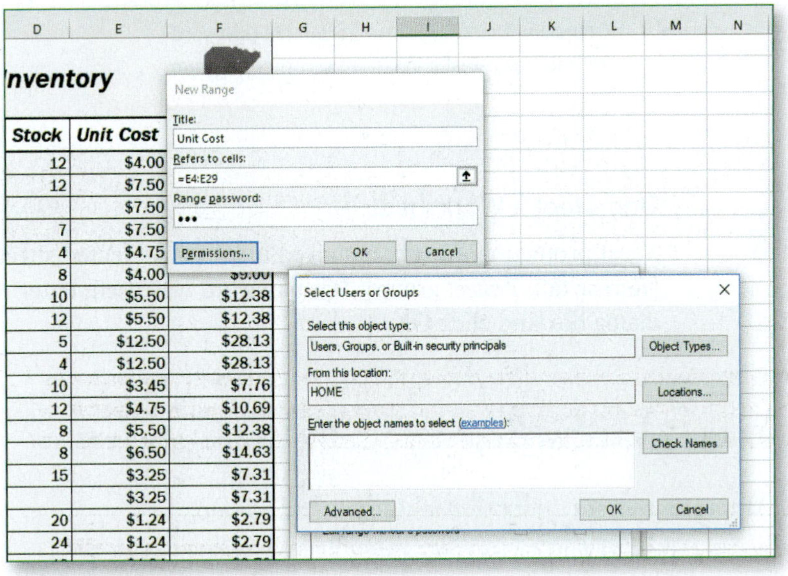

Figure 7-26 ***Allow Edit Ranges*** **requires passwords and permissions**

Protect a Worksheet

The *Locked* property and *Edit Ranges* have no effect until you add worksheet protection. The *Protect Sheet* button is in the *Protect* group on the *Review* tab. The *Protect Sheet* button becomes the *Unprotect Sheet* button when a sheet is protected. You can also protect a worksheet from the *Format* button [*Home* tab, *Cells* group] or from the *Info* command on the *File* tab.

The *Protect Sheet* dialog box has a list of editing options for locked cells, *PivotTables*, objects, hyperlinks, and more. These options include allowing cells to be selected or formatted, permitting rows and columns to be modified, and allowing *PivotTables* to be used.

As you activate worksheet protection, you can set an optional password. Worksheet protection without a password is not very secure, because you only need to know how to unprotect the sheet.

HOW TO: Protect a Worksheet

1. Unlock cells as needed.
2. Click the **Protect Sheet** button [*Review* tab, *Protect* group].
   - The *Protect Sheet* dialog box opens.
3. Type a password, as desired.
   - You see placeholders as you type a password.

4. Select the box for each editing capability that should be available (Figure 7-27).
5. Click **OK**.
   - The *Confirm Password* dialog box opens if you set a password.
6. Retype the password.
   - Passwords are case sensitive.
7. Click **OK**.
   - The *Protect Sheet* button displays *Unprotect Sheet*.

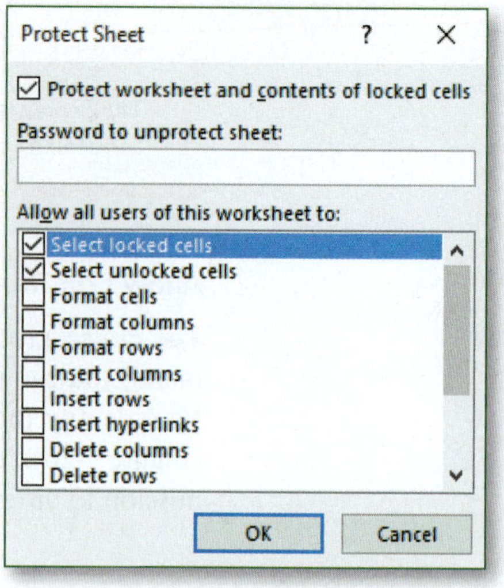

Figure 7-27 ***Protect Sheet*** **dialog box**

MORE INFO

You cannot recover a lost or forgotten password without the use of a password recovery program.

Unprotect a Worksheet

Sheet protection must be removed to edit a protected sheet. Click the **Unprotect Sheet** button [*Review* tab, *Protect* group]. If a password was used, enter the password in the *Unprotect Sheet* dialog box and click **OK**.

HOW TO: Unprotect a Worksheet

1. Click the **Unprotect Sheet** button [*Review* tab, *Protect* group].
   - Protection is removed if no password exists.
   - The *Unprotect Sheet* dialog box opens if a password exists.
2. Type the password.
3. Click **OK**.

Protect Workbook Structure

Workbook structure includes the number and arrangement of sheet tabs. By setting this protection, you prohibit others from deleting or inserting a sheet, from moving a tab, or from unhiding a worksheet. When workbook protection is active, unavailable commands are grayed out or cannot be selected.

You can protect workbook structure with or without a password. Remove workbook structure protection by clicking the **Protect Workbook** button [*File* tab].

ANOTHER WAY

Set and remove workbook protection by clicking the **Protect Workbook** button [*Review* tab, *Protect* group].

▸HOW TO: Protect Workbook Structure

1. Arrange worksheet tabs and hide sheets as desired.
2. Click the **Protect Workbook** button [*Review* tab, *Protect* group].
   - The *Protect Structure and Windows* dialog box opens.
   - The *Windows* setting is disabled by default.
3. Verify that the *Structure* box is selected (Figure 7-28).
4. Type an optional password in the *Password* box.
   - If you include a password, click **OK**, and retype it in the *Confirm Password* dialog box.
5. Click **OK** in the *Protect Structure and Windows* dialog box.
   - The *Protect Workbook* button [*Review* tab, *Changes* group] is highlighted.
6. Click the **File** tab and select **Info**.
   - The *Info* command describes the protection setting.
7. Click the **Protect Workbook** button.
8. Select **Protect Workbook Structure**.
   - Enter the password if needed and click **OK**.
   - The protection is removed.

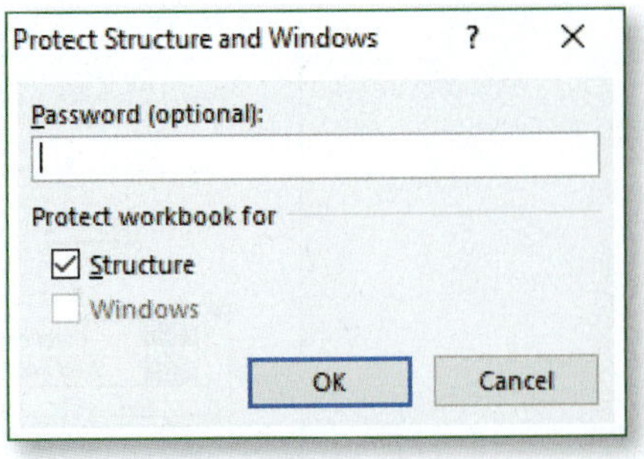

Figure 7-28 ***Protect Structure and Windows* dialog box**

PAUSE & PRACTICE: EXCEL 7-2

In this project, you create a workbook from a template, add a combo box control, unlock cells, and set worksheet protection.

File Needed: ***[your initials] PP E7-1Template.xltx***
Completed Project File Name: ***[your initials] PP E7-2.xlsx***

1. Create a workbook from a template.
   a. Click the **File** tab and select **New**.
   b. Click **Personal** (Figure 7-29).
   c. Select ***[your initials] PP E7-1Template*** completed in *Pause & Practice 7-1* to create a workbook based on the template. (If your template is not available in the *Personal* category, open it from your usual location for saving files.)
   d. Save the workbook as an Excel workbook named [your initials] PP E7-2 in your usual location.
2. Display the *Developer* tab.
   a. Click the **Customize Quick Access Toolbar** arrow at the right edge of the *Quick Access* toolbar.
   b. Choose **More Commands** to open the *Excel Options* dialog box.
   c. Click **Customize Ribbon** in the left pane.
   d. Select the **Developer** box in the *Main Tabs* group and click **OK**.

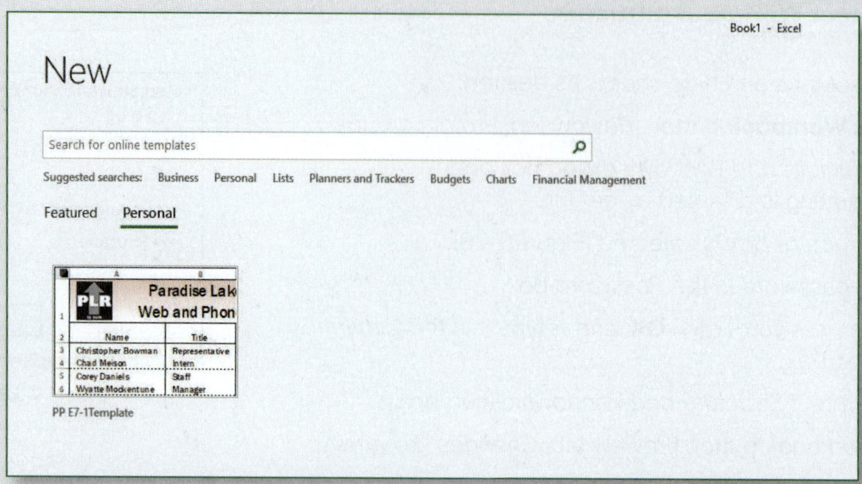

Figure 7-29 User-created templates are stored in the *Pesonal* category

3. Insert a combo box form control.
   a. Click the **Name** box arrow and choose **Location**. This range includes the four location names for Paradise Lakes Resort on the **Validation Lists** sheet.
   b. Click the **Response Log** worksheet tab.
   c. Click the **Insert Controls** button [*Developer* tab, *Controls* group].
   d. Click the **Combo Box (Form Control)** button.
   e. Draw a control directly over and the same width and height as cells **G2:H2** (Figure 7-30).

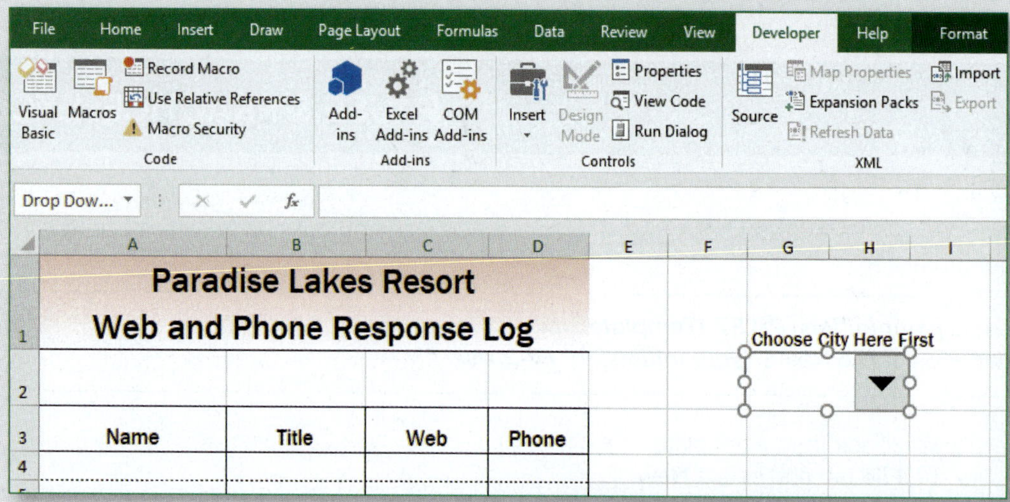

Figure 7-30 Combo box drawn on sheet

   f. Right-click any border of the control and choose **Format Control**. If the command is not listed, click a cell to deselect the control and right-click the control again.
   g. Type location in the *Input range* box on the *Control* tab.
   h. Click the **Cell link** box and select cell **I2**. The selection made in the combo box will display in this cell as a value to mark the relative position of the choice in the range.
   i. Select the **3-D shading** box (Figure 7-31).
   j. Click **OK**. Click cell **H3** to deselect the combo box control.
   k. Click the combo box arrow and choose **Baudette**. The label displays in the control and **1** displays in the linked cell (I2) because Baudette is the first item in the input range.

4. Use *INDEX* to display the city name from the combo box.
   a. Select cell **A2**. The city name associated with the *Cell link* result in cell **I2** will display here.
   b. Click the **Lookup & Reference** button [*Formulas* tab, *Function Library* group].
   c. Choose **Index** and choose the **array, row_num, column_num** argument group.
   d. Press **F3** (**FN+F3**) and select **Location** for the *Array* argument.
   e. Click the **Row_num** box, select cell **I2**, and click **OK**. The city name represented by the value in cell I2 displays in cell A2 and in the combo box.
   f. Right-click the combo box control to display its context menu.
   g. Point to a border of the control and left-click to hide the menu but maintain the selection handles.
   h. Use the four-pointed move arrow to drag the control to cells **H2:I2** so that it covers the linked cell (Figure 7-32).
   i. Deselect the combo box control.
   j. Click the combo box arrow and choose **Cass Lake**.

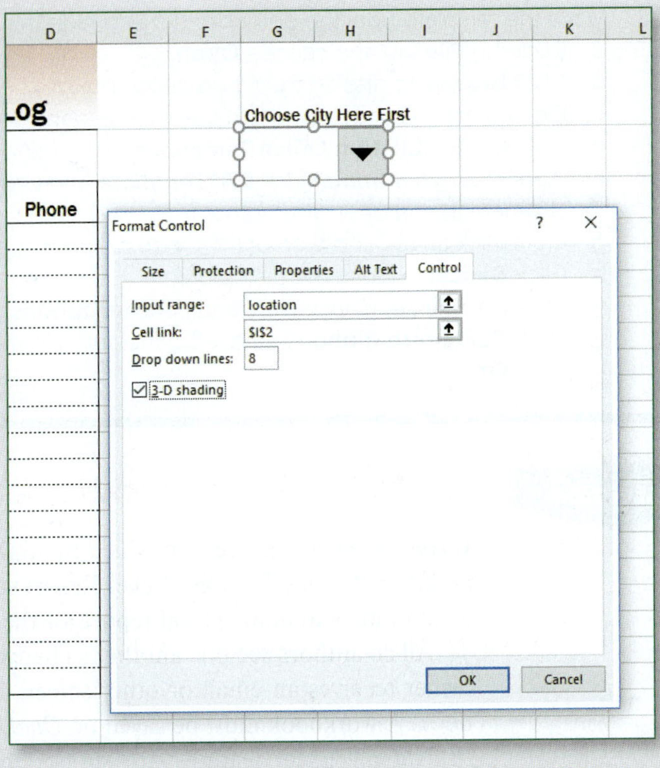

Figure 7-31 Combo box defined in *Format Control* dialog box

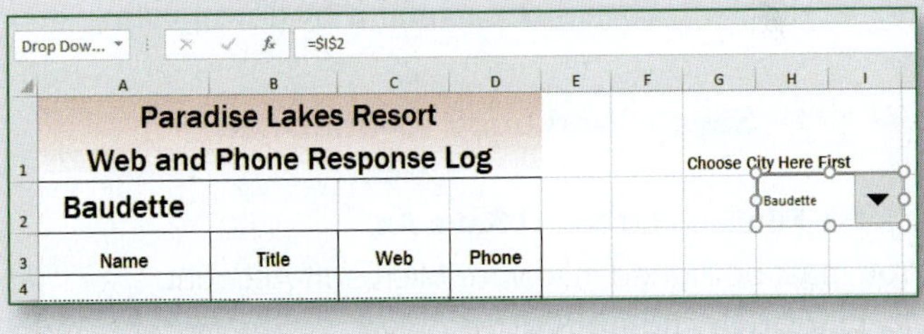

Figure 7-32 Combo box covers linked cell

5. Unlock cells and protect a sheet.
   a. Click the **Inventory** sheet tab and select cells **C5:D29**.
   b. Click the **Format** button [*Home* tab, *Cells* group] and select **Lock Cell**. All cells are locked by default; data in columns C and D are now unlocked and can be edited.
   c. Select cell **A5**.
   d. Click the **Protect Sheet** button [*Review* tab, *Protect* group].
   e. Verify that the *Select locked cells* and *Select unlocked cells* boxes are selected.
   f. Click **OK**. The command button now displays **Unprotect Sheet**.
6. Protect workbook structure.
   a. Right-click the **Validation Lists** sheet tab and choose **Hide**.
   b. Click the **File** tab and choose **Info**.
   c. Click the **Protect Workbook** button and select **Protect Workbook Structure**.
   d. Click **OK** to protect the structure without a password.
   e. Right-click a worksheet tab and note that the *Unhide* command is not available as well as the other sheet commands.
7. Save and close the workbook (Figure 7-33).

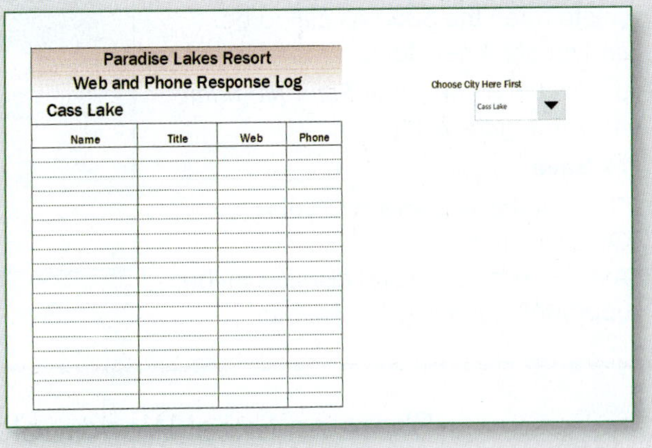

Figure 7-33 Completed worksheet for PP E7-2

8. Move the template from the default folder and hide the *Developer* tab.
   a. Click the **File** tab and choose **Open**.
   b. Click **Browse** to display the *Open* dialog box.
   c. Expand the *Quick access* list in the left pane and select **Documents**.
   d. Double-click **Custom Office Templates** in the pane on the right.
   e. Right-click ***[your initials] PP E7-1Template*** and choose **Cut**.
   f. Navigate to and open your folder for saving files.
   g. Right-click an unused area of the *Open* dialog box and choose **Paste**.
   h. Click **Cancel** to close the dialog box.
   i. Click the **File** tab if necessary and choose **Options**.
   j. Click **Customize Ribbon** in the left pane and deselect the **Developer** box in the *Main Tabs* group.
   k. Click **OK**.

SLO 7.5

Co-Authoring a Workbook

Co-authoring is a process in which multiple people edit a workbook, either simultaneously or at different times. Paradise Lakes Resort staff at various locations might co-author a workbook for inventory to build a final report for the company.

All co-authors see one another's changes immediately when working at the same time. The owner receives an email or other screen alert when a co-author has made edits to the workbook. A workbook must be saved on *OneDrive* to be co-authored.

Not all Excel features are supported in a co-authoring environment. Form controls, *SmartArt*, and charts are such examples. If you share a worbook that includes such elements, a co-author can edit it by downloading a copy to his or her computer.

HOW TO: Save a Workbook to OneDrive

1. Click the **File** tab and select **Save As**.
   - You must be signed in to your Microsoft Account.
2. Click **OneDrive - [Identifier]** to see your cloud folder names.
   - The *[Identifier]* is a domain name for an academic or business account.
   - The *[Identifier]* is *Personal* for your private account.
3. Click a folder name to store the workbook.
   - Navigate as needed to locate a folder.
   - Alternatively, click the **More options** link to open the *Save As* dialog box and create a new folder.
4. Type the file name in the *Enter file name here* box (Figure 7-34).
5. Click **Save**.
   - The workbook is saved to your *OneDrive* folder.
   - *AutoSave* is active and displays in the upper-left corner of the title bar.

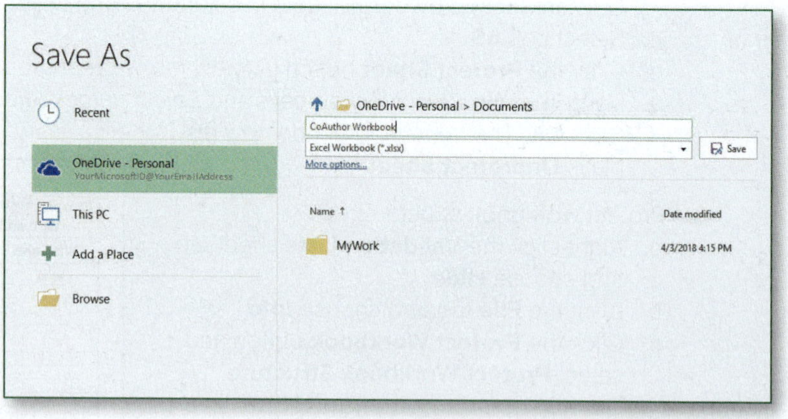

Figure 7-34 Save a workbook to *OneDrive* for co-authoring

Share an Excel Workbook

When you share a workbook, you enter email addresses and specify whether an individual can edit or simply view the document. You can also type a brief message that is included in the notification email.

▶HOW TO: Share a Workbook in Excel

1. Open the workbook from your *OneDrive* folder.
2. Click the **Share** button in the upper-right corner of the workbook window.
   - The *Send Link* window or the Share pane opens depending on your account (Figure 7-35).
3. Complete these steps in the *Send Link* window. (Go to step 4 for the *Share* pane).
   - Click the **Link settings** box at the top of the *Send Link* window.
   - Choose anyone, a work group, or specific people. Your choice determines other settings in the window.
   - Select the **Allow editing** box to permit editing; deselect the **Allow editing** box to allow viewing only.
   - Choose other settings as needed.
   - Click **Apply** to return to the *Send Link* window.
   - Type email addresses or select contacts from **Outlook**. If you choose a work group as your recipient, you need not type addresses.
   - Click **Add a message** and type an optional message for the notification email (see Figure 7-35).
   - Click **Send** and close the confirmation window.
4. Complete these steps in the *Share* pane. (Go to step 3 for the *Send Link* window).
   - Type email addresses, separated with semicolons (;) in the *Invite people* box.
   - If your account has access to your contacts list, click the **Address Book** button to the right of the entry box and choose recipient names.
   - Select **Can edit** or **Can view** from the drop-down list.
   - Click the **Include a message** box and type an optional message for the notification email (see Figure 7-35).
   - Click the **Share** button. The email is sent, and the pane lists recipient names with their permission levels.
   - Close the *Share* pane.

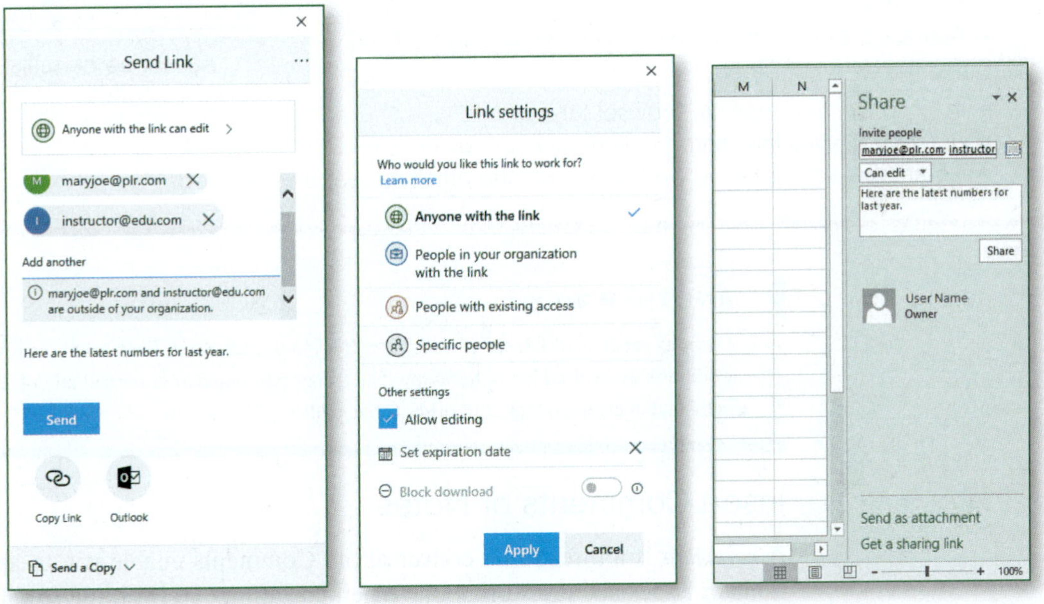

Figure 7-35 Share a workbook for co-authoring

Collaborate on a Workbook

A co-author opens a shared Excel workbook from the email message by clicking the link. The workbook opens in *Excel Online*, the free web version of Excel. The owner and co-authors see identifying icons in the upper-right corner for one another. You, the owner, see the cell in which a coworker's pointer is located, highlighted in a different color for each person, and you see all changes immediately.

AutoSave and *Excel Online* save a shared workbook after each edit so that the owner can review the development of the final document. The *Version History* command [*File* tab, *Info* group] displays a task pane that lists times and co-author edits. Click a version link in the list to open a copy of the workbook at that point in time in a separate window; you can restore a version if necessary. The *Info* page in the *Backstage* view also displays co-author identities in the *Related People* area.

> **MORE INFO**
>
> *Excel Online* is a free scaled-down version of Excel with basic features and commands for creating and editing a workbook.

▸HOW TO: Collaborate in Excel

1. Open the shared workbook from your *OneDrive* folder if you are the owner.
   - If you are a co-author, open the workbook from the email message.
   - In *Excel Online*, if you see an **Edit in Browser** button, click it. Your Microsoft account determines if this button displays.
2. Identify current co-author icons in the title bar on the right.
   - Your contact list and your browser affect how co-author information displays.
3. Edit the workbook.
   - Active cells are highlighted for each author (Figure 7-36).
4. Close the workbook.
   - In *Excel Online*, close the browser tab.
   - *AutoSave* saves the shared workbook in the owner's folder.
   - Co-authors can open the workbook from the email message as needed.

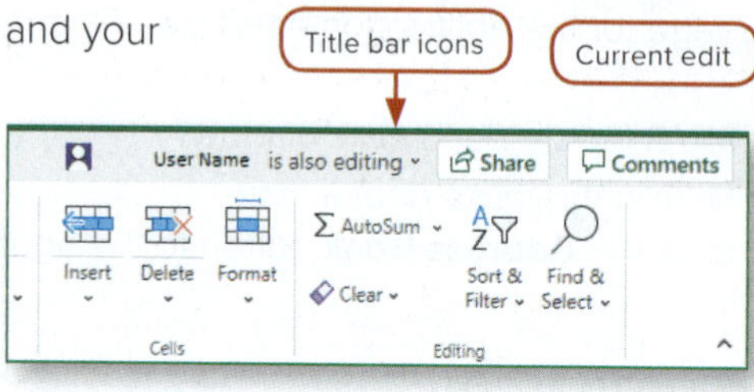

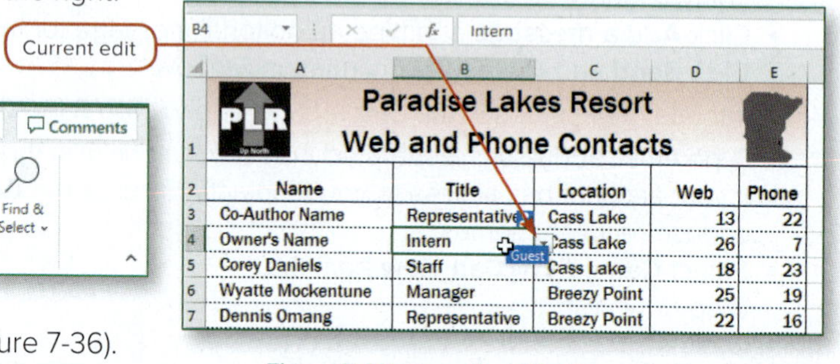

Figure 7-36 Co-author identity and edits are visible

> **ANOTHER WAY**
>
> Previous versions of Excel had the *Share Workbook* command. Each team member saved a copy of the workbook and edited his or her copy. The owner combined and merged all copies into a final workbook and accepted or rejected other users' edits.

Insert Comments or Notes

A ***comment*** is a thread in a conversation. Comments enable you to ask and respond to questions or issues about a workbook. When co-authors are working simultaneously, they see one another's comments and can reply as needed. A ***note*** is a pop-up text box attached to a cell, used for clarification or extra information. You cannot respond to a note (Figure 7-37).

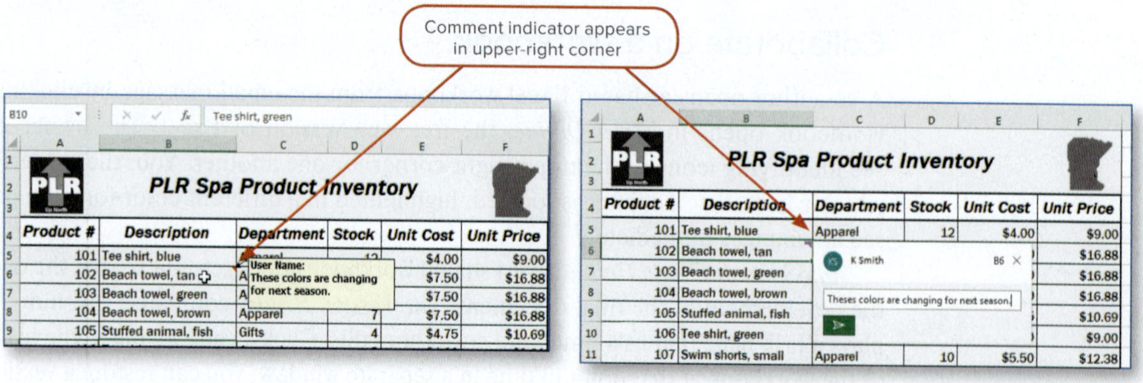

Figure 7-37 A note and a threaded comment

Insert comments or notes from the *Review* tab or from a cell's context menu, and type the text in the entry box. Comments must be posted; notes are completed by clicking any other cell. After you add a comment or note to a cell, an ***indicator*** appears in the upper-right corner of the cell. The indicator for a threaded comment is color-coded to the author/user. A note indicator is a small red triangle. To view a note or a comment, hover the pointer over a cell with an indicator.

> **ANOTHER WAY**
>
> Display the *Comments* pane by clicking the **Show Comments** button on the *Review* tab. Show all notes by clicking the ***Notes*** button on the Review tab and choosing **Show All Notes**.

You can delete a comment for which you are the owner. You can edit or delete a note, and you can convert notes to comments [**Notes** button, *Review* tab]. Select the cell with the comment or note, and choose a command on the *Review* tab. You can also execute commands by right-clicking the cell and choosing from the context menu.

> **MORE INFO**
>
> Comments and notes do not print by default. You can print notes as they appear on screen, or you can print either on a separate sheet. Choose the option to print them on the *Sheet* tab in the *Page Setup* dialog box.

To adjust how comments and notes display, open the Excel *Options* dialog box, select the *Advanced* tab, and scroll to the *Display* group.

HOW TO: Insert a Comment

1. Right-click the cell for the comment.
2. Select **New Comment**.
   - A conversation entry box opens and displays the owner's name.
   - You can edit or delete a thread if you are owner.
3. Type the text to start a conversation.
   - You cannot format text in the conversation (Figure 7-38).
4. Click **Post** to complete the comment.
5. Click any cell away from the comment cell.
6. View the comment by hovering the pointer over the cell.
7. Show the comment and click **Reply** to respond.
   - Click **Post** to complete the response.

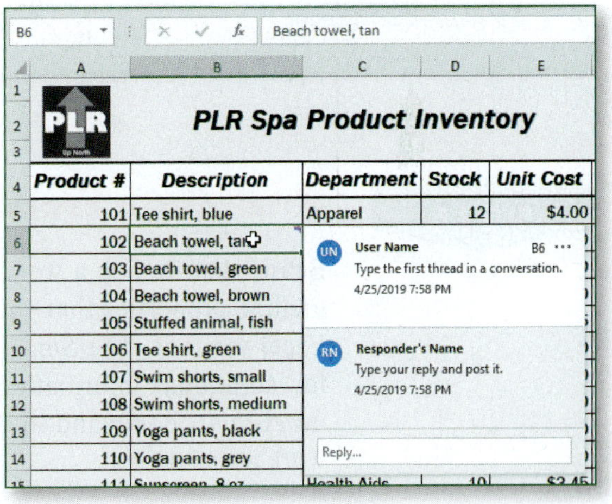

Figure 7-38 Type each thread and post

Annotate with Ink

Ink is an object drawn freehand with your finger, a stylus, or the pointer to annotate a workbook. The *Draw* tab includes a set of pens that can be customized with a color and a thickness. When you select a pen, the *Draw* tool is active so that you can complete your annotation. Your annotation is an object like a picture or shape with selection handles.

The *Draw* command tab displays by default on the *Ribbon* on a touch-enabled device. Display or hide the tab from Excel *Options* on the *File* tab.

HOW TO: Use Ink in a Workbook

1. Click the **Draw** tab and select a pen in the *Pens* group.
   - The *Draw* tool is enabled [*Tools* group].
2. Click the small arrow to the right of the pen icon.
   - A gallery of options displays.
3. Select a color and a thickness for the pen (Figure 7-39).
4. Draw a comment or annotation using the pointer, a stylus, or your finger.
5. Click the **Draw** button [*Draw* tab, *Tools* group] to toggle off the command.
6. Click the annotation object to select it.
   - The *Drawing Tools Format* tab displays.
   - Select the object and press **Delete** to remove it.
   - Select an ink object with the **Lasso Select** tool.
7. Click a worksheet cell.

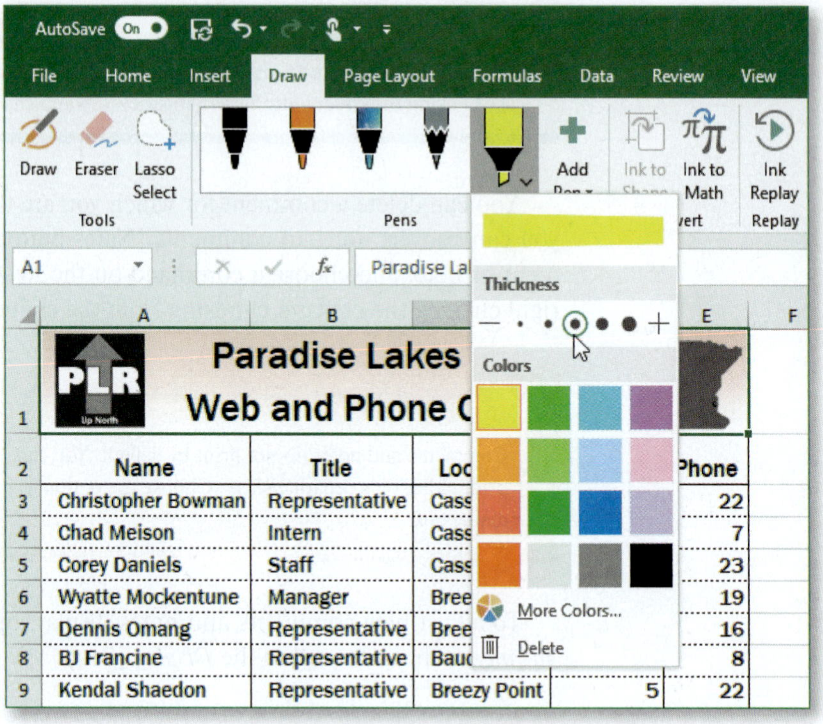

Figure 7-39 Pens can be customized

SLO 7.6

Finalizing a Workbook for Distribution

Before distributing a workbook to clients or coworkers, verify that the workbook does not include properties that should not be shared and that the workbook is compatible with all Excel versions. The *Smart Lookup* command [*Review* tab, *Insights* group] helps you search for additional information that you might need before distributing your work. Use the *Accessibility* command to gauge if your work is designed so that all users can complete their work as needed.

Smart Lookup

The ***Smart Lookup*** command is a research feature that uses Bing, an internet search engine, to find information about a label or a value. The *Smart Lookup* pane opens at the right of the window and lists content and sources for the selected data. Click a link in the pane to further research the data.

▸HOW TO: Use Smart Lookup

1. Click the cell with a label or a value to be researched.
   - Select text within a cell as needed.
2. Click the **Smart Lookup** button [*Review* tab, *Insights* group].
   - The *Smart Lookup* pane displays related data in the *Explore* group (Figure 7-40).
   - Click **Define** in the *Smart Lookup* pane to find a definition for the researched cell or text if available.
3. Click an item in the *Smart Lookup* pane to jump to the referenced site.
   - The web site opens in a new browser window.
4. Close the *Smart Lookup* pane.

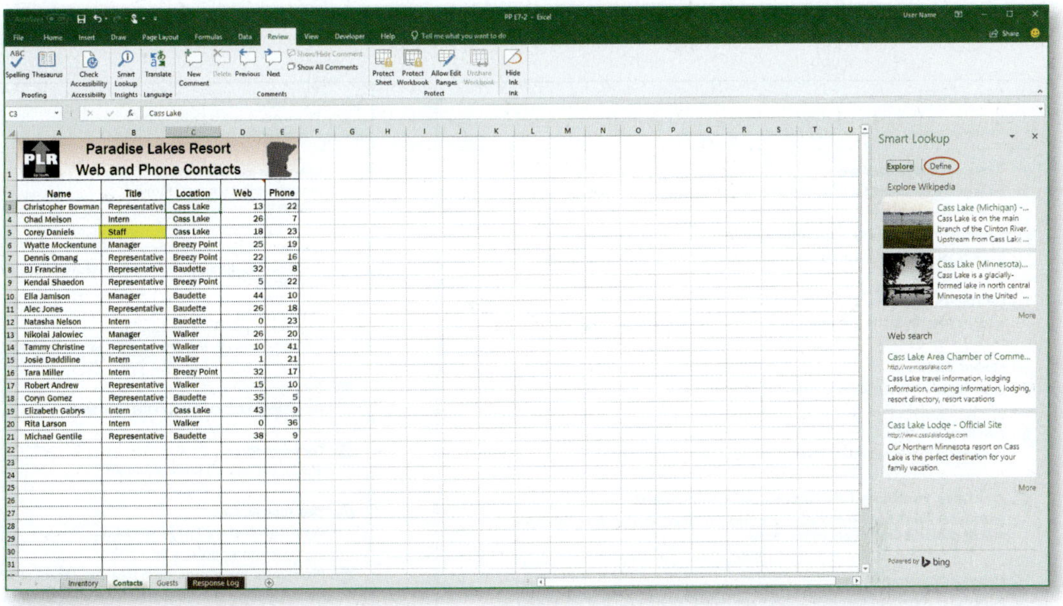

Figure 7-40 ***Smart Lookup*** **pane for label in cell C3**

> ### ANOTHER WAY
> Right-click a cell or selected text and choose *Smart Lookup* from the context menu.

Inspect a Workbook

The ***Inspect Document*** command looks for metadata and personal information in a workbook. ***Metadata*** are embedded file properties such as user name and date at the time of creation, the original file location, and user comments. Some metadata can be removed. For example, if you insert comments or notes for your team members, you can remove those comments before a customer sees the workbook. The ***Document Inspector*** is the dialog box that lists properties and data that can be removed.

▸HOW TO: Inspect a Workbook

1. Click the **Check for Issues** button [*File* tab, *Info*].
2. Choose **Inspect Document**.
   - A message box opens to save the workbook.

3. Click **Yes** to save the workbook.
   - The *Document Inspector* lists categories of content that can be searched (Figure 7-41).
   - Scroll the list to review all categories.
   - Deselect the box for any category that should not be searched.
4. Click **Inspect**.
   - The *Document Inspector* identifies content that can be removed.
   - Scroll the list to review all noted items.
5. Click **Remove All** for each category of content to be cleared (Figure 7-42).

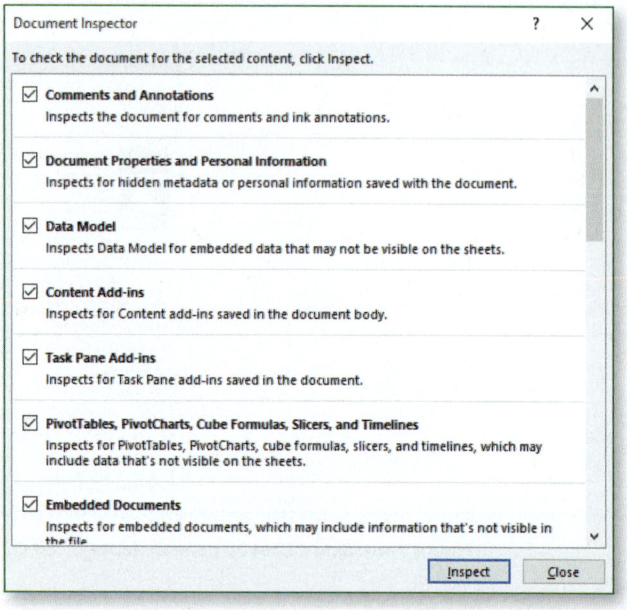

Figure 7-41 *Document Inspector* dialog box

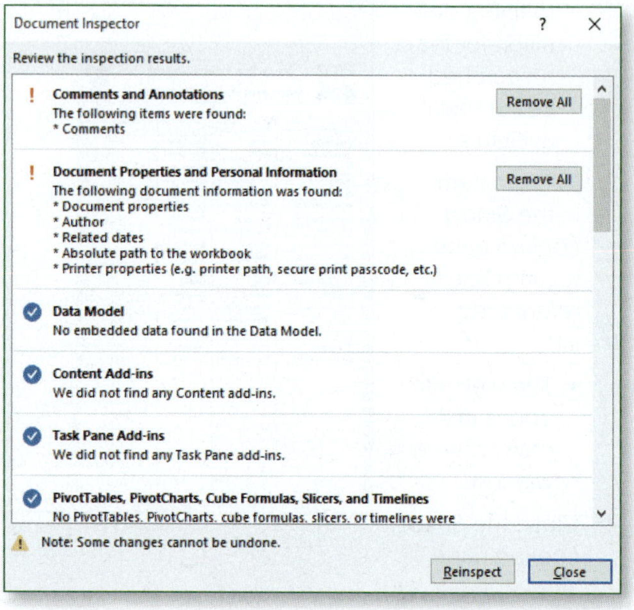

Figure 7-42 *Document Inspector* dialog box after inspection

   - You can close the dialog box to review content that needs further investigation.
   - You need not remove content.
   - Run the *Document Inspector* again when needed.
6. Click **Close**.

If you remove *Document Propertires and Personal Information*, a workbook property is set to automatically remove that metadata each time you save the file. This property may interfere with commands such as co-authoring. Disable the property by clicking *Allow this information to be saved in your file* in the *Check for Issues* group in *Backstage* view and resave workbook.

Check Accessibility and Alt Text

The ***Check Accessibility*** command opens the *Accessibility Checker* pane that identifies content in your workbook that a person with visual or literacy impairments might find difficult to understand. Such content includes pictures, shapes, and charts. For many objects, you can add alternative text, known as ***alt text***, as a property. Alt text is a brief explanation of the picture, shape, or chart. Alt text is read aloud by a ***screen reader***, such as Windows *Narrator*, to aid those who need assistance in interpreting the workbook.

▸HOW TO: Check Accessibility and Add Alt Text

1. Remove worksheet and workbook protection.
2. Click the **Check Accessibility** button [*Review* tab, *Accessibility* group].
   - The *Accessibility Checker* pane identifies *Errors* and *Warnings* about the workbook.
3. Expand the **Missing alternative text** group if it is collapsed.
   - Objects without alternative text are flagged as errors.
4. Select an item in the *Missing alternative text* list to move to the object in the workbook.
   - The object is selected.
5. Right-click the object and choose **Edit Alt Text**.
   - The *Alt Text* pane opens.
6. Type a brief explanation of the object in the entry box (Figure 7-43).
   - Select the *Mark as decorative* box for an object that a screen reader announces as simply decorative to the user.

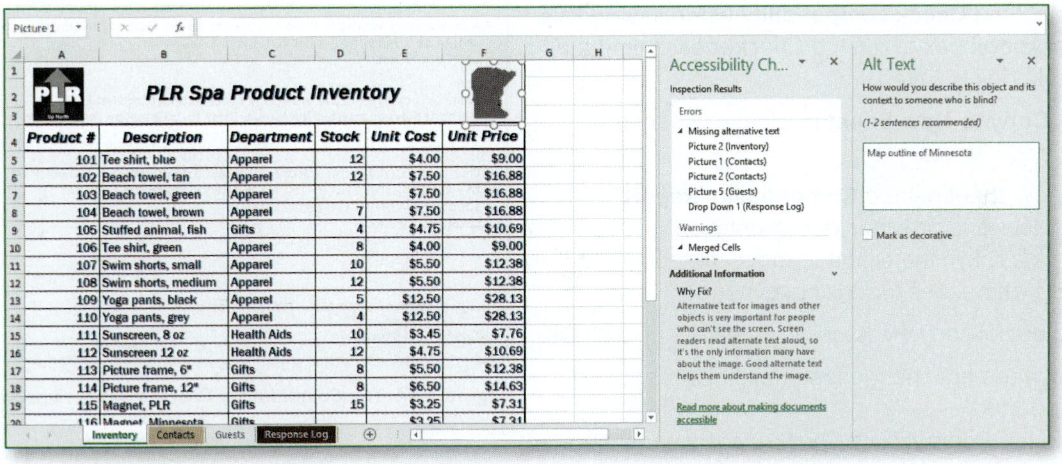

Figure 7-43 The *Accessibility Checker* locates objects that may be confusing to persons with impairments

7. Close the *Alt Text* pane and deselect the object.
8. Review *Warnings* identified in the *Accessibility Checker* pane.
   - Expand categories as needed.
   - Click an item and read the *Additional Information* area to learn how and why to fix the data.

ANOTHER WAY

Select an image and click the **Alt Text** button [*Picture Tools Format* tab, *Accessibility* group] to open the *Alt Text* pane.

Check Compatibility

The ***Check Compatibility*** command opens the *Compatibility Checker* which identifies commands, features, and objects that are not supported in earlier versions of Excel. For example, early versions of Excel did not have *SmartArt* graphics. Not all Excel functions work in earlier versions of Excel, and select formatting features are not compatible either.

The *Compatibility Checker* gives you an opportunity to edit incompatible data or objects before you save the workbook in a different file format. A few issues are significant but most are minor. When you save a workbook in Excel 97-2003 format, the *Compatibility Checker* automatically runs to alert you to potential issues. You can run the command, however, for any workbook at any time.

▸HOW TO: Check Compatibility

1. Click the **Check for Issues** button [*File* tab, *Info*].
2. Choose **Check Compatibility**.
   - The *Compatibility Checker* describes each unsupported feature (Figure 7-44).
   - All previous versions of Excel are checked.
   - Click **Select versions to show** to choose a particular Excel version.
   - The dialog box can be sized or scrolled to view all issues.
   - Select the **Check compatibility when saving this workbook** box to run the *Checker* each time the workbook is saved.
3. Click **Copy to New Sheet** to create a sheet that details the issues.
   - A new sheet named **Compatibility Report** displays and provides documentation.
   - Click a link in the report to move the pointer to the cells with issues for editing as needed.
4. If you do not copy the issues to a new sheet, click **OK**.
   - You need not change features that are not supported.
   - Run the *Compatibility Checker* again when needed.

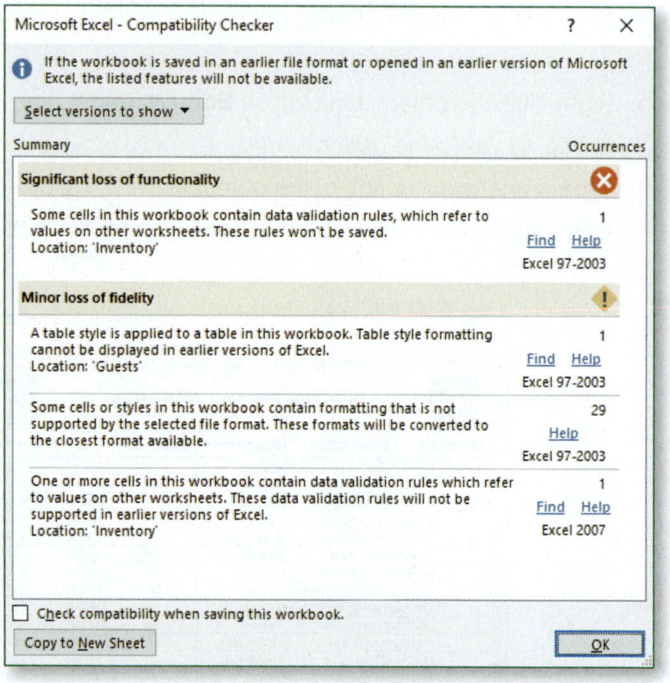

Figure 7-44 The *Compatibility Checker* locates unsupported features

Browser View Options

The *Info* pane includes the ***Browser View Options*** button which enables you to specify what can be viewed and edited for a workbook published to a *SharePoint* or similar web site. To access a *SharePoint* published workbook, a user must have *SharePoint* permissions to view and work with the workbook. If you work in a *SharePoint* environment, check with the administrator for details.

PAUSE & PRACTICE: EXCEL 7-3

In this project, you prepare a workbook for co-authoring. You inspect the workbook, check it for accessibility, save it to *OneDrive*, and share it for editing in *Excel Online*. *Note: You must have access to a secondary email address to complete this project.*

File Needed: ***[your initials] PP E7-2.xlsx***
Completed Project File Names: ***[your initials] PP E7-3.xlsx*** and ***[your initials] PP E7-3CoAuthor.xlsx***

1. Open the ***[your initials] PP E7-2*** workbook completed in *Pause & Practice 7-2* and save it as [your initials] PP E7-3.
2. Remove sheet and structure protection.
   a. Click the **Info** command on the *File* tab (Figure 7-45).
   b. Click **Unprotect** in the *Protect Workbook* group. Sheet protection is removed but workbook structure protection is still active.
   c. Click the **Protect Workbook** button and select **Protect Workbook Structure**.
   d. Click the **Check for Issues** button [*File* tab, *Info* group] and choose **Inspect Document**.
   e. Select **Yes** to save the workbook without sheet and workbook protection.
   f. Click **Inspect**. Properties and personal information that can be removed are noted.
   g. Click **Remove All** for *Document Properties and Personal Information*.
   h. Scroll the list to see the *Hidden Worksheets* tag but do not remove the sheets.
   i. Click **Close**.
   j. Click the **Info** command on the *File* tab. Note that the workbook now has a setting to remove personal information each time it is saved (Figure 7-46).
   k. Return to the workbook.

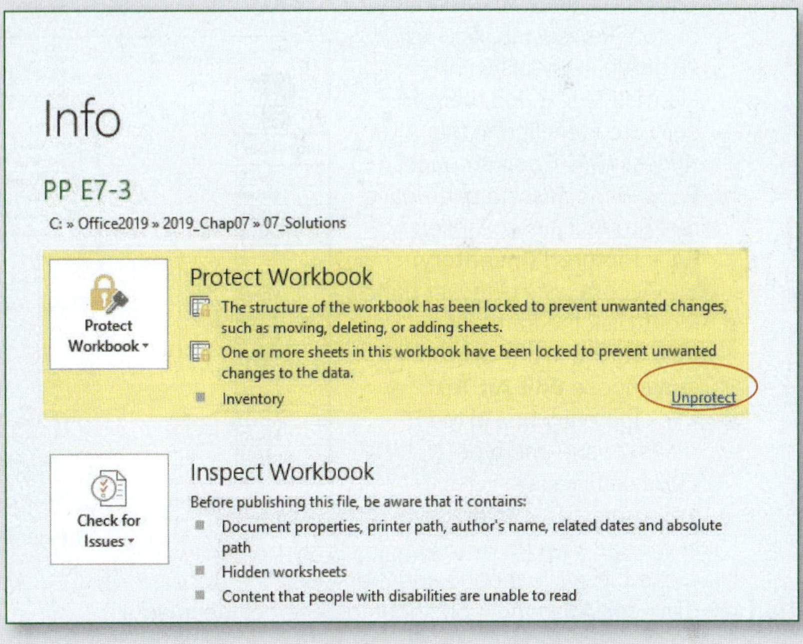

Figure 7-45 Remove sheet protection from the *File* tab

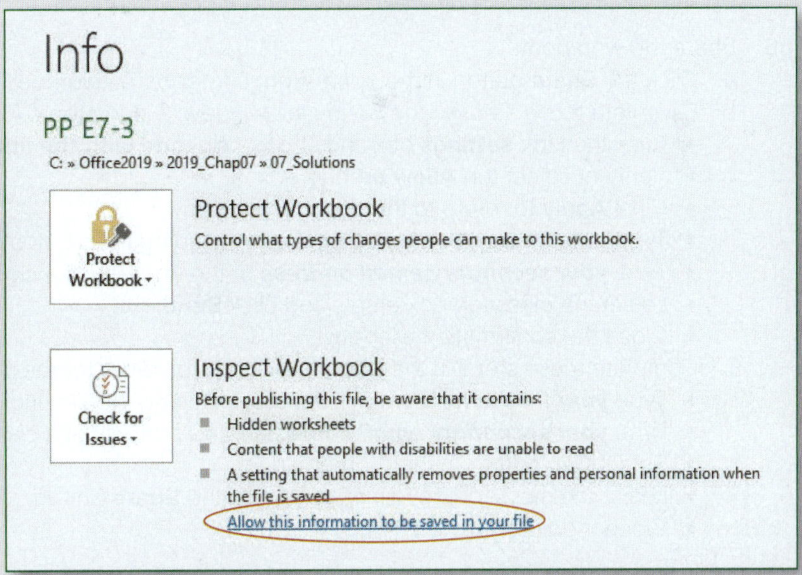

Figure 7-46 Setting removes personal information when file is saved

3. Delete sheets from the workbook so that it can be co-authored.
   a. Select the **Guests** sheet tab. This worksheet includes form controls that are not supported in a co-authored workbook.

b. Right-click the **Guests** tab and choose **Delete**.
c. Click **Delete** to remove the sheet.
d. Delete the **Response Log** sheet because it includes a form control.

4. Check accessibility.
   a. Click the **Check Accessibility** button [*Review* tab, *Accessibility* group]. Objects without alternative text and merged cells are identified in the *Accessibility Checker* pane.
   b. Expand the *Missing alternative text* group if it is collapsed.
   c. Click **Picture 1 (Inventory)** in the *Accessibility Checker* pane.
   d. Right-click the frame of the map outline in the worksheet and choose **Edit Alt Text**.
   e. Click the entry box in the *Alt Text* pane and type Filled outline map shape of Minnesota as the alternative text (Figure 7-47).

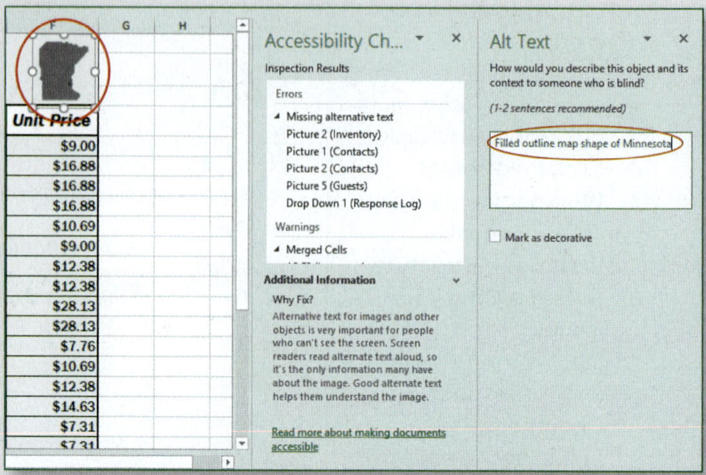

Figure 7-47 Enter alternative text for an image

   f. Close the *Alt Text* pane and then close the *Accessibility Checker* pane.
   g. Click cell **A5** in the worksheet to deselect the image.

5. Save the workbook to *OneDrive*.
   a. Click the **File** tab and select **Save As**.
   b. Click **OneDrive** – ***[Identifier]*** and then click **Documents** or another available folder in the folders list.
   c. Edit the file name to display **[your initials] PP E7-3CoAuthor** in the entry box.
   d. Click **Save**.
   e. Verify the *Saved to OneDrive* tag in the title bar and that *AutoSave* is on.

6. Share the workbook.
   a. Click the **Share** button in the upper-right corner of the workbook window.
   b. Complete these steps in the *Send Link* window. (Go to step c for the *Share* pane).
      - Click the **Link settings** box and choose **Anyone with the link**.
      - Verify or select the **Allow editing** box.
      - Click **Apply** to return to the *Send Link* window.
      - Type ***your instructor's email address***; including the semicolon.
      - Type ***your secondary email address*** or the address of a classmate or friend and press **Tab**.
      - Leave the message box empty and click **Send**.
      - Close the confirmation window.
   c. Complete these steps in the *Share* pane. (Go to step b for the *Send Link* window).
      - Type ***your instructor's email address***; including the semicolon in the *Invite people* box.
      - Type ***your secondary email address*** or the address of a classmate or friend and press **Tab**.
      - Select **Can edit** from the drop-down list.
      - Leave the message box empty and click the **Share** button.
      - Close the *Share* pane.

7. Co-author a workbook.
   a. Launch your email program and sign in to your secondary email account.
   b. Open the email message about the shared workbook and click the link.

c. Click the **Edit in Browser** button if it displays; you may not see this button in a personal account (Figure 7-48).

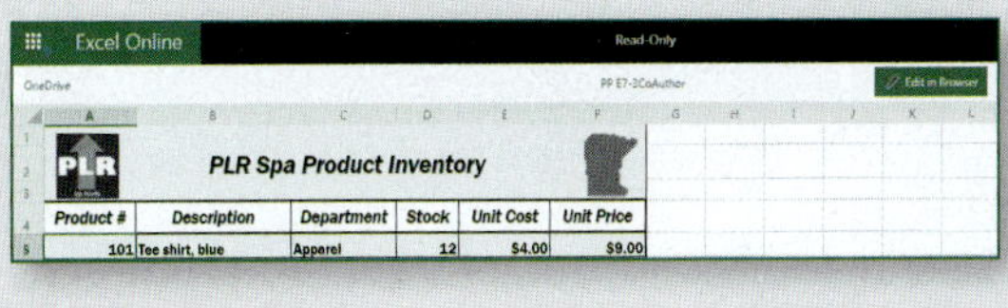

Figure 7-48 Click the Edit in Browser button to remove the *Read-Only* property

d. Select the **Contacts** sheet tab.

e. Select cell **A22**. Enter the data shown here in row 22. Use the validation list to select the title.

Jennifer Sherman	Intern	Baudette	32	12

f. Select cell **F22**.

g. Click the **New Comment** button [*Review* tab, *Comments* group]. Comments display in the *Comments* pane in *Excel Online*.

h. Type Jennifer spent two days in Baudette. in the comment box and click the **Post** button (Figure 7-49).

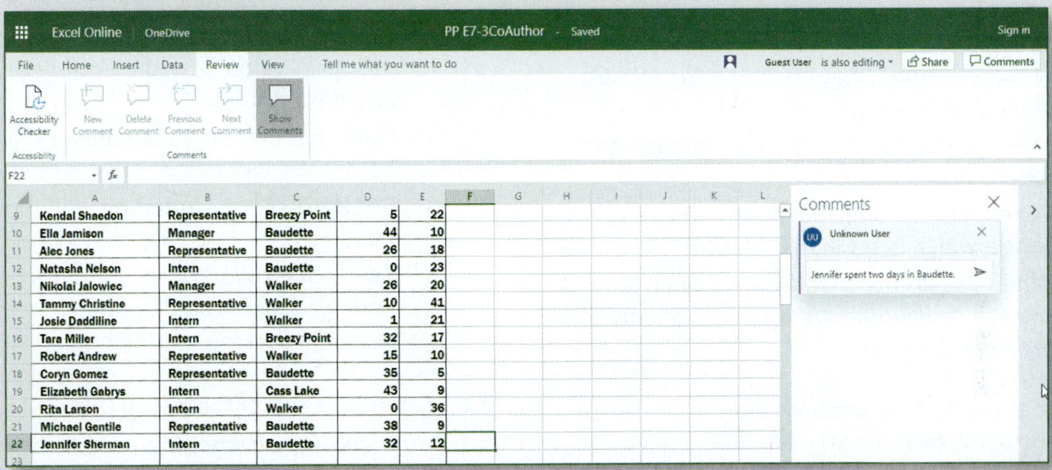

Figure 7-49 Comment entered in *Excel Online* for cell F22

i. Close the *Comments* pane and select cell **A3**.

j. Close the *Excel Online* browser window.

k. Close your secondary email message and the email client.

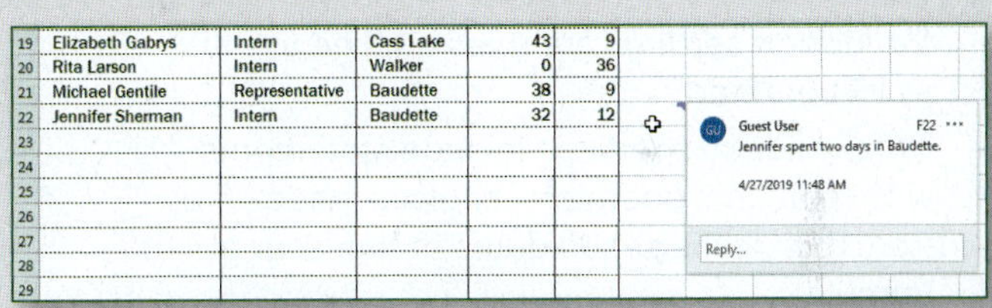

Figure 7-50 Co-author's edit in owner's workbook

8. Return to your **[your initials] PP E7-3CoAuthor** workbook in Excel.
   a. Select the **Contacts** sheet tab.
   b. Hover the pointer at cell **F22** to read the comment (Figure 7-50).
9. Save a copy of the workbook to your usual folder if instructed to do so.
10. Close the workbook. It is also saved by *AutoSave*.

Chapter Summary

7.1 Use a template to create a workbook and save a workbook as a template (p. E7-443).

- A ***template*** is a model workbook that can include data, formulas, formatting, controls, and more.
- Templates are available from the *New* pane in *Backstage* view.
- Excel templates are saved in a default folder which can be changed in the *Save* pane, Excel *Options*.
- Templates saved in the default folder are listed in the *Personal* category in the *Backstage* view.
- Template workbooks have an .xltx file name extension.
- Templates are often saved with a thumbnail image which is set in the *Save As* dialog box.
- When you create a workbook from a template, a new workbook opens as a copy of the template.

7.2 Set data validation, input messages, and error alerts (p. E7-445).

- ***Data validation*** is the process of matching data with specifications as the data is entered.
- ***Validation settings*** are rules applied to data as it is entered.
- Data validation settings include statements with relational operators, choices made from lists, limits set on dates or times, or a formula.
- An ***input message*** is a comment box that appears as soon as a cell is selected, informing the user about the validation rule.
- An ***error alert*** is a comment box that appears when invalid data is entered in a cell, and the type of alert determines whether the entry is allowed.
- If data validation is set after data has been entered, you can use the *Circle Invalid Data* command to identify those cells.

7.3 Use *Form Controls* in a workbook (p. E7-452).

- A ***form control*** is an object or shape used to display a choice, make a selection, or run a command in a worksheet.
- Form controls include option buttons, combo boxes, check boxes, and list boxes.
- The *Developer* tab on the *Ribbon* includes the *Controls* group.
- Display or hide the *Developer* tab by opening the Excel *Options* dialog box and selecting the *Customize Ribbon* pane.

7.4 Set worksheet and workbook protection to manage editing (p. E7-456).

- The *Protect Sheet* command prohibits changes to cells unless they have been unlocked.
- The ***Locked*** property is enabled for all cells but has no effect unless the *Protect Sheet* command is applied.
- Cells that can be edited must be unlocked before the worksheet is protected.
- Set ***Worksheet protection*** with or without a password.
- The *Protect Workbook Structure* command enables a user to edit data but not move, copy, delete, insert, hide, or unhide sheets.

7.5 Co-author a workbook (p. E7-462).

- A ***shared workbook*** is a workbook that is edited by multiple users, either at the same or a different time in *Excel Online*.
- To share a workbook, save it to a *OneDrive* location.
- When a workbook is saved to *OneDrive*, the *AutoSave* feature is active.
- When you share a workbook, specify whether each co-author can edit or simply view the file.
- When multiple users edit a workbook, each user sees information about co-authors in the title bar of the workbook.
- All changes are automatically saved to the owner's workbook and are immediately visible.
- Changes are highlighted on screen with color-coding and comments, depending on the browser.
- A ***comment*** is an element in a threaded conversation in a workbook.
- Comments are collaboration tools that enable you to ask or respond to questions and other issues.
- A ***note*** is a pop-up text box for a cell with explanations or questions for coworkers.
- Notes are not threaded, and you cannot respond to a note.

7.6 Finalize a workbook for distribution by inspecting it for personal information, accessibility, and compatibility (p. E7-466).

- Use ***Smart Lookup*** to research a label or a value in a workbook.
- The ***Inspect Document*** command locates metadata and personal information that can be removed from the file.
- The ***Check Compatibility*** command identifies features, commands, and objects that might not work properly in an earlier version of Excel.
- The ***Check Accessibility*** command searches a workbook for content that may be difficult to understand for an individual with visual or other impairments.
- Accessbility issues relate to objects such as images and charts as well as formatting such as merged cells.
- Alternative text can be added to an object in a worksheet to provide oral descriptions through use of a ***screen reader***.
- The *Inspect Document*, *Check Compatibility*, and *Check Accessibility* commands can be run as many times as necessary for a workbook.

Check for Understanding

The SIMbook for this text (within your SIMnet account) provides the following resources for concept review:

- Multiple-choice questions
- Short answer questions
- Matching exercises

Guided Project 7-1

In this project, you develop a template for co-instructors at Sierra Pacific Community College District (SPCCD). You add data validation, check accessibility, and share a workbook created from the template. *(Note: You must have access to a secondary email address to complete this project.)*
[Student Learning Outcomes 7.1, 7.2, 7.4, 7.5, 7.6]

File Needed: ***SierraPacific-07.xlsx*** *(Student data files are available in the* Library *of your SIMnet account.)*
Completed Project File Names: ***[your initials] Excel 7-1Template.xltx*** and ***[your initials] Excel 7-1CoAuthor .xlsx***

Skills Covered in This Project

- Set data validation with an error alert.
- Set data validation with an input message.
- Check accessibility.
- Add worksheet protection.
- Save a workbook as a template.
- Create a workbook from a template.
- Share and co-author a workbook.

---

1. Open the ***SierraPacific-07*** workbook from your student data files.
2. Save the workbook as a template.
   a. Click the **File** tab and select **Save As**.
   b. Choose **This PC** and click the **More options** link.
   c. Type the file name [your initials] Excel 7-1Template in the *File name* box.
   d. Verify that the *Save Thumbnail* box is selected or select it.
   e. Choose **Excel Template** from the *Save as type* drop-down box. The default templates folder opens.
   f. Click **Save**.
3. Set data validation for a range.
   a. Select cells **C5:C29**.
   b. Click the **Data Validation** button [*Data* tab, *Data Tools* group] and verify that the *Settings* tab is selected.
   c. Click the **Allow** arrow and choose **Decimal**.
   d. Verify that the *Data* option displays **between**.
   e. Type .1 for the *Minimum* and 20 for the *Maximum*.
   f. Do not click **OK**.
4. Create an error message for data validation settings.
   a. Click the **Error Alert** tab.
   b. Verify that the *Show error alert after invalid data is entered* box is selected.
   c. Click the **Style** arrow and choose **Warning** to allow an invalid entry.
   d. Click the **Title** box and type Class Points.
   e. Click the **Error message** box and type Enter a value between 0.1 and 20.
   f. Click **OK**.
   g. Select cell **C5**, type 21 and press **Enter** to display the error alert (Figure 7-51).
   h. Click **Cancel** to keep the current value.

5. Set data validation with an input message.
   a. Select cells **D5:D29** and click the **Data Validation** button [*Data* tab, *Data Tools* group].
   b. Click the **Allow** arrow and choose **Decimal** on the *Settings* tab.
   c. Verify that *between* is the *Data* option.
   d. Click the **Minimum** box and type 50.
   e. Enter 100 for the *Maximum*.
   f. Click the **Input Message** tab.
   g. Verify that the *Show input message when cell is selected* box is selected.
   h. Click the **Title** box and type Project Points.
   i. Click the **Input message** box and type Enter a value between 50 and 100. (Figure 7-52).
   j. Click **OK**.

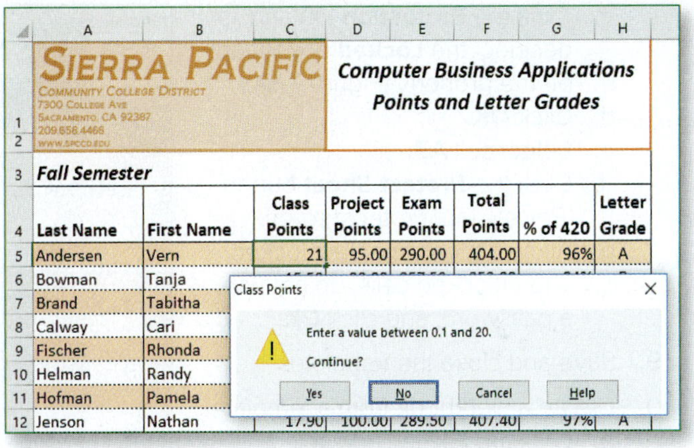

Figure 7-51 Error alert for invalid data

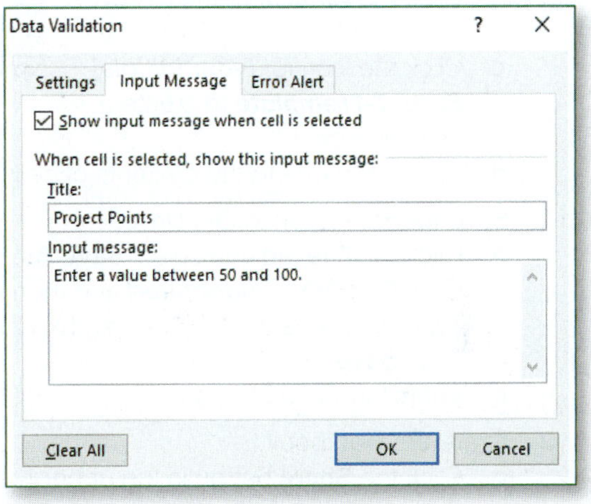

Figure 7-52 Input message for data entry

6. Select cells **E5:E29** and set data validation to limit the entry to any decimal number between 150 and 300. Do not use an input or error alert message.

7. Check accessibility.
   a. Select cell **A5**.
   b. Click the **Check Accessibility** button [*Review* tab, *Accessibility* group] and expand the *Missing alternative text* group if necessary.
   c. Choose **Picture 1 (Grade Sheet)** in the *Accessibility Checker* pane to select the image.
   d. Right-click the image in the worksheet and choose **Edit Alt Text** from the context menu.
   e. Click the entry box in the *Alt Text* pane.
   f. Type the following text (Figure 7-53):
      Sierra Pacific Community College District
      7300 College Avenue
      Sacramento, CA 92387
      209.658.4466
      www.spccd.edu
   g. Close the *Alt Text* pane and the *Accessibility Checker* pane.

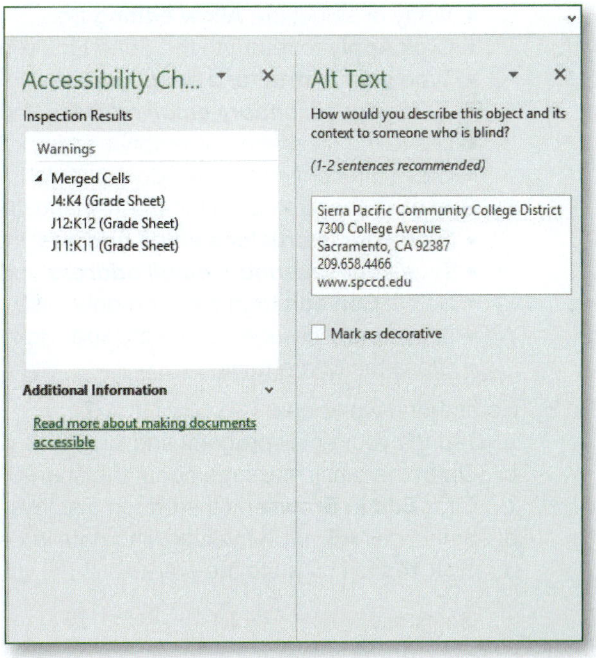

Figure 7-53 Alt text for picture

8. Unlock cells and protect the worksheet.
   a. Select cells **A5:E29**. These are cells in which co-instructors enter student names and points.
   b. Right-click cell **A5** and choose **Format Cells**.

c. Click the **Protection** tab and deselect the **Locked** box to turn off the property (Figure 7-54).
d. Click **OK**.
e. Select cell **A5**.
f. Click the **Protect Sheet** button [*Review* tab, *Protect* group].
g. Allow options to select locked and unlocked cells, do not use a password, and click **OK**.

9. Save and close the template.
10. Create a workbook from a template.
    a. Click the **File** tab and select **New**.
    b. Click **Personal** near the top of the gallery.
    c. Click the icon for ***[your initials] Excel 7-1Template*** to create a new workbook.
    d. Select and delete the contents of cells **A5:E26** and select cell **A5**.

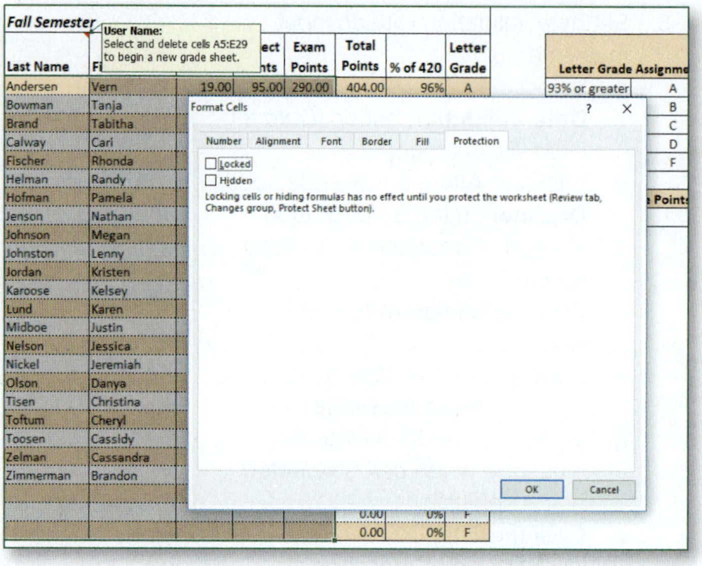

Figure 7-54 ***Protection*** **tab in the** ***Format Cells*** **dialog box**

11. Save the workbook to *OneDrive*.
    a. Click the **File** tab and select **Save As**.
    b. Click **OneDrive -** ***[Identifier]*** and then click **Documents** or any available folder.
    c. Type the file name [your initials] Excel 7-1CoAuthor in the entry box.
    d. Click **Save**.
    e. Verify that *AutoSave* is on.
12. Share the workbook.
    a. Click the **Share** button in the upper-right corner of the workbook window.
    b. Complete these steps in the *Send Link* window. (Go to step c for the *Share* pane).
        - Click the **Link settings** box and choose **Anyone with the link**.
        - Verify or select the **Allow editing** box.
        - Click **Apply** to return to the *Send Link* window.
        - Type ***your instructor's email address***; including the semicolon.
        - Type ***your secondary email address*** and press **Tab**.
        - Leave the message box empty and click **Send**.
        - Close the confirmation window.
    c. Complete these steps in the *Share* pane. (Go to step b for the *Send Link* window).
        - Type ***your instructor's email address***; including the semicolon in the *Invite people* box.
        - Type ***your secondary email address*** and press **Tab**.
        - Select **Can edit** from the drop-down list.
        - Leave the message box empty and click the **Share** button.
        - Close the *Share* pane.
13. Co-author a workbook.
    a. Launch your email program and sign in to your secondary email account.
    b. Open the email message about the shared workbook and click the file name link.
    c. Click **Edit in Browser** if the button displays; the button may not appear in a personal account.
    d. Select cell **A5**. Type the following data in cells **A5:E5**. When the error alert message displays, click **Yes** to complete the entry.

    Goldstone   Violet   29   75   295

    e. Close the *Excel Online* browser window.
    f. Close your email message and program.
    g. Return to the ***[your initials] Excel 7-1CoAuthor*** workbook in Excel.

h. Type the following data in cells **A6:E6**:

Gomez Andre 12 95 250

14. Save a copy of the workbook.
   a. Select the **Save a Copy** command [*File* tab].
   b. Click **This PC** and then click the **Up** arrow to navigate to your usual location for saving workbooks (Figure 7-55).
   c. Type or verify the file name as ***[your initials] Excel 7-1CoAuthor***.
   d. Click **Save** and close the workbook.

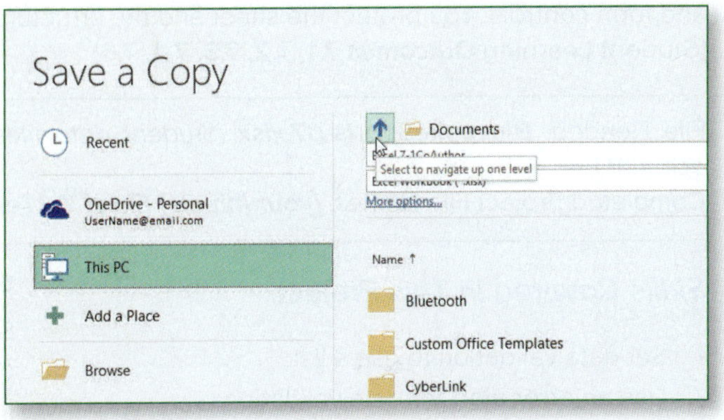

Figure 7-55 Save a copy to *This PC*

15. Move the template from the default folder.
   a. Click the **File** tab, select **Open**, and click **Folders**.
   b. Click **Custom Office Templates**. (If the *Custom Office Templates* folder is not listed, click **This PC** and select the **Documents** folder. Then click **Custom Office Templates**.)
   c. Right-click ***[your initials] Excel 7-1Template*** and choose **Cut**.
   d. In the left pane, navigate to and select your folder for saving files.
   e. Right-click an unused area of the dialog box and choose **Paste**.
   f. Click **Cancel** to close the dialog box and return to Excel.

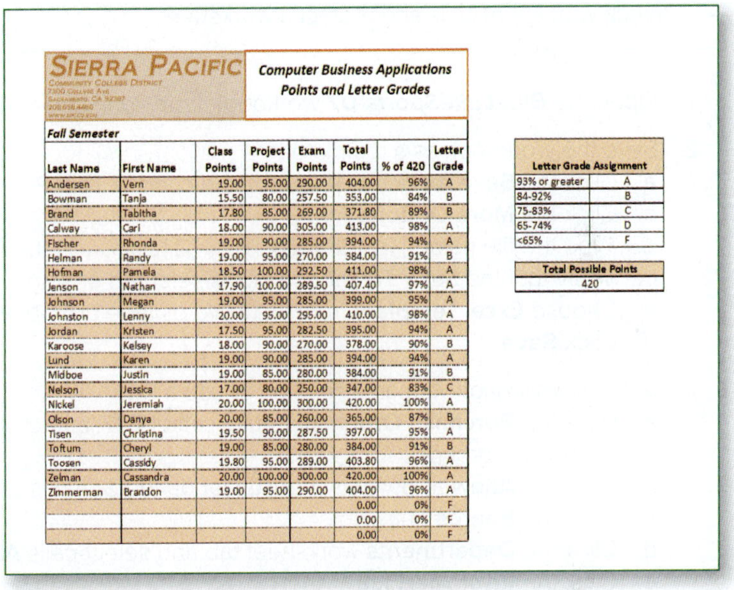

SIERRA PACIFIC

Computer Business Applications
Points and Letter Grades

Fall Semester

Last Name	First Name	Class Points	Project Points	Exam Points	Total Points	% of 420	Letter Grade
Andersen	Vern	19.00	95.00	290.00	404.00	96%	A
Bowman	Tanja	15.50	80.00	257.50	353.00	84%	B
Brand	Tabitha	17.80	85.00	269.00	371.80	89%	B
Calway	Cari	18.00	90.00	305.00	413.00	98%	A
Fischer	Rhonda	19.00	90.00	285.00	394.00	94%	A
Helman	Randy	19.00	95.00	270.00	384.00	91%	B
Hofman	Pamela	18.50	100.00	292.50	411.00	98%	A
Jenson	Nathan	17.90	100.00	289.50	407.40	97%	A
Johnson	Megan	19.00	95.00	285.00	399.00	95%	A
Johnston	Lenny	20.00	95.00	295.00	410.00	98%	A
Jordan	Kristen	17.50	95.00	282.50	395.00	94%	A
Karoose	Kelsey	18.00	90.00	270.00	378.00	90%	B
Lund	Karen	19.00	90.00	285.00	394.00	94%	A
Midboe	Justin	19.00	85.00	280.00	384.00	91%	B
Nelson	Jessica	17.00	80.00	250.00	347.00	83%	C
Nickel	Jeremiah	20.00	100.00	300.00	420.00	100%	A
Olson	Danya	20.00	85.00	260.00	365.00	87%	B
Tisen	Christina	19.50	90.00	287.50	397.00	95%	A
Toftum	Cheryl	19.00	85.00	280.00	384.00	91%	B
Toosen	Cassidy	19.80	95.00	289.00	403.80	96%	A
Zelman	Cassandra	20.00	100.00	300.00	420.00	100%	A
Zimmerman	Brandon	19.00	95.00	290.00	404.00	96%	A
					0.00	0%	F
					0.00	0%	F
					0.00	0%	F

Letter Grade Assignment	
93% or greater	A
84-92%	B
75-83%	C
65-74%	D
<65%	F

Total Possible Points
420

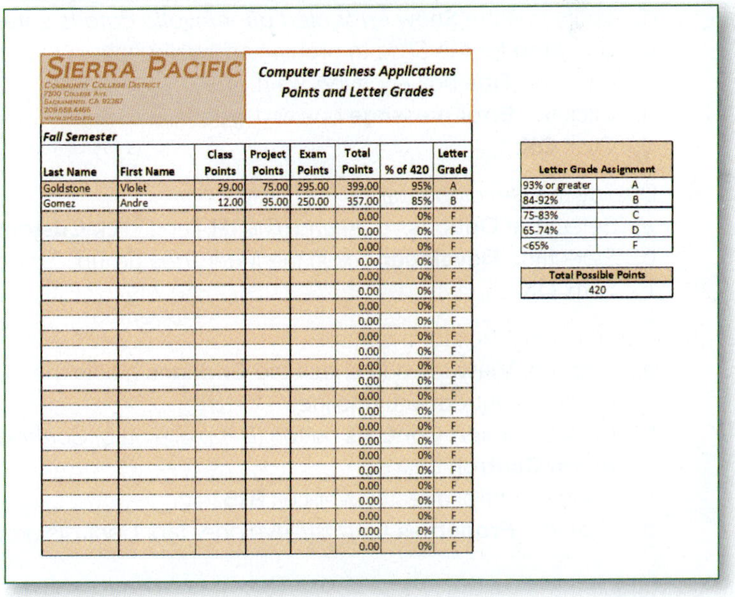

SIERRA PACIFIC

Computer Business Applications
Points and Letter Grades

Fall Semester

Last Name	First Name	Class Points	Project Points	Exam Points	Total Points	% of 420	Letter Grade
Goldstone	Violet	29.00	75.00	295.00	399.00	95%	A
Gomez	Andre	12.00	95.00	250.00	357.00	85%	B
					0.00	0%	F
					0.00	0%	F
					0.00	0%	F
					0.00	0%	F
					0.00	0%	F
					0.00	0%	F
					0.00	0%	F
					0.00	0%	F
					0.00	0%	F
					0.00	0%	F
					0.00	0%	F
					0.00	0%	F
					0.00	0%	F
					0.00	0%	F
					0.00	0%	F
					0.00	0%	F
					0.00	0%	F
					0.00	0%	F
					0.00	0%	F
					0.00	0%	F
					0.00	0%	F
					0.00	0%	F
					0.00	0%	F

Letter Grade Assignment	
93% or greater	A
84-92%	B
75-83%	C
65-74%	D
<65%	F

Total Possible Points
420

Figure 7-56 Completed template and worksheet for Excel 7-1

Guided Project 7-2

In this project, you complete the purchase order template for Blue Lake Sports by adding data validation and form controls. You protect the sheet and the structure and save the workbook as a template.
[Student Learning Outcomes 7.1, 7.2, 7.3, 7.4, 7.6]

File Needed: ***BlueLakeSports-07.xlsx*** *(Student data files are available in the* Library *of your SIMnet account.)*
Completed Project File Names: ***[your initials] Excel 7-2Template.xltx*** and ***[your initials] Excel 7-2.xlsx***

Skills Covered in This Project

- Set data validation to use a list.
- Use an error alert for data validation.
- Insert a check box form control.
- Unlock worksheet cells and protect a worksheet.
- Protect workbook structure.
- Save a workbook as a template.
- Create a new workbook from a template.
- Inspect a workbook.
- Check compatibility.

---

1. Open the ***BlueLakeSports-07*** workbook from your student data files.
2. Save the workbook as a template.
   a. Click the **Save As** button [*File* tab] and choose **This PC**.
   b. Click the **More Options** link.
   c. Type the file name [your initials] Excel 7-2Template in the *File name* box.
   d. Verify that the *Save Thumbnail* box is selected or select it.
   e. Choose **Excel Template** from the *Save as type* drop-down box.
   f. Click **Save**.
3. Set data validation with an error alert to use a list.
   a. Click the **Purchase Order** sheet tab, select **B17**, and click the **Data Validation** button [*Data* tab, *Data Tools* group].
   b. Click the **Allow** arrow and choose **List** on the *Settings* tab.
   c. Click the **Source** entry box.
   d. Click the **Departments** worksheet tab and select cells **A2:A14**.
   e. Click the **Error Alert** tab.
   f. Verify that the *Show error alert after invalid data is entered* box is selected.
   g. Use **Stop** for the *Style* to prohibit an invalid entry.
   h. Click the **Title** box and type Wait!.
   i. Click the **Error message** box and type Please choose from the list. including the period.
   j. Click **OK**.
4. Display the *Developer* tab.
   a. Select the **Options** command [*File* tab] and click **Customize Ribbon** in the left pane.
   b. Select the **Developer** box in the *Main Tabs* group.
   c. Click **OK**.
5. Insert a check box form control.
   a. Click the **View** tab and check the **Gridlines** box in the *Show* group so that you can draw and position controls with gridlines.
   b. Click the **Insert Controls** button [*Developer* tab, *Controls* group] and click the **Check Box (Form Control)** button.
   c. Draw a control directly over cell **B15**.
   d. Click the **Properties** button [*Developer* tab, *Controls* group].

e. Verify that the *Unchecked* radio button is selected on the *Control* tab.
f. Select the **3-D shading** box.
g. Click the **Protection** tab and deselect the **Locked** box.
h. Click **OK**.
i. Click near the word "Check" in the control to place an insertion point.
j. Delete **Check Box *n***, press **Spacebar**, and type Yes (Figure 7-57).
k. Click cell **E15** to deselect the control. If you accidentally placed a check mark within the control, point and click to remove it.

Figure 7-57 Edited label for check box control

6. Copy a check box form control.
   a. Point to the check box control label **Yes** and right-click.
   b. Choose **Copy** from the menu and then press **Ctrl+V** to paste the control.
   c. Point to any border of the copied control to display a move pointer.
   d. Drag the copy to cell **C15**.
   e. Press **Ctrl** and right-click while pointing to the first check box control to select both controls (Figure 7-58).
   f. Click the **Align** button [*Drawing Tools Format* tab, *Arrange* group] and choose **Align Middle**.
   g. Select cell **E15** to deselect both controls.
   h. Right-click the copied control and choose **Edit Text** to place an insertion point.
   i. Delete **Yes** and type No (Figure 7-59).
   j. Select cell **E15**. Remove check marks that you accidentally entered.

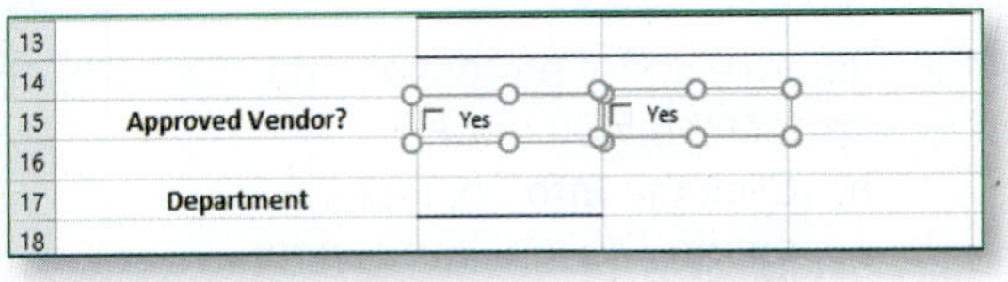

Figure 7-58 Two controls selected

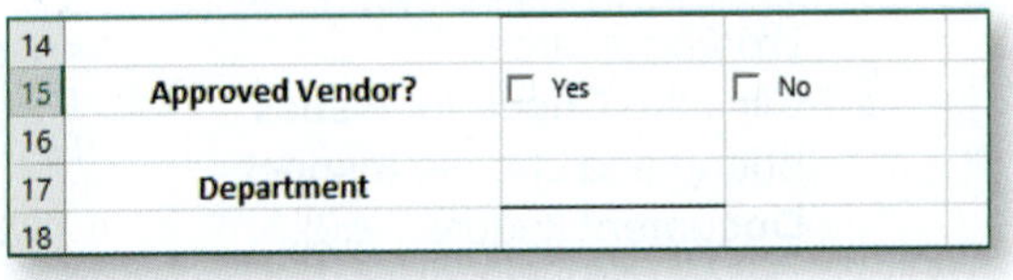

Figure 7-59 Controls are aligned

7. Protect the worksheet and the workbook structure.
   a. Select **D7**.
   b. Press **Ctrl** and select cell **D9**, cells **B11:D13**, cell **B17**, and cells **A20:D28**.
   c. Click the **Format** button [*Home* tab, *Cells* group].
   d. Select **Lock Cell** to remove the *Locked* property.
   e. Click cell **D7**.
   f. Click the **Protect Sheet** button [*Review* tab, *Protect* group].
   g. Allow the options to select locked and unlocked cells. Do not use a password.
   h. Click **OK**.
   i. Click the **Protect Workbook** button [*Review* tab, *Protect* group].
   j. Verify that the *Structure* box is selected.
   k. Do not use a password and click **OK**.
8. Save and close the template.
9. Create a workbook from a template.
   a. Click the **New** button [*File* tab] and click **Pesonal** near the top of the gallery.
   b. Click ***[your initials] Excel 7-2Template*** to create a workbook.
   c. Type BLS00120 in cell **D7** and press **Tab**.
   d. Type =to in cell **D9**, press **Tab** to select **TODAY**, and press **Enter**.

e. Type the following in cells **B11:B13**:
Outdoor Apparel, Inc.
4232 South Water Street
Omaha, NE 68107

f. Select the check box control for **Yes**.

g. Select cell **B17**, click the data validation arrow, and choose **Apparel**.

h. Type the following in cells **A20:D21**:

Ladies Parka LP10Blue 4 87

Men's Parka MP16Black 4 98

10. Save the workbook as an Excel workbook named [your initials] Excel 7-2 in your usual location for saving files.

11. Remove sheet protection and inspect the workbook.
    a. Click the **Info** command on the *File* tab. You cannot inspect a worksheet that is protected.
    b. Click **Unprotect** in the *Protect Workbook* area.
    c. Click the **Check for Issues** button and choose **Inspect Document** (Figure 7-60).
    d. Choose **Yes** to save the document before inspection.
    e. Click **Inspect** in the *Document Inspector* dialog box.
    f. Click **Remove All** to remove document properties and personal information.
    g. Click **Close**.

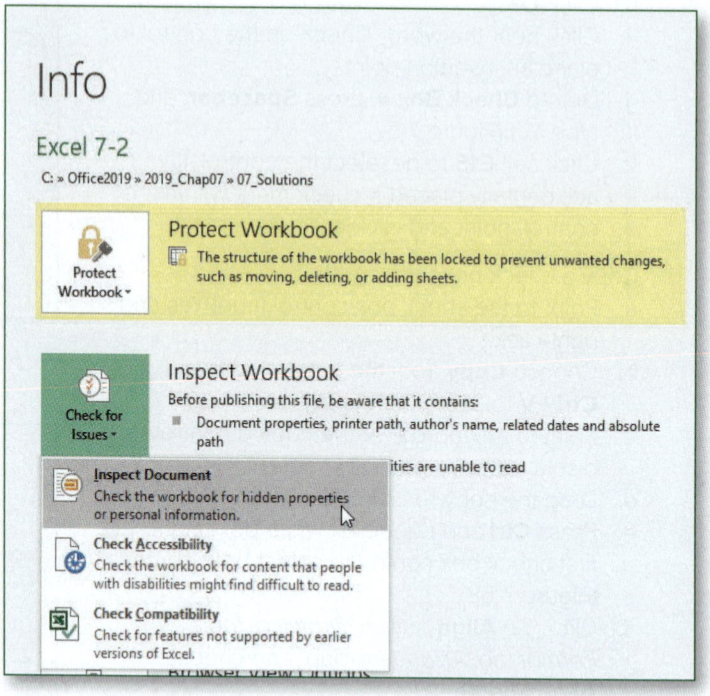

Figure 7-60 Inspect the document from the *Backstage* view

12. Check compatibility.
    a. Click the **Protect Workbook** button [*Review* group, *Protect* group]. The *Protect Workbook* property must be disabled to generate a compatibility report on a new sheet.
    b. Click the **Check for Issues** button [*File* tab, *Info* group] and choose **Check Compatibility**.
    c. Click **Copy to New Sheet**. The compatibility report displays on a new sheet.
    d. Click the **Purchase Order** sheet tab.

13. Save and close the workbook (Figure 7-61).

14. Move the template from the default folder.
    a. Click the **File** tab, select **Open**, and click **Browse** to display the *Open* dialog box.
    b. Expand the *Quick access* list if necessary and choose the **Documents** folder in the left pane.
    c. Double-click **Custom Office Templates** in the pane on the right.
    c. Right-click ***[your initials] Excel 7-2Template*** and choose **Cut**.
    d. Use the left pane to navigate to and open your folder for saving files.
    e. Right-click an unused area of the dialog box and choose **Paste**.
    f. Click **Cancel** to close the dialog box.

15. Hide the *Developer* tab.
  a. Select the **Options** command [*File* tab] pane.
  b. Click **Customize Ribbon** in the left pane.
  c. Deselect the **Developer** box in the *Main Tabs* group and click **OK**.

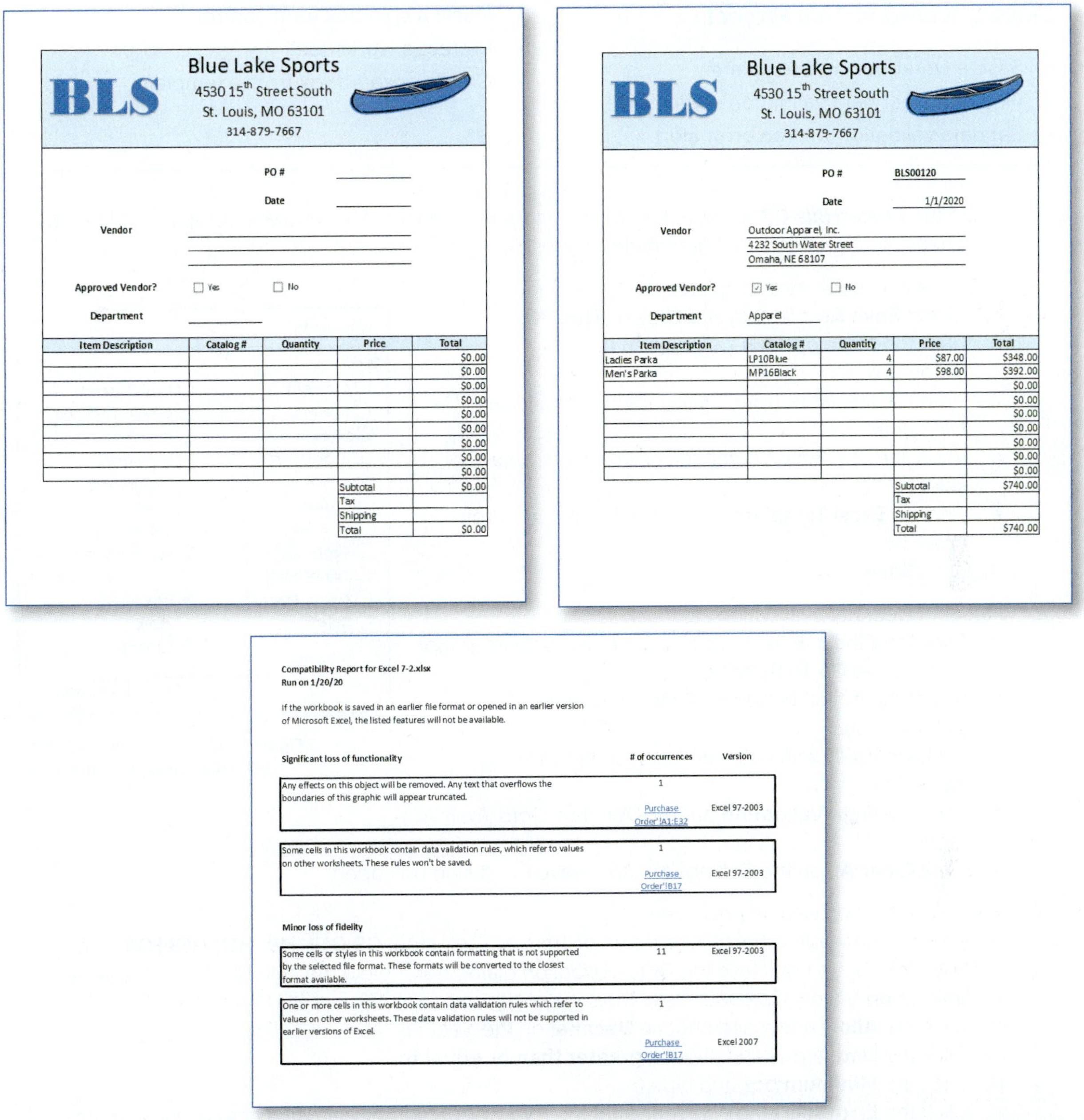

Figure 7-61 Completed template and workbook for Excel 7-2

Guided Project 7-3

Agents for Placer Hills Real Estate (PHRE) have built a worksheet to help clients compare monthly payments. You clear and reset data validation, insert a spin box form control, and save the workbook as a template.
[Student Learning Outcomes 7.1, 7.2, 7.3, 7.4]

File Needed: ***PlacerHills-07.xlsx*** *(Student data files are available in the* Library *of your SIMnet account.)*
Completed Project File Names: ***[your initials] Excel 7-3Template.xltx*** and ***[your initials] Excel 7-3.xlsx***

Skills Covered in This Project

- Save a workbook as a template.
- Find and clear data validation settings.
- Set data validation with an error alert.
- Insert a spin box form control.
- Protect a worksheet.
- Create a workbook from a template.

1. Open the ***PlacerHills-07*** workbook from your student data files. The #NUM! error appears in three cells because arguments for the formulas in those cells are missing.
2. Save the workbook as a template.
   a. Select **Save As** [*File* tab] and choose **This PC**.
   b. Click the **More options** link to open the *Save As* dialog box.
   c. Type the file name [your initials] Excel 7-3Template in the *File name* box.
   d. Verify that the *Save Thumbnail* box is selected or select it.
   e. Choose **Excel Template** from the *Save as type* drop-down box.
   f. Click **Save**.
3. Find and clear data validation settings.
   a. Click the **Find & Select** button [*Home* tab, *Editing* group] and choose **Go To Special**.
   b. Select the option button for **Data validation** (Figure 7-62).
   c. Click **OK**. Cells with data validation settings are highlighted.
   d. Click the **Data Validation** button [*Data* tab, *Data Tools* group].
   e. Click **Clear All** on the *Settings* tab and leave the dialog box open.

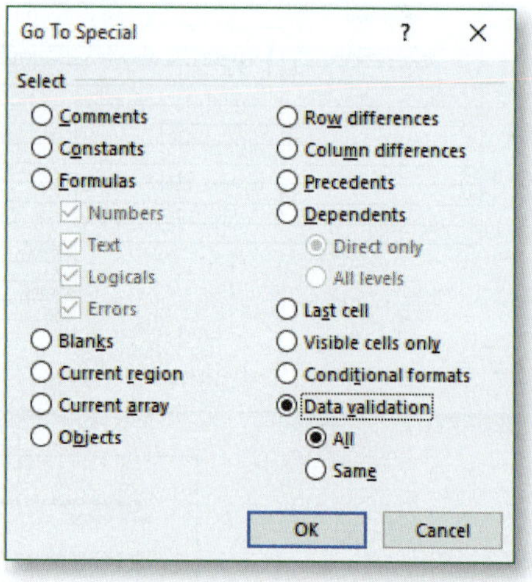

Figure 7-62 Locate cells with data validation using *Go To Special*

4. Set data validation with an error alert.
   a. Verify that the following cells in the worksheet are selected: **C9:C12**, **H9, H11, H13:H14**, and **H16**. (If they are not, close the *Data Validation* dialog box, select the cells, and click the **Data Validation** button [*Data* tab, *Data Tools* group].)
   b. Click the **Allow** arrow and choose **Decimal** on the *Settings* tab.
   c. Click the **Data** arrow and choose **greater than or equal to**.
   d. Click the **Minimum** box and type 0.
   e. Click the **Error Alert** tab and verify that the *Show error alert after invalid data is entered* box is selected.
   f. Verify that *Stop* displays as the *Style*.
   g. Click the **Title** box and type Required.
   h. Click the **Error message** box and type Please enter a positive value. including the period (Figure 7-63).
   i. Click **OK**.
5. Display the *Developer* tab on the *Ribbon* if it is not shown.
   a. Select the **Options** command [*File* tab] and click **Customize Ribbon** in the left pane.
   b. Select the **Developer** box in the *Main Tabs* group and click **OK**.

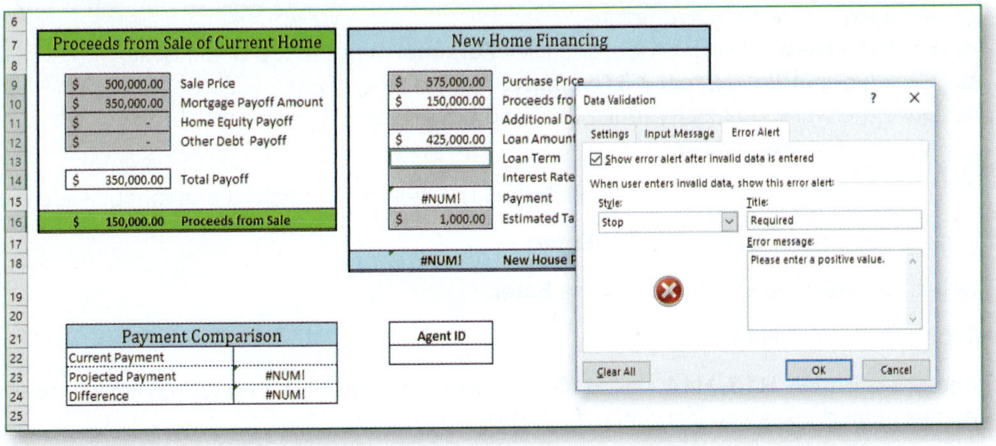

Figure 7-63 Data validation error alert

6. Insert a spin button form control.
   a. Show the gridlines on the worksheet [*View* tab].
   b. Click the **Insert Controls** button [*Developer* tab, *Controls* group].
   c. Click the **Spin Button (Form Control)** button.
   d. Draw a control directly over cells **I21:I22** (Figure 7-64).
   e. Right-click the control and choose **Format Control**.
   f. Click the **Minimum value** box on the *Control* tab and type 1.
   g. Set a maximum value of **8**. These are agent identification numbers (1 through 8).
   h. Click the **Cell link** box and select cell **H22**. The choice made by the spin button will be placed in this cell (Figure 7-65).
   i. Verify that the *3-D shading* box is selected and click **OK**. The linked cell displays the minimum value 1.
   j. Click cell **D4** to deselect the control.

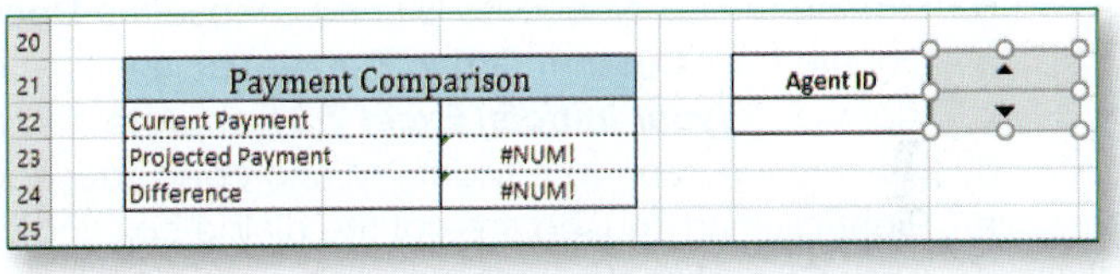

Figure 7-64 Spin button form control

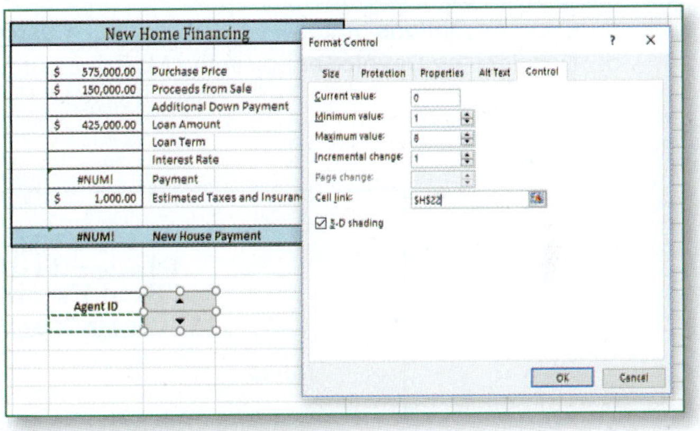

Figure 7-65 Options set for spin button control

7. Protect the worksheet for data entry.
   a. Select cells **D4:E4**.
   b. Press **Ctrl** and select cells **C9:C12**, **H9**, **H11**, **H13:H14**, **H16**, **H22**, and **E22**.
   c. Click the **Format** button [*Home* tab, *Cells* group].
   d. Select **Lock Cell** to remove the *Locked* property.
   e. Click the **Protect Sheet** button [*Review* tab, *Protect* group].
   f. Allow the options to select locked and unlocked cells. Do not use a password.
   g. Click **OK**.
8. Delete the contents of cells **C9:C10**, **H9** and **H16**.
9. Select cell **D4** to position the insertion point on the template.
10. Save and close the template.

11. Create a workbook from a template.
    a. Click the **New** button [*File* tab] and click **Personal** near the top of the gallery.
    b. Click ***[your initials] Excel 7-3Template***.
    c. Save the workbook as a regular Excel workbook named [your initials] Excel 7-3 in your usual location for saving files.
12. Select cell **C9**, type 450000, and press **Enter**. The cells are formatted and formulas are calculated.
13. Type 275000 in cell **C10** and press **Enter**.
14. Select cell **H9**, type 485000, and press **Enter**.
15. Type 75000 in cell **H11**.
16. Enter data in cells **H13**, **H14**, and **H16** as shown in Figure 7-66. The term is 30, the rate is 4.25%, and estimated taxes and insurance are $850.
17. Click the spin box control arrows to select **3** as the agent ID.
18. Select cell **E22**, type 1875, and select cell **D4**.
19. Save and close the workbook.
20. Move the template from the default folder.
    a. Click the **File** tab, choose **Open**, and click **Browse** to display the *Open* dialog box.
    b. Expand the *Quick access* list and choose the **Documents** folder.
    b. Double-click **Custom Office Templates** in the list of folder names on the right.
    c. Right-click ***[your initials] Excel 7-3Template*** and choose **Cut**.
    d. Use the left pane to navigate to and open your folder for saving files.
    e. Right-click an unused area of the dialog box and choose **Paste**.
    f. Click **Cancel** to close the dialog box.
21. Remove the *Developer* tab.
    a. Click the **Options** button [*File* tab] and click **Customize Ribbon** in the left pane.
    b. Deselect the **Developer** box in the *Main Tabs* group and click **OK**.

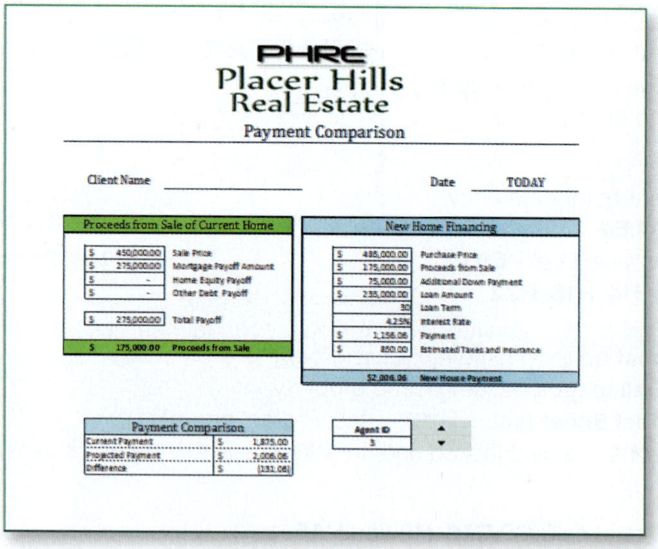

Figure 7-66 Completed worksheet for Excel 7-3

Independent Project 7-4

Classic Gardens and Landscapes (CGL) monitors employee hours by task and by day. You set validation, complete formulas, and share the workbook for co-authoring. (*Note: You must have access to a secondary email address to complete this project.*)
[Student Learning Outcomes 7.1, 7.2, 7.4, 7.5, 7.6]

File Needed: ***ClassicGardens-07.xlsx*** *(Student data files are available in the* Library *of your SIMnet account.)*
Completed Project File Names: ***[your initials] Excel 7-4Template.xltx*** and ***[your initials] Excel 7-4CoAuthor .xlsx***

Skills Covered in This Project

- Save a workbook as a template.
- Set data validation with an error alert.
- Create a workbook from a template.
- Share and co-author a workbook.
- Check accessibility and add alt text.

---

1. Open the ***ClassicGardens-07*** workbook from your student data files.
2. Save the workbook as a template with a thumbnail and name it [your initials] Excel 7-4Template in the default *Custom Office Templates* folder.
3. Set data validation with an error alert.
   a. Click the **Employee Hours** worksheet tab.
   b. Select cells **B8:G13** and set data validation to use a decimal value less than **8.1**.
   c. Use an **Information** type error alert with the title Overtime.
   d. Type the error message Overtime pay starts at greater than 8 hours. including the period.
4. Enter *SUM* formulas for the totals in column **H** and row **14**.
5. Select cells **B8:G13** and remove the **Locked** property. Select cell **B8** to cancel the selection.
6. Protect the sheet without a password.
7. Save and close the template.
8. Create a new workbook based on the template.
9. Select the **Employee Hours** tab and enter the following hours for Alvarez; accept the invalid entry.

Mon	9
Tue	8
Wed	7

10. Save the workbook as [your initials] Excel 7-4CoAuthor to your *Documents* folder on *OneDrive*.
11. Co-author a workbook.
    a. Share the workbook with ***your secondary email address***.
    b. Launch your email program and sign in to your secondary email account.
    c. Open your email message and the shared workbook.
    d. Open the workbook for editing in the browser in *Excel Online*.
12. Enter the following hours for Alvarez. Note the days of the week and accept the invalid entry to edit the hours for Wednesday.

Wed	9
Thu	8
Fri	7

13. Close the *Excel Online* browser window and your email message. Return to Excel and **[your initials] Excel 7-4CoAuthor** and close the *Share* pane.
14. Check accessibility and add the alternative text CGL Logo to the image on the **Task Hours** sheet.
15. Close the task panes.
16. Save a copy of the file to your usual location for saving files (Figure 7-67).
17. Move the **[your initials] Excel 7-4Template** file from the *Custom Office Templates* folder to your folder.

	Mon	Tue	Wed	Thu	Fri	Sat	Total
Alvarez, Tomas	9	8	9	8	7		41
Greene, Jason							0
Sylvester, Harry							0
Gomez, Jesus							0
Chajec, Mark							0
Gunn, Lester							0
Total	9	8	9	8	7	0	41

Figure 7-67 Completed worksheet for Excel 7-4

Independent Project 7-5

In the Courtyard Medical Plaza workbook, you co-author the pharmacy inventory to add items. On the *Optometry* worksheet, you find and correct invalid data. Finally, you inspect the workbook and prepare a compatibility report. *(Note: You must have access to a secondary email address to complete this project.)* [Student Learning Outcomes 7.2, 7.5, 7.6]

File Needed: ***CourtyardMedical-07.xlsx*** *(Student data files are available in the* Library *of your SIMnet account)*
Completed Project File Name: ***[your initials] Excel 7-5.xlsx*** and ***[your initials] Excel 7-5Copy.xlsx***

Skills Covered in This Project

- Share and co-author a workbook.
- Circle invalid data.
- Inspect a workbook.
- Check workbook compatibility.

1. Open the ***CourtyardMedical-07*** workbook from your student data files. It is marked as final.
2. Click **Edit Anyway** in the message bar, and save the workbook to your *Documents* folder on *OneDrive* as [your initials] Excel 7-5.
3. Share the workbook with ***your secondary email address***.
4. Co-author a workbook.
   a. Launch your email program and sign in to your secondary email account.
   b. Open your email message and the shared workbook.
   c. Select the **Pharmacy** sheet.

d. Enter data for two items shown here. Ignore the *AutoComplete* list for the Product ID values to enter new IDs as shown. The currency symbol is included in format settings.

Product ID	Description	Cost	Retail
CMP-016	Swim ear drops	4.59	6.89
CMP-017	Peptic relief tablets (25)	2.50	3.99

5. Close the *Excel Online* window and the email program and return to Excel.
6. Select the **Pharmacy** tab and *AutoFit* column **B**. Close the *Share* pane.
7. Click the **Optometry** worksheet tab and circle invalid data.
8. Review the data validation settings for any cell in column **A** and correct the invalid entries.
9. Check compatibility and copy the results to a new sheet.
10. Save a copy of the workbook named [your initials] Excel 7-5Copy on your PC in your usual folder for saving files.
11. Mark the workbook as final and close it (Figure 7-68).

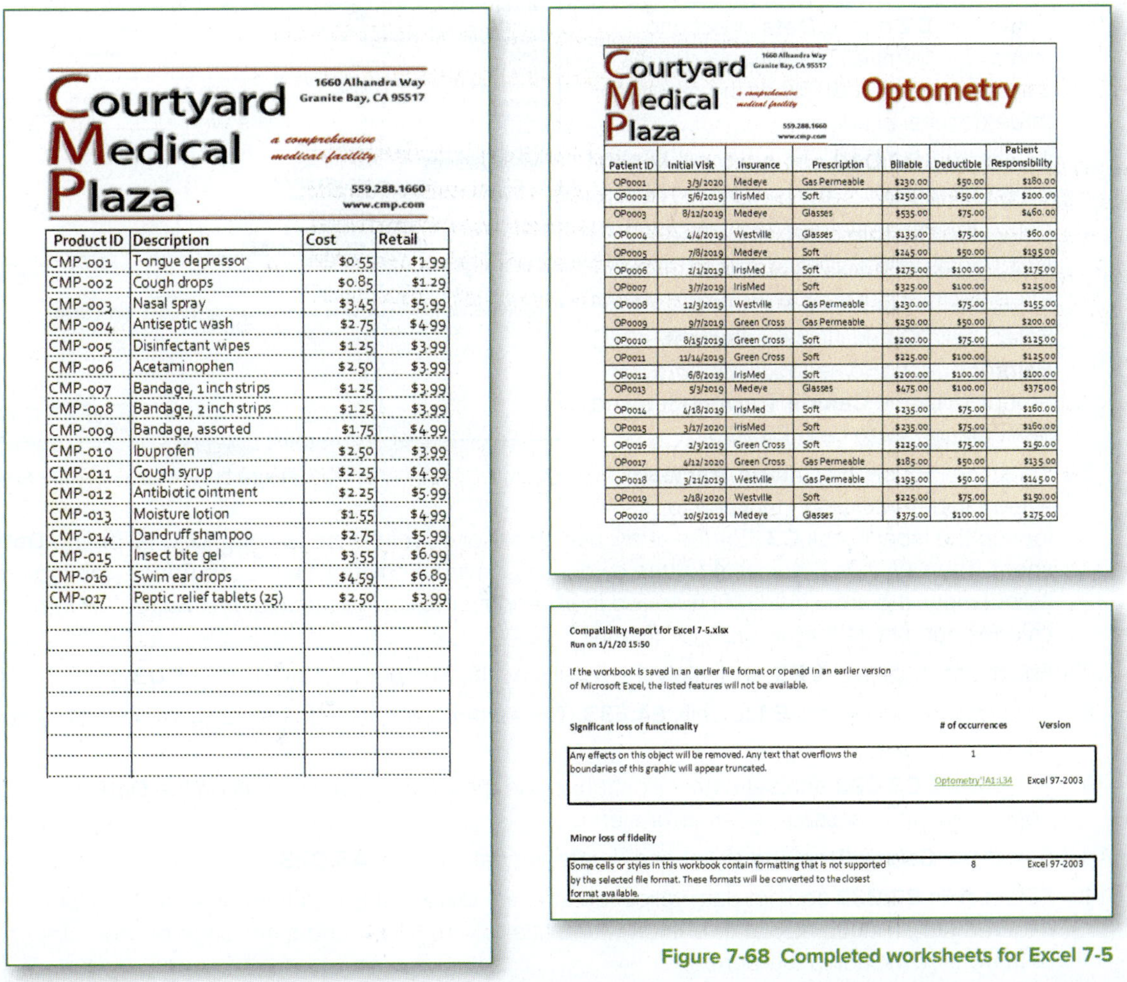

Product ID	Description	Cost	Retail
CMP-001	Tongue depressor	$0.55	$1.99
CMP-002	Cough drops	$0.85	$1.29
CMP-003	Nasal spray	$3.45	$5.99
CMP-004	Antiseptic wash	$2.75	$4.99
CMP-005	Disinfectant wipes	$1.25	$3.99
CMP-006	Acetaminophen	$2.50	$3.99
CMP-007	Bandage, 1 inch strips	$1.25	$3.99
CMP-008	Bandage, 2 inch strips	$1.25	$3.99
CMP-009	Bandage, assorted	$1.75	$4.99
CMP-010	Ibuprofen	$2.50	$3.99
CMP-011	Cough syrup	$2.25	$4.99
CMP-012	Antibiotic ointment	$2.25	$5.99
CMP-013	Moisture lotion	$1.55	$4.99
CMP-014	Dandruff shampoo	$2.75	$5.99
CMP-015	Insect bite gel	$3.55	$6.99
CMP-016	Swim ear drops	$4.59	$6.89
CMP-017	Peptic relief tablets (25)	$2.50	$3.99

Patient ID	Initial Visit	Insurance	Prescription	Billable	Deductible	Patient Responsibility
OP0001	3/3/2020	Medeye	Gas Permeable	$230.00	$50.00	$180.00
OP0002	5/6/2019	IrisMed	Soft	$250.00	$50.00	$200.00
OP0003	8/12/2019	Medeye	Glasses	$535.00	$75.00	$460.00
OP0004	4/4/2019	Westville	Glasses	$135.00	$75.00	$60.00
OP0005	7/8/2019	Medeye	Soft	$245.00	$50.00	$195.00
OP0006	2/1/2019	IrisMed	Soft	$275.00	$100.00	$175.00
OP0007	3/7/2019	IrisMed	Soft	$325.00	$100.00	$225.00
OP0008	12/3/2019	Westville	Gas Permeable	$230.00	$75.00	$155.00
OP0009	9/7/2019	Green Cross	Gas Permeable	$250.00	$50.00	$200.00
OP0010	8/15/2019	Green Cross	Soft	$200.00	$75.00	$125.00
OP0011	11/14/2019	Green Cross	Soft	$225.00	$100.00	$125.00
OP0012	6/8/2019	IrisMed	Soft	$200.00	$100.00	$100.00
OP0013	5/3/2019	Medeye	Glasses	$475.00	$100.00	$375.00
OP0014	4/18/2019	IrisMed	Soft	$235.00	$75.00	$160.00
OP0015	3/17/2020	IrisMed	Soft	$235.00	$75.00	$160.00
OP0016	2/3/2019	Green Cross	Soft	$225.00	$75.00	$150.00
OP0017	4/12/2020	Green Cross	Gas Permeable	$185.00	$50.00	$135.00
OP0018	3/21/2019	Westville	Gas Permeable	$195.00	$50.00	$145.00
OP0019	2/18/2020	Westville	Soft	$225.00	$75.00	$150.00
OP0020	10/5/2019	Medeye	Glasses	$375.00	$100.00	$275.00

Figure 7-68 Completed worksheets for Excel 7-5

Independent Project 7-6

The Hamilton Civic Center is developing a template for member exercise and off-site seminars. You create the template, set validation, enter formulas, and insert a combo box control. You then create a new workbook from the template.
[Student Learning Outcomes 7.1, 7.2, 7.3, 7.4, 7.6]

File Needed: ***HamiltonCC-07.xlsx*** *(Student data files are available in the* Library *of your SIMnet account.)*
Completed Project File Names: ***[your initials] Excel 7-6Template.xltx*** and ***[your initials] Excel 7-6.xlsx***

Skills Covered in This Project

- Set data validation to use a list.
- Set validation to restrict dates.
- Create an error alert message.
- Insert a combo box control.
- Check accessibility and add alt text.
- Protect a worksheet.
- Save a workbook as a template.
- Create a workbook from a template.

---

1. Open the ***HamiltonCC-07*** workbook from your student data files and save it with a thumbnail image as [your initials] Excel 7-6Template in the default templates folder.
2. Select cell **D2** on the **Data** sheet and review the formula. The formula divides calories by time and rounds the results to three decimal places.
3. Select cells **D2:D10** and open the *Format Cells* dialog box.
4. Select the **Custom** category on the *Number* tab and build a format to display three decimal places (Figure 7-69).
5. Select cell **D2** and click the **Format Painter** button [*Home* tab, *Clipboard* group]. Click the **Calorie Tracking** tab and paint the format to cells **E3:E33**.

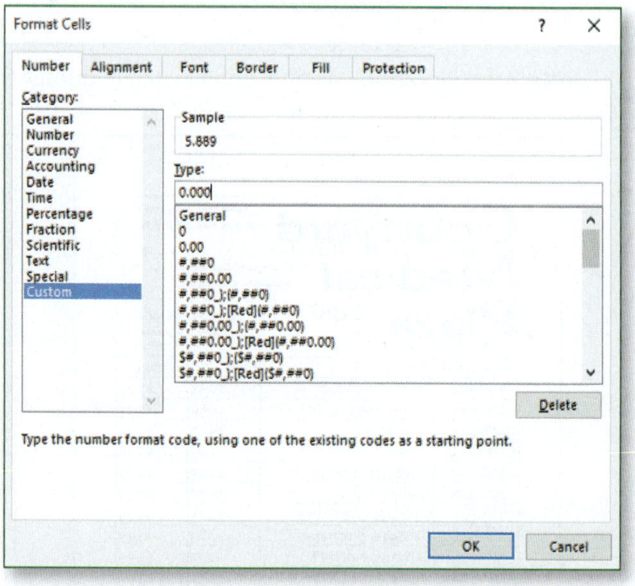

Figure 7-69 Custom format for values

6. Select cell **E3** on the **Calorie Tracking** sheet. Start a *VLOOKUP* function to lookup the label in cell **C3**. For the array, use an absolute reference to cells **A2:D10** on the **Data** sheet. The *Col_index_num* is **4** for the calories per minute column. Leave the *Range_lookup* argument empty; the array (A2:D10) is sorted in ascending order. The result of the *VLOOKUP* formula is calories per minute for the exercise (Figure 7-70).
7. Edit the formula in cell **E3** to multiply the results by the number of minutes in cell **D3**.
8. Copy the formula in cell **E3** to cells **E4:E33**. The #N/A error message displays in rows where no data displays.
9. Select cells **C3:C33** and set data validation to use the list of activity names on the **Data** sheet. Do not use an input message or an error alert.
10. Select the **Calorie Tracking** sheet and delete the data in cells **A3:D23**.
11. Select cells **B3:B33** and set data validation to use a **Date** that is less than or equal to *TODAY* (Figure 7-71). Include a *Stop* error alert with a title of Check Date and a message of Date must be today or in the past. including the period.

12. Select cells **A3:D33** and remove the **Locked** cell property. Select cell **A3** to position the insertion point.
13. Display the **Developer** tab on the *Ribbon* and click the **Data** worksheet tab.
14. Draw a combo box control to cover cell **F8** and open its *Format Control* dialog box. Select cells **G8:G11** for the *Input range* and type f8 in the *Cell link* box (Figure 7-72).
15. Deselect the control and then select **Second** from the control. The linked cell is under the control and hidden from view.

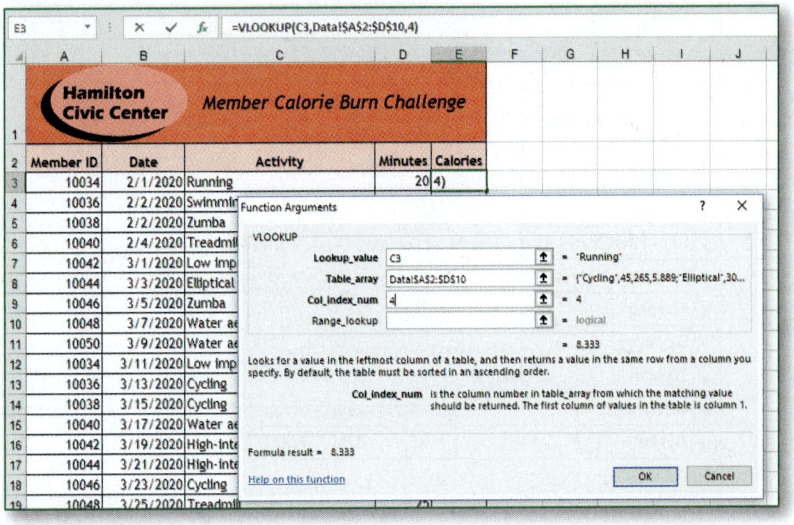

Figure 7-70 *VLOOKUP* formula

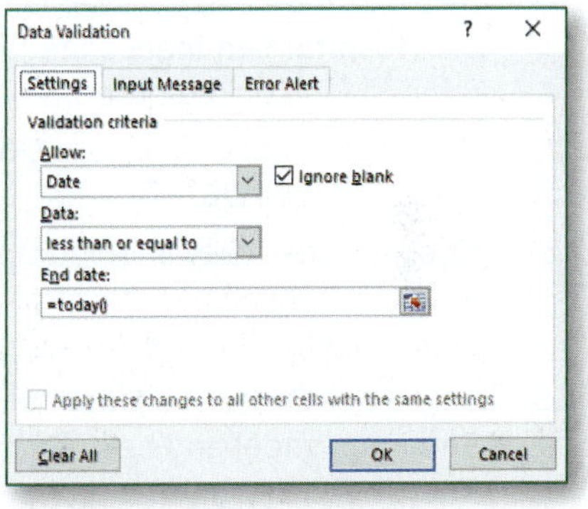

Figure 7-71 Data validation for dates

16. Click the **Hospital Seminars** tab and select cell **D4**. This cell has *Center Across Selection* alignment applied.
17. Select cell **D4** and use *CONCAT* and *INDEX* to display the result from the combo box, concatenating the *Index* results to the word "Quarter."
    a. Start a *CONCAT* function [*Text* group].
    b. Use the *INDEX* function with the first arguments list as the *Text1* argument.
    c. Choose cells **G8:G11** on the *Data* sheet for the *Array* argument and cell **F8** for the *Row_num* argument. You can select the combo box control or type f8 after the sheet name (Figure 7-73). When the array is one column, a *Column_num* argument is not necessary.
    d. Click between the two ending parentheses in the *Formula* bar to return to the *CONCAT* arguments and type a comma (,) to move to the *Text2* argument. (If you accidentally click **OK**, click the **Insert Function** button to re-open the *Function Arguments* dialog box.)
    e. Click the **Text2** box, press **Spacebar**, type Quarter, and click **OK**. (Figure 7-74).
    f. Format cell **D4** as **bold italic 16 pt**.

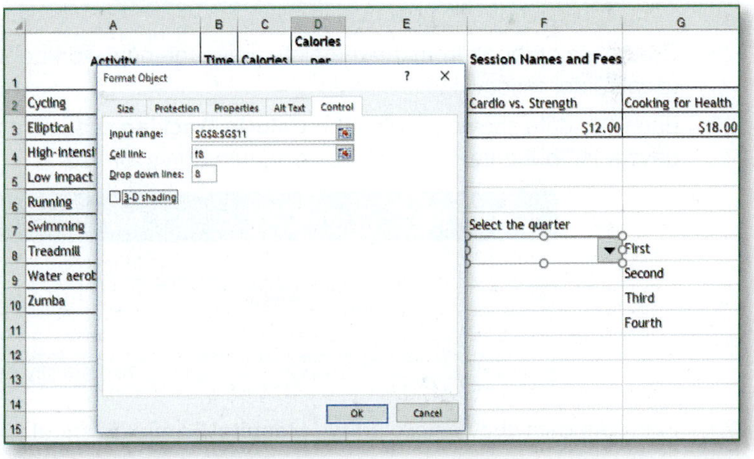

Figure 7-72 Combo box settings

18. Select the **Data** sheet, select **Third** from the combo box control, and return to the **Hospital Seminars** sheet to see the results.

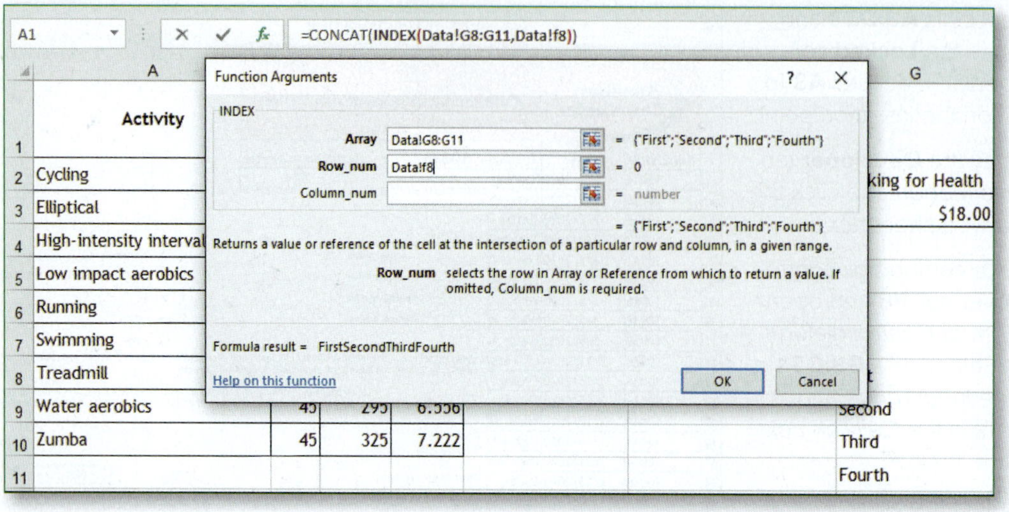

Figure 7-73 ***INDEX* is nested within *CONCAT***

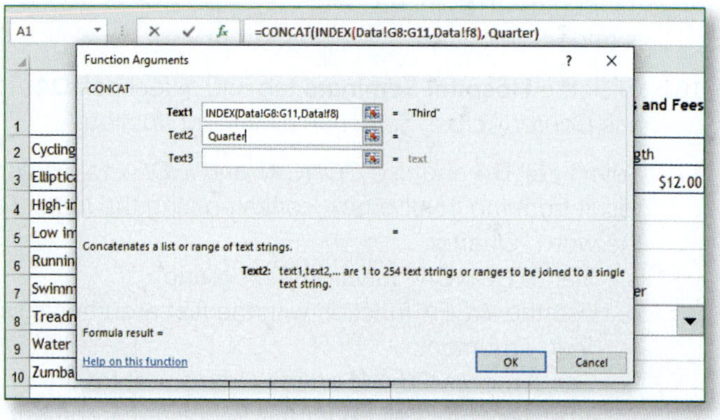

Figure 7-74 Space character is included with *Text2* argument

19. Select cell **D4** and cells **D6:G10** on the **Hospital Seminars** sheet and remove the **Locked** property.
20. Delete the contents of cells **D6:G10** and select cell **D6**.
21. Check accessibility and add the alternative text Hamilton Civic Center Logo to both pictures in the workbook.
22. Select cell **D6** on the **Hospital Seminars** sheet and cell **A3** on the **Calorie Tracking** sheet.
23. Protect the **Hospital Seminars** sheet and the **Calorie Tracking** sheet, both without passwords.
24. Save and close the template.
25. Create a workbook from the template. Save the new workbook as [your initials] Excel 7-6 in your usual folder for saving files.
26. Enter the data shown here on the **Calorie Tracking** sheet. Do not type the word "Yesterday" or "Two days ago," but enter date values using *mm/dd/yy* format.

Member ID	Date	Activity	Minutes
10001	Today	Elliptical	45
10003	Two days ago	Water aerobics	40
10007	Yesterday	Running	30
10003	Today	High-intensity interval training	40

27. Enter the data shown here on the **Hospital Seminars** sheet.

	Henderson	Advocate	Mercy	Gallatin
Cardio vs. Strength	14	22	31	15
Cooking for Health				
Know Your Numbers	32	21	18	21
Pamper Your Joints	10	20	15	18
Vitamins Are Best	14	31	27	15

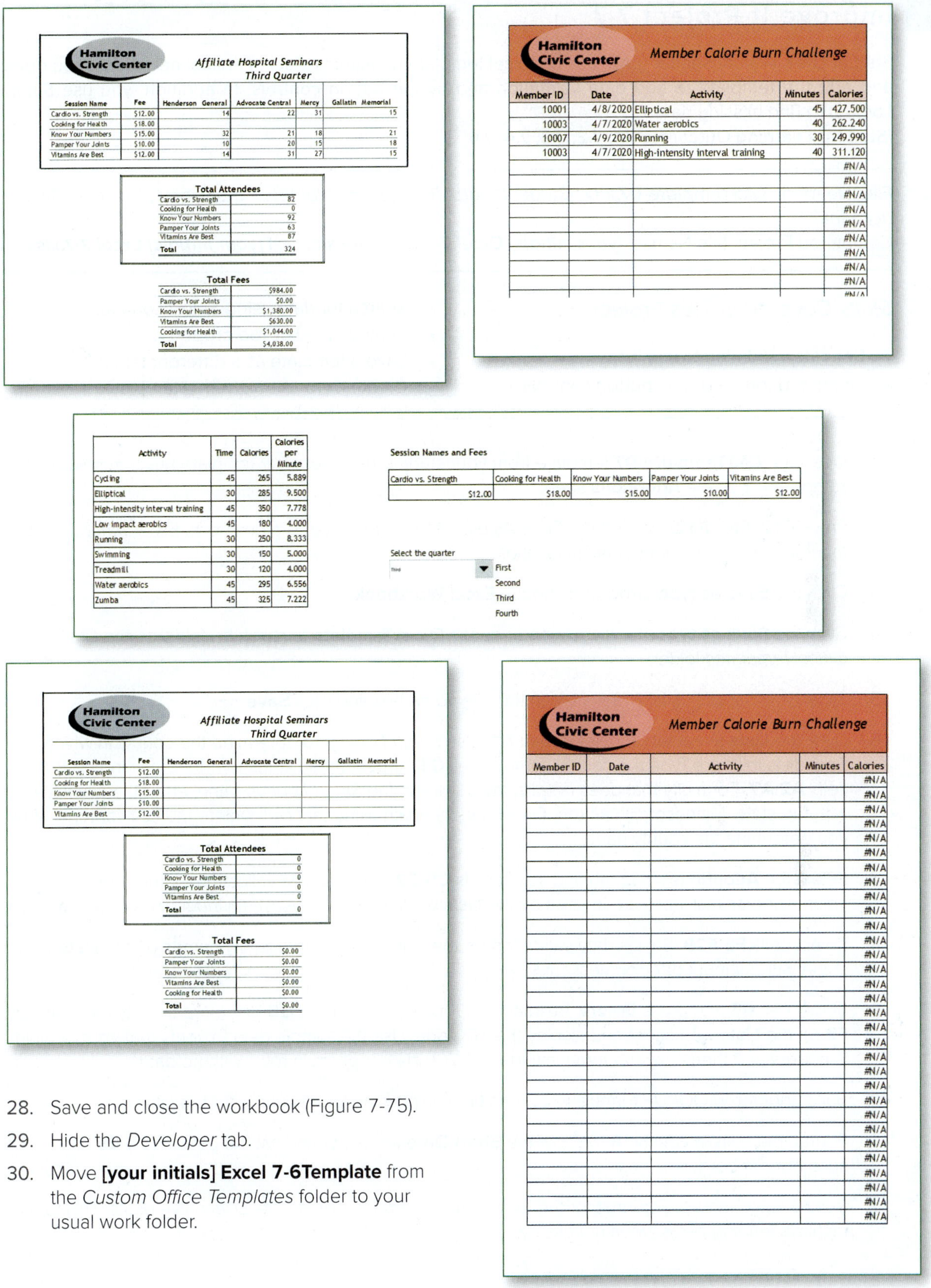

Hamilton Civic Center
Affiliate Hospital Seminars
Third Quarter
Session Name | Fee | Henderson General | Advocate Central | Mercy | Gallatin Memorial
Cardio vs. Strength | $12.00 | 14 | 22 | 31 | 15
Cooking for Health | $18.00
Know Your Numbers | $15.00 | 32 | 21 | 18 | 21
Pamper Your Joints | $10.00 | 10 | 20 | 15 | 18
Vitamins Are Best | $12.00 | 14 | 31 | 27 | 15
Total Attendees
Cardio vs. Strength 82
Cooking for Health 0
Know Your Numbers 92
Pamper Your Joints 63
Vitamins Are Best 87
Total 324
Total Fees
Cardio vs. Strength $984.00
Pamper Your Joints $0.00
Know Your Numbers $1,380.00
Vitamins Are Best $630.00
Cooking for Health $1,044.00
Total $4,038.00
Hamilton Civic Center
Member Calorie Burn Challenge
Member ID | Date | Activity | Minutes | Calories
10001 | 4/8/2020 | Elliptical | 45 | 427.500
10003 | 4/7/2020 | Water aerobics | 40 | 262.240
10007 | 4/9/2020 | Running | 30 | 249.990
10003 | 4/7/2020 | High-intensity interval training | 40 | 311.120
#N/A
Activity | Time | Calories | Calories per Minute
Cycling | 45 | 265 | 5.889
Elliptical | 30 | 285 | 9.500
High-intensity interval training | 45 | 350 | 7.778
Low impact aerobics | 45 | 180 | 4.000
Running | 30 | 250 | 8.333
Swimming | 30 | 150 | 5.000
Treadmill | 30 | 120 | 4.000
Water aerobics | 45 | 295 | 6.556
Zumba | 45 | 325 | 7.222
Session Names and Fees
Cardio vs. Strength | Cooking for Health | Know Your Numbers | Pamper Your Joints | Vitamins Are Best
$12.00 | $18.00 | $15.00 | $10.00 | $12.00
Select the quarter
First
Second
Third
Fourth
Hamilton Civic Center
Affiliate Hospital Seminars
Third Quarter
Session Name | Fee | Henderson General | Advocate Central | Mercy | Gallatin Memorial
Cardio vs. Strength | $12.00
Cooking for Health | $18.00
Know Your Numbers | $15.00
Pamper Your Joints | $10.00
Vitamins Are Best | $12.00
Total Attendees
Cardio vs. Strength 0
Cooking for Health 0
Know Your Numbers 0
Pamper Your Joints 0
Vitamins Are Best 0
Total 0
Total Fees
Cardio vs. Strength $0.00
Pamper Your Joints $0.00
Know Your Numbers $0.00
Vitamins Are Best $0.00
Cooking for Health $0.00
Total $0.00
Hamilton Civic Center
Member Calorie Burn Challenge
Member ID | Date | Activity | Minutes | Calories
#N/A

28. Save and close the workbook (Figure 7-75).
29. Hide the *Developer* tab.
30. Move **[your initials] Excel 7-6Template** from the *Custom Office Templates* folder to your usual work folder.

Figure 7-75 Completed template and worksheet for Excel 7-6

Improve It Project 7-7

Staff at Life's Animal Shelter (LAS) use an Excel template to maintain lists of animal adoptions. You open and edit the template to add data validation and option button controls. In addition, you use *Smart Lookup* to find missing data.
[Student Learning Outcomes 7.1, 7.2, 7.3, 7.4, 7.6]

File Needed: ***LASTemplate-07.xltx*** *(Student data files are available in the* Library *of your SIMnet account.)*
Completed Project File Names: ***[your initials] Excel 7-7Template.xltx*** and ***[your initials] Excel 7-7.xlsx***

Skills Covered in This Project

- Set data validation to use lists.
- Insert and format option button controls.
- Search for data using *Smart Lookup*.
- Remove the *Locked* property.
- Save a template as a different template.
- Create a workbook from a template.

1. Open the ***LASTemplate-07*** template from your student data files. The template has one row of sample data on the **Adoptions** sheet.
2. Press **F12** (**FN+F12**) to open the *Save As* dialog box. The *Save as type* shows *Excel Template*, but the folder is your student data file location.
3. Click the **Save as type** arrow and choose **Excel Workbook**.
4. Click the **Save as type** arrow again and choose **Excel Template** to reset the folder to the *Custom Office Templates* folder.
5. Type [your initials] Excel 7-7Template in the *File name* box and click **Save**.
6. Click the **Lists** sheet tab and select cell **A1**. Use *Smart Lookup* to determine the county in which Bemidji is located. Type the county name in cell **C1**. Repeat these steps for the remaining cities in cells **A2:A7**. For a city that does not display quickly in the *Smart Lookup* pane, enter the city name with the state (Minnesota) in an empty cell and try again using that cell. Delete the cell contents after you determine the county names.
7. Select the **Adoptions** sheet tab and select cells **C5:C29**. Set list data validation for the "Species" column; the animal types are located on the **Lists** worksheet. Do not use an input or an error message.
8. Select cells **F5:F29**. Set list data validation for the "City" column to use city names on the **Lists** worksheet without input or error messages.
9. Select cell **G5** and press **Delete**. Build a *VLOOKUP* formula in cell **G5** to lookup the city name in cell **F5** on the **Lists** worksheet and display the ZIP code. Use the sample data to verify that your formula is correct and then copy the formula (Figure 7-76). #NA appears in rows with no data.
10. Build another *VLOOKUP* formula in column **H** to display the county name for the city.
11. Format the cells in column **A** to show the **Short Date** format. Verify that the data in row **29** has a solid bottom border.
12. Build a custom number format for the "Animal ID" column to display the ID with five digits. This format displays leading zeros when necessary.

13. Draw an **Option Button (Form Control)** to cover most of cell **F2**. Press **Ctrl+Alt**, point at the control's border to display the copy pointer, and drag a copy of the control between cells **G2** and **H2**. Press **Ctrl** and right-click the original control so that both controls are selected. While both controls are selected, align them at the middle (*Drawing Tools Format* tab).

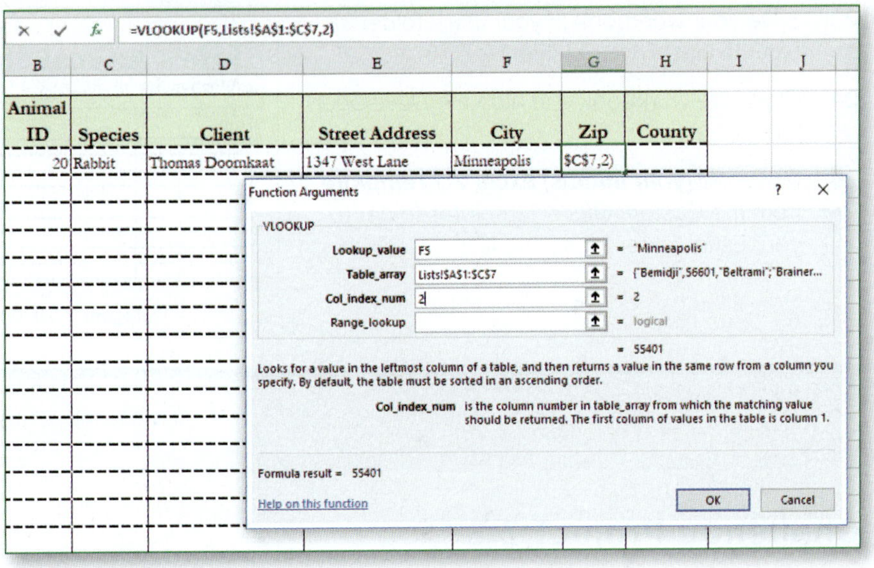

Figure 7-76 *VLOOKUP* to display ZIP code

14. While both controls are selected, right-click either one and select **Format Object** and turn off the *Locked* property. Click a worksheet cell to deselect the controls.

15. Right-click the control on the left and edit the text to display Downtown. Edit the text in the second control to display Suburban (Figure 7-77).

16. Click a worksheet cell. If you have selected one of the option buttons, right-click the control and format the button to be *Unchecked*.

17. Delete cells **A5:F5**, the test data. Data validation is not deleted when you delete cell contents, and the *VLOOKUP* formulas remain.

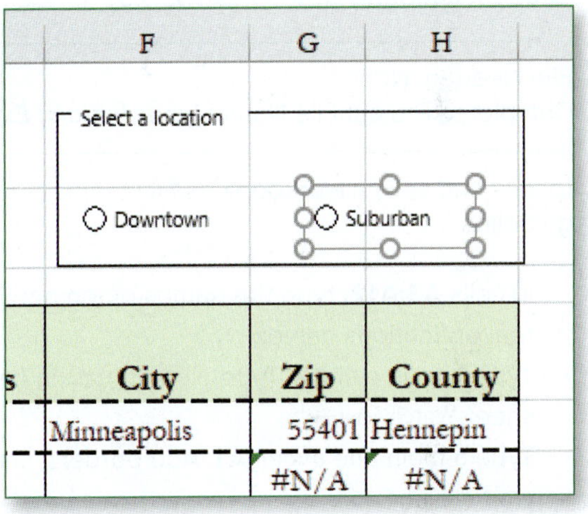

Figure 7-77 Option button controls completed

18. Remove the *Locked* property from cells **A5:H29** on the **Adoptions** sheet.

19. Select cell **A5** and protect the **Adoptions** sheet without a password.

20. Resave the template and close it.

21. Create a new workbook from the template and enter the following data:

Adoption Date	Animal ID	Species	Client	Street Address	City	Zip	County
2/5/20	10	Dog	John Doe	4567 Western Trail	Cass Lake		

22. Select the **Suburban** option button.

23. Save your workbook in your usual folder as [your initials] Excel 7-7 (Figure 7-78).

24. Close the workbook and hide the *Developer* tab.

25. Move the ***[your initials] Excel 7-7Template*** from the *Custom Office Templates* folder to your usual folder for saving files.

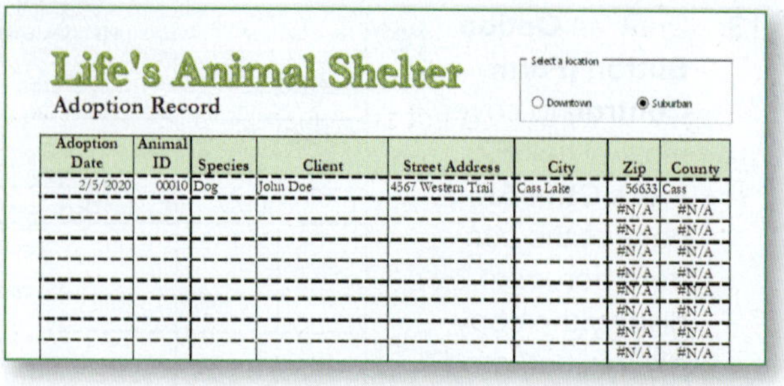

Figure 7-78 Completed worksheet for Excel 7-7

Challenge Project 7-8

In this project, you co-author a workbook with the names of television or streaming shows and series using data validation for the network or provider. *(Note: You must have access to a secondary email address to complete this project.)*
[Student Learning Outcomes 7.2, 7.5]

File Needed: None
Completed Project File Name: ***[your initials] Excel 7-8.xlsx***

Create and save a workbook as [your initials] Excel 7-8. Modify your workbook according to the following guidelines:

- In cells **A3:A12**, type the names of ten network, cable, or internet shows, series, or specials. Use real or fictitious names.
- Type Title in cell **A2**. Type Network/Site in cell **B2**, Day in cell **C2**, and Time in cell **D2**. Name this sheet Watch List.
- Type a main title in cell **A1**. Add borders, shading, or other attributes to enhance the look of the worksheet.
- On another worksheet in the same workbook, create a list of network call letters, web URLs, or other identifiers for providers of your shows. Sort the data in a logical order, or in the order in which the names should appear in your data validation list. Then use this list to set validation for the "Network/Site" column on the **Watch List** sheet.
- Complete two rows of data on the **Watch List** sheet.
- Save the workbook to *OneDrive* and share it with your instructor, your secondary email account, or a friend or colleague.
- Open the shared workbook from the email link and use *Excel Online* to add two additional rows of data to the **Watch List** sheet.
- Return to the workbook in Excel and save a copy to your usual folder.

Challenge Project 7-9

In this project, you select an Excel template from the *Featured* group and create a workbook. You explore features used in the template and edit the workbook to customize it.
[Student Learning Outcomes 7.1, 7.2, 7.3, 7.4, 7.6]

File Needed: None
Completed Project File Name: ***[your initials] Excel 7-9.xlsx***

Create a new workbook from one of the Excel templates in the *Featured* category. Save the workbook as [your initials] Excel 7-9. Modify your workbook according to the following guidelines:

- Review sample data and formulas in the workbook created from the template.
- Determine if hidden elements (worksheets, columns, rows) are included and display them.
- Use *Find & Select* and *Go To Special* to locate data validation, if any. If the workbook includes data validation, edit the settings to make a change appropriate for the worksheet. If the template has no data validation, identify a cell range and build and apply data validation.
- Enter or edit sample data to reflect your work or personal circumstances.
- Insert a comment or note to explain the purpose of the workbook.
- Identify and insert a form control that enhances an element in the workbook.
- Inspect the workbook and remove metadata that you think can be safely removed.
- Check the workbook's compatibility and copy the results to a new sheet.

Challenge Project 7-10

In this project, you create a template to keep track of your course grades. You include a combo box control to select the semester as well as data validation to select course codes and grades.
[Student Learning Outcomes 7.1, 7.2, 7.3]

File Needed: None
Completed Project File Names: ***[your initials] Excel 7-10Template.xltx*** and ***[your initials] Excel 7-10.xlsx***

Create and save an Excel template named as [your initials] Excel 7-10Template in the *Custom Office Templates* folder. Modify your workbook according to the following guidelines:

- In cells **A3:D3**, type the labels Department Code, Course Number, Course Name, and Grade. Name the sheet My Grades.
- Format cells **A3:D9** with borders or shading. This part of your template represents one semester.
- Type a main label in cell **A1** to indicate the purpose of the worksheet. Complete formatting of the data as desired.

- On another sheet in column **A**, enter data for the "Department Code" column. Department codes are indicators such as BUS, MTH, or COM. Enter codes for six departments, occupying six rows in column **A**.
- On the same sheet in column **B**, enter data for letter grades. Use A through F or other letter or number assignments. Enter at least five grade possibilities.
- In column **C**, enter a list with four semester identifiers: Fall, Winter, Spring, and Summer.
- On the **My Grades** sheet, create data validation lists for the "Department Code" and "Grade" columns.
- Insert a combo box control that covers cells **E4:F4**. Format the control to use the semester names on your second sheet and link the control to cell **E3**. Test the control and then position it to cover the linked cell.
- Copy cells **A1:D9** to start in cell **A12** for another semester. Copy the control to row **12** and then edit the copied control to use the correct linked cell.
- Save and close the template.
- Create a workbook from the template, complete data for two semesters, and save the workbook as [your initials] Excel 7-10.
- Remove the *Developer* tab and move the template from the *Custom Office Templates* folder to your work folder.

CHAPTER 8

Working with Macros

CHAPTER OVERVIEW

Routine tasks such as entering the same label or moving and copying a worksheet can often be handled by macros. A ***macro*** is a series of instructions and keystrokes that executes a command. In this chapter, you learn how to run and record a macro, how to edit and write a macro in the Visual Basic Editor, and how to create a macro-enabled workbook.

STUDENT LEARNING OUTCOMES (SLOs)

After completing this chapter, you will be able to:

SLO 8.1 Run a macro (p. E8-500).

SLO 8.2 Record and save a macro (p. E8-501).

SLO 8.3 Use form controls with macros (p. E8-505).

SLO 8.4 Edit and write macro code (p. E8-510).

SLO 8.5 Record a macro with relative references (p. E8-518).

SLO 8.6 Save a macro-enabled template (p. E8-519).

SLO 8.7 Use a macros-only workbook (p. E8-520).

CASE STUDY

In the Pause & Practice projects in this chapter, you work with a macro-enabled Excel workbook for Paradise Lakes Resort. You run and record macros, assign them to buttons, and create macro-enabled templates.

Pause & Practice 8-1: Run and record a macro.

Pause & Practice 8-2: Use form controls and edit a macro.

Pause & Practice 8-3: Record a macro with relative references and save a macro-enabled template.

EXCEL

SLO 8.1

Running a Macro

A macro is saved in an Excel macro-enabled workbook which has an ***.xlsm*** file name extension. When you open a macro-enabled workbook, a security message bar informs you that macros are disabled. You must enable macros to run or edit them.

Macro Security

Macros are targets for viruses, malware, or malicious code. The *Document Inspector* identifies macros but cannot remove them as shown in Figure 8-1. As a result, users are able to include macros in shared workbooks.

Enable macros only when you know they can be trusted. Determine and set macro security settings in the *Trust Center* [*File* tab, *Options* group]. Alternatively, the *Developer* tab has a *Macro Security* button that opens the *Macro Settings* pane in the *Trust Center*. The default option in the Excel *Trust Center* disables all macros as a workbook opens

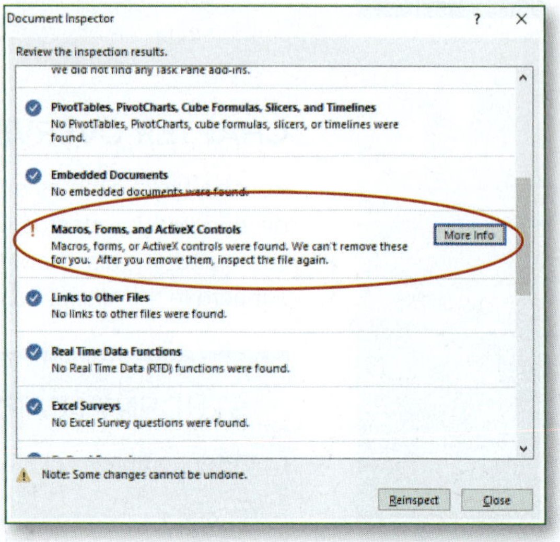

Figure 8-1 ***Document Inspector*** **does not remove macros**

▸HOW TO: Display the Developer Tab and Check Macro Settings

1. Click the **File** tab and select **Options**.
   - The *Excel Options* dialog box opens.
2. Click **Customize Ribbon** in the left pane.
3. Select the **Developer** box in the *Main Tabs* list and click **OK**.
4. Click the **Macro Security** button [*Developer* tab, *Code* group].
   - The *Trust Center* window opens to the *Macro Settings* pane (Figure 8-2).
5. Verify or select the **Disable all macros with notification** button.
6. Click **OK** to close the *Trust Center*.
   - A workbook with macros opens with a security message bar.
   - The macros cannot be run or edited.
7. Click **Enable Content** in the message bar to enable macros.

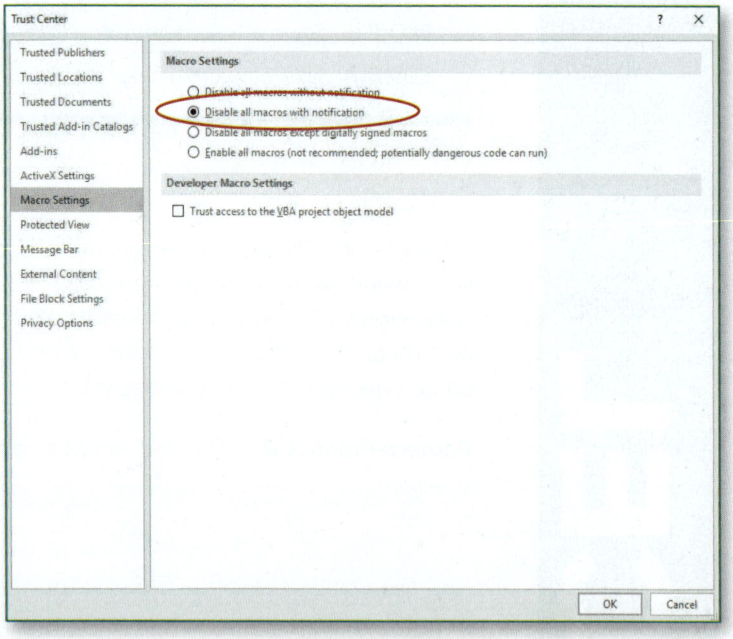

Figure 8-2 ***Macro Settings*** **in the** ***Trust Center***

MORE INFO

If you select *Enable All Macros* in the *Trust Center*, the *Security Warning* bar does not open when you open a workbook with macros.

Run a Macro

Once macros are enabled, run a macro to execute its commands. Run a macro by selecting the macro name in the *Macro* dialog box and clicking **Run** or by using the keyboard shortcut, if any, for the macro.

As long as a workbook is open, its macros are available in any open workbook. For example, run a macro stored in *Workbook 2* while working in *Workbook 1* as long as *Workbook 2* is open. The *Macro* dialog box lists the names of macros from all open workbooks. When a macro runs, it carries out the commands or enters data in the current workbook. After the macro is run, edit data entered by the macro as usual.

Macro-related commands are in the *Code* group on the *Developer* tab. You can also run and record a macro from the *Macros* button on the *View* tab.

▶HOW TO: Run a Macro

1. Open the workbook.
2. Click **Enable Content** in the security bar (Figure 8-3).
   - The security bar may not display if you enabled macros in the workbook in your current work session.
3. Click the **Macros** button [*Developer* tab, *Code* group].
   - The *Macro* dialog box lists the names of available macros.
   - The list includes macros from all open workbooks.
4. Select the macro name in the list (Figure 8-4).

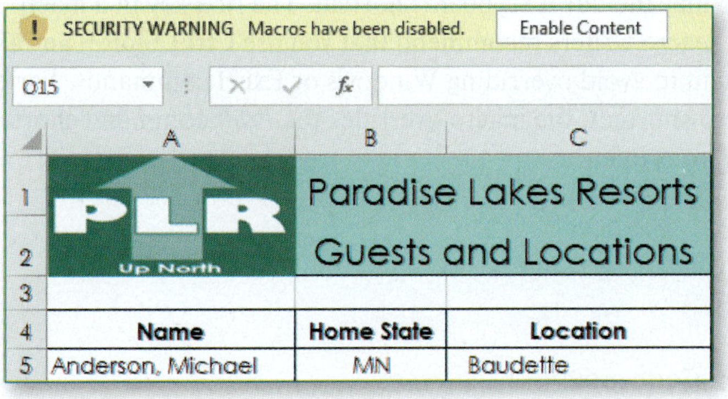

Figure 8-3 ***Security Warning*** **bar for a workbook with macros**

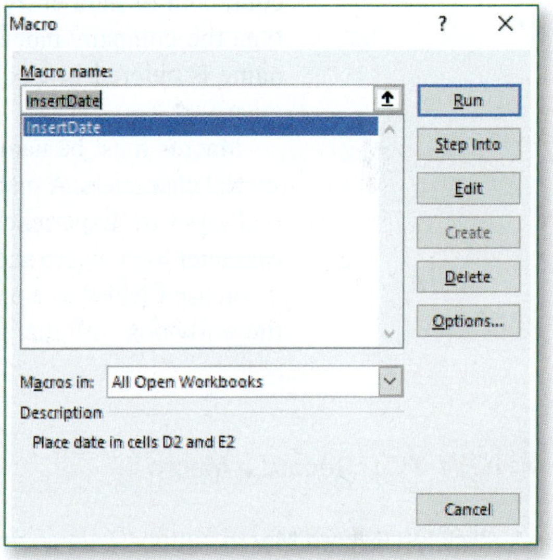

Figure 8-4 ***Macro*** **dialog box**

5. Click **Run**.
   - The macro executes its commands in the worksheet.
   - Delete a macro by selecting its name and clicking **Delete** in this dialog box.

> **ANOTHER WAY**
>
> Click the **Macros** button on the *View* tab to open the *Macro* dialog box.

SLO 8.2

Recording and Saving a Macro

Macros are programs that carry out routine, repetitive tasks. If you regularly print two copies of completed worksheets, for example, you can record a macro that performs the steps for the print command. Then, with the click of a button or a keyboard shortcut, your print command runs.

Excel macros are recorded. You perform all the steps in a worksheet, and Excel encodes each action. The code underlying a macro uses the programming language ***Visual Basic for Applications***, referred to as ***VBA***. Because you "record" a macro, you don't need to know VBA to create a macro.

Macros are saved in a workbook. You can save a macro in the current workbook, in a new workbook, or in a special macros-only workbook.

Record a Macro

Before you begin to record, practice what you want to do so that your steps while recording are error-free. For example, if you want to record a macro to open an inventory workbook, carry out the task before you record the macro to identify folder and file names. A macro records every step and every keystroke, including incorrect or unnecessary steps.

Once you know all the steps, start to record the macro. As you record, perform the commands or type the data. When you reach the last step, click the **Stop Recording** button. To test your macro, delete the data or undo the commands that you carried out during recording. Then run your macro.

By default, a macro is recorded with absolute references to the cell locations for each command or data entry task. Positioning commands are not included in the macro. If you type the company name in cell A32 while recording, the macro records that the company name is entered in cell A32. The active cell can be any worksheet cell when you run the macro.

Macros must be named. The name must begin with a letter and cannot contain spaces or special characters. A macro may include a keyboard shortcut. The first key in a macro shortcut is always **Ctrl**. Experienced macro writers recommend that you use **Ctrl+Shift+ any alphabetic character** for a macro shortcut to avoid overriding Windows or Excel commands. For example, if you use **Ctrl+P** as a macro shortcut, the macro overrides the *Print* command shortcut when the workbook with that macro is open.

▸HOW TO: Record a Macro

1. Click the **Record Macro** button [*Developer* tab, *Code* group].
   - The *Record Macro* dialog box opens.
   - A default name displays.
2. Type a name for the macro in the *Macro name* box.
   - Begin the name with a letter.
   - Do not space between words; separate words with an underscore if desired.
3. Click the **Shortcut key** box.
4. Press **Shift** and type a letter for the shortcut.
   - A shortcut is optional.
5. Click the **Store macro in** drop-down list and choose **This Workbook**.
6. Press **Tab** and type an optional explanation in the *Description* box (Figure 8-5).
   - The description displays as a comment in the VBA code.
7. Click **OK**.
   - The *Record Macro* button toggles to the *Stop Recording* button.

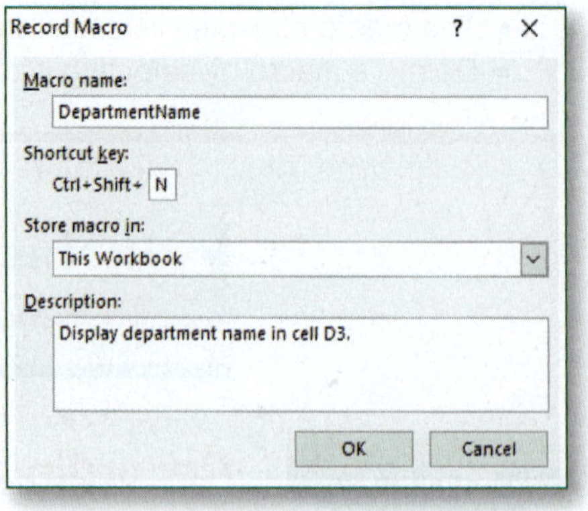

Figure 8-5 Macro name, shortcut, and description

8. Complete each task for the macro.
   - Select a cell and enter data.
   - Select cells and give a command.
   - Correct errors as usual while recording.
9. Click the **Stop Recording** button [*Developer* tab, *Code* group].
   - The data and commands performed as you recorded the macro are part of the worksheet.
10. Delete the data or undo commands that were completed while recording the macro.
11. Run the macro to test it.

ANOTHER WAY

The *Status* bar includes a *Record Macro* button next to the mode indicator. Its *ScreenTip* is *No macros are currently being recorded. Click to begin recording a new macro*. This button toggles to a button to stop recording.

MORE INFO

To change the shortcut for a macro, open the *Macro* dialog box and select **Options**.

Save a Macro-Enabled Workbook

You must save a workbook that includes macros as a ***macro-enabled workbook***. The .xlsm format allows for the inclusion of the VBA modules that store the macros. If you try to save a workbook with macros as a regular Excel workbook, a message box, shown in Figure 8-6, reminds you that your VBA work cannot be saved in a regular workbook.

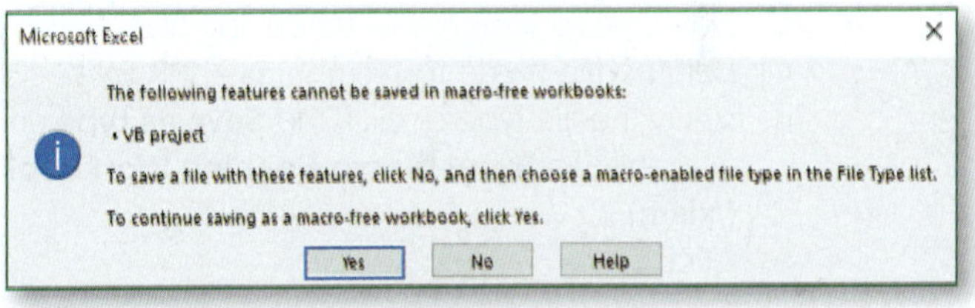

Figure 8-6 Macros can only be saved in macro-enabled workbooks

▸HOW TO: Save a Macro-Enabled Workbook

1. Click the **File** tab and select **Save As**.
2. Navigate to the desired folder location.
   - Save macro-enabled workbooks in any folder.
3. Type or edit the file name.
4. Click the **Save as type** arrow and choose **Excel Macro-Enabled Workbook (.xlsm)** (Figure 8-7).
5. Click **Save**.
   - The workbook is saved and remains open.

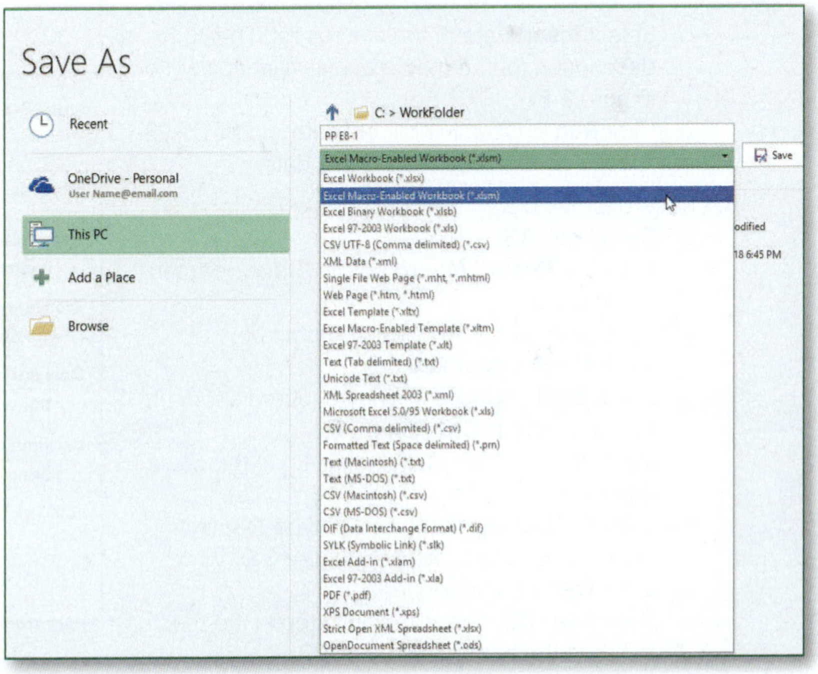

Figure 8-7 Choose the file type for a macro-enabled workbook

PAUSE & PRACTICE: EXCEL 8-1

In this project, you open a macro-enabled workbook for Paradise Lakes Resort. You enable the macros, run a macro to enter the date, and record a macro to format and enter a label.

File Needed: ***ParadiseLakes-08.xlsm*** *(Student data files are available in the* Library *of your SIMnet account.)*
Completed Project File Name: ***[your initials] PP E8-1.xlsm***

1. Check macro security and show the *Developer* tab.
   a. Click the **Options** command [*File* tab] and select **Trust Center** in the left pane.
   b. Choose **Trust Center Settings**.
   c. Click **Macro Settings** in the left pane.
   d. Verify or select the **Disable all macros with notification** button and click **OK**.
   e. Click **Customize Ribbon** in the left pane.
   f. Select the **Developer** check box in the *Main Tabs* list and click **OK**.
2. Open the ***ParadiseLakes-08.xlsm*** workbook from your student data files and click **Enable Content** in the security bar. (The message bar may not open if you have enabled macros earlier in this work session.)
3. Save the workbook as a macro-enabled workbook.
   a. Click the **File** tab and select **Save As**.
   b. Navigate to your folder for saving files.
   c. Edit the file name to [your initials] PP E8-1.
   d. Verify the file type or click the **Save as type** arrow and choose **Excel Macro-Enabled Workbook (.xlsm)**.
   e. Click **Save**.
4. Run a macro.
   a. Click the **Macros** button [*Developer* tab, *Code* group] to open the *Macro* dialog box.
   b. Select **InsertDate** in the macros list. The description for the macro explains what it will do (Figure 8-8).
   c. Click **Run** to insert the current date in cells D2:E2.
   d. *AutoFit* column **E** to display the date.
5. Record a macro.
   a. Select cell **A3**.
   b. Click the **Record Macro** button [*Developer* tab, *Code* group].
   c. Type DeptName in the *Macro name* box.
   d. Click the **Shortcut key** box.
   e. Press **Shift** and type n. The keyboard shortcut for the macro is **Ctrl+Shift+N**.
   f. Verify that *This Workbook* displays in the *Store macro in* box.
   g. Click the **Description** box and type Display department name in cell D3. (Figure 8-9).
   h. Click **OK** to begin recording.
   i. Select cell **D3**. This is the first step in the macro, to move the active cell to cell D3.

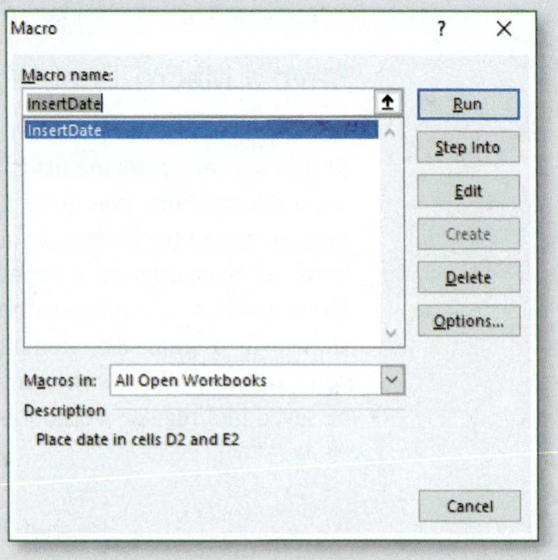

Figure 8-8 ***Macro*** **dialog box with existing macro names**

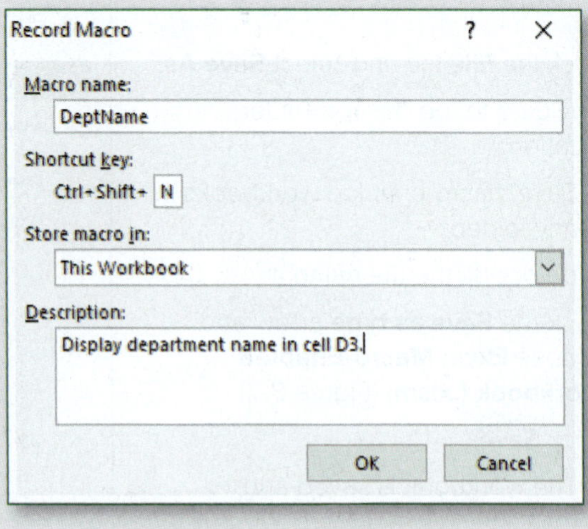

Figure 8-9 Details for the ***DeptName*** **macro**

j. Click the **Home** tab and click the **Bold** button [*Font* group].
k. Click the **Italic** button [*Font* group]. The macro will apply bold and italic.
l. Type Human Resources Department and press **Enter**. This action enters the label and moves to cell D4 (Figure 8-10).
m. Click the **Stop Recording** button [*Developer* tab, *Code* group].

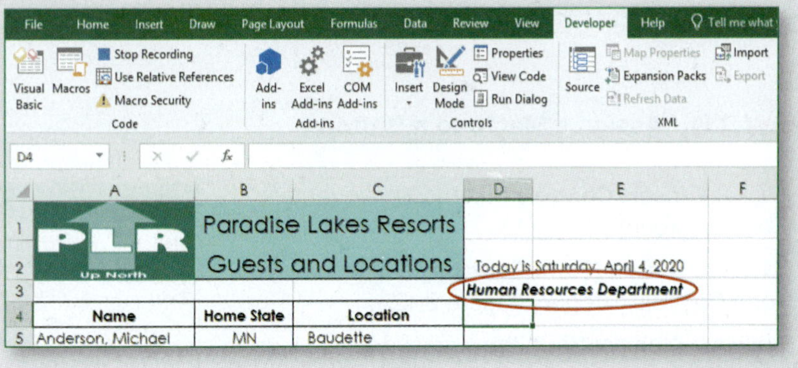

Figure 8-10 Data is entered as macro is recorded

6. Run a macro with a shortcut.
   a. Select cell **D3**.
   b. Click the **Clear** button [*Home* tab, *Editing* group] and choose **Clear All** to delete the label and the formatting.
   c. Select cell **A3**.
   d. Press **Ctrl+Shift+N** to run the macro. The macro inserts the department name in cell D3.
7. Hide the *Developer* tab.
8. Save and close the workbook (Figure 8-11).

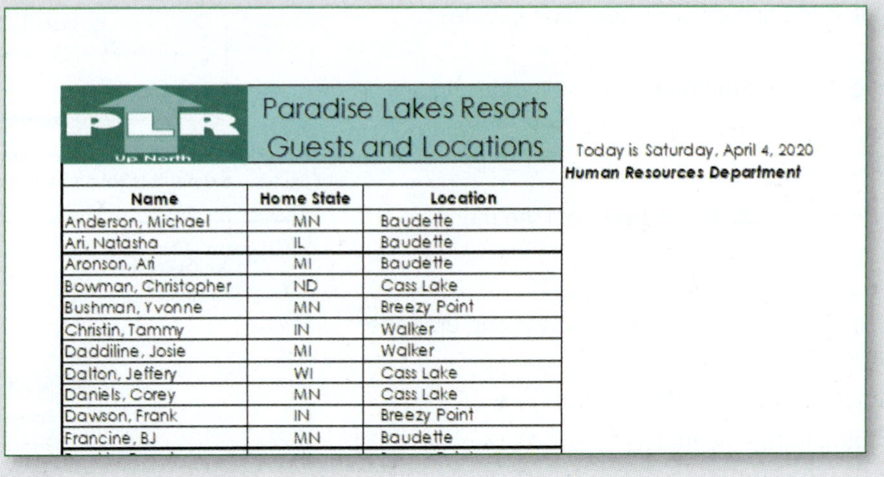

Figure 8-11 PP E8-1 completed

SLO 8.3

Using Form Controls with Macros

You worked with form controls in Chapter 7 when you inserted combo box and option button controls in a worksheet. The ***Button*** is a form control that runs a macro with a single click.

ANOTHER WAY

Choose **Quick Access Toolbar** in Excel *Options*. Select **Macros** from the *Choose commands from* list to display macro names in the open workbook. Select each name and add an icon to the *Quick Access* toolbar to run the macro.

Assign a Macro to a Button

The *Button* form control is available from the *Insert Controls* button on the *Developer* tab [*Controls* group]. As soon as you draw the control, the *Assign Macro* dialog box opens so that you can select a macro to be assigned to the control.

HOW TO: Assign a Macro to a Button

1. Click the **Insert Controls** button [*Developer* tab, *Controls* group].
2. Click the **Button (Form Control)** command in the *Form Controls* category (Figure 8-12).
3. Draw a button control in the worksheet.
   - The *Assign Macro* dialog box opens.
   - The list includes macros from all open workbooks.
4. Select the macro name to assign to the button.
5. Click **OK**.
   - The button displays the default name *Button N*, where *N* is a number.
   - The button control is selected and displays selection handles (Figure 8-13).
6. Right-click the button and choose **Edit Text** from the menu.
   - An insertion point displays within the control.
7. Delete the default label and type the new label.
8. Right-click the button and choose **Exit Edit Text** from the menu (Figure 8-14).
   - Resize the button by dragging a selection handle.
   - Point to a border to display a four-pointed move arrow and drag the button to another location.
9. Click a worksheet cell to deselect the *Button* control.
10. Click the *Button* form control to run the macro.
    - The pointer displays a hand with a pointing finger when it is ready to run the macro.
    - Right-click the control and then left-click a border to select the *Button* control without running the macro.
    - Right-click the control, left-click a border to close the menu, and then press **Delete** to delete a *Button* control.

Figure 8-12 The *Button* control is in the *Controls* group on the *Developer* tab

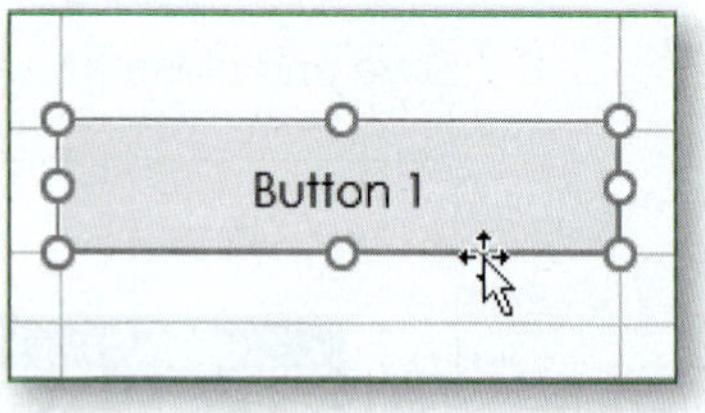

Figure 8-13 The *Button* control displays a default label and selection handles

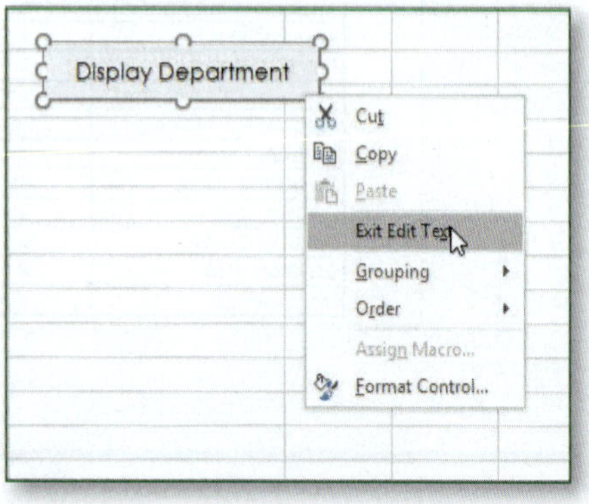

Figure 8-14 Type a new label for a *Button* control and exit editing

MORE INFO

Right-click the *Button* control and choose **Assign Macro** from the context menu to assign a different macro to the button.

Insert an ActiveX Form Control

An ***ActiveX form control*** is a worksheet object that executes VBA commands. The associated VBA commands look like macros but with subtle differences. A workbook with ActiveX controls must be saved as a macro-enabled workbook.

ActiveX controls include a button, a check box, and a combo box like Excel form controls. ActiveX controls provide greater programming power than form controls and recorded macros, but you must write the programming code. You cannot assign a macro to an ActiveX control. *ActiveX Controls* are an option on the *Insert Controls* button on the *Developer* tab [*Controls* group].

▸HOW TO: Insert an ActiveX Check Box Control

1. Click the **Insert Controls** button [*Developer* tab, *Controls* group].
2. Select the **Check Box (ActiveX Control)** command in the *ActiveX Controls* group (Figure 8-15).
3. Draw a check box control in the worksheet.
   - The object displays a default label *Check Box N*, where *N* is a number.
   - The control has selection handles and can be sized and positioned.
   - *Design Mode* is enabled [*Developer* tab, *Controls* group] (Figure 8-16).

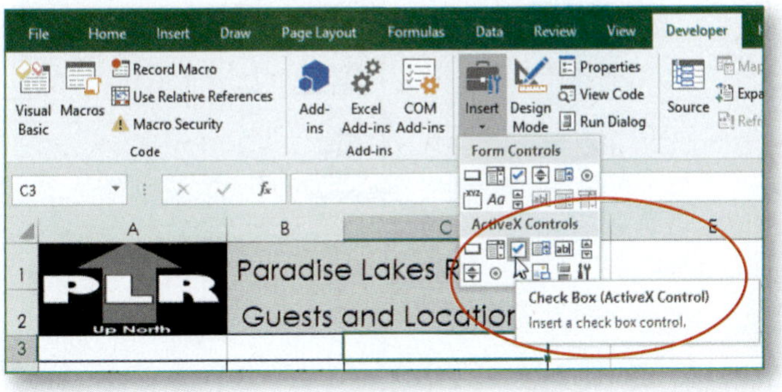

Figure 8-15 *Check Box* ActiveX control

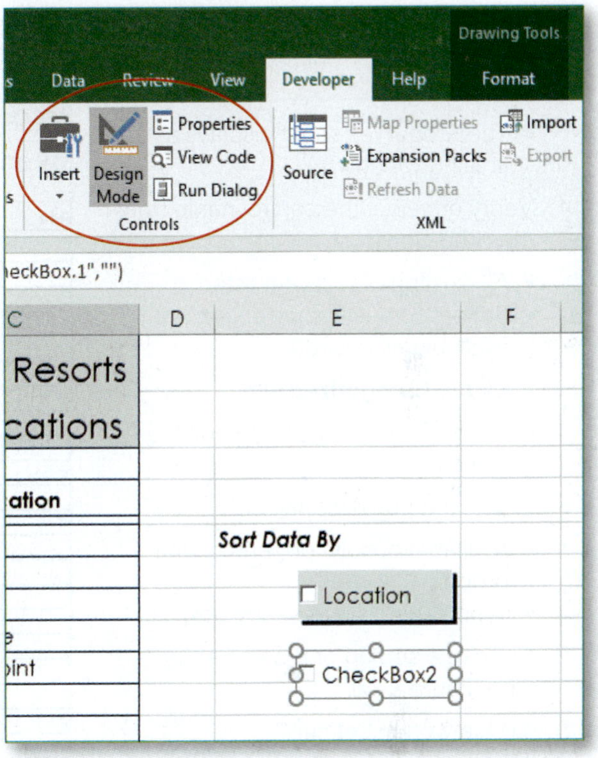

Figure 8-16 The ActiveX control has a label and selection handles

4. Click a worksheet cell to deselect the control.
   - *Design Mode* remains active [*Developer* tab, *Controls* group].
5. Click the **Design Mode** button [*Developer* tab, *Controls* group].
   - *Design Mode* cancels.
6. Click the control to run its commands.

Set Properties for an ActiveX Control

An *ActiveX* control has properties that format and direct the behavior of the control. These properties may be set from a dialog box or by programming commands in Visual Basic code. The *Format Control* dialog box is also available for basic size, protection, or similar attributes.

Use *Design Mode* to set properties or to size and position an ActiveX control. *Design Mode* is automatically enabled immediately after you insert a control and must be active to select the control. When *Design Mode* is off, click the control to run its commands.

HOW TO: Set Properties for an ActiveX Control

1. Click the **Design Mode** button [*Developer* tab, *Controls* group].
2. Select the ActiveX control in the worksheet
   - The selection handles display.
3. Click the **Properties** button [*Developer* tab, *Controls* group] (Figure 8-17).
   - The *Properties* sheet displays as a floating window.
4. Verify or select the control name from the drop-down list.
   - All existing objects are listed.
   - Set properties for any object available as desired.
5. Click the **Categorized** tab.
   - Use the *Alphabetic* list to edit the same properties.
6. Select the property name.
   - Available options depend on the property.
   - Type settings in the entry box.
7. Choose a setting or type an entry (see Figure 8-17).
8. Click a worksheet cell.
   - The control is deselected.
9. Close the *Properties* window.
10. Click the **Design Mode** button [*Developer* tab, *Controls* group] to cancel the mode.

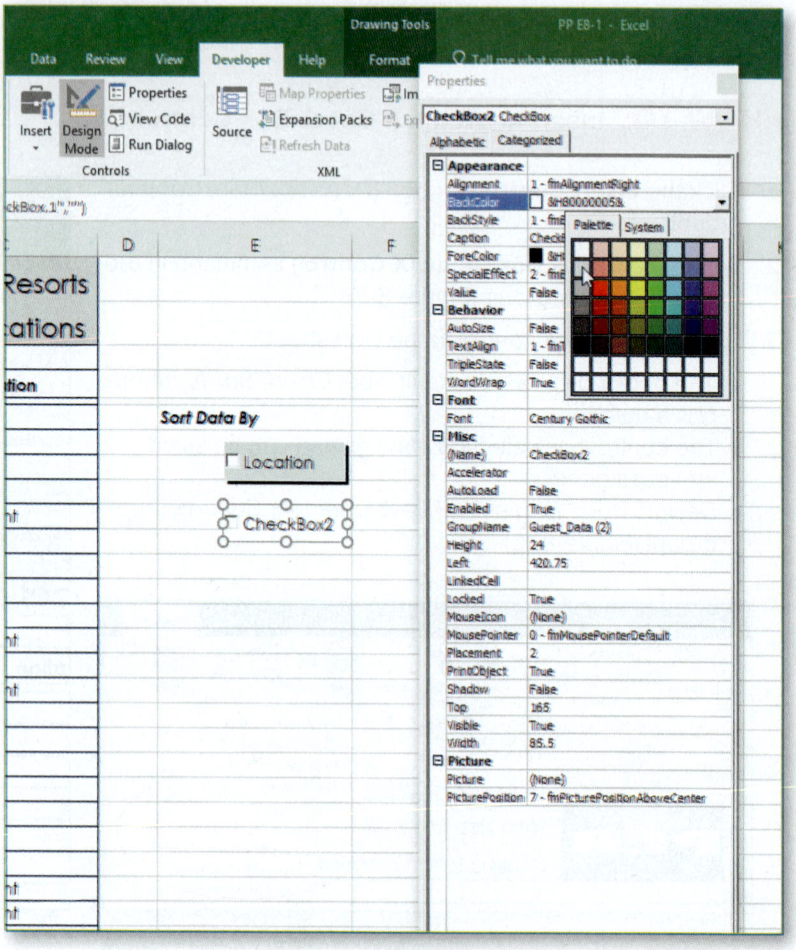

Figure 8-17 *Properties* **window for an ActiveX control**

Use a Data Input Form

A ***UserForm*** is an object created in VBA programming code for display in a workbook. A *UserForm* is a custom dialog box with ActiveX controls and VBA macros to develop an interactive workbook. *UserForms* can streamline data tasks by making it easier for users to complete the work. You can see how a *UserForm* works by adding the *Form* button to the *Quick Access* toolbar.

The *Form* button creates a data input window for list-type data. A ***data input form*** is a dialog box with controls, labels, and entry boxes in a vertical layout. It is a temporary view of worksheet data and is created each time you want to use it.

A data input form displays up to 32 fields or columns and shows one row (record) at a time. In the form, delete, add, or filter the records. After you complete a form and move to the next form, worksheet data is updated.

Display the *Form* button on the *Quick Access* toolbar or in a custom tab or group.

▸HOW TO: Create and Use a Data Input Form

1. Click the **Options** button [*File* tab] and select **Quick Access Toolbar**.
2. Choose **All Commands** from the drop-down list for the *Choose commands from* box.
3. Choose **Form** in the list of commands.
4. Click **Add** to add the command to the *Customize Quick Access Toolbar* list and click **OK** (Figure 8-18).

Figure 8-18 ***Form*** **button added to** ***Quick Access*** **toolbar**

5. Select the cell range including column headings in the worksheet.
6. Click the **Form** button on the *Quick Access* toolbar.
   - A data entry form opens and displays the first record (row) in the range.
   - When more fields exist than can be displayed at one time, a scroll bar is available for viewing all fields.
7. Click **New** to open a blank form (Figure 8-19).
8. Enter data for the new record and click **New**.
   - The row is added to the list.

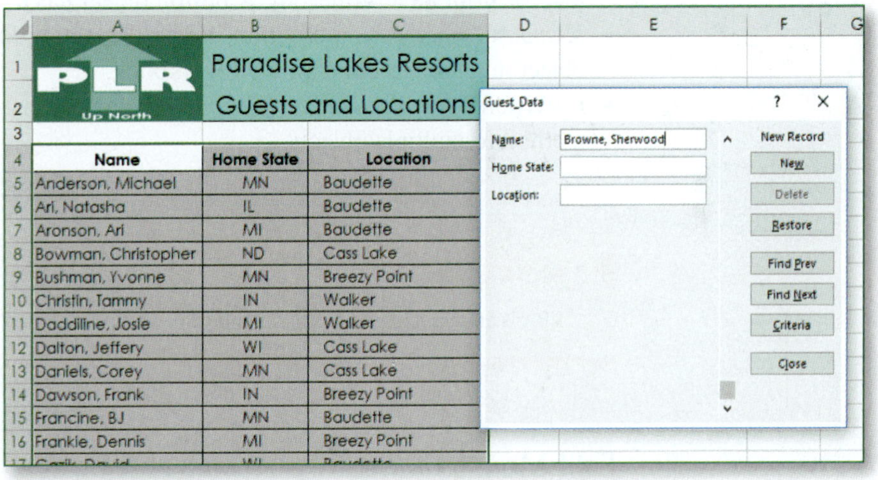

Figure 8-19 Enter a new record in the form

9. Click **Criteria** to open a blank form.
10. Click the field to be used for filtering data and type the criteria (Figure 8-20).
    - You can use wildcard characters.
    - Criteria are not case sensitive.
11. Click **Find Next** or **Find Prev** to find a matching record.
    - The first matching record displays in the form.
    - The search begins at the current form.
    - Scroll to the first or last record by using the scroll bar in the data form.
12. Click **Find Next** or **Find Prev** to find the next record.
13. Click **Close** to close the form.
14. Click the **Options** button [*File* tab] and select **Quick Access Toolbar**.
15. Choose **Form** in the list of commands on the right.
16. Click **Remove** and then click **OK**.

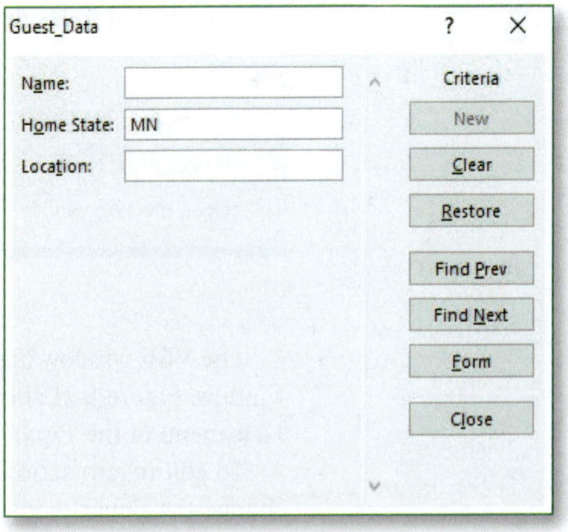

Figure 8-20 Data entry criteria form

SLO 8.4

Editing and Writing Macro Code

You need not know Visual Basic for Applications (VBA) programming to record a macro and assign that macro to an Excel form control. You must know how to write code, however, if you plan to use ActiveX controls or *UserForms* in your work. With experience and practice, you will find it relatively straightforward to make minor changes and write simple code in the Visual Basic Editor (VBE).

Visual Basic for Applications (VBA)

Visual Basic for Applications (VBA) is the programming language that underlies Excel macros and ActiveX controls. As you record a macro, Excel and VBA convert your keystrokes into VBA code. ***Code*** describes the programming commands required for a task to run. VBA uses the following concepts in code development.

- *Objects*: An ***object*** is a tool or element with functions, properties, and data. Examples of objects are *workbook*, *sheet*, *cell*, *range*, and *button*.
- *Properties*: A ***property*** is a characteristic or attribute. A worksheet object has name, default font, or print area properties. A button object has a caption property.
- *Methods*: A ***method*** is a function, service, or action for an object. A method for a workbook object might be to open another workbook.
- *Collections*: A ***collection*** is a group of similar objects. Collections enable you to apply a method to multiple objects.

MORE INFO

VBA is an object-oriented programming language.

Edit Macro Code

The ***Visual Basic Editor (VBE)*** is an application that runs in a window separate from Excel. It opens when you choose the command to edit a macro from the *Macro* dialog box or when you click the **Visual Basic** or the **View Code** button on the *Developer* tab.

ANOTHER WAY

Open the *VBE* window with the keyboard shortcut **Alt+F11**.

The VBE window has three panes, the *Code* window, the *Project Explorer*, and the *Properties* window. Figure 8-21 shows a macro with these three panes visible. Display the panes from the *View* menu in the *Visual Basic Editor* window.

To edit macro actions, you make changes in the *Code* window. In Figure 8-21, for example, change the department name by editing that line in the code. Or, change the cell where the name displays by editing the two lines that specify cell locations.

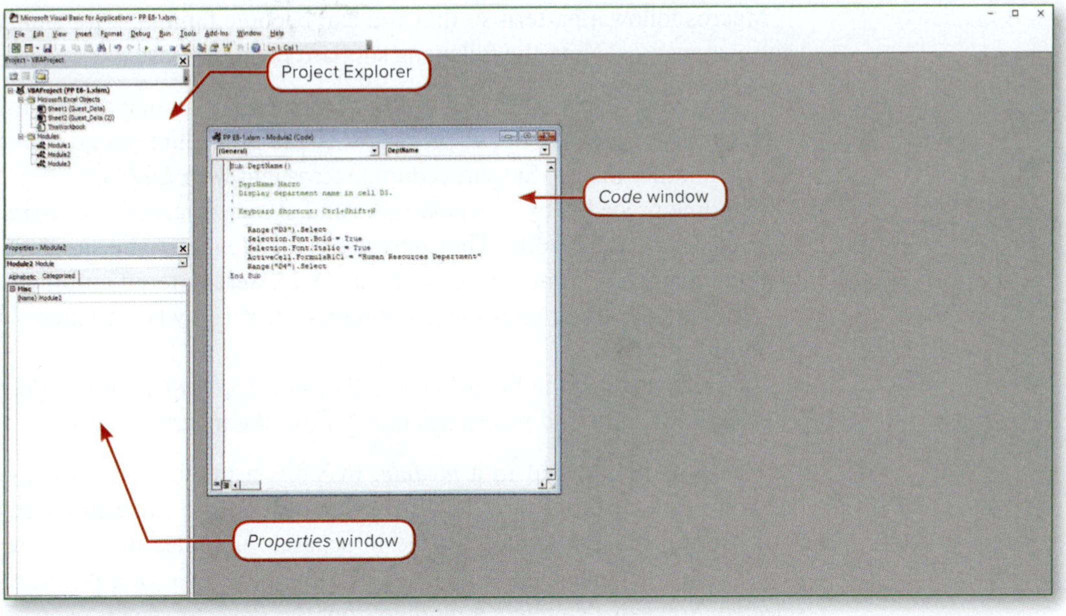

Figure 8-21 The Visual Basic Editor with *Code* window, *Project Explorer*, and *Properties* window

Be careful about punctuation, spacing, and special characters while editing code because they are part of the programming. The VBE identifies errors and highlights them in red with a message box as shown in Figure 8-22.

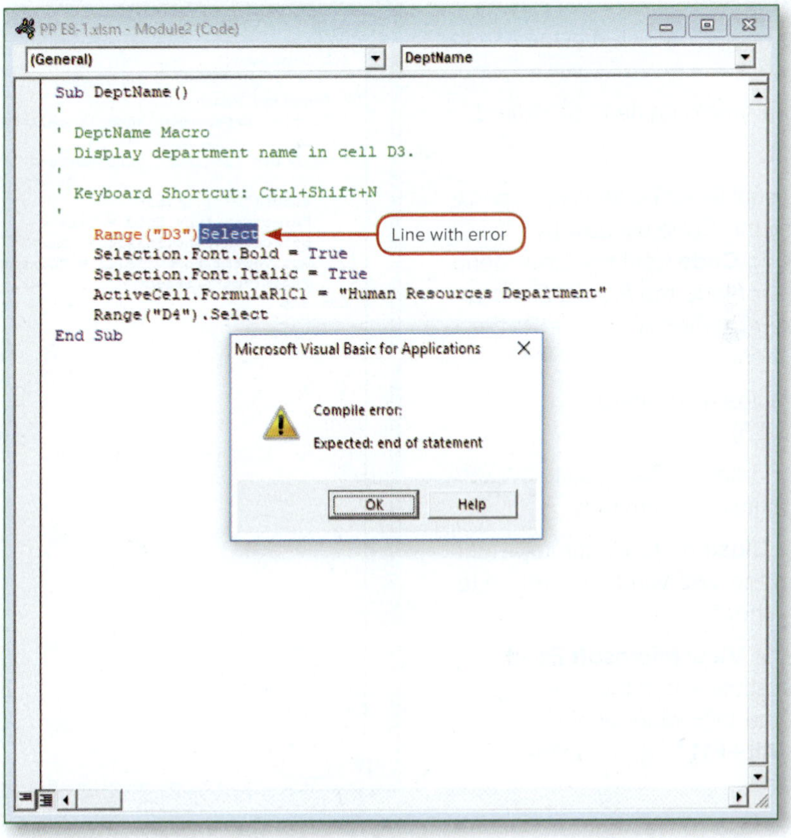

Figure 8-22 Coding error in the Visual Basic Editor

Macros follow a pattern so that you can become familiar with simple code as you analyze your own macros. Note the following similarities in macros:

- The first line displays *Sub* followed by the name of the macro and a set of parentheses. *Sub* means *subroutine* or *sub procedure*. A sub procedure macro runs from the workbook or from another macro. Sub procedure macros end with *End Sub*.
- Each line preceded by an apostrophe and shown in green is a ***comment***. Comment lines are not part of the code. They describe the code, show the shortcut, or separate sections of the macro. Comment lines in Figure 8-23 were entered automatically as the macro was recorded. Enter your own comments when you write a macro in the Visual Basic Editor.
- Lines of text shown in black between *Sub* and *End Sub* are the code. These are Visual Basic commands and properties that control the macro actions.

Macro code is stored in a ***module***. In VBA, a module is a container for the statements, declarations, and procedures. When macros are in the same module, they are separated by a solid border. Macros may also be in separate modules if they were recorded at different times. When you select a macro to be edited in the *Macro* window, the module is automatically selected. You can also select a module from the *Project Explorer* pane.

HOW TO: Edit Macro Code in the VBE

1. Click the **Macros** button [*Developer* tab, *Code* group].
   - Macro names are listed in the *Macro* dialog box.
2. Select the macro name to be edited.
3. Click **Edit**.
   - The Visual Basic Editor (VBE) opens.
   - Display the *Code* window by choosing **Code** from the *View* menu.
   - Display or hide the *Project Explorer* or the *Properties Window* from the *View* menu.
4. Edit each line as needed (Figure 8-23).
   - Add or delete code if you know VBA programming commands.
5. Click the **Close** button in the top-right corner of the *VBE* window to return to the worksheet.
   - Click the **View Microsoft Excel** button at the left of the toolbar to leave the *VBE* window open.
   - Press **Alt+F11** to return to the workbook.
6. Run the macro to test it.
   - The macro is saved with the workbook.

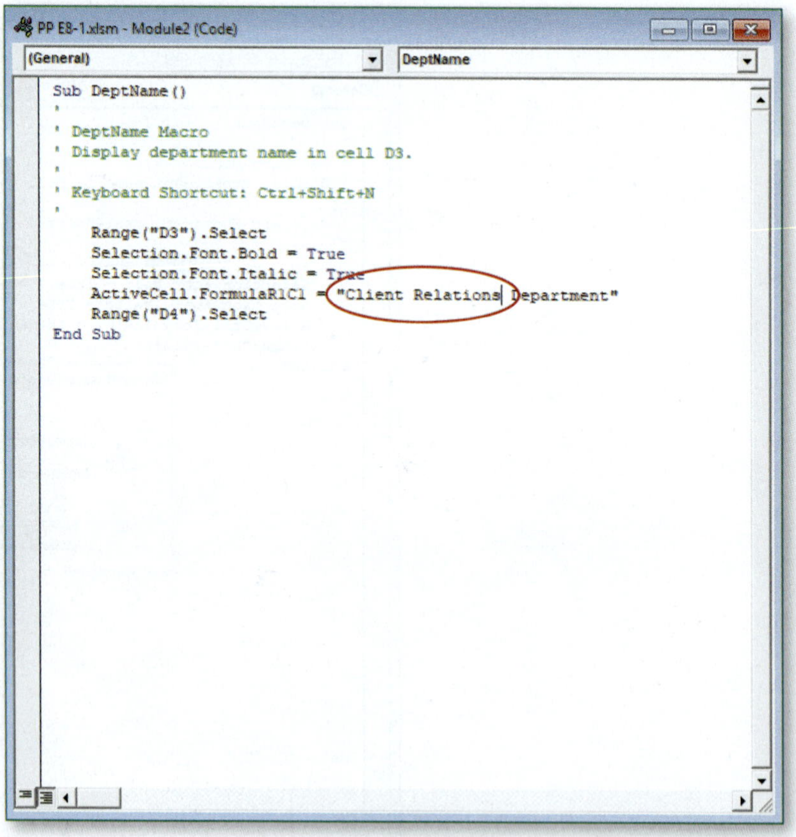

Figure 8-23 Edit code lines in the Visual Basic Editor

Write Code for an ActiveX Control

The VBA language provides sophisticated capabilities for automating tasks in a workbook through form controls. An ActiveX control requires that you write the code in the Visual Basic Editor, because you cannot assign a recorded macro to the control. You can learn programming statements and procedures by viewing the code in your recorded macros.

The worksheet must be in *Design Mode*, and an ActiveX control must be selected to write or edit the underlying code.

HOW TO: Write Code for an ActiveX Control

1. Click the **Design Mode** button [*Developer* tab, *Controls* group].
2. Select the ActiveX control in the worksheet.
3. Click the **View Code** button [*Developer* tab, *Controls* group].
   - The Visual Basic Editor (VBE) opens.
   - The insertion point displays in the code window between the *Private Sub* and *End Sub* lines.
   - Display the *Code* window by choosing **Code** from the *View* menu.
4. Type an apostrophe (') and press **Spacebar**.
5. Type a comment or explanation of the code (Figure 8-24).
   - Comments are optional.
6. Complete the code.
   - Enter code on separate lines or in grouped sections for ease of reading.
7. Close the Visual Basic Editor.
   - Click the **View Microsoft Excel** button to leave the *VBE* window open.
   - Press **Alt+F11** to return to the workbook.
8. Click the **Design Mode** button [*Developer* tab, *Controls* group].
9. Click a worksheet cell.
10. Click the ActiveX control to run the code.
    - The code is saved with the workbook.

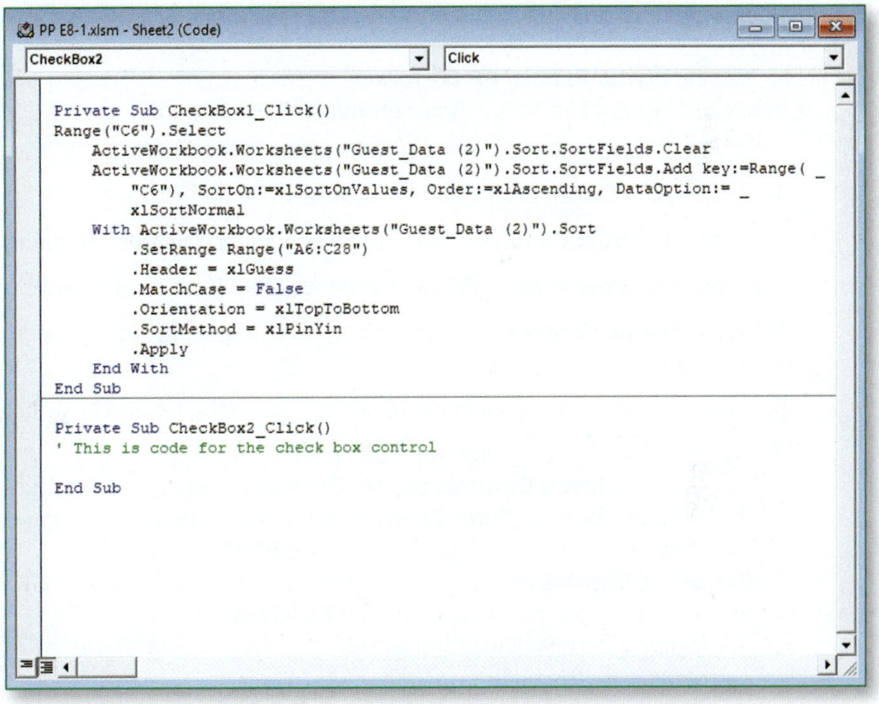

Figure 8-24 Comment line for ActiveX control code

VBA Macro Issues

Common issues arise from recording, writing, or running a VBA macro. Syntax errors display in a message box and identify code that Visual Basic does not recognize. Syntax errors result from typographical errors or incorrectly used statements. Select a problematic line in the VBE window and press **F1** to access a *Help* screen. Table 8-1 describes problems that prohibit a macro from running successfully.

Table 8-1: Common Macro Issues and Solutions

Macro Issue	Solution
Macros are disabled without notification when the workbook opens.	Select **Disable all macros with notification** from the *Macro Security* button [*Developer* tab, *Code* group].
Another macro is currently running.	End the current macro before running or recording another macro.
The worksheet is in *Edit* mode.	Press **Enter** to end *Edit* mode and then run or record the macro.
The worksheet tab is being renamed.	Press **Enter** to complete renaming the worksheet and then run or record the macro.
The workbook is protected.	Unprotect the workbook and then run or record the macro.
A dialog box is open.	Close the dialog box and then run or record the macro.

PAUSE & PRACTICE: EXCEL 8-2

In this project, you assign a macro to a button, edit a macro, and complete code for an ActiveX control.

File Needed: ***[your initials] PP E8-1.xlsm***
Completed Project File Name: ***[your initials] PP E8-2.xlsm***

1. Display the *Developer* tab if it is not shown.
2. Open the **Trust Center** and set macro security to **Disable all macros with notification**.
3. Open the ***[your initials] PP E8-1.xlsm*** workbook completed in *Pause & Practice 8-1*.
4. Click **Enable Content** in the security bar. (The security bar may not open if you completed *PP E 8-1* during the same work session.)
5. Save the workbook as a macro-enabled workbook named [your initials] PP E8-2.
6. Assign a macro to a *Button* form control.
   a. Click the **Insert Controls** button [*Developer* tab, *Controls* group].
   b. Click the **Button (Form Control)** command in the *Form Controls* category.
   c. Draw a button control that covers cells **E6:E7**.
   d. Select **DeptName** in the *Assign Macro* dialog box and click **OK**.
   e. Right-click the button and choose **Edit Text**.
   f. Delete the default text and type Display Department as the caption for the button.
   g. Right-click the button and choose **Exit Edit Text**.
   h. Right-click the button and choose **Format Control** (Figure 8-25).
   i. Select **Bold Italic** as the *Font style* on the *Font* tab and click **OK**.
   j. Select cell **A3** to deselect the control.
7. Edit a macro in the Visual Basic Editor.
   a. Click the **Macros** button [*Developer* tab, *Code* group].
   b. Select **DeptName** in the list of macro names.
   c. Click **Edit** to open the Visual Basic Editor (VBE) window. (Choose **Code** from the *View* menu to display the *Code* window if necessary.)

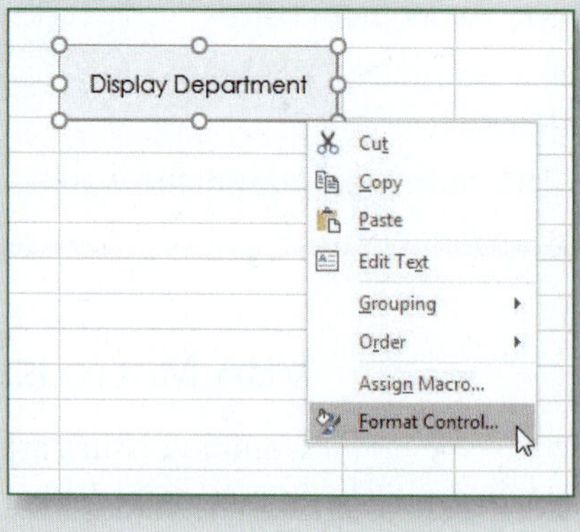

Figure 8-25 Context menu for a *Button* control

d. Select and delete "Human Resources" in the code and type Client Relationships as the department name (Figure 8-26).

e. Click the **View Microsoft Excel** button at the left side of the toolbar.

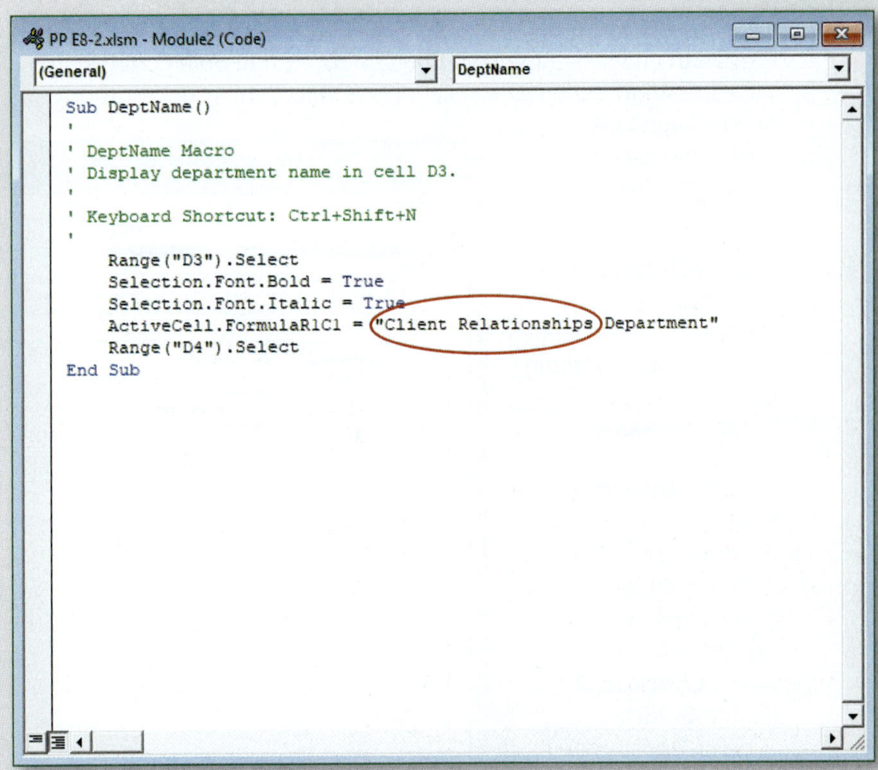

Figure 8-26 Edited code for the macro

8. Run a macro from a *Button* form control.
   a. Select cell **D3**.
   b. Click the **Clear** button [*Home* tab, *Editing* group] and select **Clear All**.
   c. Click the **Display Department** button control.
   The new department name is inserted in cell D3.

9. Insert an ActiveX check box control.
   a. Unhide the **Guest_Data (2)** worksheet.
   b. Click the **Insert Controls** button [*Developer* tab, *Controls* group].
   c. Select the **Check Box (ActiveX Control)** command in the *ActiveX Controls* group.
   d. Draw a check box control in rows **10:11** below the *Location* control.
   e. Click the **Properties** button [*Developer* tab, *Controls* group].
   f. Click the **Alphabetic** tab.
   g. Click the **BackColor** line and click the drop-down arrow.
   h. Select the **Palette** tab and click the gray color icon in the first column, second row.
   i. Click the **Caption** line and replace the default label with Name.
   j. Click the **Height** line and type 25.5, which is the height of the *Location* control.
   k. Click the **Shadow** line and choose True.
   l. Click the **Width** line and type 83.25, the width of the *Location* control (Figure 8-27).
   m. Close the *Properties* window.

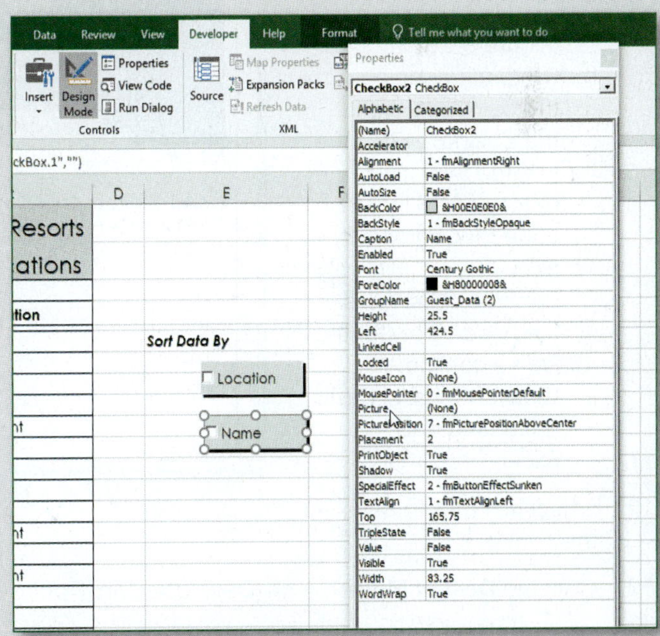

Figure 8-27 *Properties* window for the ActiveX control

10. Align controls.
    a. Press **Ctrl** and select the **Location** control so that both controls are selected.
    b. Click the **Align** button [*Drawing Tools Format* tab, *Arrange* group].
    c. Select **Align Left**.
    d. Click a worksheet cell to deselect the controls.
11. Write and edit code for an ActiveX control.
    a. Verify that *Design Mode* is active [*Developer* tab, *Controls* group].
    b. Select the **Name** control.
    c. Click the **View Code** button [*Developer* tab, *Controls* group].
    d. Click the **Object** arrow at the top of the *Code* window and select **CheckBox2** (Figure 8-28).
    e. Type an apostrophe (') and press **Spacebar**.
    f. Type Sort data by name and press **Enter**. This comment line displays in green.
    g. Select the code lines for the *CheckBox1* control starting at the word "Range" and ending at "End With" and copy it (Figure 8-29).
    h. Paste the code after the comment line for the *CheckBox2* control.
    i. Edit the two occurrences of **C6** in the code for *CheckBox2* to display A6 (Figure 8-30). Cell A6 is the header row for the *Name* column.
    j. Close the Visual Basic Editor and return to Excel.
12. Select cell **E13** to deselect the control.

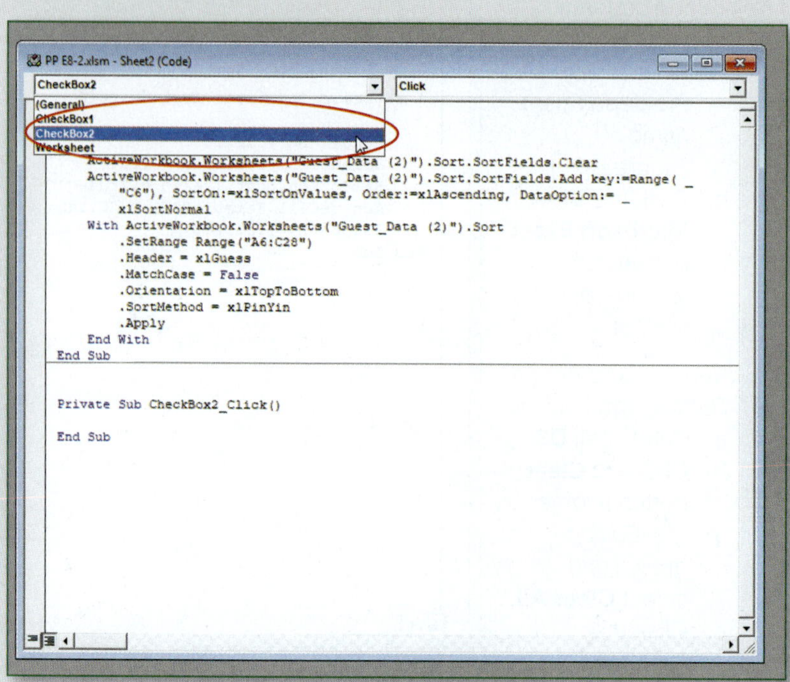

Figure 8-28 Select the object to write its code

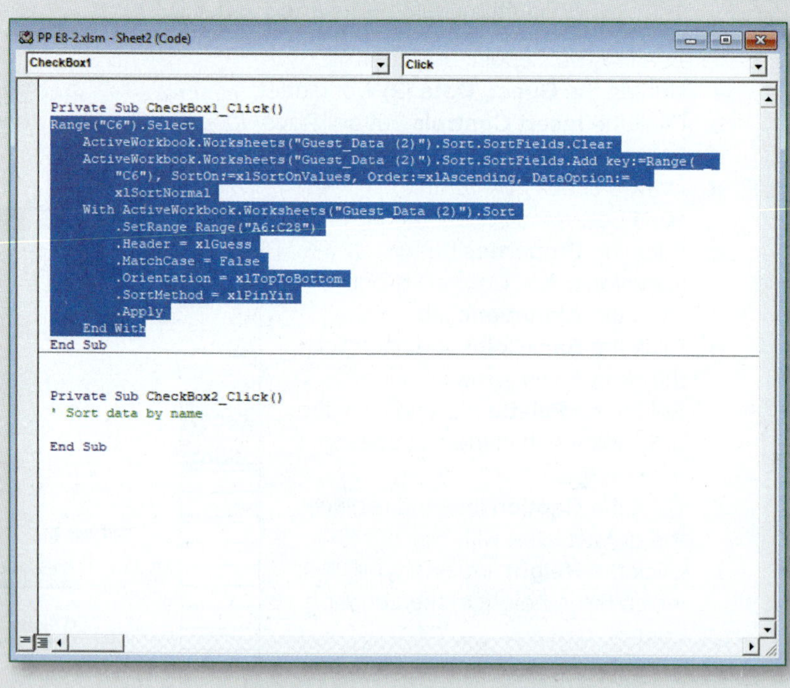

Figure 8-29 Select the code to be copied

13. Click the **Design Mode** button [*Developer* tab, *Controls* group] to turn off *Design Mode*.
14. Click the **Location** control to sort the data by city name.

15. Click the **Location** control to remove the check mark; the sort is not removed.
16. Click the **Name** control to sort the data by name.
17. Save and close the workbook (Figure 8-31).
18. Hide the *Developer* tab.

```
Private Sub CheckBox2_Click()
' Sort data by name
Range("A6").Select
    ActiveWorkbook.Worksheets("Guest_Data (2)").Sort.SortFields.Clear
    ActiveWorkbook.Worksheets("Guest_Data (2)").Sort.SortFields.Add key:=Range( _
        "A6"), SortOn:=xlSortOnValues, Order:=xlAscending, DataOption:= _
        xlSortNormal
    With ActiveWorkbook.Worksheets("Guest_Data (2)").Sort
        .SetRange Range("A6:C28")
        .Header = xlGuess
        .MatchCase = False
        .Orientation = xlTopToBottom
        .SortMethod = xlPinYin
        .Apply
    End With
End Sub
```

Figure 8-30 Edited code for *CheckBox2* control

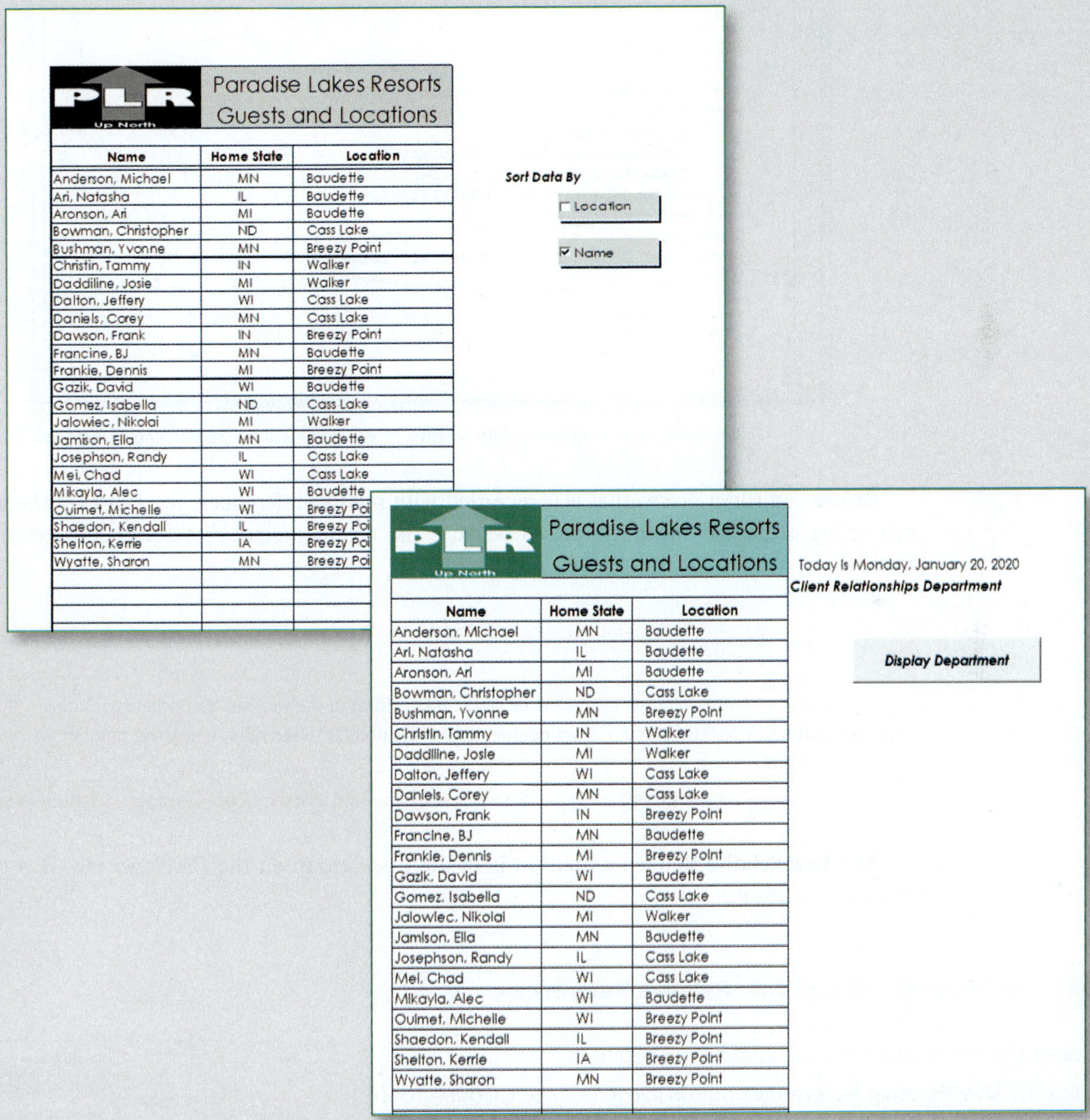

Name	Home State	Location
Anderson, Michael	MN	Baudette
Ari, Natasha	IL	Baudette
Aronson, Ari	MI	Baudette
Bowman, Christopher	ND	Cass Lake
Bushman, Yvonne	MN	Breezy Point
Christin, Tammy	IN	Walker
Daddiline, Josie	MI	Walker
Dalton, Jeffery	WI	Cass Lake
Daniels, Corey	MN	Cass Lake
Dawson, Frank	IN	Breezy Point
Francine, BJ	MN	Baudette
Frankie, Dennis	MI	Breezy Point
Gazik, David	WI	Baudette
Gomez, Isabella	ND	Cass Lake
Jalowiec, Nikolai	MI	Walker
Jamison, Ella	MN	Baudette
Josephson, Randy	IL	Cass Lake
Mei, Chad	WI	Cass Lake
Mikayla, Alec	WI	Baudette
Ouimet, Michelle	WI	Breezy Point
Shaedon, Kendall	IL	Breezy Point
Shelton, Kerrie	IA	Breezy Point
Wyatte, Sharon	MN	Breezy Point

Figure 8-31 PP E8-2 completed

SLO 8.5

Recording a Macro with Relative References

Recorded macros use absolute references, and the active cell can be anywhere in the worksheet when you run the macro. Cell addresses are included in the code. Alternatively, you can record a macro with relative references. In this type of macro, keyboard movement commands are recorded. In Figure 8-32, you can see positioning commands in the line *ActiveCell.Offset(2,0)*. The number 2 is the row offset and zero (0) is the column offset to move the insertion point down two times in the same column.

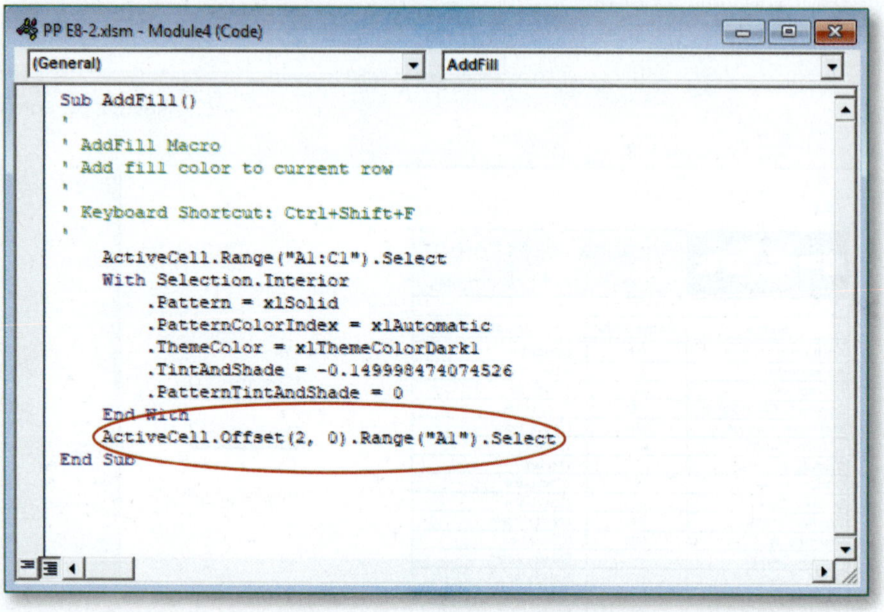
PP E8-2.xlsm - Module4 (Code)
(General)
AddFill
Sub AddFill()
'
' AddFill Macro
' Add fill color to current row
'
' Keyboard Shortcut: Ctrl+Shift+F
'
ActiveCell.Range("A1:C1").Select
With Selection.Interior
.Pattern = xlSolid
.PatternColorIndex = xlAutomatic
.ThemeColor = xlThemeColorDark1
.TintAndShade = -0.149998474074526
.PatternTintAndShade = 0
End With
ActiveCell.Offset(2, 0).Range("A1").Select
End Sub

Figure 8-32 Macro recorded with relative references includes positioning commands

Before you run a macro that was recorded with relative references, you must set the active cell at the presumed starting location because the macro executes its commands relative to that cell.

> **MORE INFO**
>
> A positive row offset number moves the insertion point down in the worksheet; a negative number moves it up. A positive column offset number moves the pointer to the right; a negative number moves it left.

The **Use Relative References** button is in the *Code* group on the *Developer* tab. It is off or inactive by default.

HOW TO: Record a Macro with Relative References

1. Select the cell at which the commands will begin.
2. Click the **Use Relative References** button [*Developer* tab, *Code* group].
   - The button is shaded when it is active (Figure 8-33).
   - The button remains active until you click to turn it off.
3. Click the **Record Macro** button [*Developer* tab, *Code* group].

Visual Basic
Macros
Record Macro
Use Relative References
Macro Security
Code

Figure 8-33 *Use Relative References* is active

4. Type a name for the macro in the *Macro name* box.
   - Begin the name with a letter and do not use spaces between words.
5. Click the **Shortcut key** box, press **Shift**, and type a letter.
   - A shortcut is optional.
6. Verify that *This Workbook* is selected in the *Store macro in* box.
7. Type an optional explanation in the *Description* box.
   - The description appears as a comment in the Visual Basic Editor.
8. Click **OK**.
   - The *Record Macro* button toggles to the *Stop Recording* button.
   - All keyboard positioning commands are recorded.
   - Position the insertion point using keyboard arrow keys or keyboard shortcuts.
9. Complete each task for the macro.
   - Enter and format data.
   - Select cells and give commands.
   - Use the keyboard to position the pointer.
10. Click the **Stop Recording** button [*Developer* tab, *Code* group].
11. Click the **Use Relative References** button [*Developer* tab, *Code* group] to turn off the feature.
12. Delete data or undo commands that were entered as the macro was recorded.
13. Save the workbook.
   - Select the starting cell before running the macro.

SLO 8.6

Saving a Macro-Enabled Template

Templates, because they are model workbooks, often include macros. A ***macro-enabled template*** is an Excel template that includes macros in addition to controls, labels, formatting, and sample data. A macro-enabled template has an ***.xltm*** file name extension and is automatically saved in the default templates folder for your computer. You can save a macro-enabled template in any folder, but its name appears in the *Personal* group in the *Backstage* view for the *New* command only when it is stored in the default folder.

Recording a macro in a template is no different from recording a macro in a regular workbook. When you create a workbook from a macro-enabled template, you must click **Enable Content** to use the macros.

HOW TO: Save a Macro-Enabled Template

1. Enter labels, controls, data, and formatting for the template.
2. Record and test macros.
3. Delete data and undo commands that were entered as macros were recorded.
4. Choose **Save As** from the *File* tab.
5. Choose **This PC**.
6. Choose **Excel Macro-Enabled Template** from the *Save as type* list.
   - The folder updates to the default macros folder.

7. Type the file name for the macro-enabled template (Figure 8-34).
8. Click **Save**.

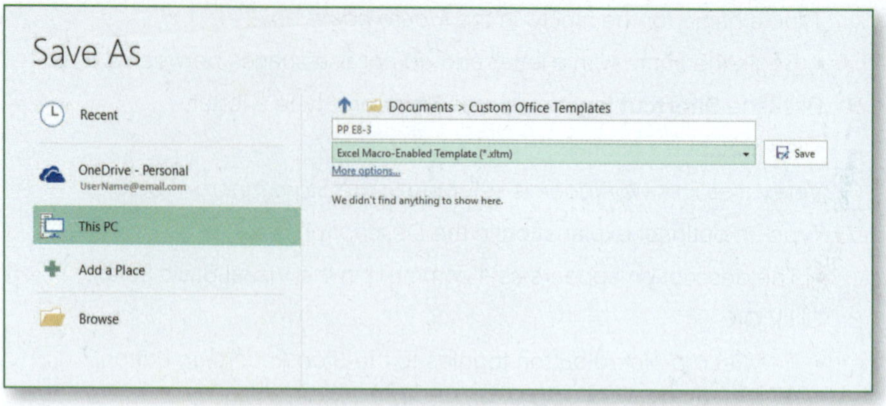

Figure 8-34 Macro-enabled templates are saved in the default templates folder

SLO 8.7

Using a Macros-Only Workbook

A ***macros-only workbook*** is an Excel workbook saved in ***.xlsm*** format that includes only macros, no data. As long as this type of workbook is open, you can use its macros in any open workbook. A macros-only workbook enables you to build a library of your macros.

> **MORE INFO**
>
> Use Microsoft Help to learn more about the *PERSONAL.XLSB* workbook.

The ***Personal Macro*** workbook is a choice in the *Record Macro* dialog box; it is a macros-only workbook. It is saved in the *XLSTART* folder for the current user with a default name of *PERSONAL.XLSB*. Once you have saved a macro in this workbook, *PERSONAL.XLSB* opens automatically as a hidden workbook each time you start Excel so that its macros are always available. If you do not share your computer with others, it is safe to use *PERSONAL.XLSB* for your macros.

> **MORE INFO**
>
> To edit macros in *PERSONAL.XLSB*, you must unhide the workbook [*View* tab, *Window* group]. After editing, hide the workbook.

You can create your own macros-only workbook, save it in your usual working folder, and open it each time you start Excel. Since a macros-only workbook includes no data, it is good practice to type a list of macro names with explanations on *Sheet1* as a reminder to not use the workbook for other work.

HOW TO: Create a Macros-Only Workbook

1. Create a new workbook.
2. Record and test macros.
3. Delete data and undo commands that were entered as macros were recorded.
4. Select cell **A1** and type Macros Workbook.

5. Select cell **A3** and type the name of the first macro.
6. Select cell **B3** and type a brief description of the macro.
   - Include the keyboard shortcut, date of creation, and information about the macro.
   - Use as many cells as necessary to document each macro.
7. Use additional rows to document macros in the workbook (Figure 8-35).
8. Choose **Save As** from the *File* tab and choose **This PC**.
9. Navigate to your folder for saving files.
10. Type a file name for the macros-only workbook.
    - Use a name such as "MacroLibrary" or "MyMacros."
11. Click the **Save as type** arrow and choose **Excel Macro-Enabled Workbook**.
12. Click **Save** and leave the workbook open.
13. Create or open another workbook and use the macros as desired.

	A	B	C	D	E	F
1	Macros Workbook					
2						
3	InsertDate	Insert the current date in cell H1				
4		Keyboard shortcut: Ctrl+Shift+D				
5						
6	AddFill	Add light green fill to the current row				
7		Keyboard shortcut: Ctrl+Shift+F				
8						
9	InsertFooter	Insert footer with company name in center section				
10						
11						

Figure 8-35 Include documentation in a macros-only workbook

PAUSE & PRACTICE: EXCEL 8-3

In this project, you record a macro with relative references to apply shading to a single row in the worksheet. You then save the workbook as a macro-enabled template.

File Needed: ***[your initials] PP E8-2.xlsm***
Completed Project File Names: ***[your initials] PP E8-3.xltm***

1. Set macro security to **Disable all macros with notification** in the *Trust Center*.
2. Open the ***[your initials] PP E8-2.xlsm*** workbook completed in *Pause & Practice 8-2* and click **Enable Content** in the security bar if necessary.
3. Save the workbook as a macro-enabled template.
   a. Choose **Save As** from the *File* tab and select **This PC**.
   b. Type [your initials] PP E8-3Template as the file name for the macro-enabled template.
   c. Choose **Excel Macro-Enabled Template** from the *Save as type* list.
   d. Verify that the default folder is *Custom Office Templates* and click **Save**.
4. Display the *Developer* tab if it is not shown.
5. Record a macro with relative references.
   a. Click the **Guest Data (2)** sheet tab and select cell **A6**. This is where the macro will start its commands.
   b. Click the **Use Relative References** button [*Developer* tab, *Code* group].
   c. Click the **Record Macro** button [*Developer* tab, *Code* group].
   d. Type ApplyFill in the *Macro name* box.
   e. Click the **Shortcut key** box, press **Shift**, and type f.

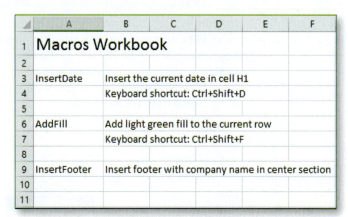

f. Verify that *This Workbook* is selected in the *Store macro in* box.
g. Click the **Description** box, type Apply fill color to current row, and click **OK**. All keyboard commands will be recorded.
h. Press **Shift +** press **right arrow** two times to select cells **A6:C6**.
i. Click the **Fill Color** arrow [*Home* tab, *Font* group] and choose **White, Background 1, Darker 15%** (first column) to apply the fill color to the selected cells.
j. Press **Home** and then press **down arrow** two times to move the active cell to cell **A8**.
k. Click the **Stop Recording** button [*Developer* tab, *Code* group].
l. Click the **Use Relative References** button [*Developer* tab, *Code* group] to turn off the command.

6. Click the **Undo** button in the *Quick Access* toolbar to remove the fill that was applied as you recorded the macro.
7. Select cell **A6** to position the active cell for the start of the macro.
8. Press **Ctrl+Shift+F** to test the macro.
9. Press **Ctrl+Shift+F** to run the macro in row 8.
10. Run the macro in the even-numbered rows with data.
11. Select cells **A6:C28** and delete the data. Select cell **A6**.
12. Select the **Name** check box control to remove the check mark (Figure 8-36).
13. Save and close the template.
14. Move the template from the *Custom Office Templates* folder to your usual folder.
15. Hide the *Developer* tab.

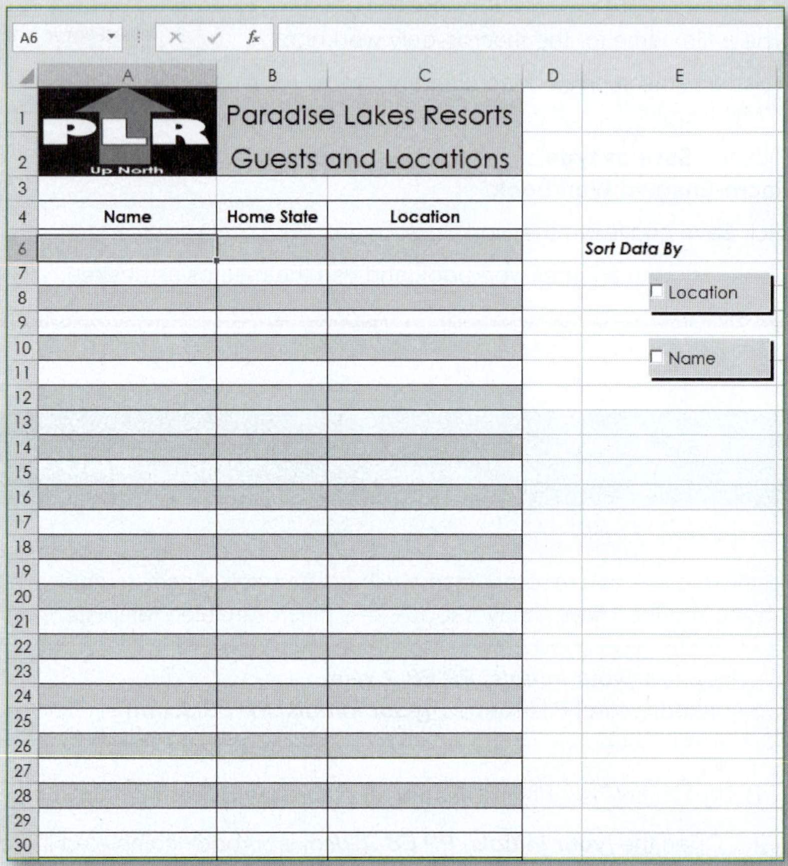

Figure 8-36 Completed template for PP E8-3 includes fill color and ActiveX controls

Chapter Summary

8.1 Run a macro (p. E8-500).

- A ***macro*** is a series of commands saved in a workbook in a ***Visual Basic for Applications (VBA)*** programming module.
- Macros must be saved in a macro-enabled workbook which has an ***.xlsm*** file name extension.
- Because macros may hide viruses and malicious code, choose the option in the *Trust Center* to disable macros as a workbook is opened.
- Macros must be enabled to be run.
- Click the *Macros* button on the *Developer* tab to open the *Macro* dialog box to see the names of existing macros for all open workbooks.
- Run a macro from the *Macro* dialog box or by pressing the macro's keyboard shortcut keys.

8.2 Record and save a macro (p. E8-501).

- A macro is recorded as you perform steps, and your actions are converted to *VBA* ***code*** automatically.
- Practice the commands that you want to record as a macro so that your actual recording is error-free.
- Enter a name for the macro and an optional shortcut in the *Record Macro* dialog. Type a description as desired.
- Macro names must begin with a letter and cannot include spaces or special characters.
- All macro shortcuts include **Ctrl** with an alphabetic character, and it is recommended to include **Shift** with the shortcut.
- While recording a macro, commands are carried out and data are entered in the worksheet. Delete or undo these commands before saving the macro-enabled workbook.

8.3 Use form controls with macros (p. E8-505).

- The ***Button*** form control runs a macro when clicked.
- The *Assign Macro* dialog box opens when you release the pointer after drawing a *Button* control.
- Assign a macro from any open workbook to the *Button* control.
- Right-click a **Button** control and choose a command from the context menu to edit or format the control.
- ActiveX controls are form controls that run VBA code when clicked or selected.
- Use *Design Mode* to select and edit an ActiveX control.
- Format an ActiveX control from its *Properties* window.
- A *UserForm* is a custom dialog box, created from objects and controls in the Visual Basic Editor (VBE).
- Display the *Form* button in the *Quick Access* toolbar to use a built-in data entry form.

8.4 Edit and write macro code (p. E8-510).

- Excel macros are saved in a *Visual Basic for Applications* module, a container for the statements, commands, and data from a macro.
- The ***Visual Basic Editor (VBE)*** is a separate application that runs in its own window.
- The Visual Basic Editor has three panes: the *Code* window, the *Project Explorer*, and the *Properties Window.*
- The *Code* window displays programming statements and properties for each command in the macro.
- The *Code* window includes ***comment*** lines that are preceded by an apostrophe and shown in green.
- For many simple changes, edit code lines in the *Code* window.
- Changes made in the Visual Basic Editor are saved when you save the workbook.
- Write code for an ActiveX control in the Visual Basic Editor.

8.5 Record a macro with relative references (p. E8-518).

- By default, a macro is recorded with cell addresses (absolute references) for each command.
- The active cell can be anywhere in the worksheet when you run a macro that was recorded with absolute references.
- Record a macro with relative references by enabling the *Use Relative References* command in the *Code* group on the *Developer* tab.

- For a macro that is recorded with relative references, select the appropriate cell before running the macro.
- View and edit positioning commands in a macro with relative references in the Visual Basic Editor *Code* window.

8.6 Save a macro-enabled template (p. E8-519).

- A template with macros must be saved as an Excel ***macro-enabled template*** with an ***.xltm*** extension.
- Macro-enabled templates are saved, by default, in the same folder as Excel workbook templates.
- Macro-enabled templates appear in the *Personal* category for the *New* command in the *Backstage* view when saved in the default templates folder.

8.7 Use a macros-only workbook (p. E8-520).

- A ***macros-only workbook*** is saved with an ***.xlsm*** file name extension.
- A macros-only workbook is a way of building a macros library for use in all workbooks.
- When a macros-only workbook is open, you can use its macros in any open workbook.
- Save a macros-only workbook in your usual folders for saving work.
- Select ***Personal Macro Workbook*** in the *Record Macro* dialog box to create *PERSONAL.XLSB* which is automatically saved in the *XLSTART* folder.
- The *Personal Macro Workbook* opens as a hidden workbook each time Excel starts so that its macros are available.

Check for Understanding

The SIMbook for this text (within your SIMnet account) provides the following resources for concept review:

- Multiple-choice questions
- Short answer questions
- Matching exercises

Guided Project 8-1

Boyd Air uses a macros-only workbook and a related template. You edit and record macros in the macros-only workbook. In the template, you record a macro and assign it to a *Button* form control.
[Student Learning Outcomes 8.1, 8.2, 8.3, 8.4, 8.5, 8.6, 8.7]

Files Needed: ***BoydAir-08.xlsx*** and ***BoydAirMacros-08.xlsm*** *(Student data files are available in the* Library *of your SIMnet account.)*
Completed Project File Names: ***[your initials] Excel 8-1Macros.xlsm***, ***[your initials] Excel 8-1Template.xltm***, and ***[your initials] Excel 8-1.xlsx***

Skills Covered in This Project

- Set macro security options.
- Use a macros-only workbook.
- Edit a macro in the Visual Basic Editor.
- Record macros.
- Run macros.
- Record a macro with relative references.
- Save a macro-enabled template.
- Assign macros to *Button* form controls.

1. Set macro security and display the *Developer* tab.
   a. Click the **Options** command [*File* tab] and click **Trust Center** in the left pane.
   b. Click the **Trust Center Settings** button and click **Macro Settings** in the left pane.
   c. Verify or select **Disable all macros with notification** and click **OK**.
   d. Click **Customize Ribbon** in the left pane, display the *Developer* tab, and close Excel *Options*.
2. Open the **BoydAirMacros-08.xlsm** workbook from your student data files, a macros-only workbook (Figure 8-37). Enable the macros if the message bar displays.
3. Save the workbook as a macro-enabled workbook.
   a. Choose **Save As** from the *File* tab.
   b. Type [your initials] Excel 8-1Macros as the file name.
   c. Verify or choose **Excel Macro-Enabled Workbook** in the *Save as type* list.
   d. Navigate to your folder and click **Save**.
4. Run and edit a macro to insert today's date.
   a. Click the **Test Sheet** worksheet tab.
   b. Press **Ctrl+Shift+D** to run the *InsertDate* macro. Today's date displays in cell E1. Widen column E as needed.

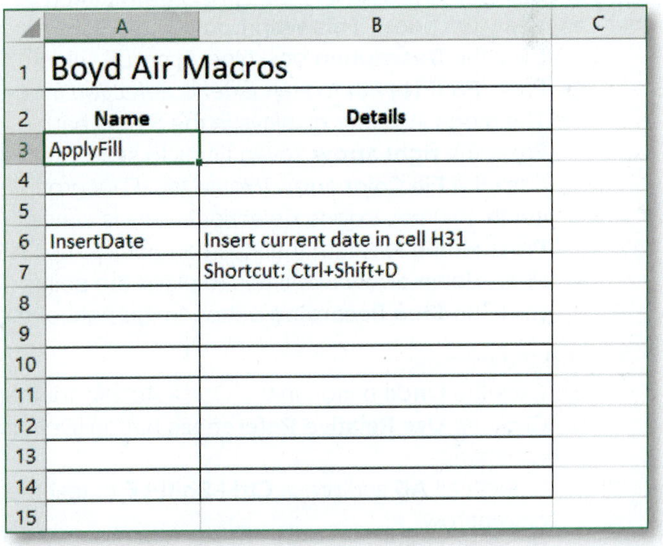

	A	B	C
1	Boyd Air Macros		
2	Name	Details	
3	ApplyFill		
4			
5			
6	InsertDate	Insert current date in cell H31	
7		Shortcut: Ctrl+Shift+D	
8			
9			
10			
11			
12			
13			
14			
15			

Figure 8-37 Workbook includes macros and documentation

c. Delete the contents of cell **E1** and press **Ctrl+Home**.
d. Click the **Macros** button [*Developer* tab, *Code* group].
e. Verify that the **InsertDate** macro name is selected and click **Edit** to open the Visual Basic Editor (VBE) window. (If the *Code* window is not displayed, select **Module1** in the *Project Explorer* pane and then choose **Code** from the *View* menu.)
f. Click between the "H" and the "1" in the second comment line and type 3 so that the address is **H31** as the cell reference.
g. Edit the code *Range("E1").Select* to show H31.
h. Edit the last line of code to show H32 instead of "E2" (Figure 8-38).
i. Click the **Close** button at the top-right corner of the VBE window.
j. Click the **Macros** button [*Developer* tab, *Code* group].
k. Verify that **InsertDate** is selected and click **Run**. The date displays in cell H31.

```
Sub InsertDate()
'
' InsertDate Macro
' Insert date in cell H31.
'
' Keyboard Shortcut: Ctrl+Shift+D
'
    Range("H31").Select
    ActiveCell.FormulaR1C1 = "=TODAY()"
    Range("H32").Select
End Sub
```

Figure 8-38 Edited code for the macro

5. Record a macro to insert text.
   a. Click the **Record Macro** button [*Developer* tab, *Code* group].
   b. Type DateText in the *Macro name* box.
   c. Click the **Shortcut key** box, press **Shift**, and type t.
   d. Verify or choose **This Workbook** in the *Store macro in* box.
   e. Click the **Description** box, type Insert date text, and click **OK**.
   f. Select cell **G31**.
   g. Click the **Align Right** button [*Home* tab, *Alignment* group].
   h. Type This report was run on and press **Enter**.
   i. Click the **Stop Recording** button to the right of the *Ready* indicator in the *Status* bar. The *ScreenTip* for the button is *A macro is currently recording. Click to stop recording*.
   j. Delete the contents of cells **G31:H31**.

6. Record a macro with relative references.
   a. Click the **Use Relative References** button [*Developer* tab, *Code* group] to enable the command.
   b. Select cell **A5** and click the **Record Macro** button [*Developer* tab, *Code* group].
   c. Type ApplyFill in the *Macro name* box.
   d. Click the **Shortcut key** box, press **Shift**, and type f.
   e. Verify or choose **This Workbook** in the *Store macro in* box.
   f. Click the **Description** box, type Apply fill color to current row, and click **OK**.
   g. Press **F8 (FN+F8)** to start *Extend Selection* mode to use directional arrows to select cells. The mode indicator displays in the *Status* bar.
   h. Press the **right arrow** seven times to select cells **A5:H5**.
   i. Click the **Fill Color** arrow [*Home* tab, *Font* group] and choose **Green, Accent 6, Lighter 80%** (tenth column). *Extend Selection* mode is canceled.
   j. Press **Home** to return the insertion point to cell **A5**.
   k. Press **down arrow** two times to place the pointer in cell **A7**.
   l. Click the **Stop Recording** button to the right of the *Ready* indicator in the *Status* bar.

7. Test the macros.
   a. Click the **Undo** button in the *Quick Access* toolbar to remove the fill color.
   b. Click the **Use Relative References** button [*Developer* tab, *Code* group] to cancel the command.
   c. Select cell **A6** and press **Ctrl+Shift+F** to test the **ApplyFill** macro. The fill applies to the current row.
   d. Press **Ctrl+Shift+T** to test the **DateText** macro.

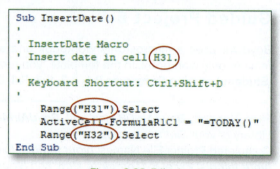

e. Press **Ctrl+Shift+D** to test the **InsertDate** macro.

8. Document and save a macros-only workbook.
   a. Click the **Documentation** sheet tab.
   b. Select cell **B3**, type Apply fill color to current row, and press **Enter**.
   c. Type Shortcut: Ctrl+Shift+F in cell **B4**.
   d. Complete documentation for the DateText macro in cells A9:B10 as shown in Figure 8-39.
   e. Save the workbook and leave it open so that the macros are available.

9. Open the **BoydAir-08.xlsx** workbook from your student data files.

	A	B
1	Boyd Air Macros	
2	**Name**	**Details**
3	ApplyFill	Apply fill color to current row
4		Shortcut: Ctrl+Shift+F
5		
6	InsertDate	Insert current date in cell H31
7		Shortcut: Ctrl+Shift+D
8		
9	DateText	Insert date text
10		Shortcut: Ctrl+Shift+T
11		
12		
13		
14		

Figure 8-39 Documentation for the macros

10. Save the workbook as a macro-enabled template.
    a. Choose **Save As** from the *File* tab.
    b. Type [your initials] Excel 8-1Template as the file name.
    c. Choose **Excel Macro-Enabled Template** from the file type list. The folder updates to the *Custom Office Templates* folder.
    d. Click **Save** to save the template.

11. Assign macros to *Button* form controls.
    a. Click the **Insert Controls** button [*Developer* tab, *Controls* group].
    b. Click the **Button (Form Control)** command in the *Form Controls* category.
    c. Draw a *Button* control that covers cells **J4:K4**.
    d. Select **DateText** in the *Assign Macro* dialog box and click **OK** (Figure 8-40).
    e. Right-click the *Button* control and choose **Edit Text**.
    f. Delete the default text and type Date Text as the label.
    g. Right-click the control and choose **Exit Edit Text**.
    h. Click the **Insert Controls** button [*Developer* tab, *Controls* group] and select the **Button (Form Control)** command.
    i. Draw a second *Button* control that covers cells **J7:K7**.
    j. Select **InsertDate** in the *Assign Macro* dialog box and click **OK**.
    k. Right-click the control and choose **Edit Text**.
    l. Delete the default text and type Date.
    m. Right-click the control and choose **Exit Edit Text**.
    n. Draw a *Button* control that covers cells **J10:K10** and assign the **ApplyFill** macro. Edit the button text to Apply Fill.

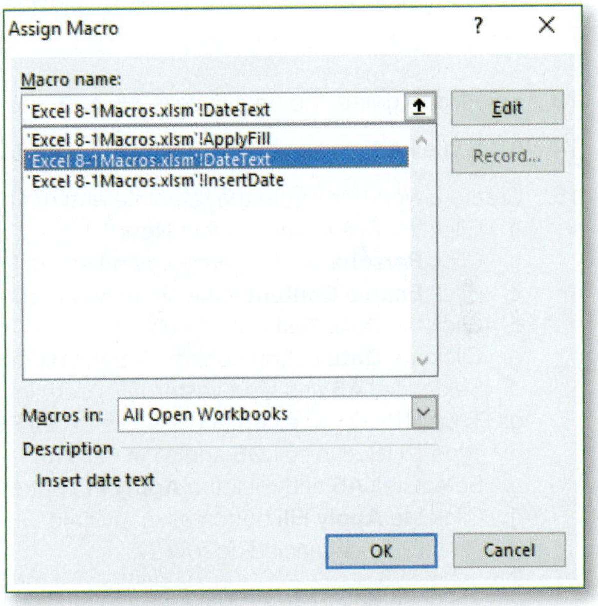

Figure 8-40 Macros are in the macros-only workbook

12. Size and align *Button* form controls.
    a. Click cell **J2** to deselect the controls.
    b. Right-click the **Date Text** button to display its selection handles.
    c. Press **Ctrl** and right-click the **Date** control and then right-click the **Apply Fill** control. Three controls are selected.
    d. Click the **Align** button [*Drawing Tools Format* tab, *Arrange* group] and select **Align Left**.
    e. Click the **Height** box [*Drawing Tools Format* tab, *Size* group] and type 0.25.
    f. Click the **Width** box [*Drawing Tools Format* tab, *Size* group], type 1.25, and press **Enter** (Figure 8-41).
    g. Click cell **J2** to deselect the controls.

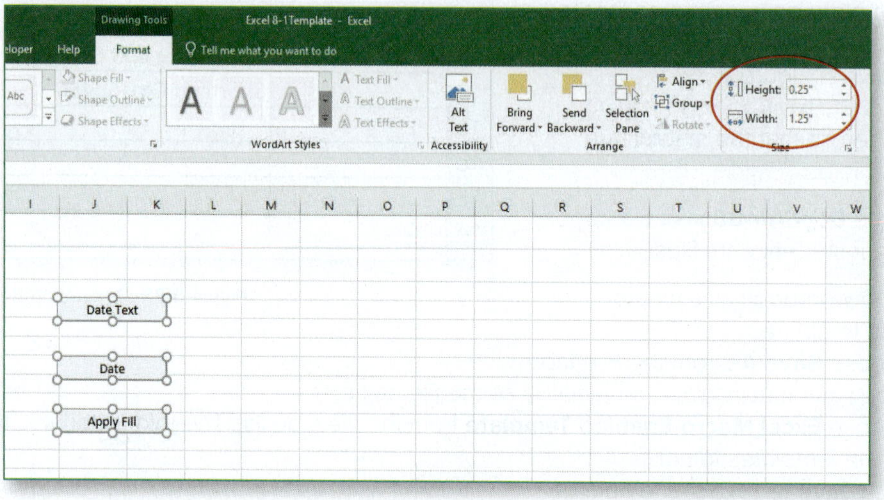

Figure 8-41 Button controls aligned and sized

13. Select and delete the data in cells **A5:A27** and **E5:H27**.
14. Select cell **A5**, and save and close the template. The macros workbook is still open.
15. Create a workbook from the template and run macros.
    a. Click the **File** tab and select **New**.
    b. Click **Personal** as the category and select **[your initials] Excel 8-1Template**.
    c. Click **Enable Content** if the security bar opens.
    d. Click the **Date Text** button control.
    e. Click the **Date** button control. Widen column H as needed to display the date.
    f. Select cell **A5** and type yesterday's date in *mm/dd/yyyy* format.
    g. Type 8:10 am in cell **E5** and 9:30 am in cell **F5**.
    h. Type Delayed in cell **G5** and 55 in cell **H5**.
    i. Select cell **A5** and click the **Apply Fill** button.
    j. Click the **Apply Fill** button as many times as necessary to apply fill color to the odd-numbered rows up to and including row 27.
16. Save the workbook as a regular Excel workbook named [your initials] Excel 8-1 in your usual location for saving files (Figure 8-42).
17. Close the workbook.
18. Save and close ***[your initials] Excel 8-1Macros***.
19. Move ***[your initials] Excel 8-1Template*** from the *Custom Office Templates* folder to your usual folder.
20. Hide the *Developer* tab.

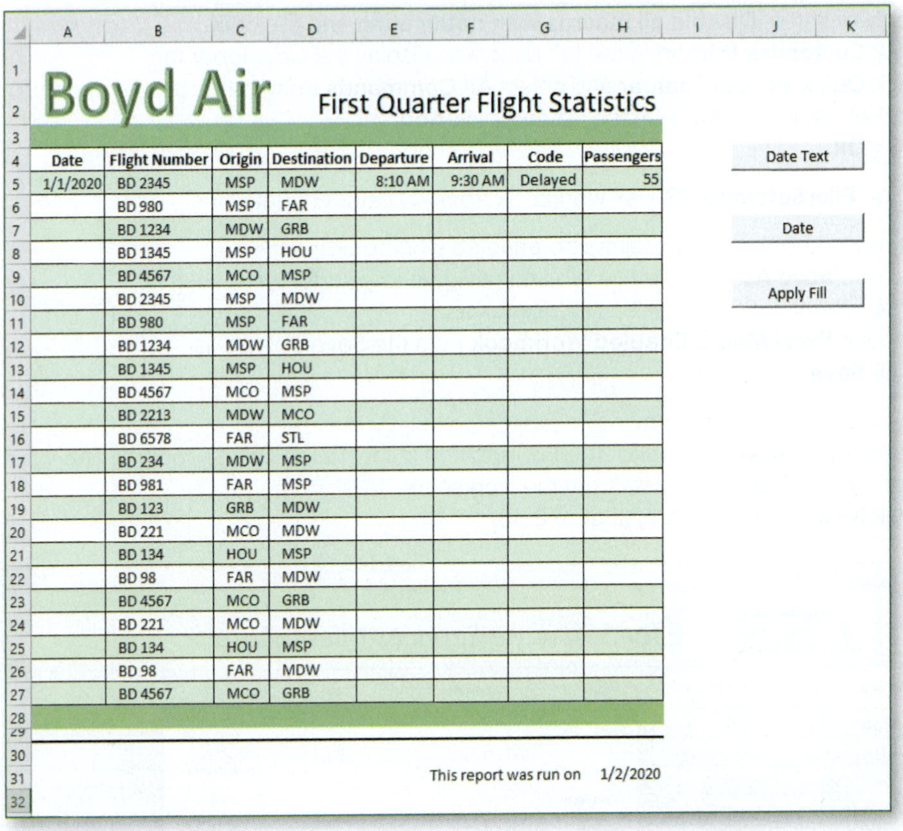

Boyd Air
First Quarter Flight Statistics
Date Text
Date
Apply Fill
Date | Flight Number | Origin | Destination | Departure | Arrival | Code | Passengers
1/1/2020 | BD 2345 | MSP | MDW | 8:10 AM | 9:30 AM | Delayed | 55
BD 980 | MSP | FAR
BD 1234 | MDW | GRB
BD 1345 | MSP | HOU
BD 4567 | MCO | MSP
BD 2345 | MSP | MDW
BD 980 | MSP | FAR
BD 1234 | MDW | GRB
BD 1345 | MSP | HOU
BD 4567 | MCO | MSP
BD 2213 | MDW | MCO
BD 6578 | FAR | STL
BD 234 | MDW | MSP
BD 981 | FAR | MSP
BD 123 | GRB | MDW
BD 221 | MCO | MDW
BD 134 | HOU | MSP
BD 98 | FAR | MDW
BD 4567 | MCO | GRB
BD 221 | MCO | MDW
BD 134 | HOU | MSP
BD 98 | FAR | MDW
BD 4567 | MCO | GRB
This report was run on 1/2/2020

Figure 8-42 Excel 8-1 worksheet completed

Guided Project 8-2

In the Eller Software Services workbook, you use a data form to enter new client information. You also record macros to filter and extract data and to clear filter results.
[Student Learning Outcomes 8.1, 8.2, 8.3, 8.4]

File Needed: ***EllerSoftware-08.xlsx*** *(Student data files are available in the* Library *of your SIMnet account.)*
Completed Project File Name: ***[your initials] Excel 8-2.xlsm***

Skills Covered in This Project

- Set macro security options.
- Display the *Developer* tab and the *Form* button.
- Enter data in a data entry form.
- Record macros.
- Run macros.
- Assign macros to *Button* form controls.
- Edit and print macro code.

1. Set macro security and display the *Developer* tab and the *Form* button.
   a. Select the **Options** command [*File* tab] and click **Trust Center** in the left pane.
   b. Click the **Trust Center Settings** button and choose **Macro Settings** in the left pane.

c. Verify or select **Disable all macros with notification** and click **OK**.
d. Click **Customize Ribbon** in the left pane and display the *Developer* tab.
e. Click **Quick Access Toolbar** and select **All Commands** from the *Choose commands from* list.
f. Find and select **Form. . .** in the list and click **Add**.
g. Click **OK**.

2. Open the **EllerSoftware-08.xlsx** workbook from your student data files.

3. Save the workbook as an Excel macro-enabled workbook.
   a. Choose **Save As** from the *File* tab and navigate to your folder.
   b. Type [your initials] Excel 8-2 as the file name.
   c. Choose **Excel Macro-Enabled Workbook** from the *Save as type* list.
   d. Click **Save**.

4. Add records using a data form.
   a. Select cells **A3:G16** and click the **Form** button in the *Quick Access* toolbar. The input form displays the first row of data from the worksheet.
   b. Click **New** in the data form (Figure 8-43).

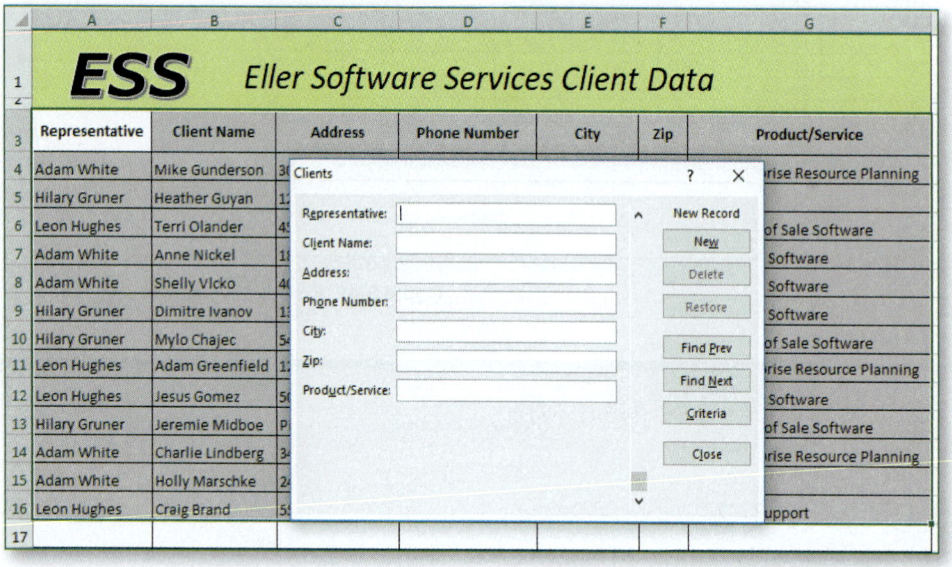

Figure 8-43 Enter data in the input form

   c. Type the following data for a new record.
      Representative: Adam White
      Client Name: Jeffrey Zander
      Address: 721 Maple Street
      Phone Number: 651-555-1321
      City: Eagan
      Zip: 55121
      Product/Service: Training
   d. Click **Close** to close the data form.
   e. Click the **Save** button in the *Quick Access* toolbar to save the workbook with the new record.
   f. Select cell **A4**.

5. Record a macro to filter clients.
   a. Verify that the **Use Relative References** button [*Developer* tab, *Code* group] is off.
   b. Click the **Record Macro** button [*Developer* tab, *Code* group].

c. Type FilterData in the *Macro name* box.
d. Do not use a shortcut key and store the macro in **This Workbook**.
e. Click the **Description** box, type Filter for selected representative, and click **OK**. All commands and selections to build an advanced filter are recorded.
f. Click the **Advanced** button [*Data* tab, *Sort & Filter* group] and select the **Copy to another location** radio button.
g. Click the **Up** arrow at the right of the **List Range** box. The arrow collapses the dialog box.
h. Select cells **A3:G17** and click the **Down** arrow to expand the dialog box.
i. Click the **Criteria range** box and select cells **A1:A2** on the **Criteria** tab.
j. Click the **Copy to** box and select cells **I12:L12** on the **Clients** tab (Figure 8-44).

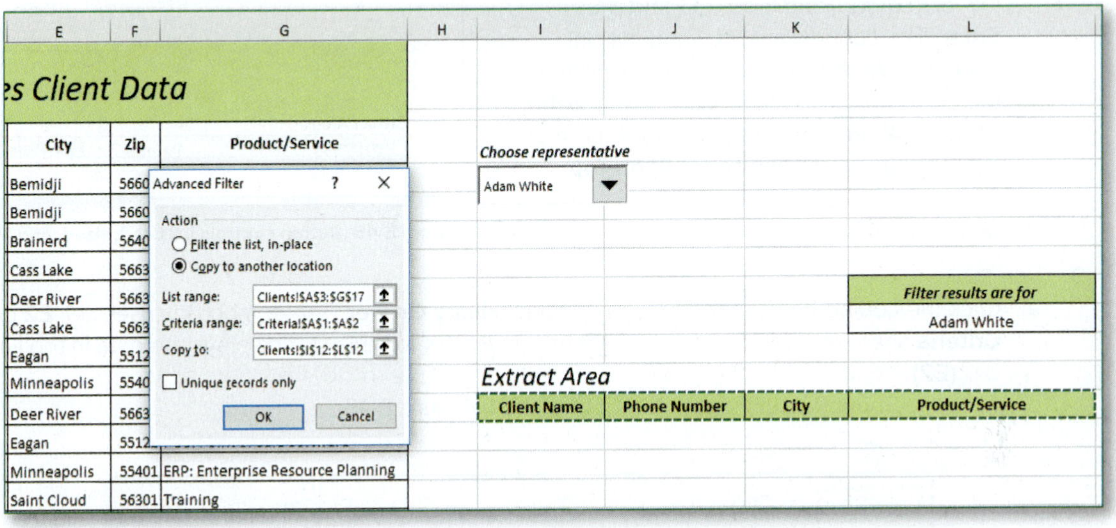

Figure 8-44 ***Advanced Filter*** **dialog box while recording macro**

k. Click **OK** to run the filter.
l. Click the **Stop Recording** button to the right of the *Ready* indicator in the *Status* bar.

6. Record a macro to clear filter results.
   a. Click the **Record Macro** button [*Developer* tab, *Code* group].
   b. Type ClearResults in the *Macro name* box.
   c. Do not use a shortcut key and store the macro in **This Workbook**.
   d. Click the **Description** box, type Clear filter, and click **OK**.
   e. Select cell **I13**, the first cell that displays filter results.
   f. Press **F8 (FN+F8)** to start *Extend Selection* mode.
   g. Press the **right arrow** three times.
   h. Press **Ctrl** and then press the **down arrow** once to highlight to the end of the filter results.
   i. Click the arrow on the **Clear** button [*Home* tab, *Editing* group] and select **Clear All**.
   j. Select cell **A4**.
   k. Click the **Stop Recording** button to the right of the *Ready* indicator in the *Status* bar.

7. Assign macros to *Button* form controls.
   a. Click the **Insert Controls** button [*Developer* tab, *Controls* group].
   b. Click the **Button (Form Control)** command in the *Form Controls* category.
   c. Draw a *Button* control that covers cell **I8**.
   d. Select **FilterData** in the *Assign Macro* dialog box and click **OK**.
   e. Right-click the button and choose **Edit Text**.
   f. Delete the default caption and type Show Results as the label.

g. Select cell **I6** to deselect the control.
h. Create another *Button* form control in cell **J8** and assign the **ClearResults** macro. Edit the caption to display Clear Results.

8. Size and align controls.
   a. Right-click the **Show Results** button to select it.
   b. Press **Ctrl** and right-click the **Clear Results** button. Both buttons display selection handles.
   c. Click the **Height** box [*Drawing Tools Format* tab, *Size* group] and type 0.35 and press **Enter**. The controls are the same height.
   d. Click the **Width** box [*Drawing Tools Format* tab, *Size* group] and type 1 and press **Enter**.
   e. Click the **Align** button [*Drawing Tools Format* tab, *Arrange* group] and select **Align Top** (Figure 8-45).
   f. Select cell **A4**.

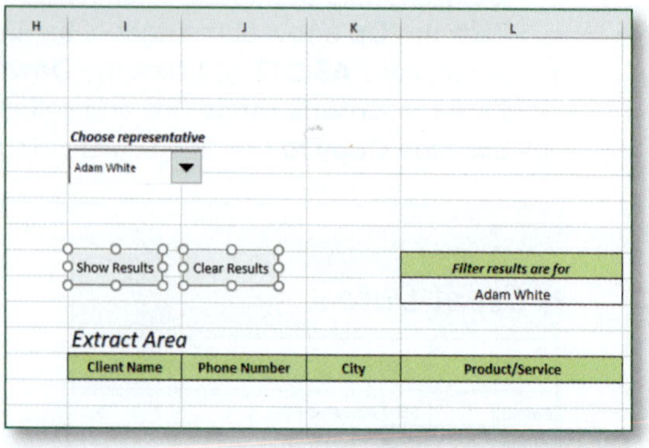

Figure 8-45 Button controls inserted, sized, and aligned

9. Run the macros.
   a. Click the combo box control arrow and select **Hilary Gruner**. The combo box uses cell **E2** on the **Criteria** sheet as its linked cell. Cell **L9** has an *INDEX* formula that displays the data in the linked cell **(E2)**.
   b. Click the **Show Results** button to run the macro (Figure 8-46).

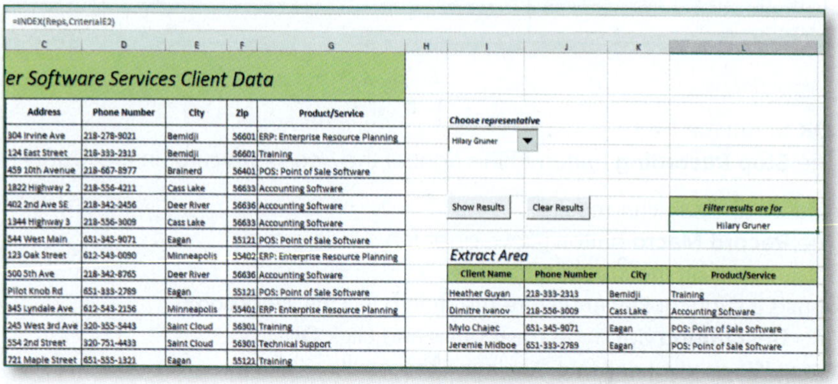

Figure 8-46 Filter results for Hilary Gruner

10. View and print macro code in the Visual Basic Editor.
    a. Click the **Macros** button [*Developer* tab, *Code* group] and select **Edit**.
    b. Display the *Code* window if necessary [*View* menu]. The code for two macros is contained in *Module 1*. (If your code is not in *Module 1*, complete the steps to print and then expand the *Module 2* to print the second macro.)
    c. Size the *Code* window to display your macros.
    d. Click **File** in the menu and select **Print**.
    e. Verify or select the **Current Module** radio button.
    f. Verify or select the **Code** box (Figure 8-47).
    g. Click **OK** to send the document to the current printer, or click **Cancel** if no printer is available.

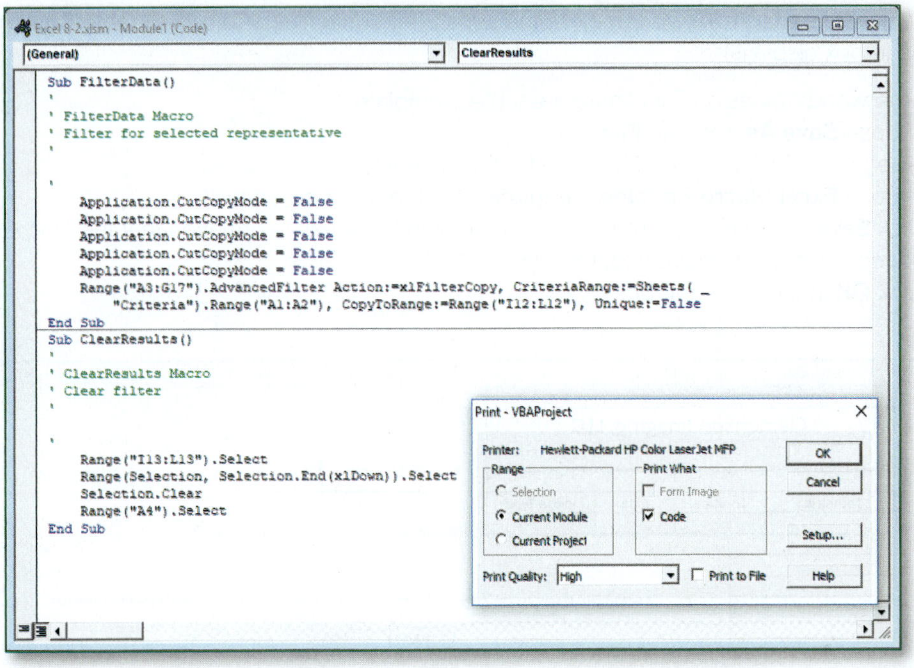

Figure 8-47 Macro code for Excel 8-2 workbook ready for printing

h. Click the **Close** button for the Visual Basic Editor and return to Excel.
i. Save and close the workbook.

11. Hide the *Developer* tab and remove the **Form** button from the *Quick Access* toolbar.

Guided Project 8-3

Clemenson Imaging is developing a macro-enabled template to track procedures. You add ActiveX controls to the procedures sheet and write a macro to print the summary report.
[Student Learning Outcomes 8.1, 8.2, 8.3, 8.4, 8.6]

File Needed: ***Clemenson-08.xlsm*** *(Student data files are available in the* Library *of your SIMnet account.)*
Completed Project File Names: ***[your initials] Excel 8-3Template.xltm*** and ***[your initials] Excel 8-3.xlsm***

Skills Covered in This Project

- Set macro security options.
- Save a macros-enabled template.
- Insert ActiveX controls.
- Edit code in the Visual Basic Editor.
- Record and run macros.
- Assign a macro to a *Button* form control.

1. Set macro security and display the *Developer* tab.
   a. Select **Options** (*File* tab) and then click **Trust Center**.
   b. Click the **Trust Center Settings** button and click **Macro Settings** in the left pane.
   c. Verify or select **Disable all macros with notification** and click **OK**.
   d. Click **Customize Ribbon** in the left pane and display the **Developer** tab.

2. Open the **Clemenson-08** workbook from your student data files and click **Enable Content** if the message box displays.

3. Save the workbook as an Excel macro-enabled template.
   a. Choose **Save As** from the **File** tab.
   b. Type [your initials] Excel 8-3Template for the file name.
   c. Choose **Excel Macro-Enabled Template** from the *Save as type* list.
   d. Click **Save**. You will see a reminder that the workbook has information that the *Document Inspector* cannot remove (Figure 8-48).
   e. Click **OK** in the message box.

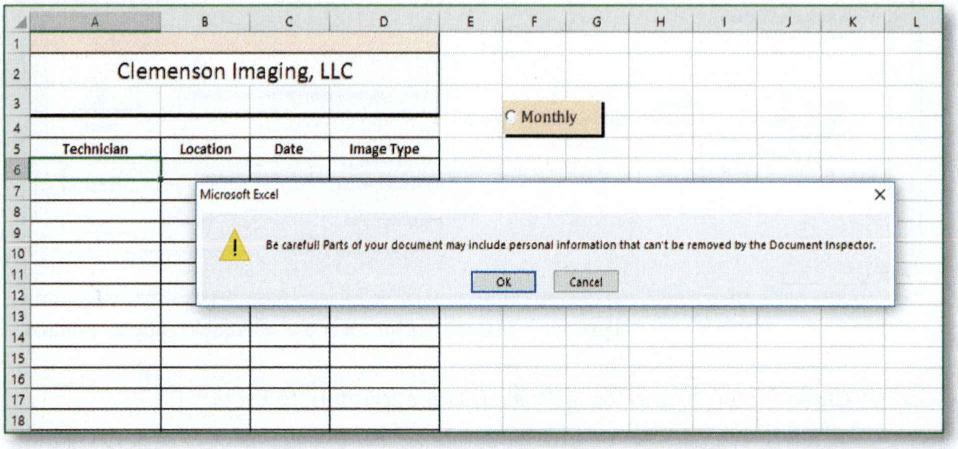

Figure 8-48 Message pertains to ActiveX control

4. Insert an ActiveX form control.
   a. Click the **Insert** button [*Developer* tab, *Code* group] and choose **Option Button (ActiveX Control)**.
   b. Draw an option button control the same width as the *Monthly* control in rows **6:7** (Figure 8-49).

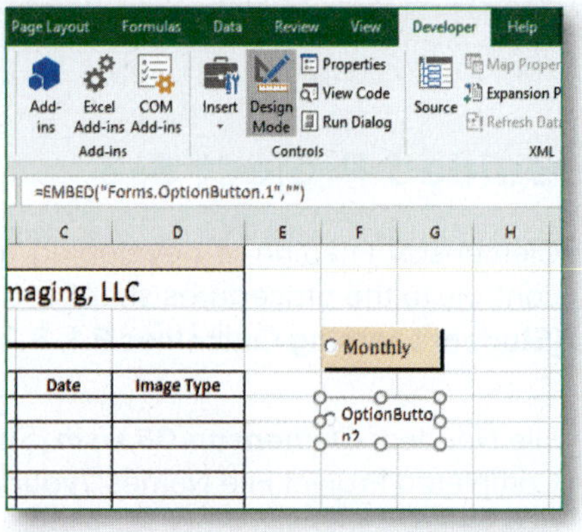

Figure 8-49 Second option button

5. Set properties for an ActiveX control.
   a. Click the **Properties** button [*Developer* tab, *Controls* group].
   b. Verify that the object displayed in the *Properties* window is **OptionButton2**.
   c. Click the **Alphabetic** tab.
   d. Click the **BackColor** line to display the drop-down list.
   e. Click the **Palette** tab.
   f. Click the color tile in the third column, first row to match the first option button.
   g. Click the **Caption** line, delete the default text, and type Weekly.
   h. Click the **Font** line and then click the ellipsis (. . .) to display the font list.
   i. Choose **Cambria**, **Regular**, and **12** for the font and click **OK**.

6. Review and copy properties for an ActiveX control.
   a. Click the **Monthly** control to display its *Properties* window. Note its *Height* setting.
   b. Click the **Weekly** control, click the **Height** line, and change the value to 24.75.
   c. Click the **Shadow** line and set its value to **True**.
   d. Click the **Width** line and select the **Monthly** control to determine its width.
   e. Click the **Weekly** control and set the *Width* value to 74.25.

7. Align controls from the *Properties* window.
   a. Click the **Monthly** control. The *Left* setting is *357*.
   b. Click the **Weekly** control.
   c. Click the **Left** line and verify or change the value to 357 (Figure 8-50).
   d. Select cell **A6** and close the *Properties* window.

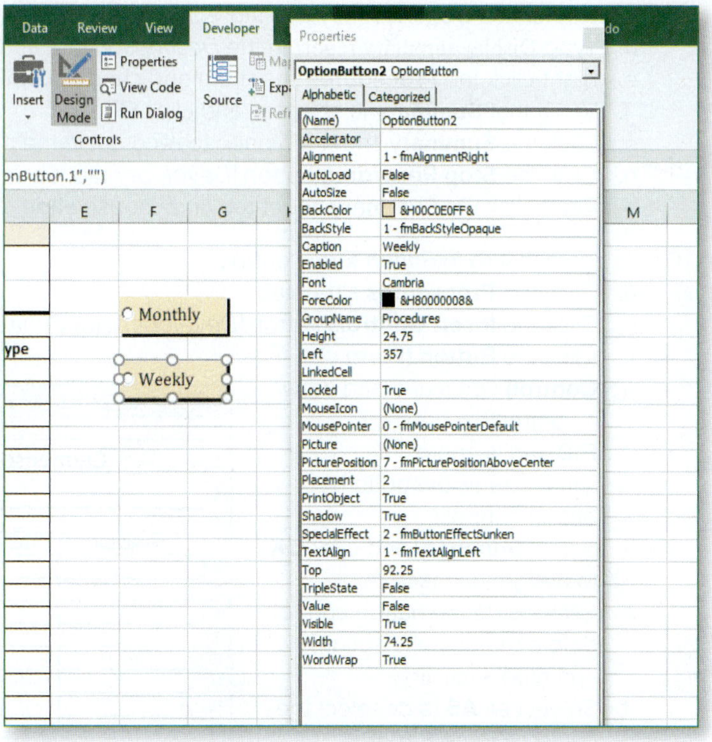

Figure 8-50 Properties window for second option button

8. Copy and write macro code in the Visual Basic Editor (VBE).
   a. Verify that *Design Mode* is enabled.
   b. Click the **Weekly** control and then click the **View Code** button [*Developer* tab, *Controls* group].
   c. Click the object list drop-down arrow and choose **OptionButton2** in the *Code* window.
   d. Type an apostrophe (') to introduce a comment and press **Spacebar**.
   e. Type Weekly Report and press **Enter** two times.
   f. Select the code for *OptionButton1* starting at the word "If" and ending at "End If" as shown in Figure 8-51.
   g. Press **Ctrl+C** to copy the code.
   h. Click the line above *End Sub* in the code for *OptionButton2*.
   i. Press **Ctrl+V** to paste the code.
   j. Replace the number "1" in "OptionButton1.Value" with 2 in the copied code.
   k. Replace the word "Monthly" in the copied code with Weekly.
   l. Click the **Close** button in the upper-right corner to close the Editor and return to Excel.

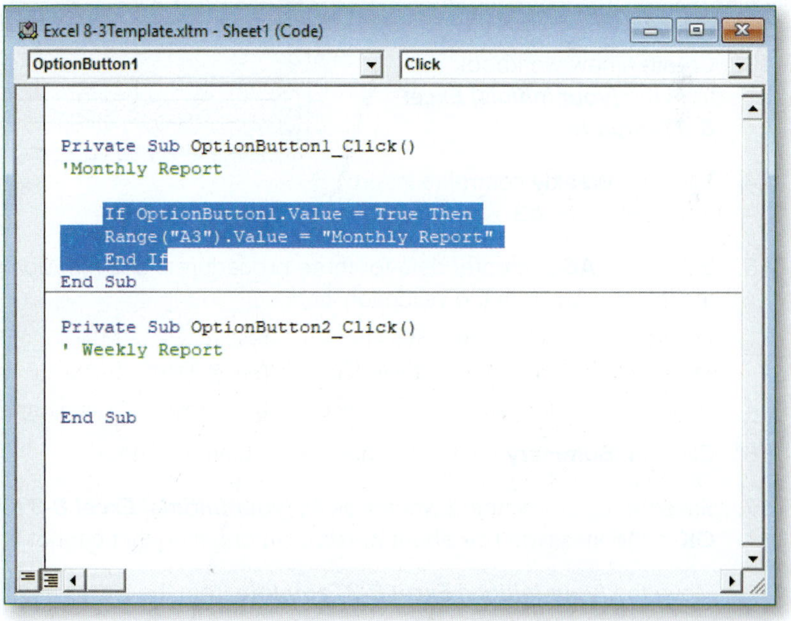

Figure 8-51 Selected code to be copied

9. Record a macro to unhide a worksheet.
   a. Select cell **A6** and click the **Record Macro** button [*Developer* tab, *Code* group].
   b. Type Summary in the *Macro name* box.

c. Do not use a shortcut key and store the macro in **This Workbook**.
d. Type Display summary report in the *Description* box and click **OK**.
e. Right-click the **Procedures** sheet tab and choose **Unhide**.
f. Verify that **Summary** is selected and click **OK**.
g. Click the **Summary** sheet tab once to record it in the macro code.
h. Click the **Stop Recording** button [*Developer* tab, *Code* group].
i. Right-click the **Summary** sheet tab and choose **Hide**.

10. Assign a macro to *Button* form control.
    a. Click the **Procedures** sheet tab.
    b. Click the **Insert Controls** button [*Developer* tab, *Controls* group].
    c. Click the **Button (Form Control)** command and draw a control that begins in cell **F10** and is approximately the same size as the option button controls.
    d. Select **Summary** and click **OK** to assign the macro.
    e. Click inside the button control, delete the default caption, and type Summary.
    f. Select cell **A6** to deselect the control (Figure 8-52).

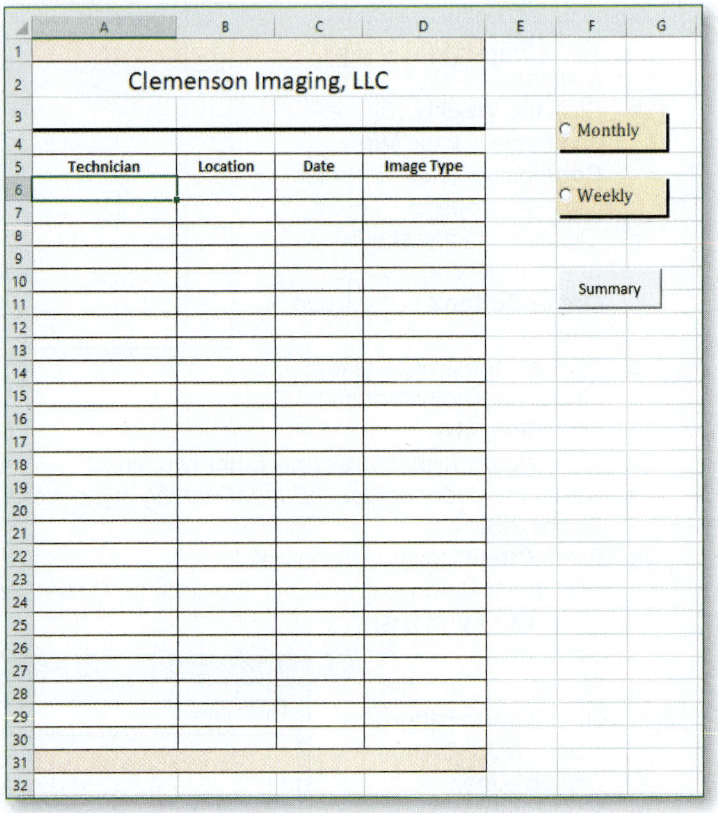

Figure 8-52 Completed template for Excel 8-3

11. Click the **Design Mode** button [*Developer* tab, *Controls* group] to turn off the command.

12. Click the **Save** button in the *Quick Access* toolbar to resave the macro-enabled template, click **OK** in the message box, and close the template.

13. Create a new workbook from the ***[your initials] Excel 8-3Template***.

14. Click the **Weekly** control to insert the label in cell **A3**.

15. Select cell **A6** and enter data for three procedures. Use *mm/dd/yy* format for the dates and choose the image type from the validation list.

Donna	McFarland	Appleton	Yesterday	MRI
Maryanne	Vonbank	Green Bay	Today	CT Scan
Jonathan	Douglas	Manitowoc	Tomorrow	Angiography

16. Click the **Summary** control to unhide the summary sheet.

17. Save the macro-enabled workbook as ***[your initials] Excel 8-3*** (Figure 8-53) in your folder and click **OK** in the message box about personal information that cannot be removed.

18. Move the ***[your initials] Excel 8-3Template*** from the *Custom Office Templates* folder to your folder.

19. Hide the *Developer* tab and close the workbook.

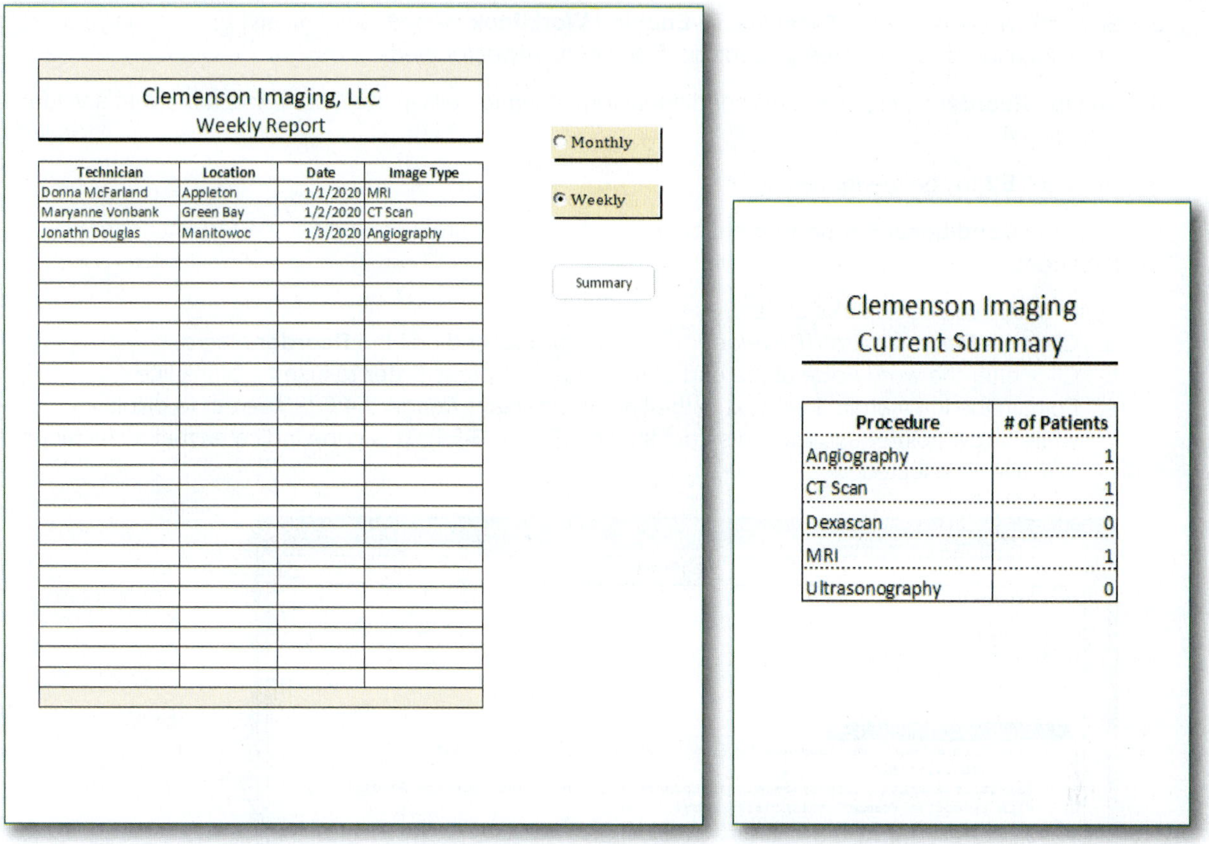

Clemenson Imaging, LLC
Weekly Report
Technician
Location
Date
Image Type
Donna McFarland
Appleton
1/1/2020
MRI
Maryanne Vonbank
Green Bay
1/2/2020
CT Scan
Jonathn Douglas
Manitowoc
1/3/2020
Angiography
Monthly
Weekly
Summary
Clemenson Imaging
Current Summary
Procedure
# of Patients
Angiography
1
CT Scan
1
Dexascan
0
MRI
1
Ultrasonography
0

Figure 8-53 Excel 8-3 completed worksheets

Independent Project 8-4

At Wear-Ever Shoes, you use a macro to identify products to be reordered. You plan to place the macro code in an ActiveX control so that you can better design the button. You also record a macro to clear conditional formatting.
[Student Learning Outcomes 8.1, 8.2, 8.3, 8.4]

File Needed: ***WearEver-08.xlsm*** *(Student data files are available in the* Library *of your SIMnet account.)*
Completed Project File Name: ***[your initials] Excel 8-4.xlsm***

Skills Covered in This Project

- Set macro security options.
- Record and run macros.
- Insert an ActiveX control.
- Edit macro code in the Visual Basic Editor.
- Enter code for an ActiveX control.

1. Set macro security to **Disable all macros with notification** and display the *Developer* tab.
2. Open the **WearEver-08** workbook from your student data files and enable macros.

3. Save the workbook as an **Excel Macro-Enabled Workbook** named [your initials] Excel 8-4 in your usual location for saving files. Accept the *Document Inspector* alert.
4. Run the **Reorder** macro. It applies conditional formatting to cells in the *Quantity* column with a value less than 4.
5. Click cell **E2** to see the formatting.
6. Click the **Conditional Formatting** button [*Home* tab, *Styles* group] and clear the formatting from the sheet.
7. Edit a macro to add a line of code.
   a. Click the **Macros** button [*Developer* tab, *Code* group] and edit the **Reorder** macro.
   b. Click after the word *False* at the end of the code and press **Enter** to insert a blank line.
   c. Point in the left margin area next to the line that displays *Range("E4:E39").Select* to display a white arrow pointer and click to select the line (Figure 8-54). This code indicates that a cell range is active or selected.

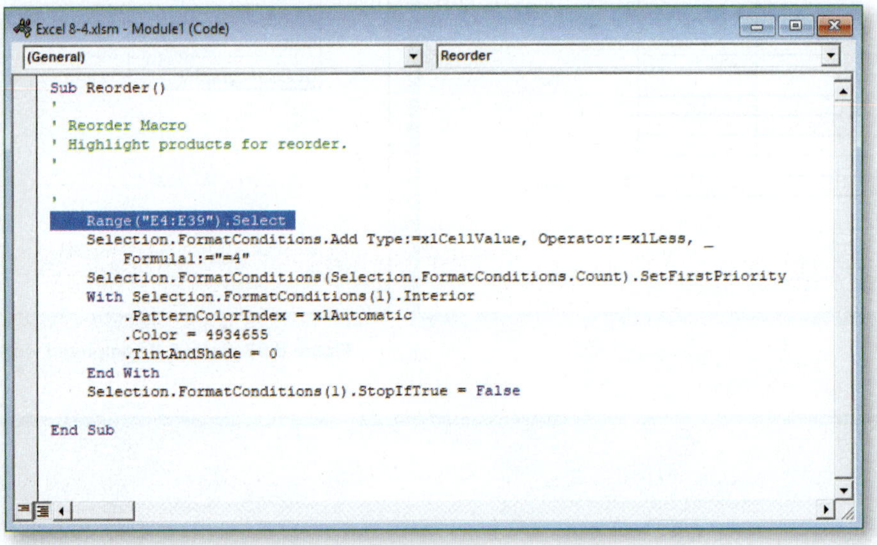
Excel 8-4.xlsm - Module1 (Code)
(General)
Reorder
Sub Reorder()
'
' Reorder Macro
' Highlight products for reorder.
'
'
Range("E4:E39").Select
Selection.FormatConditions.Add Type:=xlCellValue, Operator:=xlLess, _
Formula1:="=4"
Selection.FormatConditions(Selection.FormatConditions.Count).SetFirstPriority
With Selection.FormatConditions(1).Interior
.PatternColorIndex = xlAutomatic
.Color = 4934655
.TintAndShade = 0
End With
Selection.FormatConditions(1).StopIfTrue = False
End Sub

Figure 8-54 Code line selected in the VBE

   d. Press **Ctrl+C** to copy the line.
   e. Click the empty line that you inserted in step b and press **Ctrl+V** to copy the code.
   f. Edit the copied code to display *Range("A2").Select*. This returns the insertion point to cell A2 after conditional formatting is applied (Figure 8-55).
   g. Close the Visual Basic Editor.
8. Insert an ActiveX command button control.
   a. Insert a **Command Button (ActiveX Control)** that covers cell **J3**.
   b. Set the **BackColor** property to the green color tile in the fifth column, first row in the **Palette**.
   c. Change the **Caption** to Reorder.
   d. Set the **Shadow** property to **True**.
   e. Close the *Properties* window.
9. Copy macro code in the Visual Basic Editor.
   a. Verify that the **Reorder** control is selected and that *Design Mode* is active.
   b. Click the **View Code** button [*Developer* tab, *Controls* group].
   c. Choose **CommandButton1** from the objects list in the *Code* window.
   d. Double-click **Module1** in the *Project* window to display the *Reorder* macro code.

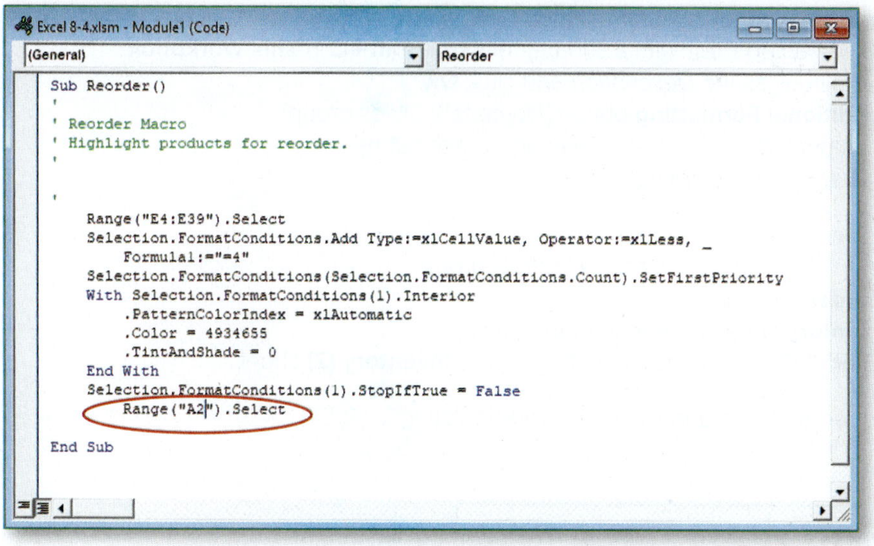
Excel 8-4.xlsm - Module1 (Code)
(General)
Reorder
Sub Reorder()
'
' Reorder Macro
' Highlight products for reorder.
'

'
Range("E4:E39").Select
Selection.FormatConditions.Add Type:=xlCellValue, Operator:=xlLess, _
Formula1:="=4"
Selection.FormatConditions(Selection.FormatConditions.Count).SetFirstPriority
With Selection.FormatConditions(1).Interior
.PatternColorIndex = xlAutomatic
.Color = 4934655
.TintAndShade = 0
End With
Selection.FormatConditions(1).StopIfTrue = False
Range("A2").Select

End Sub

Figure 8-55 Copied and edited code line

e. Arrange the code windows as shown in Figure 8-56. (Cascade the code windows (*Windows* menu) if necessary.)

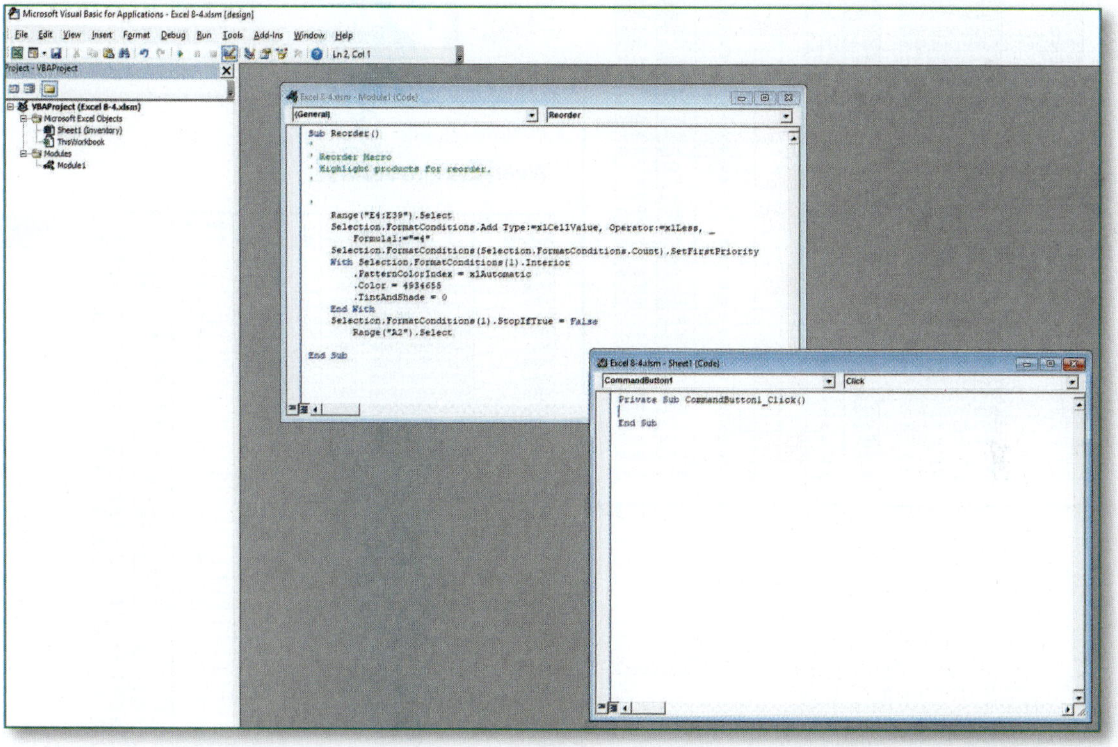
Microsoft Visual Basic for Applications - Excel 8-4.xlsm [design]
File Edit View Insert Format Debug Run Tools Add-Ins Window Help
Ln 2, Col 1
Project - VBAProject
VBAProject (Excel 8-4.xlsm)
Microsoft Excel Objects
Sheet1 (Inventory)
ThisWorkbook
Modules
Module1
Excel 8-4.xlsm - Module1 (Code)
(General)
Reorder
Excel 8-4.xlsm - Sheet1 (Code)
CommandButton1
Click
Private Sub CommandButton1_Click()
End Sub

Figure 8-56 Code windows in Editor

f. Select the code in the macro window from *Range ("E4:E39").Select* through *Range ("A2").Select* at the end of the code.
g. Copy the code.
h. Click the blank line between *Private Sub* and *End Sub* in the *CommandButton1* window and paste the code.
i. Close the Visual Basic Editor and select cell **A2**.

10. Record a macro to clear conditional formatting.
    a. Record a macro named Clear with a shortcut of **Ctrl+Shift+C** in **This Workbook**.
    b. Type Clear formatting as the *Description* and click **OK**.
    c. Click the **Conditional Formatting** button [*Home* tab, *Styles* group].
    d. Choose the command to clear the formatting from the sheet.
    e. Select cell **A2** and stop recording.

11. Test the ActiveX control and the macro.
    a. Turn off *Design Mode* [*Developer* tab, *Controls* group].
    b. Click the **Reorder** control.
    c. Copy the **Inventory** sheet to the end of the tabs.
    d. Press **Ctrl+Shift+C** to clear the formatting on the **Inventory (2)** sheet.

12. Hide the *Developer* tab. Save and close the workbook (Figure 8-57).

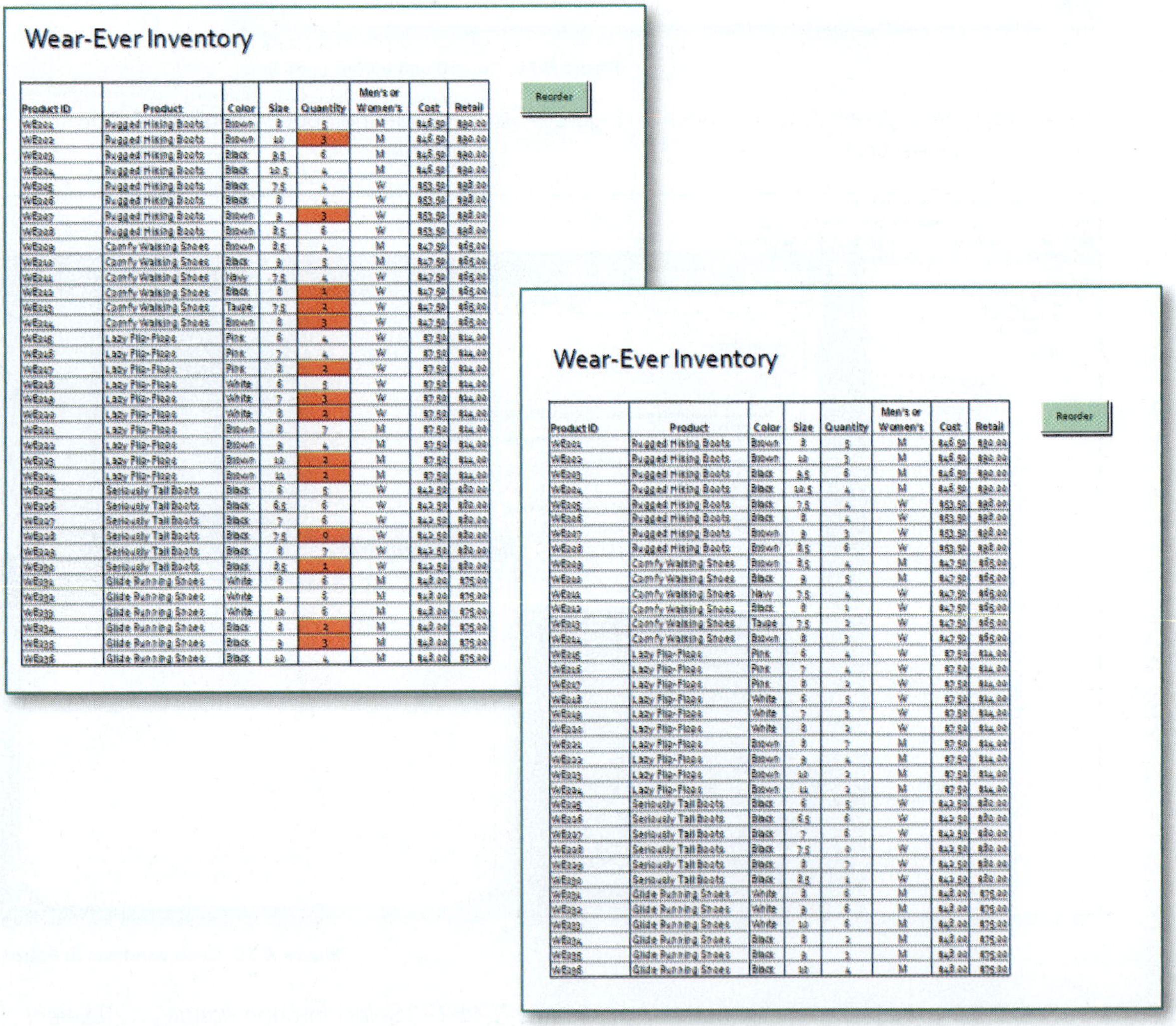

Figure 8-57 Excel 8-4 completed worksheets

Independent Project 8-5

Courtyard Medical Plaza developed a trainer's worksheet for personalized workout plans. You record and edit macros for a macros-only workbook and run the macros in the trainer's workbook.
[Student Learning Outcomes 8.1, 8.2, 8.4, 8.5, 8.7]

File Needed: ***CourtyardMedical-08.xlsx*** *(Student data files are available in the* Library *of your SIMnet account.)*
Completed Project File Names: ***[your initials] Excel 8-5Macros.xlsm*** and ***[your initials] Excel 8-5.xlsx***

Skills Covered in This Project

- Set macro security options.
- Create a macros-only workbook.
- Record a macro with relative references.
- Run macros with keyboard shortcuts.
- Edit a macro in the Visual Basic Editor.

---

1. Set macro security to **Disable all macros with notification** and display the *Developer* tab.
2. Create a new workbook and save it as an **Excel Macro-Enabled Workbook** named [your initials] Excel 8-5Macros in your usual location for saving files.
3. Activate the **Use Relative References** command and select cell **A1**.
4. Record a macro with relative references.
   a. Record a macro named Titles with a shortcut of **Ctrl+Shift+T** in **This Workbook**.
   b. Type Enter column titles for the *Description* and click **OK**.
   c. Type Activities and press the **right arrow** key.
   d. Type Calories and press the **right arrow** key.
   e. Type Times and press the **right arrow** key. Type Burned and press the **right arrow** key.
   f. Press the **left arrow** key four times to return to the "Activities" label.
   g. Select cells **A1:D1** and apply **bold** and **italic**.
   h. Stop recording.
   i. Select cell **A4** and record a macro with relative references named Activities with a shortcut of **Ctrl+Shift+A** in **This Workbook**. Type Enter activities for the *Description*.
   j. Type the labels shown here and press **Enter** after each one to move from row to row. Backspace to correct a typing error before you press **Enter**. Errors that you notice after you press **Enter** can be corrected later in the code window.
      Dance Fusion
      High Intensity Interval
      Pilates/Yoga
      Running
      Strength Training
      Swimming
      Water Aerobics
   k. Stop recording (Figure 8-58).
5. Turn off **Use Relative References**.

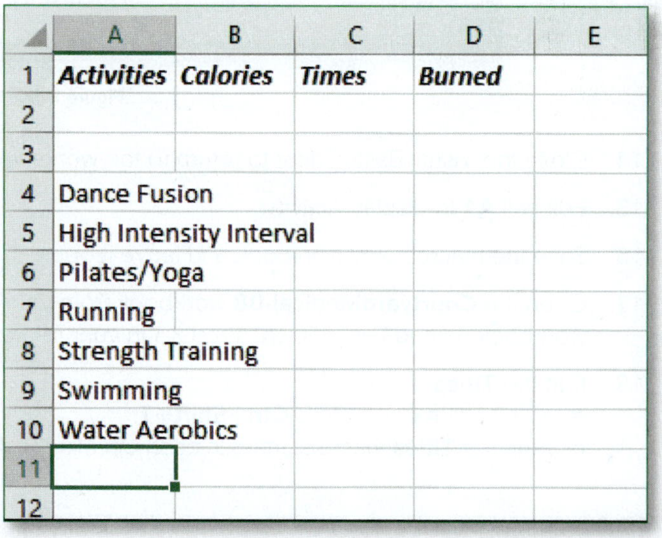

	A	B	C	D	E
1	***Activities***	***Calories***	***Times***	***Burned***	
2					
3					
4	Dance Fusion				
5	High Intensity Interval				
6	Pilates/Yoga				
7	Running				
8	Strength Training				
9	Swimming				
10	Water Aerobics				
11					
12					

Figure 8-58 Data is entered as macros are recorded

6. Select cell **F1** and type Titles Macro.
7. Remove bold and italic from cell **F1**.
8. Select cell **F2** and type Ctrl+Shift+T.
9. Select cell **F4** and type Activities Macro.
10. Type Ctrl+Shift+A in cell **F5** (Figure 8-59).
11. Edit the **Titles** macro in the Visual Basic Editor to change the word "Activities" to Activity.
12. Correct other typing errors as needed.
13. Size the *Code* window in the Visual Basic Editor so that you can see both macros. Print the code [*File* menu] if instructed to do so (Figure 8-60).

	A	B	C	D	E	F	G
1	***Activities***	***Calories***	***Times***	***Burned***		Titles Macro	
2						Ctrl+Shift+T	
3							
4	Dance Fusion					Activities Macro	
5	High Intensity Interval					Ctrl+Shift+A	
6	Pilates/Yoga						
7	Running						
8	Strength Training						
9	Swimming						
10	Water Aerobics						

Figure 8-59 Documentation for the macros workbook

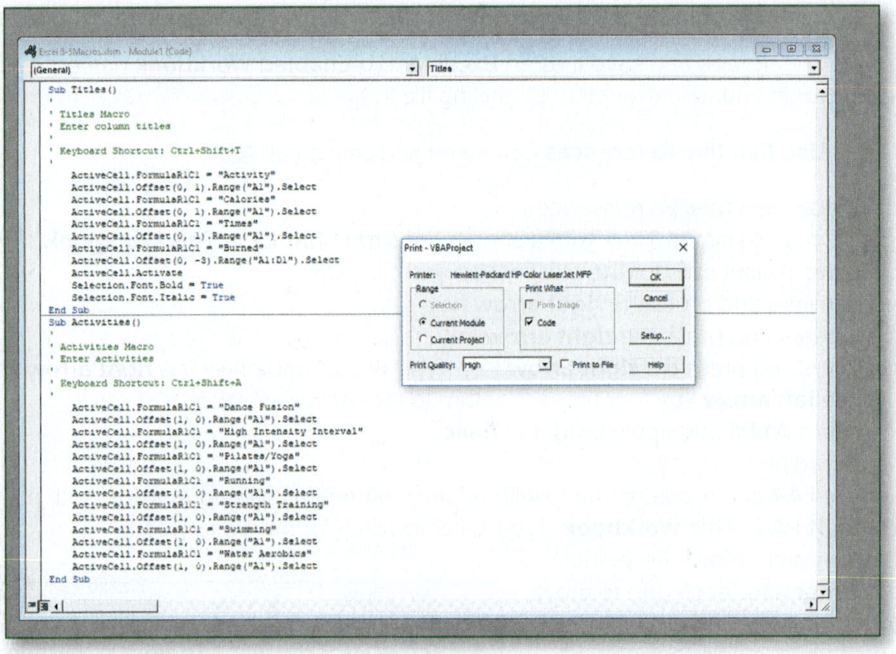

Figure 8-60 Print code from the *File* menu in the VBE

14. Close the Visual Basic Editor to return to the worksheet.
15. Edit cell **A1** to display Activity.
16. Save the macros-only workbook and leave it open.
17. Open the **CourtyardMedical-08** workbook from your student data files and save it as an Excel workbook named [your initials] Excel 8-5 in your folder.
18. Run the **Titles** macro.
    a. Click cell **A3** and press **Ctrl+Shift+T**.
    b. Run the **Titles** macro starting in each of cells **F3**, **A15**, and **F15**.

19. Run the **Activities** macro.
    a. Click cell **A4** and press **Ctrl+Shift+A**.
    b. Run the **Activities** macro starting in each of cells **F4**, **A16**, and **F16**.
20. Hide the *Developer* tab. Save and close the workbook (Figure 8-61).
21. Save and close the macros-only workbook.

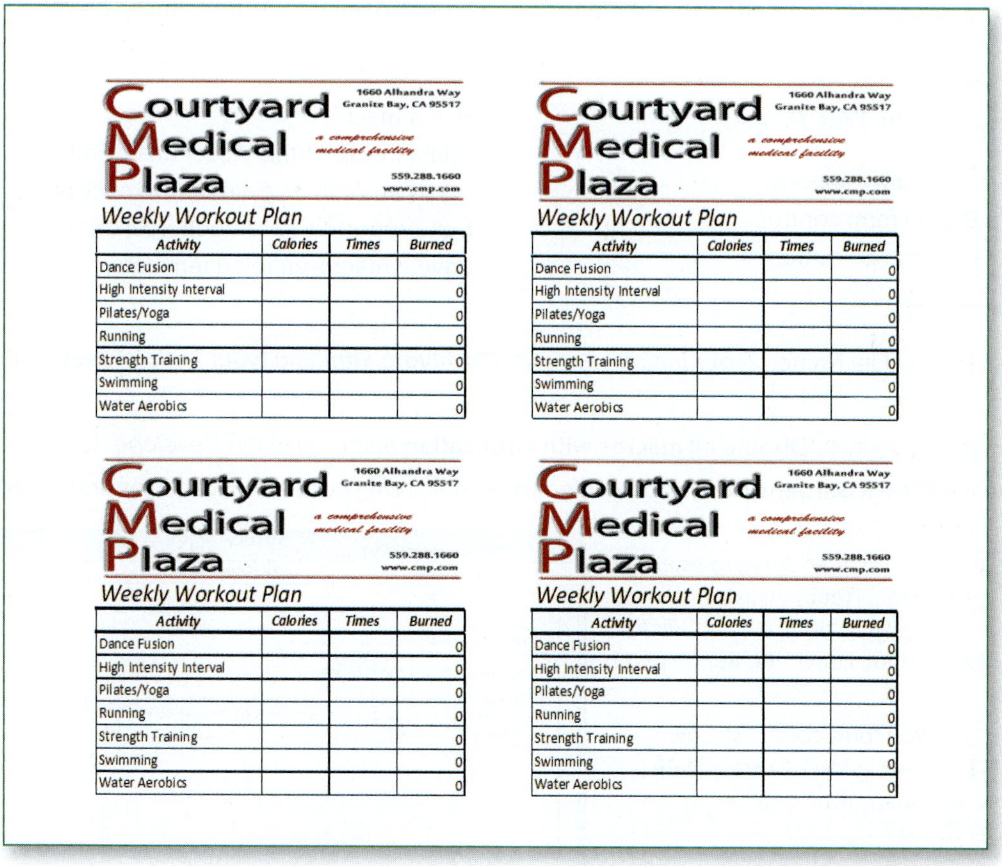

Figure 8-61 Excel 8-5 completed worksheet

Independent Project 8-6

Classic Gardens and Landscapes (CGL) monitors work hours in a macro-enabled workbook. You edit a macro that includes a *Text* function and insert an ActiveX control.
[Student Learning Outcomes 8.1, 8.3, 8.4, 8.6]

File Needed: ***ClassicGardens-08.xlsm*** *(Student data files are available in the* Library *of your SIMnet account.)*

Skills Covered in This Project

- Set macro security options.
- Insert a *Button* form control.
- Assign a macro to a button.
- Run a macro.
- Edit a macro in the Visual Basic Editor.
- Insert an ActiveX *Spin Button* control.
- Edit properties for an ActiveX control.
- Save a macro-enabled template.

Completed Project File Names: ***[your initials] Excel 8-6Template.xltm*** and ***[your initials] Excel 8-6.xlsm***

---

1. Set macro security to **Disable all macros with notification** and display the *Developer* tab.
2. Open the **ClassicGardens-08** macro-enabled workbook from your student data files and enable the macros.
3. Save the workbook as a macro-enabled template named [your initials] Excel 8-6Template in the *Custom Office Templates* folder. Leave the template open.
4. Insert a *Button* form control to cover cell **H2** and assign the **CurrentDate** macro. Edit the button caption to display "Date."
5. Deselect the *Button* control and run the macro from it. The date displays in cell F20 and in the label in row 7.
6. Delete the contents of cell **F20**.
7. Edit the **CurrentDate** macro in the Visual Basic Editor so that the format codes for TODAY() are mmmm dd. The codes spell out the month and display two digits for the date (Figure 8-62).
8. Close the Visual Basic Editor and click the **Date** button control to run the edited macro.
9. Delete the contents of cell **F20**.
10. Insert an ActiveX control.
    a. Draw a **Spin Button (ActiveX Control)** that covers cells **K4:K6** (Figure 8-63). When you draw a spin button control that is taller than it is wide, the buttons face up and down.

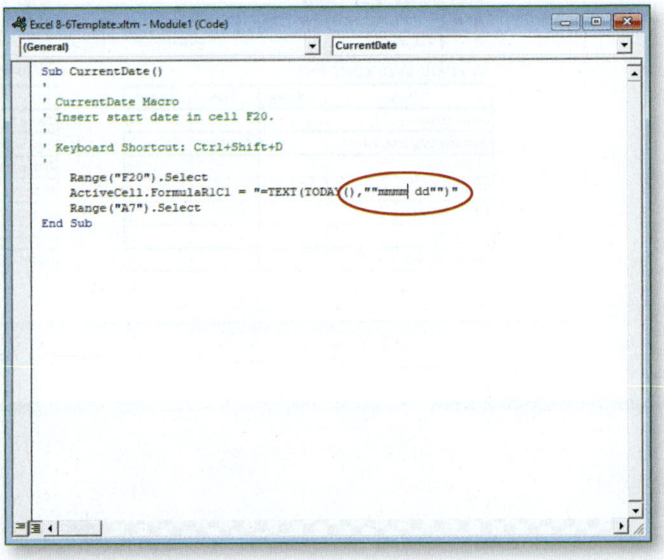

Figure 8-62 Macro includes *TEXT* function to format the date

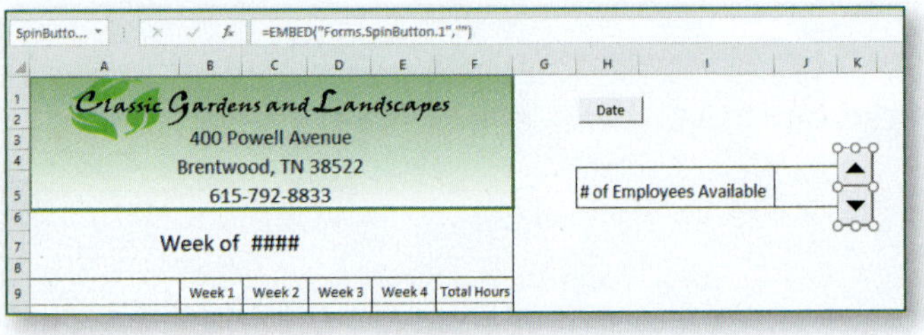

Figure 8-63 *Spin Button* ActiveX control

b. Display the *Properties* window for the control.
c. Set the **BackColor** to the green color in the fourth row, fifth column in the *Palette*.
d. Set the **Linked Cell** to cell **J5** and include a **Shadow** for the control. Close the *Properties* window.
e. Select cell **A7** and turn off *Design Mode*.

11. Save the macro-enabled template with the same name and close it.
12. Create a workbook from the template.
    a. Create a new workbook from ***[your initials] Excel 8-6Template*** and enable the macros.
    b. Click the **Button** form control to run the date macro.
    c. Click the **Spin Button** controls to display **12** in cell **J5**.
13. Save the workbook as an **Excel Macro-Enabled Workbook** named [your initials] Excel 8-6 in your usual location for saving files (Figure 8-64).
14. Close the workbook.
15. Move the template from the *Custom Office Templates* folder to your folder and hide the *Developer* tab.

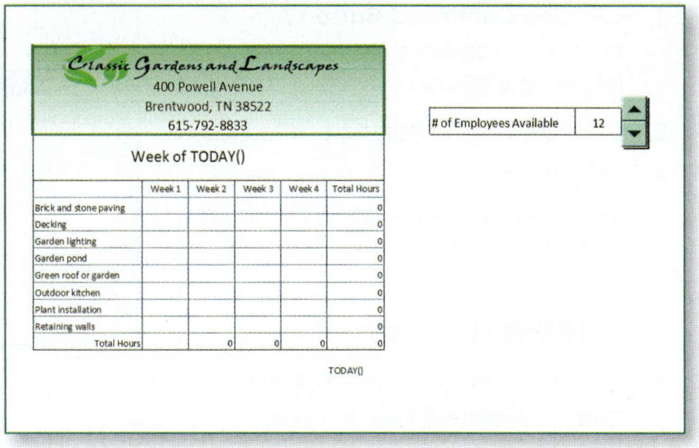

Figure 8-64 Excel 8-6 completed worksheet

Improve It Project 8-7

In the Blue Lake Sports invoice worksheet, you edit code for an ActiveX control and a macro and record a macro to copy a worksheet. You save your work in a macro-enabled template and create a new workbook. **[Student Learning Outcomes 8.1, 8.2, 8.3, 8.4, 8.6]**

File Needed: ***BlueLakeSports-08.xlsm*** *(Student data files are available in the* Library *of your SIMnet account.)*
Completed Project File Names: ***[your initials] Excel 8-7Template.xltm*** and ***[your initials] Excel 8-7.xlsm***

Skills Covered in This Project

- Set macro security options.
- Edit macro code for an ActiveX control.
- Record a macro.
- Run a macro.
- Save a macro-enabled template.

1. Set macro security to **Disable all macros with notification** and display the *Developer* tab.
2. Open the **BlueLakeSports-08** macro-enabled workbook from your student data files and enable the macros.
3. Save the workbook as a macro-enabled template named [your initials] Excel 8-7Template in the *Custom Office Templates* folder.

4. Click the **Command Button** ActiveX control. It displays a message box (Figure 8-65).
5. Click **OK** in the message box to close it.
6. Click the *Developer* tab and turn on *Design Mode*. Then select the control and view its code.
7. Edit the code to correct the shortcut to **Ctrl+Shift+D** instead of "T."
8. Edit the code to display "But first click. . ." (Figure 8-66).

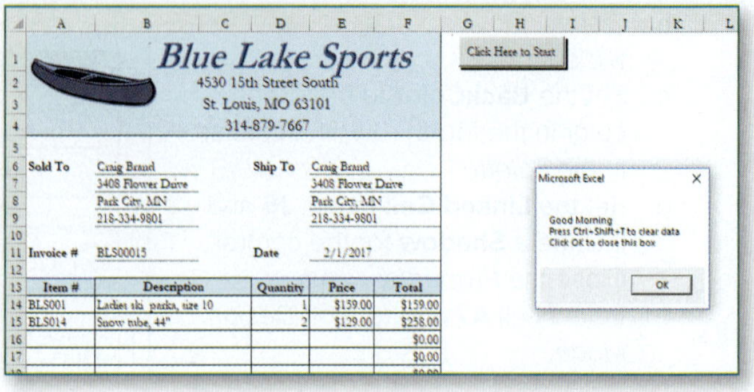

Figure 8-65 ***Command Button*** **displays a message box**

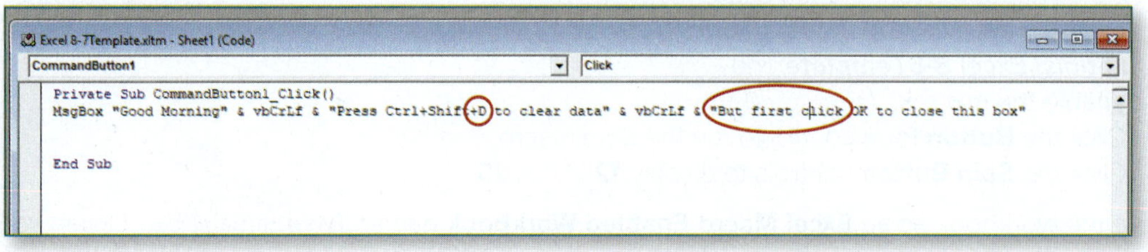

Figure 8-66 Edited code for ActiveX control

9. Close the Visual Basic Editor and turn off *Design Mode*. Then click the control to display the new message box.
10. Close the message box and select cell **A5**.
11. Edit the **DeleteData** macro so that it deletes the contents of cells **A14:E29** instead of cells A14:E15 (Figure 8-67).
12. Record a macro named **CopySheet** with a shortcut of **Ctrl+Shift+C** and no description. Record commands to copy the current worksheet to the end. Stop recording when the sheet is copied.
13. Run the **DeleteData** macro on the copied worksheet. Delete the copied sheet.

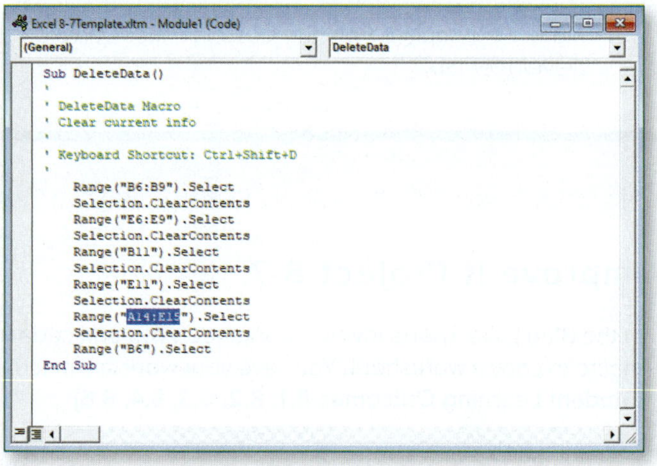

Figure 8-67 Code to be edited in ***DeleteData*** **macro**

14. Save and close the template.
15. Create a new workbook from ***[your initials] Excel 8-7Template*** and enable the macros.
16. Run the **CopySheet** macro.
17. Click the ActiveX control and close its message box.
18. Select cell **A5** and run the **DeleteData** macro.
19. Save the workbook as a macro-enabled workbook named [your initials] Excel 8-7 in your usual folder (Figure 8-68).
20. Move the template from the *Custom Office Templates* folder to your folder and hide the *Developer* tab.

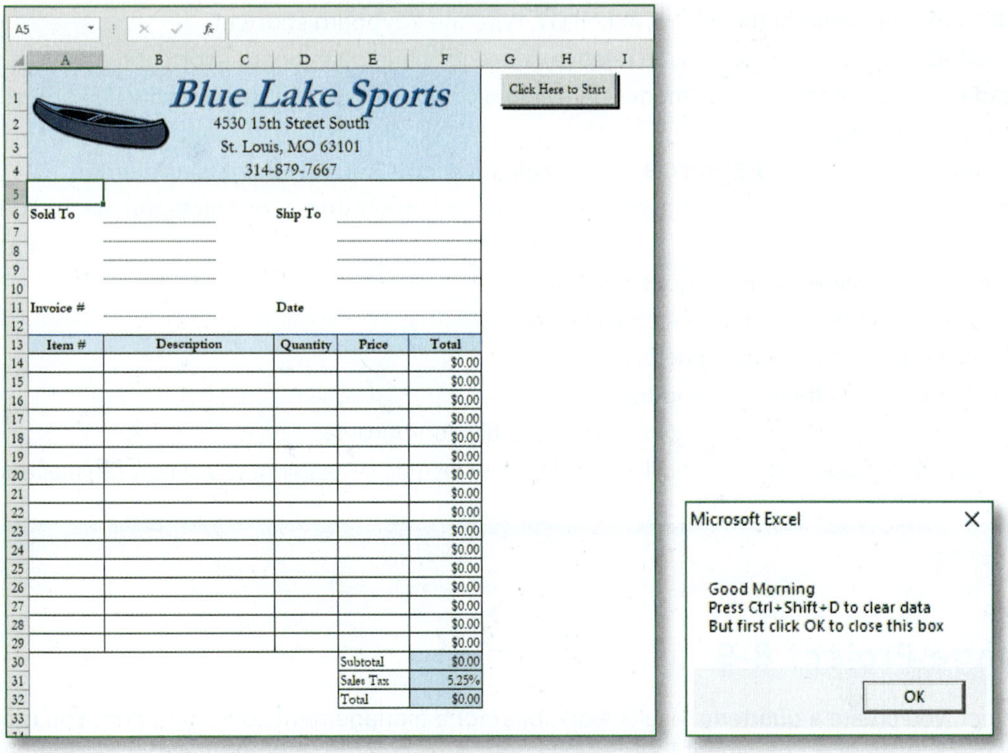

Figure 8-68 Excel 8-7 completed worksheet and edited message box

Challenge Project 8-8

In this project, you create a macros-only workbook for an automobile dealership. You record macros to enter main labels, model names, and column labels. In a separate workbook, you run these macros to build a worksheet.
[Student Learning Outcomes 8.1, 8.2, 8.4, 8.5, 8.7]

File Needed: None
Completed Project File Names: ***[your initials] Excel 8-8Macros.xlsm*** and ***[your initials] Excel 8-8.xlsx***

Create and save a macro-enabled workbook named [your initials] Excel 8-8Macros. Modify your workbook according to the following guidelines:

- Record a macro with absolute references and a keyboard shortcut to display the name of the automobile dealership, its address lines, telephone and fax numbers, and a web site address in cells **A1:A5**. Format the labels with a 14 pt font size as part of the macro.
- In cell **F1**, type the name of your macro as documentation. In cell **G1**, type its keyboard shortcut.
- Select cell **A7**. Record a macro with relative references and a keyboard shortcut that enters Week 1, Week 2, Week 3, and Week 4 in a single row. Use the *Fill* handle or the **right arrow** key to move from column to column.

- In cell **F7**, type the name of the macro. In cell **G7**, type the keyboard shortcut.
- Select cell **A9** and record a macro with relative references and a keyboard shortcut that enters the names of eight automobile makes/models in a single column. Press the **down arrow** key or **Enter** to move from row to row.
- Add documentation in cells **F9** and **G9**. Adjust column widths and row heights as needed.
- Insert a blank sheet and test your macros. Make edits to correct errors, or delete the macro and re-record it.
- Save the macros-only workbook and leave it open.
- Create a new workbook and run the labels macro.
- Select cell **B7** and run the week macro.
- Select cell **A8** and run the makes/models macro.
- Format the worksheet using font styles, alignment, fill, and borders.
- Save the Excel workbook as [your initials] Excel 8-8. It is not macro-enabled; you simply ran macros in it.

Challenge Project 8-9

In this project, you create a quarterly results worksheet for a management consulting firm. You record a macro to copy the sheet and assign it to a *Button* control. You record another macro to delete data on the copied sheet. Finally, you print your macro code.
[Student Learning Outcomes 8.1, 8.2, 8.3, 8.4]

File Needed: None
Completed Project File Name: ***[your initials] Excel 8-9.xlsm***

Create and save a macro-enabled workbook named [your initials] Excel 8-9. Modify your workbook according to the following guidelines:

- In cell **A1**, type the name of a management consulting firm. In cell **A2**, type Quarterly Results, and in cell **A3**, type the name of a city followed by Office (for example, New York Office).
- Enter three month names for any quarter, spelled out, in cells **B4:D4**.
- In cells **A5:A9**, type the names of five tasks typically billed by a consulting firm.
- Prepare formulas to show totals in column **E** and in row **10**.
- Name the sheet tab Quarter Results. Format the worksheet with fonts, styles, alignment, fill, borders, or other attributes.
- Enter values in cells **B5:D9** that indicate number of tasks or dollars billed. Format these cells based on the type of value you chose.
- Write a macro to copy the worksheet and place it at the end.
- On the copied sheet, write a macro to delete the contents of cells **B5:D9** and the cells with month names. Use a keyboard shortcut for this macro.
- Draw a *Button* form control on the **Quarter Results** sheet and assign the macro that copies the worksheet.
- Delete the copied sheet and then test both macros.
- Open the Visual Basic Editor and the *Code* window for *Module 1* to print the code. If your macros are in separate modules, open *Module 2* and print the code.

Challenge Project 8-10

In this project, you explore how to use the *PERSONAL.XLSB* workbook, an option in the *Store Macro In* list in the *Record Macro* dialog box. *PERSONAL.XLSB* is a hidden workbook that is created and named automatically when you choose it as the location for a recorded macro. The workbook opens each time you start Excel, and its macros are available in any open workbook. (Note: If you are unable to access the PERSONAL workbook, verify that it is enabled. Click **File**, **Options**, and **Add-ins**. Then choose **Disabled Items** from the *Manage* drop-down list and enable the workbook if its name displays in the list.)
[Student Learning Outcomes 8.1, 8.2, 8.4, 8.5, 8.7]

File needed: None
Completed project file names: ***[your initials] Excel 8-10.xlsx*** and ***PERSONAL.XLSB***

Open a new Excel workbook and modify your workbook according to the following guidelines:

- Select cell **A1** and record a macro with relative references named MyName. Use a shortcut of **Ctrl+Shift+N**. In the *Record Macro* dialog box, select **Personal Macro Workbook** to store the macro.
- Type your name, your street address, your city, state, and ZIP code in three rows, typical address style, and stop recording.
- Verify that a printer is available and ready.
- Write another macro named PrintIt. Use a shortcut of **Ctrl+Shift+P** and store the macro in **Personal Macro Workbook**. Record your actions to print the active sheet; the sheet will print as you record the macro.
- Close the open workbook used for recording your macros without saving it. The *PERSONAL* macro workbook includes your macros.
- Open another new workbook and confirm that your printer is ready.
- Press **Ctrl+Shift+N** and then **Ctrl+Shift+P**. The *PERSONAL.XLSB* workbook is hidden, but its macros are available.
- Click the **View** tab and note that the *Unhide* button [*Window* group] is available.
- Click the arrow on the **Macros** button [*View* tab] and choose **View Macros**. The available macros list identifies the *PERSONAL.XLSB!* workbook. Select the **MyName** macro and choose **Edit**. You cannot edit a macro in a hidden workbook. Click **OK** in the message box and close the *Macro* dialog box.
- Click the **Unhide** button [*View* tab, *Window* group] to show the **PERSONAL** workbook. It has no visible data, only your macros. (If you are using a shared computer, the *PERSONAL* workbook may also include macros and documentation from another user.)
- Click the **Macros** button [*View* tab] and choose **View Macros**. Select the **MyName** macro and choose **Edit**. The Visual Basic Editor opens.
- In the VBE, edit your address. Add a personal title or your middle initial, a street direction, or spell out the state name. Be careful when editing code to not alter punctuation or commands unless you are familiar with Visual Basic for Applications programming. Close the VBE and return to the Excel window.
- Verify that you are in the *PERSONAL* workbook. From the *View* tab, choose **Hide** to hide the *PERSONAL* workbook. It is important that this workbook be hidden so that you don't accidentally enter data or unwanted commands.
- Delete data in the open workbook (or open a new workbook) and press **Ctrl+Shift+N** to run the edited macro. Save the Excel workbook as [your initials] Excel 8-10. Close the workbook.

- The *Personal Macro Workbook* remains available until you delete it. It is usually stored in *Users\UserName\AppData\Roaming\Microsoft\Excel\XLSTART*, which may be a hidden folder. In order to find and delete the *Personal Macro Workbook*, you must exit Excel. The file name does not appear in any Explorer window until you do that.
- Exit Excel and select **Save** in the message box to save changes to the *Personal Macro Workbook*. Do not restart Excel yet.
- Use a File Explorer window so that you can unhide the *XLSTART* folder if it is hidden. Click the **File Explorer** button on the Windows taskbar or choose **File Explorer** from the *Start* menu.
- Navigate to *C:\Users\UserName*. *UserName* is the name for the computer at which you are currently working.
- If you do not see the *AppData* folder, click the **View** tab and select the **Hidden items** box. This command displays folders that are hidden.
- Continue navigating to find *C:\Users\UserName\AppData\Roaming\Microsoft\Excel\XLSTART*. You should see *PERSONAL.XLSB* in this folder; file name extensions may be hidden on your computer. (Do not delete *PERSONAL* workbook if you are using a shared computer on which other users store macros.)
- Select and delete *PERSONAL.XLSB*. You cannot delete it if Excel is running because the file is open whenever Excel is running.
- Navigate once more to *C:\Users\UserName*.
- Click the **View** tab, deselect the **Hidden items** box, and close the File Explorer window.

Source of screenshots Microsoft Office 365 (2019): Word, Excel, Access, PowerPoint.

CHAPTER 9

Exploring Data Analysis and Maps

CHAPTER OVERVIEW

Excel provides self-service business intelligence (BI) with its data analysis tools so that you can use Excel to accomplish what previously required the help of an information technology department. In this chapter, you explore scenarios, *Goal Seek*, *Solver*, data tables, maps, and more.

STUDENT LEARNING OUTCOMES (SLOs)

After completing this chapter, students will be able to:

SLO 9.1 Create and manage scenarios for worksheet data (p. E9-552).

SLO 9.2 Use *Goal Seek* to backsolve a cell value for a formula (p. E9-555).

SLO 9.3 Use *Solver* to find a solution for a formula (p. E9-556).

SLO 9.4 Build data tables with one and two variables (p. E9-564).

SLO 9.5 Create a forecast sheet for time-based data (p. E9-568).

SLO 9.6 Use the *Analysis ToolPak* to calculate statistical measures (p. E9-572).

SLO 9.7 Work with Excel maps (p. E9-576).

CASE STUDY

In the Pause & Practice projects in this chapter, you create scenarios for Paradise Lakes Resort and build a Solver *problem. You build data tables, explore the* Analysis ToolPak, *and learn about maps.*

Pause & Practice 9-1: Create scenarios and use *Goal Seek* and *Solver* to find solutions.

Pause & Practice 9-2: Build one- and two-variable data tables and create a forecast sheet.

Pause & Practice 9-3: Use the *Analysis ToolPak* and create a map chart.

EXCEL

SLO 9.1

Creating and Managing Scenarios

A ***scenario*** is a named and saved set of values in a worksheet enabling you to vary numbers and see potential results. Scenarios are simple what-if analysis tools, often used to review best and worst possibilities. Paradise Lakes Resort, for example, can change the values for two revenue categories to calculate the effect on total revenue. Each test value is an input, is saved in the scenario, and can be shown in the worksheet.

> **MORE INFO**
>
> Because each scenario input value must be typed in the *Scenario Values* dialog box, use scenarios for data with only a few sets of values.

Create a Scenario

The first scenario to create is a scenario for current data so that you can always return to those values. After that, create additional scenarios using the same cells with different values. You can display any scenario when needed, but only one scenario can be displayed at a time. Although it is optional, it is helpful to name input and result cells so that summary reports are easily understood.

Create a scenario by choosing ***Scenario Manager*** from the **What-if Analysis** button in the *Forecast* group on the *Data* tab.

HOW TO: Create and Show a Scenario

1. Click the **What-if Analysis** button [*Data* tab, *Forecast* group].
2. Select **Scenario Manager**.
   - The *Scenario Manager* dialog box opens.
   - Existing scenarios, if any, are listed in the dialog box (Figure 9-1).
3. Click **Add**.
   - The *Add Scenario* dialog box opens.
   - If cells are selected, the addresses display in the *Changing cells* box.
4. Type a name in the *Scenario name* box.
   - Name the original set of values Original or a similar name.
   - Use a short, descriptive name.
   - Use capitalization and spaces as desired.
5. Click the **Changing cells** box and select the cells whose values will be changed.
   - Press **Ctrl** to select non-contiguous cells or type a comma (,) to separate addresses.
   - If you select cells from this entry box, the addresses are absolute.
   - The dialog box displays *Edit Scenario* in its title bar when you select a contiguous cell range.
6. Click the **Comment** box to type an optional description or explanation.
   - A default comment with the user name and date displays for each scenario.

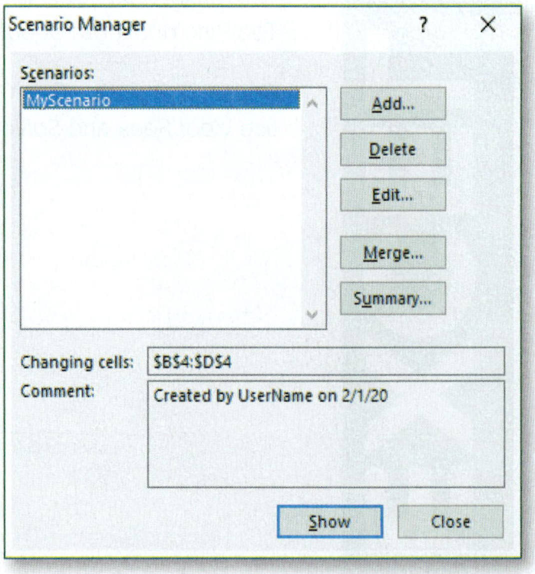

Figure 9-1 ***Scenario Manager*** **dialog box**

7. Make *Protection* choices (Figure 9-2).
   - The options pertain to a protected worksheet.
   - Select the **Prevent changes** box to prohibit edits to the scenario in a protected worksheet.
   - Select the **Hide** box to prevent a scenario from displaying in a protected worksheet.
8. Click **OK**.
   - The *Scenario Values* dialog box opens.
   - The values currently displayed in the worksheet are shown for each cell address or name in the *Changing cells* selection.
9. Type a new value for each cell name or address (Figure 9-3).
   - Leave the values unchanged when creating a scenario for the original set of values.
   - Each scenario can include up to 32 values.

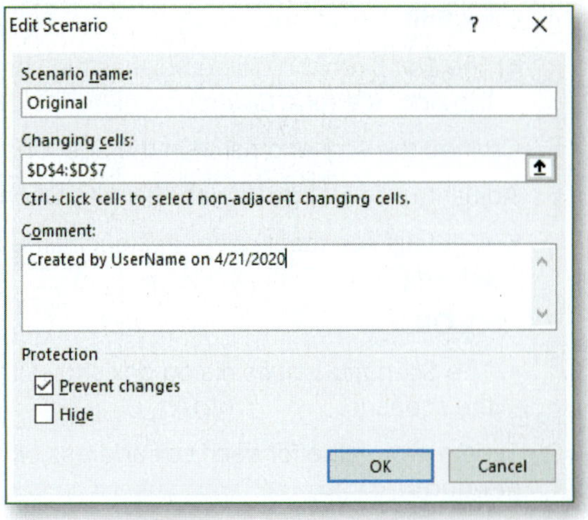

Figure 9-2 Scenario setup for original values

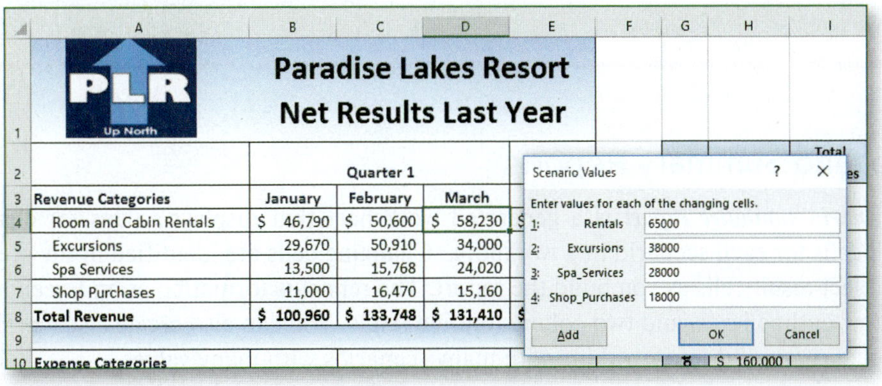

Figure 9-3 New values entered in the *Scenario Values* dialog box

10. Click **OK** in the *Scenario Values* dialog box.
    - The *Scenario Manager* dialog box shows the scenario name.
11. Click **Show**.
    - The values from the selected scenario replace the values in the worksheet.
    - Select another scenario name and click **Show**.
12. Click **Close** in the *Scenario Manager* dialog box.
    - The values currently displayed remain visible.

Edit a Scenario

When a scenario displays, you can change the values in the affected cells as a regular edit. The scenario itself is unchanged. To change the values saved in a scenario, open the *Scenario Manager*, select the scenario name, and click *Edit*. From the *Edit Scenario* dialog box, change a scenario name, redefine which cells are changed, and open the *Scenario Values* dialog box.

▸HOW TO: Edit and Display a Scenario

1. Click the **What-if Analysis** button [*Data* tab, *Forecast* group].
2. Select **Scenario Manager**.
3. Select the scenario name in the *Scenarios* list.

4. Click **Edit**.
   - The *Edit Scenario* dialog box has the same entry options as the *Add Scenario* dialog box.
5. Change the scenario name in the *Scenario name* box.
6. Adjust the cell range if needed in the *Changing cells* box.
   - A default comment generates each time the scenario is edited (Figure 9-4).
7. Click **OK**.
   - The *Scenario Values* dialog box shows the current values for the scenario.
8. Type a new value for each cell address or range name as needed.
9. Click **OK**.
10. Click **Show** to view the edited scenario in the worksheet.
11. Click **Close**.

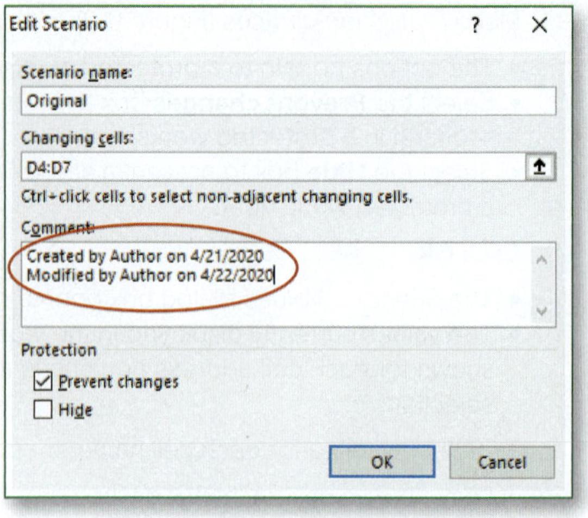

Figure 9-4 Comments are inserted each time a scenario is edited

Scenario Summary Reports

A ***scenario summary report*** is a generated worksheet that displays values for changing and result cells for each scenario in a workbook. Changing cells are identified in the scenario, and you select result cells as you build the report. The report is formatted as an Excel outline with two row outline levels and two column outline levels. You can also create a scenario summary report as a *PivotTable* for working with many scenarios with many values.

If you edit a scenario after creating a summary report, the report does not update. You can, however, generate another scenario summary report.

▸HOW TO: Create a Scenario Summary Report

1. Click the **What-if Analysis** button [*Data* tab, *Forecast* group].
2. Select **Scenario Manager**.
3. Click **Summary**.
   - The *Scenario Summary* dialog box opens.
4. Choose **Scenario summary** as the *Report type*.
5. Click the **Result cells** box and select the cell or range (Figure 9-5).
   - These are cells that are affected by the changing cells.
   - Press **Ctrl** to select nonadjacent cells or type a comma (,) to separate cell addresses.
6. Click **OK**.
   - The report is generated on a sheet named **Scenario Summary** (Figure 9-6).
   - The report is formatted as an outline in a default style.
   - Hide or display details, delete blank columns and rows, and format the sheet as desired.

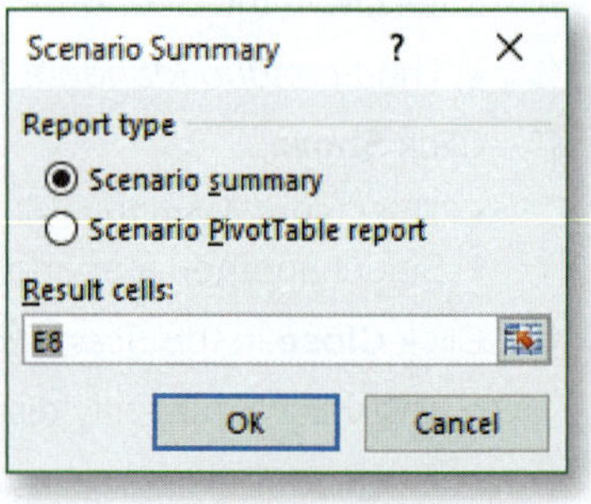

Figure 9-5 *Scenario Summary* dialog box

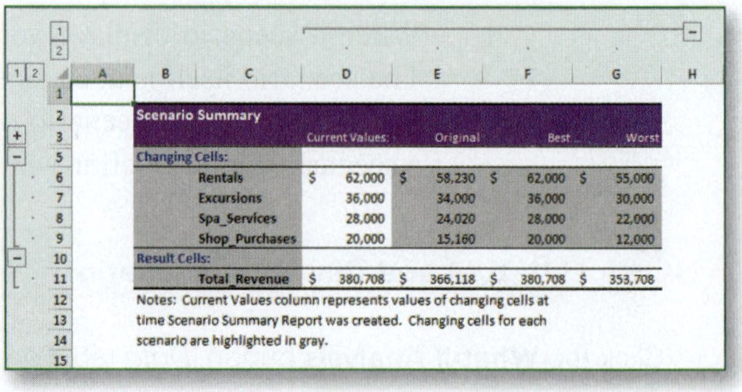

Figure 9-6 *Scenario Summary* report

> **MORE INFO**
>
> You can merge scenarios from different worksheets or workbooks when the data follows a consistent layout and pattern. Explore this option in Excel *Help*.

SLO 9.2

Using Goal Seek

Goal Seek is a what-if analysis command that tests values in a cell to *backsolve* a formula. ***Backsolving*** means knowing the results and determining the value needed to reach those results. When buying a car, use *Goal Seek* to determine your loan amount if you can afford a $500 per month payment.

Use Goal Seek

Goal Seek solves a formula for one cell (one argument) in the formula. In the *Goal Seek* dialog box, enter the cell reference for the formula in the *Set cell* box. Then type a target or goal number in the *To value* box. In Figure 9-7, the formula in cell D4 is backsolved by adjusting the value in cell B4 so that the formula result is $50. The solution appears in the *Goal Seek Status* dialog box shown in Figure 9-8 and in the worksheet. You can accept it or keep the original value.

The *Goal Seek* command is an option for the **What-if Analysis** button [*Data* tab, *Forecast* group].

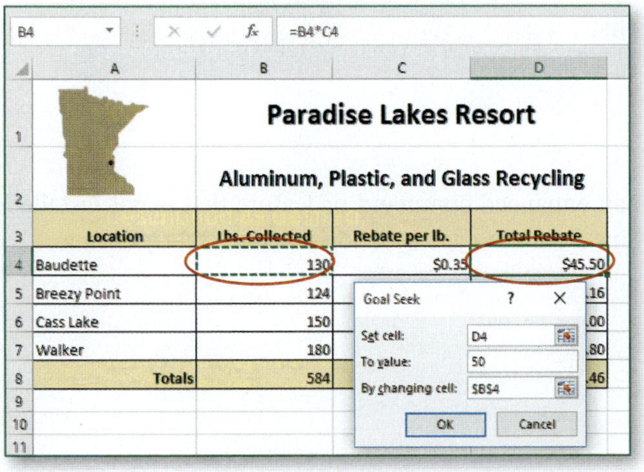

Figure 9-7 *Goal Seek* problem and dialog box

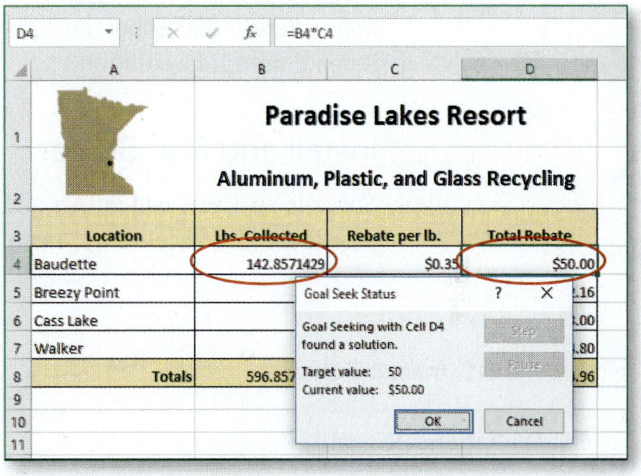

Figure 9-8 *Goal Seek Status* shows a solution

HOW TO: Use Goal Seek

1. Select the cell with the formula.
2. Click the **What-if Analysis** button [*Data* tab, *Forecast* group] and choose **Goal Seek**.
   - The *Goal Seek* dialog box opens.
   - Verify the formula address in the *Set cell* box.
3. Click the **To value** box and type the target value.
   - This is the result you want the formula to return.

4. Click the **By changing cell** box and click the cell to be adjusted (see Figure 9-7).
   - The address displays as an absolute reference.
   - *Goal Seek* can change only one cell.
   - Key the address instead of selecting the cell.
5. Click **OK**.
   - The *Goal Seek Status* dialog box indicates that a solution was calculated (see Figure 9-8).
   - The solution displays in the cell.
6. Click **OK** to accept the solution.
   - Alternatively, press **Enter** to accept the solution.
   - Choose **Cancel** to ignore the solution and keep the original data.

SLO 9.3

Using Solver

Solver is an analysis tool that finds the lowest, the highest, or a specific result for a formula by changing values in other cells within limitations that you set. Using *Solver* can be described as solving a problem in reverse, because you start with the desired answer and *Solver* calculates how to reach that answer. Paradise Lakes Resort, for example, might set a goal for quarterly revenue and use *Solver* to determine the best way to reach that goal by calculating a target for each revenue category.

Solver is a sophisticated analysis tool, but it may not be able to find a solution to every problem. When it cannot do so, the *Solver Results* dialog box informs you that it could not find a solution.

> **MORE INFO**
>
> *Solver* may be described as an optimization tool.

Install and Run Solver

Solver is an Excel ***add-in***. An add-in is an enhanced command or feature that is not installed with the initial Excel setup. Install add-ins from the *Add-ins* dialog box in Excel *Options*.

HOW TO: Install Solver

1. Select **Options** [*File* tab].
2. Click **Add-ins** in the left pane.
   - The *View and manage Microsoft Office Add-ins* dialog box opens.
   - Active applications are listed near the top of the window.
   - Inactive but available add-ins are also listed.
3. Verify that **Solver Add-in** appears in the list of *Inactive Application Add-ins* (Figure 9-9).
   - Excel applications that are available depend on your version of Excel.
4. Click **Go** near the bottom of the dialog box to open the *Add-ins* dialog box.
5. Select the **Solver Add-in** box (see Figure 9-9).
   - Remove *Solver* by deselecting the box.
6. Click **OK**.
   - The **Solver** button displays in the *Analysis* group on the *Data* tab.

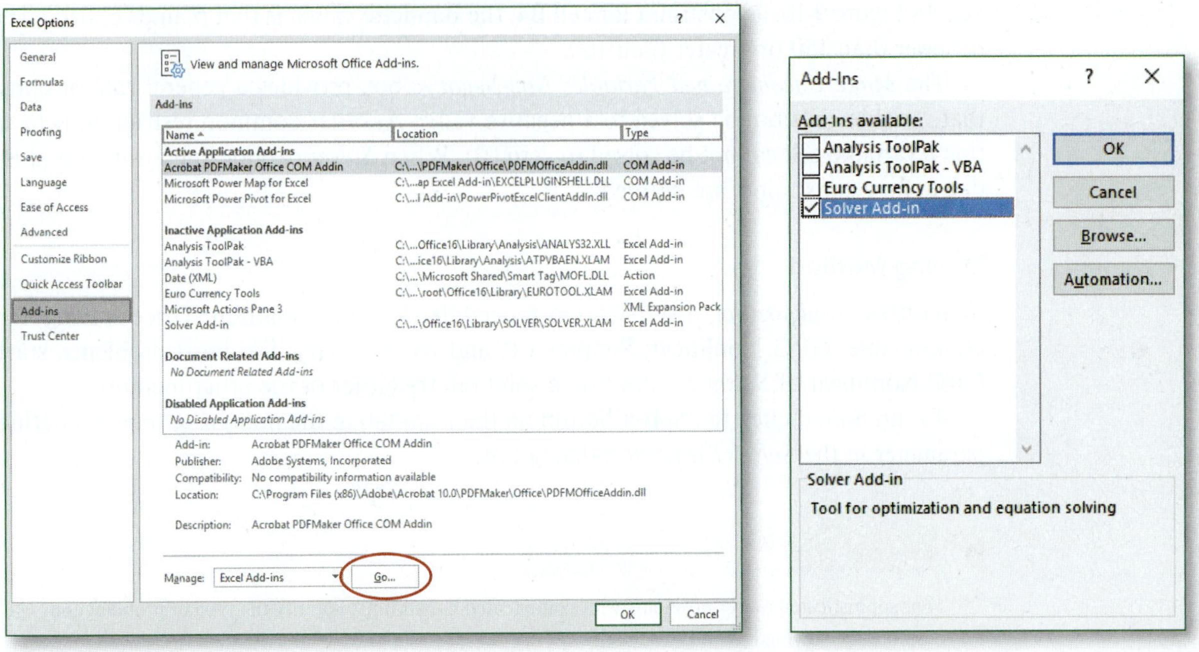

Figure 9-9 *Add-ins* dialog boxes in Excel *Options*

A *Solver* problem has three components, known as ***parameters***. A parameter is information that *Solver* needs to find a solution. The parameters are the objective cell, variable cells, and constraints.

The Objective Cell

The ***objective cell*** is a cell with a formula to be calculated to reach a desired result. It is sometimes referred to as the ***target cell***. You can set the objective cell to the maximum or minimum or to a value. In Figure 9-10, Paradise Lakes uses *Solver* to determine a maximum total rebate. The formula in cell D8 is the objective cell.

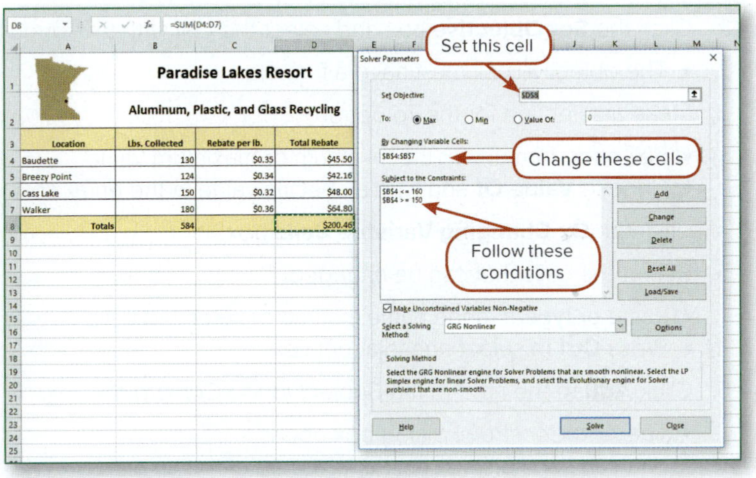

Figure 9-10 *Solver* problem for Paradise Lakes

Variable Cells

In order to reach the desired result in the objective cell, *Solver* changes the cells identified as ***variable cells***. These cells may also be called ***decision cells*** or ***changing cells***. In Figure 9-10, the variable cells are cells B4:B7.

Constraints

A ***constraint*** is a restriction or limitation. It might be a limitation on the formula, on one or more of the variable cells, or a limitation on other cells that are directly related to the objective cell. In Figure 9-10, a constraint for cell B4, the Baudette value, is that pounds collected cannot be fewer than 150 or greater than 160.

The *Make Unconstrained Variables Non-Negative* box provides a general rule or constraint that variable cells not be solved to a negative value. Another common restriction is to specify that a variable cell cannot be solved to zero (0). When *Solver* cannot find a solution, it is often due to how constraints are defined.

Solving Method

Solver uses an ***algorithm***, a step-by-step procedure, to find a solution. Three solving methods are available: GRG Nonlinear, Simplex LP, and Evolutionary. For most problems, start with GRG Nonlinear. If *Solver* cannot find a solution, try either of the other methods.

To run *Solver*, click the **Solver** button on the *Data* tab in the *Analysis* group and define each parameter in the *Solver Parameters* dialog box.

> **MORE INFO**
>
> For sophisticated *Solver* problems with complicated constraints, identify the type of problem and explore the solving methods in detail.

HOW TO: Run Solver

1. Click the **Solver** button [*Data* tab, *Analysis* group].
   - The *Solver Parameters* dialog box opens.
2. Click the **Set Objective** box and select the cell with the formula to be solved.
   - The objective cell must have a formula.
3. Make a selection for the *To* option.
   - Solve the formula for the minimum or maximum value.
   - Choose **Value Of** and type a specific value in the entry box.
4. Click the **By Changing Variable Cells** box.
5. Select the cells that can be changed.
   - Paste or type a range name instead of selecting cells.
   - Press **Ctrl** to select nonadjacent cells.
6. Click **Add** to the right of the *Subject to the Constraints* box.
   - The *Add Constraint* dialog box opens.
   - You can set multiple constraints for a cell.
7. Click the **Cell Reference** box and select the first cell or range that has a limitation.
8. Click the middle drop-down arrow and choose an operator.
   - The *int* operator limits the value to a whole number.
   - The *bin* operator requires a binary value, either 0 or 1.
   - The *dif* operator is used to specify that all values in a range must be different.
9. Click the **Constraint** box and enter a value (Figure 9-11).
10. Click **Add** in the *Add Constraint* dialog box to add another constraint.
    - If you click **OK** but want to add another constraint, click **Add** to the right of the *Subject to the Constraints* box.

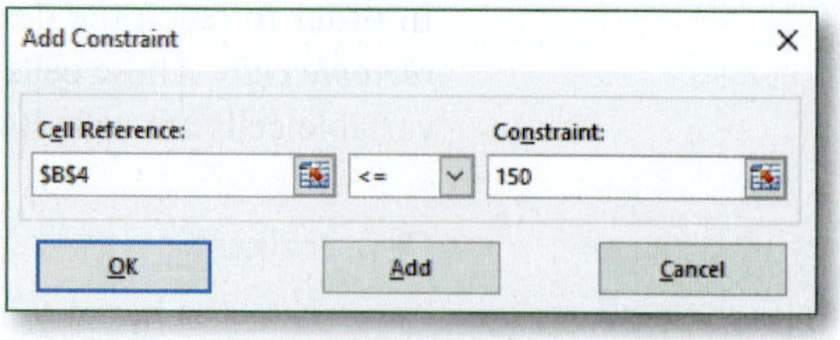

Figure 9-11 ***Add Constraint* dialog box**

11. Click **OK** in the *Add Constraint* dialog box when all constraints are identified.
    - The constraints display in the *Solver Parameters* dialog box.
12. Select the **Make Unconstrained Variables Non-Negative** box.
    - If you leave this box unchecked, a variable cell without a constraint may be solved to a negative number.
13. Click the **Select a Solving Method** arrow and choose a method (Figure 9-12).
    - If *Solver* cannot find a solution, try a different method.
14. Click **Solve**.
    - The *Solver Results* dialog box includes an option to keep the solution or to return to the original values.
    - Save the results as a scenario if desired.
    - Generate *Solver* reports as needed.
15. Click **OK** to keep the solution.

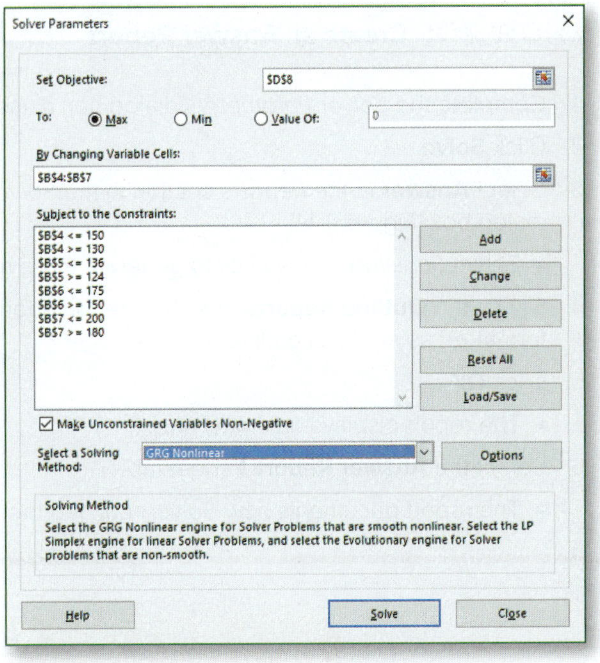

Figure 9-12 **Completed *Solver* parameters with constraints**

Solver Reports

Select an option in the *Solver Results* dialog box to generate statistical analysis reports about the problem and the solution. Three reports for a solved problem are listed: *Answer*, *Sensitivity*, and *Limits*. These reports are straightforward to generate, but you should have an understanding of statistical concepts and terms to understand and interpret the reports.

> **MORE INFO**
>
> When *Solver* cannot find a solution, print the *Feasibility* and *Feasibility-Bounds* reports to help identify constraint issues.

Answer Report

The ***Answer*** report identifies and lists each parameter and serves as documentation of your work. The report includes original values and values suggested by *Solver* as shown in Figure 9-13.

The first *Answer* report is inserted in the workbook in a sheet named **Answer Report 1**. If you run *Solver* multiple times, you can generate an answer report each time, and the sheets are named **Answer Report 2**, and so on.

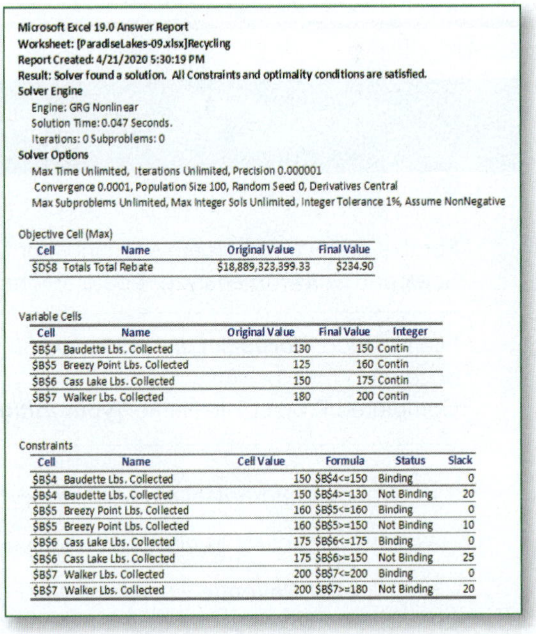

Microsoft Excel 19.0 Answer Report
Worksheet: [ParadiseLakes-09.xlsx]Recycling
Report Created: 4/21/2020 5:30:19 PM
Result: Solver found a solution. All Constraints and optimality conditions are satisfied.
Solver Engine
Engine: GRG Nonlinear
Solution Time: 0.047 Seconds.
Iterations: 0 Subproblems: 0
Solver Options
Max Time Unlimited, Iterations Unlimited, Precision 0.000001
Convergence 0.0001, Population Size 100, Random Seed 0, Derivatives Central
Max Subproblems Unlimited, Max Integer Sols Unlimited, Integer Tolerance 1%, Assume NonNegative

Objective Cell (Max)

Cell	Name	Original Value	Final Value
$D$8	Totals Total Rebate	$18,889,323,399.33	$234.90

Variable Cells

Cell	Name	Original Value	Final Value	Integer
$B$4	Baudette Lbs. Collected	130	150	Contin
$B$5	Breezy Point Lbs. Collected	125	160	Contin
$B$6	Cass Lake Lbs. Collected	150	175	Contin
$B$7	Walker Lbs. Collected	180	200	Contin

Constraints

Cell	Name	Cell Value	Formula	Status	Slack
$B$4	Baudette Lbs. Collected	150	$B$4<=150	Binding	0
$B$4	Baudette Lbs. Collected	150	$B$4>=130	Not Binding	20
$B$5	Breezy Point Lbs. Collected	160	$B$5<=160	Binding	0
$B$5	Breezy Point Lbs. Collected	160	$B$5>=150	Not Binding	10
$B$6	Cass Lake Lbs. Collected	175	$B$6<=175	Binding	0
$B$6	Cass Lake Lbs. Collected	175	$B$6>=150	Not Binding	25
$B$7	Walker Lbs. Collected	200	$B$7<=200	Binding	0
$B$7	Walker Lbs. Collected	200	$B$7>=180	Not Binding	20

Figure 9-13 **A *Solver Answer* report**

▸HOW TO: Create an Answer Report

1. Complete the *Solver Parameters* dialog box as needed.
2. Click **Solve**.
3. Select **Answer** in the *Reports* section in the *Solver Results* dialog box (Figure 9-14).
   - Select *Sensitivity* and *Limits* to generate three reports.
4. Select the **Outline Reports** box if the report should be formatted as an Excel outline.
5. Click **OK**.
   - The report displays on a new sheet.
6. Select the **Answer Report 1** sheet tab.
   - The report documents how *Solver* reached the solution.

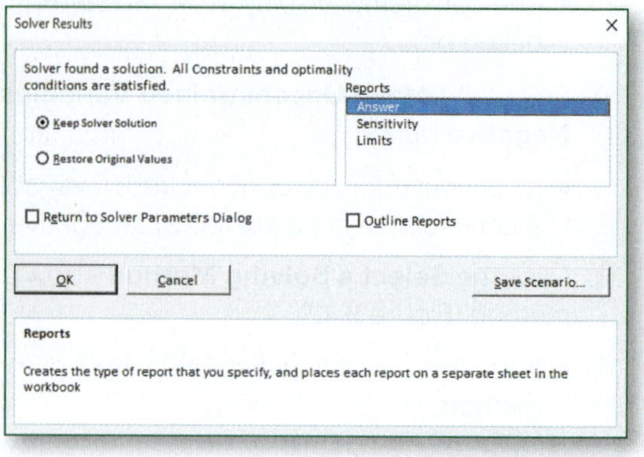

Figure 9-14 ***Solver Results*** **window**

MORE INFO

If *Solver* returns a runtime error, uninstall the command from the *Add-Ins* dialog box in Excel *Options*, and exit Excel. Then restart Excel and install *Solver* again.

▸HOW TO: Uninstall Solver

1. Select **Options** [*File* tab] and click **Add-ins** in the left pane.
   - The *View and manage Microsoft Office Add-ins* dialog box opens.
2. Select **Solver Add-in** in the list of *Active Application Add-ins*.
3. Click **Go** near the bottom of the dialog box.
4. Deselect the **Solver Add-in** box and click **OK**.

PAUSE & PRACTICE: EXCEL 9-1

For this project, you create scenarios for March revenue at Paradise Lakes Resort. You also use *Goal Seek* and *Solver* to analyze rebate amounts.

File Needed: ***ParadiseLakes-09.xlsx*** *(Student data files are available in the* Library *of your SIMnet account.)*
Completed Project File Name: ***[your initials] PP E9-1.xlsx***

1. Open the **ParadiseLakes-09** workbook from your student data files.
2. Enable content as needed and save the workbook as [your initials] PP E9-1.
3. Click the **Revenue** worksheet tab. Formulas in the "Expense Categories" section refer to cell ranges on a hidden worksheet in the workbook.

4. Create a scenario for the original revenue data.
   a. Select cells **D4:D7**, the revenue for March.
   b. Click the **What-if Analysis** button [*Data* tab, *Forecast* group].
   c. Select **Scenario Manager**. No scenarios exist in the workbook.
   d. Click **Add**.
   e. Type Original as the name in the *Add Scenario* dialog box. The *Changing cells* box displays **D4:D7** and a default comment (Figure 9-15).

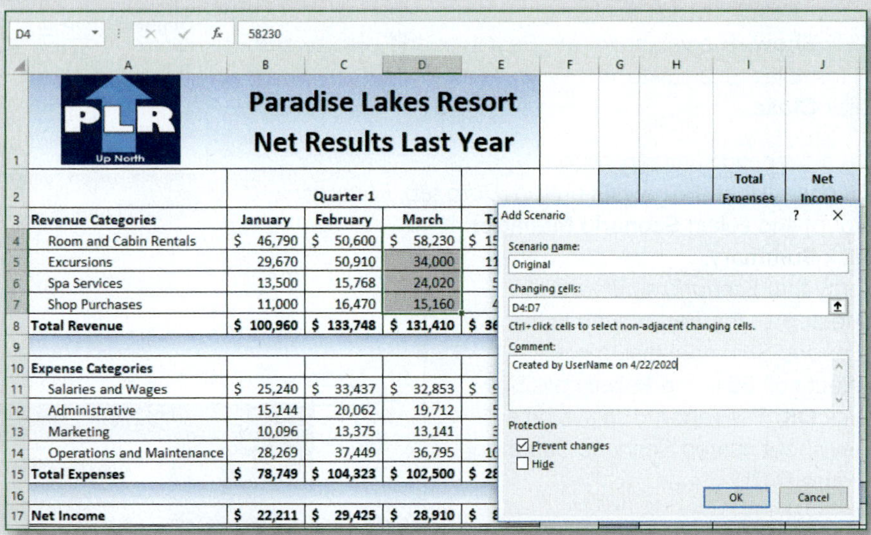

Figure 9-15 *Add Scenario Manager*

   f. Click **OK**. The *Scenario Values* dialog box displays range names for the changing cells.
   g. Do not change any values in the *Scenario Values* dialog box and click **OK**.
   h. Click **Close**.

5. Create scenarios with new data.
   a. Click the **What-if Analysis** button [*Data* tab, *Forecast* group] and select **Scenario Manager**. The *Original* scenario name is listed.
   b. Click **Add** to add a second scenario to the workbook.
   c. Type Best as the name in the *Add Scenario* dialog box.
   d. Verify that the *Changing cells* are cells **D4:D7**.
   e. Click **OK**.
   f. Type 62000 for **Rentals** in the *Scenario Values* dialog box and press **Tab**. If you accidentally press **Enter** and return to the *Scenario Manager* dialog box, select the **Best** scenario name, click **Edit**, and click **OK**.
   g. Edit the values as shown here:

Excursions	36000
Spa_Services	28000
Shop_Purchases	20000

   h. Click **OK** and then click **Add** to add a third scenario.
   i. Type Worst as the name and click **OK**.
   j. Edit the values as shown here:

Rentals	55000
Excursions	30000
Spa_Services	22000
Shop_Purchases	12000

k. Click **OK** and click **Close**. The original values still display in the workbook.
l. Select cell **A2**.

6. Show a scenario.
   a. Click the **What-if Analysis** button [*Data* tab, *Forecast* group] and select **Scenario Manager**. The three scenario names are listed (Figure 9-16).
   b. Select **Best** in the list to highlight the name.
   c. Click **Show**. The values for the *Best* scenario display and all formulas recalculate.
   d. Click **Close**.

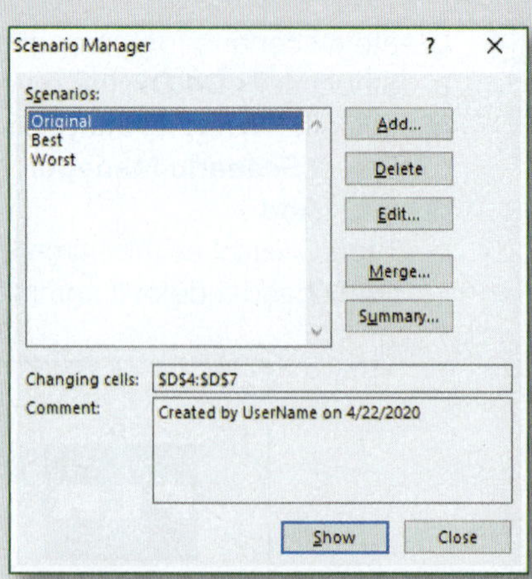

Figure 9-16 Scenario names in the dialog box

7. Create a scenario summary report.
   a. Click the **What-if Analysis** button [*Data* tab, *Forecast* group] and select **Scenario Manager**.
   b. Click **Summary**.
   c. Verify that *Scenario summary* is selected as the *Report type* in the *Scenario Summary* dialog box.
   d. Select cell **E8** in the *Result cells* box.
   e. Click **OK**. The report displays on a new sheet named *Scenario Summary* (Figure 9-17).

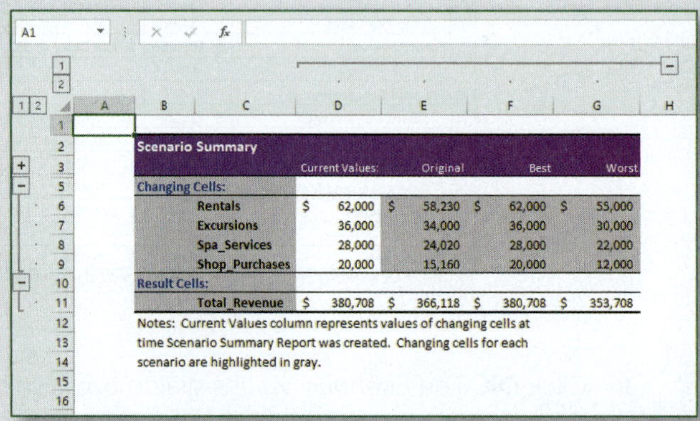

Figure 9-17 *Scenario Summary* report sheet

8. Use *Goal Seek* to determine the number of pounds of recycling.
   a. Click the **Recycling** sheet tab and select cell **D4**.
   b. Click the **What-if Analysis** button [*Data* tab, *Forecast* group] and choose **Goal Seek**.
   c. Click the **To value** box and type 50.
   d. Click the **By changing cell** box and select cell **B4** (Figure 9-18).
   e. Click **OK** to run *Goal Seek*. The solution in cell D4 calculates that recycling must increase to more than 142 pounds to reach the target.
   f. Click **OK** to accept the solution.
   g. Select cell **D5**, run *Goal Seek* to determine how many pounds must be collected to reach $50 for Breezy Point, and accept the solution.
   h. Select cells **B4:B8** and click the **Decrease Decimal** button [*Home* tab, *Number* group] five times to display all values with two decimal places.

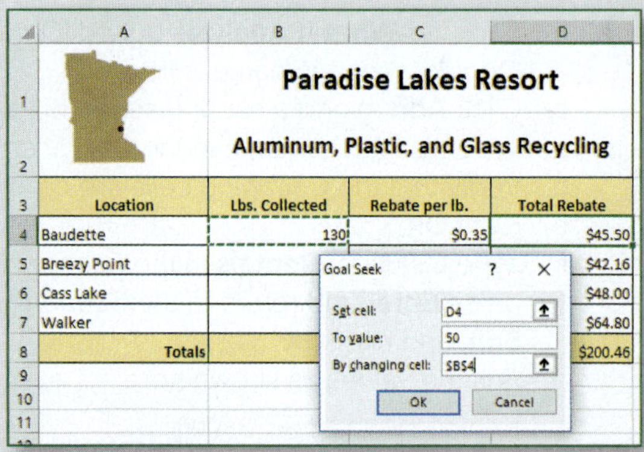

Figure 9-18 *Goal Seek* dialog box

9. Create a scenario for the *Goal Seek* solutions.
   a. Select cells **B4:B7** and click the **What-if Analysis** button [*Data* tab, *Forecast* group].
   b. Select **Scenario Manager** and click **Add**. Scenarios are associated with a worksheet, and this sheet currently has no scenarios.
   c. Type Current as the name in the *Add Scenario* dialog box.
   d. Click **OK**.
   e. Do not change any values and click **OK** and then click **Close**.

10. Install *Solver*. (Skip this step if *Solver* is already installed.)
    a. Select the **Options** command [*File* tab].
    b. Click **Add-ins** in the left pane.
    c. Click **Solver Add-in** in the *Inactive Application Add-ins* list.
    d. Click **Go** near the bottom of the window.
    e. Select the **Solver Add-in** box and click **OK**.
11. Set *Solver* parameters.
    a. Select cell **D8**. This cell has a *SUM* formula.
    b. Click the **Solver** button [*Data* tab, *Analysis* group] to open the *Solver Parameters* dialog box.
    c. Click cell **D8** for the *Set Objective* box; it is an absolute reference.
    d. Verify that the *Max* radio button is selected for the *To* option.
    e. Click the **By Changing Variable Cells** box and select cells **B4:B7**.
12. Add constraints to a *Solver* problem.
    a. Click **Add** to the right of the *Subject to the Constraints* box.
    b. Select cell **B4** for the *Cell Reference* box.
    c. Verify that **<=** is the operator.
    d. Click the **Constraint** box and type 150 (Figure 9-19).
    e. Click **Add** to add another constraint. If you accidentally closed the *Add Constraint* dialog box, click **Add** in the *Solver Parameters* dialog box.
    f. Select cell **B4** again for the *Cell Reference* box.
    g. Choose **>=** as the operator and type 130 as the constraint. The value in cell B4 must be equal to or less than 150 and equal to or greater than 130 (between 130 and 150).
    h. Add the following constraints:

B5	<=	160
B5	>=	150
B6	<=	175
B6	>=	150
B7	<=	200
B7	>=	180

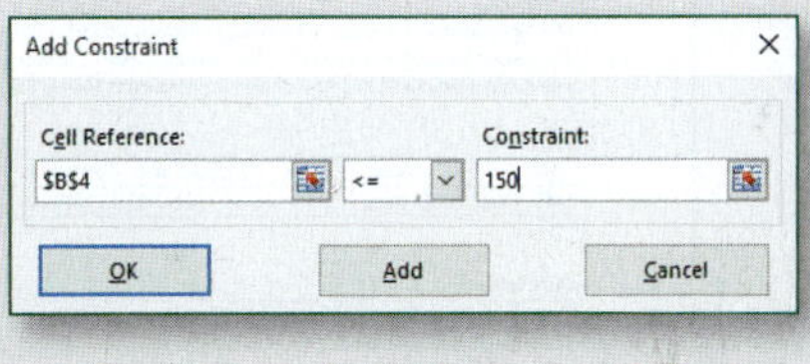

Figure 9-19 *Add Constraint* dialog box

    i. Click **OK** in the *Add Constraint* dialog box when all constraints are identified (Figure 9-20).
    j. Select the **Make Unconstrained Variables Non-Negative** box if needed.
    k. Choose **GRG Nonlinear** for the *Select a Solving Method*.
    l. Click **Solve**. A possible solution to the problem displays in the worksheet and the *Solver Results* dialog box is open.
    m. Position the *Solver Results* dialog box to see cell D8 in the worksheet.

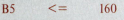

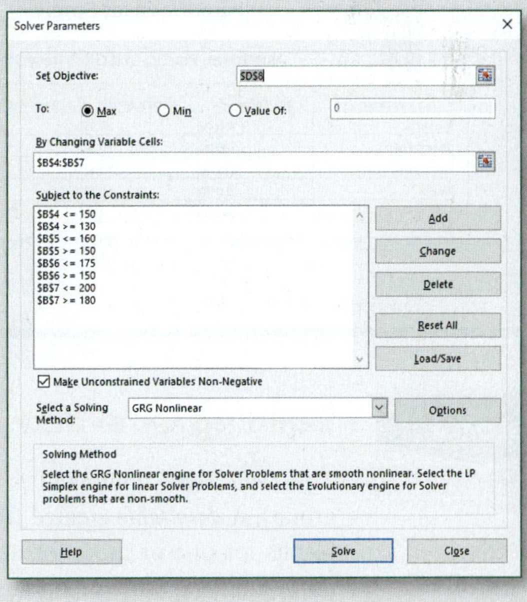

Figure 9-20 All constraints are listed

13. Manage *Solver* results.
    a. Click **Save Scenario** in the *Solver Results* dialog box.
    b. Type Max as the scenario name.
    c. Click **OK** to return to the *Solver Results* dialog box.
    d. Verify that the *Keep Solver Solution* button is selected.
    e. Select **Answer** in the *Reports* list.
    f. Click **OK**. The generated report displays on the **Answer Report 1** sheet, and *Solver* results replace original values in the worksheet.

14. Create a scenario summary report.
    a. Click the **Recycling** sheet tab, click the **What-if Analysis** button [*Data* tab, *Forecast* group], and select **Scenario Manager**.
    b. Click **Summary**.
    c. Verify that *Scenario summary* is selected as the *Report type*.
    d. Click the **Result cells** box and verify or select cell **D8**.
    e. Click **OK**. The report displays on a sheet named **Scenario Summary 2**.
15. Uninstall *Solver*.
    a. Select **Options** [*File* tab] and click **Add-ins** in the left pane.
    b. Select **Solver Add-in** in the list of *Active Application Add-Ins*.
    c. Click **Go** near the bottom of the dialog box.
    d. Deselect the **Solver Add-in** box and click **OK**.
16. Save and close the workbook (Figure 9-21).

Microsoft Excel 19.0 Answer Report
Worksheet: [PP E9-1.xlsx]Recycling
Report Created: 4/22/2020 5:14:54 PM
Result: Solver found a solution. All Constraints and optimality conditions are satisfied.
Solver Engine
Engine: GRG Nonlinear
Solution Time: 0.016 Seconds
Iterations: 5 Subproblems: 0
Solver Options
Max Time Unlimited, Iterations Unlimited, Precision 0.000001
Convergence 0.0001, Population Size 100, Random Seed 0, Derivatives Central
Max Subproblems Unlimited, Max Integer Sols Unlimited, Integer Tolerance 1%, Assume NonNegative

Objective Cell (Max)

Cell	Name	Original Value	Final Value
$D$8	Totals Total Rebate	$212.80	$234.90

Variable Cells

Cell	Name	Original Value	Final Value	Integer
$B$4	Baudette Lbs. Collected	142.86	150.00	Contin
$B$5	Breezy Point Lbs. Collected	147.06	160.00	Contin
$B$6	Cass Lake Lbs. Collected	150.00	175.00	Contin
$B$7	Walker Lbs. Collected	180.00	200.00	Contin

Constraints

Cell	Name	Cell Value	Formula	Status	Slack
$B$4	Baudette Lbs. Collected	150.00	$B$4<=150	Binding	0
$B$4	Baudette Lbs. Collected	150.00	$B$4>=130	Not Binding	20.00
$B$5	Breezy Point Lbs. Collected	160.00	$B$5<=160	Binding	0
$B$5	Breezy Point Lbs. Collected	160.00	$B$5>=150	Not Binding	10.00
$B$6	Cass Lake Lbs. Collected	175.00	$B$6<=175	Binding	0
$B$6	Cass Lake Lbs. Collected	175.00	$B$6>=150	Not Binding	25.00
$B$7	Walker Lbs. Collected	200.00	$B$7<=200	Binding	0
$B$7	Walker Lbs. Collected	200.00	$B$7>=180	Not Binding	20.00

Paradise Lakes Resort
Net Results Last Year

	Quarter 1			
Revenue Categories	January	February	March	Total
Room and Cabin Rentals	$ 46,790	$ 50,600	$ 62,000	$ 159,390
Excursions	29,670	50,910	36,000	116,580
Spa Services	13,500	15,768	28,000	57,268
Shop Purchases	11,000	16,470	20,000	47,470
Total Revenue	**$ 100,960**	**$ 133,748**	**$ 146,000**	**$ 380,708**
Expense Categories				
Salaries and Wages	$ 25,240	$ 33,437	$ 36,500	$ 95,177
Administrative	15,144	20,062	21,900	57,106
Marketing	10,096	13,375	14,600	38,071
Operations and Maintenance	28,269	37,449	40,880	106,598
Total Expenses	**$ 78,749**	**$ 104,323**	**$ 113,880**	**$ 296,952**
Net Income	$ 22,211	$ 29,425	$ 32,120	$ 83,756

Paradise Lakes Resort
Aluminum, Plastic, and Glass Recycling

Location	Lbs. Collected	Rebate per lb.	Total Rebate
Baudette	150.00	$0.35	$52.50
Breezy Point	160.00	$0.34	$54.40
Cass Lake	175.00	$0.32	$56.00
Walker	200.00	$0.36	$72.00
Totals	685.00		$234.90

Scenario Summary

	Current Values:	Current	Max
Changing Cells:			
$B$4	150.00	142.86	150.00
$B$5	160.00	147.06	160.00
$B$6	175.00	150.00	175.00
$B$7	200.00	180.00	200.00
Result Cells:			
$D$8	$234.90	$212.80	$234.90

Notes: Current Values column represents values of changing cells at time Scenario Summary Report was created. Changing cells for each scenario are highlighted in gray.

Figure 9-21 Completed worksheets for PP E9-1

SLO 9.4

Building One- and Two-Variable Data Tables

The *Data Table* command is an option on the **What-If Analysis** button [*Data* tab, *Forecast* group]. A ***data table*** created from the **What-If Analysis** button is a range of cells that calculates results for one or more formulas. The *Data Table* command inserts the function {=TABLE (row_input, column_input)} as an array formula, because the same formula is executed in each cell in the data table range. In *SLO 6.3:* Explore the *Lookup & Reference category* with *INDEX*, *MATCH*, and *TRANSPOSE*, you learned about array formulas when you used *TRANSPOSE*.

Build a One-Variable Data Table

A ***one-variable data table*** substitutes values for one argument in a formula and displays results for each substituted value. Figure 9-22 shows a data table in columns G:J with descriptive labels in column G and row 2. The data table refers to two formulas that have a relationship to cell B8. Cell I3 refers to the January expenses formula in cell B15. Cell J3 refers to the January income formula in cell B17. The *Data Table* command calculates results for those formulas in cells I4:J14 when the values in column H are substituted for cell B8.

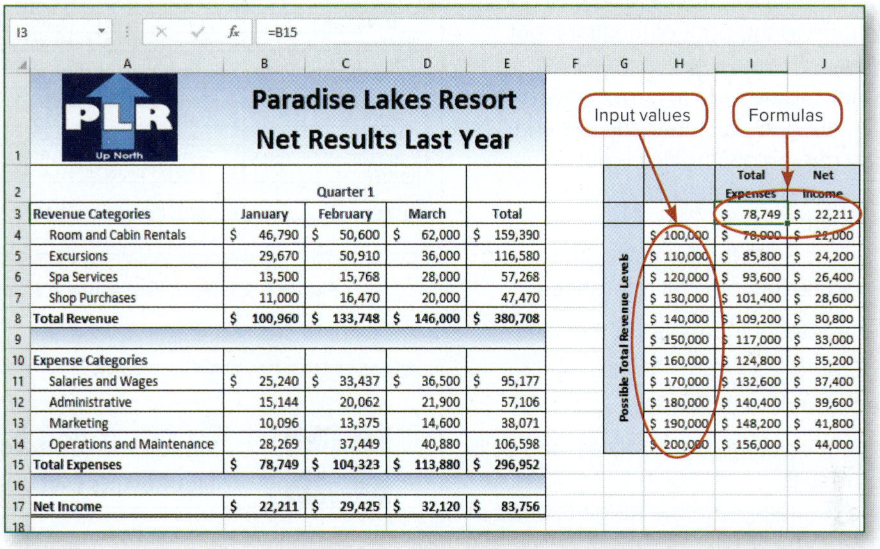

Figure 9-22 Data table shows expense and income numbers when January revenue amounts are varied

The *Data Table* command requires one or two ***input cell(s)***. A one-variable data table uses one input cell, either a column or row input based on worksheet layout. The data table in Figure 9-22 has a column input (cell B8) to use the values in column H as possible results for the formula in cell B8.

When input values are in a column, the data table formulas must start in the column to the right and one row above where the input values start. When the data table has multiple formulas, the formulas must be in the same row. Figure 9-22 has two formulas, the first in cell I3 and the other in cell J3.

> **MORE INFO**
>
> When input values are in a row, the first formula must be one column to the left of the first input value and one row below.

Select the entire data table range including the formulas, the input values, and the result cells for the *Data Table* command. In Figure 9-22, the data table range is cells H3:J14, not including descriptive text in column G and row 2.

Edit an input value after a data table is built to recalculate results. You cannot delete the contents of a single result cell in a data table, because that would "shrink" the array used in the formula. Select all result cells and delete them to rebuild a data table if necessary.

▸HOW TO: Create a One-Variable Data Table

1. Enter input values in a single column or row.
   - Fill a series of values or key specific numbers.
2. Enter the first formula.
   - If input values are in a column, enter the formula one row above and one column to the right of the first input value.
   - If input values are in a row, enter the formula one column to the left and one row below the first input value.
   - Type a reference to an existing formula.
   - Type or build the formula with sample data and sample cell references.
3. Enter additional formulas in the same row (Figure 9-23).
4. Select the data table range.
   - Select input values, formulas, and cells for results.
   - The top-left cell in the range is empty.
5. Click the **What-If Analysis** button [*Data* tab, *Forecast* group].
6. Choose **Data Table**.
   - The *Data Table* dialog box opens.
7. Enter a column or a row input cell reference (Figure 9-24).
   - In a one-variable data table, enter either a row input or a column input reference.
   - Select the cell for which the input values will be substituted or type the cell address.
8. Click **OK**.
   - The data table cells display results for each input value.
   - The *TABLE* function is an array formula in each result cell.
   - Format a data table to add number styles, fill, borders, or explanatory labels.

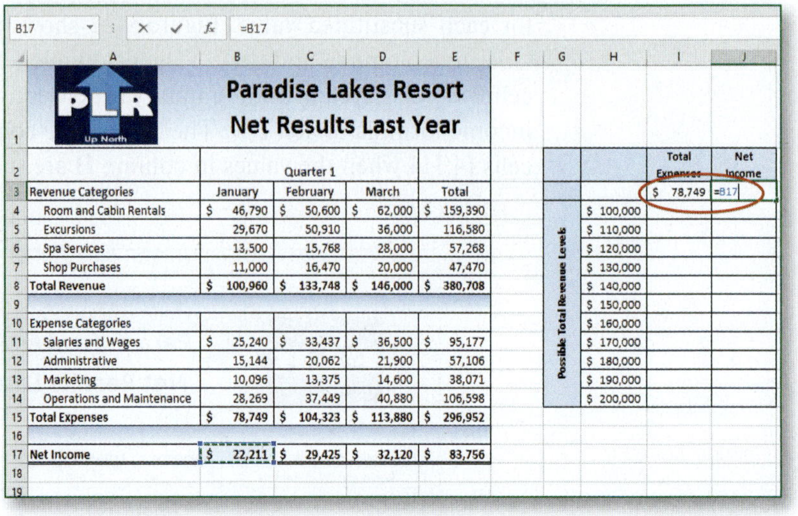

Figure 9-23 Input values are in a column; formulas are in the row above, one column to the right

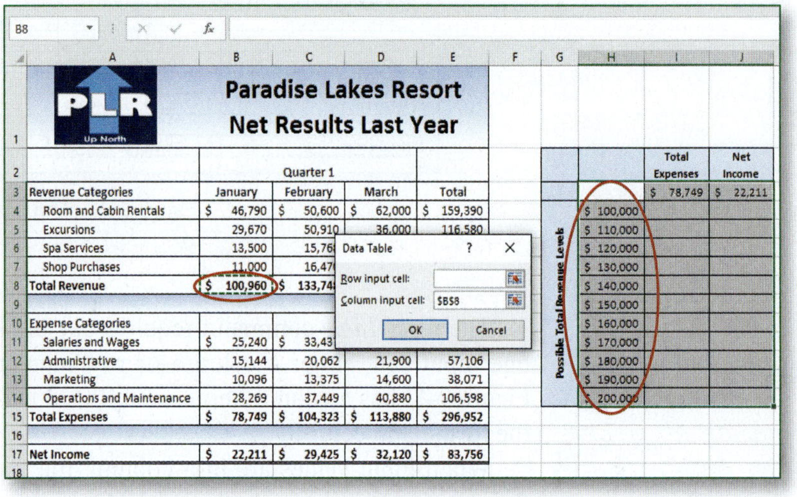

Figure 9-24 Values in column H will replace the value in cell B8 in the data table to calculate expense and income amounts

Build a Two-Variable Data Table

A ***two-variable data table*** uses two input cells and the table has one formula. Figure 9-25 shows a two-variable data table in which both January revenue *and* January expenses are varied. Cell H4 refers to the net income formula in cell B17 which is =B8-B15. Cells H5:H17 list *revenue* amounts for the column input (B8). Cells I4:P4 represent possible *expense* values; these values will be substituted for cell B15 (row input).

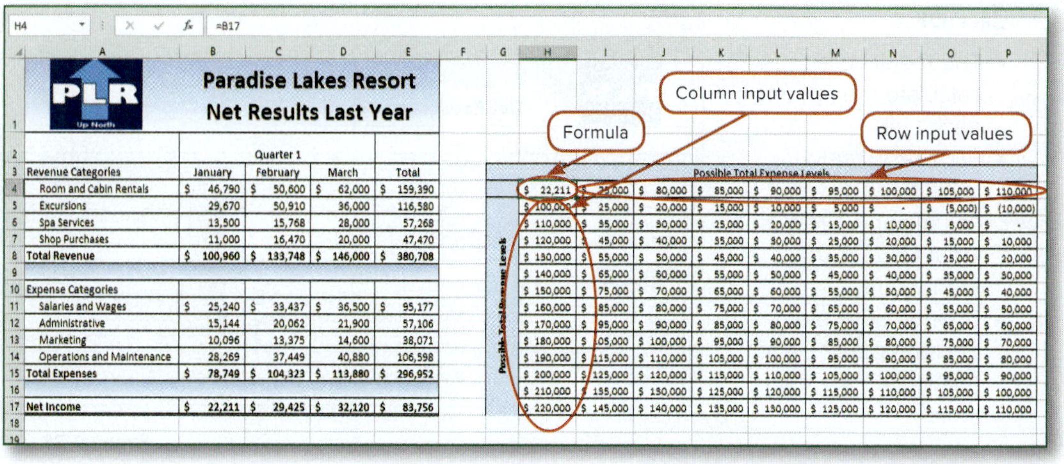

Figure 9-25 Two-variable data table

Row input values start one column to the right of the column values and one row above the first column value, cell I4 in the figure. Place the formula above the column values and to the left of the row values (cell H4 in the example).

The data table range includes the formula, the input column, the input row, and result cells (H4:P17); do not include descriptive labels. In Figure 9-25, the column input cell is cell B8 because revenue values are in *column* H. The row input cell is cell B15 because expense values are in *row* 4.

> **MORE INFO**
>
> A data table must be on the same worksheet as its formulas.

HOW TO: Create a Two-Variable Data Table

1. Enter column input values in a single column.
   - Type values or fill a series.
   - Prepare either the row or column input values first.
2. Enter row input values in a single row.
   - Start the first row value one row above and one column to the right of the first column value.
3. Enter the formula or a reference to the formula.
   - It is easier to refer to an existing formula than to re-enter the formula.
   - Place the formula reference in the cell above the column input values and to the left of the row input values.
4. Select the data table range.
   - Include the formula, column input values, row input values, and result cells.
5. Click the **What-If Analysis** button [*Data* tab, *Forecast* group].
6. Choose **Data Table**.
7. Select the row input cell or type the cell address.
   - You must know the formula to determine each input cell.
8. Select the column input cell or type the cell address (Figure 9-26).

9. Click **OK**.
   - The result cells calculate the formula in each cell.
   - Each result cell substitutes a column and a row input value in the formula.
   - Change any column or row input value to recalculate the data table.

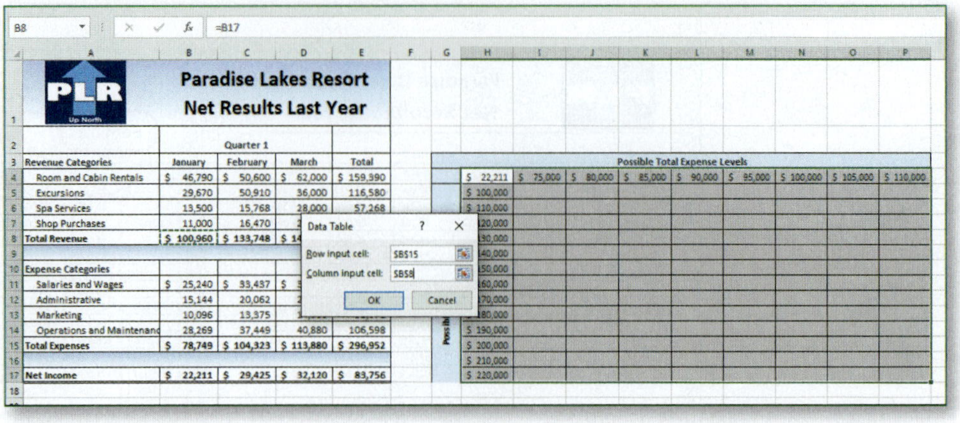

Figure 9-26 Two-variable data table setup

Creating a Forecast Sheet

SLO 9.5

A ***forecast sheet*** is a worksheet that illustrates past data and predicts future values in an Excel table and a chart. A forecast sheet is generated from data in the workbook to estimate future values for product sales, work hour requirements, expense levels, and more.

Create a Forecast Sheet

A forecast sheet uses two data series to build either a line or a column chart. One data series must be a date or time field, and the other series is the values used for forecasting. The date or time series must follow an interval, such as every hour, every other day, every month, and so on. The generated sheet is an Excel table that displays existing dates/times and values in adjacent columns. At the end of the table, forecast dates display with estimated values in a third column.

MORE INFO

A forecast sheet inserts *FORECAST* functions [*Statistical* category] in its tables. Explore these functions to learn about them.

The *Create Forecast Sheet* dialog box has options for calculating statistics such as alpha, beta, and gamma values, and more. You can also redefine the time and value ranges if needed.

After the forecast sheet is created, format the table from the *Table Tools Design* tab. The *Chart Tools Design* and *Format* tabs display for limited formatting of the chart.

HOW TO: Create a Forecast Sheet

1. Select the two data series including the header or label for each.
   - One column must be a time or date field.
   - The columns need not be adjacent.

2. Click the **Forecast Sheet** button [*Data* tab, *Forecast* group].
   - The *Create Forecast Worksheet* window opens (Figure 9-27).
3. Select the line or column chart type.
   - The chart preview displays.
4. Click the calendar icon for **Forecast End** and set the ending date or time for estimated values.
5. Select the **Options** arrow to expand the window.
   - Edit the data series ranges as needed.
   - The default confidence interval is 95% which measures how likely a value is to occur within the range of forecasted values.
6. Select the **Include forecast statistics** box to generate alpha, beta, gamma, and additional statistical measures.
7. Click **Create** (Figure 9-28).

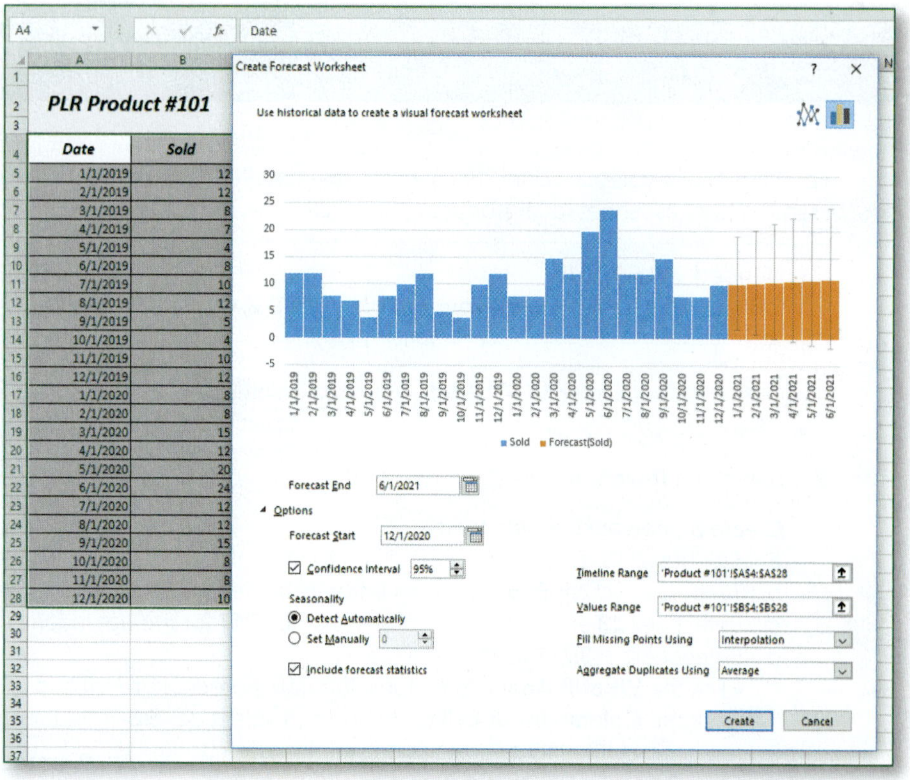

Figure 9-27 ***Create Forecast Worksheet* window**

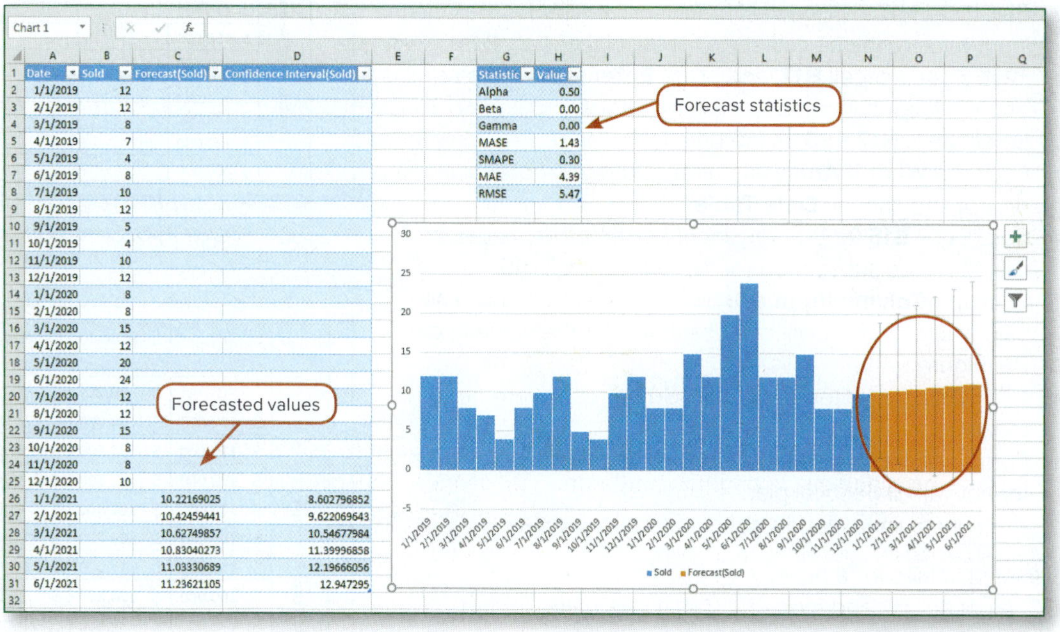

Figure 9-28 Forecast table, chart, and statistics

- The forecast sheet includes the table, forecast statistics, and the chart.
- Forecasted values display at the bottom of the table.
- Forecast statistics display in a separate table.

PAUSE & PRACTICE: EXCEL 9-2

For this project, you build one- and two-variable data tables for Paradise Lakes Resort (PLR). You also create a forecast sheet for a product sold at PLR spas.

File Needed: ***PP E9-1.xlsx***
Completed Project File Name: ***[your initials] PP E9-2.xlsx***

1. Open the ***[your initials] PP E9-1*** workbook completed in *Pause & Practice 9-1* and save it as [your initials] PP E9-2.
2. Select the **Revenue** worksheet tab.
3. Create a one-variable data table.
   a. Select cell **I3**. This cell is one column to the right and one row above the first input value (cell H4).
   b. Type =, select cell **B15**, and press **Enter** to create a reference to the total expenses formula for January.
   c. Select cell **J3** and create a reference to cell **B17** for the net income formula (Figure 9-29).
   d. Select cells **H3:J14** as the data table range.
   e. Click the **What-If Analysis** button [*Data* tab, *Forecast* group] and choose **Data Table**.
   f. Click the **Column input cell** entry box and select cell **B8**. The January revenue amount will be replaced by the input values in column H in both formulas.
   g. Click **OK** to create the data table.
   h. Select cells **I4:J14** and format them as **Accounting Number** format with **0** decimal places.
   i. *AutoFit* columns that do not display all the data (Figure 9-30).
4. Create a two-variable data table.
   a. Select cell **H17** to place the formula one row above the column input values and one column to the left of the row values.
   b. Type =, select cell **B17**, and press **Enter** to create a reference to the net income formula for January.
   c. Select cells **H17:P30** as the data table range.
   d. Click the **What-If Analysis** button [*Data* tab, *Forecast* group] and choose **Data Table**.
   e. Select cell **B15** for the *Row input cell* box. The values in row 17 will be substituted for the value in cell B15.
   f. Click the **Column input cell** box and select cell **B8**. The values in column H will be substituted for the value in cell B8 (Figure 9-31).
   g. Click **OK** to build the data table. Some results are negative, meaning a net loss.
   h. Format all cells in the data table as **Accounting Number** format with **0** decimal places.
   i. *AutoFit* columns that do not display all the data.
5. Edit input values for a table.
   a. Select cell **I17** and type 75000 as a new value.
   b. Select cell **J17** and type 80000 to start a new series.
   c. Select cells **I17:J17** and use the *Fill* handle to fill values to reach cell **P17**. The data table updates with fewer negative results (Figure 9-32). When revenue and expenses are equal, no profit exists, shown as a hyphen (-) in the *Accounting Number* format.

Possible Total Revenue Levels		Total Expenses	Net Income
		$ 78,749	=B17
	$ 100,000		
	$ 110,000		
	$ 120,000		
	$ 130,000		
	$ 140,000		
	$ 150,000		
	$ 160,000		
	$ 170,000		
	$ 180,000		
	$ 190,000		
	$ 200,000		

Figure 9-29 Formula reference in the data table

Possible Total Revenue Levels		Total Expenses	Net Income
		$ 78,749	$ 22,211
	$ 100,000	$ 78,000	$ 22,000
	$ 110,000	$ 85,800	$ 24,200
	$ 120,000	$ 93,600	$ 26,400
	$ 130,000	$ 101,400	$ 28,600
	$ 140,000	$ 109,200	$ 30,800
	$ 150,000	$ 117,000	$ 33,000
	$ 160,000	$ 124,800	$ 35,200
	$ 170,000	$ 132,600	$ 37,400
	$ 180,000	$ 140,400	$ 39,600
	$ 190,000	$ 148,200	$ 41,800
	$ 200,000	$ 156,000	$ 44,000

Figure 9-30 One-variable data table results

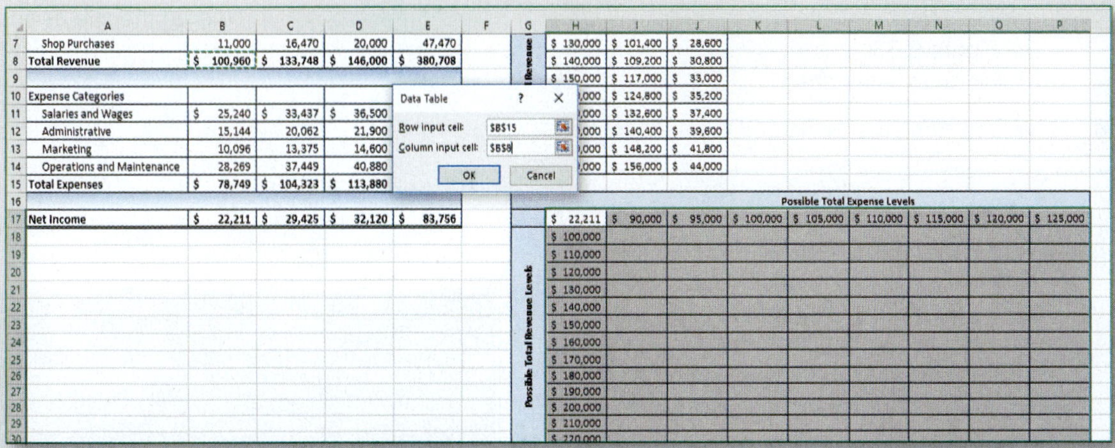

Figure 9-31 *Data Table* dialog box for a two-variable table

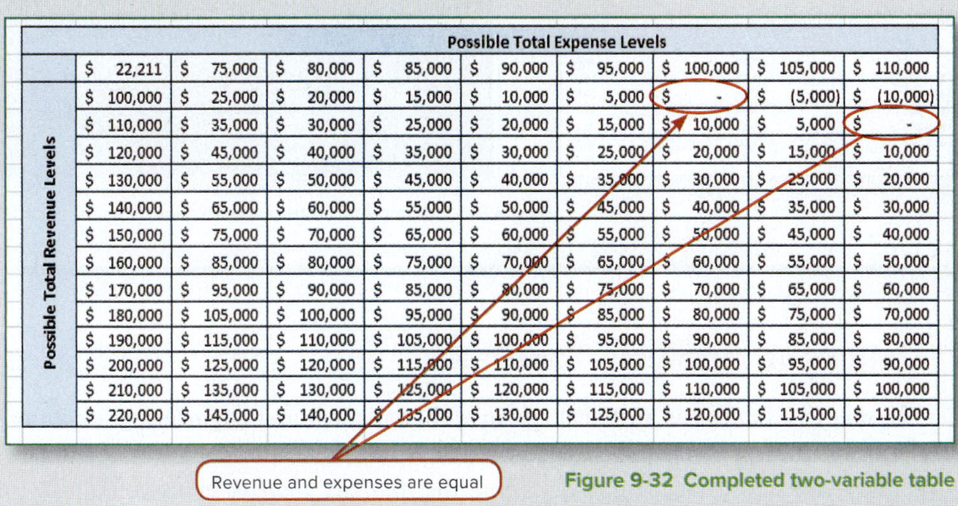

	Possible Total Expense Levels								
	$ 22,211	$ 75,000	$ 80,000	$ 85,000	$ 90,000	$ 95,000	$ 100,000	$ 105,000	$ 110,000
Possible Total Revenue Levels	$ 100,000	$ 25,000	$ 20,000	$ 15,000	$ 10,000	$ 5,000	$ -	$ (5,000)	$ (10,000)
	$ 110,000	$ 35,000	$ 30,000	$ 25,000	$ 20,000	$ 15,000	$ 10,000	$ 5,000	$ -
	$ 120,000	$ 45,000	$ 40,000	$ 35,000	$ 30,000	$ 25,000	$ 20,000	$ 15,000	$ 10,000
	$ 130,000	$ 55,000	$ 50,000	$ 45,000	$ 40,000	$ 35,000	$ 30,000	$ 25,000	$ 20,000
	$ 140,000	$ 65,000	$ 60,000	$ 55,000	$ 50,000	$ 45,000	$ 40,000	$ 35,000	$ 30,000
	$ 150,000	$ 75,000	$ 70,000	$ 65,000	$ 60,000	$ 55,000	$ 50,000	$ 45,000	$ 40,000
	$ 160,000	$ 85,000	$ 80,000	$ 75,000	$ 70,000	$ 65,000	$ 60,000	$ 55,000	$ 50,000
	$ 170,000	$ 95,000	$ 90,000	$ 85,000	$ 80,000	$ 75,000	$ 70,000	$ 65,000	$ 60,000
	$ 180,000	$ 105,000	$ 100,000	$ 95,000	$ 90,000	$ 85,000	$ 80,000	$ 75,000	$ 70,000
	$ 190,000	$ 115,000	$ 110,000	$ 105,000	$ 100,000	$ 95,000	$ 90,000	$ 85,000	$ 80,000
	$ 200,000	$ 125,000	$ 120,000	$ 115,000	$ 110,000	$ 105,000	$ 100,000	$ 95,000	$ 90,000
	$ 210,000	$ 135,000	$ 130,000	$ 125,000	$ 120,000	$ 115,000	$ 110,000	$ 105,000	$ 100,000
	$ 220,000	$ 145,000	$ 140,000	$ 135,000	$ 130,000	$ 125,000	$ 120,000	$ 115,000	$ 110,000

Figure 9-32 Completed two-variable table

6. Create a forecast worksheet.
   a. Select the **Product #101** worksheet tab.
   b. Select cells **A4: B28** and click the **Forecast Sheet** button [*Data* tab, *Forecast* group].
   c. Click the **Create a line chart** button.
   d. Click **Create** to generate the forecast worksheet.
   e. Name the new sheet tab Forecast Sheet.
7. Format a forecast chart sheet.
   a. Move the chart to its own sheet named Forecast Chart.
   b. Format the chart with **Style 9**.
   c. Click the **Chart Elements** drop-down list [*Chart Tools Format* tab, *Current Selection* group] and select **Horizontal (Category) Axis** to select the dates along the bottom axis.
   d. Click the **Format Selection** button [*Chart Tools Format* tab, *Current Selection* group].
   e. Select the **Axis Options** button in the *Format Axis* pane.
   f. Expand the **Labels** group in the task pane and set the **Specify interval unit** at **2** to show every other month.
   g. Select the **Legend** and position it at the **Bottom**.
   h. Click the **Chart Elements** button at the top-right corner of the chart and insert a **Centered Overlay** chart title.
   i. Edit the placeholder text to Forecasted Sales for Product #101.
   j. Click outside the chart to deselect the title object.

k. Point at the chart title object to display the four-pointed move pointer and drag the title as shown in Figure 9-33.
l. Click outside the chart.

8. Save and close the workbook.

	A	B	C	D	E
1	Date	Sold	Forecast(Sold)	Lower Confidence Bound(Sold)	Upper Confidence Bound(Sold)
2	1/1/2019	12			
3	2/1/2019	12			
4	3/1/2019	8			
5	4/1/2019	7			
6	5/1/2019	4			
7	6/1/2019	8			
8	7/1/2019	10			
9	8/1/2019	12			
10	9/1/2019	5			
11	10/1/2019	4			
12	11/1/2019	10			
13	12/1/2019	12			
14	1/1/2020	8			
15	2/1/2020	8			
16	3/1/2020	15			
17	4/1/2020	12			
18	5/1/2020	20			
19	6/1/2020	24			
20	7/1/2020	12			
21	8/1/2020	12			
22	9/1/2020	15			
23	10/1/2020	8			
24	11/1/2020	8			
25	12/1/2020	10	10	10.00	10.00
26	1/1/2021		10.22169025	1.62	18.82
27	2/1/2021		10.42459441	0.80	20.05
28	3/1/2021		10.62749857	0.08	21.17
29	4/1/2021		10.83040273	-0.57	22.23
30	5/1/2021		11.03330689	-1.16	23.23
31	6/1/2021		11.23621105	-1.71	24.18

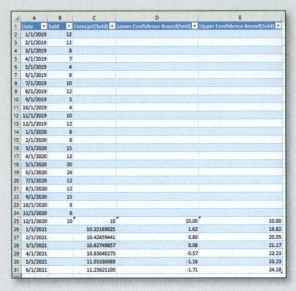

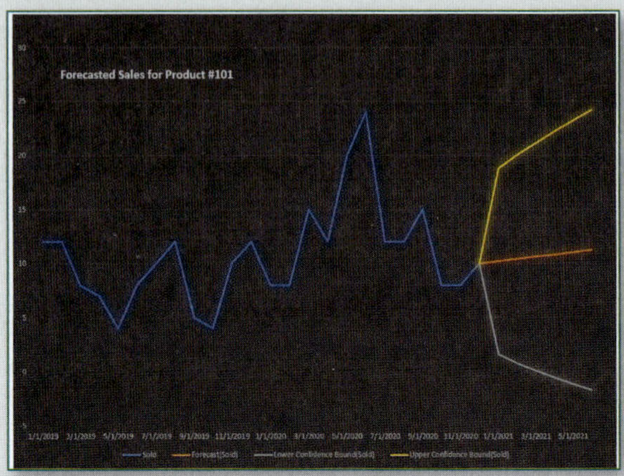

Figure 9-33 Completed forecast worksheet and chart for PP E9-2

SLO 9.6

Using the Analysis ToolPak

The *Analysis ToolPak* is an Excel add-in with statistical and engineering functions. Each tool performs its task when you provide the data and define the required components. For concepts such as covariance and regression, the *Analysis ToolPak* helps you analyze data with a minimum of steps and time.

Install the Analysis ToolPak

The *Analysis ToolPak* is installed from the *Add-ins* pane in Excel *Options*. Its button displays on the *Data* tab in the *Analysis* group.

HOW TO: Install the Analysis ToolPak

1. Select **Options** [*File* tab].
2. Click **Add-ins** in the left pane.
   - The *View and manage Microsoft Office Add-ins* dialog box opens.
   - Active applications are listed near the top of the window.
3. Select **Analysis ToolPak** in the *Inactive Application Add-ins* list.
4. Click **Go** near the bottom of the dialog box to open the *Add-ins* dialog box.
5. Select the **Analysis ToolPak** box.
   - Remove the *ToolPak* by deselecting the box.
6. Click **OK**.
   - The *Data Analysis* button displays in the *Analysis* group on the *Data* tab.

Generate Descriptive Statistics

Descriptive statistics are summary measures for a data range including the mean or average, the maximum, the minimum, a count, the mode, the standard deviation, and the range. You already know how to calculate several of these measures using functions from the *Statistical* and *Math & Trig* categories.

The ***Descriptive Statistics*** command creates a summary report about a set of values. Just select the range and indicate where results should display. The resulting report is a two-column layout of labels and values.

HOW TO: Generate Descriptive Statistics

1. Click the **Data Analysis** button [*Data* tab, *Analysis* group].
   - The *Data Analysis* dialog box lists calculations available in the *ToolPak* (Figure 9-34).
2. Choose **Descriptive Statistics** and click **OK**.
   - The *Descriptive Statistics* dialog box opens.
3. Click the **Input Range** box and select the cell range on the sheet.
   - These are cells with data points to be analyzed.
   - Include a column label if there is one and select the **Labels in first row** box.
4. Select the **Columns** radio button if the data is in a column.
   - Select the **Rows** button when the data is in a row.
5. Select the **Output Range** radio button.
6. Click the **Output Range** box and select an empty cell on the sheet.
   - Select a cell where there is room for a two-column report.
   - A worksheet ***ply*** is a new sheet tab that you can name.
7. Select the **Summary statistics** box (Figure 9-35).
   - Include a confidence interval and *Kth* values in the report.
   - *Kth* settings order the values. *Kth Largest* of 2 displays the second largest value in the range.
8. Click **OK**.
   - The two-column report displays (Figure 9-36).
   - The column label is the report title.
   - Format the report as desired.

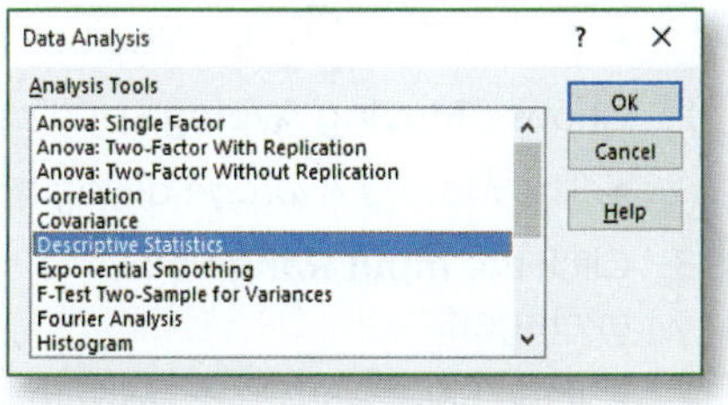

Figure 9-34 ***Data Analysis*** **dialog box**

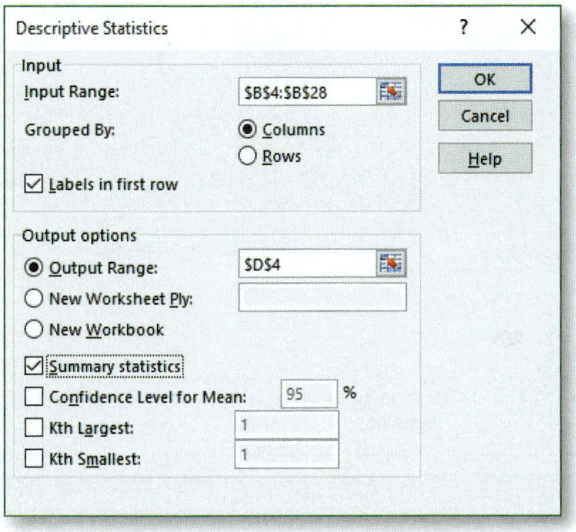

Figure 9-35 ***Descriptive Statistics*** **dialog box**

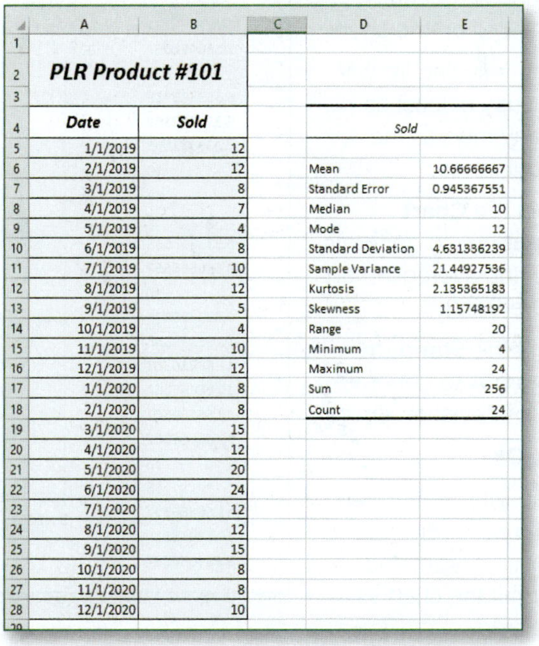

	A	B	C	D	E
1					
2	PLR Product #101				
3					
4	Date	Sold		Sold	
5	1/1/2019	12			
6	2/1/2019	12		Mean	10.66666667
7	3/1/2019	8		Standard Error	0.945367551
8	4/1/2019	7		Median	10
9	5/1/2019	4		Mode	12
10	6/1/2019	8		Standard Deviation	4.631336239
11	7/1/2019	10		Sample Variance	21.44927536
12	8/1/2019	12		Kurtosis	2.135365183
13	9/1/2019	5		Skewness	1.15748192
14	10/1/2019	4		Range	20
15	11/1/2019	10		Minimum	4
16	12/1/2019	12		Maximum	24
17	1/1/2020	8		Sum	256
18	2/1/2020	8		Count	24
19	3/1/2020	15			
20	4/1/2020	12			
21	5/1/2020	20			
22	6/1/2020	24			
23	7/1/2020	12			
24	8/1/2020	12			
25	9/1/2020	15			
26	10/1/2020	8			
27	11/1/2020	8			
28	12/1/2020	10			

Figure 9-36 Generated report

Prepare a Moving Average

A moving average calculates a series of averages for a set of values. It is also known as a rolling or running average. Paradise Lakes Resort, for example, tracks average three-month rental revenue. On April 1, they calculate an average for January-March. On May 1, they average February-April, and so on throughout the year. At the end of a year, they average all the averages. A moving average smooths out unequal measurement periods or values in the data.

The ***Moving Average*** command analyzes past results and predicts future values. It generates a column of averages and can also display a chart and a list of forecast errors.

▸HOW TO: Calculate a Moving Average

1. Click the **Data Analysis** button [*Data* tab, *Analysis* group].
   - The *Data Analysis* dialog box lists available calculations.
2. Choose **Moving Average** and click **OK**.
   - The *Moving Average* dialog box opens.
3. Click the **Input Range** box and select the values to be averaged.
   - If the values are in a row with labels directly above, select the **Labels in First Row** box.
4. Click the **Interval** box and type the number of cells to be averaged in each set.
   - An interval of 3 calculates an average for every 3 values in the list.
   - An interval of 3 shows no results for the first two values in the list.
5. Click the **Output Range** box and select an empty cell on the sheet.
   - The resulting list will occupy at least as many rows as the input range.
6. Select the **Chart Output** box to generate a moving average chart (Figure 9-37).
7. Select the **Standard Errors** box to generate a list of deviation errors.
8. Click **OK**.
   - The list is generated (Figure 9-38).
   - Position, size, and format the chart as desired.

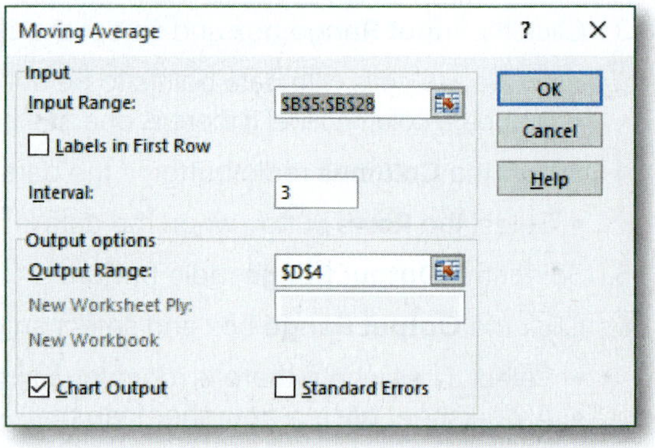

Figure 9-37 *Moving Average* dialog box

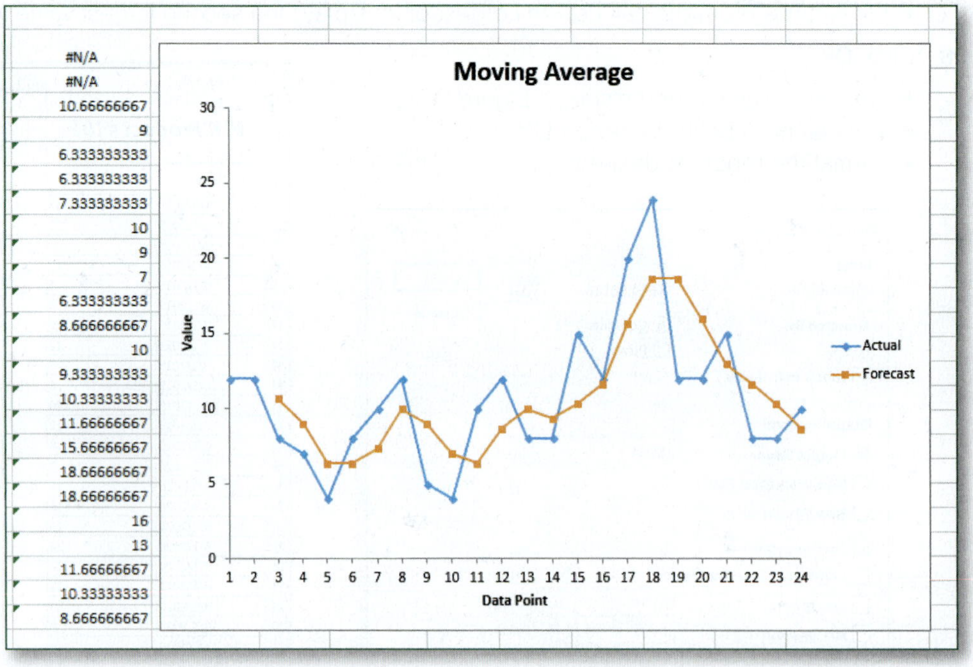

Figure 9-38 Generated moving average list and chart

Create a Histogram

A ***histogram*** is a column chart that illustrates the frequency of each data point in a data set. Build a histogram from the *Analysis ToolPak* or from the *Charts* group on the *Insert* tab. The ***Histogram*** tool in the *ToolPak* uses two sets of values, the data to be analyzed and the ***bin range***. A *bin range* is a list of values that sets low and high values for each column. Each column in a histogram is a bin. If you do not specify a bin range, Excel uses statistical formulas to create bins for your data.

> **MORE INFO**
>
> Create a histogram through the *Analysis ToolPak* because it does the work for you. Using the *Charts* group [*Insert* tab] requires more work on your part.

HOW TO: Create a Histogram

1. Click the **Data Analysis** button [*Data* tab, *Analysis* group].
   - The *Data Analysis* dialog box lists available calculations.
2. Choose **Histogram** and click **OK**.
   - The *Histogram* dialog box opens.
   - Click the **Input Range** box and select the values to be analyzed.
3. Click the **Bin Range** box and select the values that identify the upper limit for each bin.
   - Type a list of values in the workbook to create your own bins.
   - Excel creates bins if you do not select a range of values for the bin range.
   - Excel places a value in a bin when the value is equal to or less than the limit value.
4. Click the **Output Range** box and select a worksheet cell for the report and chart.
   - Place the report and chart on a new worksheet or in another workbook.
5. Select *Output options* as desired (Figure 9-39).
   - A *Pareto* chart sorts the column in descending order to draw attention to the largest values.

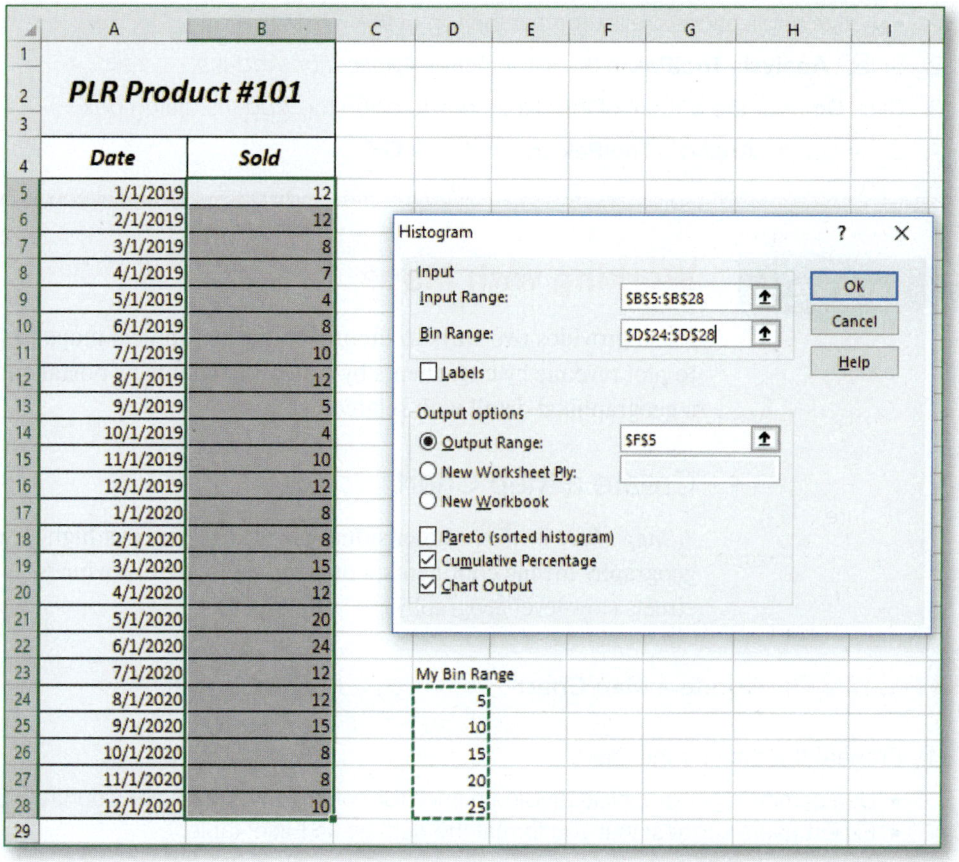

Figure 9-39 *Histogram* dialog box

- *Cumulative Percentage* displays a percentage for each frequency value in the report and the chart.
- *Chart Output* creates the histogram chart.

6. Click **OK**.
   - The output displays in the worksheet.
   - Edit labels as needed.
   - Format the chart from the *Chart Tools* tabs (Figure 9-40).

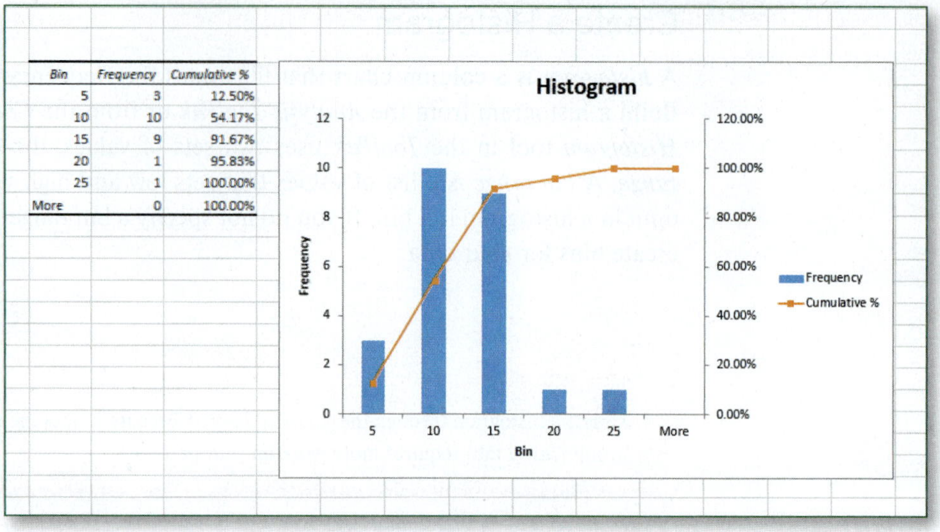

Figure 9-40 ***Histogram*** **report and chart**

The **Data Analysis** button remains on the *Data* tab until you remove the *Analysis ToolPak*. Remove the *ToolPak* from the *Add-ins* pane in Excel *Options*.

▶HOW TO: Uninstall the Analysis ToolPak

1. Select **Options** [*File* tab] and click **Add-ins** in the left pane.
   - The *View and manage Microsoft Office Add-ins* dialog box opens.
   - Active applications are listed near the top of the window.
2. Select **Analysis ToolPak** in the list of *Active Application Add-ins*.
3. Click **Go** near the bottom of the dialog box to open the *Add-ins* dialog box.
4. Deselect the **Analysis ToolPak** box and click **OK**.

SLO 9.7

Working with Maps

Excel provides two ways to incorporate geographical maps in your work. You might use maps to plot revenue by city, clients by state, or students by postal code. Data for a map must include a geographical detail with related values.

Create a Map Chart

A ***map chart*** is a one-dimensional chart that displays high-level geographic details. High-level geography means continents, countries, states, or provinces. A map chart cannot plot cities or streets (low-level geography).

▶HOW TO: Create a Map Chart

1. Prepare the data for the chart.
   - Use common geographical division names for column titles such as "Country," "State," or "Province."
   - Expert users suggest that you format the data as an Excel table.
2. Click a cell in the table.
   - Select the cell range with labels if the data is not formatted as a table.

3. Click the **Insert Map Chart** button [*Insert* tab, *Charts* group].
4. Select **Filled Map** to insert the chart object (Figure 9-41).
    - The chart plots the values in the first column to the right of the identifying geography data.
    - Hide columns to display data from another column.

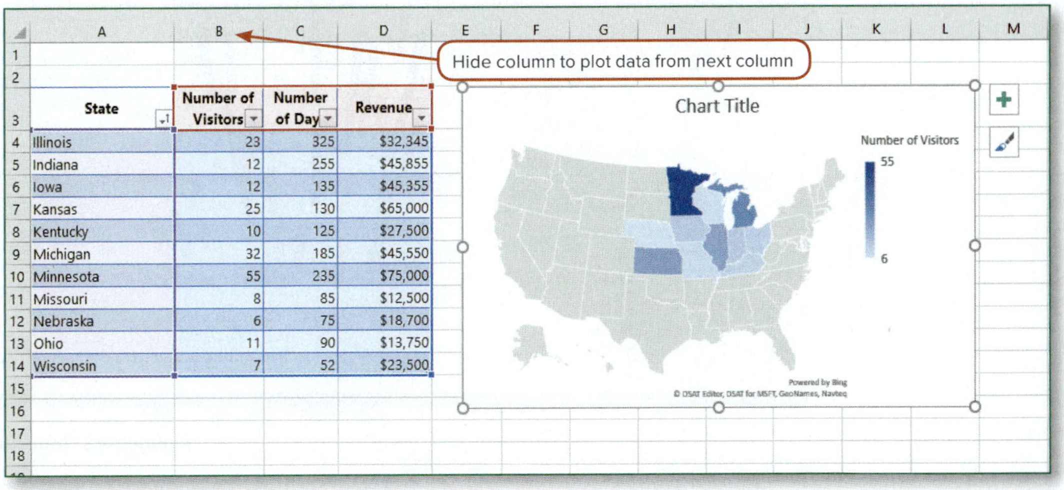

Figure 9-41 Map chart and its source data

5. Size and position the chart object.
    - Move the chart to its own sheet as desired.
6. Select a chart element and display its *Format* pane (Figure 9-42).
    - Click the **Chart Elements** arrow [*Chart Tools Format* pane, *Current Selection* group], select an element name, and click the **Format Selection** button [*Chart Tools Format* pane, *Current Selection* group].
    - Data series format options are specific to the map chart.

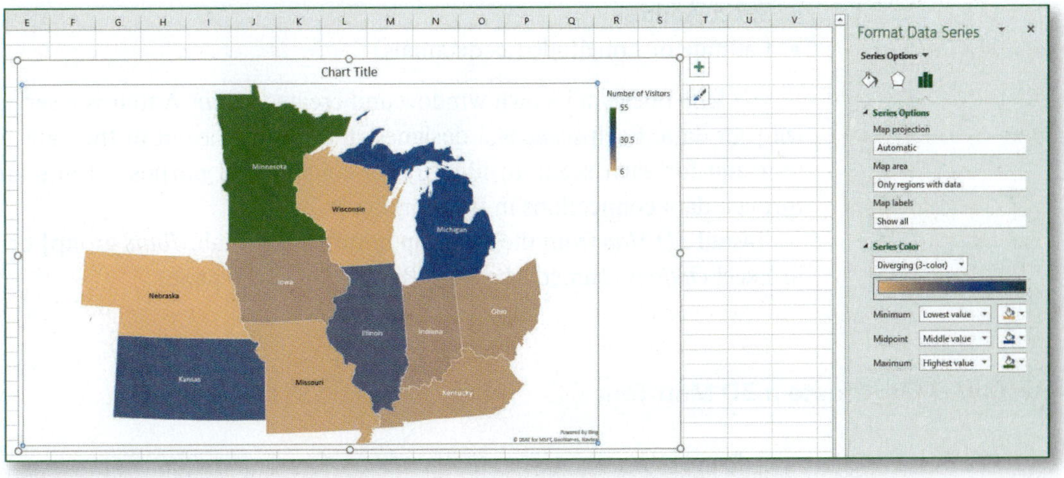

Figure 9-42 Select and format individual chart elements

7. Click a worksheet cell to deselect the chart.
    - Save the chart with the workbook as usual.

Create a 3D Map

Microsoft 3D Map is an Excel add-in that plots geographic and time data on a world map or a custom map. *3D Map* uses Bing, Microsoft's search engine, to create a three-dimensional visualization of your data. Figure 9-43 displays a tour named "PLR Inquiries" with two scenes and a column visualization. The columns (height) plot the number of inquiries for each city (category).

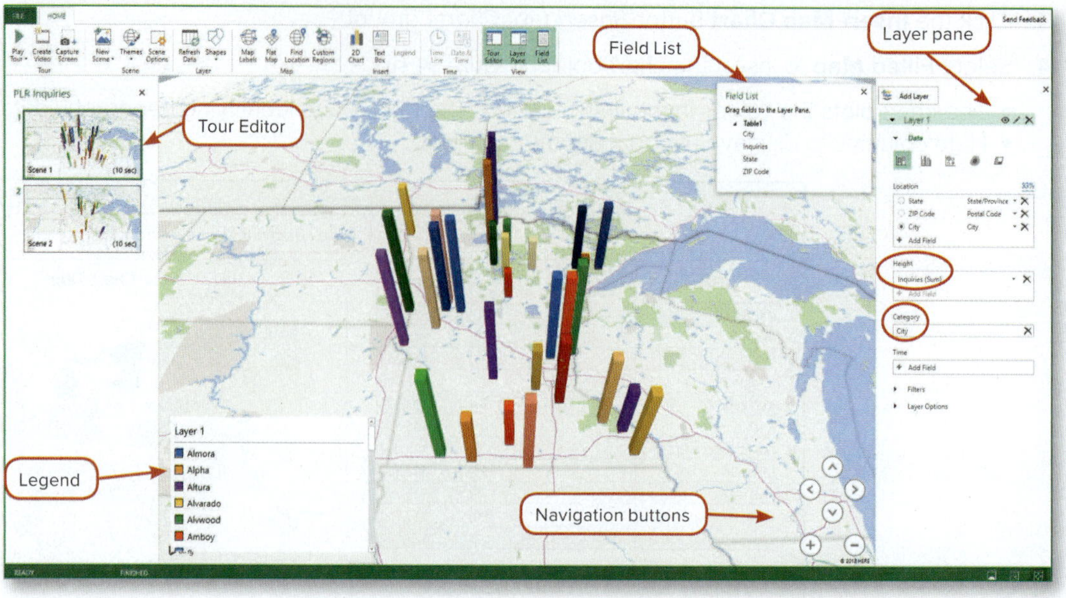

Figure 9-43 Tour with two scenes in a 3D map

Format data for a 3D map as an Excel table with at least one geographic or time value per row. *3D Map* recognizes the following labels for geocoding your data:

- Country or Region
- ZIP Code or Postal Code
- State or Province
- County
- City
- Street Address
- Latitude or Longitude (as decimals)

3D Map opens in its own window and creates a ***tour***. A tour is a series of scenes that visualize your data. Each ***scene*** is a designed and filtered layout of the data. Supply a name for the tour and for each scene to identify its content and purpose. Tours are saved automatically through data connections in the workbook.

Install *3D Map* from the **3D Map** button [*Insert* tab, *Tours* group] or from the *Add-ins* pane in Excel *Options* (named *Microsoft Power Map* in the pane).

HOW TO: Create a 3D Map Tour

1. Prepare the data as an Excel table.
   - Use one or more columns of identifying geographical data.
   - Include a date or time column to visualize data across a period of time.
2. Select a cell in the table.
3. Click the **3D Map** button [*Insert* tab, *Tours* group].
   - A tour displays with a 3D globe, the *Layer* pane, the *Field List* window, and the *Tour Editor* pane.
   - *3D Map* has a *File* tab and a *Home* tab (Figure 9-44).
   - If the workbook already includes tours, the *Launch 3D Maps* dialog box displays existing tour names.
4. Close the *Field List* window.
   - Field choices can be made from the *Layer* pane.

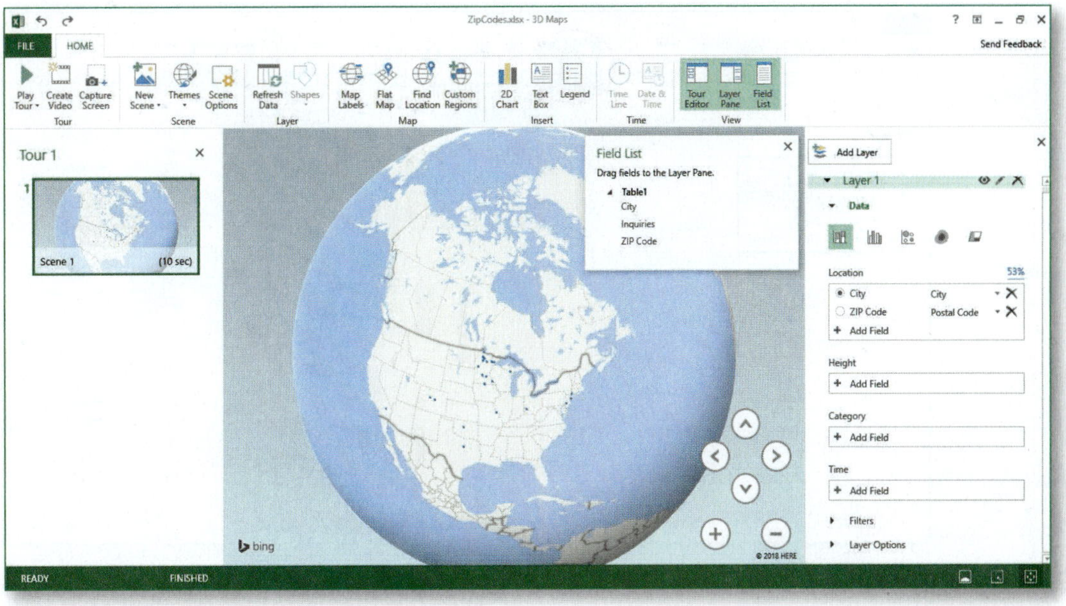

Figure 9-44 *3D Maps* window for creating a tour

5. Name the tour.
   - Point to **Tour N** in the *Tour Editor* pane and click to display the entry box.
   - Type a descriptive name and click in the white space beneath the scene icon.
6. Verify and map fields in the *Location* group.
   - Choose the field that best relates to your data.
   - The worksheet label displays on the left and the recognized geocoding label displays on the right.
   - The focus and zoom size may adjust based on your location choice.
   - Change a miscoded field type by clicking the drop-down list (Figure 9-45).
7. Click the **Add Field** box for *Height* in the *Layer* pane.
   - Select the field with values to be plotted.
   - A legend for the selected visualization type displays.
   - Size and position the legend as desired.
8. Click the **Add Field** box for *Category* in the *Layer* pane.
   - A category field may not be necessary.
   - Click the **Delete Field** button in the *Category* group to remove a field.
9. Select a visualization option.
   - Visualizations include stacked or clustered columns, bubbles, a heat map, and a region map.
   - Change the visualization as needed.
10. Click navigation buttons to zoom in or out, to tilt, or to rotate the map.
    - Size and arrange the map to highlight your area of interest.
    - Click the **Flat Map** button [*Home* tab, *Map* group] to display a two-dimensional perspective (Figure 9-46).

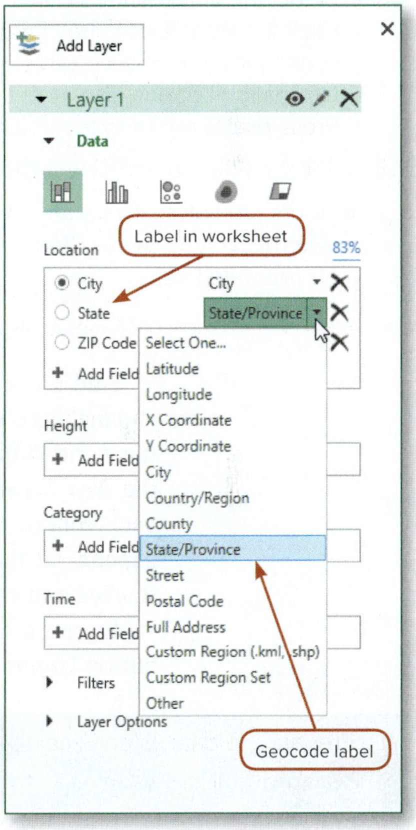

Figure 9-45 Change a miscoded field in the *Layer* pane

11. Click the **Scene Options** button [*Home* tab, *Scene* group] to change the scene's name (Figure 9-47).
    - Type a descriptive name for the scene.
    - Close the *Scene Options* dialog box.
    - Open the *Scene Options* dialog box from the button at the bottom of the scene icon.

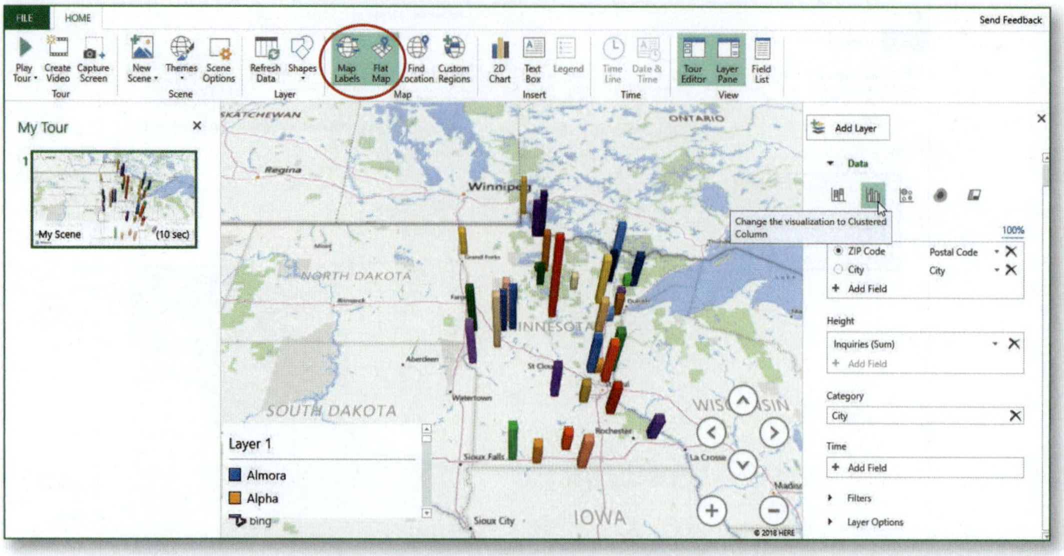

Figure 9-46 Flat map with labels

12. Play the tour.
    - Select the first scene icon in the *Tour Editor*.
    - Click the **Play Tour** button [*Home* tab, *Tour* group]. Each scene plays in full-screen mode.
    - Navigation buttons display at the bottom of the window.
    - Press **Esc** to return to the editing window.
13. Click the **File** tab and select **Close** to return to the worksheet.
    - Tours are automatically saved with the workbook.
    - Alternatively, click the **Close** button in the *3D Maps* window to return to Excel.

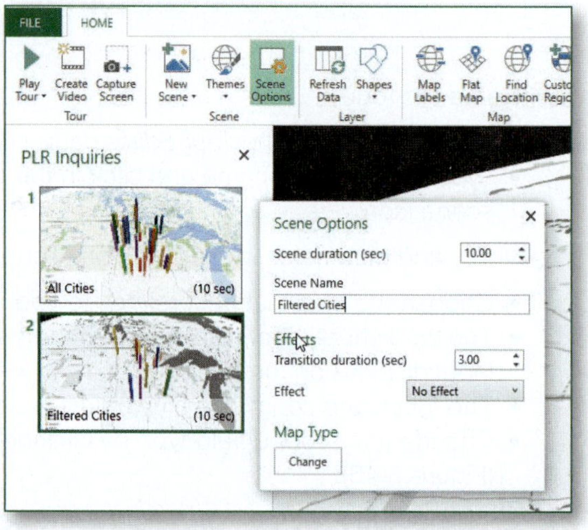

Figure 9-47 The *Scene Options* dialog box

Add scenes by copying an existing scene and making changes, or by starting anew with the world map. A custom map, an option for the *New Scene* button [*Home* tab, *Scene* group] enables you to use a different image as the background. From the *Layer* pane, you can filter data displayed in the map. *Layer Options* depend on the type of visualization and include color, opacity, and similar attributes. For stacked and clustered column maps, select from five column shapes [*Home* tab, *Layer* group].

Open an existing *3D Map* tour by clicking a cell in the worksheet, clicking the **3D Maps** button [*Insert* tab, *Tours* group], and selecting the tour name in the *Launch 3D Maps* window.

PAUSE & PRACTICE: EXCEL 9-3

For this project, you work with the *Analysis ToolPak* to display descriptive statistics and a moving average for Paradise Lakes Resort. You also create a 2D map chart.

File Needed: ***PP E9-2.xlsx***, *(Student data files are available in the* Library *of your SIMnet account.)*
Completed Project File Name: ***[your initials] PP E9-3.xlsx***

1. Open the ***[your initials] PP E9-2*** workbook completed in *Pause & Practice 9-2* and save it as [your initials] PP E9-3.
2. Install the *Analysis ToolPak*.
   a. Select **Options** [*File* tab] and click **Add-ins** in the left pane.
   b. Select **Analysis ToolPak** in the *Inactive Application Add-ins* list.
   c. Click **Go** near the bottom of the dialog box.
   d. Select the **Analysis ToolPak** box and click **OK**.
3. Right-click either tab scrolling button to open the *Activate* dialog box.
4. Select **Product #101** and click **OK** (Figure 9-48).
5. Calculate descriptive statistics for a data range.
   a. Click the **Data Analysis** button [*Data* tab, *Analysis* group].
   b. Choose **Descriptive Statistics** and click **OK**.
   c. Select cells **B4:B28** for the *Input Range* box.
   d. Verify that the *Columns* radio button is selected.
   e. Select the **Labels in First Row** box.
   f. Select the **Output Range** radio button.
   g. Click the **Output Range** box and select cell **E4**.
   h. Select the **Summary statistics** box.
   i. Select the **Kth Largest** box and type 3 in the entry box to calculate the third largest value in the range (Figure 9-49).

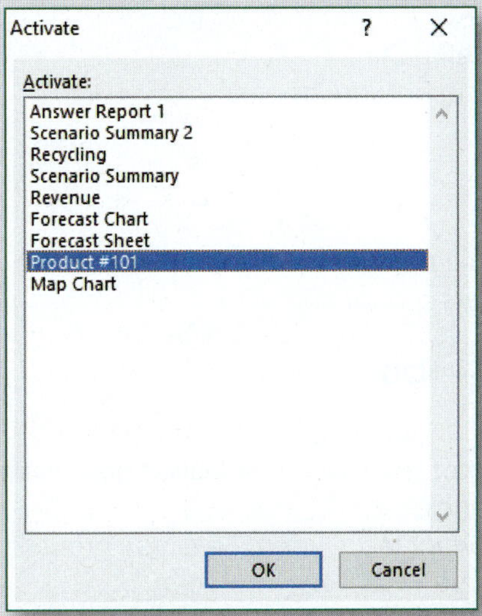

Figure 9-48 ***Activate*** **dialog box with sheet names**

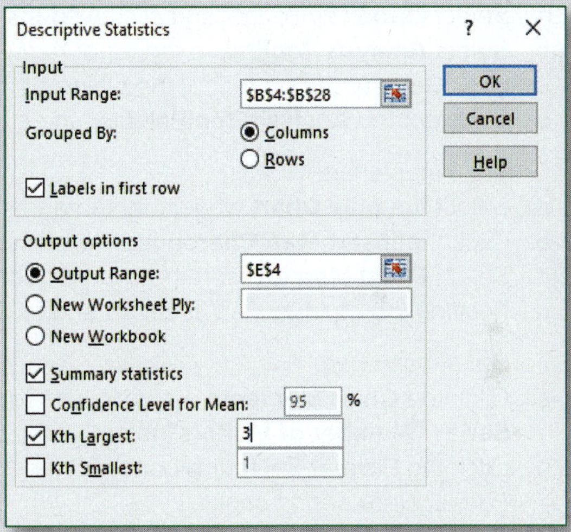

Figure 9-49 ***Descriptive Statistics*** **dialog box**

   j. Click **OK**.
   k. *AutoFit* column **E** (Figure 9-50).
6. Calculate a moving average for a data range.
   a. Click the **Data Analysis** button [*Data* tab, *Analysis* group].
   b. Choose **Moving Average** and click **OK**.
   c. Select cells **B5:B28** for the *Input Range* box.
   d. Click the **Interval** box and type 3 to average groups of three cells in the range.
   e. Click the **Output Range** box and select cell **E21**.

f. Select the **Chart Output** box.
g. Click **OK**.
h. Select the chart object and move it so that its top-left corner is at cell **G21**.
i. Size the chart object to reach cell **Q44** (Figure 9-51).

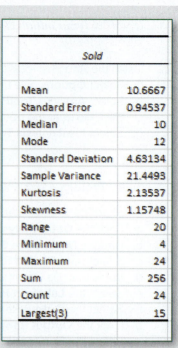

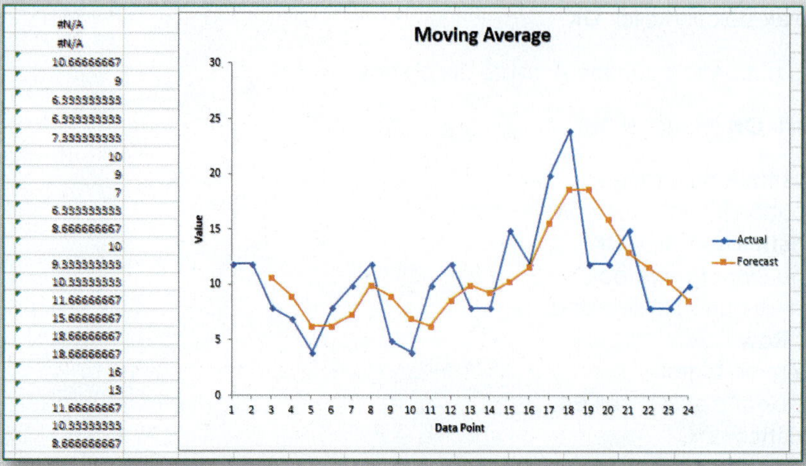

Figure 9-51 Moving average output and chart

Sold	
Mean	10.6667
Standard Error	0.94537
Median	10
Mode	12
Standard Deviation	4.63134
Sample Variance	21.4493
Kurtosis	2.13537
Skewness	1.15748
Range	20
Minimum	4
Maximum	24
Sum	256
Count	24
Largest(3)	15

Figure 9-50 Generated statistics report

7. Uninstall the *Analysis ToolPak*.
   a. Select **Options** [*File* tab] and click **Add-ins** in the left pane.
   b. Select **Analysis ToolPak** in the list of *Active Application Add-ins*.
   c. Click **Go** near the bottom of the dialog box.
   d. Deselect the **Analysis ToolPak** box and click **OK**.

8. Create a map chart.
   a. Select the **Map Chart** worksheet tab and select cell **A4**.
   b. Click the **Insert Map Chart** button [*Insert* tab, *Charts* group].
   c. Select **Filled Map** to insert the chart object.
   d. Position the chart to start at cell **F1** and to reach cell **N20**.

9. Format a map chart.
   a. Click the **Chart Elements** button [*Chart Tools Format* tab, *Current Selection* group] and choose **Series "Number of Visitors"** to select the data series.
   b. Click the **Format Selection** button [*Chart Tools Format* tab, *Current Selection* group] to open the *Format Data Series* pane.
   c. Click the **Series Options** button and expand the *Series Options* and the *Series Color* groups.
   d. Click the **Map area** box and select **Only regions with data**.
   e. Click the **Series Color** drop-down list and select **Diverging (3-color)**.
   f. Verify that the *Minimum* setting displays **Lowest value** and click the **Fill Color** arrow.
   g. Choose **Light Gray, Background 2** in the third column.
   h. Verify that the *Midpoint* setting displays **Middle value** and click the **Fill Color** arrow (Figure 9-52).
   i. Choose **Orange, Accent 2** in the sixth column.
   j. Set the *Highest value* to **Blue, Accent 1** in the fifth column.

10. Edit the chart title and chart area.
   a. Select the chart title placeholder and change the title to Visitors from Selected States.
   b. Select the chart area and format it with the preset **Light Gradient - Accent 6** fill.
   c. Select cell **A4** (Figure 9-53).

11. Save and close the workbook.

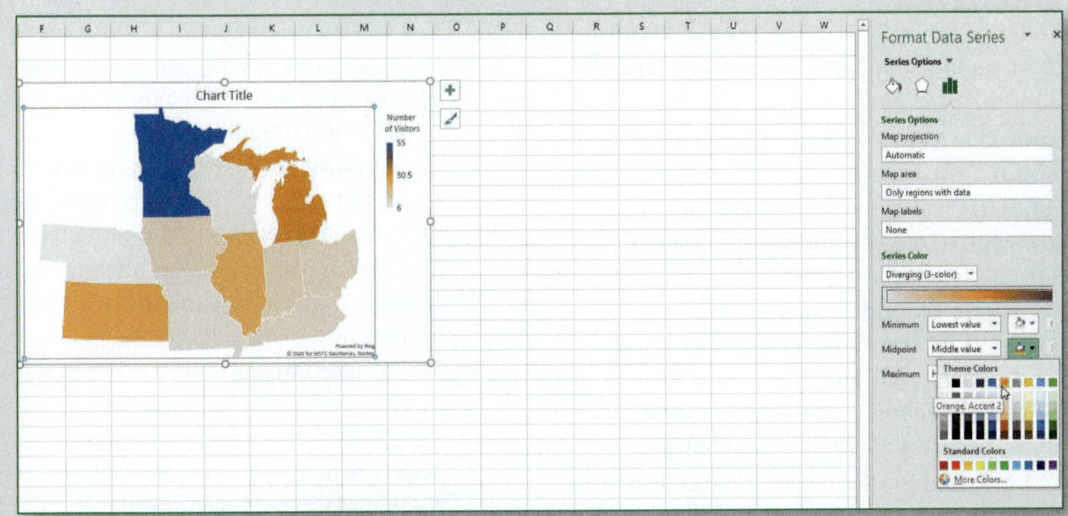

Figure 9-52 Select and format map chart elements

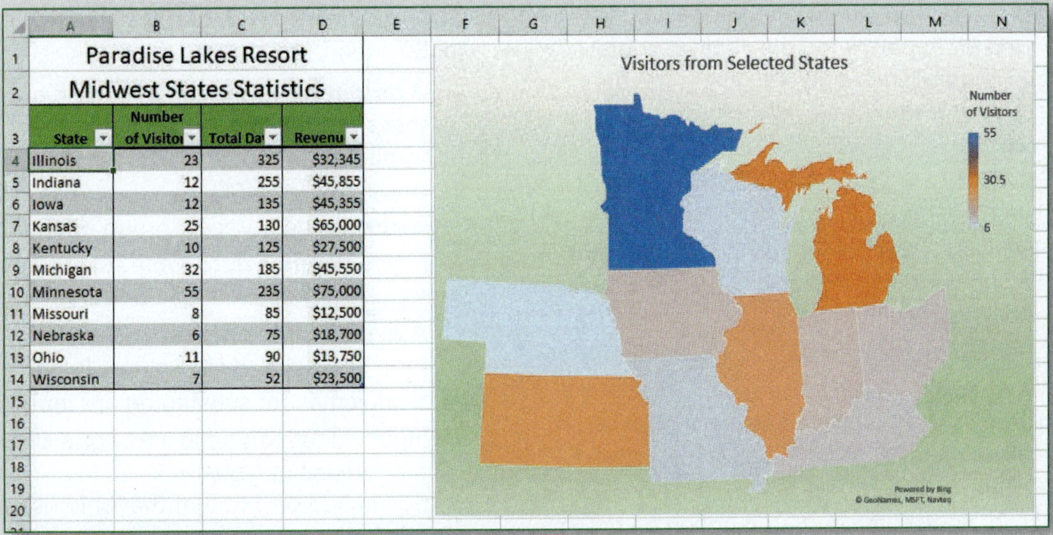

Figure 9-53 Map chart for PP E9-3

Chapter Summary

9.1 Create and manage scenarios for worksheet data (p. E9-552).

- A ***scenario*** is a saved set of values in a workbook.
- A scenario is a what-if analysis tool because it allows you to display and compare multiple data possibilities in a worksheet.
- The ***Scenario Manager*** command is available from the *What-if Analysis* button in the *Forecast* group on the *Data* tab.
- Name each scenario in the *Add Scenario* dialog box and select cells to be changed.
- Accept or type new values for each scenario in the *Scenario Values* dialog box.
- Only one scenario can be displayed in the worksheet at a time.
- Create a ***scenario summary report*** from the *Scenario Manager* dialog box that lists details about changing cells and result cells for all scenarios in a workbook.

9.2 Use *Goal Seek* to backsolve a cell value for a formula (p. E9-555).

- ***Backsolving*** is a problem-solving method that starts with the result and calculates the value to reach that result.
- The ***Goal Seek*** command tests values for one cell in a formula.
- *Goal Seek* determines what value should be in the cell so that the formula results in a specified value.
- The *Goal Seek* command is an option on the *What-if Analysis* button in the *Forecast* group on the *Data* tab.

9.3 Use *Solver* to find a solution for a formula (p. E9-556).

- The *Solver* ***add-in*** is an analysis tool that solves a problem in reverse.
- ***Solver*** determines the highest, the lowest, or a specific result for a formula by adjusting values in cells used in the formula.
- A *Solver* problem has three components known as ***parameters***, identified in the *Solver Parameters* dialog box.
- The ***objective cell*** is a cell with a formula that will be solved for specific results. It is also called the ***target cell***.
- ***Variable cells***, also known as ***decision*** or ***changing cells***, are cells that *Solver* can adjust to reach the objective.
- ***Constraints*** are restrictions or limitations on variable cells, the formula, or other worksheet cells that are related to the objective cell.
- The *Solver Results* dialog box includes options to keep the solution, to return to the original values, and to save the results as a scenario.
- The *Solver Results* dialog box has a *Reports* section with analysis reports that can be generated for each solution.
- *Solver* is activated from the *Add-ins* pane in the Excel *Options* dialog box.
- The *Solver* button displays in the *Analysis* group on the *Data* tab.

9.4 Build data tables with one and two variables (p. E9-564).

- A ***data table*** is a range of cells in a worksheet that shows multiple results for one or more formulas.
- Create a data table from the *What-If Analysis* button in the *Forecast* group on the *Data* tab.
- A ***one-variable data table*** substitutes values for one argument in one or more formulas.
- A ***two-variable data table*** substitutes values for two arguments in a single formula.
- Values that are substituted are ***input values***.
- Input values can be in a row or a column, and the formula must be entered in a specific location based on whether the table uses one or two variables.
- In the data table range, the formula can be typed or entered as a reference to the formula in the worksheet.
- Specify a single input cell in the *Data Table* dialog box for a one-variable table and specify two input cells for a two-variable table.
- The row or column input is the cell address in the formula that is replaced with input values.
- A *Data Table* command inserts the *TABLE* function in an array formula in each result cell.

9.5 Create a forecast sheet for time-based data (p. E9-568).

- A ***forecast sheet*** is a generated worksheet that uses existing data to analyze and predict results.

- A forecast sheet includes a table and a related chart.
- Two data series are required to build a forecast sheet; one series must be a date or time field.
- The date or time field must use a recognizable time interval.
- The forecast chart can be a line or a column chart.
- The *Forecast Sheet* button is in the *Forecast* group on the *Data* tab.

9.6 Use the *Analysis ToolPak* to calculate statistical measures (p. E9-572).

- The *Analysis ToolPak* is an Excel add-in with built-in statistical and engineering calculations.
- The *Data Analysis* button appears in the *Analysis* group on the *Data* tab.
- The ***Descriptive Statistics*** command calculates and generates a list of popular measures for a data range.
- The ***Moving Average*** command calculates and generates a list of running or rolling averages for a set of values with a related chart.
- A ***histogram*** is a column chart that illustrates the frequency of each data point in a data set, built from two sets of values, the data to be analyzed and the ***bin range***.
- A *bin range* is a list of values that identifies low and high values for each column in a histogram.
- Other *Analysis ToolPak* commands include covariance, regression analysis, and random number generation.

9.7 Work with Excel maps (p. E9-576).

- Plot high-level geographical data with related values in a *map chart*.
- A map chart displays data for continents, countries, states, or provinces.
- ***Microsoft 3D Map*** builds three-dimensional maps in a separate window for worksheet data.
- *3D Map* uses Microsoft Bing to geocode Excel data by country or region, ZIP code or postal code, county, state or province, city, street address, or latitude or longitude.
- *3D Map* visualizes data in a ***tour*** with ***scenes*** and can incorporate time-related values.
- Visualization options in a *3D Map* tour include columns, bubbles, heat maps, and regions.
- Create a map chart from the *Charts* group and a 3D map from the *Tours* group, both on the *Insert* tab.

Check for Understanding

The SIMbook for this text (within your SIMnet account) provides the following resources for concept review:

- Multiple-choice questions
- Short answer questions
- Matching exercises

Guided Project 9-1

Wear-Ever Shoes uses *Solver* to analyze advertising for greatest exposure. You use scenarios, a data table, and *Goal Seek* in the analysis.
[Student Learning Outcomes 9.1, 9.2, 9.3, 9.4, 9.5, 9.6, 9.7]

File Needed: ***WearEverShoes-09.xlsx*** *(Student data files are available in the* Library *of your SIMnet account.)*
Completed Project File Name: ***[your initials] Excel 9-1.xlsx***

Skills Covered in This Project

- Create and manage scenarios.
- Use *Solver.*
- Use *Goal Seek.*
- Build a one-variable data table.
- Build a two-variable data table.
- Create and format a 3D map.
- Create a bin range for a histogram.
- Generate a histogram using the *Analysis ToolPak.*
- Create a forecast sheet.

1. Open the ***WearEverShoes-09*** workbook from your student data files and save it as [your initials] Excel 9-1.
2. Review marketing formulas.
   a. Select cell **E7** on the **Marketing Analysis** tab. The *SUMPRODUCT* formula multiplies the cost per campaign (cells C7 and D7) by the number of ads (cells C13 and D13).
   b. Select cell **E10** and then cell **G4** to review the *SUMPRODUCT* formulas.
3. Create a scenario for original data.
   a. Select cells **C13:D13** and click the **What-if Analysis** button [*Data* tab, *Forecast* group].
   b. Select **Scenario Manager**. No scenarios exist in the workbook.
   c. Click **Add**.
   d. Type Original in the *Add Scenario* dialog box.
   e. Verify that the *Changing cells* box shows cells **C13:D13**.
   f. Click **OK**.
   g. Do not edit the *Scenario Values* dialog box and click **OK**.
   h. Click **Close**.
4. Install *Solver* and the *Analysis ToolPak*.
   a. Select the **Options** command [*File* tab].
   b. Click **Add-ins** in the left pane.
   c. Click **Go** near the bottom of the window.
   d. Select the **Solver Add-in** box.
   e. Select the **Analysis ToolPak** box.
   f. Click **OK**.
5. Set *Solver* parameters.
   a. Click the **Solver** button [*Data* tab, *Analysis* group].
   b. Click cell **G4** for the **Set Objective** box. This cell has a *SUMPRODUCT* formula.

c. Verify that the *Max* radio button is selected to find the maximum value.
d. Click the **By Changing Variable Cells** box and select cells **C13:D13**. *Solver* will test values for the number of social media and cable ads.

6. Add constraints to a *Solver* problem.
   a. Click **Add** to the right of the *Subject to the Constraints* box.
   b. Select cell **C13** for the *Cell Reference* box and verify that **<=** is the operator.
   c. Click the **Constraint** box and select cell **C15**. This constraint is that the number of social media ads (cell C13) be less than or equal to the value in cell C15.
   d. Click **Add**. (If you accidentally closed the dialog box, click **Add** to reopen it.)
   e. Select cell **D13** for the *Cell Reference* box and verify that **<=** is the operator.
   f. Click the **Constraint** box and select cell **D15**. The number of cable ads must be less than or equal to the value in cell D15.
   g. Add another constraint for cell **D13** that the value be greater than or equal to 2.
   h. Add a constraint for cell **E7** with **<=** as the operator and cell **G7** as the constraint so that the total spent matches the budget amount.
   i. Add another constraint that cell **E10** be greater than or equal to cell **G10**. This means that the audience reach must be at least 12 million.
   j. Add a constraint that cell **C13** be an integer (int).
   k. Add a constraint that cell **D13** be an integer.
   l. When all constraints are identified, click **OK** in the *Add Constraint* dialog box.
   m. Verify or choose **Simplex LP** for the *Select a Solving Method* box.
   n. Verify that the *Make Unconstrained Variables Non-Negative* box is selected (Figure 9-54).
   o. Click **Solve**. A solution displays in the worksheet, and the *Solver Results* dialog box is open. The maximum total exposure is **14,550**. (If *Solver* did not return that value, uninstall *Solver*, exit Excel, restart Excel, and install *Solver* again. Then repeat steps 5–6. If an error persists, go to step 7e.)

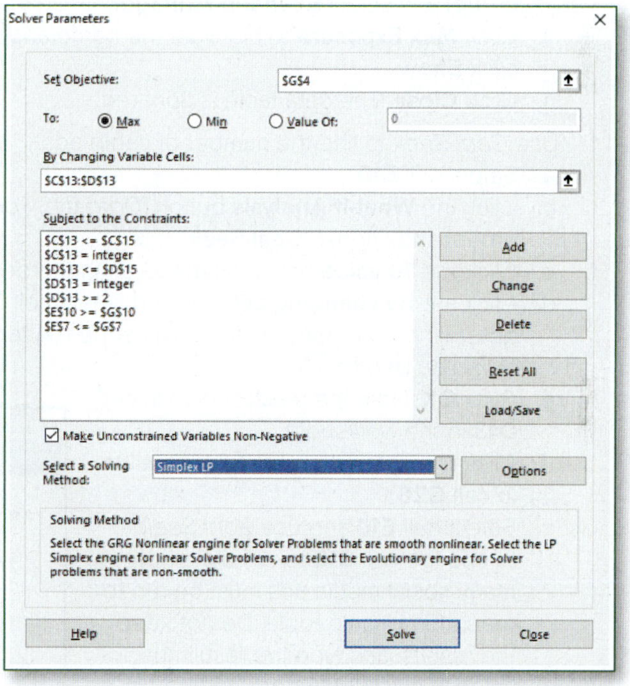

Figure 9-54 ***Solver*** **parameters**

7. Save *Solver* results as a scenario.
   a. Click **Save Scenario** in the *Solver Results* dialog box.
   b. Type Max Exposure as the scenario name.
   c. Click **OK** to return to the *Solver Results* dialog box.
   d. Select **Answer** in the *Reports* list and click **OK**. The generated report is inserted. Go to step 8.
   e. If *Solver* has not worked as indicated, type 6 in cell **C13** and type 3 in cell **C15** and proceed to step 7f. Your workbook will not have the **Answer Report 1** sheet.)
   f. Create a scenario named Max Exposure with cells **C13:D13** as the changing cells.

8. Create a scenario summary report.
   a. Click the **What-if Analysis** button [*Data* tab, *Forecast* group] and select **Scenario Manager**.
   b. Click the **Summary** button.
   c. Verify that the *Scenario summary* button is selected.

d. Select cells **C13:D13** for the *Result cells* box, type a comma (,) and then select cell **G4** (Figure 9-55).

e. Click **OK** in the *Scenario Summary* dialog box. The report displays in a new worksheet.

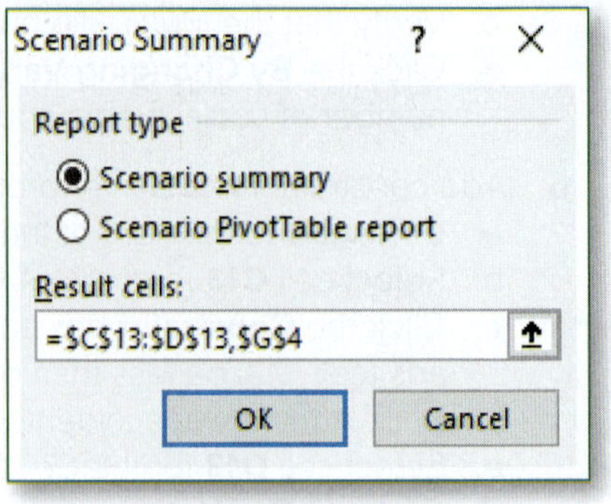

Figure 9-55 Nonadjacent cells used in the report

9. Show a scenario.
   a. Click the **Marketing Analysis** worksheet tab.
   b. Click the **What-if Analysis** button [*Data* tab, *Forecast* group] and select **Scenario Manager**.
   c. Click **Original** to highlight the name.
   d. Click **Show** and click **Close**.
10. Create a one-variable data table.
    a. Select cells **B20:B21** and fill values to reach cell **B30** as column input values.
    b. Select cell **C19**, one column to the right and one row above the first input value.
    c. Type =, click cell **E7**, and press **Enter** to reference the amount spent.
    d. Select cells **B19:C30** as the data table range.
    e. Click the **What-If Analysis** button [*Data* tab, *Forecast* group] and choose **Data Table**.
    f. Click the **Column input cell** box and select cell **C7** to indicate that the cost per ad will be replaced by the input values in column B.
    g. Click **OK** to create the data table (Figure 9-56).
    h. Click the **What-if Analysis** button [*Data* tab, *Forecast* group] and select **Scenario Manager**.
    i. Click **Max Exposure** to highlight the name and click **Show**.
    j. Click **Close**. The data table is updated.

Social Media Ad Costs	Total Spent
	$750
$500	$750
$525	$775
$550	$800
$575	$825
$600	$850
$625	$875
$650	$900
$675	$925
$700	$950
$725	$975
$750	$1,000

Figure 9-56 Data table results with *Original* scenario

11. Use *Goal Seek* to find the number of cable ads.
    a. Select cell **E10**.
    b. Click the **What-if Analysis** button [*Data* tab, *Forecast* group] and choose **Goal Seek**.
    c. Click the **To value** box and type 15 as the target.
    d. Click the **By changing cell** box and select cell **D13** to determine how many cable ads must be run to reach 15 million people.
    e. Click **OK**. Note the result shown in cell **D13** in the worksheet.
    f. Click **Cancel** and type the result value in cell **G26**.
    g. Select cell **E10** and use *Goal Seek* to change cell **C13** to calculate how many social media ads must be run to reach 15 million people. Do not keep the results, and type the resulting value in cell **G23** (Figure 9-57).

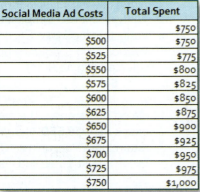

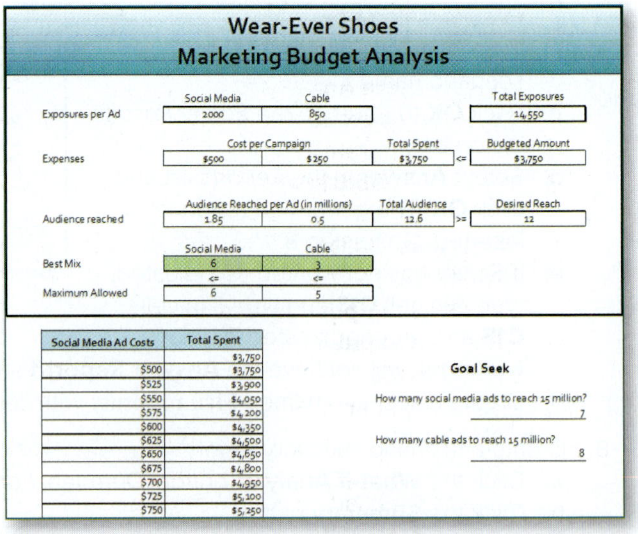

Figure 9-57 Completed *Marketing Analysis* sheet

12. Create a two-variable data table.
    a. Click the **Inventory** worksheet tab. Current costs and increase percentages are shown at the right.
    b. Select cell **K4** to place the formula one row above column input values and one column left of the row values.

c. Type =, click cell **J7**, type *(1+, click cell **J4**, and press **Enter**. The formula requires a closing right parenthesis and a message box suggests the correction.

d. Click **Yes** in the message box to accept the correction with closing right parenthesis. The formula multiplies the cost times 1 plus the percentage increase. Because cells **J4** and **J7** contain labels, the result is a standard error message (Figure 9-58).

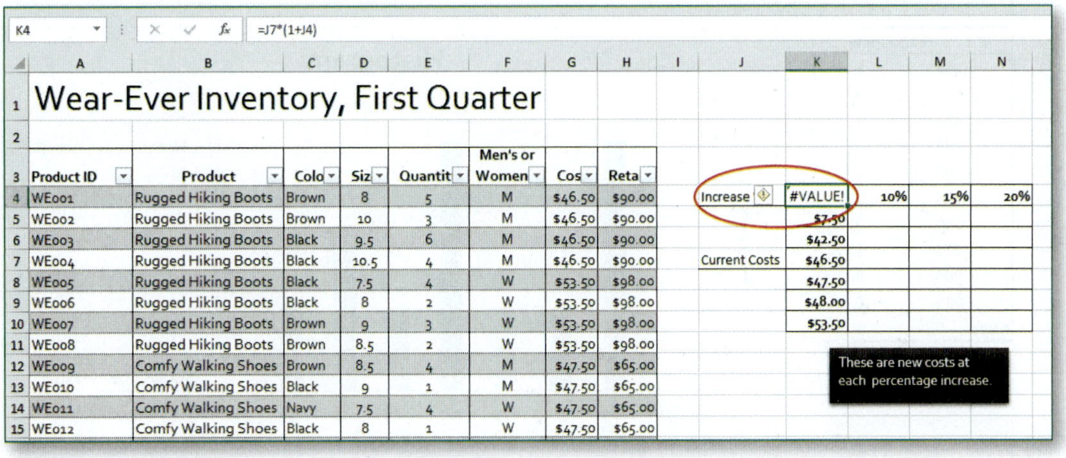

Figure 9-58 Error results from use of labels as placeholders in formula

e. Select cells **K4:N10** as the data table range.

f. Click the **What-If Analysis** button [*Data* tab, *Forecast* group] and choose **Data Table**.

g. Select cell **J4** for the *Row input cell* box because the percentage values in row 4 will replace the label in cell J4.

h. Click the **Column input cell** box and select cell **J7** so that the costs in column K replace the label in cell J7.

i. Click **OK** to build the data table.

j. Format cells **L5:N10** as **Currency** with two decimal places.

k. Format cell **K4** to use a **White, Background 1** font color.

13. Create a bin range and generate a histogram.

a. Click the **Glide History** sheet tab and select cell **D4**.

b. Type 100 and press **Enter**.

c. Type 125 in cell **D5** and press **Enter**.

d. Select cells **D4:D5** and fill a series to reach **325** in cell **D13**.

e. Click the **Data Analysis** button [*Data* tab, *Analysis* group].

f. Select **Histogram** and click **OK**.

g. Select cells **B5:B16** for the *Input Range* box.

h. Select cells **D4:D13** for the *Bin Range* box.

i. Select the **Output Range** button.

j. Click the **Output Range** box and select cell **E4**.

k. Select the **Chart Output** box (Figure 9-59).

l. Click **OK**.

m. Position the chart object with its top-left corner at cell **H4** and the bottom-right corner at **Q20**.

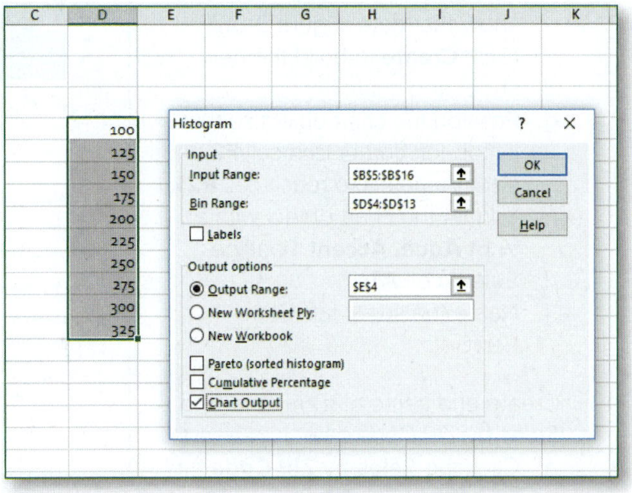

Figure 9-59 ***Histogram*** **dialog box**

n. Select and delete cells **D4:D13** (Figure 9-60).

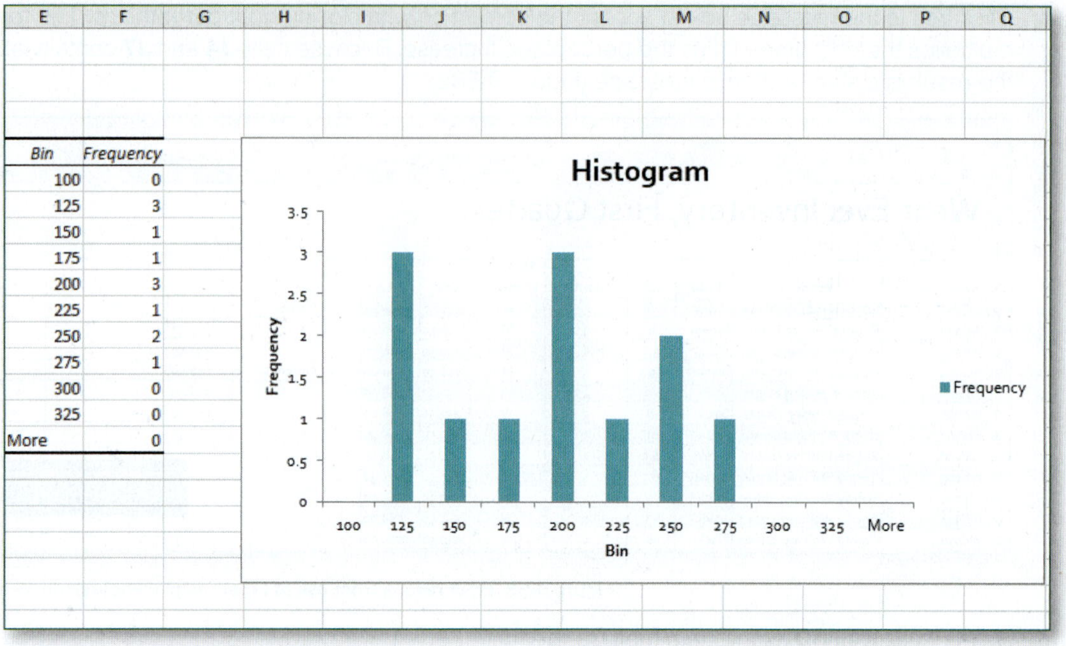

Figure 9-60 ***Histogram*** **output and chart**

14. Create a forecast sheet.
    a. Select cells **A4:B16** on the *Glide History* sheet tab. One data series is time-based, and the other represents values.
    b. Click the **Forecast Sheet** button [*Data* tab, *Forecast* group].
    c. Click the **Create a column chart** button at the top right of the window.
    d. Click the **Options** button to expand the window.
    e. Set the forecast to end at **12/31/2022** if it does not already show that date (Figure 9-61).
    f. Click **Create** to build the new sheet and chart.
    g. Position the chart object so that its top-left corner is in cell **F2** and size the object to reach cell **R21**.
    h. Format the chart object with a **¼ pt Aqua, Accent 1** outline.
    i. Select cell **A1**.
    j. Name the sheet tab Glide Forecast.

15. Create and name a 3D map for the *Sales by ZIP Code* data.
    a. Click the **Sales by ZIP Code** tab and select cell **A4**.

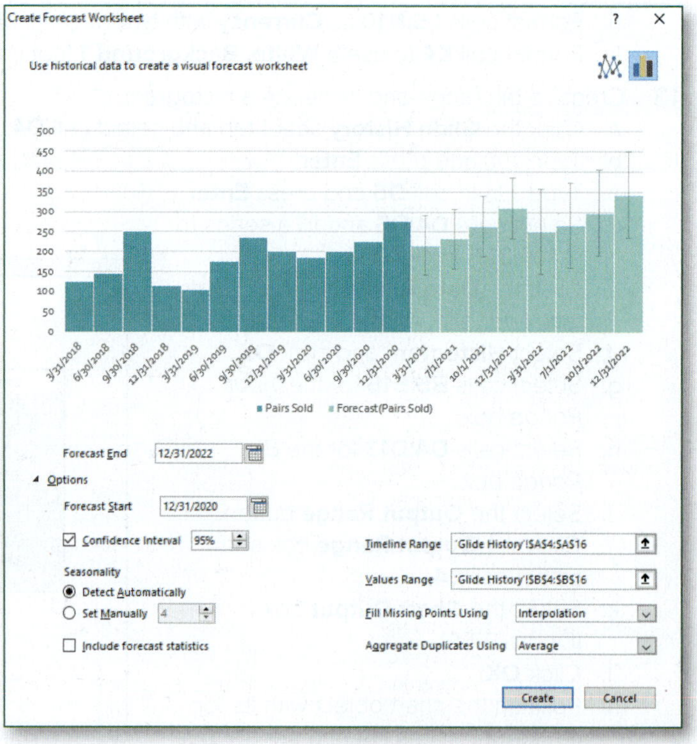

Figure 9-61 Options for a forecast sheet

b. Click the **3D Map** button [*Insert* tab, *Tours* group]. (Click **Enable** to use the *Data Analysis add-ins* if the message displays.)
c. Close the *Field List* window.
d. Click **Tour 1** in the *Tour Editor* pane.
e. Edit the name to ZIP Code Sales.
f. Click in white space in the *Tour Editor* pane.

16. Modify settings in the *Layer* pane.
    a. Verify that **City** is mapped as a *City* field type in the *Layer* pane.
    b. Verify that **ZIP Code** is mapped as a *Postal Code* field type.
    c. Verify or select the radio button for **City**.
    d. Click the **Add Field** box for *Height* and choose **Pairs**.
    e. Click the **Add Field** box for *Category* and choose **City** (Figure 9-62).

Figure 9-62 Map with *City* as the geocode and the category

17. Review and refresh data for the map.
    a. Select the radio button for **ZIP Code** in the *Location* group.
    b. Click the **Refresh Data** button [*Home* tab, *Layer* group]. The map refreshes and displays an outlier ZIP code.
    c. Click the **Zoom Out** button once so that you can see the state of Montana.
    d. Point to the single column marker in Montana. Bratsberg (actually located in Minnesota) has an incorrect ZIP code in the worksheet (Figure 9-63).
    e. Click the **File** tab and select **Close** to return to the worksheet.
    f. Select cell **A19**, change the ZIP code to 56711, and press **Enter**.

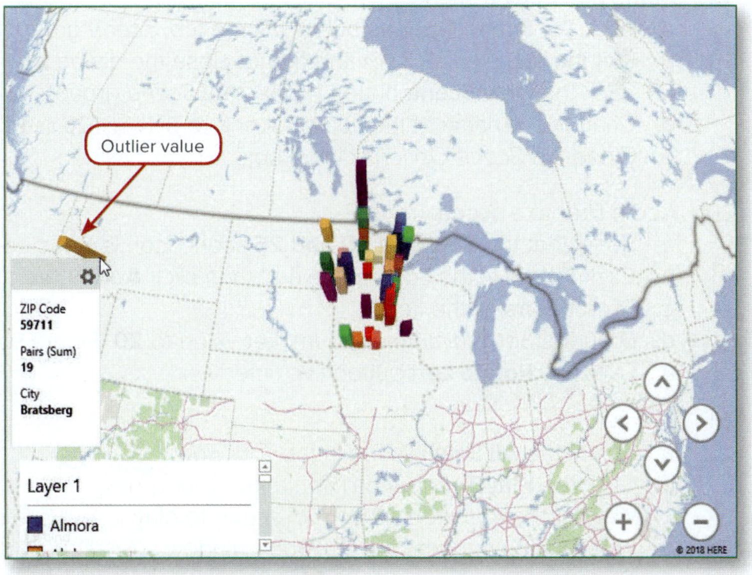

Figure 9-63 Map with ZIP code as geocode and resulting outlier column

g. Click the **3D Map** button [*Insert* tab, *Tours* group] and click the **ZIP Code Sales** icon in the *Launch 3D Maps* window.
h. Close the *Field List* window if it displays.
i. Click the **Refresh Data** button [*Home* tab, *Layer* group].
j. Select the radio button for **City** in the *Location* group. The map refreshes.

18. Change map perspective and shapes.
    a. Click the **Flat Map** button [*Home* tab, *Map* group].
    b. Click the **Tilt Down** button three times.
    c. Click the **Zoom In** button three times.
    d. Click the **Rotate Right** button three times.
    e. Click the **Shapes** button [*Home* tab, *Layer* group] and choose the round (ellipse) shape (Figure 9-64).

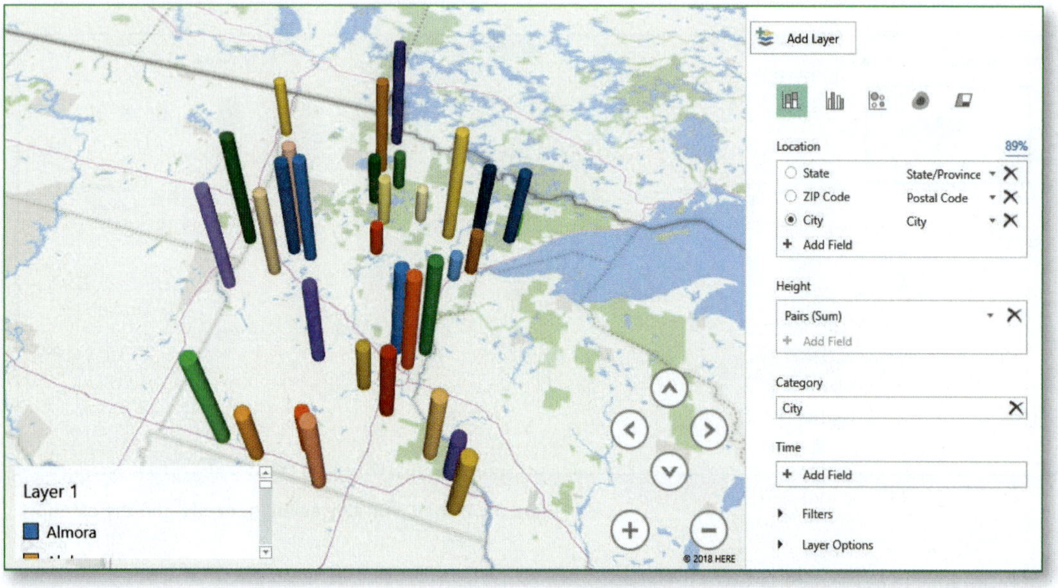

Figure 9-64 Flat map perspective and round shapes

19. Name and copy a scene.
    a. Click the **Scene Options** button [*Home* tab, *Scene* group].
    b. Edit the name to All Sales and do not close the dialog box.
    c. Click the **New Scene** button [*Home* tab, *Scene* group].
    d. Change the name of the copied scene to Between 20 and 25.
    e. Close the *Scene Options* dialog box.

20. Add a filter to a scene.
    a. Verify that the **Between 20 and 25** scene icon is selected.
    b. Click **Filters** in the *Layer* pane and then click **Add Filter**.
    c. Select **Pairs** as the field.
    d. Drag the *Set minimum value* marker value to **20** (Figure 9-65).
    e. Click the **Rotate Left** button five times.

21. Play a tour.
    a. Select the **All Sales** scene in the *Tour Editor*.
    b. Click the **Play Tour** button [*Home* tab, *Tour* group].
    c. Wait for the *Between 20 and 25* scene to play.
    d. Press **Esc** to return to the *3D Maps* window.
    e. Click the **File** tab and select **Close** to return to the worksheet. 3D maps are saved with the workbook.

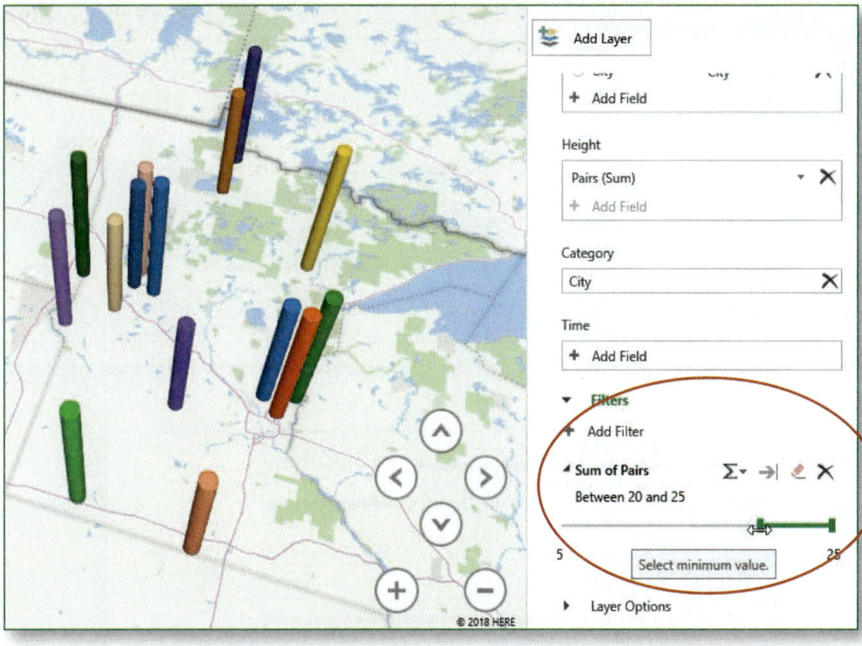

Figure 9-65 Add a filter for a values field

22. Uninstall *Solver* and the *Analysis TookPak*.
    a. Select the **Options** command [*File* tab] and click **Add-ins** in the left pane.
    b. Select **Solver Add-in** in the list of *Active Applications Add-ins*.
    c. In the *Manage* section near the bottom of the window, click **Go**.
    d. Deselect the **Solver Add-in** and **Analysis ToolPak** boxes.
    e. Click **OK**.
23. Save and close the workbook (Figure 9-66).

Wear-Ever Inventory, First Quarter

Product ID	Product	Color	Size	Quantity	Men's or Women's	Cost	Retail
WE001	Rugged Hiking Boots	Brown	8	5	M	$46.50	$90.00
WE002	Rugged Hiking Boots	Brown	10	3	M	$46.50	$90.00
WE003	Rugged Hiking Boots	Black	9.5	6	M	$46.50	$90.00
WE004	Rugged Hiking Boots	Black	10.5	4	M	$46.50	$90.00
WE005	Rugged Hiking Boots	Black	7.5	4	W	$53.50	$98.00
WE006	Rugged Hiking Boots	Black	8	2	W	$53.50	$98.00
WE007	Rugged Hiking Boots	Brown	9	3	W	$53.50	$98.00
WE008	Rugged Hiking Boots	Brown	8.5	2	W	$53.50	$98.00
WE009	Comfy Walking Shoes	Brown	8.5	4	M	$47.50	$65.00
WE010	Comfy Walking Shoes	Black	9	1	M	$47.50	$65.00
WE011	Comfy Walking Shoes	Navy	7.5	4	W	$47.50	$65.00
WE012	Comfy Walking Shoes	Black	8	1	W	$47.50	$65.00
WE013	Comfy Walking Shoes	Taupe	7.5	2	W	$47.50	$65.00
WE014	Comfy Walking Shoes	Brown	8	3	W	$47.50	$65.00
WE015	Lazy Flip-Flops	Pink	6	4	W	$7.50	$14.00
WE016	Lazy Flip-Flops	Pink	7	0	W	$7.50	$14.00
WE017	Lazy Flip-Flops	Pink	8	2	W	$7.50	$14.00
WE018	Lazy Flip-Flops	White	6	3	W	$7.50	$14.00
WE019	Lazy Flip-Flops	White	7	1	W	$7.50	$14.00
WE020	Lazy Flip-Flops	White	8	2	W	$7.50	$14.00
WE021	Lazy Flip-Flops	Brown	8	2	M	$7.50	$14.00
WE022	Lazy Flip-Flops	Brown	9	4	M	$7.50	$14.00
WE023	Lazy Flip-Flops	Brown	10	2	M	$7.50	$14.00
WE024	Lazy Flip-Flops	Brown	11	2	M	$7.50	$14.00
WE025	Seriously Tall Boots	Black	6	0	W	$42.50	$80.00
WE026	Seriously Tall Boots	Black	6.5	0	W	$42.50	$80.00
WE027	Seriously Tall Boots	Black	7	1	W	$42.50	$80.00
WE028	Seriously Tall Boots	Black	7.5	0	W	$42.50	$80.00
WE029	Seriously Tall Boots	Black	8	2	W	$42.50	$80.00
WE030	Seriously Tall Boots	Black	8.5	1	W	$42.50	$80.00
WE031	Glide Running Shoes	White	8	6	M	$48.00	$75.00
WE032	Glide Running Shoes	White	9	6	M	$48.00	$75.00
WE033	Glide Running Shoes	White	10	6	M	$48.00	$75.00
WE034	Glide Running Shoes	Black	8	2	M	$48.00	$75.00
WE035	Glide Running Shoes	Black	9	3	M	$48.00	$75.00
WE036	Glide Running Shoes	Black	10	1	M	$48.00	$75.00

Increase %		10%	15%	20%
	$7.50	$8.25	$8.63	$9.00
	$42.50	$46.75	$48.88	$51.00
Current Costs	$46.50	$51.15	$53.48	$55.80
	$47.50	$52.25	$54.63	$57.00
	$48.00	$52.80	$55.20	$57.60
	$53.50	$58.85	$61.53	$64.20

These are new costs at each percentage increase.

Scenario Summary	Current Values:	Original	Max Exposure
Changing Cells:			
$C$13	6	1	6
$D$13	3	1	3
Result Cells:			
$C$13	6	1	6
$D$13	3	1	3
$G$4	14,550	2,850	14,550

Notes: Current Values column represents values of changing cells at time Scenario Summary Report was created. Changing cells for each scenario are highlighted in gray.

Figure 9-66 Completed worksheets for Excel 9-1 (continued on next page)

Quarter	Pairs Sold	Forecast(Pairs Sold)	Confidence Interval(Pairs Sold)
3/31/2018	125		
6/30/2018	145		
9/30/2018	250		
12/31/2018	115		
3/31/2019	105		
6/30/2019	175		
9/30/2019	235		
12/31/2019	200		
3/31/2020	185		
6/30/2020	200		
9/30/2020	225		
12/31/2020	275		
3/31/2021		216.4468667	74.1538518
7/1/2021		232.9820473	74.53111385
10/1/2021		263.2816735	74.91392648
12/31/2021		308.8732127	75.30227808
3/31/2022		250.3636369	105.8407723
7/1/2022		266.8988176	106.1267792
10/1/2022		297.1984437	106.417469
12/31/2022		342.789983	106.7128549

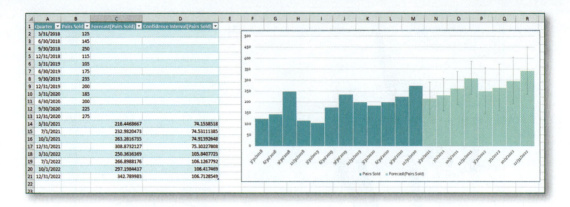

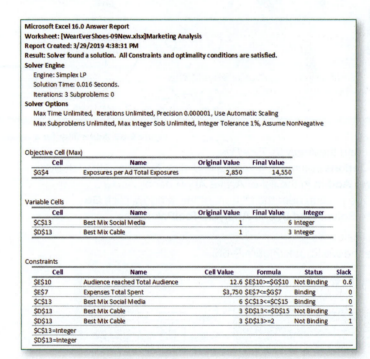

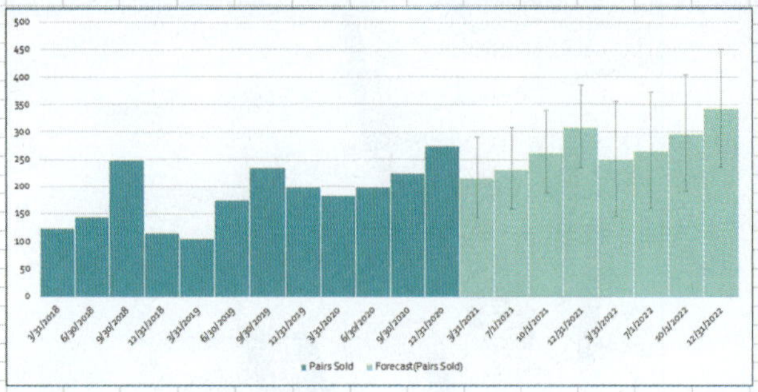

Microsoft Excel 16.0 Answer Report
Worksheet: [WearEverShoes-09New.xlsx]Marketing Analysis
Report Created: 3/29/2019 4:38:31 PM
Result: Solver found a solution. All Constraints and optimality conditions are satisfied.
Solver Engine
Engine: Simplex LP
Solution Time: 0.016 Seconds.
Iterations: 3 Subproblems: 0
Solver Options
Max Time Unlimited, Iterations Unlimited, Precision 0.000001, Use Automatic Scaling
Max Subproblems Unlimited, Max Integer Sols Unlimited, Integer Tolerance 1%, Assume NonNegative

Objective Cell (Max)

Cell	Name	Original Value	Final Value
$G$4	Exposures per Ad Total Exposures	2,850	14,550

Variable Cells

Cell	Name	Original Value	Final Value	Integer
$C$13	Best Mix Social Media	1	6	Integer
$D$13	Best Mix Cable	1	3	Integer

Constraints

Cell	Name	Cell Value	Formula	Status	Slack
$E$10	Audience reached Total Audience	12.6	$E$10>=$G$10	Not Binding	0.6
$E$7	Expenses Total Spent	$3,750	$E$7<=$G$7	Binding	0
$C$13	Best Mix Social Media	6	$C$13<=$C$15	Binding	0
$D$13	Best Mix Cable	3	$D$13<=$D$15	Not Binding	2
$D$13	Best Mix Cable	3	$D$13>=2	Not Binding	1
$C$13=Integer					
$D$13=Integer					

Figure 9-66 Completed worksheets for Excel 9-1 (continued from previous page)

Guided Project 9-2

Sierra Pacific Community College District (SPCCD) has a worksheet for evaluating student loan offerings. You build data tables, determine how to reach a goal capacity for the freshmen orientation seminar, and create a map chart for alumni data.
[Student Learning Outcomes 9.1, 9.2, 9.3, 9.4, 9.6, 9.7]

File Needed: ***SPCCD-09.xlsx*** *(Student data files are available in the* Library *of your SIMnet account.)*
Completed Project File Name: ***[your initials] Excel 9-2.xlsx***

Skills Covered in This Project

- Create and manage scenarios.
- Use *Goal Seek*.
- Build data tables with one and two variables.
- Use *Solver* to determine capacity.
- Calculate a moving average using the *Analysis ToolPak*.
- Create a map chart.
- Edit data for a map chart.
- Format a map chart.

---

1. Open the ***SPCCD-09*** workbook from your student data files and save it as [your initials] Excel 9-2.
2. Review the loan formulas on the **Loan Tables** worksheet.
   a. Select cell **C7**. The PMT function determines the monthly payment for a $10,000 loan at 4.5% for five years.
   b. Select cell **F4**. The total interest is the payment times the number of years times 12 minus the loan amount.
   c. Select cell **F6**. The total interest plus the loan amount are added.
3. Create scenarios in a worksheet.
   a. Select cell **C5** and click the **What-if Analysis** button [*Data* tab, *Forecast* group].
   b. Select **Scenario Manager**. No scenarios exist in the workbook.
   c. Click **Add**.
   d. Type 5 Year as the name in the *Add Scenario* dialog box.
   e. Verify that the *Changing cells* box displays cell **C5** as the argument to be changed.
   f. Click **OK**.
   g. Do not edit the *Scenario Values* entry and click **OK**.
   h. Click **Add** to add another scenario.
   i. Type 7 Year as the name and keep the *Changing cells* as cell **C5**.
   j. Click **OK**.
   k. Change the value to 7 in the *Scenario Values* dialog box and click **OK**.
   l. Add another scenario for a nine-year loan and close the *Scenario Manager* dialog box.
4. Display a scenario in a worksheet.
   a. Click the **What-if Analysis** button [*Data* tab, *Forecast* group] and select **Scenario Manager**.
   b. Select **7 Year** in the list and click **Show**.
   c. Click **Close**.
5. Use *Goal Seek* to find a target payment.
   a. Select cell **C7**.
   b. Click the **What-if Analysis** button [*Data* tab, *Forecast* group] and choose **Goal Seek**.
   c. Click the **To value** box and type 125 as the target.
   d. Click the **By changing cell** box and select cell **C6** to determine the interest rate that results in this payment.
   e. Click **OK** to run *Goal Seek* (Figure 9-67).
   f. Click **OK** to accept the solution.
6. Save *Goal Seek* results as a scenario.
   a. Select cell **C6** and click the **What-if Analysis** button [*Data* tab, *Forecast* group].
   b. Select **Scenario Manager** and click **Add**.

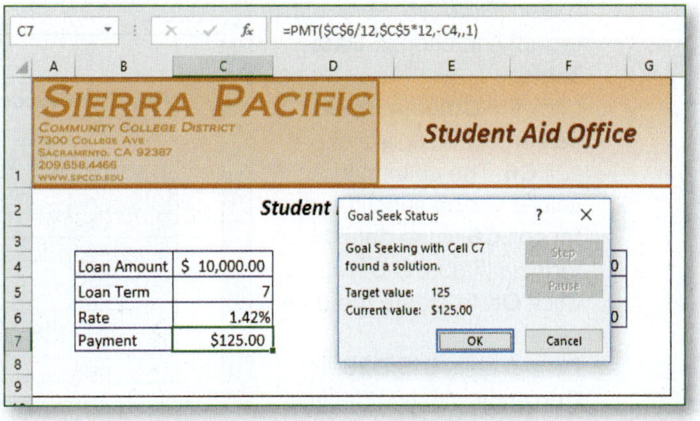

Figure 9-67 ***Goal Seek* results**

c. Type $125 Payment as the scenario name.
d. Verify that the *Changing cells* box displays cell **C6**.
e. Click **OK**.
f. Do not change the *Scenario Values* entry, click **OK**, and click **Close**.

7. Create a scenario summary report.
   a. Click the **What-if Analysis** button [*Data* tab, *Forecast* group] and select **Scenario Manager**.
   b. Click the **Summary** button.
   c. Verify that the *Scenario summary* is selected.
   d. Select cells **C5:C7** for the *Result cells* box.
   e. Click **OK** in the *Scenario Summary* dialog box. The report displays in a new worksheet (Figure 9-68).

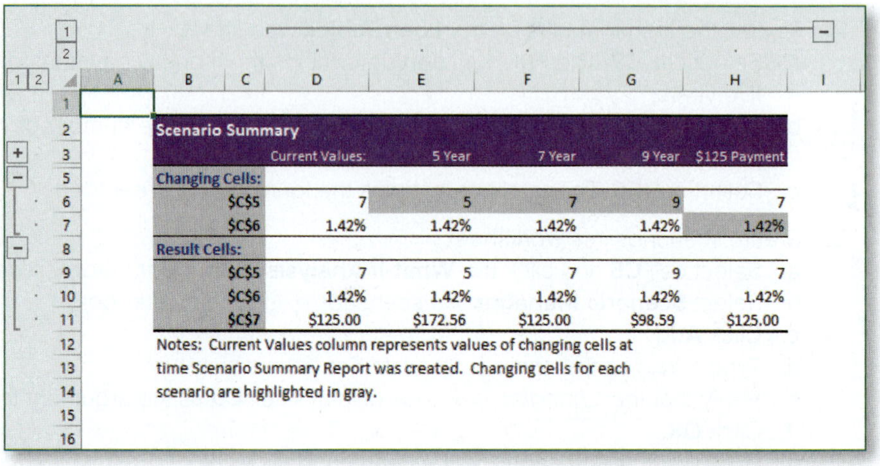

Scenario Summary
Current Values:
5 Year
7 Year
9 Year
$125 Payment
Changing Cells:
$C$5 7 5 7 9 7
$C$6 1.42% 1.42% 1.42% 1.42% 1.42%
Result Cells:
$C$5 7 5 7 9 7
$C$6 1.42% 1.42% 1.42% 1.42% 1.42%
$C$7 $125.00 $172.56 $125.00 $98.59 $125.00
Notes: Current Values column represents values of changing cells at
time Scenario Summary Report was created. Changing cells for each
scenario are highlighted in gray.

Figure 9-68 Scenario summary report results

8. Create a one-variable data table to calculate the payment and total interest charges based on different rates.
   a. Select the **Loan Tables** worksheet tab.
   b. Select cells **B15:B16** and fill percentages to reach cell **B23**. These are column input values.
   c. Select cell **C14**. The first formula must be one column to the right and one row above the first input value.
   d. Type =, select cell **C7**, and press **Enter** to reference the payment formula.
   e. Select cell **D14**. Additional formulas must be in the same row.
   f. Type =, select cell **F4**, and press **Enter** to reference the total interest formula.
   g. Select cells **B14:D23** as the data table range.
   h. Click the **What-If Analysis** button [*Data* tab, *Forecast* group] and choose **Data Table**.
   i. Click the **Column input cell** entry box and click cell **C6**. The column input values will be substituted for cell **C6** in the data table formula (Figure 9-69).
   j. Click **OK** to create the data table.
   k. Format cells **C15:D23** as **Currency** with two decimal places.

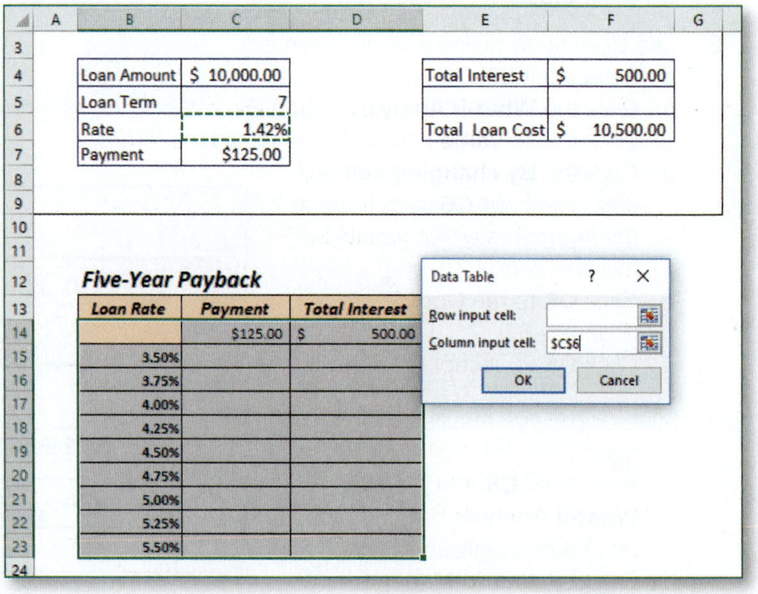

Figure 9-69 One-variable data table setup

9. Create a two-variable data table to calculate monthly payments at different rates and payback years.
   a. Select cell **B26** to place the formula one row above column input values and one column left of row values.
   b. Type =, click cell **C7**, and press **Enter**.
   c. Select cells **B26:F35** as the data table range.
   d. Click the **What-If Analysis** button [*Data* tab, *Forecast* group] and choose **Data Table**.
   e. Select cell **C5** for the *Row input cell* box. The number of years is in the row of this data table.
   f. Click the **Column input cell** box and select cell **C6**. The changing interest rates are in a column.
   g. Click **OK** to build the data table. The standard error message #VALUE! appears in all the cells.
   h. Select **C27** and click its **Trace Error** button. An *Error in Value* results because the content in row 26 is recognized as text (Figure 9-70).
   i. Click cell **C26**, type 6, and press **Tab**. The first column of the data table is refreshed.
   j. Type 8 in cell **D26** and press **Tab**.
   k. Correct the row input values in cells **E26:F26**.
   l. Format cells **C27:F35** as **Currency** with two decimal places.
   m. Format cell **B26** to use **Orange, Accent 2, Lighter 60%** as the font color.

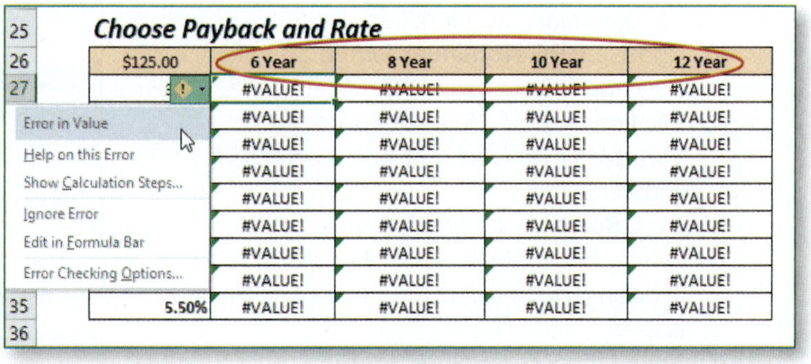

Figure 9-70 Year values were entered as text

10. Install *Solver* and the *Analysis ToolPak*.
    a. Select the **Options** command [*File* tab].
    b. Click **Add-ins** in the left pane.
    c. Click **Go** near the bottom of the window.
    d. Select the **Solver Add-in** box.
    e. Select the **Analysis ToolPak** box.
    f. Click **OK**.

11. Use *Solver* to find a capacity goal.
    a. Select the **Orientation** sheet tab. The college wants to maximize the number of students who can be accommodated in the orientation seminar.
    b. Click the **Solver** button [*Data* tab, *Analysis* group].
    c. Select cell **E9** for the *Set Objective* box. This cell has a *SUM* formula.
    d. Verify that the *Max* radio button is selected for the *To* parameter.
    e. Click the **By Changing Variable Cells** box and select cells **D5:D8**.

12. Add constraints to a *Solver* problem.
    a. Click **Add** to the right of the *Subject to the Constraints* box.
    b. Select cell **D5** for the *Cell Reference* box.
    c. Use <= as the operator.
    d. Click the **Constraint** box and type 4. The Davis campus can hold four or fewer sessions.
    e. Click **Add**. (If you accidentally closed the dialog box, click **Add** to reopen it.)
    f. Select cell **D5** again for the *Cell Reference* box.
    g. Choose >= as the operator.
    h. Click the **Constraint** box and type 1. The Davis campus must have at least one session.

i. Click **Add**. Complete constraints for the problem as shown here:

D6 <= 3
D6 >= 1
D7 <= 1
D7 >= 1
D8 <= 4
D8 >= 1

j. click **OK** in the *Add Constraint* dialog box when all constraints are identified.
k. Choose **GRG Nonlinear** for the *Select a Solving Method*.
l. Confirm that the *Make Unconstrained Variables Non-Negative* box is selected (Figure 9-71).
m. Click **Solve**. A solution is shown in the worksheet, and the *Solver Results* dialog box is open. The maximum number of students is 870.
n. Select the **Keep Solver Solution** button and click **OK**. (If you see a *Solver* run-time error message, type 4, 3, 1, and 4 in cells **D5:D8** so that you can continue.)

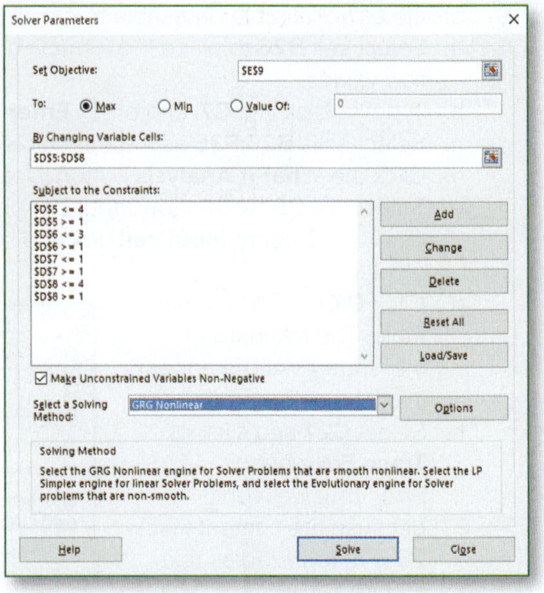

Figure 9-71 ***Solver*** **constraints for the capacity problem**

13. Calculate a moving average.
    a. Click the **Enrollment** sheet tab.
    b. Click the **Data Analysis** button [*Data* tab, *Analysis* group].
    c. Choose **Moving Average** and click **OK**.
    d. Select cells **B8:B13** for the *Input Range* box.
    e. Click the **Interval** box and type 2 so that every two years are averaged.
    f. Click the **Output Range** box and select cell **B16**.
    g. Click **OK**.
    h. Click the **Data Analysis** button [*Data* tab, *Analysis* group], choose **Moving Average**, and click **OK**.
    i. Select cells **E8:E13** for the *Input Range* box.
    j. Click the **Interval** box and verify or type 2.
    k. Click the **Output Range** box, select cell **E16**, and click **OK**.
    l. Calculate the moving average for the PHI department in column **H** (Figure 9-72).

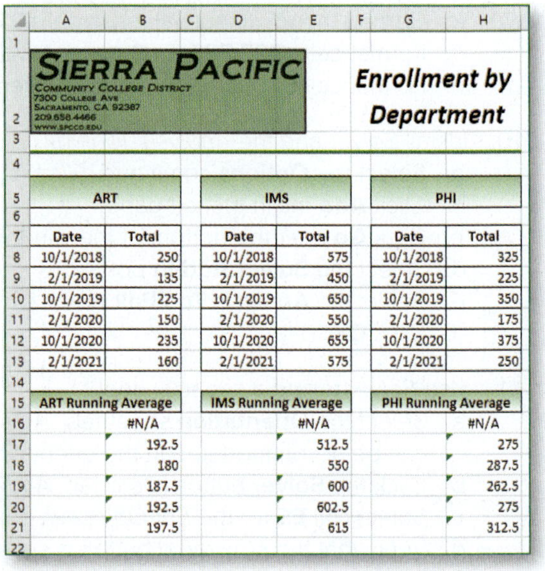

Figure 9-72 Moving average results

14. Create a map chart for alumni data.
    a. Click the **Alumni** sheet tab.
    b. Select cells **C5:D18** and click the **Maps** button [*Insert* tab, *Charts* group].
    c. Choose **Filled Map**.
    d. Move the chart to its own sheet named Alumni Map.

15. Edit the chart data source.
    a. Click the **Alumni** sheet tab and select cell **C19**.
    b. Type Alaska, press **Tab**, type 3, and press **Enter**.
    c. Click the **Alumni Map** sheet tab and display the *Chart Tools* command tabs.

d. Click the **Select Data** button [*Chart Tools Design* tab, *Data* group], select cells **C5:D19** as the *Chart data range*, and click **OK**.

16. Edit and format map chart elements.
    a. Click the **Chart Elements** button at the top-right corner of the chart and place a check mark in the **Data Labels** box.
    b. Click the **Chart Elements** drop-down list [*Chart Tools Format* tab, *Current Selection* group], **Series 1**, and click the **Format Selection** button [*Chart Tools Format* tab, *Current Selection* group].
    c. Click the **Series Option** button in the *Format Data Series* pane, click the **Map labels** arrow, and select **Show all** (Figure 9-73).

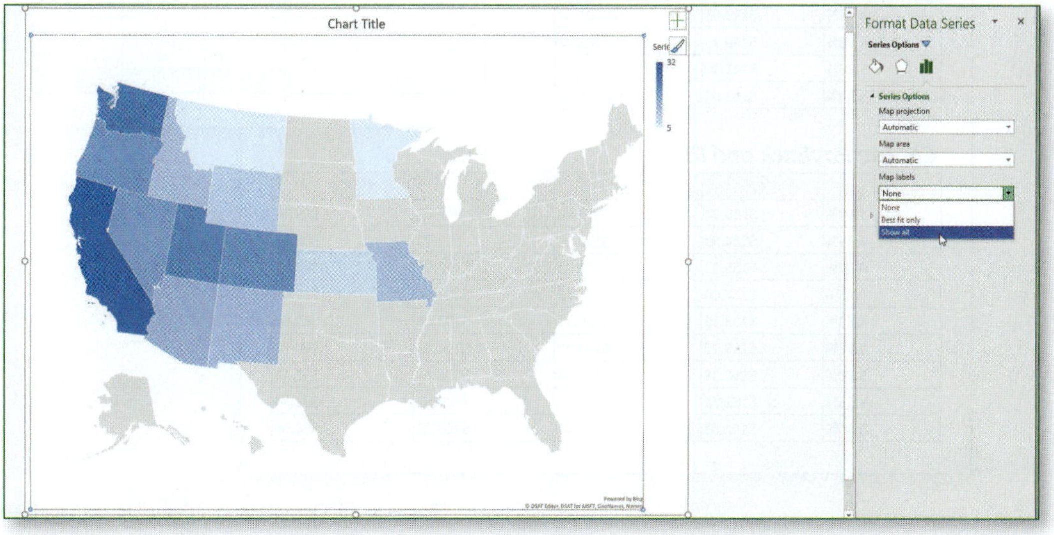

Figure 9-73 Series options for a map chart

    d. Expand the **Series Color** group and verify that **Sequential (2-color)** is selected.
    e. Verify that the *Minimum* option is **Lowest value** and set its **Fill Color** to **Gold, Accent 4, Lighter 80%** (eight column).
    f. Verify that the *Maximum* option is **Highest value** and set its fill color to **Gold, Accent 4, Darker 25%** (eight column).
    g. Select and delete the legend.
    h. Edit the chart title to display Number of Alumni by State. (Figure 9-74).

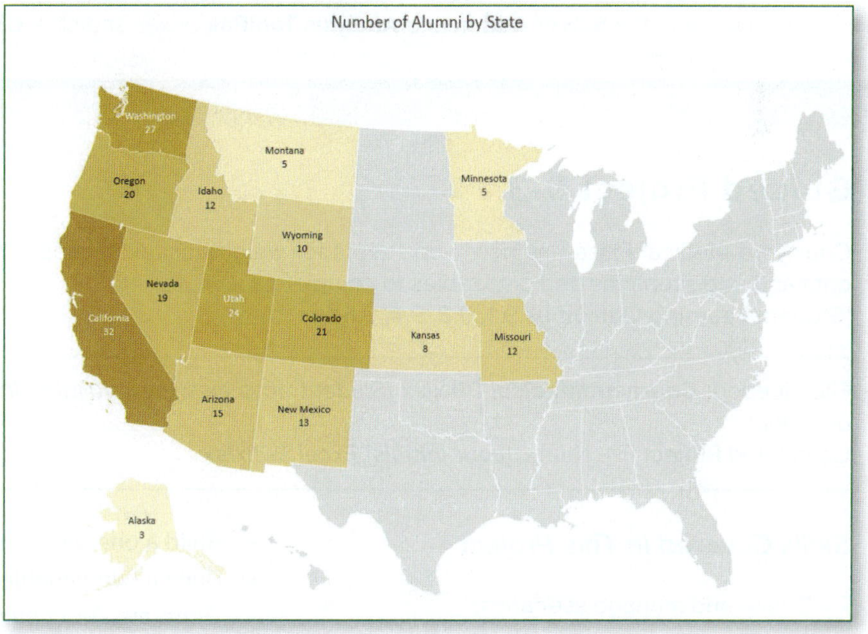

Figure 9-74 Alumni map chart

17. Save and close the workbook (Figure 9-75).

Five-Year Payback

Loan Rate	Payment	Total Interest
	$125.00	$ 500.00
3.50%	$134.01	$1,256.64
3.75%	$135.12	$1,349.92
4.00%	$136.23	$1,443.65
4.25%	$137.36	$1,537.85
4.50%	$138.48	$1,632.51
4.75%	$139.61	$1,727.64
5.00%	$140.75	$1,823.22
5.25%	$141.90	$1,919.26
5.50%	$143.04	$2,015.76

Choose Payback and Rate

	6	8	10	12
3.50%	$153.74	$119.23	$98.60	$84.90
3.75%	$154.83	$120.36	$99.75	$86.08
4.00%	$155.93	$121.49	$100.91	$87.26
4.25%	$157.04	$122.62	$102.08	$88.46
4.50%	$158.15	$123.77	$103.25	$89.66
4.75%	$159.26	$124.92	$104.43	$90.88
5.00%	$160.38	$126.07	$105.63	$92.11
5.25%	$161.50	$127.24	$106.82	$93.34
5.50%	$162.63	$128.40	$108.03	$94.58

SIERRA PACIFIC
COMMUNITY COLLEGE DISTRICT
7300 COLLEGE AVE
SACRAMENTO, CA 92387
209.658.4466
WWW.SPCCD.EDU

Freshman Orientation Capacity

Campus	Session Capacity	Sessions per Semester	Total Capacity
Davis	90	4	360
Fair Oaks	55	3	165
Granite Bay	85	1	85
Roseville	65	4	260
Total	295	12	870

Figure 9-75 Completed worksheets for Excel 9-2

18. Uninstall *Solver* and the *Analysis TookPak*.
    a. Select the **Options** command [*File* tab] and click **Add-ins** in the left pane.
    b. Select **Solver Add-in** in the list of *Active Applications Add-ins*.
    c. Click **Go** in the *Manage* section near the bottom of the window.
    d. Deselect the **Solver Add-in** and **Analysis ToolPak** boxes and click **OK**.

Guided Project 9-3

Courtyard Medical Plaza has new worksheets for weight loss workshops. You use *Solver* with sample data and add scenarios and data tables to complete a sample set.
[Student Learning Outcomes 9.1, 9.3, 9.4, 9.6]

File Needed: ***CourtyardMedical-09.xlsx*** *(Student data files are available in the* Library *of your SIMnet account.)*
Completed Project File Name: ***[your initials] Excel 9-3.xlsx***

Skills Covered in This Project

- Create and manage scenarios.
- Use *Solver* in a worksheet to find a solution.
- Build a one-variable data table.
- Build a two-variable data table.
- Generate *Descriptive Statistics* for a set of data.

1. Open the ***CourtyardMedical-09*** workbook from your student data files and save it as [your initials] Excel 9-3.
2. Install *Solver* and the *Analysis ToolPak*.
   a. Select the **Options** command [*File* tab] and click **Add-ins** in the left pane.
   b. Click **Go** near the bottom of the window.
   c. Select the **Solver Add-in** box.
   d. Select the **Analysis ToolPak** box and click **OK**.
3. Click the **Workout Plan** worksheet tab and select cell **E10**. Five activities are summed to count calories. This cell includes a *SUM* formula.
4. Add scenarios in a worksheet.
   a. Select cells **D5:D9**.
   b. Click the **What-if Analysis** button [*Data* tab, *Forecast* group] and select **Scenario Manager**.
   c. Click **Add** and type Basic Plan as the name.
   d. Verify or set the *Changing cells* box to display **D5:D9** and click **OK**.
   e. Do not edit the *Scenario Values* and click **OK**.
   f. Click **Add** to add another scenario.
   g. Type Double as the name, keep the *Changing cells* as **D5:D9**, and click **OK**.
   h. Change the values to 2, 2, 4, 2, and 2, doubling each current value, in the *Scenario Values* dialog box and click **OK** (Figure 9-76).
   i. Click **Close** and select cell **B3**.

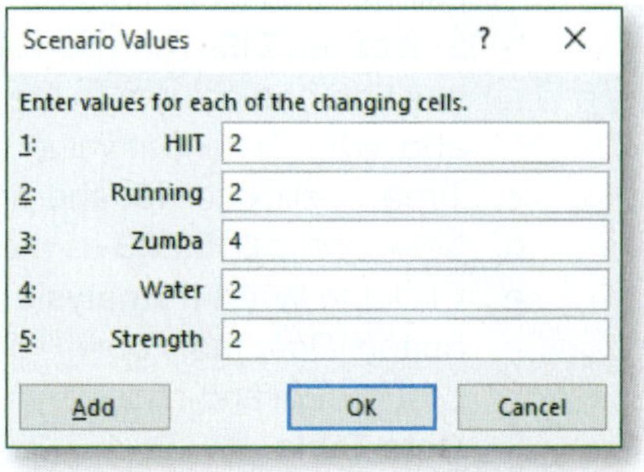

Figure 9-76 Edited scenario values

5. Use *Solver* to find a maximum calorie burn.
   a. Click the **Solver** button [*Data* tab, *Analysis* group].
   b. Select cell **E10,** the cell with a *SUM* formula, for the *Set Objective* box.
   c. Verify or select the **Max** radio button.
   d. Click the **By Changing Variable Cells** box and select cells **D5:D7** to adjust the occurrences of three activities in the workout plan.
6. Add constraints to a *Solver* problem.
   a. Click **Add** to the right of the *Subject to the Constraints* box.
   b. Select cell **D5** for the *Cell Reference* box and choose **int** as the operator. The *Constraint* box displays **integer** to require that the result be a whole number.
   c. Click **Add** to add each of constraints shown here:
      D5 <=4
      D5 >=2
      D6 int
      D6 <=3
      D6 >=1
      D7 int
      D7 <=4
      D7 >=1
   d. When all constraints are identified, click **OK** in the *Add Constraint* dialog box.
   e. Verify or select **Simplex LP** for the *Select a Solving Method* option.
   f. Confirm that the *Make Unconstrained Variables Non-Negative* box is selected (Figure 9-77).
   g. Click **Solve**. A solution displays in the worksheet, and the *Solver Results* dialog box is open.
7. Save *Solver* results as a scenario.
   a. Click **Save Scenario** in the *Solver Results* dialog box.
   b. Type Solver as the scenario name.
   c. Click **OK** to return to the *Solver Results* dialog box.
   d. Select the **Restore Original Values** button and click **OK**.

8. Create a scenario summary report.
   a. Click the **What-if Analysis** button [*Data* tab, *Forecast* group] and select **Scenario Manager**.
   b. Click the **Summary** button and verify that the *Scenario summary* button is selected.
   c. Select cells **D5:D9** for the *Result cells* box, type a comma (,) and then select cell **E10**.
   d. Click **OK** to create the report (Figure 9-78).

9. Create a one-variable data table to calculate total calories if dinner calories are adjusted.
   a. Click the **Calorie Journal** worksheet tab and select cell **I5**. The *SUM* formula calculates total calories consumed per day.
   b. Select cell **E15**. The formula for the data table must be one column to the right and one row above the first input value.
   c. Type =, click cell **I5,** and press **Enter**.
   d. Select cells **D15:E23** as the data table range.
   e. Click the **What-If Analysis** button [*Data* tab, *Forecast* group] and choose **Data Table**.
   f. Click the **Column input cell** box and select cell **G5**. The input values will be substituted for this cell in the data table formula.
   g. Click **OK** (Figure 9-79).

10. Create a two-variable data table to calculate total calories if both lunch and dinner calories are adjusted.
   a. Select cell **L15**. A two-variable table has one formula, one row above column inputs and one column left of row values.
   b. Type =, click cell **I5,** and press **Enter**.
   c. Select cells **L15:T23**.
   d. Click the **What-If Analysis** button [*Data* tab, *Forecast* group] and choose **Data Table**.
   e. Select cell **E5** for the *Row input cell* box. Lunch calories are in the row of this data table.
   f. Click the **Column input cell** box and select cell **G5**. Dinner calories are in the column.
   g. Click **OK** to build the data table (Figure 9-80).

11. Select cell **J1** and insert a page break [*Page Layout* tab, *Page Setup* group].

12. Generate *Descriptive Statistics* for a rating category.
   a. Click the **Dental Insurance** sheet tab.
   b. Click the **Data Analysis** button [*Data* tab, *Analysis* group].

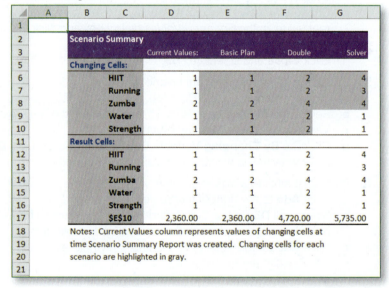

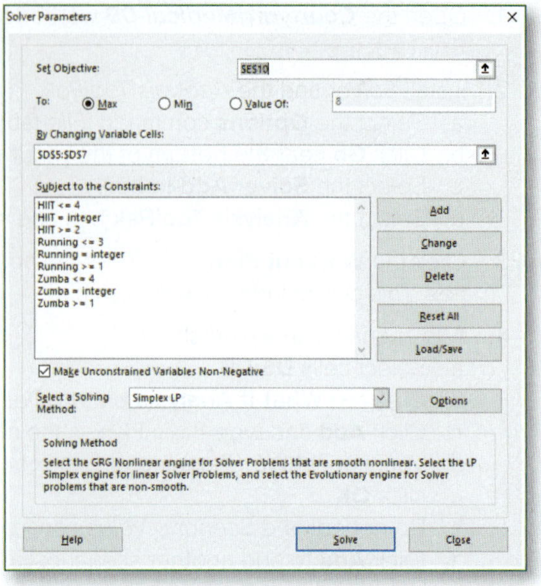

Figure 9-77 *Solver* **parameters and constraints**

	A	B	C	D	E	F	G
1							
2		Scenario Summary					
3				Current Values:	Basic Plan	Double	Solver
5		Changing Cells:					
6			HIIT	1	1	2	4
7			Running	1	1	2	3
8			Zumba	2	2	4	4
9			Water	1	1	2	1
10			Strength	1	1	2	1
11		Result Cells:					
12			HIIT	1	1	2	4
13			Running	1	1	2	3
14			Zumba	2	2	4	4
15			Water	1	1	2	1
16			Strength	1	1	2	1
17			$E$10	2,360.00	2,360.00	4,720.00	5,735.00
18		Notes: Current Values column represents values of changing cells at					
19		time Scenario Summary Report was created. Changing cells for each					
20		scenario are highlighted in gray.					
21							

Figure 9-78 Generated scenario summary

		Total Calories
Dinner Calories		2,450
	500	2,150
	600	2,250
	700	2,350
	800	2,450
	900	2,550
	1,000	2,650
	1,100	2,750
	1,200	2,850

Figure 9-79 One-variable data table with results

c. Select **Descriptive Statistics** and click **OK**.
d. Select cells **E4:E35** for the *Input Range* box.
e. Select the **Labels in First Row** box.
f. Select the **Output Range** button, click the **Output Range** box, and select cell **G4**.
g. Select the **Summary statistics** box and click **OK**.
h. *AutoFit* column **G** (Figure 9-81).

		Lunch Calories							
	2,450	500	600	700	800	900	1000	1100	1200
Dinner Calories	500	2050	2150	2250	2350	2450	2550	2650	2750
	600	2150	2250	2350	2450	2550	2650	2750	2850
	700	2250	2350	2450	2550	2650	2750	2850	2950
	800	2350	2450	2550	2650	2750	2850	2950	3050
	900	2450	2550	2650	2750	2850	2950	3050	3150
	1000	2550	2650	2750	2850	2950	3050	3150	3250
	1100	2650	2750	2850	2950	3050	3150	3250	3350
	1200	2750	2850	2950	3050	3150	3250	3350	3450

Figure 9-80 Two-variable data table with results

Courtyard Medical Plaza — Dental Services

	A	B	C	D	E	F	G	H
4	Patient ID	Insurance	Service Code	Maximum Benefit	Billed		*Billed*	
5	OP0001	CompDent	D0120	$125.00	$135.00			
6	OP0002	SIP	D1110	$185.00	$135.00		Mean	239.0323
7	OP0003	CompDent	D2751	$235.00	$250.00		Standard Error	20.75772
8	OP0004	Westville	D2751	$135.00	$100.00		Median	235
9	OP0005	CompDent	D1110	$245.00	$185.00		Mode	235
10	OP0006	SIP	D1110	$275.00	$100.00		Standard Deviation	115.5741
11	OP0007	SIP	D1110	$325.00	$425.00		Sample Variance	13357.37
12	OP0008	Westville	D0120	$175.00	$125.00		Kurtosis	0.865547
13	OP0009	BlueDent	D0120	$195.00	$145.00		Skewness	1.125652
14	OP0010	BlueDent	D1110	$200.00	$225.00		Range	450
15	OP0011	BlueDent	D1110	$225.00	$235.00		Minimum	100
16	OP0012	SIP	D1110	$200.00	$185.00		Maximum	550
17	OP0013	CompDent	D2751	$475.00	$325.00		Sum	7410
18	OP0014	SIP	D1110	$235.00	$235.00		Count	31

Figure 9-81 Summary statistics for the billed amounts

13. Save and close the workbook.
14. Uninstall *Solver* and the *Analysis TookPak*.
    a. Select the **Options** command [*File* tab] and click **Add-ins** in the left pane.
    b. Select **Solver Add-in** in the list of *Active Applications Add-ins*.
    c. Click **Go** in the *Manage* section near the bottom of the window.
    d. Deselect the **Solver Add-in** and **Analysis ToolPak** boxes and click **OK**.

Independent Project 9-4

You use data from Central Sierra Insurance to create a commission calculator with a two-variable data table. You also edit a *3D Map* tour to add and adjust scenes.
[Student Learning Outcomes 9.4, 9.7]

File Needed: ***CentralSierra-09.xlsx*** *(Student data files are available in the* Library *of your SIMnet account.)*
Completed Project File Name: ***[your initials] Excel 9-4.xlsx***

Skills Covered in This Project

- Build a two-variable data table.
- Add map labels to a scene.
- Insert a text box in a scene.
- Copy and edit scenes in a *3D Map* tour.
- Change shapes and layer options in a scene.
- Edit and refresh data for a *3D Map* tour.
- Play a *3D Map* tour.

1. Open the ***CentralSierra-09*** workbook from your student data files and save it as [your initials] Excel 9-4.
2. Click the **Commissions** worksheet tab and enter a formula in cell **E6** to calculate commission dollars (multiply the premium by the rate).
3. Build a two-variable data table to calculate commissions.
4. Format the data table results as **Currency** with no decimal places (Figure 9-82).
5. Click the **Claims** worksheet tab and select cell **A7**.
6. Click the **3D Map** button [*Insert* tab, *Tours* group] and select the **Claims** tour icon in the *Launch 3D Maps* window.
7. Close the *Field List* window if it displays.
8. Click the **Map Labels** button [*Home* tab, *Map* group].
9. Insert a text box in a scene.
   a. Click the **Text Box** button [*Home* tab, *Insert* group]. The *Add Text Box* dialog box opens.
   b. Type August Claims in the *Title* box and click **Create** (Figure 9-83).

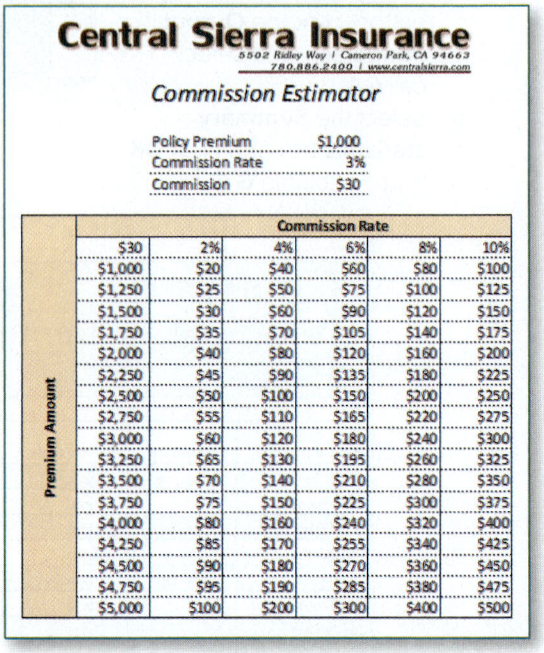

Central Sierra Insurance

5502 Ridley Way | Cameron Park, CA 94663
780.886.2400 | www.centralsierra.com

Commission Estimator

Policy Premium	$1,000
Commission Rate	3%
Commission	$30

Premium Amount / Commission Rate

$30	2%	4%	6%	8%	10%
$1,000	$20	$40	$60	$80	$100
$1,250	$25	$50	$75	$100	$125
$1,500	$30	$60	$90	$120	$150
$1,750	$35	$70	$105	$140	$175
$2,000	$40	$80	$120	$160	$200
$2,250	$45	$90	$135	$180	$225
$2,500	$50	$100	$150	$200	$250
$2,750	$55	$110	$165	$220	$275
$3,000	$60	$120	$180	$240	$300
$3,250	$65	$130	$195	$260	$325
$3,500	$70	$140	$210	$280	$350
$3,750	$75	$150	$225	$300	$375
$4,000	$80	$160	$240	$320	$400
$4,250	$85	$170	$255	$340	$425
$4,500	$90	$180	$270	$360	$450
$4,750	$95	$190	$285	$380	$475
$5,000	$100	$200	$300	$400	$500

Figure 9-82 Completed data table for commissions

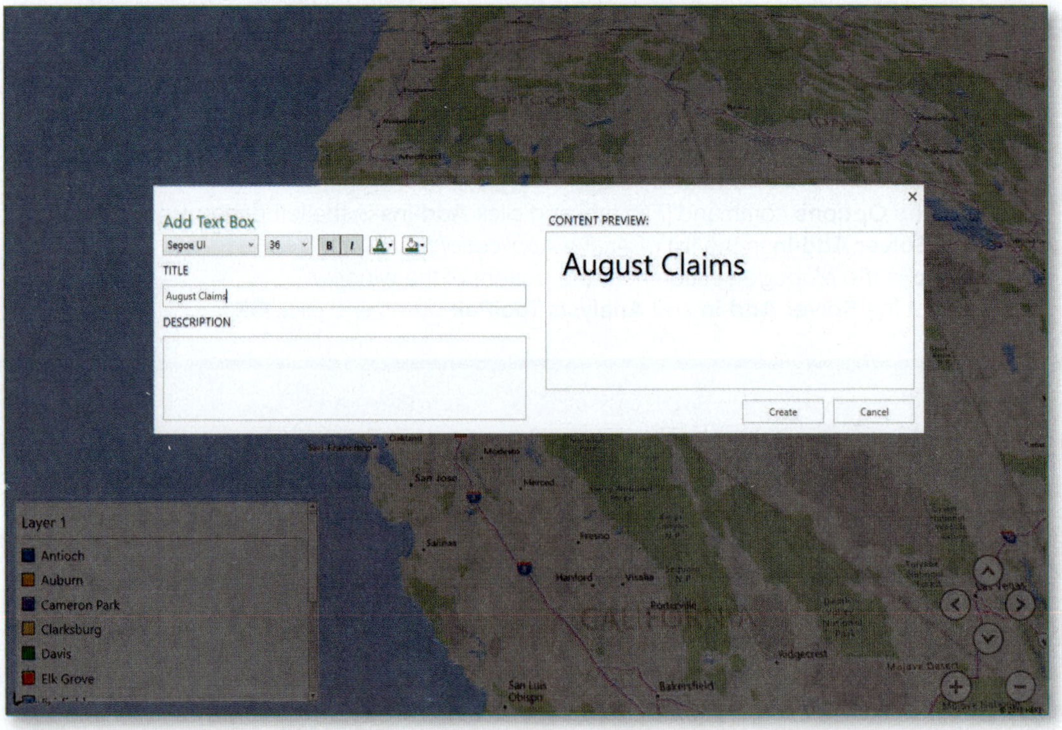

Figure 9-83 *Add Text Box* dialog box for a scene

c. Size the bounding frame to fit the text on a single line and position the text box as shown in Figure 9-84. To move a text box, point to the frame's outline and drag.

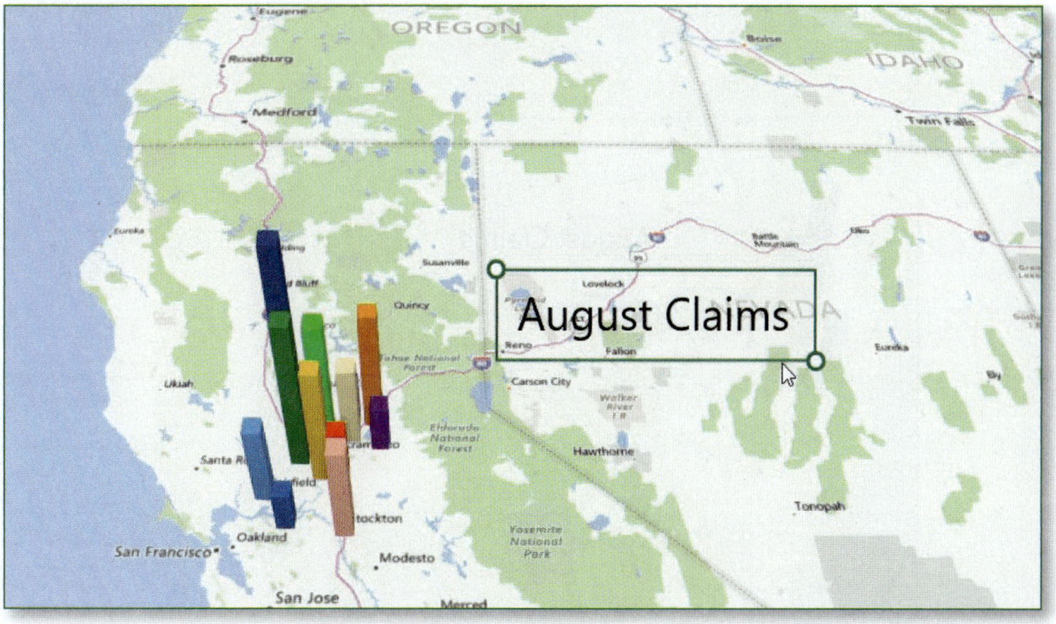

Figure 9-84 Completed text box for August scene

10. Copy the **August** scene two times so that you have three total scenes. Name the copied scenes September and October.
11. Edit the text box.
    a. Select the **September** scene in the *Tour Editor*.
    b. Point to the text box to display its two selection handles.
    c. Point near one of the selection handles, right-click, and choose **Edit**.
    d. Edit the text to display September Claims and click **OK**.
    e. Drag a selection handle to enlarge the text box as needed to display the title on a single line.
    f. Select the October scene and edit the text box to display October Claims.
12. Change shapes and layer options.
    a. Select the **September** scene and click the **Shapes** button [*Home* tab, *Layer* group].
    b. Select the round shape, the ellipse.
    c. Click the **Delete Field** button for the **Height** in the *Layer* pane to remove *August* as the field.
    d. Click **Add Field** for the *Height* box and select **September**.
    e. Select the **October** scene and change the shape to the pentagon, the five-sided figure (fourth option).
    f. Change the *Height* field to display October values.
    g. Select the **August** scene and open the *Layer Options* group in the *Layer* pane.
    h. Change the **Thickness** to **150%** (Figure 9-85).
13. Edit data in the worksheet.
    a. Click the **File** tab and select **Close** to return to the workbook.
    b. Select cell **E20** and press **Tab** to add a row to the table.
    c. Type the following data in row 21:
       Eureka California 15 20 25
    d. Click the *AutoFilter* arrow for the *City* field and sort the data in ascending order.
    e. Save the workbook.
14. Refresh data and play the tour.
    a. Click the **3D Map** button [*Insert* tab, *Tours* group] and launch the **Claims** tour.
    b. Click the **Refresh Data** button [*Home* tab, *Layer* group].
    c. Click the **Play Tour** button [*Home* tab, *Tour* group].

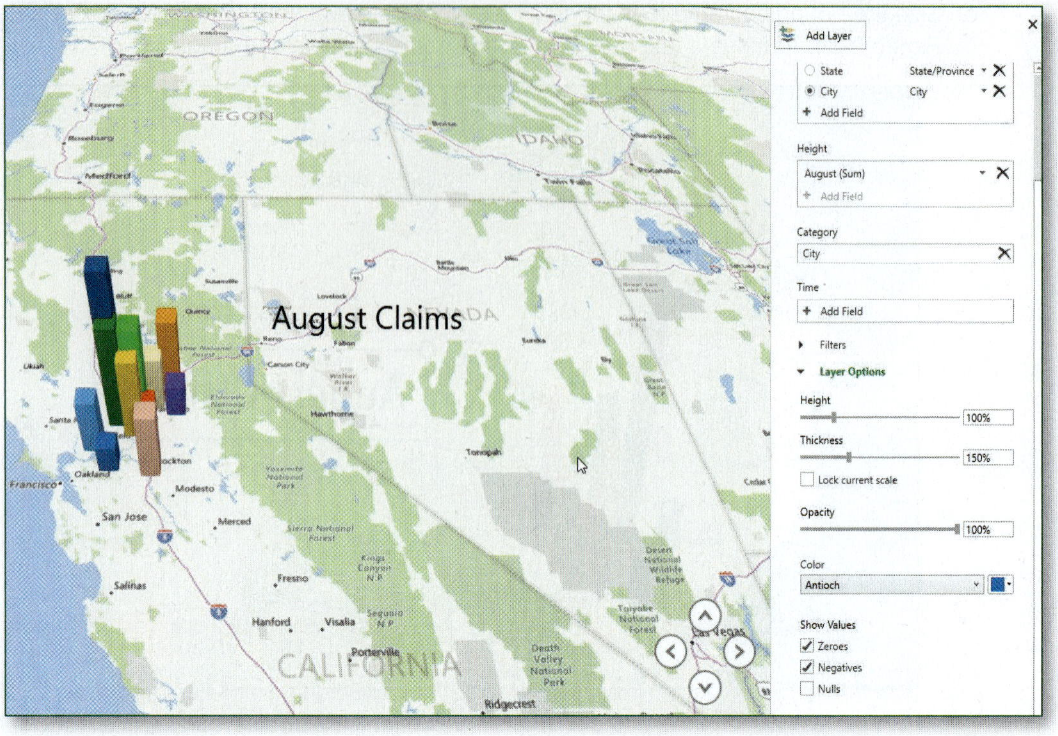

Figure 9-85 *Thickness* setting in *Layer Options*

d. Press **Esc** to return to the editing window after each scene has played.
e. Click the **File** tab and select **Close** to return to the workbook.

15. Save and close the workbook. Figure 9-86 illustrates sample maps; your scenes may vary depending on your screen size and computer settings.

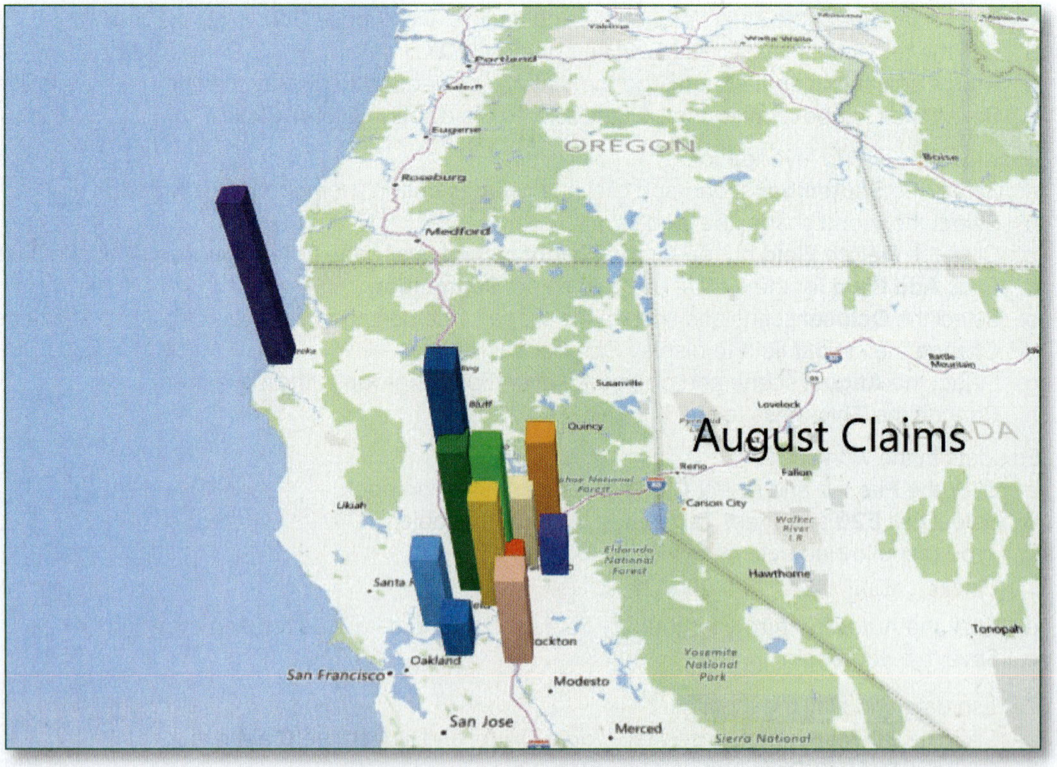

Figure 9-86 Sample *3D Map* scenes for Excel 9-4 (continued on next page)

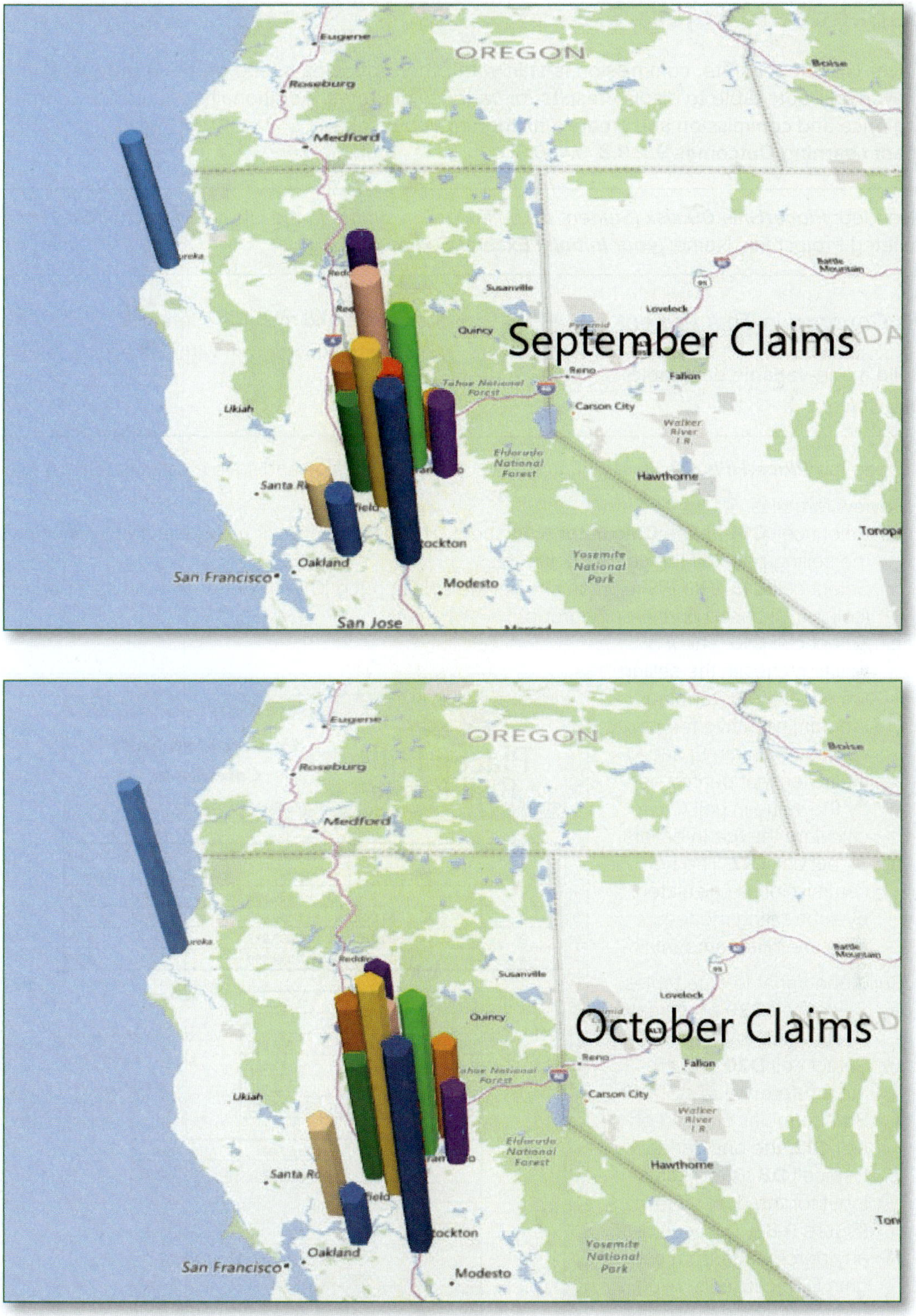

Figure 9-86 Sample *3D Map* scenes for Excel 9-4 (continued from previous page)

Independent Project 9-5

At Placer Hills Real Estate, commission is split with other agencies based on price groups. You create a one-variable data table to display results for various split rates. Additionally, you create scenarios for selling price and commission and create a histogram about sales.
[Student Learning Outcomes 9.1, 9.3, 9.4, 9.6]

File Needed: ***PlacerHills-09.xlsx*** *(Student data files are available in the* Library *of your SIMnet account.)*
Completed Project File Name: ***[your initials] Excel 9-5.xlsx***

Skills Covered in This Project

- Build a one-variable data table.
- Use *Solver*.
- Create and manage scenarios.
- Create a histogram with a chart.

1. Open the ***PlacerHills-09*** workbook from your student data files and save it as [your initials] Excel 9-5.
2. Review formulas.
   a. Select cell **C14** on the **Calculator** worksheet. The total commission is calculated by multiplying the selling price by the commission rate.
   b. Select cell **C15**. The *IFS* function checks the selling price (C12) to determine the split percentage (column D) based on the price group.
   c. Select cell **C16**. The *IFS* function checks the selling price (C12) to determine the administrative fee percentage (column E) and multiplies that percentage by the value in cell C15 to calculate the fee in dollars.
   d. Select cell **C17**. The net commission is calculated by subtracting the fees from the PHRE amount.
3. Build one-variable data tables.
   a. Select cell **C20** and create a reference to cell **C15**.
   b. Select cell **D20** and create a reference to cell **C17**. Both formulas depend on cell **C12,** the one variable.
   c. Use cell **D8** as the column input for the data table (Figure 9-87). (You can use any percentage from column D because its value is replaced by the proposed rates in column B in the data table.)
   d. Decrease the decimal two times for all values in the data table.

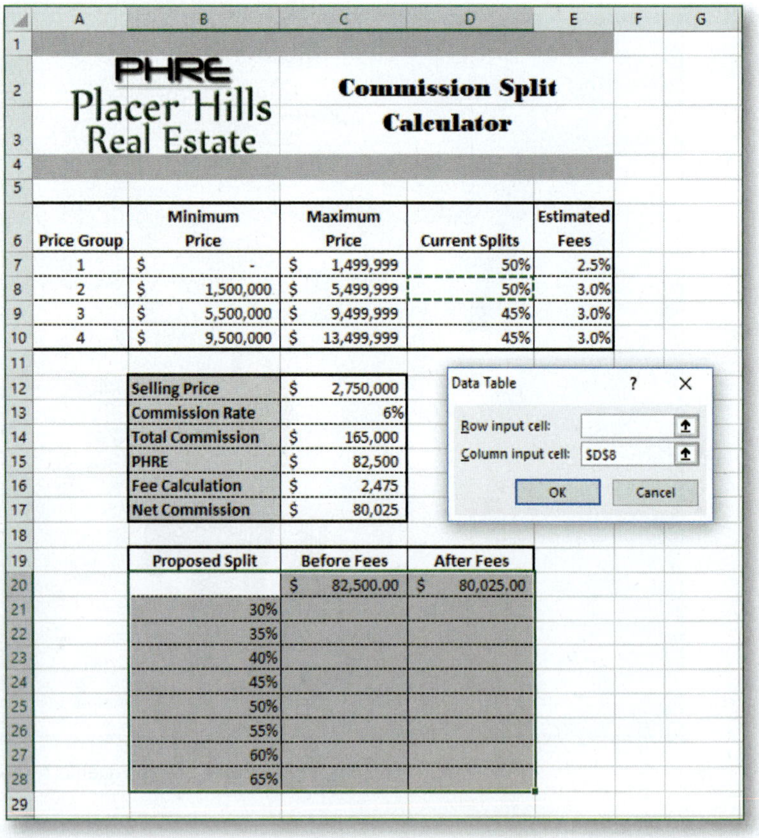

Figure 9-87 Data table setup for commission rates

4. Name cell ranges.
   a. Click the **Price Solver** worksheet tab.
   b. Click cell **C12** and name the range Selling_Price. You cannot use spaces in a range name.
   c. Name cell **C14** as Total_Commission and cell **C17** as PHRE_Commission.
5. Install the *Solver Add-in* and the *Analysis ToolPak*.
6. Use *Solver* to find target PHRE net commission amounts.
   a. Build a *Solver* problem with cell **C17** as the objective cell. For the first solution, set the objective to a value of **50000** by changing cell **C12**. Use the **GRG Nonlinear** solving method. Save the results as a scenario named $50,000.
   b. Restore the original values and run another *Solver* problem to find a selling price for a PHRE commission of 75000. Save these results as a scenario named $75,000.
   c. Restore the original values and run a third *Solver* problem to find a selling price for a net commission of $100,000. Save these results as a scenario and restore the original values.
7. Manage scenarios.
   a. Show the **$50,000** scenario in the worksheet.
   b. Create a **Scenario summary** report for cells **C12**, **C14**, and **C17**.
8. Create a histogram for recent sales.
   a. Click the **Sales Forecast** sheet tab and select cell **G13**.
   b. Create a bin range of 10 values starting at 350,000 with intervals of 50,000, ending at 800,000 in cell G22.
   c. Use the *Analysis ToolPak* to create a histogram for cells **E5:E26**. Do not check the *Labels* box and select the bin range in your worksheet.
   d. Select cell **H3** for the *Output Range* and include a chart.
   e. Position and size the chart from cell **K3** to cell **V19**.
   f. Edit the horizontal axis title to display Selling Price and edit the vertical axis title to Number of Sales.
   g. Edit the chart title to display Sales by Price Group.
   h. Select and delete the legend.
   i. Delete cells **G13:G22** (Figure 9-88).

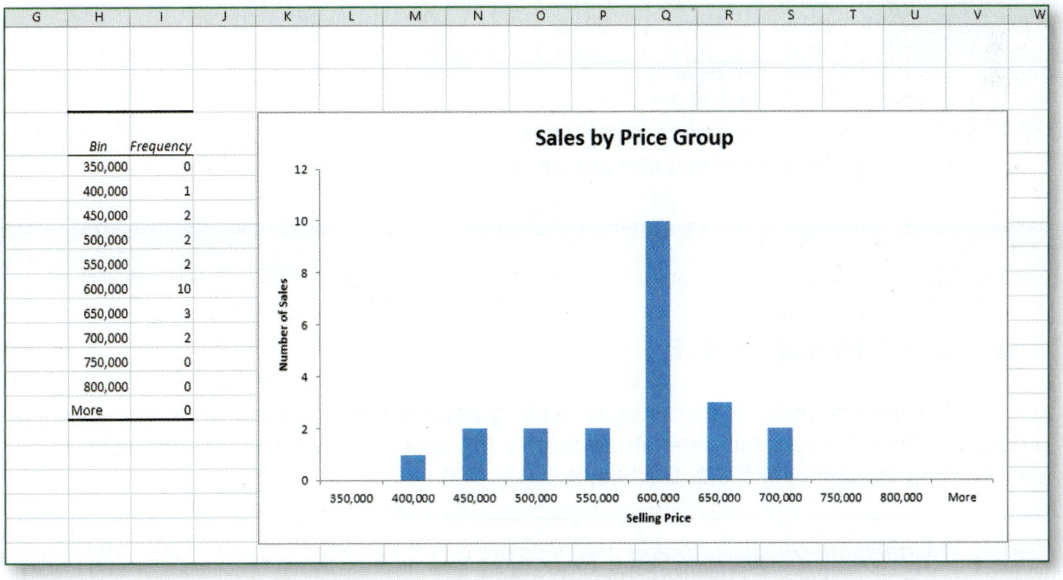

Figure 9-88 Histogram and chart for sales data

9. Save and close the workbook (Figure 9-89).

10. Uninstall the *Solver Add-in* and the *Analysis ToolPak*.

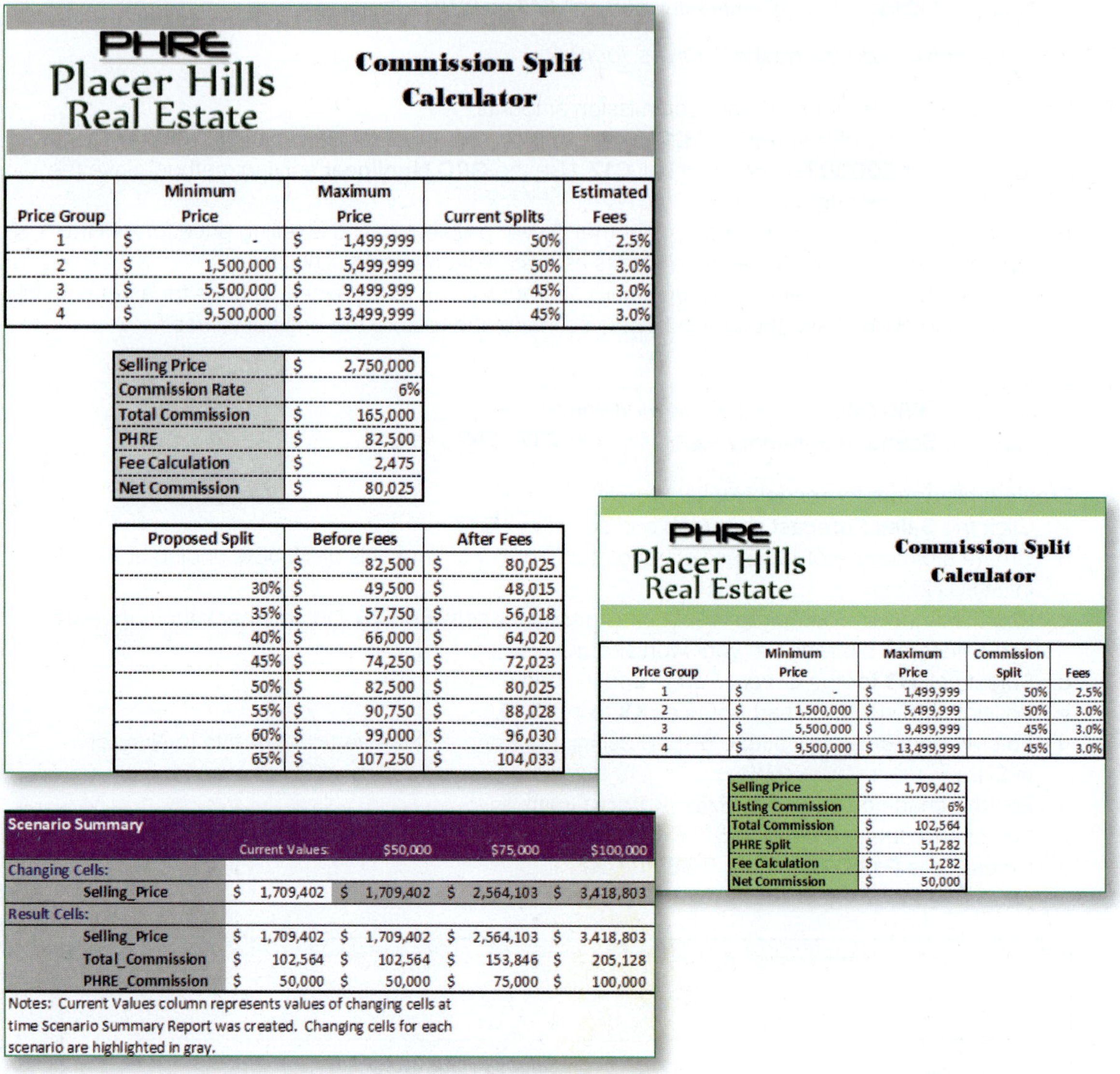

PHRE Placer Hills Real Estate — Commission Split Calculator

Price Group	Minimum Price	Maximum Price	Current Splits	Estimated Fees
1	$ -	$ 1,499,999	50%	2.5%
2	$ 1,500,000	$ 5,499,999	50%	3.0%
3	$ 5,500,000	$ 9,499,999	45%	3.0%
4	$ 9,500,000	$ 13,499,999	45%	3.0%

Selling Price	$ 2,750,000
Commission Rate	6%
Total Commission	$ 165,000
PHRE	$ 82,500
Fee Calculation	$ 2,475
Net Commission	$ 80,025

Proposed Split	Before Fees	After Fees
	$ 82,500	$ 80,025
30%	$ 49,500	$ 48,015
35%	$ 57,750	$ 56,018
40%	$ 66,000	$ 64,020
45%	$ 74,250	$ 72,023
50%	$ 82,500	$ 80,025
55%	$ 90,750	$ 88,028
60%	$ 99,000	$ 96,030
65%	$ 107,250	$ 104,033

PHRE Placer Hills Real Estate — Commission Split Calculator

Price Group	Minimum Price	Maximum Price	Commission Split	Fees
1	$ -	$ 1,499,999	50%	2.5%
2	$ 1,500,000	$ 5,499,999	50%	3.0%
3	$ 5,500,000	$ 9,499,999	45%	3.0%
4	$ 9,500,000	$ 13,499,999	45%	3.0%

Selling Price	$ 1,709,402
Listing Commission	6%
Total Commission	$ 102,564
PHRE Split	$ 51,282
Fee Calculation	$ 1,282
Net Commission	$ 50,000

Scenario Summary

	Current Values:	$50,000	$75,000	$100,000
Changing Cells:				
Selling_Price	$ 1,709,402	$ 1,709,402	$ 2,564,103	$ 3,418,803
Result Cells:				
Selling_Price	$ 1,709,402	$ 1,709,402	$ 2,564,103	$ 3,418,803
Total_Commission	$ 102,564	$ 102,564	$ 153,846	$ 205,128
PHRE_Commission	$ 50,000	$ 50,000	$ 75,000	$ 100,000

Notes: Current Values column represents values of changing cells at time Scenario Summary Report was created. Changing cells for each scenario are highlighted in gray.

Figure 9-89 Completed worksheets for Excel 9-5

Independent Project 9-6

Wilson Home Entertainment Systems calculates selling price based on cost and profit margin. You create scenarios, build a two-variable data table, create a forecast sheet, and insert a map chart.
[Student Learning Outcomes 9.1, 9.2, 9.3, 9.4, 9.5, 9.6, 9.7]

File Needed: ***WilsonHome-09.xlsx*** *(Student data files are available in the* Library *of your SIMnet account.)*
Completed Project File Name: ***[your initials] Excel 9-6.xlsx***

Skills Covered in This Project

- Create and manage scenarios.
- Create a scenario summary report.
- Build a two-variable data table.
- Create a forecast sheet.
- Use the *Analysis ToolPak* to generate a moving average.
- Use *Solver* to find a solution.
- Use *Goal Seek* to backsolve a problem.
- Insert a map chart.

1. Open the ***WilsonHome-09*** workbook from your student data files and save it as [your initials] Excel 9-6.
2. Install *Solver* and the *Analysis ToolPak*.
3. Review pricing formulas.
   a. Select cell **F5** on the **Product Pricing** worksheet. Shipping and handling charges are calculated at 10% of the manufacturer's cost.
   b. Select cell **F6**. An insurance cost is calculated at 6% of the cost.
   c. Select cell **F7**. Total investment is the sum of the cost, shipping and handling, and insurance.
   d. Select cell **F9**. The suggested selling price is the total investment multiplied by 1 plus the margin. These results are rounded to show zero (0) decimal places.

Scenario Summary					
	Current Values:	12%	13%	15%	17%
Changing Cells:					
Margin	12%	12%	13%	15%	17%
Result Cells:					
Cost	$100	$100	$100	$100	$100
Margin	12%	12%	13%	15%	17%
Selling Price	$130	$130	$131	$133	$136

Notes: Current Values column represents values of changing cells at time Scenario Summary Report was created. Changing cells for each scenario are highlighted in gray.

Figure 9-90 Scenario summary report for profit margins

4. Create and manage scenarios.
   a. Create a scenario named **12%** with cell **F8** as the changing cell but do not edit the value. This is the original data set.
   b. Add another scenario named **13**% and change the value.
   c. Add scenarios for **15%** and **17%** profit margins. Note that the original 12% scenario displays in the worksheet.
   d. Generate a scenario summary report for cells **F4**, **F8**, and **F9**.
   e. Edit the label in cells **C6** and **C9** in the *Results Cells* section of the summary report to display Margin.
   f. Edit the label in cell **C8** to display Cost and cell **C10** to display Selling Price.
   g. Right-align cells **C6** and **C8:C10** (Figure 9-90).
5. Show the **15%** scenario in the **Product Pricing** worksheet. Then select cell **B12** and create a reference to the selling price formula.
6. Build the data table and format results as **Currency** with zero (0) decimal places (Figure 9-91).

	A	B	C	D	E	F	G	H	I
2			*Pricing Calculator*						
3									
4			Manufacturer's Cost			$100			
5			Shipping and Handling			$10			
6			Insurance			$6			
7			WHES Investment			$116			
8			Preferred Margin			15%			
9			Suggested Selling Price			$133			
10									
11			Profit Margin						
12		$133	8%	10%	12%	14%	16%	18%	20%
13		$200	$251	$255	$260	$264	$269	$274	$278
14		$225	$282	$287	$292	$298	$303	$308	$313
15		$250	$313	$319	$325	$331	$336	$342	$348
16		$275	$345	$351	$357	$364	$370	$376	$383
17		$300	$376	$383	$390	$397	$404	$411	$418
18	Manufacturer's Cost	$325	$407	$415	$422	$430	$437	$445	$452
19		$350	$438	$447	$455	$463	$471	$479	$487
20		$375	$470	$479	$487	$496	$505	$513	$522
21		$400	$501	$510	$520	$529	$538	$548	$557
22		$425	$532	$542	$552	$562	$572	$582	$592
23		$450	$564	$574	$585	$595	$606	$616	$626
24		$475	$595	$606	$617	$628	$639	$650	$661
25		$500	$626	$638	$650	$661	$673	$684	$696
26		$525	$658	$670	$682	$694	$706	$719	$731
27		$550	$689	$702	$715	$727	$740	$753	$766
28		$575	$720	$734	$747	$760	$774	$787	$800
29		$600	$752	$766	$780	$793	$807	$821	$835
30		$625	$783	$798	$812	$827	$841	$856	$870
31		$650	$814	$829	$844	$860	$875	$890	$905
32		$675	$846	$861	$877	$893	$908	$924	$940
33		$700	$877	$893	$909	$926	$942	$958	$974
34		$725	$908	$925	$942	$959	$976	$992	$1,009
35		$750	$940	$957	$974	$992	$1,009	$1,027	$1,044
36									

Figure 9-91 Completed data table for *Product Pricing* sheet

7. Select the **Soundbar Sales** sheet and click cell **A16**. Note the date in the formula bar.
8. Create a forecast sheet for the data with a line chart, ending the forecast four months from the date in cell **A16**.
9. Format the chart object.
   a. Position the chart object with its top-left corner in cell **A20**.
   b. Change the outline color for the **Values** series in the chart to **Blue-Gray, Text 2** (fourth column).
   c. Change the outline color for the **Forecast** series to **Orange, Accent 4** (eighth column).
   d. Select the chart area and format the outline color as **Black, Text 1** (second column).
10. Rename the sheet tab as Forecast Sheet and select cell **A1** (Figure 9-92).

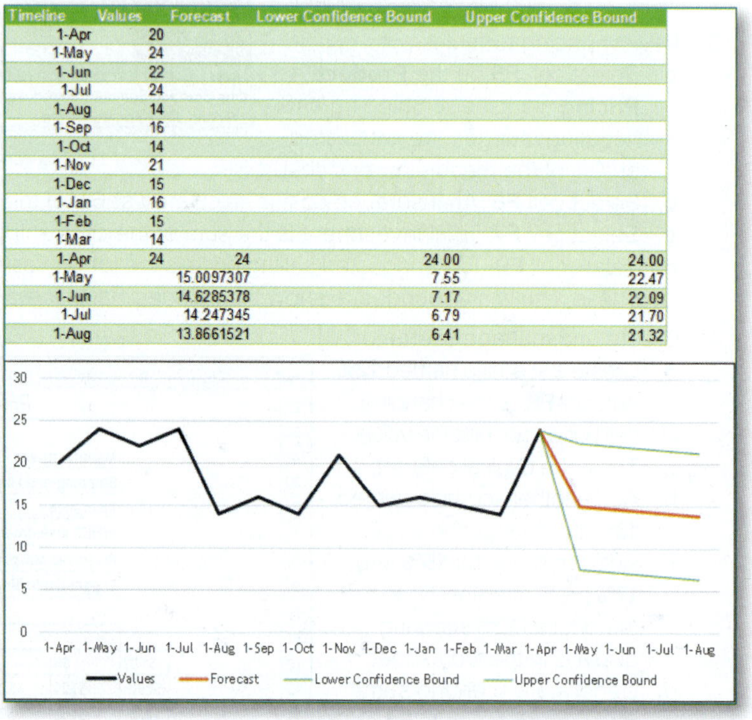

Figure 9-92 Completed forecast sheet and chart

11. Select the **Soundbar Sales** sheet. Create a moving average list and chart for cells **B4:B16** with an interval of **2** and output the results to cell **D4**.
12. Format the chart output object.
   a. Position the chart object to start at cell **E4** and size it to reach cell **M18**.
   b. Select the **Forecast** series in the chart.
   c. Change both the outline color and the shape fill color for the **Forecast** series to **Blue-Gray, Text 2** (fourth column).
   d. Select cell **A3** (Figure 9-93).

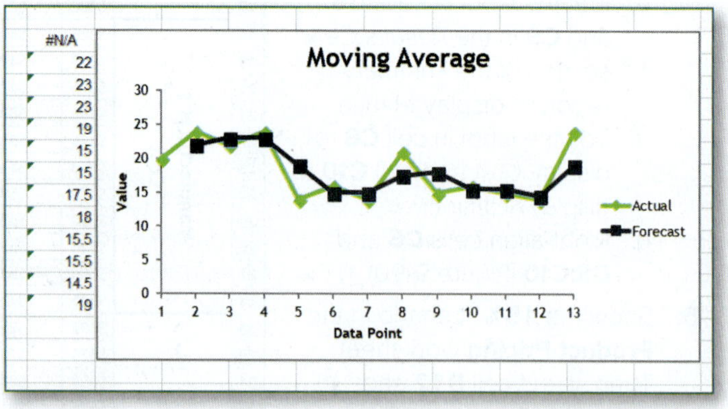

Figure 9-93 Completed moving average and related chart

13. Use *Solver* to find total wages for one day.
   a. Click the **Staffing** sheet tab.
   b. Select cells **C5:C8** and save the values as a scenario named Current.
   c. Build a *Solver* problem to find the minimum result for cell **E9** by changing cells **C5:C8**.
   d. Add the first constraint for cell **C5** as shown here which requires the value to be between 16 and 18:

      C5 >=16
      C5 <=18

   e. Add the following constraints:

      C6 Between 6 and 10
      C7 Between 12 and 15
      C8 Between 4 and 12

   f. Use the **Simplex LP** solving method and save the results ($1,841) as a scenario named Minimum.
   g. Keep the solution.

14. Use *Goal Seek* to set cell **E9** to a value of **1600** by changing cell **C5**. Accept the solution.
15. Save cells **C5:C8** as a scenario named >$1600.
16. Create a scenario summary report for cells **C5:C8** and cell **E9** (Figure 9-94).
17. Insert a map chart for Soundstand sales data.
    a. Click the **Soundstand Promotion** sheet tab.
    b. Select cells **B4:C12** and create a filled map chart.
    c. Move the chart to its own sheet named Map Chart.
    d. Format the data series to display only the regions with data [*Map area*] and show all map labels [*Format Data Series* pane, *Series Options*].
    e. Select **Diverging (3-color)** for the data series.
    f. Select **Red, Accent 5, Lighter 60%** (ninth column) for the **Minimum** (lowest) value.
    g. Select **Gold, Accent 3, Lighter 60%** (seventh column) for the **Midpoint** (middle) value.
    h. Do not change the maximum value color.
    i. Add data labels to the chart and do not display the legend.
    j. Edit the chart title to Soundstand East Coast Promotion.
18. Save and close the workbook (Figure 9-95).
19. Uninstall *Solver* and the *Analysis ToolPak*.

Scenario Summary	Current Values:	Current	Minimum	$1,600
Changing Cells:				
$C$5	9	15	16	9
$C$6	6	12	6	6
$C$7	12	16	12	12
$C$8	4	20	4	4
Result Cells:				
$C$5	9	15	16	9
$C$6	6	12	6	6
$C$7	12	16	12	12
$C$8	4	20	4	4
$E$9	$1,600.00	$3,315.00	$1,841.00	$1,600.00

Notes: Current Values column represents values of changing cells at time Scenario Summary Report was created. Changing cells for each scenario are highlighted in gray.

Figure 9-94 Scenario summary report for *Staffing* sheet

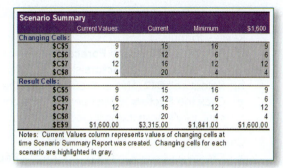

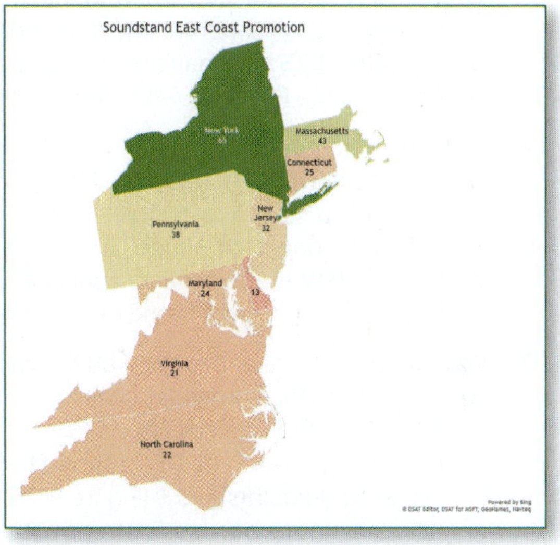

Figure 9-95 Completed map chart for Excel 9-6

Improve It Project 9-7

Pool and Spa Oasis forecasts sales for three categories of business. You create scenarios with different growth rates, build a one-variable data table, and use *Solver* to find minimum total wages for a work crew.

[Student Learning Outcomes 9.1, 9.3, 9.4]

File Needed: ***Pools&Spa09.xlsx*** *(Student data files are available in the* Library *of your SIMnet account.)*
Completed Project File Name: ***[your initials] Excel 9-7.xlsx***

Skills Covered in This Project

- Create and manage scenarios.
- Build a one-variable data table.
- Use *Solver* with constraints.

1. Open the ***Pools&Spa-09*** workbook from your student data files and save it as [your initials] Excel 9-7.
2. Review formulas.
   a. Select cell **D5** on the **Forecast** worksheet. The text box explains the formula which uses 3D references to the **Factors** sheet.
   b. Select cell **B12**. This is a reference to the growth factor in cell **F3** on the **Factors** sheet.
   c. Click the **Factors** worksheet tab. The company predicts a general growth rate, but each category's potential is increased or reduced by an adjustment factor.
3. Create scenarios for the growth rate.
   a. Create a scenario named .15% on the **Factors** sheet for the existing data with cell **F3** as the changing cell.
   b. Add another scenario named .5% and change the value to **.005**.
   c. Add scenarios for **1.25%** and **1.75%** growth rates. In the *Scenarios Values* dialog box, you must enter the decimal equivalent of the percentage (.0125 and .0175).
   d. Show the **1.25%** scenario in the worksheet.
   e. Return to the **Forecast** worksheet.
4. Build the data table.
   a. Select cell **E17**. It refers to cell **H5**. Cells F17 and G17 refer to cells H6 and H7, respectively.
   b. Use the *Fill* handle to complete the growth rate percentages in cells **D20:D27**.
   c. Select the data table range.
   d. Use cell **B12** as the column input cell. The results are incorrect because data table formulas must use data on the same worksheet as the data table.
5. Edit formulas to use a reference on the same sheet as the data table.
   a. Select cell **D5,** a precedent cell for cell **H5**. Cells E17:G17 in the data table indirectly refer to *(1+Factors!$F$3)* in cell D5.
   b. Edit the formula in cell **D5** to show **(1+$B$12)** in place *(1+Factors!$F$3)* (Figure 9-96). The data table does not use *Factors!$F$6* in its calculations, so it need not be changed.
   c. Copy the formula in cell **D5** to the cells **E5:G5** and then to cells **D6:G7**. The data table updates.
   d. Redefine the bottom borders of cells as needed.
   e. Format data table results as **Currency** with no decimal places.

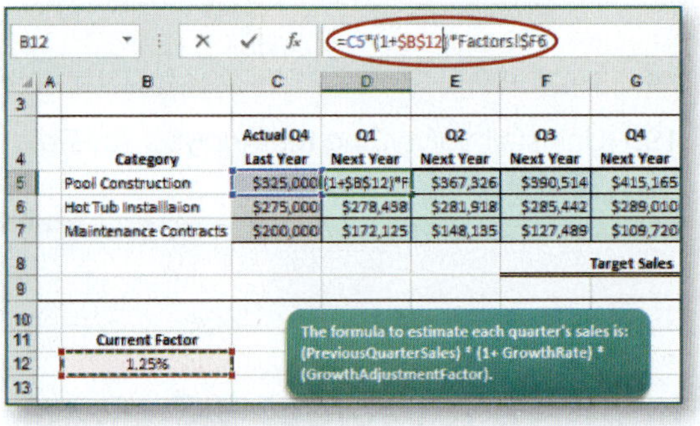

Figure 9-96 Edited formula to refer to cell on the same sheet as the data table

6. Edit a *Solver* problem to find minimum wages.
   a. Click the **Crew1** worksheet tab.
   b. Start a *Solver* problem to find the minimum value for cell **E9** by changing cells D5:D8. Constraints for cell **D8** are already entered.
   c. Add constraints for each of cells **D5:D7** that reflect the information in column C in the worksheet.
   d. Add a constraint that cell **D9** be less than or equal to 150.
   e. Use the **GRG Nonlinear** solving method (Figure 9-97).
   f. Keep the *Solver* solution.
7. Save and close the workbook (Figure 9-98).
8. Uninstall the *Solver Add-in*.

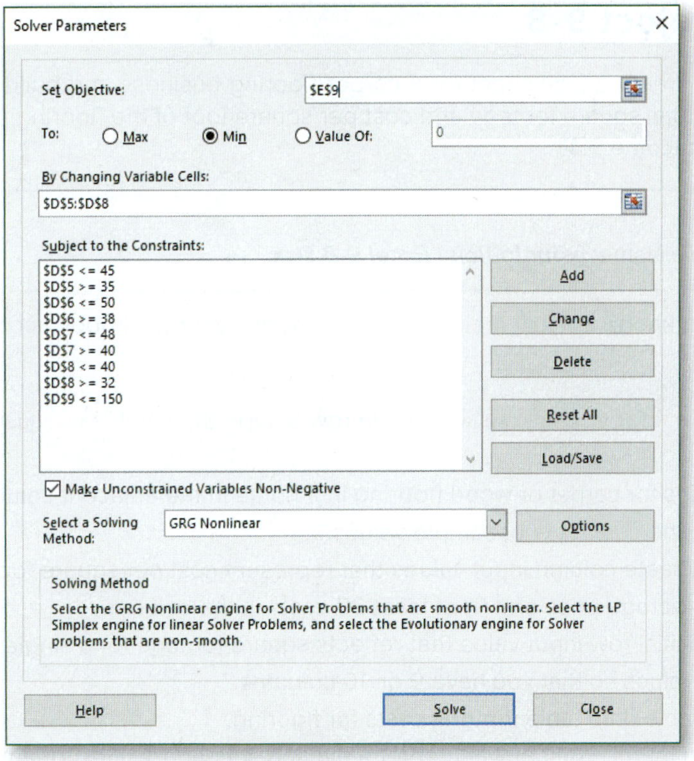

Figure 9-97 ***Solver*** **constraints for work crew problem**

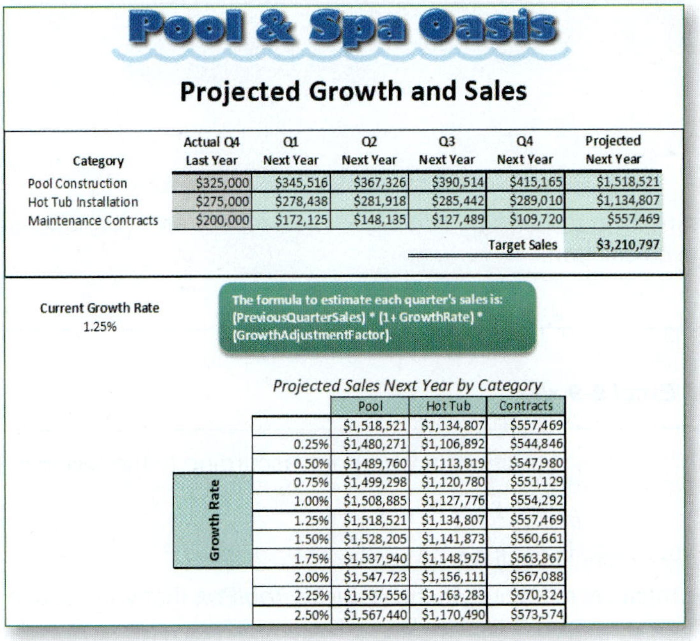

Category	Actual Q4 Last Year	Q1 Next Year	Q2 Next Year	Q3 Next Year	Q4 Next Year	Projected Next Year
Pool Construction	$325,000	$345,516	$367,326	$390,514	$415,165	$1,518,521
Hot Tub Installation	$275,000	$278,438	$281,918	$285,442	$289,010	$1,134,807
Maintenance Contracts	$200,000	$172,125	$148,135	$127,489	$109,720	$557,469
					Target Sales	$3,210,797

	Pool	Hot Tub	Contracts
	$1,518,521	$1,134,807	$557,469
0.25%	$1,480,271	$1,106,892	$544,846
0.50%	$1,489,760	$1,113,819	$547,980
0.75%	$1,499,298	$1,120,780	$551,129
1.00%	$1,508,885	$1,127,776	$554,292
1.25%	$1,518,521	$1,134,807	$557,469
1.50%	$1,528,205	$1,141,873	$560,661
1.75%	$1,537,940	$1,148,975	$563,867
2.00%	$1,547,723	$1,156,111	$567,088
2.25%	$1,557,556	$1,163,283	$570,324
2.50%	$1,567,440	$1,170,490	$573,574

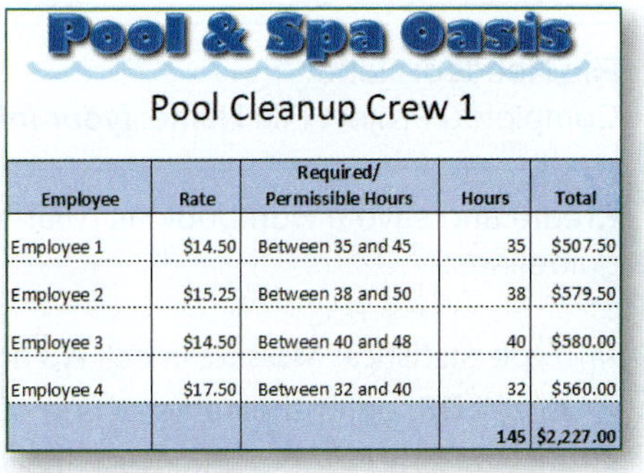

Employee	Rate	Required/ Permissible Hours	Hours	Total
Employee 1	$14.50	Between 35 and 45	35	$507.50
Employee 2	$15.25	Between 38 and 50	38	$579.50
Employee 3	$14.50	Between 40 and 48	40	$580.00
Employee 4	$17.50	Between 32 and 40	32	$560.00
			145	$2,227.00

Figure 9-98 Completed worksheets for Excel 9-7

Challenge Project 9-8

For this project, you create a worksheet for a carpet/flooring business and build a data table that displays cost based on total square footage and cost per square foot of the flooring product.
[Student Learning Outcome 9.4]

File Needed: None
Completed Project File Name: ***[your initials] Excel 9-8.xlsx***

Create and save a workbook as [your initials] Excel 9-8. Modify your workbook according to the following guidelines:

- Enter a label in row 4 for Costs per square foot. In row 5, type the label Total square footage. In row 6, type Total cost.
- Enter sample values for carpet or wood flooring in a home in the adjacent column. Build a formula in row 6 to calculate the cost for your sample values.
- Starting in row 9, create column input values that represent cost per square foot. Use an increment of $2. Start at an average price and fill at least 20 costs in the column.
- In row 8, type an initial row input value that reflects square footage for a single room. Use an increment of 5 and fill values so that you have 9 or 10 columns.
- Build the two-variable data table for total costs for flooring.
- Determine a name for the company and enter main and secondary titles for your worksheet. Add borders, shading, or other format attributes to enhance the interpretation of the worksheet.

Challenge Project 9-9

For this project, you use a statistical measure from the *Analysis ToolPak* and prepare an informational worksheet to describe and demonstrate the calculation.
[Student Learning Outcome 9.6]

File Needed: None
Completed Project File Name: ***[your initials] Excel 9-9.xlsx***

Create and save a workbook as [your initials] Excel 9-9. Modify your workbook according to the following guidelines:

- Type Statistical Measure in cell **A3** and type Purpose in cell **A4**.
- In cell **B3,** enter the name of one of the statistical measures in the *Analysis ToolPak* that you used in this chapter. Type a brief description of its use and purpose in cell **B4**.
- Starting in row 6, develop worksheet data that will illustrate the measure you have chosen, using work, school, or personal data. Include labels and values that clearly illustrate the goal of using your statistical measure.
- Calculate the measure.
- Format the sheet and related results in a professional manner.

Challenge Project 9-10

For this project, you create a 3D map for a worksheet about green roof and solar panel installations in two states or provinces.
[Student Learning Outcome 9.7]

File Needed: None
Completed Project File Name: ***[your initials] Excel 9-10.xlsx***

Create and save a workbook as [your initials] Excel 9-10. Modify your workbook according to the following guidelines:

- Enter labels in cells **A2:D2** for State/Province, City, Roofs, and Panels.
- In cell **A3,** type the two-letter abbreviation for the name of your state/province and copy it down to cell **A12**. In cell **A13,** type the two-letter abbreviation for a neighboring state/province and copy it down to cell **A22**.
- Type the names of ten cities or towns in your state/province, starting in cell **B3**. Choose locations throughout the state/province so that you can easily see the locations in your 3D map.
- Type the names of ten cities or towns in the neighboring state/province, starting in cell **B13**. Choose locations throughout the state/province.
- Fill in random values in columns C and D for the number of residential installations for each city.
- Format the data as an Excel table and sort by state/province and then by city name.
- Build a 3D map with a clustered column visualization. The *Location* and the *Category* is *City* and use *Roofs* as the *Height* in the first scene.
- If the map displays an outlier city, it is because *3D Maps* needs additional data to locate the city; substitute another city and refresh the data.
- Name the tour and the first scene and arrange the map to illustrate the data well.
- Add a scene to show the panel installations. Then add scenes with filters to show each state or province individually.
- Explore and create a video for your tour to share with your instructor or a classmate.

CHAPTER 10

Exploring Business Intelligence

CHAPTER OVERVIEW

Data analysis is essential to business, education, research, government, and personal use. Business intelligence (BI) is a suite of tools, applications, and processes for analyzing data. Business intelligence in Excel enables you to accomplish tasks that previously required the help of professional data analysts. In this chapter, you are introduced to business intelligence tools in Excel including queries and the data model.

STUDENT LEARNING OUTCOMES (SLOs)

After completing this chapter, students will be able to:

SLO 10.1 Create an Excel query (p. E10-619).

SLO 10.2 Edit a query in *Power Query* (p. E10-621).

SLO 10.3 Use external data sources (p. E10-623).

SLO 10.4 Merge and append queries (p. E10-630).

SLO 10.5 Manipulate data in a query (p. E10-633).

SLO 10.6 Work with the Excel data model (p. E10-643)

SLO 10.7 Review *PivotTable* tools (p. E10-645).

SLO 10.8 Explore *Power Pivot* (p. E10-652).

CASE STUDY

In the Pause & Practice projects in this chapter, you create and edit queries for Paradise Lakes Resort, get data from external sources, explore data models, and work with PivotTables.

Pause & Practice 10-1: Create and edit a query for Excel data.

Pause & Practice 10-2: Merge queries and manipulate data.

Pause & Practice 10-3: Use the data model to build a *PivotTable*.

EXCEL

SLO 10.1

Creating an Excel Query

A ***query*** is a combination of instructions, filters, and formats that establishes a connection to and displays data. An Excel query can get data from a workbook, a text file, a corporate database, online public data, or cloud services. Data for use in a query is always in list-type format or a table.

Get Data from a Workbook

A query can get data from one Excel workbook and display that data in another workbook for an easy way to learn about the power and capabilities of queries. Queries are saved with the workbook and can be refreshed as needed.

Create an Excel query in the *Power Query Editor*, a separate application window. The *Power Query Editor* launches when you choose a command from the *Get & Transform* group on the *Data* tab.

> **MORE INFO**
>
> Getting data is often referred to as importing data.

HOW TO: Get Workbook Data for a Query

1. Open a new workbook or the workbook that will display the data and position the pointer where the imported data should start.
2. Click the **Get Data** button [*Data* tab, *Get & Transform Data* group] and choose **From File**.
3. Choose **From Workbook**.
   - The *Import Data* dialog box opens.
4. Navigate to the folder with the workbook file.
5. Select the file name and click **Import**.
   - The *Navigator* window displays the names of tables and worksheets in the workbook.
6. Select the name of the table or worksheet.
   - The *Navigator* previews the data (Figure 10-1).
7. Launch *Power Query*.
   - Click **Transform Data** or click **Edit**. The button name depends on your Excel version.
   - The *Power Query Editor* window displays the data (Figure 10-2).
   - Load the data and bypass the *Query Editor* by clicking the **Load** button in the *Navigator* window.

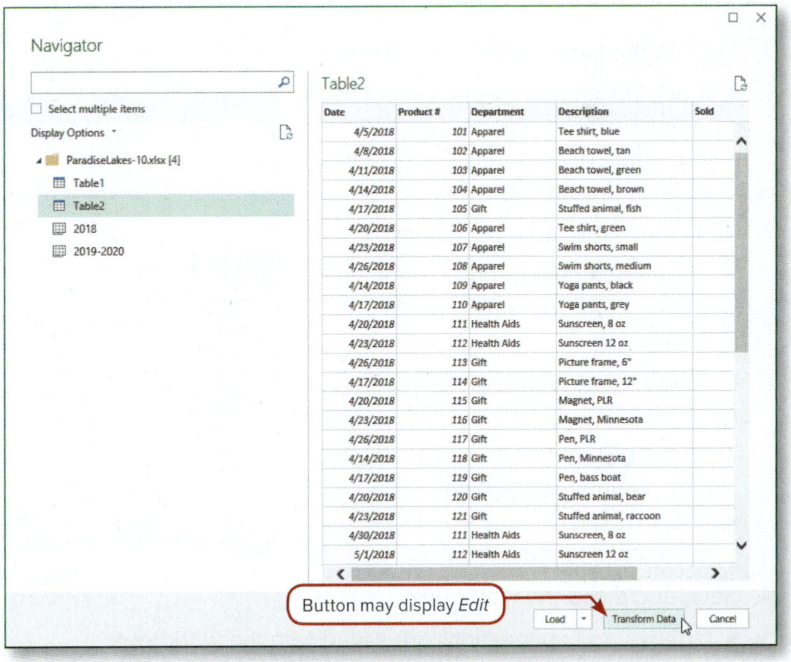

Figure 10-1 ***Navigator*** **window with data preview**

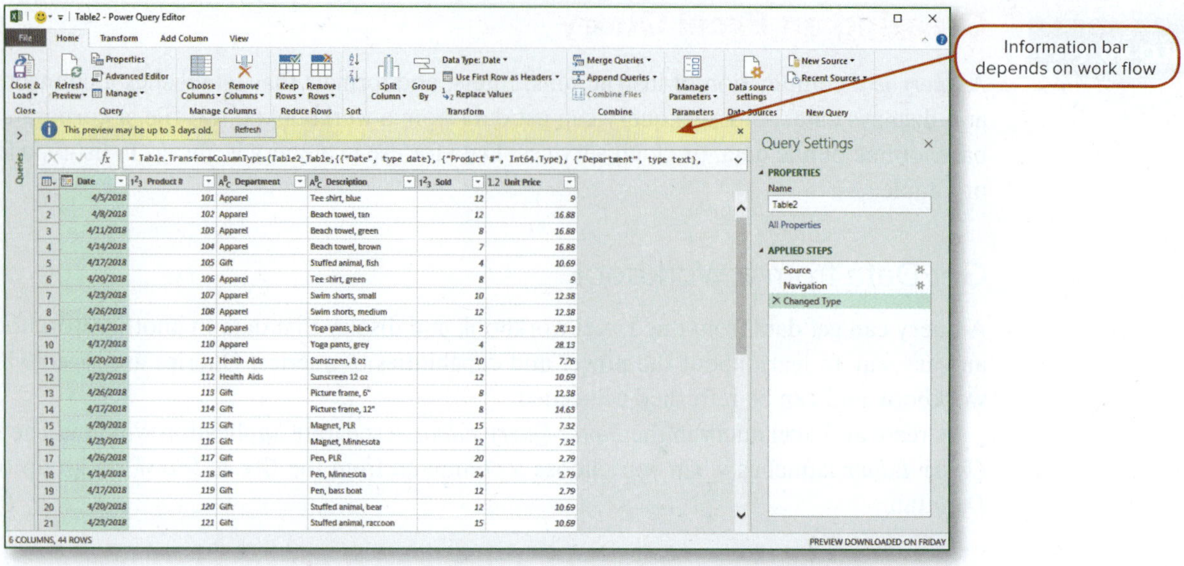

Figure 10-2 *Power Query Editor* window

8. Click **Refresh** in the *Information* bar if it displays.

Load Data from Power Query

The *Power Query Editor* connects to and displays data from the original source. You cannot edit data in the *Editor*. Make edits to the data after you load it to the workbook.

HOW TO: Load Data from Power Query to Excel

1. Click the **Close & Load** button [*Home* tab, *Close* group] in the *Power Query Editor* window.
   - The data displays in an Excel table, and the *Power Query Editor* window closes.
   - The default destination is cell A1 of the active sheet.
   - The *Queries & Connections* pane and the *Table Tools Design* and *Query Tools* command tabs display.
2. Point to the name of the query in the *Queries & Connections* pane.
   - A pop-up window displays information about the query (Figure 10-3).
   - The name of the query is the same as its data source.
3. Edit data in the table as needed.
   - If you reload the query, current source data overwrites worksheet data.
4. Delete the query to remove the data connection.
   - Select **Delete** in the pop-up window and confirm the deletion.
   - Keep the query to maintain a connection to the original source data.
5. Save and close the workbook.
   - Queries and connections are saved with the workbook.

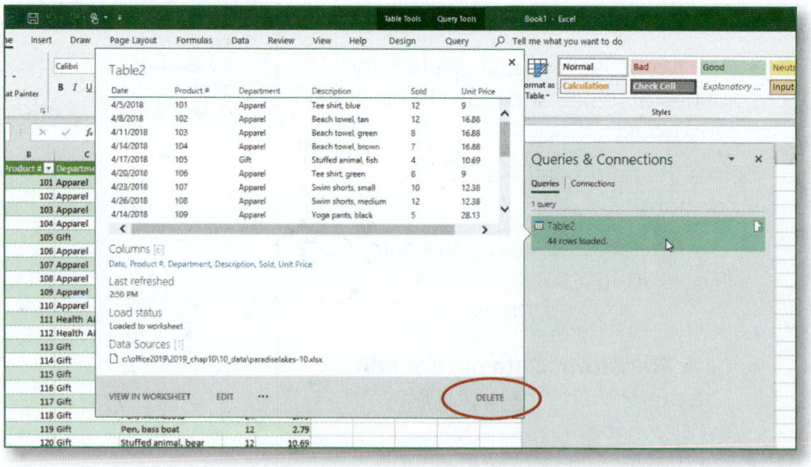

Figure 10-3 *Query & Connections* pane and pop-up information

SLO 10.2

Editing a Query

Power Query is an application that enables you to combine, filter, sort, and refine data. It is a data analysis tool that transforms, "cleans," and shapes data so that it is ready for use in Excel.

> **MORE INFO**
>
> *Power Query* is part of Microsoft's *Power BI* platform for desktop or the cloud.

The Power Query Editor

The ***Power Query Editor*** is a window that floats on top of the worksheet. It has its own *Ribbon* with command tabs and buttons, a display window, a *Navigator* pane, and the *Query Settings* pane. The *Power Query Editor* resembles Excel but is not Excel.

▸HOW TO: Navigate in the Power Query Editor

1. Select a cell in the imported data in a workbook.
2. Click the **Data** tab and click the **Queries & Connections** button [*Queries & Connections* group].
   - The *Query & Connections* pane displays.
   - The *Queries & Connections* button toggles the display of the pane.
3. Point to the query name in the *Queries & Connections* pane and click **Edit** in the pop-up window.
   - The data displays in rows and columns in the *Power Query Editor*.
4. Click the **View** tab.
5. Verify or select the **Query Settings** button [*View* tab, *Layout* group].
   - The *Query Settings* pane displays at the right of the window.
   - *Applied Steps* list each task completed in the query.
   - Expand the list as needed.
6. Select the **Formula Bar** box [*View* tab, *Layout* group] (Figure 10-4).
   - The *Formula bar* displays above the data.
   - *Power Query* formulas use M language and are different from Excel formulas.
7. Click the **Properties** button [*Home* tab, *Query* group].
   - The *Query Properties* dialog box opens.
8. Click the **Name** box and type a name for the query.
   - The default name is the same as the source data.
9. Click the **Description** box, type an explanation of the query purpose and results, and click **OK**.
10. Click the **Expand the Navigator Pane** arrow to the left of the window (Figure 10-5).
    - Use the *Navigator* pane to display another query associated with the workbook.

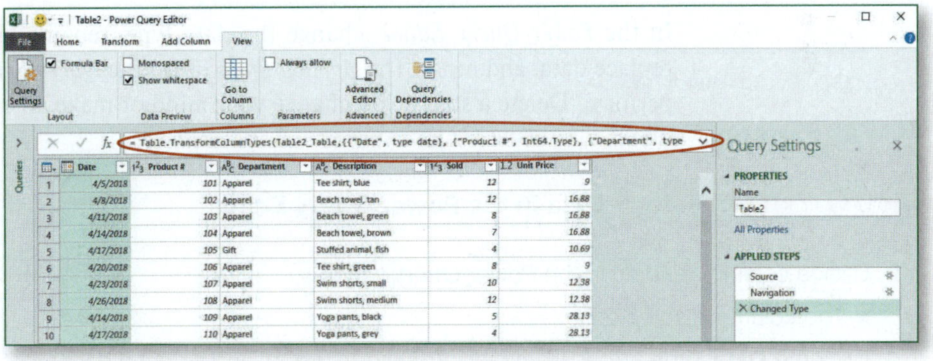

Figure 10-4 ***Power Query*** **formulas are different from Excel formulas**

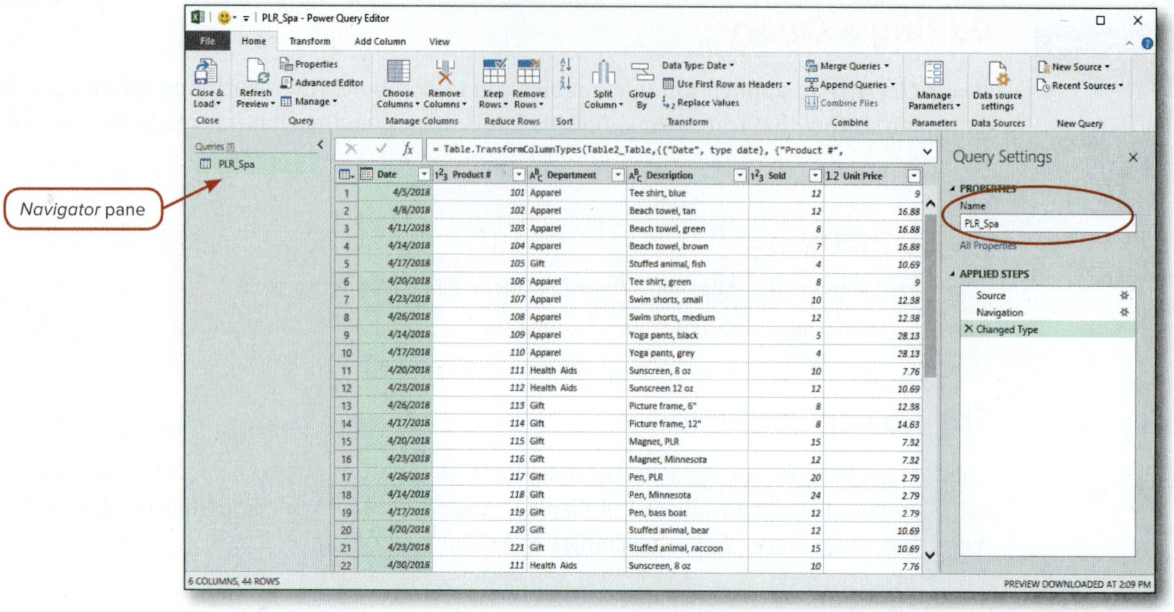

Figure 10-5 *Power Query* window and *Navigator* pane

11. Click the **Minimize the Navigator Pane** arrow.
12. Click the **File** tab and choose **Close & Load**.
    - The worksheet data is formatted as a table.
13. Close the *Queries & Connections* pane and click a blank worksheet cell.
    - The *Table Tools Design* and *Query Tools* command tabs no longer display.
14. Click a data cell within the table.
    - The *Table Tools Design* and *Query Tools* command tabs display.
    - Display or hide the *Queries & Connections* pane from the *Data* tab [*Queries & Connections* group].

Transform Data in Power Query

In the *Power Query Editor*, change the data type, rename headings, delete or split columns, replace data, and more. The *Applied Steps* list in the *Query Settings* pane displays each task you perform. Delete a step if you change your mind or make an error.

HOW TO: Transform Data in the Power Query Editor

1. Click a column heading in the *Power Query* window.
    - The column is selected.
2. Click the **Data Type** arrow [*Home* tab, *Transform* group] and select a data type.
    - *Power Query* assigns a likely data type when data is imported.
3. Click a column heading and click the **Remove Columns** button [*Home* tab, *Manage Columns* group].
    - Press **Shift** or **Ctrl** to select multiple columns.
    - Click the **Remove Columns** arrow and select **Remove Other Columns** to remove all but the selected column(s).
4. Select a column and click the **Split Column** button [*Home* tab, *Transform* group].
    - Choose **By Delimiter** or **By Number of Characters** (Figure 10-6).
    - The *By Delimiter* or the *By Number of Characters* dialog box displays.

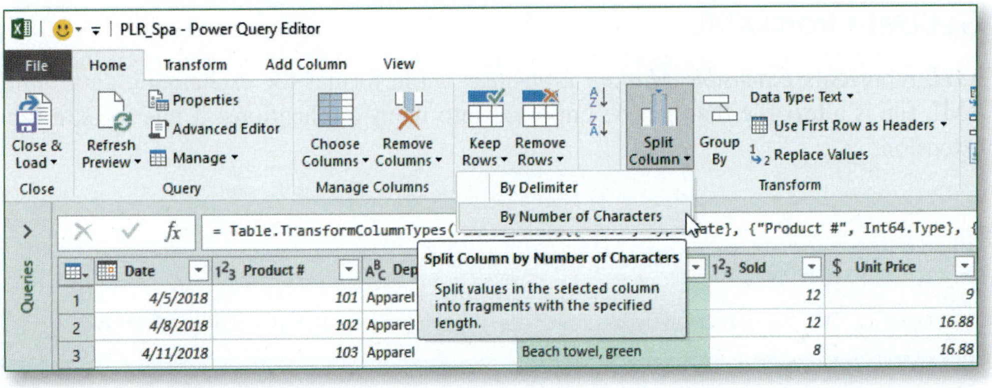

Figure 10-6 Split a column into two columns

- Select the delimiter or type the number of characters.
- Define split choices and click **OK**.
- A new column displays to the right of the column that was split.

5. Select a column and click the **Replace Values** button [*Home* tab, *Transform* group].
   - The *Replace Values* dialog box opens.
   - Replace text strings or numbers as needed and click **OK**.
6. Click a column *AutoFilter* arrow and choose a sort order.
7. Click a step name in the *Applied Steps* list in the *Query Settings* pane to display results at that point in the query.
8. Point to the **X** to the left of a step name to display a red X (Figure 10-7).
9. Click the red X to delete a step.
   - A message box reminds you that deleting a step may affect subsequent steps (Figure 10-8).

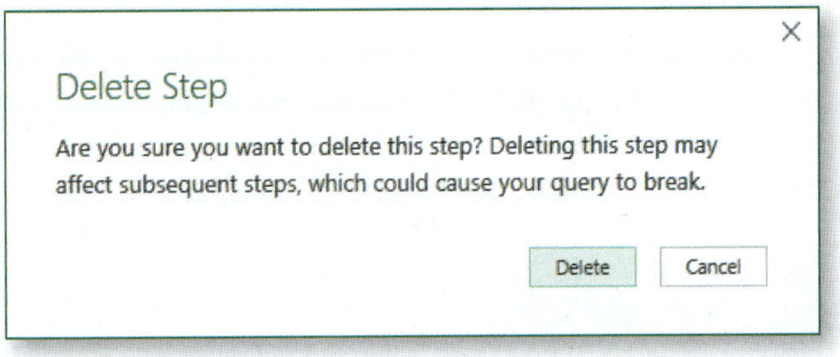

Delete Step
Are you sure you want to delete this step? Deleting this step may affect subsequent steps, which could cause your query to break.
Delete
Cancel

Figure 10-8 A broken query may not give the expected results

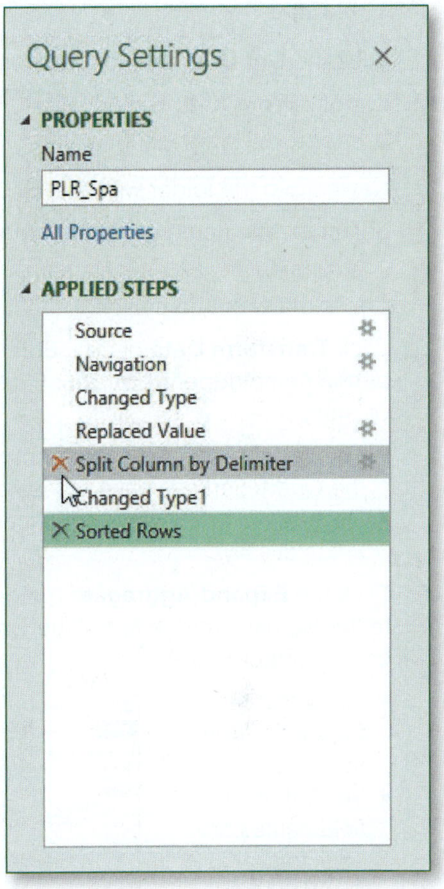

Figure 10-7 Query steps are in chronological order

10. Click the **Close & Load** button [*Home* tab, *Close* group].
    - The transformed data displays in the worksheet.

SLO 10.3

Using External Data Sources

You can use data from sources such as corporate and government databases, cloud services, data feeds, and social media sites. External data sources typically provide more than you need, not quite what you need, or a part of what you need. *Power Query* launches when you get data from external sources so that you can "clean" the data before loading it into your workbook.

Get Data from XML

XML represents *Extensible Markup Language*, a file format for exchanging data online. An XML file is a text file that can be imported into many applications; it has an .xml file name extension.

> **ANOTHER WAY**
>
> Open an XML file in Excel to bypass *Power Query*. Then save the data as a regular workbook.

▸ HOW TO: Get an XML File for a Query

1. Click the **Get Data** button [*Data* tab, *Get & Transform Data* group] and choose **From File**.
2. Choose **From XML**.
   - The *Import Data* dialog box opens.
3. Navigate to the folder with the XML file.
4. Select the file name and click **Import**.
   - A window displays the file name and a single row of information.
5. Click **Transform Data** or click **Edit**. (The button name depends on your Excel version).
   - The *Query Editor* window opens with the *Query Settings* pane at the right.
   - Data from an XML file is not expanded automatically.
6. Click the **Expand/Aggregate** button next to the file name at the top of the first column (Figure 10-9).
   - Verify that the **Expand** button is selected.
   - Verify that all field names are selected.
   - Deselect field names for data that should not be displayed.
7. Click **OK**.
   - Each data field displays.
   - An XML file includes two descriptive fields at the right of the table (Figure 10-10).

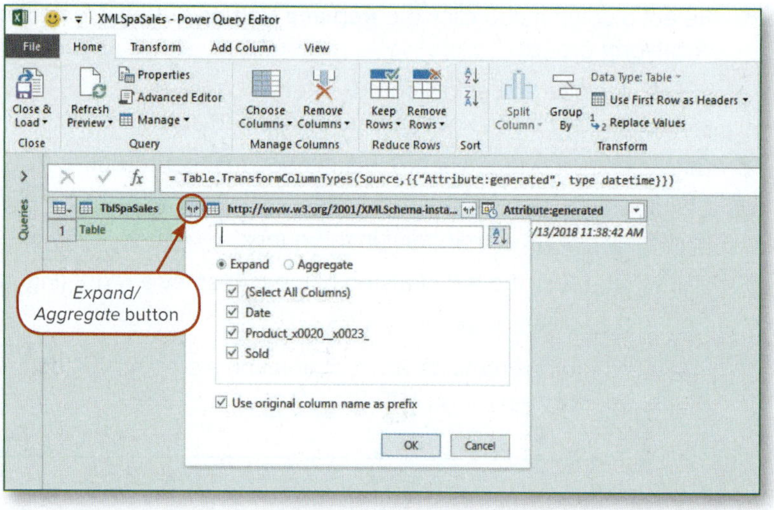

Figure 10-9 XML data does not display automatically in *Power Query*

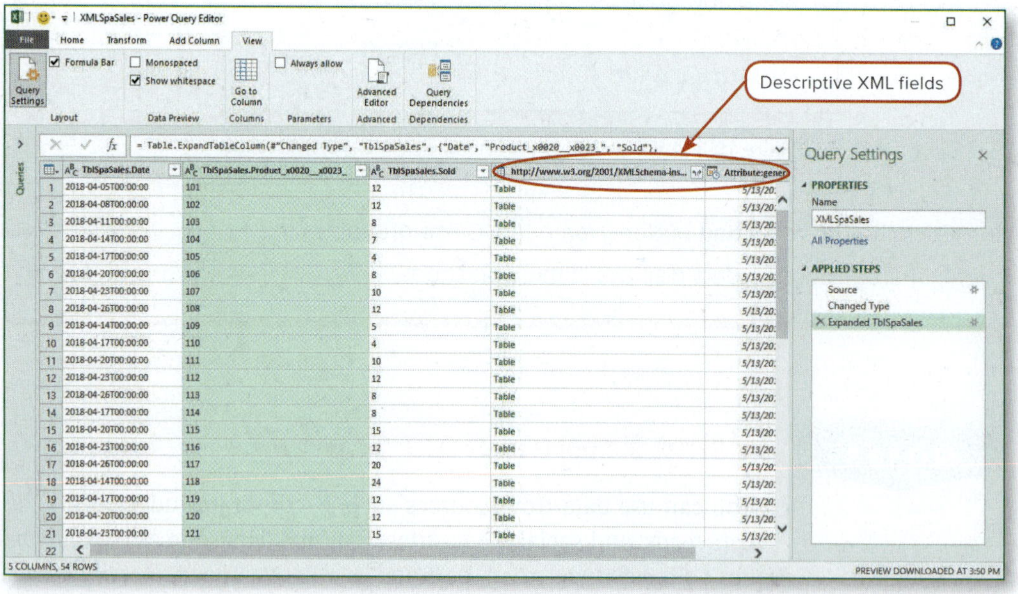

Figure 10-10 Descriptive fields are included in XML data

8. Transform the data as desired.
   - Delete the two XML descriptive fields.
   - Set data types, remove columns, replace values, filter data, and so on.
9. Click the **Close & Load** button [*Home* tab, *Close* group].
   - Query results display in an Excel table on a new sheet.
   - Rename the sheet tab and edit data as desired.

Get a Database Table

The *From Database* command [*Get Data* button] provides options for getting data from Microsoft Access, SQL Server, and Analysis Services. These are Microsoft applications and services accessible from Excel when you have permission to connect to them.

HOW TO: Build a Query for a Database Table

1. Click the **Get Data** button [*Data* tab, *Get & Transform Data* group] and choose **From Database**.
2. Choose **From Microsoft Access Database**.
   - The *Import Data* dialog box opens.
3. Navigate to the folder with the database file.
4. Select the database name and click **Import**.
   - The *Navigator* window displays the names of tables and queries in the Access database.
5. Select the name of the table or query.
   - The *Navigator* shows a preview of the data (Figure 10-11).
6. Click **Transform Data** or click **Edit** at the bottom of the window.
   - The *Power Query Editor* displays all the fields from the table or query.
   - Database field names are used in the header row.
7. Transform the data as desired.
   - If you plan to use a field in calculations, it must be a number-type field.
8. Click the **Close & Load** button [*Home* tab, *Close* group].
   - Query results display in an Excel table on a new sheet.
   - Rename the sheet tab and edit data as desired.
9. Save the workbook.
   - Data connections are saved with the workbook.

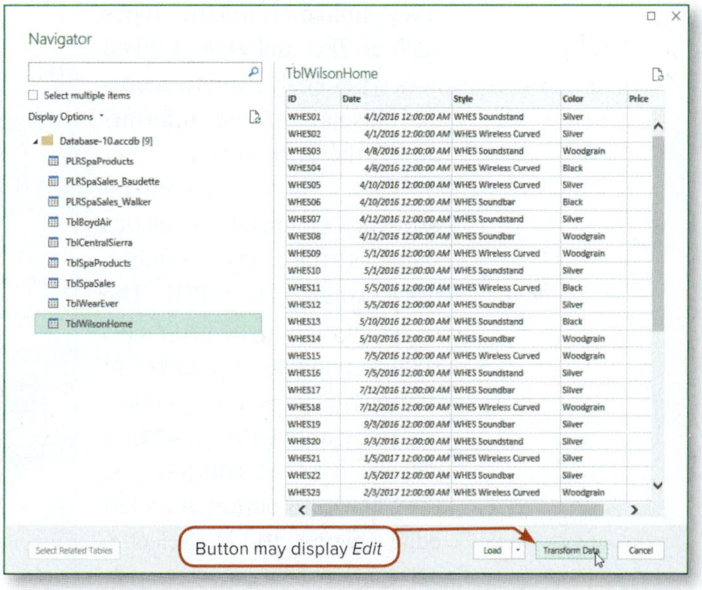

Figure 10-11 *Navigator* window for getting data from a database

Online and Other Sources

The *Get & Transform Data* group on the *Data* tab enables you to import data from online and local sources. The data can then be managed in *Power Query* for incorporation into your Excel workbook.

Database management systems (DBMS) hold large datasets with millions of records. You will see terms such as OData (Open Data Protocol), ODBC (Open Database Connectivity), and OLEDB (Object Linking & Embedding Database). SQL Server and Analysis Services are two options included for the *Get Data, From Database* button, too.

ANOTHER WAY

Microsoft Query [*Get Data* button] is a legacy wizard for importing data from Excel or Access. It does not launch *Power Query*.

Online sources include social media. You can also get data directly from a web page that has data formatted as tables for import. Web data today tends to incorporate audio and visual elements, so you may find it time-consuming to locate data that can be imported on a web page. Web content that is designed for importing, however, is generally in a format that is easily brought into Excel or *Power Query* using the *Get & Transform* group [*Data* tab].

Extracting Data through Data Types

A ***data type*** assigned to a cell from the *Data* command tab establishes a connection to an online source. The *Data Types* group has two commands, *Stocks* and *Geography*. They are *linked data types* unlike standard types such as *Text* and *Date*. Linked data types enable you to access and display related information in the worksheet.

The *Stocks* command extracts financial statistics such as the ticker symbol, price, volume, and P/E. The *Geography* data type gets fields such as population, number of households, area, and income.

You can determine when a cell has a linked data type by the **Show card** button at its left edge (Figure 10-12). Select a cell with a *Show card* button to display the **Add Column** button and choose a field to display its data.

Linked data types are evolving and may not be available in all Excel versions. Use Excel *Help* to stay current on this feature.

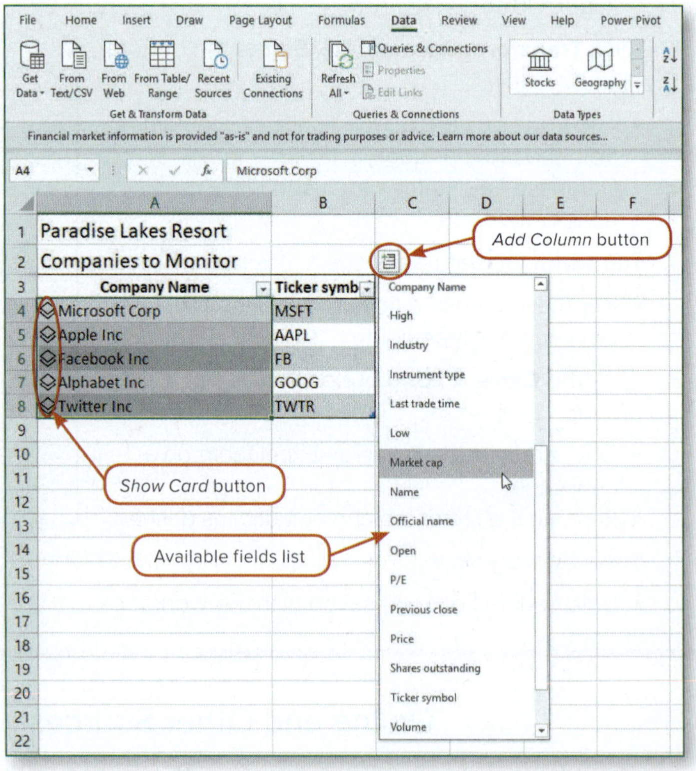

Figure 10-12 ***Stocks*** **data type assigned**

> **MORE INFO**
>
> *Power Query*, *Power Pivot*, *PivotTables*, and map charts may not work as expected when source data has linked data types.

HOW TO: Extract Data Using Data Types

1. Type geographic or stock data in a column.
   - Excel recognizes region, country, state/province, and city names for geographic data types.
   - Type a ticker symbol, company name, or fund name for stock data types.
2. Format the column as an Excel table.
   - You can apply a linked data type to plain text in a cell.
3. Select the cells for the linked data type.
   - Do not include column titles or headers.
4. Click the **Stocks** button [*Data* tab, *Data Types* group] or the **Geography** button [*Data* tab, *Data Types* group].
   - Each recognized item displays a *Show card* button at the left.
   - An unidentified item displays a question mark icon.
   - The *Data Selector* pane may open automatically when unrecognized data exists.
5. Click a question mark icon to troubleshoot an unrecognized item.
   - The *Data Selector* pane identifies the first cell with an error and offers search suggestions (Figure 10-13).

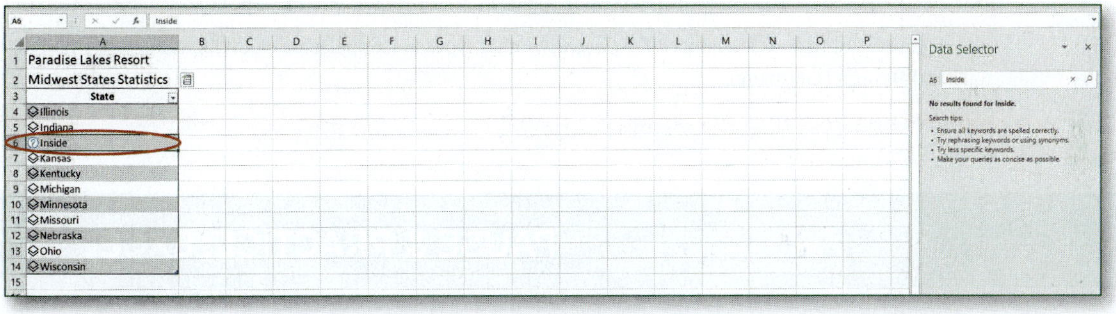

Figure 10-13 Unrecognized content for the data type

6. Select the cell, type the correct data, and press **Enter**.
   - The linked data type is updated if the data is recognized.
7. Select the cells with linked data types and click the **Add Column** button.
   - A list of field names displays.
   - Choices depend on the data type and the online source.
8. Choose a field name to place a column in the table (see Figure 10-12).
   - The data displays in the first empty column.
   - Repeat to add statistics to the table.

9. Click the **Show card** button for a cell.
   - The card is a window with field names and related data (Figure 10-14).
   - Display the card by pressing **Ctrl+Shift+F5**.
10. Point to a field name in the card and click the **Extract *[FieldName]* to grid** button to insert the field in the table.
    - Data displays for all records in the table.
    - Click a cell to hide the card.
11. Format, sort, and filter the table as needed.
    - Delete a column to remove statistics from the table.
    - Delete rows as needed.
12. Click the **Refresh All** button [*Data* tab, *Queries & Connections* group] to update the links.
    - Alternatively, select the cells, right-click the selection, and choose **Refresh**.
13. Select the cells with linked data types, right-click the selection, choose **Data Type**, and click **Convert to Text** to remove the linked data types.
    - Data connections are removed, and columns that rely on the link display *#FIELD!*.
    - Delete columns from the table as needed.
    - Undo the *Convert to Text* command to restore the linked data types.

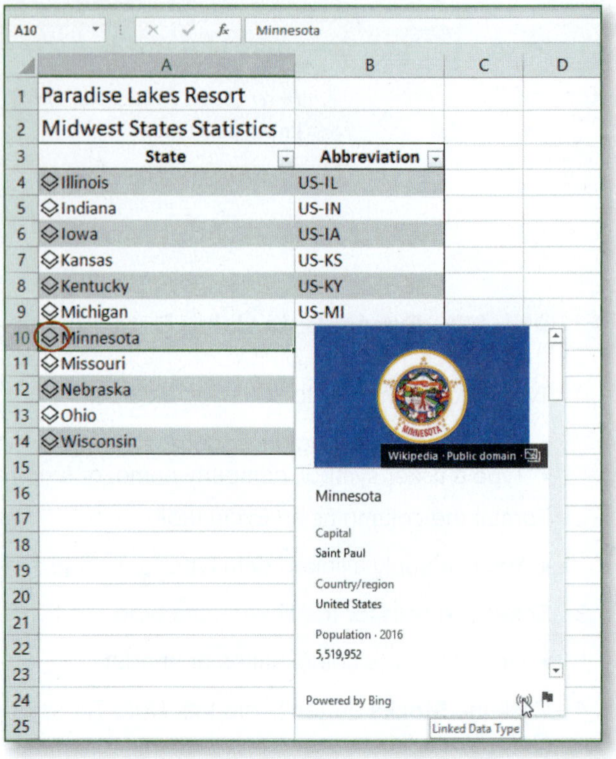

Figure 10-14 Card for a cell with a linked data type

MORE INFO

Examples of regions recognized for *Geography* data types are Appalachia (USA), Normandy (France), and Bavaria (Germany).

PAUSE & PRACTICE: EXCEL 10-1

For this project, you get data from an XML file and from an Access database. You transform each dataset before loading the data into an Excel workbook.

Files Needed: ***XMLSpaSales.xml***, ***XMLSpaSales.xsd***, and ***Database-10.accdb*** *(Student data files are available in the* Library *of your SIMnet account.)*
Completed Project File Name: ***[your initials] PP E10-1.xlsx***

1. Open a new workbook and save it as [your initials] PP E10-1.
2. Get data from an XML file.
   a. Click the **Get Data** button [*Data* tab, *Get & Transform Data* group], choose **From File**, and **From XML**.

b. Navigate to the folder with the **XMLSpaSales.xml** file from your student data files. The *XMLSpaSales .xsd* file is a support file and is included when you import the XML file.
c. Select the file name **XMLSpaSales**, click **Import**, and then click **Transform Data** or **Edit**. (The button name depends on your Excel version.)
d. Click the **Expand/Aggregate** button next to the *TblSpaSales* label at the top of the first column in the *Power Query Editor*.
e. Verify that the *Expand* button is selected, that all field boxes are selected, and click **OK**.

3. Transform XML data in *Power Query*.
a. Click the **TblSpaSales.Date** column header.
b. Click the **Data Type** button [*Home* tab, *Transform* group] and choose **Date/Time**.
c. Click the **TblSpaSales.Product_. . .** column header in the second column.
d. Click the **Data Type** button [*Home* tab, *Transform* group] and choose **Whole Number**.
e. Click the **Transform** tab and click the **Rename** button [*Any Column* group].
f. Change the column header to display TblSpaSales.ProductID. Delete unnecessary characters and press **Enter** to complete the edit.
g. Select the **TblSpaSales.Sold** column and choose the **Whole Number** data type.
h. Select the **http://. . .XMLSchema. . .** column, the fourth column.
i. Press **Ctrl** and click the **Attribute:generated** column (Figure 10-15).
j. Click the **Remove Columns** button [*Home* tab, *Manage Columns* group].

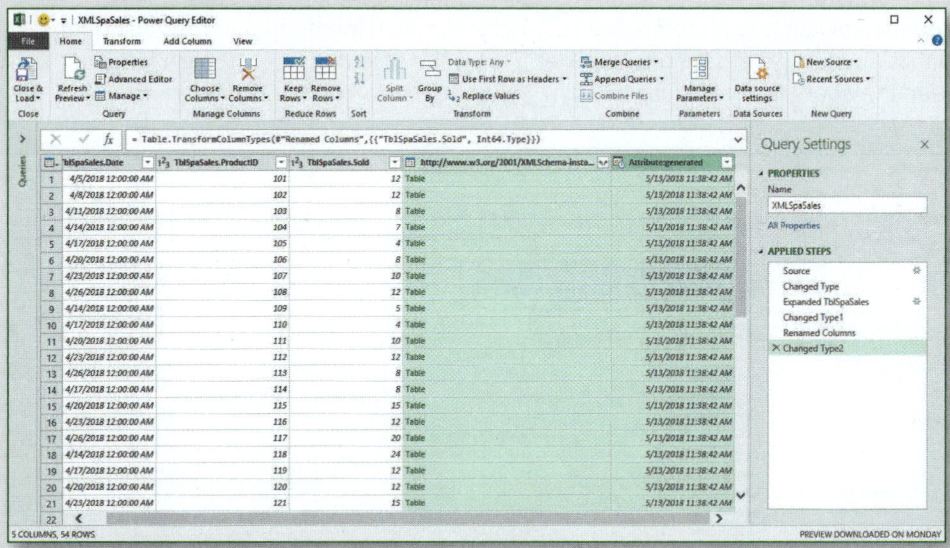

Figure 10-15 Transform XML data in *Power Query*

4. Load data to a workbook.
a. Click the **Close & Load** button [*Home* tab, *Close* group].
b. Rename the query results sheet as XML Query (Figure 10-16).

5. Get data from an Access database file.
a. Click the **Sheet1** tab.
b. Click the **Get Data** button [*Data* tab, *Get & Transform Data* group] and choose **From Database**.
c. Choose **From Microsoft Access Database**.
d. Navigate to the folder with the ***Database-10*** file from your student data files.
e. Select the **Database-10** name and click **Import**.
f. Select **TblSpaProducts** in the *Navigator* window and click **Transform Data** (or **Edit**) at the bottom of the window.
g. Click **Refresh** if an *Information* bar opens about the age of the file.

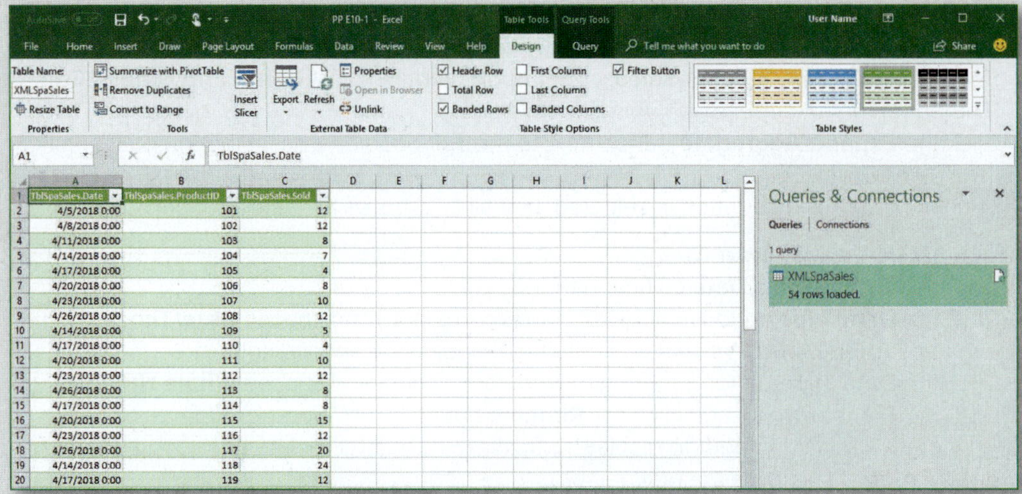

	A	B	C
1	TblSpaSales.Date	TblSpaSales.ProductID	TblSpaSales.Sold
2	4/5/2018 0:00	101	12
3	4/8/2018 0:00	102	12
4	4/11/2018 0:00	103	8
5	4/14/2018 0:00	104	7
6	4/17/2018 0:00	105	4
7	4/20/2018 0:00	106	8
8	4/23/2018 0:00	107	10
9	4/26/2018 0:00	108	12
10	4/14/2018 0:00	109	5
11	4/17/2018 0:00	110	4
12	4/20/2018 0:00	111	10
13	4/23/2018 0:00	112	12
14	4/26/2018 0:00	113	8
15	4/17/2018 0:00	114	8
16	4/20/2018 0:00	115	15
17	4/23/2018 0:00	116	12
18	4/26/2018 0:00	117	20
19	4/14/2018 0:00	118	24
20	4/17/2018 0:00	119	12

Figure 10-16 XML data loaded to Excel

6. Transform data from an Access database file.
   a. Click the **Product #** column header.
   b. Click the **Transform** tab and click the **Rename** button [*Any Column* group].
   c. Change the column header to display ProductID to match the header in the XML query.
   d. Verify that the data type is **Whole Number**. This is the field that will establish a relationship between the query tables (Figure 10-17).

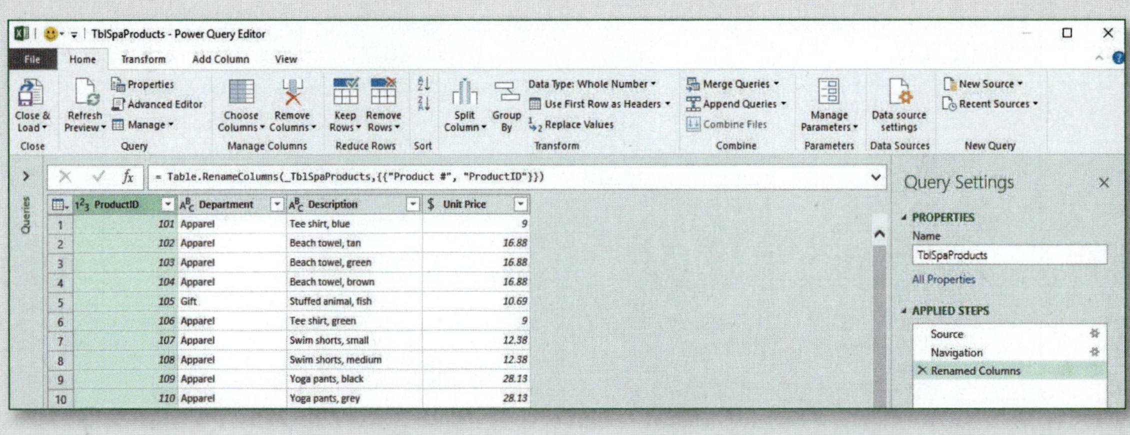

	ProductID	Department	Description	Unit Price
1	101	Apparel	Tee shirt, blue	9
2	102	Apparel	Beach towel, tan	16.88
3	103	Apparel	Beach towel, green	16.88
4	104	Apparel	Beach towel, brown	16.88
5	105	Gift	Stuffed animal, fish	10.69
6	106	Apparel	Tee shirt, green	9
7	107	Apparel	Swim shorts, small	12.38
8	108	Apparel	Swim shorts, medium	12.38
9	109	Apparel	Yoga pants, black	28.13
10	110	Apparel	Yoga pants, grey	28.13

Figure 10-17 Transform Access data in *Power Query*

7. Load data from an Access database file.
   a. Click the **Close & Load** button [*Home* tab, *Close* group]. The data loads to a new worksheet.
   b. Rename the query results sheet as Database Query.
8. Save and close the workbook.

SLO 10.4

Merging and Appending Queries

Merge or append queries to combine data from more than one table. You are then able to manipulate and analyze data from multiple sources that might be impossible to accomplish otherwise. The ***Merge*** and the ***Append*** commands display in the *Combine* group on the *Query Tools* tab.

The *Append* command combines queries that have exactly the same fields; all fields are matching fields. Append one table to the end of another table, or append them to each other in a new query.

The *Merge* command depends on a relationship between the queries. At least one field must be the same in both or all queries. You cannot merge queries at random, because each query must have a common or matching field so that a relationship can be established.

> **MORE INFO**
>
> Merge and append as many queries as necessary, but the same matching and relationship rules apply.

For your continuing work with *Power Query* in this chapter, the terms "query" and "table" are used interchangeably because a table is actually a view of query results.

Common and Key Fields

A relationship is a "***join***" between tables and is required to merge queries. A ***common field*** is data that is the same in each of the queries. In the product list for Paradise Lakes Spa, each product ID appears once with a description of the item. In a related sales query, however, the product ID appears each time a sale is recorded. The *Product ID* field is the common field and allows the queries to be joined.

The common field is described as a ***key field*** when data appears only once in the table. The *Product ID* field is a key field in the product list table. The *Product ID* field appears as many times as a sale is made in the related sales query. This is a one-to-many relationship; the key field appears once in the table on the "one" side of the relationship and many times in the other table.

> **MORE INFO**
>
> If you incorrectly identify a matching field when combining queries, the merge query displays inaccurate results.

HOW TO: Merge Queries

1. Open the workbook that contains multiple queries.
   - The matching field must be in both tables.
2. Click a cell in one of the tables to be merged.
3. Click the **Merge** button [*Query Tools* tab, *Combine* group].
   - The *Merge* dialog box opens.
4. Select a table or query name in the upper text box.
   - Click the drop-down list to display the names of queries in the workbook.
   - Select the table or query from which you want to see all the records.
5. Select the column that is the matching field in the preview.
6. Select the second table name in the lower text box.

7. Select the column with the matching field in the preview (Figure 10-18).
   - The dialog box identifies how many rows were matched initially.
8. Click the **Join Kind** drop-down list.
9. Select the matching pattern.
   - Join type names are from SQL (standard query language) and include a description of how the queries will be merged.
10. Click **OK**.
    - The combined query opens in the *Power Query Editor*.
    - The default query name is *MergeN*.
    - All fields from the first table are displayed; fields from the second table are collapsed (Figure 10-19).
11. Transform the data as desired.
    - Expand the data from the second table to work with those fields.
12. Load the data to the workbook.

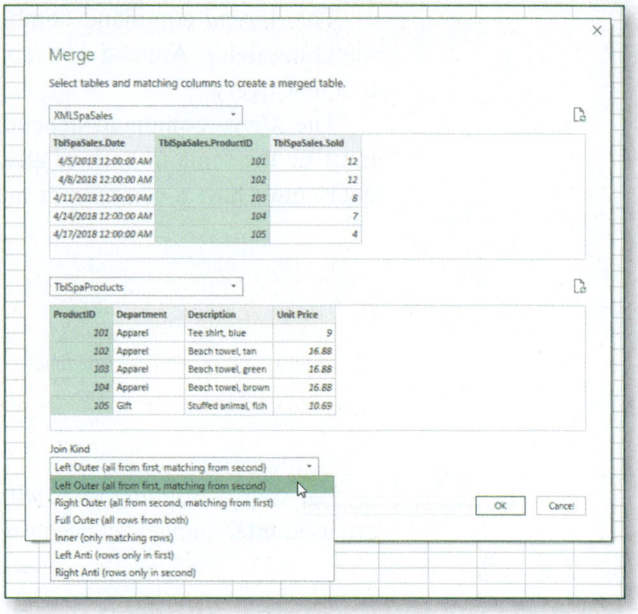

Figure 10-18 ***Merge*** **dialog box to combine queries**

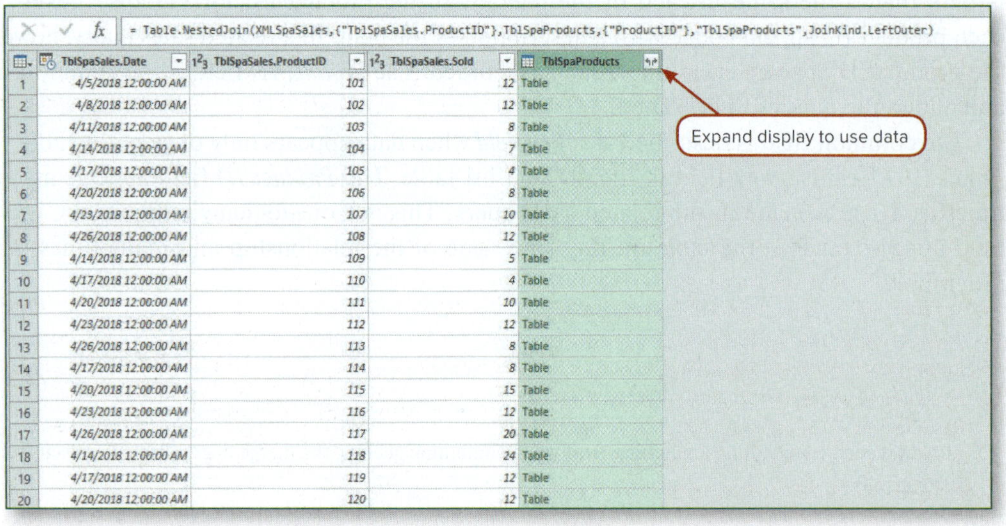

Figure 10-19 Not all fields display in the merged query

> ## ANOTHER WAY
> Merge queries in the *Power Query Editor* by clicking the **Merge Queries** button [*Home* tab, *Combine* group].

View Dependencies

Queries and tables in your workbook may have relationships or dependencies that enable you to work with the data in various layouts. Look at these dependencies in a diagram for a clear picture of how each query fits in the data and in the workbook. The *Query Dependencies* dialog box identifies locations and names of source files and illustrates how *Power Query* uses each source.

▸HOW TO: View Dependencies

1. Click a cell in one of the workbook queries.
2. Launch *Power Query*.
3. Click the **Query Dependencies** button [*View* tab, *Dependencies* group].
   - The *Query Dependencies* dialog box displays source file names and current relationships for the workbook (Figure 10-20).
4. Click the **Layout** button in the *Query Dependencies* dialog box.
   - Select a layout pattern for the window.
5. Click the **Zoom In** or **Zoom Out** button in the *Query Dependencies* dialog box to change the view size.
   - Zoom out for a workbook with many dependencies so that you can see all the relationships at once.
6. Click the **Fit to Screen** button in the *Query Dependencies* dialog box.
   - Information in the dialog box sizes to fit.
7. Close the dialog box.

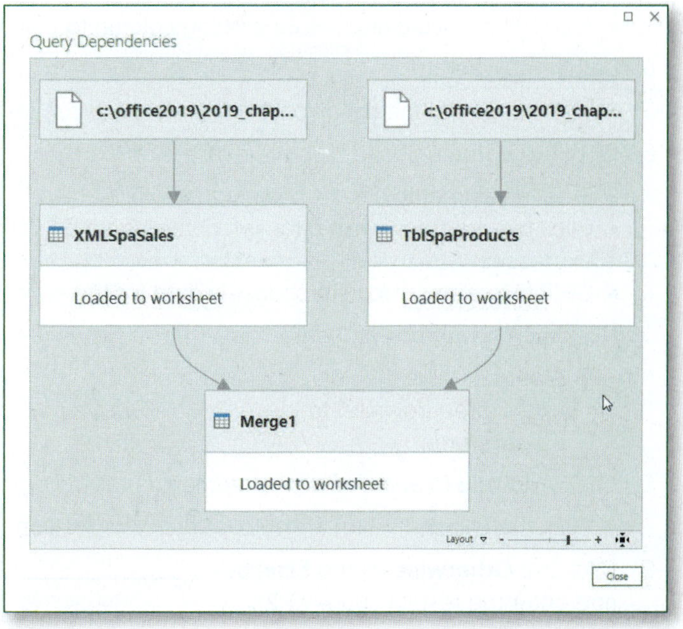

Figure 10-20 ***Query Dependencies*** **dialog box**

SLO 10.5

Manipulating Data in a Query

Power Query provides commands for arranging and transforming data quickly and easily whether in a one-table query or a merged query. These transformations include creating conditional columns, inserting a column by example, extracting data, and more. With these commands, you create new information about your existing data for enhanced analysis and reporting.

Conditional Columns

A ***conditional column*** is a generated or calculated column with an *IF* statement that determines what displays in the column. Data in a conditional column is not a field in the source data, but it uses a source field in its *IF* statement. A conditional column is loaded and refreshed in the workbook like other fields in the query.

Build the *IF* statement in the *Add Conditional Column* dialog box with common relational operators. If you have programming experience, you can build sophisticated statements to populate a new column. The conditional column displays at the right of the query columns, but you can move it to another location in the query or in the workbook.

▸HOW TO: Add a Conditional Column to a Query

1. Select a cell in the query results worksheet and launch *Power Query*.
   - Click the **Get Data** button [*Data* tab, *Get & Transform* group] and select **Launch Power Query Editor**.
   - Alternatively, point to the query name in the *Queries & Connections* pane and click **Edit** in the information pop-up window.
   - A third option is to click the **Query** command tab and then click the **Edit** button [*Edit* group].

2. Click the **Conditional Column** button [*Add Column* tab, *General* group].
   - The *Add Conditional Column* dialog box displays.
3. Click the **New column name** box and type a name for the conditional column.
4. Click the **Column Name** drop-down list and select the field name for the *IF* expression.
   - A conditional column uses an existing column to build new data.
5. Select the operator.
   - The first part of the condition is similar to a *logical_test* argument.
6. Click the **Value** box and type the expression.
   - Enter a value or text to be evaluated.
   - Click the drop-down list to the left of the *Value* box and choose **Select a column** to use another column in the expression.
   - Click the calendar icon to choose a date for the expression.
7. Click the **Output** box and enter the result.
   - The output is like the *value_if_true* argument.
   - Click the drop-down list to the left of the *Output* box and choose **Select a column** to display results from another column.
8. Click **Add rule** to add an *Else If* statement (another *logical_test*) as needed.
   - Click the ellipsis (. . .) for a row to delete or reposition the statement.
9. Click the **Otherwise** (or the **Else**) box and enter the result (Figure 10-21).
   - This result is a *value_if_false* argument.
   - Click the drop-down list for *Otherwise* (or *Else*) and choose **Select a column** to display results from another column.
10. Click **OK**.
    - The conditional column displays at the right of the query.
11. Select the column and click the **Move** button [*Transform* tab, *Any Column* group].
    - Select **Left** to move the column one column to the left at a time.
    - Move the column to the beginning and then to the right as desired.
    - Alternatively, drag the column heading to reposition it as desired.

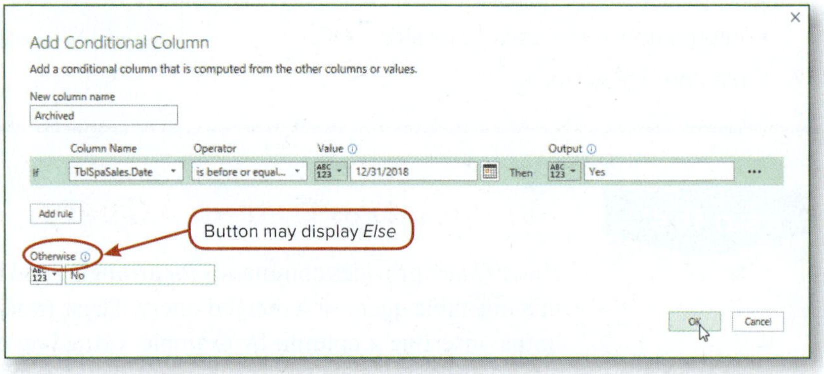

Figure 10-21 The *Add Conditional Column* dialog box

Column From Examples

Power Query can add a column to your data based on a data sample. Use ***Column From Examples*** to insert missing symbols, such as a number sign (#) with the product ID, to change uppercase data to lowercase, or to combine data from two columns.

Enter one or a few sample pieces of data to create a recognizable pattern. As soon as *Power Query* identifies the pattern, it proposes a new column. The proposed column displays at the right of the window for your acceptance or cancellation. When you accept a column, it is named and listed in the *Applied Steps* in the *Query Settings* pane. You can then rename and transform the data as usual.

▸HOW TO: Create a Column From Examples

1. Select a cell in the query results and launch *Power Query*.
   - Click the **Get Data** button [*Data* tab, *Get & Transform* group] and select **Launch Power Query Editor**.
   - Alternatively, click the **Query** tab and click the **Edit** button [*Edit* group].
   - You can point to the query name in the *Queries & Connections* pane and click **Edit** in the information pop-up window.
2. Select the column from which to build an example.
   - Select multiple columns as needed.
   - Build a column from all existing columns if necessary.
3. Click the **Column From Examples** button [*Add Column* tab, *General* group].
   - An empty column displays at the right of the window.
4. Click the first row in the empty column.
5. Type the first character for data in the new column (Figure 10-22).

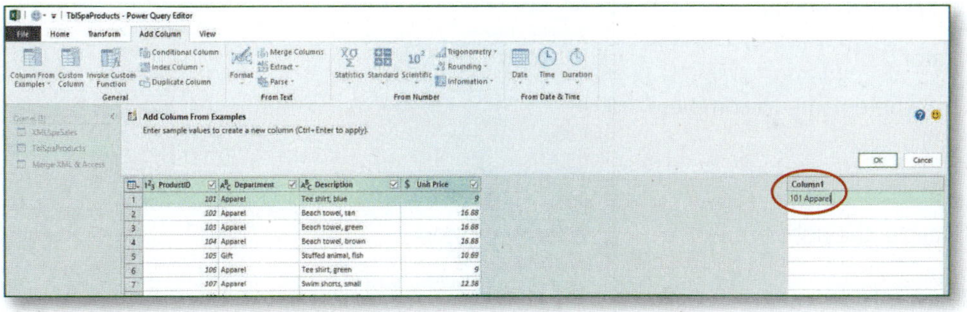

Figure 10-22 Example data to create a column from two existing columns

   - Type a new character to insert it in front of existing data.
   - Type the first character from the first item in an existing row.
6. Complete the example and press **Enter**.
   - The sample column fills if *Power Query* identifies your pattern.
   - The *Add Column From Examples* bar displays the M language code to build the column.
   - Type a second line if the pattern is not recognized, or build the example using another field.
7. Click **OK** to place the new column in the query.
   - The new column displays at the right.
   - The *Applied Steps* name and list the action.
   - Alternatively, press **Ctrl+Enter** to insert the column in the query.
8. Rename and position the column.
   - Delete the columns used to create the new column as desired.

Custom Columns

A ***custom column*** displays generated or calculated data in a new column in the query. The data is not a field in the source data. Use the same syntax and operators as Excel to create simple arithmetic formulas in the *Custom Column* dialog box. For complex calculations, learn about *Power Query* M language to access its functions and expressions.

▸HOW TO: Create a Custom Column

1. Select a cell in the query results and launch *Power Query*.
   - Click the **Get Data** button [*Data* tab, *Get & Transform* group] and select **Launch Power Query Editor**.
   - Alternatively, point to the query name in the *Queries & Connections* pane and click **Edit** in the information pop-up window.
2. Click the **Custom Column** button [*Add Column* tab, *General* group].
   - The *Custom Column* dialog box opens.
3. Type a name for the new column in the **New column name** box.
   - Edit the name after the column displays as desired.
4. Click after the = symbol in the *Custom column formula* box.
5. Double-click a field name in the *Available columns* list to insert it in the formula.
   - The field name displays in the *Custom column formula* box enclosed in square brackets.
6. Type an arithmetic operator.
7. Type a constant or select a field name to complete the formula (Figure 10-23).
8. Click **OK**.
   - The new column displays at the right of existing columns.
   - Set the data type as desired [*Home* tab].
   - Rename or position the field in the query [*Transform* tab].

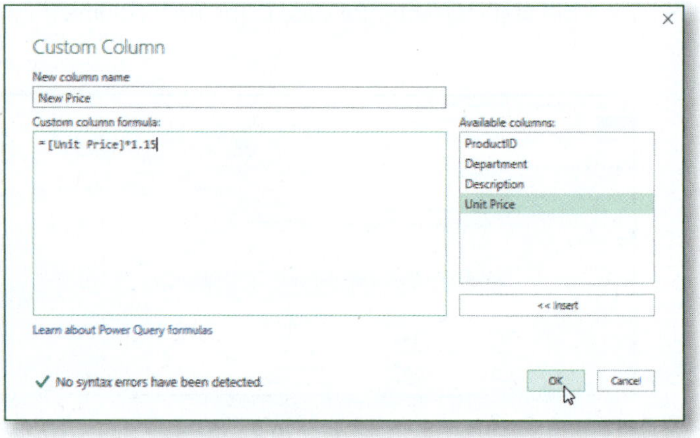

Figure 10-23 ***Custom Column* dialog box in *Power Query***

Query Language

You can learn about *Power Query* M language by reviewing formulas inserted by *Power Query* when you create custom or other user-created columns. Although M language is specific to *Power Query*, the language uses procedures, expressions, and syntax similar to SQL.

View the code for a formula in the *Formula bar*. Display the entire code for the query by clicking the **Advanced Editor** button [*View* tab, *Advanced* group].

▸HOW TO: View Query Language

1. Create a conditional or custom column in the query as desired.
   - The *Formula bar* displays the formula in M language.
   - Columns inserted from commands on the *Add Column* command tab have formulas.
2. Expand the *Formula bar* as needed to see the formula.
   - The formula is similar to but different from an Excel formula.
3. Click the **Advanced Editor** button [*View* tab, *Advanced* group].
   - The underlying code for the entire query displays (Figure 10-24).

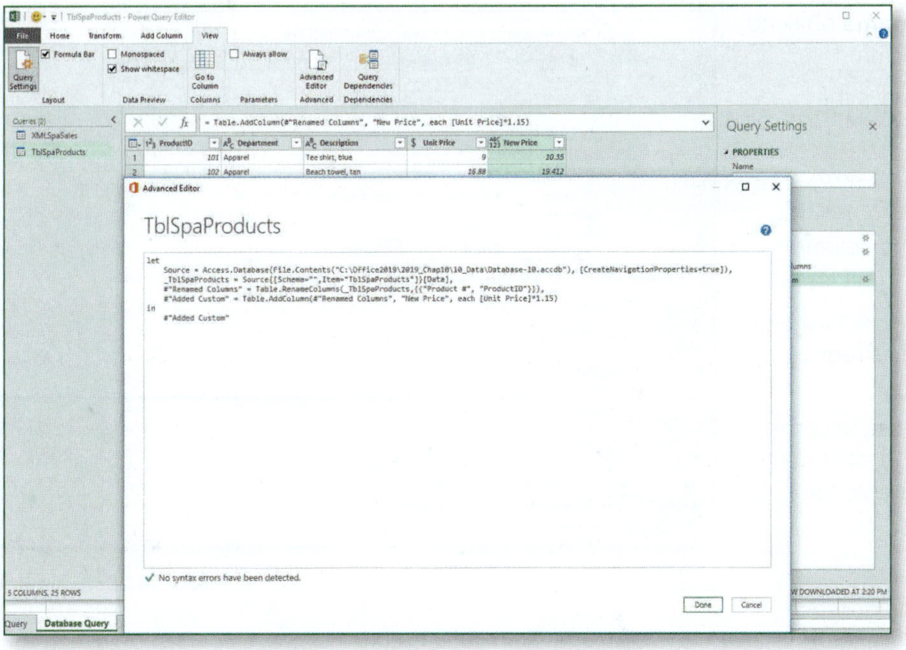

Figure 10-24 M language code in the *Formula bar* and the *Advanced Editor*

4. Click **Cancel** in the *Advanced Editor* window.
5. Collapse the *Formula bar.*

Group Rows

Group records in *Power Query* by one or more fields to categorize and summarize data. The ***Group By*** command enables you to organize millions of rows of data in a meaningful way such as revenue by state or province, number of students enrolled per year, or online sales by date. The *Group By* command is located in the *Table* group on the *Transform* tab.

ANOTHER WAY

Grouping rows in *Power Query* is similar to arranging data in a *PivotTable* or using the *Subtotal* command in a worksheet.

HOW TO: Group Rows

1. Launch *Power Query* to edit the query.
2. Select a column for grouping.
   - Press **Ctrl** to select multiple columns as needed.
3. Click the **Group By** button [*Transform* tab, *Table* group].
   - The *Group By* dialog box displays.
4. Select or verify that the **Basic** button is selected.
   - Select the **Advanced** button to use multiple columns for grouping.
5. Click the **Group By** drop-down list and choose a column name.
   - Select the column that is to be summed, averaged, or otherwise calculated.

6. Click the **New column name** box and type a name for the column.
   - The new column displays the results of the operation.
7. Click the **Operation** drop-down list and choose the operation.
   - Options depend on the column used for grouping.
8. Click the **Column** drop-down list and choose a column name as required (Figure 10-25).
   - It is not necessary to use another column in the grouping statement.
   - This option is not available for *Count* operations.
9. Click **OK**.
   - The query displays the grouped column and the results (Figure 10-26).

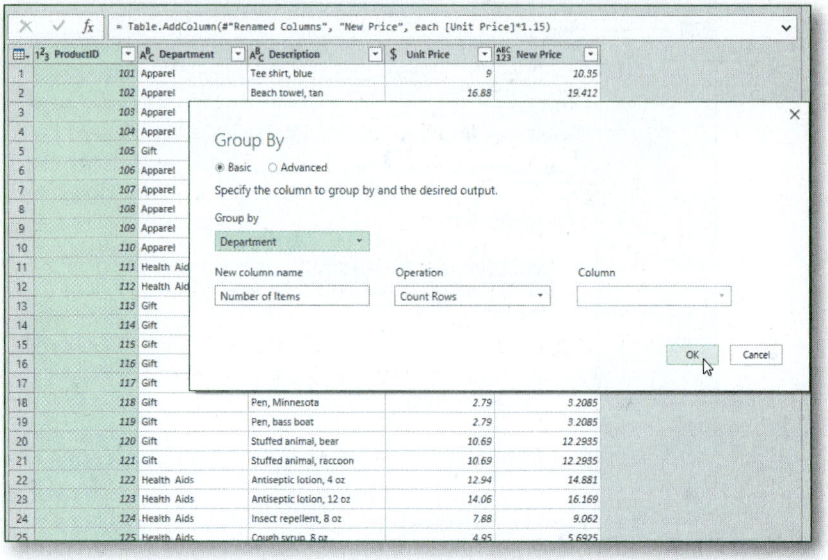

Figure 10-25 *Group By* dialog box

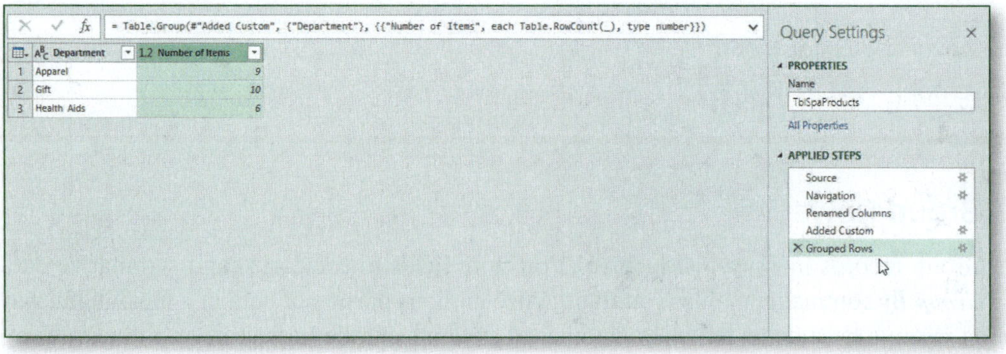

Figure 10-26 Grouped data in *Power Query*

Tips for Using Power Query

Power Query is a sophisticated data analysis tool, but keep in mind that *Power Query* is one piece of a collection of business intelligence products and services. Here are tips and suggestions for your work in *Power Query*.

- Use your data to experiment with *Power Query* commands. Remove the step from the *Applied Steps* list in the *Query Settings* pane if the command does not work as expected.
- The path to the data source file is coded in the query. This makes it difficult to move from one computer to another unless your sources are online and accessible.
- Verify data types carefully–especially when merging queries because data types must match.
- When merging queries, the common field *names* need not match, but the data *type* must be the same.
- Name each query with a descriptive name.
- Close the *Power Query Editor* and discard your work when experimenting to learn new features.
- Study SQL and M language to learn how to edit and refine queries.
- Review online tutorials, blogs, and other sources to learn about *Power Query* and related business intelligence products and services as they become available.

PAUSE & PRACTICE: EXCEL 10-2

For this project, you merge your queries from XML and Access and view dependencies. You also create a conditional column, a column from examples, and a custom column in *Power Query*.

File Needed: ***[your initials] PP E10-1.xlsx***
Completed Project File Name: ***[your initials] PP E10-2.xlsx***

Note: Depending on your work environment, the source files used in *Pause & Practice 10-1* may need to be accessible. Those files are ***XMLSpaSales.xml***, ***XMLSpaSales.xsd***, and ***Database-10.accdb***. *(Student data files are available in the* Library *of your SIMnet account.)*

1. Open the ***[your initials] PP E10-1*** workbook created in *Pause & Practice 10-1* and enable the content if prompted. Save the workbook as [your initials] PP E10-2. *Note: Click the* **Refresh** *button to update data connections when a* Power Query Information *bar displays.*

2. Merge queries.
   a. Click the **XML Query** worksheet tab and select cell **A2**.
   b. Click the **Merge** button [*Query Tools* tab, *Combine* group].
   c. Verify that *XMLSpaSales* displays as the name in the upper text box.
   d. Click the **TblSpaSales.ProductID** column heading in the table to select the column as the matching field.
   e. Click the drop-down list for the lower text box and select **TblSpaProducts** as the second query.
   f. Click the **ProductID** header in the second table as the matching field.
   g. Verify that *Left Outer* is the *Join Kind*. This join will display all records from the *XMLSpaSales* query with matching data from the *TblSpaProducts* query (Figure 10-27).
   h. Click **OK**.

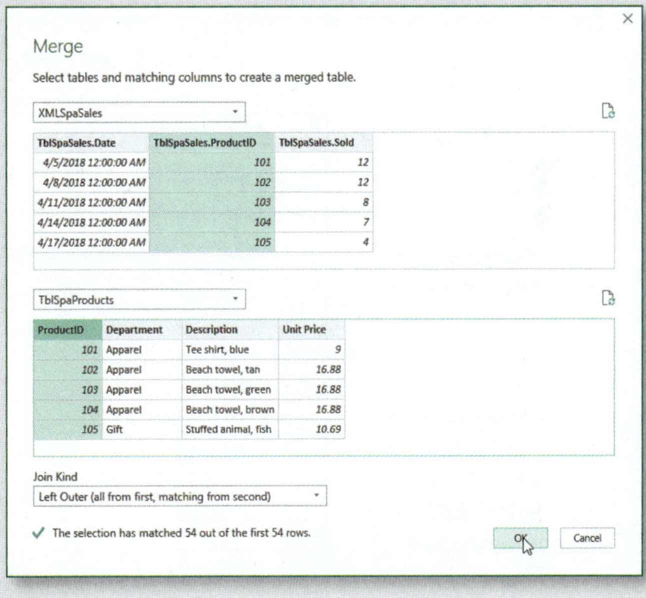

Figure 10-27 Merge query for XML and Access data

3. Display data, name the query, and load the query.
   a. Click the **Expand/Aggregate** button next to the *TblSpaProducts* column header in the merged query.
   b. Verify that the *Expand* button is selected, that all field names are selected, and that the *Use original column name as prefix box* is selected (Figure 10-28).
   c. Click **OK** to display the fields from the *TblSpaProducts* query.
   d. Click the **Name** box in the *Query Settings* pane.
   e. Delete the default name, type Merge XML & Access as the query name, and press **Enter** (Figure 10-29).
   f. Click the **Close & Load** button [*Home* tab, *Close* group].
   g. Name the worksheet Merge XML & Access to match the query name.
   h. Sort the table in ascending order by *TblSpaSales.ProductID*.

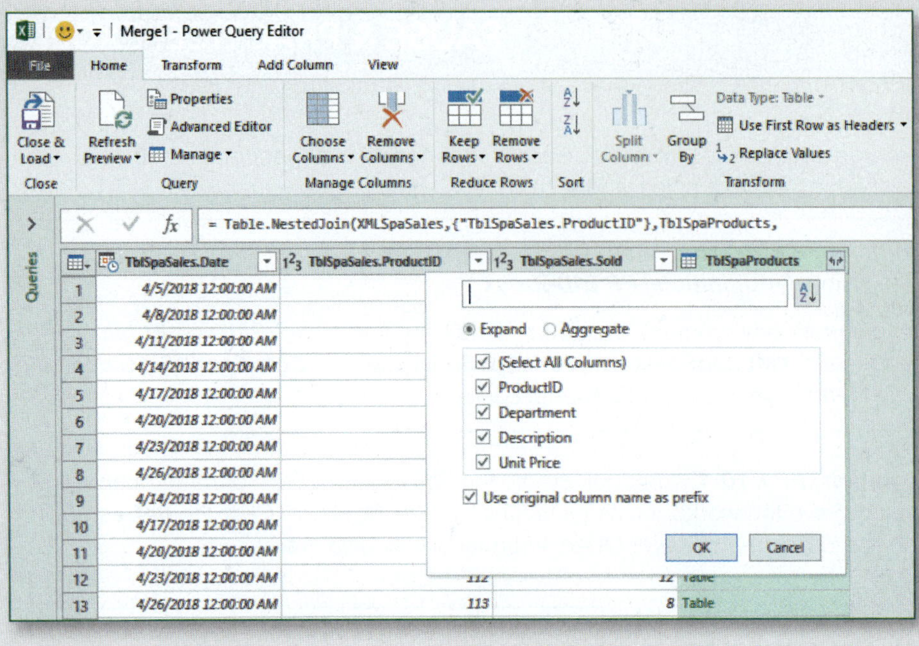

Figure 10-28 Display fields in the merged query

4. View query dependencies for the workbook.
   a. Point to the **Merge XML & Access** query name in the *Queries & Connections* pane to display the information window.
   b. Select **Edit** to return to the *Power Query Editor*.
   c. Click the **Query Dependencies** button [*View* tab, *Dependencies* group].
   d. Click the **Layout** button in the *Query Dependencies* dialog box and select **Left to Right Layout** (Figure 10-30).
   e. Close the dialog box.

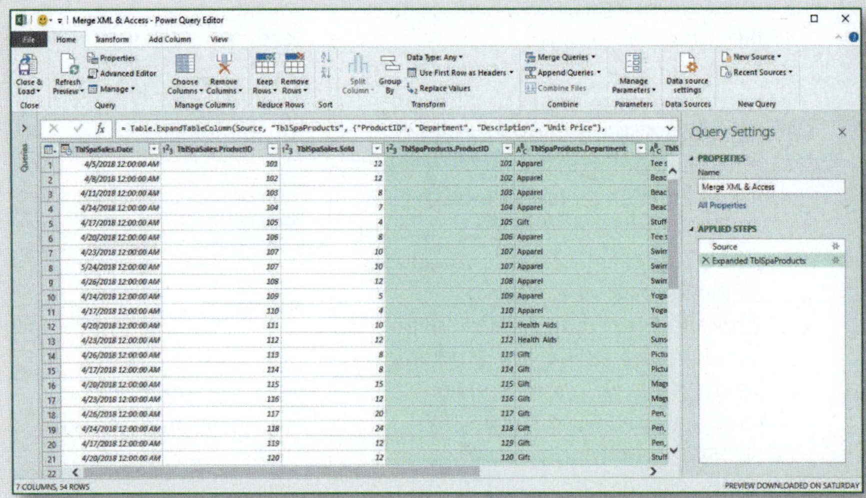

Figure 10-29 Query results after merging

5. Create a conditional column in a query.
   a. Click the **Conditional Column** button [*Add Column* tab, *General* group].
   b. Click the **New column name** box and type Archived? as the name.
   c. Click the **Column Name** drop-down list and choose **TblSpaSales.Date**.
   d. Click the **Operator** drop-down list and select **is before or equal to**.
   e. Click the calendar icon for the *Value* box and set the calendar to **December 31, 2018**.
   f. Click the **Output** box and type Yes.
   g. Click the **Otherwise** (or **Else**) box and type No.
   h. Click **OK**.

6. Move a column in a query.
   a. Verify that the *Archived?* column is selected in the query.
   b. Click the **Move** button [*Transform* tab, *Any Column* group].
   c. Select **To Beginning** to move the column to the first column position.
   d. Click the **Move** button [*Transform* tab, *Any Column* group] and choose **Right** to position the conditional column as the second column (Figure 10-31).
   e. Click the **Close & Load** button [*Home* tab, *Close* group]. The new data is included in the Excel table in the workbook, in ascending sort order for the *TblSpaSales .ProductID* field.

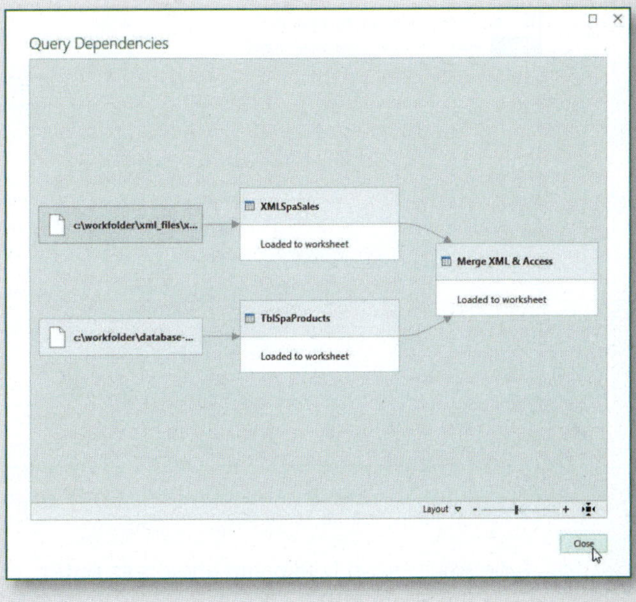

Figure 10-30 Left to right layout for query dependencies

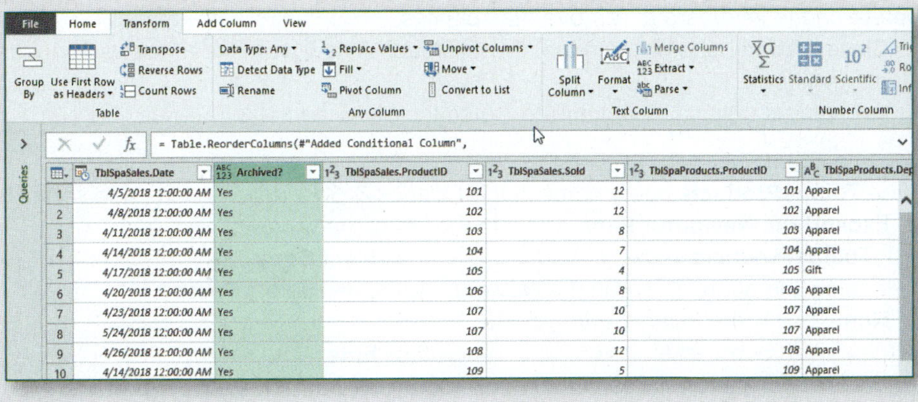

Figure 10-31 Conditional column is moved

7. Copy a query.
   a. Point to the **TblSpaProducts** query name in the *Queries & Connections* pane and select **Edit**.
   b. Click the **Manage** button [*Home* tab, *Query* group] and select **Duplicate** to copy the query.
   c. Click the **Name** box in the *Query Settings* pane.
   d. Rename the copied query as Column by Example and press **Enter**.
   e. Verify that the *Navigator* pane displays to the left of the window. If it does not, click the **Expand the Navigator Pane** arrow.

8. Create a column by example in a query.
   a. Click the **Column From Examples** button [*Add Column* tab, *General* group].
   b. Click the first row in the new empty column at the right.
   c. Type 101 and press **Spacebar** to model the data in the *Product ID* column.
   d. Type Apparel after **101** to model the department name.
   e. Press **Enter**. The column completes and is named *Merged* (Figure 10-32).
   f. Click **OK** to place the new column in the query.

9. Move and rename a column in a query.
   a. Verify that the *Merged* column is selected.
   b. Click the **Move** button [*Transform* tab, *Any Column* group] and select **To Beginning**.
   c. Click the **Rename** button [*Transform* tab, *Any Column* group].

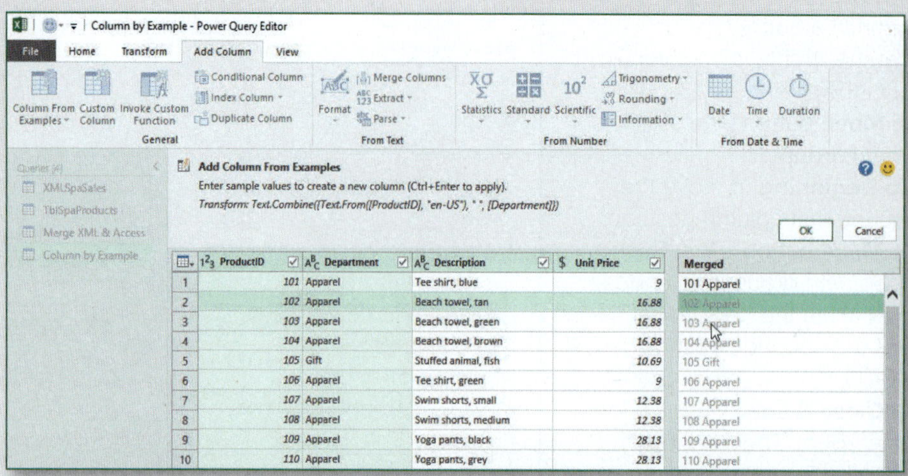

Figure 10-32 Column by example in the query

d. Type Code as the field name and press **Enter**.
e. Click the **ProductID** column heading, press **Ctrl**, and click the **Department** heading to select both columns.
f. Press **Delete** on the keyboard to remove the columns.
g. Click the **Close & Load** button [*Home* tab, *Close* group]. A new worksheet inserts for the new query in the workbook.
h. Name the worksheet Column by Example to match the query name.

10. Copy and rename a query.
    a. Point to the **TblSpaProducts** query name in the *Queries & Connections* pane and select **Edit**.
    b. Click the **Expand the Navigator Pane** arrow to the left of the window.
    c. Right-click **TblSpaProducts** in the *Navigator* pane and select **Copy**.
    d. Right-click below the query names in the *Navigator* pane and select **Paste**.
    e. Click the **Name** box in the *Query Settings* pane.
    f. Rename the copied query as Custom Column and press **Enter**.

11. Create a custom column in a query.
    a. Click the **Custom Column** button [*Add Column* tab, *General* group].
    b. Type New Price in the *New column name* box.
    c. Click after the equals sign (=) in the *Custom column formula* box.
    d. Double-click **Unit Price** in the *Available columns* list.
    e. Type *1.15 after *[Unit Price]* in the *Custom column formula* box to calculate a new price that is 115% of the current price. You must use the decimal equivalent of the value.
    f. Click **OK** to place the new column in the query (Figure 10-33).

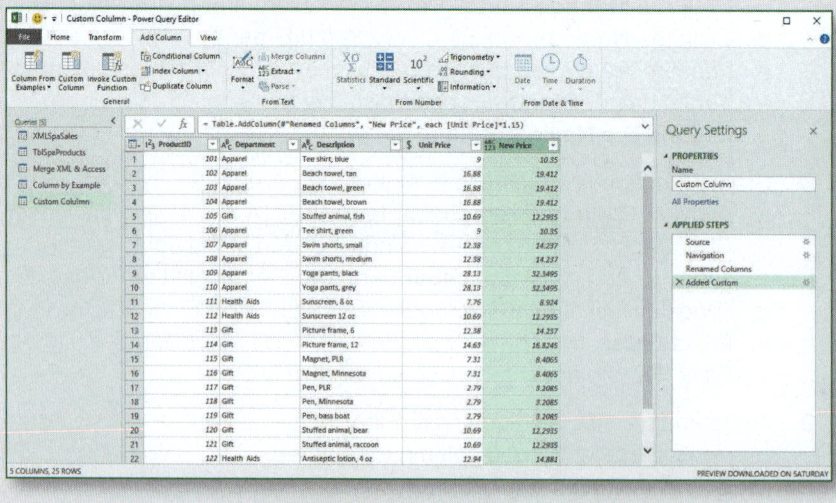

Figure 10-33 Custom column in the query

g. Click the **Close & Load** button [*Home* tab, *Close* group].
h. Name the worksheet Custom Column to match the query name.

12. Save and close the workbook.

SLO 10.6

Working with the Excel Data Model

You can create a *PivotTable* for multiple tables without launching *Power Query* when the tables have a common field. Simply indicate that you want to use multiple tables as you create the *PivotTable*.

The Data Model

A ***data model*** is a collection of tables and queries in a workbook. Excel automatically and invisibly builds a data model when you use commands in the *Get & Transform* group on the *Data* tab. You may recall from *SLO 4.6: Importing Data* that you loaded data directly into a worksheet and that the *Queries & Connections* pane was available. *Power Query* is behind the scenes, but you may not need to use it.

ANOTHER WAY

A merged query from *Power Query* is a data model that is limited to the fields in the merged query.

HOW TO: Create a PivotTable from the Data Model

1. Create a new workbook.
2. Import and load data from each source on its own sheet.
   - Data to be combined or merged must have a common field.
   - Close the *Queries & Connections* pane for more screen space.
3. Select a cell in one of the tables.
   - The *Table Tools Design* and *Query Tools* tabs open.
4. Click the **Summarize with PivotTable** button [*Table Tools Design* tab, *Tools* group].
   - The *Create PivotTable* dialog box displays the name of the table and highlights the data range.
   - Confirm or edit the data range as needed.
5. Verify or select the **New Worksheet** button.
6. Verify or select the **Add this data to the Data Model** box for the *Choose whether you want to analyze multiple tables* section.
   - Commands from the *Get & Transform Data* group [*Data* tab] automatically activate this option.
7. Click **OK**.
   - A blank *PivotTable* layout displays on a new sheet.
   - The *PivotTable Fields* pane displays *Active* and *All* at the top of the pane.
8. Select a field from the active table for the *PivotTable*.
   - Excel places the field name in the *PivotTable* layout.
   - Place at least one field from the active table before displaying other table or query lists.
   - Move the field name as needed from one area to another.

9. Click **All** at the top of the *PivotTable Fields* pane.
    - The names of tables and queries in the data model display.
10. Expand the table or query list as needed to see the field names.
11. Select fields for the *PivotTable*.
    - A message box in the *PivotTable Fields* pane states that *Relationships between tables may be needed*.
    - Fields in the *PivotTable* layout may display inaccurate data when the relationship is undefined (Figure 10-34).
12. Click **Auto-Detect** in the *PivotTable Fields* pane.
    - The *Auto-Detect Relationships* dialog box verifies that a relationship was detected and created.
13. Click **Close**.
    - The data is refreshed as needed.

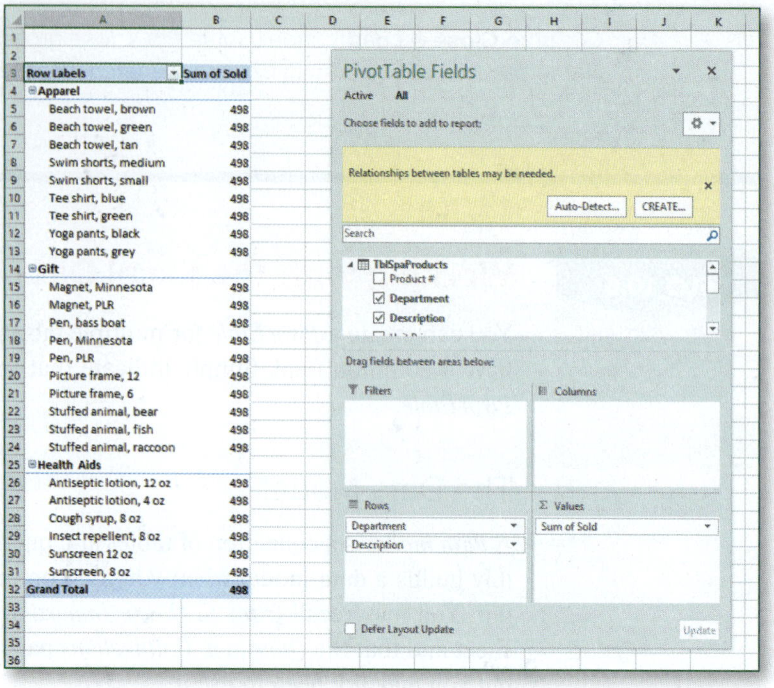

Figure 10-34 *PivotTable* **lists same total for each product because relationship is undefined**

Create a Relationship in the Data Model

The *Create Relationship* dialog box identifies a *Table* and a *Related Table*. The *Table* uses a ***foreign*** column and the *Related Table* has a ***primary*** column. The primary column is a ***key field***; it is data that appears only once in the table. The foreign column is the matching column; it holds data that can appear many times in the table.

> **MORE INFO**
>
> Relationships in the data model and *Power Query* follow database relationship logic and rules.

Excel will generally detect a relationship in the data model when field names are the same and have identical attributes (data type and size). When field names are different but have identical attributes, you can create a relationship. When no relationship is detected, review data types for the matching fields in the underlying tables; they must be exact matches. For some text fields, you may need to confirm that field sizes in the original data are identical.

HOW TO: Create a Relationship in the Data Model

1. Select a cell in the *PivotTable*.
2. Click the **Relationships** button [*PivotTable Tools Analyze* tab, *Calculations* group].
    - The *Manage Relationships* dialog box opens.
3. Click **New** to open the *Create Relationship* dialog box.
    - Click **Edit** to modify an existing relationship in the *Edit Relationship* dialog box.

4. Click the **Table** drop-down list and select the table name that includes the foreign key.
   - Select the table in which common field data appears many times.
   - Select a table from the data model when the list includes other queries or tables in the workbook.
5. Click the **Column (Foreign)** drop-down list and select the common field name.
   - The names of the primary and foreign fields need not match.
   - Data types must match.
6. Click the **Related Table** drop-down list and select the table name that includes the primary key.
   - Select the table in which common field data appears once.
7. Click the **Related Column (Primary)** drop-down list and select the common field name (Figure 10-35).

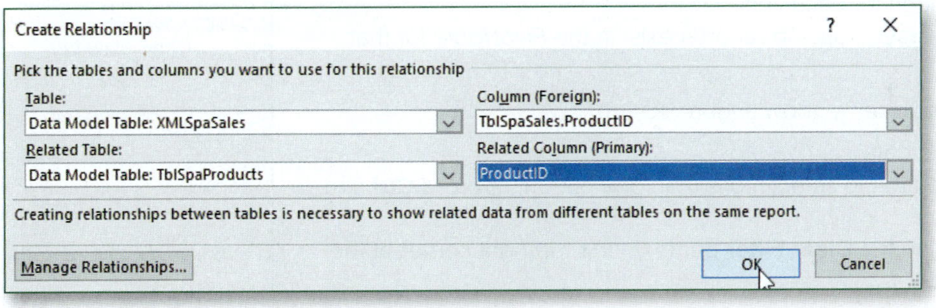

Figure 10-35 ***Create Relationships*** **dialog box**

8. Click **OK**.
   - The *PivotTable* updates the data.
   - The relationship is identified in the *Manage Relationships* dialog box.
9. Click **Close** in the *Manage Relationships* dialog box.
   - Data in the *PivotTable* is accurate when a relationship is valid.

SLO 10.7

Reviewing PivotTable Tools

PivotTables and *PivotCharts* have features that enable you to manage data for many reporting needs. These commands include timelines for date fields, values as ratios or percentages, and custom groupings.

PivotTable Slicers

The *Slicer* tool inserts a visual filter for a field in a *PivotTable*. For a *PivotTable* with thousands of records, a ***slicer*** enables you to display only the data you need at the moment. In the Paradise Lakes worksheet, for example, use a slicer to display items sold by one department at a time (Figure 10-36).

Create a slicer by clicking the **Insert Slicer** button in the *Filter* group on the *PivotTable Tools Analyze* tab. From the *Insert Slicers* dialog box, select fields to use as slicers. When you select multiple fields, each field displays in its own slicer window.

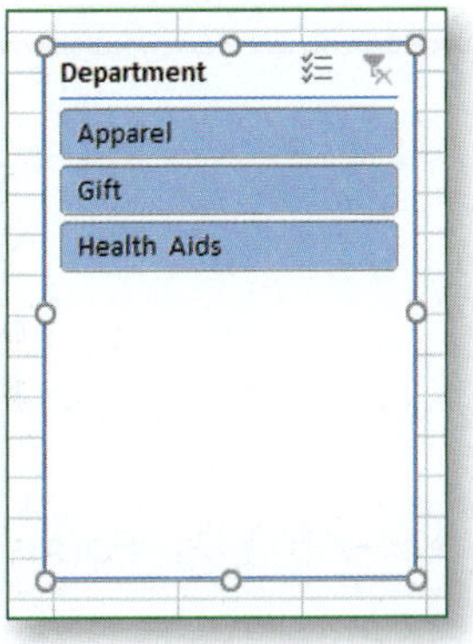

Figure 10-36 Slicer for the ***Department*** **field**

▸HOW TO: Insert a Slicer in a PivotTable

1. Click a cell in the *PivotTable*.
2. Click the **Insert Slicer** button [*PivotTable Tools Analyze* tab, *Filter* group].
   - The *Insert Slicers* window lists fields in the data model.
3. Select the box for each field to be used for filtering data (Figure 10-37).
   - Choose any field in the data model.
4. Click **OK**.
   - A *Slicer* window displays for each field.
   - The slicer displays a button for each item.
   - When a slicer button is grayed out, no records exist in the *PivotTable* for that item.
5. Click a button name in the *Slicer* window (Figure 10-38).
   - The *PivotTable* filters the data.
   - Click the **Multi-Select** button to select more than one button, or press **Ctrl** and click each button.
   - Remove a filter by clicking the **Clear Filter** button in the top-right corner of the slicer.

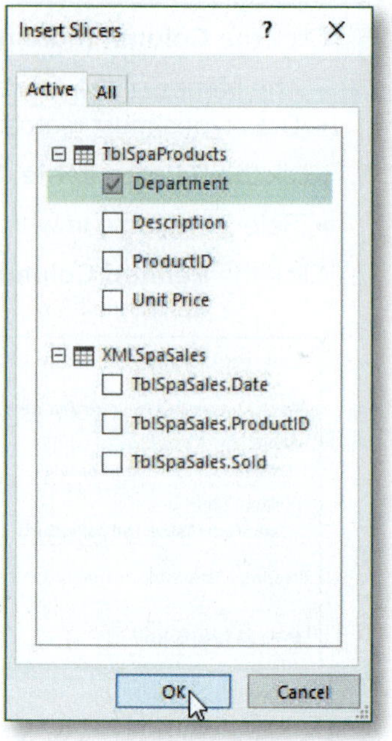

Figure 10-37 Choose one or more fields to use as slicers

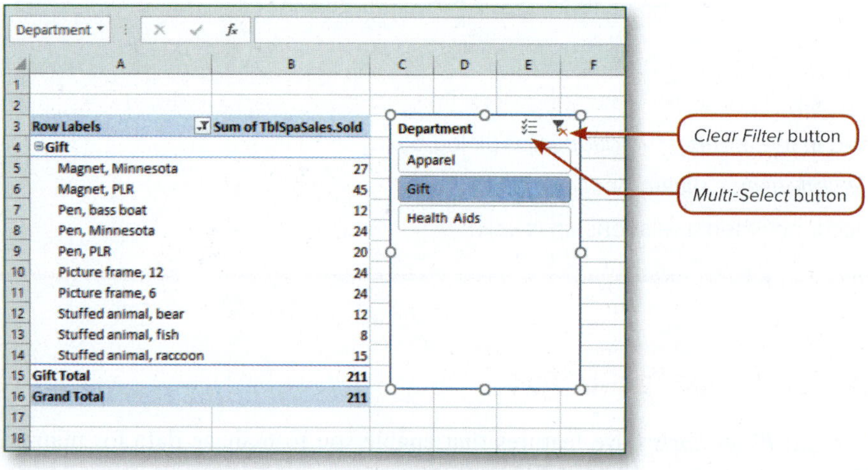

Figure 10-38 Slicer with filter

Slicer Tools Options

When a slicer window is selected, the *Slicer Tools Options* tab displays with commands to format the slicer, to change its caption, and more. A slicer is saved with the *PivotTable*. If you no longer need the slicer, select it and press **Delete** to remove it.

▸HOW TO: Format a PivotTable Slicer

1. Select the slicer.
2. Click the **More** button [*Slicer Tools Options* tab, *Slicer Styles* group].
3. Choose a style and click the icon in the gallery.
4. Click the **Columns** box [*Slicer Tools Options* tab, *Buttons* group] and type the number of columns.
   - Set a width and height for each button as desired [*Slicer Tools Options* tab, *Buttons* group].

5. Set a width and height for the slicer window.
   - Drag a border of the slicer to size it.
   - Type a width or height setting as desired [*Slicer Tools Options* tab, *Size* group].
6. Click the **Slicer Settings** button [*Slicer Tools Options* tab, *Slicer* group].
   - The *Slicer Settings* dialog box opens.
7. Click the **Caption** box and type a label for the slicer (Figure 10-39).
   - The *Name* box is the field name from the table.
8. Change the sort order of item names as desired.
   - Optionally, make choices about how to display item names in the slicer when there is no filtered data.
9. Click **OK**.

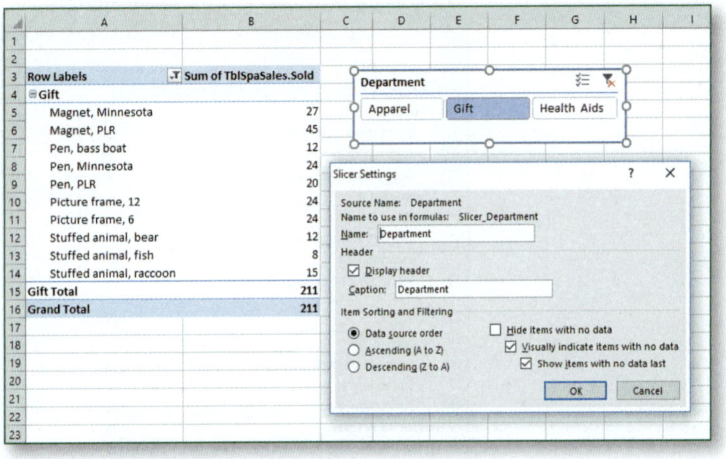

Figure 10-39 Slicer with three columns and *Slicer Settings* dialog box

Timelines

A ***timeline*** is a visual filter for a date field in a *PivotTable*. In a timeline, select days, months, quarters, or years for filtering. The *Insert Timeline* button is on the *PivotTable Tools Analyze* tab in the *Filter* group. The *Timeline Tools Options* tab appears when the timeline is selected. Timeline options include light and dark styles and height and width settings.

> **MORE INFO**
>
> You can insert a timeline for dates in an Excel table.

HOW TO: Insert and Format a Timeline in a PivotTable

1. Click a cell in the *PivotTable*.
   - The *PivotTable Tools Analyze* and *Design* tabs open.
2. Click the **Insert Timeline** button [*PivotTable Tools Analyze* tab, *Filter* group].
   - The *Insert Timelines* dialog box lists date fields in the data model.
   - Click the *All* tab to list fields from all tables.
3. Select the box for the timeline date field.
   - The date field need not display in the *PivotTable*.
   - The field must be formatted as a date.
4. Click **OK**.
   - The *Timeline* object displays with selection handles.
   - The *Timeline* displays months as the default time level.
5. Click the **Months** arrow and choose the time division as desired.
6. Click the specific time period in the timeline to filter the data.
   - The *PivotTable* displays rows based on the selected time period (Figure 10-40).

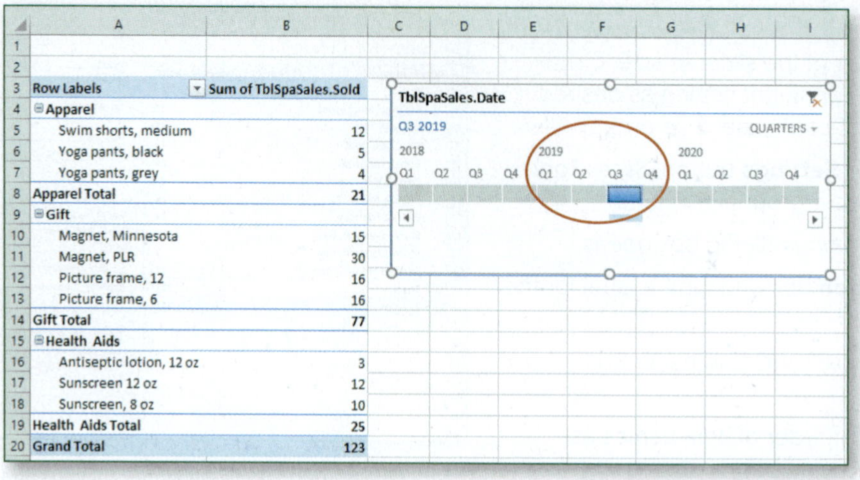

Figure 10-40 *Timeline* filter for Q3 in 2019

7. Click the **More** button [*Timeline Tools Options* tab, *Timeline Styles* group] and choose a style.
8. Point to a border to display a move pointer and drag the timeline to a new location.
9. Point to a corner handle to display a size arrow and resize the timeline.

Custom Calculations

A ***custom calculation*** displays a percentage, a ranking, or a ratio in a *PivotTable*. Custom calculations are listed in the *Value Field Settings* dialog box on the *Show Values As* tab. In Figure 10-41, the *Sold* field appears twice in the *PivotTable*, once as a value (column B) and once as a percentage of the total (column C). The field name is listed twice in the *Values* area in the *PivotTable Fields* pane.

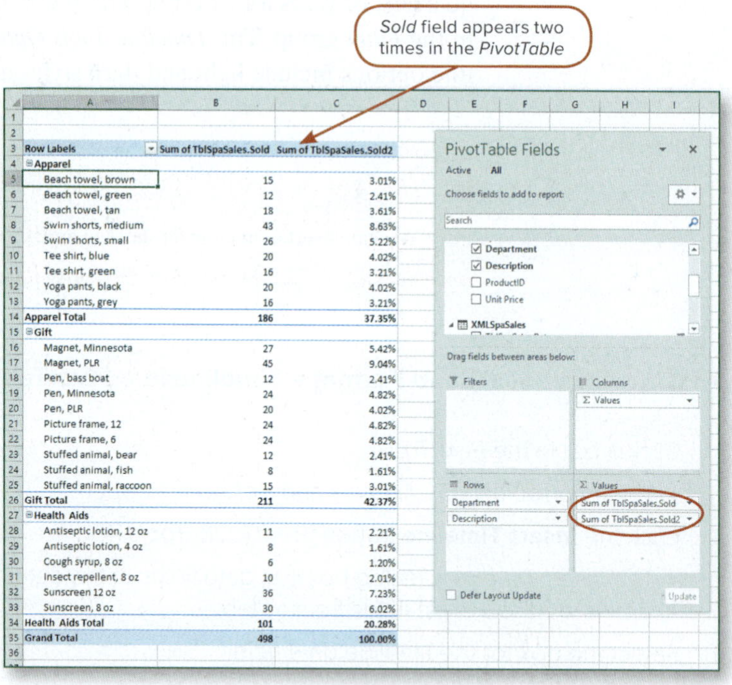

Figure 10-41 Value field displayed twice with different calculations

> **MORE INFO**
>
> You cannot insert a calculated field in a *PivotTable* that is based on a data model. Use *Power Query* to insert a custom column instead.

HOW TO: Use a Custom Calculation in a PivotTable

1. Right-click a value in the *PivotTable* column.
2. Select **Show Values As**.
   - The menu lists names of custom calculations.
   - *No Calculation* is the first option.
3. Choose a calculation (Figure 10-42).
   - The column in the *PivotTable* displays the calculation results.

ANOTHER WAY

Click a cell in the *PivotTable* column, click the **Field Settings** button [*PivotTable Tools Analyze* tab, *Active Field* group], and click the **Show Value As** tab to use a custom calculation.

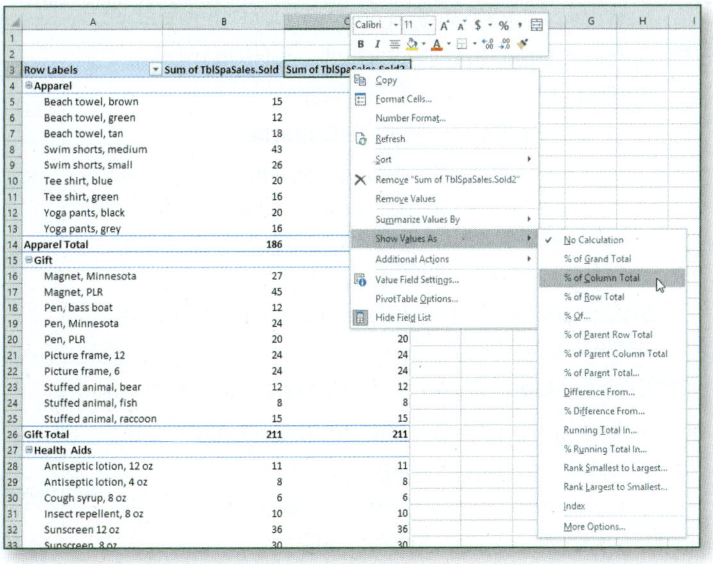

Figure 10-42 Choose a custom calculation

Named Sets in a PivotTable

A ***named set*** is a custom collection of items from a column or a row. A named set enables you to view data in ways that are otherwise not possible. Consider the *PLR Spa Products* query that lists all products in each of three departments. When you pivot the data to show one department, the *PivotTable* displays all products in that department. In a named set, however, you can create a subset of the products in the department. Results displayed by a named set are often referred to as asymmetric reports.

MORE INFO

Named sets use Multidimensional Expressions (MDX), a query language. Learn more about this language from *Microsoft Docs* and other online tutorials to build and edit custom named sets.

Named sets are available in a *PivotTable* that is based on a data model. The set name appears in a new *Sets* category in the *PivotTable Fields* pane. When you place the set in the *PivotTable*, it replaces the rows or columns on which the set is based. Undo the command to return to the original *PivotTable* layout.

HOW TO: Create and Display a Named Set

1. Click a cell in the *PivotTable*.
   - The *PivotTable* must be based on the workbook data model.
2. Click the **Fields, Items, & Sets** button [*PivotTable Tools Analyze* tab, *Calculations* group].
   - Menu command names that are dimmed are not available.
3. Select **Create Set Based on Row Items** or **Create Set Based on Column Items**.
   - The *New Set (ThisWorkbookDataModel)* dialog box displays.
   - Row or column items are listed.

4. Click the **Set name** box and type a name for the data set.
   - Use a name that describes the data grouping.
   - Type a folder name to create a custom folder in the *Sets* group in the *PivotTable Fields* pane.
5. Select an item that should not display in the named set.
6. Click **Delete Row** or **Delete Column**.
   - A named set that removes a few items is easier to create than one that removes many items.
   - Alternatively, press **Delete** on the keyboard to delete a row or column.
7. Select and remove rows or columns to create the desired grouping.
8. Click the **Up** or **Down** arrow to move items in the list.
   - Arrange the items in the desired display order.
9. Deselect the box for *Replace the fields currently in the row area with the new set* (Figure 10-43).
   - When this box is selected, the set automatically displays in the *PivotTable*.

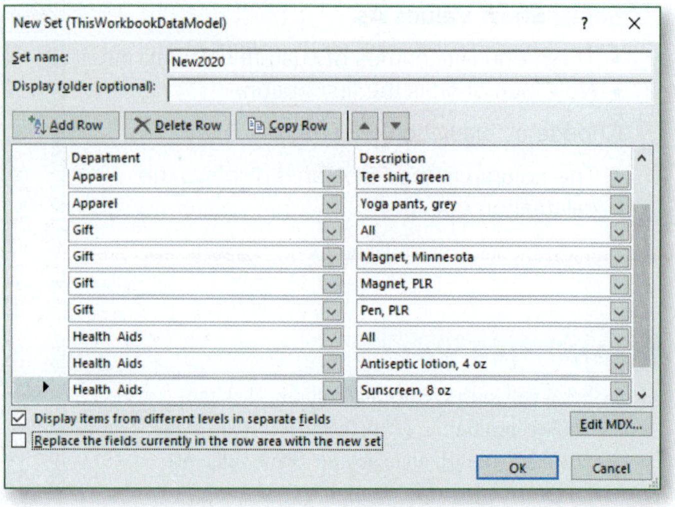

Figure 10-43 ***New Set*** **dialog box**

10. Click **OK**.
    - The *Sets* group displays at the top of the *PivotTable Fields* pane.
11. Expand the *Sets* folder and select the box for the named set.
    - A message box informs you that the set will replace current fields in the *PivotTable* (Figure 10-44).

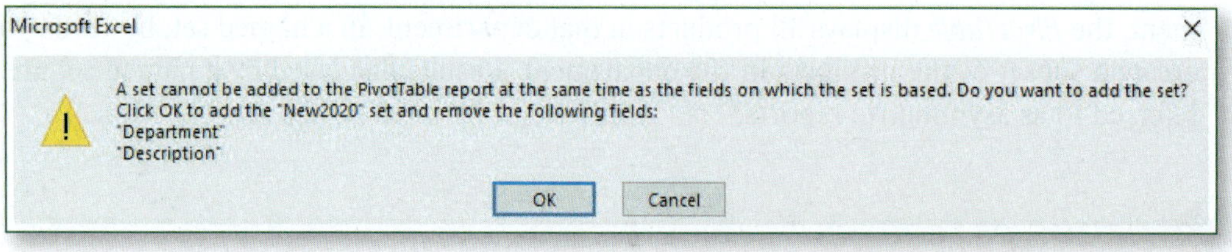

Figure 10-44 Message box that set replaces fields

12. Click **OK**.
    - The new grouping displays and replaces the previous data (Figure 10-45).
    - You cannot apply filtering or sorting to the set.
13. Click the **Undo** button [*Quick Access* toolbar] to unpivot the data.

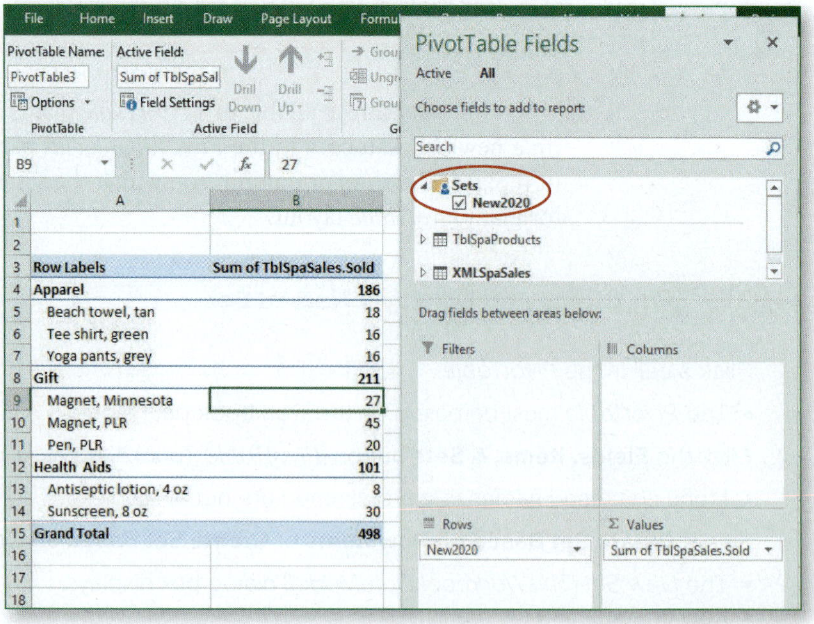

Figure 10-45 Named set displayed in *PivotTable*

GETPIVOTDATA

Use the *GETPIVOTDATA* function from the *Lookup & Reference* category to identify specific results in a *PivotTable*, regardless of cell location. When you refer to a value in a *PivotTable* in another worksheet, you cannot simply insert a 3D reference to the target cell. If the *PivotTable* is rearranged, that cell content may display in a different cell in the *PivotTable*. *GETPIVOTDATA* displays results from the original *PivotTable* layout as long as that result is still somewhere in the pivoted version.

> **MORE INFO**
>
> When the original data referenced in *GETPIVOTDATA* is no longer displayed in the *PivotTable*, the function returns the error message #REF!

The syntax for *GETPIVOTDATA* is:

=GETPIVOTDATA(Data_field,Pivot_table,Field,Item)

The function is created automatically with required arguments when you enter a 3D reference to the cell in the *PivotTable* in the dependent sheet or workbook.

HOW TO: Use GETPIVOTDATA

1. Select the cell where the *PivotTable* result should display.
   - This cell is not on the same sheet as the *PivotTable*.
   - Open the workbook with the *PivotTable* if necessary.
2. Type = to start a formula.
3. Select the workbook and tab name with the *PivotTable*.
4. Select the *PivotTable* cell with the desired result.
5. Press **Enter** (Figure 10-46).
   - The *GETPIVOTDATA* formula is a 3D reference to the *PivotTable*.
   - The result from the *PivotTable* appears in the cell.

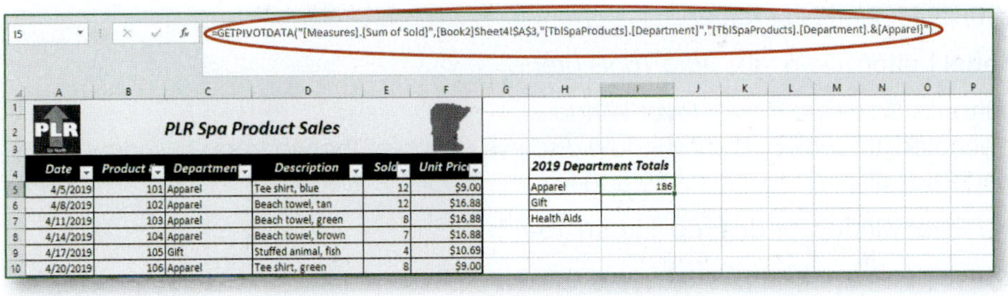

Figure 10-46 ***GETPIVOTDATA*** **inserted in the cell**

6. Return to the workbook and sheet with the *PivotTable*.
7. Pivot the table to a different arrangement as desired.
   - The result used in the *GETPIVOTDATA* formula must display somewhere in the rearranged *PivotTable*.
8. Return to the worksheet with the *GETPIVOTDATA* formula.
   - *GETPIVOTDATA* returns the same result.

SLO 10.8

Exploring Power Pivot

When you use an Excel table or query as the basis for a *PivotTable*, you are limited to 1,048,576 records, the current maximum number of rows in a worksheet. For massive data analysis in a *PivotTable*, explore the *Power Pivot* add-in for Excel.

Power Pivot

Power Pivot enables you to use millions of records in the data model for a *PivotTable*. *Power Pivot* is a COM add-in, a compiled application. It is a memory-based database that connects to local, network, or cloud services and sites to access data from public, government, and private sources.

Power Pivot is available for most versions of Excel. Install it from the *Add-Ins* dialog box [Excel *Options*] or by clicking the **Manage Data Model** button [*Data* tab, *Data Tools* group]. After you have activated the add-in, the *Power Pivot* command tab displays in the Excel *Ribbon*.

View the Data Model in Power Pivot

Power Pivot operates in a separate window. Data in a *Power Pivot* table resembles an Excel worksheet, but you cannot edit data in *Power Pivot*. The *Power Pivot* table is simply a view of the data which is maintained at its source. *Power Pivot's* primary purpose is access to large datasets, but you can use *Power Pivot* to view the data model in an Excel workbook.

> **ANOTHER WAY**
>
> Click the **Manage** button in the *Data Model* group on the *Power Pivot* command tab to launch *Power Pivot*.

HOW TO: View the Data Model in Power Pivot

1. Open the Excel workbook with a data model.
   - This workbook includes multiple queries or tables.
2. Click the **Manage Data Model** button [*Data* tab, *Data Tools* group].
   - The *ScreenTip* for the button is *Go to the Power Pivot Window*.
   - If *Power Pivot* has been enabled, the *Power Pivot* window displays on top of the workbook window.
   - Click **Enable** if the message box displays to install the add-in.
3. Size and position the *Power Pivot* window as desired (Figure 10-47).
   - The *Power Pivot Ribbon* includes *File*, *Home*, *Design*, and *Advanced* tabs.
4. Click a sheet tab name in the *Power Pivot* window.
   - Each data source in the Excel workbook displays on its own tab.
5. Click the **Manage Relationships** button [*Design* tab, *Relationships* group].
   - The *Manage Relationships* dialog box displays relationships created in the workbook.
6. Select an active relationship and click **Edit**.
   - The *Edit Relationship* dialog box shows details about the connection between the tables or queries (Figure 10-48).

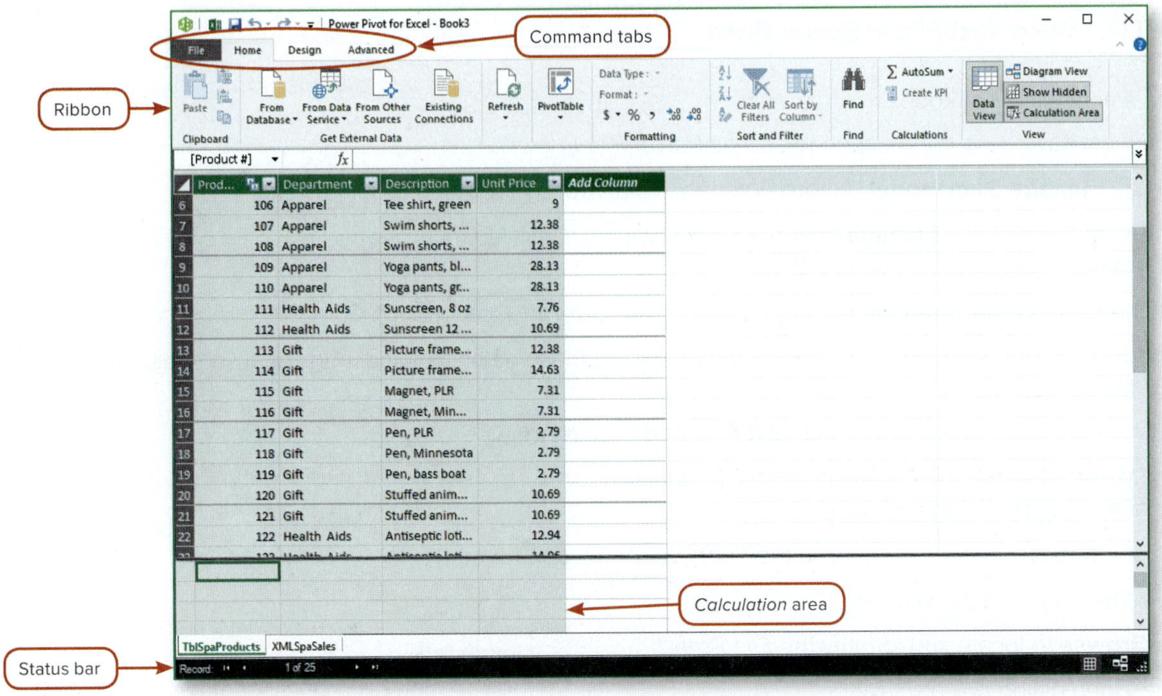

Figure 10-47 The *Power Pivot* window with a data model

7. Click **Cancel** to close the *Edit Relationship* dialog box.
8. Click **Close** to close the *Manage Relationships* dialog box.
9. Click the **File** tab and choose **Close**.
   - The *Power Pivot* window closes, and the Excel workbook displays.
   - Click the **Switch to Workbook** button in the *Power Pivot* title bar to leave *Power Pivot* open for continued work.

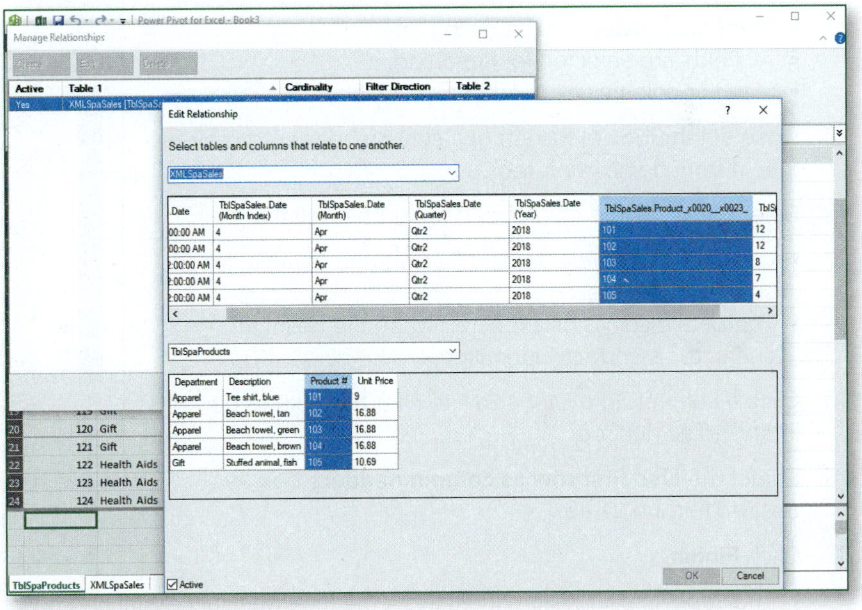

Figure 10-48 Relationships in *Power Pivot*

Get a Text File in Power Pivot

Source data types for *Power Pivot* include relational database systems such as Microsoft SQL Server and Oracle, data feeds, and online services or platforms. You can learn the basics of getting data into *Power Pivot*, however, with a text file.

> **MORE INFO**
>
> A text file is a flat file, just rows of data.

▸ HOW TO: Get a Text File in Power Pivot

1. Open a new Excel workbook.
   - You must have a workbook open to access *Power Pivot*.
2. Click the **Manage Data Model** button [*Data* tab, *Data Tools* group].
   - Alternatively, click the **Manage** button [*Power Pivot* tab, *Data Model* group].
   - The *Power Pivot* window opens with no data.
3. Click the **From Other Sources** button [*Home* tab, *Get External Data* group].
   - The *Table Import Wizard* dialog box lists relational database names, multidimensional sources, data feeds, and text file categories.
4. Scroll to the bottom of the list, select **Text File**, and click **Next**.
   - The wizard displays the *Connect to Flat File* options.
   - A flat file is a single table of data.
5. Type an optional connection name in the *Friendly connection name* box.
   - Use the default name as desired.
6. Click **Browse** to locate and identify the *File Path*.
   - The *Open* dialog box displays.
7. Navigate to and select the file name and click **Open**.
   - The data previews in the dialog box.
   - All fields are selected for importing.
   - Size the columns as needed to view the data.
8. Deselect the box to the left of a column header to prevent a field from being imported.
9. Select or verify the column separator (the delimiter).
   - Common separators for text files are the comma, tab, or space characters.
   - The data displays as expected when the delimiter character is correctly identified.
10. Click a column *AutoFilter* arrow to filter the data to be imported as desired.
11. Select the **Use first row as column headers** box as desired (Figure 10-49).

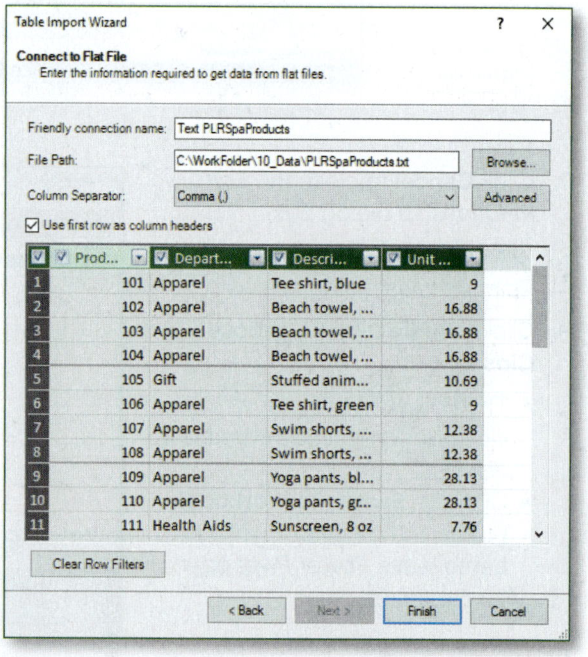

Figure 10-49 Get text data for a *Power Pivot* table

12. Click **Finish**.
    - The *Table Import Wizard* indicates if the task was successful and how many rows were imported.
13. Click **Close** in the *Table Import Wizard*.
    - The table displays in the *Power Pivot* window on a worksheet tab.
    - A *Power Pivot* table does not display column letters.

MORE INFO

For sources with millions of rows, filter data in the *Import Data* dialog box before you import it in *Power Pivot*.

Create a Relationship in Power Pivot

A data model requires a relationship between the sources. The common fields need not have the same name, but your work is easier when they do. The common fields must have the same data type and size (when size is specified in the data sources).

HOW TO: Create a Relationship in Power Pivot

1. Import the data sources in *Power Pivot*.
2. Click the **Create Relationship** button [*Design* tab, *Relationships* group].
   - The active table or query data displays.
3. Click the top drop-down list and select a table or query name.
4. Click the column that is the common field.
   - Follow the same logic as when defining a relationship in Excel.
5. Click the bottom drop-down list and select the related table or query name.
6. Click the column that is the common field.
7. Click **OK**.
8. Click the tab name for one of the related tables.
   - The data displays.
9. Point to the column heading for the common field.
   - The *ScreenTip* defines the existing relationship (Figure 10-50).
10. Click the **Diagram View** button [*Home* tab, *View* group].
    - Tables or queries display in boxes.
    - Alternatively, click the **Diagram** button at the right side of the *Status bar*.
    - The relationship shows as a line (Figure 10-51).
11. Click the **Data View** button [*Home* tab, *View* group].
    - Click the **Grid** button at the right side of the *Status bar*.

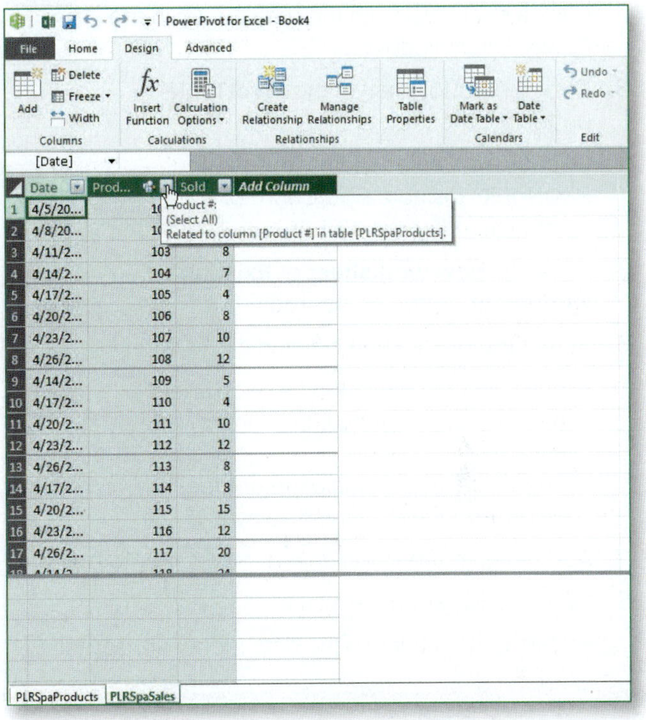

Figure 10-50 Relationship *ScreenTip* in *Power Pivot*

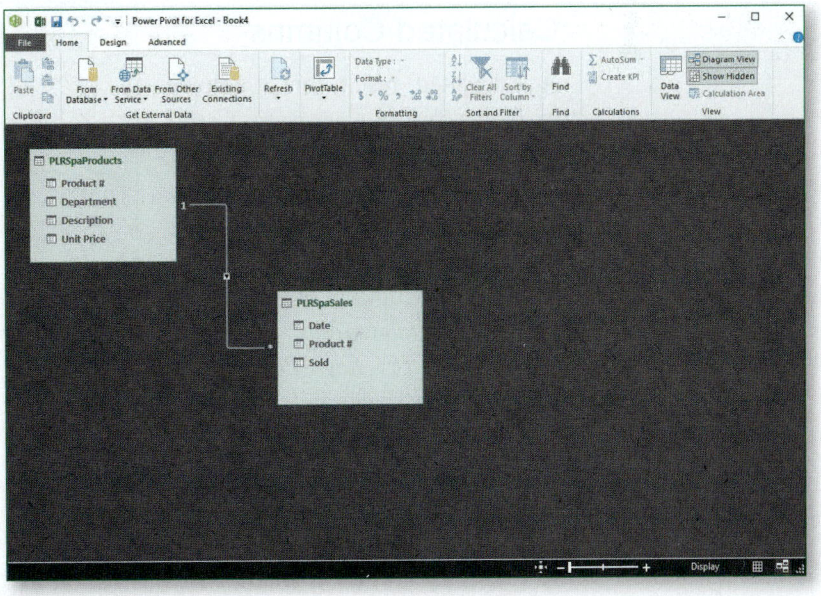

Figure 10-51 Relationship in *Diagram View*

Create a PivotTable from Power Pivot Data

Power Pivot tables do not display in Excel, but you can create a *PivotTable* that displays in Excel. The *PivotTable* button [*Home* tab] lists options for creating a single *PivotTable*, a *PivotTable* and *PivotChart*, or other combinations.

▸HOW TO: Create a PivotTable in Power Pivot

1. Import the data sources in *Power Pivot* and create the relationship.
2. Click a sheet tab from the data model in the *Power Pivot* window.
3. Click the bottom half of the **PivotTable** button [*Home* tab].
4. Choose a command to build a single *PivotTable*, a single *PivotChart*, or a combination (Figure 10-52).
5. Click the **New worksheet** or **Existing worksheet** button as desired.
6. Select the destination cell and click **OK**.
   - Blank layouts display in the worksheet based on your menu choice in *Power Pivot*.
   - The *PivotTable Fields* pane or the *PivotChart Fields* pane displays.
7. Add fields to the *PivotTable* or *PivotChart* to build the layout.
8. Save the workbook as usual.
   - Data connections to the data model are saved.

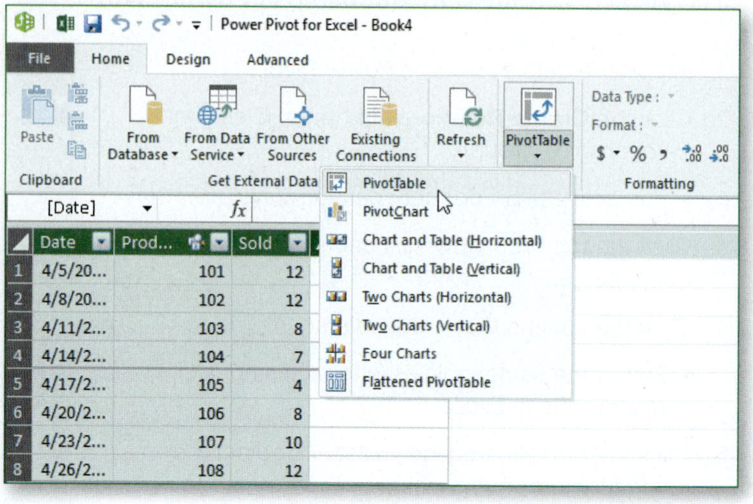

Figure 10-52 *PivotTable* **options in** *Power Pivot*

Measures, KPIs, and Calculated Columns

A calculated result for a column in *Power Pivot* is a ***measure***. Create a measure by selecting a column, clicking the **AutoSum** arrow [*Home* tab, *Calculations* group], and selecting a function name. The measure appears at the bottom of the column in the *Calculations* area.

A ***KPI*** or ***Key Performance Indicator*** is a visual representation for a column that has a measure. KPIs are only available for measures and might be compared to conditional formatting in Excel (Figure 10-53). KPIs display in the *PivotTable Fields* list pane and are placed in the *PivotTable* like other fields.

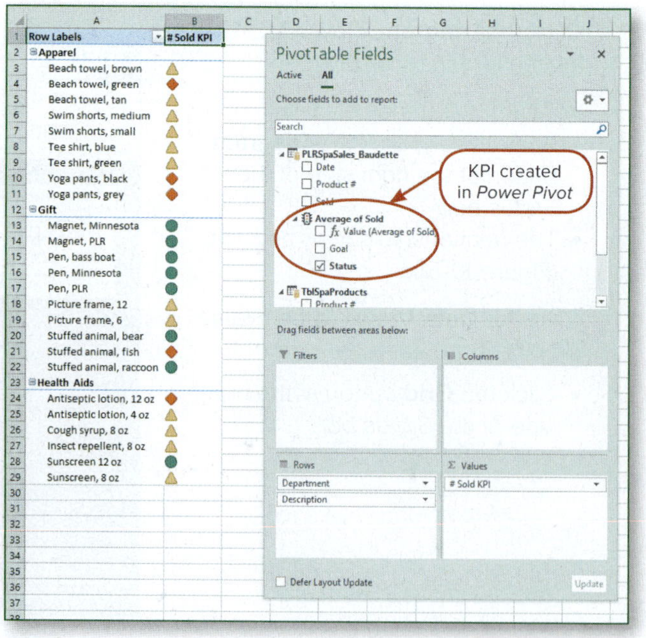

Figure 10-53 KPI in a *PivotTable*

Create a calculated column in *Power Pivot* by typing a simple formula in the *Formula bar*. The *Insert Function* button [*Home* tab, *Calculations* group] lists DAX function names (Data Analysis Expressions). DAX formulas are like Excel functions but may use different syntax or assumptions. Experiment with these functions as you develop your skills with *Power Pivot*.

Remove the Power Pivot Add-In

Remove the *Power Pivot* add-in when desired. Select **COM Add-ins** from the *Manage* button in the Excel *Options* dialog box. Then deselect the *Power Pivot* box and click **OK**.

PAUSE & PRACTICE: EXCEL 10-3

For this project, you use the data model as the source for a *PivotTable*. You also insert the *GETPIVOTDATA* function in a separate workbook to extract data from your *PivotTable*.

Files Needed: ***ParadiseLakes-10.xlsx*** and ***Database-10.accdb*** *(Student data files are available in the* Library *of your SIMnet account.)*
Completed Project File Names: ***[your initials] PP E10-3a.xlsx*** and ***[your initials] PP E10-3b.xlsx***

1. Create a new workbook and save it as [your initials] PP E10-3a.
2. Get data from an Access database file.
   a. Click the **Get Data** button [*Data* tab, *Get & Transform Data* group] and choose **From Database**.
   b. Choose **From Microsoft Access Database**.
   c. Navigate to the folder with the ***Database-10*** file from your student data files.
   d. Select the **Database-10** name and click **Import**.
   e. Select **TblSpaProducts** in the *Navigator* window.
   f. Click the **Load** arrow and select **Load To**.
   g. Import the data as a table on the **Existing worksheet** in cell **A1**.
   h. Rename the query results sheet as Spa Products.
   i. Get **TblSpaSales** from the ***Database-10*** file and load it to a **New worksheet** in your workbook.
   j. Rename the results sheet as Spa Sales.
3. Create a *PivotTable* from two queries.
   a. Select cell **A2** in the table on the **Spa Products** sheet.
   b. Click the **Summarize with PivotTable** button [*Table Tools Design* tab, *Tools* group].
   c. Select the **New Worksheet** radio button.
   d. Select the **Add this data to the Data Model** box and click **OK**.
   e. Close the *Queries & Connections* pane.
   f. Select the boxes for the **Department** and **Description** fields In the *PivotTable Fields* pane.
   g. Click **All** at the top of the *PivotTable Fields* pane.
   h. Select **TblSpaSales** to expand the field list and select the **Sold** box.
   i. Click **AutoDetect** in the warning box to create a relationship between the tables.
   j. Click **Close** in the *Auto-Detect Relationships* dialog box (Figure 10-54).
   k. Rename the sheet as Timeline.
4. Format a *PivotTable*.
   a. Click a cell in the *PivotTable*.
   b. Click the **More** button [*PivotTable Tools Design* tab, *PivotTable Styles* group] and select **White, Pivot Style Medium 8**.

c. Click the **Grand Totals** button [*PivotTable Tools Design* tab, *Layout* group] and select **On for Columns Only**.

d. Click the **Subtotals** button [*PivotTable Tools Design* tab, *Layout* group] and choose **Show all Subtotals at Bottom of Group**.

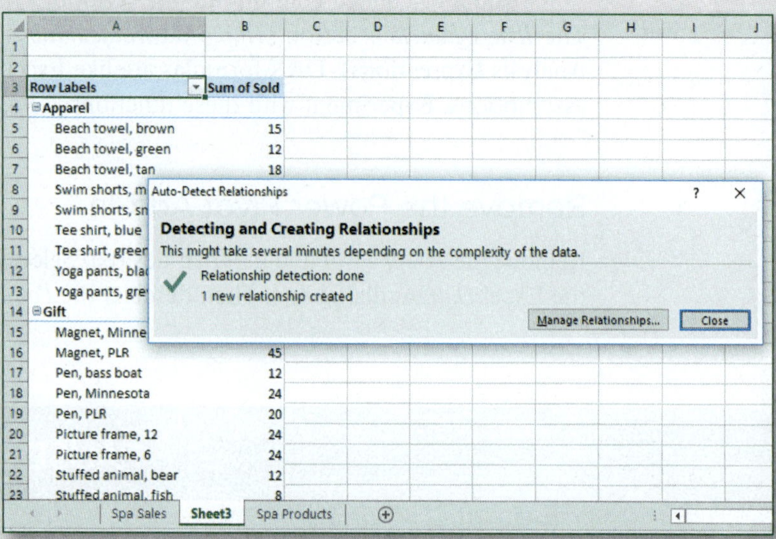

Figure 10-54 *PivotTable* created from the data model

5. Insert a timeline for a *PivotTable*.
   a. Click a cell in the *PivotTable* and click the **Insert Timeline** button [*PivotTable Tools Analyze* tab, *Filter* group].
   b. Select the **Date** box from **TblSpaSales** and click **OK**.
   c. Click the **Months** button in the timeline and select **Quarters**.
   d. Click **Q3** for 2019 in the timeline.
   e. Click the **More** button [*Timeline Tools Options* tab, *Timeline Styles* group].
   f. Find and select **Light Gray, Timeline Style Dark 3** in the gallery.
   g. Position the timeline with its top-left corner in cell **D3** (Figure 10-55).

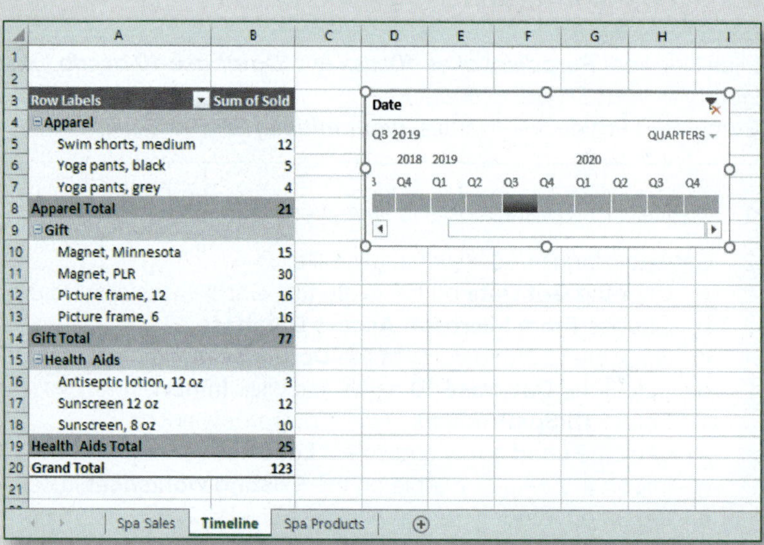

Figure 10-55 Timeline filters the data by quarter

6. Select cell **A1**, save the workbook, and leave it open.
7. Use *GETPIVOTDATA* to display results from a *PivotTable*.
   a. Open the ***ParadiseLakes-10*** workbook from your student data files and save it as [your initials] PP E10-3b.
   b. Click the **2019-2020** tab and select cell **I5**.
   c. Type = to start the formula.
   d. Switch to the ***[your initials] PP E10-3a*** workbook, click the **Timeline** sheet tab, select cell **B8**, and press **Enter**. Results displays in cell **I5**.
   e. Select cell **E5** and review the formula syntax in the *Formula* bar.
   f. Select cell **I6** and use *GETPIVOTDATA* to display the total for the *Gift* department.
   g. Select cell **I7** and use *GETPIVOTDATA* (Figure 10-56).
8. Pivot data in a *PivotTable*.
   a. Switch to the ***[your initials] PP E10-3a*** workbook, select the **Timeline** tab, and click a cell in the *PivotTable*.
   b. Drag the *Department* field name in the *Rows* area of the *PivotTable Fields* pane into the *Columns* area. The *PivotTable* is pivoted (Figure 10-57).

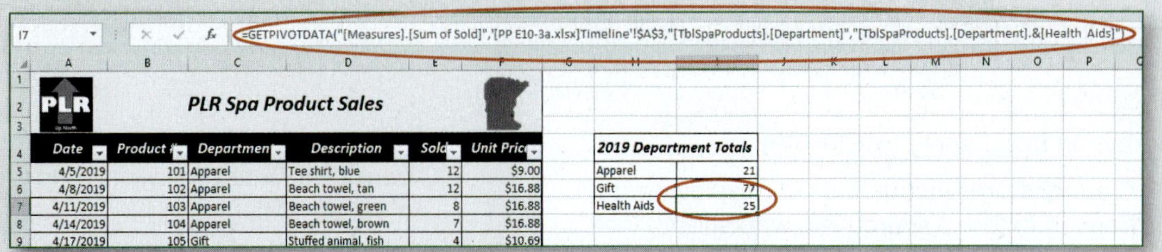

Figure 10-56 *GETPIVOTDATA* displays results from the *PivotTable*

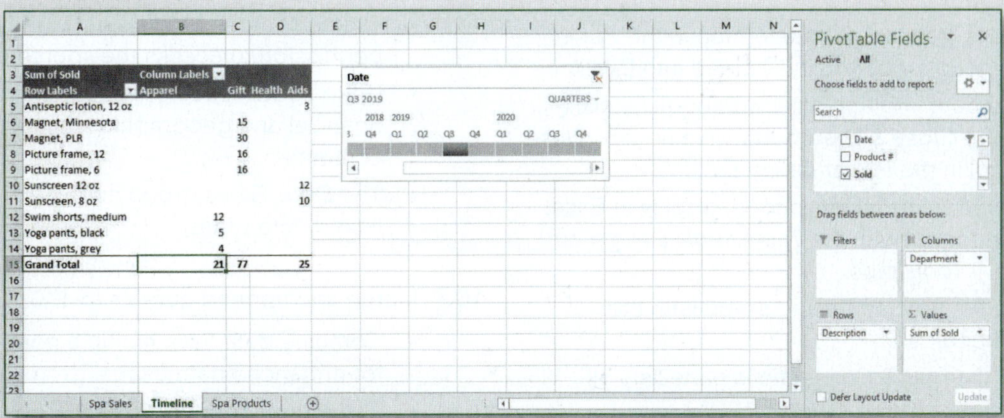

Figure 10-57 Data is pivoted

c. Reposition the timeline as needed.
d. Return to the ***[your initials] PP E10-3b*** workbook. *GETPIVOTDATA* shows the same results even though the content at the original cell locations in the *PivotTable* has changed.

9. Save and close both workbooks.

Chapter Summary

10.1 Create an Excel query (p. E10-619).

- A ***query*** stores instructions for displaying data from an external source in a worksheet.
- The *Power Query Editor* launches from commands in the *Get External Data* group on the *Data* tab.
- Data is cleaned or transformed in the *Power Query Editor* before it is loaded into Excel.
- Load data into the Excel workbook by clicking the **Close & Load** button [*Home* tab, *Close* group] in the *Power Query Editor.*
- Query results, when loaded, display in Excel table format with the *Table Tools Design* and *Query Tools* tabs.
- Queries are named and saved with the workbook.
- The *Queries & Connections* pane lists all queries in the workbook.
- Point at the query name in the *Queries & Connections* pane and click **Delete** in the pop-up information window to remove a query.

10.2 Edit a query in *Power Query* (p. E10-621).

- ***Power Query*** enables you to transform data, but you cannot edit the data content.
- The *Power Query* window floats on top of the worksheet with its own *Ribbon,* the *Query Settings* pane, and a *Navigator* pane to display available queries.
- The ***Power Query Editor*** has a *Formula bar* to display its M language formulas.
- The *Query Settings* pane lists each step or action that you perform in a query.
- Undo steps by pointing to a task name in the *Applied Steps* list and clicking its red X.
- Name the query or edit other properties in the *Query Settings* pane.
- Set the data type, remove columns, add or split columns, and replace values in the *Power Query Editor.*

10.3 Use external data sources (p. E10-623).

- External data comes from public and private databases, cloud services, data feeds, and social media sites.
- An ***XML*** file is a text file in *Extensible Markup Language* with an .xml file name extension.
- Click the **Get Data** button [*Data* tab, *Get & Transform Data* group] and choose **From File** to get an XML file.
- Get data from a Microsoft Access database or other database by clicking the **Get Data** button [*Data* tab, *Get & Transform Data* group].
- Online sources provide data when you have permission to access the source.
- Linked ***data types*** connect to and extract financial and geographic statistics for cell contents.
- The *Data Types* group on the *Data* tab creates linked data types.

10.4 Merge and append queries (p. E10-630).

- Combine data from multiple queries or tables for enhanced data usage.
- The ***Merge*** and the ***Append*** commands are available on the *Query Tools* tab [*Combine* group].
- Use the *Append* command to add one table to another when both tables have the same fields.
- Use the *Merge* command to combine different fields from multiple tables when there is a common field in both tables.
- A ***common*** field is data that is the same in both queries; it is a ***key*** field when each data piece appears once in the query.
- The common field is the basis for a relationship or a "***join***" between the queries.
- View relationships in a query by clicking the **View Dependencies** button [*View* tab, *Dependencies* group] in *Power Query.*

10.5 Manipulate data in a query (p. E10-633).

- A ***conditional column*** uses an *IF* statement to display new data in a query.
- Use ***Column From Examples*** to insert a column in a query based on sample data typed in the query.
- A column from examples uses one or more existing columns as the basis for a new column.
- A ***custom column*** in *Power Query* uses M language formulas to generate data.

- M language formulas follow SQL (structured query language) protocol and are different from Excel formulas.
- Data in a conditional column, a column from examples, or a custom column are not fields in the source data, but the columns can be refreshed.
- The ***Group By*** command in *Power Query* organizes rows by category to summarize data.
- Business intelligence applications such as *Power Query* provide improved handling of data and are constantly evolving.

10.6 Work with the Excel data model (p. E10-643).

- A ***data model*** is the collection of tables and queries in a workbook.
- Excel builds a data model when you select the option to add imported data to the data model in the *Create PivotTable* dialog box.
- A common field must be present in each query or table used in the *PivotTable.*
- The ***foreign*** column is a common field in which data can appear many times in the table. The ***key field*** is the ***primary*** column and data can display only once in the table.
- Click the **Relationships** button [*PivotTable Tools Analyze* tab, *Calculations* group] to identify the common field.

10.7 Review *PivotTable* tools (p. E10-645).

- A ***slicer*** is a visual filter for a *PivotTable,* a small window that floats on the sheet.
- A ***timeline*** is a visual filter for a date field in a *PivotTable.*
- The *Insert Slicer* and *Insert Timeline* buttons are in the *Filter* group on the *PivotTable Tools Analyze* tab.
- Slicers and timelines are objects that can be positioned, sized, and formatted.
- A ***custom calculation*** is a built-in percentage, ranking, or ratio.
- Create a ***named set*** in a *PivotTable* to save a custom grouping or subset of items.
- Named sets are available in a *PivotTable* that is based on the data model.
- The *GETPIVOTDATA* function displays results from a cell in a *PivotTable.*

10.8 Explore *Power Pivot* (p. E10-652).

- Use the ***Power Pivot*** add-in to import data from private and public database services as well as from text files or Excel workbooks.
- *Power Pivot* depicts the data model for a *PivotTable.*
- *Power Pivot* tables do not display in Excel; they are underlying data for a *PivotTable* in Excel.
- A *Power Pivot* table resembles an Excel worksheet but is not limited in the number of records that can be analyzed.
- Create a relationship between tables in *Power Pivot* before creating the *PivotTable.*
- A ***measure*** in *Power Pivot* is a calculation for a column.
- A ***KPI*** is a ***Key Performance Indicator*** which depicts how a value compares to a measure.
- Create a calculated column in *Power Pivot* by typing a formula in the *Formula bar.*

Check for Understanding

The SIMbook for this text (within your SIMnet account) provides the following resources for concept review:

- Multiple-choice questions
- Short answer questions
- Matching exercises

Guided Project 10-1

Wear-Ever Shoes keeps inventory and sales data in different formats. You get an Access table and Excel data to create a *PivotTable* that relates customer satisfaction and cost.
[Student Learning Outcomes 10.1, 10.2, 10.3, 10.5, 10.6, 10.7, 10.8]

Files Needed: ***WearEverShoes-10.xlsx*** and ***Database-10.accdb*** *(Student data files are available in the* Library *of your SIMnet account.)*
Completed Project File Name: ***[your initials] Excel 10-1.xlsx***

Skills Covered in This Project

- Get data from a workbook.
- Manipulate data in *Power Query*.
- Get data in *Power Pivot* from Microsoft Access.
- Create a measure and a KPI in a *Power Pivot* table.
- Use the data model to create a *PivotTable*.
- Create and format a *PivotTable*.
- Insert a slicer in a *PivotTable*.

---

1. Create a new workbook and save it as [your initials] Excel 10-1.
2. Get data from a workbook.
   a. Click the **Get Data** button [*Data* tab, *Get & Transform* group] and choose **From File**.
   b. Select **From Workbook** and navigate to and select the ***WearEverShoes-10*** workbook from your student data files.
   c. Click **Import** and select **InventoryTable** in the *Navigator* window.
   d. Click **Transform Data** (or **Edit**) to open *Power Query*.
3. Transform data in the *Power Query Editor*.
   a. Click the **Quantity** column header to select the column.
   b. Press **Ctrl** and click the **Men's or Women's** and the **Cost** column headers so that three columns are selected.
   c. Click the **Remove Columns** button [*Home* tab, *Manage Columns* group].
   d. Click the **Retail** column header, click the **Data Type** button [*Home* tab, *Transform Data* group] and choose **Currency** (Figure 10-58).
4. Load data to Excel.
   a. Click the **Close & Load** button [*Home* tab, *Close* group].
   b. Name the worksheet tab Workbook Data.
   c. Select the **Sheet1** tab.
5. Get data in a *Power Pivot* table.
   a. Click the **Manage Data Model** button [*Data* tab, *Data Tools* group] to start *Power Pivot*. (Click **Enable** if prompted to load the add-in).
   b. Click the **From Database** button [*Home* tab, *Get External Data* group] in the *Power Pivot* window and select **From Access**.
   c. Click **Browse**, navigate to and select **Database-10** from your student data files, and click **Open**.

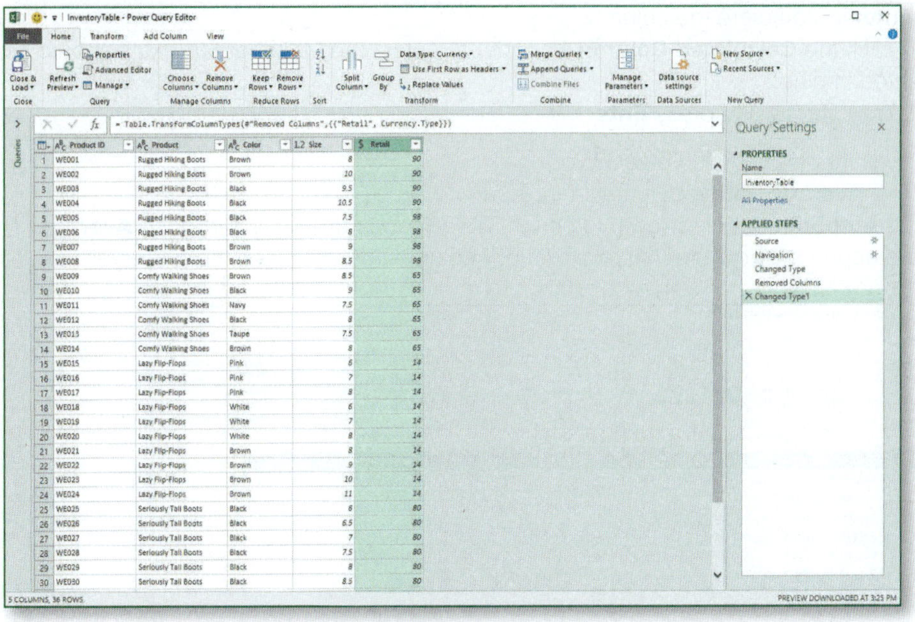

Figure 10-58 Data ready for loading from *Power Query*

d. Click **Next** in the *Table Import Wizard* dialog box.
e. Verify or choose the **Select from a list of tables and views to choose the data to import** button and click **Next**.
f. Select the box for **TblWearEver** and click **Finish**.
g. Click **Close** in the *Success* box.

6. Create a calculated column in *Power Pivot*.
   a. Click the first blank cell below the *Add Column* header.
   b. Type =(to start a formula and insert the left parenthesis in the *Formula bar*.
   c. Click the first value in the "Comfort" column to insert its reference in the formula.
   d. Type + for addition.
   e. Click the first value in the "Fit" column and type + for addition.
   f. Click the first value in the "Style" column, type +, and click the first value in the "Value" column (Figure 10-59).

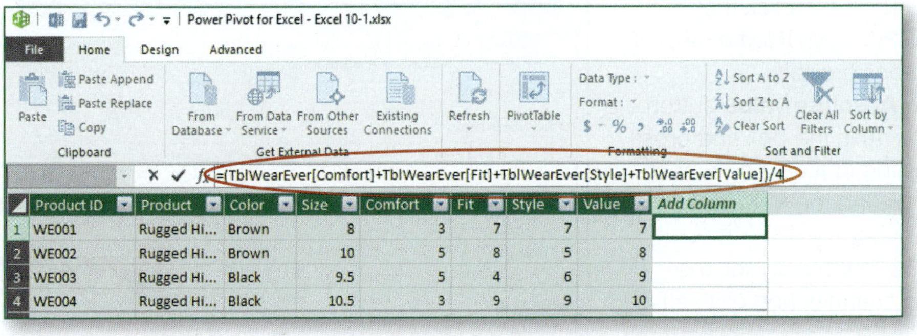

Figure 10-59 Insert a calculated column in *Power Pivot*

   g. Type)/4 to insert the closing parenthesis, a division symbol, and "4" to calculate an average of the four characteristics. Here is the DAX expression:

   =(TblWearEver[Comfort]+TblWearEver[Fit]+TblWearEver[Style]+TblWearEver[Value])/4

h. Press **Enter** to complete the column.

i. Double-click the **Calculated Column 1** header to select the placeholder text; it should be highlighted in blue.

j. Type Average Rating and press **Enter**.

7. Create a measure and a KPI in *Power Pivot*.

a. Select the **Average Rating** column if necessary.

b. Click the **AutoSum** button arrow [*Home* tab, *Calculations* group] and choose **Average**. The measure appears below the "Average Rating" column and averages the averages (Figure 10-60).

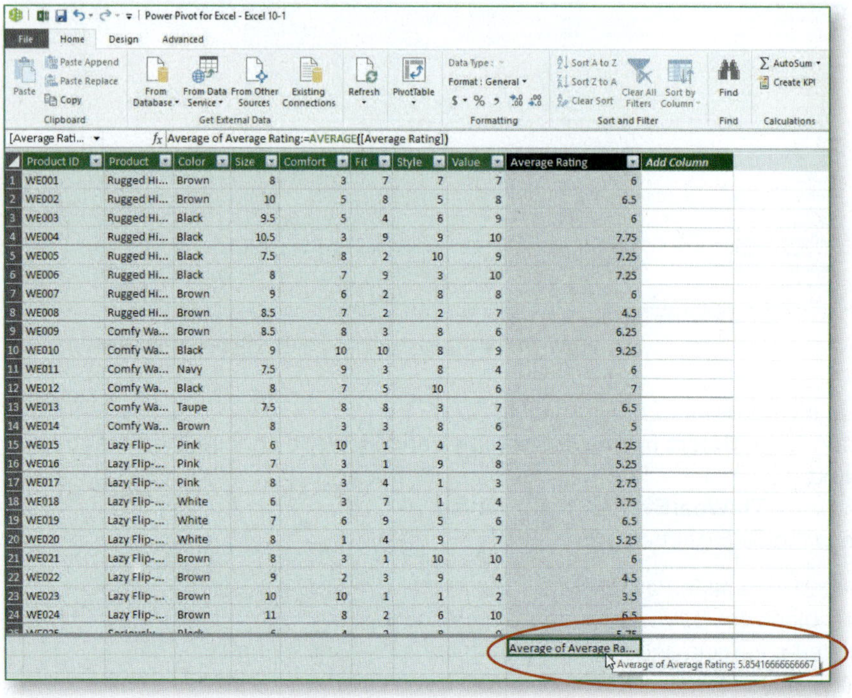

Figure 10-60 Measure in *Power Pivot*

c. Select the **Average of Average Rating** measure at the bottom of the column and click the **Create KPI** button [*Home* tab, *Calculations* group].

d. Click the **Absolute value** button and enter 10 in the box and press **Tab**. A value of 10 is the highest possible rating for WearEver shoes.

e. Select the fourth icon set, the diamond, triangle, and ellipse set (Figure 10-61).

f. Click **OK**. A *KPI* icon displays with the *Average Rating* measure at the bottom of the column.

g. Select the first cell in the "Product ID" column.

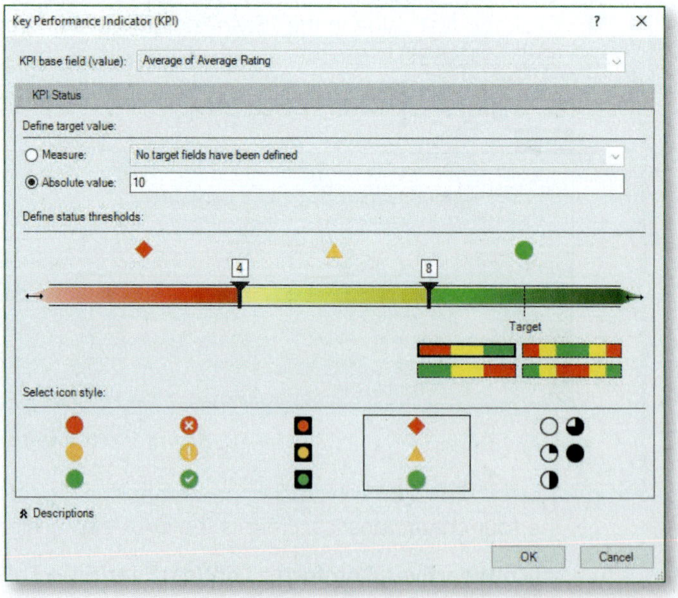

Figure 10-61 *Key Performance Indicator (KPI)* dialog box

8. Create a *PivotTable* from *Power Pivot* data.
   a. Click the **PivotTable** button [*Home* tab].
   b. Select **Existing Worksheet** and click **OK**.
   c. Close the *Queries & Connections* pane if it is open; display the *PivotTable Fields* pane if necessary.
   d. Expand the **InventoryTable** field list in the *PivotTable Fields* pane.
   e. Select the boxes for **Product ID**, **Product**, and **Retail**.
   f. Expand the **TblWearEver** field list in the *PivotTable Fields* pane and click the **Average Rating** box.

9. Create a relationship in a *PivotTable*.
   a. Click the **Auto-Detect** button in the *PivotTable Fields* List pane (Figure 10-62).
   b. Select **Manage Relationships** in the message box. The common field is *Product ID*.
   c. Click **Close**.

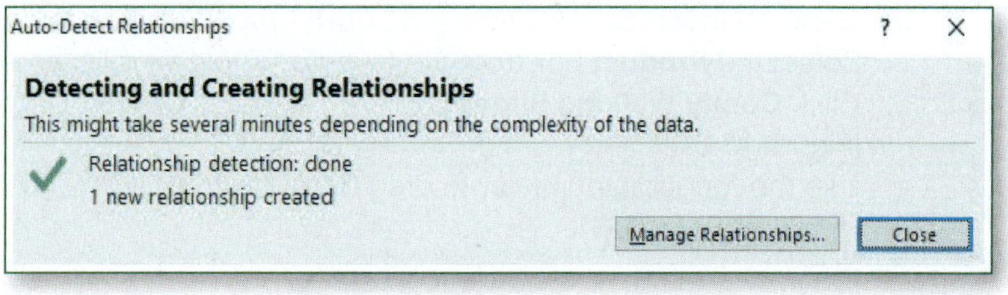

Figure 10-62 Relationship is detected

10. Place a KPI in a *PivotTable*.
    a. Expand the **TblWearEver** field list.
    b. Click the **Average of Average Rating** KPI box to expand its options.
    c. Select the **Status** box to display the icons in the *PivotTable* (Figure 10-63).

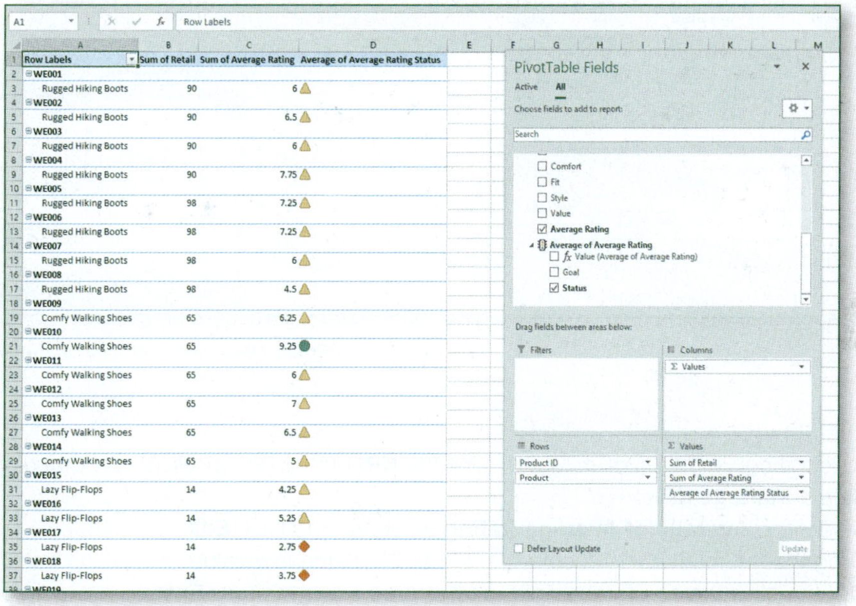

Figure 10-63 KPI displays in the *PivotTable*

11. Format the *PivotTable*.
    a. Click the **Report Layout** button [*PivotTable Tools Design* tab, *Layout* group].
    b. Choose **Show in Tabular Form**.
    c. Click the **Grand Totals** button [*PivotTable Tools Design* tab, *Layout* group].
    d. Choose **Off for Rows and Columns**.
    e. Right click **Sum of Retail** in cell **C1** and select **Value Field Settings**.

f. Type Retail Cost in the *Custom Name* box.
g. Click the **Number Format** button, select **Currency** with no decimal positions, and close the dialog boxes.
h. Right click **Sum of Average Rating** in cell **D1** and select **Value Field Settings**.
i. Type Average Score in the *Custom Name* box.
j. Click the **Number Format** button, select **Number** with two decimal positions, and close the dialog boxes.
k. Change the column header for cell **E1** to Rating vs Goal.

12. Insert a slicer.
    a. Verify that any cell in the *PivotTable* is active.
    b. Click the **Insert Slicer** button [*PivotTable Tools Analyze* tab, *Filter* group].
    c. Select the **Product** box from the *InventoryTable* field list and click **OK**.
    d. Click **Comfy Walking Shoes** in the slicer, press **Ctrl**, and click **Lazy Flip-Flops** (Figure 10-64).
    e. Use the four-pointed arrow to drag the slicer to position it as shown in Figure 10-64 with the top-left corner at cell **G1**.

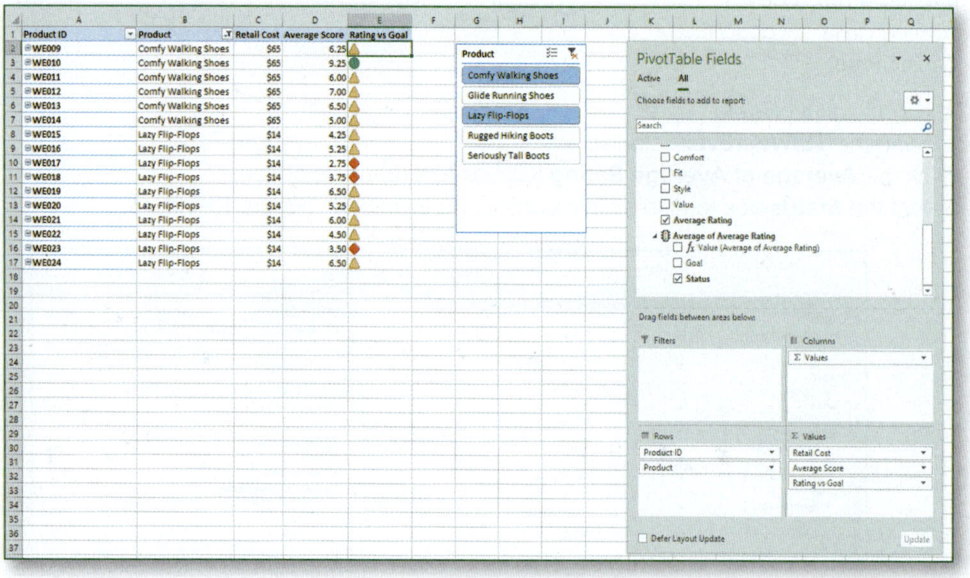

Figure 10-64 KPI and slicer in the *PivotTable*

13. Edit the KPI.
    a. Select a cell in the *PivotTable* and click the **KPI** button [*Power Pivot* tab, *Calculations* group].
    b. Select **Manage KPIs**.
    c. Select the **Average of Average Rating** measure and click **Edit**.
    d. Drag the left marker in the color bar to set 2.8 as the low value.
    e. Double-click the box for the right marker, type 6.5, and press **Enter**.
    f. Click **OK** and then click **Close**.
    g. Select cell **A19**.
    h. Name the sheet tab PivotTable.

14. Uninstall *Power Pivot* as desired.
    a. Select the **Options** command [*File* tab] and click **Add-Ins** in the left pane.
    b. Click the **Manage** drop-down list, select **COM Add-ins**, and click **Go**.
    c. Deselect the **Microsoft Power Pivot for Excel** box and click **OK**.

15. Save and close the workbook (Figure 10-65).

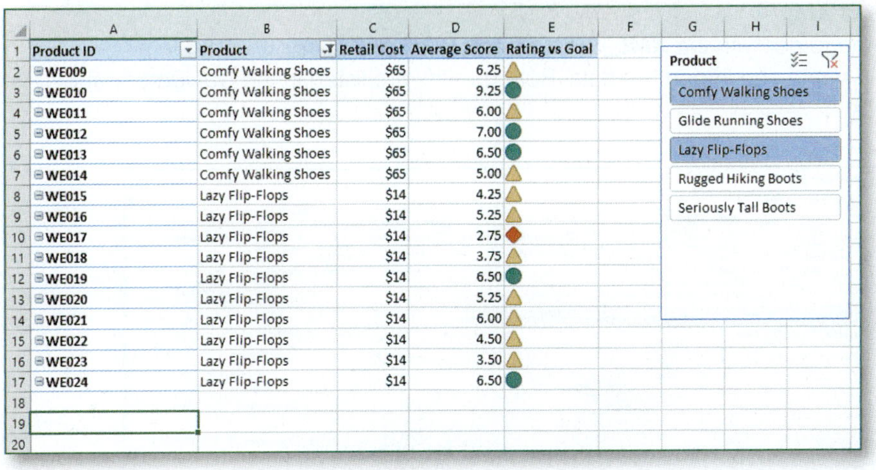

Product ID	Product	Retail Cost	Average Score	Rating vs Goal
WE009	Comfy Walking Shoes	$65	6.25	
WE010	Comfy Walking Shoes	$65	9.25	
WE011	Comfy Walking Shoes	$65	6.00	
WE012	Comfy Walking Shoes	$65	7.00	
WE013	Comfy Walking Shoes	$65	6.50	
WE014	Comfy Walking Shoes	$65	5.00	
WE015	Lazy Flip-Flops	$14	4.25	
WE016	Lazy Flip-Flops	$14	5.25	
WE017	Lazy Flip-Flops	$14	2.75	
WE018	Lazy Flip-Flops	$14	3.75	
WE019	Lazy Flip-Flops	$14	6.50	
WE020	Lazy Flip-Flops	$14	5.25	
WE021	Lazy Flip-Flops	$14	6.00	
WE022	Lazy Flip-Flops	$14	4.50	
WE023	Lazy Flip-Flops	$14	3.50	
WE024	Lazy Flip-Flops	$14	6.50	

Figure 10-65 Completed *PivotTable* for Excel 10-1

Guided Project 10-2

Sierra Pacific Community College (SPCC) analyzes departmental course fees. The source data is stored in separate XML files, and you plan to merge the queries.
[Student Learning Outcomes 10.1, 10.2, 10.3, 10.4, 10.5, 10.6, 10.7]

Files Needed: ***XML_SPCCDept10.xml***, ***XML_SPCCDept10.xsd***, ***XML_SPCCFees10.xml***, and ***XML_SPCCFees10.xsd*** (*Student data files are available in the* Library *of your SIMnet account.*)
Completed Project File Name: ***[your initials] Excel 10-2.xlsx***

Skills Covered in This Project

- Get and transform XML data.
- Create and edit a query.
- Merge queries.
- Manipulate data in *Power Query*.
- Create a custom column in *Power Query*.
- Create a *PivotTable* from the data model.
- Use *PivotTable* tools.

1. Open a new workbook and save it as [your initials] Excel 10-2.
2. Create an Excel query.
   a. Click the **Get Data** button [*Data* tab, *Get & Transform Data* group].
   b. Choose **Launch Power Query Editor**. No data displays yet.
   c. Expand the *Navigator* pane to the left of the window if it is collapsed.
3. Get XML data in *Power Query*.
   a. Click the **New Source** button [*Home* tab, *New Query* group].
   b. Select **File** and then choose **XML**.
   c. Navigate to the folder with the ***XML_SPCCDept10*** XML file.
   d. Select the file name and click **Import**. The *Navigator* window does not preview data for XML files.

e. Click **OK** to import the data. The fields are not automatically expanded in an XML file.
f. Click the **New Source** button [*Home* tab, *New Query* group] again.
g. Select **File** and **XML**.
h. Navigate to the folder with the ***XML_SPCCFees10*** XML file.
i. Select the file name and import the data. Both queries are listed in the *Navigator* pane (Figure 10-66).

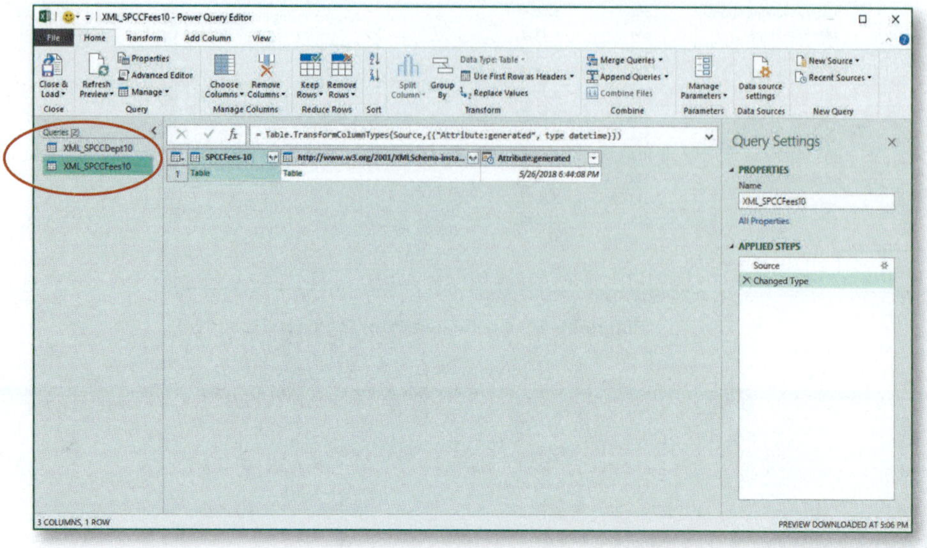

Figure 10-66 Two XML files in *Power Query Editor*

4. Transform data in *Power Query*.
   a. Click the **XML_SPCCDept10** query name in the *Navigator* pane.
   b. Click the **http://. . .Schema. . .** column header (second column), press **Ctrl**, and click the **Attribute:generated** header (third column).
   c. Click the **Remove Columns** button [*Home* tab, *Manage Columns* group].
   d. Click the **Expand/Aggregate** button next to the **XML_SPCCDept-10** column header.
   e. Verify that the **Expand** button is selected and that all fields are selected and click **OK**.
   f. Click the **XML_SPCCDept-10.ID** column label, click the **Data Type** button [*Home* tab, *Transform* group], and choose **Whole Number**.
   g. Click the **XML_SPCCDept-10.Course . . .** label in the third column. Note that the *Data Type* [*Home* tab, *Transform* group] is **Text**. Leave this field as text because you concatenate the field in a custom column in a later step.
   h. Select the **Whole Number** data type for the *Hours* and *Sections* fields in the query (Figure 10-67).
   i. Display the **XML_SPCCFees10** query.
   j. Select and remove the **http://. . .Schema. . .** and the **Attribute:generated** fields.
   k. Click the **Expand/Aggregate** button for *XML_SPCCFees-10* and display the data.
   l. Change the **ID** and the **Fees** columns to **Whole Number** data type.

5. Merge queries.
   a. Display the **XML_SPCCDept10** query.
   b. Click the **Merge Queries** button [*Home* tab, *Combine* group].
   c. Select the **ID** field as the common field in the *Merge* dialog box.
   d. Click the drop-down list for the related query and choose **XML_SPCCFees10**.
   e. Select the **ID** field as the common field.
   f. Verify that the *Join Kind* is *Left Outer* and click **OK** (Figure 10-68).

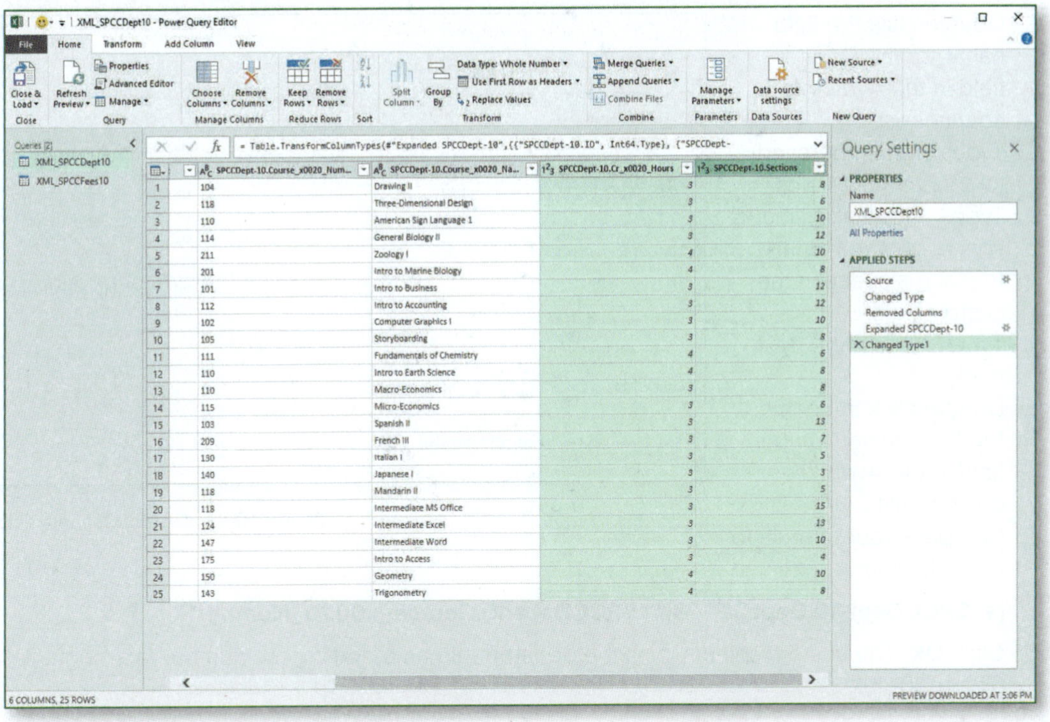

Figure 10-67 Transformed data for *Dept* query

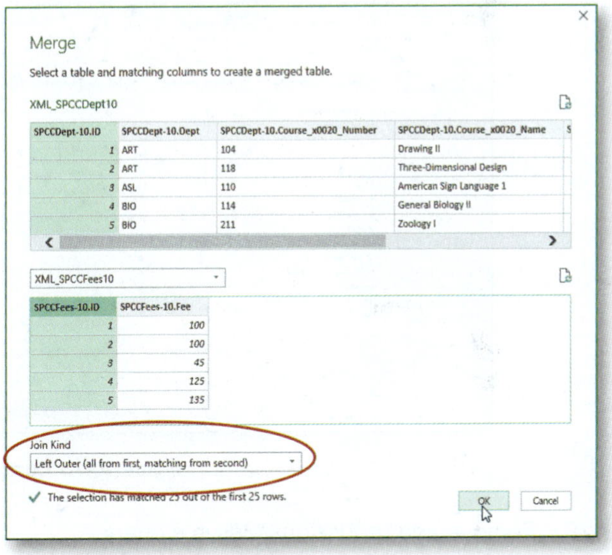

Figure 10-68 Select the common field to merge queries

g. Expand and display the data from **XML_ SPCCFees10** in the merged query. *XML_SPCCDept10* is now the merged query. (The *Fees* query still exists separately, too.)

6. Create a custom column with a multiplication formula.
   a. Select and remove the **SPCCDept-10 . . . Hours** field.
   b. Remove the **XML_SPCCFees10 . . . ID** field. The *ID* field remains in the query in the first column.
   c. Click the **Custom Column** button [*Add Column* tab, *General* group].
   d. Type Fees Collected as the *New column name*.
   e. Click after the = symbol in the *Custom column formula* box.
   f. Double-click the field name for the **Sections** field in the *Available columns* list. It displays in the formula box.
   g. Type * to multiply.
   h. Double-click the field name for the *Fee* field in the *Available columns* list (Figure 10-69).
   i. Click **OK**. The new column displays to the right of the fields.

7. Create a custom column with a concatenated text expression.
   a. Click the **Custom Column** button [*Add Column* tab, *General* group].
   b. Type Code as the *New column name*.
   c. Click after the = symbol in the *Custom column formula* box.

d. Double-click the field name for the *Dept* field in the *Available columns* list.
e. Type & (an ampersand) to concatenate fields.
f. Type " " (quotation mark, space, quotation mark) to place a space in the custom field.
g. Type & to join the next field.
h. Double-click the name for the *Course Number* field in the *Available columns* list.
i. Compare your formula to the following:

[#"SPCCDept-10.Dept"]&" "&[#"SPCCDept-10.Course_x0020_Number"]

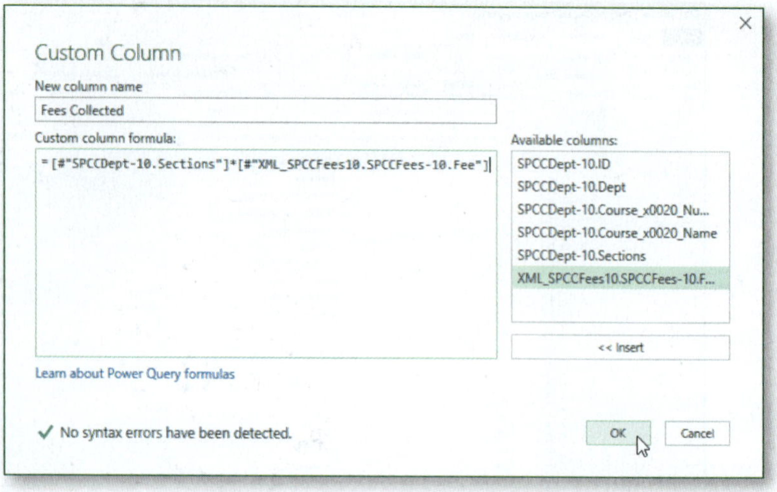

Figure 10-69 ***Custom Column* dialog box**

j. Click **OK**. The custom column joins the department name and course number in a single field (Figure 10-70).

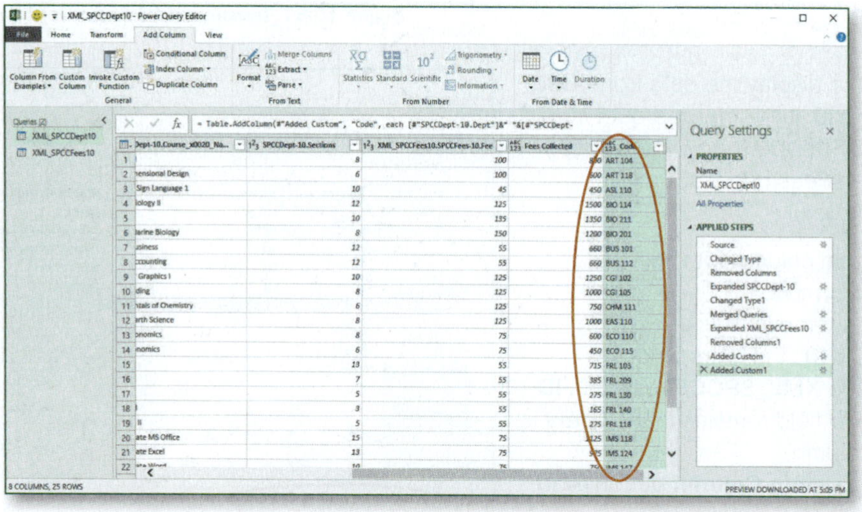

Figure 10-70 Custom column for concatenated text fields

8. Remove and reposition fields in a query.
   a. Select the **Dept** field, press **Ctrl** and select **Course Number** field (second and third columns).
   b. Remove the selected columns.
   c. Point to the **Code** column header and drag the column to be the second field in the query.
   d. Select the **Sections** field, press **Ctrl** and select **Fees** field, and remove the columns (Figure 10-71).

9. Load query data to the workbook.
   a. Click the **Close & Load** button [*Home* tab, *Close* group].
   b. Select the **XML_SPCCDept10** query name in the *Queries & Connections* pane. This is the merged query.
   c. Rename the sheet as Fee Total.

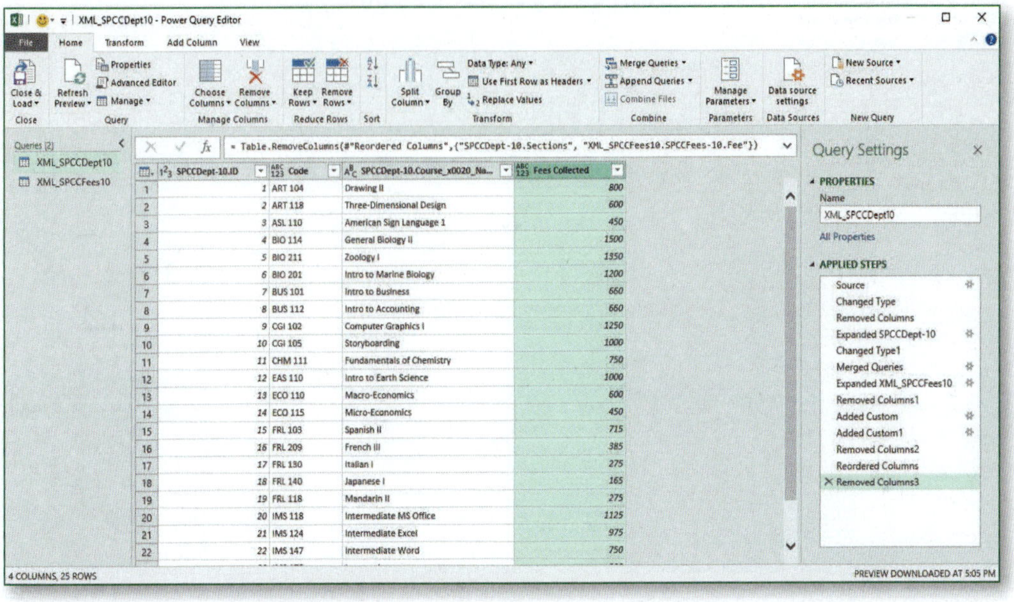

Figure 10-71 Query ready to be loaded

10. Format the Excel table.
    a. Select and delete column **A** in the Excel table.
    b. Format column **C** as **Currency** with no decimals.
    c. Edit the column header for column **B** to Course Name.

11. Copy a query.
    a. Display the *Queries & Connections* pane if necessary [*Data* tab, *Queries & Connections* group].
    b. Point to the **XML_SPCCDept10** query in the pane and select **Edit** in the information window.
    c. Expand the *Navigator* pane in *Power Query Editor* to see the names of available queries.
    d. Click the **Manage** button [*Home* tab, *Query* group] and choose **Duplicate**.
    e. Double-click **XML_SPCCDept10 (2)** in the *Navigator* pane.
    f. Type SPCC_Copy as the new name and press **Enter**.

12. Manipulate data in a query.
    a. Point to the *Removed Columns3* step, the last (bottom) task in the *Applied Steps* pane. (The *3* might be a different number based on your work.)
    b. Click the red X to delete the step, which will undo the command to remove the "Sections" and "Fee" columns. The columns are restored at the right.
    c. Delete four steps at the bottom of the list so that the last step is *Removed Columns1*. The tasks are undone so that the "Dept" and "Course Number" columns are restored, and the custom columns are removed (Figure 10-72).
    d. Close and load the query to your workbook.

13. Create a *PivotTable* from the data model.
    a. Verify that the *SPCC_Copy* query displays in the worksheet.
    b. Click the **Summarize with PivotTable** button [*Table Tools Design* tab, *Tools* group].
    c. Verify that the **New Worksheet** button is selected.
    d. Verify or select the **Add this data to the Data Model** box and click **OK**.
    e. Close the *Queries & Connections* pane.
    f. Expand the **SPCC_Copy** query list in the *PivotTable Fields* pane if it is not expanded.
    g. Select the **Course . . . Name** and **Sections** boxes to place the fields in the *PivotTable* layout. (Float the *PivotTable Fields* pane or point to a lengthy field name to see the name.)
    h. Click **All** at the top of the *PivotTable Fields* pane and expand the **XML_SPCCDept10** list.

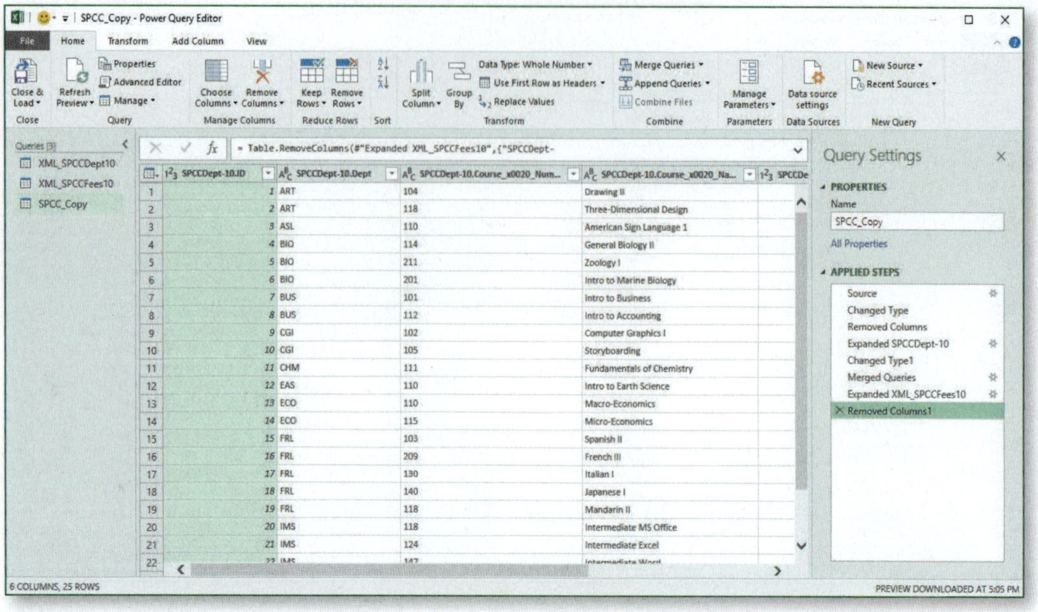

Figure 10-72 Edited query

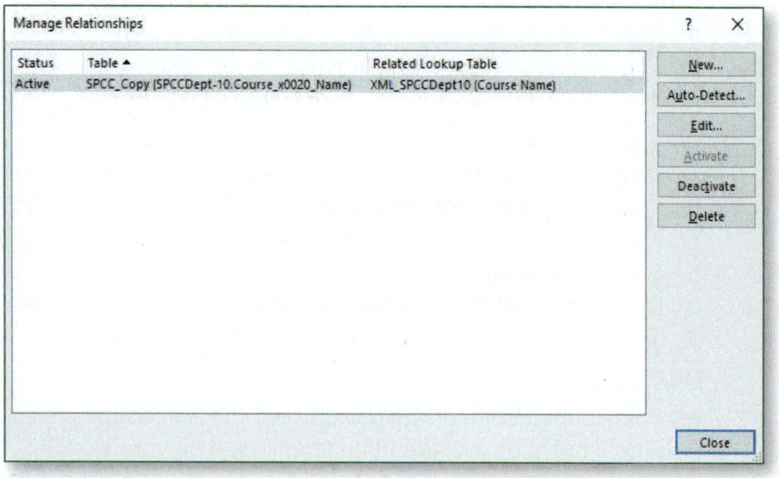

Figure 10-73 Common field was detected

i. Select the **Code** box to add it to the *PivotTable* layout.
j. Click **Auto-Detect** to create the relationship.
k. Click **Manage Relationships** in the message box. The course name field serves as a common field for these two queries (Figure 10-73).
l. Click **Close**.
m. Name the sheet tab PivotTable.

14. Pivot and format a *PivotTable*.
    a. Drag the **Code** field on top of the **Course Name** field in the *Rows* area in the *PivotTable Fields* pane to arrange the *Code* field on the left of the *Course Name* field in the *PivotTable*.
    b. Select cell **B3**, type Number of Sections, and press **Enter**.
    c. Click the **Report Layout** button [*PivotTable Tools Design* tab, *Layout* group] and choose **Show in Tabular Form**.
    d. Select cell **B3**, type Course Name, and press **Enter**.
    e. Click the **More** button [*PivotTable Tools Design* tab, *PivotTable Styles* group] and choose **White, Pivot Style Light 22**.
    f. Select the **Banded Rows** box [*PivotTable Tools Design* tab, *PivotTable Style Options* group] (Figure 10-74).

15. Save and close the workbook.

Code	Course Name	Fees Collected
ART 104	Drawing II	$800
ART 118	Three-Dimensional Design	$600
ASL 110	American Sign Language 1	$450
BIO 114	General Biology II	$1,500
BIO 211	Zoology I	$1,350
BIO 201	Intro to Marine Biology	$1,200
BUS 101	Intro to Business	$660
BUS 112	Intro to Accounting	$660
CGI 102	Computer Graphics I	$1,250
CGI 105	Storyboarding	$1,000
CHM 111	Fundamentals of Chemistry	$750
EAS 110	Intro to Earth Science	$1,000
ECO 110	Macro-Economics	$600
ECO 115	Micro-Economics	$450
FRL 103	Spanish II	$715
FRL 209	French III	$385
FRL 130	Italian I	$275
FRL 140	Japanese I	$165
FRL 118	Mandarin II	$275
IMS 118	Intermediate MS Office	$1,125
IMS 124	Intermediate Excel	$975
IMS 147	Intermediate Word	$750
IMS 175	Intro to Access	$300
MTH 150	Geometry	$550
MTH 143	Trigonometry	$440

	A	B	C
3	Code	Course Name	Number of Sections
4	ART 104	Drawing II	8
5	ART 118	Three-Dimensional Design	6
6	ASL 110	American Sign Language 1	10
7	BIO 114	General Biology II	12
8	BIO 201	Intro to Marine Biology	8
9	BIO 211	Zoology I	10
10	BUS 101	Intro to Business	12
11	BUS 112	Intro to Accounting	12
12	CGI 102	Computer Graphics I	10
13	CGI 105	Storyboarding	8
14	CHM 111	Fundamentals of Chemistry	6
15	EAS 110	Intro to Earth Science	8
16	ECO 110	Macro-Economics	8
17	ECO 115	Micro-Economics	6
18	FRL 103	Spanish II	13
19	FRL 118	Mandarin II	5
20	FRL 130	Italian I	5
21	FRL 140	Japanese I	3
22	FRL 209	French III	7
23	IMS 118	Intermediate MS Office	15
24	IMS 124	Intermediate Excel	13
25	IMS 147	Intermediate Word	10
26	IMS 175	Intro to Access	4
27	MTH 143	Trigonometry	8
28	MTH 150	Geometry	10
29	Grand Total		217

Figure 10-74 Completed table and *PivotTable* for Excel 10-2

Guided Project 10-3

Courtyard Medical Plaza has two tables with dental insurance data. You get these tables in *Power Query* to append one to the other and to create a *PivotTable* with a *PivotChart*.
[Student Learning Outcomes 10.1, 10.2, 10.3, 10.4, 10.5, 10.7]

File Needed: ***CourtyardMedical-10.xlsx*** *(Student data files are available in the* Library *of your SIMnet account.)*
Completed Project File Name: ***[your initials] Excel 10-3.xlsx***

Skills Covered in This Project

- Get data from a workbook in *Power Query.*
- Append queries.
- Create and customize a *PivotTable.*
- Insert a *PivotChart.*
- Insert a slicer in a *PivotTable.*

1. Create a new workbook and save it as [your initials] Excel 10-3.
2. Get Excel data in *Power Query*.
   a. Click the **Get Data** button [*Data* tab, *Get & Transform Data* group] and select **Launch Power Query Editor**.
   b. Expand the *Navigator* pane to the left of the window if it is collapsed.
   c. Click the **New Source** button [*Home* tab, *New Query* group].

d. Select **File** and then choose **Excel**.
e. Navigate to the folder with the **CourtyardMedical-10** workbook.
f. Select the file name and click **Import**. The *Navigator* window displays sheet and range names in the workbook (Figure 10-75).
g. Select **Data2019** to preview the data and click **OK**.
h. Click the **New Source** button [*Home* tab, *New Query* group] again and select **File** and **Excel**.
i. Navigate to the folder with the **CourtyardMedical-10** workbook, select **Data2020**, and click **OK**. Both queries display in the *Navigator* pane.

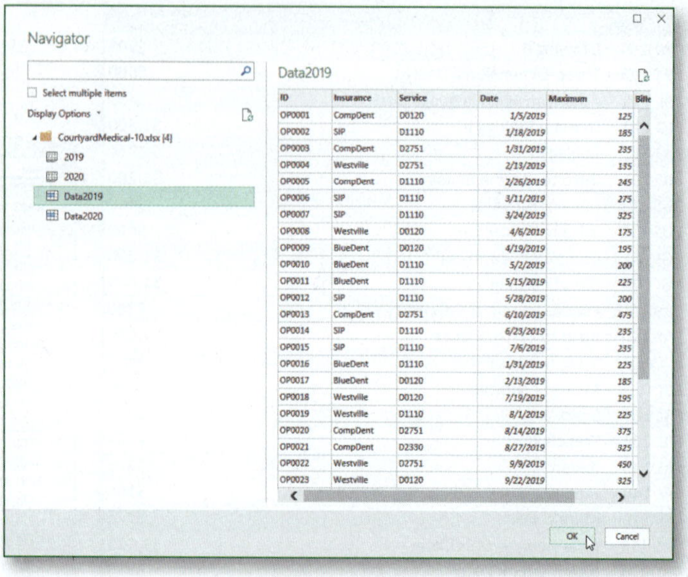

Figure 10-75 ***Navigator* window for an Excel file**

3. Append queries.
   a. Select **Data2019** in the *Navigator* pane.
   b. Click the arrow for the **Append Queries** button [*Home* tab, *Combine* group] and select **Append Queries as New**.
   c. Confirm that the *Two tables* button is selected and that **Data2019** displays as the *Primary table*.
   d. Click the drop-down list for *Table to append to the primary table* and choose **Data2020** (Figure 10-76).

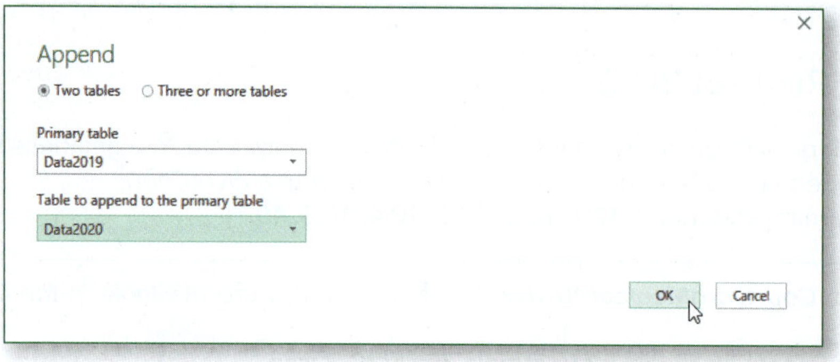

Figure 10-76 ***Append* dialog box**

   e. Click **OK**. The new query is named *Append1*.
4. Load data to Excel.
   a. Click the **Close & Load** button [*Home* tab, *Close* group]. The two source queries and the appended query are loaded to separate worksheets.
   b. Name the appended queries tab Append1. This sheet displays 60 rows of data.
   c. Select cell **A1**.
5. Create a *PivotTable* for the appended queries.
   a. Select the **Summarize with PivotTable** button [*Table Tools Design* tab, *Tools* group].
   b. Select **New Worksheet** and click **OK**.
   c. Close the *Queries & Connections* pane if it displays.
   d. Name the worksheet tab PivotTable 1.

6. Place fields in the *PivotTable*.
   a. Select the **Service Code** field name in the *PivotTable Fields* pane. Label fields display in the *Rows* area.
   b. Select the **Billed** field name. Numeric fields display in the *Values* area.
   c. Point to **Billed** in the *Choose fields to add to report* area and drag the field name to the **Values** area to show the field twice in the *PivotTable*.
7. Edit value field settings.
   a. Click **Sum of Billed** in cell **B3** and click the **Field Settings** button [*PivotTable Tools Analyze* tab, *Active Field* group].
   b. Type Total Billed as the *Custom Name*.
   c. Click **Number Format**, choose **Currency**, set **0** (zero) decimal places, and click **OK** two times to close the dialog boxes.
   d. Right-click **Sum of Billed2** in cell **C3** and select **Value Field Settings**.
   e. Type Average Billed as the *Custom Name*.
   f. Select the *Summarize Values By* tab and choose **Average** as the function.
   g. Click **Number Format**, choose **Currency**, set **0** (zero) decimal places, and close the dialog boxes.
8. Refresh data and format the *PivotTable* report.
   a. Select cell **A7** in the **PivotTable**. This code is an outlier.
   b. Click the **Append1** worksheet tab and select cell **C61**.
   c. Type D0120 and press **Enter**.
   d. Return to the **PivotTable 1** sheet. The data is not automatically updated.
   e. Click the **Refresh** button [*PivotTable Tools Analyze* tab, *Data* group].
   f. Click any cell in the *PivotTable* and apply the **Light Blue, Pivot Style Medium 6** style.
   g. Select the **Banded Rows** and **Banded Columns** boxes [*PivotTable Tools Design* tab, *PivotTable Style Options* group].
   h. Click the **Grand Totals** button [*PivotTable Tools Design* tab, *Layout* group] and choose **Off for Rows and Columns**.
9. Select cell **A1** and type Courtyard Medical Dental Services.
10. Type Billings by Service Code in cell **A2**.
11. Format both labels as **14 pt** (Figure 10-77).
12. Create a *PivotChart*.
    a. Select a cell in the *PivotTable* and click the **PivotChart** button [*PivotTable Tools Analyze* tab, *Tools* group].
    b. Choose **Combo** and **Clustered Column - Line** as the subtype and click **OK** (Figure 10-78).
    c. Drag the chart object so that its top-left corner is in cell **E3**.
    d. Size the chart object to reach cell **N25**.

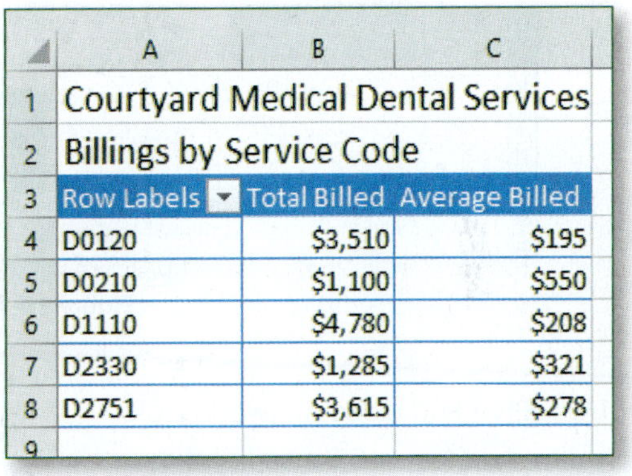

	A	B	C
1	Courtyard Medical Dental Services		
2	Billings by Service Code		
3	Row Labels	Total Billed	Average Billed
4	D0120	$3,510	$195
5	D0210	$1,100	$550
6	D1110	$4,780	$208
7	D2330	$1,285	$321
8	D2751	$3,615	$278
9			

Figure 10-77 Completed *PivotTable*

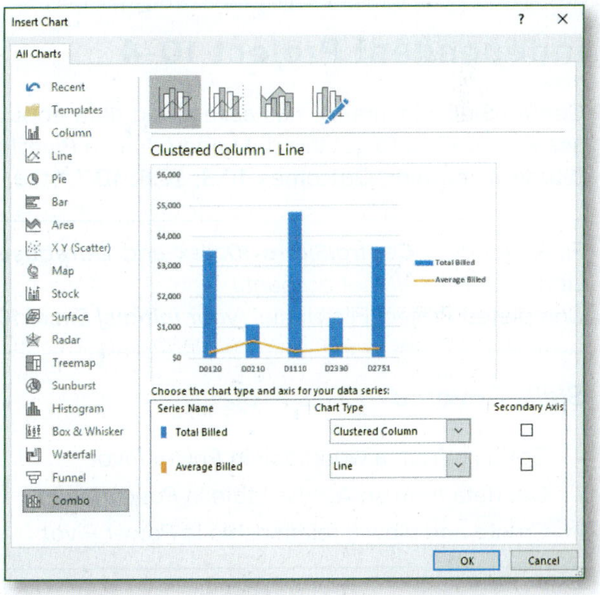

Figure 10-78 Create a combo *PivotChart*

13. Insert a slicer.
   a. Click any cell in the *PivotTable* and click the **Insert Slicer** button [*PivotTable Tools Analyze* tab, *Filter* group].
   b. Select the **Insurance** box and click **OK**.
   c. Position the slicer so that the top-right corner is in cell **B10**.
   d. Format the slicer with **Light Blue, Slicer Style Dark 5**.
   e. Click **CompDent** in the slicer to filter the *PivotTable* and *PivotChart* (Figure 10-79).
   f. Select cell **A1**.

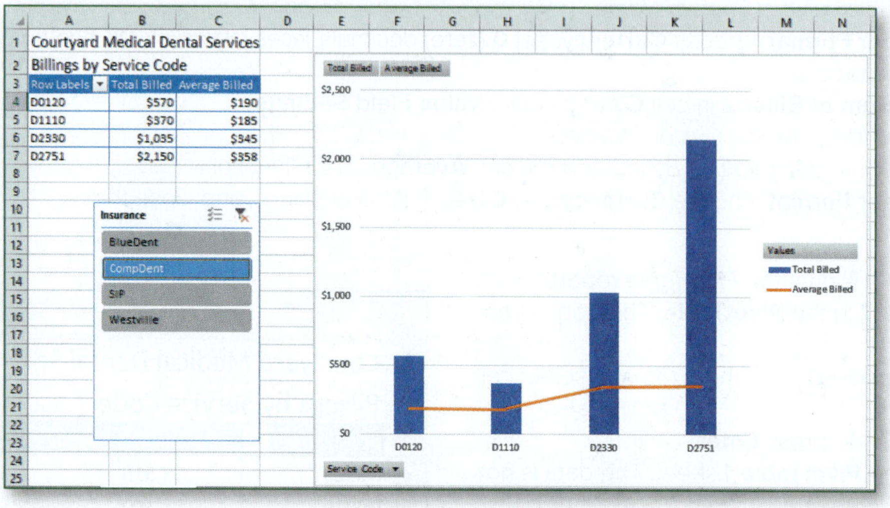

Figure 10-79 Completed *PivotTable*, *PivotChart*, and slicer

14. Save and close the workbook.

Independent Project 10-4

Central Sierra Insurance has assembled data about clients in a workbook and in an Access table. You use *Power Pivot* to get this data and create a *PivotTable*.
[Student Learning Outcomes 10.3, 10.6, 10.7, 10.8]

Files Needed: ***CentralSierra-10.xlsx*** and ***Database-10.accdb*** *(Student data files are available in the Library of your SIMnet account.)*
Completed Project File Name: ***[your initials] Excel 10-4.xlsx***

Skills Covered in This Project

- Get data from a workbook in *Power Pivot*.
- Get data from an Access table in *Power Pivot*.
- Create and view a relationship in *Power Pivot*.
- Build a formula in a *Power Pivot* table.
- Create a *PivotTable* from the data model.
- Work with *PivotTable* tools.

1. Create a new workbook and save it as [your initials] Excel 10-4.
2. Start *Power Pivot*.
3. Get **TblCentralSierra** from the Microsoft Access database named ***Database-10***. *AutoFit* the "City" and "State" columns.
4. Click the **From Other Sources** button [*Home* tab, *Get External Data* group], scroll the list, and get the ***CentralSierra-10*** workbook file. Use the first row as column headers. *AutoFit* the "City" and "State" columns.
5. Select the **F7** column header on the *Client Stats* tab and delete the column [*Design* tab, *Columns* group].
6. Select the **ID** column. Use the move pointer to drag the column to display as the first column in the table.
7. Change the data type for the "ID" column to **Whole Number** (Figure 10-80).
8. Select the **TblCentral Sierra** tab. Create a relationship between the tables using the **ID** field. The *TblCentralSierra* table name displays in the upper drop-down list.
9. View the relationship in **Diagram View** [*Home* tab, *View* group] and then return to **Data View**.
10. Follow the steps below to calculate the ratio of students to the total number of clients. The formula is the number of students divided by the total number.
    a. Select the **Client Stats** tab.
    b. Click the first cell in the *Add Column* field and type = to start the formula.
    c. Select the first cell in the "Students" column and then type / for division.
    d. Type a left parenthesis (and click the first cell in the "Females" column.
    e. Type +, click the first cell in the "Males" column, type +, click the first cell in the "Students" column, and type the right parenthesis) to order the arithmetic.
    f. Press **Enter**.
    g. Double-click **Calculated Column 1**, type Student Ratio, and press **Enter** (Figure 10-81).
11. Create a *PivotTable* in the existing worksheet on its own sheet.

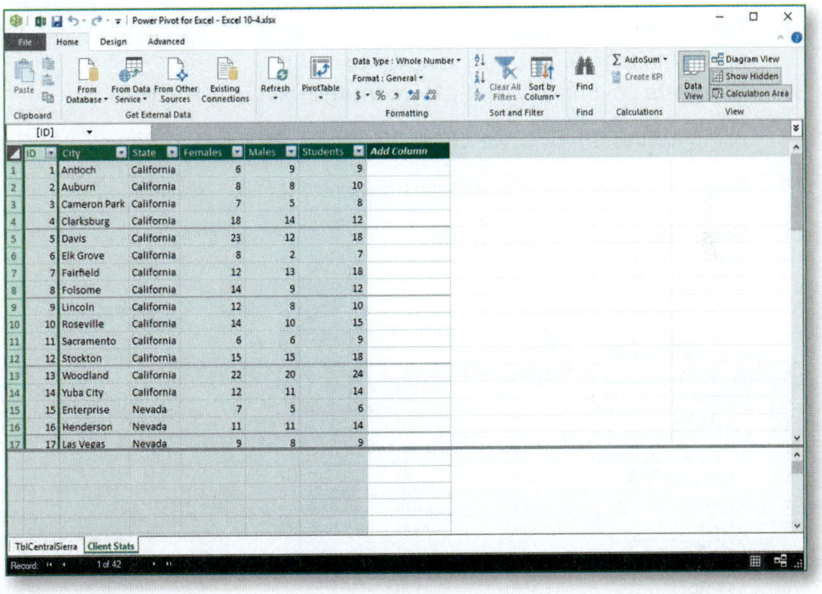

Figure 10-80 Workbook data in *Power Pivot* table

12. Select the **State** box and then the **City** box from the *Client Stats* field list in the *PivotTable Fields* pane. Both fields display in the *Rows* area.
13. Select the **Working** field from the *TblCentral Sierra* field list and the **Students** and **Student Ratio** fields from the *Client Stats* list. These are *Values* fields.
14. Edit the *PivotTable* to show # Working, # of Students, and % Students as column labels.
15. Turn off all grand totals and format the **% Students** column to display **Percentage** with 2 decimals.
16. Apply **White**, **Pivot Style Light 22** and show **Banded Rows**.
17. Name the sheet tab PivotTable 1 (Figure 10-82).
18. Save and close the workbook.

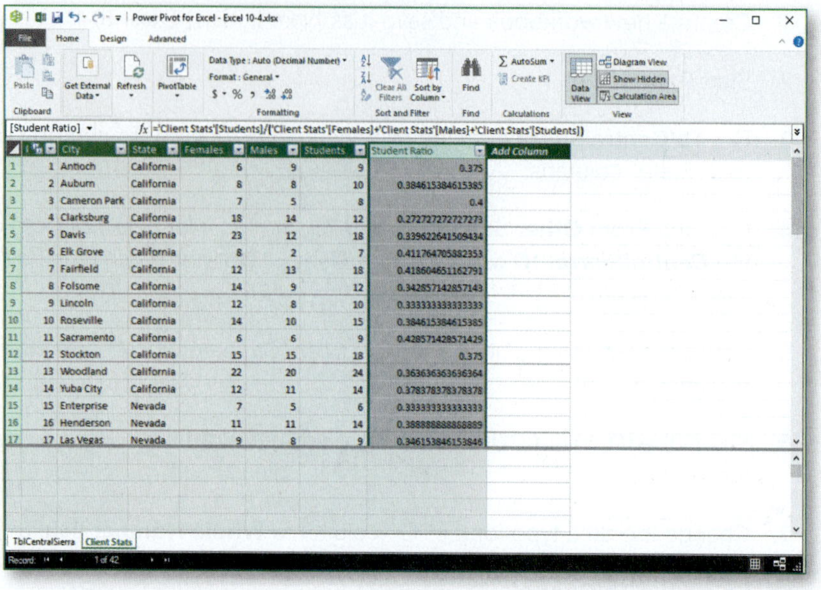

Figure 10-81 Calculated column for *Client Stats*

	A	B	C	D
1	Row Labels	# Working	# of Students	% Students
2	⊟California			
3	Antioch	6	9	37.50%
4	Auburn	8	10	38.46%
5	Cameron Park	7	8	40.00%
6	Clarksburg	18	12	27.27%
7	Davis	23	18	33.96%
8	Elk Grove	8	7	41.18%
9	Fairfield	12	18	41.86%
10	Folsome	14	12	34.29%
11	Lincoln	12	10	33.33%
12	Roseville	14	15	38.46%
13	Sacramento	6	9	42.86%
14	Stockton	15	18	37.50%
15	Woodland	22	24	36.36%
16	Yuba City	12	14	37.84%
17	⊟Nevada			
18	Enterprise	7	6	33.33%
19	Henderson	11	14	38.89%
20	Las Vegas	9	9	34.62%
21	North Las Vegas	5	8	36.36%
22	Paradise	10	9	27.27%
23	Reno	9	14	36.84%
24	Spring Valley	9	7	33.33%
25	Winchester	10	10	35.71%
26	Witney	13	13	33.33%
27	⊟Oregon			
28	Beaverton	9	15	42.86%
29	Gresham	17	23	39.66%
30	Hillsboro	5	11	45.83%
31	Milwaukie	8	9	36.00%
32	Oak Grove	7	8	40.00%
33	Portland	10	14	41.18%
34	Tigard	12	16	39.02%
35	Vancouver	10	15	42.86%
36	Walnut Grove	12	13	39.39%
37	⊟Washington			
38	Bainbridge Island	12	16	39.02%
39	Bellevue	9	14	36.84%
40	Bothell	10	9	27.27%
41	Kirkland	5	11	45.83%
42	Lynnwood	7	8	40.00%
43	Parkland	8	2	14.29%
44	Poulsbo	9	5	19.23%
45	Redmond	8	5	25.00%
46	Tacoma	11	8	27.59%
47	Yakima	14	7	24.14%

Figure 10-82 Completed *PivotTable* for Excel 10-4

Independent Project 10-5

The Department of Motor Vehicles tracks information in three database tables about citations, drivers, and officers. You import three tables in *Power Query* to merge them and create a *PivotTable* with a slicer and a timeline.
[Student Learning Outcomes 10.1, 10.2, 10.3, 10.4, 10.5, 10.6, 10.7]

File Needed: ***Database-10.accdb*** *(Student data files are available in the* Library *of your SIMnet account.)*
Completed Project File Name: ***[your initials] Excel 10-5.xlsx***

Skills Covered in This Project

- Get external data in *Power Query*.
- Build and edit queries.
- Merge queries.
- Use the data model to create a *PivotTable*.
- Work with *PivotTable* tools.

1. Create a new workbook and save it as [your initials] Excel 10-5.
2. Launch *Power Query* [*Data* tab, *Get & Transform Data* group].
3. Get three tables from the Microsoft Access ***Database-10*** file in your student data files: ***DMVDrivers-10***, ***DMVOfficer-10***, and ***DMVTicket-10***.
4. Edit the queries.
   a. Select and delete the **RecordAddedTimeStamp** field from the *DMVTicket-10* query.
   b. Select and delete the **BirthDate**, **Address**, **City**, and **State** fields from the *DMVDrivers-10* query (Figure 10-83).

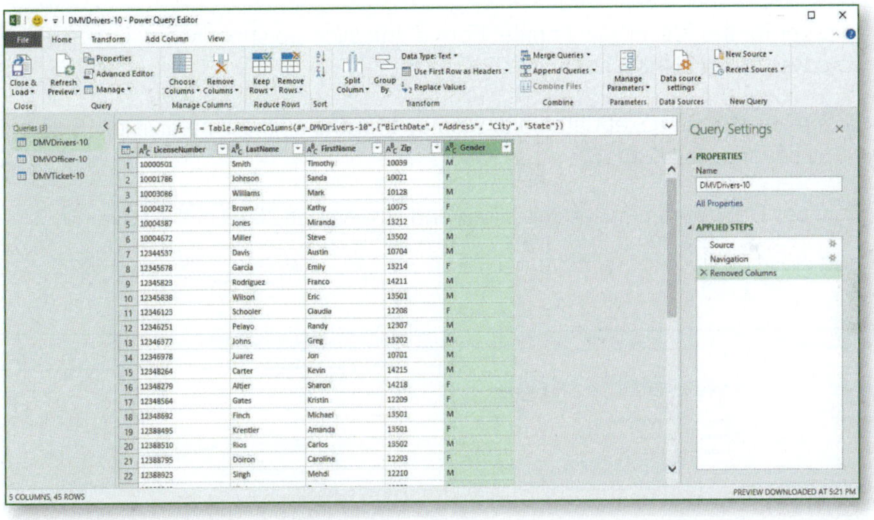

Figure 10-83 ***DMVDrivers-10*** **query**

   c. Select the **DMVTicket-10** query tab.
5. Merge the **DMVTicket-10** query with the **DMVDrivers-10** query in a new query. The driver's license number is the common field. The new query is named *Merge1* and note the *DMVDrivers-10* fields are collapsed.
6. Merge the **Merge1** query with the **DMVOfficer-10** query in a new query. The officer's badge number is the common field. The new query is named *Merge2* and the *DMVDrivers-10* and *DMVOfficer-10* fields are collapsed.

7. Click the **Expand/Aggregate** button with the *DMVDrivers-10* column header and display all the fields. Select and delete the **DMVDrivers-10.LicenseNumber** field; the same data displays from the *DMVTicket-10* fields.

8. Select and delete the **DMVDrivers-10. Gender** field.

9. Expand the **DMV Officer-10** query fields. Then select and delete the officer ID and date hired fields (Figure 10-84).

10. Close and load the **Merge2** query to your workbook. Name the worksheet tab Merge2.

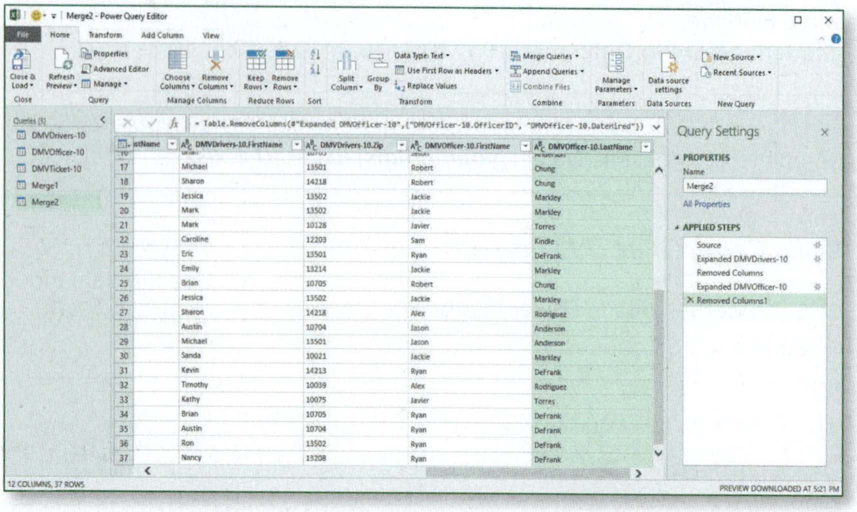

Figure 10-84 ***Merge2* query fields**

11. Summarize the data in the **Merge2** sheet with a *PivotTable* in a new worksheet. Display the ticket number, the driver's last name, and the primary factor as *Rows*. Display the fine as a *Values* field.

12. Choose tabular form for the report layout and do not show subtotals.

13. Insert a slicer for the officer's last name. Format the slicer to show two columns. Position and size the slicer to cover cells **H14:K21**.

14. Insert a timeline for the ticket date field. Display **Months** as the time division. Size and position the timeline to cover cells **H2:O10**.

15. Select Officer DeFrank's name in the slicer and November 2019 in the timeline.

16. Save and close the workbook (Figure 10-85).

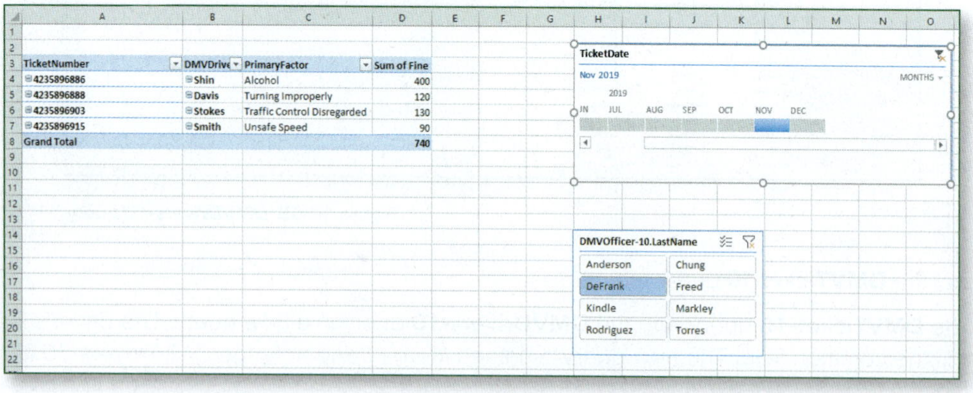

Figure 10-85 Completed *PivotTable* for Excel 10-5

Independent Project 10-6

Boyd Air keeps a text file with performance codes and a Microsoft Access table with flight details. You import the data in *Power Pivot* to use the data model for a *PivotTable*.
[Student Learning Outcomes 10.3, 10.6, 10.7, 10.8]

Files Needed: ***Text-BoydAir10.txt*** and ***Database-10.accdb*** *(Student data files are available in the* Library *of your SIMnet account.)*
Completed Project File Name: ***[your initials] Excel 10-6.xlsx***

Skills Covered in This Project

- Import a text file in *Power Pivot.*
- Get a database table in *Power Pivot.*
- Create a relationship in *Power Pivot.*
- Create a *PivotTable* from the data model.
- Format a *PivotTable.*

---

1. Create a new workbook and save it as [your initials] Excel 10-6.
2. Launch *Power Pivot.*
3. Import the ***Text-BoydAir10.txt*** file from your student data files. Use the first row as column headers.
4. Get the **TblBoydAir** table from the Microsoft Access ***Database-10*** file in your student data files.
5. Create a relationship using the date field as the common field.
6. Create a *PivotTable* from the *Power Pivot* data model in cell **A1** in your existing worksheet.
7. Display the **Flight** and the **FlightDate** fields from **TblBoydAir** in the *Rows* area with the *Flight* field first. If the date field separates to include months or quarters, drag unnecessary field names out of the *PivotTable Fields* pane to remove them.
8. Display the **Passengers** field in the *Values* area.
9. Choose tabular form for the report layout.
10. Place the **Code** field from the **Text-BoydAir10** list. It is a *Rows* field.
11. Insert a slicer for the **Arrival** field.
12. Apply **White, Pivot Style Medium 15** style to the *PivotTable* and **White, Style Slicer Dark 3** to the slicer.
13. Filter the data for **GRB** (Figure 10-86).
14. Save and close the workbook.

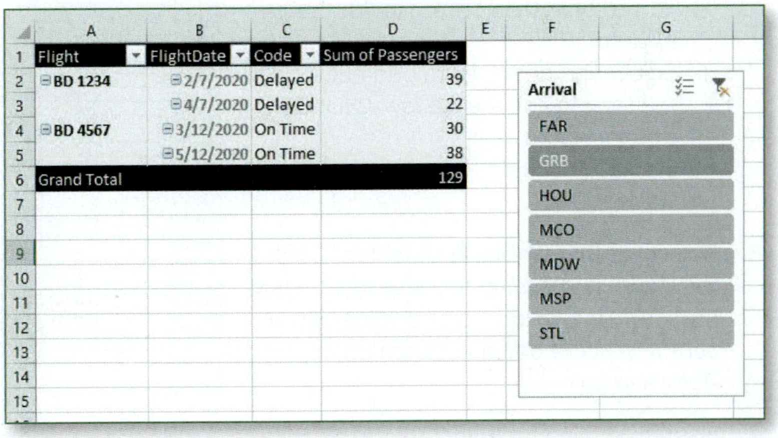

Figure 10-86 Completed *PivotTable* for Excel 10-6

Improve It Project 10-7

Wilson Home Entertainment Systems uses a *PivotTable* to combine sales and representatives' data. You copy the *PivotTable* to use one copy for named sets and one for the *GETPIVOTDATA* function. [Student Learning Outcomes 10.6, 10.7]

File Needed: ***WilsonHome-10.xlsx*** *(Student data files are available in the* Library *of your SIMnet account.)*
Completed Project File Name: ***[your initials] Excel 10-7.xlsx***

Skills Covered in This Project

- Edit fields in a *PivotTable*.
- Copy a *PivotTable*.
- Create named sets in a *PivotTable*.
- Pivot fields in a *PivotTable*.
- Use *GETPIVOTDATA* in a worksheet.

1. Open the ***WilsonHome-10*** workbook from your student data files and save it as [your initials] Excel 10-7. When the *Compatibility Checker* dialog box opens, click **Continue**.
2. Edit fields in a *PivotTable*.
   a. Select the **PivotTable** sheet tab and change the display name for cell **D3** to Sold.
   b. Change the display name for cell **A3** to Staff.
3. Copy the **PivotTable** sheet to the end and keep the default sheet name.
4. Select the **PivotTable** sheet and remove the **Staff** field from the *PivotTable*. Verify that the data is sorted in ascending order by the transaction field.
5. Create named sets in a *PivotTable*.
   a. Create a set based on row items named Odd.
   b. Deselect the **Replace the fields currently in the row area with the new set** box.
   c. Select and delete each even-numbered transaction and the row that displays **All**. Click **OK** when finished.
   d. Create a set based on row items named Even.
   e. Deselect the **Replace the fields currently in the row area with the new set** box.
   f. Select and delete each odd-numbered transaction and the **All** row. Click **OK** when finished.
   g. Display the **Odd** set in the *PivotTable* (Figure 10-87).
6. Select the **PivotTable(2)** sheet tab. Display the **Product** and **Staff** fields as rows in that order and the **Sold** field as a value. Show subtotals at the bottom of each group and *AutoFit* each column.
7. Insert a timeline for **PivotTable(2)** and choose **Quarters** as the time division. Then select the fourth quarter for 2019 in the timeline (Figure 10-88).

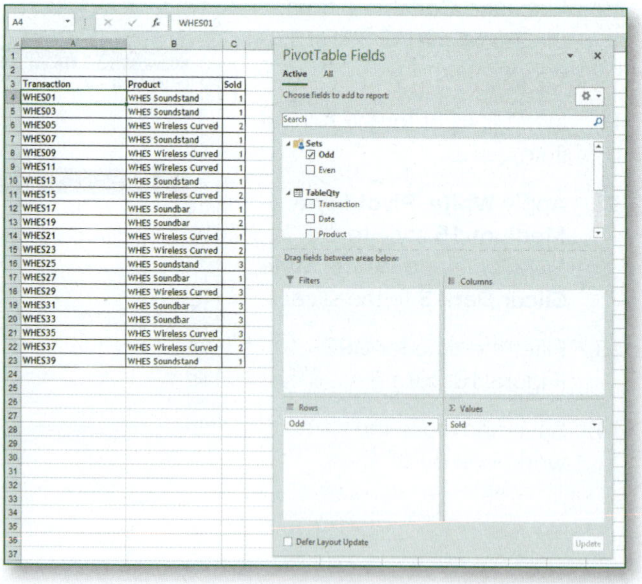

Figure 10-87 Named set for odd-numbered transactions

8. Use *GETPIVOTDATA* in cells **H4:H6** on the **Sales** sheet to display fourth quarter sales for the products.
9. Save and close the workbook (Figure 10-89).

Figure 10-88 ***PivotTable* with timeline**

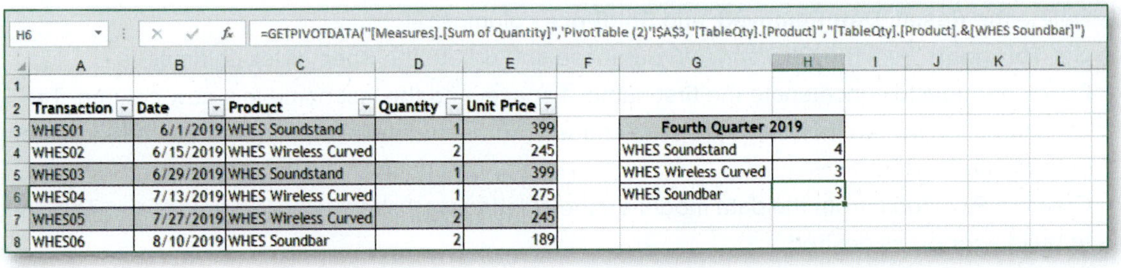

Figure 10-89 ***GETPIVOTDATA* results for Excel 10-7**

Challenge Project 10-8

For this project, you create queries for a music database. You get tables from Microsoft Access and create an Excel table to display your favorite music genre.
[Student Learning Outcomes 10.1, 10.2, 10.3, 10.4, 10.5]

File Needed: ***Challenge-10.accdb*** *(Student data files are available in the* Library *of your SIMnet account.)*
Completed Project File Name: ***[your initials] Excel 10-8.xlsx***

Create and save a workbook as [your initials] Excel 10-8. Modify your workbook according to the following guidelines:

- Launch *Power Query* and get **Music_Albums** from the *Challenge-10* Microsoft Access database in your student data files.
- Remove the **Length** and **ReleaseDate** columns.
- Get **Music_Songs** from the *Challenge-10* database and remove the **Length** column.
- Merge the queries into a new query. Remove the **FKAlbumID** field from the merged query.
- Load the merged query to your workbook.
- Sort and filter the Excel table to display your preferred music genre. Hide columns as desired.

Challenge Project 10-9

For this project, you get data from a Microsoft Access database for real estate listings. You use *Power Pivot* to build the data model and then create a *PivotTable*.
[Student Learning Outcomes 10.7, 10.8]

File Needed: ***Challenge-10.accdb*** *(Student data files are available in the* Library *of your SIMnet account.)*
Completed Project File Name: ***[your initials] Excel 10-9.xlsx***

Create and save a workbook as [your initials] Excel 10-9. Modify your workbook according to the following guidelines:

- Launch *Power Pivot* and get **TblListings** from the *Challenge-10* Microsoft Access database in your student data files.
- Delete the **Result**, **DateRemoved**, and **SoldPrice** columns.
- Get **TblAgents** from the *Challenge-10* database and delete the **Specialties** column.
- Build a formula to concatenate the first name, a space, and the last name in a new column. The concatenation symbol is **&** and the space character must be enclosed in quotation marks. Name the column Agent Name.
- Create a *PivotTable* from the data model on the existing worksheet. Choose fields from *TblListings* to build a report as desired.
- Display the **Agent Name** field from *TblAgents* and create the relationship.
- Determine how to layout and format the report. Remove or add fields as desired.

Challenge Project 10-10

For this project, you use personal or public data to build a table or a *PivotTable*. Use *Power Query* or *Power Pivot* to manipulate the data depending on your final report plans.
[Student Learning Outcome 10.1, 10.2, 10.3, 10.4, 10.5, 10.6, 10.7, 10.8]

Files Needed: Various cloud data or services
Completed Project File Name: ***[your initials] Excel 10-10.xlsx***

Create and save a workbook as [your initials] Excel 10-10. Modify your workbook according to the following guidelines:

- Search online for data that you can import as an Excel file or in a text format. Review public databases from the U.S. Census Bureau, the Bureau of Labor Statistics, data feeds you review, or media services where you have an account.
- Download the data in an acceptable format and save the file if necessary. You may also be able to get data directly from the cloud.
- Use *Power Query* to display results in a table; use *Power Pivot* to create a *PivotTable*.
- Get and transform the data as desired. Build calculated or custom columns as needed.
- Create the table or *PivotTable* and format your work.

Source of screenshots Microsoft Office 365 (2019): Word, Excel, Access, PowerPoint.

CHAPTER 11

Customizing Excel and Using OneDrive and Office Online

EXCEL

Chapter Overview

This chapter introduces you to Excel settings, your Excel working environment, and online services and tools. Excel integrates "cloud" technology so that you can store workbooks on local media, in *OneDrive*, and with *Office Online*. Cloud services enable you to access and share your work from anywhere on any computer with internet access.

STUDENT LEARNING OUTCOMES (SLOs)

After completing this chapter, you will be able to:

SLO 11.1 Customize Excel options, the *Ribbon*, and the *Quick Access* toolbar to personalize your working environment (p. E11-686).

SLO 11.2 View and modify Office account settings and install an Office add-in (p. E11-695).

SLO 11.3 Create a folder, add a file, and move and copy a file in *OneDrive* (p. E11-701).

SLO 11.4 Share *OneDrive* files and folders (p. E11-707).

SLO 11.5 Open, create, and edit an Excel workbook in *Office Online* (p. E11-712).

SLO 11.6 Explore *Office Online* applications and productivity tools (p. E11-720).

CASE STUDY

In the Pause & Practice projects in this chapter, you customize Excel settings and use cloud services to save, edit, and co-author workbooks for Paradise Lakes Resort (PLR).

Pause & Practice 11-1: Customize Excel and Office account settings and install an add-in.

Pause & Practice 11-2: Use *OneDrive* and *Excel Online* to co-author a workbook.

Pause & Practice 11-3: Create and share a form.

Customizing Excel

SLO 11.1

You have learned ways to customize an individual workbook such as changing the tab color or choosing the zoom size. The *Excel Options* dialog box includes customization choices that globally alter Excel settings and apply to all workbooks you create.

Excel Options

The *Excel Options* dialog box displays settings and commands in 12 categories. The following list shows the names of the panes or categories in the *Excel Options* dialog box. Each category is discussed in the sections that follow.

- *General*
- *Formulas*
- *Data*
- *Proofing*
- *Save*
- *Language*
- *Ease of Access*
- *Advanced*
- *Customize Ribbon*
- *Quick Access Toolbar*
- *Add-ins*
- *Trust Center*

HOW TO: Customize Excel Options

1. Click the **File** tab to open the *Backstage* view.
2. Choose **Options** to open the *Excel Options* dialog box (Figure 11-1).
3. Click the category or pane name at the left to display options at the right.
4. Make selections using check boxes, text boxes, drop-down lists, or buttons.
    - When you click a button, a dialog box with related settings opens.
5. Click **OK** to close the *Excel Options* dialog box and apply the settings.

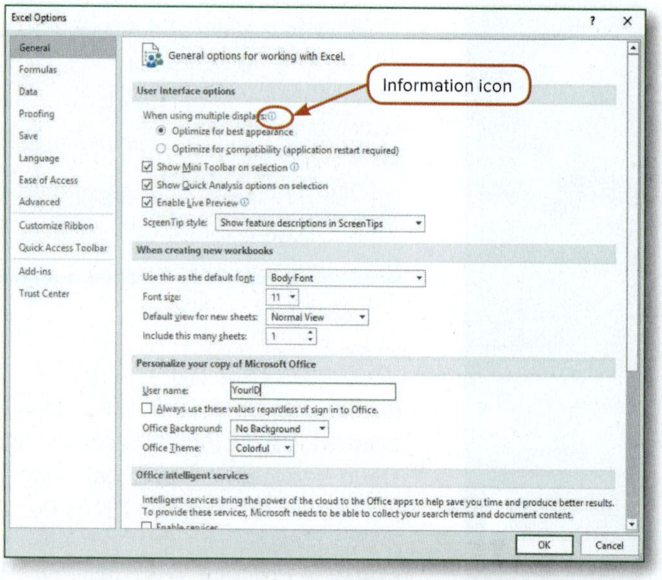

Figure 11-1 *Excel Options* dialog box, *General* pane

General

The *General* category includes the following groups: *User Interface options*, *When creating new workbooks*, *Personalize your copy of Microsoft Office*, *Office Intelligent services*, *LinkedIn Features*, and *Start up options* (see Figure 11-1).

In the *User Interface options* group, you can choose whether the mini toolbar displays for selected data and if the *Quick Analysis* button appears for selected cells. You can enable or disable *Live Preview* and customize the *ScreenTip* style.

The *When creating new workbooks* area has options to select the default font, the default view, and the number of sheets in a new workbook. Changes that you make do not affect workbooks already saved, only new workbooks created after you customize these options.

> **MORE INFO**
>
> Point to an *Information* icon at the end of an item to display a *ScreenTip* about the option.

In the *Personalize your copy of Microsoft Office* area, change your user name, enforce your Excel settings for all users on the computer, and choose the Office background and theme.

The *Office intelligent services* are cloud-based tools such as *Smart Lookup* or *Translator*, which can be turned off as desired. The *LinkedIn features*, when enabled, display *LinkedIn* information in Outlook and while co-authoring.

The *Start up options* group enables you to select compatible file name extensions for Excel, so that Excel starts when you double-click the file name in a *File Explorer* window. From this group, you can also choose whether the *Start* screen displays when Excel opens. The *Start* screen displays your recent documents and Excel templates.

Formulas

The *Formulas* pane includes settings for calculation and for formula and error handling (Figure 11-2). In the *Calculation options* area, choose automatic or manual calculation. Manual calculation can speed editing for exceptionally large worksheets, but you must calculate formulas by clicking the **Calculate Now** button [*Formulas* tab, *Calculation* group] or by pressing **F9 (FN+F9)**. Iterative calculations are used in *Goal Seek* and *Solver* problems to find a solution and affect calculation speed for a workbook.

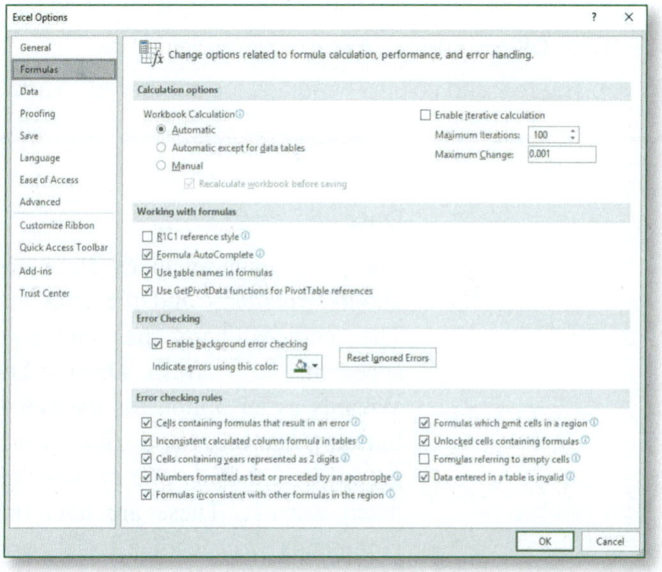

Figure 11-2 ***Formulas*** **options in the** ***Excel Options*** **dialog box**

> **MORE INFO**
>
> When you choose manual calculation, you can set the option to recalculate automatically when the workbook is saved.

Select the cell reference style in the *Working with formulas* group. The default setting is the column letter and row number convention with cell addresses such as A1, B15, and D25. The *R1C1* style identifies rows and columns by numbers with cell addresses such as R2C4 for row 2, column 4. Some macro commands use the *R1C1* style in the code.

From the *Formulas* pane, disable *Formula AutoComplete* if you prefer to not see a list of function and range names when you type an entry in a formula. Table names and structured references are supplied when you refer to a cell in a table unless you deselect the *Use table names in formulas* box. Finally, you can prohibit use of the *GETPIVOTDATA* function when you refer to a cell in a *PivotTable*.

Two groups in the *Formulas* pane affect how Excel handles formula errors. In the *Error Checking* group, disable background error checking and determine the color for the alert triangle in the cell. The rules that Excel uses for background checking display in the *Error checking rules* list. Note that the default setting does not identify formulas that refer to empty cells.

▶HOW TO: Customize the Cell Reference Style

1. Create a new blank workbook.
2. Click the **File** tab and choose **Options** to open the *Excel Options* dialog box.
3. Click **Formulas**.
4. Select the **R1C1 reference style** box in the *Working with formulas* group.
   - Point to the *Information* icon to see details about the option.
   - Deselect the box to use the standard A1 reference style.
5. Click **OK** to close the *Excel Options* dialog box.
   - The row and column headings are numbered (Figure 11-3).

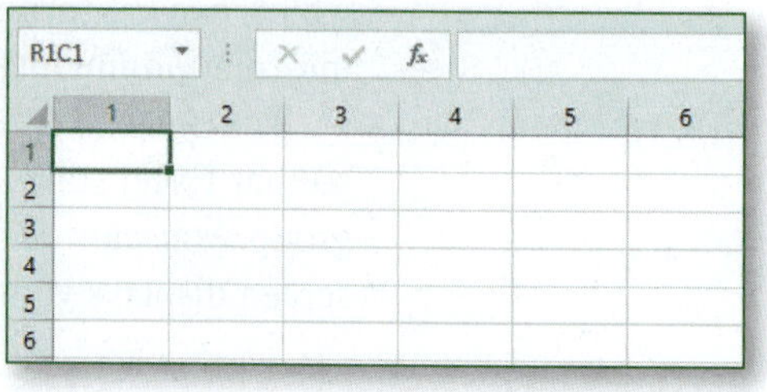

Figure 11-3 Workbook in R1C1 reference style

Data

The *Data* pane includes *Data options* about *PivotTables* and the data model. The choices here are intended to speed up data refresh. Display **Legacy Wizards** as an option for the **Get Data** button [*Data* tab, *Get & Transform* Data group] by choosing one or more of the listed wizards. These are data import commands from earlier Excel versions (Figure 11-4).

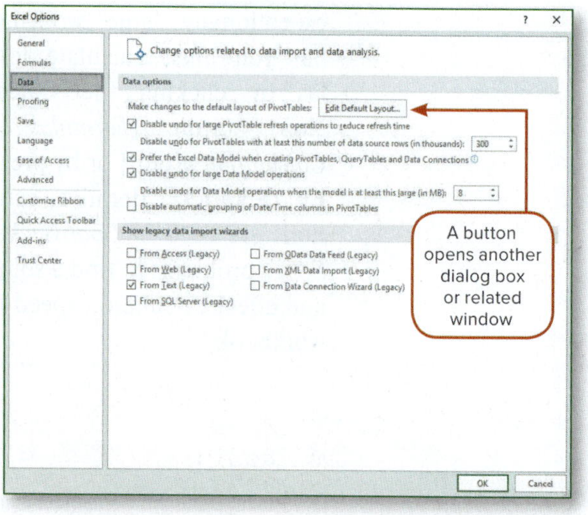

Figure 11-4 *Data* pane in the *Excel Options* dialog box

Proofing

The *Proofing* category offers settings for text entries in a workbook. Click the *AutoCorrect Options* button to open the *AutoCorrect* dialog box with tabs for *AutoCorrect*, *AutoFormat As You Type*, *Actions*, and *Math AutoCorrect*. *Math AutoCorrect* is a Word feature that converts text into math symbols; it does not apply to Excel.

The *When correcting spelling in Microsoft Office programs* list applies to all Office programs, so that a choice you make in Excel applies to a Word document. Excel does not highlight spelling errors as you type, but it does correct two initial uppercase letters in a word in a cell.

> **MORE INFO**
>
> A workbook, even if it is blank, must be open to access all choices in the *Excel Options* dialog box.

Save

In the *Save* pane, you control how and where workbooks are saved (Figure 11-5). You have seen that *AutoSave* is enabled when you save a workbook to *OneDrive*, but you can disable that command from this pane. Select the default file format in the *Save workbooks* group. The *AutoRecover* feature saves open workbooks, and you set where and how often recovery files are stored. Disable *AutoRecover* for an individual workbook in the *AutoRecover exceptions for* section.

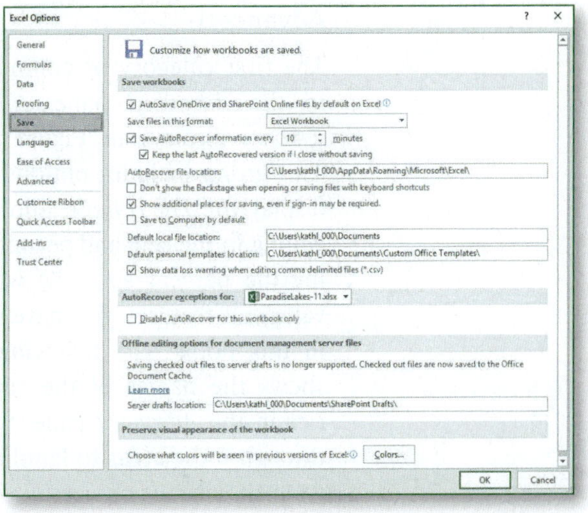

Figure 11-5 ***Save*** **options in the** ***Excel Options*** **dialog box**

The *Backstage* view displays when you press **Ctrl+O** or **Ctrl+S** to open or save a workbook unless you deselect the *Don't show the Backstage view when opening or saving files with keyboard shortcuts* box. From the *Save* pane, you can also set the default save location for files and templates.

The *Offline editing options for document management server files* group pertains to documents shared in Microsoft SharePoint. *Preserve visual appearance of the workbook* controls how colors display when a workbook is opened in earlier versions of Excel.

Language

Use the *Language* pane to set the language preference in all Office programs (Figure 11-6). The selected language affects spelling, grammar, dictionaries, and sorting. You can add a new language, set a language as the default, or remove a language. In the *Choose Display Language* group, choose the language for tabs, buttons, and *Help* screens.

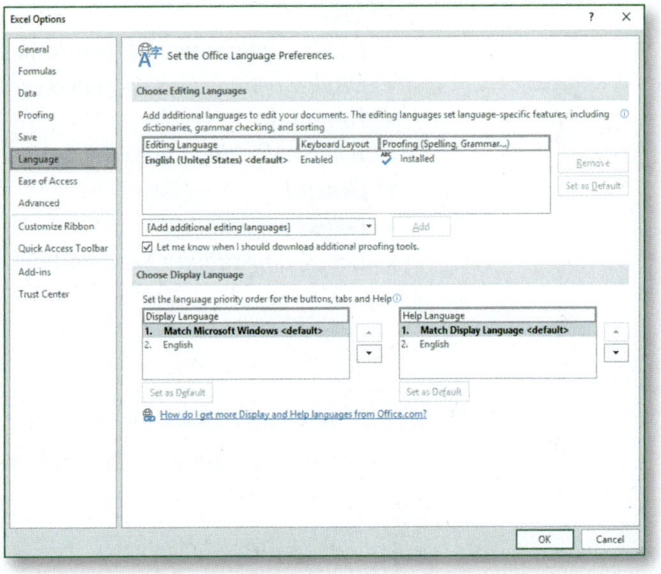

Figure 11-6 ***Language*** **options in the** ***Excel Options*** **dialog box**

> **MORE INFO**
>
> Language settings in Office are determined by the language you chose when you installed Windows.

Ease of Access

The *Ease of Access* pane has settings that help make a workbook accessible for those with sight or hearing impairment. Select sound or animation in the *Feedback options* group to provide audio and visual clues for commands and actions. Use *Application display options* to include *ScreenTips* for features and functions and to display the *Start* screen. From the *Document display options*, select the default font size. Note that you can choose to automatically create generic alt text for charts, pictures, SmartArt, and other visual content in your workbook, too.

Advanced

The first category of commands in the *Advanced* pane, *Editing options*, displays in Figure 11-7. This group includes options that display the *Fill Handle*, allow for editing in the cell, and permit typing the percent sign (%) with a value, all features you have used in this book. The following list shows the names of the categories in the *Advanced* pane. Scroll through these areas to familiarize yourself with the choices.

- *Editing options*
- *Cut, copy, and paste*
- *Pen*
- *Image size and quality*
- *Print*
- *Chart*
- *Display*
- *Display options for this workbook*
- *Display options for this worksheet*
- *Formulas*
- *When calculating this workbook*
- *General*
- *Lotus compatibility*
- *Lotus compatibility Settings for*

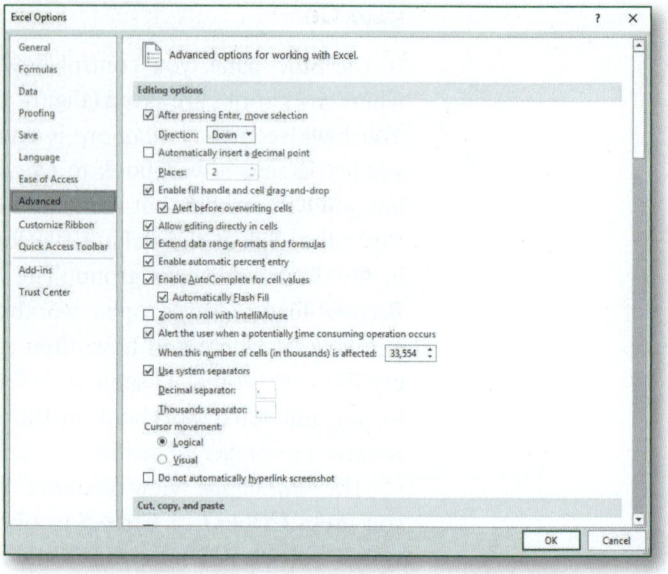

Figure 11-7 *Advanced* pane in the *Excel Options* dialog box

> **MORE INFO**
>
> The *Customize Ribbon* and *Quick Access Toolbar* panes are covered later in this section.

Add-ins

The add-in commands or programs that are available on your computer depend on your Office product and installation (Figure 11-8).

Active add-ins are listed in the top half of the *Add-ins* pane. When the *Manage* box displays *Excel Add-ins*, click **Go** to open the *Add-ins* dialog box and install an inactive feature or remove an active one. In the *Manage* list, choose *COM Add-ins* to see a list of compiled programs that are available for installation on your computer.

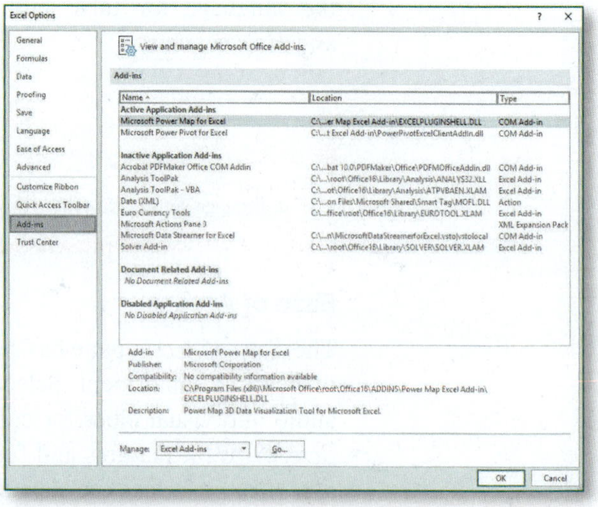

Figure 11-8 *Add-ins* pane in the *Excel Options* dialog box

Trust Center

You used the *Trust Center* in *SLO 8.1: Running a Macro* to set macro security. Additional settings in the *Trust Center* include the use of *Protected View*, the appearance of the message bar, and handling of external data (Figure 11-9). It is generally recommended that you use the default settings in the *Trust Center* to keep your files and computer safe.

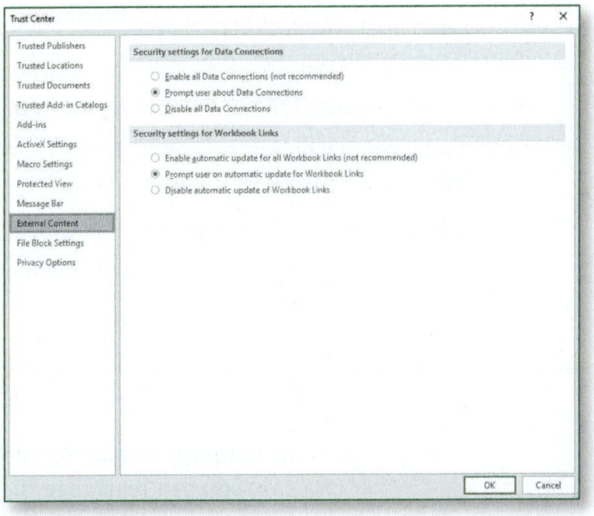

Figure 11-9 *Trust Center* dialog box for *External Content*

Customize the Ribbon

The *Ribbon* displays common commands for Excel, but not all commands. Customize the *Ribbon* to display commands you use often or create your own tabs and groups. New groups may be added to standard command tabs or to your custom tabs. Command buttons can be added only to a custom group.

▸HOW TO: Add a Tab, a Group, and a Command to the Ribbon

1. Right-click the **Ribbon** and select **Customize the Ribbon** from the context menu.
   - The *Excel Options* dialog box opens to the *Customize Ribbon* pane.
   - The leftmost list shows available commands; the rightmost list displays *Ribbon* tab and group names.
2. In the list on the right, click the tab name after which you want to insert a new tab.
3. Click the **New Tab** button.
   - A new custom tab and custom group are inserted.
4. Click **New Tab (Custom)** and then click **Rename**.
   - The *Rename* dialog box opens.
5. Type the name of the new tab and click **OK** (Figure 11-10).
6. Select **New Group (Custom)** and click **Rename**.
   - You see a custom group name on the *Ribbon* after you add a button to the group.
   - Icons are available for commands, not groups.
7. Type the name of the group and click **OK**.
8. Select the custom group name to which you want to add a command.
9. Click the **Choose commands from** drop-down list and select **All Commands**.
10. Select the command name and click **Add** to place the command in the group (Figure 11-11).

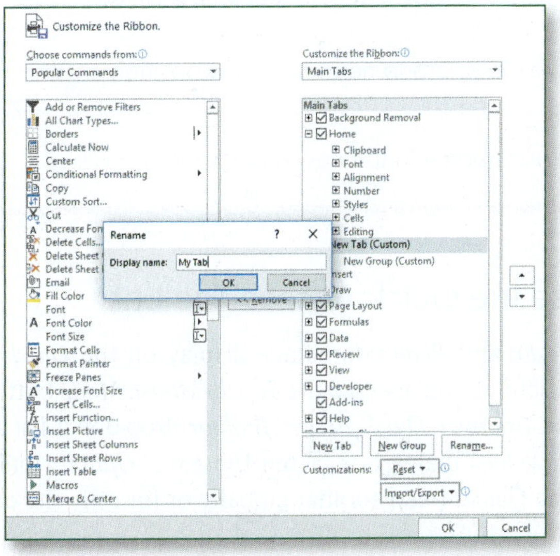

Figure 11-10 Rename a custom *Ribbon* tab

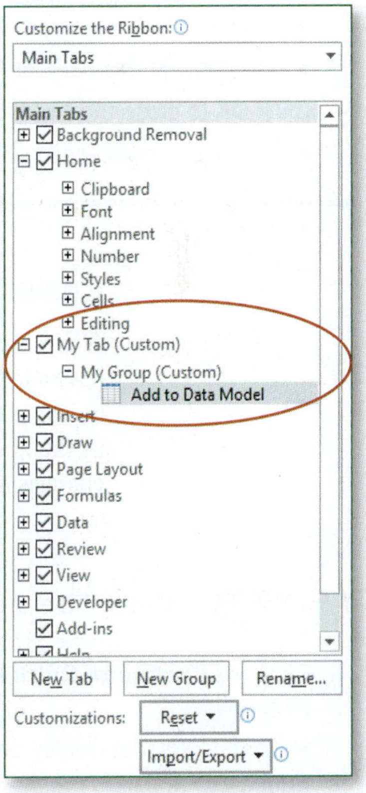

Figure 11-11 Command added to a custom group on a custom tab

11. Select the command name and click **Rename**.
12. Type a new name for the command.
    - Keep the original command name as desired.
13. Select a different icon for the command as desired and click **OK**.
14. Click **OK** to close the *Excel Options* dialog box.
    - The custom tab, group, and command display on the *Ribbon* (Figure 11-12).

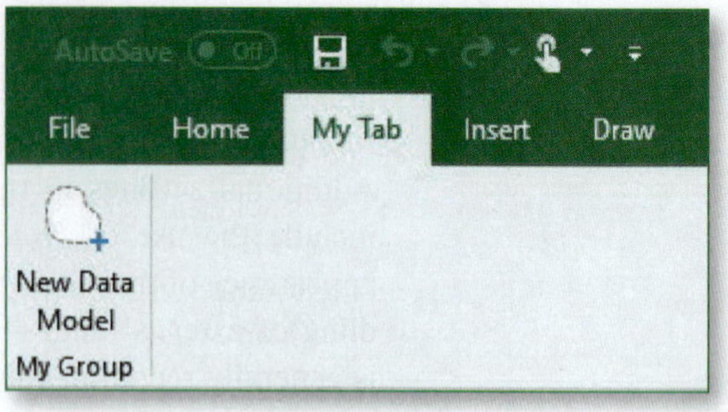

Figure 11-12 Custom tab and group on the *Ribbon*

In addition to adding tabs, groups, and commands to the *Ribbon*, you can rearrange the order of tabs or groups by dragging and dropping the tab or group names in the *Excel Options* dialog box. You can also rearrange names by clicking the *Move Up* or *Move Down* button in the *Excel Options* dialog box.

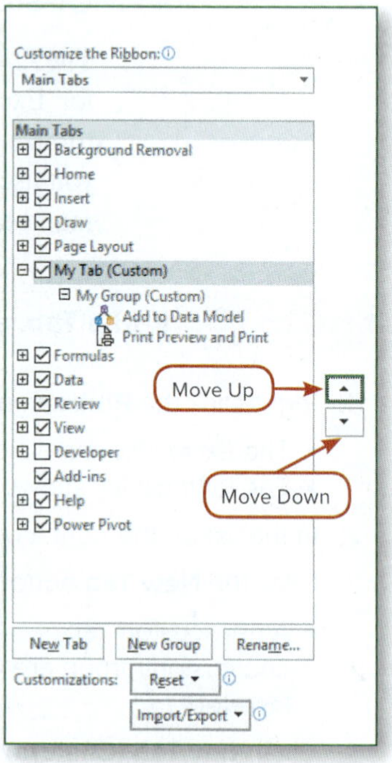

Figure 11-13 Move item names up or down to rearrange the *Ribbon*

HOW TO: Move Tabs, Groups, and Commands on the Ribbon

1. Right-click the **Ribbon** and select **Customize the Ribbon** from the context menu.
    - The *Excel Options* dialog box opens to the *Customize Ribbon* pane.
2. Select the command, group, or tab to be moved.
    - You cannot make changes to the *File* tab.
3. Click the **Move Up** or **Move Down** button to rearrange the selected item (Figure 11-13).
    - Alternatively, drag and drop the tab or group name to a new position.
4. Click **OK** to close the *Excel Options* dialog box.
    - The tabs, groups, and commands appear in the new arrangement.

Customize the Quick Access Toolbar

The *Save*, *Undo*, and *Redo* commands display on the *Quick Access* toolbar by default. If you have a touch screen, you also see the *Touch/Mouse Mode* button. Add commands to the toolbar by using the *Customize Quick Access Toolbar* drop-down list or the *Quick Access Toolbar* pane in the *Excel Options* dialog box. From the *Excel Options* dialog box, you can choose to show changes in the *Quick Access* toolbar globally or for only the current workbook.

HOW TO: Customize the Quick Access Toolbar

1. Click the **Customize Quick Access Toolbar** drop-down list on the right edge of the *Quick Access* toolbar (Figure 11-14).
    - Commands that display on the *Quick Access* toolbar include a check mark.
2. Select a command to display it on the *Quick Access* toolbar.
    - A default button for the command appears on the *Quick Access* toolbar.

3. Click the **Customize Quick Access Toolbar** drop-down list and select **More Commands**.
   - The *Excel Options* dialog box opens to the *Quick Access Toolbar* pane.
4. Select a command in the list and click **Add** (Figure 11-15).
   - The command name displays in the list on the right.
   - The list on the left is filtered to show *Popular Commands*. Display all commands by selecting **All Commands** from the **Choose commands from** drop-down list.
   - Select **For WorkbookName.xlsx** from the *Customize Quick Access Toolbar* drop-down list (above the rightmost list) to limit the changes to the current workbook.
5. Click **OK** to close the *Excel Options* dialog box.

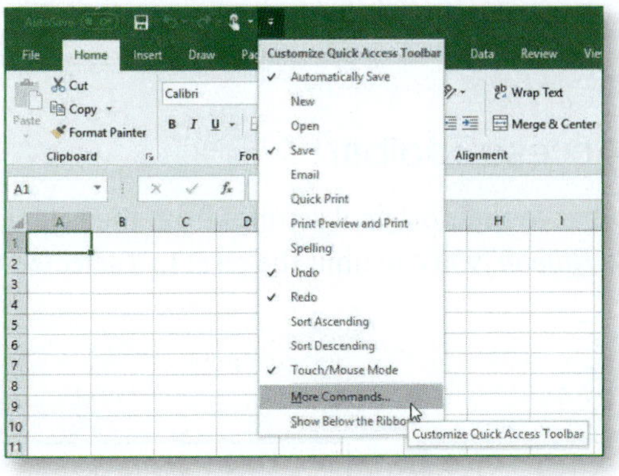

Figure 11-14 Commonly used commands are available from the drop-down list

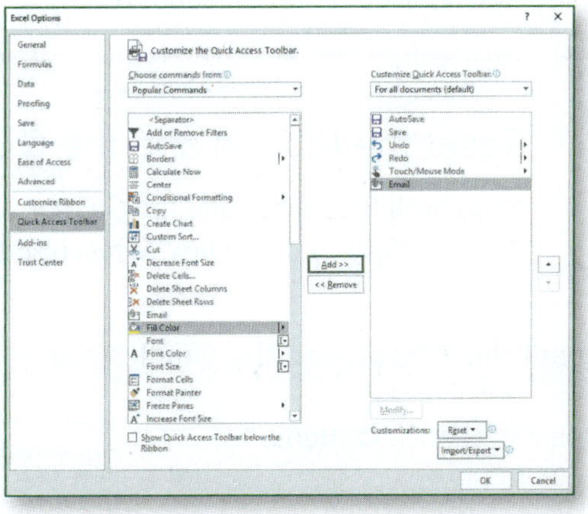

Figure 11-15 ***Customize Quick Access Toolbar***

ANOTHER WAY

Right-click a command button on a command tab and choose **Add to Quick Access Toolbar** to place the button on the toolbar.

MORE INFO

Display the *Quick Access* toolbar below the *Ribbon* by clicking the **Customize Quick Access Toolbar** drop-down list and choosing **Show Below the Ribbon**.

Remove Commands from the Ribbon and the Quick Access Toolbar

Remove commands from the *Quick Access* toolbar as desired and remove commands, groups, or tabs from the *Ribbon* if you no longer need them.

HOW TO: Remove Items from the Quick Access Toolbar and the Ribbon

1. Right-click the button to be removed in the *Quick Access* toolbar.
   - The context menu opens (Figure 11-16).
2. Select **Remove from Quick Access Toolbar**.
   - The button is removed from the toolbar.
   - Click the **Customize Quick Access Toolbar** drop-down list and deselect the command name to remove the button.

3. Right-click the **Ribbon** and select **Customize the Ribbon** from the context menu.
   - The *Excel Options* dialog box opens to the *Customize Ribbon* pane.
4. In the list on the right, select the command, group, or tab name to be removed.
   - Expand or collapse the tab or group as needed.
5. Click **Remove**.
6. Click **OK** to close the *Excel Options* dialog box.
   - The *Ribbon* displays modified groups and tabs.

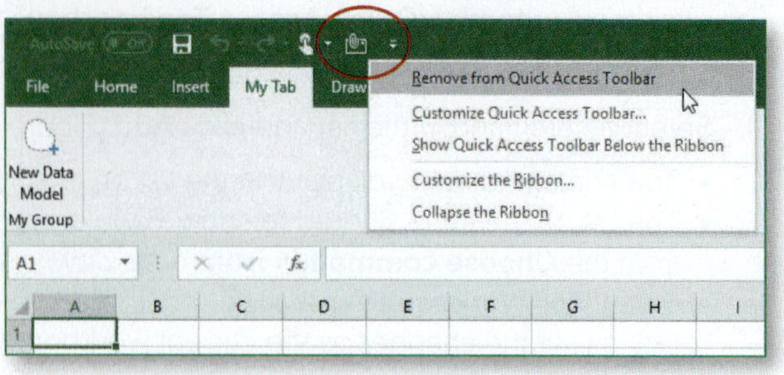

Figure 11-16 Remove a command from the *Quick Access* toolbar using the context menu

Reset the Ribbon and the Quick Access Toolbar

Reset both the *Ribbon* and the *Quick Access* toolbar to their original settings from their panes in the *Excel Options* dialog box. When resetting the *Ribbon*, you can limit the reset to a selected tab.

▶HOW TO: Reset the Ribbon and the Quick Access Toolbar

1. Click the **File** tab and choose **Options**.
2. Select *Customize Ribbon* or *Customize Quick Access Toolbar.*
   - To reset a specific *Ribbon* tab, select the tab name in the list on the right.
3. Click **Reset** and choose a command (Figures 11-17 and 11-18).
   - The *Reset only selected Ribbon tab* option is available when commands have been added to one of the default tabs.
   - The *Reset only Quick Access Toolbar* option is grayed out if only the default buttons display on the toolbar.
4. Select **Reset all customizations**.
   - A message box asks you to confirm that all customizations will be removed.
5. Click **Yes** (Figure 11-19).

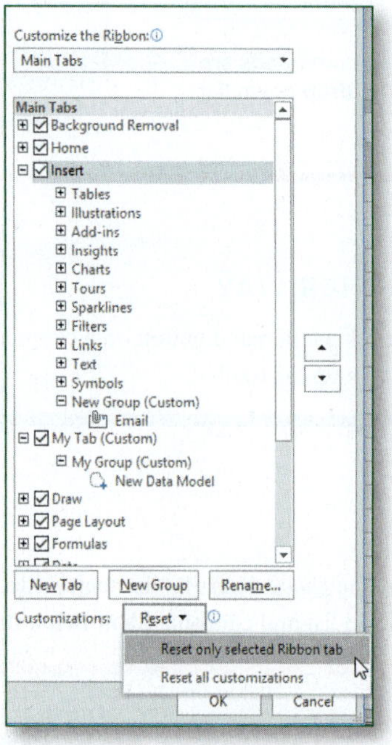

Figure 11-17 Reset the *Ribbon*

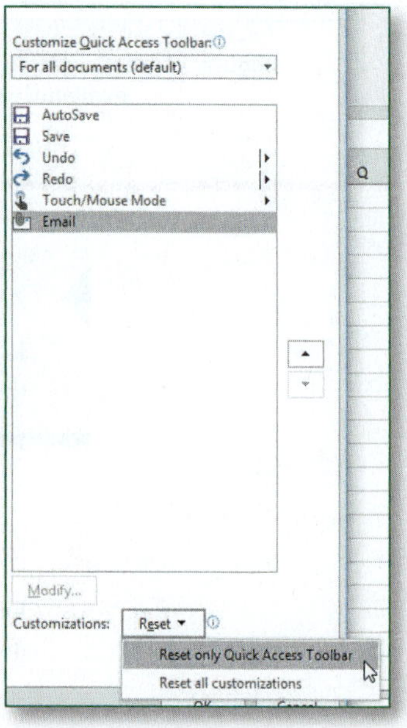

Figure 11-18 Reset the *Quick Access* toolbar

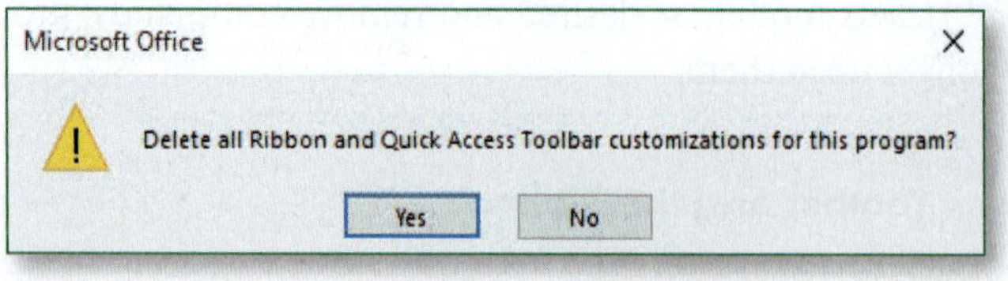

Figure 11-19 Message box to confirm resetting of the *Ribbon* and the toolbar

6. Click **OK** to close the *Excel Options* dialog box.
   - The *Ribbon* and the *Quick Access* toolbar reset to their default displays.

SLO 11.2

Customizing Office Account Settings

When you install Office, you use your Microsoft account information to set up and log in to Windows and Office. You can view and customize your Office account settings in the *Backstage* view, add connected services such as LinkedIn or Twitter, and install *Office Add-ins* for extra commands and features in all your programs.

> MORE INFO
>
> If you don't have a Microsoft account, create a free account at https://signup.live.com.

Microsoft Account Information

Your Microsoft account signs you in to Windows, Office, and other free Microsoft services such as ***OneDrive*** and ***Office Online***. You log in with your Microsoft account user name and password. Microsoft Office uses this information to apply your Office settings to the computer you are using. The *OneDrive* and *Office Online* environments are slightly different when using a personal, education, or business account.

Point to your name in the upper-right corner of the Excel window and click. Then choose **Account settings** to open the *Account* pane in the *Backstage* view (Figure 11-20).

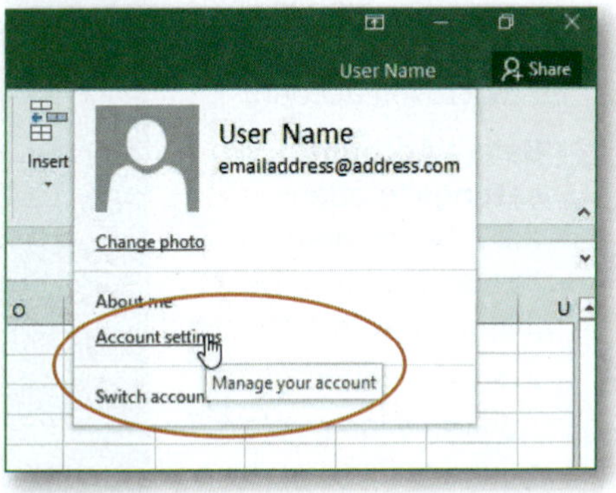

Figure 11-20 Microsoft account information

> MORE INFO
>
> When you open an Office file in an older version of Windows and Office, you may be prompted to sign in to your Microsoft account.

> MORE INFO
>
> When you use a public computer, click the **Sign out** link in the *Account* area in the *Backstage* view to log out of your Office account.

Office Background and Theme

Change the ***Office Background*** and ***Office Theme*** in the *Account* area in the *Backstage* view. The background is a graphic pattern in the upper-right corner of the Excel window. The theme controls colors on the *Ribbon*, the *Backstage* view, and dialog boxes. Your background and theme selections apply to all Office applications. The default *Office Theme* is *Colorful*.

> ANOTHER WAY
>
> Change the *Office Background* and the *Office Theme* on the *General* pane in the *Excel Options* dialog box.

Connected Services

Office enables you to quickly connect to cloud services. For some services, you may be prompted to enter your sign-in credentials. You can also remove a service from ***Connected Services*** as desired.

▸HOW TO: Change Office Account Settings

1. Click your name in the upper-right corner of the Excel window (see Figure 11-20).
   - If your name is not displayed, find and click the **Sign in** link and sign-in to your Microsoft account.
2. Select **Account settings** to open the *Account* area on the *Backstage* view (Figure 11-21).
   - Your account information displays.
   - Your settings and choices depend on your Microsoft account and may be different from Figure 11-21.
   - Alternatively, click the **File** tab and select **Account**.

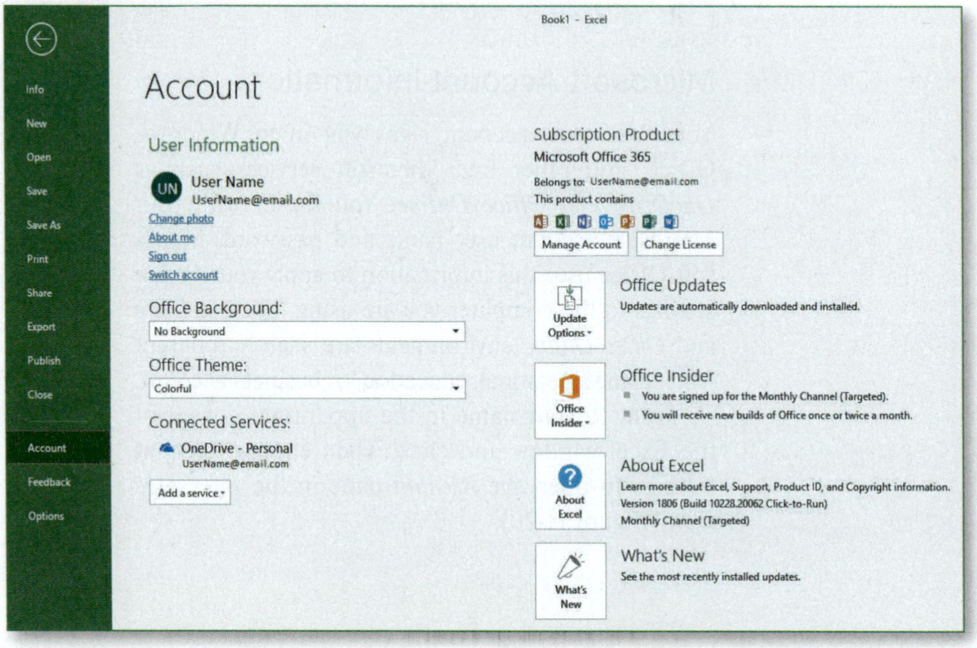

Figure 11-21 Office user information and settings

3. Select the **Office Background** drop-down list and choose a background.
   - The image appears in the upper-right corner.
4. Select the **Office Theme** drop-down list and choose a theme.
   - Theme colors display in the *Backstage* view.
5. Click **Add a service**.
   - Choose from cloud storage services listed for your account.

Office Add-ins

Office add-ins are programs that provide enhanced features and commands for your Office software, similar to apps on your smartphone. In Excel, for example, add specialized charts and graphs or a currency converter. These programs may be from Microsoft or from other suppliers and may or may not be free. Each program has its own set of commands and features, and most add-ins include help screens, instructions, or a tutorial. An add-in application displays as a floating dialog box or in a pane at the right of the Excel window.

▸HOW TO: Install an Office Add-in

1. Click the sheet tab where the add-in will be used.
2. Click the **Get Add-ins** button [*Insert* tab, *Add-ins* group].
   - The *Office Add-ins* dialog box opens and displays the names of categories and suggested add-ins (Figure 11-22).
   - Add-ins are regularly updated and featured.
   - Click the **My Add-ins** link to display add-ins currently installed for your account.
3. Select a category name to filter the list.
   - Type a keyword in the search box to locate specific types of add-in programs.
4. Select the name of an add-in.
   - A dialog box opens that contains details about the program.
5. Click **Add** to install the add-in.
   - Add-ins install in various ways because they are from different sources (Figure 11-23).
   - The add-in may display as a floating window or in a pane at the right of the window.
   - When the add-in is a floating window, select, size, and position it as desired.
   - For some add-ins, a web site may open for installation of the program.
6. Use the add-in features and commands as desired in the workbook.
7. Select the add-in window and press **Delete** or close the add-in pane.
   - The add-in window closes.
   - The add-in is available in your account for use when needed.

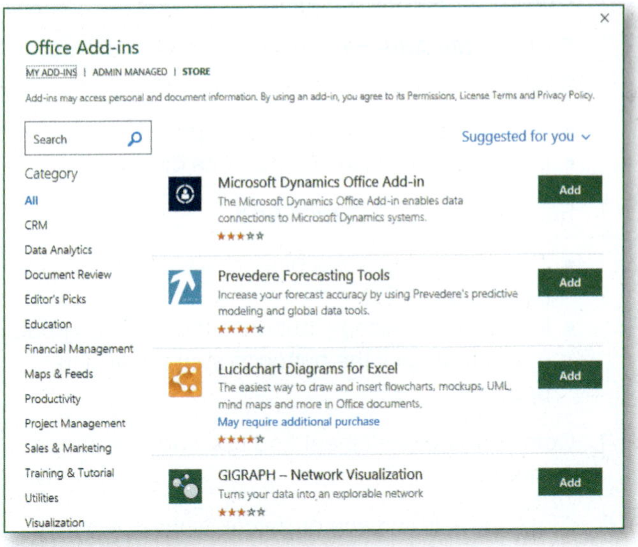

Figure 11-22 *Office Add-ins* dialog box from the *Store*

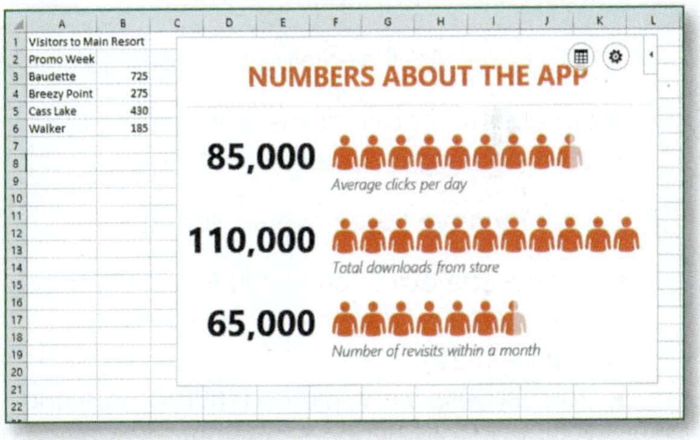

Figure 11-23 *Add-in* displayed in a window

Manage Office Add-ins

Click the **My Add-ins** button [*Insert* tab, *Add-ins* group] to review details about installed add-ins, rate or review an installed program, or remove an add-in. When you remove an add-in, it is deactivated and not shown as part of your account in the *Office Add-ins* dialog box. You can reactivate an add-in at any time. Microsoft add-ins may place a button in the *Add-ins* group [*Insert* tab] so that you can reactivate the add-in from the button.

> **MORE INFO**
>
> The add-ins in *Excel Options* [*Add-ins* pane] are not the same as those available in the *Office Store*.

▶HOW TO: Manage Office Add-ins

1. Open a workbook.
2. Click the **My Add-ins** button [*Insert* tab, *Add-ins* group] (Figure 11-24).
   - The *Office Add-ins* dialog box opens.
   - Installed add-in names and icons display.
3. Select an add-in and click **Add**.
   - The add-in opens in a pane or a window (see Figure 11-23).
   - If the add-in placed a button in the *Add-ins* group [*Insert* tab], click the button to start the add-in program.
4. Complete the worksheet and use add-in features as needed.
5. Close the add-in pane or delete its window when finished.
6. To deactivate an add-in, click the **My Add-ins** button [*Insert* tab, *Add-ins* group].
   - The *Office Add-ins* dialog box opens.
7. Right-click an add-in name or click the ellipses (**. . .**) in the upper-right corner.
8. Select **Remove** to remove an add-in.
   - A message box informs you that the add-in will be removed from your Microsoft account (Figure 11-25).
   - You can also view add-in details or rate and review the add-in from the context menu.
9. Click **Remove** in the message box.
   - The add-in is deactivated and not listed in the *Office Add-ins* dialog box.
   - Microsoft add-in buttons may remain on the *Ribbon*.
10. Close the *Office Add-ins* dialog box.

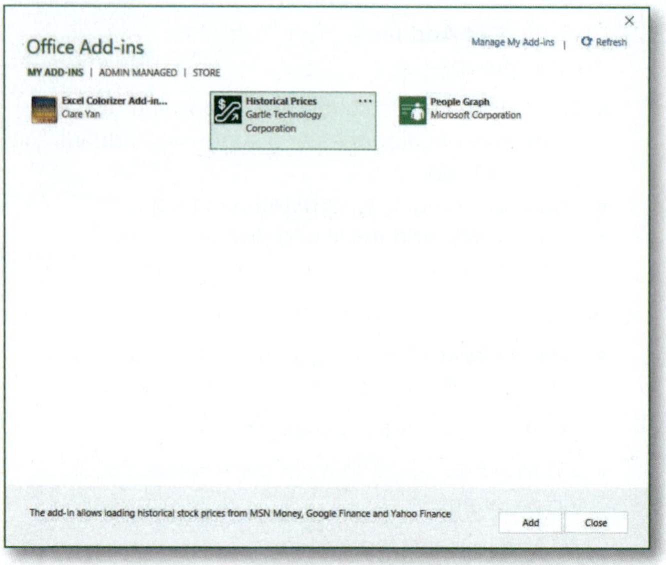

Figure 11-24 ***Office Add-ins*** **dialog box lists currently available programs**

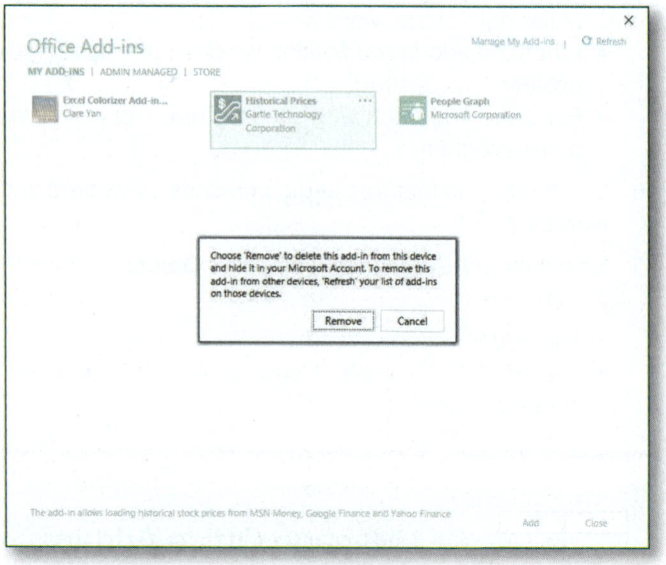

Figure 11-25 Remove an add-in from your Office account

ANOTHER WAY

Click the **Manage My Add-ins** link in the *Office Add-ins* dialog box to open your *Office Store* account. From this window, *Hide* an add-in to remove it from your account.

PAUSE & PRACTICE: EXCEL 11-1

For this project, you customize Excel options, add items to the *Ribbon* and the *Quick Access* toolbar, and customize your Office account settings.

Note: You need a Microsoft account (https://signup.live.com) to complete this project.

File Needed: ***ParadiseLakes-11.xlsx*** *(Student data files are available in the* Library *of your SIMnet account.)*
Completed Project File Name: ***[your initials] PP E11-1.xlsx***

1. Open Excel and verify that you are signed in to your Microsoft account.
2. Open the ***Paradise Lakes-11*** workbook from your student data files.
3. Customize Excel options.
   a. Click the **File** tab and select **Options** to open the *Excel Options* dialog box.
   b. Select **Formulas** at the left to open the *Formulas* pane.
   c. Select the **Manual** radio button in the *Calculation options* group.
   d. Select the **R1C1 reference style** box in the *Working with formulas* group.
   e. Click **OK** to close the *Excel Options* dialog box and apply the changes.
4. Select cell **R7C2** on the **Revenue** sheet and delete the contents. The formulas do not recalculate.
5. Click the **Formulas** tab and click the **Calculate Now** button [*Calculation* group].
6. Add a tab, a group, and commands to the *Ribbon*.
   a. Right-click the **Ribbon** and select **Customize the Ribbon**.
   b. Click **Home** in the *Main Tabs* list on the right.
   c. Click the **New Tab** button at the bottom of the list.
   d. Select **New Tab (Custom)** below the *Home* tab and click **Rename**.
   e. Type your first name for the *Display name* and click **OK**.
   f. Select **New Group (Custom)** and click **Rename**.
   g. Type My Commands as the *Display name* and click **OK**.
   h. Select the **My Commands (Custom)** group name.
   i. Select **Open** in the *Popular Commands* list on the left and click **Add**.
   j. Select **Print Preview and Print** in the list and click **Add**.
   k. Add the **Save As** command to the *My Commands* group.
7. Change the icon for a command.
   a. Select **Save As** in the *My Commands* group.
   b. Click **Rename** and type New File as the *Display name*.
   c. Click an icon in the gallery and click **OK** (Figure 11-26).
   d. Click **OK** to close the *Excel Options* dialog box.
8. Click the **[your first name]** tab on the *Ribbon*.
9. Click the **New File** button in the *My Commands* group and save the workbook as [your initials] PP E11-1 in your folder for saving files.
10. Add commands to the *Quick Access* toolbar.
    a. Click the **Customize Quick Access Toolbar** drop-down list and select **New** to add the button to create a new workbook to the toolbar.

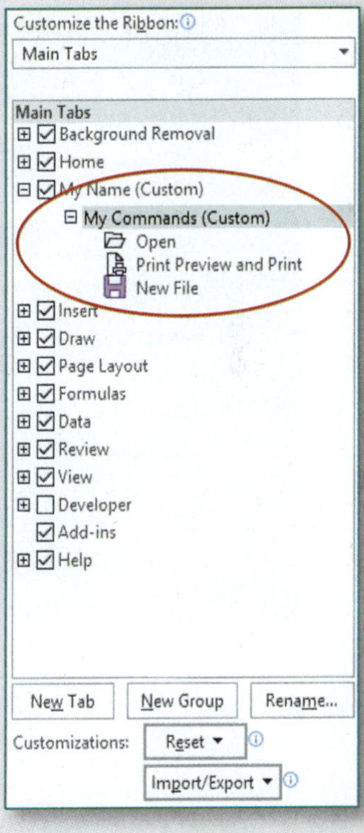

Figure 11-26 Custom tab and group with commands added in the *Excel Options* dialog box

b. Click the **Customize Quick Access Toolbar** drop-down list and select **More Commands**.
c. Click the **Choose commands from** drop-down list and select **All Commands**.
d. Find and select the first occurrence of **Insert Comment**. The *ScreenTip* for the command is *Review Tab | Comments | Insert Comment (NewThreadedComment)*. Click **Add**.
e. Click **OK** to close the *Excel Options* dialog box (Figure 11-27).

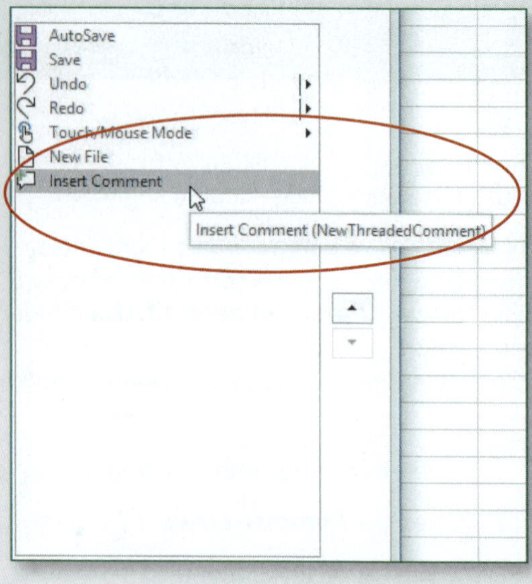

Figure 11-27 *New* and *Insert Comment* buttons added to the *Quick Access* toolbar

11. Select cell **R7C2** and click the **New Comment** button in the *Quick Access* toolbar.
12. Type Re-enter values ASAP. and click the **Post** button.
13. Hide the *Comments* pane if it displays and select cell **R2C1**.
14. Customize your Office account settings.
    a. Click the **File** tab and select **Account**.
    b. Click the **Office Background** drop-down list and choose **Circles and Stripes**.
    c. Click the **Office Theme** drop-down list and select **Dark Gray** (Figure 11-28).
    d. Return to the workbook.

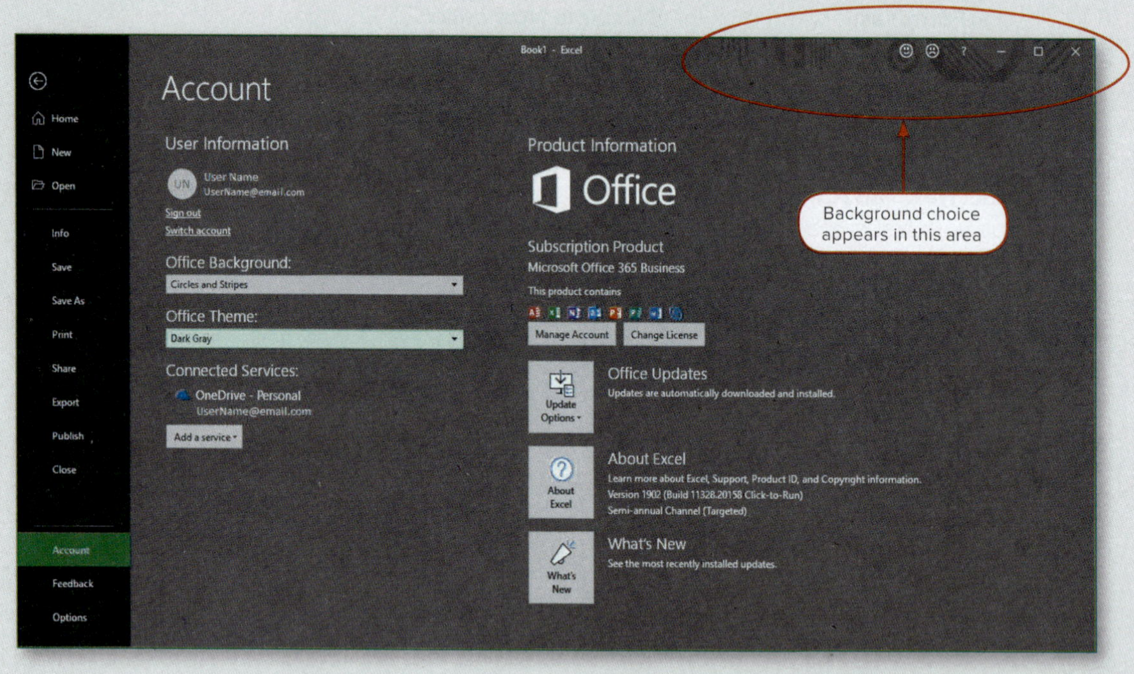

Figure 11-28 Office *Account* settings affect all Office applications

15. Save and close the workbook (Figure 11-29).
16. Reset your Office account settings.
    a. Open a new blank workbook.
    b. Click the **File** tab and select **Account**.
    c. Click the **Office Background** drop-down list and choose **No Background**.

d. Click the **Office Theme** drop-down list and select **Colorful**.
e. Select **Options** on the left and then click **Customize Ribbon**.
f. Click **Reset**, choose **Reset all customizations**, and then click **Yes**.
g. Click **Formulas** on the left.
h. Select the **Automatic** radio button.
i. Deselect the **R1C1 reference style** box.
j. Click **OK** to close the *Excel Options* dialog box.

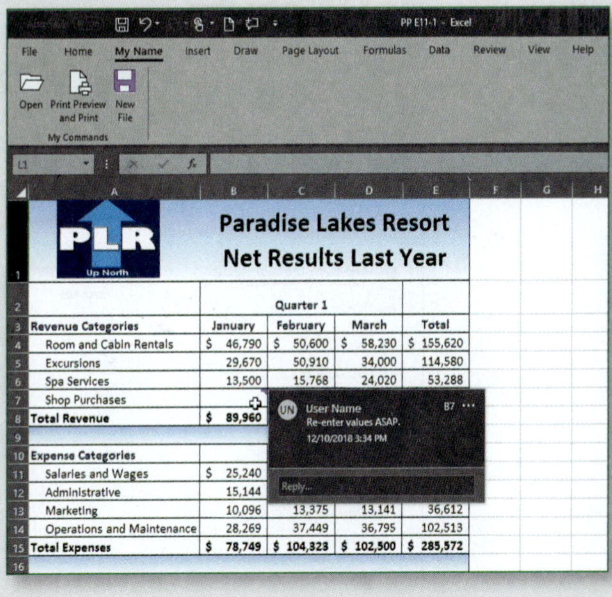

Figure 11-29 PP E11-1 completed

SLO 11.3

Using OneDrive

OneDrive is cloud storage where you store files in an online location for access from any computer. Cloud storage means that you are not limited to a single device and that you do not need to transport files on portable media. When you have a Microsoft account, you have a *OneDrive* account. If you don't have a Microsoft account, create a free account at https://signup.live.com/.

Save, open, and edit documents from your *OneDrive* account as well as create folders and rename, move, or delete files. *OneDrive* is listed in the *Open*, *Save*, and *Save As* commands in the *Backstage* view. In *Excel Options*, you can set *OneDrive* as your default save location.

> **MORE INFO**
>
> Do not store confidential or sensitive documents online. No online account is completely safe.

Use OneDrive in a File Explorer Window

In a Windows *File Explorer* window, *OneDrive* is a storage location, like your *Documents* or *Pictures* folders (Figure 11-30). The difference between your *OneDrive* folder and other folders is the physical location. When you save a workbook in the *Documents* folder on *This PC*, the file is stored on your computer. You have access to the file only from your computer. When you save a document in your *OneDrive* folder, the workbook is stored in the cloud, and you have access to the file from any device with internet access. To access your *OneDrive* folders from a *File Explorer* window, you must be logged in to your Microsoft account.

> **MORE INFO**
>
> Download and install the ***OneDrive desktop app for Windows*** for Windows 7 or 8. After installation, the *OneDrive* folder is available in the *File Explorer* window.

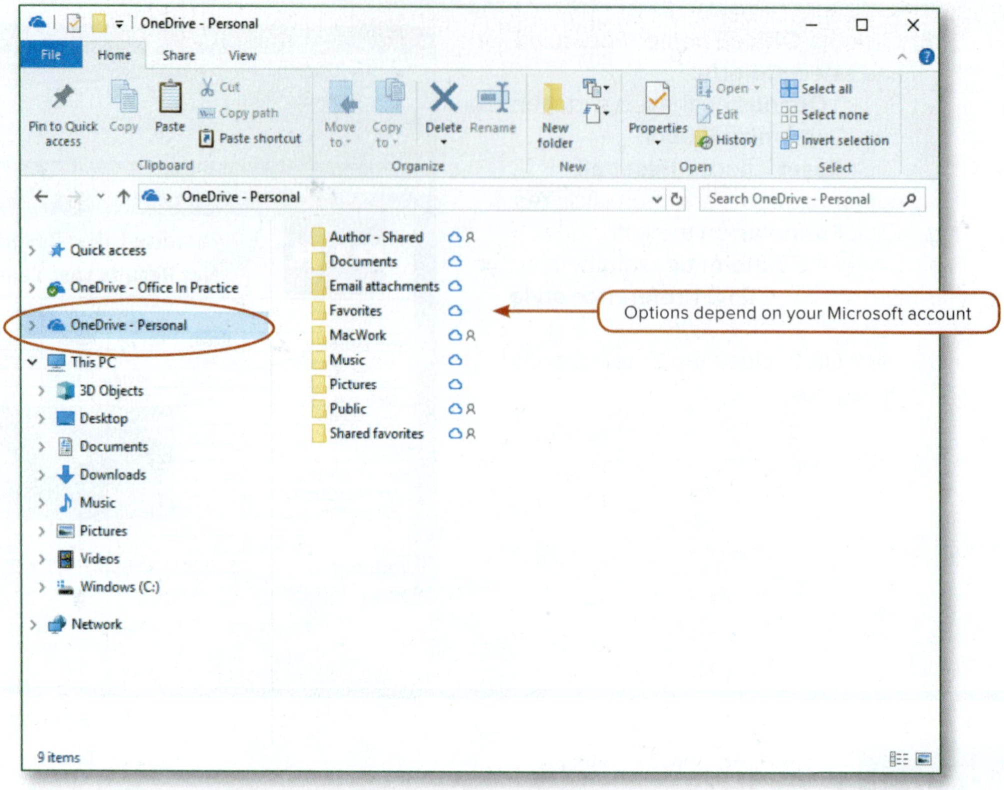

Figure 11-30 Personal *OneDrive* folder displayed in a *File Explorer* window

Use OneDrive Online

Sign-in directly to the *OneDrive* site with your Microsoft account from a browser window. Your *OneDrive* account lists default category names on the left of the window. The *Files* group displays your folders; these are the folders that are available from a *File Explorer* window or an Excel dialog box. The *PCs* category is included when you have multiple Office installations assigned to your account. The *OneDrive* online environment depends on your Microsoft account, but features are similar across platforms so that you can easily adapt.

HOW TO: Use OneDrive Online

1. Open an internet browser window and navigate to the *OneDrive* web site (www.onedrive.com).
   - Use any browser (Microsoft Edge, Google Chrome, or Mozilla Firefox).
2. Click the **Sign in** button.
   - If you are signed in to Windows with your Microsoft account and use Microsoft Edge as your browser, you may be automatically signed in to your *OneDrive* account.
3. Type your Microsoft account email address, if necessary, and click **Next**.
   - If you are signed in to Windows and Office, your email address may already be displayed.
4. Type your Microsoft account password and click **Sign in**.
   - *OneDrive* category names are listed at the left.
   - Category names depend on your Microsoft account.
   - The *PCs* category, if listed, expands to display multiple Office installation account names (Figure 11-31).
   - *OneDrive* category names do not display in a *File Explorer* window.

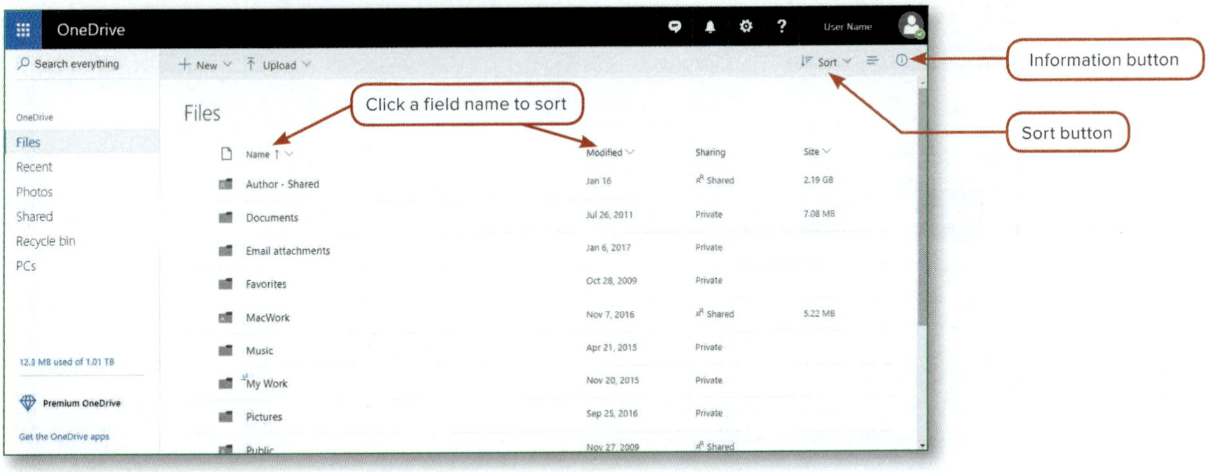

Figure 11-31 Personal *OneDrive* window in *List* view

5. Select **Files** to display folder and file names.
   - Your folder and file names may not match those shown in Figure 11-31.
6. Click the **View** button to toggle between available views.
   - In *Tiles* view, a folder that holds files shows the number of documents in the folder.
7. Click a header name (*Name, Modified, Size*) to sort folder or file names.
   - Header names and options depend on your account.
   - Click the header name arrow to apply a filter (may not be available in all accounts).
   - Header names do not appear in *Tiles* view.
   - Your account may display a **Sort** drop-down list.
8. Click a folder name to open it (Figure 11-32).
   - File names and icons display.

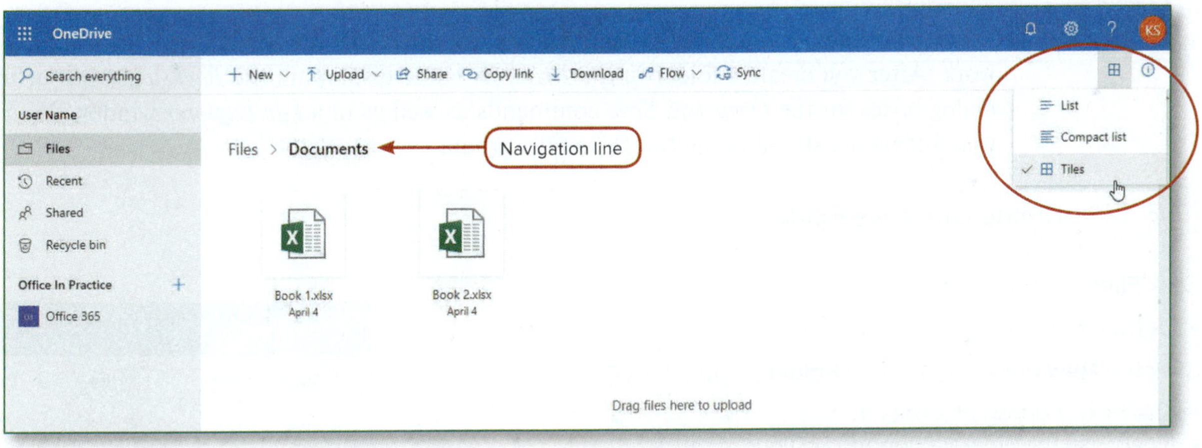

Figure 11-32 Folder contents displayed in *OneDrive* in *Tiles* view

9. Point to the folder or file icon and click its selection circle.
   - Click the **Information** button (encircled lowercase i) to display details about a selected folder or file.
10. Click a workbook name to launch *Excel Online*.
    - The workbook opens in its own browser window.
    - If the workbook has data connections, they are disabled; close the related security bar (Figure 11-33).
11. Close the workbook by closing its browser tab.
    - Do not click the **Close** button at the top-right corner of the window; this will close *OneDrive*.
    - Edits are saved automatically to the *OneDrive* folder.

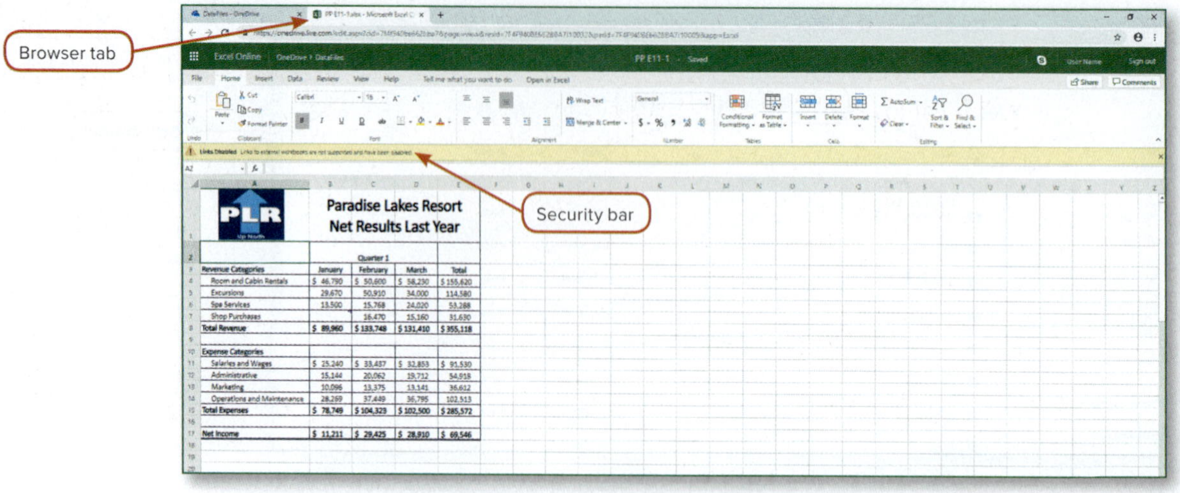

Figure 11-33 Workbook from *OneDrive* opened in *Excel Online*

12. Click **Files** to return to your *OneDrive* folder list.
    - Click **Files** in the category list on the left or in the navigation line in the center pane (see Figure 11-32).
13. Click your initials, name, or picture in the upper-right corner of the window and select **Sign out**.

> **MORE INFO**
>
> Do not check a *Keep me signed in* box when you use a public computer so that your *OneDrive* files are not available to the next person who uses the computer.

Create a OneDrive Folder

Upload workbooks to a default folder in *OneDrive* or create your own folders to organize your work. After you create a folder in *OneDrive*, its name displays in the *Backstage* view or in the dialog boxes for the *Open* and *Save* commands as well as in a *File Explorer* window. Your custom folders are stored in the *OneDrive Files* group.

HOW TO: Create OneDrive Folders

1. Click **Files** on the left in *OneDrive*.
    - Default folder and file names display.
2. Click the **New** button and select **Folder** (Figure 11-34).
    - The *Folder* dialog box opens.
    - Options in the *New* list depend on your account.
3. Type the name of the new folder and click **Create**.
4. Click a folder name to open the folder.
    - You can create a new folder inside an existing folder.
    - Right-click a folder name and select **Delete** to delete the folder from *OneDrive*.
5. Click **Files** to return to your *OneDrive* list.
    - Click **Files** in the list on the left or in the navigation line above folder names.

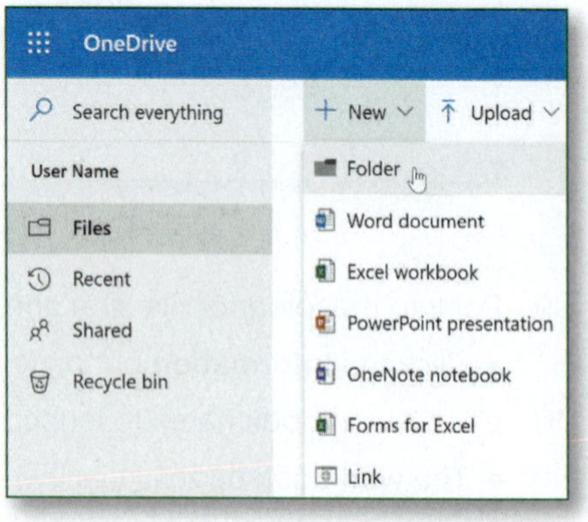

Figure 11-34 Create a new *OneDrive* folder

Upload a File or Folder

When you upload files to *OneDrive*, the files are copied to *OneDrive* and maintained in the original location. Upload files from your computer or portable media.

▶HOW TO: Upload Files to OneDrive

1. Click **Files** on the left to display file and folder names in *OneDrive*.
   - If you are uploading a file to a specific *OneDrive* folder, click the folder name to open it.
2. Click the **Upload** button (Figure 11-35).
3. Select **Files** or **Folder**.
   - If you choose *Files*, the *Open* dialog box displays.
   - If you select *Folder*, a *Select Folder* dialog box opens (Figure 11-36).
   - Some browsers may not have a command to upload a folder.
4. Select the file or folder name to upload.
   - Press **Ctrl** or **Shift** to select multiple file names.
   - You can select one folder name at a time.
5. Click **Open** or **Upload**.
   - The button name depends on the browser.
   - An uploading status message appears in the upper-right corner.
   - A confirmation dialog box may open depending on the browser.
   - The uploaded file or folder names appear in *OneDrive*.

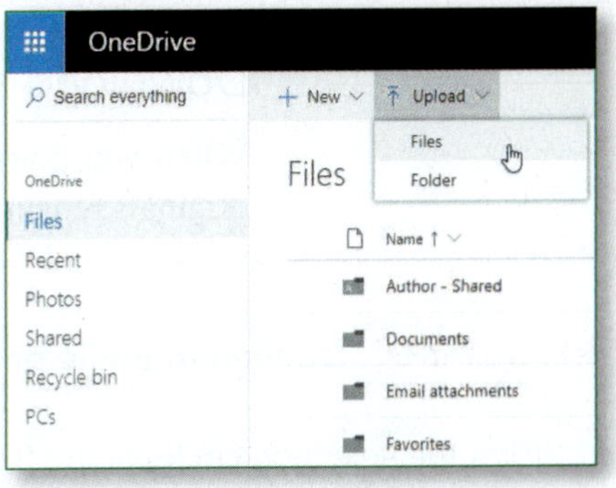

Figure 11-35 Upload a file to *OneDrive*

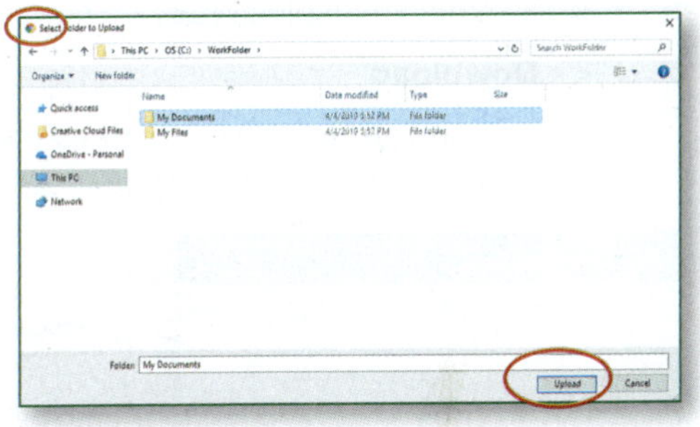

Figure 11-36 *Select a Folder* dialog box in Chrome browser

Move, Copy, or Delete a File or Folder

You can move or copy files and folders in *OneDrive* among your own folders. You can also delete files or folders for which you are the owner.

▶HOW TO: Move, Copy, or Delete OneDrive Files

1. Click the selection **circle** for the file or folder to be moved or copied.
   - In *Tiles* or *Photo* view, the selection circle is in the top-right corner of the folder or file icon.
   - In *List* or *Compact List* view, the selection circle is to the left of the folder or file name.
   - Select multiple items to be moved or copied to the same destination.
2. Click **Move to** or **Copy to** in the menu bar.
   - The task pane opens.
   - If you have multiple Microsoft accounts, verify that the desired *OneDrive* account is current.
3. Select the name of the destination folder (Figure 11-37).
   - Alternatively, click **New folder** to create a folder for moved or copied items.
4. Click **Copy here** or **Move here** (or click **Copy** or **Move**).
   - A message appears while the files are copied or moved.
5. Click the selection **circle** for a file or folder to delete.

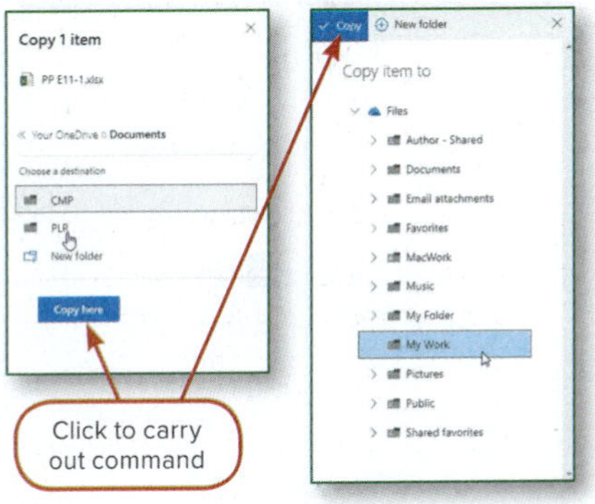

Figure 11-37 Select the destination folder

6. Click **Delete** in the menu bar and click **Delete** in the message box.
   - The file or folder is deleted.
   - If your account does not display a confirmation message, you will see a prompt with an **Undo** button to restore the item(s).

Download a File or Folder

When you download items from *OneDrive*, the items are copied to the destination, and the originals remain in the *OneDrive* folder. If you edit the file locally, you must upload the revised work to *OneDrive*.

HOW TO: Download a File or Folder from OneDrive

1. Click the selection **circle** for the file or folder to be downloaded.
   - In *Tiles* or *Photo* view, the selection circle is in the top-right corner of the icon.
   - In *List* or *Compact List* view, the selection circle is to the left of the name.
   - If you select multiple files or folders, a compressed (zipped) folder downloads with the selected files/folders.
2. Click **Download**.
   - When you use Google Chrome as your browser, the file or zipped folder is downloaded to the *Downloads* folder on your computer, and a message box appears on the *Status* bar (Figure 11-38).

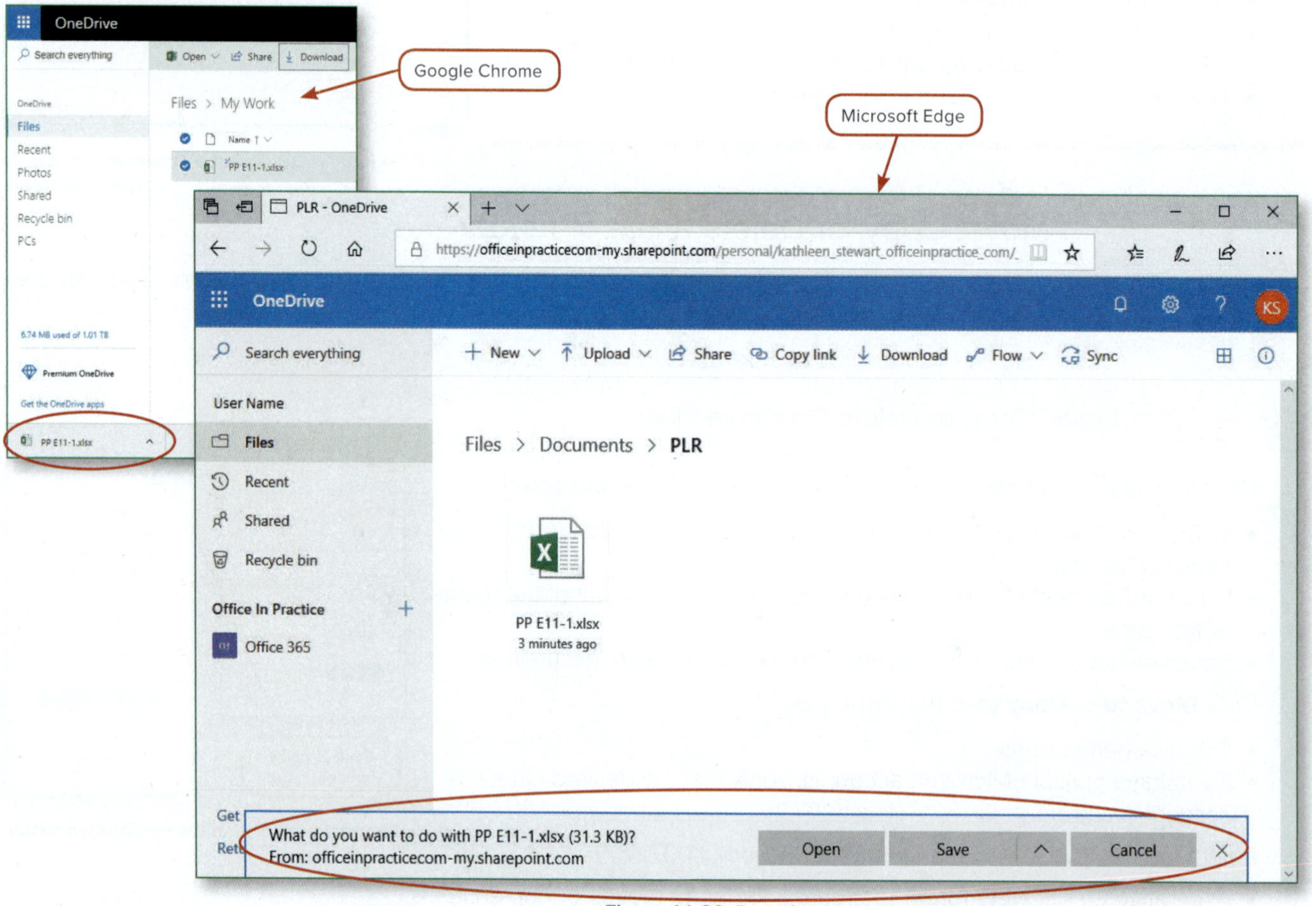

Figure 11-38 Download process and message box depend on the browser

   - If you use Microsoft Edge or Mozilla FireFox as your browser, a message box at the bottom of the screen opens with options to open or save the file (see Figure 11-38).
3. Locate and open the file in the application program.

> **MORE INFO**
>
> When you store and work directly with files in *OneDrive*, all your work is "in sync."

SLO 11.4

Sharing OneDrive Files and Folders

In addition to retrieving your *OneDrive* files from any computer or mobile device, you can share files and folders for collaboration and co-authoring. When you share a file or a folder, you determine how others can use your work, because you assign permission to view or to edit files.

Share an Excel Workbook

A workbook must be saved to your *OneDrive* account before you can share it. When you share the workbook, enter email addresses and specify whether recipients can edit or only view your file. You can also type a brief message that is included in the notification email. Your Microsoft account determines if you see a *Send Link* window or a *Share* pane after you click the *Share* button.

HOW TO: Share a Workbook in Excel

1. Save the workbook to your *OneDrive* folder.
   - Choose any folder in your *OneDrive* account.
   - Leave the workbook open in Excel.
2. Click the **Share** button in the workbook window.
   - The *Send Link* window or the *Share* pane opens depending on your Microsoft account (Figure 11-39).

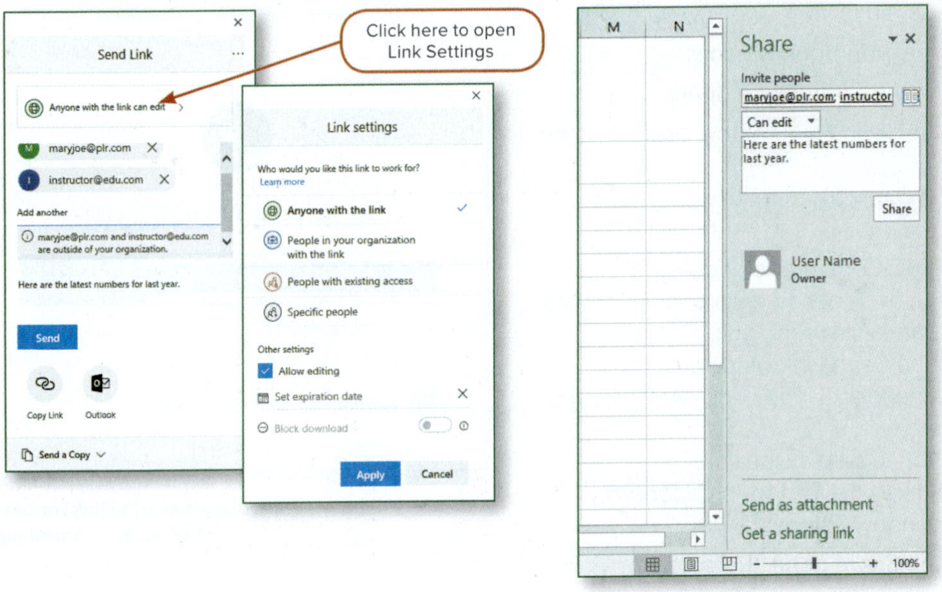

Figure 11-39 Share a workbook

3. Complete these steps in the *Send Link* window. (Go to step 4 for the *Share* pane).
   - Click the **Link settings** box at the top of the *Send Link* window.
   - Choose anyone, a work group, or specific people. Your choice determines other settings in the window.

- Select the **Allow editing** box to permit editing; deselect the **Allow editing** box to allow viewing only.
- Choose other settings as needed.
- Click **Apply** to return to the *Send Link* window.
- Type email addresses or select contacts from **Outlook**. If you choose a work group as your recipient, you need not type addresses.
- Click **Add a message** and type an optional message for the notification email (see Figure 11-39).
- Click **Send** and close the confirmation window.

4. Complete these steps in the *Share* pane. (Go to step 3 for the *Send Link* window).
   - Type email addresses, separated with semicolons (;).
   - If your account has access to your contacts list, click the **Address Book** button to the right of the entry box and choose recipient names.
   - Select **Can edit** or **Can view** from the drop-down list.
   - Click the **Include a message** box and type an optional message for the notification email (see Figure 11-39).
   - Click the **Share** button and close the *Share* pane.

ANOTHER WAY

Click the **File** button and select **Share** to open the *Send Link* window or the *Share* pane.

Create a Sharing Link for a Workbook

A ***sharing link*** is a text hyperlink that you can post on social media, in another document, or in an email. You can specify a link that permits editing or one that allows only viewing the workbook.

HOW TO: Create a Sharing Link

1. Open the workbook to be shared.
   - The workbook must be saved in your *OneDrive* account.
2. Click the **Share** button in the workbook window.
   - The *Send Link* window or the *Share* pane opens.
3. Complete these steps in the *Send Link* window. (Refer to step 4 for the *Share* pane).
   - Click the **Link settings** button to open the *Link Settings* window (see Figure 11-39).
   - Select anyone, a work group, or specific people.
   - Select the **Allow editing** box to permit editing; deselect the **Allow editing** box to create a view-only link.
   - Click **Apply** to return to the *Send Link* window.
   - Enter email addresses if needed. If you chose *Anyone*, you need not type addresses.
   - Click the **Copy Link** button to display the link.
   - Click **Copy** to copy the link to the Windows *Clipboard*.
   - Close the confirmation window (Figure 11-40).
4. Complete these steps in the *Share* pane. (Refer to step 3 for the *Send Link* window).
   - Click **Get a sharing link** at the bottom of the *Share* pane to open the second pane (see Figure 11-39).
   - Click **Create an edit link** to permit editing.
   - Alternatively, click **Create a view-only link** to prohibit editing.

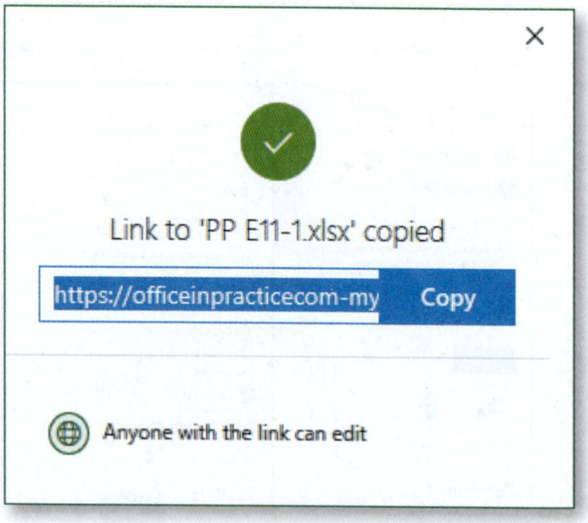

Figure 11-40 Copy a sharing link for pasting in an email or social media

- Click the **Copy** button to copy the link to the Windows *Clipboard* (Figure 11-41).
- Close the *Share* pane.

5. Paste the copied link in an email or in an online location.

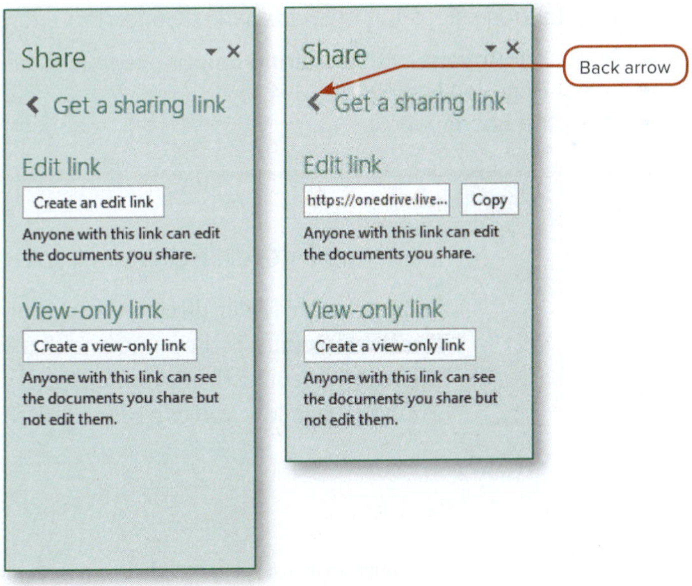

Figure 11-41 Second page of *Share* pane and link for copying

Remove or Disable a Link

After you have shared a file, you can change or remove permission to edit the file. If you created a sharing link, you can disable the link.

HOW TO: Change Sharing Permission

1. Open the shared workbook and click the **Share** button.
   - The *Send Link* window or the *Share* pane opens.
2. Complete these steps in the *Send Link* window. (Go to step 3 for the *Share* pane).
   - Verify the sharing link when multiple links are listed.
   - Click the **More options** button (**. . .**) and choose **Manage Access**.
   - Click **X** to remove the link (Figure 11-42).
   - Close the *Manage Access* window.

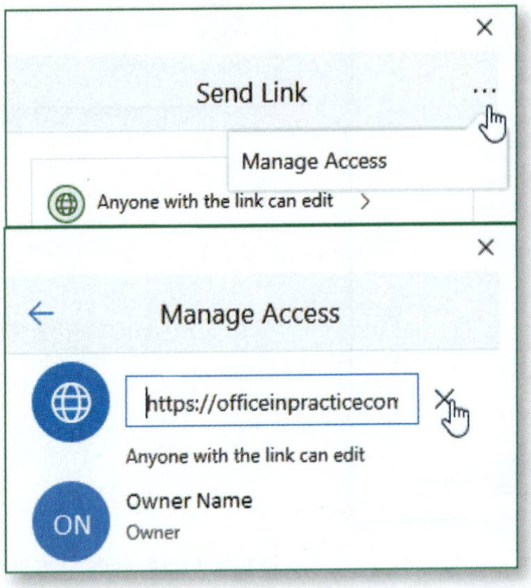

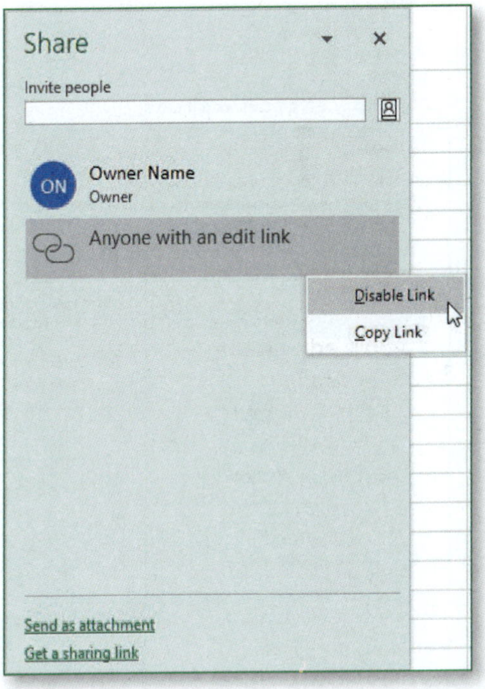

Figure 11-42 Disable a link

3. Complete these steps in the *Share* pane. (Go to step 2 for the *Send Link* window).
   - Right-click **Anyone with a sharing link** or a recipient name.
   - Select **Disable Link** (Figure 11-42).
   - Close the *Share* pane.

Share a File or Folder in OneDrive

Share a file or folder directly from your *OneDrive* account, too. The *Send Link* window in your *OneDrive* account is the same one that you see when you share a workbook from Excel. If your Microsoft account displays the *Share* pane, your *OneDrive* account displays a *Share* window. From that window, you can post a link to a social media account or send an email (Figure 11-43).

> **MORE INFO**
>
> Figures and steps in this chapter may be slightly different from your *OneDrive* account. Look for subtle differences in button names, screen prompts, or command locations.

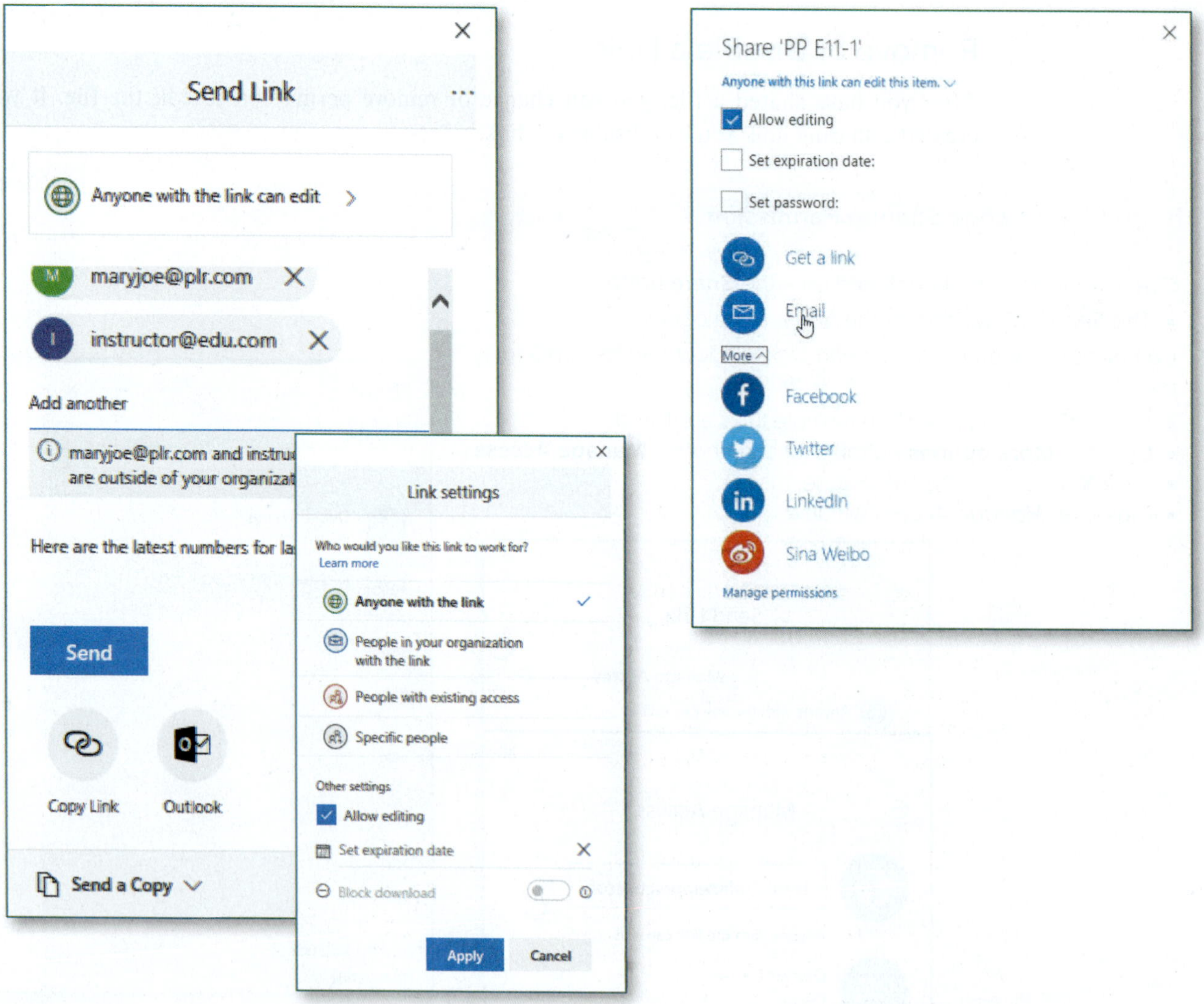

Figure 11-43 ***Send Link*** **and** ***Share*** **windows in** *OneDrive*

▸ HOW TO: Share a File in OneDrive

1. Sign in to your *OneDrive* account.
2. Check the selection **circle** for the file or folder to be shared.
   - When you share a folder, users have access to all files in the folder.
3. Click **Share** in the menu bar.
   - The *Send Link* or the *Share* window opens.
4. Complete these steps in the *Send Link* window. (Go to step 5 for the *Share* pane).
   - Click the **Link settings** box at the top of the *Send Link* window (see Figure 11-43).
   - Choose anyone, a work group, or specific people. Your choice determines other settings in the window.
   - Select the **Allow editing** box to permit editing; deselect the **Allow editing** box to allow viewing only.
   - Choose other settings as needed.
   - Click **Apply** to return to the *Send Link* window.
   - Type email addresses or select contacts from **Outlook**.
   - Click **Add a message** and type an optional message for the notification email.
   - Click **Send** and close the confirmation window. The link is sent to your recipients.
5. Complete these steps in the *Share* window. (Go to step 4 for the *Send Link* window).
   - Click **Anyone with this link can edit this item** to expand the window (see Figure 11-43).
   - Select the **Allow editing** box to permit editing; deselect the **Allow editing** box to allow viewing only.
   - Set an expiration date or a password as needed.
   - Click **Email** in the *Share* window.
   - Type email address(es) in the first text box.
   - Click the message box and type an optional message for the email.
   - Click the **Share** button to send the email (Figure 11-44).

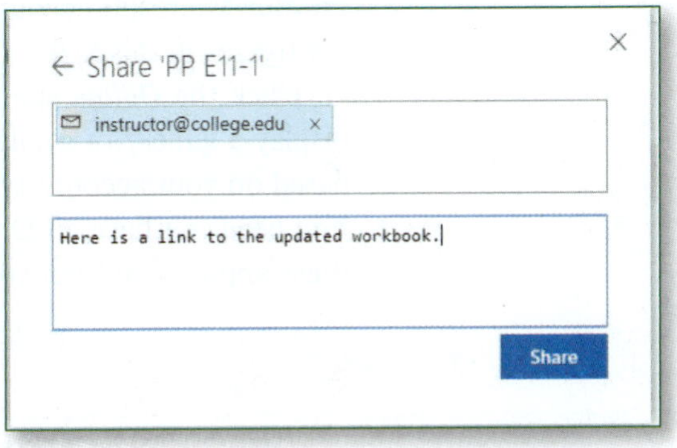

Figure 11-44 Send an email from the *Share* window in *OneDrive*

Change Sharing Permission in OneDrive

You can remove or edit the sharing permission for a file or folder from your *OneDrive* account. The *Information* pane displays properties of the selected file or folder. When you click *Manage access* in the pane, the *Manage Access* pane displays information about current links. Your *OneDrive* account determines the options for removing the link, stopping the sharing, or editing the type of access (Figure 11-45).

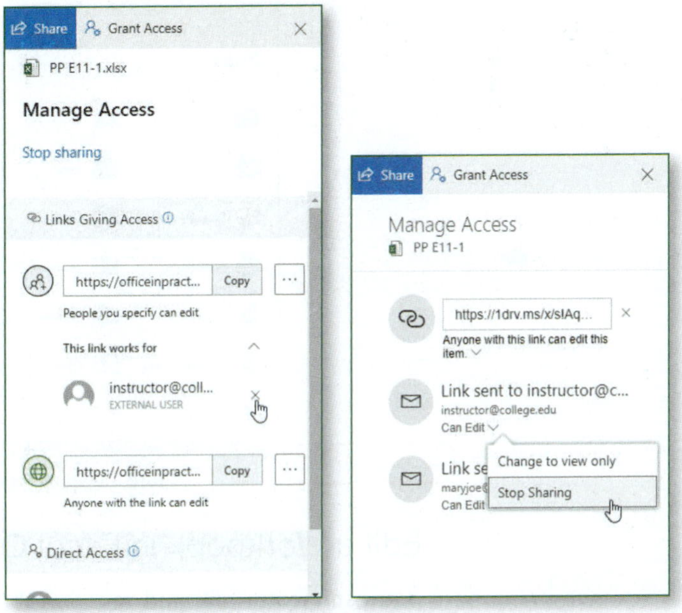

Figure 11-45 *Manage Access* pane for shared file

Export and Publish

The *Export* command [*File* tab] saves a workbook in XPS or PDF format. An XPS document is a text file that can be viewed but not easily edited. An XPS file uses Microsoft XML specifications to define layout and appearance. A PDF file uses Adobe Portable Document Format to display a workbook using a free reader. Use either format for disseminating information, not for co-authoring.

The *Publish* command [*File* tab] uploads a workbook to *Power BI*, a Microsoft business intelligence platform. *Power BI* is an analytical reporting and visualization tool for collaboration in the workplace. You need sign-in information with a business account to use *Power BI*.

SLO 11.5

Using Office Online

Office Online is a free scaled-down version of Office applications available from your Microsoft account or *OneDrive* page. *Office Online* applications look and perform like the complete programs but with fewer features and capabilities. Excel, PowerPoint, and Word are available, as well as mail, calendar, and work flow apps. These programs are updated regularly and depend on your Microsoft account, so your screen may display options different from what displays in the figures in this text.

Click the *Online app launcher* button in the upper-left corner of the *OneDrive* window to display a gallery of available applications (Figure 11-46). The *ScreenTip* on the button varies based on your account type. The same button displays in each of the online applications, too. You need not have an Office 365 subscription or a purchased version of Office to use any of these applications, but you must have a Microsoft account.

MORE INFO

Microsoft Access is currently not available in *Office Online*.

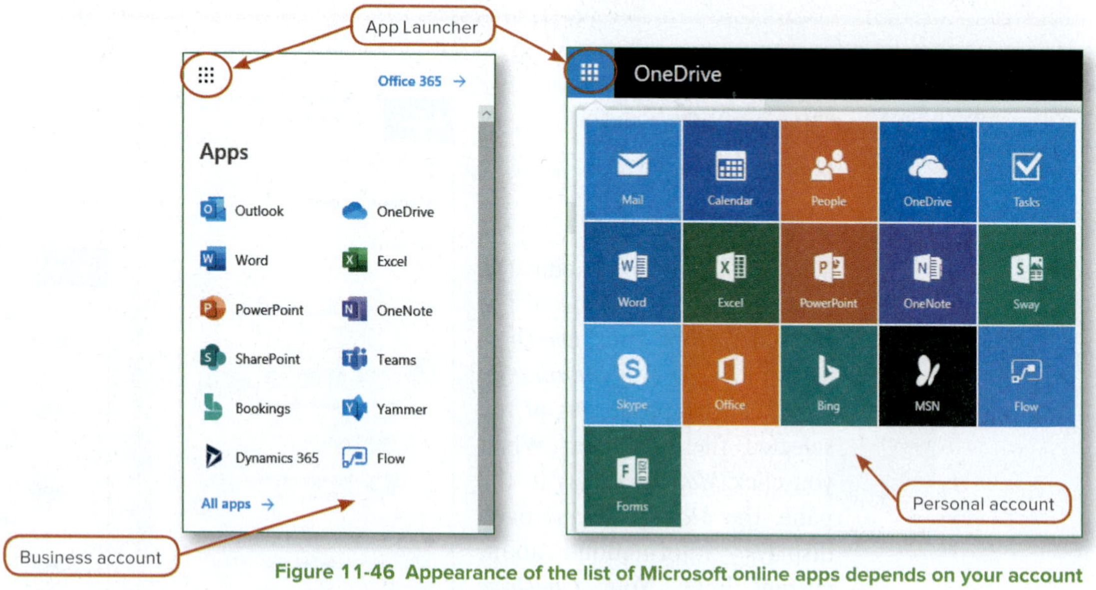

Figure 11-46 Appearance of the list of Microsoft online apps depends on your account

Edit a Workbook in Excel Online

You can create, edit, and save workbooks using *Excel Online*. Build basic formulas, use functions, create charts, and format worksheets. *Excel Online* does not have all the features and commands as Excel, but you can start a workbook in *Excel Online* and complete it in Excel if necessary. When Excel is available on the computer, *Excel Online* includes an option to open the workbook in Excel.

Excel Online has a *Ribbon* and command tabs, and you insert functions from the *Insert* tab.

▸HOW TO: Edit a Workbook in Excel Online

1. Log in to your *OneDrive* account.
2. Click the name of an Excel workbook in a *OneDrive* folder.
    - The workbook opens in *Excel Online*.
    - The workbook opens in its own browser tab, and *OneDrive* is open in the previous tab.
    - You can also right-click the file name and select **Open in Excel Online**.
    - If the workbook has links, they are disabled. Close the message bar to continue working (Figure 11-47).
3. Edit the workbook.
4. Close the browser tab to close the *Excel Online* workbook.
    - *Excel Online* automatically saves the workbook in your *OneDrive* folder.
    - The *OneDrive* tab displays.

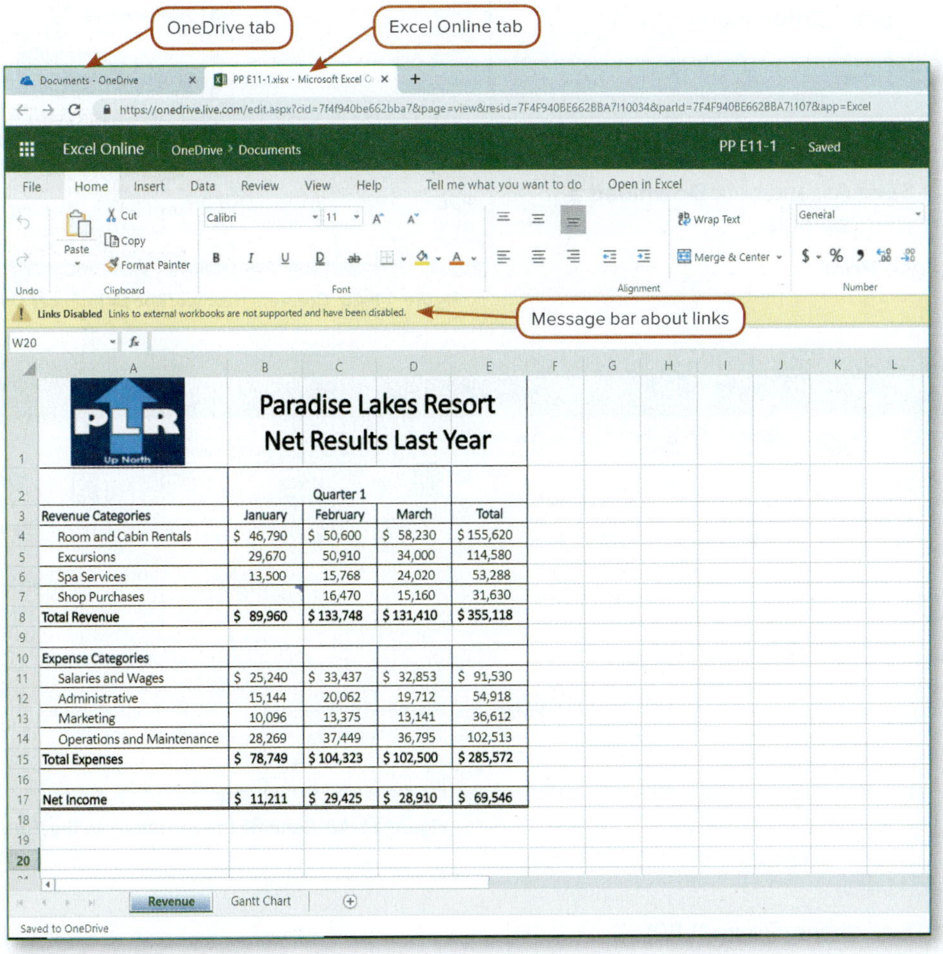

Figure 11-47 Workbook opened in *Excel Online*

Create and Print an Excel Online Workbook

A workbook created in *Excel Online* has a default name, such as **Book1** or **Book2**, and is saved automatically when you close the browser tab. Click the default name in the *Title* bar and type a new name, or click the **File** tab and choose **Save As**. Workbooks are saved to your *OneDrive* account, and the *Save As* command includes an option to download a copy of the workbook to your computer.

The *Print* command is listed in the *Backstage* view. The *Print Settings* dialog box includes options for what is printed, paper size, page orientation, and scaling. After you make your choices, the workbook displays in a preview window and uses your default Windows printer.

HOW TO: Create and Print an Excel Online Workbook

1. Log in to your *OneDrive* account.
2. Click the folder name where you want to store the workbook.
3. Click the **New** button and select **Excel workbook** (Figure 11-48).
   - *Excel Online* starts and a blank workbook is open.
4. Enter data for the worksheet.
5. Click the default **Book1** name in the *Title* bar.
6. Type the new file name and press **Enter** (Figure 11-49).
   - The workbook is saved in the folder you selected in *OneDrive*.
   - Click the **File** tab, select **Save As**, and then select **Save As** to choose a *OneDrive* folder and name the workbook.
   - Click the **File** tab, select **Save As**, and click **Download a Copy** to save a copy on your computer.
7. Click the **File** tab and choose **Print**.

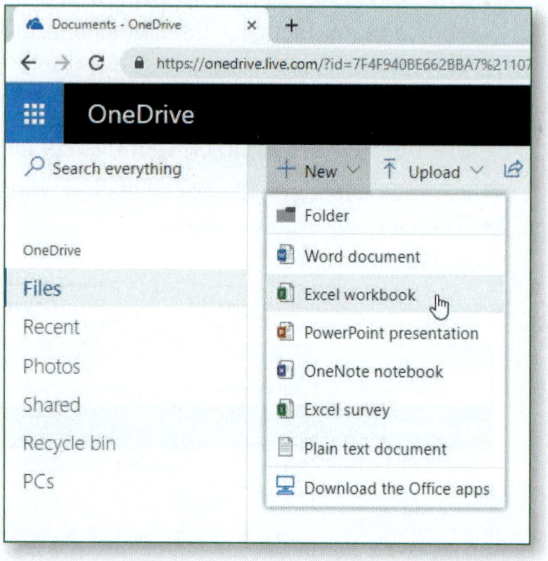

Figure 11-48 Create a new workbook in *Excel Online*

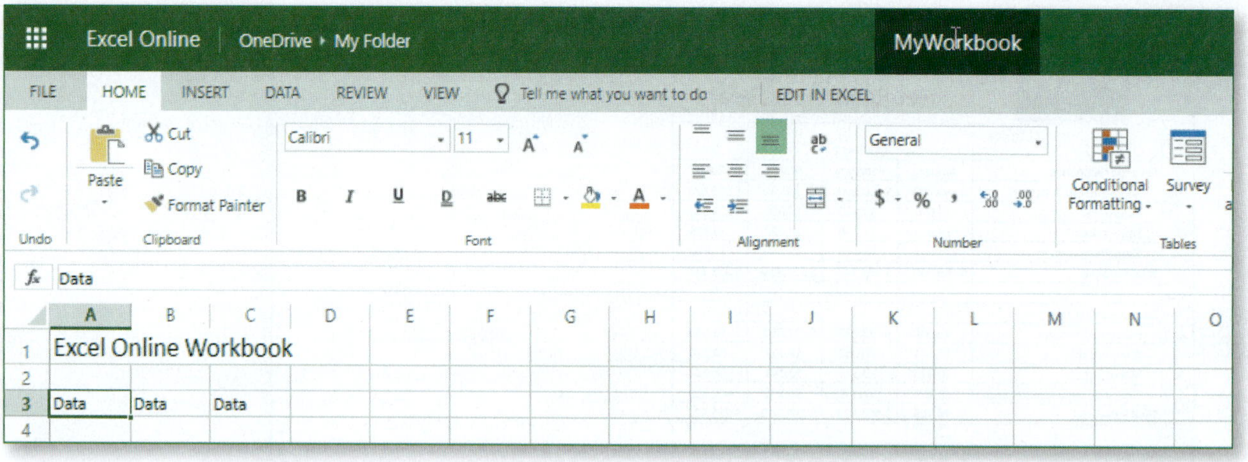

Figure 11-49 Rename the workbook in the *Title* bar

8. Click **Print** in the *Backstage* view.
   - The *Print Settings* dialog box opens (Figure 11-50).
9. Make selections and click **Print**.
   - A browser print window opens.

10. Click **Print** in the browser window to use your default printer settings.
    - A message box may inform you when printing is done; close the message box to continue.
11. Close the browser tab to save and close the workbook.

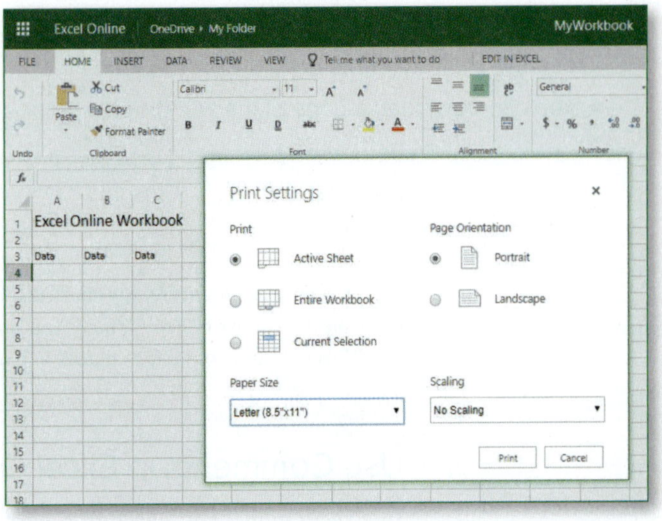

Figure 11-50 ***Print Settings*** **dialog box for an *Excel Online* workbook**

Create a Chart in Excel Online

Create a chart in *Excel Online* by selecting the source data and clicking the *Insert* tab. Most types and subtypes are available. For an active chart object, the *Chart Tools* tab displays on the *Ribbon* with options for chart layout.

MORE INFO

Excel Online does not currently support 3D charts.

HOW TO: Create a Chart in an Excel Online Workbook

1. Open the workbook in *Excel Online*.
2. Select the data for the chart.
    - The selected cells must be contiguous.
3. Click the **Insert** tab and click the desired chart type button [*Charts* group].
4. Choose the chart subtype.
    - The chart object displays in the worksheet.
    - The *Chart Tools* tab is available.
5. Size and position the chart object as desired.
    - You cannot select individual chart elements.
6. Click the **Chart Title** button [*Chart Tools* tab, *Labels* group].
7. Choose a position for the chart title.
    - The *Edit Title* dialog box opens.
8. Type the title for the chart and click **OK** (Figure 11-51).

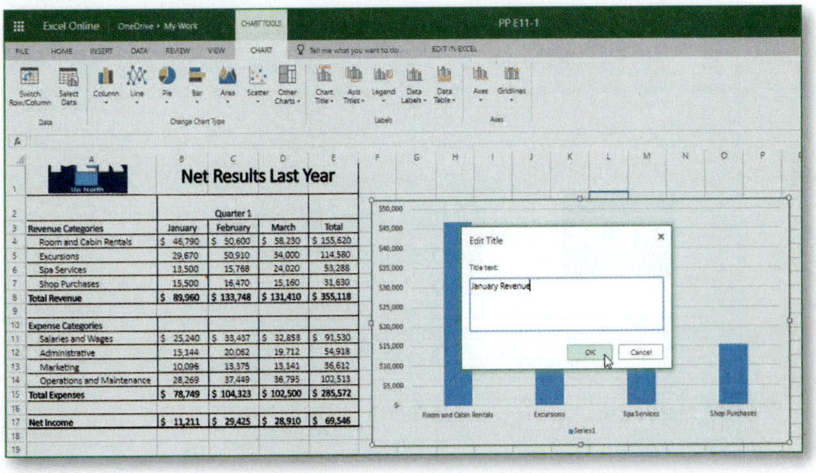

Figure 11-51 **Create a chart in *Excel Online***

9. Use commands in the *Labels* group [*Chart Tools* tab] to add or remove chart elements.
10. Close the browser tab to save the workbook.
    - You can download a copy of the workbook to your computer to enhance the chart.

MORE INFO

Keyboard and function key shortcuts in *Excel Online* are assigned by the browser, so not all Excel shortcuts work in *Excel Online*. You cannot, for example, select nonadjacent cell ranges because the **Ctrl** key does not work as it does in Excel.

Use Comments in Excel Online

In *Excel Online*, you can add a comment, review and reply to comments from co-authors, or delete a comment. Comments in *Excel Online* are threaded conversations that display in the *Comments* pane at the right of the window. A comment is attached to a cell and identified by a triangle-shaped indicator. When you select a cell with an indicator, a comment bubble displays; click the bubble to open the *Comments* pane.

HOW TO: Add a Comment in Excel Online

1. Open the workbook in *Excel Online*.
2. Right-click the cell in which you want to add a comment.
3. Choose **New Comment** from the context menu.
    - The *Comments* pane opens on the right.
    - The selected cell and your user name are indicated in the comment box.
    - Alternatively, click the **New Comment** button [*Review* tab, *Comments* group] or the **Comment** button [*Insert* tab, *Comments* group].
4. Type the text of the comment in the comment box (Figure 11-52).
5. Click the **Post** button in the *Comments* pane.
    - The comment is attached to the cell and posted to the workbook.
6. Close the *Comments* pane.

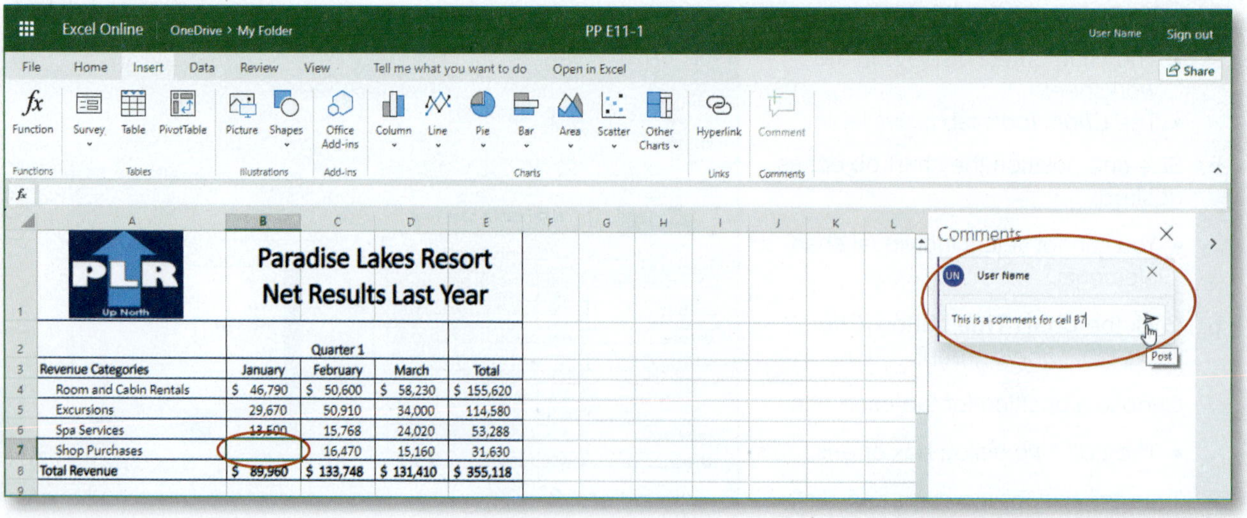

Figure 11-52 Insert a comment in *Excel Online*

Collaborate in Excel Online

Excel Online enables you to work with others on a workbook simultaneously or at different times; the workbook must be shared with the other users. If two or more of you work at the same time in *Excel Online*, everyone's sign-in information is visible in the *Excel Online* window, and you are notified when an edit is made. Changes are automatically saved and marked with the name of the person who made the edit.

PAUSE & PRACTICE: EXCEL 11-2

For this project, you create a folder in *OneDrive*, save a file to *OneDrive*, upload a file to *OneDrive*, edit a workbook in *Excel Online*, and share a *OneDrive* folder.

*Note: You need a Microsoft account (*https://signup.live.com*) to complete this project.*

File Needed: ***[your initials] PP E11-1.xlsx***
Completed Project File Names: ***[your initials] PP E11-2.xlsx***, ***[your initials] PP E11-2a.xlsx***, and ***[your initials] PP E11-1a.xlsx***

1. Open the ***[your initials] PP 11-1.xlsx*** workbook completed in *Pause & Practice 11-1*.
2. Save the workbook as [your initials] PP E11-2 in your usual location for saving files on your computer.
3. Log in to your *OneDrive* account.
   a. Open an internet browser window and go to the *OneDrive* web site (www.onedrive.live.com).
   b. Click the **Sign in** button and sign-in to your Microsoft account. (You may be signed in if you use Microsoft Edge as your browser).
4. Create a *OneDrive* folder.
   a. Click **Files** on the left to display the contents of your *OneDrive* folder.
   b. Click the **View options** button and use a *List* view.
   c. Click the **New** button and select **Folder** from the drop-down list.
   d. Type PLR as the name for the new folder (Figure 11-53).
   e. Click **Create**.
5. Save a workbook to a *OneDrive* folder.
   a. Click the Excel icon on the Windows task bar to return to ***[your initials] PP E11-2***.
   b. Click the **File** tab and choose **Save As**.
   c. Select **OneDrive – *[Identifier]*** in the locations list. (Your *OneDrive* account may show a domain name or *Personal* as an identifier.)

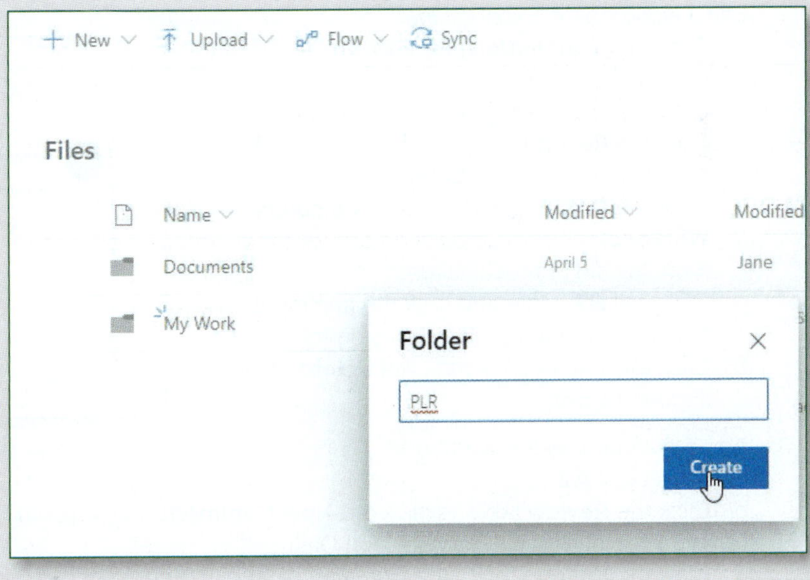

Figure 11-53 Create a folder in *List* view

d. Find and click the **PLR** folder name.
e. Edit the file name to [your initials] PP E11-2a (Figure 11-54).
f. Click **Save**.
g. Close the workbook in Excel but leave Excel running.
h. Click the browser icon on the Windows task bar to return to your *OneDrive* folder.

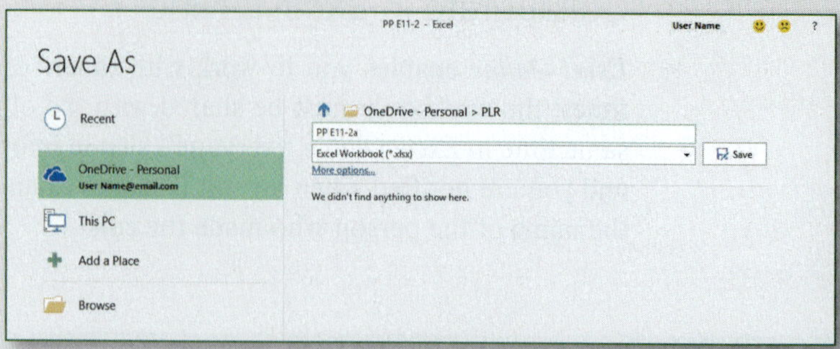

Figure 11-54 *Save As* command for a *OneDrive* folder

i. Select the **PLR** folder name to display its contents. (If the page has not refreshed, click the **Refresh** or the **Reload this page** button; the button name depends on your browser.)

6. Upload a workbook to a *OneDrive* folder.
   a. Verify that the **PLR** folder is the current folder.
   b. Click the **Upload** button and choose **Files**.
   c. Navigate to and select the ***[your initials] PP E11-1*** workbook on your computer.
   d. Click **Open** to upload the workbook to the *PLR* folder.
   e. Right-click the ***[your initials] PP E11-1*** file name in the *PLR* folder and select **Rename**.
   f. Edit the file name to [your initials] PP E11-1a in the *Rename* dialog box (Figure 11-55).
   g. Click **Save**.

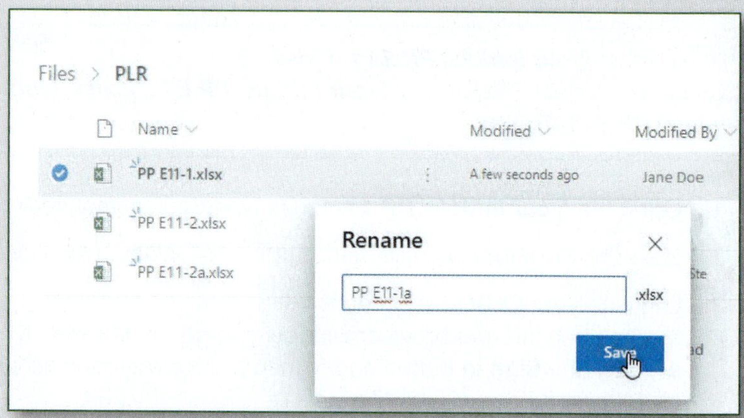

Figure 11-55 Rename a *OneDrive* file

7. Edit a workbook in *Excel Online*.
   a. Click the ***[your initials] PP E11-2a*** file name to launch *Excel Online*.
   b. Close the *Links Disabled* message bar.
   c. Click the **Revenue** sheet tab, select cell **B7**, type 15400, and press **Enter**.
   d. Click the **Data** tab and click the **Calculate Workbook** button [*Calculation* group] if the formulas did not recalculate.
   e. Click cell **B7** again and click the comment balloon to open the *Comments* pane.
   f. Click the ellipsis (**. . .**) and click **Delete thread** (Figure 11-56).

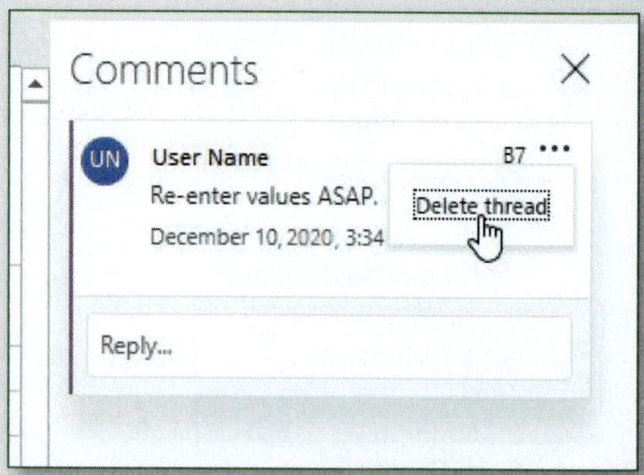

Figure 11-56 Delete a comment in *Excel Online*

8. Add a comment to the workbook.
   a. Select cell **A2**.
   b. Click the **Review** tab and click the **New Comment** button [*Comments* group].
   c. Type I completed all values in Excel Online.
   d. Click the **Post** button in the *Comments* pane (Figure 11-57).
   e. Close the *Comments* pane.
   f. Close the *Excel Online* browser tab to save and close the ***[your initials] PP E11-2a*** workbook and display the *OneDrive* tab.

9. Get a sharing link for the **PLR** folder.
   a. Select **Files** at the left to display your *OneDrive* folders.
   b. Click the selection circle for the **PLR** folder name.
   c. Click **Share** to open the *Send Link* or the *Share* window.
   d. Complete these steps in the *Send Link* window. (Go to step e for the *Share* window.)
      - Click the **Link settings** button and choose **Anyone with the link**.
      - Verify or select the **Allow editing** box and click **Apply**.
      - Click the **Copy Link** button to display the link (Figure 11-58).
      - Click **Copy** to copy the link to the Windows *Clipboard*.
      - Close the confirmation window.
   e. Complete these steps in the *Share* window. (Go to step d for the *Send Link* window.)
      - Verify or select the **Allow editing** box.
      - Select **Get a link**.
      - Click **Copy** to copy the link to the Windows *Clipboard*.
      - Close the *Share* window (Figure 11-59).

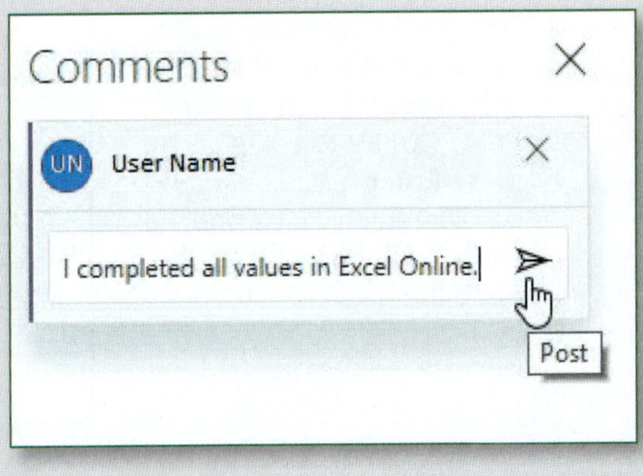

Figure 11-57 Insert a comment in *Excel Online*

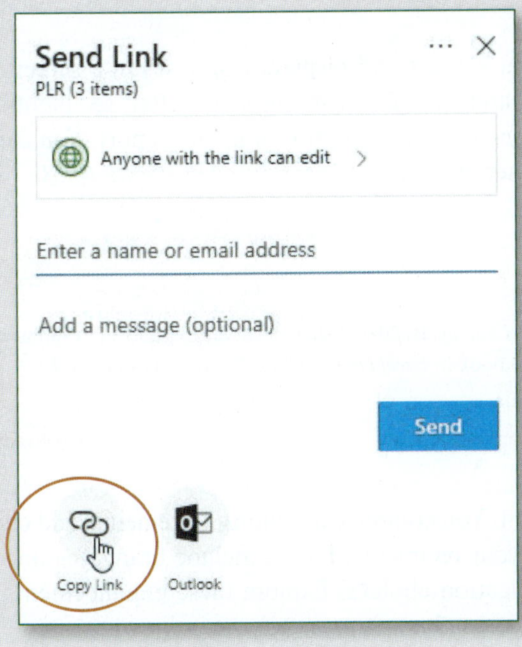

Figure 11-58 Copy the link in the *Send Link* window

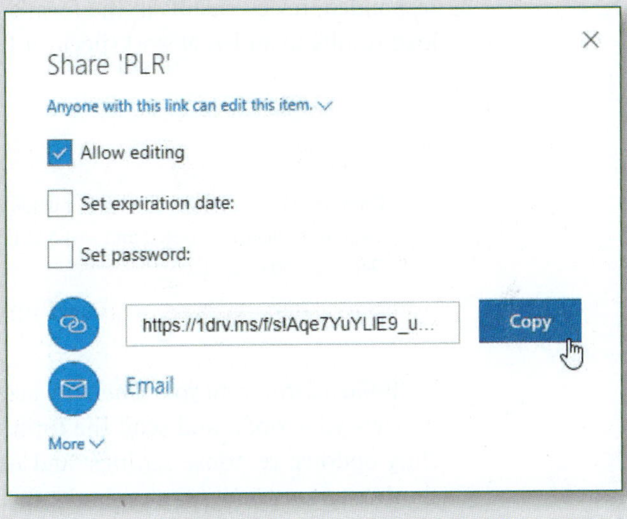

Figure 11-59 Copy the link in the *Share* window

10. Sign out of your *OneDrive* account.
    a. Click **[your name]** or picture in the top-right corner of the window.
    b. Choose **Sign out** from the *Account* drop-down list.
    c. Close the *OneDrive* browser tab.
11. Email the sharing link to your instructor.
    a. Open the email account that you use for your course.
    b. Create a new message with your instructor's email address in the *To* area.
    c. Type Your Name, Course Code, PLR as the subject line.

d. Type Here is a link to my PLR folder. in the body of the message and press **Enter**.

e. Press **Ctrl+V** to paste and press **Enter**. Your link will be different from the one shown in Figure 11-60.

f. Send the email.

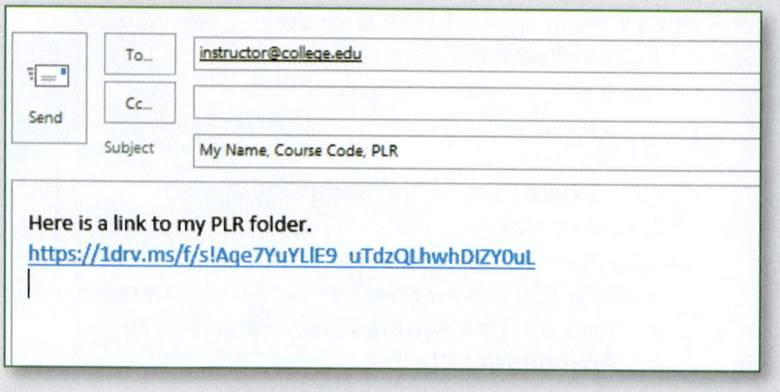

Figure 11-60 Pasted link in the email message

SLO 11.6

Exploring Office Online Applications

With your Microsoft account, you have access to multiple applications in addition to *OneDrive* and *Excel Online*. *Forms*, *Sway*, and *OneNote* are examples.

Forms

The ***Forms*** app creates a digital survey that gathers and displays responses in a screen form. Respondents complete the form online and submit their answers. After recipients have responded, review results in the form's *Responses* tab or print a summary report. You can also load results to an Excel worksheet for further analysis.

> **MORE INFO**
>
> Personal Microsoft accounts may include *Excel Survey*. Build and share a survey like a form; responses are automatically collected and saved as a workbook in *Excel Online*. Click the *Insert* tab in *Excel Online* to create a survey.

Build a form from your *OneDrive* account. You complete questions, statements, and choices, preview your work, and send the form to your recipients. Forms include branching and shuffling options, response settings, and notification choices. Explore these enhancements from the *More form settings* button in the form's menu bar.

HOW TO: Create a Form

1. Log in to your *OneDrive* account.
2. Click the **App launcher** button and select **Forms**. (Click **All apps** or **Explore all your apps** to expand the list if needed.)
   - The *My forms* window opens and displays the names of existing forms.
   - Click the ellipse (**. . .**) in an existing form icon and select **Delete** to delete a form.
3. Click **New Form**.
   - The form is untitled and has two tabs, *Questions* and *Responses*.

4. Click **Untitled form** on the *Questions* tab.
   - The form expands and shows two entry boxes.
5. Type a title or name for your form.
   - Use text that identifies your form for your recipients.
6. Click the **Insert image** button to insert an optional picture.
   - Select an image in your *OneDrive* account or upload a picture from the computer or external media.
   - The image displays above or next to the main title.
   - Point to the image and click its **Delete** button to remove it from the form.
7. Click **Enter a description** and type an optional explanation.
   - The description appears below the main title.
8. Click **Add new** (or **Add question**) to display a list of question types.
   - Click the **More** button (**. . .**) to display additional question types (Figure 11-61).
   - The name on the button depends on your Microsoft account.
9. Choose a question type.
   - Type the question or statement.
   - You can insert an image for each question.
10. Click the **Required** button to indicate that a response must be completed.
    - A question or statement with a required response displays an asterisk in the form.
11. Click the ellipsis next to the *Required* button to display more settings for the question.
    - Options depend on the question type.
    - Choose **Subtitle** to add secondary text or clarification for the question.

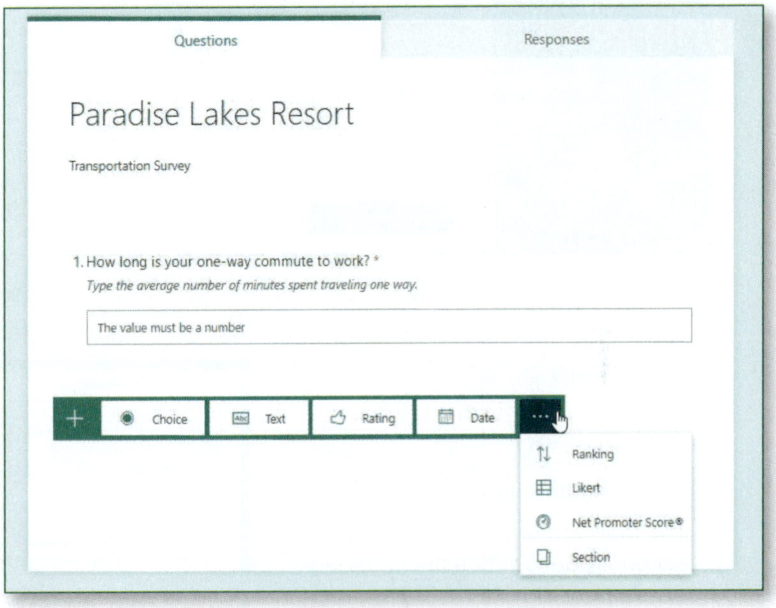

Figure 11-61 Build a form by adding and customizing questions

12. Add questions as needed in the form.
    - Questions are numbered.
    - Scroll the window to move through the items.
    - Click either side of the *Questions* or *Reponses* tab to close the editing screen.
13. Select a question in the form.
    - Edit the question as needed.
    - Click the **Move question up** or **Move question down** arrow to reorder your questions.
    - Click the **Delete question** button to remove a question from the form.
14. Click **Theme** in the menu bar to apply a background color or image.
    - Click the **Customize theme** button (or **Upload image** button) to create a custom background.
15. Click **More form settings** in the menu bar (the ellipsis) to use branching, shuffling, date criteria, and similar refinements.
16. Click **Preview** to see the form as it will appear to a recipient (Figure 11-62).
    - Select **Mobile** to preview the form on a mobile device.
17. Click **Back** to exit the preview window and return to the form.
18. Click **Share** (or **Send**) to get a link for the form. (The button name depends on your Microsoft account).
    - Verify or select **Anyone with the link can respond**.

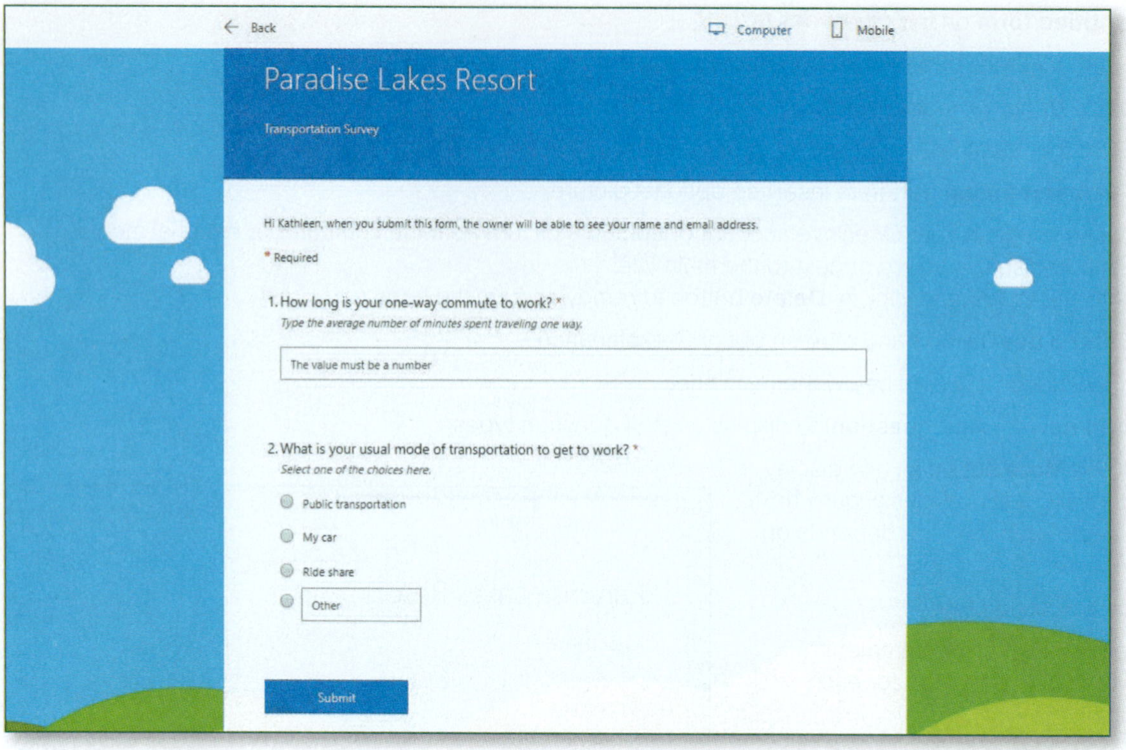

Figure 11-62 Preview the form before sharing

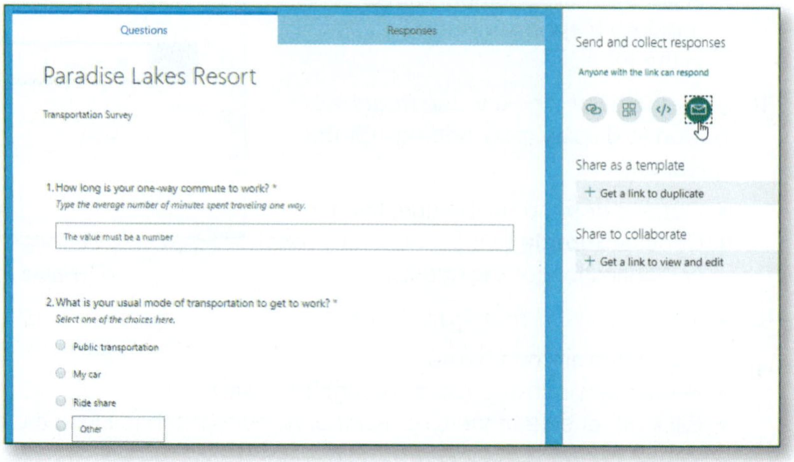

Figure 11-63 Get a link for the *Form*

19. Click the **Copy** button.
    - A *ScreenTip* notes that the link is ready to paste.
20. Click the **Email** button (Figure 11-63).
    - The mail app for your Microsoft account opens with a new message and the pasted link.
    - Alternatively, close the form, start your usual email client, compose the message, and paste the link.
    - You can also copy the link in an online location.
21. Click after the last character in the pasted link in the body of the message and press **Enter** to format the link as a hyperlink.
22. Click the **To** line and complete recipient email addresses.
    - Edit the email subject line as needed.
23. Send the message.

MORE INFO

When it is important to identify recipient responses to a form, one of your questions should request a name or other identifier.

After the form is distributed, view results in *Forms* by launching the app and opening your form. Click the *Responses* tab to see the results in a summary report or to view individual results. You can print the summary report or open the results in an Excel workbook. In the workbook, the results are formatted as an Excel table so that you can filter the data, add formulas, or apply formats.

Sway

Sway is a digital storytelling application. A *Sway* is an interactive presentation in which you can place text, images, videos, charts, tweets, and links. Your *Sways* and their associated data are stored in the cloud in central data centers. They are always available through your Microsoft account. You can share a *Sway* the same way you share a *OneDrive* file.

The *Sway* application includes tutorials and sample *Sways* to help you learn how to build your own presentations, newsletters, or stories (Figure 11-64). *Sways* can be displayed on a PC, a tablet, or a mobile device.

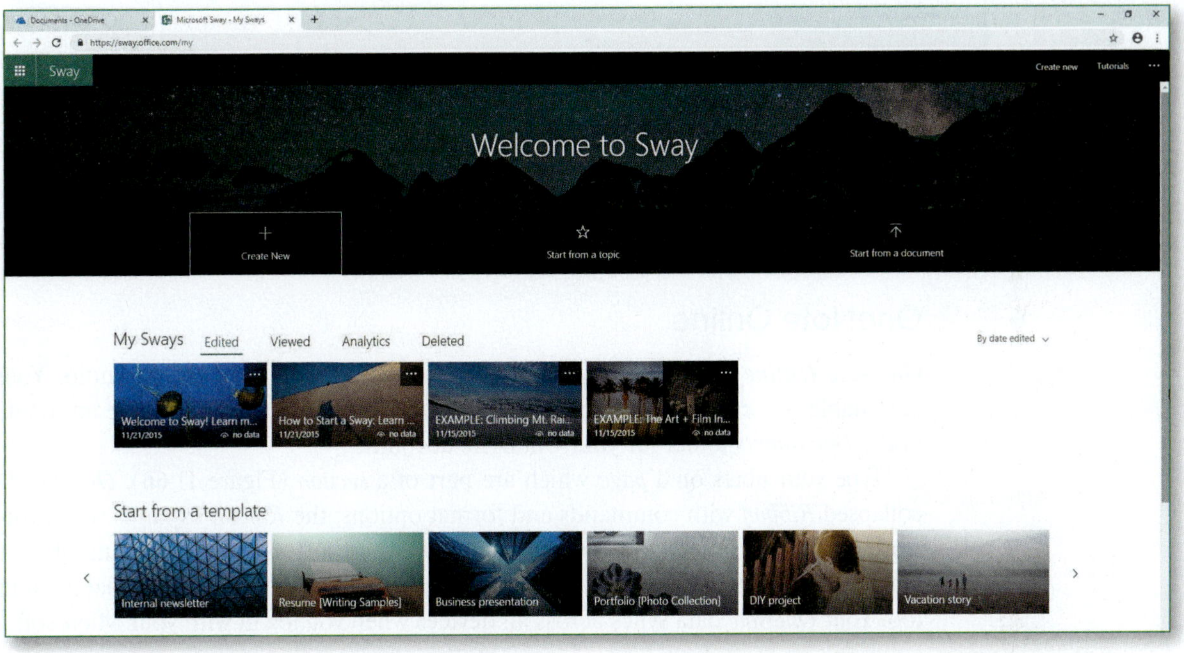

Figure 11-64 Explore *Sway* features to build a story

> **MORE INFO**
>
> The working area for a *Sway* is the ***storyline*** and each element or part is a ***card***. Cards can be grouped.

Mail

The ***Mail*** or ***Outlook*** application launches the email program that is part of your Microsoft account. Use the *Mail* application in a personal Microsoft account to organize all email from your personal addresses in one location (*Settings* button, *View all Outlook settings, Sync email*).

People

People is a service to store names and information about your contacts. Connect to social media sites to sync those contacts or import your contact list from your email service. If you have a business or education account, options and commands may be managed by an administrator.

Calendar

Calendar is an appointments and events schedule. Your *Calendar* can be shared so that others see your availability. You can view your calendar in several formats including by day, by week, or by month (Figure 11-65). In addition to the default calendar, you can add a holiday calendar or a specialty calendar from a sports team or entertainment service.

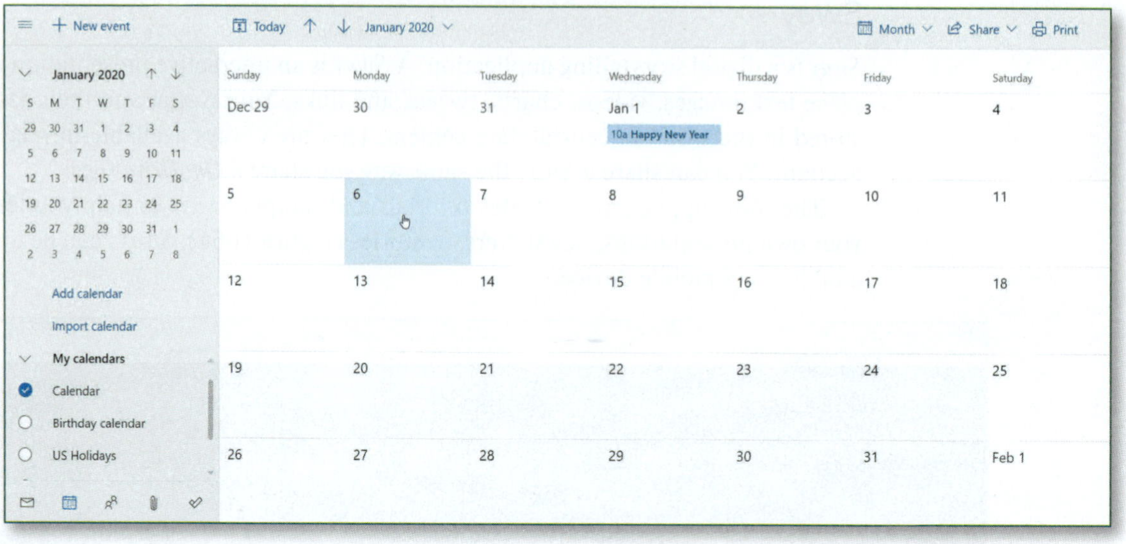

Figure 11-65 Sample calendar in a personal *OneDrive* account

OneNote Online

OneNote Online is a productivity tool for taking notes and recording audio. Your notes are searchable, stored in the cloud, and immediately available. Notebooks are automatically saved in the *Documents* folder for your *OneDrive* account.

Type your notes on a *page* which are part of a *section* (Figure 11-66). *OneNote Online* has a collapsed *Ribbon* with commands and format options; the *Ribbon* expands when you click a tab name. Your first notebook is named with your Microsoft user name; rename it from the *Documents* folder if you prefer. You can create multiple workbooks for keeping separate note groupings, too. Your *OneNote* data syncs across all devices when you log in with your Microsoft account.

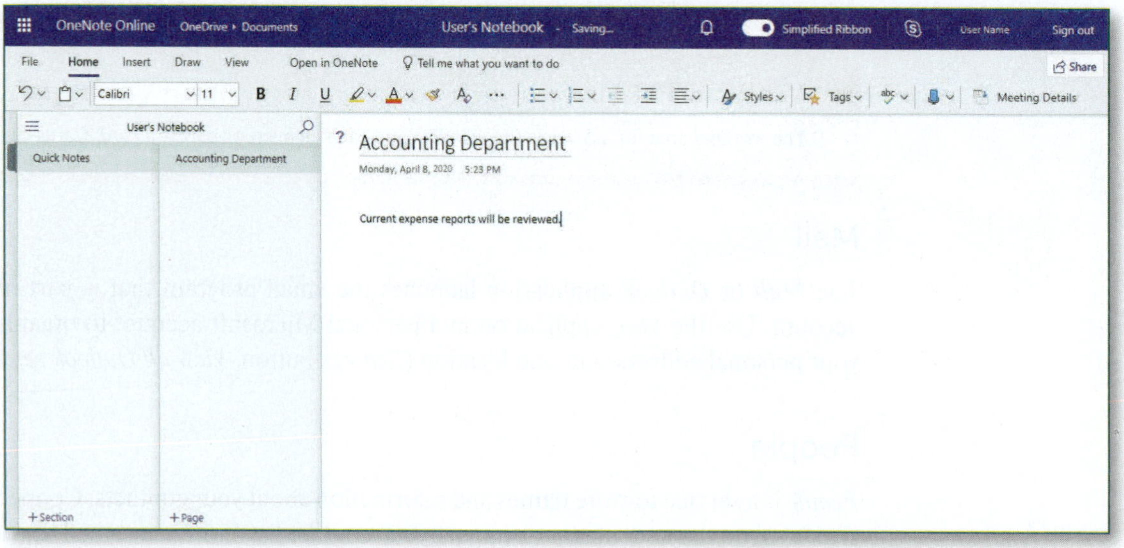

Figure 11-66 *OneNote Online* notebook in a personal account

PAUSE & PRACTICE: EXCEL 11-3

For this project, you create a *Form*, share it, and open results in Excel. You need email addresses for your instructor and two classmates or friends who are available to respond.

*Note: You need a Microsoft account (*https://signup.live.com*) to complete this project.*

File Needed: None
Completed Project File Name: ***[your initials] PP E11-3.xlsx***

1. Log in to your *OneDrive* account.
2. Create a form.
   a. Click the **App launcher** button and select **Forms**. (Click **All apps** to expand the list if needed.)
   b. Click **New Form**.
   c. Click **Untitled form** in the form window.
   d. Type [your initials] PP E11-3 in the entry box.
   e. Click **Enter a description** in the form window.
   f. Type PLR Transportation Survey in the entry box.
3. Add a *Text* question with a *Number* response.
   a. Click **Add New** (or **Add question)** and select **Text**.
   b. Click the entry box and type How long is your one-way commute to work?
   c. Click the **Required** button.
   d. Click the ellipsis next to the *Required* button and select **Subtitle**.
   e. Type Type the average number of minutes spent traveling one way. in the entry box.
   f. Click the ellipsis next to the *Required* button and select **Restrictions**.
   g. Verify that the restriction is **Number** (Figure 11-67).

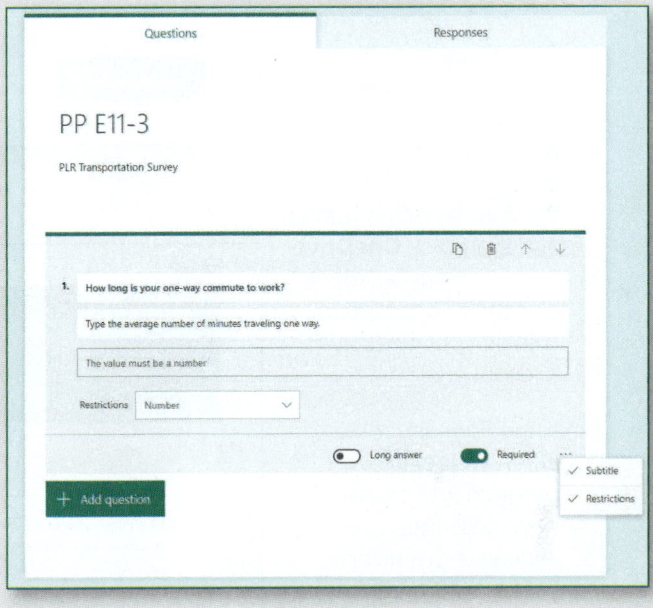

Figure 11-67 Required question that restricts responses to a number

4. Add a question with a *Choice* response.
   a. Click **Add new** (or **Add question**) and select **Choice**.
   b. Click the entry box and type What is your usual mode of transportation to get to work? as the question.
   c. Verify that the **Required** button is active; this choice is copied from your first question.
   d. Verify that the subtitle box displays. (Click the ellipsis next to the *Required* button and select **Subtitle** if needed.)
   e. Click the subtitle box and type Select one of the choices here. as the subtitle.
   f. Click the **Option 1** box and type Public transportation.
   g. Click the **Option 2** box and type My car.
   h. Click **Add option** and type Ride share.
   i. Add two additional options for Bus and Walk.

j. Click **Add "Other" option** to add a final choice.
k. Click the background area of the window, either side of the *Questions* tab (Figure 11-68).

5. Preview and share the form.
   a. Click **Preview** to preview the form (Figure 11-69).
   b. Click the **Back** button to return to the form.
   c. Click **Share** (or **Send**) to get a link.
   d. Verify or click the **Link** button.
   e. Verify that the permission is *Anyone with the link can respond*.
   f. Click **Copy** to copy the link to the Windows *Clipboard*.
   g. For an academic or business account, click the **App launcher** button and then click **OneDrive**.
   h. For a personal account, close the *Forms* tab to display your *OneDrive* account.

6. Email the *Form* link.
   a. Open your email program and create a new message.
   b. Type your instructor's, your two other recipients', and your email addresses in the *To* area for a total of four names. Separate the names by pressing **Tab** or by typing a semicolon (**;**).
   c. Type [your name] Excel Form PP E11-3 as the subject.
   d. In the message area, type Please complete the form and submit your answers., and press **Enter**.

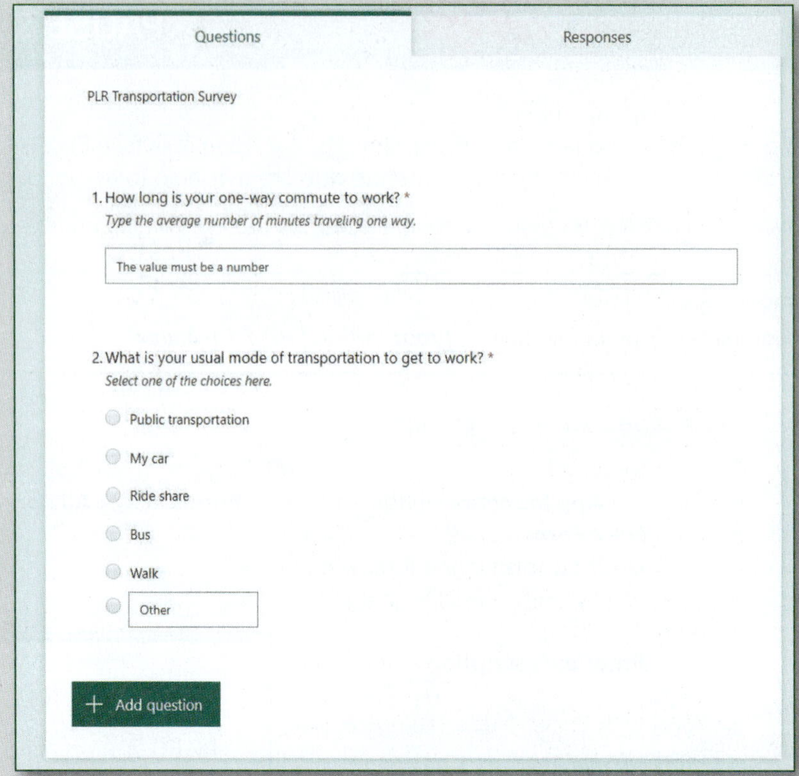

Figure 11-68 Required *Choice* question

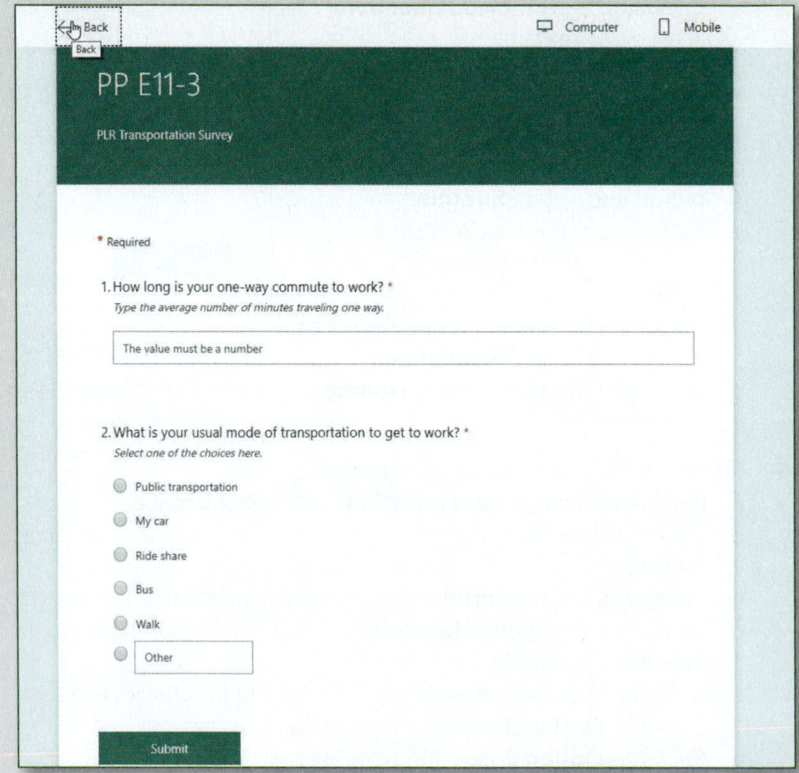

Figure 11-69 Preview the form

e. Press **Ctrl+V** to paste the link and press **Enter** to format the link as a hyperlink.
f. Send the email.

7. Review *Form* results after recipients have replied.
   a. Log in to your *OneDrive* account and start the **Forms** app.
   b. Click the ***[your initials] PP E11-3*** form to open it.
   c. Click the **Responses** tab. Responses in your form will not match those in Figure 11-70.

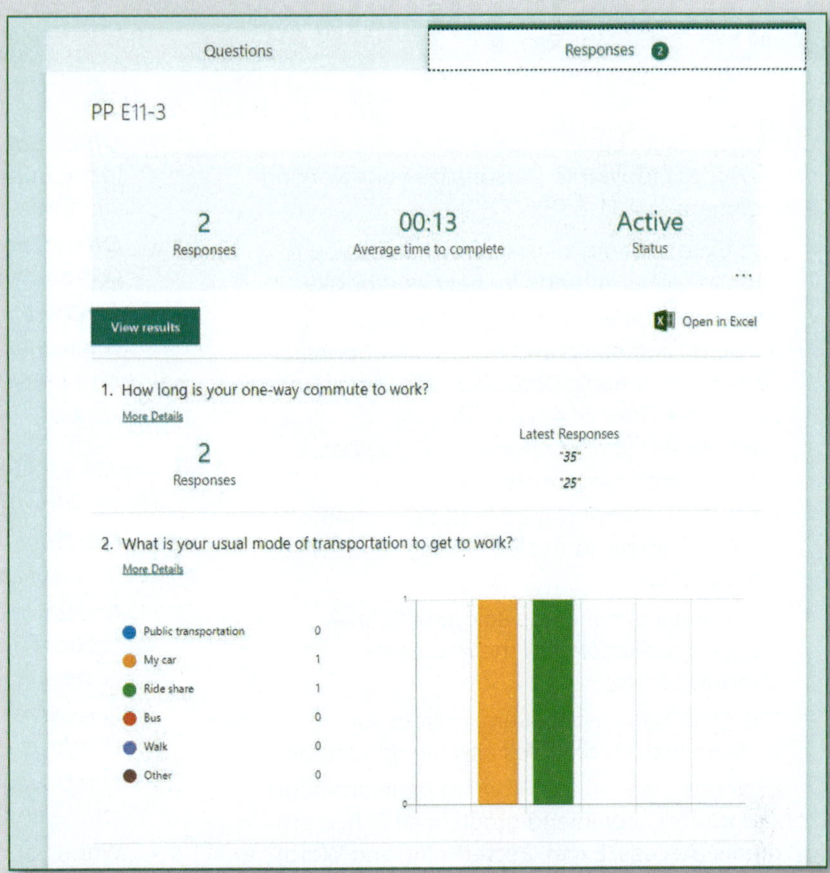

Figure 11-70 Responses in the form

8. Close the *Forms* app.
   a. For an academic or business account, click the **App launcher** button and then click **OneDrive**.
   b. For a personal account, close the *Forms* tab to display your *OneDrive* account.
9. Sign out of *OneDrive* and close the browser.

Chapter Summary

11.1 Customize Excel options, the *Ribbon,* and the *Quick Access* toolbar to personalize your working environment (p. E11-686).

- The *Excel Options* dialog box enables you to choose global settings for new workbooks.
- The *Excel Options* dialog box has the following command and feature categories: *General, Formulas, Data, Proofing, Save, Language, Ease of Access, Advanced, Customize Ribbon, Quick Access Toolbar, Add-ins,* and *Trust Center.*
- From the *General* category choose whether the *Quick Analysis* button displays and select a default font.
- The *Formulas* pane has an option to use manual calculation and the *R1C1* cell reference style.
- The *Data* pane lists several options for working with *PivotTables* and the data model.
- Changes made in the *Proofing* pane affect the *AutoCorrect* command group in all Office programs (Access, Excel, PowerPoint, and Word).
- From the *Ease of Access* pane, set audio and visual cues for your workbooks to help users with hearing or sight impairment.
- The *Advanced* pane has categories and settings for display of the *Fill Handle, AutoComplete, Flash Fill,* and more.
- You can customize the *Ribbon* to create a new tab or group, add commands to custom groups, and rearrange or rename tabs and groups.
- When you customize the *Quick Access* toolbar, choose a command from the *Customize Quick Access Toolbar* drop-down list or use the *Excel Options* dialog box to add any command.
- Both the *Ribbon* and the *Quick Access* toolbar can be reset to their original settings from the *Excel Options* dialog box.

11.2 View and modify Office account settings and install an Office add-in (p. E11-695).

- The *Account* area in the *Backstage* view displays user and product information for your Microsoft Office account.
- Your account information and settings are applied when and where you log in to your Microsoft account.
- ***Office Background*** displays a graphic pattern in the upper-right corner of the application window.
- ***Office Theme*** determines *Ribbon* and other screen colors.
- An ***Office add-in*** provides additional features and commands to Excel and other Office programs.
- Add-ins are available in the *Office Store;* many are free.

11.3 Create a folder, add a file, and move and copy a file in *OneDrive* (p. E11-701).

- ***OneDrive*** is "cloud" or online storage for your files, available with your Microsoft account.
- Access documents stored in your *OneDrive* account from any computer that has internet access.
- *OneDrive* is listed as a storage location in a *Windows File Explorer* window.
- *OneDrive* has default folders, and you can create and name new folders.
- When you upload a saved workbook to *OneDrive,* it is copied to the cloud and remains in its original location on the computer.
- When you download a file from a *OneDrive* folder, it is copied to your computer.

11.4 Share *OneDrive* files and folders (p. E11-707).

- You can share a *OneDrive* file or folder.
- Use the *Share* command to send an email with a link to a shared workbook.
- Get a ***sharing link*** to be copied into an email or to an online location.
- After a file has been shared, change the sharing permission or remove access for recipients.
- A workbook can be shared from within Excel, but it must first be saved to your *OneDrive* account.

11.5 Open, create, and edit an Excel workbook in *Office Online* (p. E11-712).

- ***Office Online*** is free online software available with your Microsoft account.
- *Office Online* includes condensed versions of Word, PowerPoint, Excel, and OneNote.
- ***Excel Online*** has features and commands similar to Excel.
- You can edit an existing Excel workbook in *Excel Online* or create a new workbook online.

11.6 Explore *Office Online* applications and productivity tools (p. E11-720).

- Your Microsoft account gives you access to productivity tools for use with *Office Online* software.
- Use the ***Forms*** application to build an online survey and gather recipient responses.
- Recipient responses to a *Form* are summarized on the *Reponses* tab.
- ***Sway*** is a digital storytelling application that can include text, images, videos, and links.
- The mail application uses your primary Microsoft account information with your connected email addresses to send and receive messages.
- The ***People*** application is a contact manager for creating an online address book.
- Use the ***Calendar*** application to maintain a schedule of events, appointments, and tasks.
- ***OneNote Online*** is a notetaking application with text and audio features.

Check for Understanding

The SIMbook for this text (within your SIMnet account) provides the following resources for concept review:

- Multiple-choice questions
- Short answer questions
- Matching exercises

Guided Project 11-1

You change Excel options, use an add-in, and upload a Courtyard Medical Plaza (CMP) workbook to *OneDrive*. After you edit the workbook in *Excel Online*, you share it. Finally, you build a form.
[Student Learning Outcomes 11.1, 11.2, 11.3, 11.4, 11.5, 11.6]

Note to Instructor and Students:

For this project, you use your Microsoft and OneDrive accounts. If you don't have a Microsoft account, create a free account at https://signup.live.com.

Microsoft regularly updates Office Online *applications and* OneDrive. *Instructions and figures in this project may differ from your working environment. The Google Chrome web browser is illustrated in this project.*

File Needed: ***CourtyardMedical-11.xlsx*** *(Student data files are available in the* Library *of your SIMnet account.)*
Completed Project File Names: ***[your initials] Excel 11-1.xlsx***, ***[your initials] Excel 11-1a.xlsx***

Skills Covered in This Project

- Customize *Excel Options* to use manual calculation.
- Customize *Excel Options* to use the *R1C1* cell reference style.
- Install and use an Office add-in.
- Create a *OneDrive* folder.
- Upload a workbook to a *OneDrive* folder.
- Edit a workbook in *Excel Online*.
- Share a *OneDrive* workbook.
- Create a form.

---

1. Open the ***CourtyardMedical-11*** workbook from your student data files.
2. Save the workbook as [your initials] Excel 11-1 in your usual location for saving files on your computer.
3. Customize Excel options to use manual calculation and the *R1C1* reference style.
   a. Click the **File** tab and select **Options** to open the *Excel Options* dialog box.
   b. Select **Formulas** on the left.
   c. Select the **Manual** radio button in the **Calculation options** group.
   d. Select the **R1C1 reference style** box in the **Working with formulas** group.
   e. Click **OK** to close the *Excel Options* dialog box.
4. Select cell **R5C5**, type 145 and press **Enter**.
5. Type 195 in cell **R6C5** and press **Enter**.
6. Click the **Formulas** tab and click the **Calculate Now** button [*Calculation* group].
7. Install an Office add-in. (If you are unable to install an add-in, go to step 8e.)
   a. Log-in to your Microsoft account if you have not already done so.
   b. Click the **Get Add-ins** button [*Insert* tab, *Add-ins* group].
   c. Click the **Search** box, type bubbles, and press **Enter**.
   d. Verify that **Bubbles** displays in the list and click **Add** to install the add-in.

8. Use an Office add-in in a workbook.
   a. Select the add-in and drag it to position the top left selection handle at cell **R2C12**.
   b. Click the **Select Table** bubble in the add-in.
   c. Select cells **R4C9:R8C10** in the worksheet (*Company* and *Billed* data) and click **OK** (Figure 11-71). The cells represent the billed amount for each company.
   d. Select cell **R3C9** to deselect the add-in (Figure 11-72). Bubbles may move as you scroll the worksheet.
   e. Save the workbook with the same file name in the same folder on your computer.

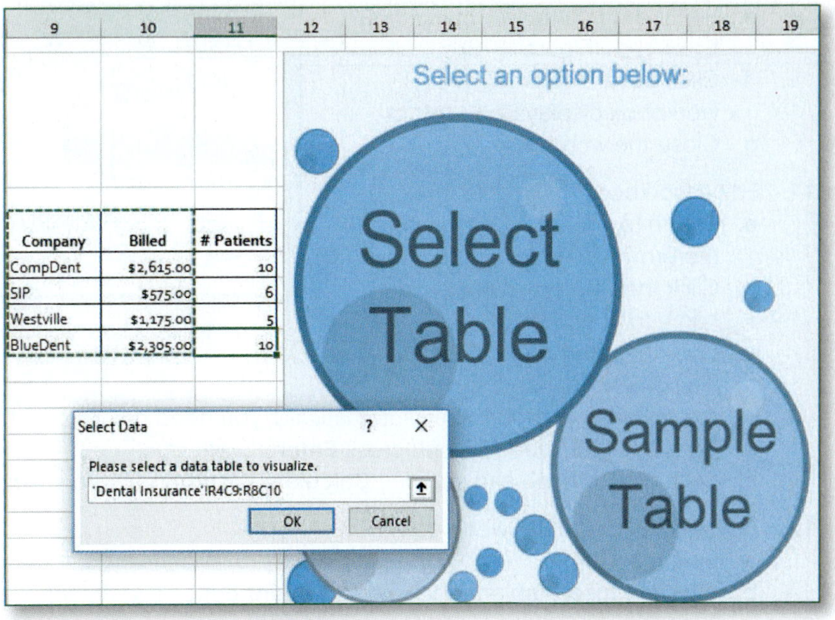

Figure 11-71 Table selected for the add-in

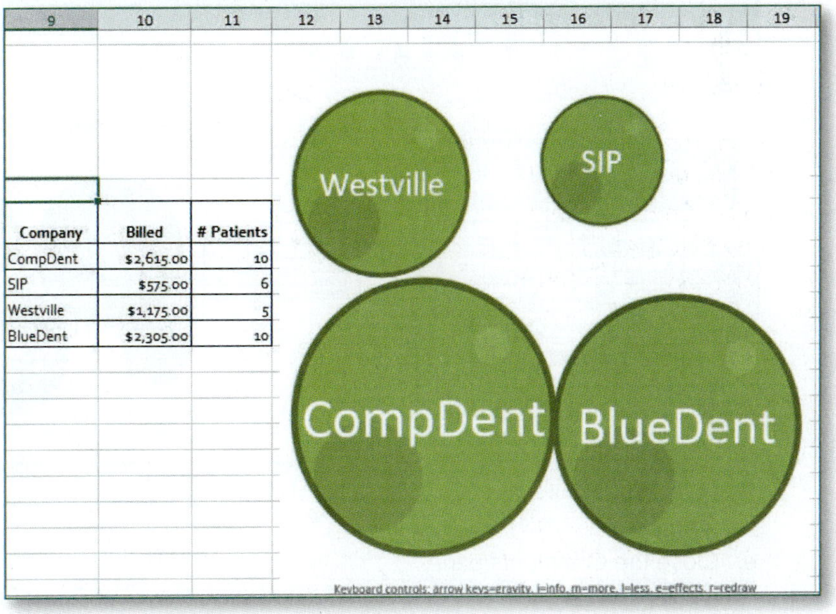

Figure 11-72 Add-in displays different bubble sizes

9. Create a *OneDrive* folder.
   a. Open a browser, go to the *OneDrive* site, and log in to your *OneDrive* account.
   b. Click **Files** to display the contents of your *OneDrive* folder.
   c. Click the **View options** button and choose a **List** view.
   d. Click the **New** button and select **Folder**.
   e. Type Courtyard Med and click **Create**.

10. Save a workbook to a *OneDrive* folder.
    a. Click the Excel icon on the Windows task bar to return to ***[your initials] Excel 11-1***.
    b. Click the **File** tab and choose **Save As**.
    c. Click **OneDrive – *[Identifier]*** in the locations list.
    d. Click the **Courtyard Med** folder name.

e. Edit the file name to [your initials] Excel 11-1a (Figure 11-73).

f. Click **Save**. The *OneDrive* workbook displays in Excel.

g. Close the workbook.

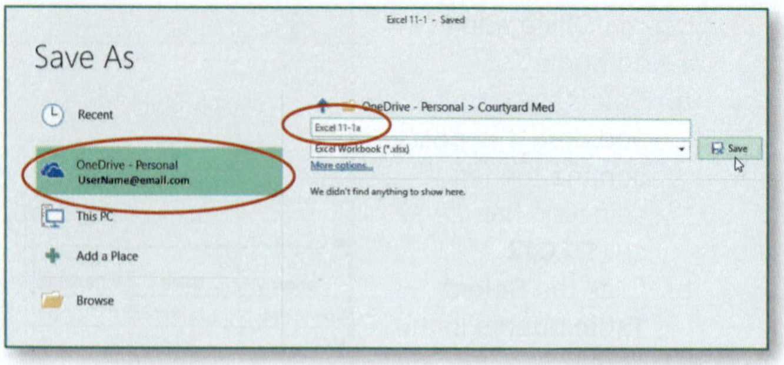

Figure 11-73 Workbook is renamed and saved on *OneDrive*

11. Edit a workbook in *Excel Online*.

a. Return to your *OneDrive* account in the browser window.

b. Click the **Courtyard Med** folder name to open it.

c. Click the ***[your initials] Excel 11-1a*** file name to launch *Excel Online*. If the add-in does not display automatically, you need not display it now.

d. Select cell **E5**, type 525, and press **Enter**.

e. Click the **Data** tab and click the **Calculate Workbook** button [*Calculation* group].

12. Add a comment to the workbook.

a. Select cell **E4**.

b. Click the **Insert** tab and click the **Comment** button [*Comments* group].

c. Type Billed amounts are still being adjusted.

d. Click **Post** in the *Comments* pane (Figure 11-74).

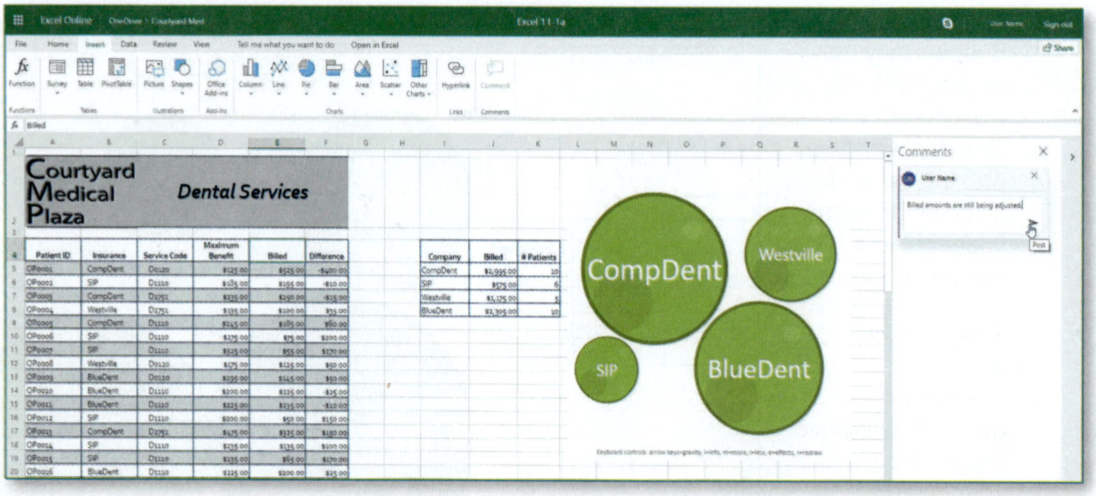

Figure 11-74 A comment in *Excel Online*

e. Close the *Comments* pane.

f. Close the *Excel Online* browser tab to save and close the ***[your initials] Excel 11-1a*** workbook and return to your *OneDrive* account.

13. Share a *OneDrive* workbook.

a. Verify or open the **Courtyard Med** folder.

b. Click the selection circle for the ***[your initials] Excel 11-1a*** file name.

c. Click the **Share** button. You will see the *Send Link* or the *Share* window depending on your Microsoft account.

d. Complete these steps in the *Send Link* window. (Go to step e for the *Share* window.)

- Click the **Link settings** box at the top of the window.
- Choose **Anyone with the link**.
- Select the **Allow editing** box to permit editing.

- Click **Apply** to return to the *Send Link* window.
- Type your instructor's email address and type a semicolon (;).
- Type your email address.
- Click **Add a message** and type Here is the insurance workbook.
- Click **Send** and close the confirmation window.

e. Complete these steps in the *Share* window. (Go to step d for the *Send Link* window.)
- Click **Anyone with this link can edit this item** to expand the window.
- Select the **Allow editing** box to permit editing.
- Click **Email** in the *Share* window.
- Type your instructor's email address.
- Click the message box and type Here is the insurance workbook.
- Click the **Share** button to send the email.

14. Create a form.
   a. Click **Files** in your *OneDrive* account.
   b. Click the **App launcher** and find and select **Forms**.
   c. Click **New Form**.
   d. Click **Untitled form** and type Courtyard Medical Plaza to replace the placeholder text.
   e. Click **Enter a description** and type Your Visits to CMP.

15. Add a *Text* question to a form.
   a. Click **Add new** or **Add question**.
   b. Click **Text** to open the entry screen.
   c. Type Number of Visits in the first entry box.
   d. Click the **Required** button.
   e. Click the **More settings** button (. . .) and choose **Restrictions**.
   f. Verify that *Number* is the restriction.
   g. Click the **More settings** button (. . .) and choose **Subtitle**.
   h. Click the subtitle box and type How many times have you met with your physical therapist? (Figure 11-75).

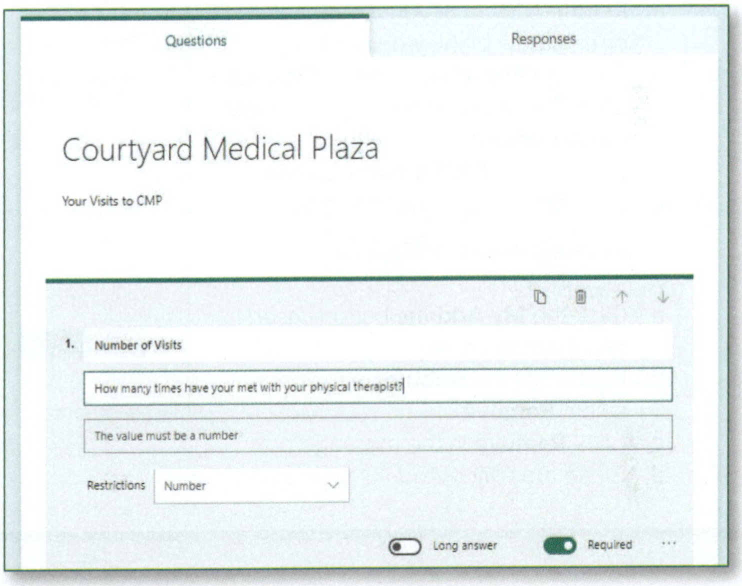

Figure 11-75 Required text question

16. Add a question with a *Yes/No* response.
   a. Click **Add new** or **Add question**.
   b. Click **Choice** to build a yes/no response.
   c. Type Are you satisfied with your progress so far?
   d. Click **Yes** in the *Suggested options* group and then click **No**.
   e. Verify that the *Required* box is active (Figure 11-76).

17. Review and edit form settings.
   a. Click the **More form settings** button (**. . .**) and select **Settings**.
   b. Select **Anyone with the link can respond** if your account displays a *Who can fill out this form* group. You will not see this group when you use a personal account.
   c. Verify or select the **Accept responses** box.

18. Preview the form.
    a. Click in the background area on either side of the *Questions* tab.
    b. Click **Preview** to view the form (Figure 11-77).
    c. Click **Back** to return to the design window.
    d. Copy and send a link to your instructor if instructed to do so.
19. Sign out of *OneDrive* and close the browser.
    a. If you have an education or business account, click the **Apps launcher** and find and click **OneDrive**.
    b. If you have a personal account, close the *Forms* browser window.
    c. Sign out and close the browser window.
20. Reset *Excel Options*.
    a. Return to Excel at your computer and open a new blank workbook.
    b. Click the **File** tab and select **Options**.
    c. Click **Formulas** on the left and select the **Automatic** radio button.
    d. Deselect the **R1C1 reference style** box.
    e. Click **OK** to close the dialog box.
21. Deactivate the add-in. (Skip this step if you did not install the add-in.)
    a. Click the **My Add-ins** button [*Insert* tab, *Add-ins* group].
    b. Right-click the **Bubbles** add-in and select **Remove**.
    c. Click **Remove** in the message box.
    d. Close the *Office Add-ins* dialog box.

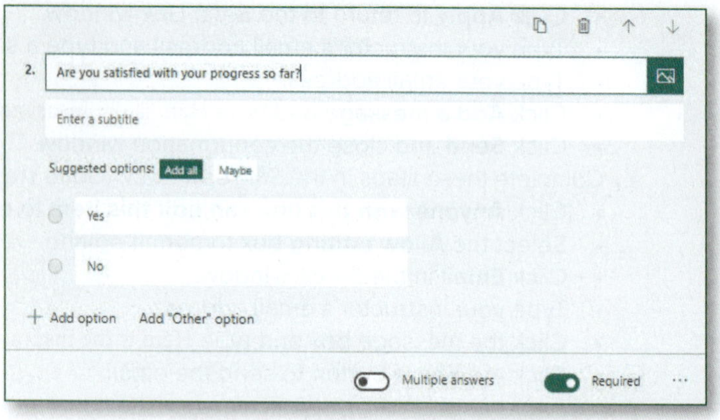

Figure 11-76 ***Yes/No*** **question**

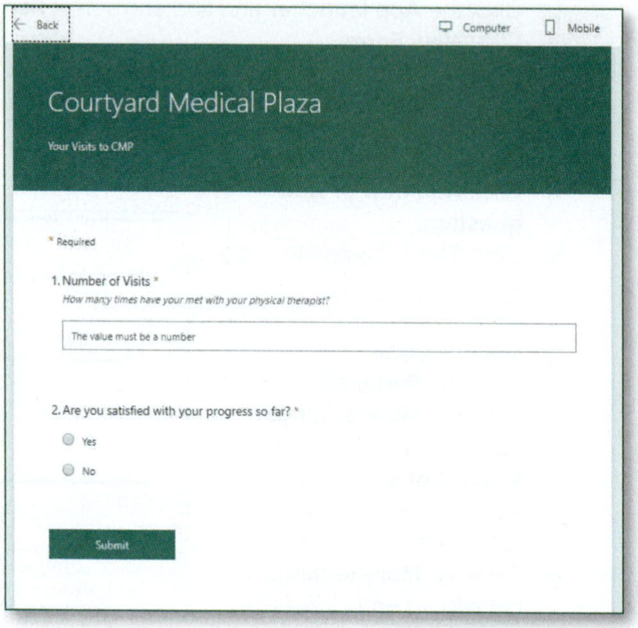

Figure 11-77 Form as it will appear to recipients

Guided Project 11-2

In the workbook for Blue Lake Sports, you customize the *Ribbon* to display your own command tab and group. You change Office settings, save the workbook to your *OneDrive* account, edit it online, and share the workbook.

[Student Learning Outcomes 11.1, 11.2, 11.3, 11.4, 11.5]

Note to Instructor and Students:

For this project, you use your Microsoft and OneDrive accounts. If you don't have a Microsoft account, create a free account at https://signup.live.com.

Microsoft regularly updates Office Online *applications and* OneDrive. *Instructions and figures in this project may differ from your working environment. The Google Chrome web browser is illustrated in this project.*

File Needed: ***BlueLakeSports-11.xlsx*** *(Student data files are available in the* Library *of your SIMnet account.)*
Completed Project File Names: ***[your initials] Excel 11-2.xlsx*** and ***[your initials] Excel 11-2a.xlsx***

Skills Covered in This Project

- Modify Office account settings to choose a theme.
- Add a custom command tab and group to the *Ribbon.*
- Add command buttons to a custom group on the *Ribbon.*
- Save a workbook to a *OneDrive* folder.
- Edit a workbook in *Excel Online.*
- Share a *OneDrive* workbook.

1. Open the ***BlueLakeSports-11*** workbook from your student data files.
2. Save the workbook as [your initials] Excel 11-2 in your usual location for saving files on your computer.
3. Customize the *Ribbon* to add a tab and a group.
   a. Right-click the **Ribbon** and select **Customize the Ribbon**.
   b. Select **Insert** in the *Main Tabs* list on the right.
   c. Click **New Tab** to insert a custom tab and group.
   d. Click **New Tab (Custom)** and click **Rename**.
   e. Type [your initials] Tab and click **OK**.
   f. Select **New Group (Custom)** and click **Rename**.
   g. Type [your initials] Group and click **OK**.
4. Add command buttons to a custom group.
   a. Select **[your initials] Group**.
   b. Select **Save As** in the *Popular Commands* list on the left.
   c. Click **Add** to place the button in the custom group.
   d. Click the **Choose commands from** drop-down list and select **All Commands**.
   e. Select **Screenshot** in the list and click **Add**.
   f. Select **Screenshot** in the **[your initials] Group** list and click **Rename**.
   g. Select the **Smiley Face** icon and click **OK**.
   h. Click **OK** (Figure 11-78).

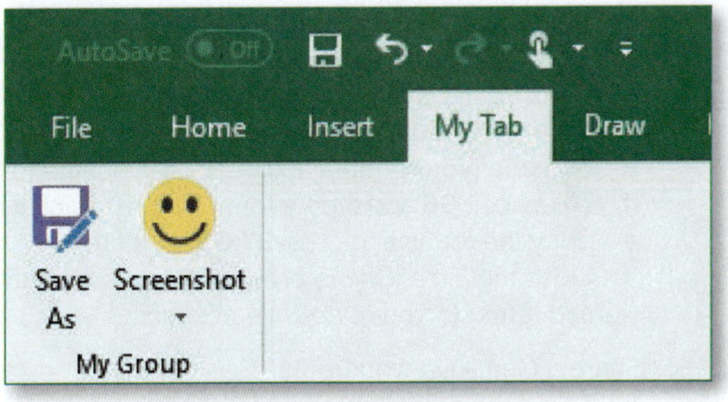

Figure 11-78 Custom tab, group, and buttons

5. Select an Office theme.
   a. Click the **File** tab and select **Account**.
   b. Click the **Office Theme** drop-down list and select **Dark Gray**.
   c. Return to the workbook.
6. Use a custom group to take a screenshot.
   a. Press **Ctrl+N** to open a new blank workbook.
   b. Click the **[your initials] Tab** command tab on the *Ribbon*.

c. Press **Ctrl+F6** to return to ***[your initials] Excel 11-2***.
d. Click the **[your initials] Tab** command tab on the *Ribbon*.
e. Click the **Screenshot** button and choose **Screen Clipping**.
f. With the crosshair pointer, select from the top-left corner of the blank workbook window to cell **K5**.
g. Click the **Height** box on the *Picture Tools Format* tab in the *Size* group.
h. Type 2 as the new height and press **Enter**. The width is proportional.
i. Select the picture object and position its top left selection handle at cell **I2**.
j. Select cell **G6** (Figure 11-79).

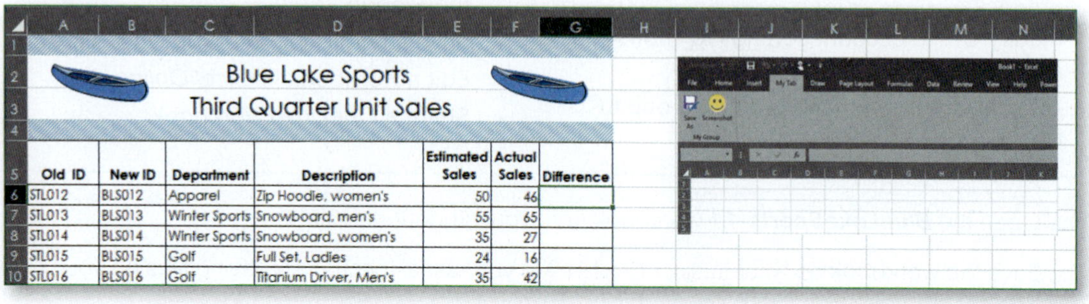

Figure 11-79 Sized and positioned screenshot

7. Save a workbook to a *OneDrive* folder.
   a. Click the **File** tab and choose **Save As**.
   b. Select **OneDrive – *[Identifier]*** in the locations list.
   c. Click the **Documents** folder name. (If your account does not have a *Documents* folder, click *More options* to open the *Save As* dialog box. Navigate to your *OneDrive* account and create the folder. Close the *Save As* dialog box, return to the workbook, and select **File**, **Save As** again.)
   d. Edit the file name to [your initials] Excel 11-2a.
   e. Click **Save**.
   f. Close the workbook.

8. Edit a workbook in *Excel Online*.
   a. Open your browser, go to the *OneDrive* page, and sign in to your *OneDrive* account.
   b. Click the **Documents** folder name to open it
   c. Click the **[your initials] Excel 11-2a** file name to launch *Excel Online*.
   d. Select cell **G6** and type a formula to subtract actual sales from estimated sales.
   e. Copy the formula to cells **G7:G20** (Figure 11-80).
   f. Close the *Excel Online* browser tab to save and close the ***[your initials] Excel 11-2a*** workbook and return to your *OneDrive* account.

9. Share a *OneDrive* workbook.
   a. Select the **selection circle** for the **[your initials] Excel 11-2a** file name.
   b. Click the **Share** button.
   c. Complete these steps in the *Send Link* window. (Go to step d for the *Share* window.)
      - Click the **Link settings** box at the top of the window.
      - Choose **Anyone with the link**.
      - Select the **Allow editing** box to permit editing.
      - Click **Apply** to return to the *Send Link* window.
      - Type your instructor's email address and type a semicolon (;).
      - Type your email address.
      - Click **Add a message** and type Excel 11-2a with screenshot.
      - Click **Send** and close the confirmation window.

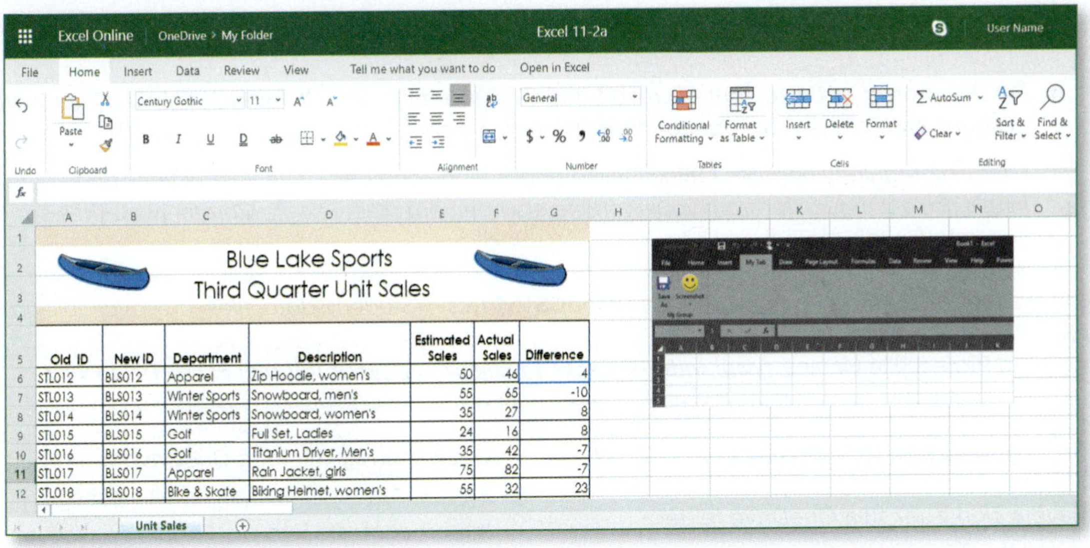

Figure 11-80 ***Excel Online*** **workbook with screenshot**

d. Complete these steps in the *Share* window. (Go to step c for the *Send Link* window.)
- Click **Anyone with this link can edit this item** to expand the window.
- Select the **Allow editing** box to permit editing.
- Click **Email** in the *Share* window.
- Type your instructor's email address and type a semicolon (;).
- Type your email address.
- Click the message box and type Excel 11-2a with screenshot.
- Click the **Share** button to send the email.

10. Sign out of *OneDrive* and close the browser.

11. Reset the *Ribbon*.
    a. Return to Excel and the blank workbook.
    b. Click the **File** tab and select **Options**.
    c. Select **Customize Ribbon** on the left.
    d. Click **Reset** and choose **Reset all customizations**.
    e. Click **Yes** in the message box.
    f. Click **OK** to close the dialog box.

12. Reset the Office theme.
    a. Click the **File** tab and select **Account**.
    b. Click the **Office Theme** drop-down list and select **Colorful**.
    c. Return to the workbook and close it.

Guided Project 11-3

The aging detail worksheet for Livingood Accounting Services has an error that you correct using *Excel Online*. You use *Mail* (*Outlook*) to send a sharing link in an email message and upload a CSV file (comma-separated values) to the *People* application.
[Student Learning Outcomes 11.3, 11.4, 11.5, 11.6]

Note to Instructor and Students:

For this project, you use your Microsoft and OneDrive accounts. If you don't have a Microsoft account, create a free account at https://signup.live.com.

Microsoft regularly updates Office Online *applications and* OneDrive. *Instructions and figures in this project may differ from your working environment. The Google Chrome web browser is illustrated in this project.*

Files Needed: ***Livingood-11.xlsx*** and ***LivingoodCSV-11.csv*** *(Student data files are available in the* Library *of your SIMnet account.)*
Completed Project File Names: ***[your initials] Excel 11-3**.xlsx* and ***[your initials] Excel 11-3a**.xlsx*

Skills Covered in This Project

- Save a workbook to a *OneDrive* folder.
- Insert the *TODAY* function in a workbook in *Excel Online*.
- Get a sharing link for a *OneDrive* workbook.
- Send a sharing link in an email message.
- Import contacts into the *People* application.

---

1. Open the ***Livingood-11*** workbook from your student data files.
2. Save the workbook as [your initials] Excel 11-3 in your usual location for saving files on your computer.
3. Save a workbook to a *OneDrive* folder.
   a. Click the **File** tab and choose **Save As**.
   b. Click **OneDrive – *[Identifier]*** in the locations list.
   d. Select **Documents** to open the folder. (If your account does not have a *Documents* folder, click **More options** to open the *Save As* dialog box. Navigate to your *OneDrive* account and create the folder. Close the *Save As* dialog box, return to the workbook, and select **File**, **Save As** again.)
   c. Edit the file name to [your initials] Excel 11-3a.
   d. Click **Save**.
   e. Close the ***[your initials] Excel 11-3a*** workbook in Excel.
4. Edit a workbook in *Excel Online* to insert the TODAY function.
   a. Open your browser and go to your *OneDrive* account.
   b. Click the **Documents** folder name.
   c. Click the **[your initials] Excel 11-3a** file name to launch *Excel Online*.
   d. Select cell **G1** and type =to to display the *Formula AutoComplete* list.
   e. Press **Tab** to select the function (Figure 11-81).

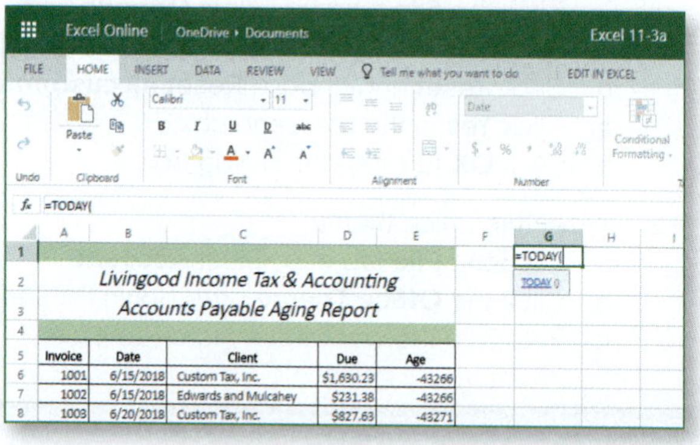

Figure 11-81 Enter the *TODAY* function in *Excel Online*

   f. Press **Enter** to complete the function. The formulas in column **E** are calculated.
   g. Close the *Excel Online* browser tab to save and close the ***[your initials] Excel 11-3a*** workbook and return to your *OneDrive* account.
5. Get a view-only link for a *OneDrive* workbook.
   a. Select the **selection circle** for the **[your initials] Excel 11-3a** file name (Figure 11-82).
   b. Click the **Share** button.

c. Complete these steps in the *Send Link* window. (Refer to step d for the *Share* pane).
   - Click the **Link settings** button.
   - Select **Anyone with the link**.
   - Deselect the **Allow editing** box to create a view-only link.
   - Click **Apply** to return to the *Send Link* window.
   - Click the **Copy Link** button to display the link.
   - Click **Copy** to copy the link to the Windows *Clipboard*.
   - Close the confirmation window.

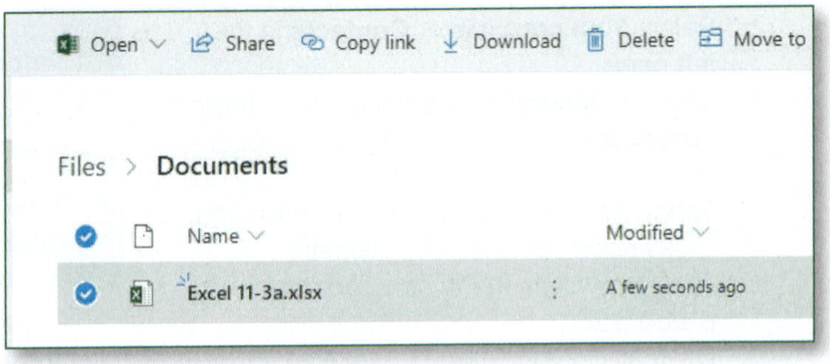

Figure 11-82 Select a workbook in *OneDrive*

d. Complete these steps in the *Share* pane. (Refer to step c for the *Send Link* window).
   - Click **Get a sharing link** at the bottom of the *Share* pane
   - Click **Create a view-only link**.
   - Click the **Copy** button to copy the link to the Windows *Clipboard*
   - Close the *Share* pane.

6. Paste the link in an *Outlook Mail* email message.
   a. Click the **App launcher** button and choose **Outlook** or **Mail**. (Your choice depends on your account.)
   b. Click the **New** button or **New message**.
   c. Select or type your instructor's email address in the *To* box.
   d. Type Updated File as the subject.
   e. Click in the message area and press **Ctrl+V** to paste the link.
   f. Press **End** to position the pointer and press **Enter** to format the hyperlink.
   g. Type Click this link for the corrected file. and press **Enter** (Figure 11-83). (Your link and mail window will be different from the figure.)
   h. Click **Send**.
   i. Close the *Outlook Mail* browser tab to return to the *OneDrive* tab.

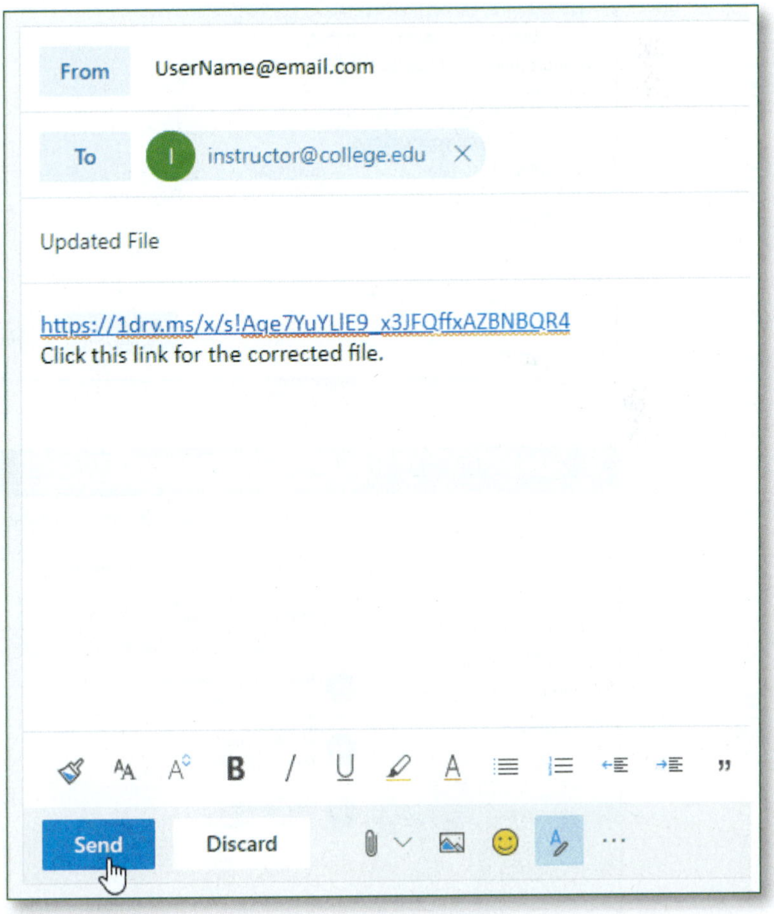

Figure 11-83 Send a link in an *Outlook Mail* message

7. Import a CSV file into the *People* application. Your screen choices and prompts depend on your Microsoft account.
   a. Click the **App launcher** button and choose **People**.

b. Select **Your contacts** or **Contacts** in the left pane.
c. Click the **Manage** button and select **Import contacts** (Figure 11-84). (If your account displays a window that lists *Gmail*, *Outlook*, *Yahoo Mail*, or other mail clients after you click *Import contacts*, click **Gmail**.)
d. Click **Browse** in the *Import contacts* dialog box.

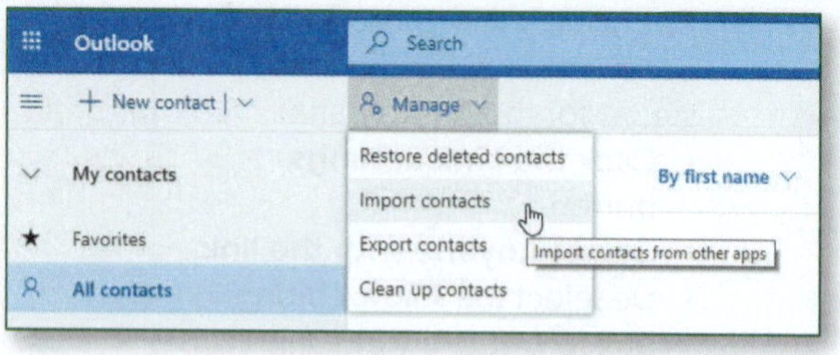

Figure 11-84 Add contacts to the *People* application

e. Navigate to your student data files folder, select ***LivingoodCSV-11.csv***, and click **Open**.
f. Click **Import** or **Upload** (Figure 11-85).
g. Close the confirmation or message window. Four contacts were imported (Figure 11-86).

8. Return to *OneDrive*, sign out, and close the browser.

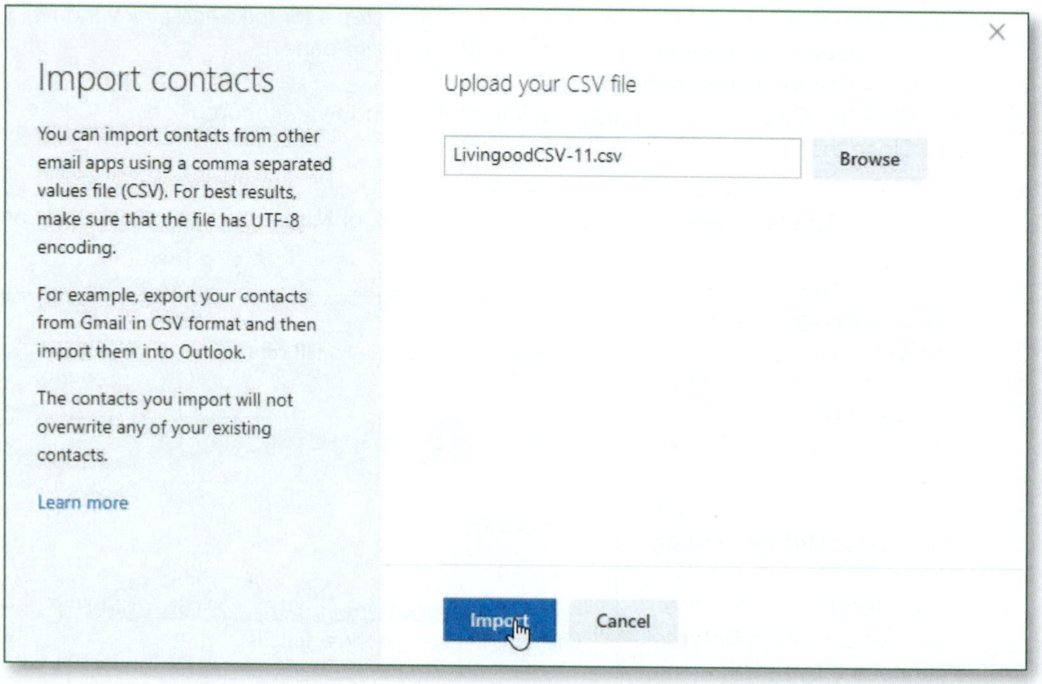

Figure 11-85 Import a *CSV* file

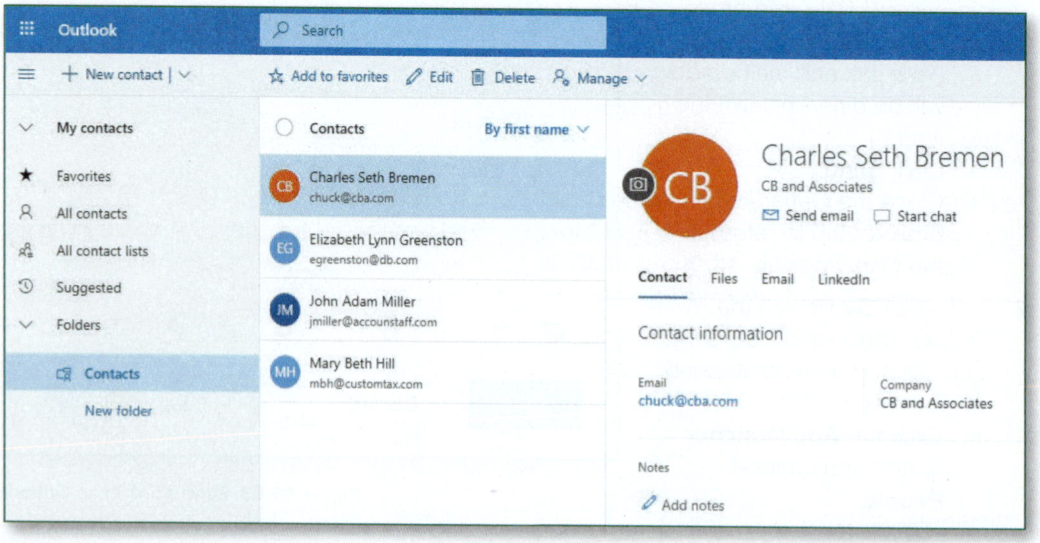

Figure 11-86 Imported contacts in a personal *OneDrive* account

Independent Project 11-4

For the Hamilton Civic Center, you customize the *Quick Access* toolbar to display a *Draw* button. After annotating the workbook, you upload the workbook and a related Word document to *OneDrive* for sharing.
[Student Learning Outcomes 11.1, 11.3, 11.4]

Note to Instructor and Students:

> *For this project, you use your Microsoft and OneDrive accounts. If you don't have a Microsoft account, create a free account at https://signup.live.com.*
>
> *Microsoft regularly updates* Office Online *applications and* OneDrive*. Instructions and figures in this project may differ from your working environment. The Google Chrome web browser is illustrated in this project.*

Files Needed: ***HamiltonCC-11.xlsx*** and ***HamiltonCCWord-11.docx*** *(Student data files are available in the* Library *of your SIMnet account.)*
Completed Project File Names: ***[your initials] Excel 11-4.xlsx*** and ***[your initials] Excel 11-4Word.docx***

Skills Covered in This Project

- Add a command to the *Quick Access* toolbar.
- Create a *OneDrive* folder.
- Upload files to *OneDrive.*
- Share a *OneDrive* folder.
- Remove a command from the *Quick Access* toolbar.

---

1. Copy the ***HamiltonCCWord-11.docx*** document from your student data files to your usual location for saving files on your computer.
2. In a *File Explorer* window, rename the copied Word file as [your initials] Excel 11-4Word.
3. Open the ***HamiltonCC-11*** Excel workbook from your student data files.
4. Save the workbook as [your initials] Excel 11-4 in your usual location for saving files on your computer.
5. Click the **Draw** tab and then click the **Pen: Red, 1 mm** button [*Pens* group]. If the *Draw* button is active, click the **Draw** button [*Tools* group] to turn it off. This sets the red pen as the selected draw option (Figure 11-87).
6. Click the **Home** tab.
7. Click the **Customize Quick Access Toolbar** drop-down list and select **More Commands**. Display **All Commands**, find and select **Draw** in the list, and add the command to the toolbar.

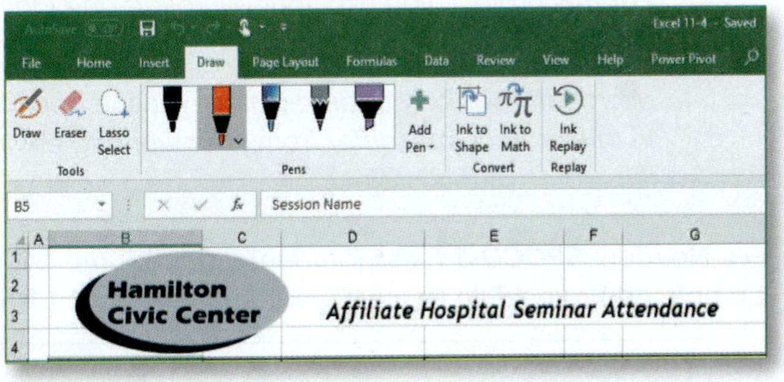

Figure 11-87 Red pen is selected and *Draw* button is deselected

8. Click the **Draw** button on the *Quick Access* toolbar.
9. Draw a check mark next to the **0** in cell **E9** and a second check mark next to the **6** in cell **G10**.
10. Click the **Draw** button on the *Quick Access* toolbar to turn off the tool (Figure 11-88).
11. Select cell **B5** and save and close the workbook.

12. Open your browser and sign-in to your *OneDrive* account.
13. Create a folder named Hamilton CC in the *Files* category and open the folder.
14. Upload ***[your initials] Excel 11-4.xlsx*** and ***[your initials] Excel 11-4Word.docx*** to the *Hamilton CC* folder on *OneDrive* from your usual folder for saving files.
15. Display the *Files* category and select the *Hamilton CC* folder.
16. Share the folder in an email to your instructor.
17. Sign out of your *OneDrive* account and close the browser.

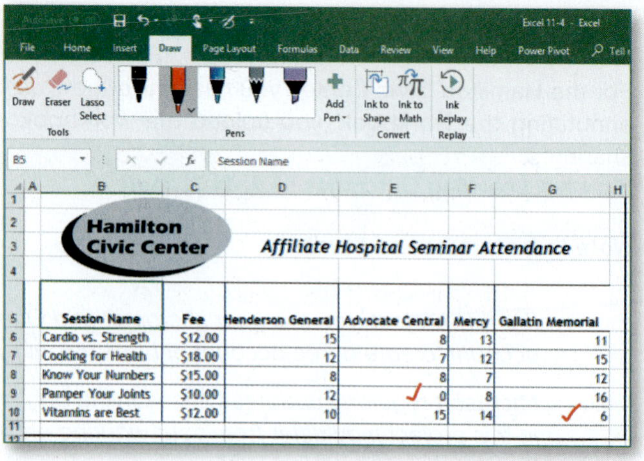

Figure 11-88 Annotated worksheet

18. Open a blank workbook in Excel. Open the *Excel Options* dialog box and remove the **Draw** command from the *Quick Access* toolbar.

Independent Project 11-5

You add two commands to the *Quick Access* toolbar so that you can complete and upload a workbook for Sierra Pacific Community College District (SPCCD). You enter labels for a new workbook using *Excel Online* and save it to the SPCCD folder.
[Student Learning Outcomes 11.1, 11.3, 11.4, 11.5]

Note to Instructor and Students:

For this project, you use your Microsoft and OneDrive accounts. If you don't have a Microsoft account, create a free account at https://signup.live.com.

Microsoft regularly updates Office Online *applications and* OneDrive. *Instructions and figures in this project may differ from your working environment. The Google Chrome web browser is illustrated in this project.*

File Needed: ***SPCCD-11.xlsx*** *(Student data files are available in the* Library *of your SIMnet account.)*
Completed Project File Names: ***[your initials] Excel 11-5.xlsx*** and ***[your initials] Excel 11-5a.xlsx***

Skills Covered in This Project

- Customize the *Quick Access* toolbar.
- Create a *OneDrive* folder.
- Upload a workbook to *OneDrive*.
- Create a new workbook in *Excel Online*.
- Share a *OneDrive* folder.

1. Open the ***SPCCD-11*** workbook from your student data files.
2. Save the workbook as [your initials] Excel 11-5 in your usual location for saving files on your computer.

3. Click the **Customize Quick Access Toolbar** drop-down list and select **More Commands**. Display **All Commands** and add the **Rename Sheet** and **Thick Bottom Border** commands to the toolbar (Figure 11-89).
4. Click the **Rename Sheet** button in the *Quick Access* toolbar and type Capacity as the new sheet name.
5. Select cells **B2:E2** and click the **Thick Bottom Border** button in the *Quick Access* toolbar.
6. Select cell **F1**. Save and close the workbook.
7. Leave Excel running. If a blank workbook is not open, press **Ctrl+N**.
8. Open your browser and sign-in to your *OneDrive* account.
9. Create a folder named SPCCD in the *Files* category and upload a copy of ***[your initials] Excel 11-5*** to the folder.
10. From the **SPCCD** folder window in *OneDrive*, create a new *Excel Online* workbook. Click the default file name in the *Title* bar and name the workbook as [your initials] Excel 11-5a.
11. Enter the data shown in Figure 11-90.
12. Close the browser tab for ***[your initials] Excel 11-5a***.
13. Share the **SPCCD** folder in an email to your instructor.
14. Sign out of your *OneDrive* account and close the browser.
15. Return to Excel on your computer and reset the *Quick Access* toolbar.

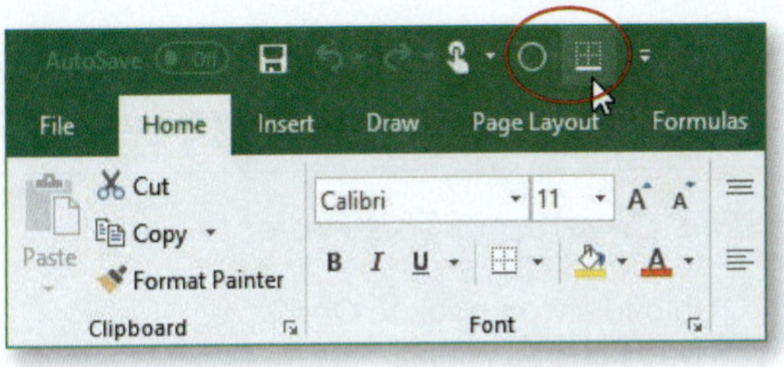

Figure 11-89 Command buttons for the *Quick Access* toolbar

	A	B	C	D
1	Sierra Pacific Community College			
2	Humanities Department			
3	Brainstorming Sessions for Next Month			
4				
5	Date	Room	Time	
6	5	A101	9:30	
7	10	A220	10:30	
8	15	B105	9:30	
9	20	B105	10:30	
10				

Figure 11-90 Data for new *Excel Online* workbook

Independent Project 11-6

You take notes using *OneNote Online* for a planning meeting at Mary's Rentals. You share your notes and attach a copy of a related workbook for completion.
[Student Learning Outcomes 11.4, 11.6]

Note to Instructor and Students:

For this project, you use your Microsoft and OneDrive accounts. If you don't have a Microsoft account, create a free account at https://signup.live.com.

Microsoft regularly updates Office Online *applications and* OneDrive. *Instructions and figures in this project may differ from your working environment. The Google Chrome web browser is illustrated in this project.*

File Needed: ***MarysRentals-11.xlsx*** *(Student data files are available in the* Library *of your SIMnet account.)*
Completed Project File Name: ***[your initials] Excel 11-6.xlsx***

Skills Covered in This Project

- Upload a workbook to *OneDrive*.
- Use *OneNote Online*.
- Share a *OneNote* notebook.

1. Open the ***MarysRentals-11*** workbook from your student data files.
2. Save the workbook as [your initials] Excel 11-6 in the *Documents* folder in the *Files* category of your *OneDrive* account. (If your account does not have a *Documents* folder, click **More options** to open the *Save As* dialog box. Navigate to your *OneDrive* account and create the folder. Close the *Save As* dialog box, return to the workbook, and select **File, Save As** again.)
3. Edit the workbook properties to show your first and last name as *Author*. Type Maintenance Costs as the *Title*.
4. Close the workbook.
5. Open your browser and sign-in to your *OneDrive* account. Display the *Documents* folder contents.
6. Click the **Apps launcher** button and select **OneNote**. Respond to and navigate through opening screens as needed. If you are using a personal *OneDrive* account, a default notebook opens and is named ***[Your User Name's] Notebook***. If you are using an academic or business account, click **New notebook** and name the notebook Your Name Notebook.
7. Click the **+ Section** at the bottom of the left pane and type Maintenance as the section name. Personal *OneDrive* accounts include a default *Quick Notes* section.
8. Type Mary's Rental Planning Meeting as the title for the page and press **Enter** (Figure 11-91).

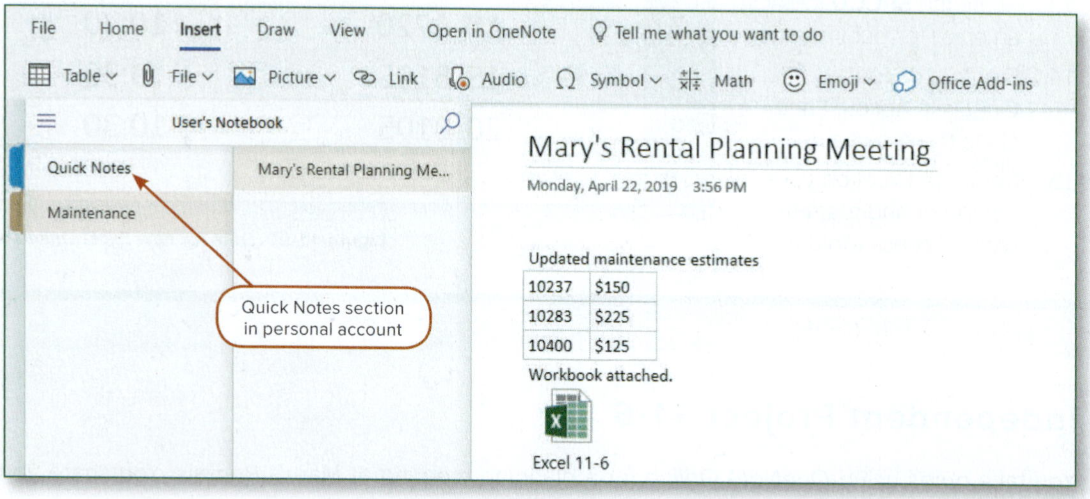

Figure 11-91 New notebook and section in *OneNote Online*

9. Type Updated maintenance estimates as the first line of text and press **Enter**.
10. To create the table, enter the first ID number and press **Tab**. Type the amount and press **Enter**. After the last item, press **Enter** and then press **Backspace** to exit the table format.
11. Type Workbook attached. below the table and press **Enter** (see Figure 11-91).
12. Click **Insert** on the *Ribbon*. Click the **File** button and choose **Insert as Attachment** in a personal account or click the **File Attachment** button in a business account. Click **Choose File** and navigate

to your *OneDrive* account. Open the *Documents* folder, select ***[your initials] Excel 11-6***, and click **Open**. Then click **Insert** to attach the workbook to the notebook.

13. Click **Share** and send an email to your instructor with the following message: Here are notes from the meeting.
14. Close the *OneNote Online* browser tab.
15. Sign out of your *OneDrive* account and close the browser.

Improve It Project 11-7

The Pool & Spa Oasis wants to use the *Calendar* application to schedule work crews. You enter the current schedule in *Calendar* and share your work.
[Student Learning Outcomes 11.3, 11.4, 11.6]

Note to Instructor and Students:

For this project, you use your Microsoft and OneDrive accounts. If you don't have a Microsoft account, create a free account at https://signup.live.com.

Microsoft regularly updates Office Online *applications and* OneDrive. *Instructions and figures in this project may differ from your working environment. The Google Chrome web browser is illustrated in this project.*

File Needed: ***Pool&Spa-11.xlsx*** *(Student data files are available in the* Library *of your SIMnet account.)*
Completed Project File Name: ***[your initials] Excel 11-7.xlsx***

Skills Covered in This Project

- Upload a workbook to *OneDrive.*
- Use the *Calendar* application.
- Share a calendar.

1. Open the ***Pool&Spa-11*** workbook from your student data files.
2. Save the workbook as [your initials] Excel 11-7 in the *Files* folder in your *OneDrive* account.
3. Enter the *TODAY* function in cell **A8**.
4. Type 1000 Street Address in cell **B8**.
5. Type ro in cell **C8** and press **Tab** to accept the *AutoComplete* suggestion.
6. Type the start time at 1 PM and the end time of 2 PM.
7. Open your browser and sign-in to your *OneDrive* account.
8. Start the **Calendar** application and verify that the calendar displays in *Month* view and that the left pane is visible.
9. Size and position the Excel window and the *Calendar* window side by side, or print a copy of the worksheet for reference as your work in the *Calendar* application.

10. Click **Add calendar** in the left pane (personal account), or click the **Add calendar** button and choose **Secondary calendar** (business account). Type PoolSpa as the name and press **Enter**. For a business account, click the **PoolSpa** calendar name in the left pane so that it is active.

11. Deselect the *Calendar* circle in the left pane to hide the calendar in a personal account. Click the **X** for **Calendar** below the current month name at the top to hide the calendar in a business account (Figure 11-92).

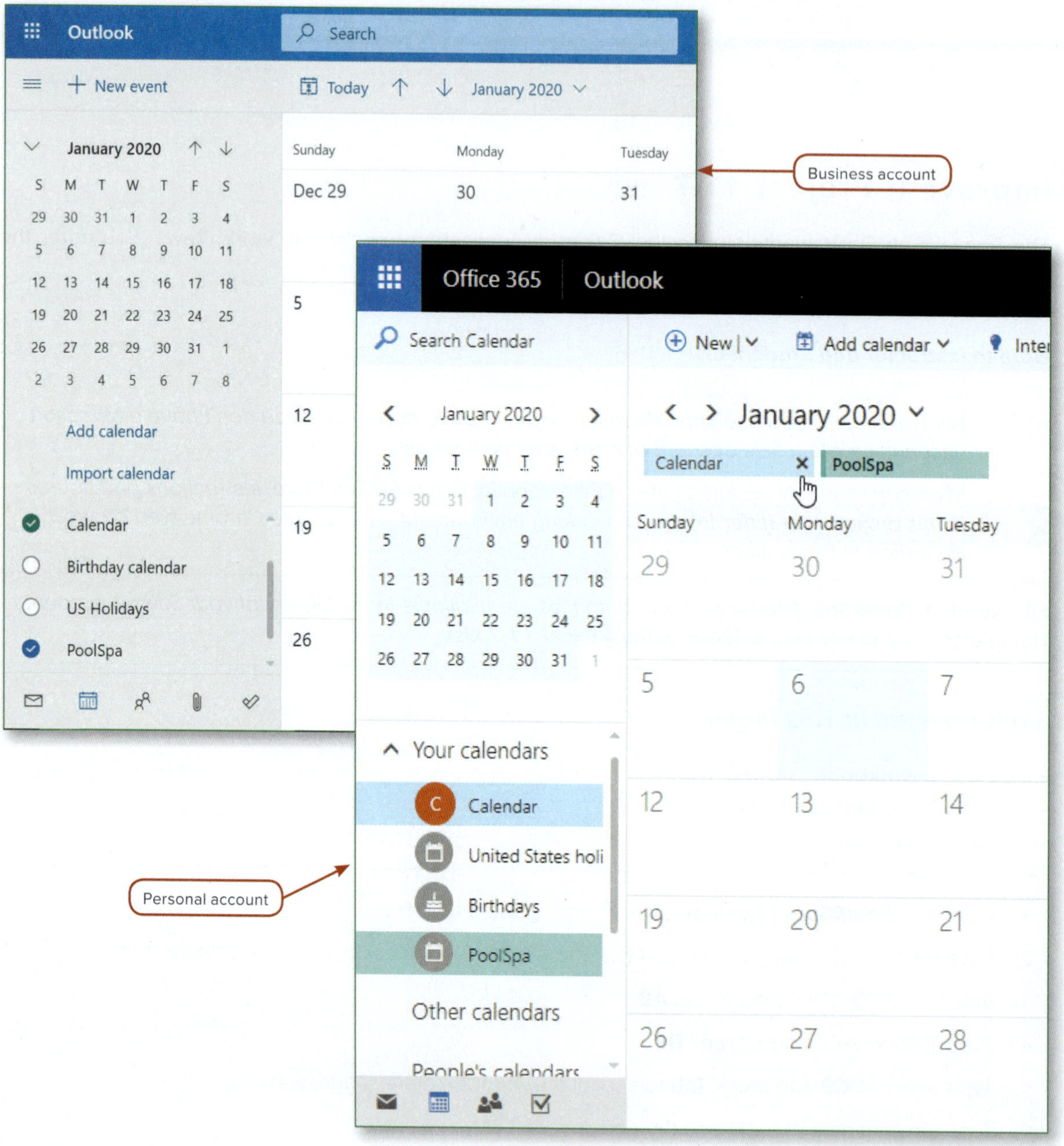

Figure 11-92 Close or hide a calendar

12. Verify that today is selected in the calendar and click **New event** or the **New** button to create an event for today.

13. Type Routine maintenance in the *Add a title* line.

14. Click the *Add a location* line, type 1000 Street Address, and ignore suggested locations.
15. Select **1:00 PM** as the start time and **2:00 PM** for the ending time box.
16. Click **Save** (Figure 11-93).

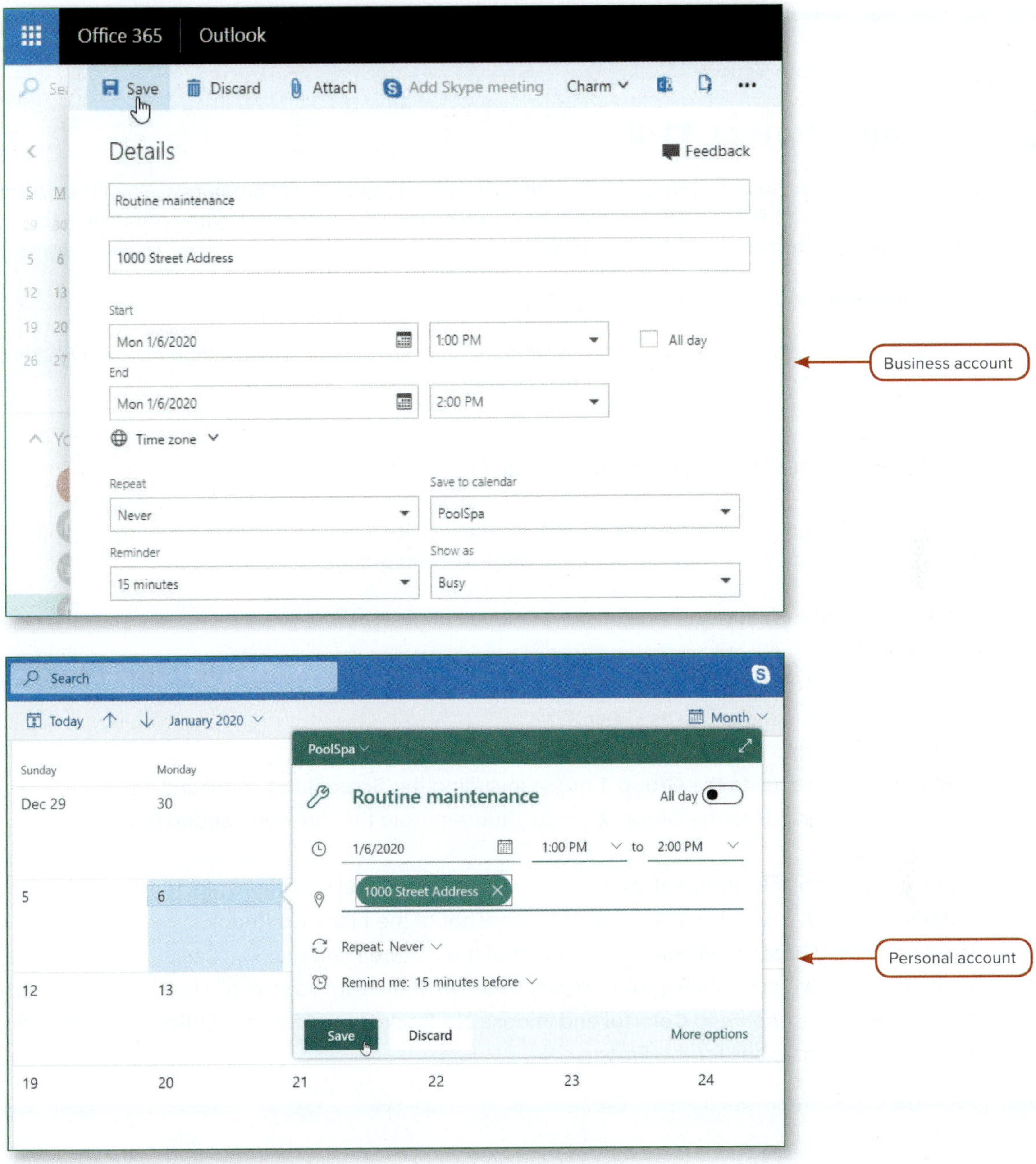

Figure 11-93 Enter and save data for an event

17. Refer to your workbook to complete data for the remaining four dates. If your dates reach into next month, locate and click the arrow that will display the next month.
18. Click **Share** when all dates are entered and select the **PoolSpa** calendar for sharing.

19. Type your instructor's email address and verify that the **Can view all details** option is selected. Then click **Share**.
20. Return to *OneDrive*, sign out, and close the browser.
21. Close ***[your initials] Excel 11-7***. It is *AutoSaved*.

Challenge Project 11-8

For this project, you add a custom tab to the *Ribbon* with two groups of commands. You insert a screenshot of the customized *Ribbon* in a new workbook and share that workbook with your instructor.
[Student Learning Outcomes 11.1, 11.2, 11.3, 11.4]

Note to Instructor and Students:

For this project, you use your Microsoft and OneDrive accounts. If you don't have a Microsoft account, create a free account at https://signup.live.com.

File Needed: None
Completed Project File Name: ***[your initials] Excel 11-8.xlsx***

Create a new workbook and save it to the *Documents* folder in your *OneDrive* account as [your initials] Excel 11-8. Modify your workbook according to the following guidelines:

- Modify the *Office Theme* to *Dark Gray* and choose an *Office Background* other than *No Background.*
- Customize the *Ribbon* to add a new tab after the *View* tab. Name the new tab [your last name] Tab. Name the new custom group as Group 1.
- Add a new group to the **[your last name]** tab and name it as Group 2.
- Add three commands to the **Group 1** group including the **Screenshot** command.
- Add three commands to the **Group 2** group, different from the three you added to the *Group 1* group.
- Open a second blank workbook and click the **[your last name]** command tab. Return to the ***[your initials] Excel 11-8*** workbook and take a screenshot of the blank workbook.
- In ***[your initials] Excel 11-8***, format the height of the picture image to **5** inches.
- From the Excel window, share ***[your initials] Excel 11-8*** file with your instructor.
- Modify the *Office Theme* to **Colorful** and choose **No Background** for your Office account settings.
- Reset all customizations for the *Ribbon.*

Challenge Project 11-9

For this project, you create a workbook that lists tasks with start and end dates for stages of a project. You search for and install an *Add-in* from the Office *Store* to create a Gantt chart.
[Student Learning Outcome 11.6]

Note to Instructor and Students:

For this project, you use your Microsoft and OneDrive accounts. If you don't have a Microsoft account, create a free account at https://signup.live.com.

File Needed: None
Completed Project File Name: ***[your initials] Excel 11-9**.xlsx*

Create a new workbook and save it to the *Documents* folder in your *OneDrive* account as [your initials] Excel 11-9. Modify your workbook according to the following guidelines:

- Type Task 1 in cell **A1**. Type Task 2 in cell **A2**. Fill the labels to "Task 5" in cell **A5**.
- Type today's date in cell **B1**. In cells **B2:B5**, enter a date for each task that is after today but within six months of today. These dates are starting dates for each task.
- Type the date for one week from today in cell **C1**. This is the end date for Task 1.
- In cells **C2:C5**, type ending dates for each task with overlapping dates for two tasks. For example, start Task 3 before Task 2 is complete.
- Search the Office *Add-ins* for a free Gantt chart application and install the add-in.
- Review guidelines, samples, or demos in the add-in to determine how to create the chart.
- Create the Gantt chart.
- Edit the task labels to display the names of tasks in an actual project. Develop tasks for a project such as remodeling your kitchen, deciding whether to buy or lease a new automobile, writing an historical novel, and so on.
- Reload or refresh the data for the Gantt chart if necessary.
- Close ***[your initials] Excel 11-9***.
- Remove the add-in from your Office account.

Challenge Project 11-10

For this project, you create and distribute a *Form* to gather information about school, work, or social activities. After recipients have responded, you review results and open a copy in Excel.
[Student Learning Outcomes 11.3, 11.4, 11.6]

Note to Instructor and Students:

For this project, you use your Microsoft and OneDrive accounts. If you don't have a Microsoft account, create a free account at https://signup.live.com.

File Needed: None
Completed Project File Name: ***[your initials] Excel 11-10.xlsx***

Assemble social media contact information or email addresses of four classmates or colleagues who agree to respond to your form within 24 hours of receiving a link. Ask questions about distance commuting to work or school, money spent on sports activities, hours spent on social media, or a similar concept of interest.

- Log in to your *OneDrive* account.
- Click the **app launcher** button and then click **Forms** to create a new form.

- Determine and enter a title and a description for your form.
- Ask the individual to identify himself or herself in the first question.
- Determine and use a question that will require a *Choice* response and develop the options.
- Create a question that will use a *Choice* response with *Yes* and *No* as the two options.
- Continue to develop a form that has a total of five questions using *Text, Rating,* or *Date* responses.
- Share the form with your classmates or colleagues and your instructor through email or other social media.
- Review the responses in the *Forms* app. Then open the responses in Excel.
- Rename the workbook as [your last name] Excel 11-10.
- Format the table with a different style and make other format choices to enhance the appearance of the results.
- Save and close ***[your initials] Excel 11-10***.

Source of screenshots Microsoft Office 365 (2019): Word, Excel, Access, PowerPoint.

appendices

- **APPENDIX A:** Office 365 Shortcuts
- **APPENDIX B:** Business Document Formats (online resource)

APPENDIX A

Office 365 Shortcuts

Using Function Keys on a Laptop

On a laptop computer, numbered function keys (**F1**, **F2**, and so on) perform specific Windows or Macintosh tasks, such as adjusting speaker volume, opening system *Settings*, or modifying screen brightness. An Office application shortcut, such as pressing the **F12** key to open the *Save As* dialog box, may require that you press the ***function key*** (**Fn** or **fn**) with the numbered function key to give the Office command. The *function key* is a modifier key typically located near the bottom left of a laptop keyboard next to the *Ctrl* key.

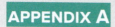

Appendix A-1 Function key

Common Office 365 Keyboard Shortcuts

Close *Start* page or *Backstage* view	Esc
Open *Help* dialog box	F1
Activate *Tell Me* feature	Alt+Q
Save file	Ctrl+S
Copy selected data	Ctrl+C
Cut selected data	Ctrl+X
Paste data	Ctrl+V
Select All	Ctrl+A
Bold selected data	Ctrl+B
Underline selected data	Ctrl+U
Italicize selected data	Ctrl+I
Switch among open applications	Alt+Tab

Excel 365 Keyboard Shortcuts

Action	Keyboard Shortcut
File Management and Navigation	
Open a new workbook	Ctrl+N
Display the *Open* pane from *Backstage* view	Ctrl+O
Open a workbook from the *Open* dialog box	Ctrl+F12 or Ctrl+O
Close the active workbook	Ctrl+W or Ctrl+F4
Open the *Save As* dialog box	F12
Save the active workbook	Ctrl+S
Move pointer to cell A1	Ctrl+Home

Action	Keyboard Shortcut
Move pointer to last cell (bottom row and rightmost column)	Ctrl+End
Complete entry and move to next cell down	Enter
Complete entry and move to next cell to the right	Tab
Complete entry and move to previous cell to the left	Shift+Tab
Complete entry and maintain current cell	Ctrl+Enter
Switch between open workbooks	Ctrl+F6
Editing and Formatting	
Start *Edit* mode	F2
Start a new line in a cell	Alt+Enter
Check spelling in active worksheet	F7
Undo last command	Ctrl+Z
Repeat or redo last command	Ctrl+Y
Copy data from cell above	Ctrl+' (apostrophe)
Open *Format Cells* dialog box	Ctrl+1
Display Quick Analysis options for selected data	Ctrl+Q
Add a note to a cell	Shift+F2
Insert chart object for selected data	Alt+F1
Insert chart sheet for selected data	F11
Open the *Create Table* dialog box for selected data	Ctrl+T
Open the *Macro* dialog box	Alt+F8
Open the Visual Basic Editor	Alt+F11
Working with Calculations	
Start a formula in a cell	= (equals key)
Insert *SUM*	Alt+=
Open *Insert Function* dialog box	Shift+F3
Expand/collapse *Formula* bar	Ctrl+Shift+U
Display/hide formulas	Ctrl+` (grave accent)
Calculate the worksheet	Shift+F9
Calculate all open workbooks	F9
Rotate through absolute or relative cell reference	F4
Open *Paste Name* dialog box	F3
Open *Name Manager* dialog box	Ctrl+F3
Cancel an entry in the cell or the *Formula* bar	Esc
Complete an array formula	Ctrl+Shift+Enter

(continued)

Action	Keyboard Shortcut
Modifying Worksheets	
Display/hide *Ribbon*	Ctrl+F1
Open the context menu for selected cell(s)	Shift+F10
Insert new worksheet	Shift+F11
Select current column	Ctrl+Spacebar
Select current row	Shift+Spacebar
Open *Insert* dialog box	Ctrl+plus sign (+)
Open *Delete* dialog box	Ctrl+minus sign (−)
Enter the current date in the cell	Ctrl+; (semi-colon)
Enter the current time in the cell	Ctrl+Shift+: (colon)

glossary

3D cell reference A cell address in another worksheet in the same workbook.

A

absolute cell reference A cell address with dollar signs such as $B$2.

active cell A cell that is ready for editing, surrounded with a solid border.

ActiveX form control Object that executes Visual Basic commands when clicked.

add-in Enhanced command or feature available for Excel.

Advanced Filter Filter process that uses a criteria range and an optional output range.

algorithm A step-by-step procedure used by *Solver* to reach a solution.

alignment Vertical and horizontal position of data in a cell.

Alt text Object property that is an oral explanation of an image, shape, or chart

Analysis Toolpak Add-in for Excel with built-in statistical and engineering calculations.

annuity A series of equal payments.

argument A cell reference, value, or other element required for a function.

array A range of cells in a row or a column.

array formula A formula that calculates and displays results across a range of cells.

ascending order Alphabetically from A to Z or from smallest to largest value.

attribute Setting or property for a cell.

Auto Outline Summary that inserts groups based on formula location.

AutoCalculate *Status* bar area that displays calculations for selected cells.

AutoComplete Feature that suggests an entry for a cell based on data already in the column.

AutoFilter Arrow in a header row used for sorting or filtering data.

AutoFit Feature that fits column or row to accommodate largest entry.

axis Horizontal or vertical boundary of plotted data in a chart.

axis title Title for categories or values in a chart.

B

backsolving Problem-solving method in which the result is known and a value necessary to reach that result is determined.

bin range List of values that specifies low and high values for each column in a histogram

border Outline for a cell or range.

business intelligence (BI) Tools, applications, and processes used to analyze data.

Button Form control that runs a macro with a single click.

C

calculated field Field in a *PivotTable* that is built from a formula with an existing *PivotTable* field.

Calendar Free time and appointment scheduling application available with a Microsoft account.

cash flow Future payment or receipt.

category axis Describes data shown in a chart; the horizontal axis in a column chart and the vertical axis in a bar chart.

category label Text label that described a data series in a chart.

cell Intersection of a column and a row in a worksheet.

cell address Column letter and row number that identifies location of cell or range; also called cell reference.

cell style Set of formatting elements for data in a cell.

change history Record of edits made in a shared workbook.

changing cells Variable cells in a *Solver* problem.

chart A visual representation of numeric worksheet data.

chart area Background rectangle area for a chart.

chart element Separate object or part in a chart that can be selected and edited.

chart floor Base or bottom for a 3D chart.

chart layout Set of charts elements and their locations.

chart object Selectable chart with clickable elements located on a worksheet.

chart sheet Chart displayed in its own tab or sheet in a workbook.

chart style Combination of colors and effects for a chart and its elements.

chart title Name or main label for a chart.

chart wall Vertical background for a 3D chart.

circular reference Formula error in which the formula refers to the cell in which it is located.

Co-Authoring Process in which multiple workers edit a workbook.

code Programming statements and commands in a Visual Basic for Applications module.

col_index_number Argument in a *VLOOKUP* functions for the column with data to be displayed in the result.

collections (VBA) Group of similar objects.

Combo Box Form control that displays as a drop-down list used to make a choice.

comment A thread in an online conversation. Also a line preceded by an apostrophe in the Visual Basic Editor that is not part of the code.

common field Data field that is the same data type and displays the same data in a query.

Compatibility Checker Dialog box that identifies commands and features that are not supported in earlier versions of Excel.

concatenate To link or join data.

conditional column Generated or calculated column in Power Query with an *IF* statement

conditional formatting Format settings that are applied based on rules, rankings, or other criteria.

connection Identifier and a link to external data in a workbook.

consolidated worksheet Worksheet that gathers and summarizes values from more than one worksheet.

constant A value used in a formula.

constraints Solver parameter that sets a restriction or limitation.

criteria Function argument which sets a restriction or condition.

criteria range Two or more rows of data used to specify advanced filter conditions.

CSE formula An array formula, executed by pressing **Ctrl+Shift +Enter**.

custom AutoFilter Criteria set in a dialog box from an AutoFilter arrow.

custom calculation *PivotTable* column that displays a percentage, a ranking, or a ratio.

custom column Generated column in a query with an M language formula

custom view Named and saved display and print settings in a workbook

D

Data Analysis Expression (DAX) Syntax for function and formulas in a *Power Pivot* table

data input form Dialog box with controls, labels, and entry boxes that displays worksheet data.

data label Object that displays value for each data marker in a chart.

data marker Bar, column, slice, or other object used to graph a value in a chart.

data model Collection of tables or queries in a workbook, available for building *PivotTables*.

data point A value in a chart represented by a cell; a single value graphed in a chart.

data series A group of related values graphed by columns, bars, slices, or other objects in a chart.

data table Columnar display of values for each data series in a chart located below the chart; also a range of cells with calculated results for one or more formulas.

data validation Process of setting rules for data entry.

Data visualization Formatting that uses colored bars, color variations, or icons based on rules or rankings.

database Software applications that use related tables, queries, forms, and reports; also a cell range in a worksheet with label and data rows.

Database function A function that performs a mathematical or statistical calculation only for data that meet its criteria.

decision cells Changing cells in a *Solver* problem.

delimited File that separates data into columns with a special character.

delimiter Character used to separate columns.

dependent Cell that is affected by the active cell.

dependent workbook Workbook that has a linking or external reference formula.

descending order Alphabetically from Z to A or from largest to smallest value.

Descriptive Statistics Group of popular statistical measures for a data range.

destination cell Cell location for pasted data.

Developer tab Ribbon command tab with tools for working with form controls, macros, and XML data.

deviation A forecast error.

dimension Number of row and columns in an array.

discount rate The cost of financing or a competing rate of return.

Document Inspector Dialog box that lists metadata in a workbook.

document property Information about a workbook such as file name, creation and edit dates, size, etc.

duplicate row Record in a table with the same content as another record in one or more columns.

dynamic data consolidation Consolidation command that inserts a formula that updates when changes are made to the source data.

E

ellipse Oval shape.

error alert Message box that appears when invalid data is entered in a cell with data validation settings.

Excel Start page Opening screen when Excel is started.

exporting Saving or copying data for use in another program or application.

external data Data that originated in another program or format.

external reference A formula or cell address that refers to cells in another workbook.

extract range One row of labels for results of an advanced filter.

F

field One column of data, a column in a database.

field name Label in a header row.

fill Color or pattern used as a background for a cell or range.

Fill handle Small square at lower right corner of a cell or range used to complete a series or copy data.

filter Requirement or condition that identifies data to be shown or hidden.

fixed width Specific number of characters assigned to a field or column.

Flash Fill Excel feature that completes column data based on first entry.

font Named design of type for characters, punctuation, and symbols.

font style Thickness or angle of characters.

footer Data that prints at the bottom of each page.

forecast error The difference between actual and predicted values.

forecast sheet Generated worksheet with a table and chart built from two data series, one of which is a time or date field.

foreign column A matching column in which data can appear many times

Form control Object used to display a choice, run a command, or perform a task.

Format Painter Tool that copies format from one cell to others.

formula A calculation in a cell that displays a result.

formula auditing Process of reviewing formulas for accuracy.

Formula AutoComplete Feature that displays a list of function and range names after a character is typed.

Formula bar Bar below the *Ribbon* that displays active cell contents.

Forms Free electronic survey application available with a Microsoft account.

function A built-in formula.

Fv Argument in *Financial* functions for the future value.

G

Goal Seek What-if analysis command that finds a value that will provide a specified formula result.

gradient Blend of two or more colors used as fill.

gridline Horizontal or vertical line across the plot area in a chart.

gridlines Vertical and horizontal lines on screen that form columns and rows in a worksheet.

group Set of rows with the same entry in at least one column.

group box Form control used to organize other form control objects

H

header Data that prints at the top of each page.

header row First row of a table with labels.

hidden worksheet Worksheet whose tab is not visible.

hierarchy Division of data into groups and related subgroups.

histogram Column chart that displays frequency of each data point in the data set.

hyperlink Clickable jump text or object in a worksheet.

I

identifier Character used in a cell address that labels a component of the address.

importing Process of getting data from an outside source.

indent Command that moves data away from the left edge of a cell.

indicator Triangle in the upper-right corner of a cell to identify a comment or a note.

Ink Object drawn freehand by a finger, a stylus, or the mouse.

input message Comment box that appears at data entry as part of a cell's data validation settings.

input value Group of values in a column or row that is substituted for a value in a formula in a data table.

invalid data Cell data that does not conform to data validation settings.

J

Join A relationship between tables or queries

K

key field Data field that is a common field but each data piece is used only once in a query.

Key performance indicator (KPI) Visual display for illustrating how a column value compares to a measure in a *PivotTable*

L

label Text data in a worksheet that is not used in calculations.

Legacy Wizard Data import commands from early versions of Excel

legend Chart element that describes colors, symbols, or textures used in a chart.

line break Start of a new line in a cell made by pressing **Alt+Enter**.

link A live data connection to another workbook.

linking Process of referring to data in another workbook.

M

macro Series of commands and keystrokes that executes a command.

macro-enabled template Excel template that includes macros.

macros-only workbook Macro-enabled workbook that includes only macros.

Mail Free email application available with a Microsoft account.

map chart An Excel chart that displays high-level geographic details such as countries or states

Mark as Final Workbook property that sets the file as read-only.

marker Data point in a sparkline.

math hierarchy Sequence of arithmetic calculations in a formula.

mathematical order of operations Sequence of arithmetic operations in a formula.

mean Value determined by adding all values in a range and dividing by the number of values.

mean absolute deviation (MAD) Popular measure of how spread out values are from the average.

measure Calculated result for a column in a *Power Pivot* table

metadata Properties and settings that are embedded in a workbook and stored with the file.

methods (VBA) Function, action, or service for an object.

Microsoft 3D Map Add-in that plots geographic and time data on a three-dimensional globe

Microsoft Access Relational database management system available with the Office suite.

Mini toolbar Collection of common commands for selected cells

mixed cell reference A cell address with one dollar sign such as $B2 or B$2.

module Container or folder for Visual Basic for Applications statements and procedures.

moving average A series of averages for a set of values.

N

Name box Area in *Formula* bar that displays cell address of the active cell.

Named set Custom grouping of items from a column or row in a *PivotTable*

nested function A function within another function; a function used as an argument in another function.

Normal view Worksheet view used to create and modify a worksheet.

nper Argument in *Financial* functions for the term of a loan or investment that specifies the number of periods.

O

objective cell Cell with a formula used as a *Solver* parameter.

Objects (VBA) Tools or elements with properties, functions, or data.

Office add-in Application programs for enhanced features and commands in Excel and other Office software.

Office Background Graphic pattern displayed in the top right corner of the application window.

Office Clipboard Storage location for cut or copied data shared by all Office applications.

Office Online Free, abbreviated versions of Office 365 applications.

Office theme Ribbon, tab, and dialog box colors for Office applications.

OneDrive Online or cloud storage available with a Microsoft account.

OneNote Online Free note-taking and audio recording application available with a Microsoft account.

one-variable data table Range of cells that calculates results by substituting values for one argument in one or more formulas.

Option Button Form control that displays as a radio button used to make one choice in a group.

Order of precedence Sequence of arithmetic calculations in a formula.

Outline Summary that groups records with collapse/expand buttons.

P

Page break Printer code to start a new page.

Page Break preview Worksheet view that shows printed pages with dashed or dotted lines to mark where new pages start.

Page Layout view Worksheet view that opens header and footer areas, indicates margin areas, and shows rulers.

parameter Information used in a Solver problem.

Paste Options Gallery of choices for how data is copied.

pattern Crosshatches, dots, or stripes used as fill.

People Free contact management application available with a Microsoft account.

***Personal Macro* workbook** Hidden macros-only workbook named PERSONAL.XLSB, saved in the XLSTART folder, that is automatically opened each time Excel is started.

PivotChart Summary chart built from a *PivotTable* or a range of data.

PivotTable Summary report for a range of data with interactive field and filter buttons.

Pixel One screen dot used as measurement.

Plot area Chart element bounded by the horizontal and vertical axes.

Pmt Argument in *Financial* functions that specifies the amount saved or invested each period

Point Font measurement of 1/72 of an inch.

population All data available for analysis.

Power Pivot Add-in for Excel that accesses and extracts data from large databases for use in *PivotTable* reports.

Power Query Data analysis tool to clean data for use in Excel

precedent Cell that contributes to a formula's result.

print area Defined data that prints.

print title Row or column that prints on each page.

product Result of a multiplication formula.

Protected View Status of a workbook opened or copied from an Internet source.

Pv Argument in *Financial* functions for the present or current value.

Q

query Set of instructions, filters, and formats that connects to and gets data for use in Excel.

Quick Analysis Tool that displays for a selected cell range with suggested command groups.

R

range Rectangular group of cells such as A1:B3.

Range Finder Feature that highlights and color-codes a formula cell range in Edit mode.

range name Label assigned to a single or a group of cells.

rate Argument in many *Financial* functions that specifies an interest rate for the time period.

record One row of data, a row in a database.

relative cell reference A cell address such as B2.

S

sample A subset of a population.

scenario Set of values saved with the worksheet.

scenario summary report Generated worksheet outline that describes scenarios for the sheet.

scene Layout, format, and perspective for a single display of data in a 3D map tour

screen reader Application that verbalizes aloud alt text explanations

scope A worksheet set as the location for a range name.

screenshot Picture of an application window or any part of the window.

selection handle Small shape on each corner and middle edge of an object or element.

serial number Value assigned to a date.

series List of labels or values that follow a pattern.

shape effects Design elements such as shadows, bevels, or soft edges for a chart element or object.

shape fill Background color for a chart element or object.

shape outline Border color and thickness for a chart element or object.

shape style Set of fill colors, borders, and effects for a chart element or object.

SharePoint Web platform designed for collaboration via the Internet.

sharing link Text hyperlink that can be copied into an email to share a file.

sheet Individual page or tab in a workbook.

Smart Lookup Research tool that searches the web to find information about a selected cell, text, or value

SmartArt Text-based line illustration available for use in a worksheet.

Solver What-if analysis command that finds lowest, highest, or specific result for a formula.

sorting Process of arranging rows of data in an identified order.

source Text, database, or other file from which data is imported.

source cell Cell data that is copied or cut.

source data Cell range with values and labels graphed in a chart.

source workbook Workbook that provided data to another workbook in a consolidation command or an external reference formula.

source worksheet Worksheet that provides data to a consolidation command or to an external reference formula.

sparklines Miniature charts embedded in a worksheet cell.

splitter bar Horizontal or vertical gray bar that divides a worksheet into panes.

spreadsheet Individual page or sheet in a workbook.

standard deviation Popular measure of how broadly values vary from the average.

static data consolidation Consolidation command that inserts a value result that does not update when changes are made to the source data.

structured reference Name assigned to specific parts of an Excel table.

subtotal Summary row for grouped data.

SUM *Math & Trig* function that adds cell values.

Sunburst chart Hierarchy chart similar to a pie chart with concentric rings for each level in the hierarchy.

Sway Free storytelling application available with a Microsoft account.

syntax Required elements and the order of those elements for a function.

T

tab Identifier at the bottom left of a worksheet that displays the name of sheet.

tab scrolling buttons Buttons to the left of tab names used to move through all worksheet tabs.

table Excel data formatted with a header row followed by data rows.

table style Predesigned set of format settings.

target cell Objective cell in a *Solver* problem.

template Model workbook with any combination of data, formulas, formatting, charts, images, controls, and more.

text file File format that includes data with no formatting.

theme Collection of fonts, colors, and special effects for a workbook.

thumbnail Small image of a worksheet in a dialog box.

tick mark Small line on a chart axis to guide in reading values.

timeline Visual filter for a date field, displayed as a floating dialog box.

tour Named and saved visualization details for data in a 3D map

trendline Chart element that averages and forecasts chart data.

two-variable data table Range of cells that calculates results by substituting values for two arguments in one formula.

type Argument in *Financial* functions for the timing of a payment.

U

UserForm Custom dialog box created using VBA and ActiveX form controls

V

validation settings Rules or requirements applied to data as it is entered.

value Numerical data in a worksheet that can be used in calculations.

value axis Shows the numbers in a chart; the vertical axis in a column chart and the horizontal axis in a bar chart.

variable cells Cells that can be changed in a Solver problem.

Visual Basic Editor (VBE) Application with three panes that displays programming for a macro.

Visual Basic for Applications (VBA) Underlying programming language used in Excel macros and ActiveX controls in a workbook.

Volatile Description for function results that depend on the date and time set in the computer.

W

Watch Window Floating dialog box that displays selected cell references.

waterfall chart A chart that depicts a running total based on negative and positive values.

WordArt Text box with font style, color, fill and effects.

workbook Saved Excel document file that contains worksheets.

worksheet Individual page or sheet in a workbook.

worksheet protection Property that sets which cells can be edited.

X

.xlsm File name extension for an Excel macro-enabled workbook.

.xltm File name extension for an Excel macro-enabled template.

.xltx File name extension for an Excel template.

.xlxs Excel file name extension and format for workbooks.

.xml Text file format that uses Extensible Markup Language.

index

Symbols

Numbers

A

B

C

D

E

F

M

N

O

P

Q

R

S

T

U

V

W

X

Z